Textbook meets Web.

Lefton means learning at a whole *new* level!

What are the advantages to you?

Fact: 100% of students want better grades.

Fact: 100% of students want to save money.

"According to the research, the Internet is the most frequently used study aid, with 65% of respondents saying they use it for their classes."

Campus Marketplace Newsletter
The Official Weekly Newsletter of
The National Association of College Stores
March 10, 2000

It's the experience you've been waiting for!

Introducing Lester Lefton's new

InterActive Psychology Online

A text/web hybrid that gives you core content in the textbook with additional content online, all at a significantly lower price!

This unique *InterActive Psychology Online* text invites you to learn both by reading the text and by using the website. With the purchase of a new book, the accompanying comprehensive password-protected Website offers additional dynamic online content such as a downloadable chapter, full-color artwork, building tables, access to the HOTTEST site in psychology – *The Psychology Place™ Website* – and more!

- @ **A new black-and-white textbook format** includes all the core content in an impressive 1-color design – with fewer photos and art – at a significantly lower price.

- @ **Cutting-edge material** includes the explosion of information on brain and behavior, coverage of diversity, sensitivity to culture and gender, and an emphasis on research in psychology.

- @ **A comprehensive password-protected website, at** www.abacon.com/leftononline contains a downloadable chapter, Statistical Methods Appendix, full-color artwork, Building Tables, learning activities, Weblinks, and access to *The Psychology Place™ Website*.

The special InterActive Psychology Online edition still relies on the backbone of teaching — the traditional textbook...

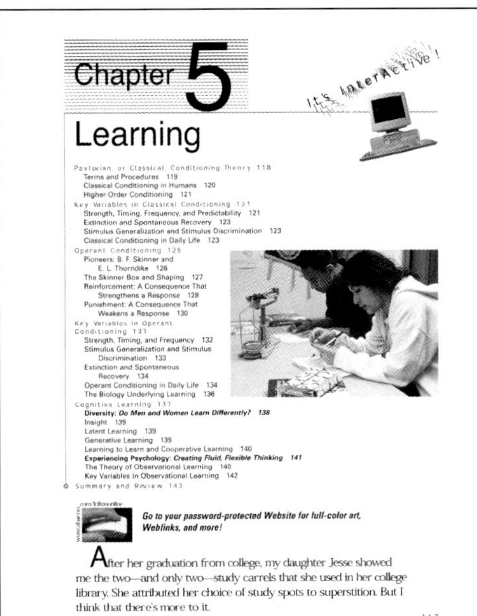

Chapter 5

It's InterActive!

Learning

Go to your password-protected Website for full-color art, Weblinks, and more!

After her graduation from college, my daughter Jesse showed me the two—and only two—study carrels that she used in her college library. She attributed her choice of study spots to superstition. But I think that there's more to it.

117

This exciting new concept in textbooks is a culmination of seven strategic goals:

1. To write a brief, interactive, web-oriented text.
2. To be sensitive to the cost issues many students face.
3. To keep current with the new directions in psychology – coverage includes the explosion of information on brain and behavior.
4. To emphasize diversity and the need for sensitivity to culture and gender in applying and doing research.
5. To demonstrate that research is a corner stone of psychology and to familiarize students with the research process.
6. To focus on critical thinking as a key to good scientific thought and research.
7. To successfully convey that applications grow from research and demonstrate psychologists build conceptual bridges between research and applications.

Content is organized by core topics and delivered in a black-and-white printed format.

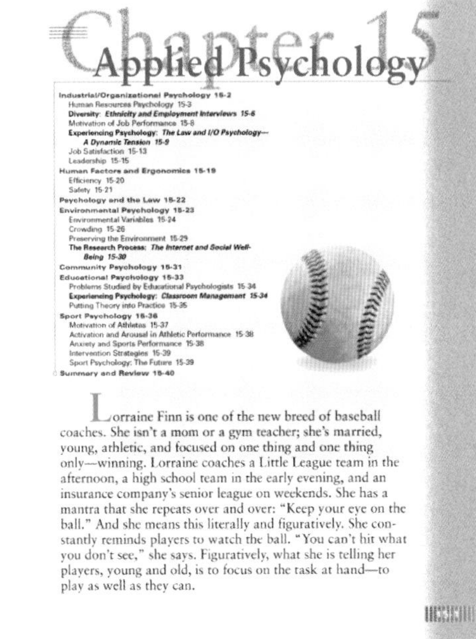

Chapter 15

Applied Psychology

Lorraine Finn is one of the new breed of baseball coaches. She isn't a mom or a gym teacher; she's married, young, athletic, and focused on one thing and one thing only—winning. Lorraine coaches a Little League team in the afternoon, a high school team in the early evening, and an insurance company's senior league on weekends. She has a mantra that she repeats over and over: "Keep your eye on the ball." And she means this literally and figuratively. She constantly reminds players to watch the ball. "You can't hit what you don't see," she says. Figuratively, what she is telling her players, young and old, is to focus on the task at hand—to play as well as they can.

Additional content appears on the Web in a dynamic full-color format.

...but with a new measure of staying current while being cost-conscious.

Providing up-to-date information between editions is a challenge.

This new format allows us to provide you with the most current information in psychology by continuously updating the accompanying website!

The cost of textbooks can be a concern for students and professors.

In order to offer competitive pricing to cost-conscious adopters and their students, we have designed this new black-and-white format with fewer photos and art. This **Online Edition** delivers core content with additional online content, but at a lower cost.

Table 4.3 Behavioral Effects Associated with Various Blood Alcohol Levels

Blood Alcohol Level*	Behavioral Effects
0.05	Lowered alertness, impaired judgment, release of inhibitions, feelings of well-being or sociability
0.10	Slowed reaction time and impaired motor function, less caution
0.15	Large, consistent increases in reaction time
0.20	Marked depression in sensory and motor capability, decidedly intoxicated behavior
0.25	Severe motor disturbance and impairment of sensory perceptions
0.30	In a stupor but still conscious—no comprehension of events in the environment
0.35	Surgical anesthesia; lethal dose for about 1% of adults
0.40	Lethal dose for about 50% of adults

*In milligrams of alcohol per 100 milliliters of blood

who also has both physiological and psychological needs to consume alcohol and to experience its effects is an **alcoholic**. All alcoholics are problem drinkers, but not all problem drinkers are alcoholics. Without alcohol, alcoholics develop physiological withdrawal symptoms. In addition, they often develop tolerance; a single drink or even a few will not affect them.

Are some people more likely than others to become alcoholics? The answer is yes, according to researchers who study the biological aspects of alcoholism. Researchers assert that genetics, blood and brain chemistry, and specific brain structures predispose some people to alcoholism (Tarter & Vanyukov, 1994). Children of alcoholics are more likely to be alcoholics, even if they are raised by nonalcoholic adoptive parents. The correlations suggest that certain individuals' physiology predisposes them to alcoholism.

From both a medical and a psychological standpoint, alcohol abuse is one of the most widespread social problems in the United States.

An important study of the inheritance factor and the vulnerability of women to alcoholism shows similar results. According to Kenneth Kendler and his colleagues (1994), the transmission of vulnerability to alcoholism from parents to their daughters is due to genetic factors. This study showed that genetic vulnerability was equally transmitted from fathers and mothers to their daughters. It may be that alcohol use affects a mother's ova or a father's sperm (Cicero, 1994). That inheritance is involved in alcoholism in both men and women is clear; how in- [...] in-fluence (Chassin et al., 1993), and especially the alcoholic's thought processes (Goldman et al., 1991) is the question researchers must answer next (Hawkins, Catalano, & Miller, 1992).

Social and Medical Problems. From both a medical and a psychological standpoint, alcohol abuse is one of the most widespread social problems in the United States. Between 30% and 40% of the homeless are people with alcohol problems (McCarty et al., 1991). Public drunkenness is the biggest law enforcement problem, accounting for millions of arrests each year. The National Highway Traffic Safety Administration estimates that alcohol is involved in more than 18,000 deaths from automobile accidents each year. Although the number of deaths caused by alcohol-related accidents has decreased in the last few years, the number likely to occur in the next 3 years will still exceed the total number of Americans killed in the Vietnam War. In addition, people who are involved in violent crimes or who attempt suicide are often found to have been drinking, and alcohol abuse is associated with marital violence (Murphy & O'Farrell, 1996).

Although alcoholism is seen as a social problem because of its devastating social consequences, it is also a medical problem. Biomedical researchers look for the effects of alcohol on the brain, as well as differences in the brains and basic genetic makeup of alcoholics that

genes and experience are important factors affecting behavior. In fact, it makes little sense to talk about one without talking about the other.

Both genes and experience are important factors affecting behavior. In fact, it makes little sense to talk about one without talking about the other.

Your genetic heritage is unaffected by day-to-day experiences. Over tens of thousands of years, however, we humans have evolved a highly organized brain that does allow us to learn, and that learning affects our behavior. Your brain acts as a library of information. Each new experience affects your later behavior. Those who consider nurture more important than nature suggest that people are not limited by genetic heritage, because experience, training, and hard work can stretch individual potential amazingly.

Psychologists know that biological makeup affects people's intelligence. But can the environment interact with and modify biological makeup? The truth is that genetic traits provide the framework for behavior; within that framework, experiences ultimately shape what individuals feel, think, and do. Let's take a closer look at the key genetic factors that shape day-to-day behavior.

The Basics of Genetics

Genetics is the study of *heredity*, which is the biological transmission of traits and characteristics from parents to offspring. Behavioral traits such as temperament and intelligence and disorders such as Alzheimer's disease and schizophrenia also have a genetic basis; this is why psychologists are especially interested in heredity (Chorney et al., 1998; Hamer, 1998). The focus of the field of *behavioral genetics* is on the influence of genetics on behavior. Behavioral geneticists ask questions about whether human characteristics such as shyness, impulsiveness, or intelligence have a genetic, inherited basis. If they do, then to what extent is the behavior biological and to what extent is it learned? Such researchers talk of the *heritability* of a trait or behavior. Many characteristics vary among individuals in a population—intelligence, dancing ability, and height are just a few heritable variables. Remember that such characteristics sometimes require a genetic contribution from both parents, and estimates of how heritable a trait or characteristic is are estimates of how likely it is to occur within a *group* (not in a specific person). We will take a closer look at heritability in Chapter 7.

Uniqueness of Human Beings. With the exception of identical twins (discussed on p. 32), every human being is genetically unique. Although each of us shares traits with our brothers, sisters, and parents, none of us is identical to them or to anyone else. The reason is that a large number of genes determine, or at least influence, each person's physical, cognitive, and emotional characteristics (Reiss, 1995, 1997).

Each human cell normally contains 23 pairs of chromosomes (46 chromosomes in all). **Chromosomes** are microscopic strands of deoxyribonucleic acid (DNA) found in the nucleus (center) of every cell in the body (see Figure 2.1). Chromosomes carry the self-

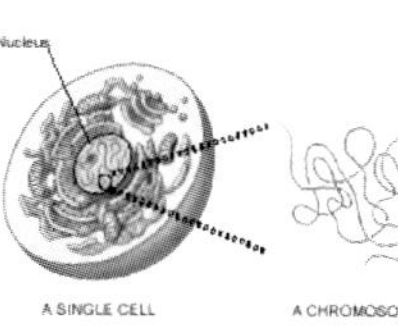

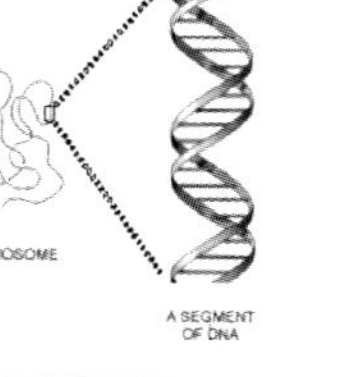

A SEGMENT OF DNA

FIGURE 2.1
Building Blocks of Genetics
Each of the trillions of cells in the human body has 23 pairs of chromosomes in its nucleus. Each chromosome is essentially a long, threadlike strand of DNA, a giant molecule consisting of two spiraling and cross-linked chains. Resembling a twisted ladder and referred to as a *double helix*, each DNA molecule carries thousands of genes—the basic building blocks of the genetic code—which direct the synthesis of all the body's proteins.

Lefton's Website delivers a unique interactive experience through an online chapter and appendix...

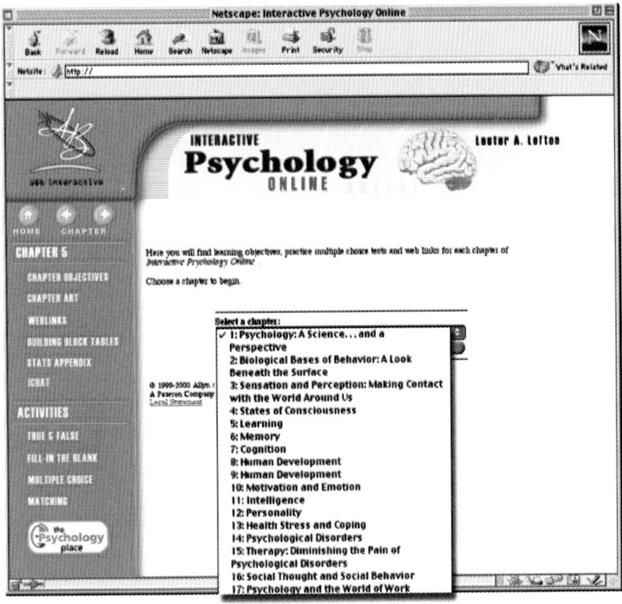

www.abacon.com/leftononline

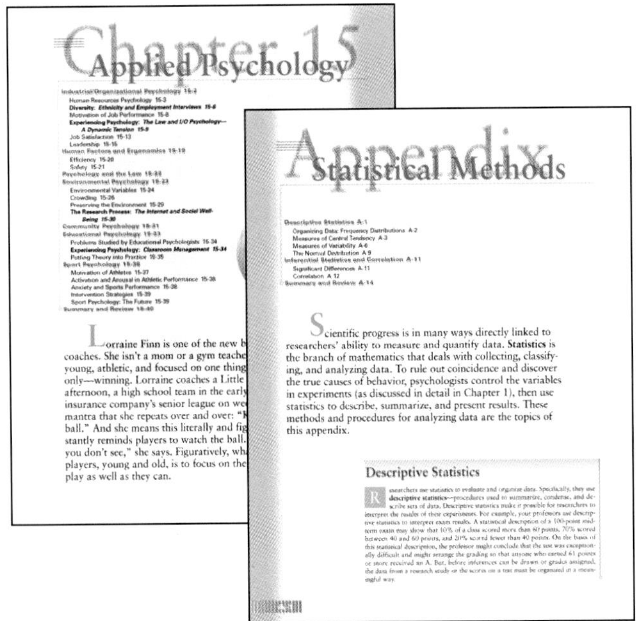
Chapter 15
Applied Psychology

Appendix
Statistical Methods

Scientific progress is in many ways directly linked to researchers' ability to measure and quantify data. Statistics is the branch of mathematics that deals with collecting, classifying, and analyzing data. To rule out coincidence and discover the true causes of behavior, psychologists control the variables in experiments (as discussed in detail in Chapter 1), then use statistics to describe, summarize, and present results. These methods and procedures for analyzing data are the topics of this appendix.

Descriptive Statistics

On the inside cover of each new textbook purchased is a PIN code allowing access to this dynamic Web resource!

This site offers additional learning tools that enhance the information presented in the printed textbook. Visit the site and you will find...

- @ An exclusive downloadable online chapter on *Applied Psychology*
- @ *Statistical Methods Appendix*
- @ Full-color artwork
- @ Building Tables
- @ Learning activities
- @ Weblinks
- @ Access to *The Psychology Place™ Website*

An Interactive Online Chapter!
Chapter 15, *Applied Psychology,* has been placed on the Web. This bonus chapter shows how psychological principles can be used to solve practical problems of everyday life — whether on the job, at school, or on the playing field.

Statistical Methods Appendix
This ready reference to basic statistical methods is available to you from any point on the Website.

...as well as animated Building Tables and full-color artwork.

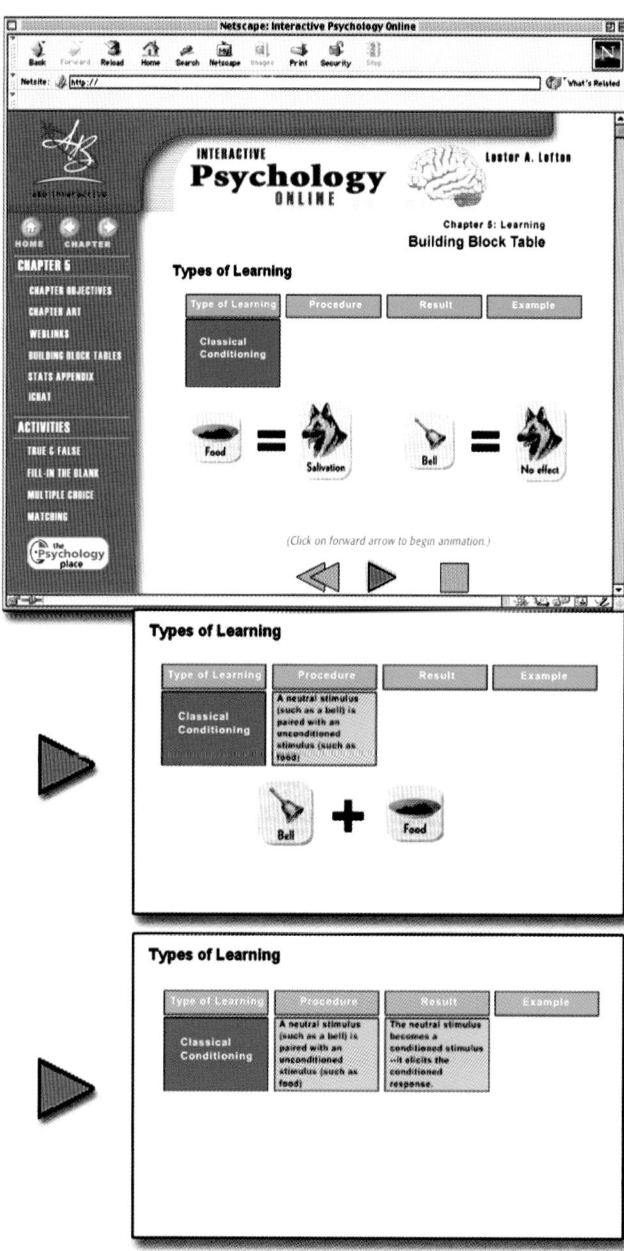

Building Tables

Presenting important theories and concepts in a way that shows the development of ideas is a major pedagogical element of the Website. Building Tables are **animated online,** showing the progression of ideas. As you master a concept, it is added to a Building Table that lists related concepts. These tables allow you to compare, contrast, and integrate concepts. They, too, are an excellent study and review aid.

Full-Color Artwork

A picture can be worth a thousand words, especially if you are a visual learner. On the Website, you will find full-color art to enhance your understanding of the text discussion. The anatomical and brain art has been drawn by a studio specializing in medical illustrations to ensure accuracy and pedagogical value.

When you use the arrow functions, Building Tables come to life on the Web through animation.

The Psychology Place™ Website
offers a multitude of helpful study aids...

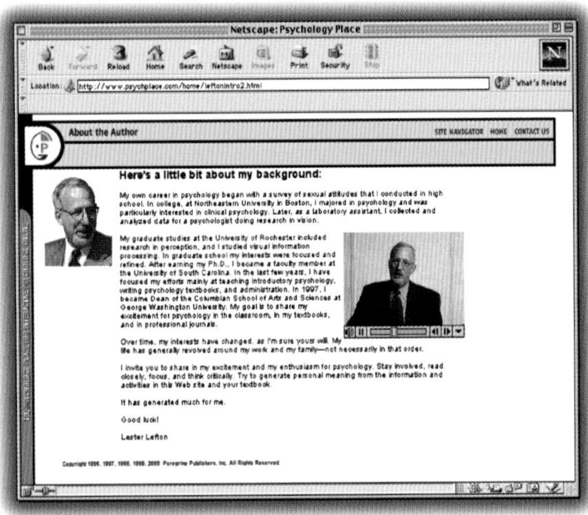

Access to *The Psychology Place™ Website* is available at www.abacon.com/leftononline.

The Psychology Place™ Website, the premier web resource for college psychology, has been expanded and customized for Lefton's *InterActive Psychology Online*.

Each student will receive...

- A six-month subscription to the HOTTEST place in psychology!
- Direct support of his/her daily coursework.
- Extensive learning activities, news updates, research reports, Weblinks, practice tests, and animations, as well as videos of Lester Lefton.

As an instructor, you will enjoy...

- An extensive selection of teaching resources for each chapter of the text.
- Recent research news and the ability to launch your students' own web investigations.
- Scientifically accurate and appropriate Web resources using *Best of the Web*.
- Integration of online investigative and collaborative *Learning Activities* into your course.
- Communication with other instructors and the ability to share your teaching ideas and challenges by participating in the *Op Ed Forum*.
- Up-to-date teaching news and resources.

Site Features Include...

NEW! Crossword Puzzle Learning Tool, which is updated twice a month.

Ask Dr. Mike... if you have a question about psychology.

Learning Activities that promote inquiry-based learning on the Web.

Op Ed Forum, which contains essays from guest contributors.

Scientific American Connection — a collection of articles from *Scientific American* magazine that are relevant to introductory psychology.

...including Test Flight, Learning Activities, Research News, and much more!

Test Flight

Students can customize their own practice tests in preparation for course exams. The student chooses the chapters and the number of questions to appear on the test, *Test Flight* grades the test automatically and indicates the correct answer for each question. A personalized Review Profile, based on the test results, identifies the topics where additional review might be needed before the actual exam.

Op Ed Forum

Each month *The Psychology Place™ Website* posts original essays by guest contributors who challenge you with important new information, ideas, or strategies pertinent to introductory psychology, and who invite you to join a collegial dialogue about issues raised.

Research News

Twice a month an article is posted summarizing important news in the field of psychology. The most recently posted items are listed for quick reference. Explore information related to your course or find materials for research projects. Each *Research News* article includes print and Web references that can be used for further research.

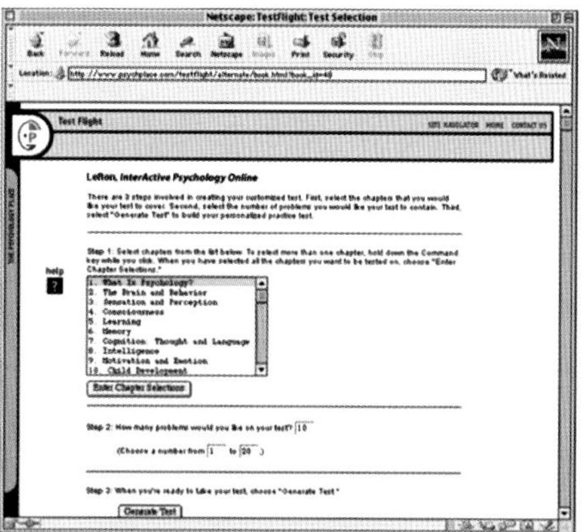

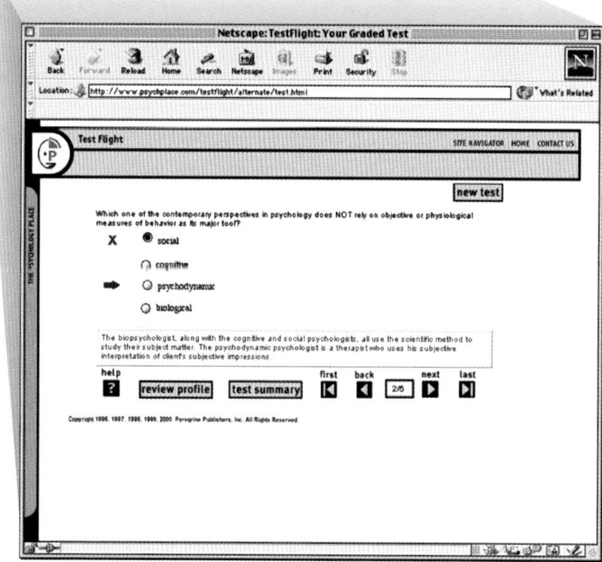

The Test Flight feature gives students the independence to test themselves chapter by chapter online, or the instructor can use this feature as an assignment and receive the results via email.

Further enhance the learning experience with these helpful supplements!

For the Instructor...

Instructor's Resource Manual and Test Bank

Computerized Test Bank
(Windows CD-ROM and disk; Mac disk; DOS disk upon request.)

Allyn & Bacon Transparencies for Introductory Psychology, 2000

Website for Lefton's Interactive Psychology Online (PIN required), with access to The Psychology Place™ Website (http://www.abacon.com/leftononline)

For the Student...

Practice Test Booklet

Psychology on the Net, 2001
Psychology on the Net, by Whitford and Gotthoffer, packaged for FREE! This guide provides students with the basics of using the Internet, activities, hundreds of Psychology-related URLs, and information on using the Internet in the classroom.
(Value-Package option only. Contact your local publisher's representative for details.)

NEW for 2001!

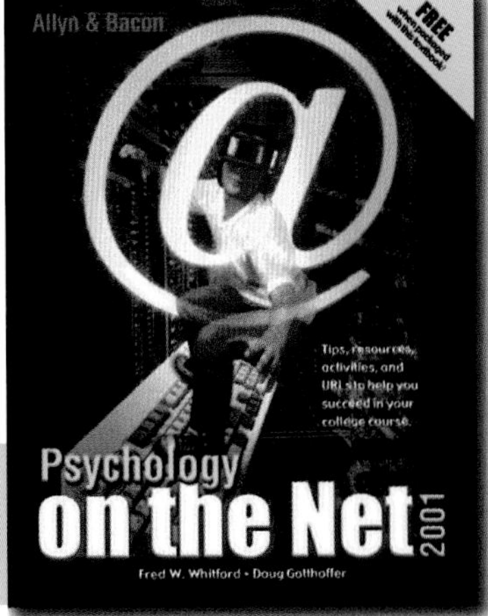

Allyn & Bacon
FREE
Tips, resources, activities, and URL sites help you succeed in your college course.
Psychology on the Net 2001
Fred W. Whitford • Doug Gotthoffer

Textbook meets Web.

Lefton means learning at a whole *new* level!

InterActive Psychology Online

InterActive Psychology Online

Lester A. Lefton *The George Washington University*

ALLYN AND BACON
Boston / London / Toronto / Sydney / Tokyo / Singapore

Executive Editor: Carolyn Merrill
Senior Development Editor: Sue Gleason
Series Editorial Assistant: Lara Zeises
Marketing Manager: Caroline Croley
Editorial Production Supervisor: Susan McIntyre
Editorial Production Service: Jane E. Hoover/Lifland et al., Bookmakers
Text Designer: Shelley Davidson
Composition: Omegatype Typography, Inc.
Composition Buyer: Linda Cox
Manufacturing Buyer: Megan Cochran
Cover Administrator: Linda Knowles

A Pearson Education Company
160 Gould Street
Needham Heights, MA 02494
Internet: www.abacon.com

Library of Congress Cataloging-in-Publication Data
Lefton, Lester A.
InterActive psychology online / Lester A. Lefton
p. cm.
Includes bibliographical references and index.
ISBN 0-205-32286-7
1. Psychology. I. Title.

BF121.L422 2000
150—dc21

00-033194

Credits appear on pages 487–488, which constitute a continuation of the copyright page.

Printed in the United States of America
10 9 8 7 6 5 4 3 2 1 02 01 00

Contents

Chapter 6
Memory and Cognition 146

Chapter 7
Intelligence 186

Chapter 8
Motivation and Emotion 208

Chapter 11 Social Psychology 307

Chapter 12 Stress and Health Psychology 339

Chapter 13 Psychological Disorders 362

Chapter 14 Therapy 392

Preface to the Student

Welcome to an interactive learning experience online! No matter who you are, this book and its accompanying website will have meaning for you because they deal with everyday issues of human thought and behavior.

- If you are having trouble with your roommate . . .
- If the adjustment to college was more difficult than you thought it would be . . .
- If you become stressed out over exams and papers . . .
- If you argue with your parents . . .
- If a friend has been depressed for a long time . . .
- If you have difficulty retaining information for tests . . .

then reading this book and engaging in its interactive activities will give you useful insights. I strongly believe in helping students retain all the insights they can from a book; therefore, I have made a special effort to make psychology both understandable and interesting. This unique **InterActive Psychology Online** text invites you to learn both by reading the text and by using the website: *www.abacon.com/leftononline*.

Be an Active Learner

The following important study tips will increase your effectiveness as a student and help to reduce your stress level as you study:

- Become actively involved in the learning process.
- Take advantage of the online opportunities that accompany the text.
- Make new information meaningful by linking it to your life experiences and knowledge.
- Be responsible for your own learning.

Use Effective Study Skills

One way to really improve your studying and to be an active learner is to use the SQ3R system, which reminds learners to *survey, question, read, recite,* and *review* when reading textbooks (Robinson, 1970). College students have used SQ3R effectively and successfully for over 50 years. It is a tried-and-true active study method, which is why it is the strategy most recommended by psychology professors. I have modified the original SQ3R method slightly to *SQ3R plus: survey, question, read, recite, review*—plus *write and reflect*. To be an effective learner of psychology, look at the SQ3R material on the book's website: *www.abacon.com/leftononline*.

Use the Pedagogical Features

Pedagogical features are integrated into *InterActive Psychology Online* to stimulate your active involvement with and critical thinking about issues, as well as to help you learn more efficiently and effectively.

Brain and Behavior. This text particularly emphasizes the relationship between biology and the environment. Psychologists now recognize that people are influenced by both genetics and the environment. I have integrated biological concepts and neuropsychology throughout the text. Graphic representations of the brain will help you locate its parts as you read about them in the text. You can also see colorful representations online.

Critical Thinking. According to learning theory, retention improves if you review and rethink what you have read. In fact, learning about psychology means learning about the thinking process itself. Developing critical thinking skills is thus a major theme—from Chapter 1's introduction to the scientific method and critical thinking (on pp. 3–5 and 8–10), to *Think Critically* questions at the end of major sections, to questions within the text that model critical thinking.

Key Terms. Key terms appear in boldface type in the text and are defined in the running glossary with a pronunciation guide where appropriate. In addition, the key terms are listed within each chapter's *Summary and Review*, to provide you with an additional opportunity to review key concepts after you have finished the chapter.

Building Tables. Presenting important theories and concepts in a way that shows the development of ideas is a major pedagogical element available on the website. As you master a set of concepts, it is added to a Building Table that lists related concepts. These tables allow you to compare, contrast, and integrate concepts. They, too, are an excellent study and review aid.

Art. A picture can be worth a thousand words, especially if you are a visual learner. Available on the website, *www.abacon.com/leftononline*, the brain and anatomical art will help bring concepts to life.

Diversity. One goal of the text is to introduce you to the growing diversity in our culture and to show you how multicultural factors must be taken into account when evaluating psychological research data. This means thinking critically about issues such as gender, ethnicity, age, and socioeconomic status. Multicultural topics are featured in special *Diversity* sections throughout the text.

Experiencing Psychology. Featuring interesting topics such as left-handedness, tickling, happiness, and proactive coping, the *Experiencing Psychology* sections focus on how psychology can be applied to everyday life. The goal is to show how psychologists build bridges between research and application. Experiencing psychology is also a recurring theme throughout the text.

Chapter Summary and Review. Every chapter ends with a *Summary and Review.* The summary is organized by section headings, and the review is set up in a study-question format, including a list of key terms.

Use the Supplements

You can further reinforce your learning by making use of a variety of supplements that are designed to enhance the learning experience. These supplements are available from Allyn and Bacon.

Practice Test Booklet. If you want extra help preparing for exams (and who doesn't?), this booklet provides sample tests so that you can practice what you've learned by taking a simulated classroom quiz. The booklet also includes answers and page references to the text.

Allyn and Bacon Interactive Website. The purchase of this new book provides you with an interactive website, as well as a direct connection to Peregrine Publishers' **Psychology Place™** website, which offers Lefton users a variety of exercises to enhance the total learning experience. The interactive website provides access to an abundance of timely and highly interesting material, including further Internet sites, activities, artwork, Building Tables, and bonus chapters, which will be updated and added to continually. The Psychology Place™ includes multiple-choice tests, learning activities, a glossary, video, audio, and links to psychologically relevant Internet sites, as well as a wealth of readings and simulations. This expanded website is available with the purchase of a new book via a PIN code in the front cover of your new text. The address for this website is *www.abacon.com/leftononline.*

One Career in Psychology

My own career in psychology began with a survey of sexual attitudes that I conducted in high school. I passed out questionnaires to the juniors and seniors, who were to respond anonymously. Then I spent days poring over, collating, and summarizing the data—which I, of course, found fascinating.

At Northeastern University in Boston, I majored in psychology and was particularly interested in clinical psychology. I took courses in traditional experimental psychology—learning, physiology, perception—but especially enjoyed abnormal psychology, child development, and personality. While in college, I worked in a treatment center for emotionally disturbed children. The work was hard, emotionally grueling, and stressful, and the pay wasn't particularly good—thus, the direct delivery of mental health services began to lose some of its appeal for me. Later, as a laboratory assistant, I collected and analyzed data for a psychologist doing research in vision. In contrast to my counseling experience, hunting for answers to scientific questions and collecting data were activities that held my interest.

My graduate studies at the University of Rochester included research in perception, and I studied visual information processing. In graduate school, my intellectual skills were sharpened, and my interests were focused and refined. After earning my PhD, I became a faculty member at the University of South Carolina. My research in cognitive psychology involved studying perceptual phenomena such as eye movements. Now at The George Washington University, I teach, do research in cognitive psychology, and write psychology textbooks. My goal is to share my excitement about psychology in the classroom, in my textbooks, and in professional journals.

Over time, my interests have changed, as I'm sure yours will. At first, I was interested in the delivery of mental health services to children. Later, I focused on applied research issues, such as eye movements in learning disabled readers. But my primary focus remains on basic research issues. My evolving interests have spanned the three major areas in which psychologists work: applied research, human services, and experimental psychology—topics I present throughout the text.

I am married to a wonderful woman and have two daughters. I have applied in my family life much of what I have learned in my profession. My family hasn't been angry about it, although from time to time my "psychologizing" about issues can be annoying, I'm sure. I'm an avid bicyclist and computer hacker and occasional photographer. My life has generally revolved around my work and my family—not necessarily in that order. You'll probably gather that from many of the stories and examples I relate in this text.

I invite you to share in my excitement and my enthusiasm for psychology. Stay focused, read closely, and think critically. As you read, think about how the text relates to your own experiences—drawing personal connections to what you read will make it more meaningful. And please feel free to write me: *lefton@gwu.edu.* Good luck!

Preface to the Instructor

This is a new text. It is a new concept in textbooks. But it grows out of my experience—in both teaching and writing—over the last three decades. Seven strategic goals guided my work on *InterActive Psychology Online*. First and foremost, I wanted to write a brief, affordable, *interactive,* web-oriented text. Second, I wanted to keep current with the new directions in psychology, so I wrote many sections of the book to reflect the new explosion of information on neuropsychology, evolutionary psychology, and behavioral genetics. Third, I wanted to stress diversity and sensitivity to culture and gender; I am particularly interested in showing that psychologists must consider the wide range of participants in research. To make reasonable generalizations about human behavior, they must consider ethnic, cultural, age, and gender bias. Fourth, I wanted to show that research is a cornerstone of psychology; this text reflects an emphasis on the role of research in psychology. In emphasizing the importance of research, I especially wanted to focus on critical thinking as a key to good scientific thought and research—my fifth goal. Sixth, I wanted to focus on how applications grow from research and how psychologists build conceptual bridges between research and applications. Last, I wanted to sustain student interest and understanding. To help accomplish this goal, I have used a highly personal voice in my writing and have often shared my own point of view.

Content and Organization

In this new brief book, I have endeavored to focus on clarity and the balance between research and application. I wanted it to be attuned to the needs of students and professors through the year 2004.

To achieve my goals, I enlisted the aid of colleagues, friends, and students who read new drafts. Psychologists read the manuscript with an eye for accuracy, current trends, sensitivity to gender and diversity issues, pedagogy, and general student interest.

The result of all the input is a new book: brief, inexpensive, web-based, and interactive, with an especially clear writing style and a direct and personal approach to student learning.

Content. This new text covers the core concepts of psychology in addition to emerging trends and topics. The materials on the biological bases of behavior, memory, and cognition are especially up to date. In addition, intelligence, development, psychological disorders, treatment, and social psychology have received special scrutiny. The most recent data and theories on neuropsychology, behavioral genetics, and evolutionary psychology are presented. The applied fields are similarly represented, with complete coverage of topics such as child development, gender differences, performance appraisal, and testing issues. The text covers high-interest topics such as therapy, codependence, substance abuse, brain plasticity, and Alzheimer's disease. These topics are presented in an integrated manner, bringing science and application together and showing how they flow directly from traditional psychology. The content of the text reflects the essential current status of psychological science without being trendy or neglecting the classics.

Organization. The content of the text is organized in a logical manner. Every chapter has been written so that it can either stand alone or be read in sequence with others. Also, every chapter has been written to provide a structured approach, with a smooth, cohesive flow of information. The internal structure of each chapter attempts to match the way teachers present material; editors at Allyn and Bacon and I talked with hundreds of psychology teachers to determine the most logical and sought-after structure.

Supplements for Instructors

- The *Instructor's Resource Manual,* written by Fred Whitford of Montana State University, contains a wealth of activities, handouts, and numerous additional teaching aids. It also contains Teaching Tips for integrating the companion website into the classroom.

- Peter Gram of Pensacola Junior College has developed a lengthy test bank, which is also available in computer-ready format (Macintosh, DOS, or Windows). Many of the items have been classroom-tested and validated at Montana State University. Over 2,000 multiple-choice questions are available in the test bank.
- A full set of color acetate transparencies is available to enhance classroom lectures and discussions, along with a supplemental set of 60 newly rendered acetates.
- An interactive video, with onscreen Critical Thinking questions, has been developed to accompany *InterActive Psychology Online;* the video segments illustrate real-life applications of the textbook topics and provide a springboard for initiating classroom discussions.
- The Digital Media Archive Version 2.0 is a CD-ROM that contains hundreds of full-color digitized images, audio, video, and lecture outlines to enhance introductory psychology lectures.
- Allyn and Bacon also makes available to instructors an extensive videotape library. Please see your local Allyn and Bacon sales representative for details regarding the video policy.

Acknowledgments

I owe a debt of gratitude to three constituencies: my students, my colleagues, and my publisher. The students who read this book constitute my most important audience. For nearly three decades, students in my classroom and in classrooms all over the country have read my texts. They have provided criticisms and pointed out areas that needed to be strengthened. I am in their debt. I also thank my colleagues and friends at so many colleges and universities around the country for their advice and guidance. Last, my publisher, Allyn & Bacon, is an educational leader and innovator, and the people I work with there are truly a superb creative team. I especially thank Sandy Kirshner and Bill Barke for their continued confidence in this project and me, and Carolyn Merrill, Executive Editor, whose dedication to creating an innovative and affordable book has resulted in this text. A tireless editor, publisher, and friend, she spent countless hours working on this project, and her vision is reflected throughout the book.

Lester Lefton
The George Washington University

Chapter 1

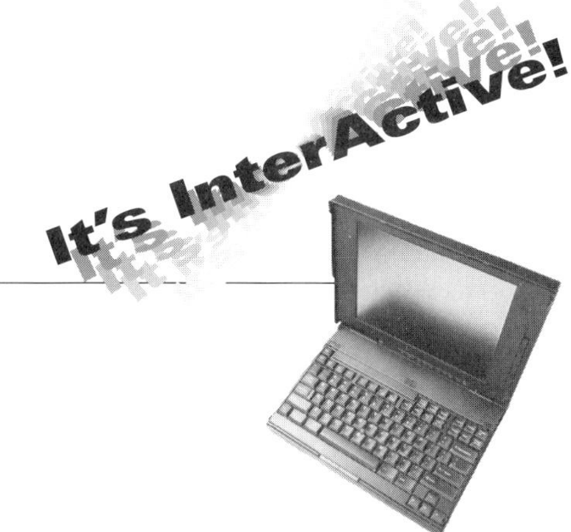

What Is Psychology?

www.abacon.com/leftononline

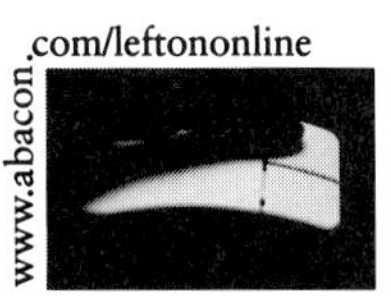

Go to your password-protected Website for full-color art, Weblinks, and more!

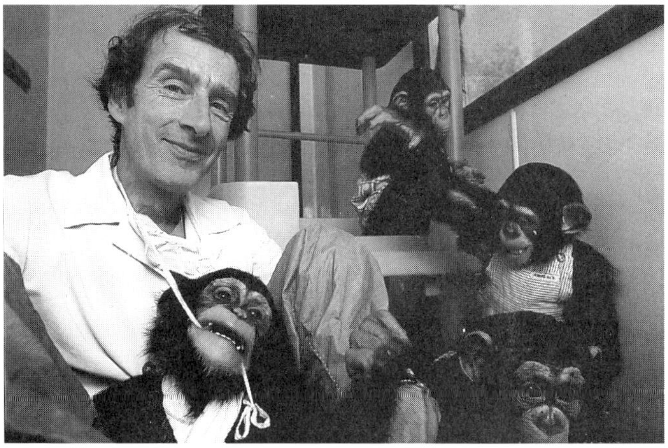

Michael Cooper knew that his girlfriend Janet was on the edge of disaster. “On the edge” is what Michael kept thinking, “on the edge.” Michael and Janet had been friends, then close friends, and now were dating seriously. They had met at their college’s freshman orientation, and the rest, as they say, was history. But Janet’s recent history was perplexing. With each passing month, she seemed more moody. At first, she passed it off as homesickness, later as exam stress, and recently as "sophomore slump." Her ups and downs were making their relationship at times rocky, at other times nearly impossible. Michael never knew what to expect, and he felt he was always walking on eggs. And then, one Saturday evening, Janet attempted suicide.

Michael was an active problem solver, not a passive worrier. He could not control Janet's moods or her actions. But he wanted desperately to gain some insight into her problem so as to offer her what help he could. He sought that insight through the Internet. Michael opened his Web browser, accessed a search engine, and typed in "Psychology." Click. 415,800 "hits," or likely sites with information, appeared. He knew he would have to refine his search, so he typed in "Depression." Click. There were still 94,000 hits. "Suicide." Click. "Behavior." Click. "Lethargy." Click. "Depressive." Click. Fifteen minutes and many leads later, Michael had learned that there was an enormous volume of research on depression, suicide, and therapy for young women. He found that the National Institutes of Health has an extensive site on depression where he learned that each year millions of dollars are spent trying to find its causes and millions more on its treatment. Michael kept returning to one site in particular, which claimed that depression is the psychiatric equivalent of the common cold. And that serious depression nearly always precedes a suicide attempt. The site noted that nearly 23% of all women suffer from serious depression at some time. Michael decided that Janet was becoming a statistic. And he decided that he wasn't going to let that happen. ■

Michael could not cure Janet. But helping Janet realize that she needed professional help was a beginning. Millions of men and women each year seek help for a complex array of emotional disorders and symptoms. You may have a friend or family member who has had a problem, and you may have done an Internet search similar to the one Michael did—or perhaps you browsed in a library or bookstore. If you did, what you found is that there is a whole array of therapeutic techniques, drugs, and combination treatments for such problems—and the good news is that they work.

Psychologists study and try to help people like Janet. Perhaps her story will help you understand why we consider psychology—the science of human behavior and mental processes—so moving, fascinating, and exciting. Before we begin to explore psychology, it is important to carefully define what it is.

I What Is This Science of Psychology?

Focus on issues and ideas

- How psychology assists people in managing their own behavior
- The relationship between your mental processes and your day-to-day behaviors

What exactly is psychology? It is as difficult for me to provide a definition of psychology that includes all its elements as it would be for you to list all the reasons why you might want to study it. We'll begin with a simple definition and gradually expand on it. Broadly defined, **psychology** is the science of behavior and mental processes.

Let's look at the first part of this definition, because it is key to understanding what sets real psychology apart from the pop psychology of talk shows and tabloids. Psychology is a *science.* Because psychology is a science, psychologists use scientific principles, carefully defined methods, and precise procedures to develop an organized body of knowledge and to draw inferences, or make predictions, about how people will behave. Predicting behavior is important, for it enables psychologists to help people anticipate their responses to certain situations and learn how to manage their reactions and express themselves in reasonable ways. For example, because excessive stress can cause anxiety, depression, and even heart attacks, psychologists use theories about stress to devise therapies to help people handle it more effectively.

Now for the second part of the definition: psychology as the science of *behavior and mental processes.* Psychologists observe not only mental processes, but also most other aspects of human functioning—overt actions or behaviors, social relationships, emotional responses, and physiological reactions. In countries other than the United States, especially in former Soviet bloc nations, psychology also embraces paranormal phenomena such as telepathy and clairvoyance.

Mental processes, which most of us consider the main grist for the psychological mill, include thoughts and ideas as well as more complex reasoning processes. *Overt actions* are directly observable and measurable movements or the results of such movements.

Walking, talking, playing, kissing, gesturing, and making facial expressions are examples of overt actions. Results of overt actions include the papers you write, the piles of unsorted laundry in your bedroom, or the body you have kept in shape through regular exercise. *Social relationships* are the behaviors we exhibit in our interactions with other people. We make assumptions about the causes of other people's behaviors; we try to change their attitudes; we avoid them or engage them; we date, marry, and have children with them. *Emotional responses* are basically feelings, such as anger, regret, lust, happiness, and depression. *Physiological reactions*—the body's reactions to stimuli—are closely associated with emotional responses. An increased heart rate when you are excited, biochemical changes in your optic nerves when light stimulates your eyes, and high blood pressure in response to stress are all examples of physiological reactions. All of these phenomena are fair game for psychological scientists.

Psychology is considered a social and behavioral science because it deals with behavior and mental process. In the late 1990s, through their national organization, the American Psychological Association (APA), psychologists launched an initiative to name the years 2000–2010 the "Decade of Behavior." The goal of the initiative is to focus attention on the contributions of the behavioral and social sciences in addressing many of society's daunting challenges—including child abuse and neglect, violence against women, and safety and security in our communities—and on the critical importance of psychology to our nation's health.

Three Principles of Scientific Endeavor

As a science, psychology is committed to objectivity, accuracy, and healthy skepticism about the study of behavior and mental processes. These three basic principles are at the very core of psychology—they are part of what makes it a science. They can also help you be a critical thinker in your day-to-day life.

Objectivity. For psychologists, objectivity means evaluating research and theory on their merits, without preconceived ideas. For example, when scientists challenged the validity and usefulness of lie detector tests to select truthful employees, both believers and skeptics stepped up offering case studies, as well as anecdotal experiences, that supported their own assessments of the usefulness of these tests. Psychologists attempt to bring scientific objectivity to the research arena; they know that anecdotal reports are seldom objective and that though they can explain events after they have happened, they are too limited to support predictions about future behavior or mental processes. Remember, scientists want to both describe *and* predict. Common sense relies heavily on looking backward—using hindsight—but is not very objective or reliable when it comes to making predictions about behavior.

Accuracy. Psychologists are concerned with gathering data from the laboratory and the real world in precise ways—that is, with accuracy. For instance, to conclude from a small number of eyewitness accounts that whole communities have been abducted by aliens falls considerably short of scientific accuracy. Might there be another plausible explanation for the astonishingly similar accounts of small, ghostly figures levitating people into flying-saucer laboratories? Might those reporting such incidents suffer from similar psychological disorders? Rather than relying on limited samples and immediate impressions, psychologists base their thinking on precise, detailed, and thorough study.

Healthy Skepticism. One needn't be a scientific researcher to realize that although life *is* full of incredible events, people's reports of strange phenomena must be taken with a grain of salt. Most people think twice when they hear stories like that of the woman who reported that she was saved from falling off an alpine precipice by an angelic rescuer who suddenly appeared and then disappeared. Intriguing as accounts of alien abductions or angelic rescues may be, psychologists maintain a healthy skepticism: a cautious view of data, hypotheses, and theory until results are repeated, verified, and established over time.

The Scientific Method in Psychology

Like other scientists, psychologists use the scientific method in developing theories that describe, explain, predict, and help manage behavior. The **scientific method** is the technique used in psychology to discover knowledge about human behavior and mental

Psychology: The science of behavior and mental processes.

Scientific method: In psychology, the techniques used to discover knowledge about human behavior and mental processes; in experimentation, the scientific method involves stating the problem, developing hypotheses, designing a study, collecting and analyzing data, replicating results, and drawing conclusions and reporting results.

processes; in experimentation, it involves *stating the problem, developing hypotheses, designing a study, collecting and analyzing data* (which often includes manipulating some part of the environment to better understand conditions that led to a behavior or phenomenon), *replicating results*, and *drawing conclusions and reporting results*.

Let's consider these six basic steps of the scientific method, so that you can have an overview of how psychologists do their work.

Stating the Problem. The question a psychologist asks must be stated in such a way that it can be answered; that is, it must be stated in a way that lends itself to investigation. For instance, if you ask the question "What is the mind?" you will make little headway toward an answer, even with the most rigorous techniques. But a question such as "To what extent is zinc effective in alleviating cold symptoms?" or "Does St. John's wort work better than Prozac in treating depression?" can be investigated with some degree of clarity.

Developing Hypotheses. In the second step of the scientific method, psychologists make an educated guess about the answer to the question they've posed. Such a formulation is called a **hypothesis**—a tentative statement or idea expressing a causal relationship between two events or variables that are to be evaluated in a research study. A hypothesis might be that a specific diet—perhaps one low in refined sugar—is more effective than any other diet in controlling or reducing hyperactive behavior in 10-year-old boys; further, the hypothesis might assert that such a diet will be 10% more effective than another diet or no special diet at all.

Most often, a hypothesis emerges from a theory, which psychologists have developed from their current knowledge and past research. A **theory** is a collection of interrelated ideas and facts put forward to describe, explain, and predict behavior and mental processes. For example, a theory that a diet high in sugar, caffeine, and red dye causes hyperactivity might put together related facts about personality, gender differences, cultural differences, and the demographics of hyperactivity. A theory must organize data well, and it must suggest testable predictions that can be used to check the theory. Such testing usually occurs within the context of a well-designed research study.

Designing a Study. Researchers next have to develop an approach to testing the hypothesis. They identify key variables, responses, and techniques that will help them understand the issue at hand. At the outset, the key elements of the study must be defined. The behaviors to be examined have to be carefully specified, and researchers must determine how they are to be measured, with what instruments, how frequently, and by whom. In children who suffer from hyperactivity, some behaviors are fairly easily specified—for example, concentrating on a task such as solving addition problems. Other behaviors, such as those that might signify anxiety or lack of self-esteem, are more difficult to define precisely—in hyperactive children or in anyone else, for that matter.

Collecting and Analyzing the Data. After researchers have specified the key elements and chosen the participants for an experiment, they conduct the experiment, hoping it will yield interpretable, meaningful results. Techniques for data collection must be carefully chosen so as not to bias the results in favor of one hypothesis or another. The data collected must also be organized, coded, and simplified in a way that allows a reasonable set of conclusions to be drawn. When a researcher has 10,000 observations on 300 participants, something must be done to organize all the information. Statistical techniques are usually called on to help summarize and condense the data. But before researchers organize their data, they often try to ensure that the results of an experiment are repeatable.

Replicating Results. Most psychologists are aware of their all-too-human tendency to bias, or subtly predetermine, the outcomes of their research so that they obtain precisely the results they expected. Thus, before they are willing to state that an experimental outcome is unbiased, researchers generally require that an experiment be repeated and that the results of each repetition be essentially the same. Repeating an experiment, often many times, to verify a result is called *replicating* the experiment. If the results of a replicated experiment are essentially the same as those of the original experiment, a researcher can generally say that the results are reliable and that they are likely to occur again, given the same set of circumstances.

Drawing Conclusions and Reporting Results. After replication, when results are organized and statistics are calculated, researchers try to organize ideas and observations to make predictions about behavior. They begin to draw conclusions about results and relate those conclusions to the data that they have collected. Ultimately, researchers report their results to the scientific community by publishing their study—they report their findings along with their interpretations of what the results mean.

Next, we'll go into the research process in more detail, examining how psychologists go about the process of scientific inquiry.

Think Critically

- You may have read that scientists have hypothesized that estrogen replacement therapy may lessen the likelihood of a woman's developing Alzheimer's disease, a progressive degenerative disorder affecting memory. What questions would you ask, and what issues would you be concerned with, in attempting to test this hypothesis?
- Why do you think replicating a research study is so important to scientists?

The Research Process

Focus on issues and ideas

- The scientific research process and its methods and purpose
- Variables and hypotheses and their relationships to experimentation
- How to avoid pitfalls and setbacks in experimentation
- Developing your critical thinking skills
- Diversity and its relationship to effective research

If you ever have the opportunity to tour a psychologist's laboratory, you should do so. Even better, if you are asked to assist a psychologist in research, say yes. Although psychologists use some of the same techniques as other scientists, they refine these techniques to deal with the uncertainties of human behavior. The typical scientific research process in psychology is systematic and begins with a specific question—the "stating the problem" step of the scientific method. Psychological research usually takes the form of an **experiment**—a procedure in which a researcher systematically manipulates and observes elements of a situation in order to answer a question and, usually, to establish causality. For example, if a researcher wants to determine the relationship between an animal's eating behavior and its weight, the researcher could systematically vary (manipulate) how much the animal ate and then weigh (observe) the animal each day to infer that eating behavior and weight are causally related.

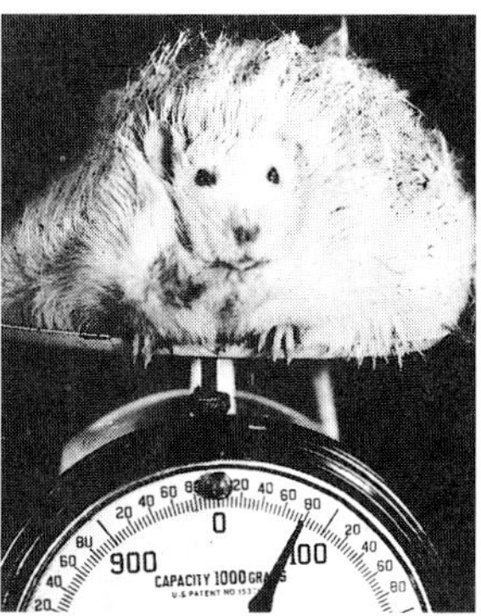

Variables, Hypotheses, and Experimental and Control Groups

Variables. A **variable** is a condition or a characteristic of a situation or a person that is subject to change (varies) either within or across situations or individuals. Researchers manipulate variables in order to measure how changes in them affect other variables. There are two types of variables in any controlled experiment: independent variables and dependent variables. The **independent variable** is the variable that the experimenter directly and purposely manipulates to see how the other variables under study will be affected. The **dependent variable** is the variable that is expected to change because of manipulation of the independent variable. For example, one characteristic of a situation that might change is temperature, and a change in temperature might affect behavior. A researcher might therefore raise the temperature in a room to determine if a person's activity level increases or decreases as a result of the change.

To see how variables come into play, imagine a simple experiment intended to determine the effects of

Hypothesis: A tentative statement or idea expressing a causal relationship between two events or variables that are to be evaluated in a research study.

Theory: In psychology, a collection of interrelated ideas and facts put forward to describe, explain, and predict behavior and mental processes.

Experiment: A procedure in which a researcher systematically manipulates and observes elements of a situation in order to test a hypothesis and make a cause-and-effect statement.

Variable: A condition or characteristic of a situation or a person that is subject to change (varies) within or across situations or individuals.

Independent variable: The variable in a controlled experiment that the experimenter directly and purposely manipulates to see how the other variables under study will be affected.

Dependent variable: The variable in a controlled experiment that is expected to change because of the manipulation of the independent variable.

sleep loss on behavior. The independent (manipulated) variable might be the number of hours college students are allowed to sleep. The dependent variable could be the students' reaction to a stimulus—for example, how quickly they push a button when a light is flashed. The participants in the study might be a large group of college students who normally sleep about 7 hours a night.

Hypotheses. As we saw earlier, a *hypothesis* is a tentative statement or idea expressing a causal relationship between two events or variables that are to be evaluated in a research study. The hypothesis for a sleep experiment might be that students deprived of sleep will react more slowly to a stimulus than will students allowed to sleep their regular 7 hours. Suppose the participants sleep in a laboratory on four successive nights and are tested each morning on a reaction-time task. The participants sleep 7 hours on each of three nights but only 4 hours on the fourth. If the response times after the first three nights are constant and if all other factors are held equal, any observed differences in reaction time on the fourth test (following the night of 4 hours of sleep) can be attributed to the reduced hours of sleep. That is, a change in the independent variable (numbers of hours of sleep) produces a change in the dependent variable (reaction time). If the results show that students deprived of sleep respond on the reaction-time task a half-second slower than they did after a normal amount of sleep, the researcher could feel justified in concluding that sleep deprivation slows down reaction time. The researcher's tentative idea is affirmed by the experiment.

Participant: An individual who takes part in an experiment and whose behavior is observed as part of the data collection process; previously known as a *subject.*

Experimental group: In an experiment, a group of participants to whom a treatment is given.

Control group: In an experiment, the comparison group—the group of participants who are tested on the dependent variable in the same way as those in the experimental group but who do not receive the treatment.

Operational definition: Definition of a variable in terms of the set of methods or procedures used to measure or study that variable.

Sample: A group of participants who are assumed to be representative of the population about which an inference is being made.

Significant difference: In an experiment, a difference that is unlikely to have occurred because of chance alone and is most likely due to the systematic manipulation of variables by the researcher.

Experimental and Control Groups. Researchers must determine whether it is actually the change in the manipulated variable—not some unknown extraneous factor—that causes a change in the dependent variable. One way to do this is to set up at the start of the experiment at least two groups of participants who are identical in important ways. **Participants** are individuals who take part in experiments and whose behavior is observed and recorded. (In previous decades, psychologists called participants *subjects.*) The attributes that participants must have in common depend on what the experimenter is testing. For example, because reflexes slow down as a person grows older, the researcher would want to ensure that the two groups in the reaction-time experiment were composed of participants of the same or nearly the same age.

Once the participants are known to be identical on important attributes, they are assigned randomly to either the experimental or the control group. *Random assignment* means that the participants are assigned by lottery rather than on the basis of any particular characteristic, preference, or situation that might have even a remote possibility of influencing the outcome. The **experimental group** is the group of participants to whom a treatment is given. Some psychologists even refer to the experimental group as the *treatment group.* The **control group** is the comparison group—the group of participants who are tested on the dependent variable in the same way as the experimental group but who do not receive the treatment. In the reaction-time experiment, students who sleep a full 7 hours on all four nights form the control group. Those who are allowed to sleep only 4 hours on the last night form the experimental group. The treatment they receive is being deprived of sleep. (Of course, in other research studies, they might be treated by being allowed to sleep longer than usual, by being given a drug, or perhaps by being trained to use some special sleep techniques.) By comparing the reaction times (the dependent variable) of the experimental and control groups, the researcher can determine whether the independent variable is responsible for any difference in the dependent variable between the groups.

If the researcher is confident that all the participants responded with the same reaction time before the experiment—that is, that the two groups are truly comparable—then he or she can conclude that sleep deprivation is the cause of the experimental group's decreased performance. Unless the researcher uses comparable groups, the effect of the treatment is not clear, and few real conclusions can be drawn from the data.

Of course, extraneous, or irrelevant, variables can also make interpretation difficult. *Extraneous variables* are factors that affect the results of an experiment but that are not of interest to the experimenter. An example of an extraneous variable is a lightning storm that occurs during an experiment in which participants' anxiety levels are being gauged by measuring a physical response such as an increase in skin conductivity. It might be impossible for the researchers to ascertain how much of the increased skin conductivity was due to their experimental treatment of the participants and how much was due to anxiety about lightning. When extraneous variables intrude during an experiment (or just before it), they may *confound results*—make data difficult to interpret.

Operational Definitions, Sample Size, and Significant Differences

Operational Definitions. For research to be successful, it is essential that all terms used in describing the variables and the experimental procedure be given operational definitions. An **operational definition** is a definition of a variable in terms of a set of methods or procedures used to measure or study that variable. For example, a researcher might be interested in the effects of hunger (the independent variable) on exploratory behavior (the dependent variable) in mice. In this case, the concepts *hunger* and *exploratory behavior* must be defined operationally. The researcher might define hunger operationally in terms of the number of hours of food deprivation and define exploratory behavior operationally in terms of the number of times the mice walk more than 2 feet down a path.

Sample Size. Another important factor in an experiment is the size and representativeness of the sample. A **sample** is a group of participants who are assumed to be representative of the population about which an inference is being made. For example, a researcher studying schizophrenia has to put together a sample of people with that disorder. A psychologist who wished to discover whether murderers have low levels of the neurotransmitter serotonin in their brains would have better luck finding a representative sample at a maximum security penitentiary than at a university.

A significant difference is an experimental difference that is statistically unlikely to have occurred because of chance alone and is most likely due to the systematic manipulation of variables by the researcher.

The number of participants in a sample is very important. If an effect is obtained consistently with a large enough number of participants, the researcher can reasonably rule out individual differences and chance as causes. The key assumption is that a large sample better represents the population to which the researcher wishes to generalize the results.

Significant Differences. Researchers want to be sure that the differences they find are significant. For psychologists, a **significant difference** is an experimental difference that is statistically unlikely to have occurred because of chance alone and is most likely due to the systematic manipulation of variables by the researcher. For example, when one therapy technique appears to be more effective than another, the researcher wants to be sure that the results achieved using the first technique are significantly different from the results achieved using the second and that the difference is enough to be important. The results are significantly different only if they could not be due to chance, to the use of only one or two participants, or to the use of a unique set of participants. If experimental results are not statistically significant, they are not considered to have established a finding or confirmed a hypothesis.

Successful Experiments Avoid Pitfalls

Good experiments often involve several experimental groups, each tested under different conditions. Another study of the effects of sleep deprivation might involve a control group and five experimental groups. The participants in each of the experimental groups might be deprived for a different number of hours of sleep (sleep deprivation operationally defined in terms of number of hours of sleep less than participants' normal number). In this way, the researcher could examine the effects on reaction time of several different degrees of sleep deprivation.

Frequently, things turn out just the way a researcher expects. Researchers are aware, however, that their *expectancies* (expectations) about results may influence their findings, particularly where human behavior is concerned. A researcher may unwittingly create a situation that leads to specific prophesied results—a **self-fulfilling prophecy.**

To avoid the risk of the self-fulfilling prophecy, researchers often use a **double-blind technique**—a research technique in which neither the experimenter nor the participants know who is in the control or the experimental group. In this situation, someone who is not connected with the research project keeps track of which participants are assigned to which group. The double-blind technique minimizes the potential effect of a researcher's subtle cues on participants.

Researchers also try to minimize the demand characteristics of their experiments. **Demand characteristics** are elements of an experimental situation that might cause a participant to perceive the situation in a certain way or might tip off a participant as to the purpose of the research and perhaps thereby elicit specific behavior from the participant. Participants who even *think* they know the real purpose of an experiment may try to behave "appropriately" and in so doing may distort the results. Even when a double-blind procedure is used and demand characteristics are minimized, participants often just behave differently when they are in a research study. This finding is known as the **Hawthorne effect.**

Correlation Is Not Causation

Consider this statement: In general, the more education you have, the higher your yearly income. This is a true descriptive statement, but only up to a point. After a person receives a college degree, adding a professional degree is less likely to add significant additional income to the person's yearly take-home pay. It is not accurate to say that each unit of education causes income to rise; rather, education opens new doors for a person and creates opportunities to earn more. At a certain point, another master's degree does little to increase opportunities. In short, more education does not *cause* more yearly income.

Only controlled laboratory experiments permit researchers to take the next step in the scientific method: drawing conclusions. They form theories and develop hypotheses in order to make *cause-and-effect statements*—inferences about the causes of behavior. Here is a key point: *Correlated events are not necessarily causally related.* Two events are *correlated* when the increased presence (or absence) of a particular situation or condition is regularly associated with a high (or low) presence of another situation, or condition. For example, a researcher who finds that children from broken homes have more emotional problems and commit more crimes than other children can state that there is a correlation between home life, emotional health, and criminal behavior. However, the researcher cannot conclude that broken homes *cause* emotional problems or crime. In contrast, events are causally related when one event or situation makes another occur—when one event or situation is contingent on another.

Correlated events are not necessarily causally related.

Before researchers suggest that one situation causes another, they have to be sure that several specific conditions are met. They pay close attention to how the data are collected and to whether the results of a study are repeatable in additional experiments. To make meaningful causal inferences, researchers must create situations in which they can limit the likelihood of obtaining a result that is simply a chance occurrence or due to other irrelevant factors. Only by using carefully formulated experiments can researchers make sound interpretations of their results and cautiously extend them to other situations. Experiments have specific components and requirements, which we'll examine next. And because the research process is so central to psychological inquiry and because it can be applied to your own thinking, it is stressed in the next section.

Thinking Critically and Evaluating Research

Psychologists, like all scientists, are trained to think, to evaluate research critically, and to put their results into a meaningful framework. Psychologists follow a traditional approach to evaluating research. To benefit from this textbook, you might find it helpful to use the same critical thinking skills and framework in order to follow psychologists' logic, to understand their approach, and to evaluate their research.

Critical thinking consists of evaluating evidence, sifting through choices, assessing outcomes, and deciding whether conclusions make sense. When you think critically, you are being open-minded but evaluative. You are not accepting glib generalizations; instead, you are determining the relevance of facts and looking for biases and imbalances, as well as for objectivity and testable, repeatable results. A critical thinker identifies central issues and is careful not to draw cause-and-effect conclusions from correlations. A critical thinker maintains a skeptical and questioning attitude. A critical thinker also has to tolerate some uncertainty and be patient—to accept that all the answers do not come at once.

When you think critically about research, you become a detective sorting through facts. You look objectively at the facts, question the hypotheses and conclusions, avoid oversimplification, and consider all the arguments, objections, and counterarguments. You evaluate all assumptions and assertively seek out conflicting points of view. You revise your opinions when the data and conclusions call for it. Whenever you have to evaluate a research study in this text, in the popular press, or in a psychological publication, you will find it helpful to focus on and ask questions about five research criteria: purpose, methodology, participants, repeatability, and conclusions.

A critical thinker identifies central issues and is careful not to draw cause-and-effect conclusions from correlations.

Purpose. What is the purpose of the research? What is the researcher trying to test, demonstrate, or prove? Has the problem been clearly defined? Is the researcher qualified to conduct this research?

Methodology. Is the methodology—the method of investigation used (for example, a case study, survey, or experiment)—the most appropriate one for the topic? Has the method been properly and carefully executed? Is there a control group? Have variables been carefully (operationally) defined? Has the researcher followed ethical guidelines (a topic considered on pp. 13–15)?

Participants. Was the sample of participants properly chosen and carefully described? How was the sample selected? Does the sample accurately reflect the characteristics of the population of individuals about which the researcher would like to make generalizations? Will any generalizations be possible from this study?

Repeatability. Are the results repeatable? Has the researcher shown the same finding more than once? Have other investigators made similar findings? Are the results clear and unambiguous—that is, not open to criticism because of poor methodology? What additional evidence will be necessary for other researchers to support the conclusions?

Conclusions. How logical are the conclusions of the study, and what are the implications and applications suggested by the study? Do the researcher's data support them? Has the researcher gone beyond the data, drawing conclusions that might fit a predisposed view rather than conclusions that follow logically from the facts? What implications do the data have for psychology as a science and as a profession? Does the research have any implications for you as an individual? Has the researcher considered alternative explanations of the results?

Think again about the sleep deprivation experiment described earlier. Let's use the five criteria to evaluate this research. The participants were college students deprived of sleep and tested on a reaction-time task.

Was the purpose of the study clear? The purpose was to assess the effect of sleep loss on reaction time.

Was the methodology appropriate? The method involved depriving participants of sleep after they had become used to sleeping in a controlled environment; participants were tested each morning. The task was operationally defined.

Was the sample of participants properly chosen? The participants were college students who were in good health. Reasonable generalizations from their reaction times to the reaction times of other people of similar age might be possible.

Are the results repeatable? If the results were obtained with several groups of participants, and if the results were consistent within each of those groups, the repeatability of the results would seem assured.

How logical are the conclusions? Limited conclusions can be drawn from such a research study. There was only one age group—college students. There were no controls on other factors in the students' environment, such as workloads, school pressure, energy expenditures, and history of sleep

Self-fulfilling prophecy: The unwitting creation by a researcher of a situation that unintentionally allows his or her expectancies to influence the participants or the situation.

Double-blind technique: A research technique in which neither the experimenter nor the participants know who is in the control and experimental groups.

Demand characteristics: Elements of an experimental situation that might cause a participant to perceive the situation in a certain way or become aware of the purpose of the study and thus bias the participant to behave in a certain way and in so doing distort results.

Hawthorne effect: The finding that people behave differently (usually better) when they know they are being observed.

loss. A simple conclusion about sleep deprivation can be drawn: In a controlled study of college students, sleep deprivation tends to slow down reaction time. However, not much more can be said, and no generalizations could be applied to, say, children, older adults, or the chronically mentally ill. The results of the study do not contradict common sense, but they add little to an overall or comprehensive understanding of sleep deprivation.

A key to thinking critically about research is to be evaluative, to question all aspects of a study. Think about the advantages as well as the limitations of the research method used. You can also apply your critical thinking skills to nonacademic material. When a TV commercial tells you that 9 out of 10 doctors recommend Brand X, think critically about that claim. What kind of doctors, for what kind of ailment, for patients of what age, and for what extent of usage? As you read this text, evaluate research findings. I will present the research in ways that will allow you to evaluate it critically and draw your own conclusions.

Other Methods of Psychological Inquiry

Experiments, with their focus on cause-and-effect relationships, are not the only way to collect data about human behavior. Techniques that provide descriptive information about behavior and that capture how well one variable predicts another are also important and useful. These techniques include questionnaires, interviews, naturalistic observation, and case studies.

Questionnaires. A **questionnaire**, or *survey*, is usually a printed form with questions that is given to a large number of people. Researchers use questionnaires to gather a large amount of information from many people in a short time. A questionnaire being used to learn the typical characteristics of psychology students might be sent to students enrolled in an introductory psychology course. It might ask each student to provide age, sex, height, weight, previous courses taken, grades in high school, SAT scores, number of brothers and sisters, and parents' financial status. There might also be questions regarding sexual activity, career goals, and personal preferences in TV shows, clothing styles, and music.

One aim of surveys is to discover relationships among variables. For example, a questionnaire designed to assess aggressiveness might ask respondents to indicate their gender, the number of physical fights they have had in the past year, how often they feel angry, and the sports they enjoy. The researcher who is analyzing the results might check to see whether men's and women's answers suggest gender differences in aggressive behavior.

The strength of the questionnaire is that it gathers a large amount of information in a short time. Its weaknesses are that it is impersonal, it gathers only the information asked by the questions, it limits the participants' range of responses, it cannot prevent respondents from leaving some questions unanswered or from being untruthful in their responses, and it does not provide a structure that allows a researcher to infer cause-and-effect relationships (although correlations may be found).

Interviews. An **interview** is typically a face-to-face meeting in which a researcher (interviewer) asks an individual a series of standardized questions. The interviewer usually tape-records or writes down the participant's responses. The advantage an interview has over a questionnaire is that it allows a wider range of responses. An interviewer who notes an exaggerated response, for example, might ask related questions to explore more fully an area that seems important to the participant. The interview technique is time-consuming, however, and, as with questionnaires, no cause-and-effect relationships can be inferred from data gathered through interviews.

Naturalistic Observation. A seemingly simple way to find out about behavior is to observe it. As was mentioned earlier, however, people who are told they are going to be observed tend to become self-conscious and to alter their natural behavior. Therefore, psychologists often use the technique of **naturalistic observation**—careful and objective observation of events from a distance, without observer intervention. The intent is to see how people or animals behave in their natural settings.

Questionnaire: A printed form with questions, usually given to a large group of people, allowing researchers to gather a substantial amount of data in a short time; also known as a *survey.*

Interview: A face-to-face meeting in which a series of standardized questions are used to gather detailed information.

Naturalistic observation: Careful and objective observation of events from a distance, without observer intervention.

Case study: A method of interviewing participants to gain information about their backgrounds, including data on such factors as childhood, family, education, and social and sexual interactions.

The strength of naturalistic observation is that the data collected are largely uncontaminated by the researcher's presence or by a laboratory setting. A major weakness is that the behavior the researcher wishes to examine might not be exhibited. For example, sometimes groups of people do not act persuasively or become aggressive; sometimes animals do not show mating behavior. Naturalistic observation is also very time-consuming.

Naturalistic observers take their data where and how they find them. They cannot manipulate the environment, because that might alter the behavior they are observing. Because variables cannot be manipulated, data from naturalistic observation, like those from questionnaires and interviews, are descriptive and do not permit cause-and-effect conclusions.

Case Studies. The case study is a method of interviewing participants to gain information about their background, including data on such factors as childhood, family, education, and social and sexual interactions. The information included in a case study describes in detail a specific person's responses to the world; a case study is often used to determine a potential method of treatment.

The strength of the case study is that the information it provides is extensive, for one individual. A weakness is that the information describes only one person's particular situation. Because the behavior of one individual may be like that of others or may be unique, researchers cannot generalize from a single case study to an entire population. They must be cautious even when generalizing from a number of case studies.

Table 1.1 summarizes the major approaches to data collection.

Avoiding Gender, Ethnic, and Cultural Bias

To do effective research, to draw meaningful conclusions, and to make generalizations that may be wide-ranging, researchers must recognize the existence and effects of diversity, even within a single society, such as that of the United States. Psychologists say that a community, organization, or nation is culturally diverse if its inhabitants exhibit differences in race, ethnicity, language, nationality, age, and religion. Each subgroup in such a society develops its own style of living, which may vary considerably from that of the majority culture and which may lead to marked differences in day-to-day behavior and in mental health.

Race and Ethnicity. *Race* refers to a person's ancestry and descent and to a heritable set of traits; race is genetically determined and is a variable that is less interesting to psychologists than ethnicity. *Ethnicity* refers to people's common traits, background, and allegiances, which are often culture-, religion-, or language-based; ethnicity is learned from family, friends, and experiences. Families of Asian American descent, for example, bring to the American experience a wealth of different worldviews and different ways of bringing up children, based on their particular heritages (Korean, Chinese, Japanese, or Vietnamese). Like most things that involve large populations of individuals, ethnic groups show enormous differences. Cultural values and ideas within a group differ, each person's subjective sense of being in a group differs, and the experience of being a minority individual has different qualities—for example, powerlessness and

Table 1.1 Five Approaches to Collecting Data

Approach	Strengths	Weaknesses
Experiment	Manipulation of variables to control outside influences; best method for identifying causal relationships	Laboratory environment is artificial; limited generalizability of findings; manipulation of some variables is unethical or impractical.
Questionnaire	Effective means of measuring actions, attitudes, opinions, preferences, and intentions of large numbers of people	Lack of explanatory power; validity of findings is limited by sample; reliability is difficult to determine; self-report may be inaccurate or biased.
Interview	Allows a wide range of responses; follow-up questions are possible	Does not enable researchers to draw conclusions about causal relationships; time-consuming
Naturalistic observation	Behavior is unaffected by a researcher's manipulations.	Little opportunity to control variables; time-consuming
Case study	Extensive evidence is gathered on a single person.	Lack of generalizability of findings; time-consuming

discrimination for some individuals or pride and uniqueness for others (Phinney, 1996).

Culture. Culture reflects a person's racial and ethnic background, religious and social values, artistic and musical tastes, and scholarly interests. Culture is the unwritten social and psychological rulebook that each of us has learned and uses to interpret ourselves and others (Landrine, Klonoff, & Brown-Collins, 1992). Various cultural factors shape behavior, values, and even mental health. One such factor that must be considered is the difference between individualist and collectivist cultures. Individualist cultures (like that of the United States) stress personal rather than group goals and value individual freedom and autonomy; collectivist cultures (like those in many Asian countries) stress group needs over individual ones and value a tightly knit social fabric and a willingness to go along with the group. Of course, it is important to remember that no society is entirely made up of people who adhere rigidly to a single set of cultural values. Most societies have a wide range of cultural values within their population; furthermore, in today's world of global travel and communications, many societies are sharing values, ideas, and traditions. It is easy, for example, to see how Western values and ideas have permeated Japan. Cultural values within a population are strong, but not homogeneous (Hermans & Kempen, 1998).

In the end, research on culture and its differences will help people understand both their differences *and* their commonalities. The ultimate goal is to eliminate the need for cross-cultural research because psychology will have taken into account the effects of culture—and not just North American or Northern European culture—on human behavior (Segall, Lonner, & Berry, 1998).

Class. Closely tied to culture is a person's class. Although the U.S. class structure is not as rigid as it was in the last century or as those are in some non-Western countries, and although class distinctions are somewhat fuzzy in the United States, Americans do fall into several socioeconomic classes. Among these classes are the economically poor, the disadvantaged, the educated, and the middle class. People in different socioeconomic classes (which include individuals of different races and cultures) may view the world differently and behave differently primarily because of their class.

Gender. Psychologists know that because of both biological factors and learned behaviors, women often react differently than men do in the same situations. This fact makes it easy to see that the gender of the sample in a research study is crucial (Denmark, 1994). For example, some research on morality shows that, in general, women see moral situations differently than men do. Also, research on brain functions shows differences in brain structure between men and women; research on communication styles, aggression, and love shows sharp differences between men and women. Further, more than half of the people seen by mental health practitioners are women—although this may be because men with mental health problems are less likely to seek therapy. These differences must be explored to find their causes.

Exceptionality and Age. The exceptional and the elderly are two other groups that shape research results in distinctive ways. The exceptional include individuals diagnosed as having mental retardation, learning disabilities, or physical disabilities. They often require special sensitivity on the part of psychologists. The elderly comprise a growing percentage of the general population. More than 30 million Americans are 65 or older, and the aging of the baby boomers means that that number will continue to rise.

Diversity Within versus Between Groups. The differing perspectives on day-to-day behavior held by diverse groups in a society have not always been appreciated, understood, or even recognized in psychological research or theory. For example, psychologists now take Freud to task for developing a personality theory that is seen as clearly sexist. (We will be evaluating Freud's theory in Chapter 10.) In Freud's day, however, the concept of sexism was unheard of. Further, ethnic minorities and special groups such as the exceptional and the elderly were rarely—if ever—included in psychological research studies intended to represent the general population.

Today, psychologists seek to study all types of individuals and groups to make valid conclusions based on scientific evidence. They see cultural diversity as an asset for both theorists and practitioners; they also recognize that they must research, learn about, and theorize about this diversity to help individuals optimize their potential (Hall, 1997). It is crucial to realize, though, that *there are usually more differences within a group than between groups.* For example, intelligence test scores differ more among Asian Americans than they do between Asian Americans and any other ethnic group (Zuckerman, 1990).

. . . there are usually more differences within a group than between groups.

Individual circumstances exist, and people's unique experiences make glib generalizations impossible. Individuals—even those who are members of special populations—often behave just as the general population does, but perhaps with a slight twist or variation. Here is the key point to remember as you read this book: Although people are very much alike and share many common, even universal, experiences and behaviors, every individual is unique; each person's behavior reflects his or her distinctive life experiences. (I)

(I) Ethics in Psychological Research

Focus on issues and ideas

- Animal and human experimentation in research
- The purpose and necessity of deception in psychological research

Some psychologists study behavior by first observing it in animals and then generalizing the principles to human behavior. Research with both animals and human beings is extensive, and all of it must be governed by ethical considerations. **Ethics** in research comprises the rules concerning proper and acceptable conduct that investigators use to guide their research; these rules govern the treatment of animals, the rights of human beings, and the responsibilities of investigators.

Research with Animals

Almost everyone has heard about white rats and pigeons being used in psychology labs. Using animals in research studies allows experimenters to isolate simple aspects of behavior and to eliminate the complex distractions and variables that arise in studies involving human beings. The use of animals also enables researchers to conduct studies that could not ethically be done with human beings.

Some people object to the use of animals in research, but for some areas of study there are no realistic alternatives. For example, experiments on laboratory rats reveal much about the addictive properties of cocaine and its adverse effects on behavior. Similar experiments with human beings would be unethical. In addition, for many diseases, such as multiple sclerosis and Alzheimer's disease, animal research and experimentation have brought almost daily breakthroughs and raised legitimate hopes for a cure. Most researchers are aware and sensitive to the needs of animals (Plous, 1996); furthermore, the American Psychological Association (APA) has strict ethical guidelines on the humane and sensitive care and treatment of animals used in research.

Human Participants

Although animal research is an important part of the psychological landscape, psychologists more often work with human participants. Researchers study many of the same processes in humans that they study in animals, as well as designing experiments specifically for human participants. The APA (1992) also has strict ethical guidelines for research with human participants: Participants cannot be coerced to do things that are physically harmful to them, that would have other negative effects, or that would violate standards of decency. The investigator is responsible for ensuring the ethical treatment of the participants in a research study; the participants are free to decline to participate or to withdraw at any time without penalty. In addition, any information gained in an experimental situation is considered strictly confidential. Before a study begins, participants must also give the researcher their **informed consent**—their agreement to

Ethics: Rules of proper and acceptable conduct that investigators use to guide psychological research; these rules concern the treatment of animals, the rights of human beings, and the responsibilities of investigators.

Informed consent: The agreement of participants to take part in an experiment and their acknowledgment, expressed through their signature on a document, that they understand the nature of their participation in upcoming research and have been fully informed about the general nature of the research, its goals, and its methods.

EXPERIENCING PSYCHOLOGY

Using Psychological Knowledge to Improve Performance

Psychology might seem to be just another academic subject, a set of theories and concepts to be learned in order to pass an exam and complete a course requirement. Not so. Psychology can be applied to everyday life in an endless variety of ways, as you'll see throughout this book. Let's look at just one example.

Did you take piano or violin or flute lessons as a child? Do you remember those dreaded days when you and your teacher's other students had to perform in recitals? I do. I remember when I had memorized a piece, knew it backwards and forwards, and had played it over and over again. But when it was my turn to play, it was as if I had never seen a piano before. I froze, staring at the keyboard. My teacher got out the music and placed it in front of me, but I had no idea what the notes meant. Somehow I eventually managed to stumble through the performance, all the while saying to myself, "But I know this piece! Why can't I play it?"

We see the same phenomenon on television during the Olympics. A high jumper who holds the world record suddenly becomes nervous and can't clear the bar even when it's set low. Or, in the middle of her program, a figure skater who has been doing triple toe loops perfectly in practice tumbles onto the ice while performing in front of judges.

How can psychological knowledge help in such situations? These kinds of episodes stem from a phenomenon called *performance anxiety,* and they can be avoided, or at least alleviated, by applying a little knowledge of psychological processes. In fact, many top athletes are assisted by sport psychologists, who help athletes maintain their focus and avoid becoming too emotionally involved in their performance. The athlete can then concentrate on the specific actions necessary, while still enjoying the experience of competing. The same principles can be applied to other types of performances, including piano recitals and public speaking.

People need to separate the judgmental part of the personality from the part that's doing the performing. The best performances occur when an athlete or musician isn't thinking about the performance—not giving the body a lot of instructions, not telling it to correct mistakes, not evaluating the action in any way. Instead, good performances occur when the performer is in a state of effortless concentration. It's a matter of not trying too hard but simply focusing on the action itself. As W. Timothy Gallwey notes in *The Inner Game of Tennis,* tennis players are most likely to hit the ball well when they focus on the seams of the ball, rather than giving themselves mental instructions such as "Now be sure to follow through or you'll hit the ball into the net." Musicians can achieve the same type of concentration by focusing on the measure being played, rather than saying to themselves, "I've got to be careful to hit all the sixteenth notes in that tough section coming up next."

Eloise Ristad, in her book *A Soprano on Her Head,* is applying psychology when she notes: "We all have inner judges who yammer at the edge of our consciousness. . . . Once we drop our preoccupation with the 'right way,' improvising freely with movement or music can provide us with a metaphor for improvising in our lives."

Psychologists and science writers like Ristad offer advice based on well-known psychological concepts that you'll encounter throughout this book. An understanding of the processes of learning and thinking (Chapters 5 and 6) can be helpful in developing ways to mute your judgmental side and allow your natural abilities to come through. Knowledge of the principles of motivation and emotion (Chapter 8) can also be helpful.

You use psychological principles all the time, and, in truth, all of human behavior is part of psychology—the subject of this book. You will see that the many subfields of psychology that affect individual performance are related. The way we as individuals can improve our performances—indeed, improve our lives—is by understanding basic psychological processes. ■

take part in the experiment and their acknowledgment, through a signature on a document, that they understand the nature of their participation in the research and have been fully informed about the general nature of the research, its goals, and its methods. At the end of the project, the participants must go through debriefing. **Debriefing** is a procedure that informs participants about the true nature of an experiment, including hypotheses, methods, and expected or potential results. Debriefing is done *after* the experiment so that the validity of the responses is not affected by participants' knowledge of the experiment's purpose.

Deception in Psychological Research

Is it ever acceptable for researchers to deceive human participants in psychological studies? Imagine a situation in which a researcher tricks a person into believing that she is causing another person pain. Is this acceptable? Or is it acceptable for a researcher to try to change a participant's views of social or political issues? The answer to these questions is generally no. Researchers must not use deception unless the study has overriding scientific, educational, or practical value. And even then, two key procedures must be followed: obtaining informed consent and providing debriefing.

Some psychologists believe deception is unacceptable under *any* circumstances. They assert that it undermines the public's belief in the integrity of scientists and that its costs outweigh its potential benefits. Most psychologists do not conduct research that involves deception; those who do are especially careful to use informed consent and extensive debriefing to minimize potentially harmful effects. Whenever deception must be used to achieve some legitimate scientific goal, psychologists go to extraordinary lengths to protect the well-being, rights, and dignity of the participants; anything less is considered a violation of APA guidelines (Fisher & Fyrberg, 1994).

You may be wondering what psychology can do for you in your daily life. *Experiencing Psychology* looks at one answer to this question. You might also be curious about the people who work in the field of psychology. Who are these people handing out questionnaires and depriving students of sleep? Next, we'll examine who psychologists are and what they do on a day-by-day basis. (I)

Think Critically

- Imagine a research study testing the effects of a low dosage of a drug that helps relieve anxiety. The participants are 50 men who suffer from job-related stress. What are the limitations of such a study? Would you say that such a study is poorly designed, or that it has a flawed methodology?
- Why do you think sample size is so important in psychological research?
- As psychologists increasingly consider themselves to be biomedical researchers, what kind of special training in ethics do you think they need?

(I) Who Are These People We Call Psychologists?

Focus on issues and ideas

- The differences among the many specialties within psychology

Psychologists are professionals who study behavior and use behavioral principles in scientific research or in applied settings. Most psychologists have advanced degrees, usually a PhD (doctor of philosophy). Many psychologists also train for an additional year or two in a specialized area such as mental health, physiology, or child development.

Founded in 1892, the American Psychological Association (APA) is the oldest and largest professional organization for psychologists. Its purpose is to advance psychology as a science, a profession, and a means of promoting human welfare. The APA is not the sole voice of psychology. Many specialty groups have emerged over the years. In 1989, the American Psychological Society (APS) was founded; it has a large membership of psychologists with academic interests and focuses on scientific research rather than on practice or applied interests. Two of its goals are to preserve the scientific base of psychology and to promote public understanding of psychology as a science.

People are often unsure about the differences among clinical psychologists, psychiatrists, and psychoanalysts. All are mental health practitioners who help people with serious emotional and behavioral problems, but each takes a different perspective. **Clinical psychologists** usually have a PhD in psychology and view behavior and emotions from a psychological perspective. In contrast, **psychiatrists** are physicians

Debriefing: A procedure to inform participants about the true nature of an experiment after its completion.

Psychologist: Professional who studies behavior and uses behavioral principles in scientific research or in applied settings.

Clinical psychologist: Mental health practitioner who views behavior and mental processes from a psychological perspective and who treats persons with serious emotional or behavioral problems or conducts research into the causes of behavior.

Psychiatrist: Physician (medical doctor) specializing in the treatment of patients with mental or emotional disorders.

DIVERSITY

Women and Ethnic Minorities Are Hidden No Longer

A helping profession with deep scientific roots, psychology is attracting increasing numbers of women and members of ethnic minorities. For example, women earn 73% of bachelor's degrees in psychology, and the number of women in graduate training programs has doubled since the mid-1970s (two out of three graduate students in psychology are women). Also, about 27% of full-time faculty are women (Kohout, Wicherski, & Cooney, 1992), and about 50% of new faculty appointments are women (APA, 1995). Proportionately more women than men are entering psychology; they are more likely than men to enter clinical practice than research fields; and women are more likely than men to be employed on a part-time basis (Pion et al., 1996).

The first women psychologists received training similar to that of their male colleagues but were much less likely to achieve equivalent professional status. Today, however, research by women is at the forefront of scientific inquiry. Among important female researchers are Judith Wallerstein and Mavis Hetherington, who have studied the impact of divorce on children; Judith Rodin, who has done important work on eating and eating disorders; Elizabeth Loftus, who has studied the ability of eyewitnesses to remember accurately; and Sandra Scarr, who studies intelligence. Women are presidents of national, regional, and local psychological organizations, and their thoughts and work are prominent in psychological journals.

Individuals from ethnic minorities comprise 28% of the membership of the American Psychological Association (APA, 1995). African Americans and Hispanic Americans each year receive about 3% of the new PhDs in psychology and have consistently done so for at least a decade. Many early African American psychologists faced harsh discrimination against members of an ethnic minority. Still, they overcame the odds; they received PhDs, published scientific research, and made lasting contributions to the discipline.

Gilbert Haven Jones was the first African American holder of a PhD to teach psychology in the

(medical doctors) who have chosen to specialize in the treatment of mental or emotional disorders. Patients who see psychiatrists often have both physical and emotional problems. As physicians, psychiatrists can prescribe drugs and can admit patients for hospitalization. In 1995, the APA voted to pursue the development of curricula that would prepare psychologists to prescribe drugs.

Clinical psychologists generally have more extensive training than psychiatrists do in research, assessment, and psychological treatment of emotional problems. Their nonmedical perspective gives them different roles from psychiatrists in hospital settings and encourages them to examine social and interpersonal variables more than psychiatrists do. Psychiatrists are physicians and thus use a medical approach, which often involves making assumptions about behavior—for example, that abnormal behavior is diseaselike in nature—that psychologists do not make. Clinical psychologists and psychiatrists often see a similar mix of clients and often work together as part of a mental health team. Most clinical psychologists and psychiatrists support collaborative efforts. However, friendly rivalry often arises from their different points of view.

Psychoanalysts are usually psychiatrists (physicians who are able to prescribe medications); they have training in the technique of psychoanalysis and use it in treating people with mental or emotional problems. As you'll see, psychoanalysis was originated by Sigmund Freud and includes the analysis of unconscious motivations and dreams. In strict Freudian psychoanalysis, a course of daily therapy sessions is required; the patient's treatment may last several years. In the past, psychoanalysts had to be physicians. In 1988, however, psychoanalytic institutes began to accept nonphysicians into their training programs.

Psychoanalyst: Psychiatrist or, occasionally, nonmedical practitioner who has studied the technique of psychoanalysis and uses it in treating people with mental or emotional problems.

United States. Albert S. Beckham was a clinician who published studies in the 1930s of socioeconomic status and adolescence among ethnic minority groups. Inez Prosser and Howard H. Long are also among the distinguished African American psychologists who published in the 1930s. Francis C. Sumner, who chaired the psychology department at Howard University, is considered the father of African American psychology. Kenneth Clark, former president of the APA (shown in the photo), achieved national prominence for his work on the harmful effects of segregation. The works of Mamie Phipps Clark on self-esteem and racial identification (with her husband, Kenneth Clark) have become classics.

There is less documentation of the role of Hispanic Americans in the history of psychology. We do know that prominent Hispanic American psychologists have focused on a variety of psychological issues. Manuel Barrera has done important work in community psychology, especially on social support systems. R. Diaz-Guerrero has examined cultural and personality variables in Hispanic Americans. Jorge Sanchez conducted exemplary research on the role of education in the achievements of members of different ethnic minority groups and on biased test scores and intelligence testing. Psychologist Clarissa Pinkola Estés became the first Mexican American author to make the *New York Times* best-seller list with her book *Women Who Run With the Wolves: Myths and Stories of the Wild Woman Archetype.*

Understanding and embracing rather than avoiding the range of people's abilities strengthens psychology. Research and theory become more complete when the multicultural nature of human beings is explored. On a practical level, the effectiveness of the helping professions is enhanced when practitioners understand their clients. The variety of psychologists' research interests and their wide-ranging socioeconomic and ethnic backgrounds are contributing to a greater recognition of diversity among people—and this diversity is a strength that today's psychologists not only recognize but celebrate. ■

As you may have gathered from the above descriptions, the three kinds of practitioners may treat similar clients. However, their training and assumptions may vary, and this variation may be reflected in their choice of treatment.

Choosing Psychology as a Career

Focus on issues and ideas

- The diversity of jobs in the practice of psychology
- The intellectual challenge of psychology as a field of endeavor

Psychology attracts many college students who like the idea of understanding human behavior and helping others. The causes and implications of behavior intrigue these students; they realize that psychology is part of the fabric of daily life. After business administration, psychology is the second most popular undergraduate major—every year, about 70,000 college graduates have majored in psychology. Today's psychology students are increasingly female, ethnically diverse, and interested in subfields such as health psychology, child psychology, and social psychology. And there is good news for students who go on to graduate school: Almost all of the approximately 3,600 recipients of PhDs in psychology each year find jobs related to their training. There are more than 120,000 psychologists in the United States. If you are considering the field of psychology, you'll be glad to hear that unemployment among psychologists is low. Most experts agree that employment opportunities will continue to be good; psychology is often cited as one of the top 10 growth areas for jobs. Furthermore, compensation for most psychologists is good.

Training, of course, is the key to employment. A psychologist who (1) obtains a PhD in clinical psychology from an accredited university, (2) does an internship in a state hospital, and (3) becomes licensed will have a wide variety of job opportunities in both the private and public sectors. Individuals with a master's degree, such as an MSW (master of social work), can function in a variety of settings, and even those with only a bachelor's degree can play an important role in delivering psychological services. Salaries, responsibilities, and working conditions tend to be commensurate with level of training in the discipline. In this era of managed care, psychologists with PhDs are increasingly filling supervisory roles in the delivery of mental health services (Humphreys, 1996).

About 63% of the members of the APA who work in the field of psychology deliver human services. About 42% are clinical psychologists who work in clinics, community mental health centers, health maintenance organizations, veterans' hospitals, public hospitals, and public and private mental health hospitals. The remainder are private practitioners who maintain offices and work in schools, universities, businesses, and numerous other public and private settings (APA, 1995).

Psychologists with doctoral degrees provide more than 50 million hours of service annually to 4 to 10 million people in the United States (Howard et al., 1986). Most psychologists employed by hospitals spend their time in the direct delivery of human services, including individual and group therapy. Business, government, and industry employ about 4% of the working psychologists. About 30% of the APA's members are employed by universities, nearly half of them in psychology departments. University psychologists spend most of their time researching and teaching.

Diversity looks at the current prevalence of women and members of ethnic minorities in the ranks of psychology's practitioners. (I)

(I) Applied Research, Human Services Psychology, and Experimental Psychology

Focus on issues and ideas

- The many community roles of applied psychologists
- The techniques used by experimental psychologists

Applied research, human services psychology, and experimental psychology have much in common. Actually, human services is a subfield of applied research, but it employs such a large proportion of psychologists that it is generally viewed as a separate field. All psychologists consider research and theory to be the cornerstones of their approach (Beutler et al., 1995). A human services provider may also do research, and a researcher who works in a university may also provide human services to people at the university or in the community at large. For example, a human services psychologist may help an alcoholic client by applying learning principles discovered in an experimental laboratory. Similarly, problems discovered by therapists challenge researchers to investigate causes in the laboratory. This cross-fertilization is stimulating. Let's look at each of these areas.

Applied Research. Applied psychologists conduct research and then use their findings to solve practical problems. Many use psychological principles in businesses, government, and institutions such as hospitals.

Engineering psychologists (sometimes called *human factors psychologists*) use psychological principles to help people design machines that are safe and efficient (for example, an easy-to-use ATM machine).

Educational psychologists focus on such topics as how learning occurs in the classroom, how intelligence affects performance, and the relationship between personality and learning.

Forensic psychologists deal with legal issues, often working in courts and correctional systems. They treat prison inmates and evaluate whether individuals are ready for parole, whether a rehabilitation program is achieving its goals, and whether a person accused of a crime has lied, has grounds for an "insanity defense," or is likely to give false testimony.

Health psychologists determine how lifestyle changes can improve health. They devise techniques for helping people avoid medical and psychological problems. We will discuss this field further in Chapter 12.

Behavioral medicine psychologists help people who suffer from chronic physical problems such as back problems and migraine headaches learn to cope and to develop pain management techniques.

Sport psychologists work in an emerging field that focuses on brain–behavior interactions, the role of sports in healthful lifestyles, and the motivation and preparation of athletes.

Industrial/organizational psychologists help employers evaluate employees; they also focus on personnel selection, employee motivation and training, work behavior, incentives, and work appraisals. They apply psychological research and theory to organizational problems such as low productivity, high turnover, and absenteeism, and negative management–labor relations. Working in human resources offices and in other departments at universities and businesses, they also evaluate organizational programs.

Human Services Psychology. Many human services psychologists use behavioral principles to teach people to cope with life more effectively. They try to help people solve problems and to promote well-being. Within the human services area are the subfields of clinical, counseling, community, and school psychology.

Clinical psychologists help clients with behavioral or emotional problems such as shyness, depression, inappropriate expressions of anger, and marital discord. They work in private practices or at hospitals, mental institutions, or social service agencies. They administer psychological tests, interview potential clients, and use psychological methods to treat clients' problems. Many universities employ psychologists to help students and staff handle the pressures of academic life.

Surprisingly, the practice of clinical psychology is a relatively recent development. It resulted from the work of Lightner Witmer (1867–1956), a charter member of the APA, who called for the establishment of a field within psychology that would focus on helping people (McReynolds, 1996). Witmer established the first psychological clinic, at the University of Pennsylvania, and coined the term *clinical psychologist.* The field of clinical psychology grew especially rapidly after World War II, when its training began to focus on professional practice and human services needs (Resnick, 1997).

Counseling psychologists, like clinical psychologists, work with people who have behavioral or emotional problems. They also help people handle career planning and marriage, family, or parenting problems. Counseling psychology began in the 1940s; at first, the problems clients presented to counseling psychologists were less serious than those clients presented to clinical psychologists. However, since the 1980s, the problems of layoffs, spousal abuse, and violence have become more serious, and counseling psychologists have increasingly used psychotherapy and other therapies that were previously used exclusively by clinical psychologists. According to many practitioners and researchers, counseling and clinical psychology are converging.

Counseling psychologists often work for public agencies such as mental health centers, hospitals, and universities. Many work in college or university counseling centers, where they help students adjust to the academic atmosphere and provide them with vocational and educational guidance. Like clinical psychologists, counseling psychologists may research the causes and treatment of maladjustment.

Community psychologists strengthen existing social support networks and stimulate the formation of new networks to meet a variety of challenges (Gonzales et al., 1983). Their goal is to help neighborhoods or communities to grow, plan for the future, and prevent problems from developing. Community psychology emerged in response to the widespread desire for an action-oriented approach to individual and social adjustment, and one of its key elements is community involvement to effect social change. For example, community psychologists have been instrumental in organizing social support groups that help AIDS patients and their families handle the stress and loss of self-esteem produced by this catastrophic illness. Community psychologists work in mental health agencies, state governments, and private organizations.

School psychologists help students, teachers, parents, and administrators to communicate effectively with one another and accomplish mutually agreed-on goals. School psychology began in 1896 at the University of Pennsylvania in a clinic founded to study and treat children considered "morally or mentally defective." Early leaders such as G. Stanley Hall and Lightner Witmer were crucial in promoting psychological interventions and techniques in schools (T. K. Fagan, 1992).

There are more than 30,000 school psychologists, most of whom work in public educational systems. They administer and interpret tests, help teachers with classroom-related problems, and influence school policies and procedures (Bardon, 1983). They foster communication among parents, teachers, administrators, and other psychologists. They also provide information to teachers and parents about students' progress and advise them on how to help students achieve more.

Experimental Psychology. Experimental psychologists try to identify and understand the basic elements of behavior and mental processes. Theirs is an approach, not a specific field. That is, experimental psychologists use a set of *techniques*; experimental psychology does not define the topics they examine. Experimental psychologists focus on basic research issues—in contrast to applied psychologists, who generally use methods perfected through experimentation or based on theories evolved through experimentation to improve a specific situation, help a mental health practitioner, or work with an employer.

Experimental psychology covers many areas of interest, some of which overlap with fields outside psychology. Experimental psychologists may do research on, for example, visual perception, how people learn language or solve problems, or how hormones influence behavior. *Physiological psychologists* (sometimes called *neuropsychologists*) try to understand the relationship between the brain and behavior. They may study the effects of drugs, hormones, and even brain transplants. We will examine some of their explorations in Chapter 2. *Cognitive psychologists* focus on thought processes, especially the relationships among learning, memory, and perception. They may, for example, examine how organisms process and interpret information on the basis of some internal representation in memory. We will discuss this field further in Chapter 6. *Developmental psychologists* focus on the emotional, physical, and intellectual changes that take place throughout people's lives. We will return to this field in Chapter 9. *Social psychologists* study how other people affect an individual's behavior and thoughts and how people interact with one another. For example, they may examine attitude formation, aggressive versus helping behavior, or the formation of intimate relationships. We will discuss this field in Chapter 11. (I)

Think Critically

- Which kinds of practitioners do you think would be best suited to work with Janet, whose story opened this chapter?
- If you were to seek help for marital conflict, what would be the key reason for choosing a psychologist rather than a psychiatrist?

(I) How Have Schools of Psychological Thought Developed?

Focus on issues and ideas

- The evolution and development of both the early and more modern schools of psychological thought
- The special influence of cognitive and biological schools of thought in contemporary psychology
- How applied psychology ties day-to-day behavior and mental processes together

Psychology would not have been recognized as a discipline and a science 200 years ago. The psychological study of human behavior has evolved over a relatively brief time span, beginning a little more than a century ago. Over that period, psychologists have subscribed to many different perspectives. Once fully developed, such a perspective serves to orient researchers and provide them with a frame of reference in which to do new work. A specific perspective is called a *school of psychological thought.* In this section, you'll see that the study of behavior and mental processes, despite its short life, has had a rich and varied history.

The Early Traditions

Structuralism—The Contents of Consciousness. Wilhelm Wundt (1832–1920) (pronounced "Voont") developed the first widely accepted school of psychological thought. In Leipzig, Germany, in 1879, the former medical student and physiologist founded the first psychological laboratory; its focus was the study of mental life (Leahey, 1992). Before Wundt, the field of psychology simply did not exist; what are now considered psychological questions lay in the domains of philosophy, medicine, and theology. Wundt was a formal, humorless man, but his lectures were extremely popular, and his dozens of graduate students were admiring followers. One of Wundt's major contributions was teaching his students to use the scientific method when asking psychological questions (Benjamin et al., 1992). Through his writing and talks, Englishman Edward B. Titchener (1867–1927) helped popularize Wundt's ideas, along with his own, in the United States and the rest of the English-speaking world.

What Wundt, Titchener, and others espoused was structuralism. **Structuralism** was the school of psychological thought that considered the structure and elements of immediate, conscious experience to be the proper subject matter of psychology. Instead of looking at the broad range of behavior and mental processes that psychologists consider today, the structuralists tried to observe only the inner workings of the mind to find the simple elements of conscious experience. They felt that all conscious experience could ultimately be reduced to simple elements or blends of those simple elements.

To discover these elements, Wundt and Titchener used the technique of **introspection,** or *self-examination,* in which an individual describes and analyzes what he or she is thinking and feeling or what he or she has just thought about. In the process of formulating this technique, they also conducted some of the first experiments in psychology. For example, they studied the speed of thought by observing reaction times for simple tasks.

By today's standards, of course, the structuralists focused too narrowly on individuals' conscious experiences. Understanding one person's conscious experience actually reveals little about another's. Thus, though their work represented a beginning, the structuralists' results allowed few generalizations, and the school made little progress in describing the nature of the mind.

Functionalism—How Does the Mind Work? Before long, a new perspective developed, bringing with it a new, more active way of thinking about behavior. Built on the basic concepts of structuralism, **functionalism** was the school of psychological thought that tried to explore not just the mind's structures but how and why the mind *functions* and is related to consciousness. It also sought to understand how people adapted to their environment.

With William James (1842–1910) at its head, this lively new school of psychological thought was the first truly American one. He argued that knowing only the contents of consciousness (structuralism) was too limited; a psychologist also had to know how those contents functioned and worked together. Through such knowledge, the psychologist could understand how the mind (consciousness) guided behavior. In 1890, James published *Principles of Psychology*, in which he described the mind as a dynamic set of continuously evolving elements. In this work, he coined the phrase *stream of consciousness,* describing the mind as a river, always flowing, never remaining still.

James broadened the scope of structuralism by studying animals, by applying psychology in practical areas such as education, and by experimenting on overt behavior, not just mental processes. James's ideas influenced the life and writing of G. Stanley Hall (1844–1924), another American psychologist who was one of Wundt's early students. Hall, the first person to receive a doctorate in psychology, was the founder of the APA and, as Titchener was for structuralism, was an organizer and promoter of functionalist psychology in the United States.

Functionalists continued to use introspection as a technique; for them, psychology was still the study of consciousness. For many proponents of emerging schools of psychological thought, however, this scope was too limiting. The early schools were soon replaced by new conceptualizations: Gestalt psychology, psychoanalysis, behaviorism, and humanistic and cognitive approaches to psychology.

Gestalt Psychology—Examining Wholes. In the early 20th century, while some psychologists were subscribing to structuralism and functionalism, others were developing very different approaches. One such approach was **Gestalt psychology**—the school of psychological thought that argued that it is necessary to study a person's total experience, not just parts of the mind or behavior (*Gestalt* is a German word that means "configuration"). Gestalt psychologists such as Max Wertheimer (1880–1943) and Kurt Koffka (1886–1941) suggested that conscious experience is more than simply the sum of its individual parts. Arguing that each mind organizes the elements of experience into something unique, by adding structure and meaning to incoming stimuli, Gestalt psychologists analyzed the world in terms of perceptual frameworks. They proposed that people mold simple sensory elements into patterns through which they interpret the world.

Eventually Gestalt psychology became a major influence in many areas of psychology—for example, in therapy. However, as broad as its influence was, Gestalt psychology seemed lacking in scientific rigor and somewhat mystical, and it never achieved as wide a following as did psychoanalysis.

Psychoanalysis—Probing the Unconscious. One of the first researchers to develop a theory about emotional disturbance was Sigmund Freud (1856–1939). Freud grew up during a difficult time in the history of central Europe; he was a dark, brooding, complex, yet charismatic figure. Freud was a physician who was interested in helping people overcome anxiety; he worked in Vienna, Austria, focusing on the causes and treatment of emotional disturbances. Working from the premise that unconscious mental processes direct daily behavior, he developed techniques to explore those unconscious processes; these techniques

Structuralism: The school of psychological thought that considered the structure and elements of immediate, conscious experience to be the proper subject matter of psychology.

Introspection: A person's description and analysis of what he or she is thinking and feeling or what he or she has just thought about; also known as *self-examination.*

Functionalism: The school of psychological thought that was concerned with how and why the conscious mind works; an outgrowth of structuralism, its main aim was to know how the contents of consciousness functioned and worked together.

Gestalt [gesh-TALT] psychology: The school of psychological thought that argued that behavior cannot be studied in parts but must be viewed as a whole; the focus was on the unity of perception and thinking.

include free association and dream interpretation. He emphasized that childhood experiences influence future adult behaviors and that sexual energy fuels day-to-day behavior.

Freud created the **psychoanalytic approach**—the school of psychological thought that assumes that psychological maladjustment is a consequence of anxiety resulting from unresolved conflicts and forces of which a person may be unaware. Its therapeutic technique is *psychoanalysis*. The psychoanalytic approach has undergone many changes since Freud devised it. At times, in fact, it has seemed only loosely connected to Freud's basic ideas. Chapter 10 discusses Freud's theory of personality, and Chapter 14 describes the therapeutic technique of psychoanalysis.

Psychological Schools Grow Broader

The early schools of psychology focused on the mind and how it functioned; for example, psychoanalysis examined how the unconscious operated and shaped later maladjustment. Yet it was not until the mid-1920s that the influences of learning were stressed, and it was not until the 1940s and 1950s that the roles of free will and self-expression were investigated. The 1970s saw the emergence of cognitive psychology, which stresses thinking processes; psychology in the 1980s and 1990s was also heavily influenced by studies of the neurological and biological foundations of behavior. Let's look at these more recent trends in the history of psychology.

Skinner is arguably the most influential psychologist ever trained in the United States.

Behaviorism—Observable Behavior. Despite their differences in focus, the structuralists, functionalists, Gestaltists, and psychoanalysts were all concerned with the functioning of the mind. They were all interested in private perceptions and conscious or unconscious activity. In the early 20th century, however, American psychology moved from studying the contents of the mind to studying overt behavior. At the forefront of that movement was John B. Watson (1878–1958), the founder of behaviorism. **Behaviorism** is the school of psychological thought that rejects the study of the contents of consciousness and focuses instead on describing and measuring only what is observable, either directly or through assessment instruments.

Watson was an upstart—clever, brash, and defiant. Trained as a functionalist, he argued forcefully that there is no objective way to study the human mind, particularly not introspection. Watson, flamboyantly and with great self-assurance, contended that behavior, not the private contents of the mind, is the proper subject matter of psychology. According to Watson, psychologists should study only activities that can be objectively observed and measured; prediction and control should be the theoretical goals of psychology. This contention was a major break with previous psychological perspectives.

After Watson, other American researchers extended and developed behaviorism to such a degree that it became the dominant and only acceptable view of psychology in the United States in the 1920s. Among those supporting the study of behaviorism, and certainly the most widely recognized, was Harvard psychologist B. F. Skinner (1904–1990). In the 1940s, Skinner attempted to explain the causes of behavior by cataloging and describing the relations among events in the environment (stimuli) and a person's or animal's reactions (responses). Skinner's behaviorism led the way for thousands of research studies on conditioning and human behavior, which focused on stimuli and responses and the controlling of behavior through learning principles.

Skinner is arguably the most influential psychologist ever trained in the United States. Skinner believed that we are what we do—that there is no "self," only a collection of possible behaviors. He was also a determinist. In his view, our actions are more a result of past experiences than of genetics. And he took the phrase "a result of" very literally. According to Skin-

ner, our environment determines completely what we do—we control our actions about as much as a rock in an avalanche controls its path.

Behaviorists focus on how observable responses are learned, modified, and forgotten. They usually emphasize how current behavior is acquired or modified rather than dealing with inherited characteristics or early childhood experiences. One of their fundamental assumptions is that disordered behavior can be replaced with appropriate, worthwhile behavior through traditional learning techniques (described in Chapter 5).

Humanistic Psychology—Free Will. Another important perspective of modern psychology is **humanistic psychology**—the school of psychological thought that emphasizes the uniqueness of each human being's experience and the idea that human beings have free will to determine their destiny. Stressing individual free choice, the humanistic approach arose in the post-World War II era. It was in part a response to the psychoanalytic and behaviorist views. Humanistic psychologists see people as inherently good and as conscious, creative, and born with an innate desire to fulfill themselves; they believe that psychoanalytical theorists misread people as fraught with inner conflict and that behaviorists are too narrowly focused on stimulus–response relations. Humanistic psychologists focus on individual uniqueness and decision-making ability; they assume that inner psychic forces contribute positively to establishing and maintaining a normal lifestyle.

Cognitive Psychology—Thinking Again. In the 1960s and 1970s, many psychologists realized that behaviorism in its strict form had limitations, particularly its narrow focus on observable behavior. As both an outgrowth of behaviorism and a reaction to it, these psychologists developed **cognitive psychology**—the school of psychological thought that focuses on the mental processes and activities involved in perception, learning, memory, and thinking. Cognitive psychology goes beyond behaviorism in considering the mental processes involved in behavior—for example, how people solve problems and appraise threatening situations and how they acquire, code, store, and retrieve information. Cognitive psychology currently exerts a strong influence on psychological thinking. It is sometimes seen as antibehaviorist, but it is not. It simply views the strict behavioral approach as missing a key component—mental processes.

The cognitive perspective asserts that human beings engage in behaviors, both worthwhile and maladjusted, because of ideas and thoughts. Cognitive psychologists may be clinicians working with maladjusted clients to help them achieve more realistic ideas about the world and then change their thoughts and behavior to adjust to the world more effectively. For example, a cognitively oriented clinician might work to help a client realize that her distorted thoughts about her own importance are interfering with her ability to get along with coworkers. Cognitive psychologists may also be researchers who study intelligence, memory, perception, and all mental processes.

Because cognitive psychology spans many psychological fields and research traditions, it is hard to identify a single person who could be called its leader. However, psychologists Albert Bandura, Albert Ellis, Aaron Beck, George Miller, Ulric Neisser, and Richard Lazarus have all taken prominent roles, and we will encounter their work in later chapters.

The Biological Perspective—Predispositions. A belief that people are born to win, lose, be fat, athletic, or outgoing might lead a researcher to focus on the biological basis of behavior. Indeed, researchers are increasingly turning to biology to explain behavior. The **biological perspective,** also referred to as the *neuroscience perspective,* is the school of psychological thought that examines psychological issues in light of how heredity and biological structures affect mental processes and behavior and focuses on how physical mechanisms affect emotions, feelings, thoughts, desires, and sensory experiences. Researchers with a biological perspective study genetic

Psychoanalytic [SYE-ko-an-uh-LIT-ick] approach: The school of psychological thought developed by Freud, which assumes that psychological maladjustment is a consequence of anxiety resulting from unresolved conflicts and forces of which a person may be unaware; includes the therapeutic technique known as *psychoanalysis.*

Behaviorism: The school of psychological thought that rejects the study of the contents of consciousness and focuses on describing and measuring only what is observable either directly or through assessment instruments.

Humanistic psychology: The school of psychological thought that emphasizes the uniqueness of each human being and the idea that human beings have free will to determine their destiny.

Cognitive psychology: The school of psychological thought that focuses on the mental processes and activities involved in perception, learning, memory, and thinking.

Biological perspective: The school of psychological thought that examines psychological issues in light of how heredity and biological factors affect mental processes and behavior and that focuses on how physical mechanisms affect emotions, feelings, thoughts, desires, and sensory experiences; also known as the *neuroscience perspective.*

abnormalities, central nervous system problems, brain damage, and hormonal changes, for example. Michael Gazzaniga (perception), Noam Chomsky (language), Irving Gottesman (schizophrenia), and Robert Plomin (intelligence) are often cited as leaders of the biological perspective. You'll be hearing more about their work later.

The growing importance of the biological perspective has lifted it to a prominent position in psychology—which you will see reflected in this text. We will revisit it many times, on many topics, in later chapters.

Evolutionary Psychology. Is your sense of humor shaped by the same processes that shaped adaptive physical features such as your opposable thumb and your erect posture? Did Stone Age men and women laugh at life the way we do? Some psychologists think so; a distinctly psychobiological approach is **evolutionary psychology**—the psychological perspective that seeks to explain and predict behaviors by analyzing how specific behaviors, over the course of many generations, have led to adaptations that allow the species to survive. Evolutionary psychology assumes that behavioral tendencies that help organisms adapt, be fit, and survive are the ones that will be passed on to successive generations, because adaptable, fit individuals have a greater chance of reproduction. Using ideas such as survival of the fittest, these researchers argue that human beings have evolved not only physically, but also in other respects that might be referred to as psychological. Evolutionary psychology argues that significant portions of human behaviors and mental abilities are directly coded in the genome—they are innate. Language is but one example. Human beings may learn language from one another, but they do so at about the same rate and about the same age, in a wide variety of cultures. Thus, psychologists conclude that language learning is a universal behavior and ability that is encoded in the genome. Evolutionary psychologists assert that certain psychological traits represent evolved heredity; they argue that these traits were not always what they are today. For example, in the early stages of human evolution, language consisted merely of grunts, groans, and crude gestures. But through the course of generations, those who grunted good directions, warnings, and other communications were more likely to survive in difficult circumstances. Those who did live taught their offspring, and over successive generations, language developed and was ultimately encoded in the human genome.

Today, psychologists realize that there are complex relationships among the factors that affect both overt behavior and mental processes. Therefore, most . . . who practice applied psychology . . . are eclectic in their perspective.

Evolutionary psychologists argue (and most psychologists agree) that human behavior and mental processes are *plastic,* or subject to change. The design of the brain and its functioning have been shaped by previous experiences—not only those in an individual's lifetime, but also those of the species. From an evolutionary perspective, this constant change serves as an adaptive mechanism allowing individuals, and their brains, to continue to evolve (Buss et al., 1998).

Eclecticism. Today, psychologists realize that there are complex relationships among the factors that affect both overt behavior and mental processes. Therefore, most American psychologists who practice applied psychology, especially clinical and counseling psychology, are eclectic in their perspective. **Eclecticism** is a combination of theories, facts, or techniques. In clinical and counseling psychology, eclecticism means evaluating the appropriateness of a variety of theories and therapies for an individual client, rather than relying exclusively on the techniques of one school of psychology.

Eclecticism allows a researcher or practitioner to view a problem from several orientations. For example, consider depression, the disabling psychological disorder that affects 10–20% of men and women in the United States at some time in their lives (Chapter

Evolutionary psychology: The psychological perspective that seeks to explain and predict behaviors by analyzing how specific behaviors, over the course of many generations, have led to adaptations that allow the species to survive; it assumes that behaviors that help organisms adapt, be fit, and survive are the ones that will be passed on to successive generations, because adaptable, fit individuals have a greater chance of reproduction.

Eclecticism [ek-LECK-tih-sizm]: In psychology, a combination of theories, facts, or techniques; the practice of using whatever theories and therapies are appropriate for an individual client rather than relying exclusively on the techniques of one school of psychology.

13 discusses depression at length). From a biological perspective, people become depressed because of changes in brain chemistry. From a behavioral point of view, people learn to be depressed and sad because of faulty reward systems in their environment. From a psychoanalytic perspective, people become depressed because their early childhood experiences caused them to form a negative outlook on life. From a humanistic perspective, depression is often caused when people choose inaction because they had or have poor role models. From a cognitive perspective, depression is fostered by the interpretations (thoughts) an individual adopts about a situation. An eclectic practitioner recognizes the complex nature of depression and acknowledges the possible contributions of each point of view; the practitioner evaluates not only the person but the depression and the context in which it occurs.

Think Critically

- Think about the historical events occurring around the time each school of psychological thought emerged. How might the historical era have helped give birth to each school?
- John B. Watson ultimately went into the advertising business. How might he have applied behaviorist principles in that field?
- Which school of psychology is most likely to be free of cultural biases? Why?

www.abacon.com/leftononline

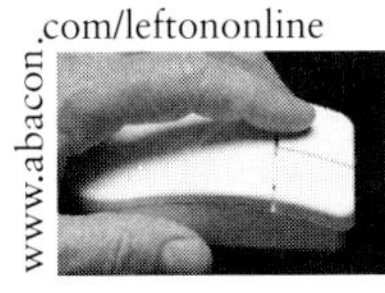

Your password-protected Website allows you access to the most comprehensive set of materials in The Psychology Place.

Summary and Review

What Is This Science of Psychology?

What do psychologists study?

Describe the steps in the scientific method.

KEY TERMS

psychology, p. 2; scientific method, p. 3; hypothesis, p. 4; theory, p. 4

The Research Process

Describe an experiment and indicate its key components.

How do researchers ensure objectivity?

What are the various other methods of research?

When is a group considered culturally diverse?

KEY TERMS

experiment, p. 5; variable, p. 5; independent variable, p. 5; dependent variable, p. 5; participant, p. 6; experimental group, p. 6; control group, p. 6; operational definition, p. 7; sample, p. 7; significant difference, p. 7; self-fulfilling prophecy, p. 8; double-blind technique, p. 8; demand characteristics, p. 8; Hawthorne effect, p. 8; questionnaire, p. 10; interview, p. 10; naturalistic observation, p. 10; case study, p. 11

Ethics in Psychological Research

Describe the ethical considerations in psychological research.

KEY TERMS

ethics, p. 13; informed consent, p. 13; debriefing, p. 14

Who Are These People We Call Psychologists?

Distinguish the various types of professionals in psychology.

KEY TERMS

psychologist, p. 15; clinical psychologist, p. 15; psychiatrist, p. 15; psychoanalyst, p. 16

Choosing Psychology as a Career

In what fields are psychologists likely to be employed?

Applied Research, Human Services Psychology, and Experimental Psychology

Identify the focuses of applied research, human services psychology, and experimental psychology.

How Have Schools of Psychological Thought Developed?

Identify the key assumptions underlying each school of psychological thought.

KEY TERMS
structuralism, p. 20; introspection, p. 20; functionalism, p. 21; Gestalt psychology, p. 21; psychoanalytic approach, p. 22; behaviorism, p. 22; humanistic psychology, p. 23; cognitive psychology, p. 23; biological perspective, p. 23; evolutionary psychology, p. 24; eclecticism, p. 24

Self-Test

1. Of the following, the definition that most effectively captures the broad scope of the term *psychology* is that it is the study of ____________.
   A. social relationships and physiological reactions
   B. emotional responses and overt actions
   C. behavior and mental processes
   D. mental processes and physiological reactions

2. ____________ is not a principle of scientific endeavor.
   A. Accuracy
   B. Hypothesis development
   C. Objectivity
   D. Healthy skepticism

3. In an experiment, the ____________ variable is manipulated by the experimenter, and the ____________ variable is expected to change as a result of that manipulation.
   A. dependent, extraneous
   B. extraneous, independent
   C. independent, dependent
   D. dependent, independent

4. The use of ____________ as a method of psychological inquiry allows for the collection of a large amount of data from many people in a small amount of time.
   A. questionnaires
   B. interviews
   C. naturalistic observation
   D. case studies

5. A(n) ____________ is conducted at the conclusion of an experiment and serves to inform the participants as to the true nature of the study.
   A. informed consent
   B. demand characteristic
   C. self-fulfilling prophecy
   D. debriefing

6. A medical doctor who has chosen to devote his or her efforts to the treatment of emotional or mental disorders is known as a ____________.
   A. clinical psychologist
   B. psychiatrist
   C. counseling psychologist
   D. psychoanalyst

7. Roughly ____________ individuals earn their PhDs in psychology each year, and each year psychologists with PhDs provide in excess of ____________ million hours of service to people in the United States.
   A. 1,800; 100
   B. 7,200; 25
   C. 3,600; 50
   D. none of the above

8. Individuals working in the fields of engineering, educational, forensic, and industrial/organizational psychology demonstrate skills in ____________ psychology.
   A. applied
   B. human services
   C. experimental
   D. health

9. ______________ was a school of psychological thought that was based on the premise that it is necessary to examine the total experience of the individual, not parts of the mind or behavior.
   A. Structuralism
   B. Functionalism
   C. Gestaltism
   D. Behaviorism

10. ______________ is a field of psychology that focuses on the mental processes involved in behavior, which are viewed as a key component missing from ______________.
    A. Cognitive psychology, behaviorism
    B. Evolutionary psychology, cognitive psychology
    C. Cognitive psychology, humanistic psychology
    D. Biological psychology, behaviorism

Chapter 2

Biological Bases of Behavior

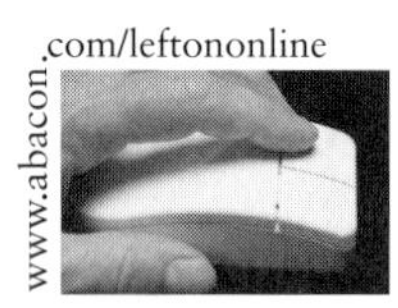

Go to your password-protected Website for full-color art, Weblinks, and more!

Andy Mendelsohn felt sick to his stomach at the devastating news he had just heard. His wife, Charlotte, lay in a fetal position, sobbing with grief. When confronted with the possibility of having a child born with a serious abnormality, Andy and Charlotte were beyond consolation. Soon to follow was a barrage of self-doubt—including questions of whose "fault" the abnormality was, why this was happening to them, and ultimately, a pervasive sense of anger and sorrow.

Most babies are born healthy, so when Andy and Charlotte were told that something was wrong, their reaction was quite normal—indeed, predictable. Andy and Charlotte's unborn child was growing too slowly, and fetal monitoring suggested a heart and lung defect. Subsequent tests suggested that a faulty heart valve was preventing the child's brain from receiving sufficient oxygen. Through microsurgery, physicians could repair the damage, even before birth. The likelihood of success was high, and permanent damage was unlikely. The Mendelsohns were going to have doctors perform the procedure—after which they would pray and then wait and see.

The causes of abnormalities in newborns are myriad: Genetic defects are caused when something goes wrong in the earliest cell divisions after conception. Biochemical abnormalities create malformations of developing organs. There are toxins (poisons) consumed during pregnancy—alcohol and other drugs, for example. There are accidents. And sometimes otherwise healthy and genetically normal fetuses are born too early to sustain life.

When brain damage exists, the behavioral problems that result can be extensive. Heart and circulation problems can restrict normal, day-to-day activities, and even minimally disfigured body parts can have serious effects on a person's development. Today, the problems that can lead to physical malformation are being corrected through medical procedures, and the behavioral problems that children might develop because of such malformations are being averted. All parents hope and pray for healthy children; when they are born with problems, surgical and medical interventions can often help them grow normally. Medical interventions will not help when behavioral problems emerge, however. Children and adults can grow up shy or verbose, can suffer from low self-esteem, or can develop personality problems. Surgery, drugs, and other medical interventions are not always, or even usually, effective against these problems. ■

Psychologists know that biology plays a large role—although not necessarily the determining role—in shaping human behavior. However, there is a complex interplay between biology and experience, between inherited traits and encounters in the world—that is, between nature and nurture. **Nature** consists of a person's inherited characteristics, determined by genetics; **nurture** refers to a person's experiences in the environment. For example, you can lift weights for years to build up your physical strength, but your efforts will be limited by your inherited body structure. Similarly, people try to maximize their intellectual skills through education; yet not everyone can become a nuclear physicist. A person's inherited traits may not become evident in behavior unless the environment supports and encourages them. For example, people with special talents must be given opportunities to express and develop them. If Mozart had not had access to musical instruments, his talent might never have surfaced.

In this chapter, we first examine the issue of nature versus nurture, in order to lay a strong foundation for studying the biological processes that underlie all human behavior and mental processes. Beginning with the smallest of the biological building blocks of behavior—genes and neurons—we go on to the structure and functioning of the brain. We then look at how scientists study brain activity and how chemical substances in our bodies affect our behavior. Remember that our focus will be on how biological processes, especially brain activity, affect behavior; this focus is coming to dominate much of psychological thinking.

(I) Nature versus Nurture

Focus on issues and ideas

- How nature and nurture shape human behavior
- How genetics plays a role in individual human characteristics
- How research on twins can help unravel the nature-versus-nurture issue

My father always insisted that I was a born athlete and that my sister was the scholar in the family. My father reasoned that each of his children had to be born *either* athletic *or* scholarly. He was assuming that what we were was fixed; he allowed little room for environmental influences. My father's beliefs highlight a major question in psychology: What is the relationship between biological mechanisms and environmental mechanisms—between nature and nurture? The debate over what determines abilities and behavior is often thought of as concerning the contributions of these biological and environmental variables. How much of what we are depends on the genes we inherited from our parents? How much is related to the environment in which we are raised—or to our

Nature: A person's inherited characteristics, determined by genetics.

Nurture: A person's experiences in the environment.

parents' expectations for us? As we shall see, *both* genes and experience are important factors affecting behavior. In fact, it makes little sense to talk about one without the other.

Both genes and experience are important factors affecting behavior. In fact, it makes little sense to talk about one without talking about the other.

Your genetic heritage is unaffected by day-to-day experiences. Over tens of thousands of years, however, we humans have evolved a highly organized brain that does allow us to learn, and that learning affects our behavior. Your brain acts as a library of information. Each new experience affects your later behavior. Those who consider nurture more important than nature suggest that people are not limited by genetic heritage, because experience, training, and hard work can stretch individual potential amazingly.

Psychologists know that biological makeup affects people's intelligence. But can the environment interact with and modify biological makeup? The truth is that genetic traits provide the framework for behavior; within that framework, experiences ultimately shape what individuals feel, think, and do. Let's take a closer look at the key genetic factors that shape day-to-day behavior.

The Basics of Genetics

Genetics is the study of *heredity,* which is the biological transmission of traits and characteristics from parents to offspring. Behavioral traits such as temperament and intelligence and disorders such as Alzheimer's disease and schizophrenia also have a genetic basis; this is why psychologists are especially interested in heredity (Chorney et al., 1998; Hamer, 1998). The focus of the field of *behavioral genetics* is on the influence of genetics on behavior. Behavioral geneticists ask questions about whether human characteristics such as shyness, impulsiveness, or intelligence have a genetic, inherited basis. If they do, then to what extent is the behavior biological and to what extent is it learned? Such researchers talk of the *heritability* of a trait or behavior. Many characteristics vary among individuals in a population—intelligence, dancing ability, and height are just a few heritable variables. Remember that such characteristics sometimes require a genetic contribution from both parents, and estimates of how heritable a trait or characteristic is are estimates of how likely it is to occur within a *group* (not in a specific person). We will take a closer look at heritability in Chapter 7.

Uniqueness of Human Beings. With the exception of identical twins (discussed on p. 32), every human being is genetically unique. Although each of us shares traits with our brothers, sisters, and parents, none of us is identical to them or to anyone else. The reason is that a large number of genes determine, or at least influence, each person's physical, cognitive, and emotional characteristics (Reiss, 1995, 1997).

Each human cell normally contains 23 pairs of chromosomes (46 chromosomes in all). **Chromosomes** are microscopic strands of deoxyribonucleic acid (DNA) found in the nucleus (center) of every cell in the body (see Figure 2.1). Chromosomes carry the self-

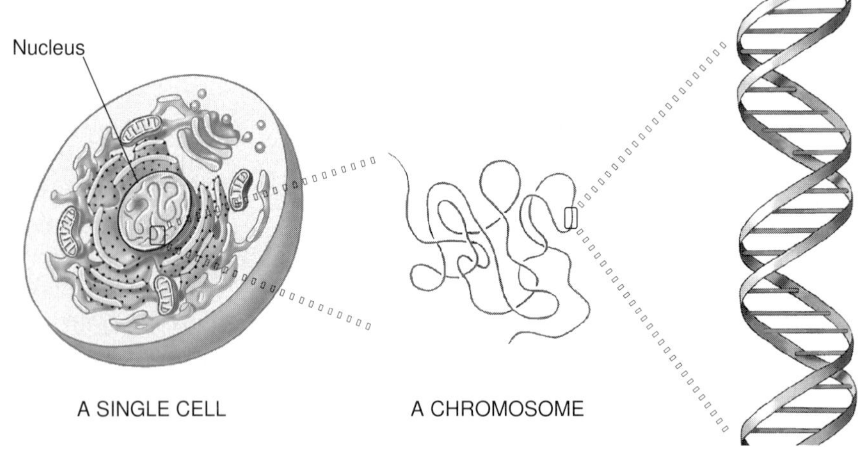

FIGURE 2.1
Building Blocks of Genetics
Each of the trillions of cells in the human body has 23 pairs of chromosomes in its nucleus. Each chromosome is essentially a long, threadlike strand of DNA, a giant molecule consisting of two spiraling and cross-linked chains. Resembling a twisted ladder and referred to as a *double helix,* each DNA molecule carries thousands of genes—the basic building blocks of the genetic code—which direct the synthesis of all the body's proteins.

replicating genetic information in their basic functional units, the genes—thousands of which line up along each chromosome. **Genes** are the fundamental units of hereditary transmission, consisting of DNA and protein. Genes control various aspects of a person's physical makeup, including eye color, hair color, and height—and perhaps basic intellectual abilities as well. Every such trait is determined by a pair of genes, located in parallel positions on a pair of chromosomes. Both of these corresponding genes influence the same trait, but they often carry different forms of the genetic code for that trait, and one of them may be dominant over the other. For example, if an individual's two genes for eye color carry the genetic codes for blue and brown, the individual will be brown-eyed, because the brown gene is *dominant*. Different, alternative forms of a gene that occupy the same position on paired chromosomes are called **alleles.** Each allele on a chromosome has a corresponding allele on the other chromosome of the pair; one of the alleles is inherited from each parent. Although a pair of genes may control a specific trait, most traits are determined by more than one gene pair.

Each parent's sperm or ovum (egg) contains 23 chromosomes—half of the total of 46 contained in all other body cells. Of these 23 pairs of chromosomes, 22 carry the same types of genetic information in both males and females. The 23rd pair differs, and it determines a person's sex. In females, the 23rd pair contains two X chromosomes; in males, it contains one X and one Y chromosome. (The photo shows the 23 pairs of chromosomes for a male.) At the moment of conception, a sperm and an ovum, each containing 23 chromosomes, combine, and the chromosomes form 23 new pairs. There are 8,388,608 possible ways for the 23 pairs of chromosomes to form, with 70,368,744,000,000 possible combinations of genes. Since most traits are determined by multiple gene pairs, you can see that the chance of any two individuals being exactly alike is exceedingly slim.

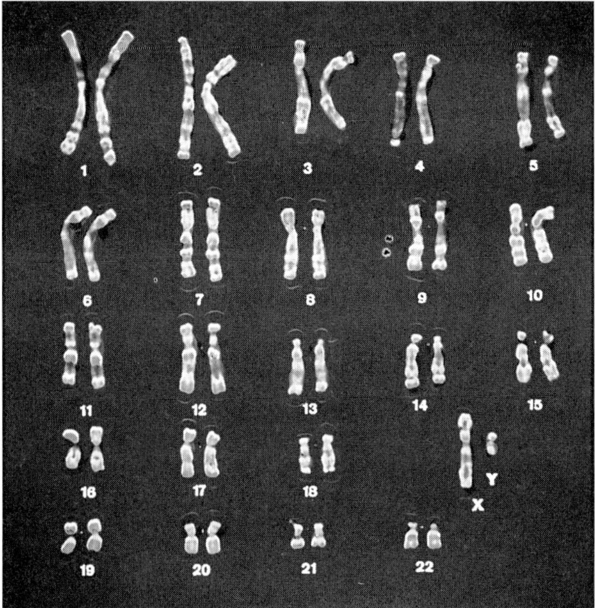

Mapping the Genome. In an exciting research revolution that began in the 1980s and was completed in the year 2000, biologists have associated specific traits with specific genes. That is, they have mapped the human *genome*—the total DNA blueprint of heritable traits contained in every cell of the body. Mapping involves first dividing the chromosomes into smaller fragments that can be characterized and then ordering (mapping) the fragments to reflect their respective locations on the chromosomes. Researchers have identified the exact location of genes contributing to muscular dystrophy, Huntington's disease, some cancers, and some psychological disorders, such as schizophrenia. The focus of research has shifted from demonstrating the existence of genetic influence to exploring its extent and significance.

Of course, researchers in this area face the crucial question of what to do with the expanding knowledge of the human genome. When scientists understand the basic genetic and biological mechanisms and their relationship to behavior, they will be better able to predict situations in which maladjustment and behavior disorders may occur. Yet this ability to predict will no doubt create some perplexing ethical dilemmas. Ethical considerations and legislation to guard people's rights must be high on the agenda of genetic researchers. As the ethical debate continues, it will be important to remember that genetics only lays the framework for behavior; so many events, life experiences, and cultural influences affect us that genetic influences must not be considered *the* determiner of behavior. Genes may bias us to respond in a specific way, but they do not determine the response.

Genetics: The study of heredity, which is the biological transmission of traits and characteristics from parents to offspring.

Chromosome: Microscopic strands of DNA found in the nucleus of every cell in the body and carrying the self-replicating genetic information in their basic functional units, the genes.

Gene: The functional unit of hereditary transmission, consisting of DNA and protein.

Allele [a-leel]: One of two alternative forms of a gene that occupies a particular place on a pair of chromosomes.

Twins and the Nature-versus-Nurture Issue

One of the best ways psychologists have found to assess the contributions of nature and nurture is to study twins. Twins make ideal subjects for such studies because they begin life in the same uterine environment and share similar patterns of nutrition and other prenatal influences. **Fraternal twins** occur when two sperm fertilize two ova (eggs) and the two resulting *zygotes* (fertilized eggs) implant themselves in the uterus and grow alongside each other. The genes of these twins are not identical, so the siblings are only as genetically similar as any brothers and sisters are. Fraternal twins can be the same or different sexes. Only about 12 sets of fraternal twins occur in every 1,000 births. **Identical twins** occur when one zygote splits into two identical cells, which then separate and develop independently. The multiplication of these cells proceeds normally, and the cells become two genetically identical organisms, always the same sex. Only 4 sets of identical twins occur in every 1,000 births.

Twins' genetic factors (nature) are fixed; but if the twins are reared apart—that is, grow up in different families—their environments (nurture) are different. By comparing psychological characteristics of identical twins reared apart, researchers can assess the extent to which environment affects behavior and perhaps untangle a bit more of the nature–nurture issue. Researchers have concluded that significant psychological similarities between identical twins are probably due to biological variables, and significant psychological differences are probably due to environmental variables. They ask the question "How much of the difference, or variability, between twins (or between any two individuals, for that matter) is due to inherited characteristics?"

By comparing psychological characteristics of identical twins reared apart, researchers can assess the extent to which environment affects behavior and perhaps untangle a bit more of the nature–nurture issue.

There are striking similarities in identical twins, even those separated for their entire lives (Wright, 1997). For example, a long and famous series of studies, called the *Minnesota adoption studies,* show that young adopted twins are similar intellectually and in personality to other children in their adoptive families. This suggests that family environment exerts a great influence on young children. By adolescence, however, there is greater variation. Plomin (1989, 1994b), Bouchard et al. (1990), and Turkheimer (1991) assert that even though environmental influences, especially on intelligence, are strong, heredity exerts a stronger influence. But psychologists meet this assertion with healthy skepticism, because the whole story is yet to be told. For example, experiences outside the family are known to play a powerful role (Wright, 1999). Further, heredity may lay a pattern for negative parenting—which in turn places children at greater risk for various disorders. A family is an interactive system (Ge, Conger, Cadoret, et al., 1996). We will consider identical twins again in Chapter 7. (I)

Fraternal twins: Twins that occur when two sperm fertilize two eggs; fraternal twins are only as genetically similar as any brothers or sisters are.

Identical twins: Twins that occur when one zygote splits into two identical cells, which then separate and develop independently; identical twins have exactly the same genetic makeup.

Nervous system: The structures and organs that facilitate electrical and chemical communication in the body and allow all behavior and mental processes to take place.

Neuron [NEW-ron]: The single cell that is the basic building block of the nervous system and comprises dendrites (which receive neural signals), a cell body (which generates electrical signals), and an axon (which transmits neural signals); also known as a *nerve cell.*

Afferent neurons: Neurons that send messages to the spinal cord and brain.

Efferent neurons: Neurons that send messages from the brain and spinal cord to other structures in the body.

Dendrites: Thin, bushy, widely branching fibers that extend outward from the neuron's cell body and that receive signals from neighboring neurons and carry them back to the cell body.

Axon: A thin, elongated structure that transmits signals from the neuron's cell body to the axon terminals, which pass them on to adjacent neurons, muscles, or glands.

Think Critically

- What are some environmental influences that can potentially alter people's inherited characteristics? Can such influences be limited? Should they be?
- The effort to map the human genome and understand the biological characteristics associated with particular gene patterns has ethical implications. What if scientists find genes strongly associated with criminality, for example? What should be done with this knowledge?

(I) Communication in the Nervous System

Focus on issues and ideas

- How neurons send messages throughout the body
- The relationship between neurotransmitters and human behavior
- The significance of neurotransmitters relative to disease, mood swings, and psychological disorders

Even the simplest task requires smooth functioning of the communication system we call the nervous system. When there is a misfire, a glitch, in the communication process, people have trouble. For example, a recent research study showed that people with dyslexia, who have difficulty with reading and who often reverse letters and words, don't use the same pathways and regions of the brain that nondyslexics do (Shaywitz et al., 1998). I'll have more to say about dyslexia and this study later; for now the key idea is that the nervous system underlies all of your behavior, including tasks like reading. Singing in a choir or even in the shower involves paying attention to the pattern of the music, producing the right sounds, keeping up with the rhythm, perhaps tapping a foot or clapping your hands. That's a lot of activity, just to sing along! By studying how the nervous system's components work together and how they are integrated, psychologists learn a great deal about the nature and diversity of human behavior.

The **nervous system** consists of the structures and organs that facilitate electrical and chemical communication in the body and allow all behavior and mental processes to take place. The nervous system has two divisions: the *central nervous system* (the brain and spinal cord) and the *peripheral nervous system* (all the other parts). We'll examine these two divisions shortly. First, however, you need to understand how communication proceeds within the nervous system as a whole. The nervous system is composed of hundreds of billions of cells, each of which receives information from thousands of others. The most elementary unit in the nervous system is the neuron, which is where we will begin.

The Neuron

The basic building block of the nervous system is a single cell—the **neuron**, or *nerve cell.* There are billions of neurons throughout the body (as many as 100 billion in the brain alone), differing in shape, size, and function. Some neurons operate quickly, some relatively slowly. Some neurons are large; others are extremely small. Neurons are often grouped together in bundles; these bundles of neuron fibers are called *nerves* if they are in the peripheral nervous system and *tracts* if they are in the central nervous system.

Not all of the neurons in your body are active at once. Nonetheless, each neuron is always on alert, ready to convey information and signals to some part of the nervous system. Nerve pathways allow signals to flow (1) to the brain and spinal cord from the sense organs and muscles, and (2) from the brain and spinal cord to the sense organs and muscles, carrying messages that initiate new behavior. Each type of neuron involved in this two-way neuronal firing has a name: **Afferent neurons** (from the Latin *ad,* "to," and *ferre,* "carry") are neurons that send messages to the spinal cord and brain; **efferent neurons** (from the Latin *ex,* "out of," and *ferre,* "carry") are neurons that send messages from the brain and spinal cord to other structures in the body.

Types of Neurons. There are three types of neurons: sensory neurons, motor neurons, and interneurons. *Sensory neurons* are afferent neurons that convey information from the body's sense organs to the brain and spinal cord. *Motor neurons* are efferent neurons that carry information from the brain and spinal cord to the muscles and glands. *Interneurons* connect other types of neurons and combine the activities of sensory and motor neurons. There are many more interneurons than sensory or motor neurons; the interneurons form a network that allows the other neurons to interact with one another. The millions of neurons that work together are surrounded by *glial cells,* which nourish the neurons and help hold them in place. Glial cells are small—and ten times more numerous than sensory or motor neurons or interneurons. Glial cells help insulate the brain from toxins and form the *myelin sheath.* Many neurons, especially the longer ones, are *myelinated,* or covered with a thin white substance (the myelin sheath) that allows them to conduct signals faster than unmyelinated neurons.

Parts of a Neuron. Typically, neurons are composed of four primary parts: dendrites, a cell body, an axon, and axon terminals (see Figure 2.2 on p. 34). **Dendrites** (from the Greek word for "tree," because of their branchlike appearance) are thin, bushy, widely branching fibers that extend outward from the neuron's cell body. Dendrites receive signals from neighboring neurons and carry them back to the cell body. At the *cell body,* the signals are transformed and then continue to travel along the axon. The **axon** is a thin, elongated structure that transmits signals

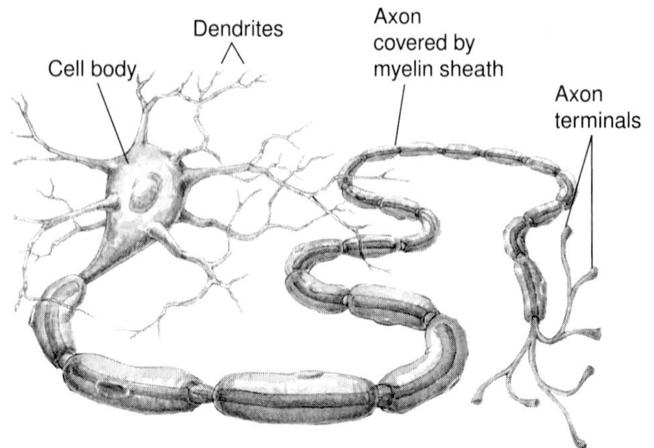

FIGURE 2.2
The Basic Components of a Neuron
Neurons appear in many forms, but all possess the basic structures shown here: a cell body, an axon (with myelin sheath and axon terminals), and dendrites.

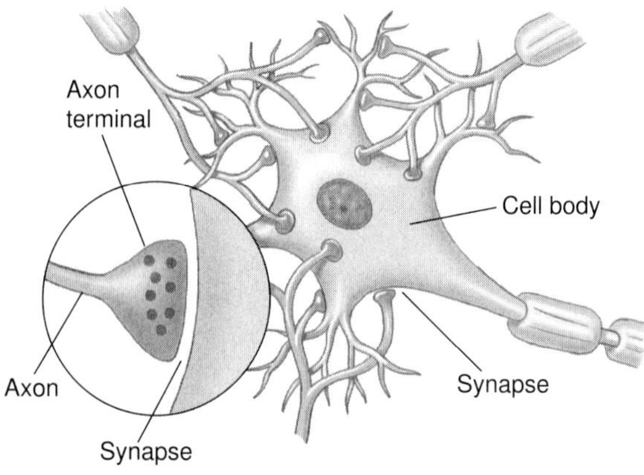

FIGURE 2.3
The Synapse
The synapse is very small. Chemicals released by the axon terminals cross the synapse to stimulate the cell body or the dendrites of another neuron.

from the neuron's cell body to the *axon terminals* (the end points of each neuron). Like dendrites, axons have branches at their endings.

Neuronal Synapses. The axon terminals of almost all neurons lie very close to receptor sites (dendrites, cell body, or axons) of other neurons. The microscopically small space between the axon terminals of one neuron and the receptor sites of another is called a **synapse** (see Figure 2.3). This small region is considered by most researchers to hold the key to understanding how the nervous system can allow the wide variability seen in behavior. You can think of many neurons strung together in a long chain as a relay team sending signals, conveying information, or initiating some action in a cell, muscle, or gland. Each neuron receives information from about 1,000 neighboring neurons and may "synapse on" (transmit information to) anywhere from 1,000 to 10,000 other neurons.

Synapse [SIN-apps]: The microscopically small space between the axon terminals of one neuron and the receptor sites of another neuron.

Action potential: An electrical current that is sent down the axon of a neuron and is initiated by a rapid reversal of the polarization of the cell membrane; also known as a *spike discharge.*

All-or-none: Either at full strength or not at all; the basis on which neurons fire.

Refractory period: Amount of time needed for a neuron to recover after it fires; during this period, an action potential is much less likely to occur.

Neurotransmitter [NEW-roh-TRANS-mitt-er]: Chemical substance that resides in the axon terminals within synaptic vesicles and that, when released, moves across the synaptic space and binds to a receptor site on an adjacent cell.

Electrochemical Processes. How do neurons communicate? What kind of signals do they transmit? Neuroscientists know that nerves are not as simple as electrical relay circuits, but rather are affected by a wide array of electrical and chemical variables. Two types of electrochemical process take place. The first involves activity within a neuron; the second involves transmitter substances (chemicals) that are released from the axon terminals of one neuron and act on neighboring neurons or other targets.

Understanding the electrochemical processes within a cell is essential to understanding the role of neurons in behavior. A widely accepted explanation of these electrochemical processes is that an extremely thin membrane (less than 0.00001 millimeter thick) surrounds every neuron; and there are channels, or "gates," in this permeable membrane through which electrically charged ions and other small particles can pass. The neuron is normally in a resting state, in which its interior is negatively charged relative to its exterior environment. This resting state is maintained by the cell membrane. The difference in electrical charge between the inside and the outside of the cell creates a state of *polarization* across the cell membrane.

Action Potential. When the neuron has been stimulated (its resting state has been disturbed) to the point where it reaches a *threshold* (a level of stimulation intensity below which nothing happens), it is said to be *depolarized.* At this point, the "gates" of the cell

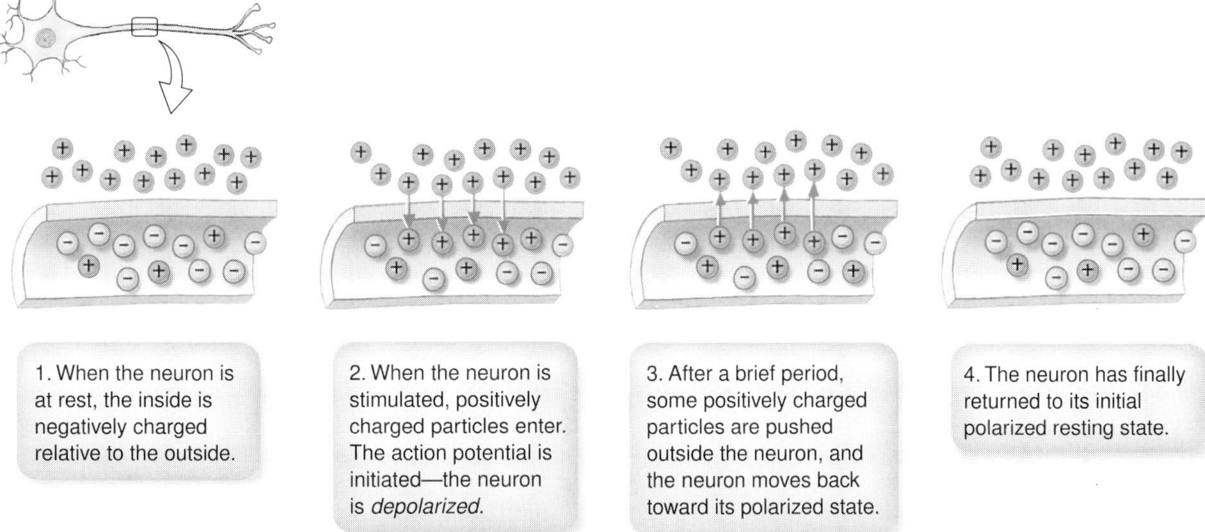

1. When the neuron is at rest, the inside is negatively charged relative to the outside.
2. When the neuron is stimulated, positively charged particles enter. The action potential is initiated—the neuron is *depolarized.*
3. After a brief period, some positively charged particles are pushed outside the neuron, and the neuron moves back toward its polarized state.
4. The neuron has finally returned to its initial polarized resting state.

FIGURE 2.4
Generation of an Action Potential

membrane open, a rapid reversal of electrical polarity occurs, and positively charged ions rush through the membrane into the neuron, thereby disturbing the resting state and generating an action potential (see Figure 2.4). The **action potential,** or *spike discharge,* is an electrical current that is sent down the axon of a neuron and is initiated by a rapid reversal of the polarization of the cell membrane.

A neuron does not necessarily *fire,* or produce an action potential, every time it is stimulated. If the level of polarization across the cell membrane has not been disturbed enough to generate an action potential—in other words, if the neuron has not reached its threshold—the cell will not fire. Neurons that are highly stimulated are more likely to fire than those that are less stimulated. For example, a bright flash from a camera will stimulate cells in the visual areas of the brain, but a flicker of a candle may affect far fewer cells. When a neuron fires, it generates an action potential in an **all-or-none** fashion—that is, the firing of the neuron, like the firing of a gun, occurs either at full strength or not at all. Action potentials occur in 2 to 4 milliseconds; therefore, neurons cannot normally fire more than 500 times per second. After each firing, a neuron needs time to recover (generally just a few thousandths of a second); the time needed for recovery is called the **refractory period.** During this period, an action potential is much less likely to occur.

When a neurotransmitter has affected an adjacent cell, it has accomplished its main mission; the neurotransmitter is then either neutralized by an enzyme or taken back up by the neuron that released it, in a process called reuptake.

Neurotransmitters and Behavior

When an action potential moves down to the end of an axon, it initiates the release of **neurotransmitters**—chemical substances that reside in the axon terminals within synaptic vesicles (small storage structures in each axon terminal) (Dunant & Israel, 1985) The neurotransmitters that are released into the synapse move across the synaptic space and bind to receptor sites on an adjacent cell, thereby conveying information to that cell (see Figure 2.5 on p. 36). We will examine the various types of neurotransmitters shortly.

When a neurotransmitter has affected an adjacent cell, it has accomplished its main mission; the neurotransmitter is then either neutralized by an enzyme or taken back up by the neuron that released it, in a process called *reuptake.* Sometimes neurotransmitters excite receiving neurons, or cause them to fire more easily; sometimes they inhibit receiving neurons, or cause them to fire less easily. A change in the membrane potential of a neuron after it has received neurotransmitters

FIGURE 2.5 Major Steps in Neuronal Transmission

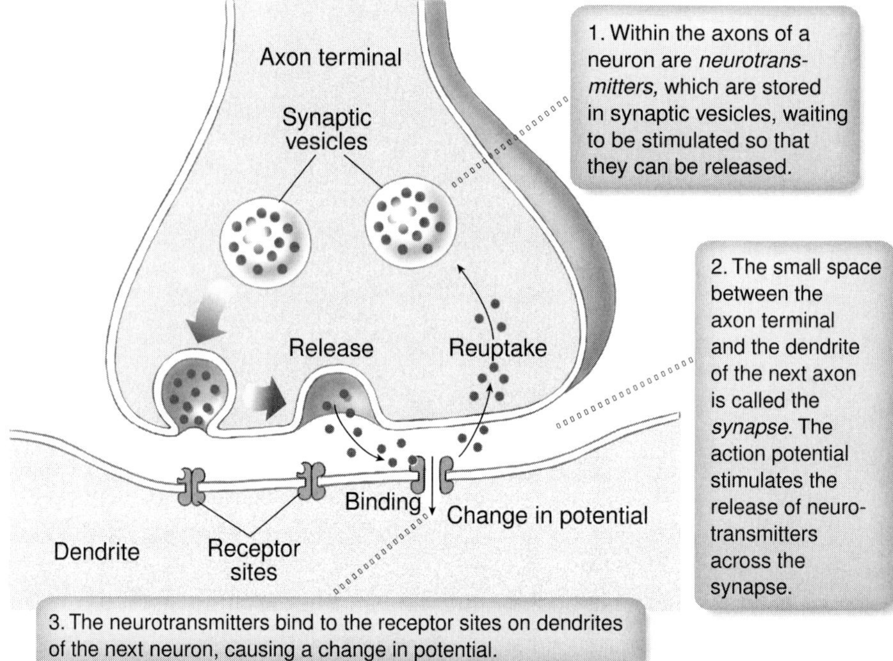
Axon terminal
Synaptic vesicles
1. Within the axons of a neuron are *neurotransmitters,* which are stored in synaptic vesicles, waiting to be stimulated so that they can be released.
Release
Reuptake
2. The small space between the axon terminal and the dendrite of the next axon is called the *synapse.* The action potential stimulates the release of neurotransmitters across the synapse.
Binding
Change in potential
Dendrite
Receptor sites
3. The neurotransmitters bind to the receptor sites on dendrites of the next neuron, causing a change in potential.

from another neuron is called a *postsynaptic potential (PSP).* An *excitatory PSP* makes it easier for the cell to fire; an *inhibitory PSP* makes it harder for the cell to fire. Because thousands of neurons may synapse on a single cell, a single neuron can receive both excitatory and inhibitory PSPs at once (Abbott et al., 1997).

There are a large number of neurotransmitters; at least 50 have been identified. One of them, gamma-aminobutyric acid (GABA), is involved in virtually every behavior, including anxiety states. Another important neurotransmitter, *serotonin,* is distributed throughout the brain and is especially important in regulating sleep. The most well-studied neurotransmitter, however, is *acetylcholine,* which is found in neurons throughout the brain and spinal cord. Table 2.1 describes five key neurotransmitters and their effects.

Research on Neurotransmitters. Although scientists have known about the existence of neurotransmitters for a long time, they have only recently realized the significance of these substances for human behavior. For example, researchers have found that serotonin affects motivation and mood. Serotonin is implicated in the debilitating disorder of autism. Other researchers have found that people with Parkinson's disease, whose symptoms include weakness and uncontrollable shaking, have low levels of the neurotransmitter dopamine. When clinicians give these people drugs (such as L-dopa) that have the same effects as dopamine, many of their symptoms are

Table 2.1 Five Key Neurotransmitters

Neurotransmitter	Location	Effects
Acetylcholine	Brain, spinal cord, autonomic nervous system, selected organs	Excitation in brain and autonomic nervous system; excitation or inhibition in certain organs
Norepinephrine	Brain, spinal cord, selected organs	Inhibition in brain; excitation or inhibition in certain organs
Dopamine	Brain	Inhibition
Serotonin	Brain, spinal cord	Inhibition
GABA	Brain, spinal cord	Inhibition

temporarily alleviated. Schizophrenia is associated with increased levels of activity in neural circuits that use dopamine. Although it is unlikely that one neurotransmitter alone can cause a disorder such as autism, Parkinson's disease, or schizophrenia, a single neurotransmitter may play an important role in the onset or maintenance of such an illness.

Neuropeptides are short chains of amino acids that act much like neurotransmitters. The effects of one type of naturally produced neuropeptide called *endorphins* (perhaps best known for inducing "runner's high") are mimicked by the actions of the narcotic morphine. As morphine does in hospitalized patients, endorphins inhibit certain synaptic transmissions—particularly those involving pain—and generally make people feel good (e.g., Miller et al., 1993). We will examine pain, endorphins, and pain management in more detail in Chapter 3.

Earlier researchers thought that only one type of neurotransmitter existed in each neuron and that each neurotransmitter acted on only one type of receptor. Today, researchers know that neurons often hold more than one type of neurotransmitter, and these may act on more than one type of receptor. Some neurotransmitters (especially neuropeptides) are released into the bloodstream, so their effects may be far-reaching. Researchers now think of such neurotransmitters as neuromodulators. **Neuromodulators** are chemical substances that function to increase or decrease the sensitivity of widely distributed neurons to the specific effects of other neurotransmitters. A neuropeptide released into the bloodstream, for example, affects whole classes or groups of cells, such as those within the limbic system, a brain structure known to be involved in emotional responses.

Chemicals can be used to mimic or facilitate the actions of neurotransmitters; such chemicals are called **agonists**. When an agonist is present, it is as if the neurotransmitter itself has been released. Other chemicals, called **antagonists**, oppose the actions of specific neurotransmitters. When an antagonist is present, receptor sites are blocked, and the neurotransmitter cannot have its usual effect. Schizophrenia, a disabling mental disorder, is often treated with antagonists. Cells that normally respond to dopamine are blocked from doing so by being exposed to certain drugs that act as antagonists and symptoms of schizophrenia are thereby alleviated. (Dopamine and schizophrenia will be discussed in more detail in Chapter 13.) Some drugs block the reabsorption, or reuptake, of neurotransmitters from their receptor sites. This blocking of reuptake has proved highly useful in the treatment of depression, which affects millions of people worldwide.

When neurons fire, information is transferred from the sense organs to the brain and from the brain to the muscular system and the glands. If psychologists knew precisely how this transfer occurred, they could more successfully predict and manage the behavior of people with neurological damage, mood disorders, or epilepsy, for example. However, the firing of neurons and the release of neurotransmitters and neuromodulators do not in themselves completely explain the biological bases of human behavior. The firing of individual neurons is only a part of the picture—because it is the brain as a whole that receives, interprets, and acts on neuronal impulses. We'll turn next to the brain and the nervous system.

Think Critically

- Should scientists try to apply their increasing knowledge of neuronal transmission to improving the human body—perhaps creating one that would not experience pain?
- What is the disadvantage of the increasing availability of drugs for the treatment of mental disorders?

Neuromodulator: Chemical substance that functions to increase or decrease the sensitivity of widely distributed neurons to the specific effects of other neurotransmitters.

Agonist [AG-oh-nist]: Chemical that mimics or facilitates the actions of a neurotransmitter.

Antagonist: Chemical that opposes the actions of a neurotransmitter.

(I) Organization of the Peripheral and Central Nervous Systems

Focus on issues and ideas

- The structure and function of the two major subsystems of the peripheral nervous system
- How the CNS is the main processing system for sensory information

It is a dark, wet evening; you are driving down a deserted road, listening to some 1980s oldies. A truck appears out of nowhere, heading straight toward you. You swerve, brake, swerve again, pump the brakes, and then pull over to the side of the road—all within a matter of seconds. On just such a second-by-second basis, the nervous system controls behavior. It is therefore essential for psychologists to understand the organization and functions of the nervous system and its mutually dependent systems and divisions. Recall that the nervous system is made up of the peripheral nervous system and the central nervous system. The central nervous system consists of the brain and spinal cord; the peripheral nervous system connects the central nervous system to the rest of the body. Let's examine both systems in detail.

The Peripheral Nervous System

The **peripheral nervous system** is the part of the nervous system that carries information to and from the central nervous system through spinal nerves attached to the spinal cord and through 12 cranial nerves, which carry signals directly to and from the brain. The peripheral nervous system contains all the nerves that are not in the central nervous system; its nerves focus on the *periphery*, or outer parts, of the body. Its two major divisions are the somatic nervous system and the autonomic nervous system.

Peripheral [puh-RIF-er-al] nervous system: The part of the nervous system that carries information to and from the central nervous system through spinal nerves attached to the spinal cord and through 12 cranial nerves.

Somatic [so-MAT-ick] nervous system: The part of the peripheral nervous system that carries information from sense organs to the brain and from the brain and spinal cord to skeletal muscles, and thereby affects bodily movement; it controls voluntary, conscious sensory and motor functions.

Autonomic [au-toe-NOM-ick] nervous system: The part of the peripheral nervous system that controls the vital and automatic activities of the body, such as heart rate, digestive processes, blood pressure, and functioning of internal organs.

Sympathetic nervous system: The part of the autonomic nervous system that responds to emergency situations by activating bodily resources needed for major energy expenditures.

Parasympathetic [PAR-uh-sim-puh-THET-ick] nervous system: The part of the autonomic nervous system that controls the normal operations of the body, such as digestion, blood pressure, and respiration.

The Somatic Nervous System. The **somatic nervous system** is the part of the peripheral nervous system that both responds to the external senses of sight, hearing, touch, smell, and taste and acts on the outside world. Generally considered to be under the individual's voluntary control, the somatic nervous system is involved in perceptual processing (processing information gathered through the senses) and in control of movement and muscles. Because it carries information from the sense organs to the brain and from the brain and spinal cord to the consciously controlled muscles, the somatic nervous system consists of both sensory (afferent) and motor (efferent) neurons. It is the somatic nervous system that allows you to see an oncoming truck and get out of its way.

The Autonomic Nervous System. The **autonomic nervous system** is the part of the peripheral nervous system that controls the vital and automatic activities of the body, such as heart rate, digestive processes, blood pressure, and functioning of internal organs. In contrast to the somatic nervous system, the autonomic nervous system operates continuously and involuntarily (although the technique of biofeedback, discussed in Chapter 4, has sometimes proved to be effective in bringing some of these processes under partial voluntary control). The system is called *autonomic* (from the Greek word meaning "independent") because many of its subsystems are self-regulating, focused on the utilization and conservation of energy resources. The autonomic nervous system is made up of two divisions: the sympathetic nervous system and the parasympathetic nervous system, which work together to control the activities of muscles and glands (see Figure 2.6).

The **sympathetic nervous system** is the part of the autonomic nervous system that responds to emergency situations by activating bodily resources needed for major energy expenditures. Activation results in a sharp increase in heart rate and blood pressure, slowing of the digestive processes, dilation of the pupils, and general preparation for an emergency, like a possible head-on collision with a truck. Together, these bodily changes are sometimes called the *fight-or-flight response*. These changes are usually accompanied by

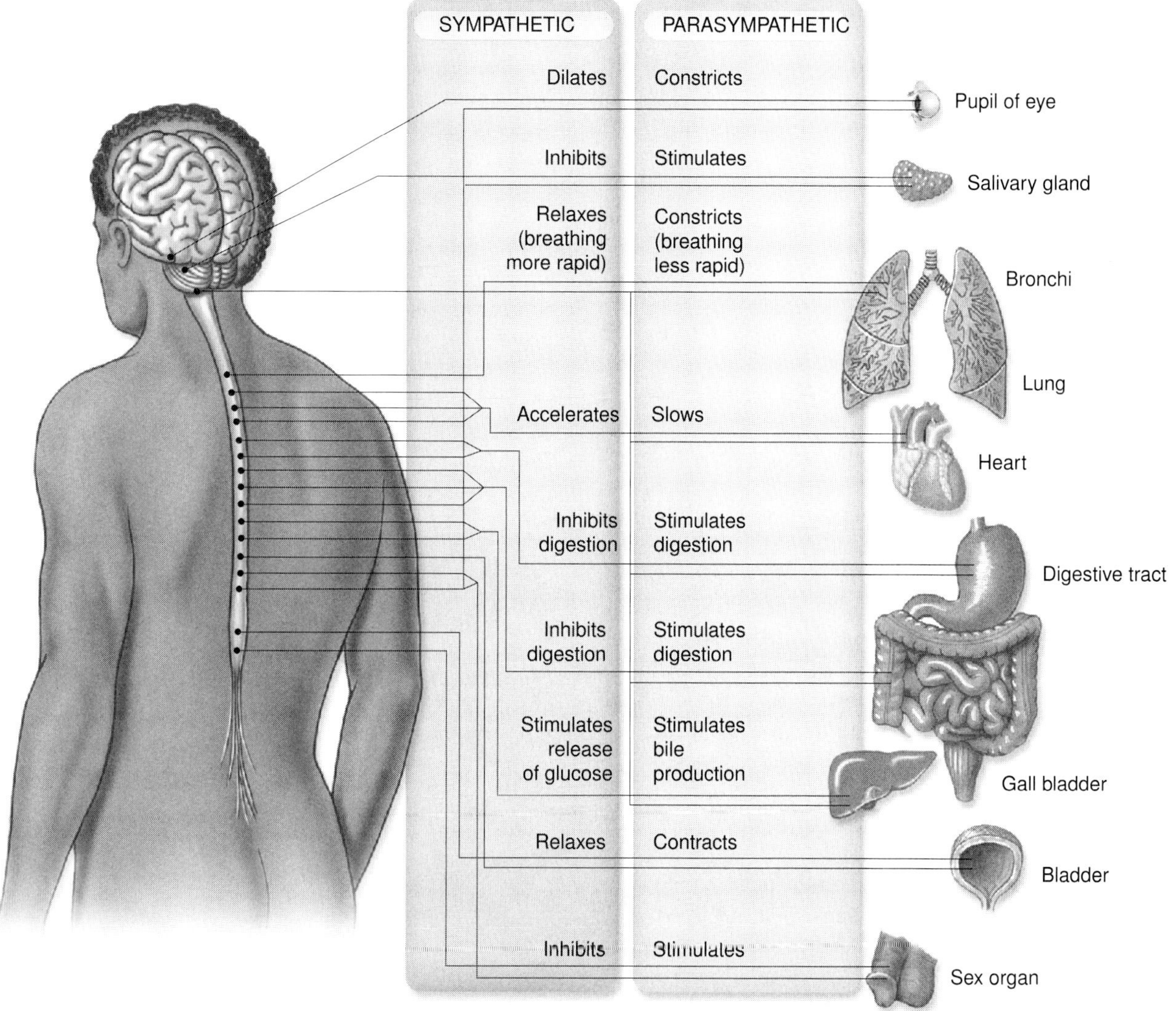

FIGURE 2.6
The Two Divisions of the Autonomic Nervous System

an increased flow of epinephrine, or adrenaline, which is a substance released by the adrenal gland (to be discussed later in this chapter), and they are regulated by a set of neurons in the hypothalamus and brain stem (to be discussed shortly) (Jansen et al., 1995). Increased activity of the sympathetic nervous system is what makes your heart pound and your mouth go dry when your car narrowly misses hitting an oncoming truck.

When the sympathetic nervous system is active and the organism is in a fight-or-flight state, the somatic nervous system is also activated. For example, when a large, snarling dog chases a cyclist, the cyclist's adrenal gland is stimulated by the sympathetic nervous system; the burst of energy produced by epinephrine (released by the adrenal gland) affects the somatic nervous system, making the cyclist's muscles respond strongly and rapidly. Thus, changes in the sympathetic nervous system can produce rapid changes in the organism's somatic nervous system; these changes are usually seen in emotional behavior and in stress reactions (discussed in detail in Chapters 8 and 12). Even simple automatic responses, such as blushing from embarrassment, are regulated by the sympathetic nervous system.

The **parasympathetic nervous system,** which is active most of the time, is the part of the autonomic nervous system that controls the normal operations of the body, such as digestion, blood pressure, and respiration (breathing). In other words, it keeps the body running smoothly. This system calms everything down and moves the heartbeat back to normal after an emergency. Parasympathetic activity does not show sharp changes from minute to minute.

The Central Nervous System

The **central nervous system** is the other of the two major parts of the nervous system. Consisting of the brain and the spinal cord, it serves as the body's main processing system for information (see Figure 2.7).

Although exactly how the brain functions still remains a mystery, neuroscientists know that the brain operates through many mutually dependent systems and subsystems to affect and control behavior (see Figure 2.8). As you've seen in our discussion of neuronal activity, millions of brain cells are involved in the performance of even simple activities. When you walk, for example, the visual areas of the brain are active and your sight guides you, the brain's motor areas help make your legs move, and the cerebellum helps you keep your balance. It is the central nervous system communicating with the muscles and glands, under the control of the brain, that allows all these things to happen so effortlessly.

The brain is the control center, but it receives much of its information from the spinal cord, the main communication line to the rest of the body, and from the cranial nerves. The **spinal cord,** contained within the spinal column, receives signals from the sensory organs, muscles, and glands and relays these signals to the brain. Some behaviors do not involve the brain directly. Among them are *spinal reflexes*—automatic responses that are controlled almost solely by the spinal cord. The knee jerk, elicited by a tap on the tendon below the kneecap, is a spinal reflex. A sensory input (the tap) is linked to a motor response (the knee jerk) without passing through the brain. Most sensory signals eventually make their way up the spinal cord to the brain for further analysis, but the knee jerk response happens at the level of the spinal cord, before the brain has had time to register and act on the tap.

The spinal cord's importance cannot be overstated. When a person's spinal cord is severed, the information exchange between the brain and the muscles and glands below the point of damage is halted. Spinal reflexes still operate, and knee jerk responses are evident. However, individuals who suffer spinal cord damage, like actor Christopher Reeve, lose voluntary control over muscles in the parts of their bodies below the site of the injury. This shows that the spinal cord serves a key communication function between the brain and the rest of the body; it is the chief trunk line for neuronal activity. Let's turn next to the brain itself. *I*

I Brain Structures

Focus on issues and ideas

- The structure and function of the brain and its unique organization
- The structure and function of the three main divisions of the brain: hindbrain, midbrain, and forebrain

A person's intelligence, personality traits, and ability to communicate through language reside in a small organ protected by the skull—the brain. The human

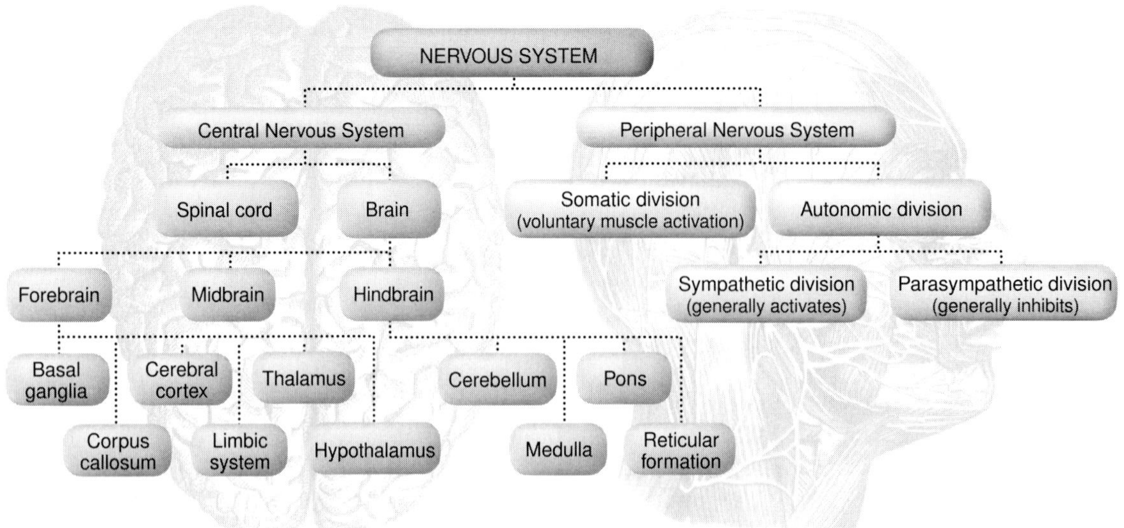

FIGURE 2.7
The Basic Divisions of the Nervous System

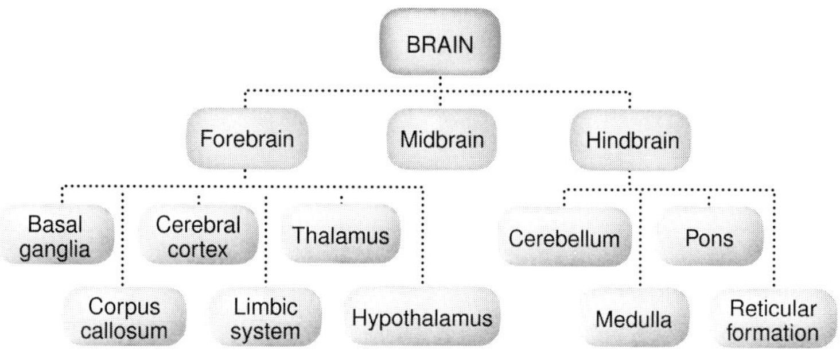

FIGURE 2.8
The Human Brain
The human brain is divided into three major sections: the forebrain, the midbrain, and the hindbrain.

brain is highly evolved, complex, and specialized. It is this specialization that allows humans—in contrast to other animals—to think about the past and the future and to communicate possibilities. Scientists know much about the structure and functions of the brain itself, yet they still have a great deal to learn. They have studied its structure, its functions, its interconnections, and what happens to it when it is damaged. Let's examine the brain's structure in detail.

The **brain** is the part of the central nervous system that regulates, monitors, processes, and guides other nervous system activity. Located in the skull, the human brain is an organ weighing about 3 pounds and composed of two large *cerebral hemispheres,* one on the right side and one on the left. A large, thick dividing structure, the *corpus callosum,* connects the two hemispheres and permits the transfer of information between them. Besides being divided into right and left halves, the brain has areas with special functions. Some parts are specialized for visual activities; others govern hearing, sleeping, breathing, eating, and other important functions. Some brain activities are localized. Most speech and language activity, for example, can be pinpointed to a specific area, usually on the left side of the brain. Other activities may occur in both hemispheres. For example, visual activity occurs in the visual cortex, which occupies both sides of the brain. You will see later in this chapter, however, that psychologists disagree on the extent to which functions are localized within the brain.

In examining the brain, we begin where the spinal cord and the brain meet. Many structures at this juncture deep within the back of the brain are responsible for basic bodily processes, such as breathing, sleeping, and eating. As we move higher up and toward the front of the brain, we find structures with more complicated functions. In both embryonic and evolutionary development, the brain grows organizationally and functionally into three fairly discrete sections (see Figure 2.9): the hindbrain, the midbrain, and the forebrain (which includes the cortex). Structures in the hindbrain and midbrain are organizationally more primitive than structures in the forebrain and are responsible for more basic, reflexive actions. Structures in the lower portions of the forebrain are organizationally somewhat more complex and involve higher mental functions. Finally, the cortex—the deeply fissured gray surface matter that covers the cerebral hemispheres (see Figure 2.10)—exhibits the highest level of functioning. The cortex is the location of thought processing—one of the most advanced abilities of humans.

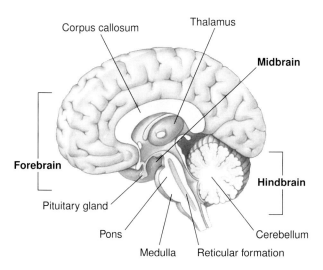

FIGURE 2.9
A Cross-Section of the Human Brain

Central nervous system: One of the two major parts of the nervous system, consisting of the brain and the spinal cord.

Spinal cord: The portion of the central nervous system that is contained within the spinal column, and transmits signals from the sensory organs, muscles, and glands to the brain, controls reflexive responses, and conveys signals from the brain to the rest of the body.

Brain: The part of the central nervous system that is located in the skull and that regulates, monitors, processes, and guides other nervous system activity.

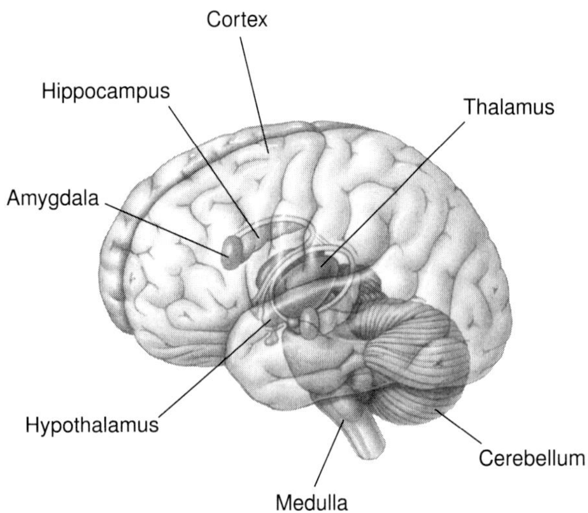

FIGURE 2.10
Structures of the Brain

Hindbrain

When Mark McGwire sent his 70th home run over the fence, I couldn't help but think, "What a cerebellum on that guy!" The cerebellum, part of the hindbrain, is what helped McGwire fine-tune the swing of his bat to power the ball into the stands. The four main structures of the hindbrain receive afferent signals from other parts of the brain and from the spinal cord; they interpret the signals and either relay the information to more complex parts of the brain or immediately cause the body to act. The **hindbrain** (refer to Figure 2.9) consists of the medulla, the reticular formation, the pons, and the cerebellum.

The **medulla,** through which many afferent and efferent signals pass, is the dense package of nerves lying just above the spinal cord that controls heartbeat and breathing. Within the medulla is a latticelike network of nerve cells, the **reticular formation,** which directly controls a person's state of arousal, waking, and sleeping, as well as responsive bodily functions; damage to it can result in coma and death. The reticular formation extends into and through the pons and the midbrain, with projections toward the cortex. The **pons** provides a link between the hindbrain and the rest of the brain; like the medulla, the pons affects sleep and dreaming.

The **cerebellum** (or "little brain"), a large structure attached to the back surface of the brain stem (the area from the medulla up to the midbrain), influences balance, coordination, and movement, including single joint actions such as the flexing of an elbow or knee. The cerebellum allows you to do such things as walk in a straight line, type accurately on a keyboard, and coordinate the many movements involved in dancing—and if you're Mark McGwire, hit an unbelievable number of home runs. The cerebellum may also be involved in some cognitive (thinking) operations, including learning, although its functions in this area are not yet clearly established (Daum et al., 1993; Leiner, Leiner, & Dow, 1986).

Midbrain

The **midbrain** (refer to Figure 2.9) consists of nuclei (collections of cell bodies) that receive afferent signals from other parts of the brain and from the spinal cord. Like the hindbrain, the midbrain interprets the signals and either relays the information to a more complex part of the brain or causes the body to act at once. One portion of the midbrain governs smoothness of movement, another temperature regulation, and yet another reflexive movement. Movements of the eyeball in its socket, for example, are controlled by the *superior colliculus,* a structure in the midbrain. The reticular formation continues in the midbrain.

Forebrain

The **forebrain** is the most advanced brain structure organizationally and structurally; it is also the largest and most complicated of the brain structures because of its many interrelated parts: the thalamus and hypo-

Hindbrain: The most primitive organizationally of the three functional divisions of the brain, consisting of the medulla, the reticular formation, the pons, and the cerebellum.

Medulla [meh-DUH-lah]: The most primitive and lowest portion of the hindbrain; controls basic bodily functions such as heartbeat and breathing.

Reticular [reh-TICK-you-lar] formation: A latticelike network of neurons within the medulla that directly controls a person's state of arousal, waking, and sleeping, as well as responsive bodily functions.

Pons: A structure of the hindbrain that provides a link between the medulla and the cerebellum and the rest of the brain; it affects sleep and dreaming.

Cerebellum [seh-rah-BELL-um]: A large structure that is attached to the back surface of the brain stem and that influences balance, coordination, and movement.

Midbrain: The second level of the three organizational structures of the brain, which receives afferent signals from other parts of the brain and from the spinal cord, interprets the signals, and either relays the information to a more complex part of the brain or causes the body to act at once; considered important in the regulation of movement.

Forebrain: The largest, most complicated, and most advanced organizationally and functionally of the three divisions of the brain, with many interrelated parts: the thalamus and hypothalamus, the limbic system, the basal ganglia and corpus callosum, and the cortex.

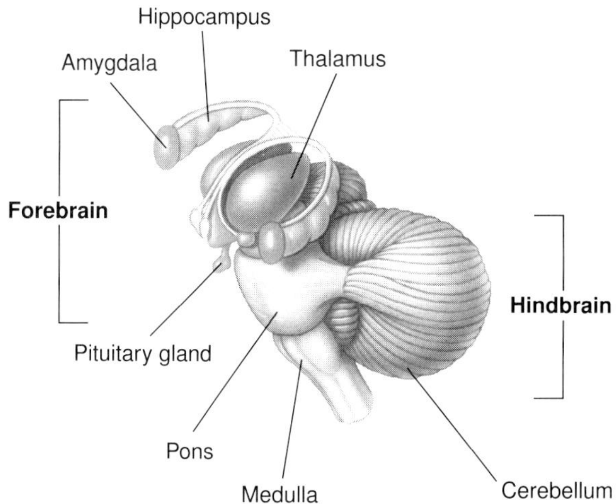

FIGURE 2.11
The Forebrain and the Hindbrain

thalamus, the limbic system, the basal ganglia and corpus callosum, and the cortex (see Figure 2.11).

Thalamus and Hypothalamus. The **thalamus** acts primarily as a routing station for sending information to other parts of the brain, although it probably also performs some interpretive functions. Nearly all sensory information proceeds through this large structure before going to other areas of the brain. The **hypothalamus,** which is relatively small (the size of a pea) and located just below the thalamus, has numerous connections with the rest of the forebrain and the midbrain and affects many complex behaviors, such as eating, drinking, and sexual activity. It plays a crucial role in the regulation of food intake; disturbances in the hypothalamus often produce sharp changes in eating and drinking behavior. We will examine these topics in more detail in Chapter 8.

Limbic System. One of the most complex and least understood structures of the brain is the **limbic system.** This system, located deep within the temporal lobe, is an interconnected group of structures (including parts of the cortex, thalamus, and hypothalamus) that influence emotions, memory, social behavior, and brain disorders such as epilepsy. Within the limbic system are the hippocampus and the amygdala. In human beings, the *hippocampus* is involved in learning, memory, navigating about the world, and some emotional functions (Maguire et al., 1998).

The *amygdala* is a set of cells that also control some emotional behaviors. Stimulation of the amygdala in animals, for instance, produces attack responses; surgical removal of the amygdala in human beings was once a radical way of treating people who were extremely violent. The amygdala is now considered important in learning, in the recognition of fear, and in a wide range of other emotions (Bechara et al., 1995; Damasio, 1994).

Stimulation of several areas of the limbic system in rats produces what appear to be highly pleasurable sensations. Olds and Milner (1954) discovered that rats, when given small doses of electrical current in some of the limbic areas as a reward for bar pressing, chose bar pressing over eating, even after having been deprived of food for long periods. The researchers called the areas of the brain being stimulated *pleasure centers.*

The Basal Ganglia and Corpus Callosum. The *basal ganglia* are a series of nuclei located deep in the forebrain to the left and right of the thalamus. They control movements and posture and are also associated with Parkinson's disease. Parts of the basal ganglia influence muscle tone and initiate commands to the cerebellum and to higher brain centers. Damage to this important neurological center can have severe behavioral consequences. The *corpus callosum* is a thick band of 200 million or so nerve fibers, which provide connections that convey information between the two cerebral hemispheres; damage to it results in essentially two separate brains within one skull. We'll return to the corpus callosum shortly.

Cortex. The brain has two major portions, referred to as the left and right cerebral hemispheres (we'll discuss brain specialization in more detail shortly). The exterior covering of these hemispheres, called the **cortex** (or *neocortex*), is about 2–3 millimeters thick and

Thalamus: A large structure of the forebrain that acts primarily as a routing station to send information to other parts of the brain but probably also performs some interpretive functions; nearly all sensory information proceeds through the thalamus.

Hypothalamus: A relatively small structure of the forebrain, lying just below the thalamus, which acts through its connections with the rest of the forebrain and the midbrain and affects many complex behaviors, such as eating, drinking, and sexual activity.

Limbic system: An interconnected group of structures (including parts of the cortex, thalamus, and hypothalamus) located deep within the temporal lobe and influencing emotions, memory, social behavior, and brain disorders such as epilepsy.

Cortex: The convoluted, or furrowed, exterior covering of the brain's hemispheres, which is about 2 millimeters thick, consists of six thin layers of cells, and is divided into several lobes, or areas, each with characteristic structures; thought to be involved in both sensory interpretation and complex thought processes; also known as the *neocortex.*

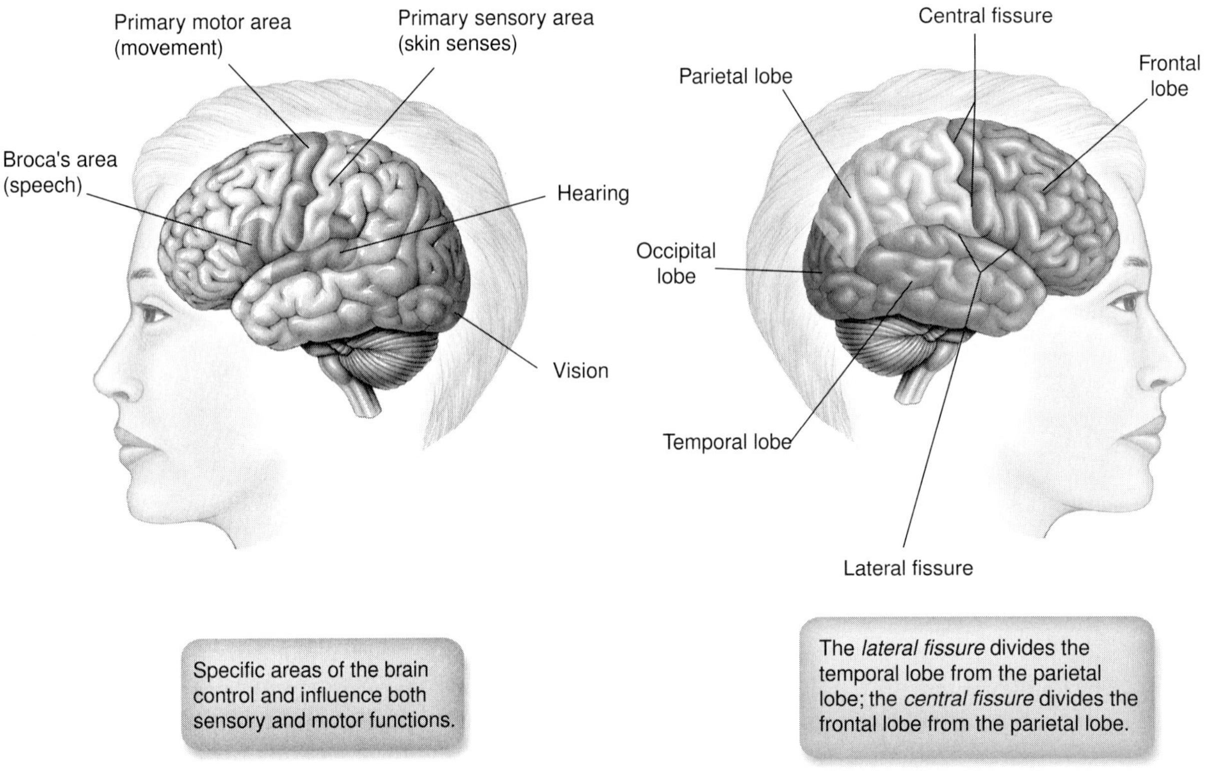
Primary motor area (movement)
Primary sensory area (skin senses)
Broca's area (speech)
Hearing
Vision
Specific areas of the brain control and influence both sensory and motor functions.
Central fissure
Parietal lobe
Frontal lobe
Occipital lobe
Temporal lobe
Lateral fissure
The *lateral fissure* divides the temporal lobe from the parietal lobe; the *central fissure* divides the frontal lobe from the parietal lobe.

FIGURE 2.12
The Cortex and the Lobes of the Brain
The cortex is the exterior covering of the cerebral hemispheres. It consists of four major lobes and the association cortex. The cortex plays a special role in behavior because it is directly involved in thought.

consists of six thin layers of cells. It is *convoluted,* or furrowed. These **convolutions,** folds in the tissue of the cerebral hemispheres and the overlying cortex, have the effect of creating more surface area within a small space. The overall surface area of the human cortex is at least 1.5 square feet. Human beings have a highly developed cortex, but most other mammals' brains are less deeply furrowed. The cortex plays a special role in behavior because it is intimately involved in thought.

A traditional way to study the cortex is to consider it as several *lobes,* or areas, each with characteristic structures and functions. The most prominent structures are two deep fissures (very deep furrows, or folds)—the *lateral fissure* and the *central fissure*—that divide the lobes. These easily recognizable fissures are like deep ravines that run among the convolutions, separating the lobes. The *frontal lobe* is in front of the central fissure; the *parietal lobe* is behind it. Below the lateral fissure and the parietal lobe is the *temporal lobe.* And at the back of the head, behind the parietal and temporal lobes, is the *occipital lobe.* Figure 2.12 illustrates the various lobes; Table 2.2 describes each lobe and its primary functions. (I)

Convolutions: Folds in the tissue of the cerebral hemispheres and the overlying cortex.

(I) Studying the Brain

Focus on issues and ideas

- How neuroanatomy helps us understand the brain and its relationship to human behavior
- How scientists measure, evaluate, and monitor neuronal activity
- The different diagnostic information derived from CT, PET, MRI, and fMRI

Knowledge of the brain and its relationship to behavior comes in part from the study of *neuroanatomy*—the structures of the nervous system. Some

Table 2.2 Lobes of the Brain

	Location	Function
Frontal lobe	In front of the central fissure; contains the motor cortex and Broca's area	Memory Movement Speech and language production
Parietal lobe	Behind frontal lobe	Sense of touch and body position
Temporal lobe	Below lateral fissure and parietal lobe	Speech, hearing, and some visual information processing
Occipital lobe	Back of the brain, next to and behind parietal and temporal lobes	Visual sense
Association cortex	Areas between parietal, temporal, and occipital lobes	Believed to be responsible for complex behaviors that involve thinking and sensory processes

neuroanatomists study the brains of people who have died of tumors, brain diseases, and trauma (injury) to the brain, hoping to correlate the type of brain damage with the loss of specific abilities, such as seeing, reading, or writing. Observing the behaviors and mental processes of individuals with damage known to have been caused by accidents, strokes, or brain tumors provides further information. Neuroanatomists who study behavior often use a technique called *ablation.* In ablation, researchers remove or destroy a portion of an animal's brain and study the animal to determine which behaviors have been disrupted. Today, in addition to ablation, neuroanatomists use electrical recording techniques such as EEGs, MRIs, and CT and PET scans. Still other researchers study brain–behavior relationships by watching animals or children as they interact with their environment and solve problems.

Monitoring Neuronal Activity

Though nonliving brains can be dissected, neuroscientists are becoming more interested in exploring the functions and interconnections of the active central nervous system, a more difficult task. Much of what scientists know about the electrical activity in the nervous system comes from laboratory studies of abnormalities in brain structure and function. In conducting such studies, scientists use several basic procedures to measure neuronal activity.

One measuring technique is *single-unit recording,* in which researchers insert a thin wire, needle, or glass tube containing an electrolyte solution into or next to a single neuron to measure its electrical activity. Because neurons fire extremely rapidly, the data are often fed into a computer, which averages the number of times the cell fires in 1 second or 1 minute. Scientists usually perform this type of recording technique on the neurons of rats, cats, or monkeys. There are widely scattered neuronal clusters that act together, in synchrony, and identifying all of them is a task of Herculean proportions. But synchronized firing of neurons is essential to movement and perception; synchronized output from widely spaced neurons may be at the heart of perception and thought and of consciousness itself (Crick & Koch, 1998; Riehle et al., 1997; Rodriguez et al., 1999). Synchronized firing of diverse cells allows both specialization of different brain regions and combination of neuronal output for higher-order thinking.

Another technique, *electroencephalography,* can measure electrical activity in the nervous systems of either animals or human beings. As the photo shows, this technique produces a graphical record of brain-wave activity called an **electroencephalogram,** or EEG

Electroencephalogram (EEG) [ee-LECK-tro-en-SEFF-uh-low-gram]: A graphical record of brain-wave activity obtained through electrodes placed on the scalp.

(*electro* means "electrical," *encephalon* means brain," and *gram* means "record"). Small electrodes placed on the scalp record the activity of thousands of cells beneath the skull to produce an EEG. EEGs, which are generally analyzed by computer, are used for a variety of purposes, including the assessment of brain damage, epilepsy, tumors, and other abnormalities. Erratic patterns in brain waves that are normally synchronized are usually evidence of an abnormality requiring further investigation.

In normal, healthy human beings, EEGs show a variety of characteristic brain-wave patterns, depending on the level and kind of mental activity the person is engaged in. Researchers usually describe brain waves in terms of their *frequency* (the number of waves in a unit of tiı .e) and *amplitude* (the relative height or size of the waves). If people are awake, relaxed, and not engaged in active thinking, their EEGs are predominantly composed of *alpha waves*, which occur at a moderate rate (frequency) of 8 to 12 cycles per second and are of moderate amplitude. When people are excited, their brain waves change dramatically from alpha waves to *beta waves*, which are of high frequency and low amplitude. At different times during sleep, people show varying patterns of high-frequency and low-frequency waves correlated with dreaming activity and restorative functions, both of which are discussed in Chapter 4.

Functional MRI (fMRI), an imaging technique that registers changes in the metabolism (energy consumption) of cells in various regions of the brain, . . . allows observation of activity in the brain as it takes place.

CT (computerized tomography) scans: Computer-enhanced X-ray images of the brain (or any area of the body) in three dimensions—essentially a series of X-rays that show photographic slices of the brain (or other part of the body).

PET (positron emission tomography): Imaging technique that tracks radioactive markers injected into the bloodstream, enabling researchers to monitor marked variations in cerebral activity, which are correlated with mental processes.

MRI (magnetic resonance imaging): Imaging technique that uses magnetic fields instead of X-rays to produce scans of great clarity and high resolution, distinguishing brain parts as small as 1 or 2 millimeters.

fMRI (functional magnetic resonance imaging): Imaging technique that allows observation of brain activity as it takes place by registering changes in the metabolism (energy consumption) of cells in various regions of the brain.

Three significant techniques for measuring the activity of the nervous system have emerged in the last two decades: CT, PET, and MRI scanning. **CT (computerized tomography) scans** are computer-enhanced X-ray images of the brain (or any area of the body) in three dimensions—essentially a series of X-rays that show photographic slices of part of the brain or body. CT scans are especially helpful in locating specific damaged areas or tumors in the brain.

PET (positron emission tomography) tracks radioactive markers injected into the bloodstream, enabling researchers to monitor marked variations in cerebral activity, which are correlated with mental processes. PET scans are a relatively new tool for neuroscientists, but research is proceeding rapidly. For example, Alivisatos and Petrides (1997) used PET scans to trace regional blood flow during simple cognitive tasks and found a relationship between blood flow and cognitive activity. Specific brain regions have been found to be associated with specific types of memory or thought processes, and those areas show more blood flow for some tasks (for example, recall compared to recognition) than do other areas (Cabeza et al., 1997). The potential of PET scans has yet to be fully unleashed, but researchers are using them to study a wide range of psychological coding processes as well as disorders such as schizophrenia (Andreasen, 1997). The biggest problem with PET scans is that although they display cortical function efficiently, they do not have high enough resolution to allow precise location of the activated region.

MRI (magnetic resonance imaging) uses magnetic fields instead of X-rays to produce brain scans that have far greater clarity and resolution than CT scans. MRI can distinguish brain parts as small as 1 or 2 millimeters, providing highly detailed images of the brain's tissue and revealing many kinds of abnormalities. Because nothing, radioactive or otherwise, needs to be injected to provide results, MRI scans are often preferred to CT or PET scans.

Only a few years ago, observing the brain actually functioning was the stuff of science fiction. Today, scientists use **functional MRI (fMRI)**, an imaging technique that registers changes in the metabolism (energy consumption) of cells in various regions of the brain and thus allows observation of activity in the brain *as it takes place*. A person performs a particular task while the imaging is being performed. The area of the brain responsible for this task experiences an increase in metabolism that ultimately shows up on the fMRI image as a color change. By having a person perform specific tasks that correspond to different functions, it is possible to locate the corresponding regions of brain activation. Unlike PET, which requires a break between scans (to allow radioactive traces to leave the system), fMRI allows for alternating experimental conditions in the same individual over time—a distinct and important advantage. And the newest fMRI techniques are exploiting its ability to track changes in brain activity over time (D'Esposito, Zarahn, & Aquirre, 1999).

Table 2.3 summarizes the four important imaging techniques we have just discussed.

Remember that imaging techniques such as PET and fMRI do not detect mental activity directly—rather, they measure changes in blood flow or metabolism that are related to energy consumption by cells in the brain. Nevertheless, these techniques, especially fMRI, are creating a revolution in neuroscience—allowing researchers not only to explore anatomy but also to learn how the brain operates. For example, researchers have been able to show that small brain lesions (small areas of damaged brain tissue, often due to disease or injury) are common in elderly people and are a natural part of aging. Further, researchers are establishing tentative links among brain lesions, illness, neurochemistry, and depression (Nemeroff et al., 1988). Ground is being broken every day with even newer techniques, including some that induce lesionlike disruption of brain activity that allows researchers to investigate attention, discrimination, and plasticity. *I*

I Brain Specialization—The Left and Right of Things

Focus on issues and ideas

- How left or right brain dominance may affect your interactions in the environment
- The impact of brain dominance on mental and behavioral processes
- The ability of the brain to learn and relearn over time

Did David Helfgott—the sensitive, cigarette-smoking, brilliant pianist with psychiatric problems, portrayed in the film *Shine*—have a disorder in a particular lobe? Are there specific places in the brain that control specific behaviors and thoughts? Does one side of the brain have more control over certain behaviors (for example, handedness—see *Experiencing Psychology* on p. 48) than the other side does? Is there a gender difference in which side of the brain controls which behaviors? Some science writers have concluded that brain hemisphere dominance may affect your choice of occupation, and even your worldview. Let's explore the evidence.

Splitting the Brain. Many body organs or structures exist bilaterally (arms, legs, kidneys), and in such instances, each member of the pair does the same thing. We know that a human being can lose one kidney and still function well. The body's general

Table 2.3 Four Important Imaging Techniques

Technique	Function and Application
CT (computerized tomography)	Produces computer-enhanced, three-dimensional, X-ray images of the brain (or any part of the body), essentially a series of X-rays showing photographic slices of the brain (or other part of the body)
PET (positron emission tomography)	Tracks radioactive markers that were injected into the bloodstream, enabling researchers to monitor marked variations in cerebral activity, which are correlated with mental processes
MRI (magnetic resonance imaging)	Uses magnetic fields instead of X-rays to produce highly detailed images of brain tissue that have far greater clarity and resolution than CT scans; can distinguish brain parts as small as 1 or 2 millimeters
fMRI (functional MRI)	Registers changes in the metabolism (energy consumption) of cells in various regions of the brain and thus allows observation of activity in the brain as it takes place

EXPERIENCING PSYCHOLOGY

Left-Handed in a Right-Handed World

What do James Garfield, Harry Truman, Gerald Ford, Ronald Reagan, George Bush, and Bill Clinton have in common? Aside from being presidents of the United States, all are (or were) left-handed, as were Joan of Arc, Alexander the Great, and C. P. E. Bach. So are Lisa Kudrow, Bruce Jenner, and Monica Seles. In fact, about 10% of the population is left-handed, depending on how you define left-handed. People's handedness—left-handedness especially—affects their lives in many ways.

It is most likely that a couple of different genes control whether you use principally the left or the right hand—what psychologists call "handedness" (Klar, 1996). One of the genes probably controls whether your left or right hemisphere is dominant; the other most likely controls whether your brain dominance controls your handedness. Most left-handed people are right-brain dominant, and most right-handed people are left-brain dominant. Left-handedness is genetically determined before birth, appears in all cultures, has been recorded for thousands of years, and is a uniquely human trait, as most other animals are ambidextrous.

There is also a strong cultural contribution to handedness; parents reinforce right-handed behavior, and the world is set up for right-handers. School desks are made to support your right arm and hand for writing. Computer mice are shaped for people who use their right hand. Safety levers on mechanical equipment are placed for right-handers. Eating at a crowded table can be an elbow-clashing ordeal for those who are left-handed. And until recent decades, lefties were discriminated against and heavily encouraged to switch hands. I remember my first-grade teacher using a ruler on the knuckles of those who wrote with their left hand.

Despite such recent accommodations as specially designed (and more expensive) computer mice, which have buttons that are reversible for lefties, the world is still structured for the right-handed. As a consequence, left-handed people are more likely to have accidents (Graham & Cleveland, 1995). Perhaps because their accidents are more frequent and severe, they also suffer more pain from accidents and Coren has argued that left-handed people die at a younger age (Halpern & Coren, 1991)—although this assertion is hotly disputed.

The research on left-handedness, especially on accidents and death rates, is controversial for a number of reasons, many of which reflect methodological problems. First, to do good research, psychologists should separate people who are predominately right-handed, or "strong right-handers," from those who are predominately left-handed, or "strong left-handers"—and this often has not been done. Second, how do you define people as lefties or righties? By which hand they use for writing? Drawing? Throwing a ball? Perhaps dealing cards? So, depending on how you define left-handedness, it turns out that some people are solely left-handed—they do everything with their left hand. Others are right-handed, and many people are ambidextrous, using either hand. Up to half of left-handed writers throw a ball with their right hand! Furthermore, research shows that most right-handed people (about 95%) process speech and language exclusively with their left hemisphere; they are clearly left-hemisphere dominant for many activities. In contrast, only 50% of left-handers process speech and language exclusively in the right hemisphere; the other 50% show a mixed dominance and are likely to use both hemispheres to process language.

So what do we know for sure about handedness? We know that handedness is partly, but not solely, biological. We know that since the brain is plastic, those who might be solely lefties may learn to modify their behavior and become ambidextrous—and that when this happens, ultimately the neuronal workings are modified as well. We also know that despite accommodations to the lefties of the world, the work and home environments are organized for righties, and this affects the way lefties live and work in both minor and major ways. Lefties of the world, unite! ■

symmetry may be misleading, however. Studies of brain structure show that different areas of the two-sided brain are responsible for different functions. Noted brain and consciousness expert Robert Ornstein (1997) likens the two sides of the brain to the cities in Charles Dickens's *A Tale of Two Cities*—in the sense that complex and related operations take place in two hemispheres that in some ways are as unlike as London and Paris.

Since the early 1970s, Nobel Prize winner Roger Sperry (1913–1994) and Michael Gazzaniga have been at the forefront of research in brain organization.

Gazzaniga has concluded that the human brain has a modular organization—that it is divided into discrete units that interact to produce mental activity (Gazzaniga, 1989). Research shows that the more experience an organism has with a particular event, situation, or concept, the more the brain does indeed become specialized (Jacobs, 1997).

Studies by Sperry (1985) and Gazzaniga (1983) show that in most human beings one cerebral hemisphere, usually the left, is specialized for the processing of speech and language; the other, usually the right, appears better able to handle spatial tasks and musical and artistic endeavors. Some of the evidence comes from studies monitoring brain-wave activity in normal participants exposed to different kinds of stimuli. For example, when normal participants are asked to look at or think about letters, or perhaps to rehearse a speech, some characteristic brain-wave activity can be detected on the left side of the brain. When these participants are asked to do creative tasks or are told to reorganize some spatial pattern, brain-wave activity is apparent on the right side of the brain. Although studies of brain waves do not yield complete or thoroughly convincing knowledge of brain function or brain structure, evidence of hemispheric specialization is mounting. For example, research using MRI scans supports a left—right distinction for pitch and music perception and indicates a difference between individuals who have perfect pitch and the rest of us (Schlaug et al., 1995). Similarly, an array of studies asserts a right dominance for men in spatial tasks but a left dominance for women in reading comprehension (Ornstein, 1997).

. . . the popular press and TV newscasters oversimplify the specificity of functions and, in some cases, overgeneralize their significance to account for school problems, marital problems, artistic abilities, and even baseball batting averages.

What happens to behavior and mental processes when connections between the left and the right sides of the brain are cut? Several important studies have involved **split-brain patients**—many of whom are people with uncontrollable, life-threatening epilepsy who have undergone an operation to sever the corpus callosum (the band of fibers that connects the left and right hemispheres of the brain) to prevent seizures from spreading across the hemispheres. After the operation, testing revealed that there was little or no perceptual or cognitive interaction between the hemispheres; the patients seemed to have two distinct, independent brains, each with its own abilities. Studies of split-brain patients are invaluable to scientists seeking to understand how the brain works—in particular, how the left and right sides function together (e.g., Blanc-Garin, Fauré, & Sabio, 1993).

Each cerebral hemisphere is neurologically connected to the opposite side of the body; thus, the left hemisphere normally controls the right side of the body (Johnson, 1998). Split-brain patients are unable to use the speech and language capabilities located in the left cerebral hemisphere to describe activities carried out by the right one. When stimulus information is presented exclusively to a participant's left hemisphere (by presenting it in the right visual field while a participant stares straight ahead), the person can describe the stimulus (tell whether two items are identical) and can perform matching tasks in essentially normal ways. But when the same stimulus is presented to the right cerebral hemisphere, the person is unable to describe the stimulus verbally (a left-hemisphere task). (See Figure 2.13 on p. 50.)

Studies of split-brain patients reveal two key features of brain function: (1) localization of specific functions, and (2) the fact that not every behavior is traceable to a single structure in the central nervous system. Most behaviors involve the combined work of several areas. There do seem to be some specifically left-brain and right-brain activities (Baynes et al., 1998). And certain key functions may develop early in life and may be slightly different for men and women (Zaidel et al., 1995). Nevertheless, the two halves of the brain still work together.

There is no doubt that both human beings and other animals exhibit lateralization and specificity of functions (Hopkins, 1997; Scalaidhe, Wilson, & Goldman-Rakic, 1997). Unfortunately, the popular press and TV newscasters oversimplify the specificity of functions and, in some cases, overgeneralize their significance to account for school problems, marital problems, artistic abilities, and even baseball batting averages. The extent of hemispheric specialization is yet to be determined, and most scientists and critical thinkers maintain a healthy skepticism about the existence of "two minds" in one. They realize, for example, that the left side of the brain may recognize

Split-brain patients: People whose corpus callosum, which normally connects the two cerebral hemispheres, has been surgically severed.

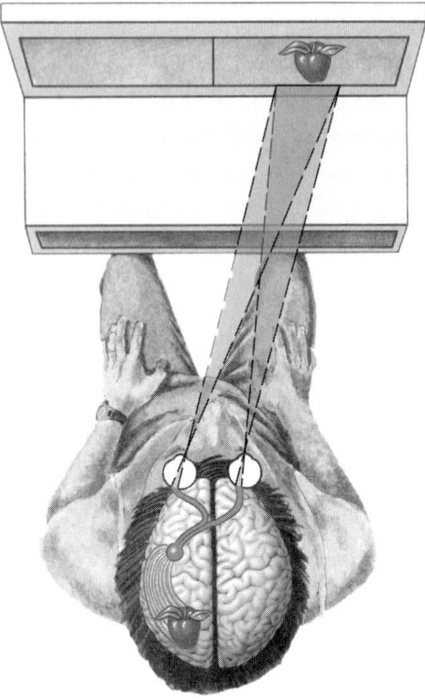

"I see an apple."

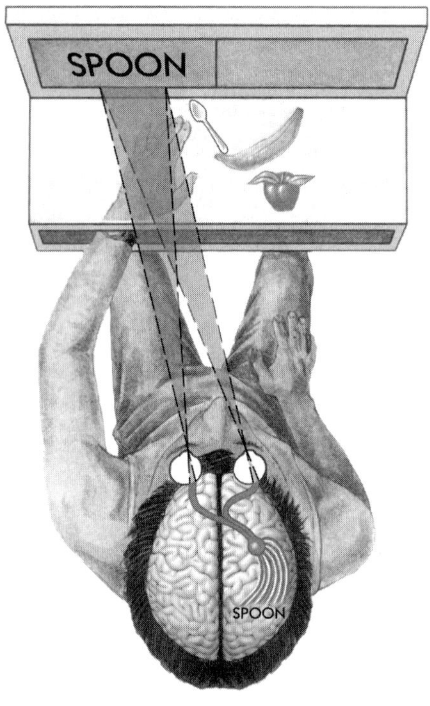

"I don't know what the image is."

FIGURE 2.13
The Effects of Severing the Corpus Callosum
Imagine that a man whose corpus callosum (but not his optic nerves) has been severed is staring directly before him at a screen on either side of which a researcher can flash words or pictures. The researcher flashes a picture of an apple on the right side of the screen. The man is able to name the image because it has been sent via his optic nerves only to his brain's left hemisphere—where verbal processing occurs. When the researcher flashes the word *spoon* on the left side of the screen, the man's optic nerves send an image exclusively to his right hemisphere—which predominantly processes nonverbal stimuli. Now, because the right hemisphere is nonverbal, when the man is asked to name what he sees on the screen, he is unable to name the image as the word *spoon*. If he is asked to use his right hand, which is controlled by the left hemisphere, to pick out the object named on the screen (a spoon) from several objects, by touch alone, he will not be able to do so. However, if the man is asked to use his left hand to touch the object named on the screen, he can do so. The left hand is controlled by the right hemisphere, which is spatially adept and has been exposed to the word *spoon*.

a stimulus, but the right side is necessary to put that recognition into context (Ornstein, 1997).

Plasticity and Change

Does your brain stay the same from birth to death, or can it change through experience or simply through the passage of time? Basic brain organization is established well before birth and does not change in any substantial way after birth; but details of brain structure and functions, particularly in the cerebral cortex, are subject to continued growth and development. What happens in one cell affects what happens to neighboring cells, so psychologists recognize that the brain is still *malleable* (teachable), especially during the formative years. This ability to change is often referred to as *plasticity*. Within limits, the nervous system can be modified and fine-tuned by experience that people acquire over many years—and the brain can be trained to relearn, or to simulate previous learning that was lost through an accident or some other brain trauma (Singer, 1995). The relearning typically involves some type of brain reorganization that establishes new representations of information in the brain (Florence, Taub, & Kaas, 1998; Jones & Pons, 1998).

Experience with specific stimuli reinforces the development of neural structures (Kilgard & Merzenich, 1998). You can liken the developing brain to a highway system that expands with use. Less-traveled roads are abandoned, but popular ones are broadened and new ones are added when needed. When neural structures are used, reused, and constantly updated, they become faster and more easily accessed. During early fetal and infant development, the neural links, connections, and interconnections are embellished and if the links remain unused, they may begin to disappear (Colman, Nabekura, & Lichtman, 1997). Such elaboration and even reorganization may occur (Florence, Taub, & Kaas, 1998), but are more likely when organisms are placed in complex, superenriched (e.g., visually stimulating) environments (Kempermann, Kuhn, & Gage, 1998). One study showed that children with language-based learning impairments can be taught to use repetitive and adaptive training exercises to overcome their problems. The exercises are assumed to change neuronal structures and allow improvement in speech and language processing (Merzenich et al., 1996).

You can liken the developing brain to a highway system that expands with use. Less-traveled roads are abandoned, but popular ones are broadened and new ones are added when needed.

In the end, we know that human beings are amazingly adaptable and can adjust to a changing world by reorganizing both brain structure and behavior (Houde & Jordan, 1998; Moser et al., 1998).

Neurotransplants

The idea of replacing body parts is no longer science fiction; physicians routinely perform kidney and heart transplants. But could the theme of the science fiction movie *Donovan's Brain* be a reality—could you take a brain or a portion of a brain and move it to another organism? Researchers are focusing on this question in an effort to help patients with brain disorders such as epilepsy and Parkinson's disease. The research is complicated; it also has serious ethical implications.

Can brain tissue that is transplanted from one organism to another survive and develop normally? Research shows the answer depends on the type of tissue and the site where it is transplanted. Some sites prove to be good locations; others are less successful at fostering normal growth. Transplantation is most likely to be successful if the transplanted cells are clearly organized, as in the visual cortex (Raisman, Morris, & Zhou, 1987). In a series of studies, researchers Fine (1986) and Mikhailova and colleagues (1991) successfully grafted (attached) brain tissue to the central nervous system in rats and other organisms and were able to observe behavior changes associated with the grafts. Yet research with animals, however successful, is not the same as research with human beings. People with Parkinson's disease (in which brain tissue no longer secretes sufficient levels of dopamine, causing muscular rigidity and tremors) have been treated with implants of healthy fetal brain tissue and have shown positive results (Bekhtereva et al., 1990). The implants survive, grow naturally, and secrete dopamine, and the patient's condition improves (Lindvall, 1991; Lindvall et al., 1990).

In the future, neurotransplants may open up a world of therapeutic possibilities. Victims of head injuries, brain diseases, and birth defects could all benefit. But should the medical and psychological community be allowed to create a more perfect human being? There are surgical risks; many techniques are dangerous and as yet unproven. Physicians and researchers must establish procedures for selecting the best candidates for such experimentation. And what about the source of the transplanted tissue? Implants that have been successful have come from human fetal tissue. Researchers and ethicists alike are unsure under what conditions, if any, fetal tissue should be made available. One possibility that skirts some of the ethical issues is the use of a patient's own dopamine-producing healthy tissue. This procedure is being explored with some success (Madrazo et al., 1987).

Think Critically

- What do you think would happen to behavior if the pons were damaged?
- What might be one possible function of the convolutions of the cortex?
- Given that the brain is malleable and sensitive to change, what—if anything—can individuals do to optimize their own growth and potential?

Hormones and Glands

Focus on issues and ideas

- The significance of glands and their effect on human development and specific behaviors

In 1978, Dan White fatally shot both San Francisco mayor George Moscone and city supervisor Harvey Milk. In court, White's attorney successfully argued that a diet of junk food had jumbled his client's brain and reduced his capacity for moral behavior.

DIVERSITY

Gender Differences in Brain Organization?

Some people believe that men and women are essentially the same; however, research does show some important biological and behavioral differences. In recent years, research on gender differences in brain organization has created a volatile debate.

Let's look at some facts. Sex hormones are present during the fetal development of animals and human beings and help create sexual differentiation (Breedlove, 1997). Sex hormones are also thought to create permanent changes in brain development that become evident in later behavior. Research shows that, on average, men do better than women on some spatial tasks—for example, the mental rotation of objects (Linn & Petersen, 1985). Numerous research studies have confirmed that men also do better, on average, in mathematical reasoning and in some motor tasks, such as guiding projectiles through space (Halpern, 1986).

In contrast, women do better than men at some perceptual tasks—for example, the rapid matching of items. Women have greater verbal fluency than men and outperform men in some arithmetic calculations (Hyde, Fennema, & Lamon, 1990). They also do better than men at reading emotions from photographs. On certain other tasks—for example, rhyming—both sexes do equally well, but men and women use different areas of the brain to do the task (Shaywitz et al., 1995).

Women and men perform some tasks differently. Women tend to use both sides of the brain in cognitive tasks such as spelling, for example; men use primarily the left side. Women use both ears equally; men favor the right ear. Not all gender differences appear at all ages and at all phases of learning, however. Gender differences in problem solving, for ex-

White spent only 3 years in prison for committing the double homicide. Although lawyers are no longer allowed to use the "Twinkie defense" in California, White's lawyer capitalized on the fact that a person's body chemistry—even an imbalance in blood sugar levels—can have a dramatic impact on behavior. It is true that body chemistry, hormones, and learned experiences can work together to influence behavior. But does this interaction render people unaccountable for their own actions, as Dan White's lawyer claimed?

Endocrine Glands

Throughout each day, the secretions of glands—groups of cells that form structures and secrete substances—affect many of our behaviors. Psychologists are particularly interested in the **endocrine glands**—ductless glands that secrete hormones directly into the bloodstream, rather than through a specific duct, or opening, into a target organ. **Hormones** are chemicals that are produced by the endocrine glands and regulate the activities of specific organs or cells; a hormone travels through the bloodstream to target organs containing cells that respond specifically to that hormone. Although researchers do not know the extent to which hormones control people's behavior, there is no doubt that the glandular system is interconnected. Each hormone affects behavior and eventually other glands. A disorder in the thyroid, for example, affects not only the body's metabolic rate but also the pituitary gland, which in turn affects other behaviors. The glands, the hormones, and the target organs interact; the brain initiates the release of hormones, which affect the target organs, which in turn affect behavior, which in turn affects the brain, and so on. *Diversity*

ample, tend to favor females in elementary school and males after puberty (Hyde, Fennema, & Lamon, 1990).

At birth, human brains are remarkably alike. Kimura (1992) asserts that differing patterns of abilities probably reflect hormonal influences after birth and structural asymmetries. In males, male hormones predominate; they may affect the size and function of brain structures such as the hypothalamus. For example, when newborn rats are administered large doses of male hormones, their brains develop differently than when they are administered large doses of female hormones, and this difference alters their behavioral abilities permanently.

Of course, making the leap to human beings is difficult, because ethics preclude the manipulation of hormone levels of newborns. However, researchers have been able to measure simultaneously the abilities of human adults and their levels of the hormone testosterone. Testosterone is evident in all human beings, although men have significantly higher levels than women do. Valerie Shute measured these levels in men and women and found that women with high levels of testosterone performed better on spatial tasks than women with low levels; in men, the reverse was true. Her conclusion was that testosterone levels in men and women affect performance (Shute et al., 1983).

But are gender differences also influenced by the way individuals are raised? The answer to this question is certainly yes. Some gender differences may be biologically based, but Western culture emphasizes and encourages them. Psychologist Sandra Lipsitz Bem (1993) asserts that many traditionally held gender stereotypes are embedded in cultural and social institutions. For example, boys have traditionally been encouraged to participate in physically rough-and-tumble sports; girls have been encouraged to take part in domestic activities. Men have traditionally been expected to be the providers—the wage earners and problem solvers—and women the caregivers for children.

Today, however, many men and women in Western societies are sharing roles and responsibilities; many parents are showing a greater understanding that boys and girls should have equal opportunities. The effects of changing societal values are becoming more evident in individual behavior. In some Western cultures, some differences between men and women are diminishing; access to and enrollment in courses that encourage problem solving—for example, engineering or physics—are no longer limited to boys. Unfortunately, many girls—themselves influenced by stereotypes—still shy away from science courses; stereotypes and discrimination are slow to die. In Chapter 7, you'll see that many of the differences between males and females in mathematical ability are exceedingly small, and those differences are shrinking each year.

Most important is the fact that *there are usually more differences within a gender than between genders.* For example, there are more differences among individual women's spatial abilities than between women's and men's spatial abilities. This idea is especially important for the relevance of data. It becomes impossible to generalize results to all people if the data are taken from only a small sample of women or men. ■

explores the question of whether gender differences are caused by hormones.

Sexual Behavior. In newborn animals, hormones have an irreversible effect on sexual behavior—they set specific behavior patterns in motion by permanently affecting brain development. In human adults, sexual behavior is to some extent under hormonal control. One study, for example, showed a significant correlation between married couples' hormone levels and frequency of intercourse (Persky, 1978). Hormones such as testosterone and estrogen, whose release is affected by the pituitary gland, the adrenal gland, the testes, and the ovaries, are certainly involved in sexual activity.

Pituitary Gland. The most important endocrine gland is the **pituitary gland,** which is often called the body's master gland because it regulates the actions of many other endocrine glands (see Figure 2.14 on p. 54). The pituitary is located at the base of the brain and is closely linked to the hypothalamus, and one of its major functions is control of growth hormones.

Endocrine [END-oh-krin] glands: Ductless glands that secrete hormones directly into the bloodstream, rather than through a specific duct, or opening, into a target organ.

Hormones: Chemicals that are produced by the endocrine glands and regulate the activities of specific organs or cells.

Pituitary [pit-YOU-ih-tare-ee] gland: The body's master gland, which is located at the base of the brain and closely linked to the hypothalamus, regulates the actions of other endocrine glands, and controls growth hormones.

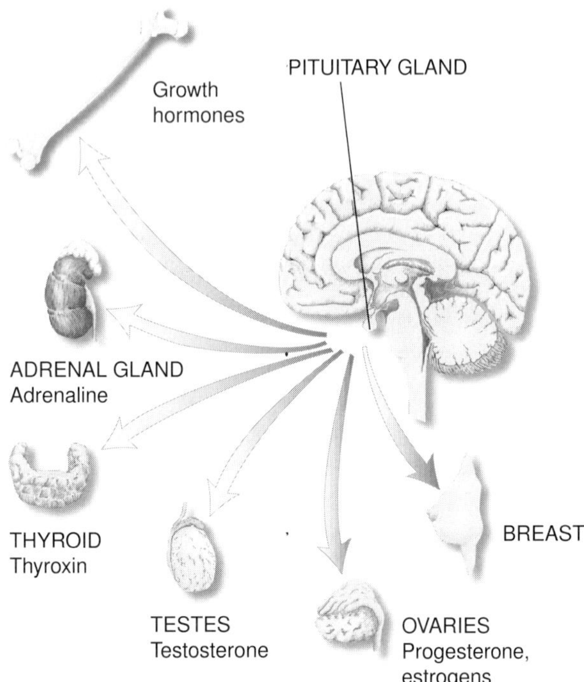

FIGURE 2.14
The Pituitary Gland
The pituitary gland is often called the body's master gland because it regulates many of the other endocrine glands. Located at the base of the brain, the pea-sized pituitary gland affects behavior indirectly through control of other glands and directly through release of hormones—including growth hormones and sex hormones—into the bloodstream.

The pea-sized pituitary gland is divided into two lobes, the anterior and the posterior. Secretions from the lobes produce direct changes in bodily functions, such as growth, and affect other glands. The *anterior lobe* produces a number of hormones—including hormones that stimulate the thyroid and adrenal glands, each of which controls specific behaviors; growth hormones (called *somatotrophins*), which control the body's development; and sex hormones (called *gonadotrophins*), which are involved in sexual behavior. A person's psychological state influences the secretions from the anterior pituitary; for example, viewing sexually explicit films raises the level of gonadotrophins in men (LaFerla, Anderson, & Schalch, 1978). The *posterior lobe* of the pituitary gland stores and secretes two major hormones, antidiuretic hormone (ADH) and oxytocin. ADH acts on the kidneys to increase fluid absorption and decrease the amount of urine produced by the body. Oxytocin stimulates uterine contractions in pregnant women and causes labor to begin. It also helps nursing mothers release milk.

Insulin: Hormone that is produced by the pancreas and facilitates the transport of sugar from the blood into body cells, where it is metabolized.

Diabetes mellitus [mel-LIGHT-us]: A condition in which the pancreas produces too little insulin, causing sugar to be insufficiently transported out of the blood and into body cells.

Hypoglycemia [hi-po-gly-SEE-me-uh]: A condition in which overproduction of insulin results in very low blood sugar levels.

Pancreas. Another endocrine gland, the *pancreas,* is involved in regulating the body's sugar levels. Sugar in the blood determines a person's energy level. When blood sugar is high, people are energetic; when it is low, they feel weak and tired. Cells in the pancreas called the *islets of Langerhans* control the production of **insulin**—the pancreatic hormone that facilitates the transport of sugar from the blood into body cells, where it is metabolized. Two insulin-related problems are diabetes and hypoglycemia. **Diabetes mellitus** is a condition in which the pancreas produces an insufficient amount of insulin, causing sugar to be inefficiently transported out of the blood into the cells and thus allowing too much sugar to accumulate in the blood. If the pancreas errs in the opposite direction, the result is **hypoglycemia**—a condition in which overproduction of insulin results in very low blood sugar levels. Hypoglycemic patients have little energy. The condition can usually be controlled through diet, with careful monitoring of types of food eaten and daily calorie intake.

Adrenal Glands. The *adrenal glands,* which also affect behavior, are located just above the kidneys and are divided into two parts. The *adrenal medulla,* located deep within each adrenal gland, produces epinephrine (adrenaline), a substance that dramatically alters energy levels and affects a person's reactions to stress through stimulation of the sympathetic nervous system. Imagine that you are being chased through a dark alley. The release of epinephrine makes your heart pound and gives you a burst of energy to help you outdistance your pursuer. The *adrenal cortex,* the outer layer that covers each adrenal gland, secretes one hormone that influences growth and development as well as others that affect cardiovascular functions. *I*

Think Critically

- What are the social implications of the conclusions researchers have reached about gender differences in intellectual and other abilities? Should men and women be expected to do things differently?

Summary and Review

Nature versus Nurture

What is the distinction between nature and nurture?

What is genetics, and why do psychologists study it?

KEY TERMS
nature, p. 29; nurture, p. 29; genetics, p. 30; chromosome, p. 30; gene, p. 31; allele, p. 31; fraternal twins, p. 32; identical twins, p. 32

Communication in the Nervous System

Describe the structures and processes that allow communication in the nervous system.

What is the focus of psychopharmacology?

KEY TERMS
nervous system, p. 33; neuron, p. 33; afferent neuron, p. 33; efferent neuron, p. 33; dendrites, p. 33; axon, p. 33; synapse, p. 34; action potential, p. 35; all-or-none, p. 35; refractory period, p. 35; neurotransmitter, p. 35; neuromodulator, p. 37; agonist, p. 37; antagonist, p. 37

Organization of the Peripheral and Central Nervous Systems

Describe the subdivisions of the nervous system.

KEY TERMS
peripheral nervous system, p. 38; somatic nervous system, p. 38; autonomic nervous system, p. 38; sympathetic nervous system, p. 38; parasympathetic nervous system, p. 39; central nervous system, p. 40; spinal cord, p. 40

Brain Structures

What are the major sections of the brain, and what are its structures?

KEY TERMS
brain, p. 41; hindbrain, p. 42; medulla, p. 42; reticular formation, p. 42; pons, p. 42; cerebellum, p. 42; midbrain, p. 42; forebrain, p. 42; thalamus, p. 43; hypothalamus, p. 43; limbic system, p. 43; cortex, p. 43; convolutions, p. 44

Studying the Brain

Describe several techniques for studying brain activity and functions.

KEY TERMS
electroencephalogram (EEG), p. 45; CT scans, p. 46; PET, p. 46; MRI, p. 46; fMRI, p. 46

Brain Specialization—The Left and Right of Things

To what extent are the cerebral hemispheres specialized for the processing of speech and language?

What happens when connections between the left and right sides of the brain are cut?

KEY TERMS
split-brain patient, p. 49

Hormones and Glands

How does the endocrine system affect behavior?

KEY TERMS
endocrine glands, p. 52; hormones, p. 52; pituitary gland, p. 53; insulin, p. 54; diabetes mellitus, p. 54; hypoglycemia, p. 54

Self-Test

1. Which of the following (is)are prominent area(s) of study focusing on the influence of nature on individual differences?

   A. genetics C. heredity
   B. twin studies D. all of the above

2. Composed of protein and DNA, ______________ are the basic units of hereditary information.

   A. genomes C. alleles
   B. chromosomes D. genes

3. ______________ carry information from the central nervous system to the glands and muscles.
   A. Interneurons
   B. Sensory neurons
   C. Afferent neurons
   D. Motor neurons

4. The ______________ is the small space that separates the axon terminals of one neuron and the receptor sites of another neuron.
   A. axon
   B. dendrite
   C. synapse
   D. action potential

5. The ______________ nervous system is part of the peripheral nervous system and transmits sensory information through both afferent and efferent neurons.
   A. somatic
   B. autonomic
   C. sympathetic
   D. parasympathetic

6. The ______________ includes brain structures such as the cortex, a thought-oriented structure, and the thalamus, which routes information to different parts of the brain.
   A. corpus callosum
   B. hindbrain
   C. midbrain
   D. forebrain

7. ______________ is a brain-imaging technique that uses radioactive markers to track the regional blood flow during various mental tasks.
   A. Magnetic resonance imaging
   B. Computerized tomography
   C. Positron emission tomography
   D. Electroencephalography

8. Which of the following is not knowledge garnered from studying split-brain patients?
   A. Not every behavior or function is associated with a single part of the brain.
   B. Severing of the corpus callosum produces ambidextrous abilities.
   C. Specific localization of certain functions.
   D. Performance on certain tasks is decremented due to the inability of the left and right hemispheres to communicate.

9. The central nervous system effects the release of ______________ which then impact ______________ to ultimately impact human behavior.
   A. glands, organs
   B. organs, hormones
   C. hormones, glands
   D. hormones, organs

10. The ______________ is directly related to the development of disorders involving the overproduction or underproduction of insulin.
    A. pituitary gland
    B. pancreas
    C. adrenal gland
    D. salivary gland

Sensation and Perception

Go to your password-protected Website for full-color art, Weblinks, and more!

Jean-Claude is typical of many second-graders—smart, eager, and energetic. He has a loving home, where he receives lots of stimulation and is well nourished and well cared for. But life for Jean-Claude is becoming frustrating. School is difficult; doing homework is a parent-child wrestling match. Jean-Claude is being stereotyped and is becoming alienated. It is happening slowly, day by day, but nevertheless it is happening. His problem is perceptual, and his teachers are just beginning to realize it.

"Bright and intelligent, quick at games, as able in most areas as his or her peers" is a typical prelude from many psychologists before they announce that Jean-Claude or Jessica is unable to read—a diagnosis that is often called a "reading disability." A reading disability is one of the most common of various learning disabilities. In some school districts, 15–20% of all children are diagnosed with a learning disability, and many—if not most—have a reading disability. Children with reading problems have trouble decoding words, distinguishing one syllable from another, and figuring out new and unfamiliar words. Individuals with such a disability are at a real disadvantage, as Jean-Claude and his family are finding out. ■

The causes of reading disability are complex, and no single answer satisfies researchers. Some assert that far too many children have been identified as reading-disabled; indeed, definitions of *reading-disabled* and *learning-disabled* are blurred. Research is focusing on various types of deficits in processing, from the processing of the visual stimulus at the beginning of reading to the more complex processing that involves decision making and elaborate decoding. The point at which one starts to investigate—at the beginning or the end of the process, at the bottom or at the top—has an effect on the kind of information obtained. Some of the newest physiological research shows anatomical differences in brain structure and functioning between men and women and between disabled readers and normal ones (Shaywitz et al., 1998). In this chapter, we explore how such differences affect all of the senses.

(I) The Perceptual Experience

Focus on issues and ideas

- The structure, anatomy, and anomalies of the eye
- How receptive fields process information
- Eye movements and their role in the perceptual span
- The three key dimensions of color and the theories that explain color vision

Whenever you are exposed to a stimulus in the environment—a word on a page or a breeze through your hair—the stimulus initiates an electrochemical change in sensory receptors in your body. That change in turn initiates the processes of sensation and perception. Psychologists study sensation and perception because what people sense and perceive determines how they will understand and interpret the world. Such understanding depends on a combination of stimulation, past experiences, and current interpretations. Although the relationship between perception and culture has not been extensively researched, it is clear that culture can affect perception—by establishing what people believe, pay attention to or ignore, and expect in their environments. For example, composers have long known that a person exposed only to Western music will find non-Western melodies unfamiliar and dissonant.

Sensation and Perception: Definitions

Traditionally, psychologists have studied sensation and perception together—as we do in this chapter. **Sensation** is the process in which the sense organs' receptor cells are stimulated and relay initial information to higher brain centers for further processing. **Perception** is the process by which an organism selects and interprets sensory input so that it acquires meaning. Thus, sensation provides the stimulus for further perceptual processing. For example, when light strik-

Sensation: Process in which the sense organs' receptor cells are stimulated and relay initial information to higher brain centers for further processing.

Perception: Process by which an organism selects and interprets sensory input so that it acquires meaning.

Psychophysics [SYE-co-FIZ-icks]: Subfield of psychology that focuses on the relationship between physical stimuli and people's conscious experiences of them.

Absolute threshold: The statistically determined minimum level of stimulation necessary to excite a perceptual system.

Subliminal perception: Perception below the threshold of awareness.

ing your eyeball initiates electrochemical changes, you experience the sensation of light. But your interpretation of the pattern of light and its resulting neural representation as an image are part of perception.

Some researchers who examine sensation and perception start at the most fundamental level of sensation—where the stimulus meets the receptors—and work up to more complex perceptual tasks involving interpretation. This approach is often called *bottom-up analysis.* Other researchers examine perceptual phenomena starting from the more complex level—not surprisingly, called *top-down analysis.* This type of analysis focuses on such aspects of the perceptual process as selective attention and active decision making, which are top-down processes. Perception is more than a reflexive discrimination process; rather, it involves integration of current sensory experiences with past experiences and even cultural expectations.

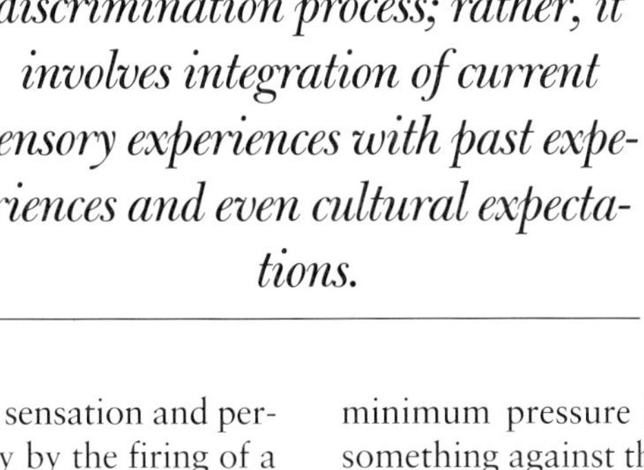
Perception is more than a reflexive discrimination process; rather, it involves integration of current sensory experiences with past experiences and even cultural expectations.

These two approaches, from the top down and from the bottom up, are both useful, because sensation and perception are not accomplished merely by the firing of a single group of neurons but involve whole sets of neurons, as well as previous experiences and stimulation that occurs at the eyes, ears, or other sense organs. Today, perceptual psychologists generally think in terms of *perceptual systems*—the sets of structures, functions, and operations by means of which people perceive the world around them. And psychologists know that perceptual systems interact. Sensory and perceptual processes rely so heavily on each other that many researchers think about them together. So, sensation and perception together form the entire process through which an organism acquires sensory input, converts it into electrochemical energy, and interprets it so that it gains organization, form, and meaning. It is through this complex process that people explore the world and discover its rules. Doing so involves the nervous system and one or more of the perceptual or sensory systems: vision, hearing, taste, smell, and touch.

Psychophysics

Although perceptual systems differ, they share a common process. In each case, the environment provides an initial stimulation. Receptor cells translate that stimulus into neural impulses, and the impulses are then sent to specific areas of the brain for further processing. Psychologists who study this process are using **psychophysics**—the subfield of psychology that focuses on the relationship between physical stimuli and people's conscious experiences of them.

Psychophysical studies attempt to relate the physical dimensions of stimuli to psychological experiences. This effort often begins with studying sensory thresholds. A *threshold* can be thought of as a dividing line, a point at which things become different. In perception, a threshold is the value of a sensory event at the point where things are perceived as different. Some early researchers, such as Ernst Weber and Gustav Fechner, investigated absolute thresholds, the minimum levels of stimulation necessary to excite a perceptual system, such as vision. They asked, for example, what minimum intensity of light is necessary to make a person say, "I see it," or what minimum pressure is necessary for a person to feel something against the skin. It turns out that a true absolute threshold is impossible to determine, because no two individuals see, hear, or feel at exactly the same intensity. The absolute threshold for vision, or any other sense, is thus an average of the responses of a range of normal people. So, for a psychologist, the **absolute threshold** is the statistically determined minimum level of stimulation necessary to excite a perceptual system. Closely related is the *difference threshold*—the amount of change necessary for an observer to report 50% of the time that a value of a stimulus (say, a sound) has changed (has become louder or softer) or is different from another value (is the chirping of a cricket rather than a bird).

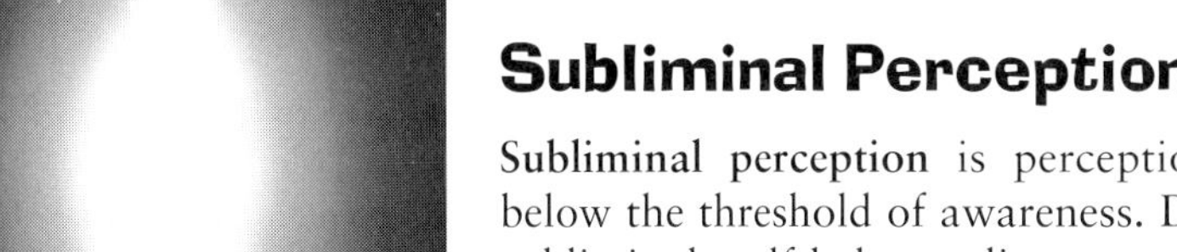

Subliminal Perception

Subliminal perception is perception below the threshold of awareness. Do subliminal self-help audiotapes do what that they claim? If a visual or auditory stimulus is presented so quickly or at such a low intensity or volume that you cannot consciously perceive it, can it affect your behavior? Is it affecting your brain organization?

Talk of this type of perception began in the 1950s with tales of an innovative advertising ploy. The story was that a marketing executive superimposed on a movie messages that said, among other things, "Buy popcorn." Enterprising advertisers claimed that movie theaters could induce audiences to buy more popcorn by flashing advertisements on the screen too briefly to be consciously observed. Many psychologists dismissed the popcorn marketing story as fraudulent, but it did create a stir.

Subliminal perception is possible. In fact, many cognitive scientists take unconscious perception for granted and build theories around it (e.g., Kihlstrom, Barnhardt, & Tataryn, 1992). However, research on this kind of perception has had a controversial history. Many of the studies in the 1960s lacked control groups and did not specify the variables being manipulated. Some presented stimuli for durations in which one participant might easily perceive several words and another participant no words at all. Other studies presented "dirty" words to see if they affected responses more than neutral or emotionally uncharged words did. Would the dirty words be threatening and emotionally arousing and thus lead participants to perceptually block them out? Initial results showed that participants did indeed show increased thresholds and higher autonomic activity, indicating arousal. Of course, some participants were too embarrassed to repeat the words to the experimenter (often a person of the opposite sex) and denied having seen them.

Subliminal perception, and any learning that results from it, is subtle at most and is strongly affected by such variables as expectation, motivation, previous experience, personality, and learned, culturally based behaviors.

To avoid some of these methodological problems, later experiments presented participants with both threatening and neutral words for very brief durations. The participants responded by repeating the words or by pressing a button as soon as they saw each word. In these experiments, threatening words had to be presented for a longer time or at a higher illumination than nonthreatening words in order to be identified.

In some controlled situations, subliminal stimuli can influence perception, attitudes, and behavior (Greenwald, Klinger, & Schuh, 1995). In the real world, however, we are constantly faced with many competing sensory stimuli. Therefore, what grabs our attention depends on many variables, such as the importance, prominence, and interest of a stimulus. Should we fear mind control by advertisers? The answer is probably no, because advertisements have to compete with so many other stimuli. Can backward speech in rock songs be interpreted and understood? Again, the answer is no. Can tapes listened to while you are asleep help you learn Greek or Latin? Once more, the answer is no. In the end, subliminal perception, and any learning that results from it, is subtle at most and is strongly affected by such variables as expectation, motivation, previous experience, personality, and learned, culturally based behaviors (Pratkanis, Eskenazi, & Greenwald, 1994). However, most psychologists argue that more research is needed to determine exactly what is taking place when subliminal perception occurs and to what degree subliminal stimuli can influence us.

Selective Attention

If you think that you see just because your eyes are open and hear just because you are awake, you may be wrong. Both vision and hearing are senses that require attention, which is an active process. Two perception researchers (Mack & Rock, 1998) assert that there is no perception without attention. Attention has long been a key element in the study of sensation and perception because researchers have always recognized its complex role.

Consider what happens when you face competing tasks that require attention. For example, have you ever tried to study while listening to quiet music? You may have thought that the music barely reached your threshold of awareness. Yet you may have found your attention wandering. Did melodies or words start to interrupt your studying? Research on attention shows that human beings constantly extract signals from the world around them. Although we receive many different messages at once, we can usually attend to only a single selected one.

Because people can pay attention to only one or two things at a time, psychologists sometimes call the study of attention the study of *selective attention.* Early researchers in this area discovered the *cocktail party phenomenon,* whereby a person who cannot discern the content of conversations across a crowded and noisy room can nevertheless hear his or her name mentioned by someone in the crowd.

Perceptual psychologists are interested in the complexities of the processes through which people extract information from the environment. These psychologists hope to answer this question: Which stimuli do people choose to attend to? They focus on the *allocation* of a person's attention. For example, in selective-

listening experiments, participants wearing a pair of headphones receive different messages simultaneously in each ear. Their task is often to shadow, or repeat, a message heard in one ear. Typically, they report that they are able to listen to a speaker in *either* the left ear or the right ear (but not both) and provide information about the content and quality of that speaker's voice.

The filter theory and the attenuation theory are two of the several theories about how people are able to listen selectively. The *filter theory* states that human beings possess a limited capacity to process information and that perceptual "filters" screen out information presented to one or the other of the two ears. The *attenuation theory* states that all the information a person receives is analyzed but that intervening factors inhibit (attenuate) attention so only selected information reaches the highest centers of processing. Hundreds of selective-listening studies have examined the claims of the competing theories, and recent research favors attenuation theory (Wood & Cowan, 1995). But regardless of whether people filter or attenuate information, selective-attention studies show that human beings must select among the available stimuli. It is impossible, for example, to pay attention to four lectures at once. A listener can extract information from only one speaker at a time. Admittedly, you can do more than one task at a time—for example, you can drive a car and talk on a cell phone—but you cannot use the same channel (such as vision) for several tasks simultaneously. You cannot drive a car, read a book, and look at photographs at the same time because you have to direct your attention (Kastner et al., 1998).

Clearly, both the auditory and visual systems have limited capacities. People have limited ability to divide their attention between tasks and must allocate their perceptual resources for greatest efficiency. But what happens when it is not necessary to divide your attention? What occurs when stimuli in the environment are restricted?

Restricted Environmental Stimulation

Imagine utter loneliness . . . darkness . . . complete lack of light and sound. Imagine being in an isolation tank where you don't have to adapt to the light—because there is absolutely none. This was the situation described in a compelling novel, a page-turner by Paddy Chayefsky called *Altered States*. I recommend it to all of my students; it raises provocative questions about human perceptual systems and consciousness—and the relationship between the two.

In 1954, neurophysiologist John Lilly enlisted modern technology to find out what would happen if the brain were deprived of all sensory input—if a person were to be placed in a situation much like that described by Chayefsky. Lilly actually constructed an isolation tank (similar to the one in the photo) that excluded all light and sound and was filled with heavily salted water, which helps the body to float. In this artificial sea, deprived of all external stimuli, Lilly experienced dreams, reveries, hallucinations, and other altered mental states. Throughout the ages, mystics of all kinds have claimed to achieve such trance states by purposely limiting their sensory experiences—taking vows of silence, adhering to austere lifestyles, meditating while sitting as still as a stone for hours, and so on.

Psychologists refer to what Lilly experienced as restricted environmental stimulation. And some researchers argue that there are psychological benefits to be derived from sensory restriction (deprivation)—isolation from sights, sounds, smells, tastes, and most tactile stimuli. The benefits may have been exaggerated, but such restriction can have profound effects on animals and humans. One team of researchers (Bexton, Heron, & Scott, 1954) studied the effects of sensory restriction by isolating individual college students in a comfortable but dull room. The researchers allowed the students to hear only the continuous hum of an air conditioner; the participants wore translucent plastic visors to limit their vision and tubes lined with cotton around their hands and arms to limit sensory input to their skin. The results were dramatic. Within a few hours, the participants' performance on tests of mental ability was impaired. The students became bored and irritable, and many said they saw "images."

Several fascinating follow-up studies placed participants in identical conditions *except* that they were told that the sensory restriction would serve as an aid to meditation. How do you think this information affected their responses? The participants did not hallucinate or become irritable; in fact, their mental abilities actually improved (Lilly, 1956; Zuckerman, 1969). These studies suggest that people do not necessarily become bored because of lack of stimulation. Rather, when people evaluate their situation as monotonous, they become bored. Given the opportunity to relax in a quiet place for a long time, many people meditate; they find the "deprivation" relaxing. Such findings indicate the need for caution in interpreting data from sensory deprivation studies involving human beings, because participants approach these situations with powerful expectations (recall the effects of self-fulfilling prophecies mentioned in Chapter 1).

Sensory restriction has proved to have positive effects on some people (Harrison & Barabasz, 1991). Many participants experience a profound relaxation in an environment of extreme sensory restriction (Sakata et al., 1995), which can be highly effective in modifying some habits, such as smoking, and in treating such problems as obesity (Suedfeld, 1990) and addiction (Borrie, 1991). Men, older individuals, and people with strongly religious backgrounds may be more likely to benefit than others, and some people may be adversely affected. Further, previous experience with sensory restriction may produce a cumulative effect; that is, each time a person experiences the restricted environment, it may have a greater effect. In general, the benefits of restricted environmental stimulation are probably underestimated (Suedfeld, 1990). *I*

Electromagnetic [ee-LEK-tro-mag-NET-ick] radiation: The entire spectrum of waves initiated by the movement of charged particles.

Light: The small portion of the electromagnetic spectrum that is visible to the human eye.

Myopic [my-OH-pick]: Able to see clearly things that are close but having trouble seeing objects at a distance; nearsighted.

Hyperopic [HY-per-OH-pick]: Able to see objects at a distance clearly but having trouble seeing things up close; farsighted.

Photoreceptors: The light-sensitive cells in the retina—the rods and the cones.

Transduction: Process by which a perceptual system analyzes stimuli and converts them into electrical impulses; also known as *coding.*

Think Critically

- How does the culture influence how and where individuals focus their attention?
- What fundamental assumption is a researcher making when depriving an organism of sensory experience and then measuring its behavior?

I The Visual System

Focus on issues and ideas

- The structure of the eye and its relationship to visual perception
- The duplicity theory of vision and the functions of the two types of receptor cells in the retina
- How the brain processes electrochemical signals and uses receptive fields to interpret stimuli
- How information from both central and peripheral vision determines subsequent eye movements
- How our ability to perceive color depends on the wavelength and other physical properties of visible light

Imagine that you are in an unfamiliar house at night when the power goes out. Left in total darkness, you hear creaking sounds but have no idea where they are coming from. You stub your toe on the coffee table, then frantically grope along the walls until you reach the kitchen, where you fumble through the drawers in search of a flashlight. You quickly come to a full appreciation of the sense of sight when you suddenly lack it.

Human beings derive more information through sight than through any other sense. By some estimates, the eyes contain 70% of the body's sense receptors. Although the eyes do respond to pressure, the appropriate stimulus for vision is **electromagnetic radiation**—the entire spectrum of waves initiated by the movement of charged particles. The electromagnetic spectrum includes gamma rays, X-rays, ultraviolet rays, visible light, infrared rays, radar, broadcast bands, and AC currents. Note that the **light** that is visible to the human eye is a very small portion of the electromagnetic spectrum. Light may come directly from a source or may be reflected from an object.

We begin our analysis of the visual system with a bottom-up analysis of the effect of light on the structure of the eye. Such an analysis will show that the visual system is exceedingly intricate. Although often likened to a camera, which records images, the visual system is interpretive, and a later top-down analysis will show that the camera analogy explains only part of the process.

The Structure of the Eye

Figure 3.1 shows the major structures of the human eye. Light first passes through the *cornea*—a small, transparent bulge covering both the *pupil* (the dark opening in the center of the eye) and the pigmented *iris*. The iris either constricts to make the pupil smaller or dilates to make it larger. Behind the pupil is the *lens*, which is about 4 millimeters thick. Together, the cornea, the pupil, the iris, and the lens form images in much the same way as a camera shutter and camera lens do. The *retina*, which lines the back of the eye, is like the film in a camera: It captures an image. Constriction of the iris makes the pupil smaller, improving the quality of the image on the retina and increasing the depth of focus—the distance to the part of the visual field that is in sharp focus. The action of the lens also helps control the amount of light entering the eye.

When people's eyeballs are not perfectly shaped, their vision is affected. People with elongated eyeballs are **myopic**, or *nearsighted;* they see clearly things that are close but have trouble seeing objects at a distance, because the image of an object falls short of the retina. **Hyperopic**, or *farsighted*, people have shortened eyeballs. They see objects at a distance clearly but have trouble seeing things up close, because the image of an object is focused behind the retina.

The *retina* consists of 10 layers of cells. Of these, the most important are the **photoreceptors** (the light-sensitive cells), the bipolar cells, and the ganglion cells. After light passes through several layers of bipolar and ganglion cells, it strikes the photoreceptor layer, which consists of *rods* (rod-shaped receptors) and *cones* (cone-shaped receptors); these will be described in detail later. In this layer, the light breaks down *photopigments* (light-sensitive chemicals), which causes an electrochemical change in the rods and cones. The process by which the perceptual system analyzes stimuli and converts them into electrical impulses is **transduction**, or *coding*. After transduction of the light stimulus by the retina, the resulting electrical energy is transferred back out to the next major layer, the *bipolar cells*.

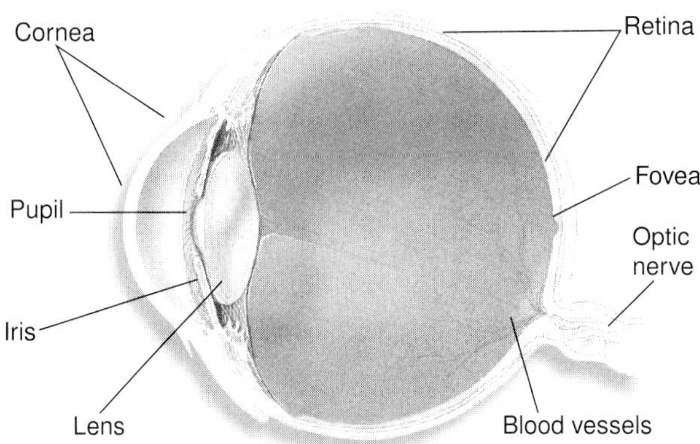

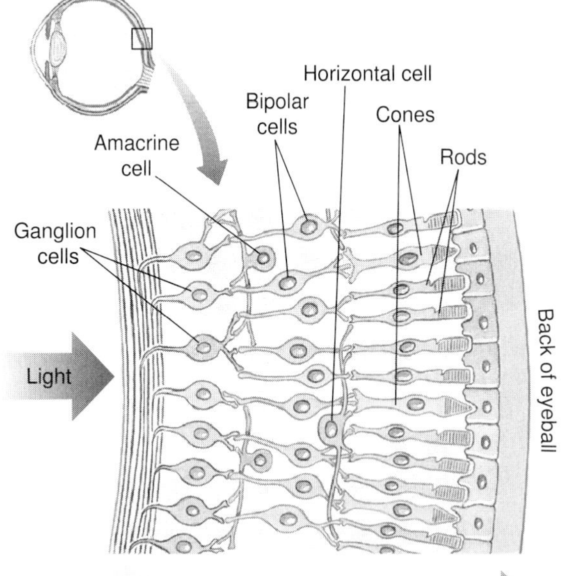

FIGURE 3.1
The Main Structures of the Eye
The photoreceptors of the retina are connected to higher brain pathways through the optic nerve. Light filters through layers of retinal cells before hitting the receptors (rods and cones), located at the back of the eyeball and pointed away from the incoming light. The rods and cones pass an electrical impulse to the bipolar cells, which in turn relay the impulse back out to the ganglion cells. The axons of the ganglion cells form the fibers of the optic nerve.

Each eye contains more than 120 million rods and 6 million cones. These millions of photoreceptors do not have individual pathways to the higher visual centers in the brain. Instead, through the process of *convergence,* electrochemical signals from many rods come together onto a single bipolar cell. At the same time, hundreds of cones synapse and converge onto other bipolar cells. From the bipolar cells, electrochemical energy is transferred to the *ganglion cell layer* of the retina. Dozens of bipolar cells synapse and converge onto each ganglion cell (there are about 1 million ganglion cells). The axons of the ganglion cells make up the *optic nerve,* which carries information that was initially received by the rods and cones to higher pathways in the nervous system. Still further coding takes place at the brain's **visual cortex,** or *striate cortex.* The visual cortex, the most important area of the brain's occipital lobe, further processes information from the *lateral geniculate nucleus* (one of the major visual projection areas in the visual system).

Rods and Cones. The *duplicity theory of vision* (sometimes called the *duplexity theory*), which is now universally accepted, asserts that there are two separate receptor systems in the retina: the rods and the cones. It also states that rods and cones are structurally different and accomplish different tasks. Cones are for the most part tightly packed in the center of the retina, at the *fovea,* and are used for day vision, color vision, and fine visual discrimination. Rods (together with some cones) are found on the rest of the retina (the periphery) and are used predominantly for night vision (see Figure 3.2). The functioning of the cones is demonstrated in the visual acuity test you take

\+ ●

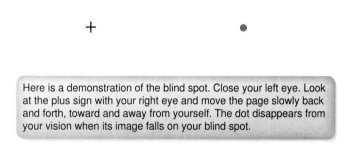

Here is a demonstration of the blind spot. Close your left eye. Look at the plus sign with your right eye and move the page slowly back and forth, toward and away from yourself. The dot disappears from your vision when its image falls on your blind spot.

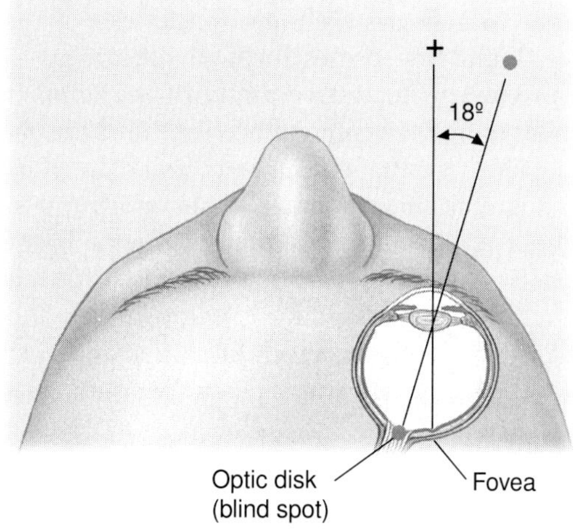

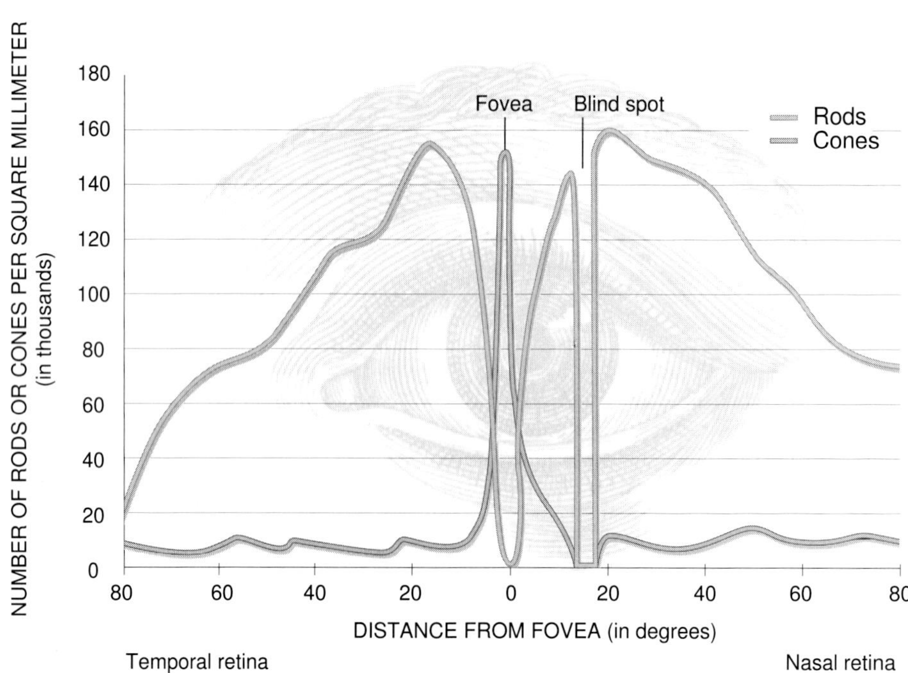

FIGURE 3.2
The Distribution of Rods and Cones and the Blind Spot
The center of the retina (the fovea) contains only cones. At about 18° of visual angle (a measure of the size of images on the retina), there are no receptors at all. This is the place where the optic nerve leaves the eye, called the *blind spot.* Because the blind spot for each eye is on the nasal side of the eyeball, there is no loss of vision; the two blind spots do not overlap.

when you apply for a driver's license. A *visual acuity test* measures the resolution capacity of the visual system—the ability to see fine details. Cones principally mediate this ability. You do best on such a test in a well-lit room (cones operate at high light levels) and when looking directly at the test items (again, more cones are in the center of the retina than in any other place).

Your eyes are always in some state of light or dark adaptation. Rods and cones are sensitive to light, but they are less sensitive in a well-lit room than they are after having been in the dark. **Dark adaptation** is the increase in sensitivity to light that occurs when the illumination level changes from high to low. In dark adaptation, chemicals in the photoreceptors (rods and cones) regenerate and return to their inactive state, increasing the eyes' light sensitivity. If you go from a well-lit lobby into a dark theater, for example, you experience a brief period of low light sensitivity, during which you are unable to distinguish empty seats. Your ability to discern objects and people in the theater increases with each passing moment. Within 30 minutes, your eyes will have almost fully adapted to the dark and will be far more light-sensitive. Of course, after leaving a dark theater and returning to the afternoon sunlight, you must squint or shade your eyes until they become adapted to the light.

Figure 3.3 shows a dark adaptation curve. The first part of the curve is determined by the cones, the second part by the rods. The speed at which the

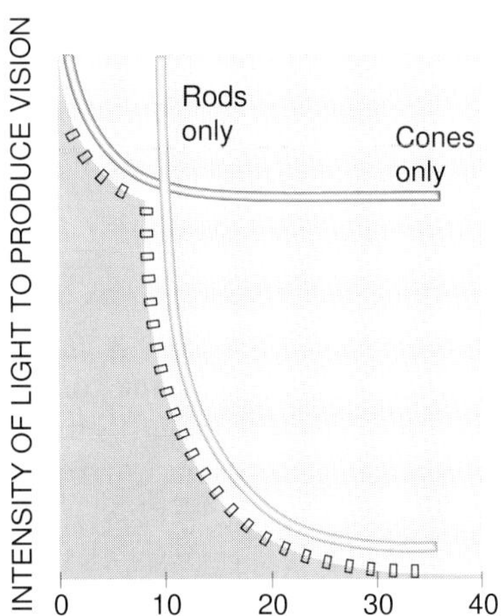

FIGURE 3.3
A Dark Adaptation Curve
The dashed line represents a typical overall dark adaptation curve. The two solid lines represent separate dark adaptation for rods and cones. Most dark adaptation occurs within 10 minutes. Rods, however, continue to adapt for another 20 minutes, reaching greater levels of sensitivity.

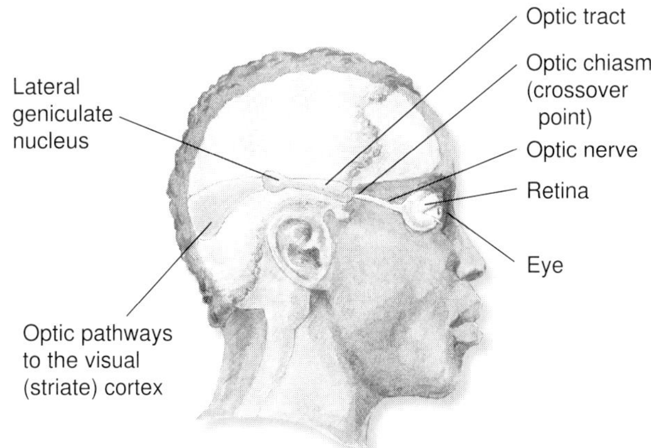

FIGURE 3.4
The Major Components of the Visual System

photochemicals in these receptors regenerate determines the shape of the two parts of the curve. The data for such curves are obtained from experiments with participants who possess only rods or cones. Typically, a participant is first shown bright light for 2 minutes. The light is then turned off, and the participant waits in a totally dark room for 15 seconds. Next, a very dim test spot of light is turned on for half a second, and the participant is asked if he or she sees it. Usually, the participant will report seeing the test spot only after several successive presentations, because dark adaptation occurs gradually. This is why, when you are driving at night, you may have trouble seeing clearly for a brief time after a car drives toward you with its high beams on; the photochemicals in the rods take some time to regenerate.

Higher Pathways. As electrical impulses leave the retina through the optic nerve, they proceed to higher centers of the brain, including the lateral geniculate nucleus and the visual cortex, or striate cortex (see Figure 3.4). These connections are quite specific. Knowledge about the way visual structures are connected to the brain aids not only psychologists but also physicians, who can determine, for example, whether a stroke victim with poor vision has a blood clot that is obstructing circulation in one hemisphere of the brain.

Visual cortex: The most important area of the brain's occipital lobe, which receives and further processes information from the lateral geniculate nucleus; also known as the *striate cortex.*

Dark adaptation: The increase in sensitivity to light that occurs when the illumination level changes from high to low, causing chemicals in the rods and cones to regenerate and return to their inactive state.

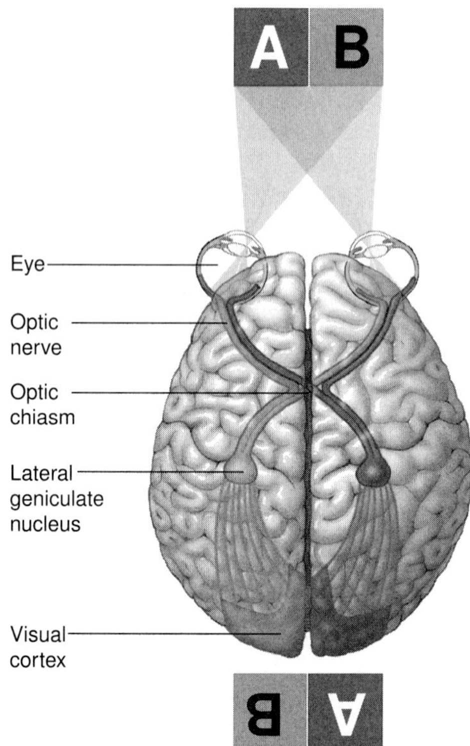

FIGURE 3.5
A Visual Image Is Projected to Both Hemispheres of the Brain

Each eye is connected to both sides of the brain, with half of its optic nerve fibers going to the left side of the brain and the other half connecting to the right side. The point at which the crossover of half of the optic nerve fibers from each eye occurs is called the **optic chiasm** (see Figure 3.5). This crossover of impulses allows the brain to process two sets of signals from an image and helps human beings perceive form in three dimensions. Severing of the optic nerves at the optic chiasm results in tunnel vision—a condition in which peripheral vision is severely impaired and a person can only see items whose images fall on the central area of the eye, the fovea.

The Electrical Connection

You can probably find your way around your room in the dark; you know where light switches and doorknobs are. You can reach out and touch just about any object when you need it. Your memory for object locations and how to reach out is coded electrochemically, and scientists know which neurons are involved (Graziano, Hu, & Gross, 1997). In fact, vision and all other perceptual processes are electrochemical in nature. When receptors in the perceptual systems are stimulated, the information is coded and sent to the brain for interpretation and further analysis. Using this basic information about electrochemical stimulation, researchers are working on a visual prosthesis—a device to help the blind see—that bypasses the eyes and directly stimulates the visual cortex (Bak et al., 1990).

Current knowledge about how the brain processes electrochemical signals comes from studies of receptive fields and associated pathways. **Receptive fields** are the areas of the retina that, when stimulated, produce a change in the firing of cells in the visual system. For example, specific cells in the retina will fire, or become active, if a vertical line is presented to a viewer but not if a horizontal line is presented. Many perceptual psychologists refer to these stimulated visual system cells as *feature detectors.* Hubel and Wiesel (1962) found receptive fields that are sensitive to such features of a stimulus line as its position, length, movement, color, and intensity. Hubel and Wiesel characterized the feature detectors as simple, complex, or hypercomplex cells. *Simple cells* respond to the shape and size of lights that stimulate the receptive field. *Complex cells* respond most vigorously to the movement of light in one direction. *Hypercomplex cells* are the most specific; they respond only to a line of the correct length and orientation that moves in the proper direction. From Hubel and Wiesel's point of view, electrical coding becomes increasingly more complex as information proceeds through the visual system. The work of Hubel and Wiesel earned them a Nobel Prize in 1981 and has been supported and extended by other noted researchers (e.g., Heeger, 1994).

Scientists now know that receptive fields also help link visual perception of space to body movements—as when Jackie Chan judges just the right time to leap from a helicopter to a floating barge, or when you see a ball and then slide to catch it (Graziano & Gross, 1994). Receptive fields are associated not only with every area of the visual cortex but with some nonvisual areas as well; for example, receptive fields stimulate cells in the parietal cortex, which is adjacent to the visual cortex and is associated with the control of movement (Corbetta et al., 1995). Receptive fields not only help you recognize vertical and horizontal lines and balls flying through the air, but also seem to be critically involved in the recognition of faces and other common objects (Allison et al., 1994). Receptive fields may be linked together in complex ways and probably not by direct, strong connections between individual cells—the perceptual system is just too complicated and flexible (Hoffman, 1999).

Receptive fields may be a key to an understanding of perception, but it is also known that the visual system processes an object's form and color—*what* it is—separately from its spatial location—*where* it is. Both behavioral and neural evidence supports this distinction. Kirkpatrick and Wasserman (1997) found evidence of "what" and "where" information in a visual discrimination task with animals. In humans, Mecklinger and Muller (1996) found distinctions in memory stores.

Researchers' study of electrochemical changes in the visual system shows that the brain simultaneously processes many components of an image—what it is, where it is, when it is perceived, colors, movement, and so on. Such simultaneous processing of information taking place in multiple locations of the brain is referred to as *parallel processing*, in contrast to *serial processing*, which occurs in a step-by-step, linear fashion. Parallel processing allows for fast recognition of complexities in the world; it also explains why brain-damaged individuals can recognize some elements of a scene and not others.

Eye Movements

Your eyes are constantly in motion. They search for familiar faces in a crowded classroom, scan the headlines on a page in a newspaper, or follow a baseball hit high into right field for a home run. You notice when someone else's eye is caught by something over your shoulder. You know when someone is fixating on a spot on top of your head. (Is there a spider there?) Research on eye movements reveals what people are looking at, how long they look at it, and perhaps where they will look next. It also helps psychologists understand some visual problems, such as reading disabilities.

Saccades are the most common type of eye movement—in fact, your eyes make at least 100,000 saccades per day. These are rapid voluntary movements of the eyes when you are reading, driving, or looking for an object. The eye can make only four or five saccades in a second. Each movement of the eye takes only about 20 to 50 milliseconds, but there is a delay of about 200 to 250 milliseconds before the next movement can be made. During this delay, the eye fixates on some part of the visual field. People use eye *fixations* to form representations of the visual world, probably by integrating successive glances into memory. This integration requires that observers move their eyes, pay attention to key elements of a visual scene, and exert careful, systematic control over eye movements (Rayner & Pollatsek, 1992).

Eye movements have been used to determine the *perceptual span*—the size of the region a person sees when fixating visually; for example, the perceptual span is the number of letters you see when you fixate on a specific point on this page. Research shows that people use information gathered by both central vision (at the fovea) and peripheral vision (at noncentral regions of the eye) to determine the location of their next eye movements; this information ultimately affects the size of the perceptual span (Rayner, 1998). Like so many other psychological phenomena, the size and nature of the perceptual span depends on the situation and personal variables. People also tend to direct their gaze to a point just to the left of center of words when they are reading. This site (left of center) may help them make inferences about the rest of the word (Reichle et al., 1998). A key benefit of this whole line of research is that eye movements can reveal a great deal about cognitive processes in general, about reading and language in particular, and, as we'll see next, about the perception of scenes and pictures.

Color Vision

Think of all the different shades of blue (navy blue, sky blue, baby blue, royal blue, turquoise, aqua). If you are like most people, you have no trouble discriminating among a wide range of colors. Color depends on the wavelengths of the visible light that stimulates the photoreceptors. It has three psychological dimensions: hue, brightness, and saturation. These dimensions correspond to three physical properties of light: wavelength, intensity, and purity.

When people speak of the color of an object, they are referring to its **hue**—whether the light reflected from the object looks red, blue, orange, or some other color. *Hue* is a psychological term, because objects themselves do not possess color. Rather, a person's perception of color is determined by how the eyes and brain interpret reflected wavelengths. In the visible spectrum, a different hue is associated with each range of wavelengths. Light with a wavelength of 400–450 nanometers looks blue; light with a wavelength of 700 nanometers looks red.

The second psychological dimension of color is **brightness**—how light or dark the hue of an object

Optic chiasm [KI-azm]: Point at which half of the optic nerve fibers from each eye cross over and connect to the other side of the brain.

Receptive fields: Areas of the retina that, when stimulated, produce a change in the firing of cells in the visual system.

Saccades [sack-ADZ]: Rapid voluntary movements of the eyes.

Hue: The psychological property of light referred to as color, determined by the wavelengths of reflected light.

Brightness: The lightness or darkness of reflected light, determined in large part by the light's intensity.

appears. Brightness is affected by three variables: (1) The greater the intensity of reflected light, the brighter the object; (2) the longer the wavelength of reflected light, the less bright the object; (3) the nearer the wavelengths are to the 500 to 600 nanometer (yellow) range, the more sensitive the photoreceptors. This is why school buses are often painted yellow—it makes them more visible to motorists.

The third psychological dimension of color is **saturation**, or *purity*—the depth and richness of the hue, determined by the homogeneity of the wavelengths contained in the reflected light. Few objects reflect light that is totally pure. Usually objects reflect a mixture of wavelengths. Pure, saturated light has a narrow band of wavelengths and, thus, a narrow range of perceived color. A saturated red light with no blue, yellow, or white in it, for example, appears as a very intense red. Unsaturated colors are produced by a wider band of wavelengths. Unsaturated red light can appear to be light pink, dark red, or rusty brown, because its wider range of wavelengths makes it less pure.

Theories of Color Vision. How does the brain code and process color? Two 19th-century scientists, Thomas Young and Hermann von Helmholtz, working independently, proposed that different types of cones provide the basis for color coding in the visual system. *Color coding* is the ability to discriminate among colors on the basis of differences in wavelength. According to the **trichromatic theory**, or the *Young–Helmholtz theory*, all colors can be made by mixing three basic colors: red, green, and blue. (*Trichromatic* means "three colors"—*tri*, from "three," and *chroma*, "color.") All cone cells in the retina are assumed to respond to all wavelengths of light; but there are three types of cones that are especially likely to respond to red, green, or blue wavelengths. The combined neural output of the red-sensitive, green-sensitive, and blue-sensitive cones provides the information that enables a person to distinguish color. If the neural output from one type of cone is sufficiently greater than that from the others, that type of color receptor will have a stronger influence on a person's perception of color. Because each person's neurons are unique, it is likely that each of us sees color somewhat differently.

Unfortunately, the trichromatic theory does not account for some specific visual phenomena. For example, it does not explain why some colors look more vivid when placed next to other colors (color contrast). It does not explain why people asked to name the basic colors nearly always name more than three. Further, the trichromatic theory does not do a good job of explaining aspects of **color blindness**—the inability to perceive different hues (described below). For example, many people with color blindness cannot successfully discriminate colors in two areas of the visual spectrum. In 1887, to solve some of the problems left unsolved by the trichromatic theory, Ewald Herring proposed another theory of color vision—the **opponent-process theory.** This theory assumes that there are six basic colors to which people respond and that there are three types of receptors: red–green, blue–yellow, and black–white. Every receptor fires in response to all wavelengths; but in each pair of receptors, one fires more strongly in response to one wavelength. Strong firing in response to red, for example, is accompanied by weak firing in response to green. Opponent-process theory explains color contrast and color blindness better than the trichromatic theory does.

Both the trichromatic theory and the opponent-process theory have received support from research (e.g., Hurvich & Jameson, 1974). Physiological studies of the retina do show three classes of cones. Thus, the trichromatic theory seems to describe accurately the coding at the retina (Marks, Dobell, & MacNichol, 1964). Support for the opponent-process theory comes from microelectrode studies of the lateral geniculate nucleus in monkeys. Cells in this nucleus respond differently to various wavelengths. When the eye is stimulated with light of a wavelength between 400 and 500 nanometers, some cells in the lateral geniculate nucleus decrease their rate of firing. If the eye is stimulated with light of a longer wavelength, their firing rate increases (DeValois & Jacobs, 1968). This change is predicted by the opponent-process

Saturation: The depth and richness of a hue determined by the homogeneity of the wavelengths contained in the reflected light; also known as *purity.*

Trichromatic [try-kroe-MAT-ick] theory: Visual theory, stated by Young and Helmholtz, that all colors can be made by mixing the three basic colors: red, green, and blue; also known as the *Young–Helmholtz theory.*

Color blindness: The inability to perceive different hues.

Opponent-process theory: Visual theory, proposed by Herring, that color is coded by stimulation of three types of paired receptors; each pair of receptors is assumed to operate in an antagonistic way so that stimulation by a given wavelength produces excitation (increased firing) in one receptor of the pair and also inhibits the other receptor.

Trichromats [TRY-kroe-MATZ]: People who can perceive all three primary colors and thus can distinguish any hue.

Monochromats [MON-o-kroe-MATZ]: People who cannot perceive any color, usually because their retinas lack cones.

Dichromats [DIE-kroe-MATZ]: People who can distinguish only two of the three basic colors.

theory. Exactly how color information is transferred from the retina to the lateral geniculate nucleus remains to be discovered.

Color Blindness. In 1794, John Dalton, formulator of the atomic theory of matter, believed he had figured out why he couldn't distinguish his red stockings from his green ones. He reasoned that something blue in his eyeball absorbed red light and prevented him from seeing red. Although Dalton was the first to try to describe color blindness scientifically, he was not the first—or the last—person to suffer from it. In fact, about 30 million Americans have some type of color perception problem.

Most human beings have normal color vision and can distinguish among about 100 different hues; they are considered trichromats. **Trichromats** are people who can perceive all three primary colors and thus can distinguish any hue. A very few people (less than 1%) do not see any color. These people, known as **monochromats**, are totally color-blind and cannot discriminate among wavelengths, often because they lack cones in their retinas (Boynton, 1988). The lack of the specific color-absorbing pigment or chemical in the cones makes accurate color discriminations impossible. Fortunately, most people with color vision deficiencies (about 8% of men and 1% of women) are only partially color-blind (Nathans, 1989). **Dichromats** are people who can distinguish only two of the three basic colors; they have difficulty distinguishing between either red and green or blue and yellow. About 2% of men cannot discriminate between reds and greens (Wyszecki & Stiles, 1967). What does the world look like to a person who is a dichromat? Such a person sees all the colors in a range of the electromagnetic spectrum as the same. For example, to a person with a blue–yellow deficiency, all greens, blues, and violets look the same; a person with a red–green deficiency may see red, green, and yellow as yellow. Many color-blind individuals have distorted color responses in several areas of the electromagnetic spectrum; that is, they have trouble with several colors.

The precise role of genetics in color blindness is not clear, but this perceptual problem is transmitted genetically from mothers to their male offspring. The fact that more men than women are color-blind is due to the way the genetic information is coded and passed on to each generation. Color blindness results from inherited alterations in the genes that are responsible for cone pigments; these genes are located on the X chromosome. Since girls have two X chromosomes and boys have only one, a girl will be color-deficient only if she inherits the defective gene from both parents. (I)

Think Critically

- Viewing 3-D comics through special glasses creates the perception of depth. Explain how you think the perception is created.
- Why do you think that psychologists prefer to use the term *color-deficient* rather than *color-blind* when describing people who have trouble seeing colors?

(I) Visual Perception

Focus on issues and ideas

- How our ability to monitor constancy is related to the perception of form
- How depth cues help us understand the environment
- Visual illusions that operate in everyday experiences
- How culture affects illusions

Many perceptual experiences depend on past events as well as current stimulation. Integrating previous experiences with new events makes perceptual encounters more meaningful. For example, it is only through experience that children learn that an object stays the same size and shape when it is moved farther away from them. In this section, we look at a range of visual perceptual phenomena that rely heavily on the integration of past and current experiences.

Perception of Form: Constancy

If your friend is wearing dark glasses that conceal much of her face, you will probably still recognize her. Similarly, impressionist artists count on people's ability to infer a complete object from dots of paint on canvas, and cartoonists use exaggerated features to portray well-known people. Understanding how human beings perceive form and space helps architects to design buildings and designers to create furniture and clothes. Perception of form involves the interpretation of stimuli conveying information about size, shape, and depth to create a unified image. Two important aspects of form perception are recognizing forms at a distance and recognizing forms that appear to have changed size or shape.

Size Constancy. People can generally judge the size of an object, even if the size of its image on the retina changes. For example, you can estimate the height of a 6-foot man who is standing 50 feet away and casts a small image on the retina; you can also estimate his height from only 5 feet away, when he casts a much larger image on the retina. **Size constancy** is the ability of the visual perceptual system to recognize that an object remains constant in size regardless of its distance from the observer or the size of its image on the retina. Infants attain size constancy by the age of 6 months and probably as early as 4 months.

Three variables determine the ability to maintain size constancy: (1) previous experience with the true size of objects, (2) the distance between the object and the person, and (3) the presence of surrounding objects. As an object moves farther away, the size of its image on the retina decreases and its perceived distance from the viewer increases (see Figure 3.6). These two effects always work together. Moreover, as an object moves away, its perceived size does not change in relation to that of objects around it. This is why knowing the size of surrounding objects helps people determine a perceived object's distance from them as well as its actual size. Hollywood special effects artists have used the brain's tendency to judge an object's size by comparing it with surrounding objects to convince moviegoers that, for example, a 6-inch clay model of an ape is the giant King Kong.

Shape Constancy. Another important aspect of form perception is **shape constancy**—the ability of the visual perceptual system to recognize a shape despite changes in its orientation or the angle from which it is viewed (see Figure 3.6). For example, even though you usually see trees standing perpendicular to the ground, you can recognize a tree that has been chopped down and is lying in a horizontal position. Similarly, an ice cream cone looks triangular when you view it from the side; yet you perceive it as an ice cream cone even when you view it from above, where it appears more circular than triangular.

Depth Perception

For centuries, Zen landscape artists have used the principles of perception to create seemingly expansive, rugged gardens out of tiny plots of land. Although a Zen landscape can fool the eye, you normally judge distances accurately when you drive a car, catch a ball, or take a picture. Depth perception allows you to estimate your distance from an object and the distance between that object and another one. Closely associated with these two tasks is the ability to see in three dimensions—that is, to perceive height, width, and depth. Both monocular cues (using one eye) and binocular cues (using two eyes) are used in depth perception.

FIGURE 3.6
Perceptual Constancies
Size constancy is the perceptual system's ability to recognize that an object remains the same size regardless of its distance from an observer or the size of its image on the retina. *Shape constancy* is the perceptual system's ability to recognize a shape despite changes in the angle or position from which it is viewed.

SIZE CONSTANCY: The size of the image on the retina gets larger or smaller as you move closer to or farther away from an object. But thanks to size constancy, you still perceive the object as being the same size.

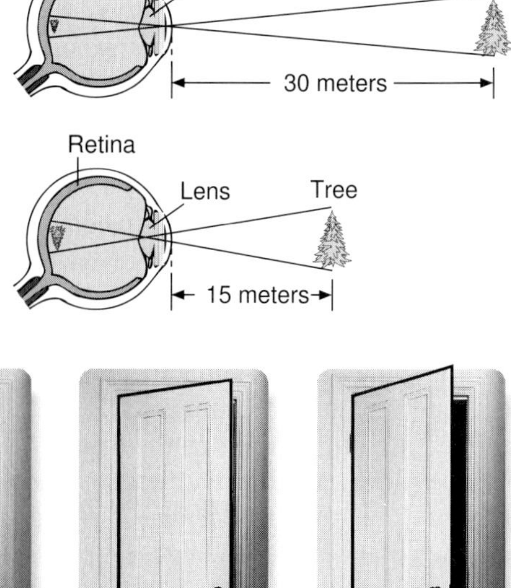

SHAPE CONSTANCY: A door is a door is a door . . . whether it is open, shut, or viewed at an angle.

Binocular cues predominate at close distances, and monocular cues are used for distant scenes and two-dimensional fields of view, such as paintings.

Monocular Depth Cues. Depth cues that do not depend on the use of both eyes are **monocular depth cues** (see Figure 3.7 on p. 72). Two important monocular depth cues arise from the effects of motion on perception. The first cue, *motion parallax,* occurs when a moving observer stares at a fixed point. The objects behind that point appear to move in the same direction as the observer; the objects in front of the point appear to move in the opposite direction. For example, if you stare at a fence while riding in a moving car, the trees behind the fence seem to move in the same direction as the car (forward) and the bushes in front of the fence seem to move in the opposite direction (backward). Motion parallax also affects the speed at which objects appear to move. Objects at a greater distance from the moving observer appear to move more slowly than objects that are closer. The second monocular depth cue derived from movement is the *kinetic depth effect.* Objects that look flat when stationary appear to be three-dimensional when set in motion. When two-dimensional projections—such as images of squares or rods shown on a computer screen—are rotated, they appear to have three dimensions.

Other monocular depth cues arise from the stimulus itself; these are often seen in photographs and paintings. For example, because of the depth cue of *linear perspective* larger or taller objects are usually perceived to be closer than smaller ones, particularly in relation to surrounding objects. In addition, because distant objects appear to be closer together than nearer objects, a painter shows distance by making parallel lines converge as they recede. Another monocular cue for depth is *interposition.* When one object blocks out part of another, the first appears to be closer. A fifth monocular cue is *texture;* surfaces that have little texture or detail seem to be in the distance. Artists often use the additional cues of *highlighting* and *shadowing.* Highlighted (light) objects appear close; shadowed (dark) objects appear to be farther away. In addition, the perceptual system picks up other information from shadowing, including the curvature of surfaces (Cavanagh & Leclerc, 1989). Still another monocular depth cue is *atmospheric perspective,* which relates to the wavelengths of reflected light. Distant mountains often look blue, for example, because long (red) wavelengths are more easily scattered as they pass through the air, allowing more short (blue) wavelengths to reach our eyes. Leonardo da Vinci used this phenomenon in his paintings; he even developed an equation for how much blue pigment to mix with the close-up color of an object to make the object appear as far away as he wished. Similarly, Michelangelo's figures seem to float off the ceiling of the Sistine Chapel because he used color so effectively to portray depth.

Another monocular depth cue that is not derived from the stimulus is accommodation. If a person looks from one object to another that is at a different distance, the lenses of the eye accommodate—that is, change shape to adapt to the depth of focus. This cue is available from each eye separately. **Accommodation** is the change in the shape of the lens of the eye that enables the observer to keep an object in focus on the retina when the object is moved or when the observer focuses on an object at a different distance. Muscles attached to the lens control this change and provide information about the shape of the lens to the higher processing systems in the brain.

Binocular Depth Cues. Most people, even infants, also use **binocular depth cues**—cues for depth perception that require the use of both eyes. One important binocular depth cue is **retinal disparity,** which is the slight difference between the visual images projected on the two retinas. Retinal disparity occurs because the eyes are physically separated (by the bridge of the nose), which causes them to see an object from

Size constancy: Ability of the visual perceptual system to recognize that an object remains constant in size regardless of its distance from the observer or the size of its image on the retina.

Shape constancy: Ability of the visual perceptual system to recognize a shape despite changes in its orientation or the angle from which it is viewed.

Monocular [mah-NAHK-you-ler] depth cues: Depth cues that do not depend on the use of both eyes.

Accommodation: The change in the shape of the lens of the eye that enables the observer to keep an object in focus on the retina when the object is moved or when the observer focuses on an object at a different distance.

Binocular depth cues: Cues for depth perception that require the use of both eyes.

Retinal disparity: The slight difference between the visual images projected on the two retinas.

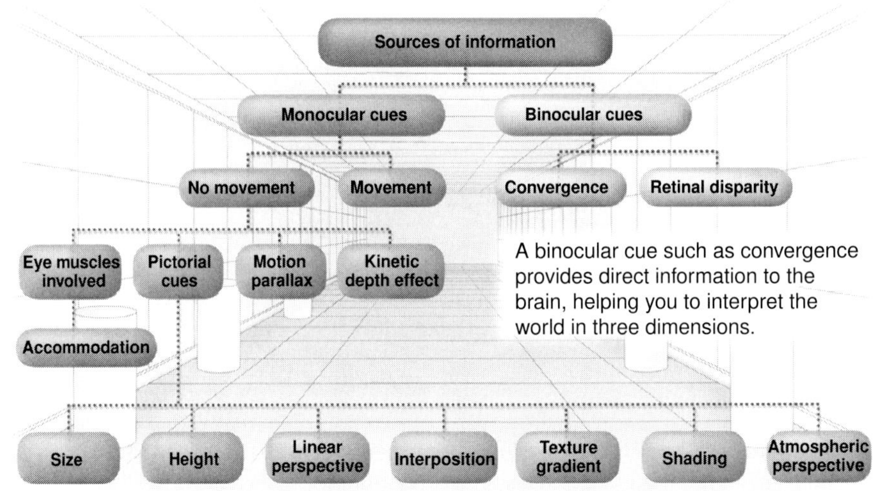

FIGURE 3.7
Depth Perception
The ability to see in three dimensions—height, width, and depth—depends on both monocular and binocular cues.

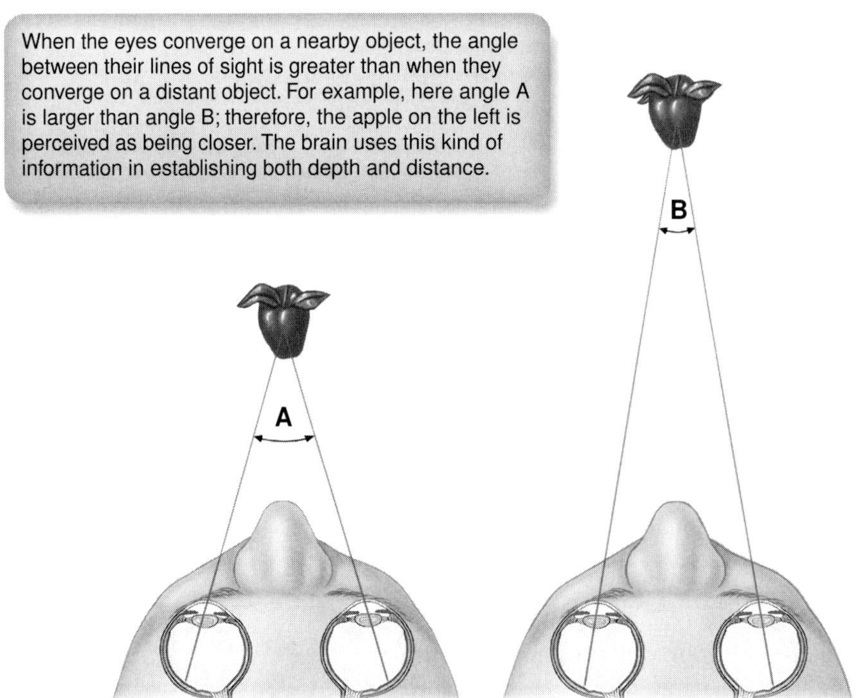

slightly different angles. To see how retinal disparity works, hold a finger up in front of your face and look at some object across the room first with one eye and then with the other eye; your finger will appear in different positions relative to the object. The closer objects are to the eyes, the farther apart their images on the retinas will be—and the greater the retinal disparity. Objects at a great distance produce little retinal disparity.

When the eyes converge on a nearby object, the angle between their lines of sight is greater than when they converge on a distant object. For example, here angle A is larger than angle B; therefore, the apple on the left is perceived as being closer. The brain uses this kind of information in establishing both depth and distance.
A
B

Another binocular depth cue is convergence. **Convergence** is the movement of the eyes toward each other in order to keep visual stimulation at corresponding points on the retinas as an object moves closer to the observer. Like accommodation, convergence is controlled by eye muscles that convey information to the brain. For objects beyond 20 or 30 feet away, the eyes are aimed pretty much in parallel, and the effect of convergence diminishes.

Illusions

At some time, you have probably seen what looks like water ahead on the road, only to find it has disappeared when you drive by that point. You most likely

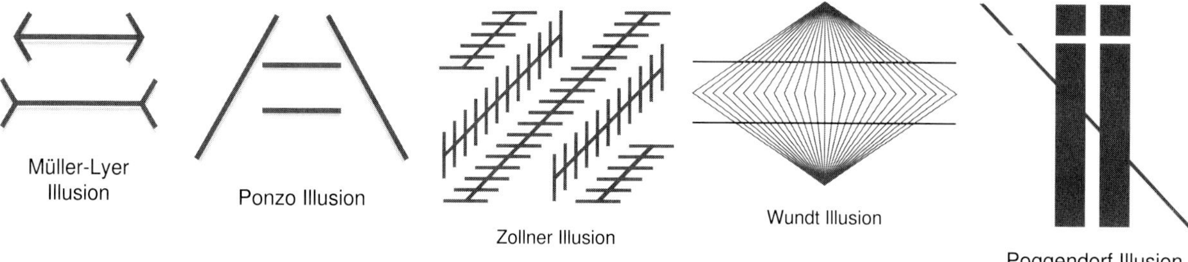

FIGURE 3.8
Five Well-Known Illusions
In the Müller-Lyer and Ponzo illusions, lines of equal length appear to differ in length. In the Zollner illusion, the short lines make the longer ones seem not parallel, even though they are. In the Wundt illusion, the center horizontal lines are parallel, even though they appear bent. In the Poggendorf illusion, the line disappears behind a solid and reappears in a position that seems wrong.

also have seen railroad tracks appear to converge in the distance. When normal visual process and depth cues seem to break down, you experience an optical illusion. An **illusion** is a perception of a physical stimulus that differs from measurable reality or from what is commonly expected.

A common illusion is the *Müller-Lyer illusion*, in which two lines of equal length with arrows on the ends appear to be of different lengths. A similar illusion is the *Ponzo illusion* (sometimes called the railroad illusion), in which two horizontal lines of the same length, bracketed by slanted lines, appear to be of different lengths. (See Figure 3.8 for examples of these two illusions and three others).

The *moon illusion* is a natural illusion. Although the actual size of the moon and the size of its image on the retina do not change, the moon appears about 30% larger when it is near the horizon than when it is overhead. The moon illusion is quite striking—in just a few minutes, the moon appears to change from quite large to quite small. The moon illusion is even seen in photographs and paintings (Coren & Aks, 1990).

How do visual illusions work? No completely satisfactory explanations have been found. Recent theories account for these illusions in terms of the backgrounds against which the objects are seen. These explanations assume that the observer has had previous experiences with a particular stimulus and has well-developed perceptual constancies. (*Diversity,* on p. 74, explores how cultural experiences affect the experience of illusions.) For example, the moon illusion is explained by the fact that, when seen overhead, the moon is against a featureless background, whereas, when at the horizon, objects are close to it. Objects in the landscape provide cues about distance that change the observer's perception of the size of the moon (Baird, Wagner, & Fuld, 1990). To see how the moon illusion depends on landscape cues, try this: When the moon is at the horizon, bend over and look at it from between your legs. Since that position screens out some of the horizon cues, the magnitude of the illusion is reduced.

The Ponzo illusion is similarly accounted for by the linear perspective provided by the slanted background lines. The Müller-Lyer illusion occurs because of the angles of the short lines attached to the ends of the longer lines. Short lines angled like arrow tails are often interpreted as far corners—corners distant from the observer. Short lines angled like arrow heads are commonly interpreted as corners that are close to the observer. Therefore, lines with far-corner angles attached to them appear longer because their length is judged in a context of distance.

These are not the only ways of explaining illusions. Some researchers assert that the moon looks different sizes on the horizon and overhead because people judge its size the same way they judge that of other moving objects that pass through space. Because the moon does not get closer to them, they assume it is moving away. Objects that move away get smaller; hence the illusion of a change in the size of the moon (Reed, 1984). This explanation focuses on constancies but also takes account of movement and space.

Gestalt Laws of Organization

Gestalt psychologists (see p. 21) suggest that people's conscious experience is more than the sum of its parts. They argue that the mind organizes the elements of

Convergence: The movement of the eyes toward each other to keep visual stimulation at corresponding points on the retinas as an object moves closer to the observer.

Illusion: A perception of a physical stimulus that differs from measurable reality or from what is commonly expected.

DIVERSITY

Cross-Cultural Research on Illusions

A wonderful advertisement a number of years ago showed a 12-year-old African American boy eating a thick deli sandwich. The caption was "You don't have to be Jewish to like Levy's rye bread." You also don't have to be Russian to appreciate Tchaikovsky; nor do you have to be from Ireland to like U2. Yet there is no doubt that artists bring to their work a nationalistic tone. George Gershwin's *Rhapsody in Blue* sounds distinctly American, as does New Orleans jazz.

Each person brings a lifetime of experiences to his or her perceptions. This becomes especially clear from research conducted cross-culturally. Cross-cultural research on illusions, for example, shows that the Müller-Lyer and Ponzo (railroad) illusions are perceived differently by different cultures. Leibowitz (1971) conducted a series of studies on the Ponzo illusion using both American participants and participants from Guam, where there are no railroads and perspective cues are far less prevalent than in the United States. Leibowitz had his participants judge the Ponzo illusion presented as simple line drawings and also in photographs. He found that the illusion was more pronounced for the American participants as he added more pictorial depth cues. The participants from Guam showed few differences when more pictorial cues were added. There were other differences between the groups; for example, the participants from Guam viewed depth differently than did their American counterparts. The different cultures viewed the world in dissimilar ways.

Other illusions have been investigated with different cultural groups. For example, Pedersen and Wheeler (1983) compared the reactions of two groups of Navajos to the Müller-Lyer illusion. One group lived in rectangular houses; these participants had extensive experience with corners, angles, and oblique lines. The other group lived in traditional Navajo round houses, and their early experiences included far fewer encounters with angles. The researchers found that those who lived in angular houses were more susceptible to the Müller-Lyer illusion, which depends on angles. Some researchers say such illusions depend on the *carpenter effect,* because in Western cultures carpenters use lines, angles, and geometry to build houses.

Research shows that people's auditory perceptions are also culturally dependent. Although there is little systematic scientific evidence on the topic, musicians have long known that a person's experiences with Western music make 12-tone music and Indian and Asian melodies sound unfamiliar and dissonant. The perception of music, like the perception of illusions, depends on early experiences. Deregowski (1980) asserts that there is a dearth of studies of perception in non-Western cultures; yet he concludes from his review of studies of language, pictures, smell, and illusions that there are cross-cultural differences in perception that reflect people's cultures. Individuals from non-Western cultures do not initially see many visual illusions and some features of depth; but when key characteristics of pictures and scenes are pointed out, they often exclaim, "Oh, now I see it!" Yet initially they fail to recognize visual cues that individuals from Western cultures do perceive. Cross-cultural research is exciting and illuminating, though unfortunately limited in its extent. For psychologists to develop truly comprehensive theories of perception, they must incorporate cross-cultural differences into their research. ■

experience to form something unique; each individual views the world in terms of perceptual frameworks. Analyzed as a whole experience, the patterns of a person's perceptions make sense. The first Gestalt psychologists—including Max Wertheimer, Kurt Koffka, and Wolfgang Köhler—greatly influenced early theories of form perception. These psychologists assumed (wrongly) that human perceptual processes *solely* reflect brain organization and that they could learn about the workings of the brain by studying perception. Researchers now know, of course, that the relationship between brain structure and function is much more complex—perception is a process that not only represents current stimuli but reflects past experiences as well.

Perception is a process that not only represents current stimuli but reflects past experiences as well.

The early Gestaltists focused their perceptual studies on how people experience form and organization. These early researchers

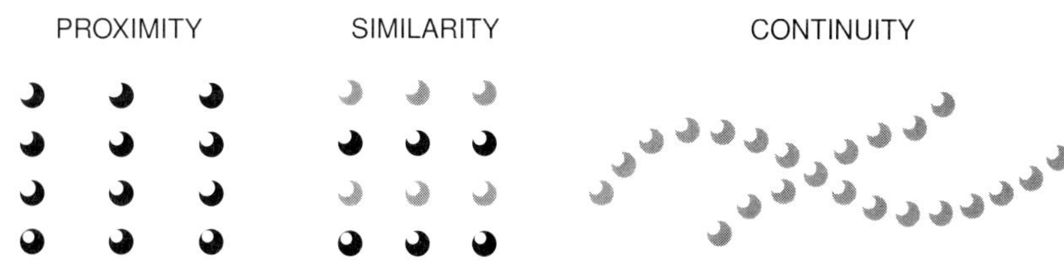

According to the Gestalt law of proximity, the circles on the left appear to be arranged in vertical columns because items that are close together tend to be perceived as a unit. According to the law of similarity, the lighter and darker circles in the middle appear to be arranged in horizontal rows because similar items tend to be perceived in groups. According to the law of continuity, an observer can predict where the next item should occur in the arrangement on the right because the grouping of items projects lines into space.

The law of Prägnanz: Items or stimuli that *can* be grouped together as a whole *will* be. These 16 dots are typically perceived as a square.

In a study asking people to divide these objects into two groups, Beck (1966) found that participants generally placed the boundary between upright and tilted Ts rather than between the backward Ls and the upright Ts because the latter appear more similar. Beck argued that this result supports the law of Prägnanz.

FIGURE 3.9
Gestalt Laws
Gestalt principles are the organizing elements humans use to group perceptual fragments into the coherent wholes by which they perceive the world.

believed people organize each complex visual field into a coherent whole rather than seeing individual, unrelated elements. That is, they believed people see groups of elements, not fragments or parts. According to this idea, called the **law of Prägnanz,** items or stimuli that *can* be grouped together and seen as a whole, or a form, *will* be seen that way; viewers see the simplest shape consistent with available information. So, for example, people tend to see the series of 16 dots in the lower left portion of Figure 3.9 as a square. Not only did Gestaltists believe that perception is organized by grouping and form, but they also assumed that retinal stimulation was directly reflected in physiological processing.

The law of Prägnanz was based on principles of organization for the perception of figures, especially contours, which help define *figure–ground relationships.* Gestalt psychologists focused on the nature of these relationships, contending that people perceive *figures* (the main objects of sensory attention—the foregrounds) as distinct from the *grounds* (the backgrounds) on which they are presented (see Figure 3.10). Gestalt psychologists developed the following series of laws, the first three of which are illustrated in the upper part of Figure 3.9, for predicting which areas of an ambiguous pattern would

FIGURE 3.10
The Figure–Ground Relationship
Gestalt psychologists studied the figure–ground relationship. In this drawing, figure and ground can be reversed. You can see either two faces against a white background or a goblet against a dark background.

Law of Prägnanz [PREG-nants]: The Gestalt notion that when items or stimuli *can* be grouped together and seen as a whole, they *will* be.

be seen as the figure (foreground) and which as the ground (background):

- *Law of proximity:* Elements close to one another in space or time will be perceived as groups.
- *Law of similarity:* Similar items will be perceived in groups.
- *Law of continuity:* A string of items will project the probable location of the next item.
- *Common fate principle:* Items that move or change together will be perceived as a whole.
- *Law of closure:* Parts of a figure that are not presented will be filled in by the perceptual system.

Beck (1966) conducted a well-known study that examined Gestalt principles (see the lower right part of Figure 3.9). However, Beck's work showed that Gestalt principles are vague: They apply whether participants choose orientation or shape to break up the figure, but they do not explain why orientation predominated in Beck's study. Apparently, not all people use the same criteria in applying Gestalt laws under the same circumstances. Nor are Gestalt laws always consistent with current knowledge of brain organization—for example, when a figure is made up of other figures, there is little consistency among people as to what they pay attention to, the larger figure or the embedded smaller ones (Rock & Palmer, 1990). Furthermore, the fact that "what" and "where" processing cells are located throughout the brain shows that processing is multistage and complex—not merely bottom up, but also top down. Nevertheless, early investigations by Gestaltists offered enough glimpses into the true nature of perception that they continue to influence perceptual psychologists, serving as springboards to further research. (I)

Think Critically

- What do Gestalt researchers mean when they say that the whole is greater than the sum of its parts?
- How do you think culture exerts its influence on your perceptual systems?

(I) Hearing

Focus on issues and ideas

- The structural components of the ear and their relationship to hearing
- The differences between place and frequency theories of hearing
- Hearing impairments and the varying levels of deafness

You may have heard the oft-repeated statement that blind people can hear better than sighted individuals—and at least on some tasks, it turns out to be true (Lessard et al., 1998). Although our sense of sight is powerful and gives texture to our experience, we rely enormously on our sense of hearing for many perceptual experiences, even more than on sight. Nevertheless, most of us take hearing for granted, but the task of listening is exceedingly complex. Consider music. Listening closely to a Beethoven symphony is delightful and intriguing, but it is difficult because so much is going on at once. The listener must simultaneously process the sounds, rhythms, and intensities produced by more than 20 instruments playing at once. Like seeing, hearing is a complex process that involves converting physical stimuli into a psychological experience.

Sound

When a tuning fork is struck or a stereo system booms out a bass note, sound waves are created and air is moved. You can place your hand in front of a stereo speaker and feel the displacement of the sound waves when the volume rises. The movement of the air and the accompanying changes in air pressure (physical stimuli) cause a listener's eardrum to move back and forth rapidly. The movement of the eardrum triggers a series of electromechanical and electrochemical changes that the person experiences as sound. **Sound** is the psychological experience that occurs when changes in air pressure affect the receptive organ for hearing; the resulting tones, or sounds, vary in frequency and amplitude. Sound is often thought of in terms of two psychological aspects, pitch and loudness, which are associated with the two physical attributes of frequency and amplitude.

As shown in Figure 3.11, **frequency** is the number of complete changes in air pressure occurring during a given unit of time. Within 1 second, for example, there may be 50 complete changes (50 cycles per second) or 10,000 complete changes (10,000 cycles per second). Frequency is usually measured in hertz (Hz); 1 Hz equals 1 cycle per second. Frequency determines the pitch, or *tone*, of a sound; **pitch** is the psychological experience that corresponds with the frequency of an auditory stimulus. High-pitched tones usually have high frequencies. When a piano hammer strikes a short string on the right-hand end of a piano keyboard, the string vibrates at a high frequency and sounds high in pitch; when a long string (at the left-hand end) is struck, it vibrates less frequently and sounds low in pitch.

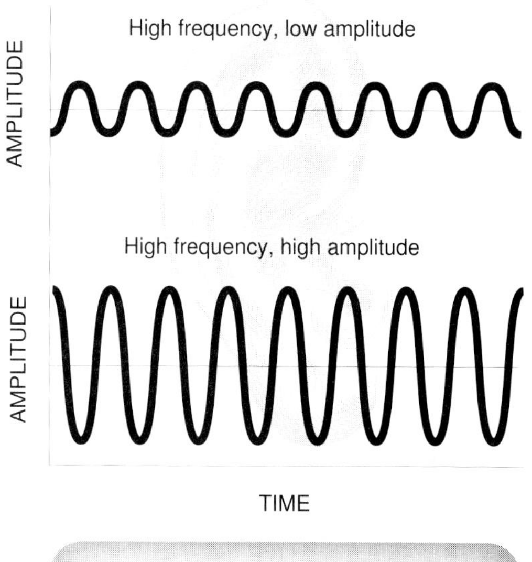

High-frequency sound waves have a large number of complete cycles per second and a high pitch; they can be of low amplitude (soft sound) or high amplitude (loud sound).

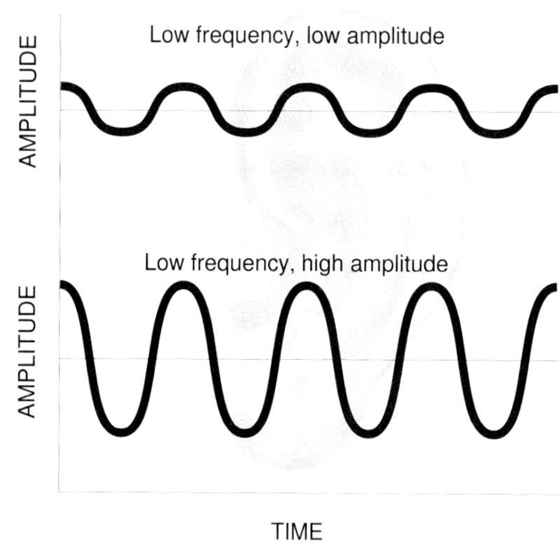

Low-frequency sound waves have a small number of complete cycles per second and a low pitch; they can be of low amplitude (soft sound) or high amplitude (loud sound).

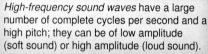

FIGURE 3.11
The Frequency and Amplitude of Sound Waves
A person's psychological experience of sound depends on the frequency and amplitude of sound waves.

Amplitude, or *intensity*, is the total energy of a sound wave, which determines the loudness of the sound. High-amplitude sound waves have more energy than low-amplitude waves; they apply greater force to the ear (see Figure 3.11). Amplitude is measured in *decibels*. Every increase of 20 decibels corresponds to a tenfold increase in perceived intensity. (Decibels are measured on a logarithmic scale, which is exponential, not linear; thus, increases in sound intensity measured in decibels are quite large.) As Figure 3.12 (on p. 78) shows, normal conversation has an amplitude of about 60 decibels, and sounds above 120 decibels are painfully loud.

Amplitude and frequency are not correlated. A low-frequency sound can be very loud or very soft; that is, it can have either high or low amplitude. Middle C on a piano, for example, can be played loudly or softly. The frequency (and thus the pitch) of the sound stays the same—it is still middle C; only its amplitude (and corresponding loudness) varies. The psychological perception of loudness depends on other factors, such as the amount of background noise and whether the person is paying attention to the sound. Another psychological dimension, *timbre*, is the quality of a sound—the specific mixture of amplitudes and frequencies that make up the sound. People's perceptions of all these qualities depend on the physical structure of their ears.

Structure of the Ear

The receptive organ for *audition*, or hearing, is the ear: It translates physical stimuli (sound waves) into electrical impulses that the brain can interpret. The ear has three major parts: the outer ear, the middle ear, and the inner ear (see Figure 3.13 on p. 78). The tissue on the outside of the head is part of the outer ear. The eardrum (*tympanic membrane*) is the boundary between the outer and middle ear. When sound waves enter the ear, they produce changes in pressure on the eardrum. The eardrum responds to these changes by vibrating. Pressure on the eardrum can sometimes be problematic, as *Experiencing Psychology* (on p. 79) illustrates.

Sound: The psychological experience that occurs when changes in air pressure stimulate the receptive organ for hearing; the resulting tones, or sounds, vary in frequency and amplitude.

Frequency: The number of complete changes in air pressure occurring per unit of time; measured in hertz (Hz), or cycles per second.

Pitch: The psychological experience that corresponds with the frequency of an auditory stimulus; also known as *tone*.

Amplitude: The total energy of a sound wave, which determines the loudness of the sound; also known as *intensity*.

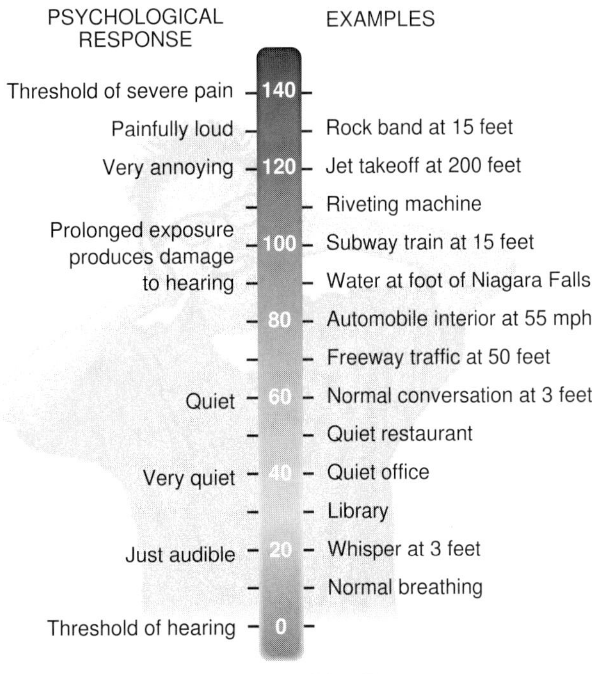

FIGURE 3.12
Psychological Responses to Various Sound Intensities
High-amplitude sound waves, such as those generated by a rock band, have greater energy than low-amplitude waves and a greater impact on the sensitive structure of the ears.

The middle ear is quite small. Within it, tiny bones (*ossicles*) known as the *hammer, anvil,* and *stirrup,* help convert the relatively large forces striking the eardrum into small forces. Two small muscles are attached to the ossicles; these muscles contract involuntarily when they are exposed to intense sounds. They help protect the delicate mechanisms of the inner ear from the damaging effects of an intense sound that could overstimulate them (Borg & Counter, 1989). Ultimately, the middle ear bones stimulate the *basilar membrane,* which runs down the middle of the *cochlea,* a spiral tube in the inner ear (see Figure 3.14).

In the cochlea, which is shaped like a snail's shell and comprises three chambers, sound waves of different frequencies stimulate different areas of the basilar membrane. These areas, in turn, stimulate the hair cells, which initiate the electrical coding of sound waves. That is, these cells are responsible for the transduction of mechanical energy into electrochemical energy. The hair cells are remarkably sensitive. Hudspeth (1983), for example, found that hair cells respond when they are displaced as little as 100 picometers (trillionths of a meter).

Electrical impulses make their way through the brain's auditory perceptual system in much the same way as visual information proceeds through the visual perceptual system. The electrical impulses proceed through the auditory nerve to the midbrain and finally to the auditory cortex. Studies of single cells in the auditory areas of the brain show that some cells are

FIGURE 3.13
The Major Structures of the Ear

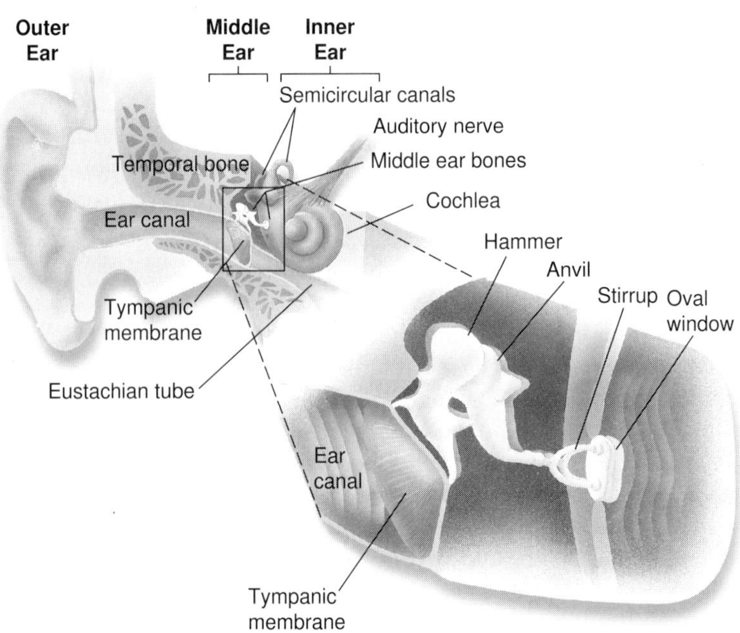

EXPERIENCING PSYCHOLOGY

The Pressures of Flying in Airplanes

When you fly anywhere in a large passenger plane, you are often at altitudes of 33,000 to 40,000 feet above sea level. Since airliner cabins are pressurized to the equivalent of between 5,000 and 8,000 feet, you won't need canisters of oxygen. But this is still well above sea level and equivalent to the height of many ski slopes in Oregon or Colorado.

When you fly, as the plane gains altitude, air pressure inside the cabin drops, gas in the body expands, and you feel a "popping" sensation in your ears. Gas expansion raises the pressure in your sinuses and middle ear cavities; this pressure must be equalized with that of the air pressure inside the plane; this is accomplished by the escape of air through the nose, throat, and Eustachian tubes. The ear popping is quite normal and will occur without your having to do anything special such as swallowing, gum chewing, or yawning.

During the descent before the plane lands, the situation is reversed. The pressure in the middle ear gradually becomes lower than the pressure in the cabin. If your Eustachian tubes in the middle ear are clear, air passes easily and pressure is equalized. But if you are ill and your tubes are blocked (for example, with an infection), you may feel pressure on your eardrums. If this occurs, a reasonable and relatively safe technique to help equalize the pressure is to yawn and move the lower jaw from side to side.

Many well-traveled individuals advise not flying if you have a head cold. If you must fly, take an antihistamine/decongestant to help clear your ears before you leave—the pain of the unequal pressure in an infected ear is quite severe! ■

more responsive to certain frequencies than to others. Some cells are highly sensitive to certain narrow frequency ranges; if a frequency is outside their range, these cells might not fire at all. This finding is analogous to the findings reported by Hubel and Wiesel, who discovered receptive visual fields in which proper stimulation brought about dramatic changes in the firing of a cell; research supports a highly structured cellular organization in the auditory system, much like that of the visual system (DeCharms, Blake, & Merzenich, 1998).

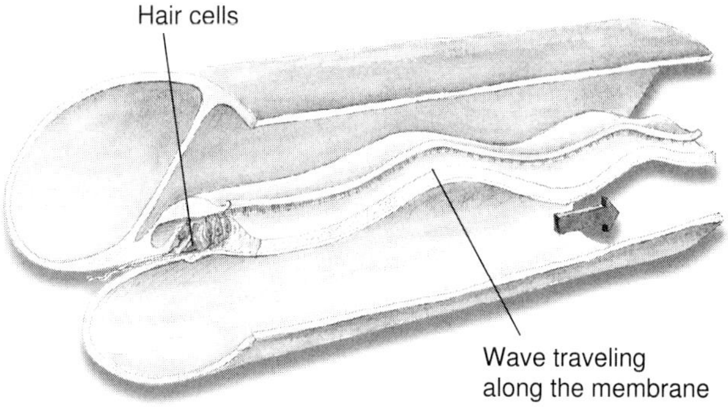

Hair cells

Wave traveling along the membrane

FIGURE 3.14
The Basilar Membrane
In this view, the cochlea has been unwound and cut open to reveal the basilar membrane, which is covered with thousands of hair cells. Pressure variations in the fluid that fills the cochlea cause oscillations to travel in waves along the basilar membrane, stimulating the hair cells.

Theories of Hearing

Most theories of hearing fall into two major classes: place theories and frequency theories. *Place theories* claim that the analysis of sound occurs in the basilar membrane, with different frequencies and intensities affecting different parts (places) of the membrane. Such theories assert that each sound wave causes a traveling wave on the basilar membrane, which in turn causes displacement of hair cells on the membrane. The displacement of individual hair cells triggers specific information about pitch.

In contrast, *frequency theories* maintain that the analysis of pitch and intensity occurs at higher centers (levels) of processing, perhaps in the auditory area of the cortex, and that the basilar membrane merely transfers information to those centers. These theories suggest that the entire basilar membrane is stimulated and its overall rate of responding is somehow communicated to higher centers for analysis.

Like the theories that attempt to explain color vision, both place theories and frequency theories present theoretical problems. And neither type of theory explains all the data about pitch and loudness. For example, the hair cells do not act independently (as place theories suggest) but instead act together (as frequency theories suggest). And the rate at which hair cells fire is not fast enough to keep up with sound waves (which typically have frequencies of 1,000 to 10,000 cycles per second), as frequency theories suggest.

To get around the difficulties, modern researchers have developed theories of auditory information processing that attempt to explain pitch in terms of both specific action in parts of the basilar membrane and generalized frequency analyses at higher levels. Theories that seem at odds with one another can work together to explain pitch and loudness when the best parts of them are combined. (Does this remind you of the debate over the trichromatic and opponent-process theories of color vision discussed earlier?)

Sound Localization

How do you know where to turn when you hear a baby crying? Although not as direction-sensitive as many animals, human beings have amazingly efficient sound-localization (direction-determining) abilities. Researchers have learned much about these abilities by presenting sound through headsets, with one sound going to one ear and another sound to the other ear. Such experiments have revealed that two key factors influence sound localization: interaural time differences and interaural intensity differences. Because you have two ears, a sound produced to the left of your head will arrive at the left ear before the right. Thus, you have an *interaural time difference.* In addition, the sound will reach the two ears at different intensities. A sound produced at your left will be perceived as slightly more intense by the left ear than the right; thus, there is an *interaural intensity difference.* These two pieces of information are analyzed in the brain at nuclei (collections of cell bodies) that are especially sensitive to time and intensity differences between the ears.

Time and intensity differences are not the sole factors that determine sound localization, however. What happens when the sound source is just in front of you, and thus is equidistant from your two ears? It turns out that head and body movements help resolve the source of a sound. You rotate your head and/or move your body when you are unsure of the source of a sound. In addition, the external ear has ridges and folds that bounce sounds around just a bit, creating slight delays that help you localize sounds. Finally, visual cues and previous experiences help in localizing sounds in space.

Conduction deafness: Deafness resulting from interference with the transmission of sound to the neural mechanism of the inner ear.

Sensorineural [sen-so-ree-NEW-ruhl] deafness: Deafness resulting from damage to the cochlea, the auditory nerve, or higher auditory processing centers.

Hearing Impairments

Sixteen percent of adults and more than one-third of people over age 60 have a hearing loss. In total, about 13 million people in the United States have hearing impairments, ranging from minor hearing loss to total deafness. Older individuals are often discriminated against because of their hearing problems. The numerous causes of hearing impairments include both environmental and genetic factors, which can lead to varying degrees of conduction deafness, sensorineural deafness, or a combination of the two (Vahava et al., 1998).

Conduction deafness is deafness resulting from interference with the transmission of sound to the neural mechanism of the inner ear. The interference may be caused by something temporary, such as a head cold or a buildup of wax in the outer ear canal. Or it may be caused by something far more serious, such as hardening of the tympanic membrane, destruction of the tiny bones within the ear, or diseases that create pressure in the middle ear. If sound can somehow be transmitted past the point of the conduction problem, hearing can be improved.

Sensorineural deafness is deafness resulting from damage to the cochlea, the auditory nerve, or higher auditory processing centers. The most common cause of this type of deafness is ongoing exposure to very high-intensity sound, such as that of rock bands or jet planes. Listening to even moderately loud music for longer than 15 minutes a day can cause permanent deafness.

An audiometer, which presents sounds of different frequencies through a headphone, is used to evaluate hearing; results are presented as an *audiogram,* which is a graph showing hearing sensitivity at selected frequencies. The audiogram of the person whose hearing is being tested is compared with that of an adult with no known hearing loss. One less technical way to assess hearing is to test a person's recognition of spoken words. In a typical test of this sort, a person listens to a tape recording of speech sounds that are standardized in terms of loudness and pitch. Performance is rated in terms of the number of words the participant can repeat correctly at various intensity levels. Nonmedical personnel often administer these types of tests and then refer individuals who may have hearing problems to a physician.

You can easily see that there are many similarities in the perceptual mechanisms for hearing and vision. In both perceptual systems, physical energy is transduced into electrochemical energy, coding takes place at several locations in the brain, and impairments can affect people's abilities.

Think Critically

- Why do scientists consider sound a psychological experience rather than a physical one?
- Why might an inner ear infection cause lightheadedness?

Taste and Smell

Focus on issues and ideas

- How taste and smell—both chemical senses—are psychologically determined
- The relationship of past experience to sensory adaptation
- The role of the visual and olfactory systems in communication

Try the following experiment. Cut a fresh onion in half and inhale its odor while holding a piece of raw potato in your mouth. Now chew the potato. You'll most likely find that the potato tastes like an onion. This experiment demonstrates that taste and smell are closely linked. Food contains substances that act as stimuli for both taste and smell.

There is one taste most people have a special fondness for—sweetness. Babies prefer sweet foods, and so do great-grandmothers. But researchers know that a sweet tooth involves a craving for more than the taste of sugar. People with a sweet tooth crave candy, cake, ice cream, and sometimes liquor. Their bodies perceive the sweetness and learn that it is associated with many foods that are high in carbohydrates. Carbohydrates act almost as sedatives. So your cravings for some substances—your desire to taste or smell or eat or drink them—are affected by a number of variables, including the chemical composition of the substance, what it ultimately does to you, and your previous experiences with it.

Taste

Taste is a chemical sense. Food placed in the mouth is partially dissolved in saliva, which releases chemicals in the food that stimulate the *taste buds,* the primary receptors for taste stimuli (see Figure 3.15). When substances contact the taste buds, you experience taste. The taste buds are found on small bumps on the tongue called *papillae.* Each hill-like papilla is separated from the next by a tiny trench, or moat; located on the wall of this moat are the taste buds, which can be seen only under a microscope. Each taste bud (human beings have about 10,000 of them) consists of 5 to 150 *taste cells.* These cells last only about 10 to 14 days and are constantly being renewed.

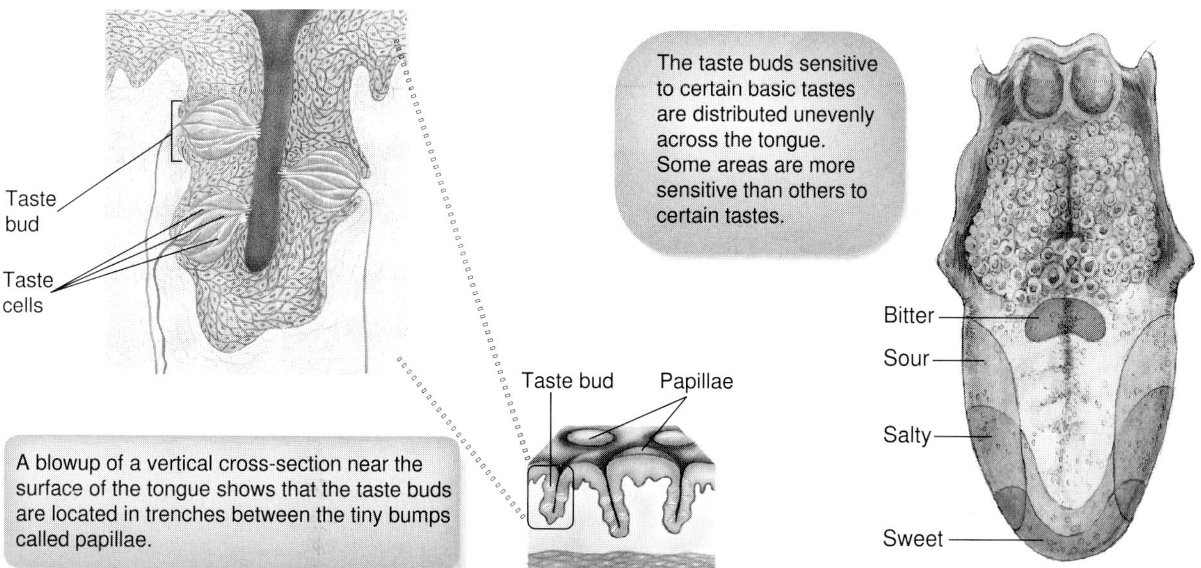

Taste bud
Taste cells
Taste bud
Papillae
A blowup of a vertical cross-section near the surface of the tongue shows that the taste buds are located in trenches between the tiny bumps called papillae.
The taste buds sensitive to certain basic tastes are distributed unevenly across the tongue. Some areas are more sensitive than others to certain tastes.
Bitter
Sour
Salty
Sweet

FIGURE 3.15
Taste Buds Are Found on the Surface of the Tongue

Although psychologists do not know exactly how many tastes there are, most agree that there are four basic ones: sweet, sour, salty, and bitter. Most foods contain more than one primary taste; Hawaiian pineapple pizza, for example, offers a complex array of taste stimuli and also stimulates the sense of smell. All taste cells are sensitive to all taste stimuli, but some cells are more sensitive to some stimuli than to others. (In this regard, they are much like the cones in the retina, which are sensitive to all wavelengths but are especially sensitive to a specific range of wavelengths.) By isolating stimuli that initiate only one taste sensation, psychologists have found that some regions of the tongue seem to be more sensitive than others to particular taste stimuli. The tip of the tongue, for example, is more sensitive to sweet tastes than the back of the tongue is, and the sides are especially sensitive to sour tastes.

Some people are more sensitive to tastes than others, and sensitivity seems to be genetically determined. In fact, there are vast differences in taste sensitivity—with some individuals even being considered nontasters, most being considered medium tasters, and some being considered supertasters. Well-known taste researcher Linda Bartoshuk and her colleagues (Bartoshuk et al., 1996), investigating the taste buds of the different groups, found that nontasters had as few as 11 buds per square centimeter on the tip of the tongue, whereas supertasters had as many as 1,100 taste buds per square centimeter. Supertasters taste sweet things as too sweet, bitter things as too bitter, and so forth. Nontasters cannot distinguish among basic tastes and require additional samplings to discern a flavor. Interesting, and not yet explained, is the finding that women are more likely to be supertasters (Bartoshuk et al., 1994).

The taste of a particular food depends not only on its chemical makeup and the number of taste buds you have, but also on your past experiences with this or similar foods, on how much saliva is being mixed into the food as you chew, and on how long you chew the food.

The taste of a particular food depends not only on its chemical makeup and the number of taste buds you have, but also on your past experiences with this or similar foods, on how much saliva is being mixed into the food as you chew, and on how long you chew the food. Food that is chewed well has a stronger taste. Food that rests on the tongue for a long time loses its ability to stimulate. This phenomenon is called *sensory adaptation*, or the temporary decrease in responsiveness of a receptor, often due to repeated high levels of stimulation. A food that loses its texture by being mashed up, or blended, with other foods has less taste and is less appealing to most adults. Thus, a taste experience, much like other perceptual experiences, depends not only on a sensory stimulus but also on past experiences and other variables.

Olfaction [ole-FAK-shun]: The sense of smell.

Smell

There's a good reason, other than etiquette, not to talk when your mouth is full—you lose some of the smells that help you experience the taste of food. The nose is the external section of the olfactory system, and it houses a complex array of receptors that allow us to smell (Vroon, 1997). Try eating chunks of raw potato and raw onion while holding your nose, and you will quickly see that they taste alike, as do chunks of carrot and apple. Smell is such an important sense that those who lose it permanently feel disabled. Like the sense of taste, **olfaction**—the sense of smell—is a chemical sense. That is, the stimulus for smell is a chemical in the air. The human olfactory system is remarkably sensitive: Humans can distinguish approximately 10,000 different scents and can recognize a smell from as few as 40 or 50 molecules of the chemical. For the sensation of smell to occur, the molecules must move toward the receptor cells located on the walls of the nasal passage. This happens when you breathe molecules in through your nostrils or take them in through the back of your throat when you chew and swallow. When a chemical substance in the air moves past the receptor cells, it is partially absorbed into the mucus that covers the cells, thereby initiating the process of smell.

For human beings to perceive smell, information must be sent to the brain. At the top of the nasal cavity is the *olfactory epithelium*, a layer of cells that contains the olfactory receptor cells—the nerve fibers that process odors and transmit information about smell to the olfactory bulbs (the enlargements at the end of the olfactory nerve) and on to higher centers of the brain. There can be as many as 30 million olfactory receptor cells in each nostril, which is what makes the olfactory system so sensitive. The sensitivity of the human sense of smell is dramatically illustrated by perfume manufacturing, which is a complex process.

Perfume makers may combine hundreds of substances to make one new perfume; dozens of perfumes have the same basic scent, varying only slightly.

Theories of smell involve both the stimulus for smell and the structure of the olfactory system. Some theories posit a few basic smells; others suggest that there are many smells—including flowery, foul, fruity, resinous, spicy, and burnt. Psychologists have not agreed on a single classification system for smells; nor do they completely understand how odors affect the receptor cells. Research into the coding of smell is intense, and physiological psychologists make headway each year; for example, they have shown that our memory for odors is long-lasting and that odors can evoke memories of past events, childhood, and especially emotional times in our lives (Herz & Engen, 1996). Another important question researchers are studying is whether and how odors affect human behavior. We consider this issue next.

Smell and Communication

Animals secrete *pheromones* (pronounced FER-uh-moans)—chemical substances that are detected as scents by other animals and act as a means of communication. In fact, scents released by one animal may even influence the physiology of another animal.

Pheromones are widely recognized as initiators of sexual activity among animals. For example, female silkworms release a pheromone that can attract male silkworms from miles away. Similarly, when female hamsters are sexually receptive, they emit a highly odorous substance that attracts males (Montgomery-St. Laurent, Fullenkamp, & Fischer, 1988); mice behave similarly (Coppola & O'Connell, 1988).

Many animals emit pheromones to elicit specific behavioral reactions; others, notably dogs and cats, use scents from their feces and urine to maintain territories and identify one another. Beavers attempt to keep strangers out of their territory by depositing foul-smelling substances emitted by sacs near the anus. Reindeer have scent glands between their toes that leave a trail for the rest of the herd. Communication via pheromones is found throughout the animal world. But do human beings share this ability?

Although people have always believed that a kind of "chemistry" exists between close friends, few really believed that one person's secretions might alter another person's behavior. Until relatively recently, scientists assumed that human beings do not communicate through smell. However, groundbreaking research in the 1970s began to change psychologists' thinking about smell and communication. McClintock (1971) found that the menstrual periods of women living in a college dormitory who were either roommates or close friends became roughly *synchronous*. That is, after the women lived together for several months, their menstrual cycles began and ended at about the same time. McClintock and others began to question whether the synchronization of the menstrual cycles was due to some type of chemical message. In more recent experimental research, Stern and McClintock (1998) found that women emit a whole array of chemical signals that affect synchronicity and behavior.

The effects of pheromones on animals are profound, but the role of pheromones in human life remains somewhat obscure and even controversial. Nevertheless, perfume makers have been working frenetically to make a perfume with pheromonelike capabilities. Is it reasonable for them to assert that perfumes, like pheromones, can attract members of the opposite sex? Probably not. Pheromones are not likely to be as powerful for human beings as they are for animals, because so many other environmental stimuli affect human behavior, attitudes, and interpersonal relations. *I*

I The Skin Senses

Focus on issues and ideas

- The role of the skin as a sensory receptor
- The gate control theory of pain and pain suppression
- Pain management techniques

Your skin, an organ of your body, contains a wide range of receptors for relaying information about the *skin senses*—pain, touch, and temperature. In each case, a stimulus is converted into neural energy, and then the brain interprets that energy as a psychological experience. Skin receptors ultimately send information to the somatosensory cortex of the brain.

Touch

The skin is more than just a binding that holds your body together. It is the location of your *sense of touch*—your tactile system. The skin of an adult human being measures roughly 2 square yards and comprises three layers: the epidermis, the dermis, and the hypodermis. The top layer, the *epidermis* (*epi* means "outer"), consists primarily of dead cells and varies in thickness. It is thin on the face and quite thick on the elbows and the heels. The epidermis is constantly regenerating; in fact, all of its cells are replaced every

28 days or so. The layer underneath the epidermis—the *dermis* (from *derma,* or "skin")—contains live cells as well as a supply of nerve endings, blood, hair cells, and oil-producing (sebaceous) glands. Together, the dermis and epidermis are resilient, flexible, and quite tough. They protect the body against quick changes in temperature and pressure, and the epidermis in particular guards against pain from small scratches, cuts, and bumps. The deepest layer—the *hypodermis* (*hypo* means "under")—is a thick, insulating cushion.

The specialized receptors for each of the skin senses—pain, touch, and temperature—vary in shape, size, number, and distribution. For example, the body has many more cold receptors than heat receptors; it has more pain receptors behind the knee than on the top of the nose. In the most sensitive areas of the hand, there are as many as 1,300 receptors per square inch.

The skin sense receptors appear to interact with one another; sometimes one sensation seems to combine with or change to another. Thus, increasing pressure can become pain. Similarly, an itch seems to result from a low-level irritation of nerve endings in the skin; however, a tickle can be caused by the same stimulus and can produce a reflexlike response (a response that is also dependent on psychological and social variables, as *Experiencing Psychology* points out). Further, people are far more sensitive to pressure in some parts of their bodies than in other parts (compare your fingers to your thigh); the more sensitive areas, such as the neck and the back of the knees, have more receptors than do the less sensitive areas. Complicating matters further, women have greater sensitivity to some pain stimuli than do men, and they are better able to discriminate among painful stimuli (Berkley, 1997).

EXPERIENCING PSYCHOLOGY

A Ticklish Subject

There's no one who hasn't been tickled at some point in his or her life. Some of us are especially ticklish. We smile, laugh, squirm, and, sometimes, howl when tickled. But why?

Nineteenth-century speculations suggested that people laugh and are ticklish because of a "pleasant state of mind." But recent research is showing that tickling and its results are in part physical but in larger part psychological. People respond to a light touch on the sole of the foot or on the spine, but if they anticipate the touch, if they are with a friend or relative, or if there is an element of surprise, the response is much stronger. That's why people can't tickle themselves—there is no element of surprise, and tickling requires a social interaction and a psychological tension that requires at least two people (Claxton, 1975).

Think back to your childhood. When your mom or dad said, "I'm going . . . to . . . *tickle* you!" and started to wiggle her or his fingers, you were likely to wiggle and giggle even before you were touched. Once you were actually tickled, you may have convulsed in laughter. Those of us who laugh easily at humor are more likely to respond to tickling (Harris & Christenfeld, 1997), our physiological responses to tickling are likely to be stronger when we are with friends (Christenfeld et al., 1997), and we are more likely to experience touch as tickling if we feel comfortable with our bodies and are disposed to perceive pleasurable stimuli (Ruggieri et al., 1983).

When researchers used "tickle machines" to lightly stimulate the soles of participants' feet, they found that people were far more likely to respond as if being tickled when the stimulation was preceded by something else that was funny, or when they were with another person. Although a tickle response may be a reflexive one, it is highly enhanced by social interactions (Christenfeld et al., 1997). Think of it as top-down *and* bottom-up processing; we laugh because laughing is a reflexive response to being tickled (bottom up) *and* because of the situation in which we find ourselves (top down).

Our response to humor and our ability to be tickled seem to be somewhat related. Both tickling and humor are universal behaviors found in human beings and in some chimpanzees. These behaviors occur at an early age and can be linked to specific neural pathways—these are elements of an evolved response. Indeed, the responses to both humor and tickling may serve an evolutionary purpose—some evidence suggests that those with a humorous outlook on life may live longer (Weisfeld, 1993). Laughter is a good antidote for the blues, and those who take a lighter view of the world suffer less from stress than those who tend to look on the dark side. Be tickled and live longer? Well, not exactly—but you'll have more fun! ■

Many of your determinations of how something feels are relative. When you say a stimulus is cold, you mean it is cold compared to normal skin temperature. When you say an object is warm, you mean it feels warmer than normal skin temperature. When you feel a child's head with the back of your hand and say the child has a fever, you are comparing normal skin temperature to a sick child's elevated skin temperature (and you wouldn't make such a determination immediately after coming in from outdoors on a winter day when it was 20°F outside).

Pain

Everyone has experienced acute pain at one time or another: a severe headache, the pain of childbirth, dental or arthritic pain, or perhaps a kidney stone or appendicitis. For most of us, pain comes and then goes, and we look back, thankful for the relief. Pain is a perceptual experience with particular negative qualities (Fernandez & Turk, 1992). Pain is the most common symptom that doctors deal with, but despite its association with illness and disease, pain is adaptive and necessary. In rare cases, children have been born without the ability to feel pain, which places them in constant danger. Their encounters with caustic substances, violent collisions, and deep cuts elicit no painful responses that could teach them to avoid such experiences. Further, they do not recognize serious conditions that would send most of us to the doctor for attention—for example, broken bones, deep burns, or the sharp pains that signal appendicitis.

Studying pain is difficult, because pain can be elicited in so many ways. For example, hunger or the flu may cause stomach pains, a toothache can be caused by a cavity or an abscess, and headaches can be caused by stress or eyestrain. Myriad kinds of pain exist, including sunburn pain, pain from terminal cancer, labor pains, low back pain, pain from frostbite, and even pain in a "phantom limb" after trauma or surgery. Psychologists use several kinds of stimuli to study pain. Among them are chemicals, extreme heat and cold, and electrical stimulation.

Most researchers believe the receptors for pain are free nerve endings. *Free nerve endings* are the microscopic ends of afferent neurons that are distributed throughout the body's tissues and are not connected to any specific sensory organ. There are various types of these receptors, each especially sensitive to a certain type of intense or potentially harmful stimulation. Some areas of the body are more sensitive to pain than others. For example, the sole of the foot and the ball of the thumb are less sensitive than the back of the knee and the neck. Also, though an individual's pain threshold remains fairly constant, different individuals show varying sensitivities to pain. Some people have a low threshold for pain; they will describe a comparatively low-level stimulus as painful. Others have a fairly high pain threshold. When you experience pain, you know where it hurts, how much it hurts, and the quality of the pain (sharp, burning, localized); your body responds with autonomic nervous system activity—increased heart rate and blood pressure, sweating, and so forth. You then, in turn, respond in a certain way, depending on whether you are frightened, anxious, or merely annoyed.

You can see that the perception of pain is both physical and psychological; much depends on a person's attitudes, previous experiences, and culture. For example, athletes often report not feeling the pain of an injury until after the competition has ended. Some cultures teach individuals to be stoical about pain and to endure individual suffering without complaint; in Western cultures, many people believe that pain and suffering are ennobling (Berkowitz, 1993). Also, boys and girls within Western cultures are often taught to respond differently to pain.

What allows pain suppression? How does the body process, interpret, and stop pain? Gate control theory may offer an answer.

Gate Control Theory. One explanation of how the body processes pain is the Melzack—Wall gate control theory (Melzack & Wall, 1970). The theory is complex, taking into account the sizes of nerve fibers, their level of development, and the interplay of excitatory cells that initiate pain sensations and inhibitory cells that can diminish such sensations. The theory contends that when a signal that might normally indicate a painful stimulus is sent to the brain, the signal goes through a series of "gates." These gates can be either fully or partially open or closed. How far each gate is open determines how much of the original pain signal gets through. A chemical called *substance P* (for pain), which is released by the sensory nerve fibers, transmits pain impulses across the gates. A variety of drugs, as well as electrical stimulation and acupuncture needles, are thought to close some of the gates, making the original painful stimulus far less potent. Research support for gate control theory is sparse, and Melzack (1993) acknowledges the shortcomings of his idea and its inability to explain problems such as chronic pain. His most recent formulations suggest that initial, or "early," pain can be blocked at "gates," but continuous, or "late," pain can be sustained by the brain and might only be relieved through nonsensory mechanisms—for example, endorphins.

Endorphins. There have been some exciting breakthroughs in research on pain receptors and the nature of pain. Consider, for example, the study of endorphins. **Endorphins** (from *endogenous,* meaning "naturally occurring," and *morphine,* which is an opiate painkiller) are painkillers that are produced naturally in the brain and the pituitary gland. There are many kinds of endorphins, and they help regulate several bodily functions, including blood pressure and body temperature (Bloom, 1981). Endorphins also can produce euphoria and a sense of well-being—to an even greater extent than morphine does. Engaging in athletic activities can bring about an increased endorphin level. During and after running, runners often report experiencing "runner's high," a sensation many believe is related to their body's increased endorphin level.

Endorphins bind themselves to receptor sites in the brain and spinal cord, thereby preventing pain signals from passing on to higher levels of the nervous system. Some endorphins increase tolerance to pain, and others actually reduce pain sensations. *Enkephalin,* for example, is a brain endorphin that blocks pain signals. Another endorphin, nocistatin, is being tested on a variety of painful conditions, and scientists may eventually be able to produce it synthetically (Okuda-Ashitaka et al., 1998). Physicians prescribe synthetic endorphins or endorphinlike substances, such as morphine, to block pain when traditional medications are ineffective.

Acupuncture. Many people who suffer chronic, unrelieved pain have sought help from acupuncture. Initially developed in China thousands of years ago, *acupuncture* is a technique that uses long, slender needles, inserted into the body at specific locations, to relieve particular kinds of pain. Controlled studies of acupuncture have yielded varying results. Acupuncture seems to help when needles are placed near the site of pain; this is in contrast to the traditional Chinese view that the key sites are located along life-force meridians found on acupuncture charts. It is possible that the needles stimulate endorphins that may help block the pain (Murray, 1995) or alter serotonin levels (Nash, 1996). For some people, acupuncture may be a reasonable option and an effective treatment (Baischer, 1995). The National Institutes of Health concludes that acupuncture may be effective with some kinds of pain—migraines, arthritis, and postoperative pain from dental surgery—but that more research is needed because controlled studies on acupuncture are inconclusive.

Endorphins [en-DOR-finz]: Painkillers produced naturally in the brain and the pituitary gland.

Pain Management. Usually the pain resulting from a headache, toothache, or small cut is temporary and can be alleviated with a simple pain medication such as aspirin. For millions of people, however, aspirin is not enough. For those who suffer from constant pain caused by back injury, arthritis, or cancer, drug treatment either is not effective or is dangerous because of the high dosages required; in addition, each type of pain may require a different treatment. Sometimes painkillers are not prescribed because of fear of addiction—a fear that is often exaggerated by caring, well-meaning family and friends (Melzack, 1990).

New technologies are emerging to help people manage pain. Leaders in pain research reason that something must happen at the site of an injury to trigger endorphin production. What if a drug could stop the whole pain perception process at the place where the injury occurred, before endorphin production even started? In an effort to find such a compound, researchers are studying the receptor sites in skin tissue and observing how chemicals bind to them. The compounds they discover may not relieve pain completely, but may be effective in combination with other pain medications, such as aspirin. The latest pain-relief techniques involve local electrical stimulation with a procedure called *TENS,* or transcutaneous electrical nerve stimulation. Brief pulses of electricity are applied to nerve endings under the skin; at just the right frequency and voltage, these electrical pulses can help patients with chronic pain.

Practitioners who deal with pain recognize that although it may arise initially from physical complaints, it sometimes continues even after the physical cause abates because it provides other benefits to the sufferer (Fernandez & Turk, 1992). For example, pain may provide the sufferer with attention, which is reinforcing, or it may act as a distraction from other problems. Treatment focuses on helping people cope with pain regardless of its origins and on increasing a patient's pain-controlling skills (Hardy, 1995).

Hypnosis (which will be examined in more detail in Chapter 4) has been used to treat pain. Patients may be instructed to focus on other aspects of their lives and may be told that their pain will be more bearable after the hypnotic session. Although some claim that two-thirds of patients who are considered highly susceptible to suggestion can experience some relief of pain through hypnosis, the National Institutes of Health concluded that a more accurate estimate was 15–20%.

Anxiety and worry can make pain worse. People who suffer from migraine headaches, for example, often make their condition worse by becoming fearful when they feel a headache coming on. Researchers find that biofeedback training, which teaches people how to relax and cope more effectively, can help those who suffer from chronic pain or migraine headaches gain some relief—although, again, results are mixed. (Biofeedback will be discussed further in Chapter 4.) Other treatments, closely related to biofeedback, involve cognitive coping strategies (discussed in Chapters 12 and 14). A negative attitude can make pain worse. Cognitive coping strategies teach patients to have a better attitude about their pain. Patients learn to talk to themselves in positive ways, to divert attention to pleasant images, and to take an active role in managing their pain and transcending the experience. (I)

(I) Kinesthesis and the Vestibular Sense

Focus on issues and ideas

- How the kinesthesis and vestibular systems operate in information processing
- How studies of the sensory systems help us understand day-to-day behavior

If you are a dancer or an athlete, you rely mightily on your body to provide you with information about hand, arm, and leg movements. You try to keep your balance, be graceful, and move with coordination and smoothness. Two sensory systems allow for skilled, accurate, and smooth movement—the often ignored, but vitally important, kinesthetic and vestibular systems.

Kinesthesis is the awareness aroused by movements of the muscles, tendons, and joints. It is what allows you to touch your finger to your nose with your eyes closed, leap over hurdles during a track-and-field event, and dance without stepping on your partner's feet. The study of kinesthesis provides information about bodily movements. The movements of muscles around your eye, for example, help you know how far away objects are. Kinesthesia and other internal sensations (such as an upset stomach) are *proprioceptive cues* (kinesthesia is sometimes called *proprioception*)—sensory cues that come from within the body.

The **vestibular sense** is the sense of bodily orientation and postural adjustment. It helps you keep your balance and sense of equilibrium. The structures essential to these functions are in the ear. Vestibular sacs and semicircular canals, which are linked indirectly to the body wall of the cochlea, provide information about the orientations of the head and the body (Parker, 1980). The vestibular sense allows you to walk on a balance beam without falling off, to know which way is up after diving into the water, and to sense that you are turning a corner when riding in a car, even when your eyes are closed.

Rapid movements of the head cause changes in the semicircular canals. These changes induce eye movements to help compensate for head changes and changes in bodily orientation. They may also be accompanied by physical sensations ranging from pleasant dizziness to unbearable motion sickness. Studies of the vestibular sense help scientists understand what happens to people during space travel and under conditions of weightlessness. (I)

(I) Extrasensory Perception

Focus on issues and ideas

- The reality underlying extrasensory perception

Sights, sounds, tastes, smells, touches, and even pain are all part of the normal sensory experience of human beings. Some people, however, claim there are other perceptual experiences that not all human beings recognize as normal. People have been fascinated by *extrasensory perception (ESP)* for hundreds of years. The British Society for the Study of Psychic Phenomena has investigated reports of ESP since the 19th century. Early experimenters tested for extrasensory perception by asking participants to guess the symbols on what are now called ESP cards, each marked with a star, a cross, a circle, a square, or a set of wavy lines. One of the most consistently successful guessers once guessed 25 cards in a row, an event whose odds of happening by chance are nearly 300 quadrillion to 1.

ESP includes telepathy, clairvoyance, precognition, and psychokinesis. *Telepathy* is the transfer of thoughts from one person to another. *Clairvoyance* is the ability to recognize objects or events, such as the contents of a message in a sealed envelope, that are not discernible by normal sensory receptors. *Precognition* is unexplained knowledge about future events, such as knowing when the phone is about to ring. *Psychokinesis* is the ability to move objects using only one's mental powers.

Kinesthesis [kin-iss-THEE-sis]: The awareness aroused by movements of the muscles, tendons, and joints.

Vestibular [ves-TIB-you-ler] sense: The sense of bodily orientation and postural adjustment.

Experimental support for the existence of ESP is generally weak, and results have not been repeated very often. Moreover, ESP phenomena such as "reading people's minds" or bending spoons through mental power cannot be verified by experimental manipulations in the way that other perceptual events can be. In addition, the National Research Council has denounced the scientific merit of most of these experiments. None of these criticisms means that ESP does not exist. Research using scientific methods continues, including new techniques such as the use of sophisticated electronic detection devices. Attempts to relate ESP phenomena to traditional psychology (as is common in nations of the former Soviet bloc) are underway. However, most psychologists see so much trickery and falsification of data and so many design errors in experiments on this subject that they remain skeptical.

Think Critically

- Some individuals are born without a sense of smell. What effect would this have on their sense of taste, and why?
- How do you think research on endorphins might be relevant to your life?

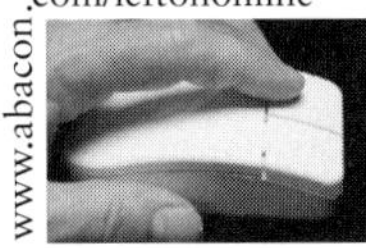

Your password-protected Website allows you access to the most comprehensive set of materials in The Psychology Place.

Summary and Review

The Perceptual Experience

How does the study of the psychological aspects of perception help explain individuals' attending to and attaching meaning to stimuli?

KEY TERMS
sensation, p. 58; perception, p. 58; psychophysics, p. 59; absolute threshold, p. 59; subliminal perception, p. 59

The Visual System

Describe the structures of the visual system.

What is the duplicity theory of vision?

What do receptive fields tell researchers about the perceptual process?

What are the trichromatic and opponent-process theories of color vision?

KEY TERMS
electromagnetic radiation, p. 63; light, p. 63; myopic, p. 63; hyperopic, p. 63; photoreceptors, p. 63; transduction, p. 63; visual cortex, p. 64; dark adaptation, p. 65; optic chiasm, p. 66; receptive fields, p. 66; saccades, p. 67; hue, p. 67; brightness, p. 67; saturation, p. 68; trichromatic theory, p. 68; color blindness, p. 68; opponent-process theory, p. 68; trichromats, p. 69; monochromats, p. 69; dichromats, p. 69

Visual Perception

What is size constancy?

What are the monocular and binocular depth cues that help people see depth?

What is an illusion?

What did the Gestalt psychologists contribute to scientists' understanding of perception?

KEY TERMS
size constancy, p. 70; shape constancy, p. 70; monocular depth cues, p. 71; accommodation, p. 71; binocular depth cues, p. 71; retinal disparity, p. 71; convergence, p. 72; illusion, p. 73; law of Prägnanz, p. 75

Hearing

What are the key characteristics of sound?

Describe the anatomy of the ear and how sound is processed.

Distinguish between conduction deafness and sensorineural deafness.

KEY TERMS
sound, p. 76; frequency, p. 76; pitch, p. 76; amplitude, p. 77; conduction deafness, p. 80; sensorineural deafness, p. 80

Taste and Smell

Describe the anatomy of the tongue and explain how it allows for taste differences.

Why are taste and smell called chemical senses?

KEY TERM
olfaction, p. 82

The Skin Senses

Describe the anatomy of the skin.

What is the most prominent theory of pain?

What are the body's naturally produced painkillers?

KEY TERM
endorphins, p. 86

Kinesthesis and the Vestibular Sense

What sense involves the orientation of the entire body?

KEY TERMS
kinesthesis, p. 87; vestibular sense, p. 87

Extrasensory Perception

Is there a "sixth sense"—ESP?

Self-Test

1. When an incoming stimulus is interpreted and acquires meaning, the process is called:
   A. threshold
   B. adaptation
   C. sensation
   D. perception
2. The photoreceptors for the visual system are contained in the:
   A. lens
   B. retina
   C. iris
   D. cornea
3. When a person describes a car as red, he or she is describing the psychological dimension of hue. Which physical property corresponds to huo?
   A. wavelength
   B. intensity
   C. purity
   D. saturation
4. Pedersen and Wheeler (1983) found that one group of Navajos was more susceptible to the Müller-Lyer illusion than another group. Why was one group less sensitive to the illusion?
   A. They were less technologically advanced.
   B. They were not as intelligent.
   C. Their houses were round.
   D. Their houses were rectangular.
5. In the auditory system, transduction occurs at the:
   A. eardrum
   B. cochlea
   C. outer ear
   D. ossicles
6. Sensorineural deafness results from damage to the:
   A. eardrum
   B. ossicles
   C. tympanic membrane
   D. cochlea
7. Jack has a stuffed-up nose. His taste buds are:
   A. more sensitive
   B. less sensitive
   C. sensitive only to sour tastes
   D. unaffected
8. Which chemical is released by sensory nerve fibers to transmit pain?
   A. substance P
   B. endorphins
   C. enkephalin
   D. nocistatin
9. Charmagne felt dizzy and disoriented during a roller coaster ride. Her loss of balance and equilibrium was a function of her ______________ sense.
   A. kinesthetic
   B. vestibular
   C. proprioceptor
   D. olfactory
10. Carrie says that she is able to move dishes and books simply by concentrating on doing so. What ability is Carrie claiming she has?
    A. telepathy
    B. clairvoyance
    C. psychokinesis
    D. precognition

Chapter 4

Consciousness

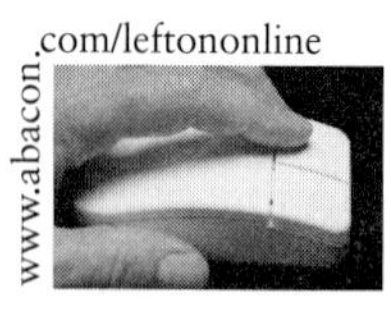

Go to your password-protected Website for full-color art, Weblinks, and more!

I've always slept well. My head hits the pillow and I'm out. I wake in the morning refreshed and ready to go. But one particular night, I lay in bed for an hour and a half, unable to drift off. I wasn't stressed or anxious; in fact, I was in a fine mood after a productive and restful day at home. But something was off. As I lay there listening to my wife's quiet, regular breathing and wondering why I was unable to sleep, I grew restless. And then it hit me. The previous night had been the last Saturday in October—the end of daylight savings time. Saturday night I had slept an extra hour. This had thrown off my normal rhythm and was affecting my sleep.

I should have recognized right away that altering my sleep pattern for one night would affect other bodily rhythms as well—and my next night's sleep. Drink alcohol, and you don't sleep normally. Allow yourself to become especially stressed, and the same thing happens. Your hormones, moods, and overall physical health affect your sleep patterns—and vice versa. In some ways, sleep can be considered a barometer of mental and physical health; if you tinker with your normal routine, the change can be reflected in your sleep. Lose too much sleep or sleep badly, and the effects spill over to the next day.

Some lucky people need only 5 hours of sleep per night—but they are in the minority. Others are able to take an occasional "power nap" to revive themselves—but opportunities for napping are rare, and, again, this solution works for only a small minority. Most people need a solid 7 to 9 hours of sleep every night.

For many Americans, though, sleep deprivation has become a way of life. They start their mornings before dawn and don't crawl into bed until after midnight. The day is filled with commuting, work, a night class at the community college, aerobics class, shopping, household chores. Child-rearing moms and dads must also get the kids off to school, drive them to after-school activities, oversee their homework, and spend "quality time" with them and with each other. And then there is the enticing entertainment that is available at all hours—cable TV, computer games, and the Web.

So, when they finally do get to bed, it's no wonder many people have trouble sleeping. Part of the problem is that they are constantly on the go, having irregular meals and too few hours in which to relax. Feeling tired each morning, they take stimulants such as coffee for a quick jolt of energy. Then they stumble through the day, doing what has to be done. Unfortunately, sleep deprivation can be dangerous. Many auto accidents happen because drivers fall asleep briefly at the wheel. And the lack of sleep often causes people to make small mistakes as well—from missed appointments to typing errors. ■

When people are deprived of sleep, their normal awareness and responsiveness are altered. For these and other reasons, psychologists are interested in sleep, dreams, and other altered states of consciousness. By studying such states and how people move from one state of consciousness to another, researchers learn more about the relationship between brain and behavior.

I Consciousness

Focus on issues and ideas

- Understanding the various theories of consciousness
- How theories of consciousness help psychologists understand day-to-day human behaviors

Data, the humanoid robot in *Star Trek: The Next Generation,* is always seeking to be more human, to experience feelings and emotions the way human beings do. He keeps trying to be sentient, to have subjective feelings and an awareness of them. Data is trying to develop a human consciousness.

Part of Data's problem, besides not being programmed to be aware of feelings, is that consciousness is difficult even to describe. Psychologists are acutely aware of this difficulty. Almost all psychologists agree that a person who is conscious is aware of the immediate environment; for example, you are conscious when you listen to a lecture (at least some of the time!). However, consciousness also refers to inner awareness, your knowledge of your own thoughts, feelings, and memories (sentience)—your mental list of errands for the day, your anger at a rude driver, and the scent of lilac that reminds you of your fourth-grade teacher.

Most psychologists—including the early structuralists, Freud, and today's cognitive researchers—have acknowledged that people experience different *levels* of consciousness. They agree that consciousness can be seen as a continuum—ranging from the alert attention required to read this textbook to dreaming, hypnosis, or drug-induced states. According to this view of consciousness, a person who is not paying attention or is not alert may be said to be conscious, but not "as conscious" as one who is vigilant and alert. Researchers who favor this view of a continuum of awareness suggest, for example, that a person who is drinking heavily temporarily enters a lower (deeper) *level* in the range—that of intoxication. A person who is in a state of consciousness that is dramatically different from ordinary awareness and responsiveness is said to be in an *altered state of consciousness.* A person who is asleep has pretty much "turned off" consciousness (Hobson, 1994).

Not only are there various levels of consciousness, but some people are more able than others to think about their own thinking—a process called *metacognition*—which may allow them to access levels of consciousness or thought processes that are not available to other people. Researchers examine consciousness and metacognition by asking individuals to track their consciousness, their levels of alertness, and their moods in some detail over a period of days or even weeks. Not surprisingly, there is a rhythm to consciousness; for example, I get drowsy at around 4 P.M. and am most alert at about 9 A.M. What about you?

What is the function of consciousness? Clearly, consciousness allows us to monitor our bodily and mental states. It also allows us, to a certain extent, to control those states. When you feel anxious, you can breathe more deeply. When you are falling asleep at your desk, you can stretch, yawn (to take in some extra oxygen), and perhaps blink. The extent to which consciousness allows us to monitor and control our daily activities depends on how aware we are, whether we are at a low level of consciousness—such as asleep—or in some altered state such as hypnotized, meditating, or drugged. Before getting further into theories of consciousness, though, let's define **consciousness** as the general state of being aware of and responsive to events in the environment, as well as one's own mental processes.

Theories of Consciousness

As in other areas of psychology, theory guides research. Several researchers have proposed biologically based theories of consciousness, in which an understanding of the evolution of the human brain is key. Jaynes (1976) believes that consciousness originates in the differing functions and physiology of the two hemispheres of the brain. In a similar view based on physiology and brain structure, Robert Ornstein (1977) proposes two modes of consciousness, each controlled by its own side of the brain: the active-verbal-rational mode (or active mode) is left-dominated, and the receptive-spatial-intuitive-holistic mode (or receptive mode) is right-dominated. Ornstein believes evolution has made the active mode automatic; this is the "default," or normal, mode of operation for human beings. Human beings limit their awareness automatically in order to shut out stimuli that do not directly relate to their ability to survive. When people need to gain perspective on and evaluate what they are doing, however, they can expand their normal awareness by using the receptive mode. According to Ornstein, techniques such as meditation, biofeedback, and hypnosis, and even the use of certain drugs, can help people learn to use the receptive mode, as their primitive ancestors did, to balance the active mode.

Ornstein and his collaborator, David Galin, support many of their ideas with laboratory data showing that the brain is divided and specialized in significant ways. They point out that the left-dominated and the right-dominated modes of consciousness operate in a complementary and alternating fashion, one working while the other is inhibited (Galin, 1974; Ornstein, 1976). The integration of these two modes underlies the highest human accomplishments. But, since the brain's functioning cannot be fully explained by its structure, support for this model is still modest.

Among the newest explanations of consciousness are those from Daniel Dennett (1991, 1996) and neurologist Richard Restak (1994). In his book *Consciousness Explained,* Dennett asserts that human beings have access to many sources of information, which together create conscious experiences. He argues that the brain creates multiple drafts (copies) of experiences, which are constantly being reanalyzed. According to Dennett, the brain develops a sense of consciousness as well as a sense of self through this constant updating and reanalysis of experience. The theory is as yet untested, is not widely accepted, and has been criticized (Mangan, 1993); however, it takes a new path in suggesting that perceptual, physiological, and historical information come together in each individual to create that person's consciousness. Such ideas are supported by Restak, who asserts in his book *The Modular Brain* that it is the brain's various sections, or parts, that control behavior. Consciousness is not centrally organized but rather resides in these modules; lose a module through a car crash or a sports accident and you will lose certain, but not all, key abilities. Damasio (1994) also follows this line of reasoning and suggests that the modules are hierarchically organized; Calvin (1996) asserts that the modules are at work generating and synthesizing through-

Consciousness: The general state of being aware of and responsive to events in the environment, as well as one's own mental processes.

Circadian [sir-KAY-dee-an] rhythms: Internally generated patterns of body functions, including hormonal signals, sleep, blood pressure, and temperature regulation, which have approximately a 24-hour cycle and occur even in the absence of normal cues about whether it is day or night.

out our lives, whether we are awake, asleep, at work, or at play. Calvin argues that it is this activity—which does not always work well—that creates interesting, and in many cases, ingenious thought patterns.

Pinker asserts that the mind is what the brain does—nothing more—and that it has evolved as an evolutionary response to the world.

Steven Pinker (1997, 1999) maintains that even the best theorists tend to confuse terms when talking about consciousness. Pinker asserts that the mind is what the brain does—nothing more—and that it has evolved as an evolutionary response to the world. That is, the mind is a system of organs of computation, designed by natural selection to solve the kinds of problems our ancestors faced in their foraging way of life. Pinker dismisses many psychological issues—guilt, remorse, and fear, for example—as nonsense, arguing that we must look only at the machine we call the brain. He argues that the "problem" of consciousness can be broken into three issues: sentience, access, and self-knowledge. *Sentience* refers to subjective experience and awareness—feelings. *Access* refers to the ability to report on the content and product of rational thought—to take deliberate, reasoned actions based on memory, rational ideas, and past experiences. *Self-knowledge* refers to the ability of individuals to recognize that their experiences are uniquely their own and to be aware that they are experiencing as they are doing it. Sentience is difficult to assess, but access and self-knowledge are cognitive activities that can be analyzed from a variety of vantage points, including the physiological, such as through fMRI scans and even biofeedback. From Pinker's view, such an analysis is crucial, because it is the only way for scientists to understand the true nature of consciousness. Remember, Pinker argues that the mind is little more than a neural computer, fitted by natural selection with systems for reasoning.

Pinker's focus on physiology contrasts sharply with the position of philosophers such as Chalmers (1996), who focus on the role of subjective experience. Consciousness theorists abound, and there is no lack of alternative explanations. Much of the analysis is biobehavioral—an attempt to explain the nature of consciousness through a description of the brain's structure and functions and a corresponding analysis of behavior. For example, Damasio (1997, 1999) attempts to explain and understand consciousness as an interaction between neurology and the environment. Damasio argues that understanding consciousness requires understanding the *self* and its relationship to objects and events. The larger issues are difficult to frame, and the answers far from complete. To work toward a more complete overall understanding of consciousness, researchers often focus on particular states of consciousness. So, in the remainder of this chapter, we look at many of those states. Some of them are desirable and normal; others alter human behavior in less desirable ways. We begin with a very familiar state of consciousness—sleep. (I)

Think Critically

- Take a few minutes to jot down the contents of your consciousness right now. How would your list be different if loud music had been playing while you compiled it? How about soft background music?

(I) Sleep

Focus on issues and ideas

- How circadian rhythms affect sleep patterns and wakefulness
- The implications of sleep deprivation for individuals, especially in the workforce
- The development of sleep cycles from infancy to adulthood
- The effects of REM sleep deprivation
- The origin and effects of sleep disorders

In the casinos of Las Vegas, it is difficult to tell night from day. Activity is at fever pitch 24 hours a day, and there are no windows and few clocks. People never seem to sleep; it is as if there *is* no day or night. But even in Las Vegas, people do sleep; they give in to their bodily urge to rejuvenate themselves. Their bodies tell them they are tired even if there is no clock on the wall to give a reminder. Humans seem to have an internal biological clock that controls the sleep–wakefulness cycle. This clock runs on about a 24-hour cycle; thus, the term *circadian* arose from the Latin *circa diem* ("around a day"). **Circadian rhythms** are internally generated patterns of body functions, including hormonal signals, sleep, blood pressure, and temperature regulation, which have approximately a 24-hour cycle and occur even in the absence of normal cues about whether it is day or night.

Human beings are sensitive to light, which helps keep their biological clocks in sync (Boivin et al.,

1996). However, when time cues (clocks, natural light windows, temperature changes as the sun goes down) are missing from the environment for a long time, an interesting thing happens: Circadian rhythms run a bit slow. When human beings are placed in artificially lit environments and are allowed to sleep and eat whenever they want to, they sleep the same amount of time each "day" but go to sleep a bit later (Foster, 1993). This is because the full sleep–wakefulness cycle runs about 24.5 to 25.5 hours. Body temperature and other bodily functions tend to follow a similar circadian rhythm.

Because you are exposed to daylight and have clocks and an arbitrary schedule, however, your circadian rhythms alone do not control sleep and wakefulness. You can see the impact of circadian rhythms when your routine is thrown off by having to work through the night and sleep during the day—your body's clock may not match your work clock. This disruption is apparent for airline pilots, surgeons, and firefighters—some of the approximately 7 million Americans who work at night (Czeisler et al., 1990). When you put in long hours that stretch through the night and into the dawn, and especially when these hours are not regular, you become less attentive, think less clearly, and may even fall asleep from time to time. Thus, employers, workers, and consumers need to be aware of the potential decreased efficiency of night workers who vary their schedules, especially airline pilots and medical interns. Research shows that circadian rhythms can be reset by shining lights on people's bodies, even while they are asleep (Campbell & Murphy, 1998)—this is an important finding for those who are perpetually readjusting their internal clock.

Consider the traveler's common problem—jet lag. If you travel by jet from, say, New York City to London, the trip will take about 6 hours. If you leave at 9:00 P.M., you will arrive in London 6 hours later—at 3:00 A.M.—as far as your body is concerned. It will seem very late at night. But local London time will be 8:00 A.M. You experience exhaustion and disorientation, a set of feelings referred to as *jet lag*. You may want to sleep during the first day and stay up at night.

Sleep: Nonwaking state of consciousness characterized by general unresponsiveness to the environment and physical immobility.

Electroencephalogram [eel-ECK-tro-en-SEFF-uh-low-gram] (EEG): Graphical record of brain wave activity obtained through electrodes placed on the scalp and forehead.

Non–rapid eye movement (NREM) sleep: Four distinct stages of sleep during which no rapid eye movements occur.

If you are experiencing jet lag, your circadian rhythms will be disrupted, and your performance will not be at its peak. Sleep deprivation also adversely affects performance, as we'll see next.

The Sleep of Long-Haul Truckers: Research Tells an Interesting Story

Have you ever driven a car for more than 6 hours? If you have, you probably can remember feeling tired and perhaps even fighting sleep. Fatigue is a major cause of automobile accidents in the United States, and 5,000 people are killed each year in accidents involving truckers. One possible explanation is that too many truckers are driving when they are not properly rested.

Driver fatigue due to sleep deprivation and a shift in circadian rhythms is often cited as the number-one problem in commercial transportation. Are there data to back up such a claim? A team of researchers (Mitler et al., 1997) from the Scripps Clinic and Research Institute undertook a study of long-haul truck drivers to assess the issue. The researchers reasoned that such truckers, whose livelihood depends on delivering goods in a timely fashion, would sleep less than they needed to. Further, their sleep patterns, measured physiologically, would be altered while they were on the road. Such alterations might lead to situations that could cause accidents on the highway. What's particularly significant about this study is that studies of sleep patterns are usually conducted in sleep laboratories, rarely in real, everyday work environments.

Mitler and his colleagues conducted round-the-clock monitoring of the physiological performance of 80 truck drivers who drove long distances in workdays lasting at least 10 hours. The researchers measured the truckers' sleep behavior, including how long they slept, how long it took them to fall asleep, brain wave activity, and eye movements; they also continuously monitored respiration during sleep and waking activity. Video monitors recorded the truckers' facial expressions while they were driving. Drivers were given little advice about when or how to sleep and were offered no financial incentives to sleep or not to sleep. The participants were driving 10 to 13 hours per day, and performance on the various measures was repeatedly tested over a 5-day period on over 200 trips totaling 204,000 miles.

Younger drivers slept more than older drivers did; their average sleep time (at night plus naps) was 5.18 hours. Overall, drivers slept only 4.78 hours per day, about 2 hours less than their average ideal amount (as reported in a questionnaire). Drivers who drove during the day slept longer than those who drove at night. For 7% of the time while they were actually driving, drivers exhibited signs of being in the first stage of sleep, the lightest sleep—that is, they were drowsy, and they showed slow-wave EEGs and slow, rolling eye movements. In addition, 56% of the participants had at least one 6-minute period of drowsiness. The most likely times for such drowsy episodes were late at night and early in the morning, or between 11 P.M. and 5 A.M.

Professional drivers who spend long days or nights on the road put themselves (and the rest of us) at risk because of their altered sleep cycles and sleep deprivation.

Professional drivers who spend long days or nights on the road put themselves (and the rest of us) at risk because of their altered sleep cycles and sleep deprivation. In Mitler's study, all long-haul drivers slept less than an optimal amount. Research like this demonstrates that sleep-deprived drivers may lapse dangerously into sleep from time to time. Although these truckers did not get into any accidents during this experiment, their lapses into sleep provided evidence that impaired performance can result from sleep deprivation. The implications of this study for airline pilots, emergency room physicians, and those who monitor nuclear weapons seem clear: People who affect the lives of others need to get a good night's sleep every night.

Sleep: A Restorative Process

Sleep is a nonwaking state of consciousness characterized by general unresponsiveness to the environment and physical immobility. It is a natural state experienced by everyone. Some psychologists think sleep allows the body to recover from the day's expenditure of energy; they see it as a restorative process. Others perceive sleep as a type of hibernation. They believe an organism conserves energy by sleeping when it would be inefficient to expend energy (night is not a good time for some animals to catch or produce food). Still others see sleep as a time when the brain itself recovers from exhaustion and overload; they believe sleep has little effect on basic physiological processes in the rest of the body. Horne (1988) asserts that sleep can be divided into two major types: core and optional. *Core sleep* repairs the effects of waking wear and tear on cerebral functions; it is thus restorative. *Optional sleep* fills the time from the end of core sleep until waking.

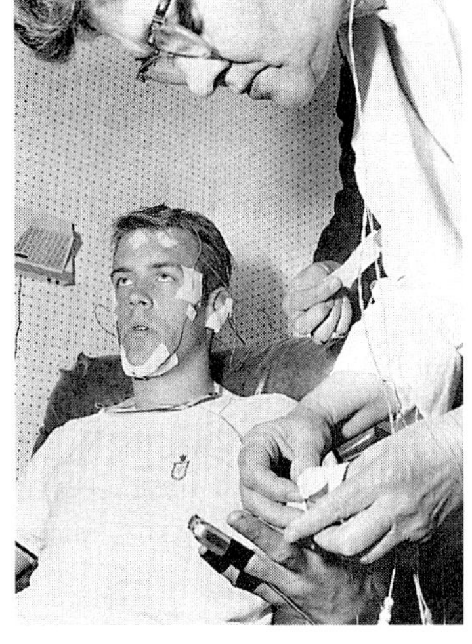

How much sleep do people really need? Most people require about 8 hours during a 24-hour period, but some can function with only 4 or 5 hours, while others need as many as 9 or 10. Young teenagers tend to need more sleep than college students, and elderly people tend to sleep less than young people do. Most young adults (65%) sleep between 6.5 hours and 8.5 hours a night, and about 95% sleep between 5.5 hours and 9.5 hours (Horne, 1988). Do you think people who are active and energetic require more sleep than those who are less active? Surprisingly, this is not always the case. Bedridden hospital patients, for example, sleep about the same amount of time as people who are on their feet all day. Although the average amount of sleep a person needs is determined genetically, heavy exercise seems to increase the need for sleep on any particular day (Youngstedt, O'Connor, & Dishman, 1997).

Sleep Stages: REM and NREM Sleep

The sleep–wakefulness cycle is repetitive, determined in part by circadian rhythms and in part by daily schedules and a host of other events. When early sleep researchers such as Nathaniel Kleitman and William Dement studied the sleep–wakefulness cycle, they found stages of sleep that could be characterized by eye movements that occur during sleep and by **electroencephalograms (EEGs)**—graphical records of brain wave activity obtained through electrodes placed on the scalp and forehead. Researchers working in sleep laboratories study the EEG patterns that occur in the brain while participants are sleeping. Portable devices allow the recording of brain waves throughout the day as well (Broughton, 1991).

Recordings of the brain waves of sleeping participants have revealed that during an 8-hour period, people typically progress through five full cycles of sleep. A full sleep cycle lasts approximately 90 minutes and has stages marked by the absence or presence of a key characteristic—rapid eye movements. The first four stages within a cycle are characterized as **non–rapid eye movement (NREM) sleep**—because no rapid eye movements occur.

The other, very different, stage is **rapid eye movement (REM) sleep**—characterized by high-frequency, low-voltage brain-wave activity, rapid and systematic eye movements, and more vivid dreams.

When people first fall asleep, they are in stage 1; their sleep is light, and they can be awakened easily. Within the next 30 to 40 minutes, they pass through stages 2, 3, and 4. Stage 4 is very deep sleep. When sleepers leave that stage, a curious event occurs. People move back through stages 3, 2, and sometimes stage 1, and then nearly awaken before going into REM sleep for about 10 minutes. In REM sleep, breathing and heart rate increase, eye movements become rapid, other physiological excitement becomes evident, and mental imagery becomes vivid. Also, the longer people sleep (and the more sleep cycles they go through), the more REM sleep they experience (Agnew & Webb, 1973; Barbato et al., 1994).

The waking brain-wave pattern exhibits a fast, regular rhythm. In stage 1, light sleep, the brain waves are of low amplitude (height) but are relatively fast, with mixed frequencies. Sleepers in stage 1 can be awakened easily. Stage 2 sleep shows low-amplitude, nonrhythmic brain-wave activity combined with two special patterns: sleep spindles and K complexes. A *sleep spindle* is a rhythmic burst of brain waves that wax and wane for 1 or 2 seconds. A *K complex* is a higher-amplitude burst of activity seen in the last third of stage 2. Sleep spindles and K complexes appear only during NREM sleep. Sleepers in stage 2 are in deeper sleep than those in stage 1 but can still be easily awakened. Stage 3 sleep is a transitional stage between stages 2 and 4, with brain waves slower but of higher amplitude than in stage 2. Stage 4 sleep, the deepest sleep, has even higher-amplitude brain-wave traces, called *delta waves.* During this stage, people breathe deeply, their heart rates are slower, and their blood pressure is lower. People in stage 4 sleep have two well-documented behavioral characteristics. First, they are difficult to awaken. People awakened from stage 4 sleep often appear confused and disturbed and take several seconds to rouse themselves fully. Second, people in this stage generally do not dream as much as they do in REM sleep. Early research on sleep and dreaming suggested that dreams occurred only during REM sleep, but, in fact, dreams do occur during NREM sleep and have many of the same characteristics of dreams during REM sleep (Foulkes, 1996).

Rapid eye movement (REM) sleep: Stage of sleep characterized by high-frequency, low-voltage brain-wave activity, rapid and systematic eye movements, and more vivid dreams.

Insomnia: Prolonged inability to sleep.

Research participants who are awakened, especially during REM sleep, can report in great detail the imagery and mental activity they have been experiencing. Because REM sleep is considered to be restorative, even necessary for normal physiological functioning and behavior, it might also be expected to be a deep sleep; however, it is an active sleep, during which the sleeper's brain-wave activity resembles that of an aware person. For this reason, REM sleep is often called *paradoxical sleep.* In REM sleep, participants seem agitated; their eyes move and their heart rate and breathing are variable. And yet, they are difficult to awaken.

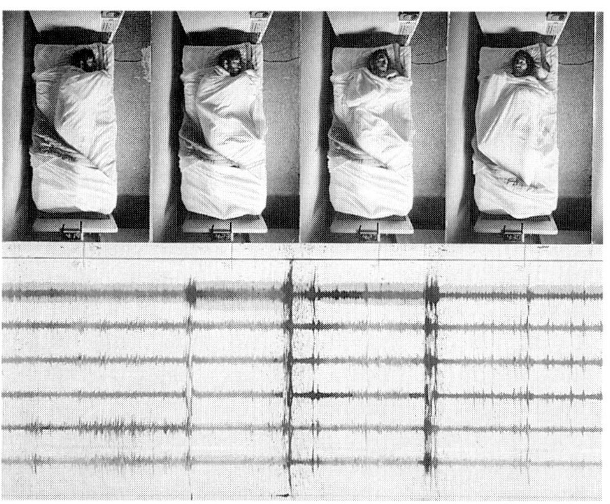

In an EEG recorded during a transition from NREM stage 2 sleep to REM sleep, the first part of the tracing shows a clear K complex, indicating stage 2 sleep; the last part shows waves characteristic of REM sleep. Researchers can identify what stage a sleeper is in by watching an EEG recording. If delta waves are present, the participant is in stage 4 sleep. To confirm this, an experimenter may awaken the participant and ask whether he or she was dreaming.

Sleep cycles develop before birth, and they continue to change into adulthood. Initially, sleeping fetuses show no eye movements. Later, they show eye, facial, and bodily movements. Newborns spend nearly half their sleep time in REM sleep. From age 1 to age 10, the ratio of REM sleep to stage 4 sleep decreases dramatically; in later adulthood, there is increased fragmentation of sleep patterns.

Although REM sleep is active sleep at all ages, PET scans show that not all areas of the brain are equally active. Braun and his colleagues (1998) found that the primary visual cortex is nearly shut down during REM sleep, but that other key visual areas are highly active. This lack of integration of visual areas may account for some of the confused nature of dreams and their bizarre content. Without interpretation from important visual areas, dreaming is like looking at a map that doesn't show key exits, roads, or directional arrows.

Sleep Deprivation: Doing without REM

When people who normally sleep 8 hours a night miss a few hours on a particular night, they may be tired the following day but can function quite well. Many Americans are sleep-deprived—not to an extreme degree, but enough to give them periods of drowsiness each day. How many times have you seen another student nod off in class? Why are coffee shops so popular?

What happens to people who are regularly deprived of REM sleep? Research shows that they become anxious and irritable, report difficulty in concentrating, and do worse than normal on tests that involve attention and originality. As soon as experimental participants deprived of REM sleep are allowed to catch up again, these psychological ill effects disappear.

One study deprived participants of all sleep for 205 hours (8.5 days). Researchers found that on the nights immediately after the experiment, participants spent a greater-than-normal amount of time in REM and stage 4 sleep and the least amount of time in stages 1 and 2—the lightest stages of sleep (Kales et al., 1970; Webb & Agnew, 1975). Similar results were obtained in a study in which participants were partially deprived of REM sleep by being awakened when they showed rapid eye movements. They reported feeling sleepy and spent more time in REM sleep on a subsequent night (Dement, Greenberg, & Klein, 1966). According to Horne (1988), people need to make up for only about 30% of lost sleep, mostly as stage 4 and REM sleep. Think of your sleep needs as a checkbook, with the total amount of REM sleep having to be in balance at the end of a week. After sleep deprivation, on the next night, your body alters its normal sleep patterns to bring you into balance—the more sleep you lose, the more recovery you need on the next night (Lucidi et al., 1997). *Experiencing Psychology* suggests some ways to sleep well.

Some researchers used to believe that people might suffer serious disruptions of personality as a result of prolonged REM sleep deprivation. But today researchers know that sleep deprivation does not lead to maladjustments (Bonnet, 1980). With the exception of brain function effects, especially in the cortex, mild sleep deprivation has surprisingly few effects on the

EXPERIENCING PSYCHOLOGY

Get Some Sleep

Sleeping is universal; every human being spends about a third of his or her life sleeping, generally while lying down with the eyes closed. How can we get the right amount of good sleep? Sleep researchers and theorists all agree on a few basic principles of sleep. Maas (1998), Coren (1996), and Lavie (1996) offer practical advice to all of us. Their suggestions are based on thousands of research studies.

- *Get enough sleep each night.* Sleep is essential, and a lack of it will impair performance and attention.
- *Make sure your sleep habits are regular.* Go to sleep at about the same time each night, sleep for about the same number of hours, and get up at the same time each day.
- *Sleep in one continuous stretch.* Disrupted, noncontinuous sleep isn't as good as a single uninterrupted stretch.
- *A full night's sleep is best.* Short naps in mid-day can help, but a full night's sleep is still better.
- *Make up for lost sleep.* The effects of sleep deprivation are cumulative. Don't let your sleep debt get too big; you need to keep your sleep accounts balanced.
- *Reduce stress, and eat a proper diet.*
- *Exercise regularly.* Get daily exercise, but allow at least 4 hours between such activity and bedtime (6 hours, if you exercise vigorously).
- *Avoid alcohol, caffeine, and nicotine, as well as late meals or snacks.* Omit those midnight trips to the kitchen—many foods have a stimulative effect.
- *At bedtime, try to relax, clear your mind, and follow a ritual* (fluffing the pillow, turning out lights, reading a boring book). ■

rest of the body (Harrison & Horne, 1996). Even more important, any changes in cerebral functions that result from sleep deprivation are quickly reversed once a person is able to get some sleep (Horne, 1988; Lucidi et al., 1997).

Sleep Disorders

Do you snore so loudly that you keep others awake or fall asleep at inappropriate times, such as when driving a car? Do you ever have trouble falling asleep, or find yourself sleepwalking? If you answer yes, you may have a sleep disorder. People who fall asleep suddenly and unexpectedly have a disorder known as *narcolepsy.* Narcolepsy is probably a symptom of an autonomic nervous system disturbance resulting in lowered arousal, but it may also reflect neurochemical problems (Mamelak, 1991). It is relatively rare, affecting only about 1 in 1,000 people.

Another sleep disorder, *sleep apnea,* causes airflow to stop for at least 15 seconds; the sleeper ceases breathing and wakens briefly. People with this disorder often have as many as 100 apnea episodes in a night; during the day, they are exceedingly sleepy and sometimes have memory losses. Because their sleep is interrupted so often, people with severe apnea may have work-related accidents and severe headaches, and they may fall asleep during the day. Drug therapy and some minor surgical techniques for creating better airflow have been used to treat those with sleep apnea—and also may relieve the loud snoring that accompanies the disorder. Monitoring equipment that can sense prolonged breathing pauses and wake the sleeper has also been used (Sheridan, 1985). Sleep apnea affects about 40 in 1,000 individuals, and males are more likely than females to suffer from it (Ingbar & Gee, 1985). Use of alcohol or other drugs that have a depressant effect on the central nervous system often contributes to sleep apnea in adults. Sleep apnea has also been proposed as a possible explanation for sudden infant death syndrome (SIDS), in which sleeping infants die suddenly for no obvious reason.

Insomnia, a prolonged inability to sleep, is a very common sleep disorder, often caused by anxiety or depression; 1 in 10 people report suffering from it at some time in their lives. Sleep disturbances and insomnia are especially common among older adults (Prinz et al., 1990). Insomniacs tend to be listless and tired during the day and may use sleeping pills or other drugs to induce sleep at night. Ironically, researchers have found that these drugs do not induce natural sleep; instead, they reduce the proportion of REM sleep (Webb & Agnew, 1975). (Recall that the body's normal response to sleep deprivation is to *increase* REM sleep.) Since researchers such as Dement have found that lack of REM sleep may alter normal behavior, people with chronic insomnia should not regularly use drugs to induce sleep. Various researchers have proposed behavioral methods that do not rely on drugs to help solve the problem; among these methods are relaxation training, thought restructuring, and self-hypnosis (e.g., Morin et al., 1994). Vitiello (1989) asserts that diet has an effect on sleep by affecting sympathetic nervous system activity, which may stimulate a person in the middle of the night. Research on diet and insomnia is still in its early stages. But since diet affects mood and sleepiness, this idea does have experimental support. Another promising option for insomniacs is discussed in the next section.

Night terrors, another sleep disorder, consist of panic attacks that occur within an hour after a person falls asleep. Sitting up abruptly in a state of sheer panic, a person with a night terror may scream, breathe rapidly, and be in a state of total fright. Night terrors are especially common in young children between the ages of 3 and 8. They usually disappear as a child grows older and do not seem to be a symptom of any psychological disorder. The cause of night terrors is not fully established, but they may be a result of an electrochemical overload of some part of the brain during NREM sleep.

Sleepwalking is a disorder that tends to run in families and is common among children. A sleepwalker appears both asleep and awake at the same time—a sleepwalking child may reach out to a parent for a hug, navigate a darkened room, avoid a piece of furniture, walk into the street, or seem to be trying to accomplish a task—yet still be asleep. More boys sleepwalk than girls, and children who sleepwalk tend to outgrow it as they mature. Brain activity of sleepwalkers, when recorded with an EEG, shows stage 4 sleep. Research shows that different parts of a sleepwalker's brain display different levels of activity: More primitive motor portions of the brain are active; higher-level cognitive portions show little activity. Contrary to popular belief, there is no danger in waking a sleepwalker. More likely, you may not be able to wake the sleepwalking individual because he or she is so deeply asleep (Hobson, 1994).

Sleep disorders probably have several origins, and devising treatments for them will require the development of a research methodology, a theory, and a set of treatment plans that reflect the complexity of the

Dream: A state of consciousness that occurs during sleep and is usually accompanied by vivid visual, tactile, or auditory imagery.

problem. To date, no single approach has been found to be universally successful.

Melatonin—A Drug That Induces Sweet Dreams?

If you were a drug researcher seeking a new drug that could make you a billionaire, you might look for one that has the effect of melatonin. Melatonin induces a sweet and easy sleep without side effects, even among people with insomnia. Currently, it is available as a nutritional supplement, not yet as a prescription drug.

Melatonin is a natural nightcap; it is a hormone normally released by the pea-sized pineal gland at the base of the brain. This hormone helps keep the biological clock in sync, among other things (Middleton, Arendt, & Stone, 1997); melatonin levels in the bloodstream vary when the amount of light in a person's environment changes (Mishima et al., 1994) and when circadian rhythms are disturbed (Dollins et al., 1993). But research shows that melatonin given in small doses to human beings induces sleep quickly and easily, even at mid-day. Richard Wurtman of the Massachusetts Institute of Technology has reported that, given in very small doses, the hormone is a sleep inducer without the side effects often brought about by sleeping pills, such as feeling hungover and losing REM sleep (Dollins et al., 1993a). Melatonin has proved especially effective in the treatment of sleep disorders (Jan, Espezel, & Appleton, 1994) and is widely used for jet lag (Brown, 1994). It has been claimed that melatonin has positive effects on sex drive, life span, heart disease, and even cancer outcomes—although little evidence exists to support these claims.

Researchers are not sure how melatonin works. It may fool the body into thinking that it's nighttime. It may act on brain centers that govern sleep. It may affect other natural sleep-inducing hormones. All researchers know is that people who take melatonin in small doses have less trouble sleeping.

Should you take melatonin? Lots of people do. But, as a critical thinker, you have to be wary of unproven drugs. Clinical trials of melatonin using double-blind procedures have yet to be conducted. Dosage levels are untested, and people report using dosages ranging from as little as 0.1 milligram to 200 milligrams. About 10% of those who have taken the hormone report negative side effects, including nightmares, headaches, and lowered sex drives. Researchers do not know whether the effects of the hormone differ in people of various ages. Do men and women respond differently? (There is reason to believe that they do.) What about older men versus younger women? Does the hormone have any long-term side effects? The potential of melatonin is enormous: It may help people who suffer from sleep disorders; it may aid those who work shifts of varying lengths, including physicians, nurses, and airline pilots. This drug may revolutionize how and when people sleep—but the operative word is *may*. The decision must await carefully controlled, scientific double-blind research.

Think Critically

- Describe your own daily sleep–wakefulness cycle. Sleep specialists have a name for "morning people" (*larks*) and "night people" (*owls*). Are you a lark or an owl?

Dreams

Focus on issues and ideas

- Developing an understanding of the content of dreams
- The evolution of dream analysis
- The effects of culture on dream content

Why do some people rarely remember their dreams while other people can recall theirs in vivid detail? Do dreams contain hidden meanings and mysterious symbols to be deciphered? Sometimes lifelike, sometimes surreal, and sometimes incoherent, dreams may seem to replay a person's life history or venture into the unknown. Dreams have long occupied an important place in psychology, but only since the 1950s have they come under close scientific scrutiny. Dream research is difficult to conduct. In addition, because the data from dream research are always memories of past events, they are sometimes difficult to quantify and verify (Koulack, 1991), and this is especially true with youngsters, who have difficulty reporting dreams from their own perspective (Foulkes & Kerr, 1994).

What Is a Dream?

A **dream** is a state of consciousness that occurs during sleep and is usually accompanied by vivid visual imagery, although the imagery may also be tactile or auditory. During a dream, there is an increase in heart rate, the appearance of rapid eye movements, a characteristic brain-wave pattern, and a lack of bodily movement. Although dreams occur more often in REM sleep, they also occur during NREM sleep; during NREM sleep, they tend to be less visual and less bizarre and to contain less action imagery (Casagrande et al., 1996). Dreams during REM sleep are intensely visual, may be action-oriented, and are more likely to be emotional than are NREM dreams. NREM dreams, such as the dreams that occur at the beginning of sleep (Vogel, 1991), are more like waking thoughts (Foulkes, 1985).

Most people dream four or five times a night, and the dreams last from a few seconds to several minutes. The first dream of a typical night occurs 90 minutes after a person has fallen asleep and lasts for 10 minutes. More dreaming occurs during the second part of the night than at the beginning (Casagrande et al., 1996). With about four dreams per night and 365 days per year, the average person is likely to have more than 100,000 dreams in a lifetime. However, people remember only a few of their dreams. Usually, they recall a dream because they woke in the middle of it or because the dream had powerful emotional content or imagery.

Content of Dreams

Sometimes the content of a dream is related to day-to-day events, to an unfulfilled desire, or to an unpleasant experience. Sometimes a person experiences the same dream or a sequence of related dreams over and over again. Dreams are mostly visual, and most are in color. Most dreams focus on events and people with whom the dreamer comes into contact frequently—family, friends, or coworkers. Common dream themes include sex, aggressive incidents, and misfortunes. Sounds and other sensations from the environment that do not awaken a sleeper are often incorporated into a dream. For example, when a researcher sprayed water on the hands of sleepers, 42% of those who did not awaken later reported dreaming about swimming pools, baths, or rain (Dement & Wolpert, 1958).

When my younger daughter was 6 years old, she told me about a dream in which she was being chased by a monster. In the dream, she realized that she was dreaming, and so she turned around and made friends with the monster. Like my daughter, people sometimes report that they are aware of dreaming while it is happening; this type of dream is a **lucid dream.** Most people have had a lucid dream at one time or another, particularly as children. Often people who have experienced a lucid dream report that they felt as though they were inside and outside the dream at the same time. For some people, this feeling is upsetting, and they may wake themselves up.

Dream Theories

Some psychologists assume that dreams express desires and thoughts that may be unacceptable to the conscious mind. Many therapists who interpret and analyze dreams assume that dreams represent some aspect of the personality that is seeking expression; this view—widely held—suggests that dreams put emotions into a context and that dreaming allows the safe expression of emotions (Hartmann, 1995, 1996). Some psychologists find dreams meaningless. Others see much symbolism in dreams and assert that the content of a dream hides its true meaning. The suggested meaning of a dream depends on the psychologist's orientation. Two theorists who made much of the meaning of dreams are Freud and Jung; both wrote extensively on the meaning of dreams and have influenced current thinking significantly. Yet there is little or no scientific support for their theories of dreams and much evidence to the contrary (Blagrove, 1996). Others see dreams as a physiological phenomenon with little meaning; the fact that dreams are often disconnected and incoherent is cited as evidence for this view. (See Table 4.1.)

Psychodynamic Views. Sigmund Freud described dreams as "the royal road to the unconscious." For Freud, a dream expressed desires, wishes, and unfulfilled needs that exist in the unconscious (see Chapter 10 for more on Freud and the unconscious). In his book *The Interpretation of Dreams* (1900/1953), Freud spoke about the manifest and latent content of dreams. The **manifest content** of a dream consists of its overt story line, characters, and setting—the obvious, clearly discernible events of the dream. The **latent content** of a dream is its deeper meaning, usually involving symbolism, hidden meaning, and repressed or obscured ideas and wishes—often wishes that might make the dreamer uncomfortable if they were ex-

Table 4.1 Theories of Dreaming

Theory	Explanation
Psychodynamic theory	Psychodynamic theorists such as Freud view dreams as expressions of desires, wishes, and unfulfilled needs that exist in the unconscious.
Jungian theory	Jungian theorists see dreams not only as expressions of needs and desires, but as reflections of people's collective unconscious.
Physiological model	Physiological models of dreaming view dreams as combinations of neural signals that are randomly generated and see analysis of dreams as a futile effort to make sense out of random events.

pressed overtly. Freud would say that at the latent level, a dream about a tunnel is definitely *not* about a tunnel. You will see in Chapters 10 and 14 that Freud used dreams extensively in his theory of personality and in his treatment approach. Freudian psychoanalysts use dream analysis as a therapeutic tool in the treatment of emotional disturbance. Many contemporary therapists use patients' dreams to help them understand current problems but may see the dreams as a starting point only.

Some contemporary researchers believe that dreams are connected to reality, have meaning, and even have a "grammar" of their own, without having a hidden, or latent, content.

Carl G. Jung (1875–1961) was trained in Freudian approaches to therapy and personality analysis, and he, too, considered dreams a crucial means for understanding human nature. However, Jung took it for granted that a dream was nature's way of allowing humans access to their own unconscious, and he focused on the meaning of dreams. Each thing a person dreams has a meaning; dreams are the language through which an individual expresses in an uncensored form his or her deepest feelings. Dreams, for Jung, were very self-oriented and were a dreamer's attempt to make sense of life's tasks, compensate for unconscious urges, and predict the future (McLynn, 1997). Jung asserted that dreams give visual expression to instincts and that all humans share in the **collective unconscious,** a storehouse of primitive ideas and images inherited from one's ancestors. These inherited ideas and images, whose representations in the individual emerge in dreams, are termed *archetypes,* are emotionally charged and rich in meaning and symbolism. Jungian therapy focuses on dream analysis as an approach to understanding and accepting one's humanity. We will consider how Jungians focus on dreams and the collective unconscious of humankind in more detail in our study of personality in Chapter 10.

Today, psychoanalytic theorists still see dreams as keys to the unconscious, but they also suggest that dreams integrate past experiences with current ones to produce a structure of ideas and feelings that are organized so as to help restore psychological balance. Thus, theorists such as Fosshage (1997) assert that dreams speak to the dreamer and tell stories of the person's ongoing psychological transformation. As appealing as these ideas are to some psychologists, there are scant data to suggest that they are correct.

Cognitive Views. Some contemporary researchers believe that dreams are connected to reality, have meaning, and even have a "grammar" of their own, without having a hidden, or latent, content. These cognitive researchers (e.g., Foulkes, 1985, 1996) suggest that dreams express current wishes, desires, and issues with which a person is dealing. Dieters dream of food; smokers trying to quit dream of (actual) cigars; people who are depressed dream of bleak futures (Hajek & Belcher, 1991). Similarly, young lovers dream of the future, and the aged dream of the past. According to this view, not only do we dream of what is currently concerning us, but our culture and language affect dream content; for example, the dream content of those who are bilingual is related to the language that was dominating their waking hours before sleep (Foulkes et al., 1993). Foulkes (1990) argues that the creation of a dream depends on active, integrative intelligence and that studying the content of dreams allows researchers to learn more about development, intelligence, and language, as well as how cognitive processes develop. *Diversity* (pp. 102–103) explores cultural influences on the content of dreams.

Biological Views. Researchers know that dreaming is neither solely a right-hemisphere nor solely a left-hemisphere function—both hemispheres are involved (McCormick et al., 1997). But both sides of the brain may not be operating simultaneously or even in congruence. Is it possible that this lack of coordination means that dreams have no underlying meaning and are just random fleeting images? Two researchers from Harvard Medical School, Allan Hobson and Robert McCarley (1977), believe dreams (and, for that matter, all consciousness) have a physiological basis but that dreams represent little more than incoherent, haphazard, transient images. They argue that during periods of REM sleep, the parts of

Lucid [LOO-sid] dream: Dream in which the dreamer is aware of dreaming while it is happening.

Manifest content: The overt story line, characters, and setting of a dream—the obvious, clearly discernible events of the dream.

Latent content: The deeper meaning of a dream, usually involving symbolism, hidden meaning, and repressed or obscured ideas and wishes.

Collective unconscious: Jung's concept of a storehouse of primitive ideas and images that are inherited from one's ancestors; these inherited ideas and images, called *archetypes,* are emotionally charged and rich in meaning and symbolism.

DIVERSITY

Does Culture Influence Dream Content?

Freud wrote that dreams were "the royal road to the unconscious." Like many other psychoanalysts, then and now, he held that dreams express desires and wishes that spring from deeply held values and past experiences. But most cognitive researchers, and even some biological scientists, assert that dreams are more a reflection of culture and current experiences. Do our dreams reflect our past or our daily lives?

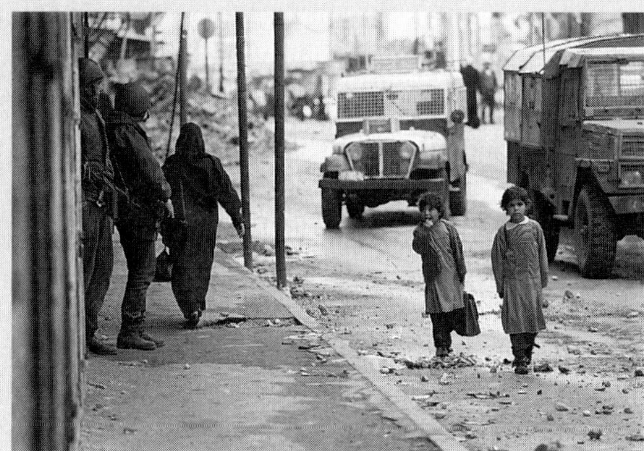

Punamäki and Joustie (1998), two researchers from the University of Helsinki, compared the dreams of participants from Finland and Palestine—two cultures that differ in how dream content is viewed. Finnish society does not value or explore dreams as part of the development process; religion, schools, and families focus on consciousness and real work—practical applications. In contrast, Palestinian culture values and explores multiple levels of reality and consciousness and prepares children to anticipate and interpret dream experiences. The researchers hypothesized that more Palestinian dreams than Finnish ones would be likely to incorporate bizarre and unreal images. Punamäki and Joustie argued that family background, living circumstances, and religious upbringing shape people's characters, giving them tendencies that might be referred to as individualistic or collectivist, and that these tendencies would show up in dreams—with the Finns being individualistic and the Palestinians more collectivist. Furthermore, they argued that Western dreams are likely to be considered private messages from a person's inner core, but Middle Eastern dreams are more likely to be seen as external messages from sacred forces.

The researchers had over 200 Finnish and Palestinian children, aged 7 through 12, keep sleep diaries over a period of a week. Each diary sheet began "Last night I dreamt that . . . ." Dreams were analyzed to assess themes such as anxiety and aggression, bizarreness, vividness, atmosphere, and quality of human relationships. Among the Palestinian children, some lived in violent neighborhoods (in Gaza, an area where opposition to Israeli occu-

the brain responsible for long-term memory, vision, audition, and perhaps even emotion are spontaneously *activated* (stimulated) by cells in the hindbrain, especially the pons. The cortex tries to *synthesize,* or make sense out of, the messages. But, because the messages do not arise from real external stimuli, the resulting dream is often fragmented and incoherent (Hobson, 1989, 1994). Activation–synthesis theory is supported by researchers who assert that the brain (especially the cortex) basically does its daily "housecleaning" during sleep, scanning previous memories, refreshing storage mechanisms, and maintaining active memories. Other researchers, however, point out that dreamlike activity occurs even when cells in the pons are not active. In this view, a dream is a random collection of images with little or no importance. Research by Braun and others (1998) lends support to the idea of disconnected brain activity; not all parts of the brain are activated during sleep. This lack of integration of brain activity may account for the random nature of images and dream content. *I*

Think Critically

- What, if anything, would happen to you if you cut your normal daily amount of sleep by 2 hours for a period of several months?
- Keep a notepad at your bedside, and record several nights' dreams immediately on awakening. (Otherwise, you're likely to forget them by the time you have breakfast.) Which theory of dreaming seems to explain your dreams best?

pation is strong) and some lived in a peaceful town (Galilea).

The results showed that the Palestinians living in violent neighborhoods reported far more dreams of persecution and aggression than did the Palestinians from nonviolent areas or the Finnish children. This was no surprise: Violence in daily life was reflected in dream content. Interestingly, the researchers' analysis revealed that gender was also an important variable—boys were more likely than girls to report bizarre imagery or imagery of death, terror, and unhappy ends. Both Finnish girls and Palestinian girls living in peaceful areas were more likely to dream of guilt and shame. Age, which the researchers hypothesized would have a large effect, was not a potent variable—the dreams of the younger children and the older ones varied little in content.

But contrary to the researchers' assumptions, the results failed to show that Palestinian dreams incorporated multiple levels of reality more than Finnish ones did. In general, the study failed to show that culture had a strong influence on dream content. What it did show was daily life experiences, especially negative events such as violence, intruding vividly on dreams. Punamäki and Joustie (1998) quoted what one 10-year-old girl wrote:

> I went to school, and on my way I saw a masked man carrying a knife and axe, and I felt afraid of him and I ran away until I reached my mother in the house. I told her why I was shaking: "Mother, mother, on the way to school I saw a masked man." She told me not to be afraid of them, because they do not do anything. So in the dream I felt calm. (p. 338)

In a real-world setting, not a laboratory, Punamäki and Joustie (1998) showed that the environment in which a dreamer lives and the person's gender affect dream content. Daily experiences far surpassed cultural themes in the children's recorded dreams. Since culture affects people's religion, values, and even daily habits so greatly, this surprised the researchers. Perhaps the cultural difference revealed by the children's dreams is in the ways societies encourage or allow the expression of fear, anger, or aggression. The children from Gaza live in a region where people are engaged in a national struggle for independence; as a result, they may have developed cultural expectations concerning violence that differ from those of their peers in Galilea and Finland. The impact of that daily struggle may dominate their dreams and mask cultural differences; among the children from Galilea and Finland, cultural differences in dreams could not be observed.

Is it possible that dreams do not reflect culture? Perhaps this study did not adequately measure the effects of culture on dreaming. Perhaps the difficulty lies in defining "culture." Or it may be that dream content, as assessed through diaries, does not fully reveal repressed desires or even cultural values. Perhaps the content of dream diaries is only one of several measures necessary to reveal cultural influences on dreaming, and in this study, it was an inaccurate measure, because children were doing the recording. Whether culture has an impact is yet to be proved; what was proved, and quite decisively, was that daily experiences dominate the dreams of children. ■

I Controlling Consciousness: Biofeedback, Hypnosis, and Meditation

Focus on issues and ideas

- The various methods of controlling consciousness
- The characteristics of biofeedback training
- The effects of hypnosis and meditation as therapeutic tools

Can you learn to control your own consciousness? Can you manipulate your mental states in order to achieve certain bodily reactions? Research and anecdotal data suggest that you can. For centuries, people have learned to relax and breathe in special ways so as not to experience pain—for example, during childbirth. Contestants have won marathons through intense mental concentration that allowed them to endure especially difficult physical circumstances. Laboratory research also shows that people can bring some of their autonomic bodily states, such as blood pressure, under conscious control through the technique of biofeedback.

Biofeedback

Imagine a special clinic where people could be taught to treat themselves for headaches, high blood pressure, stress-related illnesses, even nearsightedness. By learning to influence consciously what are normally involuntary reactions, patients might be able to cure their own physical problems. Such a psychological–medical clinic may exist in the future if biofeedback proves to be the healing tool some researchers predict it will be.

Physicians and psychologists once assumed that most biological functions, especially those involving the autonomic nervous system, could not be controlled voluntarily except through drugs or surgery. Since the 1960s, however, studies have explored the extent to which people can learn to control these functions through biofeedback. **Biofeedback** is a general technique by which a person can monitor and learn to control the involuntary activity of some of the body's organs and functions. A well-known psychologist, Neal E. Miller, was one of the first researchers to train rats to control certain glandular responses. Miller (1969) suggested human beings might benefit from the same techniques.

We do not normally control functions such as blood flow and may not have any conscious awareness of where blood actually flows. But, in theory, biofeedback gives us that awareness and allows us to directly modify brain systems that control it. The appropriate brain changes are reinforced by the feedback. A relaxed person viewing his or her own brain waves on a monitor, for example, can increase the frequency of those waves by becoming more alert and paying attention. Similarly, a participant whose heart rate is displayed on a monitor can see the rate decrease as he or she relaxes, thereby learning about the physiological states that allow the body to work easily and efficiently. The person can learn which behaviors relax the heart and lower blood pressure and, in time, can learn to reproduce those behaviors and control heart rate and blood pressure.

Some researchers contend that biofeedback training is not effective (Drennen & Holden, 1984); other researchers point out that the same effects can be obtained without real feedback (Plotkin, 1980). Some are skeptical about the long-term effectiveness of biofeedback to improve health or regulate pain. Can a person continue to achieve a particular goal over many years using biofeedback—or might the body become habituated to it, as to some medications, so that eventually it wouldn't work as well? Still other researchers claim to have used biofeedback successfully to treat people with stress-related symptoms, hyperactivity, stuttering, depression, nearsightedness, and learning disabilities.

Many laboratory studies have demonstrated biofeedback's effectiveness in helping people manage a wide range of physiological problems; however, only carefully controlled research will answer persistent questions about its usefulness. For example, under what conditions, with what kinds of problems, and with what types of individuals is biofeedback effective (Middaugh, 1990)? Methodological issues such as those described in Chapter 1 (expectancy effects or attempts to please a researcher, for example) make this research challenging.

Biofeedback: Technique by which a person can monitor and learn to control the involuntary activity of some of the body's organs and functions.

Hypnosis: Altered state of consciousness brought about by procedures that may induce a trance.

Hypnosis

"You are falling asleep. Your eyelids are becoming heavy. The weight on your eyes is becoming greater and greater. Your muscles are relaxing. You are feeling sleepier and sleepier. You are feeling very relaxed." These instructions are typical of those used in *hypnotic induction*—the process used to hypnotize people. **Hypnosis** is an altered state of consciousness brought about by procedures that may induce a trance. The generally accepted view of hypnosis is that hypnotized individuals are in an altered state of consciousness and give up control over much of their behavior. They are aware of their surroundings and are conscious, but their level of awareness and responses to others are altered. A person's ability to be hypnotized or willingness to follow instructions given by the hypnotist to do unconventional things, such as to strike unusual poses (see the photo), is called *hypnotic susceptibility*, or *suggestibility*. Most people can be hypnotized to some extent (Hilgard, 1965). Children between 7 and 14 are the most susceptible; daydreamers are also especially susceptible (Hoyt et al., 1989). Crawford (1994) argues that highly hypnotizable people have stronger attention-focusing abilities than those who are not suggestible—children certainly fit that characterization.

Effects of Hypnosis. People who have been hypnotized report that they know they have been hypnotized and are aware of their surroundings. Some report being in a special, almost mystical state, and most report a sense of time distortion (Bowers, 1979). One reported time-distortion effect of hypnosis is *age regression*—the ability to recount details about an experience that took place many years earlier or to feel and act like a child. Because few studies that report age regression during hypnosis have been controlled for accuracy of recall, the authenticity of age regression has been questioned (Nash, 1987). The age at which the events being recalled occurred is important,

because it is generally difficult to remember events experienced before age 3 (Perner & Ruffman, 1995). It is possible that individuals report what they believe might have happened at the earlier age.

Heightened memory is another purported effect of hypnosis. Evidence indicates that hypnosis helps participants recall information (e.g., McConkey & Kinoshita, 1988). However, techniques that do not involve hypnosis may work just as well for this purpose. In fact, in a study by Putnam (1979), hypnotized and nonhypnotized participants were asked to recall events they had seen earlier on a videotape. Hypnotized participants made more errors when answering leading questions than did nonhypnotized participants. Such research suggests that hypnotized participants not only make more errors (misrecollection) but also mistakenly believe their memories are accurate (Sheehan & Tilden, 1983). These results have led researchers to question the use of hypnosis in courtroom settings; in fact, some states do not admit the testimony of hypnotized persons as evidence.

Hypnosis is also used for pain reduction. However, few studies on this use of hypnosis have been experimentally rigorous. Critics of the use of hypnosis for pain management note that most patients show signs of pain even when hypnotized. Also, in many cases, analgesic drugs (pain relievers) are used along with hypnosis. Some researchers challenge the ability of hypnosis to reduce pain, reasoning that relaxation and a patient's positive attitude and lowered anxiety account for reported reductions in pain.

Hypnosis continues to be widely used as an aid in psychotherapy—to help patients relax, enhance their memory, reduce stress and anxiety, lose weight, or stop smoking. Most clients report that, if nothing else, being hypnotized is a pleasant experience. Therapists assert that in some cases hypnosis can (1) help focus a client's energy on a specific topic, (2) aid memory, or (3) help a child cope with the aftereffects of abuse. Some psychologists assert that hypnosis can help athletes concentrate (Morgan, 1992). Research into the process and effects of hypnosis continues, with emphasis on defining critical variables in the process of hypnotic induction and in the participants who are the most and the least easily hypnotized (e.g., Nilsson, 1990) and on ascertaining potential negative effects (e.g., Lynn et al., 1997; Sapp, 1996).

Challenges to Hypnosis. The traditional view of hypnosis is sometimes referred to as a "state" view because it argues that hypnotized individuals are in a state that is qualitatively different from normal waking consciousness. The traditional view suggests that a sleep-like state occurs in hypnosis and that hypnotized individuals experience significant alterations in consciousness, including highly selective attention, and willingness to engage in role playing and to follow posthypnotic suggestions (Kihlstrom, 1998). This view is sometimes distinguished from more social-cognitive views, sometimes referred to as "nonstate" views. But as you will see, such dichotomies are blurred by the data: Hypnosis is neither a distinct state nor merely a social phenomenon (Kirsch & Lynn, 1995, 1998a, 1998b); nor does it necessarily rely on special conscious mechanisms (Woody & Sadler, 1998).

The traditional state view is that responses of hypnotized individuals are due to a division of consciousness into two or more simultaneous streams that are separate, distinct, and inaccessible to each other. Hilgard (1994) presents this idea, and Bowers (1992) offers a related theory, but there are little supportive data, physiological or otherwise. Far more evidence supports the long-held view of T. X. Barber, one of the major skeptics concerning the traditional state view of hypnosis. Barber (1991) and Spanos (1991) contend that the concepts of hypnosis and the hypnotic trance are meaningless and misleading. According to them, behaviors of hypnotized participants are no different from behaviors of participants willing to think about and imagine themes suggested to them. If participants' attitudes toward a situation lead them to expect certain effects, those effects will be more likely to occur. This social-cognitive view is sometimes called the *cognitive-behavioral view;* it stresses the role of social processes in changing people's thoughts and behavior during hypnosis (Lynn, 1992).

Barber's studies show that participants who undergo hypnotic induction and participants given task-motivating instructions (such as to concentrate deeply, fix their attention, or breathe deeply) perform similarly. Typically, more than half of the participants in experimental groups showed responsiveness to task suggestions, in contrast to 16% in control groups that were given no special instructions. From the results, Barber concluded that task-motivating instructions are almost as effective as hypnotic induction in increasing participants' responsiveness.

Barber's studies have received support from other research. Salzberg and DePiano (1980), for example, found that hypnosis did not facilitate performance any more than task-motivating instructions did. In fact, they argued that for cognitive tasks, task-motivating instructions are more effective than hypnosis. But the evidence showing that the effects achieved through hypnosis can be achieved in various ways (e.g., Bryant & McConkey, 1989) does not mean that psychologists must discard the use of hypnosis. It simply means they should reconsider traditional assumptions and stop thinking about hypnosis as either one thing or another. Rather, they should see it as a topic for continuing research and debate. The ultimate view of hypnosis is unlikely to be strictly state or social-cognitive, but instead will consider motivation, intention, expectancy, memory, and automated responses (Kirsch & Lynn, 1998b).

Meditation

Meditation has become an important daily routine for one of my colleagues. Previously, searing migraines, stomach pains, and high blood pressure had afflicted her during stressful periods. Despite prescription drugs and frequent visits to the doctor, she had found little relief. Then, at a stress-management clinic, she discovered how to ease her tensions through meditation. Now, instead of taking a pill when she feels a migraine coming on, she meditates.

Meditation is the use of a variety of techniques including concentration, restriction of incoming stimuli, and deep relaxation to produce a state of consciousness characterized by a sense of detachment. For centuries, meditation has been used to alter consciousness and help relieve health problems. Those who practice it use a variety of positions—sitting, lying, or reclining—and report that it can reduce anxiety, tension headaches, backaches, asthma, and the need for sleep. It can also increase self-awareness and feelings of inner peace (West, 1980, 1982). Meditation is not relaxation—rather, relaxation is a by-product of meditation.

Practitioners distinguish between two major types of meditation: *mindful* and *concentrative*. Each type uses different techniques to induce an altered state of awareness. Both direct the focus of attention away from the outside world through intense concentration. A person begins *mindful meditation* by trying to empty the mind and just be still. As random and intrusive thoughts arise, the meditator notices them (becomes mindful of their content) without reacting to them, judging them, or dwelling on them. They eventually become mere wisps of thought that pass through consciousness while the meditator remains serene. Eventually, a mindful meditator becomes aware that it is reactions to thoughts that cause suffering, and that one can entertain thoughts without having to react.

In *concentrative meditation,* a meditator concentrates on a visual image or a mantra (a word or a phrase repeated over and over). When the mind wanders to a random thought, the meditator brings the mind back to the image or mantra, without noticing the content of the thought. In this case, the image or mantra is the important thing. Concentrative meditation is closely tied to religions such as Tibetan Buddhism and Hinduism; but it has also been commercially exploited and has thus acquired a bad reputation in some circles.

One concentrative approach, *Zen,* is especially popular among people interested in healing and holistic approaches to health. People using Zen techniques seek to attain the experience of enlightenment. Teachers of Zen techniques urge people to concentrate on their breathing and count their breaths. The immediate aim is to focus attention on a specific visual stimulus; the ultimate aim is to achieve a spiritual state of being.

Supporters of meditation claim that it is a unique state, capable of causing profound physiological and psychological changes. They argue that mindful meditation produces a different mode of cognitive processing, by training people to maintain awareness of ongoing events and increase their attention. But a study comparing the physiological responses of meditators with those of hypnotized participants found the responses to be nearly identical (Holmes, 1984). Experimental studies also show that individuals trained simply to relax and concentrate have been able to achieve bodily states similar to those of meditators (Fenwick et al., 1977).

Although most theories that explain the nature and effects of meditation rely on concepts that are not scientifically measurable or observable, some con-

Meditation: The use of a variety of techniques including concentration, restriction of incoming stimuli, and deep relaxation to produce a state of consciousness characterized by a sense of detachment.

Drug: Any chemical substance that alters normal biological processes.

Psychoactive [SYE-koh-AK-tiv] drug: A drug that alters behavior, thought, or emotions by altering biochemical reactions in the nervous system, thereby affecting consciousness.

Addictive drug: A drug that causes a compulsive physiological need in the user and whose absence produces withdrawal symptoms.

Substance abuser: A person who overuses and relies on drugs to deal with everyday life.

Psychological dependence: A compelling desire to use a drug, along with an inability to inhibit that desire.

trolled studies have been done. The data from these studies have shown that meditators can alter their physiological responses, including oxygen consumption, brain-wave activity, and sleep patterns (Pagano et al., 1976). Such evidence encourages some scientists to continue to investigate meditation as a means of relieving tension, anxiety, and arousal.

Think Critically

- If daydreamers and those who fantasize easily are ideal candidates for hypnosis, does this imply that hypnotized individuals are "faking it" somehow?
- In courtroom testimony, do you think it is reasonable to use statements made while under hypnosis? Why or why not?
- Can you think of a physiological explanation for the effects of rhythmic breathing in meditation?

Altering Consciousness with Drugs

Focus on issues and ideas

- The behaviors associated with substance abuse
- The sedative–hypnotic effects of alcohol consumption
- The social, medical, and psychological issues concerning alcohol treatment programs
- The effects of opiates and psychostimulants on psychological functioning
- The prevalence of cocaine and marijuana use and its effects on society

In each of the past few years, U.S. physicians have written more than 2 billion prescriptions for drugs. Of those, almost 50 million were for the tranquilizer diazepam (Valium). At least one-third of all U.S. citizens between the ages of 18 and 74 regularly use some kind of consciousness-altering drug that changes both brain activity and daily behavior. There is no doubt that the United States is a drug-using culture. Americans take drugs to wake up in the morning, to get through the stresses of the day, and to get to sleep. Drugs may be legal or illegal; they may be used responsibly or abused with tragic consequences. A **drug** is any chemical substance that alters normal biological processes. Many widely used drugs are both psychoactive and addictive. A **psychoactive drug** is a drug that alters behavior, thought, or emotions by altering biochemical reactions in the nervous system, thereby affecting consciousness. An **addictive drug** is a drug that causes a compulsive physiological need in the user and whose absence produces withdrawal symptoms. Addictive drugs also usually produce tolerance (discussed shortly). Basically, addiction is a physiological phenomenon; repeated exposure to a substance, over time, affects the functions of the brain, and, consequently, the body (Nestler & Aghajanian, 1997).

There is no single explanation for substance use and abuse. Societal factors, individual family situation, medical problems, and genetic heritage are all potentially part of a person's reasons for using or abusing drugs. Further, the drug itself, its properties, and the context of its use must be taken into consideration. For example, not all people respond in the same way to the same drug, and one person may respond differently on different occasions. There are two important questions to ask: Does the drug produce dependence? Are there adverse consequences of using the drug for the user, other people, or society in general?

What Is Substance Abuse?

A **substance abuser** is a person who overuses and relies on drugs to deal with everyday life. Most substance abusers turn to alcohol, tobacco, and other readily available drugs such as cocaine and marijuana; but substance abuse is not confined to these drugs. A growing number of people abuse legal drugs such as tranquilizers and diet pills, as well as illegal drugs such as amphetamines and heroin. A person is a substance abuser if all three of the following statements apply:

- The person has used the substance for at least a month.
- The use of the substance has caused legal, personal, social, or vocational problems.
- The person repeatedly uses the substance even in situations when doing so is hazardous, such as when driving a car.

Substance abuse can lead to psychological dependence, pathological use, or both. **Psychological dependence** is a compelling desire to use a drug, along with an inability to inhibit that desire. *Pathological use* involves out-of-control episodes of use, such as alcohol binges. Excessive use of most drugs leads to a physiological reaction that becomes evident when the body no longer receives the drug; in general, this reaction is evidence of physical dependence. Without the drug, a dependent person suffers from withdrawal symptoms. **Withdrawal symptoms** are the physiological reactions an addict experiences when he or she stops using an addictive drug. The reactions may include headaches, nausea, and an intense craving for the drug. In addition, addictive drugs usually produce **tolerance**—progressive insensitivity to repeated use of a drug taken in the same dosage and at the same frequency. Tolerance forces an addict to use more of the drug or to use the drug more often to achieve the same effect. For example, alcoholics must consume larger and larger amounts of alcohol to become drunk. Most addictive drugs produce both dependence and tolerance.

Psychoactive drugs change behavior by altering a person's physiology and thoughts, needs, and normal state of consciousness. Some drugs increase alertness and performance; others relax the user and diminish high levels of arousal and tension. Some drugs produce physical and psychological dependence.

Why Do People Abuse Drugs?

Some people are likely to become substance abusers for physiological or genetic reasons; others may have emotional problems caused by stress, poverty, boredom, loneliness, or anxiety. People may turn to drugs to relax, be sociable, forget their worries, feel confident, or lose weight. Parental drug use, peer drug use, poor self-esteem, stressful life changes, and social isolation have all been implicated.

In any culture, determining the causes of drug abuse is complicated by the definition of addiction. Addictive drugs are generally defined as those that are habit-forming (reinforcing) or that produce a physiological dependence—for example, alcohol or barbiturates. These two processes are not independent, however; physiological processes may lead to addictive reinforcement patterns. Many drugs that affect the brain differently are addictive—alcohol and cocaine are two examples. In order to help develop drug policies, researchers are currently attempting to devise models that incorporate psychological variables such as cravings, physiological variables such as changes in brain structures and neural firing patterns, and social variables such as family support and therapy.

Substance abusers rarely have identical abuse patterns. Some people use only one drug. Others are *polydrug abusers,* taking several drugs; a heroin addict, for example, might also take amphetamines. When amphetamines became difficult to obtain, the person might switch to barbiturates. Some researchers assert that many people are addiction-prone (Sutker & Allain, 1988). Others note that addicts are often ambivalent about whether they want to give up their drug (Bradley, 1990). Still other researchers have found that adults' addictive behaviors can be predicted from antisocial childhood behavior (Nathan, 1988; Shedler & Block, 1990).

Let's take a closer look at some of the most commonly used drugs and their consciousness-altering properties (see Table 4.2). We begin with alcohol, the source of one of the most critical drug problems in the United States today.

Alcohol

Alcohol consumption in the United States has been at an all-time high for more than a decade. According to the U.S. Department of Health and Human Services, about 80% of urban U.S. adults report having used alcohol at some time; it is estimated that 10 million people over age 18 in the United States are problem drinkers or alcoholics (defined and discussed shortly). Each year, surveys show that about one-fourth of 8th-grade students and more than one-third of 10th-grade students report having had five or more drinks on at least one occasion during the previous 2 weeks.

Alcohol is the most widely used sedative–hypnotic. A **sedative–hypnotic** is any of a class of drugs that relax and calm a user and, in higher doses, induce

Withdrawal symptoms: Physiological reactions an addict experiences when he or she stops using an addictive drug.

Tolerance: Progressive insensitivity to repeated use of a drug taken in the same dosage and at the same frequency.

Sedative–hypnotic: Any of a class of drugs that relax and calm a user and, in higher doses, induce sleep; also known as a *depressant.*

Alcoholic: A problem drinker who also has both physiological and psychological needs to consume alcohol and to experience its effects.

Table 4.2 Commonly Abused Drugs

Type of Drug	Examples of Drug	Effects of Drug	Tolerance?	Physiological Dependence?
Sedative–hypnotics	Alcohol	Reduces tension	yes	yes
	Barbiturates (e.g., Seconal)	Reduce tension; induce sleep	yes	yes
	Tranquilizers (e.g., Valium)	Alleviate tension; induce relaxation	yes	yes
Opiates	Opium Morphine Heroin	Alleviate pain and tension; induce a high	yes	yes
Psychostimulants	Amphetamines	Increase excitability, alertness, and talkativeness; decrease appetite	yes	yes
	Cocaine	Increases alertness, decreases fatigue, stimulates sexual arousal	yes	yes
Psychedelics	Marijuana	Changes mood and perception	no	no

Note: Even though a drug may not produce physiological dependence, it may produce a psychosocial need that compels repeated use.

sleep (sometimes they are referred to as *depressants*). Because alcohol is readily available, relatively inexpensive, and socially accepted, addiction to it is easy to establish and maintain. In fact, most Americans consider some alcohol consumption appropriate in a variety of situations: before, during, and after dinner, at weddings and funerals, at religious ceremonies, and during sports events.

Effects of Alcohol. Alcohol is a depressant that dampens arousal and decreases inhibitions; it encourages some behaviors that are normally under tight control (Stritzke, Lang, & Patrick, 1996). For example, it may diminish people's social inhibitions and make them less likely to restrain their aggressive impulses (Ito, Miller, & Pollock, 1996). The physiological effects of alcohol vary, depending on the amount of alcohol in the bloodstream and the gender and weight of the user. After equal amounts of alcohol consumption, women have higher blood alcohol levels than men do, even allowing for differences in body weight; this occurs because men's bodies typically have a higher percentage of fluid than do women's. With less blood and other fluids in which to dilute the alcohol, a woman may end up with a higher blood alcohol concentration after the same number of drinks as a man (Frezza et al., 1990; York & Welte, 1994).

With increasing amounts of alcohol in the bloodstream, people typically exhibit progressively slower responses; they often exhibit severe motor disturbances, such as staggering. A blood alcohol level greater than 0.10 (0.1 milligram of alcohol per 100 milliliters of blood) usually indicates that the person has consumed too much alcohol to function responsibly. In most states, a blood alcohol level of 0.10 legally defines intoxication; police officers may arrest drivers who are found to have this level of blood alcohol. Table 4.3 (on p. 110) shows the behavioral effects associated with various blood alcohol levels.

The nervous system becomes less sensitive to, or accommodates to, alcohol with increased usage. After months or years of drinking, drug tolerance develops, and a person has to consume ever-increasing amounts of alcohol to achieve the same effect. Thus, when not intoxicated, a heavy drinker develops anxiety, cravings, and other withdrawal symptoms (Levin, 1990).

Problem Drinkers versus Alcoholics. *Alcohol-related problems* are medical, social, or psychological problems associated with alcohol use. A person with an alcohol-related problem such as missing work occasionally because of hangovers, spending a paycheck to buy drinks for friends, or losing a driver's license because of drunk driving is abusing alcohol. Problems caused by chronic (repeated) alcohol abuse may include liver deterioration, memory loss, and significant mood swings (Nace, 1987). A person with alcohol-related problems, a problem drinker,

Table 4.3 Behavioral Effects Associated with Various Blood Alcohol Levels

Blood Alcohol Level*	Behavioral Effects
0.05	Lowered alertness, impaired judgment, release of inhibitions, feelings of well-being or sociability
0.10	Slowed reaction time and impaired motor function, less caution
0.15	Large, consistent increases in reaction time
0.20	Marked depression in sensory and motor capability, decidedly intoxicated behavior
0.25	Severe motor disturbance and impairment of sensory perceptions
0.30	In a stupor but still conscious—no comprehension of events in the environment
0.35	Surgical anesthesia; lethal dose for about 1% of adults
0.40	Lethal dose for about 50% of adults

*In milligrams of alcohol per 100 milliliters of blood

who also has both physiological and psychological needs to consume alcohol and to experience its effects is an **alcoholic.** All alcoholics are problem drinkers, but not all problem drinkers are alcoholics. Without alcohol, alcoholics develop physiological withdrawal symptoms. In addition, they often develop tolerance; a single drink or even a few will not affect them.

Are some people more likely than others to become alcoholics? The answer is yes, according to researchers who study the biological aspects of alcoholism. Researchers assert that genetics, blood and brain chemistry, and specific brain structures predispose some people to alcoholism (Tarter & Vanyukov, 1994). Children of alcoholics are more likely to be alcoholics, even if they are raised by nonalcoholic adoptive parents. The correlations suggest that certain individuals' physiology predisposes them to alcoholism.

An important study of the inheritance factor and the vulnerability of women to alcoholism shows similar results. According to Kenneth Kendler and his colleagues (1994), the transmission of vulnerability to alcoholism from parents to their daughters is due to genetic factors. This study showed that genetic vulnerability was equally transmitted from fathers and mothers to their daughters. It may be that alcohol use affects a mother's ova or a father's sperm (Cicero, 1994). That inheritance is involved in alcoholism in both men and women is clear; how inheritance interacts with the environment, parental influence (Chassin et al., 1993), and especially the alcoholic's thought processes (Goldman et al., 1991) is the question researchers must answer next (Hawkins, Catalano, & Miller, 1992).

From both a medical and a psychological standpoint, alcohol abuse is one of the most widespread social problems in the United States.

Social and Medical Problems. From both a medical and a psychological standpoint, alcohol abuse is one of the most widespread social problems in the United States. Between 30% and 40% of the homeless are people with alcohol problems (McCarty et al., 1991). Public drunkenness is the biggest law enforcement problem, accounting for millions of arrests each year. The National Highway Traffic Safety Administration estimates that alcohol is involved in more than 18,000 deaths from automobile accidents each year. Although the number of deaths caused by alcohol-related accidents has decreased in the last few years, the number likely to occur in the next 3 years will still exceed the total number of Americans killed in the Vietnam War. In addition, people who are involved in violent crimes or who attempt suicide are often found to have been drinking, and alcohol abuse is associated with marital violence (Murphy & O'Farrell, 1996).

Although alcoholism is seen as a social problem because of its devastating social consequences, it is also a medical problem. Biomedical researchers look for the effects of alcohol on the brain, as well as differences in the brains and basic genetic makeup of alcoholics that may predispose them to alcoholism. Researchers have established that chronic excessive drinking is associated with loss of brain tissue, liver malfunctions, and impaired cognitive and motor abilities (e.g., Ellis & Oscar-Berman, 1989).

Treatment Programs. For some alcoholics, psychological and medical treatment is successful. The most widely known program is Alcoholics Anonymous, which helps individuals abstain from alcohol by providing a therapeutic and emotionally nurturing environment. Treatment programs make abstinence their goal. The fundamental assumptions made by most treatment providers, based on the difficulty alcoholics have controlling their drinking, are that an alcoholic is an alcoholic forever and that alcoholism should be considered an incurable disease (McCrady, 1994).

Some practitioners, on the other hand, believe that getting a client to a point where he or she can indulge in limited, nonproblem drinking should be the goal of treatment programs. This view assumes that alcohol abuse is a learned behavior, which can therefore be unlearned. Those who prefer controlled use with the goal of minimizing the harmful effects of alcohol consumption claim that alcohol abuse is merely a symptom of a larger underlying problem, such as poor self-esteem or family instability. Some claim that a controlled drinking model should be preferred to an abstinence-only or "zero tolerance" approach because it supports any behavior change that reduces the problems due to alcohol. However, most researchers hold that controlled drinking is not a reliable answer for most alcoholics, although it may be a reasonable alternative for young heavy drinkers who are not yet alcoholics (Rosenberg, 1993).

A desire and belief on the part of the patient that he or she can change turns out to be an important element in treating alcohol-related disorders. Family therapy is also generally considered an important part of treatment for alcoholism, because the alcohol problem of one family member becomes a problem for the entire family. A multimodal treatment approach (one involving several modes) is often the best plan; the objective is to combine individual or group therapy with participation in Alcoholics Anonymous or some other self-help group (Levin, 1990). There have been few systematic, carefully controlled studies of treatments for alcoholism. Some researchers are investigating the use of behavioral therapies and drugs to control alcohol intake—including drugs such as naltrexone, which has been used to treat heroin addiction but shows positive effects on alcoholism (Kranzler & Anton, 1994). Others are studying whether and how detoxification centers and halfway houses can help alcoholics. Still others are trying to determine who is at risk (who is likely to become an alcoholic), in the hope that early intervention can prevent alcoholism. Table 4.4 presents some of the warning signs of developing alcoholism.

Table 4.4 Warning Signs of Alcoholism

You drink more than you used to and tend to gulp your drinks.

You try to have a few extra drinks before or after drinking with others.

You have begun to drink alone.

You are noticeably drunk on important occasions.

You drink the "morning after" to overcome the effects of previous drinking.

You drink to relieve feelings of boredom, depression, anxiety, or inadequacy.

You have begun to drink at certain times, to get through difficult situations, or when you have problems.

You have weekend drinking bouts and Monday hangovers.

You are beginning to lose control of your drinking; you drink more than you planned and get drunk when you do not want to.

You promise to drink less but do not.

You often regret what you have said or done while drinking.

You are beginning to feel guilty about your drinking.

You are sensitive when others mention your drinking.

You have begun to deny your drinking or lie about it.

You have memory blackouts or pass out while drinking.

Your drinking is affecting your relationships with friends and relatives.

You have lost time at work or school because of drinking.

You are beginning to stay away from people who do not drink.

Other Sedative-Hypnotics

Like alcohol, most barbiturates and tranquilizers are considered to be in the sedative–hypnotic class of drugs. They relax or calm people and often induce sleep when taken in higher doses. *Barbiturates* decrease the excitability of neurons throughout the nervous system. They calm the user by depressing the central nervous system. The use of barbiturates as sedatives, however, has diminished; they have largely been replaced by another class of drugs—tranquilizers.

Tranquilizers are drugs (technically, benzodiazepines) that also sedate and calm people. With a somewhat lower potential for abuse, they are sometimes called *minor tranquilizers*. Valium and Xanax are two of the most widely used tranquilizers prescribed by physicians for relief of mild stress. Such drugs have been abused by all segments of society because of their availability.

Opiates: Heroin

Perhaps among the oldest drugs known to human beings are derivatives of the drug morphine, which is a component of the opium produced naturally by some poppy plants. In general, drugs that have such a derivation are referred to as opiates. **Opiates** are drugs with pain-relieving and sedative properties that are addictive and produce tolerance. Heroin is an opiate that dulls the senses, relieves pain, tranquilizes, and induces euphoria. Like many other addictive drugs, heroin is considered highly habit-forming.

Opiates have been used for everything from relieving children's crying to reducing pain from headaches, surgery, childbirth, and menstruation. Today, most opiates are illegal; but heroin and other opiates (such as morphine, which is illegal when not prescribed by a physician) are available from drug dealers. The high cost of these illegal drugs leads many addicts to engage in crime to support their habits.

Heroin can be smoked, or eaten or, more typically, injected into a vein, sometimes as often as four times a day. A newly popular and especially dangerous method, because of the likelihood of overdose, is for the user to snort heroin. Although most come from poor and undereducated backgrounds, heroin addicts span the entire socioeconomic spectrum. Most who become addicts at a young age do so as a result of peer pressure. Estimates of the number of heroin addicts in the United States vary dramatically, but the most reliable is about 850,000, with about another 115,000 in some form of treatment program. Heroin addicts often use other drugs in combination with heroin, including alcohol, barbiturates, amphetamines, and cocaine. This usage pattern makes it difficult to classify the users as addicts of one drug or another. Moreover, even when classification is possible, treatment is complicated by the medical, psychological, and social problems associated with using many drugs at once.

Opiate: Drugs with pain-relieving and sedative properties that are addictive and produce tolerance.

The major physiological effect of heroin is impaired functioning of the respiratory system. Other effects are some detrimental changes in the heart, arteries, and veins, as well as constipation and loss of appetite. Contrary to popular belief, few heroin addicts actually die of an overdose from an injection. A lethal dose of the drug would be much larger than that injected even by a heavy user. More often than not, heroin addicts die from snorting lethal doses of pure heroin, from taking a mixture of drugs (such as heroin and alcohol), or from a disease—especially AIDS—contracted from nonsterile needles and other paraphernalia used in injecting the substance into the bloodstream. Some lawmakers advocate community programs to distribute sterile needles to drug users to prevent the spread of AIDS. But, as you might expect, such programs are extremely controversial.

The only widely used treatment program for heroin addiction that has had some success is methadone maintenance. Like heroin, methadone is an addictive drug and must be consumed daily or withdrawal symptoms will occur. Unlike heroin, however, methadone does not produce euphoria or tolerance in the user, and daily dosages do not need to be increased. Because methadone blocks the effects of heroin, a normal injection of heroin has no effect on individuals on methadone maintenance. As a result, many methadone treatment patients (there are about 115,000 in the United States) who might be tempted to use heroin to achieve a high do not do so. Moreover, because methadone is legal, many of the patients are able to stay out of jail and hold jobs to support themselves. Research suggests that methadone treatment combined with psychotherapy and behavior modification techniques to reduce illicit drug use may be far more effective than methadone by itself (Stitzer, 1988). Unfortunately, most methadone treatment programs simply prescribe methadone. Thus, they have been criticized as being unethical because they make money by perpetuating addictive behavior.

Psychostimulants: Amphetamines and Cocaine

Amphetamines and cocaine are highly addictive psychostimulants. A **psychostimulant** is any drug that increases alertness, reduces fatigue, and elevates mood when taken in low to moderate doses. *Amphetamines* are a group of chemical compounds that act on the central nervous system to increase excitability, depress appetite, and increase alertness and talkativeness. They also increase blood pressure and heart rate. After long-term use of an amphetamine, a person has cravings for the drug and experiences exhaustion, lethargy, and depression without it.

Cocaine is a central nervous system stimulant and an anesthetic. It acts on neurotransmitters such as norepinephrine (noradrenaline) and especially dopamine (it interferes with the reabsorption of dopamine). It also stimulates sympathetic activity in the peripheral nervous system, causing dilation of the pupils; increases in heart rate, blood pressure, and blood sugar; and decreased appetite. The drug produces euphoria—a light-headed feeling combined with a sense of alertness, increased energy, sexual arousal, and sometimes a sense of infallibility—but this euphoria is short-lived.

Cocaine can be snorted, smoked, or injected. Snorting is the most popular method of consumption. Once inhaled, the drug is absorbed into the tiny blood vessels that line the nose. Within 5 minutes, the user starts to feel the effects; the peak effect comes in 15 minutes and may last for 20–30 minutes. The processed, smokable form of cocaine, *crack* (so called because a crackling sound often occurs when the drug is heated), delivers an unusually large dose and induces euphoria in a matter of seconds. This method of using cocaine seems to bring about the fastest effect and turns out to be the most addictive. Cocaine can also be injected if it is dissolved in water. However, because of concerns about contracting AIDS through infected needles, intravenous injections are less common than they used to be.

Cocaine is widely abused. About 7% of high school seniors have used it at least once (down from about 15% in the mid-1980s). Crack is readily available, especially in schools. Admissions to cocaine treatment centers have increased, as have deaths associated with cocaine abuse. Why is cocaine use so prevalent in the United States? First, the positive feelings of being high on cocaine are powerfully rewarding. In laboratory studies, for example, animals will work incessantly, even to the point of exhaustion, to obtain it. Further, cocaine produces both tolerance and potent urges and cravings. A cocaine high is pleasurable but also brief; users wish to repeat the sensation almost immediately. When the cocaine wears off, its effects give way to unpleasant feelings (an experience known as "crashing"). These feelings can be alleviated only through more cocaine (Washton, 1989).

What are some of the problems of cocaine use? At a minimum, the drug is extremely addictive and produces irritability and eating and sleeping disturbances. It also seems to precipitate other disturbances, such as panic attacks. Further, cocaine can produce serious mental disorders, including paranoia, agitation, and suicidal behavior. Overdosing may cause heart attacks, hemorrhages, and stroke. Physical problems associated with cocaine use include nose sores, lung damage, infections at injection sites, and even AIDS. Those who stop using cocaine often experience medical problems later as a result of damage done to their bodies while they were abusing the drug. Using cocaine during pregnancy may result in premature birth, malformations of the fetus, and even spontaneous abortion. Last, although the effects of cocaine are enhanced by combining it with alcohol, the consequences of doing so are severe: When people mix cocaine with alcohol, they significantly increase the risk of sudden death.

About 43% of admissions to drug treatment centers are for cocaine addiction. Treatment requires first getting the addict into therapy (which is difficult, because addicts feel invulnerable), providing a structured program, and making sure the addict refrains from using any mood-altering addictive drugs, including alcohol. Blocking the pleasure centers with a drug such as methadone is not a feasible treatment for cocaine addiction. Unlike heroin, cocaine works through almost all of the major neurotransmitter systems; so, even if such a replacement drug could be found, it would probably make the addict listless, since other pleasure centers might be blocked. Because a drug treatment for cocaine addiction has not been developed, psychological therapy is the sole option. Treatment usually includes education, family involvement, group and individual therapy, a focus on abstinence, and long-term follow-up; it is time-intensive and expensive (Hall, Havassy, & Wasserman, 1991).

Psychedelic Drugs

A consciousness-altering drug that affects moods, thoughts, memory, judgment, and perception and that is consumed for the purpose of producing those results is called a **psychedelic.** (The term *psychedelic* means "mind-expanding.") Psychedelic drugs are sometimes called *hallucinogens;* but by any name they have as their principal action creating mind-altering and vivid imagery. The impact of psychedelics varies widely, depending on the individual user. A range of drugs from LSD to Ecstasy fall within this category. LSD, or lysergic acid diethylamide, commonly referred to as "acid," is sold as tablets or capsules or occasionally in liquid form. Along with increases in respiration, sweating, and dry mouth, the user experiences rapid

Psychostimulant: A drug that in low to moderate doses increases alertness, reduces fatigue, and elevates mood.

Psychedelic: Consciousness-altering drug that affects moods, thoughts, memory, judgment, and perception and that is consumed for the purpose of producing those results.

mood swings and visual imagery; time and distance perception changes. The drug-induced perceptual imagery can be frightening. Although LSD is not considered an addictive drug, many users have reported "flashbacks"—recurring experiences of being high without having taken the drug. About 7% of high school seniors have taken the drug.

Closely related to LSD is Ecstasy (also called "Adam" or "X-TC"), which has both hallucinogenic and amphetaminelike properties; users report feelings of excitement and bonding with other people. Ecstasy is considered a "designer drug"—so named because it has been specifically synthesized to have particular effects, often by professionally trained chemists eager to cash in on a lucrative underground market. Many designer drugs are more dangerous and potent than the drugs from which they were derived. Ecstasy was derived from methamphetamine, which has long been known to cause brain damage. Ecstasy interferes with dopamine reabsorption by destroying cells that use that neurotransmitter. Like other widely abused drugs (especially cocaine), Ecstasy produces psychological difficulties, including confusion, depression, and paranoia—which sometimes occur weeks after the drug was taken. Like cocaine, it puts people at risk for heart attacks. Because many different recipes are used to manufacture Ecstasy, other substances that may be lethal can be inadvertently created during its production, leading to the deaths of users who think they are taking Ecstasy.

Long-term use of marijuana can produce lasting brain changes—including problems with attention, memory, and learning.

Marijuana

Perhaps the most widely used psychedelic drug is marijuana, the dried leaves and flowering tops of the *Cannabis sativa* plant, whose active ingredient is *tetrahydrocannabinol (THC)*.

Marijuana can be ingested (eaten), but in the United States it is most commonly smoked, a process in which 20–80% of the THC is lost. Whether smoked as a cigarette (called a *joint* or a *nail*), in a pipe, or as a cigar (a *blunt*), marijuana is used to alter consciousness, to alleviate depression, or simply to "get high." Most users report a sense of elation and well-being; others assert that the drug induces wild flights of fancy. Some users report adverse reactions, such as sleeplessness, bad dreams, paranoia, and nausea. There is likely a genetic basis for a person's reaction to the drug; people react differently and some individuals are far more susceptible. Marijuana's effects are felt about 1 minute after smoking, begin to diminish within an hour, and disappear almost completely after 3–5 hours—although traces of THC can be detected in the body for weeks. Individuals under the influence of marijuana demonstrate impaired performance on simple intellectual and psychomotor tasks. They become less task-oriented and have slower reaction times. Marijuana also interferes with attention and memory. Little is known about how marijuana affects fetal development and reproductive abilities or about its long-term effects on those who use it from early adolescence on. Marijuana has been widely used only since the late 1960s; it will take a couple of generations before researchers know all of its long-term effects. However, recent research suggests that long-term use of marijuana can produce lasting brain changes—including problems with attention, memory, and learning—similar to those caused by other major drugs that are abused (Solowij, 1998; Tanda, Pontieri, & DiChiara, 1997).

Although researchers agree that marijuana is not physiologically addictive, many argue that it produces psychological dependence. People use and become dependent on marijuana for a variety of reasons. One is that it is more easily available than such substances as barbiturates and cocaine. Another is the relief of tension that marijuana users experience. Further, most users assume that the drug has few, if any, long-lasting side effects.

Despite considerable social acceptance of marijuana use in the United States, its sale and possession are still against the law in most states. About 20% of 8th-graders have tried marijuana and about 45% of high school seniors have tried it—these numbers have steadily increased in recent years. In several states, the decriminalization of marijuana has meant that possession is treated as a civil violation instead of a crime; although its use is still illegal, there are no arrests, trials, or jail sentences for users. For the most part, laws against the sale and possession of marijuana have been ineffective, and the drug is widely available across the United States in both urban and rural areas. Legalization is considered a good idea by some experts, although few legislators are willing to consider such a controversial move. (I)

Think Critically

- If you were a psychologist evaluating whether someone was a substance abuser, what would you look for?
- What do you think is the best way to treat alcoholism, and why? Would you treat cocaine addiction with the same procedures? Why or why not?

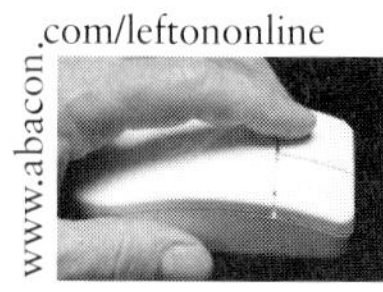

Your password-protected Website allows you access to the most comprehensive set of materials in The Psychology Place.

Summary and Review

Consciousness

What are the key characteristics of consciousness?

KEY TERM
consciousness, p. 92

Sleep

Describe the cycles of sleep and wakefulness.

What characterizes some common sleep disorders?

KEY TERMS
circadian rhythms, p. 93; sleep, p. 95; electroencephalogram (EEG), p. 95; non–rapid eye movement (NREM) sleep, p. 95; rapid eye movement (REM) sleep, p. 96; insomnia, p. 98

Dreams

What is a dream?

How have key theorists explained dreaming?

KEY TERMS
dream, p. 99; lucid dream, p. 100; manifest content, p. 100; latent content, p. 100; collective unconscious, p. 101

Controlling Consciousness: Biofeedback, Hypnosis, and Meditation

Differentiate three key means of controlling consciousness.

KEY TERMS
biofeedback, p. 104; hypnosis, p. 104; meditation, p. 106

Altering Consciousness with Drugs

What are the different broad categories of drugs?

What are the defining characteristics of a substance abuser?

How does alcohol affect behavior, and who is an alcoholic?

Describe the risks and effects of different classes of drugs.

KEY TERMS
drug, p. 107; psychoactive drug, p. 107; addictive drug, p. 107; psychological dependence, p. 107; withdrawal symptoms, p. 108; tolerance, p. 108; sedative–hypnotic, p. 108; alcoholic, p. 110; opiate, p. 112; psychostimulant, p. 112; psychedelic, p. 113

Self-Test

1. When a person is able to think about his or her own thought processes, the process is called:
   A. consciousness
   B. altered consciousness
   C. metacognition
   D. self-consciousness

2. Which of the following is important for keeping the circadian rhythm regular?
   A. jet lag
   B. sleep spindle
   C. K complex
   D. natural light

3. Research has shown that after people have been deprived of sleep, they are likely to spend a larger proportion of sleep in:
   A. REM sleep and stage 4 sleep
   B. stage 1 and stage 4 sleep
   C. REM sleep and stage 1 sleep
   D. stage 3 and stage 4 sleep

4. Donald briefly stops breathing while he sleeps, sometimes as often as 100 times per night. Which sleep disorder does he probably have?
   A. insomnia
   B. sleep apnea
   C. narcolepsy
   D. night terrors

5. Frank's psychoanalyst suggests that the images in Frank's dreams actually represent important people and events in his life. She works with Frank to try to uncover the hidden meaning, or _______________ content, of the dream images.
   A. latent
   B. lucid
   C. manifest
   D. restorative

6. According to _______________ theory, dreams are a result of the cortex trying to make sense of the spontaneous stimulation of brain cells.
   A. psychoanalytic
   B. cognitive
   C. activation–synthesis
   D. biosynthesis

7. Sharon is learning to relax her heart in order to lower her blood pressure. This method of monitoring and controlling involuntary bodily functions is called:
   A. meditation
   B. hypnotic induction
   C. biofeedback
   D. meditation

8. Bob attempts to empty his mind of all thoughts while he meditates. He is practicing:
   A. concentrative meditation
   B. zen meditation
   C. mantra meditation
   D. mindful meditation

9. A drug that produces psychological dependence in the user and whose absence produces withdrawal symptoms is a(n):
   A. psychoactive drug
   B. addictive drug
   C. psychedelic drug
   D. psychostimulant

10. Alcohol is an example of a(n):
   A. sedative–hypnotic
   B. psychostimulant
   C. psychedelic
   D. opiate

Learning

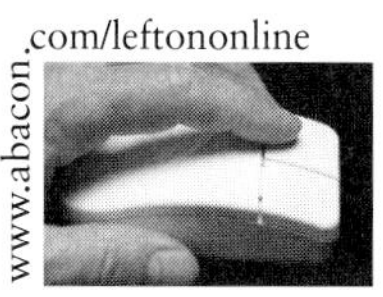

Go to your password-protected Website for full-color art, Weblinks, and more!

After her graduation from college, my daughter Jesse showed me the two—and only two—study carrels that she used in her college library. She attributed her choice of study spots to superstition. But I think that there's more to it.

If you're like many of my students, you find studying in a library difficult. You may think it's too quiet, too bright, or too hot, or too crowded. If you have problems studying in the library, you're probably wise to find someplace else—the environment in which you regularly study becomes associated with learning. My daughter associated her two special study spots with intense concentration in preparation for some final examinations on which she did well. After she did well on those exams, she kept going back to the same two spots to study. Psychologists have learned that we develop associations between places and events, between experiences and emotions. Some associations, or learned responses, are a long time developing; others develop quickly, and at a young age.

As a psychologist, I think that people can be taught new behaviors and new associations. In fact, humans exhibit few totally reflexive behaviors; most human behaviors can be learned, unlearned, and modified. Unlike the proverbial dog, we *can* be taught new tricks. The ability to think about past events and to modify future behavior is part of what distinguishes human beings from other organisms: We learn and can think about and reflect on that learning. ■

Learning is at the core of psychology. It affects personality, social behavior, and development. Much of our learning takes place effortlessly, simply as a result of experience. By the time we reach adulthood, experience has taught us a large number of simple, predictable associations. We know, for example, that a long day at the beach may result in a painful sunburn and that a gas station should be our next stop when the fuel gauge reads empty. We have also learned many complicated processes, such as how to drive a car and how to appreciate music ranging from Bach to Phish. Some people learn socially deviant behaviors, such as stealing and drug abuse.

In general, learning is the process by which people acquire new knowledge. Psychologists define **learning** as a relatively permanent change in an organism that occurs as a result of experiences in the environment and that is often *exhibited in overt behavior.* This last point means that, because the internal processes of learning cannot be seen, psychologists study the *results* of learning. To do so, they may examine such overt behavior as solving an algebra problem or throwing a ball. They may also measure physiological changes, such as those in brain-wave activity, heartbeat, and temperature. This definition of learning has three other important parts: (1) experiences in the environment (Jesse succeeded after studying in her favorite carrels), (2) change in the organism (once she had done well on her exams after studying in those particular carrels, she stopped using other carrels), and (3) permanence (she never studied anywhere else after she found her special study spots).

Behavior is always being modified; new experiences affect learning, and what is learned may be forgotten. And, along with the external environment, an organism's internal motivation, abilities, and physiological state influence its ability to learn. For example, if you are tired, learning the material in this chapter will be especially difficult. Also, practice and repeated experiences ensure that you will readily exhibit newly acquired learning. Furthermore, when learning has occurred, physiological changes—for example, in synapse organization or levels of dopamine—have occurred as well, so that after you learn, you're no longer the same.

The factors that affect learning are often studied using animals as subjects, because the genetic heritage of animals is easy to control and manipulate and because all details of their life history and environmental experiences can be known. Although some psychologists claim that different processes underlie animal and human learning, most believe—and experiments show—that the processes are similar. Differences do become apparent, however, when complex behaviors and language use are being studied. (I)

Learning: Relatively permanent change in an organism that occurs as a result of experiences in the environment.

(I) Pavlovian, or Classical, Conditioning Theory

Focus on issues and ideas

- The terms and procedures of *conditioning*
- The characteristics of higher-order conditioning and it's impact on behavior

It is easy to see that my daughter had developed an association between specific study carrels and success in exams. It was a small self-deception on Jesse's part, but one that helped relieve the stress of preparing for examinations. To a real extent, Jesse had become conditioned.

Psychologists use the term *conditioning* in a general sense, to mean learning. But **conditioning** is actually a systematic procedure through which associations and responses to specific stimuli are learned. It is one of the simplest forms of learning. For example, consider what generally happens when you hear the theme from *The X-Files*. You expect that something supernatural or otherworldly will appear on your TV screen, because the theme music introduces a program that usually includes aliens or weird events—and if you're a fan of the show, you probably feel a pleasant sense of anticipation. You have been *conditioned* to feel that way. In the terminology used by psychologists, *The X-Files* theme music is the *stimulus,* and your excitement and anticipation is the *response.*

When psychologists first studied conditioning, they found relationships between specific stimuli and responses. They observed that each time a certain stimulus occurs, the same reflexive response, or behavior, follows. For example, the presence of food in the mouth leads to salivation; a tap on the knee results in a knee jerk; a bright light in the eye produces contraction of the pupil and an eye blink. A **reflex** is an automatic behavior that occurs involuntarily in response to a stimulus and without prior learning and usually shows little variability from instance to instance. Conditioned behaviors, in contrast, are learned. Dental anxiety—fear of dentists, dental procedures, and even the dentist's chair—is a widespread conditioned behavior (De Jongh et al., 1995). Many people have learned to respond with fear to the stimulus of sitting in a dentist's chair, since they associate the chair with pain. A chair by itself (a neutral stimulus) does not elicit fear, but a chair associated with pain becomes a stimulus that can elicit fear. This is an example of *conditioning.*

Conditioned behaviors may occur so automatically that they appear to be reflexive. Like reflexes, conditioned behaviors are involuntary; unlike reflexes, they are learned. In classical conditioning (to be defined shortly), previously neutral stimuli such as chairs and buzzers become associated with specific events and lead to responses such as fear and anxiety.

In 1927, Ivan Pavlov (1849–1936), a Russian physiologist, summarized a now-famous series of experiments in which he uncovered a basic principle of learning—conditioning. His study of conditioning began quite accidentally while he was studying saliva and gastric secretions in the digestive processes of dogs. He knew it is normal for dogs to salivate when they eat—salivation is a reflexive behavior that aids digestion—but the dogs were salivating *before* they tasted their food. Pavlov reasoned that this might be happening because the dogs had learned to associate the trainers, who brought them food, with the food itself. Anxious to know more about this form of learning, Pavlov abandoned his research on gastric processes and redirected his efforts into studying dogs' salivary reflex.

Terms and Procedures

The terminology and procedures associated with Pavlov's experiments can seem confusing, but the basic ideas are actually quite straightforward. Let's explore them systematically. What Pavlov described was **classical conditioning,** or *Pavlovian conditioning,* in which an originally neutral stimulus, through repeated pairing with a stimulus that naturally elicits a response, comes to elicit a similar or even identical response. For example, when a bell, buzzer, or light (a neutral stimulus) is associated with the presentation of food, a stimulus that normally brings about a response (salivating), the neutral stimulus over time comes to elicit the same response as the normal stimulus. Pavlov termed the stimulus that normally produces the reflexive response the **unconditioned stimulus** (as its name implies, it elicits the relevant response without conditioning). He termed the response to this stimulus the **unconditioned response.** The unconditioned response occurs involuntarily, without learning, in response to the unconditioned stimulus.

Pavlov started his study of conditioning in dogs with a relatively simple experiment—teaching the dogs to salivate in response to a bell. First, he surgically moved each dog's salivary gland to the outside of the dog's cheek to make the secretions of saliva accessible. He attached tubes to the relocated salivary glands so that he could collect and then measure precisely the amount of saliva produced by the food—the unconditioned stimulus. The dog was restrained in a harness and isolated from all distractions in a cubicle. Then Pavlov introduced a bell—the new stimulus. He called the bell a neutral stimulus, because the sound of a bell is not normally related to salivation and generally elicits only a response of orientation (an attempt

Conditioning: Systematic procedure through which associations and responses to specific stimuli are learned.

Reflex: Automatic behavior that occurs involuntarily in response to a stimulus and without prior learning and usually shows little variability from instance to instance.

Classical conditioning: Conditioning process in which an originally neutral stimulus, by repeated pairing with a stimulus that normally elicits a response, comes to elicit a similar or even identical response; also known as *Pavlovian conditioning.*

Unconditioned stimulus: Stimulus that normally produces a measurable involuntary response.

Unconditioned response: Unlearned or involuntary response to an unconditioned stimulus.

to locate the sound) or attention. Pavlov measured the amount of saliva the dog produced when a bell was rung by itself; the amount was negligible. He then began the conditioning process by ringing the bell and immediately placing food in the dog's mouth. After he did this several times, the dog salivated in response to the sound of the bell alone.

Pavlov reasoned that the dog had associated the bell with the arrival of food. He termed the bell, which elicited salivation as a result of learning, a conditioned stimulus. A **conditioned stimulus** is a neutral stimulus that, through repeated association with an unconditioned stimulus, becomes capable of eliciting a conditioned response. As its name implies, a conditioned stimulus becomes capable of eliciting a response because of (conditional on) its pairing with the unconditioned stimulus. He termed the salivation—the learned response to the sound of the bell—a **conditioned response** (the response elicited by a conditioned stimulus). (Pavlov originally called the conditioned response a "conditional" response because it was conditional on events in the environment—it depended on them. An error in translating his writings created the term used most often today—conditioned response.) From his experiments, Pavlov discovered that the conditioned stimulus (the bell) brought about a similar but somewhat weaker response than the unconditioned stimulus (the food).

The key characteristic of classical conditioning is the use of an originally neutral stimulus (here, a bell) to elicit a response (here, salivation) through repeated pairing of the neutral stimulus with an unconditioned stimulus (here, food) that elicits the response naturally. On the first few trials of such pairings, conditioning is unlikely to occur. With additional trials, there is a greater likelihood that conditioning will occur. After dozens or even hundreds of pairings, the neutral stimulus yields the conditioned response. Psychologists generally refer to this process as an *acquisition process* and say that an organism has *acquired* a response.

Classical conditioning occurs regularly in the everyday world. You may have learned to associate the distinctive smell of a sandalwood aftershave with a cousin whom you see infrequently but think of warmly. If you walk into a room and smell his unique brand, you may think of him or expect him to be there. Classical conditioning doesn't always involve associations of positive things. When you enter a dentist's office, your heart rate may increase and you may begin to feel anxious because of learned associations you have developed. When classical conditioning occurs, behavior changes.

Conditioned stimulus: Neutral stimulus that, through repeated association with an unconditioned stimulus, begins to elicit a conditioned response.

Conditioned response: Response elicited by a conditioned stimulus.

Classical Conditioning in Humans

After Pavlov's success with conditioning in dogs, psychologists were able to see that conditioning also occurs in human beings. Marquis (1931) showed classical conditioning in infants. Marquis knew that when an object touches an infant's lips, the infant immediately starts sucking, because the object is usually a nipple, from which the infant gets milk. The nipple, an unconditioned stimulus, elicits sucking, an unconditioned response. After repeated pairings of a sound or light with a nipple, infants were conditioned to suck when only the sound or light was presented.

Sucking is one of many reflexive behaviors in human beings; thus, it is one of many responses that can be conditioned. For example, newborns respond reflexively to loud noises. (We'll examine newborns' reflexes in Chapter 9.) A loud noise naturally elicits a startle response—an outstretching of the arms and legs and associated changes in heart rate, blood pressure, and breathing. Through conditioning procedures, all kinds of neutral stimuli can become conditioned stimuli that elicit a reflexive response of this sort. A puff of air delivered to the eye, for example, produces the unconditioned response of an eye blink. When a light or buzzer is paired with the puff of air, it will eventually elicit the eye blink by itself; this conditioned eye blink is a robust response, one that is retained for long periods of time, particularly among younger adults (Solomon et al., 1998). This effect can be produced in many other animals besides humans.

The complex process of learning is not automatic; it depends on a whole array of events, including an organism's past experiences with the conditioned and unconditioned stimulus. This is especially true for complex conditioned responses. Both pleasant and unpleasant emotional responses can be classically conditioned. Consider this example: If a child who is playing with a favorite toy is repeatedly frightened by a sudden loud noise, the child may be conditioned to be afraid each time he or she sees the toy. John B. Watson and Rosalie Rayner explored this type of relationship in 1920 in a now-famous experiment with an 11-month-old infant named Albert. (Today, such an experiment would be considered unethical.) Albert was given several toys and a live white rat to play with. One day, as he reached for the rat, the experi-

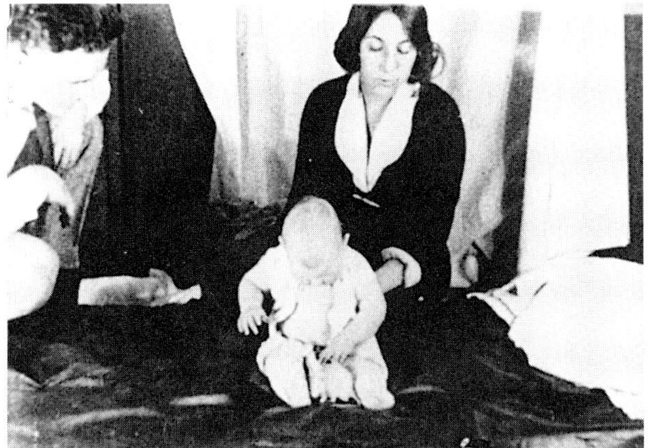

menters suddenly made an ear-splitting noise that frightened the child. After repeated pairing of the noise and the rat, Albert learned the relationship. The rat served as a conditioned stimulus and the loud noise as the unconditioned stimulus; on each subsequent presentation, the rat evoked a conditioned response of fear in Albert.

Higher-Order Conditioning

After a neutral stimulus becomes a conditioned stimulus, it generally elicits the conditioned response whenever it is presented. Another phenomenon that may occur is **higher-order conditioning**—the process by which a neutral stimulus takes on conditioned properties through pairing with a conditioned stimulus. Suppose a dog is conditioned to associate a light with a mild electric shock. On seeing the light, the dog exhibits fear; the light has become a conditioned stimulus that elicits a fear response. If a bell is now paired with or presented just before the light, the new stimulus (the bell) can also take on properties of the conditioned stimulus (the light). After repeated pairings, the dog associates the two events (the light and the bell), and either event by itself will elicit a fear response. When a third stimulus—say, an experimenter in a white lab coat—is introduced, the dog may learn to associate the experimenter with the bell or light. After enough trials, the dog may show a conditioned fear response to each of the three stimuli: the light, the bell, and the experimenter (Pavlov, 1927; Rescorla, 1977).

Thus, higher-order conditioning permits increasingly remote associations, which can result in a complex network of conditioned stimuli and responses. At least two factors determine the extent of higher-order conditioning: (1) the similarity between the new stimulus and the original conditioned stimulus, and (2) the frequency and consistency with which the two stimuli are paired (Rescorla, 1978). You can see that successful pairing of conditioned and unconditioned stimuli—that is, successful classical conditioning—is influenced by many variables. 

Think Critically

- Provide examples of classical conditioning and higher-order conditioning from your own life.
- Can you think of a situation in which you might want to facilitate higher-order conditioning? How might you increase the likelihood of this kind of learning taking place?

Key Variables in Classical Conditioning

Focus on issues and ideas

- The terms, procedures, and results of higher-order conditioning
- The role of time variables in extinction and spontaneous recovery
- How we discriminate and generalize in our everyday behaviors
- The four key concepts of classical conditioning
- The effects of classical conditioning on the immune system

Classical conditioning is not as simple a process as Pavlov might have thought. As I noted earlier, such learning is not automatic; it depends on a matrix of events, including an organism's past experiences with the conditioned and unconditioned stimuli as well as key variables concerning those stimuli. For example, how bright must the oil light in your car be? How loud does the buzzer have to be? How long does the bell have to ring? How sinister must movie music be? How many times must someone experience pain in a dentist's chair, and how strong does the pain have to be? As with other psychological phenomena, situational variables affect whether and under what conditions classical conditioning will occur. Cultural variables are also important; while the principles of conditioning are the same in every culture, what constitutes a fear-producing stimulus, for example, varies from culture to culture.

Higher-order conditioning: Process by which a neutral stimulus takes on conditioned properties through pairing with a conditioned stimulus.

Some of the most important variables in classical conditioning are the strength and timing of the unconditioned stimulus and the frequency of its pairings with the neutral stimulus. When these variables are optimal, conditioning occurs easily.

Strength, Timing, Frequency, and Predictability

Strength of the Unconditioned Stimulus. A puff of air delivered to the eye will readily elicit a conditioned response to a neutral stimulus paired with it, but only if the puff of air (the unconditioned stimulus) is sufficiently strong. Research shows that when the unconditioned stimulus is strong and constantly elicits the reflexive (unconditioned) response, conditioning to a neutral stimulus is likely to occur. On the other hand, when the unconditioned stimulus is weak, it is less likely to elicit the unconditioned response, and conditioning to a neutral stimulus is unlikely to occur. Thus, pairing a neutral stimulus with a weak unconditioned stimulus will not reliably lead to conditioning.

Timing of the Unconditioned Stimulus. For conditioning to occur, an unconditioned stimulus must usually be paired with a neutral stimulus close enough in time for the two to become associated; that is, they must be temporally contiguous. For optimal conditioning, the neutral stimulus should occur a short time (often cited as one-half second) before the unconditioned stimulus and overlap with it, particularly for reflexes such as the eye blink. (In Pavlov's experiment, conditioning would not have occurred if the bell and the food had been presented an hour apart.) The two stimuli may be presented together or separated by a brief interval. Some types of conditioning can occur with fairly long delays, but the optimal time between the two stimuli varies from one study to another and depends on many things, including the type of conditioned response sought (e.g., Schwarz-Stevens & Cunningham, 1993).

Frequency of Pairings. Occasional or rare pairings of a neutral stimulus with an unconditioned stimulus, even at close intervals, usually do not result in conditioning; generally speaking, frequent pairings that establish a relationship between the unconditioned and the conditioned stimulus are necessary. If, for example, food and the sound of a bell are paired on every trial, a dog is conditioned more quickly than if the stimuli are paired on every other trial. The frequency of the natural occurrence of the unconditioned stimulus is also important. If the unconditioned stimulus does not occur frequently but is *always* associated with the conditioned stimulus, more rapid conditioning is likely, because one stimulus predicts the other (Rescorla, 1988). Once the conditioned response has reached its maximum strength, additional pairings of the stimuli do not increase the likelihood of a conditioned response. There are exceptions to this general rule, though, in which specific one-time pairings can produce learning.

Predictability. A key factor that determines whether conditioning will occur is the predictability of the association of the unconditioned and conditioned stimuli. Closeness in time and regular frequency of pairings promote conditioning, but these are not enough. Predictability—the ability to anticipate future events—turns out to be a central factor in facilitating conditioning (Rescorla, 1988).

Pavlov thought that classical conditioning was based on timing. Research has shown, however, that if the unconditioned stimulus (such as food) can be predicted by the conditioned stimulus (such as a bell), then conditioning is rapidly achieved. Conditioning depends more on the reliability with which the conditioned stimulus predicts the unconditioned stimulus. Pavlov's dogs learned that bells were good predictors of food; the conditioned stimulus (bell) reliably predicted the unconditioned one (food), and so conditioning was quickly achieved.

Predictability—the ability to anticipate future events—turns out to be a central factor in facilitating conditioning.

In Rescorla's (1988) view, what an organism learns through conditioning is the predictability of events—bells predicting food, light predicting puffs of air to the eye, dentist chairs predicting pain. An organism learns that there is some sort of relationship between the conditioned stimulus and the unconditioned stimulus. Many learning researchers consider predictability a cognitive concept; human beings and many animals make predictions about the future based on past events in a wide range of circumstances (Siegel & Allan, 1996). As you will see in the next chapter (on memory and cognition), such thought is based on simple learning but becomes even more complex. You'll also see how the predictability and relationship of events become important in phenomena such as extinction and spontaneous recovery, considered next.

Extinction and Spontaneous Recovery

Some conditioned responses last for a long time; others disappear quickly. Much depends on whether the conditioned stimulus continues to predict the unconditioned one. Consider the following: What would have happened to Pavlov's dogs if he had rung the bell each day but never followed it with food? What would happen if you went to the dentist every day for 2 months, but the dentist only brushed your teeth with pleasant-tasting toothpaste and never drilled?

If a researcher continues Pavlov's experiment by presenting the conditioned stimulus (bell) but no unconditioned stimulus (food), the likelihood of a conditioned response (salivation) decreases with every trial; the response undergoes extinction. In classical conditioning, **extinction** is the procedure of withholding the unconditioned stimulus—presenting the conditioned stimulus alone. This procedure gradually reduces the probability (and often the strength) of a conditioned response. Imagine a study in which a puff of air is associated with a buzzer that consistently elicits the conditioned eye-blink response. If the unconditioned stimulus (the puff of air) is no longer delivered in association with the buzzer, the likelihood that the buzzer will continue to elicit the eye-blink response decreases over time. When presentation of the buzzer alone no longer elicits the conditioned response, psychologists say that the response has been *extinguished*.

But an extinguished conditioned response may not be gone forever. It can recur, especially after a rest period, and this recurrence is termed **spontaneous recovery.** If the dog whose salivation response has been extinguished is placed in the experimental situation again after a rest period of 20 minutes, its salivary response to the bell will recur briefly (although less strongly than before). This behavior shows that the effects of extinction are not permanent and that the learned association is not totally forgotten.

Stimulus Generalization and Stimulus Discrimination

Imagine that a 3-year-old child pulls a cat's tail and gets a painful scratch in return. It will not be surprising if the child develops a fear of that cat; but the child may actually develop a fear of all cats, and even of dogs and other four-legged animals. Adults may respond in a similar way—through a process that psychologists call stimulus generalization.

Stimulus generalization occurs when an organism develops a conditioned response to a stimulus that is similar but not identical to the original conditioned stimulus. The extent to which an organism responds to a stimulus similar to the original one depends on how alike the two stimuli are. If, for example, a loud tone is the conditioned stimulus for an eye-blink response, somewhat lower but similar tones will also produce the response. A totally dissimilar tone will produce little or no response.

Stimulus discrimination is the process by which an organism learns to respond only to a specific stimulus and not to other stimuli. Pavlov showed that animals that have learned to differentiate between pairs of stimuli display frustration or even aggression when discrimination is made difficult or impossible. He trained a dog to discriminate between a circle and an ellipse and then on successive trials changed the shape of the ellipse to look more and more like the circle. Eventually, the animal was unable to discriminate between the shapes but randomly chose one or the other; it also became aggressive.

Human beings exhibit similar disorganization in behavior when placed in situations in which they feel compelled to make a response but don't know how to respond correctly. On such occasions, when choosing a response becomes difficult or impossible, behavior can become stereotyped and limited in scope; people may choose either not to respond to the stimulus or always to respond in the same way (Lundin, 1961; Maier & Klee, 1941). For example, a supervisor confronted by an angry employee may either respond in kind, by blowing up, or withdraw from the situation. Often, therapists must help maladjusted people learn to be more flexible in their responses to situations.

Table 5.1 (on p. 124) summarizes four important concepts in classical conditioning: extinction, spontaneous recovery, stimulus generalization, and stimulus discrimination.

Classical Conditioning in Daily Life

I have to admit it. I respond to the sound of music with classically conditioned responses over and over

Extinction: In classical conditioning, the procedure of withholding the unconditioned stimulus and presenting the conditioned stimulus alone, which gradually reduces the probability of the conditioned response.

Spontaneous recovery: Recurrence of an extinguished conditioned response, usually following a rest period.

Stimulus generalization: Process by which a conditioned response becomes associated with a stimulus that is similar but not identical to the original conditioned stimulus.

Stimulus discrimination: Process by which an organism learns to respond only to a specific stimulus and not to other stimuli.

Table 5.1 Four Important Concepts in Classical Conditioning

Property	Definition	Example
Extinction	The process of reducing the probability of a conditioned response by withholding the unconditioned stimulus (the reinforcer).	An infant conditioned by the stroking of its lips to suck in response to a light is no longer given the unconditioned stimulus of stroking the lips; the infant stops sucking in response to the conditioned stimulus.
Spontaneous recovery	The recurrence of an extinguished conditioned response following a rest period.	A dog's conditioned salivary response has been extinguished. After a rest period, the dog again salivates in response to the conditioned stimulus, though less than before.
Stimulus generalization	The occurrence of a conditioned response to stimuli that are similar but not identical to the original conditioned stimulus.	A dog conditioned to salivate in response to a high-pitched tone also salivates in response to a somewhat lower-pitched tone.
Stimulus discrimination	The process by which an organism learns to respond only to a specific reinforced stimulus.	A goat is conditioned to salivate only in response to lights of high intensity, not to lights of low intensity.

again: Play the national anthem, and I well up with pride. Play the theme from *Titanic,* and I get teary-eyed. All of us become conditioned to respond to all kinds of stimuli, and much of that conditioning is Pavlovian classical conditioning. Let's consider some important examples that have helped psychologists understand both human behavior and conditioning.

The Garcia Effect. My daughter Sarah has hated mustard ever since her sixth birthday party. After the guests left the party, we sat down for ham sandwiches with lettuce and mustard. Two hours later, she was ill—fever, vomiting, chills, and swollen glands. It was the flu. But as far as Sarah was concerned, it was the mustard that had made her sick; 19 years later, she still refuses to eat mustard.

This association of mustard and nausea is an example of a conditioned taste aversion. In a famous experiment, John Garcia gave animals specific foods or drinks and then induced nausea (usually by injecting a drug or by exposing the animals to radiation). He found that after only one pairing of a food or drink (the conditioned stimulus) with the drug or radiation (the unconditioned stimulus), the animals avoided the food or drink that preceded the nausea (e.g., Garcia & Koelling, 1971; Linberg et al., 1982).

Two aspects of Garcia's work startled the research community. First, Garcia showed that a conditioned taste aversion could be established even if the nausea was induced several hours after the food or drink had been consumed. This contradicted the previously held assumption that the time interval between the unconditioned stimulus and the conditioned stimulus must be short, especially for conditioning to occur quickly. More recent research confirmed Garcia's finding (Schafe, Sollars, & Bernstein, 1995). Garcia also showed that not all stimuli can become associated. He tried to pair bells and lights with nausea to produce a taste aversion in rats, but he was unable to do so—learning depended on the relevance of the stimuli to each other. This led Garcia to conclude that "strong aversions to the smell or taste of food can develop even when illness is delayed for hours after consumption [but] avoidance reactions do not develop for visual, auditory, or tactile stimuli associated with food" (Garcia & Koelling, 1971, p. 461). The appropriateness of stimuli may depend on whether they "belong" together in nature: Bells and nausea have little to do with each other; smells and nausea are far more likely to be related in the real world, and so a smell might quickly become a conditioned stimulus for nausea (Hollis, 1997). Ultimately, Garcia's work disproved two accepted principles of learning.

Conditioned taste aversion, sometimes called the *Garcia effect,* has survival value and practical applications. In one trial (instance), through classical conditioning, animals associate a food with illness—and then they avoid that food. For example, coyotes often attack sheep and lambs. Garcia laced lamb meat with a substance that causes a short-term illness and put the food on the outskirts of sheep ranchers' fenced-in areas. Coyotes who ate the lamb meat became sick and developed an aversion to it. After this experience, they approached the sheep as if ready to attack but nearly always backed off (e.g., Garcia et al., 1976). By using conditioned taste aversion, Garcia deterred coyotes from eating sheep.

Learning and Chemotherapy. Cancer patients often undergo chemotherapy, and an unfortunate side effect of the therapy is vomiting and nausea. The patients often develop a lack of appetite and lose weight. Is it possible that they lose weight because of a conditioned taste aversion? According to researcher Ilene Bernstein (1991), some cancer patients become conditioned to avoid food. They check into a hospital, have a meal, are given chemotherapy, become sick, and thereafter avoid the food that preceded the therapy. Bernstein conducted research with children and adults who were going to receive chemotherapy. Her research showed that patients given foods before therapy developed specific aversions to those foods; control groups who were not given any food before their therapy did not develop taste aversions. Tomoyasu, Bovbjerg, and Jacobsen (1996) found similar results.

A comprehensive theory of drug use, abuse, tolerance, and withdrawal will have to incorporate environmental cues and bodily reactions that are Pavlovian in origin.

Patients develop the food aversions even when they know it is the chemotherapy that induces the nausea. Bernstein suggested an intervention based on learning theory: Patients could be given a "scapegoat" food, such as coconut or root beer Lifesavers, just before chemotherapy; then, any conditioned aversion that developed would be to an unimportant and easily avoided food rather than to nutritious foods. When Bernstein (1988, 1991) tried this procedure, she found that both children and adults were far less likely to develop food aversions to nutritious foods.

Conditioning of the Immune System. Classical conditioning explains a wide range of human behaviors, including some physical responses to the world, such as accelerations in heart rate and changes in blood pressure. Substances such as pollen, dust, animal dander, and mold initiate allergic reactions in many people. Cat fur, for example, may naturally elicit an allergic reaction, such as an inability to breathe, in someone with asthma. Asthma attacks, like other behaviors, can be conditioned to occur. If Lindsay's asthmatic friend has *always* found cat fur in Lindsay's house (a regular pairing), classical conditioning theory predicts that even if all the cat hair is removed, the asthmatic friend may have an allergic reaction when she enters Lindsay's house. (A conditioned stimulus, the house, predicts an unconditioned response, the allergic reaction.) Researchers have shown that people with severe allergies can have an allergic reaction after merely seeing a cat, even if there is no cat fur present, or upon entering a house that used to have a cat, even long after the cat's demise.

Even the body's immune system can be conditioned. Normally, the body releases disease-fighting antibodies when toxic substances appear in the blood. This is an involuntary activity that is not controlled by the nervous system. In a striking series of studies, animals were classically conditioned in a way that altered their immune responses (Ader & Cohen, 1985, 1993). The experimenters paired a sweet-tasting solution with a drug that produced illness and, as a side effect, also suppressed the immune response. The animals quickly learned to avoid the sweet-tasting substance that seemed to predict nausea. When later presented with the sweet-tasting substance alone, they avoided it but still showed a reduction in immune system response. The experimenters had classically conditioned an immune system response that was thought not to be under control of the nervous system. This is an intriguing finding.

Conditioning in Addicts. Research also shows that drug users become conditioned. When addicts inject heroin, their bodies produce an antiopiate substance to protect them from an overdose; this is a natural response. Siegel (1988) argues that if the addict always injects the drug in the same room, the place itself may serve to initiate an antiopiate response, without any use of the drug. That is, the location of heroin use can serve as a conditioned stimulus for the antiopiate response. When the user injects the drug in a different location, the well-developed antiopiate response does not occur—the body is not doing something that it has become accustomed to. As a consequence, the user may inject too much of the drug, leading to an overdose. The stimulus for the increased use may have been merely the location of the drug consumption. A comprehensive theory of drug use, abuse, tolerance, and withdrawal will have to incorporate environmental cues and bodily reactions that are Pavlovian in origin—addicts' bodies react not only to effects of the drug but also in an anticipatory way to the sight of needles, drugs, and locations (Siegel & Allan, 1996).

Think Critically

- What led Garcia to conclude that taste aversion can occur after one trial or one instance? What other examples of learning could occur in one trial or one instance?
- What are some conditioned responses—other than antiopiate responses—that might lead to drug overdoses in addicts?

Ⓘ Operant Conditioning

Focus on issues and ideas

- A comparison between Pavlov's research and Skinner's research
- The use of the Skinner box and the critical role of shaping in operant conditioning
- The role of reinforcement and punishment in increasing or decreasing responses
- The limitations of punishment in shaping behavior

An organism can be exposed to bells, whistles, or lights and may form associations between stimuli and events—but in these kinds of situations the organism, the learner, has little control over the events. A light is presented before food is delivered, and an association is formed. But what happens when a child is scolded for playing with and breaking a valuable camera or receives a pat on the back after doing well in class? Does learning take place? From the point of view of many learning psychologists, the consequences of behavior have powerful effects that change the course of subsequent behavior. Unlike classical conditioning, this view sees the organism as actively operating on and within the environment and, as a result, experiencing rewards or punishments. Let's explore this distinction further because it helps explain the how and why of what we do.

Pioneers: B. F. Skinner and E. L. Thorndike

In the 1930s, B. F. Skinner (1904–1990) began to change the way psychologists think about conditioning and learning. Skinner questioned whether the passive Pavlovian (classical) conditioning that focused on reflexive, automatic responses should be studied at all. Instead, he focused solely on an organism's observable behavior and did not consider thought processes, consciousness, brain–behavior relationships, and the mind to be proper subject matter for psychological research. At best, private events—thoughts, feelings, and emotions—are the early stages of overt behavior and are not readily accessible for scrutiny. Skinner's early work was in the tradition of such strict behaviorists as Watson, although Skinner ultimately modified some of his own most extreme positions. His 1938 book, *The Behavior of Organisms,* continues to have an impact on studies of conditioning.

According to Skinner, most behaviors can be explained through operant conditioning, rather than through Pavlov's classical conditioning. Skinner used the term *operant conditioning* because the organism *operates* on the environment, with every action followed by a specific event, or consequence. **Operant conditioning,** or *instrumental conditioning,* is conditioning in which an increase or decrease in the probability that a behavior will recur is affected by the delivery of reinforcement or punishment as a consequence of the behavior. The conditioned behavior is usually voluntary, not reflexive as in classical conditioning. Another key difference between classical conditioning and operant conditioning is that a consequence *follows,* rather than coexists with, the behavior.

Consider what happens when a boss rewards and encourages her overworked employees by giving them unexpected cash bonuses. If the bonuses improve morale and induce the employees to work harder, then the employer's conditioning efforts will be successful. In turn, the employees could condition the boss's behavior by rewarding her paying of bonuses with further increases in productivity, thereby encouraging her to continue giving bonuses. In the laboratory, researchers have studied similar sequences of behaviors followed by rewards. One of the most famous experiments was conducted by the American psychologist E. L. Thorndike (1874–1949), who pioneered the study of operant conditioning during the 1890s and first reported on his work in 1898. Thorndike placed hungry cats in boxes and put food outside the boxes. The cats could escape from the boxes and get food by hitting a lever that opened a door in each box. The cats quickly performed the behavior Thorndike was trying to condition (hitting the lever), because doing so (at first by accident and then deliberately) gave them access to food. Because the response (hitting the lever) was essential to (instrumental in) obtaining the reward, Thorndike used the term *instrumental conditioning* to describe the process and called the behaviors *instrumental behaviors.*

Although Skinner spoke of operant conditioning and Thorndike of instrumental conditioning, the two terms are often used interchangeably. What is important is that both Skinner and Thorndike acknowledged that first the behavior is *emitted* (displayed), and then a consequence (for example, a reward) follows. This is unlike classical (Pavlovian) conditioning, in which

Operant [OP-er-ant] conditioning: Conditioning in which an increase or decrease in the probability that a behavior will recur is affected by the delivery of reinforcement or punishment as a consequence of the behavior; also known as *instrumental conditioning.*

Skinner box: Named for its developer, B. F. Skinner, a box that contains a responding mechanism and a device capable of delivering a consequence to an animal in the box whenever it makes the desired response.

Shaping: Selective reinforcement of behaviors that gradually approach (approximate) the desired response.

there is first a change in the environment (for example, bells and food are paired) and then the conditioned behavior (usually a reflexive response) is *elicited.*

In operant conditioning, such as in Thorndike's experiment with cats, the type of consequence that follows the behavior is a crucial component of the conditioning, because it determines whether the behavior is likely to recur. The consequence can be either a reinforcer or a punisher. A reward acts as a *reinforcer,* increasing the likelihood that the behavior targeted for conditioning will recur; in Thorndike's experiment, food was the reinforcer for hitting the lever. A *punisher,* on the other hand, decreases the likelihood that the targeted behavior will recur. If an electric shock is delivered to a cat's paws each time the cat touches a lever, the cat quickly learns not to touch the lever. Parents use a reinforcer when they make use of the family car contingent on responsible behavior. A teenager on a date is more likely to return home at an appropriate hour if doing so will ensure future use of the car. (We will discuss reinforcement and punishment—consequences—in more detail on p. 130.)

The Skinner Box and Shaping

Much of the research on operant conditioning has used an apparatus that most psychologists call a Skinner box—even though Skinner himself never approved of the name. A **Skinner box** is a box that contains a responding mechanism (often a lever or a bar) and a device capable of delivering a consequence to an animal in the box whenever it makes a desired response (one the experimenter has chosen). In experiments that involve rewards, the delivery mechanism is often a small lever or bar in the side of the box; the animal receives a food reward for its pressing behavior. Punishment often takes the form of electric shocks delivered through a grid on the floor of the box.

In a traditional operant conditioning experiment, a rat that has been deprived of food is placed in a Skinner box. The rat moves around the box, seeking food or a means of escape; eventually, it stumbles on the lever and presses it. Immediately following that action, the experimenter delivers a pellet of food into a cup. The rat moves about some more and happens to press the lever again; another pellet of food is delivered. After a few trials, the rat learns that pressing the lever brings food. A hungry rat will learn to press the lever many times in rapid succession to obtain food. Today, psychologists use computerized devices to quantify behavior such as bar pressing and to track the progress an organism makes in learning a response.

Teaching an organism a complex response takes many trials because most organisms need to be taught in small steps, through *shaping.* **Shaping** is the gradual process of selectively reinforcing behaviors that come closer and closer to (approximate) a desired response. To teach a hungry rat to press a bar in a Skinner box, for example, a researcher begins by giving the rat a pellet of food each time it enters the half of the box where the bar is located. Once this behavior is established, the rat receives food only when it touches the wall where the bar is located. Next, it receives food only when it approaches the bar—and so on, until it receives food only when it actually presses the bar. At each stage, the reinforced behavior (entering the half of the box nearest the bar, touching the wall that has the bar, and so on) more closely approximates the desired behavior (pressing the bar). The sequence of stages used to elicit increasingly closer approximations of a desired behavior is sometimes called the *method of successive approximations* (which means basically the same thing as *shaping*). Somewhat controversially, Skinner used these procedures in a controlled environment called a "baby box" to shape the behaviors of his infant daughter.

Shaping is effective for teaching animals new behaviors; for example, shaping is used to train a dog to sit on command. The trainer generally does this by

pushing down on the dog's rear while verbally commanding "Sit!" and then immediately giving the dog a treat. With a treat as reinforcer following the sitting, the dog begins to sit with less and less pressure applied to its rear; eventually, it sits on command.

Shaping is also helpful in teaching people new behaviors. For example, were you taught how to hit a baseball? If so, you were probably first taught, with reinforcing praise from your coach, how to hold the bat correctly, then how to swing it, then how to make contact with the ball, how to shift your weight, how to follow through, and so on. Similarly, a father who wants his son to make his bed neatly will at first reinforce *any* attempt at bed making, even if the results are sloppy. Over successive weeks, the father will reinforce only the better attempts, until finally he reinforces only neat bed making. Patience is important, because it is essential to reinforce all steps toward the desired behavior, no matter how small. Shaping embodies a central tenet of behaviorism: Reinforced behaviors recur. Skinner is the individual responsible for forcefully advancing that notion; psychologists attribute to him the idea that various consequences can redirect the natural flow of behavior. Among the most important of these consequences is reinforcement.

Reinforcement: A Consequence That Strengthens a Response

To really understand operant conditioning, you need to study the basic principles of reinforcement. To psychologists, a **reinforcer** is any event that increases the probability of a recurrence of the response that preceded it. Thus, a behavior followed by a desirable event is likely to recur. Examples of reinforcement abound in daily life: A person works hard at his job and is rewarded with high pay; a student studies long hours for an examination and is rewarded with a top grade; sales agents call on hundreds of clients and sell lots of their products; young children behave appropriately and receive affection and praise from their parents. The specific behaviors of working hard, studying a great deal, calling on clients, and behaving appropriately are established because of reinforcement. Such behaviors can be made to recur by using either or both of two kinds of reinforcers: positive and negative.

Reinforcer: Any event that increases the probability of a recurrence of the response that preceded it.

Positive reinforcement: Presentation of a stimulus after a particular response in order to increase the likelihood that the response will recur.

Negative reinforcement: Removal of a stimulus (usually an aversive one) after a particular response to increase the likelihood that the response will recur.

Positive Reinforcement. Most people have used positive reinforcement at one time or another. **Positive reinforcement** is the presentation of a stimulus after a particular response in order to increase the likelihood that the response will recur. When you are teaching your dog tricks, you reward it with a biscuit or a pat on the head. A parent who is toilet training a 2-year-old may applaud when the child uses the toilet rather than messing his diaper; the applause is a reinforcer. The dog and the child continue the behaviors because they have been rewarded with something desirable; their behaviors have been positively reinforced.

Some reinforcers are more powerful than others, and a reinforcer that rewards one person may not have reinforcing value for another. A smile from an approving parent may be a powerful reinforcer for a 2-year-old; high grades may be the most effective reinforcer for a student; money may be effective for one adult, a trip to Hawaii for another, position or status for someone else.

Negative Reinforcement. Whereas positive reinforcement increases the probability of a response through delivery of a stimulus, **negative reinforcement** increases the probability of a response through removal of a stimulus, usually an *aversive* (unpleasant or noxious) one. Negative reinforcement is still reinforcement, because it strengthens or increases the likelihood of a response; its reinforcing properties are associated with removal of an unpleasant stimulus. For example, suppose a rat is placed in a maze whose floor is an electrified grid that delivers a shock every 50 seconds, and the rat can escape the shock by turning to the left in the maze. The behavior to be conditioned is turning to the left in the maze; the reinforcement is termination of the painful stimulus. In this case, negative reinforcement (termination of the painful stimulus) increases the probability of the response (going to the left), because that response removes the unpleasant stimulus.

Noxious or unpleasant stimuli are often used in animal studies of escape and avoidance. In *escape conditioning*, a rat in a Skinner box receives a shock just strong enough to cause it to thrash around until it bumps against a bar, thereby stopping the shock. In just a few trials, the rat learns to press the bar to escape being shocked, to bring an unpleasant situation to an end. In *avoidance conditioning*, the same apparatus is used, but a buzzer or some other cue precedes the shock by a few seconds. In this case, the rat learns that when it is presented with a stimulus or cue such as a buzzer, it should press the bar to avoid the shock—to prevent it from occurring. Avoidance conditioning generally involves escape conditioning as well: First the animal learns how to escape the shock by pressing the bar; then it learns how to avoid the shock by pressing the bar when it hears the buzzer that signals the oncoming shock.

In avoidance conditioning, the organism learns to respond in such a way that the noxious stimulus is never delivered. For example, to avoid receiving a bad grade on an English exam, a student may study before the exam. And when an adult develops an overwhelming fear of plane crashes, the person may avoid air travel entirely. Thus, avoidance conditioning can explain both adaptive behaviors, such as studying before an exam, and irrational fears, such as the fear of flying.

Most children master both escape and avoidance conditioning at an early age; appropriate signals from a disapproving parent often elicit a response intended to forestall punishment. Similarly, just knowing the possible effects of an automobile accident makes most cautious adults wear seatbelts. Both positive and negative reinforcements *increase* the likelihood that an organism will repeat a behavior. If the reinforcement is strong enough, is delivered often enough, and is important enough to the organism, it can help maintain behaviors for long periods.

Some reinforcers are more powerful than others, and a reinforcer that rewards one person may not have reinforcing value for another.

The Nature of Reinforcers. The precise nature of reinforcers is somewhat murky. Early researchers recognized that anything that satisfies biological needs is a powerful reinforcer. Later researchers defined as reinforcers things that satisfy various nonbiological needs—for example, conversation relieves boredom, and sounds relieve sensory deprivation. Then, in the 1960s, researchers acknowledged that *probable behaviors*—behaviors likely to happen, including biological behaviors such as eating and social behaviors such as playing tennis, writing letters, or talking—can reinforce less probable or unlikely behaviors such as cleaning closets, studying calculus, or pressing levers. Researchers call this idea the *Premack principle,* after David Premack, whose influential writings and research fostered it (Premack, 1962, 1965). Parents employ the Premack principle when they tell their children that they can go outside to play *after* they clean their rooms.

The Premack principle and its refinements focus on the problem of determining what is a good reinforcer. Therapists and learning theorists know, for example, that something that acts as a reinforcer for one person may not do so for another person (especially if that person is from a different culture) or for the same person on another day. Therefore, they are very careful about identifying aspects of a client's life—or a rodent's environment—that act as reinforcers. If someone were to offer you a reinforcer to perform some fairly difficult task, what would be the most effective reinforcer? Do reinforcers change with a person's age and experiences, or do they depend on how often the person has been reinforced? Today, researchers are trying to discover what reinforcers will work best in practical settings such as the home and the workplace (Timberlake & Farmer-Dougan, 1991).

A reinforcer that is known to be successful may work only in specific situations. The delivery of food pellets to a hungry rat that has just pressed a lever increases the likelihood that the rat will press the lever again. But this reinforcer works only if the rat is hungry; the food pellets are not reinforcing for a rat that has just eaten. Psychologists studying learning and conditioning create the conditions for reinforcement by depriving animals of food or water before an experiment. In doing so, they motivate the animals and allow the food or water to take on reinforcing properties. In most experiments, the organism is motivated in some way. Chapter 8 discusses the role of an organism's needs, desires, and physiological state in determining what can be used as a reinforcer.

A **primary reinforcer** is a reinforcer that has survival value for an organism (for example, food, water, or the termination of pain); its value does not have to be learned. Food can be a primary reinforcer for a hungry rat, water for a thirsty one. A **secondary reinforcer** is a neutral stimulus (such as money or grades) that initially has no intrinsic value for the organism but that becomes rewarding when linked with a primary reinforcer. Many of our pleasures are secondary reinforcers that have acquired value—for example, leather coats keep us no warmer than cloth ones, and sportscars take us where we want to go no faster than four-door sedans.

Secondary reinforcers are generally used to modify human behavior. Approving nods, unlimited use of the family car, and job promotions are secondary reinforcers that can establish and maintain a wide spectrum of behavior. Salespeople may work 72-hour weeks when their manager, using basic psychology,

Primary reinforcer: Reinforcer (such as food, water, or the termination of pain) that has survival value for an organism; this value does not have to be learned.

Secondary reinforcer: Any neutral stimulus that initially has no intrinsic value for an organism but that becomes rewarding when linked with a primary reinforcer.

offers them bonuses for increasing their sales by a specific percentage during a slow month. The manager may reason that increasing the amount of the secondary reinforcer (money) may promote better performance (higher sales). Research shows that increasing or decreasing the amount of a reinforcer can significantly alter an organism's behavior.

Superstitious Behaviors. Because the process of reinforcement plays a key role in the learning of new behaviors, parents and educators intentionally and regularly try to reinforce children and students. But what happens when a person or animal is *accidentally* rewarded for a behavior—when a reward has nothing to do with the behavior that immediately preceded it? Under this condition, people and animals may develop **superstitious behavior**—behavior learned through coincidental association with reinforcement. For example, a baseball player may try to extend his hitting streak by always using the same "lucky" bat. My daughter studied in the same library carrels because she earned good grades after studying there before. Many superstitious behaviors—including fear responses to the number 13, black cats, and walking under ladders—are centuries old and have strong cultural associations. Individual superstitious behaviors generally arise from the purely random association of some object or event and a particular behavior. Thus, a person who happens to wear the same pair of shoes in three bicycle races and wins the races may come to believe there is a causal relationship between wearing that pair of shoes and winning.

Punishment: A Consequence That Weakens a Response

You already know that consequences—whether rewards or punishments—affect behavior. Clearly, rewards can establish new behaviors and maintain them for long periods. How effective is punishment in manipulating behavior? **Punishment** is the process of presenting an undesirable or noxious stimulus, or removing a desirable stimulus, to decrease the probability that a preceding response will recur. Punishment, unlike reinforcement, aims to *decrease* the probability of a particular response. Thus, people commonly use this technique to try to teach children and pets to control their behavior. For example, when a dog growls at visitors, its owner chastises it; when a child writes on the walls with crayons, the parents may scold him harshly or make him scrub the walls. In both cases, people indicate displeasure by delivering a stimulus intended to suppress an undesirable behavior.

Researchers use the same technique to decrease the probability that a behavior will recur. They deliver a noxious or unpleasant stimulus, such as a mild electric shock, when an organism displays an undesirable behavior. If an animal is punished for a specific behavior, the probability that it will continue to perform that behavior decreases.

Another form of punishment involves removal of a pleasant stimulus. For example, if a teenager stays out past her curfew, she may be grounded for a week. If a child misbehaves, he may be forbidden to watch television that evening. One effective punishment is the *time-out,* in which an individual is removed from an environment containing positive events or reinforcers. For example, a child who hits and kicks may have to sit in a corner with no toys, television, books, or people.

Thus, punishment can involve either adding a noxious stimulus, such as scolding, or subtracting a positive stimulus, such as watching TV. In both cases, the aim is to decrease the likelihood of a behavior.

The Nature of Punishers. Like reinforcers, *punishers* can be primary or secondary. A **primary punisher** is a stimulus that is naturally painful or unpleasant to an organism; two examples are an electric shock to an animal and visible parental rage to a small child. A **secondary punisher** is any neutral stimulus that initially has no intrinsic negative value for an organism but acquires punishing qualities when linked with a primary punisher. Examples are the word "No," a shake of the head, or indifference. Secondary punishers can be effective means of controlling behavior, especially when used in combination with reinforcers for desired behaviors. But, as with reinforcement, what is punishing for one person or in one culture may not have the same properties for another person or in another culture. A show of indifference may punish some behaviors for some people, but a display of disapproval from a stern authority figure may be a far more powerful punishment for others.

Punishment plus Reinforcement. Psychologists have long known that punishment by itself

Superstitious behavior: Behavior learned through coincidental association with reinforcement.

Punishment: Process of presenting an undesirable or noxious stimulus, or removing a desirable stimulus, to decrease the probability that a preceding response will recur.

Primary punisher: Any stimulus or event that is naturally painful or unpleasant to an organism.

Secondary punisher: Any neutral stimulus that initially has no intrinsic negative value for an organism but acquires punishing qualities when linked with a primary punisher.

Learned helplessness: The behavior of giving up or not responding to punishment, exhibited by people or animals exposed to negative consequences or punishment over which they have no control.

is not an effective way to control or eliminate behavior. Punishment can suppress simple behavior patterns; once the punishment ceases, however, animals and human beings often return to the previous behavior. To be effective, punishment must be continuous, and the desired alternative behavior should be reinforced at the same time. Therefore, those who study children's classroom behavior recommend a combination of punishment for antisocial behavior and reinforcement for prosocial behavior. A combination of private reprimands for disruptive behaviors and public praise for cooperative behaviors is often the most effective method for controlling classroom behavior.

Disciplinary techniques that lead to a perception of control on the part of the child being disciplined—a sense of how to avoid future discipline—are much more likely to prevent recurrence of undesired behavior.

Limitations of Punishment. A serious limitation of punishment as a behavior-shaping device is that it suppresses only existing behaviors. It cannot be used to establish new, desired behaviors. Punishment also has serious social consequences (Azrin & Holtz, 1966). If parents use excessive punishment to control a child's behavior, for example, the child may try to escape from the home so that punishment cannot be delivered. Further, children who receive physical punishments often demonstrate increased levels of aggression when they are away from the punisher. Punishment may control a child's behavior while the parents are nearby, but it may also alienate the child from the parents.

Research also shows that children imitate aggression. Thus, parents who punish children physically are likely to have children who are physically aggressive (Mischel & Grusec, 1966). A child may strike out at the person who administers punishment in an attempt to eliminate the source of punishment, sometimes inflicting serious injury. Punishment can also bring about generalized aggression. For example, if two rats in a Skinner box both receive painful shocks, they will strike out at each other. Similarly, human beings who have been punished are often hostile and aggressive toward other members of their group. This is especially true of prison inmates, whose hostility is well recognized, and of class bullies, who are often the children most strictly disciplined by their parents or teachers. Skinner (1988) believed that punishment in schools is unnecessary and harmful; he advocated nonpunitive techniques, which might involve developing strong bonds between students and teachers and reinforcing school activities at home (Comer, 1988). In general, disciplinary techniques that lead to a perception of control on the part of the child being disciplined—a sense of how to avoid future discipline—are much more likely to prevent recurrence of undesired behavior, even when the disciplining agent (teacher or parent) is not around.

Further, if punishment is delivered inconsistently or without reference to the organism's behavior, it may lead to **learned helplessness**, the reaction of a person or animal that feels powerless to control the punishment and so stops making any response at all. Martin Seligman (1975) and his colleagues showed, for example, that dogs first exposed to a series of shocks and then given a chance to escape further punishment fail to learn the escape response. *(I)*

Think Critically

- What is the fundamental difference between positive reinforcement and negative reinforcement? Give an example of each.
- Your neighbor tells you, "Punishment just doesn't work with my kids anymore. I keep escalating the punishments, and they keep acting worse and worse! I don't know what to do!" What do you think is going on here, and what would you advise your neighbor to do?

(I) Key Variables in Operant Conditioning

Focus on issues and ideas

- The critical importance of the strength, timing, and frequency of consequences in operant conditioning
- The process of generalization and discrimination in daily behaviors
- The role of extinction and spontaneous recovery in operant conditioning
- How basic learning principles apply to behavioral self-regulation
- The potential role of consolidation in the brain's physiological development

As with classical conditioning, many variables affect operant conditioning. The most important of these are the strength, timing, and frequency of consequences (either reinforcement or punishment).

Strength, Timing, and Frequency

Strength of Consequences. Studies comparing productivity with varying amounts of reinforcement show that the greater the reward, the harder, longer, and faster a person will work to complete a task. For example, if you were a landscape contractor, the more money you received for mowing lawns, the more lawns you would want to mow. Similarly, the stronger the punishment, the more quickly a behavior can be suppressed and the longer it will remain suppressed. If you knew you would be imprisoned for speeding, you would probably obey the speed limit.

The strength of a consequence can be measured in terms of either time or degree. For example, the length of time a child stays in a time-out chair without positive reinforcements can affect how soon and for how long an unacceptable behavior will be suppressed. Thus, for a given child, a 2-minute stay might not be as effective as a 10-minute stay. Likewise, a halfhearted "Please don't do that, sweetie" is not as effective as a firm "Don't do that again."

Punishment, whatever its form, is best delivered in moderation; too much may be as ineffective as too little. If too much punishment is delivered, it may cause panic, decrease the likelihood of the desired response, or even elicit behavior that is contrary to the punisher's goals.

Timing of Consequences. Just as the interval between presenting the conditioned stimulus and the unconditioned stimulus is important in classical conditioning, the interval between a desired behavior and the delivery of the consequence (reward or punishment) is important in operant conditioning. Generally, the shorter the interval, the greater the likelihood that the behavior will be learned.

Fixed-interval schedule: A reinforcement schedule in which a reinforcer (reward) is delivered after a specified interval of time, provided that the required response occurs at least once in the interval.

Variable-interval schedule: A reinforcement schedule in which a reinforcer (reward) is delivered after predetermined but varying amounts of time, provided that the required response occurs at least once after each interval.

Fixed-ratio schedule: A reinforcement schedule in which a reinforcer (reward) is delivered after a specified number of responses has occurred.

Variable-ratio schedule: A reinforcement schedule in which a reinforcer (reward) is delivered after a predetermined but variable number of responses has occurred.

Frequency of Consequences. How often do people need to be reinforced? Is a paycheck once a month sufficient? Will people work better if they receive reinforcement regularly or if they receive it at unpredictable intervals? Up to this point, our discussion has generally assumed that a consequence follows each response. What if people are reinforced only some of the time, not continually? When a researcher varies the frequency with which an organism is reinforced, the researcher is manipulating the *schedule of reinforcement*—the pattern of presentation of the reinforcer over time. The simplest and easiest reinforcement pattern is *continuous reinforcement*—reinforcement for every occurrence of the targeted behavior. However, most researchers, or parents for that matter, do not reinforce a behavior every time it occurs; rather, they reinforce occasionally or intermittently. What determines the timetable for reinforcement? Schedules of reinforcement generally are based either on intervals of time or on frequency of response. Some schedules establish a behavior quickly; however, quickly established behaviors are more quickly extinguished than are behaviors that are slower to be established. (We'll discuss extinction in operant conditioning in more detail on p. 134.) Researchers have devised four basic schedules of reinforcement; two are *interval schedules* (based on time periods), and two are *ratio schedules* (based on work output).

Interval schedules can be either fixed or variable. Imagine that a rat in a Skinner box is being trained to press a bar in order to obtain food. If the experiment is on a **fixed-interval schedule,** the reward will follow the first bar press that occurs after a specified interval of time. That is, the rat will be given a reinforcer if it presses the bar at least once after a specified time interval and will receive the same reward regardless of whether it works a great deal (presses the bar repeatedly) or just a little. A fixed-interval schedule produces a scalloped graph. Just after reinforcement both animals and human beings typically respond slowly; just before the reinforcement is due, there is an increase in performance.

Under a **variable-interval schedule,** the reinforcer is delivered after predetermined but varying amounts of time, as long as an appropriate response is made at least once after each interval. The organism may be reinforced if it makes a response after 40 seconds, after 60 seconds, and then after 25 seconds. Rats reinforced on a variable-interval schedule work at a slow, regular rate; the graph of a variable-interval schedule does not have the scalloped effect of a fixed-interval graph. The work rate is relatively slow, because the delivery of the reinforcer is tied to time intervals rather than to output. Nevertheless, rats on a variable-interval schedule have a better overall rate of response than those on a fixed-interval schedule.

Ratio schedules, which can also be either fixed or variable, are based on output instead of time. In a **fixed-ratio schedule,** the organism is reinforced for a specified number of responses (amount of work). For example, a rat in a Skinner box might be reinforced after every 10th bar press. In this case, the rat will work at a fast, regular rate. It has learned that hard work brings regular delivery of a reinforcer. The work rate of a rat on a fixed-ratio schedule is much higher than that of a rat on an interval schedule. In the same way, a teenager who is paid for each lawn mowed (for the amount of work completed) will probably mow more lawns than one who is paid by the hour.

Variable-ratio schedules can bring about very high rates of response. In contrast to a fixed-ratio schedule, a **variable-ratio schedule** reinforces the responder for a predetermined but variable number of responses (amount of work). Thus, a rat learns that hard work produces a reinforcer, but it cannot predict when the reinforcer will be delivered. Therefore, the rat's best bet is to work at a regular, high rate, thereby generating the highest available rate of response. Sales agents for insurance companies know that the more prospects they approach, the more insurance they will sell. They may not know who will buy, but they do know that a greater number of selling opportunities will ultimately result in more sales. Similarly, gamblers pour quarters into slot machines because they never know when they will be reinforced with a jackpot. Table 5.2 summarizes the four schedules of reinforcement.

Using Schedules of Consequences. The study of reinforcement has many practical implications. Psychologists use the principles of reinforcement to study such frequently asked questions as these: How can I change my little brother's rotten attitude? How can I get more work out of my employees? How do I learn to say no? How do I get my dog to stop biting my ankles? To get your brother to shape up, you can shape his behavior. Each time he acts in a way you like, however slightly, reward him with praise or affection. When he behaves annoyingly, withhold attention or rewards and ignore him. Continue this pattern for a few weeks; as he becomes more pleasant, show him more attention. Remember, reinforced behaviors tend to recur.

Most workers get paid a fixed amount each week. They are on a fixed-interval schedule—regardless of their output, they get their paycheck. One way to increase productivity is to place workers on a fixed-ratio schedule. A worker who is paid by the piece, by the report, by the page, or by the widget is going to produce more pieces, reports, pages, or widgets than one who is paid by the hour and whose productivity therefore does not make a difference. Automobile salespeople, who are known for their persistence, work for commissions; their pay is linked to their ability to close a sale. Research in both the laboratory and the businessplace shows that when pay is linked to output, people generally work harder.

Stimulus Generalization and Stimulus Discrimination

Stimulus generalization and *stimulus discrimination* occur in operant conditioning much as they do in classical conditioning. The difference is that in operant conditioning the reinforcement is delivered only after the animal correctly discriminates between the stimuli. For example, suppose an animal in a laboratory is shown either a vertical or a horizontal line and is given two keys to press—one if the line is vertical, the other if the line is horizontal. The animal gets rewards for correct responses. The animal will usually make errors at first; but after repeated presentations of the vertical

Table 5.2 Types of Reinforcement Schedules

Schedule	Description	Effect
Fixed-interval	Reinforcement is given for the first response after a fixed time.	Response rate drops right after reinforcement but then increases near the end of the interval.
Variable-interval	Reinforcement is given for the first response after a predetermined but variable interval.	Response rate is slow and regular.
Fixed-ratio	Reinforcement is given after a fixed number of responses.	Response rate is fast and regular.
Variable-ratio	Reinforcement is given after a predetermined and variable number of responses.	Response rate is regular and high.

and horizontal lines, with reinforcements given only for correct responses, the animal will learn to discriminate between stimuli. Stimulus discrimination can also be established with colors, tones, and more complex stimuli.

The processes of stimulus generalization and discrimination are evident daily. Children often make mistakes by overgeneralizing. For example, a baby who knows that cats have four legs and a tail may call all four-legged animals "cat." With experience and with guidance and reinforcement from his or her parents, the child will learn to discriminate between dogs and cats, using body size, shape, fur, and sounds. Similarly, once you may have been unaware of distinctions among various Chinese cuisines; but after several experiences, you may have learned to discriminate among Cantonese, Hunan, and Szechuan specialties.

Extinction and Spontaneous Recovery

In operant conditioning, if a reinforcer or punisher is no longer delivered—that is, if a consequence does not follow an instrumentally conditioned behavior—the behavior either will not be well established or, if it is already established, will undergo extinction. **Extinction,** in operant conditioning, is the process by which the probability of an organism's emitting a response is reduced when reinforcement no longer follows the response. One way to measure the extent of conditioning is to measure how resistant a response is to extinction. *Resistance to extinction* is a measure of how long it takes, or how many trials are necessary, before extinction occurs. Suppose, for example, that a pigeon is trained to peck a key whenever it hears a high-pitched tone. Pecking in response to the high-pitched tone brings reinforcement, but pecking in response to a low-pitched tone does not. If the reinforcement process ceases entirely, the pigeon will eventually stop pecking the key. If the pigeon has been on a variable-ratio schedule and thus expects to work for long periods before reinforcement occurs, it will probably keep pecking for a very long time before stopping. If it has been on a fixed-interval schedule and thus expects reinforcement within a short time, it will stop pecking after just a few unreinforced trials.

People also show extinction; when researchers removed reinforcers from children who were exhibiting self-injurious behavior, the self-injuries decreased (Iwata et al., 1994). Many parents know that when they stop reinforcing a child's misbehaviors with lots of attention (even if that attention consists of scolding), the misbehaviors often decrease. Note that the decrease in response is not always immediately apparent, however. When a reinforcer is withheld, organisms sometimes work harder—showing an initial increase in performance. In such cases, the curve depicting the extinction process shows a small initial increase in performance, followed by a decrease.

Extinction: In operant conditioning, the process by which the probability of an organism's emitting a response is reduced when reinforcement no longer follows the response.

As in classical conditioning, *spontaneous recovery* also occurs in operant conditioning. If an organism's conditioned response has undergone extinction and the organism is given a rest period and then retested, the organism will show spontaneous recovery of the response. If the organism is put through this sequence several times, its overall response rate in each session will decrease. After one rest period, the organism's rate will almost equal what it was when the conditioned response was reinforced. However, after a dozen or so rest periods (with no reinforcements), the organism may make only one or two responses; the level of spontaneous recovery will have decreased markedly. Eventually, the response will disappear completely.

People also show spontaneous recovery. When you answer a question in class, reinforcement or punishment often follows: The instructor may praise you for your intelligence or grill you about your lack of understanding. However, if the instructor stops reinforcing correct answers or does not call on you when you raise your hand, you will probably stop responding (your behavior will be extinguished). After a vacation, you may start raising your hand again (spontaneous recovery), but you will quickly stop if your behavior remains unreinforced. Instructors learn early in their careers that if they want to have lively classes, they need to reinforce not just correct answers but also attempts at correct answers. In doing so, they help shape their students' behavior.

Table 5.3 summarizes four important concepts in operant conditioning: extinction, spontaneous recovery, stimulus generalization, and stimulus discrimination.

Operant Conditioning in Daily Life

Our world is full of reinforcers and punishers. We can work for rewards such as money. We can volunteer our time for such worthy causes as the Red Cross, homeless shelters, and AIDS research. Of course, sometimes people feel that they are helpless in the face of the punishers. The costs of living keep rising; random violence seems to increase; the environment

Table 5.3 Four Important Concepts in Operant Conditioning

Property	Definition	Example
Extinction	The process of reducing the probability of a conditioned response by withholding the reinforcer after the response.	A rat trained to press a bar stops pressing when it is no longer reinforced.
Spontaneous recovery	The recurrence of an extinguished conditioned response following a rest period.	A rat's continued bar-pressing behavior has undergone extinction; after a rest period, the rat again presses the bar.
Stimulus generalization	The process by which an organism learns to respond to stimuli that are similar but not identical to the original conditioned stimulus.	A cat presses a bar when presented with either an ellipse or a circle.
Stimulus discrimination	The process by which an organism learns to respond only to a specific reinforced stimulus.	A pigeon presses a key only in response to red lights, not to blue or green ones.

is in serious trouble. But, by and large, most of us feel in control of our reinforcers and punishers. We know that many of our rewards and punishments are contingent on our behaviors. Each of us, to various extents, experiences operant conditioning in daily life.

Intrinsically Motivated Behavior. Psychologists have shown that reinforcement is effective in establishing and maintaining behavior. But some behaviors are intrinsically rewarding—they are pleasurable in themselves. People are likely to repeat *intrinsically motivated behaviors* for their own sake; for example, they may work on craft projects for the feeling of satisfaction they bring. People are likely to perform *extrinsically motivated behaviors,* such as working for a paycheck, for the sake of the external reinforcement alone. Interestingly, if a person is offered reinforcement for an intrinsically motivated behavior, performance may actually decrease. Imagine, for example, that a man does charity work because it makes him feel good. Being paid could cause the man to lose interest in the work, because it would no longer offer the intrinsic reinforcement of feelings of selflessness. A student pianist may lose her desire to practice if her teacher enters her in a competition; practice sessions become ordeals, and the student may wish to stop playing altogether. For every person and in every culture, reinforcers differ and are determined by a host of learning experiences. Chapter 8 considers this issue at greater length, especially the topic of the potential hidden costs of rewards.

Electrical Brain Stimulation. Until the 1950s, researchers assumed that reinforcers were effective because they satisfied some need or drive in an organism, such as hunger. Then James Olds (1955, 1969) found an apparent exception to this assumption. He discovered that rats find electrical stimulation of specific areas of the brain to be rewarding in itself. Olds implanted an electrode in the hypothalamus of each rat and attached the electrode to a stimulator that provided a small voltage. The stimulator was activated only when the rat pressed a lever in a Skinner box. Olds found that the rats pressed the lever thousands of times in order to continue the self-stimulation. In one study, the rats pressed it at a rate of 1,920 times per hour (Olds & Milner, 1954). Rats even crossed an electrified grid to get to the lever and obtain this reward. Animals who were rewarded with brain stimulation performed better in a maze, running faster with fewer errors. And hungry rats often chose the self-stimulation over food.

Stimulation of specific areas of the brain initiates different drives and activities. In some cases, it reinforces behaviors such as bar pressing; in others, it increases eating, drinking, or sexual behavior. Psychologists are still not sure how electrical stimulation reinforces a behavior such as lever pressing; but they do know that certain neurotransmitters play an important role. The area of the brain stimulated (initially thought to be the medial forebrain bundle but now recognized to include large parts of the limbic system), the state of the organism, its particular physiological needs, and the levels of various neurotransmitters are all important. A hungry rat, for example, will self-stimulate faster than a rat that is not hungry. In addition, a hungry rat will generally choose electrical brain stimulation over food but not to the extent of starving itself.

The fact that electrical stimulation can initiate behavioral responses is a reflection of the basic electrochemical nature of brain activity, which underlies all learning. The next section explores this biological connection.

Behavioral Self-Regulation. *Behavioral regulation theorists* assume that people and animals will choose, if possible, activities that seem optimal to them. Rats, for example, will spend their time eating, drinking, and running on a wheel—activities they find pleasurable. An experiment by Bernstein and Ebbesen (1978) showed that human beings readjust their activities in a systematic manner. The researchers paid participants to live in an isolated room 24 hours a day, 7 days a week, for several weeks. The room had all the usual amenities of a home—bed, tables, bathroom, books, cooking utensils, and so forth. The experimenters observed the participants through a one-way mirror and recorded their baseline activity—the frequency of their specific behaviors when no restrictions were placed on them. The researchers found, for example, that one participant spent nearly twice as much time knitting as studying. The experimenters used the participant's baseline activity to determine the reinforcer—in this case, knitting.

The experimenters then imposed a contingency. In the case of the participant who liked to knit, for example, they insisted that she study for a specific amount of time before she could knit. If she studied only as much as she did before, she would be able to knit for much less time. As a consequence, the woman altered her behavior so that she could ultimately spend more time knitting. She began to study for longer periods of time—eventually more than doubling the time she spent studying. In other words, she regulated her own behavior through application of the Premack principle (see p. 129).

Other techniques of behavioral self-regulation are derived from the basic learning principles of reinforcement. According to Wing and his colleagues, if individuals with medical conditions that require daily attention are to regulate themselves, they must self-observe, self-evaluate, and then self-reinforce. The researchers assert that when people *self-observe* the target behavior, they are better able to *self-evaluate* their progress. After evaluating their progress, it is crucial that they receive *reinforcement* for adhering to their medical regimen—perhaps by going out to a concert with a friend or buying themselves a present. When these procedures are followed, adherence to the medical regimen improves.

Behavioral self-regulation has other practical applications. It is effective within classrooms and in other social situations where it can modulate disruptive behavior (Cavalier, Ferretti, & Hodges, 1997). Members of the diet program Weight Watchers may be told to keep track of when and what they eat, when they have the urge to eat, and what feelings or events precede those urges. The program's organizers seek to help people identify the events that lead to eating so that they can control it. The aim is to help people think clearly, regulate themselves, and thus manage their lives better. This decision process and the focus on thinking are clearly seen in studies of cognitive learning, considered soon.

The Biology Underlying Learning

Whenever there is learning, there is a relatively permanent change in behavior; and this change is reflected in the nervous system. Donald O. Hebb (1904–1985), a Canadian psychologist, was one of the first to suggest that, with each learning situation, the structure of the brain changes. He argued that certain groups of neurons act together, and their synaptic transmissions and general neural activity form a recurring pattern—he referred to such a group of coordinated neurons as a *reverberating circuit.* The more the circuit that represents a concept or experience is stimulated, the better that concept or experience is remembered and the more the structure of the brain is altered.

Remember that learning is a process that occurs because of unique interactions among hundreds of thousands of neurons in the brain. Using this fact, Hebb (1949) suggested that stimulation of particular groups of neurons causes them to form specific patterns of neural activity. The evolution of a temporary neural circuit into a more permanent circuit is known as *consolidation.* According to Hebb, consolidation serves as the basis of learning and memory. If Hebb is correct, when people first sense a new stimulus, only temporary changes in neurons take place; but repetition of the stimulus causes consolidation, and the temporary circuit becomes a permanent one.

Many psychologists today believe that the consolidation process provides the key to understanding learning—that individual differences in ability to learn (or remember) may be due to differing abilities to consolidate neural circuits. Confirmation of this notion comes from studies using electroconvulsive shock therapy (discussed in Chapter 14) to disrupt consolidation, which results in impaired learning and memory in both human beings and animals. Further support comes from studies showing that recent (less consolidated) memories are more susceptible to loss through amnesia than are older (more consolidated) memories (Milner, 1989).

The consolidation process may even play a role in the brain's physiological development. Researchers have compared the brains of animals raised in enriched environments, where toys and other objects are available for the animals to play with and learn from, with the brains of animals raised in deprived environments. The brains of animals raised in rich environments have more elaborate networks of nerve cells, with more dendrites and more synapses with other neurons (Chang, Isaacs, & Greenough, 1991). This means that stimulating a neuron over and over again may cause it to branch out and become more easily accessible to additional synaptic connections. These findings may indicate that when key neurons are stimulated, the events that cause the stimulation may be better remembered and more easily accessed—this may be part of the reason why practice makes perfect (Kandel & Abel, 1995). Although there is less work with human beings, Jacobs and his colleagues (1993) found that people with more education have more dendritic elaboration; and Scheibel's research team (1990) found that parts of the body that are used more (fingers versus the wall of the chest) have more elaborate dendritic organization in the brain.

If a neuron is stimulated and fires, the biochemical processes involved make it more likely to respond again later; further, its number of dendrites increases because of previous stimulation. Synaptic plasticity allows associations to be learned (Moser et al., 1998; Tracy et al., 1998); repetition, as in repeated pairings of a conditioned and unconditioned stimulus in classical conditioning, may make learning and remembering easier (Kandel & Abel, 1995)—a conception that fits perfectly with Hebb's original suggestions.

Not only does a single neuron have many synaptic sites on its dendrites, but it can be active in more than one network of functions. Some neurons may be involved in more activities and exert a stronger influence than others—for example, those neurons involved in behaviors in which visual and motor activities interact may become especially elaborate. Alkon (1989) showed that there is extensive interaction among a neuron's synaptic sites and with the sites of other neurons. He argued that the spread of electrical and chemical activity from one site to another is critical for initiating learning and memory. He asserted that a given neuron can receive and store a huge number of different incoming signals. More recently, Alkon has been developing mathematical and computer models to simulate neuronal encoding for memory. This exciting work also extends Hebb's ideas.

Also in its infancy, but very promising, is the finding that specific genes are necessary for the formation of learning and memory. One research team has isolated a gene, dubbed the *CREB gene,* which is crucial in the consolidation process. Without this gene, certain proteins are not activated, and memories are fleeting (Bourtchuladze et al., 1994). The genetic causes of memory and memory loss are yet to be fully understood; the presence of the CREB gene is only one link in the complex chain of events from experience to recall, but it seems to be an essential one. *I*

Think Critically

- Would you agree or disagree with the view that all intrinsically motivated behaviors must at some point have been reinforced? Why?
- When doing research on human or animal learning, researchers often record baseline activity. Why is such evidence important?

I Cognitive Learning

Focus on issues and ideas

- The impact of insight on latent learning
- How learning is affected by the generative process model
- The essential elements in the cognitive learning process
- The key variables in observational learning
- The role of reinforcement in observational learning

"Enough!" Patrick shouted, after 4 grueling hours of trying to write a program for his personal computer. The program was full of bugs, all resulting from the same basic problem—but he didn't know what the problem was. After dozens of trial-and-error manipulations, Patrick turned off the computer and went off to study for his history exam. Then, while staring at a page in the text, he noticed a phrase set off by commas—and suddenly he realized his programming mistake. He had mistakenly put commas in his program's if–then statements. It was correct English, but incorrect computer syntax.

Patrick solved his problem by thinking. His discovery was not a matter of simple conditioning of a simple response with a simple reinforcer. As you've seen, learning researchers have actively focused on learning that involves reinforcement. Studies by Pavlov, Thorndike, and Skinner revealed that conditioning processes require a reinforcer for behavior to be maintained. Much of the learning literature has focused on stimuli and responses and their relationship, timing, and frequency. But is a reinforcer always necessary for learning? Can a person learn new behaviors as a result of thinking or using the imagination? These questions are problematic for traditional learning researchers—but not for cognitive psychologists or learning researchers with a cognitive emphasis.

Thinking about a problem allows you to solve the problem and makes other behaviors possible; thus, thinking and imagination become crucial to learning and problem solving (Skinner, 1989). The importance of thinking—the focus of cognitive research—is evident even in early learning studies and will be demonstrated over and over again as we examine such areas of psychology as motivation, maladjustment, and therapy. Some of the most famous psychologists of the early part of the 20th century examined learning when reinforcement was not evident and behavior was not observable. These early studies focused on insight and latent learning, and some of them led to modern studies of cognitive mapping. Recent research has focused on generative learning and observational learning, as well as problem solving, creativity, and concept formation (which we will cover in Chapter 6). All of this work indicates that there are many different aspects to what is learned and how learning takes place, as *Diversity* clearly shows.

DIVERSITY

Do Men and Women Learn Differently?

At George Washington University's Mount Vernon campus, women are taking classes called "Women in Power" and "Women in Business," as well as traditional literature and math classes in which the students are all women. Educators are recognizing that women students work better in groups, in cooperative efforts that stimulate connections among their ideas and emphasize critical thinking (Gillies & Ashman, 1996). Critical thinking, which focuses on integrating ideas rather than memorizing information, is at the core of such efforts. It builds on the idea that women take advantage of cooperative learning more than men do (Kohn, 1993). Where possible and appropriate, colleges are finding unique approaches to educating women. All around the world, curricula in various disciplines are reflecting the idea that gender differences in learning are real.

Psychologists have been assessing cognitive learning styles for decades; in doing so, they have found that males and females seem to learn differently. Boys and girls are taught different behavior on the playground, at home, and in the classroom—and these behaviors affect the way they learn, at least according to some experts. In general, psychologists argue that boys are more independent and aggressive than girls; girls, in contrast, are more cooperative than boys. In general, boys are taught to win, whereas girls are encouraged to enjoy the game and the process of playing and are taught to get along, communicate, and cooperate (Kohn, 1993). As a consequence, females tend to learn better in cooperative learning situations, whereas males tend to learn better independently.

Research on the role of learning styles confirms some differences between men and women—although there are still more differences among women and among men than between men and women. In a study of the test-preparation strategies of college students, Speth and Brown (1990) found that men and women differ in how they prepare for multiple-choice versus essay examinations. The women described multiple-choice tests as being more difficult and challenging than did the men. This probably reflects the different approaches to acquiring knowledge, according to Meece and Jones (1996) and Magolda (1990). Magolda found that men tended more than women to view learning as an active, task-oriented process. Magolda also found that men enjoyed the challenge more than the process of learning. Furthermore, according to Crawford and MacLeod (1990), men take a more active role in classrooms than do women, and this participation facilitates learning. However, such gender differences in learning styles tend to be small, to be focused on a narrow range of abilities, and to emerge primarily when special types of processing are encouraged by test developers, teachers, or employers (Dweck, 1986; Meyers-Levy & Maheswaran, 1991).

It is not surprising that men and women learn about the world differently, that they develop distinctly different worldviews, and that these worldviews affect their learning styles and their abilities and desires to determine their own destiny (Severiens & Ten-Dam, 1997). Some researchers are calling for a radical transformation of classroom dynamics (Meece & Jones, 1996). Some feminist scholars assert that an approach that teaches women differently than men reinforces differences between men and women and encourages sexism. Psychologists know that men and women use different approaches to many life situations. However, there is no evidence that males and females are born with these differences. Certainly a person's learning style is not predetermined by his or her gender (Severiens & Ten-Dam, 1997). There is evidence that Americans are raised in a culture that exhibits and reinforces gender bias. Even in American culture, however, the extent to which anyone takes a masculine or a feminine approach to learning varies tremendously. ■

Insight

When you discover a relationship among a series of events, you may say that you have had an *insight*. Insights are usually not taught but rather are discovered. Like Patrick's discovery of his extra commas, many learning experiences involve both sustained thought and insight.

Discovering the sources of insight was the goal of researchers working with animals during World War I. Wolfgang Köhler, a Gestalt researcher, showed that chimpanzees developed insights about how to retrieve food that was beyond their reach. The chimps discovered that they could pile up boxes or make a long stick out of several shorter ones. They were never reinforced for these specific behaviors; insight showed them how to get the food. Insight results from thought, without direct reinforcement. Once a chimp learns how to pile boxes, or once Patrick realizes his comma error, the insight is not forgotten, and no further instruction or training is necessary. The role of insight is often overlooked in studies of learning; however, it is an essential element in problem solving (discussed in Chapter 6).

Latent Learning

After a person has an insight, learns a task, or solves a problem, the new learning is not necessarily evident. Researchers in the 1920s placed hungry rats in a maze and recorded how many trials it took the rats to reach a particular spot, where food was hidden. It took many days and many trials, but the hungry rats learned the mazes well. Other hungry rats were put into the maze but were not reinforced with food on reaching the same spot; instead, they were merely removed from the maze. A third group of hungry rats, like the second group, was not reinforced at first but, after 10 days, were given food on reaching the goal. Surprisingly, after 1 day of receiving reinforcement, the rats in the third group were reaching the goal with few errors. During the first 10 days of maze running, they must have been learning something but not showing it. Receiving a reward gave them a reason to use what they had learned.

Researchers such as E. C. Tolman (1886–1959) argued that the rats were exhibiting **latent learning**—learning that occurs in the absence of direct reinforcement and that is not necessarily demonstrated through observable behavior. Tolman showed that when a rat is given a reason (such as food) to show learning, the behavior will become evident. In other words, a rat—or a person—that is given no motivation to do so may not demonstrate learned behavior even if learning has occurred. Tolman's work with rats led him to propose the idea that animals and human beings develop (or *generate*) a kind of mental map of their world, which allows them to navigate a maze or city streets. Tolman's idea of latent learning was especially significant because the definition of learning at that time was strictly behavioral—observable behavior was an essential part of the definition. Tolman laid the foundation for later studies of latent learning and of generative learning and learning to learn. We will consider them in turn.

Generative Learning

Modern cognitive psychology is changing the way in which educational psychologists think about classroom learning. According to most cognitive psychologists, in addition to organizing new information in neural structures resembling maps, each individual gives a unique meaning to information being learned. The individual uses his or her existing cognitive maps to interpret the new information. Cognitive psychologists thus see learning as a *generative process*—that is, the learner generates (constructs) meaning by building relationships between familiar and unfamiliar events. According to the *generative learning model,* when people are exposed to new information or experiences, their perception is affected by their existing knowledge or previous experiences. They then generate meaning about (or interpret) the new information or experiences in ways that are consistent with their prior learning. In other words, they access existing ideas and link new ideas and experiences to them. As a result, their brain structures are modified. These modifications are encoded in memory and can be accessed later to interpret additional new information. Generative learning is thus seen as a constructive process—a process of constantly remodeling and building on existing knowledge.

According to the generative learning model, classroom learning is not so much a matter of engaging in activities and receiving external reinforcement from the teacher or even of receiving knowledge that is transferred from the teacher to the learner. Rather, it is the result of an active process in which the learner plays a critical role in generating meaning. No one else can build relationships between what the learner already knows and what he or she is currently learning. As a result, what each person actually learns is unique to that person.

Latent learning: Learning that occurs in the absence of direct reinforcement and that is not necessarily demonstrated through observable behavior.

Learning to Learn and Cooperative Learning

Most college seniors believe they are much better students than they were when they started college. What makes the difference? How do students learn to learn better? Today, educators and cognitive researchers are focusing on *how* information is learned, as opposed to *what* is learned.

Human beings learn how to learn; they learn specific strategies for particular topics, and they devise general rules that depend on their goals (McKeachie, 1988). The techniques for learning how to fish are different from those for learning a foreign language or those for learning mathematics. McKeachie, Pintrich, and Lin (1985) have argued that lack of effective learning strategies is a major cause of low achievement by university students. They suggest that students can benefit from the use of certain general cognitive techniques:

. . . cooperative interactions among students—not just between students and teachers or between students and books—play a significant role in learning.

- *Elaboration*—translating concepts into one's own language and trying actively to relate new ideas to old ones
- *Attention*—focusing one's concentrative abilities and staying on task
- *Organization*—developing skills that allow one to perform the tasks of learning and concept formation in an orderly manner
- *Scheduling*—developing routine times for studying (this turns out to be a key element of both organization and managing anxiety)
- *Managing anxiety*—learning to focus anxiety on getting a task done, rather than becoming paralyzed with fear
- *Expecting success*—developing an expectation of success rather than failure
- *Note taking*—acquiring the skills necessary to take notes that will be a worthwhile learning tool
- *Learning in groups*—developing cooperative learning styles that make the most of interactions with other students

Making students aware of the processes used in learning and remembering is vitally important. This awareness (thinking about thinking and learning about learning) is called *metacognition.* When students think about their own learning, they do better; when they act strategically to modify their own strategies, they learn more (Wynn-Dancy & Gillam, 1997) and are able to do better across a curriculum (Perkins & Grotzer, 1997). Different subjects require different learning strategies. Students can better grasp history, chemistry, or economics if they understand *how* to go about studying each of these topics. After people learn *how* to learn, the differences become obvious; indeed, some researchers think of creativity as a metacognitive process involving thinking about one's own thoughts (Pesut, 1990).

Individual learning can also be enhanced through techniques that involve cooperative learning. In the past, many American teachers attempted to motivate students by having them compete against one another. However, research shows that cooperative interactions among students—not just between students and teachers or between students and books—play a significant role in learning. Cooperation helps students think about how they learn. There is no question that classroom learning has changed. No longer are students taken to task for helping one another with their work, because they are now expected to collaborate in the learning process—breaking down barriers between learner and teacher. Teachers who overlook student-to-student teaching may be failing their own courses (Kohn, 1992).

In fact, studies show that forming teams of students in which no one gets credit until everyone understands the material is far more effective than competitive or individualized learning. Whether the students are preschoolers or college age, studying English or physics, they have more fun, enjoy the subject matter more, and learn more when they work together (Karabenick & Collins, 1997). Students' achievements and attitudes are both improved through cooperative learning (Leikin & Zaslavsky, 1997; Whicker, Bol, & Nunnery, 1997). Another approach to improving learning skills is described in *Experiencing Psychology.*

The Theory of Observational Learning

A truly comprehensive learning theory of behavior must

EXPERIENCING PSYCHOLOGY

Creating Fluid, Flexible Thinking

If you drive to school or work the same way every day, you probably use shortcuts that you think get you there sooner. People develop shortcuts in a whole array of behaviors, and some researchers (as we will see in Chapter 11) believe that mental shortcuts help account for a limited view of learning. We can learn new routes to work, and new ways to view the world, if we take novel approaches to learning.

Some researchers and practitioners argue that people need to be more flexible in their approach to learning and not be mindless or passive. Ellen Langer has argued that even the classroom basics of reading, writing, and arithmetic need to be taught "mindfully." Langer (1993, 1997) argues that essential information must be placed in a context and used in novel and important ways in order for learners to make the most of it. Mathematics, for example, can be shown to be important in music, logic, and writing. She has taken on the educational community in arguing that students must take an active role in learning to become aware adults. She has identified seven myths that stunt people's intellectual and learning growth and keep them trapped in tight categorical thinking:

- *The basics should become second nature.* She argues that people "overlearn" basic information and skills so much that they don't really think about key ideas.
- *Paying attention means staying focused.* Langer contends that noticing new, diverting ideas and events is important to help a learner place information in multiple contexts.
- *Delaying gratification is important.* Educators often take the fun out of learning by saying students should learn now and have fun later. Rather, according to Langer, learning is fun, and it should be encouraged as fun.
- *Rote memorization is necessary.* Memorized material is often not retained. When students critically analyze and think about information—rather than merely memorizing—they learn it better and remember it.
- *Forgetting is a problem.* Sometimes forgetting information can free you to learn new, more important, or more relevant information. Drive the same route every day, so to speak, and you won't consider other alternatives.
- *Intelligence is knowing skills and information.* Intelligence, for Langer, is thinking flexibly and looking at the world from many perspectives.
- *There are right and wrong answers.* From Langer's view, what is correct is context-dependent. Is there a correct way to drive to school? It depends on what your goals are—getting there quickly, a scenic drive, the fewest turns? Is capitalism the correct way to run an economic system? If you are a Westerner, you will view capitalism differently than if you live in a more socialist country.

The truth is that people do need to learn the basics and to memorize some key pieces of information, but how they learn and what they do with the basics is what Ellen Langer is concerned about. Langer would say, for example, that everyone needs to know how to read, but students need to think about what they are reading. Teachers can help children develop thinking skills by asking them questions such as "Was this a good ending?" and "Do you think that if Hamlet had been a princess, rather than a prince, the story would have unfolded differently? Why?"

Langer worries that people may become trapped by categories and distinctions that are context-dependent and become oblivious to alternative aspects of the situations they encounter (Langer, 1992). Researchers and educators are reviewing Langer's ideas. Let's hope they'll be flexible enough to consider them. ■

be able to explain how people learn behaviors that are not taught through reinforcement. For example, everyone knows that smoking cigarettes is unhealthy. Smokers regularly try to stop smoking, and most people find the first experience with smoking unpleasant. Nonetheless, 12-year-olds light up anyway. They inhale, cough for several minutes, and feel nauseated. There is no doubt that it is a punishing experience for them, but they try again. Over time, they master the technique of inhaling and, in their view, look "cool" smoking a cigarette. That's the key to the whole situation: The 12-year-olds observe other people with cigarettes, think they look cool, want to look cool themselves, and therefore imitate the smoking behavior.

Such situations present a problem for traditional learning theorists, whose theories give a central role to the concept of reinforcement. There is little reinforcement in establishing smoking behavior; instead, there is punishment (coughing and nausea). Nonetheless, the behavior recurs. To explain this type of learning, Stanford University psychologist Albert Bandura has contended that the principles of classical and operant conditioning are only two of the many ways in which people learn.

During the past 30 years, Bandura's ideas, known as observational learning theory, or *social learning theory*, have expanded the range of behaviors that can be explained by learning theory (Woodward, 1982). **Observational learning theory** suggests that organisms learn new responses by observing the behavior of a model and then imitating it. This theory focuses on the role of thought in establishing and maintaining behavior. Bandura and his colleagues conducted important research to confirm their idea that people can learn by observing and then imitating the behavior of others (Bandura, 1969, 1977b; Bandura, Ross, & Ross, 1963). In their early studies, these researchers showed a group of children some films with aggressive content (an adult punched an inflated doll); they showed another group of children some films that had no aggressive content. They then compared the play behavior of both groups. The researchers found that the children who had viewed the aggressive films tended to be aggressive afterward, whereas the other children showed no change in behavior (Bandura, Ross, & Ross, 1963b; Bandura & Walters, 1963). Bandura's research and many subsequent research studies have shown that observing aggression creates aggression in children, although children do not imitate aggressiveness when they also see the aggressive model being punished.

> *. . . many . . . research studies have shown that observing aggression creates aggression in children. . . .*

Everyday experience also shows that people imitate the behavior of others, especially those whom they hold in high esteem. Parents regularly say to children "Now watch me . . ." or "Yes, that's the right way to do it." They provide a seemingly endless string of situations for children to watch and copy, and then reinforce the children for imitation (Masia & Chase, 1997). Children emulate soldiers dressed in army fatigues, carry toy machine guns, and pretend to launch missiles. Countless young girls became interested in gymnastics or ice skating after watching Olympic stars Shannon Miller and Tara Lapinski. Unfortunately, not all observational learning is positive. Alcohol and other drug use often begins when children and teenagers imitate people they admire.

Laboratory studies of observational learning show that people can learn new behaviors merely by observing them, without being reinforced. For example, in a study by Bernal and Berger (1976), participants watched a film of other participants being conditioned to produce an eye-blink response. The filmed participants had a puff of air delivered to their eyes; this stimulus was paired with a tone. After a number of trials, the filmed participants showed an eye blink response to the tone alone. The participants who watched the film also developed an eye blink in response to a tone. Other studies show that people who stutter can decrease their stuttering by watching others decrease their stuttering (Martin & Haroldson, 1977). Even children who fear animals can learn to be less fearful by watching other children interact with animals (Bandura & Menlove, 1968). Animals, too, learn by observing. John and colleagues (1968) found that cats can learn to avoid receiving a shock through a grid floor by watching other cats successfully avoid the shocks by performing a task.

A key point to remember is that if a person observes an action that is punished, the person will not imitate that action—at least not right away. Children who observe aggression that is punished do not immediately behave aggressively; nevertheless, they may learn aggressive responses and evince them in the future. Learning may take place through observation, but performance of specific learned behaviors may depend on a specific setting and a person's expectations about the effect of exhibiting the learned behaviors.

Key Variables in Observational Learning

Whether a person learns a behavior depends on the extent to which he or she actually does it—a child who directly experiences smoking, for example, is far more likely to remember and copy the behavior than a child who merely hears about it or watches a film showing it. Direct experience will always be a far more potent way for a person to remember and learn (Murachver et al., 1996). In real-world learning situations—classrooms, playgrounds, and homes—children and adults learn best when they are engaged in doing and observing. They are reinforced in some cases, observe

Observational learning theory: Theory that suggests that organisms learn new responses by observing the behavior of a model and then imitating it; also known as *social learning theory.*

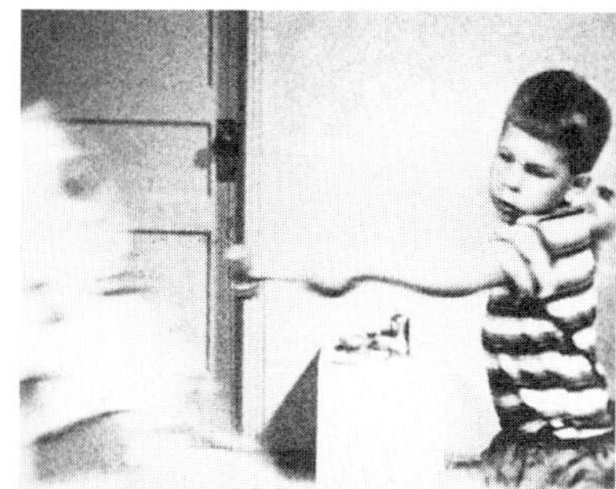

and imitate in other cases, and sometimes change the way they are learning in midstream. Greeno (1998) maintains that all learning is active, takes place within a context, constantly changes, and depends on the active participation (whether undertaken consciously or unconsciously) of the learner.

Given that people can learn in many ways, psychologists know that the effectiveness and likelihood of learning are affected by certain key elements. One is the *type and power of the model* employed. Nurturing, warm, and caring models, for example, are more likely to engage and be imitated than indifferent, angry ones; authoritative parents are more likely to be imitated than passive ones. In a classroom, children are more likely to participate with and imitate peers whom they see as powerful and dominant.

Another element is the *learner's personality and degree of independence.* Dependent children are more likely to learn from and imitate models than are independent children. Generally, the less self-confidence a person has, the more likely the person is to imitate a model.

A third factor is the *situation.* People are more likely to imitate others when they are uncertain about correct behavior. A teenager going on a first date, for example, takes cues about dress from peers and imitates their behavior. A person who has never before been exposed to death and watches a family member or close friend die may not know what to say or how to express feelings. Watching other people express their grief provides a model for behavior. But not everyone learns well, and there are sharp differences in how people learn. (I)

Think Critically

- What might be a way for a college to facilitate learning in a history class or a biology laboratory?

www.abacon.com/leftononline

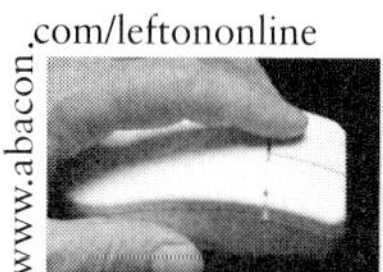

Your password-protected Website allows you access to the most comprehensive set of materials in The Psychology Place.

(I) Summary and Review

Pavlovian, or Classical, Conditioning Theory

Identify the fundamental difference between learning and reflexes.

Describe how classical conditioning works.

KEY TERMS

learning, p. 118; conditioning, p. 119; reflex, p. 119; classical conditioning, p. 119; unconditioned stimulus, p. 119; unconditioned response, p. 119; conditioned stimulus, p. 120; conditioned response, p. 120; higher-order conditioning, p. 121

Key Variables in Classical Conditioning

What are the most important variables in classical conditioning?

How may conditioned responses vary depending on the situation?

What are the key findings in studies of conditioned taste aversion?

KEY TERMS

extinction, p. 123; spontaneous recovery, p. 123; stimulus generalization, p. 123; stimulus discrimination, p. 123

Operant Conditioning

What takes place in operant conditioning?

How do reinforcement and punishment work?

KEY TERMS
operant conditioning, p. 126; Skinner box, p. 127; shaping, p. 127; reinforcer, p. 128; positive reinforcement, p. 128; negative reinforcement, p. 128; primary reinforcer, p. 129; secondary reinforcer, p. 129; superstitious behavior, p. 130; punishment, p. 130; primary punisher, p. 130; secondary punisher, p. 130; learned helplessness, p. 131

Key Variables in Operant Conditioning

What are the most important variables affecting operant conditioning?

Distinguish between extrinsic and intrinsic motivation.

KEY TERMS
fixed-interval schedule, p. 132; variable-interval schedule, p. 132; fixed-ratio schedule, p. 133; variable-ratio schedule, p. 133; extinction, p. 134

Cognitive Learning

What is the focus of cognitive learning psychologists?

What fundamental assumptions do observational learning theorists make about the learning process?

KEY TERMS
latent learning, p. 139; observational learning theory, p. 142

Self-Test

1. In classical conditioning, the stimulus that is neutral prior to conditioning is referred to as the:
   A. unconditioned stimulus
   B. unconditioned response
   C. conditioned stimulus
   D. conditioned response
2. Pavlov's dogs were trained to salivate in response to a bell. After the bell was repeatedly paired with a light, the dogs began to salivate in response to the light. This is an example of:
   A. extinction
   B. higher-order conditioning
   C. stimulus generalization
   D. acquisition process
3. Classical conditioning occurs more easily if:
   A. the unconditioned stimulus is strong
   B. there is a long delay between the presentation of the unconditioned stimulus and the neutral stimulus
   C. the unconditioned stimulus and the neutral stimulus are rarely paired together
   D. the neutral stimulus cannot be predicted by the unconditioned stimulus
4. When the conditioned stimulus is repeatedly presented without the unconditioned stimulus, in order to reduce the probability of the conditioned response occurring, ____________ will occur.
   A. spontaneous recovery
   B. operant conditioning
   C. extinction
   D. stimulus discrimination
5. The Richardsons are trying to get their son to study more. They give him money for every test at school on which he does well. This is an example of:
   A. positive reinforcement
   B. negative reinforcement
   C. positive punishment
   D. negative punishment
6. Punishment and negative reinforcement are:
   A. different terms for the same concept
   B. different in terms of their effect on behavior
   C. the same because both reduce behaviors
   D. the same because both increase emotions
7. Which is an example of a secondary reinforcer?
   A. food
   B. praise
   C. termination of pain
   D. spanking
8. A rat is being trained to press a lever. The rat is given a food pellet after pressing the lever five times. The rat is on a ____________ schedule of reinforcement.
   A. fixed-interval
   B. variable-interval
   C. fixed-ratio
   D. variable-ratio
9. Research on schedules of reinforcement suggests that when reinforcement is linked to ____________ people work harder to achieve.

A. interval
B. time
C. output
D. frequency

10. An organism's conditioned response has undergone extinction. When that organism is given a rest period and then retested, it demonstrates the conditioned response again. This is called:
A. spontaneous recovery
B. stimulus generalizability
C. renewed response
D. stimulus discrimination

11. A fitness program that requires the participants to chart their own nutrition, exercise, and aerobic activity is using the principles of:
A. self-stimulation
B. negative reinforcement
C. observational learning
D. behavioral self-regulation

12. Learning that occurs in the absence of direct reinforcement and is not necessarily demonstrated through observable behavior is called:
A. generative learning
B. insight
C. cooperative learning
D. latent learning

13. Which is not an element of observational learning?
A. the power of the model
B. the independence of the learner
C. the personality of the learner
D. the appearance of the learner

14. Research on learning styles suggests that:
A. more differences exist among men and among women
B. more differences exist between men and women
C. fewer differences exist among men and among women
D. fewer differences exist between men and women

15. The model that suggests that learning occurs as a result of the learner generating meaning between past experiences and the present is called:
A. latent learning
B. generative learning
C. insight
D. cooperative learning

Chapter 6

Memory and Cognition

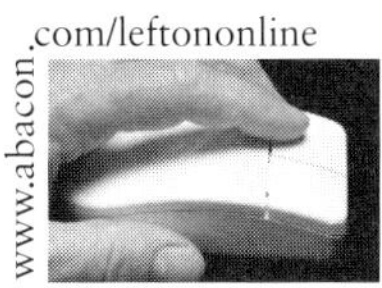

Go to your password-protected Website for full-color art, Weblinks, and more!

Most of us have a variety of personal identification numbers and other passwords that we use all the time. I have more than a half-dozen: There's the password to my office computer, my mainframe login account number, my email password, my bank PIN, the code to my home alarm system, the default code to my car alarm, my Social Security number, and my bank account number. There are still others that I use less frequently. I sometimes wonder why I can't have *one* universal number for everything.

I found myself wishing very hard for that universal number when I stood before my bank's ATM recently and my mind went blank as I tried to remember my PIN. I shook my head and recited the account number, my email password, and my Social Security number. I tried to jog my memory but failed. I really needed some cash, so I resorted to calling home (at least I remembered my phone number!) and asking my wife what the PIN was.

Everyone experiences memory failure from time to time. Most of the time, these lapses don't fall at critical moments, and we can make up for them by looking up a fact, asking a friend, or simply moving on to some other task. Often, later, we somehow remember what we'd forgotten earlier—though we may no longer need it. ■

Psychologists have long recognized that recalling well-learned facts can sometimes be difficult. Even though something has been *learned,* it may not always be *remembered.* You may be able to recite the Pledge of Allegiance, for example, but forget the name of someone you were introduced to last weekend by a friend. Chapter 5 pointed out that learning is a *relatively* permanent change in an organism that occurs as a result of experience and is often, but not always, seen in overt behavior. **Memory** is the ability to recall past events, images, ideas, or previously learned information or skills; memory is also the storage system that allows a person to retain and retrieve previously learned information. You may learn something, but it will do you little good without your memory—your ability to reconstruct the past. And memory is just the beginning—intricately involved with your memory is your ability to think about ideas and events. This study of thinking is the study of cognition. We will first consider memory and then cognition. *I*

Memory: The ability to recall past events, images, ideas, or previously learned information or skills; the storage system that allows for retention and retrieval of previously learned information.

I Memory: The Brain as Information Processor

Focus on issues and ideas

- The components of memory and how the brain processes information

Memory is not some physical structure found in one corner of the brain, with some people having more and others having less of it. Rather, memory is an ability and a process, and it can be examined from many different perspectives. Traditionally, psychologists have examined memory solely from a psychological/behavioral perspective, focusing on issues such as what people remember and what affects memory. Early memory studies, at the turn of the century, focused on how quickly people learned lists of nonsense words and how long they remembered them or how quickly they forgot them. Physiological psychologists thought of the brain as a huge map with certain areas that code vision, others that code auditory events, and still others that code and store memories. Their research goal was to discover the spatial layout and associated functions of the brain. Later studies, after World War II, became more practical, focusing on variables such as how the organization of material might affect retention. Today, research is focusing on how people code information and use memory aids, imagery, and other learning cues to retrieve information from memory. Researchers are also examining the neuroscience of memory and asking what variables determine what is remembered and what is forgotten. Under what conditions is memory enhanced? When are people most likely to forget?

In this age of computers and information technology, it is not surprising that researchers have likened the brain to a computer—an information processor. This analogy has guided the study of memory since the 1960s and 1970s, when researchers began to recognize the brain's complex interconnections and information-processing abilities. The truth, of course, is that human brains are not computers; nor do they work exactly as computers do. They make mistakes, and they are influenced by biological, environmental, and interpersonal events. Nevertheless, enough similarities exist between human brains and computers for psychologists to discuss learning and memory in terms of information processing.

Psychologists use the term *information processing* to refer to organizing, interpreting, and responding to information coming from the environment. The information-processing approach typically describes and analyzes a sequence of stages for key memory processes. This approach assumes that the stages and processes are separate, though related, and can be analyzed by scientific methods. Although psychologists once considered memory a step-by-step, linear process, they now recognize that many of these steps take place simultaneously, in parallel.

Virtually every approach to understanding memory that has been offered by researchers has proposed that memory involves three key processes. The names of these processes derive from information technology and will sound familiar to you if you know how computers work. The first process is *encoding;* the second is placement of information in some type of *storage,* either temporary or permanent; the third is making the information available through *retrieval.* We will use this three-process model to guide our exploration of memory. You will see that memory involves all three of these processes. (I)

(I) Encoding

Focus on issues and ideas

- Similarities between computer information processing and human memory models
- The process of encoding according to the level of processing theory

Last year, I had the opportunity to attend an informative conference held at a hotel in Germany. Luckily for me, since I don't speak German, the proceedings were conducted mostly in English, the menus were in English, and the hotel staff was multilingual. When you go to a foreign country, however, it is much better if you know the language. You have to be able to understand what you hear and read and respond in a meaningful way; this requires encoding.

The conversion of a sensory experience into electrochemical energy—coding—is the first step of encoding and establishing a memory. *Encoding* means getting information into the system to be processed, converting it into a usable form. In the language of memory, **encoding** is the organizing of sensory information so that the nervous system can process it, much as a computer programmer devises code that a computer can understand. The sensory information can be of any type: visual, auditory, olfactory, and so on.

Sometimes, encoding is automatic; at other times, it requires effort and concentration. We encode various kinds of information in a range of ways and to different extents. You will see that what we encode and how well we encode it determine what we remember.

Levels of Processing

Does the human brain encode and process some information at a deeper, more complex level than it does other information? Do thinking processes depend on the depth of analysis? Researchers Fergus Craik and Robert Lockhart (1972) argued that the brain can encode and process stimuli (information) in different ways, to different extents, and at different levels. They called their theory a **levels-of-processing approach.** For example, a person presented with a poster urging her to "Cast your vote for Smith, the candidate of distinction" will analyze what she sees on several levels, in several ways. The lines and shapes of the poster (letters, artwork, and the like) will be encoded at one level; the words will be encoded for basic meaning and categorized at another level; and the meaning of the poster will be encoded, analyzed, and stored at still another, deeper level. According to this view, how information is processed determines how it will be stored for later retrieval.

Cognitive psychologists began to equate the level of processing with the depth of analysis involved. When the level of processing becomes more complex, they theorized, the code goes deeper into memory. Thus, the memory for the lines and shapes of the poster may be fleeting and short-lived, the memory for the words themselves may last longer, and the memory for the meaning conveyed by the words may last the longest.

Encoding is not a discrete step that happens all at once, before memory stores information. Rather, some levels of encoding happen quickly and easily, whereas other levels take longer and are more complex. You may continue to encode information while previously encoded information is being stored. According to Craik and Lockhart, encoding of various memory levels involves different operations, and various kinds of information are stored in different ways and for different durations.

The levels-of-processing approach generated an enormous amount of research. It explained why you retain some information, such as your family history, for long periods, whereas you quickly forget other information, such as the dry cleaner's phone number. It showed that when people are asked to encode information in only one way, they do not encode it in other ways. For example, when people are asked to encode words not for meaning, but only so that they can quickly repeat them (say, to remember a list of items to buy at the supermarket), they can later recall very few of them.

However, some researchers did not fully accept the levels-of-processing approach, which dealt primarily with establishing memories. These researchers suggested refinements based on their work on how memories are elaborated on or made distinctive and how recall takes place. For example, the link between encoding and the later process of retrieval is explained by the **encoding specificity principle**, which asserts that the effectiveness of a specific retrieval cue depends on how well it matches up with the originally encoded information. The more sharply your retrieval cues are defined and the more closely they are paired with memory stores, the better your recall will be and the less likely you will be to experience retrieval failures. If you learn word processing on a Macintosh, writing a term paper on an IBM or Unix system may be more difficult. To facilitate your access to information stored in memory, you should match the retrieval situation to the original learning situation as much as possible.

Derived from the encoding specificity principle is the idea of **transfer-appropriate processing**, which occurs when the initial processing of information is similar to the process of retrieval. When there is a close relationship between encoding and retrieval in terms of the modality of the information (whether it is visual, auditory, or in some other form) and the processing required, retrieval is enhanced. Researchers have given participants instructions to encode words either for sound or for meaning; if a participant codes for sound but is then asked to recall the meaning, recall is far less extensive than if retrieval task and coding task are equivalent (McDermott & Roediger, 1996; Morris, Bransford, & Franks, 1977; Mulligan, 1996; Srinivas, 1996). Such studies suggest that when you study for a test you should study the same way you will be tested: If a test will be in essay format, study by writing essays; if a test will consist of geometry problem sets, study by doing problem sets.

The landmark levels-of-processing research and its subsequent refinements and extensions shape the way cognitive researchers think about memory. These researchers argue that the way information is encoded may determine how it is stored, processed, and later recalled. They are aware that encoding processes are flexible; they are affected by both the cues provided and the retrieval tasks at hand. The processes of encoding are also affected by preconceived biases people have; humans tend to notice and encode information that confirms beliefs they already hold—a tendency called *confirmation bias* (Silverman, 1992).

Neuroscience and Parallel Distributed Processing

Memories are retained in electrochemical form in the brain. Researchers are exploring the neurobiological bases of memory: How does the brain store memories? Where are memories stored? Are memory traces localized or distributed? Neuroscience researchers are having some success using positron emission tomography (PET) techniques (described in Chapter 2) to explore the location, extent, and timing of processing in the brain as it occurs. We will explore the neuroscience approach to memory in more detail later in this chapter.

It should come as no surprise that many researchers believe that the connections within the human brain are so sophisticated and numerous that any simple multistep model of memory is inadequate. The concept of **parallel distributed processing (PDP)** is an alternative to the levels-of-processing approach that

Encoding: The organizing of information so that the nervous system can process it.

Levels-of-processing approach: Theory of memory that suggests that the brain processes and encodes stimuli (information) in different ways, to different extents, and at different levels.

Encoding specificity principle: Notion that the effectiveness of a specific retrieval cue depends on how well it matches up with the originally encoded information.

Transfer-appropriate processing: Initial processing of information that is similar in modality or type to the processing necessary in the retrieval task.

Parallel distributed processing (PDP): Conception of the brain as being organized in neural networks, with many operations taking place simultaneously and at many locations.

developed from the notion that the brain is organized in neural networks. The PDP concept suggests that many operations take place simultaneously and at many locations within the brain. This idea is appealing because it is analogous to the way in which information processing occurs in the modern world. At telephone companies, thousands of calls arrive at switching stations simultaneously. Mainframe computers deal simultaneously with jobs from hundreds of users. The PDP model asserts that humans, too, can process and store many stimuli simultaneously.

The PDP concept is a model not only of memory but also of perception and learning. Focusing on the biological bases of memory, the PDP model is difficult to characterize in traditional terms and hard to test experimentally. Thus, it has not achieved as wide an acceptance as the information-processing approach. Nevertheless, in various forms, it has influenced the way psychologists think about memory.

As we continue to examine the process and structures of memory, try thinking of information stored in the brain as being like books in a library. Many kinds of books can be found in a library—hardbacks, paperbacks, books on tape, books on CDs, and on-line books. Books can be checked out and new ones added in parallel—many at a time. Similarly, some books deteriorate with age and are discarded; others may be misplaced and thus difficult to locate. Books that you use frequently are the easiest to find—you know exactly where to look for them. Sometimes librarians reorganize the books, storing them differently. We'll return to this library analogy later. (I)

Think Critically

- What do you think researchers who focus on parallel distributed processing see as the weakest aspect of the information-processing approach?

(I) Storage

Focus on issues and ideas

- Distinguish the functions of the three-stage storage system consisting of sensory memory, short-term working memory, and long-term memory
- The active role of short-term working memory
- How Hebb's consolidation process helps to explain both memory and learning

When my daughter Jesse went off to study abroad for a year, she stored almost everything she owned at our home. She stacked box after box in the basement and labeled each one with a number. She also drew up a master list that she posted on the door to the basement. I was informed that she would also keep a copy of the master list, and that I would easily be able to locate books, tapes, or clothes if she needed anything. Because of her organizational efforts, neither of us had to keep track of what she had brought home or in which box or trunk it was stored. Jesse had developed an elaborate storage system.

In many important ways, memory uses such a storage system. **Storage** is the process of maintaining or keeping information readily available; it also refers to the locations where information is held, which researchers call *memory stores*. The duration of storage may be for a few seconds or many years. When people think about memory, they often think solely of storage; they may not consider encoding data into memory, which we've just discussed, or retrieving data from storage, which we'll consider soon.

Researchers have conceptualized a three-stage storage system: sensory memory, short-term working memory, and long-term memory. *Sensory memory* is the mechanism by which sensory information is initially encoded and briefly stored in the brain. When you hear a rock song or touch a piece of silk, the sensory memory process starts entering, coding, and storing the auditory or tactile information temporarily. After the information is stored for a very short time, it is acted on for a longer period in *short-term working memory,* just the way a computer keeps your work in temporary random access memory. If the electricity goes off before you save your work, you lose it. Similarly, if you look up a word in a dictionary, for example, but do not process it adequately, you quickly lose its meaning. The storage mechanism of short-term working memory is fragile; repetition, further encoding, and transfer of information to a final storage place are required. In a computer, information is stored for longer periods of time on the hard disk or on a floppy disk. In the brain, information is stored in *long-term memory,* from which a person can recall, retrieve, and reconstruct previous experiences.

Sensory Memory

As George Sperling demonstrated in the early 1960s, **sensory memory,** sometimes called the *sensory register,* is the storage mechanism that performs initial encoding and provides brief storage of sensory stimuli. The brief image of a stimulus appears the way lightning does on a dark evening: The lightning flashes, and you retain a brief visual image of it. In his experiments, Sperling (1960) briefly presented research participants with a visual display consisting of three rows of letters. He asked the participants to recite from memory the letters in one of the three rows and cued them as to which row to recite by following the visual display with a tone that varied in pitch. Sperling found that participants were able to recall three out of four letters after just a 50-millisecond presentation; as he delayed the cue further, recall decreased. From Sperling's studies and others that followed, researchers concluded that a brief (250 milliseconds, or 0.25 second), rapidly decaying sensory memory exists. (*Decay* refers to loss of information from memory as a result of disuse and the passage of time.) Although some researchers have challenged the existence and physiological basis of sensory memory (Sakitt & Long, 1979), most researchers still see it as the first stage of encoding.

Sensory memory captures a visual, auditory, tactile, or chemical stimulus (such as an odor) in a form the brain can interpret. Consider the visual system. The initial coding usually contains information in the form of a picture. Sensory memory establishes the visual stimulus in an electrical form and stores it for 0.25 second with little interpretation, in an almost photographic manner. This visual sensory representation is sometimes called an *icon,* and the storage mechanism is called *iconic storage.* For the auditory system, the storage mechanism is called *echoic storage;* it holds an auditory representation for about 3 seconds.

Sensory memory is temporary and extremely fragile. Once information is established there, it must be transferred elsewhere for additional encoding and storage, or it will be lost. For example, when you locate a phone number you need in a rapidly scrolling computer screen display, the number is established in your visual sensory memory (iconic storage); but unless you quickly transfer it to short-term working memory by writing it down, repeating it over and over to yourself, or elaborating on it by associating it with something else in your memory, you will forget it.

Short-Term Working Memory

Once they are captured in sensory memory, stimuli either decay or are transferred to a second stage—short-term working memory. Initially, researchers spoke of "short-term memory," to emphasize its brief duration. After extensive research, however, the nature of short-term memory became clearer, and researchers began to recognize its active nature. The name was expanded to acknowledge this quality.

Early Research on Short-Term Memory. Thousands of research studies have been done on the components and characteristics of storage in short-term memory. Early research focused on its duration, its capacity, and its relationship to rehearsal. Researchers had been studying memory and retrieval for decades, but it was not until 1959 that Lloyd and Margaret Peterson presented experimental evidence for the existence of short-term memory. In a laboratory study, the Petersons asked participants to recall a three-consonant sequence, such as *xbd,* either immediately following its presentation or after a time interval ranging from 1 to 18 seconds. During the interval, the participants were required to count backward by threes; the purpose of this activity was to prevent them from repeating (rehearsing) the consonant sequence; the Petersons wanted to examine recall when rehearsal was not possible. As the interval between presentation and recall increased, accuracy of recall decreased, until it fell nearly to levels that could have been due to chance. The Petersons' experiment, like many others that followed, showed that information contained in short-term memory is available for 20–30 seconds at most. After that, the information must be transferred to long-term memory, or it will be lost.

Researchers agree that a key operation called *rehearsal* is especially important in memory. Rehearsal usually involves more than simply repeating information to keep it from decaying. **Rehearsal** is the process of repeatedly verbalizing, thinking about, or otherwise acting on or transforming information in order to keep that information active in memory. Psychologists distinguish two important types of rehearsal: maintenance and elaborative. **Maintenance rehearsal** is the repetitive review of information with little or no interpretation. This shallow form of rehearsal involves only the physical stimuli, not their underlying meaning. It generally occurs just after initial encoding has taken place—for example, when you repeat a phone number you need to recall. **Elaborative rehearsal** involves repetition plus analysis, in which the stimulus may be associated with (linked to) other information and further processed. When a grocery shopper attempts to remember the things she needs in order to

Storage: Process of maintaining or keeping information readily available; also, the locations where information is held, or the *memory stores.*

Sensory memory: Mechanism that performs initial encoding and brief storage of sensory stimuli; also known as the *sensory register.*

Rehearsal: Process of repeatedly verbalizing, thinking about, or otherwise acting on or transforming information in order to keep that information active in memory.

Maintenance rehearsal: Repetitive review of information with little or no interpretation.

Elaborative rehearsal: Rehearsal involving repetition and analysis, in which a stimulus may be associated with (linked to) other information and further processed.

make dinner, she may organize them in a meaningful mental pattern, such as according to the aisles where they can be found in the supermarket. Elaborative rehearsal, when information is made personally meaningful, is especially important in the encoding processes. This type of rehearsal allows information to be transferred into long-term memory. Maintenance rehearsal alone is usually not sufficient to allow information to be permanently stored. Actively rehearsed items can be maintained in short-term memory almost indefinitely. In general, however, information held in short-term memory is either transferred to long-term memory or lost.

The Emergence of Working Memory. It was in the 1970s and 1980s that researchers first began formally to think about short-term memory as working memory. Alan Baddeley and Graham Hitch (1974, 1994) reconceptualized short-term memory as a more complex *working memory* containing several substructures that operate simultaneously to maintain information while it is being processed. Earlier psychologists often concentrated on single memory tasks, trying to understand the stages of encoding, storage, and retrieval. But the concept of working memory goes beyond individual stages to describe the active integration of both conscious processes (such as repetition) and unconscious processes. The emphasis of this model of memory is on how human memory meets the demands of real-life activities such as listening to the radio, reading, and mentally calculating the sum of 74 plus 782.

Working memory goes beyond individual stages to describe the active integration of both conscious processes (such as repetition) and unconscious processes.

Short-term working memory is the storage mechanism that temporarily holds current or recently attended-to information for immediate or short-term use. In short-term working memory, information is not simply stored, of course; it is further encoded and then maintained for about 20–30 seconds while active processing takes place. A person may decide that a specific piece of information is important; if it is complicated or lengthy, the person will need to actively rehearse it. As we saw earlier, *rehearsal* is the process of repeatedly verbalizing, thinking about, or otherwise acting on or transforming information in order to keep it in memory.

The addition of new information may also *interfere* with the recall of other information in short-term memory. Baddeley and Hitch (1974) demonstrated the limited capabilities of several components, or subsystems, of working memory by having participants recall digits while doing some other type of reasoning task. If one subsystem is given a demanding task, the performance of the others will suffer. One subsystem in working memory encodes, rehearses, and holds auditory information such as a person's name or phone number. Another subsystem is a visual–spatial scratch pad or blackboard, which stores visual and spatial information, such as the appearance and location of objects, for a brief time and then is erased to allow new information to be stored. A third subsystem is a central processing mechanism, like an executive, that balances the information flow and allows people to solve problems and make decisions. This executive controls the processing flow and adjusts it when necessary. Research shows that the type of information being processed by short-term memory—for example, textual information versus textual information with pictures—affects the accuracy of the processing (Kruley, Sciama, & Glenberg, 1994).

Long-Term Memory

Information about names, faces, dates, places, smells, and events is stored in relatively permanent form in **long-term memory.** The duration of information in long-term memory is indefinite; much of it lasts a lifetime. The capacity of long-term memory is seemingly infinite; the more information a person acquires, the easier it is to acquire more information. Using the library analogy again, we can say that long-term memory includes all the books in the library's collection. And, as in a library, information can be lost ("misshelved") or unavailable for some other reason. In fact, the information in the human brain is far more fragile than the books in a library.

The information that is typically encoded and stored in long-term memory is either important (a parent's or spouse's birthday, for example) or used frequently (your telephone number). Getting information into long-term memory often involves rehearsal, but a vivid event or experience can be immediately etched into long-term memory (Schmidt, 1991).

A wide variety of information is stored in long-term memory—for example, the words to "The Star Spangled Banner," the meaning of the word *sanguine,* and how to operate a CD player. Different types of information seem to be stored and called on in different ways. On this basis, psychologists divide long-term memory into two types: procedural and declarative.

Procedural memory is memory for the perceptual, motor, and cognitive skills required to complete complex tasks. Driving a car, roller blading, or cooking a meal involves a series of steps that include perceptual, motor, and cognitive skills—and thus procedural memory. Acquiring such skills is usually time-consuming and difficult at first; but once the skills are learned, they are relatively permanent and automatic. **Declarative memory** is memory for specific facts, such as when Bill Clinton was first elected president (in 1992) or who accompanied Neil Armstrong to the moon (Buzz Aldrin and Michael Collins). Declarative memories are established quickly, but the information is more likely to be forgotten over time than is the information in procedural memory.

The Neuroscience of Coding

Remember, memories are not physical things; rather, they are made up of unique interactions among hundreds and thousands of neurons in the brain. Researchers have sought to understand how these processes take place and where in the brain such coding occurs.

Canadian psychologist Donald Hebb (1904–1985) presented one of the major physiological theories of memory. Hebb (1949) suggested that when groups of neurons are stimulated, they form patterns of neural activity. If a specific group of neurons fires frequently, a regular neural circuit is established. This evolution of a temporary neural circuit into a more permanent one is known as **consolidation.** According to Hebb, consolidation serves as the basis of short-term memory and permits the encoding of information into long-term memory. When key neurons and neurotransmitters are repeatedly stimulated by various events, those events may be better remembered and more easily accessed—this may be part of the reason practiced behaviors are so easily recalled (Kandel & Abel, 1995).

Many psychologists believe that consolidation is the key to understanding both learning and memory—that individual differences in the ability to learn or remember may be due to differing abilities to consolidate neural circuits. Confirmation of this notion comes from studies using electroconvulsive shock therapy (discussed in Chapter 14) to disrupt consolidation; disruption results in impaired memory both in human beings and in animals. Further support comes from studies showing that recent memories are more susceptible to loss due to amnesia than are older memories (Milner, 1989).

If a neuron is stimulated, the biochemical processes involved make it more likely to respond again later; this increase in responsiveness is referred to as *long-term potentiation,* a phenomenon that is especially evident in areas of the brain such as the hippocampus (which, as you will see in a moment, is important in working memory). In addition, clear evidence exists that specific protein synthesis occurs just after learning and that long-term memory depends on this synthesis (Kandel & Abel, 1995; Matthies, 1989). Psychologists now generally accept the idea that the structure of synapses changes after learning, and especially after repeated learning experiences. As Hebb said, "Some memories are both instantaneously established and permanent. To account for the permanence, some structural change seems necessary" (1949, p. 62).

Consolidation theory has been refined, extended, and supported by research. For example, researchers know that a single neuron has many synaptic sites on its dendrites. Alkon (1989) has shown that there is extensive interaction among the sites on a single neuron and between its sites and the sites of other neurons. He argues that the spread of electrical and chemical activity from one site to another—without activity or

Short-term working memory: Storage mechanism that temporarily holds current or recently attended-to information for immediate or short-term use and that is composed of several subsystems: a component to encode and rehearse auditory information, a visual–spatial "scratch pad," and a central processing mechanism, or executive, that balances and controls information flow.

Long-term memory: Storage mechanism that keeps a relatively permanent record of information.

Procedural memory: Memory for the perceptual, motor, and cognitive skills required to complete complex tasks.

Declarative memory: Memory for specific facts.

Consolidation [kon-SOL-ih-DAY-shun]: Evolution of a temporary neural circuit into a more permanent circuit.

firing of the neurons—seems to be critical for initiating memory storage. He asserts that a given neuron can receive and store a huge number of different incoming signals.

Think Critically

- Explain how consolidation plays a role in the development of the brains of animals, and discuss the implications of this process for human beings.
- Do you think it makes evolutionary or adaptive sense to have memory representations all over the brain? Or would it be better if memory were located in a specific place? Explain your reasoning.

Retrieval

Focus on issues and ideas

- The key differences between explicit and implicit memories
- Possible causes of retrieval failure
- How memory enhancement techniques can help you study

When I had to find my daughter's tape of Phish's first recording to send to her—the one that had been autographed by drummer Jon Fishman—the task was relatively easy because of her master list itemizing the contents of her stored boxes. Most memory retrieval is fairly easy; we consciously and explicitly try to remember something, and it becomes available more or less effortlessly. But things *can* get in the way of remembering—you realize when you take a test and cannot remember a fact or concept. What makes retrieval possible?

Retrieval is the process by which stored information is recovered from memory. Recalling your Social Security number, remembering the details of a phone call, and listing the names of all of the Seven Dwarfs are retrieval tasks. A person may encode information quickly, develop a well-defined working memory, and enter the information into long-term memory. But once information is coded and stored, the person must be able to retrieve the information and use it in a meaningful way. It turns out that the ability to retrieve information depends on how the information is encoded and stored and what type of information it is. Based on the information content and on the storage and retrieval tasks, psychologists have classified types of memory—episodic and semantic memory and explicit and implicit memory.

Episodic and Semantic Memory. **Episodic memory** is memory of specific events and situations that are usually personally relevant; an episodic memory includes recall of where, when, and how the information was obtained. The information remembered is chronologically dated, or tagged. Examples include what you had for breakfast this morning, the movie you saw last night, and what you did on vacation two summers ago. Studies of memory for events in the past show that people remember them well, especially events involving themselves. Episodic memory is often highly detailed. A person can describe not only when something happened but also where it happened and the circumstances surrounding it.

When researchers have examined the ability to remember real-world events (rather than events created artificially in a laboratory), the results have shown that people have amazingly good memories. These studies are often referred to as *autobiographical memory studies,* because they examine people's memories for their own pasts. People can accurately remember a person, situation, or event years later. Autobiographical memory studies suggest that long-term memory is durable and fairly easy to access if a helpful retrieval cue is available. A defining characteristic of autobiographical memories is their organization by temporal markers (Shum, 1998). The more clearly and sharply defined retrieval and time cues are and the more often the memories have been recalled or reconstructed, the more vivid the memories are and the less likely retrieval failures are (Friedman, 1993). (We will look into this issue later in this chapter when we examine forgetting.)

Semantic memory is memory of ideas, rules, and general concepts about the world. It is based on a set of generalizations about previous events, experiences, and learned knowledge. It is not time-specific; it refers to knowledge that may have been gathered over days or weeks, and it continues to be modified and expanded over a lifetime. Semantic memory develops earlier in childhood than does episodic memory (Tulving, 1993).

Semantic memory seems to be stored at different levels of memory, like sections or floors of a library; so retrieval involves different levels of processing. The immediate sensory cues are interpreted at superficial levels of processing. At deeper levels, the cues are encoded and categorized according to the kind of information they give and their meanings. At still deeper levels, the meanings are analyzed and synthesized. For example, is the following sentence true or false? "In the late 1990s, the federal government was spending $267 billion a year on defense, as much as it ever spent during the Cold War and twice as much as the next biggest spender, Great Britain." To decide on your answer, you need to access several classes of information, including interrelations among dates, countries, and historic events—which may be complex. The time and effort needed to retrieve a semantic memory depend on the number of levels of processing required (Tilley & Warren, 1983) and on the complexity of the information.

Explicit and Implicit Memory. Explicit **memory** is conscious memory that a person is aware of, such as a memory of a word in a list or an event that occurred in the past; generally speaking, most of the memory tasks we have been looking at require explicit recall of information. Explicit memory is a voluntary, active memory store that is relatively easily accessed. When you tap semantic memory, you are accessing explicit memory. In contrast, **implicit memory** is memory a person is not aware of possessing; considered an almost unconscious process, implicit memory is accessed almost automatically and unintentionally.

Researchers use different tasks to examine explicit and implicit memory. Explicit memory is usually studied using recall or recognition tasks. Participants are asked to recall a date, fact, or process. Implicit memory tasks *indirectly* test whether a person has knowledge of a previously experienced event that the individual did not consciously try to remember. Thus, you may remember things that you are supposed to, but you are also likely to recall things you did not deliberately attempt to learn—the color of a book you are studying or the name of the book's publisher, the size of a piece of cake you were served, or perhaps the make of a computer in the office of a professor you have visited. Implicit memory occurs without conscious awareness; it demonstrates that people can learn without intentional effort (Boronat & Logan, 1997), and what they learn explicitly and how they are asked to recall it may affect their implicit memories (Nelson et al., 1998).

The distinction between explicit and implicit memory adds another dimension to researchers' understanding of long-term memory, refining their understanding of its subtleties. This distinction also suggests that processes of attention and learning of which people are not aware may affect memory.

Retrieval Success and Failure: Encoding Specificity

Some contemporary researchers believe that every memory is retained and available but that some memories are less accessible than others. Think of the library analogy: Some of the books in the library cannot be found (perhaps because they are misshelved); retrieval is difficult or impossible. When retrieval of information is blocked, the information is effectively forgotten.

Research on retrieval focuses on how people encode information and on the cues that help them recall it. If you are given a cue for retrieval that relates to some aspect of the originally stored information, retrieval is easier, faster, and more accurate. For example, if I asked you who set up the first psychological laboratory in 1879 in Leipzig, Germany, you might find it fairly easy to recall because you may have associated the date and the place with Wilhelm Wundt's name. But, if I asked you to tell me what subject matter the early researcher named Wundt studied, the task would be much harder because the question contains fewer specific cues to help you recall the information. When a retrieval cue is present, retrieval is easier. This evidence supports the *encoding specificity principle,* which asserts that the effectiveness of a specific retrieval cue depends on how well it matches up with information in the original encoded memory (see p. 148). This principle is also supported by studies of state-dependent learning.

State-Dependent Learning. Psychologists find that information learned while a person is in a particular physiological state is recalled most accurately when the person is again in that physiological state. This phenomenon, known as **state-dependent learning,** is associated with states involving drugs, time of day (Holloway, 1977), mental illness (Weingartner, 1977), and electroconvulsive therapy (discussed in Chapter 14).

Several theories attempt to explain state-dependent learning. A widely accepted explanation focuses

Retrieval: Process by which stored information is recovered from memory.

Episodic [ep-ih-SAH-dick] memory: Memory of a specific event or situation that is usually personally relevant; it includes recall of when, where, and how the information was obtained.

Semantic memory: Memory of ideas, rules, and general concepts about the world.

Explicit memory: Conscious memory that a person is aware of, such as a memory of a word in a list or an event that occurred in the past.

Implicit memory: Memory a person is not aware of possessing; considered an almost unconscious process, implicit memory occurs almost automatically.

State-dependent learning: The tendency to recall information learned while in a particular physiological state most accurately when one is again in that physiological state.

EXPERIENCING PSYCHOLOGY

Practice Makes Perfect

In studying learning, we saw that reinforced behavior tends to recur; it is learned and thus remembered. Clearly, practice is critical to remembering, but there are several other—often loosely related—techniques that can improve memory. Here are some of the most powerful ones; they move from simple strategies to more complex overall approaches. Try using them to help you remember this chapter's concepts.

Rehearse, Rehearse, Rehearse. If you want to remember something, there is no substitute for rehearsal. Maintenance rehearsal, in which you simply repeat information without attaching any meaning to it, will facilitate recognition or rote recall if you do not have to remember the information for very long. However, if you want to remember ideas for a long time, you need to understand them, and this requires the use of elaborative rehearsal. With elaborative rehearsal, you generate meaning as you repeat and think about the material you are learning.

Be an Active Learner. Becoming an active learner means actively participating in the learning process; when you interact with new information, it becomes alive and interesting. By simply pursuing your own thoughts, asking and answering your own questions, and organizing information in ways that make sense to you, you become an active learner. Once you are an active learner, the facts become more than facts—they become meaningful and stay with you.

Generate Personal Meaning. To generate personal meaning out of new material (so that it becomes relevant to your needs), you must find ways to connect yourself, your knowledge, and your life experiences to the material you are studying. Although we all have a natural tendency to do this, knowing that learning and memory are enhanced when you create personal meaning should motivate you to do it intentionally. When you can relate to new information by connecting it to your past, to problems you need to solve, or to events around you, you are much more likely to understand and remember it.

Distribute Practice. When you study, distributing practice and rehearsal over time is important. Distributing practice means studying a particular subject for a relatively short time every day or every other day, instead of trying to cram all your studying into one long session. Using distributed practice to avoid cramming will increase the amount of material you can learn and remember within the same total amount of study time.

Plan on Relearning. Memory studies show that most forgetting occurs right after something has been learned. You will benefit if you review your class notes soon after class or write a summary of an article right after reading it. Studies also show that if you relearn (rehearse) material, you learn it more quickly and forget less of it. Whenever you sit down to study, go back and review what you have already studied before you move forward to learn more.

Take Advantage of the Primacy and Recency Effects. Research concerning the primacy and recency effects shows that you are most likely to remember information from the beginning and the end of a study session or lecture. So instead of forcing yourself to endure a long, drawn-out study session, take a short (5–10 minutes) break after you have studied for 20–30 minutes. Taking breaks will enhance your learning and memory because it will increase the number of times that the primacy and recency effects can work for you.

Focus to Prevent Interference. You can facilitate storage in long-term memory by doing whatever you can to avoid unnecessary interference. For ex-

on how altered or drugged states affect the storage process. According to this view, part of learning involves the encoding of stimuli in specific ways at the time of learning (the encoding specificity principle); to access the stored information, a person must evoke the same context in which the encoding occurred (Schramke & Bauer, 1997). When you study for an examination with music in the background but are tested in quiet conditions, your recall may not be as good. The reasons for retrieval failures are not completely clear, but studies of mood and its impact on memory and of state-dependent learning may hold the key (Eich, 1995; Izquierdo & Medina, 1997). Studying after exercise, when in a good mood, or when well rested is likely to lead to better recall.

Experiencing Psychology suggests how you can use the information presented in this chapter to help improve your own memory.

What Facilitates Recall?

Long-term memory studies have brought forth some interesting findings about retrieval and have generated hundreds of other studies focusing on factors

ample, when you are studying, focus on one course or one learning task at a time. If you are studying for a big test on Shakespeare's plays, stick with Shakespeare until you feel confident you have learned the material.

Use Chunking. Chunking allows you to increase the capacity of working memory. For instance, consider the word *psychoneuroendocrinology.* This long word refers to the subfield of psychology ("psycho . . .ology") that investigates the influence on the nervous system ("neuro") of hormones ("endocrin"). What if you had to learn the spelling and definition of this word so that you could use it on an essay exam? How would you do it, given the limited capacity of your short-term memory? You would be smart to use chunking. To remember the long word, you would break it into small chunks: *psycho-neuro-endocrin-ology.*

Another way to use chunking is to group ideas together in organized ways. For example, one chunk of things to remember might be a list of some factors that increase recall and another chunk might be some factors that contribute to forgetting.

Use Mnemonics. If you relate information that is abstract, difficult, or still unlearned to information that is more meaningful or memorable, the new information will be easier to remember. Using *mnemonics,* or memory aids, allows you to easily remember a series of unfamiliar items by associating them with some organized format or rhyme. For example, as a child you may have learned the notes of the treble-clef musical staff, EGBDF, by using the mnemonic "Every Good Boy Does Fine." If you can relate unfamiliar information that you want to recall to some more easily remembered pattern, the more likely you will be able to remember it.

Use Mediation. *Mediation* is a bridging technique that allows you to link two items to be remembered with a third item (or image) that ties them together and serves as a cue for retrieval. Cermak (1975) gives an example: Suppose you are introduced to a couple named John and Tillie. John reminds you of *bathroom,* which can be associated with the image of *tiles,* a word that is spelled somewhat like Tillie. Therefore, remembering a tiled bathroom helps you remember the names John and Tillie.

Use the von Restorff Effect. If one item in a group of things to be learned stands out because it differs from the other items, it will be easier to learn and remember; this is known as the *von Restorff effect.* You can make use of this effect by deliberately making an idea you want to remember stand out. Do this by using a colored highlighter on your notes, by exaggerating the meaning of the idea you want to remember, by making the idea seem funny or bizarre, or by otherwise emphasizing its distinctiveness somehow as you think about it.

Review in Different Contexts and Modalities. The place where you learned something can act as an important retrieval cue. For example, if you see a familiar face at the gym, you may not be able to identify the person as the receptionist from your dentist's office, because you aren't seeing her in the same place where you first met her. Try to review and rehearse in different settings in order to increase the number of retrieval cues associated with what you want to remember. Also, try learning through more than one sensory modality. For example, if you hear (auditory modality) a lecture, write down (tactile–kinesthetic and visual modalities) what you heard. If you have been developing mnemonics on paper, try saying them out loud. If you have been outlining a chapter, read the key ideas aloud.

Prepare the Environment. Because there is so much to learn and remember, you can facilitate the task if you prepare your environment (Brown, 1989). Limit the number of opportunities for distractions: Study in a quiet place where there are few people; avoid visual clutter in your study area. Limit the number of tasks you are working on during one session so as to focus your attention and thus stay tuned in. Finish whatever tasks you start so that they will not take further attention. Keep a notebook handy to jot down ideas, insights, and potential mnemonics. ■

that can facilitate or inhibit accurate recall. Two of these factors are primacy and recency effects and imagery. You use both every day.

Primacy and Recency Effects. In a typical memory experiment, a participant may be asked to study 30 or 40 words, with a word presented every 2 seconds. A few seconds or minutes later, the person is asked to recall the words so that the researcher can determine whether the information was transferred from short-term to long-term memory. Such experiments typically show an overall recall rate of 20%. However, recall is higher for words at the beginning of a series than for those in the middle, a phenomenon termed the **primacy effect.** This effect occurs because no information related to the task at hand is already stored in short-term memory; at the moment a new task is assigned, a person's attention to new stimuli is at its peak. In addition, words at the beginning of a series get to be rehearsed more often, allowing them to be

Primacy effect: The more accurate recall of items presented at the beginning of a series.

transferred to long-term memory. Thus, the primacy effect is associated with long-term memory processes. However, recall is *even higher* for words at the end of a series—a phenomenon termed the **recency effect.** This effect results because these more recently presented items are still being held in short-term memory, where they can still be actively rehearsed, and are not being subjected to any interference from newer information prior to being encoded into long-term memory. The recency effect is thus thought to be related to short-term memory. A *serial position curve* presents the probability of recall as a function of an item's position in a list (series) of presented items.

Imagery. People use perceptual imagery every day as a long-term memory retrieval aid. **Imagery** is the creation or recreation of a mental picture of a sensory or perceptual experience. People constantly invoke images to recall things they did, said, read, or saw. People's imagery systems can be activated by visual, auditory, or olfactory stimuli or by other images (Tracy & Barker, 1994). Even a lack of sensory stimulation can produce vivid imagery. Imagery helps you answer questions such as these: Which is darker green, a pea or a Christmas tree? Which is bigger, a tennis ball or a baseball? Does the person you met last night have brown eyes or blue?

One technique researchers use to study imagery is to ask participants to imagine objects of various sizes—for example, an animal such as a rabbit next to either an elephant or a fly. In a 1975 study by Stephen Kosslyn of Harvard University, participants reported that when they imagined a fly, plenty of room remained in their mental image for a rabbit. However, when they imagined an elephant, it took up most of the space. One particularly interesting result was that the participants required more time and found it harder to see a rabbit's nose when the rabbit was next to an elephant than when it was next to a fly, because the nose appeared to be extremely small in the first instance.

Although they are mental, not physical, phenomena, images have "edges" like those on a photograph—points beyond which visual information ceases to be represented (Kosslyn, 1987). These and other properties of mental images have been useful in a wide variety of studies designed to measure the nature and speed of thought.

Recency effect: The more accurate recall of items presented at the end of a series.

Imagery: The creation or recreation of a mental picture of a sensory or perceptual experience.

Imagery is an important perceptual memory aid. In fact, a growing body of evidence suggests that it is a means of preserving perceptual information that might otherwise decay. According to Paivio (1971), a person told to remember two words may form an image combining those words. Someone told to remember the words *house* and *hamburger,* for example, might form an image of a house made of hamburgers or of a hamburger on top of a house. When the person is later presented with the word *house,* the word *hamburger* will come to mind. Paivio suggests that words paired in this way become conceptually linked, with the crucial factor being the image.

How images facilitate recall and recognition is not yet fully understood, but one possibility is that an image may add another code to semantic memory. With two codes, semantic and imaginal, a person has two ways to access previously learned information. Some researchers argue that imagery, verbal encoding mechanisms, and semantic memory operate together to encode and to aid in retrieval (Marschark et al., 1987). *I*

Think Critically

- Is procedural memory more explicit or implicit? What about flashbulb memory? Explain.
- Provide three examples of information that you have chunked to facilitate its recall.

I Forgetting: When Memory Fails

Focus on issues and ideas

- How schema development organizes information for retention
- The key causes of forgetting
- The role of the hippocampus in memory and amnesia

Quick! Name your first-grade teacher. Recite your Social Security number. Tell where you went on your last vacation. In general, your memory serves you amazingly well. Nevertheless, at times you may have trouble recalling the name of someone you know, where you read an interesting article, or the phone number of a close friend. And have you ever started taking an exam only to have your mind suddenly go blank? In some ways, forgetting is the opposite of remembering—it's the inability to recall information or reconstruct past events.

Forgetting has many causes, including not rehearsing information well enough, not making good elaborative associations (links), or not using information for a long time. Forgetting also occurs because of interference from newly learned or previously learned information, because the information forgotten was unpleasant, or because of physiological problems. Moreover, forgetting occurs with both short- and long-term memory.

Starting with the pioneering work of Hermann Ebbinghaus and others in the latter part of the 19th century, many psychologists have studied forgetting. Such research has revealed a great deal about memory processes—in particular, those processes that affect learning and the ability to recall what has been learned.

Early Studies

Some of the first experimenters in psychology studied forgetting—and their work has not been forgotten! Some of the memory tasks used in their studies involved paper and pencil, but most merely involved the experimenter, a participant, and some information to be learned. Computers were unheard of, and many current research techniques would not have made sense.

Relearning. Using the technique of *relearning*, Hermann Ebbinghaus (1850–1909) studied how well people retain stored information. Ebbinghaus earnestly believed that the contents of consciousness could be studied by scientific principles. He tried to quantify how quickly participants could learn, relearn, and forget information. Ebbinghaus was the first person to investigate memory scientifically and systematically, which made his technique as important as his findings.

In his early studies, in which he was both researcher and participant, Ebbinghaus assigned himself the task of learning lists of letters in order of presentation. First, he strung together groups of three letters to make nonsense syllables such as *nak, dib, mip,* and *daf*. He recorded how many times he had to present lists of these nonsense syllables to himself before he could remember them perfectly. Ebbinghaus found that when the lists were short, his learning was nearly perfect after one or two trials. When they contained more than seven items, however, he had to present them over and over to achieve accurate recall.

Later, Ebbinghaus did learning experiments with other participants. He had them learn lists of syllables and then, after varying amounts of time, measured how quickly the participants relearned the original list. If participants relearned the list quickly, Ebbinghaus concluded that they still had some memory of it. He called this learning technique the *saving method*, because what was initially learned was not totally forgotten.

Practice. Following Ebbinghaus's lead, from the 1930s through the 1960s, many researchers investigated the best ways for people to learn new material and relearn forgotten skills. In one 1978 study, Baddeley and Longman wanted to learn which of two types of practice resulted in more optimal learning and retention: intensive practice at one time (massed practice) or the same amount of practice divided into several intervals (distributed practice). To answer this question, they taught postal workers to touch-type.

The participants were divided into four groups, each member of which practiced the same number of hours using either distributed practice or massed practice: One group practiced typing 1 hour a day; the second practiced 2 hours a day; the third practiced 1 hour twice a day; the fourth practiced 2 hours twice a day. Given the same total number of hours of practice, did the distribution of those practice hours make a difference? The dependent variable was how well they learned to type—that is, the number of accurate keystrokes per minute. A typing test showed that distributed practice (typing 1 hour a day for several days) was more effective. From this experiment and others, researchers have learned that the effectiveness of distributed practice depends on many variables, including the method, order, and speed of presentation. Distributed practice is especially effective for improving perceptual motor skills, where eye–hand coordination is important.

Presentation of Information. In the 1970s, researchers began to study the best way to present information to ensure that it will be learned and remembered. (This interest paralleled the innovations being carried out at that time in public schools, including open classrooms, the "new math," and cooperative learning.) They found, for example, that if one item in a list differs from the others (say, one plant name in a list with nine animal names), the one different item is learned more easily. This is the phenomenon called the *von Restorff effect*.

Measures of Retention

As a teacher, I hope my students will be able to recall key ideas, reconstruct highlights of my lectures, and be able to visualize important graphs and other images. I hope that students will take facts and concepts and associate them in meaningful, personally relevant ways. But first, they have to be able to access the information. Recall, recognition, reconstruction, and pictorial memory are all measures of *retention.* When a person retains information, presumably he or she has acquired (learned) something that was not there previously, and this retained information can later be accessed. The most widely investigated measures of retention have been recall and recognition. *Recall* is remembering the details of a situation or idea and placing them together in a meaningful framework (usually without any cues or aids). Asking someone to name the spacecraft that exploded with U.S. astronauts aboard is a test of recall. *Recognition* is remembering whether one has seen a stimulus before—whether the stimulus is familiar. Asking someone who has just walked into the room whether he or she ever saw the movie that is on TV at the moment is a test of recognition. *Reconstruction* is the procedure of remembering a sequence of events (for example, a series of events in a person's life) in its original order.

Recall. In recall tasks, participants have to remember previously presented information. (Most kinds of exams require you to recall information.) In experiments, the information usually comprises strings (lists) of digits or letters. A typical study might ask participants to remember 10 nonsense syllables, one of which is presented on a screen every half-second. The participants would then try to repeat the string of 10 syllables at the end of the 5-second presentation period.

Three widely used recall tasks are free recall, serial recall, and paired associate tasks. In *free recall tasks,* participants are to recall items in any order, much as you might recall the items on a grocery list. *Serial recall tasks* are more difficult; the items must be recalled in the order in which they were presented, as you would recall the digits in a telephone number. In *paired associate tasks,* participants are given a cue to help them recall the second item of a pair of items. In the learning phase of a study, the experimenter might pair the words *tree* and *shoe.* In the testing phase, participants would be presented with the word *tree* and would have to respond with the correct answer, *shoe.* People are amazingly good at such tasks.

Recognition. In a multiple-choice test, you are asked to recognize relevant information. Psychologists have found that recognition tasks can help them measure subtle differences in memory ability better than recall tasks can. That's because, although a person may be unable to recall the details of a previously learned fact, he or she may recognize the fact. Asked to name the capital of Maine, you would probably have a better chance of answering correctly if you were given four names to choose from: Columbus, Annapolis, Helena, or Augusta.

Reconstruction. Here's a test of your memory: What did Neil Armstrong say when he first set foot on the moon? Few Americans can recall Armstrong's words exactly, but most can recognize them or reconstruct them approximately. Researchers have shown that people often "construct" memories of past events; the constructions are close approximations but not exact memories. For example, you might reconstruct the gist of Armstrong's words as being something about man's first steps on the moon being important for all mankind. (His exact words were "That's one small step for man, one giant leap for mankind.")

In 1932, English psychologist Sir Frederick Bartlett reported that when college students tried to recall stories they had just read, they changed them in several interesting ways: They shortened and simplified details, a process Bartlett called *leveling;* they focused on or emphasized certain details, a process he called *sharpening;* they altered facts to make the stories fit their own views of the world, a process he called *assimilation.* In other words, the students constructed memories that to some degree distorted the events.

Contemporary explanations of this *reconstructive memory* have centered on the nature of the memory process and on how people develop a **schema**—a conceptual framework that organizes information and allows a person to make sense of the world. Because people cannot remember *all* the details of an event or situation, they keep key facts and lose minor details. Schemas group together key pieces of information. In general, people try to fit an entire memory into some framework that will be available for later recall. For example, my schema for life in the United States during 1969, the year the first U.S. astronauts landed on the moon, might include memories of such events as listening to the Beatles' *Abbey Road* album, going on my honeymoon, and reading about the continuing urban unrest in Watts.

Key Causes of Forgetting

We forget for a myriad of reasons, and information can be lost from both short-term and long-term memory. Two concepts, decay and interference, help explain losses from memory.

Decay of Information. **Decay** is the loss of information from memory as a result of disuse and the passage of time. Decay theory asserts that unimportant events fade from memory, and details become lost, confused, or fuzzy if not called up every once in a while. Another way to look at decay theory is this: Memory exists in the brain in a physiological form known as a *memory trace*. With the passage of time and a lack of active use, the trace disintegrates or fades and is lost. *Diversity* (on p. 162) explores the decline of memory functions with age.

. . . the limited capacity of short-term memory makes it susceptible to interference from, or confusion among, other learned items.

Decay theory was popular for many years but is not widely accepted today. Many early studies did not consider several important variables that affect memory processes, among them the rate and mode of stimulus presentation. Although decay does form a small part of the final explanation of forgetting, it is probably less important than other factors, such as interference.

Interference in Memory. **Interference** is the suppression of one bit of information by another received either earlier or later or the confusion of the two pieces of information. Interference theory suggests that the limited capacity of short-term memory makes it susceptible to interference from, or confusion among, other learned items. That is, when competing information is stored in short-term memory, the crowding that results affects a person's memory for particular items. For example, if someone looks up a telephone number and is then given another number to remember, the effort to remember the second number will probably interfere with the ability to remember the first one. Moreover, interference in memory is more likely to occur when a person is presented with a great deal of new information. (In this text, you are being provided with a great deal of new information. Organizing it into coherent chunks when studying will help you avoid interference in long-term memory.)

Research on interference theory shows that the extent and nature of a person's experiences with a learning task both before and after learning are important. For example, someone given a list of nonsense syllables may recall 75% of the items correctly. However, if the person had earlier been given 20 similar lists to learn, the number of items correctly recalled would be lower; the previous lists would interfere with recall. If the person were subsequently given additional lists to learn, recall would also be lower. Psychologists call these interference effects proactive and retroactive interference (or inhibition). **Proactive interference**, or *proactive inhibition*, is a decrease in accurate recall of information as a result of the effects of previously learned or presented information. **Retroactive interference**, or *retroactive inhibition*, is a decrease in accurate recall as a result of the subsequent presentation of different information. Proactive and retroactive interference help explain failures to recall information in long-term memory.

Interference in Attention. Interference has long been a potent explanatory factor in memory and perception studies. For many years, it was used to explain what is called the *Stroop effect* (Stroop, 1935). The Stroop test is a procedure in which people are presented with the names of colors, printed in ink that is not the color named; for example, the word *red* may be printed in blue ink. Participants are asked to name the color of the ink. Most people find it difficult to attend to the ink color alone (the Stroop effect), because of an apparently automatic tendency to read the word, which produces interference. This explanation has been popular—but attention, rather than interference, is now considered more important in explaining the Stroop effect (MacLeod, 1991).

Schema [SKEEM-uh]: A conceptual framework that organizes information and allows a person to make sense of the world.

Decay: Loss of information from memory as a result of disuse and the passage of time.

Interference: Suppression of one bit of information by another received either earlier or later or the confusion of two pieces of information.

Proactive [pro-AK-tiv] interference: Decrease in accurate recall of information as a result of the effects of previously learned or presented information; also known as *proactive inhibition.*

Retroactive [RET-ro-AK-tiv] interference: Decrease in accurate recall of information as a result of the subsequent presentation of different information; also known as *retroactive inhibition.*

DIVERSITY

Does Memory Have to Decline with Age?

At Thanksgiving last year, my daughters asked me the names of my elementary school teachers. Although I could easily remember my first-, third-, and sixth-grade teachers, the other names were gone. This amazed my daughters because they could recall, in order, every teacher they had ever had. The truth is that such recall can be difficult, and as time passes, perhaps impossible. Daniel Schacter (1996) points out the complexity of naming people and especially of piecing together a story from the past or recalling a college experience: Who was there? When did it happen? Was it when I was a sophomore? What happened first? Was I living in the dorm that semester? There are often so many intervening people and events that recall is difficult.

Do memories inevitably fade away when you get older? Does memory become fuzzy? Disjointed? Here today, gone tomorrow? Like many things psychological, the answer isn't simple. After age 30, there are slight declines in some types of memory skills, such as free recall of lists of syllables. Recall and some other memory abilities show deterioration after age 50, and still more deterioration after age 75. The frontal lobe has been implicated in this deterioration in older adults, at least for some tasks (West, 1996).

But, like many things, all memory tasks are not created equal. Some memory tasks are far more difficult than others. Knowing how to captain a 35-foot sailboat is a different kind of knowledge from knowing the first name of the Kramer character from *Seinfeld.* Further, many memory tasks depend on a speedy response. How do you respond when you're in a left-hand turn lane and the signal turns yellow? When someone says to you, "Quick, name the 38th president," you may know the answer—but not right away. (It was Gerald Ford.) Requiring speedy responses from participants may affect the results of memory research because age-related problems such as atherosclerosis can cause older individuals to respond more slowly, even though they know the answer. Another complicating factor is that memory research is often done with groups of participants of different ages—500 people at age 30, another 500 at age 50, and still a third group of people at age 75. But such research, which does not follow young people as they get older, makes interpretations difficult, because there are many differences among those three groups of people and differing environmental situations affect participants.

When Lars-Goran Nilsson undertook a study that examined the same individuals over a 10-year period, he and his colleagues found that deterioration depends on the question the researcher asks. Older individuals forget the source of information more often than the facts that were learned (Erngrund, Mantyla, & Nilsson, 1996). Nilsson also found that educational level is important. Although there are age-related deficits in semantic memory (memory for ideas, concepts, and rules), higher levels of education forestalled the effects of age on problem solving (Backman & Nilsson, 1996; Diehl, Willis, & Schaie, 1995).

In general, the memories of older adults (especially of the oldest adults) are not as good as those of younger ones. There are things you can do to minimize age-related declines in memory skills. People who make a conscious effort to learn new things as they continue to get older lose less—it is a matter of "use it or lose it!" Also, research shows that if you think you are forgetful, you will be (Erber et al., 1997)—so think positively. Research also shows that active involvement in learning and memory—for example, through elaborative rehearsal—facilitates recall; so, stay involved, be creative, and don't get passive. Older adults do not monitor their day-to-day activities and abilities as well as younger people do, and often, even when given more study time, do not use it as effectively as do younger adults; decline in recall can be offset by better time management techniques (Dunlosky & Connor, 1997). In addition, talking about learning and doing—planning to act—facilitates recall; so, plan for the future. Since it is predicted that there may be as many as 2.5 million Americans over age 100 in the 21st century, research into ways to improve people's memories will continue to be important in that future. ■

Special Types of Forgetfulness

Psychologists have learned that there are special kinds of forgetting that are not so easily explained by mere decay or simple interference. You have probably heard about these kinds of forgetting in the popular press, but psychologists have given them special attention in studies of eyewitness testimony and of motivated forgetting.

Eyewitness Testimony. The police and the courts have generally accepted *eyewitness testimony* as some of the best evidence that can be presented. Eyewitnesses are people who saw the crime, have no

bias or grudge, and are sworn to tell (and recall) the truth. But can the witness to an accident or crime accurately report the facts of the situation to the police or the courts? The answer is yes and no.

If memory is a reconstructive process, as many psychologists contend, then it is not a literal reproduction of the past (Schacter, 1996). In fact, research shows that eyewitnesses often forget; they recall events incorrectly, make mistakes, and sometimes identify the wrong people as being involved in the events (Bekerian & Bowers, 1983; Loftus, 1979). Misidentification of a criminal, even in a lineup, is not uncommon (Navon, 1990), although techniques have been developed to improve the accuracy of lineup identifications (Sporer, 1993; Wells, 1993). And when making such misidentifications, people are often confident in their judgments (Wells, Luus, & Windschitl, 1994). Nevertheless, eyewitnesses of the same event often report seeing different things. Langman and Cockburn (1975) recorded the 1968 eyewitness testimony of people who were present when Sirhan Sirhan assassinated Senator Robert F. Kennedy. Even though many of the eyewitnesses were standing next to each other, they reported seeing different things.

To complicate the matter, the memories of eyewitnesses often become enhanced over time (recall Bartlett's theory of assimilation). Harvard law professor Alan Dershowitz (1986) asserts that the memories of witnesses—particularly those with a stake in the eventual outcome—tend to get more detailed with the passage of time. Dershowitz calls this process *memory enhancement* and argues that it occurs when people fit their hazy memories into a coherent pattern that seems realistic and likely. Ironically, the more detailed a witness is (even about irrelevant details), the more credible that witness is assumed to be, even if the witness is recalling things inaccurately (Bell & Loftus, 1989).

Repeated interrogation of a witness can modify the witness's memory—enhancing the recall of some details and even inducing the person to forget other details—even when no misinformation is contained in the questioning (Shaw, Bjork, & Handal, 1995). Whether this occurs because the witness's memory is weakened, clouded, or confused or because retrieval processes are impaired is still not clear. It is also the case that when a person feels that another eyewitness has corroborated an identification, his or her confidence increases. However, a witness's confidence is not necessarily related to the accuracy of his or her identification (Sporer et al., 1995); when another witness identifies someone else, that confidence quickly decreases (Luus & Wells, 1994).

Motivated Forgetting: Memory and Childhood Abuse. Freud (1933) was the first to suggest formally the idea of *motivated forgetting*—that unwanted or unpleasant events might be forgotten simply because people want to forget them. He stated that such memory loss occurs through repression—the burying of unpleasant ideas in the unconscious, where they remain inaccessible. Most researchers agree that motivated forgetting probably is a real phenomenon. But they have found it hard to measure and difficult to demonstrate experimentally, even though anecdotal clinical evidence abounds.

For nearly two decades, Elizabeth Loftus (1991, 1993, 1997) has been asking if recall of previously forgotten, traumatic events—for example, being sexually abused as a child—is due to memory enhancement, overinflation of facts, or the planting of such memories. She has extrapolated her laboratory findings to real-life situations involving old memories—and has caused a furor by viewing with skepticism professionals who treat victims of sexual abuse. These professionals assert that their clients' memories, often from many years before, are accurate and truthful. The research is inconclusive: Children and adults can be led to enhance their memories (Lindsay, 1993); false memories can be implanted (Loftus, 1997; Pezdek, Finger, & Hodge, 1997; Seamon, Luo, & Gallo, 1998); such memories can remain well preserved over time (Brainerd, Reyna, & Brandse, 1995) and are reported with confidence (Zaragoza & Mitchell, 1996). Ceci and Bruck (1993) hold that adults and even very young children are capable of accurately recalling events that occurred early in their lives; however, how far back people can recall events is debated, because most people have few recollections before age 6 and even fewer before age 3 (Eacott & Crawley, 1998).

The debate over motivated forgetting has become intense and divisive, pitting clinical psychologists against researchers. Some memory researchers have asserted that victims of sexual abuse could not forget their childhood events for long durations (Garry & Loftus, 1994; Pendergrast, 1997) and that there is nothing special about a traumatic memory (Shobe & Kihlstrom, 1997). Others disagree (Williams, 1994). Some researchers assert that some misguided therapists are helping people "recover" events that never occurred (Ofshe & Singer, 1994; Poole et al., 1995).

Others argue that "a thoughtful review of scientific findings does not support a quick embrace of the simplistic explanation that disclosures of childhood abuse are the result of therapist suggestion" (Olio, 1994, p. 442).

Many have pointed out that three key questions need to be addressed: First, can someone forget horrible experiences and remember them years later? Second, is there a potential physiological basis for such recall? And third, is memory fallible? Clinical psychologists are concerned with the first issue; physiologists, the second; and memory researchers, the third. Research shows that memory is indeed fallible: People do forget and make mistakes; they can be led on and can attribute information to the wrong source. And there may be perceptual and physiological explanations for these findings (Payne et al., 1997; Schacter, 1997). But a long history of clinical experience and many case reports from ethical therapists indicate that many men and women have been abused as children, that such events can be corroborated, and that while there are some misguided therapists (as in any profession), children can repress memories of horrific experiences and regain their memories when they are adults and can better cope with them.

To be the critical thinkers that they were trained to be, researchers and clinicians need to stop talking past one another, focus on the evidence, and conduct a sober examination of this contentious issue (Pope, 1996). Is there such a thing as repressed memory? Sure there is. Are all people who claim that they have been abused making it all up? Surely not. Is memory fallible? Yes. Are some people's memories unreliable and subject to suggestion? Yes, again. The pain of individuals who recover unpleasant repressed memories of their childhood is real; psychologists are trying to help them while working toward resolving the larger issue.

Neuroscience of Forgetting: Studies of Amnesia

Much of the early work on the neuroscience of memory began with the study of patients in hospitals who for one reason or another had developed amnesia, often as the result of an accident. Daytime TV dramas, or soaps, frequently portray people with amnesia, but in fact the condition is relatively rare. **Amnesia** is the inability to remember information, usually because of physiological trauma (such as a blow to the head). Typically, amnesia involves loss of memory for all events within a specific period.

There are two basic kinds of amnesia: retrograde and anterograde. **Retrograde amnesia** is the inability to remember events and experiences that preceded a traumatizing event. The loss of memory can cover a period ranging from a few minutes to several years. Recovery tends to be gradual, with earlier events being remembered before more recent ones. **Anterograde amnesia** is the inability to remember events and experiences that occur *after* an injury or brain damage. People suffering from anterograde amnesia are stuck in the lives they lived before being injured; new events are often completely forgotten. For example, if the onset of the amnesia occurred in 1996, the person may be able to remember clearly events of 1995 or earlier, but have a difficult time recalling what he or she did only a half-hour ago. The person may meet someone for the hundredth time, yet believe the individual is a perfect stranger. People with anterograde amnesia are able to learn some new information, but whether they do or not is highly dependent on how the information is presented (Hamann & Squire, 1995). Amnesia most typically affects the transfer of information from working memory to long-term memory. Ultimately, most patients with amnesia have difficulty forming new long-term memories.

Most people who develop amnesia do so because of head injury; others develop symptoms because of Korsakoff's syndrome, an affliction resulting from drinking too much alcohol and eating too little, which leads to vitamin deficiencies and brain damage. Diseases, especially viral ones, can also cause amnesia. These types of causes for amnesia may seem completely unrelated, but research shows that head injury, Korsakoff's syndrome, and viral disease affect a group of loosely related neural circuits that link the temporal lobes, hippocampus, and frontal lobes. In studying patients with brain damage or those who have undergone surgery for major epileptic attacks, researchers have found that the hippocampus may play a critical role in the transfer of new information to long-term memory. Milner showed that if certain regions of the brain are damaged or removed, people can remember old information but not new information (Milner, 1966; Milner, Corkin, & Teuber, 1968). The ability to remember events far in the past seems to depend on brain mechanisms that are separate and distinct from those required for new learning of recent events (Shimamura & Squire, 1986). These studies do not conclusively

Amnesia [am-NEE-zhuh]: Inability to remember information (typically all events within a specific period), usually due to physiological trauma.

Retrograde [RET-ro-grade] amnesia: Loss of memory of events and experiences that preceded an amnesia-causing event.

Anterograde amnesia: Loss of memory of events and experiences occurring after an amnesia-causing event.

confirm the existence of separate places or processes in the brain for different types of memory, but they are suggestive. Moreover, research on learning and memory of emotional responses by Kim and Fanselow (1992), along with other research (Shallice et al., 1994; Shen & McNaughton, 1996) supports the idea that memory is not a single process or one encoded in a single place. MRI studies are showing that men and women who have undergone traumas show changes in the size of various parts of the brain, especially the hippocampus. All this research supports an important point: Memories may be coded in one or many places, and they may be affected by a range of physical events, past experiences, and current ones—thus, memory is as much a process as it is an event or thing.

Think Critically

- Why do you think distributed practice is more effective than massed practice for learning?
- In situations involving recovery of traumatic memories—for example, parental sexual abuse—what events do you think might trigger a person who has forgotten past events to recall them?

Cognitive Psychology: An Overview

Focus on issues and ideas

- The eclectic methodology of cognitive psychology

Have you ever seen a tiger? You remember going to a zoo or a circus, and thus this is largely a memory task. But what if I ask: How are a tiger and a domestic cat similar? Who is the U.S. Secretary of State? How do you make an omelet? Answering each of these questions requires a different mental procedure. To answer the first question, you probably formed mental images of both felines and then compared the images. In answering the second question, you may simply have recalled the right name from recent news stories. The third question may have required you to mentally review the preparation of an omelet and describe each step. The thinking you used to answer all three questions required the use of knowledge, language, and images.

Cognitive psychology is the study of the overlapping fields of perception, learning, memory, and thought; it is the study of how people attend to, acquire, transform, store, and retrieve knowledge. Cognitive psychology includes the topics of consciousness, learning, and memory, which we have been discussing in this and the past two chapters, and it is basic to other topics, such as intelligence (Chapter 7). In the remainder of this chapter, however, we will focus on two core subjects of cognitive psychology: thought and language. The word *cognition* derives from the Latin *cognoscere,* "to know." Cognitive psychologists are interested primarily in mental processes that influence the acquisition and use of knowledge as well as the ability to *reason*—to generate logical and coherent ideas, evaluate situations, and reach conclusions. Cognitive researchers assume that mental processes exist, that people are active processors, and that cognitive processes can be studied using techniques that measure the speed and accuracy of responses (Ashcraft, 1989).

It is sometimes hard to pinpoint exactly what cognitive psychology is. But understanding human thought and reasoning continues to be a central concern of cognitive researchers; this means understanding not only how thought takes place, but how it takes place within a context—the environment—and how people extract information from the environment (Gibson, 1992; Neisser, 1992). The next sections demonstrate the breadth of cognitive psychology and describe its growth since its origins in the 1950s. We begin with the study of concept formation, which is crucial for all cognition.

Concept Formation: The Process of Forming Mental Groups

Focus on issues and ideas

- The role of language in concept formation

Each day, we all solve problems, make decisions, and reason logically, often following steps that are complicated but orderly. Many researchers conceive of reasoning itself as an orderly process that takes place in discrete steps, one set of ideas leading to another (Rips, 1990). To perform this process, people need to be able to form, manipulate, transform, and interrelate concepts. **Concepts** are the mental categories people

Cognitive psychology: The study of the overlapping fields of perception, learning, memory, and thought with a special emphasis on how people attend to, acquire, transform, store, and retrieve knowledge.

Concept: Mental category used to classify an event or object according to some distinguishing property or feature.

DIVERSITY

Sexist Language Affects Thinking

In churches, synagogues, and mosques around the country, people are trying out, and getting used to, gender-neutral language. In some liturgies, God is no longer referred to as "father," and "forefathers" are called "ancestors." Research shows that such changes affect listeners' responses to liturgy and sermons (Greene & Rubin, 1991). Gender-neutral language is becoming accepted and commonplace—these days, the original *Star Trek* series wouldn't get away with saying, "To boldly go where no *man* has gone before."

Over the last three decades, psychologists have revealed the role of language in shaping people's conceptual structures. If you have a concept of "nurses" as being women, then you assume that a man who walks into your hospital room wearing a white lab coat is a doctor. In general, the English language has evolved in such a way that its words define many roles as male, except for roles that traditionally have been played by women (nurses, teachers) (Bem, 1993). Walk down any street where work is being done on potholes or telephone lines and you may still see the warning sign "Men Working." Even though you are likely to see women as part of the work crews, the sign probably still reads the same.

Concepts of the world first form in childhood, as children hear stories from parents and teachers. Some stories tell of pioneers who settled the West with their wives, children, and livestock. In fairy tales, it is usually the king who rules the castle, and the princess who is saved from the evil wizard or the dragon. Language with a sexist bias expresses stereotypes and expectations about men and women. For example, men are often described using active, positive words (for example, *successful, strong, independent,* and *courageous*). Women have traditionally been described with words implying passiveness (such as *gentle, loving,* or *patient*), or even with negative terms (*the weaker sex, timid, frail*). When language indicative of strength or courage is applied to a woman, it is often in the context of incongruity—for example, "She thinks like a man." Katie Couric, the popular TV talk show host, is often described as "perky"; when asked about the term, she replied that sports commentator Bob Costas is also short and funny, but no one calls him "perky."

That women tend to be thought of as loving and patient and men as successful and strong is important to psychologists who study concept formation, problem solving, and language, because such concepts establish attitudes and underlie a whole range

use to classify events and objects according to common properties. Many objects with four wheels, a driver's seat, and a steering wheel are automobiles; "automobiles" is a concept. More abstract is the concept of "justice," which has to do with legality and fairness. "Animal," "computer," and "holiday" are all examples of concepts that have various *exemplars,* or specific instances. The study of *concept formation* is the examination of the way people organize and classify events and objects, usually in order to solve problems.

Concepts make people's experience of the world more meaningful by helping them to organize their thinking. Individuals develop progressively more complex concepts throughout life. Early on, infants learn the difference between "parent" and "stranger." Within a year, they can discriminate among objects, colors, and people and comprehend such simple concepts as "animal" and "flower." By age 2, they can verbalize these differences.

Much of what young children learn involves *classification*—the process of organizing things into categories—which is crucial to understanding the complex world. Think back to your early school years and to TV shows such as *Sesame Street.* You were taught the letters of the alphabet, different colors, farm animals and their sounds, and shapes such as triangles, circles, and squares. This process of developing concepts through classification continues throughout life. It involves separating dissimilar events and finding commonalities (Medin, 1989). But what is the best way to study the processes by which children and adults classify and organize information? And are there gender-based considerations? *Diversity* examines how words can affect behavior.

As a type of thinking, concept formation is relatively easy to study in controlled laboratory situations. Psychologists design laboratory studies whose objective is to observe participants forming and using concepts through a wide range of tasks. If you were a participant in a such an experiment, you might be asked to respond to questions like this: Is a bicycle a toy or a vehicle? The experimenter might time your re-of behaviors. Bem (1993) asserts that people see the world through a male frame of reference and that this is assumed to be the preferred value system. For example, men in business have been assumed to be task-oriented problem solvers; women, in contrast, have been assumed to be people-oriented rather than problem-oriented. And, in fact, many men and women do fit such stereotypes; since they were raised in environments where the stereotypes were accepted, it is not surprising that they exhibit them in day-to-day behavior.

Research supports the idea that men and women are perceived and treated differently and that they speak differently. Frable (1989) concluded that if people believe in gender-specific abilities, they are likely to apply that belief to their decision making. Frable found that people with strong gender-typed ideas were especially likely to pay attention to the gender of job applicants and then to devalue the interview performance of the females. McDonaugh (1992) found that interviewers not only devalue the resumes of women in general but devalue even more the resumes of African American women and women who are not beautiful. Thus, racial and physical stereotyping adds to gender stereotyping. Gender differences in language use are usually context-dependent; researchers know that men's and women's language is different (Ariel & Giora, 1992), but they also know that the differences must be considered within a larger context of ethnicity, class, age, and gender—not to mention social norms (Wodak & Benke, 1997).

Although gender stereotypes continue to exist, some women and men are becoming more androgynous. (*Androgyny* is the state of possessing both male and female characteristics.) Today, most people are more accepting of individuals who express androgynous characteristics—for example, men who cook and women who are engineers. Even more importantly, people are becoming more sensitive to how language shapes their concept of the world and their problem-solving abilities. McMinn and colleagues (1990) found that those who used gender-neutral language in writing were also likely to use gender-neutral language in conversation; however, they also found that it is difficult to change the use of sexist language (McMinn et al., 1991). Further, avoiding sexist language is just a beginning; sexism and the behavior that follows from it are deeply embedded in people's attitudes.

Western culture has made progress, however. No longer do only men fight fires and only women work as nurses; people have more of a chance to be whatever they want to be, without regard for gender. Astronauts are both male and female. If Neil Armstrong, the first moon walker, were making his famous comment "One giant leap for mankind," we might hope he would say, "One giant leap for humankind." Sexism is still a problem, but today boys *and* girls in primary school are more likely to be encouraged to solve problems creatively, to approach science and math with confidence, and to be caring human beings. ■

sponses and also ask you to express your thought processes out loud.

A key requirement for laboratory studies of concept formation is that participants be able to form rules—statements of how stimuli are related. In a common task used in laboratory investigations of concept formation, an experimenter tells the participants that something about the stimuli to be presented makes them similar. Participants are asked to identify this characteristic—this rule about the relationship between the stimuli. Each time a stimulus is presented, participants are told whether or not it has the characteristic being targeted. For example, suppose the first stimulus is a picture of a large bird. The experimenter says that it is a *positive instance* (an example that has the characteristic under study). The participant now knows that the characteristic may be either largeness or being a bird. The second picture shows a small red bird; the experimenter says that this, too, is a positive instance; the participant now knows that size is not important. The third picture shows a large blue bird; it, too, is a positive instance. Although the characteristic could be the ability to fly or being an animal, the participant may guess that the relevant characteristic is being a bird. When, on the fourth trial, the picture is of a small blue toy car and the experimenter says it is a *negative instance* (not an example of the concept), the participant might say with conviction that "bird" is the concept.

The laboratory example we have just considered allows careful examination of how people form or recognize concepts. But concepts are not always clear-cut. For example, you know that a professor is a teacher and a high school instructor is a teacher, but are ministers teachers? Are den leaders? Is the President of the United States? Each of these individuals acts as a teacher from time to time. Or consider the concept "family." One concept of a family is Mom, Dad, and 2.4 kids. But what of single-parent families, blended families, adoptive families, communal families, and extended families? Some researchers consider a family to be any group of people who care about each other in significant ways. You can see that concepts are often fuzzy. Often you must think about concepts carefully in order to understand and define them.

Eleanor Rosch has asserted that when people are presented with *fuzzy concepts,* they tend to define them in terms of *prototypes,* or best examples of a class of items (Rosch, 1973, 1978). A **prototype** is an abstraction, an idealized pattern of an object or idea that is stored in memory and used to decide whether similar objects or ideas are members of the class of items. A high school English teacher may be a prototype of "teacher"; ministers, den leaders, and psychologists are also examples, but not "best" examples. Some concepts have easily defined prototypes; others are hard to define. When you think about the concept "furniture," you easily recognize that chairs, sofas, and tables are good examples. But telephones, stoves, pianos, and mirrors are all furniture as well; this is a concept that is fuzzy. The concept "computer modem" is much less fuzzy: There may be a few shapes and sizes, but nearly all computer modems do the same thing, in pretty much the same way. Of course, many variables affect how easily concepts are defined, including properties of the concept as well as an individual's unique experiences with its exemplars. It is these experiences that help people build strategies and solve problems. (I)

Think Critically

- What are the implications for psychologists of the fact that cognitive psychology is so broad and covers so many aspects of psychology?

(I) Problem Solving: Confronting Situations That Require Solutions

Focus on issues and ideas

- The distinction between the algorithmic and heuristic approaches to problem solving
- Types of barriers to problem solving
- How Sternberg's theory of creativity differs from past theories

You are generally unaware of your cognitive processes; you don't usually think about thinking. And yet you are thinking all the time—sorting through choices, deciding where to go, what to do, and when to do it. When you think, you engage in a wide variety of activities, from daydreaming to planning your next few steps on a mountain path.

How can you manage to study for your psychology exam when you have an English paper due tomorrow? How can you fit all your clothes and other belongings into your room's tiny closet? What should you do when your car gets a flat tire on the interstate? These are all problems to be solved. Your approaches to these dilemmas represent some of the highest levels of cognitive functioning. Human beings are wonderful at **problem solving,** at confronting and resolving situations that require insight or determination of some unknown elements. Because you can form concepts and group things together in logical ways, you are able to organize your thoughts and attack a problem.

There are huge differences in people's problem-solving abilities, but psychologists can help individuals become more effective problem solvers. Recall from Chapters 1 and 3 that Gestalt psychologists analyzed the world in terms of perceptual frameworks and argued that the mind organizes the elements of experience to form something unique. As we saw in Chapter 5, Wolfgang Köhler (1927/1973), a Gestalt researcher, showed that chimps developed *insights* into methods for retrieving food that was beyond their reach. They discovered they could pile up boxes to reach the food or attach short poles to make a long stick with which to grab the food. Once the insight occurred, no further instruction, investigation, or training was necessary. Insight is not essential to problem solving; but hints, cues, and prior experience all support the process of developing insight and recognizing essential elements—an advantage in problem solving (Kaplan & Simon, 1990).

When people (or machines, for that matter) solve problems, they tend to use two basic approaches: algorithms and heuristics. An **algorithm** is a procedure for solving a problem by implementing a set of rules over and over again until the solution is found. Many mathematics problems (for example, finding a square root) can be solved by using an algorithm. Algorithms are also used for a wide variety of real-life tasks, from increasing the yield of a recipe (say, by doubling each ingredient) to writing a computer program (even a relatively simple program requires several algorithms). To implement an algorithm, you follow the rules regarding which task to implement at which point in the procedure. For example, an algorithm for doubling a recipe might be: "Find the recipe's list of ingredients. Find the amount of a given ingredient, multiply that amount by 2, and use the product as the new amount for that ingredient. Repeat this procedure for each ingredient listed in the recipe." It's monotonous, but it works. However, because you *must* follow every step in an algorithm in order to use it, the necessary time and effort may make algorithms impractical for some uses. Human problem solvers learn to use rules-of-

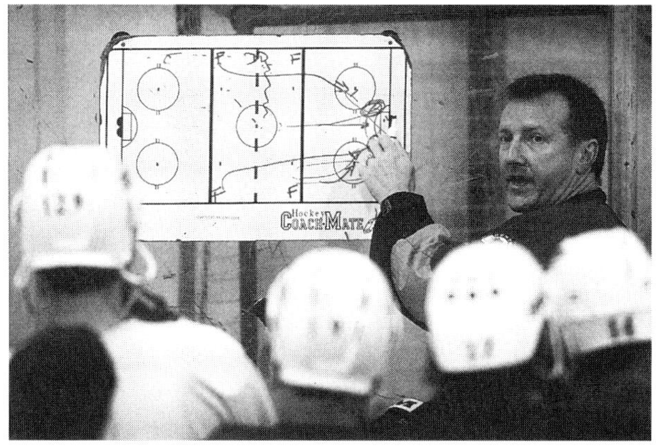

thumb so that they do not have to follow algorithms rigidly. These rules-of-thumb are integral to heuristic problem-solving strategies.

Heuristics are sets of strategies that act as flexible guidelines—not strict rules and procedures—for discovery-oriented problem solving. Heuristics reflect the processes used by the human brain; they involve making rough guesses and subjective evaluations that might be called hunches or intuitions (Bowers et al., 1990). For example, the coach of a hockey team might evaluate the team's first-period performance and intuit that different plays might better its chances against that opponent. To contrast heuristics and algorithms, let's consider the game of chess. When deciding on a move, a person (or computer) using an algorithm would consider every possible move in terms of its statistical probability of success, then choose the one with the highest likelihood of success. A person using a heuristic (for example, chess master Garry Kasparov) would consider only the moves he or she believed most likely to be successful, based on past experience. These moves would not be given statistical probabilities of outcomes; instead, the heuristic strategist would ask, "Which move has usually enhanced my strategic position in the game?"

Heuristics are sets of strategies that act as flexible guidelines—not strict rules and procedures—for discovery-oriented problem solving.

Most heuristic approaches focus on the goal that is to be achieved. For example, in **subgoal analysis,** a problem is taken apart or broken down into several smaller steps, each of which has a subgoal. In **means–ends analysis,** the person compares the current situation or position with the desired end (the goal) in order to determine the most efficient means for getting from one to the other. The objective is to reduce the number of steps needed to reach the goal. A **backward search** involves working backward from the goal, or endpoint, to the current position, both to analyze the problem and to reduce the steps needed to get to the goal. Human beings often use all three of these heuristic approaches; but a psychological set may sometimes limit an individual to only one problem-solving approach.

Table 6.1 (on p. 170) summarizes the major advantages and disadvantages of both algorithms and heuristics.

Barriers to Problem Solving

People's problem-solving abilities vary, and they may be subject to certain limitations, among which are functional fixedness and mental set. Researchers study these limitations to gain a better understanding of the processes of problem solving.

Functional Fixedness: Cognition with Constraints. When my daughter Sarah was 4 years old, she saw me taking her raincoat out of the closet before our trip to the zoo. Sarah insisted that it was not raining outside and that raincoats are for rain. I explained that the coat could also be used as a windbreaker or a light spring jacket. Reluctantly, she put it on. In this exchange, Sarah was exhibiting a basic human characteristic—functional fixedness. **Functional fixedness** is the inability to see that an object can have a function other than its stated or usual one. When people are functionally fixed, they have limited their conceptual framework; they see too few functions for an object. In many ways, this fixedness constitutes a barrier to problem solving.

Prototype: An abstraction, an idealized pattern of an object or idea that is stored in memory and used to decide whether similar objects or ideas are members of the same class of items.

Problem solving: The behavior of individuals when confronted with a situation or task that requires insight or determination of some unknown elements.

Algorithm [AL-go-rith-um]: Procedure for solving a problem by implementing a set of rules over and over again until the solution is found.

Heuristics [hyoo-RISS-ticks]: Sets of strategies, rather than strict rules, that act as guidelines for discovery-oriented problem solving.

Subgoal analysis: Heuristic procedure in which a problem is broken down into smaller steps, each of which has a subgoal.

Means–ends analysis: Heuristic procedure in which the problem solver compares the current situation with the desired goal to determine the most efficient way to get from one to the other.

Backward search: Heuristic procedure in which a problem solver works backward from the goal or end of a problem to the current position, in order to analyze the problem and reduce the steps needed to get from the current position to the goal.

Functional fixedness: Inability to see that an object can have a function other than its stated or usual one.

Table 6.1 Algorithms and Heuristics: Two Approaches to Problem Solving

Approach	Procedure	Advantages	Disadvantages	Example
Algorithm	Exhaustive, systematic consideration of all possible solutions; a set of rules.	Solution is guaranteed.	Can be very inefficient, effortful, time-consuming.	Computer chess programs are typically based on a set of predefined rules and moves.
Heuristics	Strategies; rules-of-thumb that have worked in the past.	Efficient; saves effort and time.	Solution is not guaranteed.	Person attempting to repair a car uses past experience to rule out a whole range of potential problems.

Studies of functional fixedness show that the name or meaning given to an object or tool often limits its function. In a typical study, a research participant is presented with a task and provided with tools that can be used in various ways. One laboratory problem used to show functional fixedness is the two-string problem. In this task, a person is put in a room that has two strings hanging from the ceiling and some objects lying on a table. The task is to tie the two strings together, but it is impossible to reach one string while holding the other. The only solution is to tie a weight (one of the objects on the table) to one string and set it swinging back and forth, then take hold of the second string and wait until the first string swings within reach. This task is difficult for some people because their previous experiences with objects may prevent them from considering them as potential tools in an unusual situation.

Mental Set. Psychologists have found that most individuals are flexible in their approaches to solving problems. In other words, they do not use preconceived, or "set," solutions but think about objects, people, and situations in new ways. A flexible approach would allow an astronaut to make an air-filtering device out of duct tape and other spare parts (as in a scene from the film *Apollo 13*). This kind of solution requires limber thought processes. However, sometimes people develop a rigid strategy, or approach, to certain types of problems.

Creative thinking requires breaking out of one's *mental set*—limited ways of thinking about possibilities. Having a mental set is the opposite of being creative. Prior experience predisposes a person to make a particular response in a given situation. Most of the time, this predisposition, or readiness, is useful and adaptive; for the most part, what worked in the past will work in the future. Sometimes, however, the biasing effect of a mental set is counterproductive; it limits innovation and prevents a person from solving new and complex problems. In an increasingly complex and changing world, such limitations are problematic.

Experiencing Psychology offers suggestions for overcoming barriers to problem solving and improving your critical thinking skills.

Creativity: A quality of thought and problem solving that is generally considered to include originality, novelty, and appropriateness.

Convergent thinking: In problem solving, the process of narrowing down choices and alternatives to arrive at a suitable answer.

Divergent thinking: In problem solving, the process of widening the range of possibilities and expanding the options for solutions.

Brainstorming: Problem-solving technique that involves considering all possible solutions without making prior evaluative judgments.

Creative Problem Solving

The owners of a high-rise professional building were deluged with complaints that the building's elevators were too slow. The owners called in a consultant, who researched the problem and discovered that, indeed, tenants often had to wait several minutes for an elevator. Putting in new, faster elevators would cost tens of thousands of dollars, more than the owners could afford. Eventually, the consultant devised a creative solution that ended the complaints but cost only a few hundred dollars: He installed wall mirrors at each elevator stop. Evidently, being able to check out one's appearance while waiting made the time go faster.

Creativity is a quality of thought and problem solving that is generally considered to include originality, novelty, and appropriateness. An *original response* to a problem is one that doesn't copy or imitate another response; that is, it originates from the problem solver. A *novel response* is a response that is new or that has no precedent. Unless an original and

EXPERIENCING PSYCHOLOGY

Be a Critical Thinker

Every day, you have to make judgments, classify ideas, and follow logic—that is, engage in reasoning—to solve problems. Being able to think critically will improve your reasoning and thus your problem-solving skills. Besides the guidelines presented in Chapter 1 (p. 9), several other tips can make you a better critical thinker:

Don't fixate on availability. Things that come to mind quickly are not necessarily the best solutions to problems. Don't choose the first answer just because it's there.

Don't generalize too quickly. Just because most elements in a group follow a pattern does not mean all elements in the group will follow the pattern. For example, just because the florist removed the thorns from most of the red roses you bought for Valentine's Day does not mean she didn't miss one.

Don't settle for an easy solution. People often settle for a solution that works, even though other solutions may work even better. Look at all the alternatives.

Don't choose a solution just because it fits preexisting ideas. People often accept too quickly ideas that conform to their previously held views. This is a serious mistake for researchers, who need to be open to new ideas, a state of mind that often requires conscious effort.

Don't fail to consider any possible solution. If you do not evaluate *all* of the available alternatives, you are likely to miss the correct, or most logical, answer.

Don't be emotional. Sometimes people become emotionally tied to a specific idea, premise, or conviction. When this happens, the likelihood of being able to critically evaluate the evidence drops sharply. Critical thinkers are cool and evaluative, not headstrong and emotional. ■

novel response is also an appropriate response to a given problem, however, psychologists do not call it creative. An *appropriate response* is a response that is reasonable in terms of the situation. An important question in studies of creativity is how people can become more creative in their thinking (Greeno, 1989).

You don't have to be an Einstein or a Picasso to be creative—as the building consultant demonstrated. On the other hand, being exceptionally bright and having novel responses, even appropriate ones, does not make someone creative. According to well-known creativity researcher Mihalay Csikszentmihalyi (1996), creative individuals are those who have changed the culture in some way that involves original thinking. He cites Michael Jordan, who, by everyone's definition, is a talented, gifted athlete—but who is not creative, according to Csikszentmihalyi. Csikszentmihalyi asserts that creativity is the process of redefining or transforming your domain (either in your professional field or in an area of interest such as gardening, music, or painting) or creating a new domain.

Morris Stein (1974) defined the creative process as involving three stages: hypothesis formation, hypothesis testing, and communication of results. In hypothesis formation, a person tries to formulate a new response to a problem, which is not an easy task. A person must confront the situation and think of it in nonstereotyped ways, exploring paths not previously explored. This sometimes involves making guesses based on intuition.

When people sort through alternatives to try to solve a problem, they attempt to focus their thinking, discarding inappropriate solutions until a single appropriate option is left. In this way, they *converge* on an answer (or use convergent thinking skills). **Convergent thinking** is narrowing down choices and alternatives to arrive at a suitable answer. **Divergent thinking,** in contrast, is widening the range of possibilities and expanding the options for solutions; doing so lessens the likelihood of functional fixedness or mental set. Guilford (1967) defined creative thinking as divergent thinking. According to other psychologists, any solution to a problem that can be worked out only with time and practice is not a creative solution. To foster creativity, people need to rethink their whole approach to a task. Successful entrepreneurs know this to be the case, and those who develop new technologies, products, and services are often well rewarded for their creativity. Business schools are paying closer attention to developing creativity in marketing courses, and researchers are examining the roles of creativity and insight in solving problems (Kaplan & Simon, 1990).

Another way to stimulate creative problem solving is a technique called brainstorming. In **brainstorming,** people consider all possible solutions without making any initial judgments about the worth of those solutions. This procedure can be used to generate alternative solutions to problems as diverse as how a city can dispose of its waste and how a topic for a group project can be selected. The rationale behind brainstorming is that people will produce more high-quality ideas if they do not have to evaluate the suggestions immediately. Brainstorming attempts to release the potential of the participants so as to increase the diversity of ideas and promote creativity.

Robert Sternberg has developed a novel approach to studying creativity. He argues that a person brings six interactive resources to problem solving: intelligence, thinking style, knowledge, personality, motivation, and environment. When people get involved with a solution that others have ignored or dismissed, they can be creative and productive and later "sell" their idea. This notion of working on undervalued problem solutions and marketing them later is why Sternberg calls his approach an *investment theory of creativity* (Sternberg & Lubart, 1993, 1996). Sternberg argues that if people emphasize their interactive resources like thinking style and motivation, they can be more creative; he contrasts this approach with traditional ideas of creativity that often define truly creative people as those with exceptionally high levels of certain personality attributes. From Sternberg's point of view, anyone who brings all six interactive resources to bear on a problem can be creative. *(I)*

Think Critically

- What do you think leads to functional fixedness? How do you think you could help yourself break through it to solve a problem?
- In school settings, people solve verbal problems and answer questions that might be considered silly in many other settings. What does this say about school experiences?

(I) Reasoning and Decision Making: Generating Ideas and Reaching Conclusions

Focus on issues and ideas

- How people estimate the likelihood of events in their lives
- How decision making can be hampered by different barriers

Deciding whether to go for a run at lunchtime, have a sandwich and soft drink, or catch up on my correspondence is a daily decision for me. Each choice carries with it benefits, and each has costs; but because I make this decision day in and day out, the process usually occurs quickly. And more often than not, I choose the sandwich rather than the run or the writing. But how do I make such decisions? When cognitive psychologists study *thinking*, they generally attempt to study the systematic day-to-day processes of reasoning and decision making (Galotti, 1989). **Reasoning** is the purposeful process by which a person generates logical and coherent ideas, evaluates situations, and reaches conclusions. The system or principles of reasoning used to reach valid conclusions or make inferences is called **logic.** You can think about reasoning as either an ordered process or an unstructured process in which ideas and beliefs are continuously updated (Rips, 1990)—both approaches are valid, and people use both types of reasoning.

Decision making means assessing and choosing among alternatives. You make decisions that involve the probability of some event (will my friends want to go on this trip with me?) and others that involve expected value (how important is *this* trip, rather than some other one?). Your decisions vary from the trivial to the complex—what to eat for breakfast, which courses to take, what career to pursue. The trivial decisions are usually made quickly, without much effort or even conscious thought. The complex ones require conscious, deliberate, effortful consideration. Sometimes, your decision making is logical; at other times, you are not sure whether your choices are valid.

Psychologists have devised numerous approaches for looking at decision-making processes. We examine formal reasoning (or syllogisms), used when there is a single correct answer, and estimating probabilities, used in situations in which the answer or decision is less certain.

Syllogisms: Formal Reasoning

One of the traditional ways to study reasoning and decision making is to provide research participants with deduction tasks that use syllogisms. A **syllogism** is a sequence of statements, or *premises* (usually two), which are assumed to be true and are followed by a conclusion. The task is to decide (deduce) whether the conclusion is valid, given the premises.

By asking participants to describe their thinking while they contemplate syllogisms, a psychologist can trace and analyze their cognitive processes. People are not especially good at solving abstract syllogisms; more concrete ones are easier to evaluate. Consider the following syllogism.

Premise 1: All poodles are dogs.

Premise 2: All dogs are animals.

Conclusion: All poodles are animals.

Is the conclusion logical? Do the two premises allow you to conclude that poodles are animals? It is easy to see that the conclusion in this example is true because the premises are clearly true. However, you could devise a syllogism in which the conclusion validly follows from the premises but is really false—because one or more of the premises are false. For example, if you changed Premise 1 above to "All flowers are dogs," you could logically come to the valid (but false) conclusion "All flowers are animals."

You can learn how to use logic and how to be a better critical thinker and decision maker. One way is to be skeptical about the premises on which conclusions are based. A second way is to evaluate premises systematically for truth. A third way is to think the way a detective does, using logical decision-making skills to eliminate possible alternatives one by one.

Uncertainty: Estimating Probabilities

How do people decide what to wear, where to go on vacation, or how to answer a question on the SAT? How do they decide when something is bigger, longer, or more difficult than something else? Many decisions are based on formal logic, some on carefully tested hypotheses, and some on educated guesses. An *educated* guess is one based on knowledge gained from past experience. When you see dark thunderheads, for example, you can guess that it will rain—but you cannot be 100% sure. Weather forecasts express likelihood of rain as a percentage—that is, as a probability.

People make probability estimates about all types of events and behaviors. They guess about the likelihood of a Democratic or a Republican victory in an election or of their favorite team's chances in the playoffs. On the basis of past experience, they estimate the probability that they will stay on their diet or get stuck in a traffic jam on the way to work. People can judge whether a particular event increases or decreases the probability of another event. When several factors are involved, their effects may compound or mitigate one another to alter the probability of an outcome. For example, the probability that there will be rain when there are thunderclouds, high winds, and low barometric pressure is much higher than the probability of rain when it is merely cloudy.

Research participants who are asked to make probability judgments about the real world, particularly about fairly rare events such as airplane crashes, are less likely to make accurate judgments than are participants who are given laboratory problems (Swets, 1992). People may act irrationally or ignore key pieces of data and thus make bad (or irrational) decisions that are not based on probability. The further in the future the event being predicted is, the more likely people are to make bad predictions (Payne, Bettman, & Johnson, 1992). Sometimes, people's worldviews color their probability decision making. Having strong religious or political views can influence a person's strategies and decision estimates.

Finally, people are not machines or computers; their past experiences, personalities, and cultural backgrounds can influence their thought processes—sometimes in unpredictable ways. However, cognitive psychologists have suggested ways for individuals to become the most efficient learners and thinkers they can be, and researchers have found that people can be taught to weigh costs and benefits more accurately and to be less influenced by their frames of reference (Larrick, Morgan, & Nisbett, 1990; Payne, Bettman, & Johnson, 1992). One way to break out of traditional frames of reference is to use analogies. When researchers examined how students could best learn scientific concepts, they found that analogies and metaphors are especially useful. Students can learn factual details well through traditional teaching methods, but analogies—especially creative ones—provide conceptual bridges that facilitate learning, memory, and concept development (Donnelly & McDaniel, 1993).

Barriers to Sound Decision Making

In the same way that people's problem solving can be hampered by mental sets, their decision making can be hindered by a range of stumbling blocks.

Gambler's Fallacy. If you know about probability, you know that people have misconceptions about the probabilities of events. A common fallacy is the *gambler's fallacy*—the belief that the chances of an event's occurring increase if the event has not recently occurred. This fallacy has brought millions of dollars to the casinos of Las Vegas and Atlantic City. In reality, *every time* you flip a coin, the chance of getting "heads" is 1 in 2, or .5—regardless of what happened on the last flip, or the last ten flips; and every pull of

Reasoning: The purposeful process by which a person generates logical and coherent ideas, evaluates situations, and reaches conclusions.

Logic: The system or principles of reasoning used to reach valid conclusions or make inferences.

Decision making: Assessing and choosing among alternatives.

Syllogism [SILL-oh-jiz-um]: A sequence of statements, or premises (usually two), which are assumed to be true and are followed by a conclusion; the task is to decide (deduce) whether the conclusion is valid, given the premises.

a slot machine has the same likelihood of making you a winner, regardless of what happened on the last pull.

Belief in Small Numbers. Limiting the number of observations we make because of a *belief in small numbers* also contributes to poor decision making. A small sample of observations is likely to be highly variable and not reflective of the larger population. However, the truth is that people are willing to draw conclusions from a small sample—say, 10 neighbors—and assume that such a sample is representative of an entire town, state, or country.

Availability Heuristic. Even though my wife knows that flying in planes is quite safe—safer than walking through the parking lot of a nearby shopping mall—she is still hesitant to fly for fear the plane will crash. Like my wife, most people overestimate the probability of unusual events occurring in their lives and may make poor decisions based on those probabilities. The overestimation of the probability is probably due to the wide media attention given to infrequent catastrophic events; information about them is more "available" than other information, and it is easy to think of examples. Psychologists refer to the *availability heuristic*—the tendency to judge the probability of an event by how easy it is to think of examples of it. The number of fatalities due to plane crashes, tornadoes, and icebergs is overestimated.

Overconfidence. People often become overconfident and overestimate the soundness of their judgments and the accuracy of their knowledge. Such *overconfidence* is another major stumbling block to sound decision making. Imagine the surprise of a student when he was rejected from the only law school he applied to because he was sure—convinced—that he would get into it. Individuals become so committed to their ideas and beliefs—especially political ones—that they are often more confident than correct and, when challenged, may become even more rigid and inflexible. For example, a person who believes that the only solution to local traffic problems is new roads may steadfastly refuse to even consider mass transit as an alternative solution.

The greatest challenge to making good decisions is that people tend to cling to preexisting beliefs despite contradictory evidence.

Confirmation Bias. Perhaps the greatest challenge to making good decisions is that people tend to cling to preexisting beliefs despite contradictory evidence; psychologists call this phenomenon the *confirmation bias*. People tend to discount information that does not fit with their pre-existing views. Individuals rarely dwell on missed opportunities to make money from an investment; more often they seek to confirm their good judgment by telling how they made money (or did not lose any) on the investments they did make. As you will see when we study social psychology in Chapter 11, reliance on past experience and reluctance to seek information (or listen to it) that might disconfirm one's beliefs leads to stereotypes and prejudices that are often ill-informed and wrong. (I)

Think Critically

- What might be the main reason people are not very good at estimating the probability of real-world events?
- Can you think of a political situation or crisis in which overconfidence or confirmation bias contributed to bad decisions?

(I) Artificial Intelligence

Focus on issues and ideas

- How the concept of *convergence zones* is influencing the development of new models of problem solving
- The similarities of the human brain and neural networks in computers

There is no question that computers have transformed what we do and how we do it. And because human beings invented computers, it is not surprising that computers handle information in much the same way as the human brain does—though the brain has far more options and strategies for information processing than a computer. By simulating specific models of the human brain, computers help psychologists understand human thought processes. For example, computers help shape the development of hypotheses about information processing and about perception, assist researchers in investigating how people solve problems, and enable psychologists to test models of certain aspects of behavior, such as memory. Computers also perform many tasks that humans find too time-consuming or complicated. Computer programs that mimic some type of human cognitive activities are said to use *artificial intelligence (AI)*.

The Computer as Information Processor

In Chapter 3, you learned how researchers break down many perception problems into small steps, using the information-processing approach. The information-processing approach to perception, memory, and problem solving is a direct outgrowth of computer simulations. Flowcharts showing how information from sensory memory reaches working memory and long-term memory rely implicitly on a computer analogy. Those who study memory extend the computer analogy further by referring to storage areas as "buffers" and information-processing mechanisms as "central processors." The information-processing approach is widely used, although it has come under attack because it tends to reduce memory processes to small mechanistic elements (Bruner, 1990).

The most widely investigated aspect of computer simulation and artificial intelligence is problem solving. Playing chess was one of the first human activities that researchers tried to duplicate with computers, and ever since then, human beings like Garry Kasparov have been challenging computers for dominance—with some modest successes and some notable failures! Computers have been taught to play other games, such as checkers and backgammon, and to solve simple number completion tasks. They can also solve complicated problems involving large amounts of memory. The most sophisticated programs mimic aspects of human memory and decision-making systems and have been used to solve a wide array of problems including the design of computer chips and management of human resources (Lawler & Elliot, 1996).

Although computers can be programmed to process information the way human beings do, they lack human ingenuity and imagination. In addition, computers cannot interpret information by referring to or analyzing its context. When you say to a grocer, "Halibut?" and the grocer responds, "Wednesday, after 4, downtown only," you understand the meaning of this answer: Halibut will be available on Wednesday, after 4 o'clock in the afternoon, when the shipment has arrived at the downtown branch of the grocery chain. Human beings understand the context in which fish are shipped only occasionally, to some stores, at certain times during the week. They understand the concepts of branch stores, fresh fish, and selective shipments. Computers do not have such contexts. Further, they cannot evaluate their own knowledge or improve their own problem-solving abilities by developing heuristics.

Neural Networks

The comparison of the brain to a computer is a compelling one, and interesting research has been focusing on the brain's ability to represent information in a number of locations simultaneously. Take a moment and imagine a computer. You may conjure up an image of an IBM or a Macintosh, a laptop or a mainframe. You may also start thinking about programming code, monitor screens, or even your favorite computer game. Your images of a computer or representations of what the computer can do are stored and coded at different places in your brain. No one suggests that you have a "computer corner," where all information about computers is stored. Since various pieces of information are stored in different parts of the brain, the electrical energy representing them must be combined at some point, in some way, for you to use the word *computer*, understand it, and visualize what it stands for.

Because the brain has specific processing areas, in different physical locations, a *convergence zone*, or center, is necessary to mediate and organize the information, according to University of Iowa researchers Damasio and Damasio (1992). Signals from widely separated clusters of neuronal activity come together in convergence zones to evoke words and allow a person to develop sentences and fully process ideas and images about the subject at hand. That convergence zones are not located in the same place as specific pieces of information helps explain why some stroke victims and patients with various brain lesions (injuries) can tell you some things about a given topic—say, pianos—but not everything they once knew. For example, a stroke victim may be able to look at a picture of a piano and tell you that it has keys and pedals but be unable to say that it is a picture of a piano. According to Damasio and Damasio's view, in such a case a key convergence zone has been corrupted.

The idea of convergence zones has led to the development of models of where and how the brain operates to represent the world, develop concepts, solve problems, and process day-to-day tasks like reading and listening (Posner & Pavese, 1998). It also helps explain why a person whose visual cortex has been damaged can sometimes have knowledge of things that she or he is unaware of having seen. This residual vision—sometimes referred to as *blindsight*—is attributed to secondary, less important visual pathways. Wessinger, Fendrich, and Gazzaniga (1997) reported cases of individuals who demonstrated blindsight. Such multistage models of knowledge of the world—

with multiple sources of input—suggest convergence zones and multiple levels and layers of processing.

In recent years, mathematicians, physiologists, and psychologists have joined forces to develop specific models of how neural structures represent complicated information (e.g., Hinton, 1992). Their work is often based on the concept of *parallel distributed processing (PDP),* which suggests that many operations take place simultaneously and at many locations within the brain (an idea introduced earlier in this chapter). Most computers can perform only one operation at a time—admittedly very quickly, but still only one at a time. In contrast, the largest of modern computers can operate hundreds or even thousands of processors at once. Today's supercomputers are made up of many powerful computers that operate simultaneously (in parallel) to solve problems. PDP models assert that the brain can similarly process many events simultaneously, store them, and compare them to past events (Grossberg, 1995). PDP models also incorporate perception and learning; they combine data from studies of eye movements, hearing, the tactile senses, and pattern recognition to present a coherent view of how the brain integrates information to make it meaningful. PDP models can even account for nodes, units, or (in the Damasios' terminology) convergence zones that store different types of information in different ways (McClelland, 1994).

For studying parallel distributed processing, researchers have devised artificial neural networks. These networks are typically composed of interconnected units that serve as model neurons. Each unit, or artificial neuron, receives signals of varying and modifiable weight, to represent signals that would be received by a real neuronal dendrite. Activity generated by a unit is transmitted as a single outgoing signal to other neural units. Both input and output to units can be varied electronically, as can the interconnections among units. Layers of units can be connected to other layers, and the output of one layer may be the input to another.

A neural network can be a physical entity, but researchers are tending to use computers to create complex electronic representations of neural networks that simulate specific activities. For example, such electronic neural networks have sophisticated pattern-recognition abilities and can be taught to recognize handwritten letters—say, the letter A—and other simple patterns. In addition, such a network can learn to recognize a range of forms that look like the letter A. In this case, the network has learned a *prototype.* The prototypes may constitute the network's basis of form and letter perception.

An interesting aspect of networks is what happens when one portion of a network is destroyed. The network does not crash, but it makes some mistakes, much as the brain would. When portions of the brain are surgically destroyed or removed or injured in an accident, the person is still able to complete some tasks. (Remember the split-brain patients who could name an object presented to one hemisphere but could only point to the object presented to the other hemisphere—see pp. 49–50.)

Neural networks, like the brain, learn and remember. A neural network learns by noting changes in the weights or values associated with various connections. Sophisticated networks learn quickly and easily and modify themselves based on experience. The connections between various units within the network are changed because of experience in a way that reflects Hebb's theory: Those units that are frequently activated will become more pronounced, have a lower threshold of activation, and be more easily accessed in the future (Posner, DiGirolamo, & Fernandez-Duque, 1997). This access is part of the retrieval process; easy access means easy retrieval, and both are dependent on clear, unambiguous learning.

Although neural networks operate efficiently and can learn to recognize speech and handwriting, chess moves, and spatial layouts, they are subject to error (see Nass et al., 1995). Furthermore, they do not have the creativity and personality that human beings possess. They lack a sense of humor and the ingenuity that arises from perseverance, motivation, and intelligence. Neural networks help us understand human cognition, but they are not going to take its place. *I*

Think Critically

- What do you think has made the human brain develop in such a way that it exhibits creativity and humor, which a computer cannot do?
- What are the implications of the Damasios' idea that information is stored all over the brain and brought together in convergence zones for neuroscientific studies of memory and thought? For locating the memory store?

I Language

Focus on issues and ideas

- The influence of culture on language
- The three basic components of any language
- The fundamental idea of Chomsky's transformational grammar

The doorbell rings. You open the door and see someone wearing sunglasses, a T-shirt, and neon pink and green swim trunks. The person says, "Tell your roommate to get her stick. It's 6 foot and glassy." Some people might interpret this to mean that the roommate owns some kind of long Plexiglas pogo stick. A surfer, however, would grab a surfboard (a "stick") and head out to the beach, where 6-foot-high waves are breaking on a beautiful, windless day (making the ocean's surface "glassy"). Although the words sound the same to surfer and nonsurfer, surfers know how to interpret these special expressions when talking about their sport. Linguists even have a name for the study of how the social context of a sentence affects its meaning—*pragmatics.* A **language** is a system of symbols, usually words, that convey meaning; in addition to the symbols, a language also has rules for combining symbols to generate an infinite number of messages (usually sentences). The key elements of this definition are that language is symbolic, it is a structured system, it is used to represent meaning, and it is generative, allowing an infinite number of sentences to be created. We'll examine these key elements in a moment. For now, think about how amazing it is that we are able to process such a system so effortlessly, despite its complexity. Some researchers have wondered: If two people who speak the same language use different expressions to describe the same event or situation, does this mean they think about the world in different ways? Does language determine thought, or do all people think alike, regardless of their language? Ultimately, what is the influence of culture on language?

Thought, Culture, and Language

In the 1950s, researchers discovered that Eskimo languages had many more nouns to refer to snow than English does. From this finding, anthropologist and linguist Benjamin Whorf reasoned that the Eskimos' language shaped their thinking about snow—that is, that verbal and language abilities must affect thought directly. In Whorf's view, the structure of the language that people speak directly determines their thoughts and perceptions (Whorf, 1956).

Researchers such as Eleanor Heider Rosch have put to rest Whorf's idea that language determines thought (Lillo-Martin, 1997). But psychologists do realize that culture, however, has a great influence on both language and thought. In France, for example, fairly rigid linguistic customs reflect hundreds of years of history; so, in the French language, there are formal and informal means of address. The word "you" for friends is *tu;* in more formal settings, one uses *vous.* Japan has even greater culturally determined distinctions in formality of language; who a person is in the workplace—boss, manager, supervisor, worker—affects how he or she is addressed and whether he or she will be shown deference. Language is thus an expression of ethnic, geographic, cultural, and religious tendencies (Williamson, 1991).

Americans are in a minority, in that most speak only one language; in most other developed countries, people are bilingual, speaking at least two languages. Although bilingualism promotes cognitive flexibility, research shows that when bilingual people are asked to respond to a question, take a personality test, or otherwise interact in the world, they do so in a culturally bound way—depending on the language in which they respond. When responding to a personality inventory written in Chinese, native speakers of Chinese are likely to reflect Chinese values; when they respond to an English version of the same personality test, their responses are more likely to reflect Western values (Dinges & Hull, 1993).

As Matsumoto (1994) asserts, language and culture are intertwined. Along with studies of culture, Rosch's studies suggest that language does not determine thought, but rather subtly influences it. Recall from *Diversity* (on pp. 166–167) that a person's language can shape his or her worldview and expectations of gender roles. Various languages have developed specific grammars, probably in response to specific environments, events, and cultures. It may be adaptive to discriminate among many kinds of snow or supervisors, but language does not directly determine thoughts. Rather, thoughts about snow and supervisors help shape language, which is used to express those thoughts. As Hunt and Agnoli (1991, p. 377) assert, "The language people speak is a guide to the language in which they think."

Linguistics

Throughout the ages and in every culture, human beings have rendered their thoughts into language and have employed words to order their thoughts. Without this ability, human civilization could never exist. In many ways, language and thinking define humanity.

Linguistics is the study of language, including speech sounds, meaning, and grammar. **Psycholinguistics** is the study of how language is acquired,

Language: A system of symbols, usually words, that convey meaning and a set of rules for combining symbols to generate an infinite number of messages.

Linguistics [ling-GWIS-ticks]: The study of language, including speech sounds, meaning, and grammar.

Psycholinguistics: The study of how language is acquired, perceived, understood, and produced.

perceived, understood, and produced. We will examine three major areas of psycholinguistic study: *phonology,* the study of the sounds of language; *semantics,* the study of the meanings of words and sentences; and *syntax,* the study of the relationships among words and how they combine to form sentences. In each of these areas, researchers have tried to identify the universal characteristics that exist in all languages, not just English.

Language Structure

The basic components of any language are its sounds, the meaning of the sounds, and its overall organization. Let's consider these elements, known more formally as phonology, semantics, and syntax.

Phonology. The gurgling, spitting, and burping noises infants first make are caused by air passing through the vocal apparatus. At about 6 weeks, infants begin to make speechlike cooing sounds. During their first 12 months, babies' vocalizations become more varied and frequent, until eventually they can combine sounds into pronounceable units. As psychologists have studied people's speech patterns, they have helped define the field of **phonology:** the study of the patterns and distribution of speech sounds in a language and the tacit rules for their pronunciation.

The basic units of sound that compose the words in a language are called **phonemes.** In English, phonemes are the sounds of single letters, such as *b, p, f,* and *v,* and of simple combinations of letters, such as *th* in *these.* All the sounds in the English language are expressed in 45 phonemes; of those, just 9 make up nearly half of all words.

Phonology: The study of the patterns and distribution of speech sounds in a language and the tacit rules for their pronunciation.

Phoneme [FOE-neem]: A basic unit of sound in a language.

Morpheme [MORE-feem]: A basic unit of meaning in a language.

Semantics [se-MAN-ticks]: The analysis of the meaning of language, especially of individual words.

Syntax [SIN-tacks]: The way words and groups of words combine to form phrases, clauses, and sentences.

Grammar: The linguistic description of how a language functions, especially the rules and patterns used for generating appropriate and comprehensible sentences.

Transformational grammar: An approach to the study of language that assumes that each sentence has both a surface structure and a deep structure associated with it.

Surface structure: The organization of a sentence in its written or spoken form.

Deep structure: The underlying meaning of a sentence.

Words consist of **morphemes,** the basic units of meaning in a language. A morpheme consists of one or more phonemes combined into a meaningful unit. The morpheme *do,* for example, consists of two phonemes, the sounds of the letters *d* and *o.* Adding prefixes and suffixes to morphemes can form other words. Adding *un-* or *-er* to the morpheme *do,* for example, gives *undo* or *doer. Morphology* is the study of these meaningful sound units.

No matter what language people speak, one of their first meaningful utterances is the morpheme *ma.* It is coincidental that *ma* is a word in English. Other frequently heard early words of English-speaking children are *bye-bye, dada,* and *baby.* In any language, the first words often refer to a specific person or object, especially food, toys, or animals. At about 1 year of age, children make the first sounds that can be classified as real speech. Initially they utter only one word, but soon they are saying as many as four or five words. Once they have mastered 100 or so words, there is a rapid increase in the size of their vocabulary. Interestingly, there is considerable variation when this "vocabulary spurt" takes place; some children exhibit it far earlier than others (Dromi, 1997). In the second year, a child's vocabulary may increase to more than 200 words, and by the end of the third year, to nearly 900 words.

Semantics. At first, babies do not fully understand what their parents' speech means. But as more words take on meaning, the growing child develops semantic capability. **Semantics** is the analysis of the meaning of language, especially of individual words, the relationships among them, and their significance within particular contexts.

Consider how a 4-year-old child might misconstrue what her father says to her mother: "I've had a terrible day. First, the morning traffic made me a nervous wreck. Then, I got into an argument with my boss, and he almost fired me." The child might think her dad got into a car accident and was nearly set on fire. In trying to understand what is being said, a child must decipher not only the meanings of single words but also their relationships to other words. As everyone who has attempted to learn a new language knows, the meaning of a sentence is not always the same as the definitions of the individual words added together. Although children acquire words daily, the words they learn mean different things, depending on their context. Of course, even adults use only a small set of words over and over again; most other words are used rarely. People who learn a new language usually concentrate on the most widely used words. Teachers of French or Spanish rarely attempt to have students learn the words for *aura* or *modality.* The focus tends to be on basic, utilitarian vocabulary and syntax.

Syntax. Young children start out by using single words to represent whole sentences or ideas. They say "peas" or "hungry," and adults understand that they mean they want more peas or that they are hungry. We call such one-word utterances *holophrases*. Eventually, children begin to combine words into short sentences, such as "Mama look" or "Bye-bye, Mama." This kind of slightly expanded, but still reduced, speech in which words are left out is referred to as *telegraphic speech*, or *telegraphese*. Over a period of weeks and months, children show syntactic capability. **Syntax** is the way words and groups of words combine to form phrases, clauses, and sentences. Syntactic capability enables children to convey more meaning. For example, children acquire a powerful new way of making their demands known when they learn to combine the words *I want* or *Give me* with appropriate nouns. Suddenly, they can ask for cookies, toys, or Mommy, without any of them being within pointing range. The rewards that such linguistic behavior bring children are powerful incentives to learn more language. Children do not really need external rewards to want to learn language, though. Children begin to use sentences at different ages; but once they begin, they tend to improve at similar rates (Brown, 1970). Moreover, the average length of sentences increases at a fairly regular rate as children grow older.

Early studies of children's short sentences suggested that early speech could be characterized by descriptions of the positions and types of words they used. However, later investigations showed these descriptions to be inadequate and suggested that young children possess an innate grammar and that they use grammatical relationships in much the same ways as adults do (McNeill, 1970). **Grammar** is the linguistic description of how a language functions, especially in terms of the rules and patterns used for generating appropriate and comprehensible sentences.

Table 6.2 summarizes some of the early linguistic milestones in a child's life.

Table 6.2 Early Linguistic Milestones

Age	Language Activity
12 weeks	Smiles when talked to; makes cooing sounds spontaneously
16 weeks	Turns head in response to human voices
20 weeks	Makes vowel and consonant sounds while cooing
6 months	Changes from cooing to babbling
12 months	Imitates sounds; understands some words
18 months	Uses from 3–50 words (some babies use very few words at this age—as few as 3—while others use as many as 100); understands basic speech
24 months	Uses between 50 and as much as 250 words; uses two-word phrases
30 months	Uses new words daily; has good comprehension of speech; vocabulary of about 500 words
36 months	Has vocabulary of more than 850 words; makes grammatical mistakes, but their number decreases significantly with each passing week

Transformational Grammar

In 1957, linguist Noam Chomsky, a brilliant theoretician, described a radical approach to grammar that changed many psychologists' views of language development. When it was first introduced, Chomsky's theory was seen as extreme, even reactionary, and, from a behaviorist perspective (then dominant), too "mentalistic." Today, Chomsky is widely considered to be the father of modern linguistics. His original theory claimed that each person is born with the ability to transform a particular kernel of meaning into an infinite number of meaningful sentences. In Chomsky's view, the meaningful message of a sentence is stored differently from the words used to compose it (Chomsky, 1986, 1990). Psychologists are especially interested in this theory because it helps to explain unique features of human language. Recently, Chomsky has focused on how sound and meaning are related to one another. Like his earlier constructs, his newer idea is straightforward: We possess an innate word–sound–sentence generational mechanism capable of forming meaningful sentences. This idea awaits new research to support it.

Surface and Deep Structures. The fundamental idea of Chomsky's **transformational grammar** is that each sentence has both a surface structure and a deep structure. The **surface structure** is the organization of a sentence in its written or spoken form. The words and phrases that make up surface structure can be analyzed through the diagramming procedures often taught in junior high school. The **deep structure** is the underlying meaning of the sentence. Thus, the sentences *Alex gave Mary a dog* and *Mary was given* *a dog by Alex* have different surface structures but the same deep structure.

To understand transformational grammar more clearly, consider this sentence: *Visiting relatives can be a pain.* Although the sentence is simple, it has two distinct meanings: (1) Relatives who visit can be annoying guests, or (2) going to visit relatives is an annoying chore. Transformational grammar accounts for these two meanings by showing that for the same surface structure, there are two possible deep structures. To a great extent, the deep structure, or meaning, of a word or a sentence is far more important than its surface structure.

Think Critically

- If a person is going to learn a second language, where is the best place to do it, and when? Why?

Language Acquisition

Focus on issues and ideas

- The major theories of language acquisition
- How chimp language is a vital research area in psychology

That human beings acquire language is one of their defining characteristics. Acquiring language is a major achievement in the life of a child, and language continues to define us as adults and separates us from other species (Bickerton, 1995). All of our cultural achievements, including the arts and advances in science, technology, and even warfare, depend on the use of language. Language development is an individual achievement, but it is also a social process that involves people communicating with one another (Clark, 1996).

Since language is a unique human gift, a special ability, was there an evolutionary turn of events that set humans apart in this respect (MacWhinney, 1998)? If language were solely an evolutionary unfolding, the story would be simple, but research shows that language and thought are sensitive to both genetic inheritance (nature) and experience (nurture). As in other areas of human behavior, the debate continues about the relative contribution of each factor. If language is based on evolution and biology, two things should be true: (1) Many aspects of language ability should be evident early in life. (2) All children, regardless of their culture or their language, should develop grammar (an understanding of language patterns) in a similar way. If environmental factors account for language acquisition, the role of learning should be preeminent. Consider what happens when a person decides to learn a foreign language. The person recognizes that the new language includes a new grammar, new written forms, and new pronunciation. The person may buy study aids: books, dictionaries, and tapes. She or he may read about the country in which the new language is spoken, talk to someone who speaks the language, and rely on foreign language teachers. In general, the person *prepares* to acquire the new language. But when you learned your very first language, how were you prepared for learning it? Were you prepared at all?

In trying to resolve the nature–nurture debate with respect to language acquisition, researchers use observational studies of infants and children, case histories of sensory-deprived infants, studies of reading-disabled or brain-damaged individuals, and experiments with chimpanzees.

Learning Theories

The learning approach to language acquisition is quite simple. Early learning researchers such as Skinner argued that people speak and understand language because specific language behaviors are reinforced and repeated from the moment of birth. Skinner would argue that vocalizations that are not reinforced decrease in frequency. Children in Paris learn French because that's what they hear and are reinforced for. As babies learn language, they watch models produce language, imitate the models, and then are reinforced for their language behavior (Bates & Elman, 1996). Infants are attentive listeners, and parents adjust their speech to provide them with well-spaced information (Kuhl et al., 1997). Babies attend in a focused way, listening intently and repeating the sounds they hear, especially those they have heard before (Saffran, Aslin, & Newport, 1996).

As parents become better able to untangle a baby's babble and make sense of it, they often repeat the baby's sounds in proper English so that the baby can hear them pronounced correctly. Parents often then reinforce the baby by responding in some way to the baby's utterance. A baby might say, "Daddy, baby, wasue," and the parent may say, "You want Daddy to give you water?" The baby smiles, receives a drink, and the process continues—until eventually, over days and weeks, the baby learns correct pronunciation and proper word order. Thus, learning approaches use traditional learning (operant conditioning) theories and more modern (social/observational learning) theories to explain the acquisition of language.

Biological Theories

Learning theories emphasize the role of environmental influences, or nurture, in language acquisition. The basic idea is that language is acquired in a process that reflects traditional concepts of learning. But people have the ability to generate an almost infinite number of correctly formed sentences in their native language. Because this ability cannot be acquired solely through imitation or instruction, many researchers, such as psychologist George Miller (1965), assert that human beings are biologically equipped at birth with an innate, unique capacity to acquire and develop language. Such nativist positions assume that human beings are born with a mental *language acquisition device,* or *LAD,* to process and facilitate the learning of language.

Although Miller and Chomsky (1957) do not exclude experience as a factor in shaping children's language, they claim that human nature itself, through a LAD, allows children to pay attention to language in their environment and ultimately to use it. Nonetheless, even the strongest proponents of the nature (biological) argument do not contend that a specific language is inborn. Rather, they agree that a predisposition toward language use exists and that human beings are born with a "preprinted" blueprint for language (Pinker, 1999). As a child matures, this blueprint provides the framework through which the child learns a specific language and its rules (e.g., Marcus et al., 1999). Three major sources of evidence support the nature side of the nature versus nurture debate: (1) studies of brain structure, lateralization, and convergence zones, (2) studies of learning readiness, and (3) studies of language acquisition in children and chimpanzees.

Brain Structure, Lateralization, and Convergence Zones. Even as early as 1800, researchers knew that the human brain was specialized for different functions. At that time, researchers began mapping the brain and discovering that if certain areas were damaged (usually through accidents), the injured person exhibited severe disorders in language abilities. Later work, some of it by Norman Geschwind (1972), led to the idea of *lateralization*—the localization of a particular brain function primarily in one hemisphere. As Chapter 2 showed, considerable evidence suggests that the left hemisphere and the right hemisphere of the brain (normally connected by the corpus callosum) have some distinct functions.

Some researchers argue that the brain has unique processing abilities in each hemisphere. For example, important language functions are predominantly, but not exclusively, left-hemisphere functions (Corina, Vaid, & Bellugi, 1992). However, the available data do not make an airtight case; each hemisphere seems to play a dominant role in some functions and to interact with the other hemisphere in the performance of others (Baynes et al., 1998).

Learning Readiness. Researcher Eric Lenneberg (1921–1975) claimed that human beings are born with a grammatical capacity and a readiness to produce language (Lenneberg, 1967). He theorized that language simply develops as people interact with their environment. One important aspect of this theory is that a child's capacity to learn language depends on the maturation of specific neurological structures. Lack of maturity of certain brain structures limits infants' ability to speak in the first months of life. But the structural maturation that has occurred by about 18 to 24 months permits children to acquire grammar. Lenneberg's view derives in part from observations that most children learn the rules of grammar at a very early age.

Lenneberg believed that the brain continues to develop from birth until about age 13, with the greatest developmental leap taking place around age 2. During this period, children develop grammar and learn the rules of language. After age 13, there is little room for improvement or change in an individual's neurological structure. Lenneberg supported his argument with the observation that brain-damaged children can relearn some speech and language, whereas brain-damaged adolescents or adults who lose language and speech are unable to regain the lost ability completely. Lenneberg's view is persuasive, but some of his original claims have been seriously criticized—particularly his idea of the role of a critical time period in language development (e.g., Kinsbourne, 1975).

Some researchers claim that not only human beings but also other animals—for example, chimpanzees—are born with a grammatical capacity and a readiness for language.

Language Studies with Chimpanzees

Clearly, many animals communicate with one another. Whales use clicks and wails, monkeys have various sounds to signal one another, especially when predators appear, wolves howl—the examples are nearly endless. But do animals communicate with one another through language? If they do, is that language the same as, similar to, or totally different from the language of human beings? Most important, what can scientists learn from animals about the inborn aspects of language?

The biological approach to language suggests that human beings are "prewired"—born with a capacity for language. Experience is the key that unlocks this existing capacity and allows its development. The arguments for and against the biological approach to language acquisition use studies showing that chimpanzees naturally develop some language abilities. Chimpanzees are generally considered among the most intelligent animals; in addition, they resemble human beings more closely than any other animal does. Playful and curious, chimps share many common physical and mental abilities with human beings. Their brains have a similar organization; and some languagelike functions may even be lateralized in chimpanzees (Gannon et al., 1998). This is an important and interesting finding, because psychologists have generally believed that only human beings exhibited brain asymmetries related to lateralization of language functions. Researchers are not sure what this lateralization in chimps means, but it will most likely provide some hints into their language abilities. What it does *not* mean is that chimps have human language—a similar structure does not necessarily imply a similar function.

Chimps are especially valuable to study because researchers can also control and shape the environment in which chimps learn language, something they cannot do in studies involving human beings. For these reasons, chimpanzees have been the species of choice when psychologists have studied language in animals.

However, all attempts to teach animals to talk have failed. Until recently, this failure had led most psycholinguists to conclude that only human beings have the capacity to acquire language. Two decades ago, however, some major research projects showed that even though chimpanzees lack the physical vocal apparatus necessary to produce speech, they can learn to use different methods to communicate with humans. Scientists have studied chimpanzees both in near-natural environments and in laboratory settings using computer technology. With results from sharply different environments, studies of chimps show that their language usage is similar to that of very young children: It is concrete, specific, and limited. However, chimps do not show the ability to generate an unlimited number of grammatically correct sentences, an ability that human beings begin to acquire at a fairly young age. Not only is chimp language different from that of human beings but also the purpose of chimp language is different. Unlike young children, who spontaneously learn to name and to point at objects (often called *referential naming*), chimps do not spontaneously develop such communication skills. Terrace (1985) agrees that the ability to name is a basic part of human consciousness. He argues that, as part of socialization, children learn to refer to various inner states: feelings, thoughts, and emotions. Chimps can be taught some naming skills, but the procedure is long and tedious. Children, on the other hand, develop these skills easily and spontaneously at a young age. Researchers question the comparability of human and chimp language.

Although few psychologists are completely convinced that chimpanzees can learn to use language the way humans do, their criticisms do not diminish the chimps' language abilities or their accomplishments in other areas, such as mathematics (Boysen & Berntson, 1989; Brannon & Terrace, 1998) and comprehension (Sevcik & Savage-Rumbaugh, 1994). Chimp language remains a vital research area for psychologists; researchers such as Savage-Rumbaugh assert that basic ideas about the nature of language must be reevaluated—the linguistic feats of the chimps are just too impressive. The answers to researchers' questions about language acquisition are far from complete, but the quest is exciting and is being extended to other species, including dolphins (Herman, Kuczaj, & Holder, 1993; Schusterman & Gisiner, 1988).

Social Interaction Theories: A Little Bit of Each

The debate over language acquisition is a wonderful example of how issues in psychology emerge, grow, and contribute to an understanding of human behavior. Early learning theorists took an unbending view of the role of reinforcement in language development. Later, biologically based researchers assumed that the biological and physical underpinning of language was just too strong to deny the role of physiology in language. But neither view by itself is correct. Children are born with a predisposition to language—there is no doubt about that. And nearly everybody agrees that children are reinforced for their language behavior. But children's use of language takes place within a social setting that changes daily—the child's differing moods and needs may be met by different caretakers with their own moods and needs. So language is in part innate and in part reinforced—and rigid polarized views of innate grammars or reinforced behaviors are probably too limited in their conceptions of language acquisition (Seidenberg, 1997).

A key to understanding language acquisition is to consider not only the structure of language, but also its function and the context in which it is learned, expressed, and practiced.

Like so many other behaviors, language use is affected by the context in which it occurs. At feeding time, babies are far more likely to express hunger vocally. While playing, babies are far more likely to be self-centered, making utterances that do not necessarily have communicative functions. Parents often use a teaching mode and articulate words, sentences, and emotional expressions especially strongly when talking to a child because they want the child to learn something particular. In the early months of life, infants acquire the phonetic properties of their native language by listening to adults speak. Interestingly, mothers exaggerate—they produce vowel sounds acoustically more extreme—when talking with infants than when taking to adults (Kuhl et al., 1997).

A key to understanding language acquisition is to consider not only the structure of language, but also its function and the context in which it is learned, expressed, and practiced. Human beings are very much social organisms, and language serves a vital function as a way for children to get attention and make their needs known. So, although a child may be prewired for language acquisition and reinforced for using language correctly, language nearly always is used in a social setting—whose importance cannot be underestimated.

Think Critically

- The two learning approaches to language acquisition—conditioning and imitation—differ with respect to what key underlying principle? (Think back to Chapter 5.)

www.abacon.com/leftononline

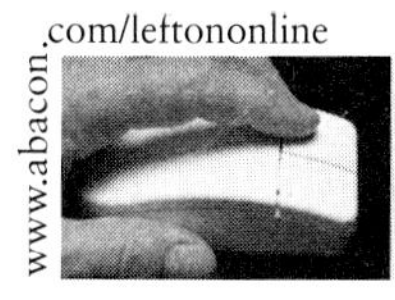

Your password-protected Website allows you access to the most comprehensive set of materials in The Psychology Place.

Summary and Review

Memory: The Brain as Information Processor

Define memory.

KEY TERM
memory, p. 147

Encoding

What is the information-processing approach to memory, and what is encoding?

What are the underlying assumptions of the levels-of-processing approach and the parallel distributed processing concept?

KEY TERMS
encoding, p. 148; levels-of-processing approach, p. 148; encoding specificity principle, p. 149; transfer-appropriate processing, p. 149; parallel distributed processing, p. 149

Storage

Describe the role of sensory memory.

Describe short-term working memory.

What is rehearsal?

What is long-term memory?

What is consolidation?

Can stimulation of specific cortical areas prompt recall from memory?

KEY TERMS
storage, p. 150; sensory memory, p. 150; rehearsal, p. 151; maintenance rehearsal, p. 151; elaborative rehearsal, p. 151; short-term working memory, p. 152; long-term memory, p. 152; procedural memory, p. 153; declarative memory, p. 153; consolidation, p. 153

Retrieval

Distinguish between episodic and semantic memory.

Differentiate between implicit and explicit memory.

What distinguishes the primacy effect from the recency effect?

What is imagery?

KEY TERMS
retrieval, p. 154; episodic memory, p. 154; semantic memory, p. 154; explicit memory, p. 155; implicit memory, p. 155; state-dependent learning, p. 155; primacy effect, p. 157; recency effect, p. 158; imagery, p. 158

Forgetting: When Memory Fails

What are recall, recognition, and reconstruction?

How and why is information lost from memory?

Distinguish retrograde from anterograde amnesia.

KEY TERMS
schema, p. 160; decay, p. 161; interference, p. 161; proactive interference, p. 161; retroactive interference, p. 161; amnesia, p. 164; retrograde amnesia, p. 164; anterograde amnesia, p. 164

Cognitive Psychology: An Overview

What is the focus of cognitive psychology?

KEY TERMS
cognitive psychology, p. 165;

Concept Formation: The Process of Forming Mental Groups

What is involved in the process of concept formation?

KEY TERMS
concept, p. 165; prototype, p. 168

Problem Solving: Confronting Situations That Require Solutions

What are the fundamental differences between algorithms and heuristics?

What are some barriers to effective problem solving?

KEY TERMS
problem solving, p. 168; algorithm, p. 168; heuristics, p. 169; subgoal analysis, p. 169; means–ends analysis, p. 169; backward search, p. 169; functional fixedness, p. 169; creativity, p. 170; convergent thinking, p. 171; divergent thinking, p. 171; brainstorming, p. 171

Reasoning and Decision Making: Generating Ideas and Reaching Conclusions

Differentiate between reasoning and decision making.

What are two approaches to decision making?

KEY TERMS
reasoning, p. 172; logic, p. 172; decision making, p. 172; syllogism, p. 172

Artificial Intelligence

What is artificial intelligence?

Describe how neural networks work.

Language

How are language, thought, and culture interrelated, and what are the key elements of language?

KEY TERMS
language, p. 177; linguistics, p. 177; psycholinguistics, p. 177; phonology, p. 178; phoneme, p. 178; morpheme, p. 178; semantics, p. 178; syntax, p. 179; grammar, p. 179; transformational grammar, p. 179; surface structure, p. 179; deep structure, p. 179

Language Acquisition

How do theorists explain language acquisition?

Self-Test

1. According to the levels-of-processing approach, people will remember the meaning of a word better if they are asked to ____________ when learning the word.
   A. recite the word many times
   B. think of synonyms for the word
   C. think of rhymes for the word
   D. think of the shape of the letters

2. Which type of memory can be described as lasting for only a brief period of time and being the place where initial encoding occurs?
   A. sensory memory
   B. short-term memory
   C. working memory
   D. long-term memory

3. Your ability to do well on these self-test questions depends on:
   A. short-term memory
   B. maintenance memory
   C. semantic memory
   D. episodic memory
4. When material must be remembered in a specific order, ______________ is required.
   A. serial recall
   B. free recall
   C. fixed recall
   D. recognition
5. Little Carrie has just learned that German shepherds and golden retrievers are different types of dogs. She has learned that they are ______________ of the dog category.
   A. concepts
   B. classifications
   C. prototypes
   D. exemplars
6. David does not change the lightbulb in the hallway because he cannot find the ladder. He does not think to use a chair instead. This is an example of:
   A. novel responding
   B. functional fixedness
   C. originality
   D. creative set
7. The belief that an event is more likely to happen if it has not happened recently is the:
   A. belief in small numbers
   B. availability heuristic
   C. gambler's fallacy
   D. overconfidence mindset
8. ______________ are certain areas where activity from different regions in the brain comes together:
   A. Blindsight areas
   B. Intelligence zones
   C. Processing centers
   D. Convergence zones
9. The study of the sounds of a language is:
   A. morphology
   B. phonology
   C. semantics
   D. syntax
10. The main difference between language in chimps and language in humans is that:
    A. chimps cannot learn the meaning of words
    B. chimps cannot comprehend spoken language
    C. chimps cannot generate an unlimited number of new sentences
    D. chimps cannot combine words to create simple phrases

Chapter 7

Intelligence

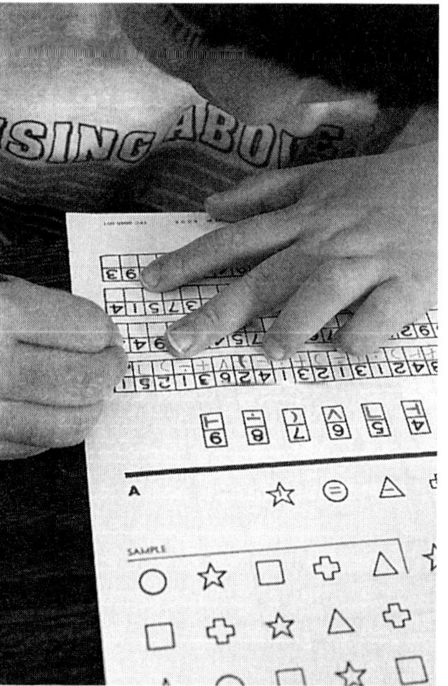

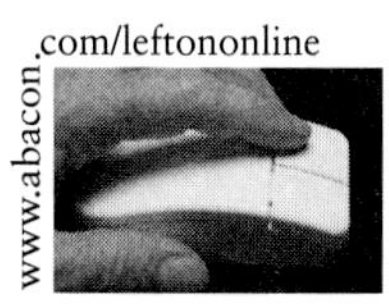

Go to your password-protected Website for full-color art, Weblinks, and more!

My nephew Corey is obsessed with increasing his SAT scores by 25 points, which may mean getting only two or three more questions right. Now, I know (and so does he) that 25 more points won't mean a great deal. No college is going to base its entire decision on such a small difference. In fact, Cory's stellar record in high school will guarantee him a spot in every school to which he has applied. The 25 extra points are an important goal for a different reason. If he improves his score by that much, his state scholarship for 75% of his tuition will increase to 100%. Those points translate into cold, hard cash; for Cory, they mean the difference between working 15 hours a week while attending college and having that much more time to study and socialize.

How to get the points? What will Corey have to learn? Will learning something particular make any difference? There are books on test taking. There are courses at Corey's local community college, as well as more expensive courses offered by a local company and costing as much as $900 for seven weeks of pre-SAT instruction. Last weekend, my nephew asked me, "What does the SAT measure?" Since this is a long-standing and important question in psychology, my answer was appropriately professorial (and possibly a bit long-winded). It began, "Corey, it's not so simple. You have to ask, can special training boost a person's score? Do results of an achievement test, like the SAT, reflect intelligence? Can achievement be improved in a person of limited intelligence—or are intelligence and achievement the same thing? There are also social policy questions: Is it fair to train some students for such tests? Should economically comfortable students be allowed an advantage because they can seek out specialized training? Should economically disadvantaged students be given some special consideration?" In the end, I fear I didn't really answer Corey's question.

Should Corey's scholarship depend on a 25-point SAT spread? It sounds like a bet on a basketball game rather than a question about a student's intellectual acuity. For a psychologist, Corey's situation raises several essential issues about testing—not the least of which is "What is intelligence?" ■

Evaluating intellectual capabilities is a complex task, for there is more to intelligence than test scores. Intelligence tests (which the SAT, by the way, is *not*) do not measure other characteristics that are important to success, such as motivation, creativity, and leadership skills. People demonstrate effective and intelligent behavior in many ways, but not in the same ways. Some people, for example, can write a complicated computer program but not a short story. Moreover, intelligence must be defined in terms of the situations in which people find themselves. Intelligent behavior for a dancer is very different from intelligent behavior for a scientist, and both of these are different from intelligent behavior for a child with a learning disability.

No single set of test questions—whether they focus on verbal ability, knowledge of English literature, or math skills—is a clear measure of intelligence. Psychologists therefore use a variety of test results, as well as other data, including interviews, teacher evaluations, and writing and drawing samples, to evaluate an individual's current intellectual status, to make predictions about future performance or behavior, and to offer suggestions for remedial work or therapy. In spite of their drawbacks, tests do have strong predictive value; for example, intelligence tests can generally predict academic achievement, and achievement tests can generally predict whether someone will profit from further training in a specific area.

In this chapter, we consider individual differences in intelligence and examine theories, tests, and controversies. We also examine two special populations: the gifted and the mentally retarded. But first, let's begin with that basic, but difficult, question: What is intelligence? (I)

(I) What Is Intelligence?

Focus on issues and ideas

- Understanding the various theories of intelligence as one ability or many abilities

Although most psychologists, and the public, accept the idea that intelligence exists, it has been measured and described quite differently, or not at all, in various societies. Clearly, agricultural societies that depend on skills related to planting and harvesting do not have standard tests that measure the speed or quality of those skills. But today's fast-paced technological society requires specialized computational and linguistic skills, generating a need to evaluate people as good or bad on specific tasks involving that set of skills, which has been named intelligence (Kagan, 1998).

For some psychologists, intelligence is all mental abilities; for others, it is the basic general factor necessary for all mental activity; for still others, it is a group of specific abilities. Most agree, however, that intelligence is a capacity, not a thing. Reaching this point of agreement involved a convoluted process. Early psychologists sought to separate normal children from mentally retarded children. They developed tests to do so. Later researchers refined the tests and developed elaborate theories of the "factors" that make up intelligence. From the beginning, researchers have sought to know the source of intelligence. Does it come from parents through the genes, or from learning and the environment? The history of psychology has been punctuated with thousands of research papers on intelligence and its nature. Part of the problem is defining what intelligence is and is not. Part is deciding whether intelligence has one or many components. And part is determining whether nature or nurture is primarily responsible for intelligent behavior.

Recognizing these complexities, we can still formulate a working definition of intelligence: **Intelligence** is the overall capacity of an individual to act purposefully, to think rationally, and to deal effectively with the environment. It is a person's ability to learn and understand. By this definition, intelligence is expressed behaviorally. It is shown in a person's actions and abilities to learn new things and to use previously learned knowledge. Most important, intelligence has to do with a person's ability to adapt to the social and cultural environment. Intelligence is thus not a thing but a capacity, which is affected by a person's day-to-day experiences in the world. Intelligence is *not* a person's IQ, which is merely a score derived from a test.

Theories of Intelligence—One Ability, or Many?

A key issue has been, and continues to be, whether there is one intelligence or many. Is intelligence a singular property, or does it consist of many, more or less independent components? Today, the most influential views on this issue are Wechsler's theory, factor theories, Jensen's two-level theory, Vygotsky's view, Gardner's theory of multiple intelligences, and Sternberg's triarchic theory proposed.

Wechsler's Theory. David Wechsler viewed intelligence from the perspective of a tester. As one of the developers of a widely used and respected intelligence test (which we will examine later), Wechsler knew that such tests are made up of many subparts, each measuring a fairly narrow aspect of a person's functioning and resourcefulness. He argued that intelligence tests involving spatial relations and verbal comprehension reveal little about someone's overall capacity to deal with the world. In Wechsler's view, psychologists need to remember that intelligence is more than simply mathematical or problem-solving ability; it is the broader ability to deal with the world.

Factor Theories. Factor theories of intelligence use a correlation technique known as *factor analysis* to explore what makes up intelligence. **Factor analysis** is a statistical procedure designed to discover the independent elements (factors) in any set of data. With regard to intelligence testing, factor analysis attempts to find a cluster of items that measure a common ability. Results of tests of verbal comprehension, spelling, and reading speed, for example, usually correlate highly, suggesting that some underlying attribute of verbal abilities (a factor) determines a person's score on those three tests.

In the early 1900s, Charles E. Spearman (1863–1945) used factor analysis to show that intelligence consists of two parts: a general factor affecting all tasks, which he termed the *g* factor, and specific factors associated with particular tasks. This view of intelligence is known as the *two-factor theory of intelligence*. Experts argue about whether this theory is well-grounded, but many continue to assert that a general factor underlies the diverse cognitive abilities (Brody, 1997).

Louis L. Thurstone (1887–1955) further developed Spearman's work by postulating a general factor analogous to Spearman's, as well as seven other basic factors, each representing a unique mental ability: verbal comprehension, word fluency, number facility, spatial visualization, associative memory, perceptual speed, and reasoning. Known as the *factor theory of intelligence,* Thurstone's theory included a computational scheme for sorting out these seven factors. The factor theory is not universally accepted.

Jensen's Two-Level Theory. Arthur Jensen approaches intelligence testing not from the viewpoint of a test constructor but from that of a theoretician. Jensen (1969, 1970, 1987) suggests that intellectual functioning consists of associative abilities and cognitive abilities. *Associative abilities* enable people to connect stimuli and events; they involve little reasoning or transformation. Items testing associative abilities might, for example, ask someone to repeat from memory a seven-digit number sequence and to identify geometric shapes or classify them into categories. *Cognitive abilities,* on the other hand, involve reasoning and problem solving. Solving word problems and explaining new concepts are examples of tasks that test cognitive ability. Jensen's idea is not new; even the founders of the testing movement (to be discussed shortly) believed that different kinds of intellectual functioning are involved in intelligence. What is new is Jensen's claim that associative and cognitive abilities are inherited, which adds fuel to the nature-versus-nurture controversy about intelligence (which we'll consider later in this chapter).

Vygotsky's View. While various researchers sought to enumerate the factors that make up "true" intelligence, others argued that there are multiple pro-

Intelligence: The overall capacity of an individual to act purposefully, to think rationally, and to deal effectively with the environment.

Factor analysis: Statistical procedure designed to discover the independent elements (factors) in any set of data.

cesses and systems involved in intelligent thinking and that a person's early development and environment are especially important in shaping intelligence. Lev Vygotsky (1896–1934) was a Russian psychologist who saw intellectual development as occurring in a social context that includes communication, with the self and with others. Intelligence is not one task, but many, which are interwoven. Children, for example, engage in private speech to plan their own actions and behavior; when they use such speech, they do better at various intellectual tasks. Vygotsky suggested that private speech helps a child understand his or her world. For Vygotsky (1934/1962), even the earliest speech is essentially social and useful and a key part of intelligence; in fact, he asserted that social speech comes first, followed by egocentric (self-centered) speech, then inner speech. In 1930, Vygotsky wrote, "the most significant moment in the course of intellectual development . . . occurs . . . when speech and practical activity, two previously completely independent lines of development, converge" (Vygotsky, 1930/1978, p. 24). Psychologists must, according to Vygotsky, examine the dynamics, the interactions, of these two lines of development. Since many tasks are involved, intelligence is not so much a product as a process; this argument is supported by a number of contemporary thinkers who assert the existence of multiple intelligences.

Gardner's Multiple Intelligences. Many researchers have proposed that there are multiple types of intelligence and that traditional intelligence tests do not measure them. Howard Gardner has been at the leading edge of those theoreticians (1983/1993, 1995; Gardner & Hatch, 1989). Gardner argues that human competencies, of which there are many, do not all lend themselves to measurement on a standard test. He maintains that people have multiple intelligences—"an intelligence" being an ability to solve a problem or create a product within a specific cultural setting. Gardner's eight types of intelligence are summarized in Table 7.1.

Gardner's view has been widely praised and criticized. It has been praised for its recognition of the cultural context of intelligence, its consideration of

Table 7.1 Gardner's Multiple Intelligences

Type of Intelligence	Exemplar	Core Components
Linguistic	Poet Journalist	Sensitivity to the sounds, rhythms, and meanings of words; sensitivity to the different functions of language
Logical–mathematical	Scientist Mathematician	Sensitivity to and capacity to discern logical or numerical patterns; ability to handle long chains of reasoning
Musical	Composer Violinist	Ability to produce and appreciate rhythm, pitch, and timbre; appreciation of the forms of musical expressiveness
Spatial	Navigator Sculptor	Capacity to perceive the visual–spatial world accurately and to perform transformations on initial perceptions
Bodily–kinesthetic	Dancer Athlete	Ability to control bodily movements and to handle objects skillfully
Naturalist	Botanist Chef	Ability to make fine discriminations among the flora and fauna of the natural world or the patterns and designs of human artifacts
Interpersonal	Therapist Salesperson	Capacity to discern and respond appropriately to the moods, temperaments, motivations, and desires of other people
Intrapersonal	Person with detailed, accurate, self-knowledge	Access to one's own feelings and the ability to discriminate among them and draw on them to guide behavior; knowledge of one's own strengths, weaknesses, desires, and intelligence

Source: H. Gardner & T. Hatch, Multiple intelligences go to school: Educational implications of the theory of multiple intelligences, *Educational Researcher, 18(8)* (1989), 6; with adaptation based on personal communication from H. Gardner (1996).

multiple human competencies, and the framework it offers in which to analyze intelligence in school and other applied settings. The criticisms of his multiple intelligences approach focus on terminology—for example, are talents one type of intelligence? Some critics assert that Gardner's "intelligences" are all highly correlated with one another, essentially measuring the same thing. Still other critics assert that his eight intelligences are merely descriptions of competencies and will lead to eight IQ test scores rather than one. The scientific jury is still out, but Gardner's work on multiple intelligences has certainly influenced other theorists, including Sternberg.

Sternberg's Triarchic Theory. Robert J. Sternberg of Yale University takes an information-processing view of intelligence. He argues (1986a) that "the essence of intelligence is that it provides a means to govern ourselves so that our thoughts and actions are organized, coherent, and responsive to both our internally driven needs and to the needs of the environment." He maintains that the traditional tests used by colleges to make admissions decisions—including the SAT, GRE, and even IQ tests—measure only limited aspects of behavior and do not predict future success very well (Sternberg & Williams, 1997).

Sternberg argues that researchers have focused for too long on how to measure intelligence, rather than on several more important questions: What is intelligence? How does it change? What can individuals do to enhance it? Sternberg claims that some tests measure individual mental abilities, while others measure the way an individual operates in the environment. He asserts that a solid theory of intelligence must account for both by focusing on *successful intelligence,* or the ability to adapt to, shape, and select environments to accomplish one's goals and those of society. Sternberg (1985, 1997a) has proposed a *triarchic theory* in which intelligence has three dimensions: analytic, practical, and creative.

The *analytic dimension* of intelligence involves an individual's ability to use intelligence for problem solving in specific situations where there is one right answer. This part of the triarchic theory focuses on how people shape their environments so that their competencies can be used to best advantage. The *practical dimension* has to do with a person's application of his or her experience with the external world and with everyday tasks. According to this part of Sternberg's theory, a test measures intelligence if it assesses a person's ability both to handle novel tasks and to master tasks so that they can be performed in an automatic manner. The *creative dimension* of Sternberg's triarchic intelligence is the glue that holds the other two dimensions together. It describes the mental mechanisms underlying what are commonly considered intelligent behaviors. Tasks involving analogies, vocabulary, and syllogisms can be used to measure the elements of creative intelligence.

Few behaviors engage all three dimensions of intelligence, so Sternberg asserts that various tasks measure intelligence to a different extent. Thus, from Sternberg's point of view, new batteries of tests are needed to fully analyze the three basic dimensions of intelligent behavior. Good predictors of a person's academic achievement will take into account knowledge of the world—practical intelligence or common sense—in addition to verbal comprehension and mathematical reasoning (Sternberg et al., 1995). Too often, children do poorly in school and in life despite having obvious intellectual skills. These individuals often do not know how to allocate their time or how to work effectively with other people. Such skills need to be taught, because some students do not develop them on their own (Sternberg, 1997c). As Ceci (1991) asserts, schools foster the learning of specific skills, not necessarily general problem-solving abilities. In addition, schools often promote specific ways of thinking about problems, but researchers and tests need to value alternative modes of thought and creativity. For example, tests—especially IQ tests—should begin to probe for wise responses. In life, people seek to develop wisdom, an intellectual facility that allows one to apply tacit knowledge of the

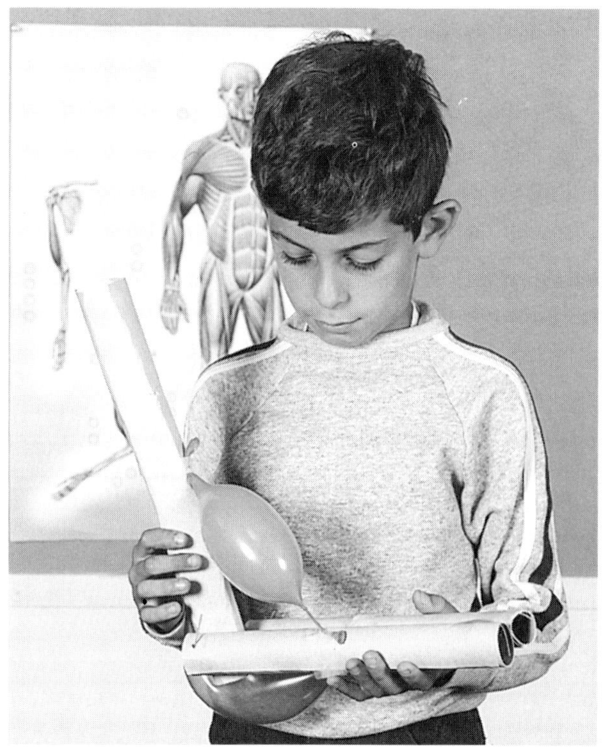

world to seek a goal (often some common good) by achieving a balance among interests and alternatives in light of personal values (Sternberg, 1998). Sternberg and Gardner have teamed up to develop a curriculum to help students improve their practical intelligence by learning to think without boundaries (brainstorm), to break down mindsets (free themselves from functional fixedness), and to recognize novel solutions (exercise creativity). (I)

Think Critically

- What might be the implications for researchers of Vygotsky's claim that scientists must examine the process of intelligence, not just its products?
- What might you add to a school curriculum to foster thinking without boundaries, breaking down of mindsets, and recognition of novel solutions?

(I) The Process of Test Development

Focus on issues and ideas

- Understanding what an intelligence test measures and how it is developed
- Distinguishing between the reliability and the validity of tests

You probably have taken one or more intelligence tests during your school years. Whether or not you were aware of the results of these tests, they may have determined your educational track from elementary school onward. But psychologists are among the first to admit that intelligence tests have shortcomings, and researchers continue to revise these tests to correct the inadequacies and to maximize the tests' practical benefits in educational, occupational, and clinical settings (Daniel, 1997).

Intelligence tests have a long history. In the late 19th and early 20th centuries, Frenchman Alfred Binet (1857–1911), became interested in psychology and began to study behavior. He later hired Theodore Simon (1873–1961), a 26-year-old physician to assist him; their friendship and collaboration became famous. Binet and Simon are best known as the founders of the psychological testing movement. Interestingly, however, their first intelligence tests weren't developed for the general population. In 1904, Binet was commissioned to devise procedures for identifying and educating children in Paris who suffered from mental retardation. Binet coined the phrase *mental age,* meaning the age level at which a child is functioning cognitively, regardless of chronological age. Binet and Simon applied everyday tasks, such as counting, naming, and using objects, to determine mental age. The scale they developed is widely considered to be the first practical measure of intelligence. One of the most influential intelligence tests in use today is the Stanford–Binet test, a direct descendant of Binet's and Simon's early tests.

Developing an Intelligence Test

Imagine you are a 7-year-old child taking an intelligence test, and you come to this question: "Which one of the following tells you the temperature?" Below the question are pictures of the sun, a radio, a thermometer, and a pair of mittens. Is the thermometer the only correct answer? Suppose there are no thermometers in your home, but you often hear the temperature given on radio weather reports. Or imagine that you estimate the temperature each morning by standing outside to feel the sun's strength, or that you know it's cold outside when your parents tell you to wear mittens. Based on your experiences, any one of the answers to the question might be appropriate.

What Does a Test Measure? The predisposition to respond to almost any test question based on experiences—social and cultural biases—illustrates the complexity of intelligence test development. In general, a *test* is a standardized device for examining a person's responses to specific stimuli, usually questions or problems. Because there are many potential pitfalls in creating a test, psychologists follow an elaborate set of guidelines and procedures to make certain that questions are properly constructed. First, a psychologist must decide what the test is to measure. For example, will it measure musical ability, knowledge of geography, or math skills? Second, the psychologist needs to construct items for the test such that answering them successfully reflects the kind of ability being measured. Third, the test must be standardized.

Standardization. Standardization is the process of developing uniform procedures for administering and scoring a test and for establishing norms.

Standardization: Process of developing uniform procedures for administering and scoring a test and for establishing norms.

Norms are the scores and corresponding percentile ranks of a large and representative sample of individuals from the population for which the test is designed. A **representative sample** is a sample of individuals who match the population with whom they are to be compared with regard to key variables such as socioeconomic status and age. Thus, a test designed for all U.S. college freshmen might be given to a sample of 2,000 freshmen, including an equal number of males and females, between the ages of 16 and 20, who graduated from large and small high schools, come from different areas of the United States, and represent different ethnic groups and socioeconomic levels.

Standardization ensures that there is a basis for comparing all future test results with those of a standard reference group. After a test has been designed and administered to a representative sample, the test developers examine the results to establish norms for different segments of the test population. Knowing how people in the representative sample have done allows psychologists and educators to interpret future test results properly. In other words, the scores of those in the representative sample serve as a reference point for comparing individual scores.

The Normal Curve. Test developers generally plot the scores of the representative sample on a graph that shows how frequently each score occurs. On most tests, some people score very well, some score very poorly, and most score in the middle. Psychologists say that test scores distributed in that way are *normally distributed,* or fall on a normal curve. A **normal curve** is a bell-shaped graphic representation of data that shows the percentage of the population that falls under each part of the curve. Most people fall in the middle range, with a few at each extreme. Tests are often devised so that individual scores can be compared to a normal distribution.

Norms: The scores and corresponding percentile ranks of a large and representative sample of individuals from the population for which a test was designed.

Representative sample: A sample of individuals who match the population with whom they are to be compared with regard to key variables such as socioeconomic status and age.

Normal curve: A bell-shaped graphic representation of data showing what percentage of the population falls under each part of the curve.

Raw score: A test score that has not been transformed or converted in any way.

Standard score: A score that expresses an individual's position relative to the mean, based on the standard deviation.

Percentile score: A score indicating what percentage of the test population would obtain a lower score.

Deviation IQ: A standard IQ test score whose mean and standard deviation remain constant for all ages.

Reliability: Ability of a test to yield very similar scores for the same individual over repeated testings.

Validity: Ability of a test to measure what it is supposed to measure and to predict what it is supposed to predict.

Scores. The simplest score on a test is the **raw score**—the number of correct answers, not converted or transformed in any way. The raw score, however, is seldom a true indicator of a person's ability. Raw scores on many tests, particularly intelligence tests, must be adjusted to take into account a person's age, gender, and grade level. An adjusted score is commonly expressed as a **standard score**—a score that expresses an individual's position relative to those of other test takers, based on the mean score and how scores are distributed around it. If, for example, a 100-item intelligence test is administered to students in the 3rd and 11th grades, test developers expect those in 11th grade to answer more items correctly than those in 3rd grade. To adjust for the differences, scoring procedures allow each student's score to be compared to the score typically achieved by other students at the same grade level. Thus, if 11th-graders typically answer 70 questions correctly, an 11th-grader who answers 90 questions correctly has done better than most other students at that grade level. Similarly, if 3rd-graders usually answer 25 questions correctly, a 3rd-grader who answers 15 questions correctly has done worse than most other 3rd-grade students. A standard score is generally a **percentile score**—a score indicating what percentage of the test population obtained a lower score. If, for example, someone's percentile score is 84, then 84% of those taking the test obtained a lower score than that person did.

Intelligence Quotients. Binet's and Simon's test to determine mental age clearly qualifies as an intelligence test—even though it was a relatively crude one. In the early 20th century, intelligence was measured by a simple formula. To obtain an intelligence quotient (IQ), a psychologist divided a person's mental abilities, or mental age, by the person's chronological age and multiplied the result by 100. (See Table 7.2 for examples.) Children's mental ages were estimated from the number of correct answers on a series of test items; the higher the number, the higher the mental age.

A problem with the traditional formula—divide mental age by chronological age and multiply the result by 100—is that young children's answers to test items vary far more than do older children's or adults'; it is as if their intelligence were less stable, less repeatable, and more subject to change. This variability makes predictions and comparisons difficult. To sim-

Table 7.2 Traditional Calculation of Intelligence Quotient for Three People

	Person 1	Person 2	Person 3
Mental Age (MA)	6 years	15 years	15 years
Chronological Age (CA)	6 years	18 years	12 years
MA ÷ CA	6 ÷ 6 = 1	15 ÷ 18 = 0.83	15 ÷ 12 = 1.25
(MA ÷ CA) × 100	1 × 100 = 100	0.83 × 100 = 83	1.25 × 100 = 125
IQ	100	83	125

plify measures of IQ, psychologists and testers began using **deviation IQ**—a standard IQ test score whose mean and standard deviation remain constant for all ages. If a child of 9 and an adolescent of 16 each have a deviation IQ of 116, they are in the same percentile relative to others of their respective ages who have taken the same IQ test.

Perhaps the most important goal of developers of IQ tests is to ensure that tests are both reliable and valid. If a student obtains different scores on two versions of the same test, which score is correct? Furthermore, does the test measure what it is supposed to measure and only that?

Perhaps the most important goal of developers of IQ tests is to ensure that tests are both reliable and valid.

Reliability

Reliability refers to the consistency of test scores. **Reliability** is a test's ability to yield very similar scores for the same individual over repeated testings. (When a researcher says that test scores have consistency, the researcher is assuming that the person taking the test is in approximately the same emotional and physiological state each time the test is administered.) If a test's results are not consistent over several testing sessions or for two comparable groups of people, useful comparisons are impossible. Of course, a single person's score is likely to vary from one administration of a test to another; this is unavoidable, as human beings are not machines. Thus, a test is rarely perfectly reliable; the question is, is it *generally* consistent and does it yield *similar* results on multiple testings?

Among the ways to determine whether a test is reliable, the simplest, termed the *test–retest* method, is to administer the same test to the same person on two or more occasions. If, for example, the person achieves a score of 87 one day and 110 another, the test is probably not reliable (see Table 7.3 on p. 194). Of course, the person might have remembered some of the items from the first testing to the next. To avoid that problem, testers use the *alternative-form method* of determining reliability, which involves giving two different versions of the same test. If the two versions test the same characteristic and differ only in the test items used, both should yield very similar results. Another way to evaluate reliability is to use the *split-half method,* which involves dividing a test into two parts; the scores from the two halves of a reliable test yield similar, if not identical, results.

A reliable test has a relatively small standard error of measurement. The *standard error of measurement* is the number of points by which a score varies because of imperfect reliability. Consider an IQ test that has a standard error of measurement of 3. If someone scores 115 on that test, the test developer can state with a high degree of confidence that the individual's real IQ is between 112 and 118—within 3 points above or below the score obtained.

Validity

If a psychology exam included questions such as "What is the square root of 647?" and "Who wrote *The Grapes of Wrath?*" it would not be a valid measure of the students' knowledge of psychology. That is, it would not be measuring what it is supposed to measure. To be useful, a test must have not only reliability, but also **validity**—the ability to measure only what it is supposed to measure and to predict only what it is supposed to predict.

Types of Validity. *Content validity* is a test's ability to measure the knowledge or behavior it is intended to measure. A test designed to measure musical

Table 7.3 Test–Retest Reliability

Test–retest reliability indicates whether people who are given the same or a similar test on repeated occasions achieve similar scores each time.

	Test with High Reliability		Test with Low Reliability	
	First Testing	Second Testing	First Testing	Second Testing
Person 1	92	90	92	74
Person 2	87	89	87	96
Person 3	78	77	78	51

aptitude should not include items that assess mechanical aptitude or personality characteristics. Similarly, an intelligence test should measure only intelligence, not musical training, cultural experiences, or socioeconomic status.

In addition to content validity, a test should have *predictive validity*—the ability to predict a person's future achievements with at least some degree of accuracy. Critics of tests like to point out that scores on tests are not always accurate predictors of people's performance. Tests cannot take into account high levels of motivation or creative abilities. Nevertheless, many colleges use standard scores to decide which high school students should be accepted for admission—thus assuming that the scores accurately predict ability to do college-level work.

Two additional types of validity are *face validity,* the extent to which a test's appropriateness can be gauged by reading or examining the test items, and *construct validity,* the extent to which a test actually does measure the particular quality or trait it is supposed to measure, such as intelligence, anxiety, or musical ability.

Criticisms of Intelligence Test Validity. Critics cite six basic problems concerning the validity of intelligence tests. The first is that there is no way to measure intelligence because no clear definition of intelligence has been agreed on. The defense against this argument is that, although different intelligence tests seem to measure different abilities, the major tests have face validity. Face validity is the appropriateness of test items at face value—that is, from simply examining the items. Intelligence tests generally contain items requiring problem solving and rational thinking, which are widely considered appropriate measures of intelligence.

The second criticism is that because intelligence test items usually refer to *learned information,* they reflect the quality of a child's schooling rather than the child's actual intelligence. The response to this challenge is that most vocabulary items on intelligence tests are learned in the child's general environment, not only in school; moreover, the ability to learn vocabulary terms and facts seems to depend on a general ability to reason verbally. Further, scores on other measures of ability, including Raven's Progressive Matrices (a nonverbal, untimed test that requires inductive reasoning about perceptual patterns), seem independent of schooling and correlate highly with traditional intelligence test scores.

The third criticism is that the administration of intelligence tests in school settings may adversely affect test scores—not only because the tests are often administered inexpertly, but also because of the halo effect (e.g., Crowl & MacGinitie, 1974). The **halo effect** is the tendency for one particular or outstanding characteristic about an individual (or a group) to influence the evaluation of other characteristics. A test administrator can develop a positive or negative feeling about a person, a class, or a group of students that may influence the administration of tests or the interpretation of test scores (Nathan & Tippins, 1990). People who defend intelligence testing against this charge acknowledge that incorrectly administered tests are likely to result in inaccurate scores, but they claim that this occurs less often than opponents think.

Two other criticisms of intelligence tests are less directly related to the issue of validity. One of these is that some people are *test-wise.* These individuals make better use of their time than others do, guess the tester's intentions, and find clues in the test. Practice

Halo effect: The tendency for one characteristic of an individual to influence a tester's evaluation of other characteristics.

in taking tests improves such individuals' performance. The usual responses to this criticism are that the items on intelligence tests are unfamiliar even to experienced test takers and that the effects of previous practice are seldom or never evident in test scores. Another criticism is that test takers' scores often depend on their *motivation to succeed* rather than on actual intelligence. Claude Steele (1997; Steele & Aronson, 1995) has argued that whenever members of ethnic or other minorities concentrate explicitly on a scholastic task, they worry about confirming negative stereotypes of their group. This extra burden may drag down their performance, through what Steele calls *stereotype threat*—people fear being reduced to a stereotype and then do worse because of the fear. Stereotype threat probably occurs in part because of subtle instructional differences and in part because of situational pressure that may undermine a test taker's self-confidence; unless members of minority groups (African Americans, older adults) are resilient to such threats, their performance is likely to suffer (Steele, 1997). (We will discuss this issue further in Chapter 11, on p. 318.) Defenders of intelligence tests agree that examinees' motivation and attitudes toward being tested are important; however, they deny that the tests themselves may influence motivation.

Test scores must be put into a context that is relevant to the situation of the person who took the test.

Last, success in the United States—both economic and social—is heavily influenced by academic achievement. Most opportunities for prestigious or well-paying jobs emerge only after a person has earned a college degree. But entry into college is determined by success on standardized tests (Sternberg, 1997a), and these tests are affected by schooling. Thus, the system is self-reinforcing and circular. So, the criticism is that society *creates* the correlation between academic success and intelligence test scores. The defense against this criticism, again, is that the scores also correlate with measures of intelligence that seem independent of schooling.

Critics of intelligence tests are concerned about the interpretation of scores. It is important to remember that intelligence tests are generally made up of different subtests or subscales, each yielding a score. There may also be one general score for the entire test. All these scores require knowledgeable interpretation; that is, test scores must be put into a context that is relevant to the situation of the person who took the test. Without such a context, a score is little more than a number. The interpretation of test scores is the key; without such interpretation, a single score can be biased, inaccurate, or misleading.

Table 7.4 summarizes some misconceptions about intelligence tests and testing. 

Table 7.4 Some Misconceptions about Intelligence Tests and Testing

Misconception	Reality
Intelligence tests measure innate intelligence.	IQ scores measure some of an individual's interactions with the environment; they never measure only innate intelligence.
IQs never change.	People's IQs change throughout life, but especially from birth through age 6. Even after this age, significant changes can occur.
Intelligence tests provide perfectly reliable scores.	Test scores are only estimates. Every test should be reported as a statement of probability, such as "There is a 90% chance that the test taker's IQ falls within a 6-point range of the reported score (from 3 points above to 3 points below)."
Intelligence tests measure all aspects of a person's intelligence.	Most intelligence tests do not measure the entire spectrum of abilities related to intellectual behavior. Some stress verbal and nonverbal intelligence but do not adequately measure other areas, such as mechanical skills, creativity, or social intelligence.
A battery of tests reveal everything necessary to make judgments about a person's competence.	No battery of tests can give a complete picture of any person. A battery can only illuminate various areas of functioning.

Source: Adapted from Sattler, 1992.

Think Critically

- Which of the criticisms of intelligence tests and testing is most significant, in your opinion? Why?
- Why might a psychologist not want parents to know their child's IQ score?

Three Important Intelligence Tests

Focus on issues and ideas

- The key characteristics of three important IQ tests
- The strengths and weaknesses of three important IQ tests

What is the best intelligence test? What does it measure? Can you study for an intelligence test and get a higher score? As in other areas of science, theory leads to application; many theorists applied their ideas to the development of intelligence tests. The three tests we examine here—the Stanford–Binet Intelligence Scale, the Wechsler scales, and the Kaufman Assessment Battery for Children—are all widely used, were developed by well-known and respected researchers, and predict performance well. Their results all correlate well with one another, and research shows that they are reliable and valid. We'll begin by examining the first real IQ test, the Stanford–Binet Intelligence Scale.

Stanford-Binet Intelligence Scale

Most people associate the beginning of intelligence testing with Alfred Binet and Theodore Simon. As noted earlier, the two men collaborated to develop the Binet–Simon Scale in 1905. The original test was actually 30 short tests arranged in order of difficulty and consisting of such tasks as distinguishing food from nonfood and pointing to objects and naming them. The Binet–Simon Scale leaned heavily toward verbal questions and was not well standardized.

From 1912 to 1916, Lewis M. Terman revised the scale and developed the test now known as the Stanford–Binet Intelligence Scale. (Terman was teaching at Stanford University when he revised the test.) With the Stanford–Binet, a child's mental age (intellectual ability) is divided by chronological age and multiplied by 100 to yield an intelligence quotient (IQ). Decades of psychologists have used the original and revised versions of the Stanford–Binet. This test has traditionally been a good predictor of academic performance, and many of its simplest subtests correlate highly with one another.

A new version of the Stanford–Binet Intelligence Scale, published in 1986, contains items designed to avoid favoring either men or women or stressing ethnic stereotypes. It is composed of four major subscales that test verbal reasoning, quantitative reasoning, abstract visual reasoning, and short-term memory. Within the four major subscales, there are 15 possible subtests, which vary greatly in content. The Stanford–Binet can be used to test anyone from age 2 through 23, yielding one overall IQ score. The test administration time varies with the examinee's age, because the number of subtests given is determined by age. All examinees are first given a vocabulary test; along with their age, this test determines the level at which all other tests begin. Each of the subtests consists of a series of levels, with two items at each level. The tester begins by using entry-level items and continues until a higher level on each subscale is established (until the test taker fails a prescribed number of items).

Raw scores, determined by the number of items passed, are converted to a standard score for each age group. The new Stanford–Binet Intelligence Scale is a potent test; one of its great strengths is that it can be used over a wide range of ages and abilities. Nonetheless, like all tests, it has limitations. One of these limitations is that examinees of different ages are not given the same battery of subtests; this makes it difficult to monitor changes in performance on subtests (Sattler, 1992). However, the new Stanford–Binet correlates well with the old one, as well as with the

Wechsler scales and the Kaufman Assessment Battery for Children.

Wechsler Scales

David Wechsler (1896–1981), a Rumanian immigrant who earned a PhD in psychology from Columbia University, was influenced by Charles Spearman and Karl Pearson, two English statisticians with whom he studied. In 1932, Wechsler was appointed chief psychologist at Bellevue Hospital in New York City; there, he began making history. Wechsler recognized that the Stanford–Binet Intelligence Scale was inadequate for testing adults. He also maintained that some of the Stanford–Binet items lacked validity. In 1939, Wechsler developed the Wechsler–Bellevue Intelligence Scale to test adults. In 1955, the Wechsler Adult Intelligence Scale (WAIS) was published; it eliminated some technical difficulties inherent in the Wechsler–Bellevue scale. The 1981 revision of the test is the WAIS–R.

Wechsler also developed the Wechsler Intelligence Scale for Children (WISC), which covers children aged 6 through 16. It was revised in 1974, becoming the WISC–R; the 1991 revision is the WISC–III. Table 7.5 shows some typical subtests included in the WISC–R. In 1967, the Wechsler Preschool and Primary Scale of Intelligence (WPPSI) was developed for children aged 4 through 6½; it was revised in 1989, becoming the WPPSI–R.

The Wechsler scales group test items by content; for example, all the information questions are presented together, all the arithmetic problems are presented together, and so on. The score on each subtest is calculated and converted to a standard (or scaled) score, adjusted for the test taker's age. The scaled scores allow for a comparison of scores across age levels. Thus, an 8-year-old's scaled score of 7 is comparable to an 11-year-old's scaled score of 7. An overall IQ score is reported, as well as subscale scores. Thousands of studies have been conducted to assess the reliability and validity of the Wechsler scales.

Kaufman Assessment Battery for Children

Many intelligence tests have been criticized for being biased, in that some of their questions are geared toward the experiences of white middle-class males. Psychologists Alan and Nadeen Kaufman contend that their Kaufman Assessment Battery for Children (K–ABC) uses tasks that tap the experiences of all individuals, regardless of background. A memory task in the K–ABC, for example, might ask a child to look at a picture of a face and, a few moments later, to pick it out from among pictures of other faces.

The K–ABC was designed especially for assessment of school problems. School psychologists, who are the primary users of the K–ABC, evaluate scores on the K–ABC and act as consultants to families and schools, helping them to set and achieve appropriate educational goals for particular children. The K–ABC consists of four global scales. Three measure mental

Table 7.5 Typical Subtests of the WISC–R

Verbal Test		Performance Test	
Subtest	**Type of Task**	**Subtest**	**Type of Task**
Information	When questioned, recall a general fact that has been acquired in a formal or informal school setting.	Picture completion	Point out the part of an incomplete picture that is missing.
Similarities	Use another concept in describing how two ideas are alike.	Picture arrangement	Put a series of pictures that tell a story in the right sequence.
Arithmetic	Solve a word problem without pencil and paper.	Block design	Use real blocks to reproduce a picture of a block design.
Digit span	Recall an orally presented string of digits.	Object assembly	Put the pieces of a jigsaw-like puzzle together to form a complete object.
Vocabulary	Define a vocabulary word.	Coding	Given a key that matches numbers to geometric shapes, fill in a form with the shapes that go with the listed numbers.
Comprehension	Answer a question requiring practical judgment and common sense.		

processing abilities (sequential processing, simultaneous processing, and a composite of the two); the fourth assesses achievement. The Kaufmans believe that the sequential- and simultaneous-processing scales measure abilities synonymous with intelligence—that is, the ability to process information and the ability to solve problems (Kaufman, 1983). A sequential task requires the manipulation of stimuli in sequential order; for example, a child might be asked to repeat a series of digits in the order in which the examiner presented them. A simultaneous-processing task involves organizing and integrating many stimuli presented at the same time; for example, a child might be asked to recall the placement of objects on a page that was presented only briefly.

The K–ABC assesses not only how a child solves problems on each task, but how well she or he does so; the test thus minimizes the role of language and of acquired facts and skills. A separate part of the test—the achievement scale—addresses such skills as reading comprehension, letter and word identification, and computation. Being heavily influenced by language experience and verbal ability, these tasks resemble those typically found on other IQ tests.

Although early research on the K–ABC showed it to be a promising IQ test (German, 1983; Zins & Barnett, 1983), it is not without its critics. Sternberg (1984) has been especially critical of the assumptions on which the K–ABC is founded, particularly the assumptions about how sequential processing proceeds and whether it reflects important elements of thought. Although many practitioners consider it child-oriented and easy to administer, a final evaluation of the K–ABC is still probably a decade away.

Experiencing Psychology discusses changes in IQ scores over the past several decades.

Environmental and Biological Factors in Intelligence

Focus on issues and ideas

- The impact of culture on the results of an intelligence test
- The stability of intelligence test scores

In 1986, a federal court in California upheld a 1979 ruling barring the administration of IQ tests to African American students in the state. According to the judge who made the original ruling, the tests were culturally biased and therefore discriminated against African Americans who were being evaluated for special education; the result was that a disproportionate number of African Americans were assigned to classes for the mentally retarded. The California court case illustrates the kinds of political, cultural, and scientific issues involved in the debate about what intelligence is and what intelligence tests actually measure. Ethnic and other minority groups have joined psychologists and educators in challenging the usefulness of IQ tests. Underlying public concern and scientific debate is the fundamental issue of how much of intelligence is due to heredity and how much is due to a person's upbringing and culture. Further, if culture is a major factor, are tests biased?

Cultural Biases?

A major argument against IQ testing is that the tests are culturally biased and thus effectively discriminate against people who do not resemble the test makers, who are usually white, male, middle-class suburbanites. A test item or subscale is considered culturally biased if, with all other factors held constant, its content is more difficult for members of one group than for those of other groups. To understand how a test can be culturally biased, imagine that the child of an impoverished migrant worker is given the temperature problem posed earlier. If the child is unfamiliar with thermometers and radios, the child might choose the sun as the best answer. But if the test designer has deemed "thermometer" the correct answer, the migrant child's answer would be discounted.

On the basis of experiments that have shown some IQ tests to be culturally biased, some educators and parents have urged a ban on such tests in all public schools. They argue that some groups of individuals who are not exposed to the same education and experiences as the middle-class group for whom the tests were designed are bound to perform less well. Table 7.6 (on p. 200) lists some questions that might bias an intelligence test. (How many children could answer the questions on Test B? Yet a person who *did* know the answers would clearly have intelligence of a particular type.)

Clearly, those who interpret IQ test scores must be particularly sensitive to any potential biases in the tests. Nonetheless, although researchers find differences among the IQ scores of various racial, ethnic, and cultural groups, they have found no consistent and conclusive evidence of bias in the tests themselves. Differences between siblings are usually as great as differences between ethnic groups; there is as great a variability between individuals as between groups. It is simply not the case that IQ tests systematically discriminate on the basis of ethnicity. Biases may exist,

EXPERIENCING PSYCHOLOGY

Why Your IQ Is Up and Your SAT Is Down

Apparently, IQs are up, but SATs are down. That's the paradox researchers are reporting. To some, this observation appears perplexing, but when you analyze what an IQ test and the Scholastic Achievement Test (SAT) measure, as well as the test takers themselves, it isn't really so surprising (Neisser et al., 1996).

Data from the last eight decades indicate that IQ test scores in the United States have risen by as much as 25 points. This rise in IQ test scores is called the *Flynn effect*, after James R. Flynn, who first noted the substantial rise in scores (Flynn, 1987, 1998, 1999). Are Americans smarter now? Or were they less intelligent years ago? As we've seen, IQ tests are not a measure of innate ability; rather, they measure vocabulary and how well people have learned analytical, critical thinking, and reasoning skills. Consider what is covered on a current IQ test: analogies, antonyms, complex puzzle solutions, spatial logic, and basic geometry and trigonometry. Such tasks would have baffled the average person when IQ tests were first developed at the turn of the 20th century; similarly, all of us would look pretty smart if we took the IQ tests developed by Binet.

Several factors might be at work. Americans are healthier and better nourished than in previous generations. Schools now focus more on critical thinking skills than on rote information learning. Many students are very test-wise, having been tested constantly in school settings. Further, today's students are challenged with everything from video games to computers to complex puzzles—all of which require higher levels of reasoning and much practice. So, it isn't so amazing that test scores are up on IQ tests whose questions have remained stable—especially those on puzzle and spatial abilities.

But what about the SAT, on which average scores have decreased by nearly 100 points since the 1970s? Has the high school curriculum gotten "softer"? The SAT focuses on achievement and what students have learned. The more learning one has, the more high-level courses one has taken, the more books one has read, the greater the likelihood of a higher score on the SAT. The difference is that, now more than ever before, a broader range of students take the SAT. Prior to the 1970s, primarily only the fraction of high school seniors going on to college took the test. Today, almost all high school seniors go on to some kind of higher education, so a much broader range of people—with far different abilities and levels of training—take the test. It isn't surprising that, with a much more varied test-taking population, the overall scores have decreased. If you tested just those headed off to the best universities, the average score would certainly be higher. And research shows that, state by state, SAT scores correlate highly with the percentage of high school students taking the test—the higher the percentage of students taking the test, the lower the overall scores (Powell & Steelman, 1996). ■

but well-respected psychologists (Sattler, 1992; Vernon, 1979) support the view that they do not exist in such tests as the WISC–R. It is possible that any bias that appears to exist in an IQ test actually arises from how the results are used (a point to be examined shortly).

IQ tests cannot predict or explain all types of intellectual behavior. They test a small sample of a restricted range of cognitive activities. Intelligence can be demonstrated in many ways; an IQ test tells little about someone's ability to be flexible in new situations or to function maturely and responsibly. Intelligence tests do reflect many aspects of people's environments—how much they are encouraged to express themselves verbally, how much time they spend reading, and the extent to which they are encouraged to engage in academic pursuits (e.g., Barrett & Depinet, 1991).

Table 7.6 Tests Can Be Constructed to Have a Bias

Test A	Test B
1. What are the colors in the American flag?	1. Of what is butter made?
2. Who is the President of the United States?	2. Name a vegetable that grows above ground.
3. What is the largest river in the United States?	3. Why does seasoned wood burn more easily than green wood?
4. How can banks afford to pay interest on the money you deposit?	4. About how often do we have a full moon?
5. What is the freezing point of water?	5. Who was President of the United States during World War II?
6. What is a referendum in government?	6. How can you locate the pole star?

Since the early 1970s, educators and psychologists have scrutinized the weaknesses of IQ tests and have attempted to eliminate cultural biases in testing by creating better tests and establishing better norms for comparison. The newer tests have attempted to control for the influences of different cultural backgrounds (Helms, 1992). However, even the courts acknowledge the complexity of the issues involved in IQ testing (Elliott, 1987). In isolation, IQ scores mean little. Information about an individual's home environment, personality, socioeconomic status, and special abilities is crucial to understanding intellectual functioning. *Diversity* (on pp. 202–203) further examines cultural differences in test scores.

Information about an individual's home environment, personality, socioeconomic status, and special abilities is crucial to understanding intellectual functioning.

Genetic and Environmental Impact

Today, psychologists recognize that both the genetic heritage established before birth (nature) and a person's life experiences (nurture) play an important role in intelligence. Few would debate the idea that the environment, and especially schooling, has a potent effect on performance of intellectual tasks (Ceci & Williams, 1997). But efforts to unravel the fixed genetic component from the environmental impact have required some sophisticated research and statistical techniques. The main goal of such studies has been to determine various traits' **heritability**, the genetically determined proportion of a trait's variation among individuals in a population. The heritability of some traits is fairly obvious; for example, height is a highly heritable trait. Children who have two tall parents have a strong likelihood of being tall—the heritability of height is high, and thus scientists state that heredity is a key factor in determining height. When scientists say that a trait is heritable, especially when they attach a percentage to that heritability—for example, 50%—they mean that 50% of the variation (differences) among *a group* of people is attributable to heredity. Note that this is *not* the same as saying that 50% of a *specific person's* intelligence, height, or any other variable is determined by heredity. One last caution: Although heritability is a biological phenomenon, even highly heritable traits, such as height, can be modified by the environment. Deprive the child of tall parents of a nutritious diet during the growth years, and the child will be less likely to be tall. So, even highly heritable traits are modifiable by the environment.

Heritability: The genetically determined proportion of a trait's variation among individuals in a population.

Estimates of the heritability of intelligence have varied widely, as have research techniques that attempt to measure it. To establish how much of intelligence is heritable, several researchers have studied adopted children, who are raised apart from their biological parents (e.g., Scarr & Weinberg, 1994). Researchers compare an adopted person's intelligence test scores and other measures of cognitive ability with those of biological parents, adoptive parents, biological siblings, and adoptive siblings. The goal is to see if scores later in life more greatly resemble those of biological relatives or adoptive relatives. Interestingly, most of the data about IQ scores and the role of genetics come from studies of identical twins and their performance early in life; only recently have data emerged from studies of older identical twins, who have lived full lives and had a wide range of experiences (McClearn et al., 1997; Pedersen et al., 1992). All of these data, taken together confirm the idea that about half of the similarity in scores of identical twins—even into old age—can be accounted for by genetics (Petrill et al., 1998).

Although heritability is a biological phenomenon, even highly heritable traits, such as height, can be modified by the environment.

So, in general, research shows that, to a great extent, heredity and environment contribute equally to IQ scores (Pedersen et al., 1992; Pedersen, Plomin, & McClearn, 1994). However, to frame nature versus nurture as a debate with a winner and a loser is a mistake; the two work together in a partnership. The idea that a genetic behavior or characteristic cannot be changed is a myth. Genes do not fix behavior; instead, they establish a range of possible reactions. Environments determine the extent to which the range of genetic potential will be expressed (Ceci & Williams, 1997). Thus, the study of nature and nurture together is essential to an understanding of intelligence (Neisser et al., 1996; Plomin, 1994a).

Stability of Intelligence Test Scores

Correlations of the IQ scores of school-age children and adults show that such scores can change, sometimes substantially. Yet some research indicates that to a certain extent infant IQ can predict school-age IQ (Rose & Feldman, 1995). What seems to remain stable is a person's score in relation to those of his or her peers of the same age.

Do IQ scores remain stable throughout adulthood? In general, psychologists have shown that intelligence and achievement test scores at first increase with age, then level off in adulthood, only to decline in late adulthood (Schaie, 1993). The results of a 40-year study of IQ showed that, in general, the intellectual functioning of men increased a bit around age 40 and then gradually declined to its earlier level when the men were in their 50s (Schwartzman et al., 1987). In other words, despite the passage of years, cognitive performance remained relatively stable. The effect of aging on IQ scores is difficult to assess, because some aspects of the scores decrease more with age than others. For example, scores on numerical portions of IQ tests tend to show a more significant decrease with advancing age than do scores on verbal portions (Schaie, 1993). In addition, not everyone shows age-related IQ declines; people who continue to further their education throughout their lives show relatively small decreases.

There is now ample evidence that IQ scores remain relatively stable once test subjects reach adulthood. However, the scores of infants and children are so prone to change that they are not reliable predictors of later IQ scores. Of course, a child who achieves a high score on an IQ test at age 9 is likely to do well or perhaps even better at age 18. The data show enough fluctuation, though, especially at younger ages, to make predictions uncertain.

Are There Gender Differences?

Many psychologists believe there are gender differences in verbal ability, with girls surpassing boys in most verbal tasks during the early school years. However, most differences have been found to be due to the expectations of parents and teachers. For example, parents and teachers have long encouraged boys to engage in spatial, mechanical tasks. Two interesting trends have been observed in the United States in recent decades, though. First, many parents have been encouraging both girls and boys to acquire math, verbal, and spatial skills; that is, they have endeavored to avoid gender stereotyping. Second, the observed cognitive differences between boys and girls have been diminishing each year (American Association of University Women, 1998).

In fact, the old consensus about gender differences is at least exaggerated, if not simply wrong (Halpern, 1997). Hyde and Linn (1988) examined 165 research studies on gender differences in verbal ability; these studies had tested more than 1 million individuals. Although Hyde and Linn found a gender difference in favor of females, it was so small that they claimed it was not worth mentioning. They further argued that more refined tests and theories of intelligence are needed to examine any gender differences that may exist. The differences found today exist only in certain special populations; for example, among the very brightest

DIVERSITY

Cultural Dimensions of Intelligence

Cross-cultural differences in IQ scores, SAT scores, and other measures of achievement or ability are narrowing (Fan, Chen, & Matsumoto, 1997). This narrowing may be due to more equal opportunities under the law, to federal intervention programs for the culturally disadvantaged, or to socioeconomic factors that affect home environments. As more minority-group students enroll in mathematics courses in high school, minority groups do better on achievement tests. Consistent with this observation is a cross-cultural study comparing Mexican Americans with Caucasian Americans; it showed that as they become increasingly acculturated to U.S. society, Mexican Americans achieve IQ scores comparable to those of Caucasian Americans (Gonzales & Roll, 1985). In addition, differences between ethnic groups have tended to decrease over the last two decades (Williams & Ceci, 1997). Furthermore, differences among individuals within a group are often greater than differences between groups, a fact that minimizes the importance of between-group differences (Zuckerman, 1990).

There are three factors that may create observed differences between groups, but their relative importance has yet to be established. As a case in point, consider African Americans, who as a group and on average—do somewhat less well on intelligence tests than do whites. The first factor being debated is the possibility of a genetic component. The second is that African Americans are disproportionately represented among those who live in culturally impoverished areas. The third is that IQ tests may contain a built-in vocabulary bias against African Americans.

People from different ethnic backgrounds and cultures differ on a whole variety of dimensions—there

mathematics students, boys continue to outscore girls, although the boys' scores are quite variable (Hedges & Nowell, 1995). Boys are motivated to achieve more and strive harder at math, in part because more of them have career aspirations that involve mathematical skills. As a consequence of these aspirations, boys tend to take more math courses and more advanced ones—this puts them still further ahead on standardized tests. It is important to remember the small gender differences (and ethnic differences) that do exist are based on group averages and say nothing about individual abilities (Halpern, 1997; Suzuki & Valencia, 1997). In general, differences between the test scores of males and those of females are disappearing, and this trend has been observed in many cultures (Geary, 1996; Skaalvik & Rankin, 1994).

In 1998, under pressure from the federal government, the SAT and the PSAT underwent revision intended to narrow the gap between the genders as much as possible. The government got involved because merit scholarships based on SAT scores were more likely to go to men than women; it was assumed that biases in the test favored men. An outcome of Hyde and Linn's analysis is the realization that since verbal ability tests provide gender-unbiased measures of cognitive ability, perhaps they should be used to select students for academic programs. Sound selection procedures are especially important for academic programs for special students, such as the gifted (Halpern, 1997).

Think Critically

- What conclusions about the nature-versus-nurture question can be drawn from data on correlations between IQ scores and child-rearing environments for both related children and unrelated children?
- If you had to design a series of selection procedures for a college or a program for gifted students, what procedures would you choose?

is no doubt about that. A cross-cultural study of 320 Israeli children whose parents had emigrated from Europe, Iraq, North Africa, or Yemen showed that the four groups tended to exhibit four different patterns of cognitive abilities (Burg & Belmont, 1990). Differing patterns of cognitive ability are not surprising; cultures vary considerably in their worldviews, their value systems, and their conceptions of time, space, and other aspects of reality. Thus, historical and cultural background has a significant effect on people's patterns of mental ability and achievement (Geary, 1996). The culture of a child from Texas or California is clearly different from that of a child from New Guinea, and so the instrument used to test any child must be culturally relevant (Greenfield, 1997). Flynn (1987) showed that IQ scores are changing around the world, and he concluded that schooling, educational emphasis, and family values in various cultures were affecting the test scores—not that people in certain cultures were getting smarter. Schooling clearly fosters the cognitive processes that contribute to high IQ scores (Ceci & Williams, 1997).

One conclusion is strikingly clear: *Rather than measuring innate intellectual capacity, IQ tests measure the degree to which people adapt to the culture in which they live.* In many cultures, to be intelligent is to be socially adept. In Western society, because social aptitude is linked with schooling, the more schooling you have, the higher your IQ score is likely to be (Ceci & Williams, 1997). All individuals have special capabilities (not necessarily intellectual ones), and how those capabilities are regarded depends on the social environment. Being a genius in traditional African cultures may include being a good storyteller; in the United States, it may mean being astute and aggressive (Eysenck, 1995). In the United States, however, the concept of genius is too often associated solely with high academic achievement. Concern about the implications of this limited conception of intelligence is one reason why some educators are placing less emphasis on IQ scores.

Critics of IQ testing have been vocal and persuasive, and their arguments cannot be discounted. Researchers now assert that the typical intelligence test is too limited because it does not take into consideration the many forms of intelligent behavior that occur outside the testing situation, within the diverse culture of the United States (Frederiksen, 1986; Sternberg & Wagner, 1993). Frederiksen suggests that real-life problem situations might be used to supplement the usual psychological tests. This view is consistent with Sternberg's (1986a) idea that intelligence must be evaluated on many levels, including the environment in which a person lives and works. Many believe that if this type of evaluation were used, IQ scores could become better at predicting both academic and occupational success (Wagner, 1997). Yet, in spite of all the limitations of IQ scores, research continues to show that they are the best overall predictor of school and job performance (Ree & Earles, 1992, 1993). ■

(I) Exceptionality and Education

Focus on issues and ideas

- The definitions of giftedness and mental retardation
- The education of exceptional children

The American educational system is oriented toward testing for and teaching special or exceptional children. As early as the first weeks of the first grade, most children take some kind of reading readiness test; by the end of the fourth grade, students are usually classified and labeled as to their projected future development, again largely on the basis of tests. Educators often use the term *exceptional* to refer to individuals who are gifted or those who suffer from learning disabilities, physical impairments, and mental retardation.

Giftedness

Gifted individuals represent one end of the continuum of intelligence and talent. The phenomenon of gifted children has been recognized and discussed for centuries. Some gifted children, like Mozart, display their genius musically. Others display it in science; many great scientists made their most important theoretical discoveries very early in their careers. Although there is no universally accepted definition of giftedness (just as there is no universally agreed-on definition of intelligence), Section 902 of the federal government's Gifted and Talented Children's Act of 1978 provides the following:

> The term *gifted and talented* means children and, whenever applicable, youth who are identified at the preschool, elementary, or secondary level as possessing demonstrated or potential abilities that give evidence of high performance responsibility in areas such as intellectual, creative, specific academic or leadership ability, or in the performing or visual arts and who by reason

> thereof require services or activities not ordinarily provided by the school.

Thus, gifted children may have superior cognitive, leadership, or performing arts abilities. Moreover, they require special schooling that goes beyond the ordinary classroom; their instruction needs to be individualized (Detterman & Thompson, 1997). Without individualized attention, these children may not realize their potential. In truth, all children may be in need of individualized instruction because most of them—but especially the gifted—are underchallenged by school (Winner, 1997). Even though the federal government acknowledges the need for special education for gifted individuals, states and communities must fund about 92% of the cost of such education. Some states—including California, Pennsylvania, and Illinois—spend more per year on educating gifted and talented students than the federal government spends nationwide. Nearly every state has a special program for the gifted; however, some school systems have none, and others provide special instruction only in brief periods or to small groups and still do not challenge the extraordinarily gifted. Some school districts provide special schools for children with superior cognitive abilities, performing talents, or science aptitude—most do not offer gifted programs for all grades. The special needs of gifted students (and of those with mental retardation—considered next) should not be addressed only 1 day a week or only in grades 1 through 6, or with traditional teaching techniques.

Mental Retardation

The term *mental retardation* covers a wide range of behaviors, from slow learning to severe mental and physical impairment. Many people with mental retardation are able to cope well. Most learn to walk and to feed and dress themselves; many learn to read and are able to work. In 1992, the American Association on Mental Retardation adopted a new formal definition of mental retardation:

> **Mental retardation** refers to substantial limitations in present functioning. It is characterized by significantly subaverage intellectual functioning, existing concurrently with related limitations in two or more of the following applicable adaptive skill areas: communication, self-care, home living, social skills, community use, self-direction, health and safety, functional academics, leisure, and work. Mental retardation manifests before age 18.

Psychologists and other practitioners who work with the mentally retarded must consider (1) the community's cultural and linguistic diversity, (2) how a person's adaptive skills interact with the community setting, (3) the fact that specific skills often exist but have limitations, and (4) the likelihood that life functioning will generally improve with age.

There are a variety of causes for mental retardation—from deprived environments (especially in the case of those with mild retardation) to genetic abnormalities, infectious diseases, and physical trauma (including that inflicted on a fetus by drugs taken during pregnancy). There are two broad ways to classify retardation. The first focuses on biological versus environmental causes; the second, more prevalent, approach focuses on levels of retardation reflected in behavior.

Levels of Retardation. A diagnosis of mental retardation involves three criteria: a lower-than-normal (below 70) IQ score on a standardized test such as the WISC–R or the WAIS–R, difficulty adapting to the environment, and the presence of such problems before age 18. There are four basic levels of mental retardation: mild, moderate, severe, and profound—each corresponding to a different range of scores on a standardized IQ test (see Table 7.7).

Mild Retardation. Approximately 90% of those classified as mentally retarded have mild mental retardation (Wechsler IQ score of 55–69). Through special programs, they are able to acquire academic and occupational skills, but they generally need extra supervision of their work (e.g., Allington, 1981). As adults, people with mild mental retardation function intellectually at about the level of 10-year-olds. Thus, with some help from family and friends, most people with mild mental retardation can cope successfully with their environment.

Moderate Retardation. People with moderate mental retardation (Wechsler IQ score of 40–54) account for approximately 6% of those classified as mentally retarded. Most moderately retarded people live in institutions or as dependents of their families. Those who are not institutionalized need

Table 7.7 Mental Retardation as Measured on the Wechsler Scales

Classification	Wechsler IQ Score	Percentage of the Mentally Retarded
Mild	55–69	90
Moderate	40–54	6
Severe	25–39	3
Profound	Below 25	1

special classes; some can hold simple jobs, although few are employed. People with moderate mental retardation are able to speak, write, and interact with friends, but their motor coordination, posture, and social skills are clumsy. Their intellectual level is equivalent to that of 5- to 6-year-olds.

Severe Retardation. Only about 3% of people with mental retardation are severely retarded (Wechsler IQ score of 25–39). People with severe mental retardation show great motor, speech, and intellectual impairment and are almost totally dependent on others to take care of their basic needs. Severe retardation often results from birth disorders or traumatic injury to the brain.

Profound Retardation. Only 1% of people with mental retardation are classified as profoundly retarded (Wechsler IQ score below 25). These people are unable to master even simple tasks and require total supervision and constant care. Their motor and intellectual development is minimal, and many are physically underdeveloped or have physical deformities or other congenital defects (such as deafness, blindness, and seizures).

Educating Those with Mental Retardation. Prior to the 1980s, thousands of children were given a substandard education after doing poorly on an intelligence test. Labeled as slow learners or perhaps even as mentally retarded, these children received neither special education nor special attention. In 1975, however, the U.S. Congress passed Public Law 94–142 (PL 94–142), the Education for All Handicapped Children Act. Originally intended to improve school programs for physically handicapped children, the law ensures individualized testing and educationally relevant programs for all children.

The law requires that all school-age children be provided with an appropriate, free public education. After testing, children with special needs are not to be grouped separately unless they have severe handicaps. Tests for identification and placement must be unbiased. Further, educational programs for special needs children must be arranged so as to make them as close to normal as possible, with the unique needs of each child considered. The school, in consultation with the parents, must arrange an individualized educational program or plan (IEP). The law also mandates that schools must follow specific procedures for conducting evaluation procedures and regular reevaluations and explaining to parents their child's rights and any changes in the child's status. PL 94–142 has significantly increased the amount of testing in public school systems, leading to more classification and labeling. Many see this as a disadvantage. However, the law has also guaranteed that thousands of children with special needs will receive an appropriate education. This is costly for local school districts; but when students need a special education, they can rely on the courts to make sure that the school system provides it.

Since the passage of PL 94–142, there has been a shift toward **mainstreaming**—the integration of all children with special needs into regular classroom settings, whenever appropriate, with the support of professionals who provide special education services. Technically, the law requires students to be placed in the least restrictive or least unusual environment feasible. The purpose is to make life as normal as possible for children with mental retardation by requiring that they and their teachers and classmates cope with their current skill levels while trying to expand them as much as possible. In mainstreaming, children are assigned to a regular class for at least half of their

Mental retardation: Below-average intellectual functioning, as measured on an IQ test, accompanied by substantial limitations in functioning that originate before age 18.

Mainstreaming: Practice of placing children with special needs in regular classroom settings, with the support of professionals who provide special education services.

school day. For the rest of the day, they are in special education classrooms or in vocational training situations. Although research studies have produced conflicting data on the effectiveness of mainstreaming, psychologists and educators generally support it (Zigler & Hodapp, 1991).

Although real progress has been made, mainstreaming has been problematic in many school settings. Too often, children are mainstreamed not into the academic (classroom) aspects, but only into the social side (athletics, lunch). One consequence is a lack of delivery of adequate special academic services to children who require them (Zigler & Hodapp, 1991). Because of such problems, some schools now keep students with special education needs in regular classrooms and bring support to them rather than bringing the children to supportive services—an approach called *inclusion.* Not without its critics, the inclusionary approach focuses on the needs of individual children in new ways; research on its success is yet to be conducted.

The federal government has taken an extensive role in the education and support of individuals with mental retardation. Advocates for people with mental retardation are concerned because the costs of such support programs are rising very quickly. Some states are directing funds formerly used for institutionalizing the retarded to businesses and colleges to pay for training mentally retarded workers. *I*

Think Critically

- A diagnosis of mental retardation involves a lower-than-normal IQ score. What does this imply about IQ tests as predictors of behavior? What might be some characteristics of a different kind of test for diagnosing mental retardation?

I Summary and Review

What Is Intelligence?

Identify the key features of a definition of intelligence.

Describe several different approaches to intelligence.

KEY TERMS
intelligence, p. 188; factor analysis, p. 188

The Process of Test Development

Why were Binet and Simon significant in the development of intelligence tests?

What criteria must be addressed in order to develop a fair and accurate intelligence test?

KEY TERMS
standardization, p. 191; norms, p. 192; representative sample, p. 192; normal curve, p. 192; raw score, p. 192; standard score, p. 192; percentile score, p. 192; deviation IQ, p. 193; reliability, p. 193; validity, p. 193; halo effect, p. 194

Three Important Intelligence Tests

Describe the Stanford–Binet Intelligence Scales, the Wechsler scales, and the Kaufman Assessment Battery for Children (K–ABC).

Environmental and Biological Factors in Intelligence

What is the effect of cultural variables and gender on intelligence test scores?

KEY TERM
heritability, p. 200

Exceptionality and Education

Describe the ends of the continuum of intelligence—giftedness and mental retardation—and their implications for educational settings.

KEY TERMS
mental retardation, p. 204; mainstreaming, p. 205

Self-Test

1. Which theory of intelligence uses correlations between items to uncover common underlying abilities?
   A. Jensen's two-level theory
   B. Gardner's multiple intelligences
   C. factor theories
   D. Wechsler's theory

2. According to Sternberg's triarchic theory of intelligence, someone who has common sense is high in ____________ intelligence.
   A. analytic
   B. practical
   C. creative
   D. successful

3. Todd wants to know what proportion of the people who took the SAT scored better than he did. Which type of score should he look at?
   A. percentile score
   B. raw score
   C. standard score
   D. deviation score

4. Which is a characteristic of an intelligence test that consistently produces the same score on different occasions?
   A. norms
   B. reliability
   C. validity
   D. standardization

5. According to the Stanford–Binet Intelligence Scale, IQ is based on:
   A. mental age
   B. chronological age
   C. both A and B
   D. neither A nor B

6. Who was responsible for an intelligence test designed to test adults?
   A. Binet
   B. Stanford
   C. Kaufman
   D. Wechsler

7. Which set of percentages most accurately describes the relative contributions of heredity and environment in determining intelligence?
   A. 10% heredity : 90% environment
   B. 75% heredity : 25% environment
   C. 50% heredity : 50% environment
   D. 90% heredity : 10% environment

8. IQ tests are especially good at predicting:
   A. verbal expression of emotion
   B. time spent doing math problems
   C. spatial maneuvering abilities
   D. academic success

9. The majority of all retarded persons are classified at the ____________ level of retardation.
   A. profound
   B. moderate
   C. mild
   D. severe

10. The passage of Public Law 94–142 states that all school-age children must be provided with appropriate and free public education. For those with mental retardation, this means:
    A. special schools must be created for mentally retarded children
    B. mainstreaming must occur when possible
    C. mentally retarded children must be included in the social aspect of schooling
    D. they must not be tested any more than normal children

Motivation and Emotion

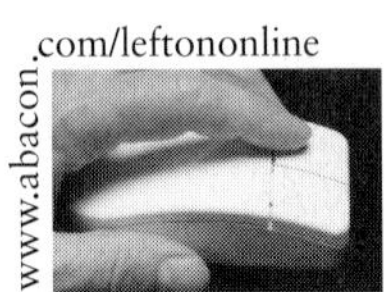

Go to your password-protected Website for full-color art, Weblinks, and more!

I work out at a gym at least three times a week, and I also ride 75 miles a week on my mountain bike. My goals are to push my 50-something body to do things it hasn't done before and to burn enough calories to keep my weight down. I am motivated by the fact that my dad had heart problems. With that family history, along with a tendency to put on weight too easily, I have some real reasons to work out. I want to live to a ripe old age and do it in good health. I also want to feel stronger and thus more self-confident and to be part of the group who work out regularly at the gym; the atmosphere is very positive and supportive. My workouts make me feel like a 16-year-old, if I ignore the crackling joints. And my regular exercise regimen also means that I can now eat just about anything I want without gaining weight.

You can see that my motivation to work out is personal and powerful, and it brings to mind several questions. Why do some people continue to strive for success while others give up after a single failure? Why will one person spend a free afternoon watching old movies and munching potato chips, while another will use the time for a 5-mile run and a quick study session before dinner? Why do some people crave the excitement of competition, while others seem to shy away from it? What drives people to take action, and what makes them react emotionally? ■

I Theories of Motivation

Focus on issues and ideas

- How the different theories of motivation attempt to explain behavior
- The effects of extrinsic and intrinsic rewards on behavior

Researchers have always sought to discover what impels people to take various actions—from simple, almost instinctual actions such as eating to complex actions such as learning to juggle. Many theories of motivation have been developed to explain human behavior, but no single theory can explain all of it. An understanding of the interacting forces that impel us must begin with a definition of *motivation*. The word derives from the Latin *movere*, meaning "to move." **Motivation** is any condition, although usually an internal one, that can be inferred to initiate, activate, or maintain an organism's goal-directed behavior.

Let's examine the four basic parts of this definition of motivation. First, motivation is usually an *internal condition*, which cannot be directly observed. The condition may develop from physiological needs and drives or from complex desires, such as the desire to help others, to obtain approval, or to earn a higher income. Second, motivation is *inferred* to be the link between a person's internal conditions and external behaviors; an observer can only infer its presence from the behavioral effects. Third, motivation *initiates, activates,* or *maintains* behavior. Because I am motivated to control my weight and keep fit, I have initiated an exercise regimen, which I hope to maintain. Finally, motivation generates *goal-directed behavior*. Individuals' goals vary widely. Some are concrete and immediate—for example, to get up and eat something, to remove a painful stimulus, or to win a diving match. Other goals are more abstract—the behavior of someone who studies hard, for example, may be motivated by a desire to learn more or to get a good job.

The study of motivation can be considered the study of what people choose to do, why they choose to do it, and how much energy they spend doing it (Edwards, 1999). Motivation theories fall into six broad categories, each of which has generated research activity: evolutionary theories, drive theory, arousal theory, expectancy theories, cognitive theory, and humanistic theory. Let's examine each of these categories in turn and then look at some basic types of motivation, before turning to how emotions and motivation are intertwined.

Evolutionary Theories

In the earliest days of psychology, theorists such as Konrad Lorenz spoke of *instincts*, meaning fixed behavioral patterns that animals produce without learning. What these researchers studied were often elaborate stereotyped behavior patterns associated with hunting and mating. They quickly realized that the study of such rigid behavior patterns—whether of geese or of wolves—had little relevance to human beings. But their early theorizing did give way to a more contemporary, *evolutionary perspective* that asserts that natural selection, the process of selective reproduction of the fittest animals, explains certain basic human behaviors. Animals (and human beings for that matter) that are motivated to stay alive and reproduce are more likely to have their genes represented in the population. Ultimately, only the fittest organisms contribute to the gene pool.

Evolutionary theorists have examined basic motivations that help an organism survive—for example, eating, drinking, and sleeping. They have studied reproductive behavior, pain avoidance, and temperature regulation and examined emotions such as fear, as we'll see later in this chapter. In each case, they wind up concluding that the organisms that develop and

Motivation: Any internal condition that can be inferred to initiate, activate, or maintain an organism's goal-directed behavior.

flourish are those that have evolved physically and mentally through natural selection; further, and most importantly, these evolutionary changes are evident in brain structure and function. Evolutionary theorists do not discount learning; rather, they assert that organisms that have learned well ultimately code that learning in brain structures. Through successive generations, over millions of years, evolution creates better adapted organisms, which are motivated to live and pass on their genetic heritage.

Drive Theory

Some of the most influential and best-researched motivation theories are forms of drive theory. **Drive theory** is an explanation of behavior that assumes that an organism is motivated to act because of a need to attain, reestablish, or maintain some goal that helps with the survival of the organism or the species. Stimuli such as hunger and pain energize and initiate such behavior. A person who is starving, perhaps a homeless person, may spend most of his or her time looking for food; that individual is *driven* to seek food.

A **drive** is an internal aroused condition that directs an organism to satisfy some physiological need. Drive theory focuses on **need**—a state of physiological imbalance usually accompanied by arousal. (We will explore arousal in greater depth in the next section.) Physiological needs are said to be *mechanistic,* because an organism is pushed and pulled by them, almost like a machine. The organism motivated by a need is said to be in a *drive state.* Both animals and human beings in such a state show goal-directed behavior. The ultimate goal is **homeostasis**—maintenance of a constant state of inner stability or balance. The processes by which organisms seek homeostasis are a key part of drive theory. For example, a thirsty animal will seek out water to reestablish its normal body fluid level. (Psychologists refer to any normally maintained level as a *steady state.*) Motivation theorists often refer to the goal that satisfies a need as an *incentive.* Incentives can be positive and lure us, as does food or a sexually attractive person; they can also repel us and cause us to act to avoid a painful situation or someone we dislike. Behavior such as eating or drinking, which reduces a biological need (and promotes homeostasis), is reinforced when its incentive is attained; such behaviors are therefore especially likely to recur. Behaviors such as juggling, which do not reduce a biological need, are less likely to recur—if they ever happen in the first place.

The Yerkes–Dodson law explains why some baseball players perform exceptionally well at the beginning of the season, when pressure is only moderately high, and then commit numerous errors when pressure mounts.

Arousal Theory

A characteristic of all motivational systems is that they involve arousal. **Arousal** is generally thought of as activation of the central nervous system, the autonomic nervous system, and the muscles and glands. Some motivational theorists suggest that organisms seek to maintain optimal levels of arousal by actively varying their exposure to arousing stimuli.

Unlike hunger and thirst, the lack of sensory stimulation does not result in a physiological imbalance; yet both human beings and animals seem impelled to seek such stimulation. When deprived of a normal amount of visual, auditory, or tactile stimulation, some people become irritable and consider their situation or environment intolerable. Kittens like to explore their environment; young monkeys investigate mechanical devices and play with puzzles. (However, in some situations, people and animals attempt to avoid stimulation—for example, when they are sick or in need of rest.)

But a lack of sensory stimulation or a need to reduce some drive fails to explain many basic behaviors. *Arousal theory* attempts to bridge the gap by explaining the link between a behavior and a state of arousal. R. M. Yerkes and J. D. Dodson first scientifically explored the link between performance and arousal in 1908. They described a relationship involving arousal and performance that has become known as the *Yerkes–Dodson law.* This law suggests that arousal and level of task difficulty are related: On easy tasks, moderate to high levels of arousal produce maximum performance; but, on difficult tasks, low levels of arousal yield better performance. Think of athletics: In a 100-meter sprint, a swimmer cannot be too aroused; but, in a triathlon, where strategy is necessary, too much arousal may yield poor decision making, for example, by causing the athlete to go all-out too soon in an event that lasts many hours. Contemporary researchers have refined the Yerkes–Dodson law by suggesting that when a person's level of arousal is either too high or too low, performance will be poor, especially on complex tasks.

Thus, people who do not care about what they are doing have little anxiety but also have low arousal and therefore usually perform poorly. If arousal increases to the point of high anxiety, performance also suffers. The Yerkes–Dodson law explains why some baseball players perform exceptionally well at the beginning of the season, when pressure is only moderately high, and then commit numerous errors when pressure mounts—for instance, in the playoffs or the World Series. It also explains why essentially the same task brings different levels of arousal at different times. High school varsity soccer players are far more concerned about their games and feel more pressured during them than 5-year-old beginning players or college graduates enjoying a weekend pickup game.

Expectancy Theories

Expectancy theories are explanations of behavior that focus on people's expectations about reaching a goal and their need for achievement as energizing factors; such theories connect thought and motivation. A key element of these theories, as expressed by achievement researcher David McClelland (1961), among others, is that people's thoughts, their expectations, guide their behaviors. The motives and needs they develop are not initiated because of some physiological imbalance. Rather, people learn through their interactions in the environment to have needs for mastery, affiliation, and competition. These needs are based on their expectations about the future and about how their efforts will lead to various rewarding outcomes.

To understand some important concepts related to expectancy theory, consider my desire to improve my cycling endurance. That desire means hours of practice, requiring me to deprive myself of other pleasures. According to expectancy theory, my motive for cycling originates partly in social needs. A **motive** is a specific (usually internal) condition, typically involving some form of arousal, which directs an organism's behavior toward a goal. Unlike a drive, which always has a physiological origin, a motive does not necessarily have a physiological basis. Thus, although I may be motivated to be thin and fit, there is no physiological need for me to be. A **social need** is an aroused condition that directs people to behave in ways that allow them to feel good about themselves and others and to establish and maintain relationships. The need to feel good about oneself often leads to specific behaviors that the individual hopes will be evaluated positively by others (Geen, 1991).

We will explore this topic in more detail when we discuss achievement later in this chapter and when we consider social psychology in Chapter 11.

Cognitive Theory

In the study of motivation, **cognitive theory** is an explanation of behavior that asserts that people actively and regularly determine their own goals and the means of achieving them. Like expectancy theory, cognitive theory focuses on thought as an initiator and determinant of behavior. However, cognitive theory emphasizes the role of conscious decision making more than expectancy theory does. For example, you are actively involved in deciding how much time you will spend studying for a psychology exam, how hard you will work to become an accomplished pianist, or how committed you will remain to a new exercise routine.

As early as 1949, Donald Hebb anticipated the influence on psychology of cognitive theory by suggesting that it is unsatisfactory to equate motivation with biological need. Other factors, such as arousal and attention, are also important determinants of motivation. Moving away from mechanistic views of motivation and behavior, contemporary researchers consider, and many emphasize, the role of active decision making and the human capacity for abstract thought. These cognitive theorists assume that individuals set goals and decide how to achieve them.

Cognitive Controls. Cognitive theory holds that if you are aware of—if you think about—your behavior, motivation, and emotions, you can alter your thoughts and control your behavior. You will see in

Drive theory: An explanation of behavior that assumes that an organism is motivated to act because of a need to attain, reestablish, or maintain some goal that helps with survival.

Drive: An internal aroused condition that directs an organism to satisfy a physiological need.

Need: State of physiological imbalance usually accompanied by arousal.

Homeostasis: Maintenance of a constant state of inner stability or balance.

Arousal: Activation of the central nervous system, the autonomic nervous system, and the muscles and glands.

Expectancy theories: Explanations of behavior that focus on people's expectations about reaching a goal and their need for achievement as energizing factors.

Motive: A specific (usually internal) condition, usually involving some form of arousal, which directs an organism's behavior toward a goal.

Social need: An aroused condition that directs people to behave in ways that allow them to feel good about themselves and others and to establish and maintain relationships.

Cognitive theory: In the study of motivation, an explanation of behavior that asserts that people actively and regularly determine their own goals and the means of achieving them through thought.

Chapter 14 that this idea is used extensively by therapists to help people with various maladjustments. In explaining motivation, cognitive psychologists show that arousal can be under voluntary cognitive control. Through instruction and self-help techniques, people can alter their behavior by changing their thoughts and thus their expectancies. That thoughts can alter behavior is also evident from studies of intrinsic and extrinsic motivation.

Intrinsic and Extrinsic Motivation. A child may love playing checkers, doing puzzles, or coloring in coloring books, yet need to be coaxed or ordered to practice the piano or do homework. Why do some activities seem like fun, and others seem like work? What are the critical variables?

In general, psychologists find that some activities are intrinsically fun—people like to do them because they provide their own reward. Other activities, however, are not nearly as much fun; people need to be motivated to perform them, either with reinforcers or with threats of punishment. Psychologists talk about *intrinsic* and *extrinsic* motivation. **Extrinsic motivation** is supplied in the form of rewards that come from the external environment. Praise, a high grade, or money given for a particular behavior are extrinsic rewards. Such rewards can strengthen existing behaviors, provide people with information about their performance, and increase feelings of self-worth and competence. In contrast, behaviors engaged in for no apparent reward except the pleasure and satisfaction of the activity itself arise from **intrinsic motivation.** Edward Deci (1975) suggests that people engage in such behaviors for two reasons: to obtain cognitive stimulation and to gain a sense of accomplishment, competence, or mastery over the environment. Individuals vary widely with respect to the need for cognitive stimulation; each person's experiences and genetic makeup affect the strength of this need (Cacioppo et al., 1996).

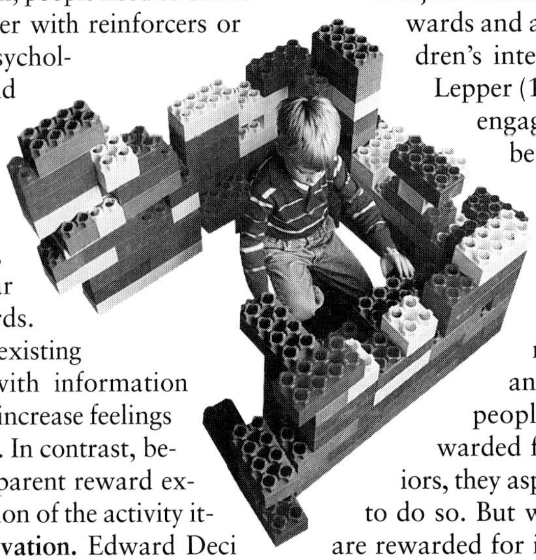

In studies focusing on intrinsic motivation, Deci (1972) compared two groups of college-age participants who engaged in puzzle solving. One group received no extrinsic rewards throughout the experiment, and the other group received rewards at first but later did not. Deci found that participants who were initially given rewards generally spent less time solving puzzles when rewards were no longer given. Those who were never rewarded, on the other hand, spent the same amount of time solving puzzles on all trials. Lepper and Greene (1978) referred to this phenomenon as the *hidden cost of rewards;* it is now known as the *overjustification effect.* The **overjustification effect** is the decrease in likelihood that an intrinsically motivated task, after having been extrinsically rewarded, will be performed when the reward is no longer given.

Research on the overjustification effect has been extensive and controversial. The earliest research focused on the basic finding that extrinsic rewards can have detrimental effects; however, newer research suggests that these detrimental effects occur only in restricted and avoidable situations (Eisenberger & Cameron, 1996; Pittenger, 1997; Snelders & Lea, 1996). In fact, Eisenberger and Cameron assert that when goals are attainable, extrinsic rewards have negligible effects on intrinsic motivation, but that some study participants report liking the task better after being given verbal extrinsic rewards. Cialdini and others (1998) have developed techniques to undermine the overjustification effect by giving children rewards and attributing the rewards to the children's internal abilities. And Cordova and Lepper (1996) found that a child's depth of engagement in learning could indeed be enhanced by giving the child feedback and by personalizing the task.

Psychologists continue to explore the effects of providing extrinsic rewards for intrinsically motivated behaviors. Baumeister and Tice (1985) showed that when people with high self-esteem are rewarded for intrinsically motivated behaviors, they aspire to excel and seek opportunities to do so. But when people with low self-esteem are rewarded for intrinsically motivated behaviors, they aspire to be only adequate or satisfactory. Thus, intrinsic motivation is, at least in part, related to a person's past experiences and current level of self-esteem. Other variables, such as the type of task and the type of reward, can influence the level of intrinsic motivation. The combination of intrinsic motivation, external rewards, self-esteem, and perhaps new and competing needs affect day-to-day behavior. (We will consider in Chapter 12 what happens when goals and needs conflict and how animals and human beings behave in situations that have both positive and negative aspects.)

Humanistic Theory

One of the appealing aspects of humanistic theory is that it recognizes the interplay among behavioral theories and incorporates some of the best elements of the drive, arousal, expectancy, and cognitive approaches for explaining motivation and behavior. **Humanistic theory** is an explanation of behavior that emphasizes the entirety of life rather than individual components of behavior. It focuses on human dignity, individual choice, and self-worth. Humanistic psychologists believe that a person's behavior must be viewed within the framework of the person's environment and values.

One of the founders and leaders of the humanistic approach was Abraham Maslow (1908–1970), who assumed that people are essentially good—that they possess an innate inclination to develop their potential and to seek beauty, truth, and harmony. Maslow believed that people are born open and trusting and can experience the world in healthy ways. In his words, people are naturally motivated toward self-actualization. **Self-actualization** is the final level of psychological development, in which a person strives to realize his or her uniquely human potential—to achieve everything he or she is capable of. This includes attempts to minimize ill health, to attain a superior perception of reality, and to feel a strong sense of self-acceptance. Maya Angelou (shown in the photo) is an example of a self-actualized person.

Maslow's influential theory conceives of motives as forming a hierarchy, which can be represented as a pyramid, with fundamental physiological needs at the base and the needs for love, achievement, understanding, and self-actualization near the top. According to Maslow, as lower-level needs are satisfied, people strive for the next higher level; the pyramid culminates in self-actualization.

Although Maslow's theory provides an interesting way to organize aspects of motivation and behavior, its global nature makes experimental verification difficult. Moreover, his levels of motivation seem closely tied to middle-class American cultural experiences. Western cultures are highly individualistic; other cultures are more collectivist. So Maslow's theory may not be valid for all cultures or socioeconomic strata. His theory, like many other motivation theories, does not explain how other components of people's lives affect behavior. For example, how does a person fulfill a need for privacy and independence and still satisfy a need to be with other people? Also, humanistic theory does not deal with how people fulfill the need to seek beauty, truth, and harmony. Again, this reveals its culture-bound Western approach—Eastern cultures and religions incorporate ways to meet this need, including meditation and exercise. 

Think Critically

- How is humanistic theory related to cognitive theory? What connections do you see between expectancy theory and drive theory?
- Why are humanistic theories difficult to test experimentally?

(I) Hunger: A Physiological Need

Focus on issues and ideas

- The role of the hypothalamus in eating behavior
- The psychological and physiological bases of obesity and eating behaviors

Now that you understand some of the theoretical work that has been done on motivation, let's look at a few *types* of motivation. All of us have been hungry, felt sexually aroused, and experienced learned motives such as the need for achievement. These three motivators—food, sex, and achievement—illustrate how motivation leads to both basic biological behaviors and some complex and culturally determined ones. Let's begin with perhaps the most fundamental, drive-based motivation—hunger. You will see that motivation, like other areas of psychology, involves a complex interplay of biology and learning, with one or the other predominating at different times.

Extrinsic [ecks-TRINZ-ick] motivation: Motivation supplied by rewards that come from the external environment.

Intrinsic [in-TRINZ-ick] motivation: Motivation that leads to behaviors engaged in for no apparent reward except the pleasure and satisfaction of the activity itself.

Overjustification effect: Decrease in likelihood that an intrinsically motivated task, after having been extrinsically rewarded, will be performed when the reward is no longer given.

Humanistic theory: An explanation of behavior that emphasizes the entirety of life rather than individual components of behavior and focuses on human dignity, individual choice, and self-worth.

Self-actualization: In humanistic theory, the final level of psychological development, in which one strives to realize one's uniquely human potential—to achieve everything one is capable of achieving.

Physiological Determinants of Hunger

Unlike animals, humans eat not only for sustenance, but also to experience tastes. We know the power of tastes, sights, and smells—they evoke hunger, or at least a desire to eat. When you are hungry, you may feel stomach pangs or become weak or dizzy—sensations that impel you to seek food. What causes these sensations? Physiological explanations of hunger focus on the concept of homeostasis and on hormones. A delicate balance—homeostasis—of food and fluid intake is necessary for proper physiological functioning; any imbalance results in a drive to restore the balance. For example, when a person experiences fluid deprivation and the resulting cellular dehydration, a homeostatic mechanism—almost like a thermostat—is activated. The person enters a drive state in which the mouth and throat become dry, cueing the person to drink. Thirst is not a result of dryness in the mouth or throat—in fact, the reverse is true. Simply placing water in the mouth will not reduce thirst; the water must rehydrate the body's cells.

A delicate balance—homeostasis—of food and fluid intake is necessary for proper physiological functioning; any imbalance results in a drive to restore the balance.

The *glucostatic approach* to explaining hunger argues that the principal physiological cause of hunger is a low level of blood sugar (glucose), which results from food deprivation and creates a chemical imbalance. In the body, foods are quickly broken down into glucose, which is crucial to cellular activity; the glucose is distributed to all cells in the body via the blood. When the blood glucose level is low, the body sends warning signals to the brain; the brain immediately responds by generating hunger pangs in the stomach. Thus, hunger is stimulated directly by insufficient levels of blood sugar (and other metabolites), a condition that triggers the central nervous system circuits that control eating. Experiments with animals in which nerves between stomach and brain were severed so that the animals did not feel stomach pangs showed that they continued to eat at appropriate times—when their blood sugar levels were low. These experiments provide evidence for the glucostatic approach.

The amount of food people eat does not necessarily affect the feeling of hunger—at least not right away. A hungry adult who eats steadily for 5 minutes may still feel hungry after stopping. But 30 minutes later, after the food has been converted into blood glucose, the person may no longer feel hungry. The type of food eaten determines how soon the feeling of hunger disappears. A candy bar loaded with sugar, which is easily converted into glucose, will ease hunger faster than will high-protein foods such as meat, cheese, and milk, which take longer to be broken down to glucose.

Much of current knowledge about hunger and eating behavior comes from studies of the hypothalamus, a region of the forebrain (see Chapter 2, p. 43). Researchers have argued that two areas of the hypothalamus are partly responsible for eating behavior: the ventromedial hypothalamus and the lateral hypothalamus. The *ventromedial hypothalamus* (the "stop eating" center) is activated to stop an organism from eating when the blood sugar level is high or when this part of the hypothalamus is electrically stimulated. The *lateral hypothalamus* (the "start eating" center) is activated to drive the organism to start eating when the blood sugar level is low or when this part of the hypothalamus is electrically stimulated. The lateral hypothalamus has been shown to play a direct role in eating behavior (both hunger and satiety); the ventromedial hypothalamus has a more indirect role. For example, the ventromedial hypothalamus may influence eating by stimulating the hormonal and metabolic systems (Powley, 1977). Researchers have used surgical techniques to destroy (ablate) the ventromedial and lateral areas of the hypothalamus in rats. This destruction caused the opposite effects to those observed with stimulation.

Hunger and Obesity: What Causes Overeating?

Despite widespread signs of health-consciousness—low-fat foods, health clubs, strong sales of sports gear—it seems there is an ever-growing tendency for Americans to be ever growing. Over one-third of Americans are overweight, and 22.5% of the population is clinically obese—a rate almost twice as high as it was two decades ago (Taubes, 1998). No one tries to be obese—the increase in obesity is clearly not due to some fad. Is it because Americans are eating too much, too often? Is it junk food, time spent watching television, not enough exercise? How do psychologists explain obesity? Two types of explanations are physiological and psychological.

Physiological Explanations of Obesity. If you have an overweight parent, your likelihood of being overweight as an adult increases dramatically, even if your weight was normal as a youngster. Some researchers insist that the reason is genetic and that behavioral and biological patterns are inherited (Bar-Or et al., 1998; Comuzzie & Allison, 1998). Researchers offer a number of biobehavioral explanations for obesity, including faulty homeostatic mechanisms (Woods et al., 1998), lack of specific proteins (Hotamisligil et al., 1996), and lower metabolic rates (Laessle, Wurmser, & Pirke, 1996). In the 1990s, the scientific journals were reporting findings of an "obesity" gene, which was said to hold the key to overeating and obesity. Researchers suggested that the gene directs the production of a hormone that tells the brain how much fat is stored in the body; this information ultimately governs eating behavior and energy expenditures (Puigserver et al., 1998). The researchers reported that if the protein product of the obesity gene was injected into animals, it caused the animals to lose weight and to maintain weight loss. The research on obesity genes may ultimately lead to a pill that may help some individuals lose weight and keep it off (Campfield, Smith, & Burn, 1998); but obesity-gene theories may not be the final word on the subject. Over the years, researchers have found other physiological reasons for obesity.

The body's genetic predisposition and physiology work at keeping weight the same—pursuing homeostasis—and therefore attempts to lose weight through intake regulation alone (such as dieting) are prone to failure.

One of the first to offer a physiological explanation for obesity was Richard Nisbett (1972) who proposed an explanation based on *fat cells.* He asserted that people are born with different numbers of fat cells and that the number of fat cells a person is born with determines the person's eating behavior and propensity toward obesity. Body fat is stored in fat cells, so people born with many fat cells are more likely to be obese than those born with few fat cells. Although the number of fat cells a person has is genetically determined, the size of each cell is affected both by genetics and by nutrition early in life. Dieting, in this explanation, decreases only the size, not the number, of fat cells. Moreover, the body attempts to maintain the size of fat cells at a constant level, so people who have shrunk their fat cells by dieting experience a constant sense of food deprivation. Thus, permanent weight loss becomes extremely difficult. This explanation accounts for the finding that about two-thirds of people who lose weight gain it all back within a year.

Closely associated with the fat cell explanation of obesity is some researchers' view that each person has a *set point*—a predetermined weight that is maintained by the body. The central idea of the set point explanation is that the body will always try to reestablish this weight. The set point, which differs from person to person, is determined by many factors, including genetics, early nutrition, current environment, and learned habits.

Further, some studies suggest that individuals can inherit both a tendency to overeat and a slow (or low) metabolism. A slow metabolism uses available energy (calories) from food efficiently; unused calories tend to be stored as fat. For example, members of the Pima tribe of Arizona are prone to obesity; 80–90% of the tribe's young adults are dangerously overweight. According to Ravussin and his colleagues (Norman et al., 1998; Ravussin et al., 1988), who spent years researching their habits, the Pima have unusually low metabolisms. During any 24-hour period, the typical Pima (who is as active as the average American) burns about 80 calories less than is considered normal for his or her body size. Ravussin's view is that the Pima, whose ancestors spent generations in the desert, where they went through periods of famine, developed a metabolism that coped with on-again, off-again eating patterns. But, in the 20th century, the Pima abandoned their traditional diet (which was low in fat) and ate like other Americans. Their genes, which had developed a disposition to being "thrifty" and storing fat, became a liability as the proportion of fat in their diet increased.

The body's genetic predisposition and physiology (Woods et al., 1998) work at keeping weight the same—pursuing homeostasis—and therefore attempts to lose weight through intake regulation alone (such as dieting) are prone to failure and tend to lead to what is called *yo-yo dieting*, or recurring cycles of dieting and weight gains. People don't have the luxury of choosing their genetic heritage, but that does not mean that those who inherit a predisposition toward obesity are condemned to become fat. Weight control—even small changes in set point—can be achieved through significant increases in physical activity.

Luckily, when most people take in too much food—when they overeat—they start to fidget and move about. In general, when people eat more, they become more active—contrary to popular opinion. When the obese overeat, they don't expend any extra energy, which makes the extra calories likely to be stored as fat. Obese individuals exercise less, walk around less, and even fidget and move their limbs less than normal-weight people. This behavior pattern may be genetically based (Levine, Eberhardt, & Jensen, 1999). Levine and his colleagues assert that even small bodily movements count—they use up calories, and over the course of a day, those calories add up. Their advice to stay trim: Keep moving.

Psychological Explanations of Obesity. Physiological makeup isn't the only important factor in eating behavior. All of us are bombarded with food-oriented messages that have little to do with nutritional needs. Advertisements proclaim that merriment can be found at a restaurant or a supermarket. Parents coax good behavior from their children by promising them desserts or snacks. Thus, eating acquires a significance that far exceeds its role in satisfying physiological needs: It serves as a rationale for social interaction, a means to reward good behavior, and a way to fend off unhappy thoughts and reduce stress (Greeno & Wing, 1994).

The obese tend to be oversensitive to food cues when compared to normal-weight individuals; furthermore, obese individuals underestimate their food intake.

Consider my own attempts to maintain my weight after losing 75 pounds through diet and exercise. Suddenly, I was more aware of food than ever before. Every time I saw food advertised on billboards or television, I wanted to eat. All the social events I attended seemed to feature a spread of delectable appetizers, which I was tempted to sample in order to be "sociable." And whenever I became anxious, my first impulse was to seek the comfort of food. However, by separating eating behaviors linked to hunger from those that were learned responses to emotions, I controlled my eating behavior and avoided gaining back the weight I had lost. Researchers continue to explore the causes of overeating. Their efforts have led to some interesting findings, especially when dieters are compared to nondieters.

Researchers know that the body seeks to maintain weight, to attain a homeostatic position (Woods et al., 1998). They also know that the American environment promotes excessive food intake, while both encouraging physical activity and offering multiple opportunities to avoid it. The problem is that the human body has developed effective mechanisms for gaining weight and weak ones for shedding pounds that are no longer needed (Hill & Peters, 1998). Researchers through the last five decades have identified four key factors that contribute to overeating. First, food is readily available—from drive-through windows and vending machines, restaurants and street vendors, at home, at work, and everywhere in between. Second, portion sizes are growing ever bigger—fast-food restaurants have super-size meals. Third, the average person's diet is higher in fat than ever before—fat provides nearly twice the calories per gram as protein or carbohydrates. Fourth, most children and adults do not engage in regular, sustained physical activity. Put all of this together—low physical activity, eating too much, too often, of the wrong things, and the result is an overweight population that has trouble losing weight.

When researchers such as Stanley Schachter and his colleagues (1968) investigated eating patterns, they found evidence that led them to infer that the mere sight of food motivates overweight people to eat more than normal-weight people. These researchers contended that the availability of food, its prominence, and other external cues tell individuals when to eat, and obese people respond more readily to such cues than normal-weight individuals do. Schachter's work set off wide-ranging research into the psychological variables that cause overeating in the obese.

The eating habits of obese and normal-weight individuals do differ; however, research shows that the differences are small and inconsistent (Rodin, 1981). The obese tend to be oversensitive to food cues when compared to normal-weight individuals; furthermore, obese individuals underestimate their food intake (Laessle, Wurmser, & Pirke, 1997). Anyone who is on a diet will tell you that external cues trigger food cravings. But think about this: Many obese individuals are nearly always on a diet, so it is not surprising that they constantly have food cravings. It may not be that the obese are more sensitive to external cues than normal-weight individuals, but rather that *those who are di-*

eting (which the obese often are) are more sensitive to such cues.

The unfortunate truth is that people who have lost weight often must take in fewer calories to maintain their lower weight than do those who have never been obese. This means that formerly obese people have an especially difficult time keeping their weight down. A cycle of dieting and regaining weight makes permanent weight loss difficult because the body burns fewer calories after weight loss. To make matters worse, even small disorders of the autonomic nervous system might play a role in keeping obese people fat (Klesges, Isbell, & Klesges, 1992).

The newest research implies that physiological mechanisms may play a much larger role than psychological ones in eating behavior. This research is forcing a critical evaluation of all previously collected data. There is no simple answer to the nature-versus-nurture question with respect to obesity, and attempts to treat obesity must incorporate the concept of a "reasonable weight" that is based on aesthetic and health standards for the particular individual with the problem. Such treatment must also take into account biological and environmental factors as well as cognitive states—the thoughts that the obese have when they are overeating (Grilo & Shiffman, 1994).

Eating Disorders

In 1994, Christy Henrich, a world-class gymnast, died because of an eating disorder. Henrich, who started training at age 4, was so fiercely competitive that she was nicknamed E. T.—for Extra Tough. An almost obsessive competitor, Henrich dealt with another obsession as well: She always felt that she was too fat. Henrich's eating disorder grew so severe that she was eventually too weak to compete. At her death at age 22, she weighed 60 pounds. Although athletes tend, on average, to be more satisfied with their body image than nonathletes, those in "lean" sports such as gymnastics and figure skating are known to be driven to stay thin. And, in some cases, this drive leads to eating disorders.

Eating disorders are psychological disorders characterized by gross disturbances in eating behavior and in the way individuals respond to food. Two important eating disorders are anorexia nervosa and bulimia nervosa. These disorders are very much culture-bound, Western diseases. Other cultures have their own disorders, but eating disorders such as anorexia nervosa and bulimia nervosa are found in wealthy Western industrialized societies. Eating disorders affect about 3% of women in such societies at some time during their lives.

Anorexia Nervosa. Anorexia nervosa, which affects as many as 40 out of every 10,000 young women in the United States, is an eating disorder characterized by an obstinate and willful refusal to eat. Individuals with the disorder, usually adolescent girls from middle-class families, have a distorted body image. They perceive themselves as fat if they have any flesh on their bones or deviate from their idealized body image. They intensely fear being fat and relentlessly pursue thinness. The anorexic's refusal to eat eventually brings on emaciation and malnutrition (which may bring about a further distortion of body image). Victims may sustain permanent damage to their heart muscle tissue, sometimes dying as a result.

Many therapists believe that anorexia nervosa has strictly psychological origins. They cite poor mother–daughter relationships, excessively protective parents, other negative family interactions, and efforts to escape self-awareness as the main causes (Walters & Kendler, 1995), as well as prejudice against the obese (Crandall, 1994). Others are exploring possible physiological contributions to the disorder (Walsh & Devlin, 1998), including the many changes taking place at puberty that might influence its emergence (Attie & Brooks-Gunn, 1989). Some psychologists believe that people with eating disorders may lack a hormone that is thought to induce a feeling of fullness after a meal.

Individuals with anorexia nervosa need a structured setting, and therapists often hospitalize them to help them regain weight. To ensure that the setting is reinforcing, hospital staff members are always present at meals. Individual and family therapy is provided. Patients are encouraged to eat and are rewarded for consuming specified quantities of food. Generally, psychotherapy is also necessary to help anorexics attain a healthy self-image. Even with treatment, however, as many as 50% suffer relapses within a year.

Bulimia Nervosa. Bulimia nervosa is an eating disorder characterized by repeated episodes of binge eating followed by purging. It tends to occur in women of normal weight with no history of anorexia nervosa. The binge eating (which the person recognizes as being abnormal) is accompanied by a fear of not being able to stop. Individuals who engage in

Eating disorders: Psychological disorders characterized by gross disturbances in eating behavior and in the way individuals respond to food.

Anorexia nervosa [an-uh-REX-ee-uh ner-VOH-suh]: An eating disorder characterized by an obstinate and willful refusal to eat, a distorted body image, and an intense fear of being fat.

Bulimia nervosa [boo-LEE-me-uh ner-VOH-suh]: An eating disorder characterized by repeated episodes of binge eating (and a fear of not being able to stop eating) followed by purging.

binge eating become fearful of gaining weight; they become preoccupied with how others see them (Striegel-Moore, Silberstein, & Rodin, 1993). Therefore, they often purge themselves of unwanted calories, mostly through vomiting and the use of laxatives and diuretics. Other methods include compulsive exercising and use of weight-reduction drugs. The medical complications of bulimia are serious. They include cardiovascular and gastrointestinal problems, menstrual irregularities, blood and hormone dysfunctions, muscular and skeletal problems, and sharp swings in mood and personality.

Men and women are affected by eating disorders in similar ways (Olivardia et al., 1995), but the ratio of female to male bulimics is 10 to 1. Researchers theorize that women believe, more readily than men, that fat is ugly and thin is beautiful. Women of higher socioeconomic classes are at greater risk of becoming bulimic, as are professionals whose weight is directly related to career achievement, such as dancers, athletes, and models. Disharmonious family life and maladjusted parents who inflict psychological and physical abuse on a child are correlated with the incidence of bulimia—although there is by no means a causal relationship (Rorty, Yager, & Rossotto, 1994). Whether dieting plays a role in bulimia is unclear because many bulimics don't regularly engage in dieting (Lowe, Gleaves, & Murphy-Eberenz, 1998). Bulimics are often depressed (Specker et al., 1994). Women with bulimia have lower self-esteem than women who eat normally, and they may have experienced some kind of clinical depression in the past (Klingenspor, 1994). Alcohol dependency and a family history of bulimia are sometimes reported (Garfinkel et al., 1996; Kozyk, Touyz, & Beumont, 1998). Some bulimics may become so wrapped up in food-related behaviors that they avoid contact with other people.

Not only physiology, but ideas, past behaviors, emotions, expectations, and goals all enter into the sexual behavior of human beings.

Bulimia may have a biological basis, taking the form of an imbalance of neurotransmitters, but most researchers have focused on psychological explanations. Some bulimics may eat as a means of lightening their mood, regulating tension, and escaping from self-awareness (Heatherton & Baumeister, 1991). After binges, however, they feel guilty. To lessen their guilt and avoid the potential consequence of eating (gaining weight), they purge themselves. Researchers believe the purges reduce post-binge guilt feelings. The problems of bulimics may not disappear completely when treated; one study found that after not being diagnosed as bulimic for an entire decade, women who had once been so diagnosed were much thinner than others in their communities (Sullivan et al., 1998). 

Think Critically

- Individuals respond to food in different ways depending on the time of day. How might this factor have affected Schachter's research participants, causing obese and normal-weight participants to behave differently?
- If, as some researchers claim, anorexia has a physiological basis, why do you think it is less prevalent in other cultures?

Sexual Behavior: Physiology plus Thought

Focus on issues and ideas

- The initiators and controls of human sexual behavior
- How beliefs about what is normal sexual behavior change

Fascinating and powerfully motivating as sex is, it is not physiologically necessary to sustain a person's life. In lower organisms, sexual behavior is controlled largely by physiological and hormonal systems. In human beings, in contrast, the sex drive is to a great extent under psychological control. This means that not only physiology, but ideas, past behaviors, emotions, expectations, and goals all enter into the sexual behavior of human beings. The relative contributions of these factors vary depending on an array of variables. Let's look at some of the initiators of human sexual behavior, at the physiology of that behavior, and then at its range.

What Initiates the Sex Drive?

Hardly a day goes by when you are not bombarded with sexually suggestive advertisements. Perfume ads abound in magazines; attractive, and often half-clad, models sell cars. Youthful, sexually desirable men and women sell sports equipment and even toothpaste. Advertisers use learning principles to pair attractive people and situations with products in the hope that the products will take on an arousing glamour—and to hint that if you use the product, you may become as alluring as the models. The advertisers are seeking to initiate buying activity by activating the sexual drive. They know, of course, that people's thoughts direct buying behavior. But sexual behavior is affected by hormones.

Sex Hormones. Sexual behavior in human beings is in part under hormonal control, and the sex hormones differ for men and women. In males, the testes are the principal producers of androgens, the male sex hormones. In females, the ovaries are the principal producers of estrogens, the female sex hormones. (In fact, there are many different male and female sex hormones, but generically they are known as androgens and estrogens.) It is the release of androgens (especially testosterone) or estrogens (especially estradiol) that first signals and accelerates the onset of the secondary sex characteristics in developing teenagers (see Chapter 9, p. 259). Once they are postpubescent, their bodies generate sufficient levels of androgens or estrogens to create the desire and ability to engage in sexual behaviors. In men, androgens (especially testosterone) stay at pretty much the same level from day to day; in women, estrogen levels vary throughout the menstrual cycle, and when the menstrual cycle ceases (at menopause), estrogen levels fall. Both men and women can be sexually receptive and active regardless of their hormone level.

People share with other animals a hormonally based sexual urge that is determined, in part, by brain structures such as the hypothalamus (Swaab & Hofman, 1995). But in other animals, hormones exert profound effects on behavior, activating an organized set of sexual responses. Most of these responses in animals do not occur without hormonal activation. So, for example, if the testes of male rats are removed, the animals show a marked decrease in sexual activity. Similarly, most female animals are sexually responsive *only* when hormones are released into the bloodstream (when they are "in heat"). Human beings, on the other hand, can choose whether or not to respond sexually at any given time. In fact, in human beings, the removal of hormone-generating organs may not affect sexual behavior at all (depending on the person's age at removal), because sexual motivation is influenced by social and psychological factors as much as by physiological ones—if not more so.

Sights, Sounds, Smells, and Fantasy. In animals, a receptive female may show her receptivity by releasing pheromones; the pheromones trigger sexual activity in the male (see Chapter 3, p. 83). A specific movement or set of actions may also signal female receptivity and trigger sexual behavior from the male animal. But human beings, because their sexuality is not so directly under hormonal control, can be aroused by the sight or sound of something with erotic associations or the smell of a familiar perfume. Thought plays an enormous role in human sexuality; people's thoughts, fantasies, and emotions initiate and activate sexual desire and behavior. And PET studies have recently located specific areas of the brain that are activated when people are experiencing sexual arousal (Stoléru et al., 1999).

The Sexual Response Cycle

When human beings become sexually aroused, they go through a series of four phases (stages). The phases, which together are known as the *sexual response cycle,* are the excitement phase, the plateau phase, the orgasm phase, and the resolution phase.

The **excitement phase** is the first phase of the cycle, during which there are increases in heart rate, blood pressure, and respiration. A key characteristic of this phase is **vasocongestion**—engorgement of the blood vessels, particularly in the genital area, due to increased blood flow. In women, the breasts and clitoris swell, the vaginal lips expand, and vaginal lubrication increases; in men, the penis becomes erect. The excitement phase is anticipatory and may last from a few minutes to a few hours.

The **plateau phase** is the second phase of the sexual response cycle, during which physical arousal continues to increase as the partners' bodies prepare for orgasm. Autonomic nervous system activity increases, causing a faster heart rate. In women, the clitoris withdraws, the vagina becomes engorged and fully extended; in men, the penis becomes fully erect, turns a darker color, and may secrete a bit of fluid, which may contain sperm.

The **orgasm phase** is the third phase of the sexual response cycle, during which autonomic nervous system activity reaches its peak and muscle contractions

Excitement phase: The first phase of the sexual response cycle, during which there are increases in heart rate, blood pressure, and respiration.

Vasocongestion: In the sexual response cycle, engorgement of the blood vessels, particularly in the genital area, due to increased blood flow.

Plateau phase: The second phase of the sexual response cycle, during which physical arousal continues to increase as the partners" bodies prepare for orgasm.

Orgasm phase: The third phase of the sexual response cycle, during which autonomic nervous system activity reaches its peak and muscle contractions occur in spasms throughout the body, but especially in the genital area.

occur in spasms throughout the body, especially in the genital area. An *orgasm* is the peak of sexual activity. In men, muscles throughout the reproductive system contract to help expel semen; in women, muscles surrounding the vagina contract. Although men experience only one orgasm during each sexual response cycle, women are capable of multiple orgasms. An orgasm lasts only a few seconds and is an all-or-none activity; once the threshold for orgasm is reached, the orgasm occurs.

The **resolution phase** is the fourth phase of the sexual response cycle following orgasm, during which the body returns to its resting, or normal, state. This return takes from one to several minutes; the time required varies considerably from person to person. During this phase, men are usually unable to achieve an erection for some amount of time, called the *refractory period.*

Like many other physiological events, the sexual response cycle is subject to considerable variation, with longer or shorter phases and different signs of arousal, depending on the person and his or her age.

Human Sexual Behavior

While American culture is saturated with sexually suggestive advertisements and sexually explicit movies, it also shows considerable reluctance to examine and talk about sexual behavior scientifically. Efforts to examine sexuality in a systematic way are often viewed with skepticism; in 1994, Congress even sought to ensure that a federally funded sex survey was not conducted.

Sex Surveys: What's Normal? Despite this reluctance to look at sex objectively, various sexual surveys, attitude questionnaires, and in-depth interviews have been conducted over the years. One of the first and most famous was conducted by a biologist, Alfred Kinsey, and his colleagues (1948, 1953). Contemporary researchers such as Morton Hunt (1974), Masters, Johnson, and Kolodny (1994), and Laumann and his colleagues (1994; Michael et al., 1998) have extended and refined the early research by Kinsey.

In general, reports about sexual practices show that individuals engage in sexual behaviors more when they are younger than when they are older. For example, the frequency of intercourse decreases from the early 20s to the 50s or 60s (Call, Sprecher, & Schwartz, 1995). Similarly, the duration of any specific sexual activity decreases with increasing age. Among couples in Western culture, patterns of sexual practices are predictable; one element of sexual activity, such as petting, often or at least usually precedes another, such as intercourse. Compared with other industrialized countries, the United States has a lower median age of onset of sexual activity, and American adolescents have a pregnancy rate five times greater than that in other developed countries (Nakkab, 1997). While the sex lives of Americans are predictable, and not as active as many assume, they are reported by most people as being satisfactory (Laumann et al., 1994).

Resolution phase: The fourth phase of the sexual response cycle, following orgasm, during which the body returns to its resting, or normal, state.

The Laumann study (Laumann et al., 1994; Michael et al., 1998) of sexual practices in the United States is the most recent and most comprehensive of the last four decades. Laumann's team administered questionnaires to and conducted face-to-face interviews with 3,432 men and women aged 18 to 59 in randomly selected households throughout the country. The results showed that men and women are more likely today than in the 1940s to have intercourse before marriage and that there has been a slow and steady decrease in the age of first intercourse (see also Feldman et al., 1997; Wadsworth et al., 1995). Men think about sex more than women do; about 54% of men think about sex daily, compared to only 19% of women. Interestingly, married men and women have more sex than do nonmarried young people—shattering a myth that the young and unattached are the most active sexually. The truth is that only one-third of people aged 18 to 59 have sex with a partner as often as twice a week. Many behavioral scientists found the results of the Laumann study predictable—but there were some surprises. Most women (90%) and most men (75%) reported that they had not had extramarital sexual affairs (Laumann et al., 1994). These high percentages may in part reflect a fear of sexually transmitted diseases; in any case, this society is not as sexually promiscuous as daytime TV dramas would have us believe. Another finding that surprised some researchers was that only 5.3% of men and 3.5% of women reported having had homosexual relations since puberty. More important, only 2.8% of men and 1.4% of women identified themselves as exclusively homosexual. The Laumann percentages are substantially less than the 10% that Kinsey reported in the 1950s, and they have been substantiated by similar estimates from other researchers (Cameron & Cameron, 1998; Sell, Wells, & Wypij, 1995).

An important aspect of the Laumann study was that it defined sexuality and sexual behavior within the context of people's lives. The researchers found that most individuals have sex with someone they know and live with (usually a spouse) and that people who are sexually active think about and desire sex more than do individuals who are not sexually active. Further, when people do engage in an extramarital affair, it is usually not a one-night stand with a stranger but a relationship with one person they know (Wadsworth et al., 1995). The Laumann study shows that contemporary sexual behavior is indeed different from what Kinsey observed. Today, people express their sexuality more often and more openly—and seek to understand their own feelings and behaviors. Laumann's team (Michael et al., 1998) reports a wide variety in sexual behaviors among Americans, compared with other cultures.

The picture is not completely happy, however. Despite the high incidence of sexually transmitted diseases, and especially the spread of AIDS (discussed in Chapter 12), engaging in risky sexual behaviors, such as not using condoms, is still disconcertingly prevalent in the United States (Downey & Landry, 1997). Also, older people are more likely to be unhappy with their sex lives, and young women and older men are more likely to suffer from various sexual problems, including inability to experience orgasm, low sexual desire, problems attaining an erection in men, and painful intercourse in women; the causes of such problems are physical and emotional (Laumann, Paik, & Rosen, 1999). The rates of *sexual dysfunction*—the generic term for such disorders—are high: 43% for women and 31% for men. But the incidence of each type of disorder is dependent on age, marital status, education, and other demographic characteristics. Unfortunately, many people do not seek treatment from their physicians or psychologists out of embarrassment. Laumann, Paik, and Rosen assert that sexual problems are widespread in American society and are influenced by both health-related and psychological factors.

Sexual Orientation. One's sexual orientation is the direction of one's sexual interest. A person with a *heterosexual orientation* has an erotic attraction and preference for members of the opposite sex; a person with a *homosexual orientation* has an erotic attraction to and preference for members of the same sex. A *bisexual orientation* is an erotic attraction to members of both sexes. Before the Kinsey studies, people were considered either heterosexual or homosexual. Kinsey, however, introduced the idea of a continuum of sexual behaviors ranging from exclusively homosexual behaviors through some homosexual behaviors, to mostly heterosexual behaviors, to exclusively heterosexual behaviors. Kinsey was the first researcher of sexual behavior to recognize that a homosexual encounter does not make a person homosexual. Also, a person may have a homosexual or bisexual orientation without ever having had a homosexual sexual experience. It is thus an overgeneralization to define a person's sexual orientation based solely on a single, or even on multiple, sexual encounters (Haslam, 1997).

The Kinsey report startled psychologists when it announced a high frequency of homosexual behavior among men (37%) and suggested that 1 in 10 men was primarily homosexual in orientation. The Laumann study came up with lower numbers, and researchers and the public are more willing to accept as reasonable estimates the 2.8% of men and 1.4% of women Laumann found who identify themselves as exclusively homosexual (Laumann et al., 1998). But Americans, perhaps more than people in other cultures, still have great difficulty with homosexuality. Having gays in the military causes intense debate. In addition, the high incidence of AIDS among gay men has placed the issues of prevention and homosexuality on the public agenda. However, some people have drawn unwarranted cause-and-effect conclusions from correlations between AIDS incidence and sexual orientation.

The causes of homosexuality have been debated for decades, and the argument has developed into a classic nature-versus-nurture one. The nurture side asserts that homosexual behavior is to a great extent under voluntary control, that it is learned, and that it can be changed by means of long-term therapy. Bem (1996) developed a theory that suggested that childhood temperament leads to atypical gender activities and preferences. These are then followed by feeling different from same-sex peers; such a feeling leads to heightened autonomic activity. Bem suggests that such arousal by people you are not like—the exotic—leads to sexual arousal, and so, the exotic becomes erotic. Bem's ideas have not yet been put to experimental tests. Bem and others who support a nurture view of homosexuality see a basic flaw in conclusions from genetic studies, family studies, and research on brain chemistry—they assert that researchers have mixed up the causes of sexual orientation with the effects (Byne, 1994).

Those on the nature side of the debate assert that homosexuality is indeed inborn, fixed, and genetically determined. They cite data showing that homosexual men and women knew when they were young children that they were "different" and point out that attempts to change gay men and women through therapy, prayer, or drugs are mostly ineffective. The weight of the evidence leans toward the physiological—or nature—side of the debate. Studies isolating brain structures, genes, and familial patterns of homosexuality (even among twins separated at birth) increasingly lend support to that side (LeVay & Hamer, 1994). Twin studies show a high concordance rate for homosexuality among fraternal and identical twins. Gay men tend to come from extended families where there have been other gay men; further, Hamer found unique DNA markers on the X chromosomes of gay men (Hamer et al., 1993). High levels of specific hormones have been found at birth among babies who later became male homosexuals. Last, both LeVay (1991) and Swaab and Hofman (1995) found that portions of the hypothalamus in gay men differ from those in heterosexual men. The impact of this evidence has been profound: Gay men and lesbians are leaving mental health counseling, seeking civil rights protection, and feeling more positive about their sexuality.

Think Critically

- Do you think the federal government should study sexual behavior? Why or why not?
- Many scientific discoveries concerning genetics raise ethical questions: For example, should parents be allowed to prescreen their unborn child for a genetic marker for homosexuality? Can you think of others?

Achievement: A Social Need

Focus on issues and ideas

- The relationship between expectancy, need for achievement, and goal attainment

Personality psychologists such as Henry Murray assert that key events and situations in a person's environment determine behavior. Murray used the word *press* to indicate how environmental situations may motivate a person (Murray, 1938): The environment may press an individual to excel at sports, to be a loving caretaker to a grandparent, or to achieve great wealth. The press of poverty may produce a social need for financial security; it may therefore cause a person to work hard and become educated so as to earn a comfortable living.

The most useful theories for measuring these kinds of motivation are expectancy theories that focus specifically on the **need for achievement**—a social need that directs a person to strive constantly for excellence and success. According to such achievement theories, people engage in behaviors that satisfy their desires for success, mastery, and fulfillment. Tasks that do not further these goals are not motivating and either are not undertaken or are performed without energy or commitment. There may be even more negative effects when people feel that making an effort is useless.

One of the leaders in studies of achievement motivation was David C. McClelland, whose early research focused on the idea that people have strong social motives for achievement (McClelland, 1958). McClelland showed that a person learns achievement motivation in the home environment during childhood. People with a high need for achievement had parents who stressed excellence and who provided physical affection and emotional rewards for high achievement. Such people also generally walked early, talked early, and had a high need for achievement even in elementary school (e.g., Teevan & McGhee, 1972). A high need for achievement is most pronounced in first-born children, perhaps because parents typically have more time to give them direction and praise. It is also especially evident in cultures, such as many Asian cultures, that stress achievement-related activities and foster in children a fear of academic failure (Eaton & Dembo, 1997).

Achievement motives are often measured by analyzing the thought content of imaginative stories. Early studies of people's need for achievement used the *Thematic Apperception Test (TAT)*. In this test, people are shown uncaptioned pictures of scenes in which it is unclear what is happening; the pictures are thus open to interpretation. Test takers are instructed not to think in terms of right or wrong answers but to answer four basic questions for each scene:

1. What is happening?
2. What has led up to this situation?
3. What are those in this situation thinking?
4. What will happen next?

Using a complex scoring system, researchers analyze participants' descriptions of each scene. They have found that persons with a high need for achievement tell stories that stress success, getting ahead, and competition (Spangler, 1992).

With tests such as the TAT, a researcher can differentiate individuals with a high need for achievement from those with a low need. Lowell (1952) found that when he asked participants to rearrange scrambled letters (such as *wtse*) to construct a meaningful word (*west*), those with a low need for achievement improved only slightly at the task over successive testing periods. In contrast, participants who scored high in the need for achievement showed increasing improvement over several periods of testing. The researchers reasoned that, when presented with a com-

Need for achievement: A social need that directs a person to strive constantly for excellence and success.

Emotion: A subjective response, usually accompanied by a physiological change, which is interpreted in a particular way by the individual and often leads to a change in behavior.

plex task, persons with a high need for achievement find new and better ways of performing the task as they practice it, whereas those with a low need for achievement try no new methods. People with a high need for achievement constantly strive toward excellence and better performance; they have developed a belief in their self-efficacy and in the importance of effort in determining performance (Carr, Borkowski, & Maxwell, 1991; McClelland, 1961).

The goals people set and the amount of risk they are willing to take are also affected by the kinds of needs that motivate them, their experiences, and even their moods (Hom & Arbuckle, 1988). The expression *self-fulfilling prophecy* suggests that those who expect to succeed will do so and those who don't, won't. Expectations for success and failure can influence the outcome of an effort if those expectations help shape the person's behavior (Elliott & Dweck, 1988). A teacher who expects a student to fail, for example, may treat the student in ways that increase the likelihood of the student's failure; things tend to turn out just the way the teacher expected (or prophesied) they would. Expectancy thus becomes a key component in explaining behavior, especially that of people with a high need for achievement. For example, a person pushed toward success by parents, drama instructors, or sports coaches may develop a high need for achievement; after positive experiences, such an individual will typically set challenging but attainable performance goals (Dweck & Leggett, 1988).

Think Critically

- Do you think that second- and third-born children have needs that are different from or greater than those of first-born children? What might those needs be?

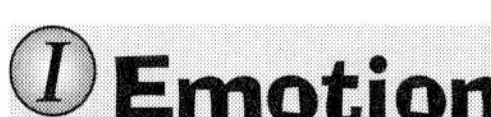

Emotion

Focus on issues and ideas

- The defining elements of an emotion
- How people display emotion through body language
- The evolution of different theories of emotion and how they explain emotional behavior

That motivation and emotion are interconnected should come as no surprise. Anger can cause you to hurl an object across a room or to lash out at a friend. When a loud noise startles you, you may freeze up. Happiness can make you smile all day or stop to help a motorist with a flat tire. Although emotions, including love, joy, and fear, can motivate behavior, emotional categories remain fuzzy (Rosch, 1978). As *Experiencing Psychology* (on p. 224) shows, even such a seemingly universal state as happiness has yet to be fully understood. Psychologists find that people in therapy just want to be happy, to have some joy in their lives. Nevertheless, as a topic of study, happiness has received relatively little attention—at least compared with fear, anger, or depression.

What Is Emotion?

The word *emotion* is an umbrella term referring to a wide range of subjective states, such as love, fear, sadness, and anger. We all have emotions, talk about them, and agree on what represents them; but this agreement is not scientific. The psychological investigation of emotion has led to a more precise definition. Most psychologists acknowledge that emotion consists of three elements: feelings, physiological responses, and behaviors. An **emotion** is a subjective response (a feeling), usually accompanied by a physiological change, which is interpreted in a particular way by the individual and often leads to a change in behavior. People cry when they are sad and breathe faster, sweat, and salivate less when they are afraid. Some physiological changes precede an emotional response. For example, just before an automobile crashes, the passengers may show physiological arousal, muscle tension, and avoidance responses—that is, they may brace themselves against the seat in front of them or put their arms up in anticipation. Other changes are evident only after an emotion-causing event. It is only after an accident that people shake with fear, disbelief, or rage.

Psychologists focus on different aspects of emotional behavior. The earliest researchers cataloged and described basic emotions (Bridges, 1932; Wundt, 1896). Others tried to discover the physiological bases of emotion (Bard, 1934). Still others focused on how people perceive the bodily movements of others and on how they convey emotions to others through gestures or eye contact (Ekman, 1992). Research has revealed that people experience the same *kinds* of emotions, but the intensity and quality vary. One person's sense of joy is different from another's. Thus, emotions have a private and personal component. These subjective feelings are difficult to measure, so most researchers focus on the physiological and behavioral aspects of emotions. Recent research has studied a range of observable and measurable aspects of emotions: the possibility that one hemisphere of the brain dominates emotion (Davidson, 1992); the biochemical components of emotions,

EXPERIENCING PSYCHOLOGY

Happy Days

What is happiness? Is it tranquility, satisfaction, joy, or contentment? Psychologists tend to refer to happiness as a state of subjective well-being, based on a person's evaluation of his or her life. Such evaluations are both cognitive, realistic judgments of facts (one's level of wealth or health, for example) and affective, or feeling-based, reactions (an evaluation of the facts as pleasant or unpleasant). In fact, most people report fairly positive subjective well-being—they are happy (Veenhoven, 1993)—despite the fact that objective measures of their situation may show them to be disadvantaged economically (Diener & Diener, 1996). Worldwide, people report overall happiness in work, leisure, and marriage, with the exception of those in the very poorest societies. Happy people tend to be optimistic, to have high self-esteem, to feel good, and to sleep well; happiness seems unrelated to some variables that many people think are important—age, gender, ethnicity, educational level, financial status, and physical attractiveness.

Like all things human, happiness shows great variation; some people are happier than others. The happiest individuals have close personal relations with other people, are interested in their work, are well-rested, and are goal-oriented (Aron & Aron, 1997; Myers & Diener, 1995). When people are happy, fluctuations in their life circumstances tend to make little difference. Happy people, whether rich or poor, seem to have a stable set of feelings about their situations, so that problems—for example, financial setbacks—do not tend to change their level of happiness. Similarly, research shows that as people's financial and other circumstances improve, their happiness level—their subjective well-being—remains stable (Diener, 1998). People adapt to being more wealthy; they wear better clothes and live in bigger houses, but then they come to take those things somewhat for granted. Thus, their relative level of subjective well-being stays the same.

Perhaps subjective well-being is randomly distributed among people, as height is; just as very few people are extremely short or tall, perhaps very few people are extremely miserable or ecstatic. Lykken and Tellegen (1996) make such an argument: "It may be that trying to be happier is as futile as trying to be taller and therefore is counterproductive" (p. 189). They argue that although most people are happy, this is genetically determined and that individual differences in happiness are a matter of chance.

Still, people *want* to be happy; in fact, people seek happiness above all other things—money, fame, even health. According to psychologist Mihaly Csikszentmihalyi (1997), with so many emotional responses available, happiness can be achieved only if people find *flow.* Flow occurs when a person's skills are engaged in overcoming a challenge that is reasonable. When people are engaged in an activity, they feel less self-conscious, and hours pass by in minutes. From Csikszentmihalyi's view, happiness follows from flow, from engagement—whether a person is a physician or a clerk in a department store. Csikszentmihalyi argues that each of us can transform our lives, find flow, and then achieve happiness by complete engagement with what we do and those we do it with.

Although it is true that happiness stays pretty stable over life and that most people report being happy, like Csikszentmihalyi, most psychologists believe that happiness can be increased through personal striving, maintenance of close relationships, and a positive attitude (e.g., DeNeve & Cooper, 1998). They argue that if you can be positive, you can brighten your life and other people's and better the human condition. In a sense, psychology is an unabashedly optimistic profession; psychologists don't assume that trying to do or be better is counterproductive. ■

including blood glucose levels and hormone changes (Baum, Grunberg, & Singer, 1992); physiological responses such as heart rate and blood pressure; and behavioral responses such as smiling and crying.

Feelings, Physiology, and Behavior. Each of the three central elements of emotions—feelings, physiology, and behavior—has been examined extensively.

Over the years, researchers have tried to identify the "basic" emotional expressions of feeling. But such cataloging is difficult because emotional responses are molded by strong cultural expectations. Fear, for example, can be praised or punished, depending on the culture, and children may learn to hide some "basic" emotions. One noted researcher (Izard, 1997) isolated ten such basic emotions (joy, interest, surprise, sadness, anger, disgust, contempt, fear, shame, and guilt). Different accounts of emotion emerge every few years and add or subtract, for one reason or another, one or two emotional states (e.g. Keltner & Buswell, 1997).

Among psychologists, the most widely studied emotional state has been fear, largely because fear has a strong physiological basis and is evident among all primates.

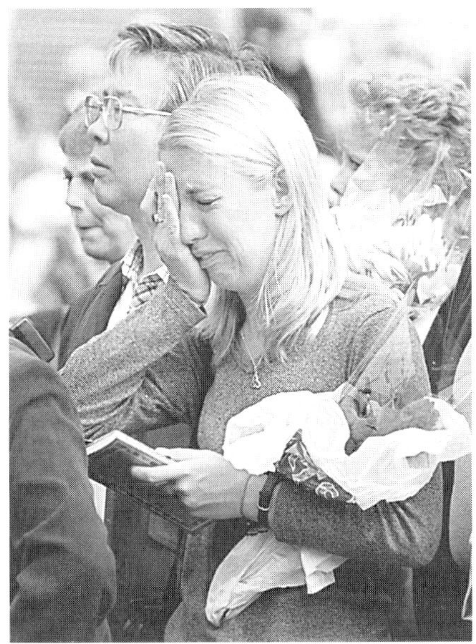

In many of the early studies of emotion, fear was studied both behaviorally and physiologically. Behaviorally, fear is evident in children and adults; in fact, it is the principal symptom of maladjusted people. People who are depressed and anxious report feeling afraid. They are afraid of life, of work, of taking action, and even of inaction. The maladjusted fear punishment, and often success. Fear leads to worry and anxiety and to inaction, which only increases the worries and anxieties—thereby setting up a vicious cycle that only compounds the problem.

Recent research has revealed that physiologically, the amygdala, within the limbic system, is crucial to fear. That is, when the amygdala is damaged, removed, or chemically altered with drugs, fear responses are altered. Fear can be initiated by stimulating the amygdala, and symptoms associated with fear can be initiated or suppressed by altering it. The amygdala is physically near and loosely connected to the hippocampus. In human beings, when the amygdala or the hippocampus is altered, people may feel fear but not know why, or they may recognize that they feel fearful but not show emotional reactions. LeDoux (1996) showed that subcortical responses of the amygdala that seem automatic are, in fact, tied into the more complex memory systems that tell people about the past, the present, and how to interpret physiological arousal.

In considering behavioral aspects of emotion, psychologists have recognized that facial expressions provide reliable clues to people's feelings. Facial expressions are easily observed and interpreted by others and are thought of as an accurate index of a person's emotional states. People are extremely good at detecting changes in facial expressions (Edwards, 1998; Farah et al., 1998). Also, there are asymmetries in facial expressions in both infants and adults, and adults can easily discern those differences. Several studies (Best & Queen, 1989; Rothbart, Taylor, & Tucker, 1989) have found that the left side of the face (controlled by the right side of the brain in most people) may be more expressive than the right side of the face, especially in adults. Researchers argue that the right side of the face may be more directly under the control of the left hemisphere of the brain, and so people are able to inhibit right-face expression more easily than left-face expression. Research also shows that upper portions of the face may be more expressive than lower portions (Asthana & Mandal, 1997). Nevertheless, though facial expressions (either side) are good indicators of emotion, they are only indicators; a happy face or a turned-down mouth can mask real emotions.

People also display emotion through gestures, body language—a lowered head, shaking fists, clenched teeth, or limpness—as well as voice tone and volume (Izard & Saxton, 1988). The autonomic nervous system responds differently to different emotions (Levenson, 1992). Researchers have studied the smiling responses of infants, children, and adults by examining the conditions under which smiling is evoked and then lost (Carlson, Gantz, & Masters, 1983). Researchers have also studied smiling cross-culturally (Levenson et al., 1992), and some have found commonalities in what brings about emotional responses such as smiling. However, not all researchers find that responses are the same (Ekman, 1992) or that they occur to the same extent in every culture (Pittam et al., 1995). Most emotions are expressed in most cultures, but the expressions vary in degree. Thus, it is crucial to note that when the anthropologist Ruth Benedict characterized Japanese culture as a shame culture and the United States as a guilt culture, she overstated the case. The Japanese know guilt, and Americans know shame; the guilt/shame distinction is not an either/or distinction, but rather part of a gradation of emotional response (Heider, 1994).

The expression of emotion is affected by situational context and by subtle variables. Facial characteristics are important; people like more feminine faces in both men and women—the Leonardo DeCaprio look—and this is a powerful determinant of attractiveness (Perrett et al., 1998). But looks are only part of the story. For example, we have all stood in lines at a grocery store and observed how the clerks behave with different customers. Psychologists have, in fact, studied the emotional expressions of store clerks and their responses to customers. One study (Rafaeli, 1989) considered a range of variables: the clerk's gender, whether the clerk wore a smock with nametag, the presence of other clerks, and the customer's gender. Although the results were complicated, the emotional expressions of clerks were affected by nearly all the variables. Female clerks displayed positive emotions more often than male clerks, male customers received positive emotional responses more often than female customers, and clerks who were especially aware of their role (because they were wearing smocks) were more expressive than other clerks. Complex emotional behavior is not likely to be explained by one simple variable such as gender or dress.

Can We Control Emotions? Psychologists know that physiological arousal created by one event can lead to an enhanced emotional arousal in response to another—they call this effect *excitation transfer.* Does this happen without a person's awareness? People do not respond automatically to environmental or internal stimuli—and they can learn to control emotional expression (for example, to hold in rage or excitement). This view asserts that people manage their emotional states in purposeful ways by constantly evaluating their environment and feelings.

Arousal is an essential component in emotion, as we've seen, and researchers show that people can use cognitive means to control their arousal level and therefore their emotions. Even young infants show some forms of emotional restraint and control, and control of emotions continues to develop, especially after the first year (Kopp, 1989).

Central to the notion that arousal affects emotion is the concept that people can read, or evaluate, their own physiological signals. People learn to evaluate their arousal, understand what it means, and use that information to modulate their responses. Understanding the flush of sexual excitement or the adrenaline rush of a challenge to a fight can lead to a variety of behaviors. The first step is to discern what the excitement is about. For psychologists studying the behavior of disturbed individuals, an understanding of the interaction of arousal, emotion, and thought has become increasingly important. Even in normal individuals, too high a level of arousal can produce extreme emotional responses and lead to disorganized, less effective behavior. Many maladjusted individuals, such as those suffering from the manic stages of bipolar disorders, have so high a level of arousal that they cannot organize their thinking or behavior (see Chapter 13, p. 377).

Some studies show that people can control their body's biochemistry. Participants in a study by Lazarus and Alfert (1964) were able to manipulate their electrodermal response (a measurement of skin conductivity that is assumed to be a physiological indication of anxiety) when told in advance about a painful procedure shown in a film. Thus, the expression of emotion is affected by both a person's motivations and her or his basic biochemistry (Carver & Scheier, 1990). People also control their emotions because of strong cultural expectations. In the United States, for example, children and women are expected to cry and express emotion more often than men do; in Latin America, men are expected to be emotional.

Expectations and cognitive appraisals of situations seem to be key elements in physiological and subsequent behavioral expressions of emotion (Smith, 1989). Unrealistic expectations can lead to some unusual consequences; for example, if a person suffers from hypochondriasis (see Chapter 13, p. 373), any ache, pain, or shortness of breath may lead to feelings of fear about his or her health.

Some aspects of emotion may be culture-specific and others may be universal.

Varieties of Emotional Experience. Robert Plutchik (1980) suggests that emotions can be mixed (just as colors are) to yield new varieties of emotional experience. He devised a way of representing emotional responses within a circle. Neighboring primary emotions mix to yield more complex emotions. So, for instance, a person experiencing joy and anticipation (which are neighboring emotions within the circle) may feel a sense of optimism; similarly, a mixture of surprise and sadness (also neighboring emotions) may be experienced as disappointment. Such models are interesting ways to think about the range of human emotional responses; however, there is as yet little data to support them.

Phillip Shaver and his colleagues have sought to identify the basic emotions that all people experience and the ways in which they are experienced. Shaver suggested that, when asked to identify emotions, almost all people will describe six basic categories of emotions, but these six basic categories can overlap, and many other emotional states can be grouped under them. Schwartz and Shaver (1987) contend that people's emotional knowledge is organized around these emotional categories and that people exhibit characteristic behaviors with each emotion. Along with others (Ekman, 1994; Izard, 1994), Schwartz and Shaver assert that these emotions appear cross-culturally. Each culture may put a different value on an emotion, and different events or experiences may trigger a given emotion, depending on the culture. For example, love is an extremely powerful emotion in the United States, but in Sumatra, one of the chief islands of Indonesia, nostalgia is the most powerful emotion (Heider, 1991). Shaver believes that psychologists must better understand the overall structure of

DIVERSITY

Stereotypes about Emotion and Gender

In this society, it is widely believed that women are more emotionally expressive than men, and that they more readily express warmth and affection as well as fear, vulnerability, and sadness. And men are believed to express less warmth and affection and to be more angry. These beliefs about men and women are widely accepted. However, research shows that the degree to which these stereotypes reflect reality may be due to the fact the stereotypes themselves help shape it! People who do not conform to generally held beliefs might be punished through social rejection, and people who do conform are rewarded for such behaviors.

Most people do not recognize that gender differences are primarily social constructs rather than biological facts. Consider, for example, the gender stereotype that males express more anger than females. This stereotype is largely inaccurate, because it focuses on the behavioral expression of anger through aggression but ignores anger expressed in other ways. For example, women often verbalize more intense anger and for longer periods of time than do men—especially women who are in close heterosexual relationships. Men in a similar situation more frequently "stonewall" by inhibiting facial expressions and minimizing listening behaviors as well as eye contact. Although research data do confirm some stereotypical behaviors, research by Leslie Brody (1997) suggests that gender differences can be either minimized or maximized depending on the social and cultural context. Brody asserts that the reason women continue to be stereotyped as expressing less anger is a failure to consider multiple modes of expression. She also points out that the context in which anger is expressed affects how it is perceived; for example, Hall (1984) suggests that people moderate their behavior with the opposite sex so that it approaches the other sex's norms.

Expression of anger also depends on where a person is in the life cycle and whether he or she is rearing children. People's expression of anger diminishes during the child-rearing years, and men who are principal caregivers tend to be similar to women in their emotional expressiveness toward children and less expressive of anger than males who are not engaged in child-rearing. Further, women (even those in Western cultures) still tend to be in positions of low power and status. Women may thus be more likely to interpret situations as being less controllable and having higher risk for expressing anger (Lips, 1994). In cross-cultural studies in Africa, LeVine (1966) showed that because of labor migration and changes in workloads, power and status levels between the two sexes began to shift—as a consequence, both sexes begin to express the emotions stereotypically associated with the other.

Clearly, stereotypes about gender and emotion tend to be imprecise and exaggerated. They tend to ignore the context in which an emotion is expressed, the way it is expressed, and the culture of the person expressing it. ■

emotion before they can propose a comprehensive theory. Paul Ekman (1993) concurs and asserts that some aspects of emotion may be culture-specific and others may be universal. Researchers have just begun to use the appropriate techniques and ask the proper questions to explore the extent to which emotional expression is universal (Izard, 1994; Russell, 1994).

Diversity explores the extent of emotional differences between men and women.

Not all researchers consider all elements of emotion in their studies. One study may focus on emotional expression; another on physiological reactions. Certain basic emotions—fear, anger, sadness, joy, disgust, and surprise—appear to be innate; these are often considered "survival" emotions. More complex emotions—pride, love, and envy—are more likely to be learned, thought about, and evaluated; these are thought to be more cognitively based. Not surprisingly, the theories researchers have developed to help explain emotions are either physiologically based theories that tend to explain a few simple emotions very well or more complex cognitive theories that tend to explain feelings that are learned.

Physiological Theories of Emotion

Many researchers feel that happiness, rage, and even romantic love are physiologically based. They argue that the wide range of emotions that human beings experience and express are in large part controlled by neurons located in an area deep within the brain, the limbic system. The *limbic system* is composed of cells in the hypothalamus, the amygdala, and other cortical and subcortical areas. Studies of these crucial areas began in the 1920s, when Bard (1934) found that the removal of portions of the cortex of cats produced sharp emotional reactions to simple stimuli such as a touch or a puff of air. The cats would hiss, claw, bite, arch their backs, and growl—and their reactions did not seem directed at any specific person or target. Bard referred to this behavior as *sham rage.* Later researchers stimulated portions of the brain with electrical current and found that many brain centers were implicated in the experiencing of emotions—they deduced that the cortex was integrating information. Two major physiological (biological) approaches to the study of emotion dominated psychology for decades: the James–Lange theory and the Cannon–Bard theory. Both are concerned with the physiology of emotions and with whether physiological change or emotional feelings occur first. More recent theories, like that of LeDoux (1996), focus on specific brain structures.

The James-Lange Theory. According to a theory proposed by both William James (1842–1910) and Carl Lange (1834–1900) (who are given joint credit because their approaches were so similar), people experience physiological changes and *then* interpret them as emotional states. People do not cry because they feel sad; they feel sad because they cry. People do not perspire because they are afraid; they feel afraid after they perspire. In other words, the James–Lange theory says that people do not experience an emotion until after their bodies become aroused and begin to respond with physiological changes; that is, feedback from the body produces feelings or emotions (James, 1884; Lange, 1922). For this approach, in its most simplified form, *feeling* is the essence of emotion. Thus, James (1890, p. 1006) wrote, "Every one of the bodily changes, whatsoever it be, is felt, acutely or obscurely, the moment it occurs."

A modern physiological approach suggests that facial movements, by their action, can create emotions. Called the *facial feedback hypothesis,* this approach suggests that sensations from the face provide cues or signals to the brain that act as feedback to help a person determine an emotional response. In some ways, this approach derives from the James–Lange theory. For example, when specific facial movements create a change in the blood flow to and thus the temperature of the brain, pleasant feelings occur. According to this theory, a facial movement such as a smile or an eye movement may release the appropriate emotion-linked neurotransmitters (Izard, 1990; Ekman, 1993; Zajonc, Murphy, & Inglehart, 1989). Some neurotransmitters may bring about pleasant emotions and others unpleasant ones. Crying, for example, is associated with a mixture of sympathetic, parasympathetic, and somatic activation (Gross, Fredrickson, & Levenson, 1994). Zajonc and his colleagues argue that facial movements alone are capable of inducing emotions; anecdotally, children (and adults) often do feel a bit happier when their parents or friends coax them to smile. This theory is still relatively new and has not yet been tested extensively by other researchers.

The Cannon-Bard Theory. Physiologists, notably Walter Cannon (1871–1945), were critical of the James–Lange theory. Cannon and Philip Bard, a colleague, argued that the physiological changes associated with many emotional states were identical. They reasoned as follows: If increases in blood pressure and heart rate accompany feelings of both anger and joy, how can people determine their emotional state simply from their physiological state? Cannon spoke of undifferentiated arousal—it is the same for fight and flight.

Cannon argued that when a person is emotional, two areas of the brain—the thalamus and the cerebral cortex—are stimulated simultaneously (he did not know the whole story about the limbic system). Stimulation of the cortex produces the emotional component of the experience; stimulation of the thalamus produces physiological changes in the sympathetic nervous system. According to Cannon (1927), emotional feelings *accompany* physiological changes; they neither produce nor result from such changes. The truth is that when Cannon and Bard were putting together their theory, they knew relatively little about how the brain operates. For example, physiological changes in the brain do not happen exactly simultaneously. Further, people report that they often have an experience and then have physiological and emotional reactions to it. Neither the James–Lange nor the Cannon–Bard approach considered how a person's thoughts about a situation might alter physiological reactions and emotional responses. But the James–Lange and Cannon–Bard approaches provided a conceptual bridge to newer, more modern approaches.

LeDoux's Emotional Brain. Joseph LeDoux (1993, 1995, 1996) has been investigating the physiological bases of emotions—especially fear—and discovering the central role of the amygdala and the structures to which it is connected. LeDoux asserts that a person's feelings and subjective experiences are initiated by primitive subcortical brain mechanisms. He maintains in his popular book, *The Emotional Brain,* that through the process of natural selection, the human brain has evolved the ability to detect fear-inducing situations and respond rapidly, with increases in heart rate and muscle tension, for example. His view is that responses such as the fear response are hard-wired into the brain's circuits, and that subjective feelings follow them, along closely associated but different routes. LeDoux reasons that fear responses—such as freezing up at the sight of a natural predator—are nature's evolutionary strategy. They occur automatically without thought. Referring to a prairie dog that sees its natural predator, the bobcat, LeDoux (1996, p. 176) states: "The sight or sound of the bobcat goes straight to [the] amygdala and out comes the freezing response." But such automatic responses are only the first, most immediate behaviors; in human beings, fear initiates control and thought, and *they* determine subsequent actions. LeDoux asserts that humans use their memory system, especially working memory, to make decisions about current situations and what to do next.

For LeDoux, emotional experiences are determined first by stimulation of the amygdala. Second, the amygdala creates arousal in various other brain structures. Next, the arousal and automatic responses created by the amygdala initiate changes in the body—release of hormones, sweating, facial changes—and these bodily changes provide feedback to the brain. The higher centers in the brain sense basic bodily reactions and interpret them (Kleinke, Peterson, & Rutledge, 1998). Thoughts and past experiences thus affect the emotional response. In the end, LeDoux (1996) asserts that there may be two routes for emotions, one subcortical and one cortical. His view is very much an evolutionary one; evolution has prepared humans to respond in certain basic emotional ways to some stimuli. Fear of heights, snakes, or insects has an evolutionary basis, as encountering any of these can be dangerous. Of course, the modern world is drastically different from that of our ancestors, and such fears today may lead to unnecessary phobias—cobras and tarantulas are not part of most people's everyday experiences.

For biopsychologists, the underpinnings of emotions are biochemical and based in evolution. But even the staunchest supporters of this approach recognize that the human brain has developed a wide range of emotional states. Our emotional repertoire is far too complex to be explained solely as a set of automatic evolutionary responses.

Cognitive Theories of Emotion

Fear, sadness, rage, and excitement all have readily recognizable emotional and physiological manifestations. But what about more complex emotions? Consider, for example, pride, embarrassment, or guilt. All of these require a far more subtle and complex analysis—one that focuses on thought (Lewis, 1995). Cognitive theories of emotion focus on mental interpretation as well as physiology. Cognitive theorists argue that emotion theories must incorporate interpretation, anticipation, and even problem solving (Parrott & Schulkin, 1993).

The Schachter-Singer Approach. The Schachter–Singer view of emotion is a cognitive approach that focuses on emotional activation and incorporates elements of both the James–Lange and the Cannon–Bard theories. Stanley Schachter and Jerome Singer observed that people do indeed interpret their emotions, but not solely from bodily changes. They argued that people interpret physical sensations within a specific context. They knew that bodily states, including chemically induced states brought on by alcohol or other drugs, can change moods. But observers cannot interpret what a person's emotional behavior means unless they know the situation in which it occurs. If a man cries at a funeral, observers suspect he is sad; if he cries at his daughter's wedding, they suspect he is joyful. Thus, according to the Schachter–Singer view, an emotion is created by cognitive factors as a person tries to account for a state of perceived activation (Lang, 1994).

To demonstrate their contention, Schachter and Singer (1962) injected volunteers with epinephrine (adrenaline), a powerful stimulant that increases physiological signs of arousal such as heart rate, energy level, and even sensations of butterflies in the stomach. The participants who got the epinephrine were not aware of its usual effects, however. Schachter and Singer compared these participants to a control group who weren't injected with epinephrine. To see if they could affect how participants interpreted their aroused state, Schachter and Singer manipulated the settings in which the volunteers experienced their arousal. These researchers hired undergraduates to act either happy and relaxed or sad, depressed, and angry. The hired students—called "stooges"—pretended that they were volunteers in the drug study; however, they were given injections of salt water, not epinephrine. Their emotional behavior was strictly an act. The "happy" stooges shot wads of paper into a wastebasket and flew paper airplanes around the room. The "angry" ones complained about the questionnaire they had to fill out and voiced their dissatisfaction with the experiment.

All the experimental participants showed increased physiological arousal when compared to the control participants. Those who interacted with the happy stooges reported that the drug made them feel good; those who interacted with the angry ones reported feeling anger. Schachter and Singer reasoned that when people see no immediate external cause for their physiological arousal (especially when arousal levels are low), they will label their feelings in terms of the thoughts available to them—in this case, thoughts stimulated by their interactions with the stooges.

Schachter and Singer had the kernel of an important idea: Arousal does intensify emotions. However, it does not work alone. People don't live in an experiential vacuum. For example, when people first smoke marijuana or take other psychoactive drugs, they tend to approach the experience with definite expectations. If told the drug produces feelings of hunger, new users report feeling hungry; if told the drug is a downer, new users often interpret their bodily sensations as depressed. In Schachter and Singer's view, people experience internal arousal, become aware of the arousal, seek an explanation for it, identify an external cue, and then label the arousal. In an important way, arousal provides the fuel—the energy—of emotion, but the labeling determines the emotion that is felt.

Valins (1966) and Reisenzein (1983) challenged Schachter and Singer's view. Valins showed that thoughts alone are sufficient to produce emotional behavior and that people can be misled about how aroused they are. He showed a group of men slides of nude women and simultaneously played a soundtrack of what participants thought were their own heartbeats but were actually previously recorded heartbeats, which were speeded up or slowed down as the slides were shown. This meant that the participants were being cued by the heartbeats as to their supposed arousal level. A control group of men saw the same slides and heard the same sounds, but were told that the sounds were meaningless and to ignore them. When the two groups were asked to judge the attractiveness of the nude women, the experimental group rated them more positively than did the control group. Valins argued that physiological arousal is not a prerequisite for labeling of emotion; cognitive processes alone will suffice (see Harris & Katkin, 1975). Reisenzein (1983) argues that Schachter and Singer's theory overestimates the role of arousal and that arousal, at best, merely intensifies an emotional experience. Today, psychologists recognize that Schachter and Singer's view probably overstated the role of cognitive processes as the determinants of emotion, but it stimulated researchers such as Damasio (1994) to think about this important component and make it part of their theories.

Detection of Deception

Many psychological changes are caused by an increase in activity in the sympathetic branch of the autonomic nervous system. When the sympathetic nervous system is activated, many different responses take place almost simultaneously. Fear, for example, may slow or halt digestion, increase blood pressure and heart rate, deepen breathing, dilate the pupils, decrease salivation, and tense the muscles. Researchers recognized that the autonomic nervous system provides direct, observable, measurable responses that can be quantified in a systematic manner. This realization led to the development of the *polygraph instrument,* commonly called the *lie detector.* The process of lie detection is known as the *psychological detection of deception.* Developed in the 1940s, the *comparison question test* is the most common kind of polygraph exam administered today. The test can be numerically scored, increasing both its validity and its reliability (Raskin, Barland, & Podlesny, 1978).

A polygraph exam involves recording many physiological responses that indicate changes in the activity of the sympathetic branch of a person's autonomic nervous system. Most autonomic nervous system activity is involuntary, and deception is usually associated with an increase in such activity. A trained polygraph operator compares the level of a person's autonomic activity while answering critical questions (for example, "Did you stab that woman?") to the level while answering comparison questions (for example, "Have you ever hurt anyone else you haven't told me about?"). Research has shown that an innocent person tends to show a higher level of autonomic activity for comparison questions than a guilty person does, perhaps because an innocent person cannot be sure that a simple "yes" or "no" is a completely truthful answer. A guilty person, on the other hand, usually reacts more strongly to the critical questions, because they evoke specific memories, which are accompanied by arousal.

Not all people, however, show marked autonomic nervous system changes when they are emotionally aroused (Bashore & Rapp, 1993). Habitual liars show little or no change in autonomic activity when they lie; they seem to be able to lie without becoming emotionally aroused (Honts, 1994). Psychopaths (individuals suffering from antisocial personality disorder, to be discussed in Chapter 13) feel no guilt about committing crimes or telling lies to avoid punishment. Can psychopaths beat the polygraph? A number of studies (e.g., Hammond, 1980; Raskin & Hare, 1978) have showed that the lies of a psychopath can be detected with as much accuracy as the lies of anyone else. Equally important is the finding that some people who are telling the truth may register changes in autonomic nervous system activity because of anxiety. This means that a truthful person who takes a polygraph exam may falsely appear to be deceptive. In a study of deception, researchers examined innocent and guilty individuals accused of theft (Kleinmuntz & Szucko, 1984). Although guilty people were often identified as guilty by the polygraph and innocent people were often identified as innocent, 37% of innocent people were found guilty!

Today, most states do not accept the results of polygraph exams as evidence in court, especially in criminal cases. A federal law restricts private businesses from using polygraph exams to test prospective employees. The American Psychological Association has expressed strong reservations about polygraph exams, asserting that their use may inflict psychological damage on innocent persons.

In summary, like any diagnostic test, polygraph exams can show errors. Their accuracy remains a controversial issue, despite decades of research. Some (e.g., Kleinmutz & Szucko, 1984; Lykken, 1998; Saxe, 1994) assert that about half of all truthful people are mistakenly identified as deceptive; others (e.g., Raskin, 1986) claim that polygraph exams are about 90% accurate in detecting truthfulness. The truth may lie somewhere between these extremes. However, like other physiologically based techniques, the psychophysiological detection of deception is being continually refined. Computers score many of the exams, and psychophysiological researchers are looking for unique physiological responses that are associated with deception. (I)

Think Critically

- Do you think using lie detectors should be permitted in the public or private sector? Why or why not?
- Are there are any universal emotions? Why? Which ones are they?

www.abacon.com/leftononline

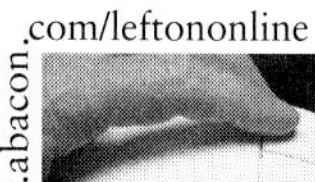

Your password-protected Website allows you access to the most comprehensive set of materials in The Psychology Place.

(I) Summary and Review

Theories of Motivation

Distinguish between a motivation and a need.

KEY TERMS
motivation, p. 209; drive theory, p. 210; drive, p. 210; need, p. 210; homeostasis, p. 210; arousal, p. 210; expectancy theories, p. 211; motive, p. 211; social need, p. 211; cognitive theory, p. 211; extrinsic motivation, p. 212; intrinsic motivation, p. 212; overjustification effect, p. 212; humanistic theory, p. 213; self-actualization, p. 213

Hunger: A Physiological Need

What causes hunger?

KEY TERMS
eating disorders, p. 217; anorexia nervosa, p. 217; bulimia nervosa, p. 217

Sexual Behavior: Physiology plus Thought

What are the roles of thought and of hormones in human sexual behavior?

What are the phases in the sexual response cycle?

How have Americans' sex lives changed over the last 40 years?

KEY TERMS
excitement phase, p. 219; vasocongestion, p. 219; plateau phase, p. 219; orgasm phase, p. 219; resolution phase, p. 220

Achievement: A Social Need

How does expectancy theory explain the need for achievement?

KEY TERM
need for achievement, p. 222

Emotion

What is an emotion?

Identify the fundamental ideas that distinguish various theories of emotion.

KEY TERM
emotion, p. 223

Self-Test

1. Motivation is considered an internal condition that initiates behavior, but the link to external behavior is inferred. Motivation generates behavior that is:
   A. abstract
   B. concrete
   C. goal-directed
   D. arousal-based

2. Which theory of motivation assumes a need for balance, or homeostasis?
   A. drive theory
   B. cognitive theory
   C. arousal theory
   D. humanistic theory

3. The __________ theory of motivation assumes that people take an active role in determining their goals and choosing the means to achieve them.
   A. expectancy
   B. cognitive
   C. social
   D. drive

4. When you engage in behavior for some external gain, the behavior is said to be __________ _________. When you engage in behavior for the internal pleasure, the behavior is said to be ________ ________.
   A. a social need; motive-driven
   B. extrinsically motivated; intrinsically motivated
   C. goal-directed; pleasure-directed
   D. self-actualization; overjustification effect

5. The ________ approach argues that hunger is caused by a low level of blood sugar and that quick relief from hunger is accomplished by consuming ___________.
   A. physiological; food
   B. set point; snacks
   C. obesity; water
   D. glucostatic; candy

6. Stimulation of the ventromedial hypothalamus will result in:
   A. the cessation of eating
   B. the start of eating
   C. hunger
   D. low blood sugar

7. Sexual behavior in humans can be initiated by:
   A. fantasy, thoughts, emotions
   B. hormones, smells, need
   C. excitement, hormones, desire
   D. pheromones, desire, excitement

8. The largest difference in the results of the Kinsey report (1950) and the Laumann report (1998) was that the later report found:
   A. more female homosexuals
   B. more male homosexuals
   C. more bisexual behavior
   D. less male homosexuality

9. Caitlin spends numerous hours practicing her guitar because she wants to be in the school band. Caitlin has a:
   A. strong intrinsic motivation
   B. strong extrinsic motivation
   C. strong musical talent
   D. strong need for achievement

10. Most psychologists agree that emotions consist of three basic elements. These are:
    A. subjective response; physical behavior; cognition
    B. feelings; physiological response; behavior
    C. love; fear; anger
    D. fear; anger; sadness

11. In his book *The Emotional Brain,* LeDoux suggests that emotions are
    A. cognitively based
    B. learned
    C. observed, then learned
    D. inherited

12. Which theory of emotion contends that emotions are cognitively based and thought alone can elicit an emotion?
    A. Cannon–Bard theory
    B. Schacter–Singer approach
    C. LeDoux's physiological perspective
    D. James–Lange theory

Development

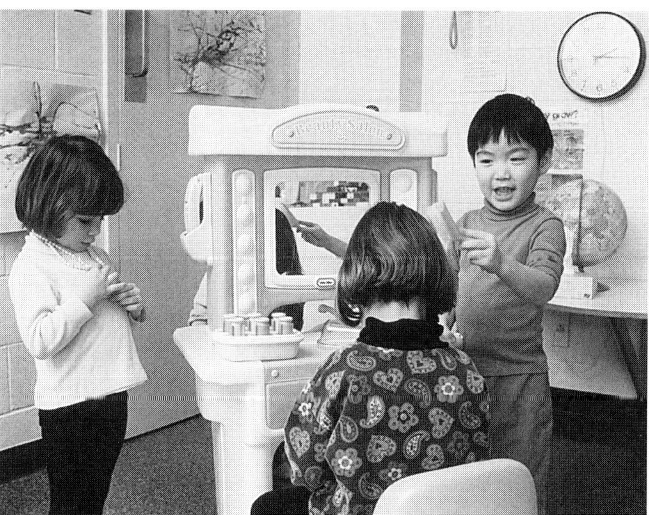

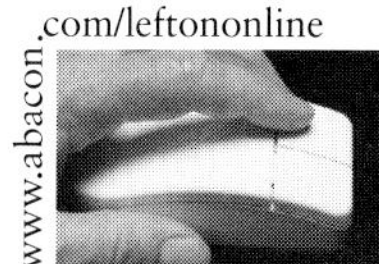

Go to your password-protected Website for full-color art, Weblinks, and more!

To tell the truth, I wasn't sure whether either of us would make it through my daughter Sarah's 14th year. She was having a rough time, and I found myself rocked as much as she was by her turmoil. She was always a delightful child—and continues to be a wonderful daughter—but that year her hormones were raging, and her emotions were running wild. And because she was our first-born, my wife and I didn't know how to deal with her frequent and massive mood swings. The big issues were staying out late, her allowance, and cleaning her room. Sarah insisted that we weren't giving her enough freedom, her allowance wasn't big enough, and it was her business if she wanted her room to look like a tornado had hit it.

I had thought the "terrible twos" were bad enough—all those emotional outbursts from a cranky and obstinate little girl. But now I was dealing with an adolescent who could express her all-too-frequent anger with great energy and quite a flare for the dramatic. It all seems so simple now, a decade later. A curfew, a couple of dollars, and some junk on the floor seem like small issues. But all that time while Sarah was slamming her door, my blood pressure was going up, and I thought we'd end up hating each other. Now that it's all behind us, Sarah and I can laugh together about that tumultuous year. Although it seemed exceptionally difficult, in fact, every age—infancy, childhood, adolescence, adulthood, and late adulthood—brings its own challenges. ■

Psychologists see human development as a process of growth and change that is influenced by a person's biological inheritance, life experiences, thoughts—and, to a certain extent, chance. For example, moving from one state to another changes people's lives; a divorce is unsettling; a death in the family can be devastating; winning the lottery can jolt a person from poverty and anonymity to luxury and fame. So, in addition to normal, predictable developmental changes, once-in-a-lifetime events can permanently alter physical, social, and personality development. *Normative* life events are those that are typical for most men and women in a culture; they are commonly experienced major events, such as having children or retiring from work. Other life events are *idiosyncratic;* they are unique to an individual, such as the death of a sibling or a major health problem. Idiosyncratic life events are often compelling, but because normative life events affect most people, psychological theories have focused on them.

This chapter discusses some of the developmental changes that occur during infancy, childhood, adolescence, and adulthood and traces the psychological processes underlying these changes. As you read, remember that a person's *chronological age* (age in years) is sometimes different from his or her *functional age* (age the person acts or seems). For example, some adolescents act older and wiser than their age-matched peers. Among older adults—especially those over 65—some function more like what would be expected of people in their 40s and 50s (Neugarten, 1968). (I)

Developmental psychology: The study of the lifelong, often age-related, processes of change in the physical, cognitive, moral, emotional, and social domains of functioning; such changes are rooted in biological mechanisms that are genetically controlled, as well as in social interactions.

Zygote [ZY-goat]: A fertilized egg.

(I) Key Issues, Theories, and Research Designs

Focus on issues and ideas

- The key issues that shape developmental researchers' point of view
- The impact of differences in research design on data
- Prenatal development and possible harmful environmental effects during this critical period

Developmental psychology is the study of the lifelong, often age-related, processes of change in the physical, cognitive, moral, emotional, and social domains of functioning; such changes are rooted in biological mechanisms that are genetically controlled (for example, maturational processes involved in the growth of the nervous system), as well as in social interactions. Developmental psychologists study all of these changes—biological, maturational, and social—to find out how people grow and become transformed from young children to mature, functioning adults and to learn what causes those changes.

Developmental psychologists recognize that development involves gains and losses over time, because people can respond in either positive or negative ways to life's experiences. They also recognize that development must be viewed from multiple perspectives and within a historical context. Developmental psychologists have focused on a few key issues, theories, and research methods to unravel the causes of behavior. Their goal is always the same: to describe, explain, predict, and potentially help manage human development.

Several key issues help developmental researchers order their questions and shape their point of view. Three of the most important of these are nature versus nurture, stability versus change, and continuity versus discontinuity.

Nature versus Nurture. One way to look at individual development is to consider to what extent the developing person's abilities, interests, and personality are determined primarily by biological influences *(nature)* or primarily by environmental influences *(nurture)*. Separating biological from environmental causes of behavior is a complicated matter; the answer to any specific question about human behavior usually involves some interaction between nature and nurture.

Stability versus Change. Do individuals stay pretty much the same throughout their lives—cognitively, emotionally, and socially—or do they change and adapt in response to events in their environment? The issue of stability versus change is a recurring theme in developmental psychology. It is closely associated with the nature–nurture issue, because when a researcher assumes stability, he or she often assumes that stable traits—for example, shyness—are inherited and genetically determined. Those who favor an environmental view are more likely to believe that people change over the course of a lifetime because of unique life events—for example, the loss of a sibling in a car accident.

Continuity versus Discontinuity. A third issue revolves around whether development is continuous or discontinuous. Some see development as *continuous,* as a process of gradual growth and change with skills and knowledge added one bit at a time and one skill building on another. But development can also be viewed as *discontinuous,* with growth, maturation, and understanding of the world occurring at various critical periods and with changes appearing abruptly—almost suddenly.

Research Designs. Good researchers know that the method they use to study a problem often influences the results. In order to interpret what results might mean, a researcher must take into account the particular research design used. In developmental research, two widely used designs are the cross-sectional and the longitudinal. A psychologist using a *cross-sectional research design* compares many individuals of different ages to determine how they differ on some important dimension. The psychologist using a *longitudinal research design* studies a specific group of individuals at different ages to examine changes that have occurred over a long period of time.

Each research design has its advantages and disadvantages. For example, the cross-sectional design suffers from the fact that the participants' backgrounds differ; they may have learned various things in different ways. Further, a participant's behavior, performance in a specific task, or ability may reflect a predisposition, a liking of the task, or some other variable unrelated to changes that come from development or aging. Most important, the age groups that are being examined may have had different life experiences—for example, one generation may have received substantially less education than the next, and education level will affect results on standardized tests. Individual differences are impossible to assess with the cross-sectional design. But the longitudinal research design also has problems. For one thing, it requires the researcher to have access to the same people repeatedly, but some participants may move, withdraw from the study, or even die. Also, after repeated testing on the same task (even though the tests are months or years apart), participants may do better because of practice. Moreover, longitudinal research sometimes takes years to complete; during that time, important changes may occur in the participants' environment (personal or social). Finally, such research is time consuming and expensive. I

I The First Ten Months

Focus on issues and ideas

- The reflexes and abilities of newborns
- Understanding an infant's perceptual abilities

Psychologists refer to developmental events that occur before birth as *prenatal;* those that occur in the month after birth are *neonatal.* Both terms derive from the Latin word *natus,* meaning "born."

Prenatal Development

The lifelong journey of human development begins with conception. Conception occurs when an ovum and a sperm join in a woman's fallopian tube to form a **zygote**—a fertilized egg. Within 10 hours of conception, the zygote divides into four cells. During the

Table 9.1 Life Stages and Approximate Ages in Human Development

Period	Life Stage	Approximate Age
Prenatal period	Zygote	Conception to day 5 to 7
	Embryo	To day 49
	Fetus	Week 8 to birth
Postnatal period	Infancy	Birth to 18 months
	Toddlerhood	18 months to 3 years
	Early childhood	3 to 6 years
	Middle childhood	6 to 13 years
	Adolescence	13 to 20 years
	Young adulthood	20 to 40 years
	Middle adulthood	40 to 65 years
	Late adulthood	65 plus

next 5 days or so, the zygote floats down the fallopian tube and implants itself in the wall of the uterus. From implantation until the 49th day after conception, the organism is called an **embryo.** Then, from the 8th week until birth, the organism is called a **fetus.** On the average, maturation and development of a full-term human infant requires 266 days, or about 9 months; this length of time is often divided into three *trimesters* (3-month periods). Table 9.1 summarizes the prenatal (before birth) and postnatal (after birth) periods of development.

In the United States, birth defects are the leading cause of death during the first year of life.

Embryo [EM-bree-o]: The prenatal organism from the 5th through the 49th day after conception.

Fetus [FEET-us]: The prenatal organism from the 8th week after conception until birth.

Placenta [pluh-SENT-uh]: A mass of tissue that is attached to the wall of the uterus and connected to the developing fetus by the umbilical cord; it supplies nutrients and eliminates waste products.

Teratogen [ter-AT-oh-jen]: Substance that can produce developmental malformations (birth defects) during the prenatal period.

Although the prenatal environment—especially the mother's diet (Sigman, 1995)—can have an influence, a person's basic characteristics are established as the zygote is formed; these include the color of the hair and eyes, the sex (gender), the likelihood that the person will be tall or short, fat or lean, and perhaps basic intellectual abilities and personality traits. There, the cells begin the process of *differentiation*: Organs and other parts of the body begin to form. Some cells form the *umbilical cord*—a group of blood vessels and tissues that connect the zygote to the placenta. The **placenta** is a mass of tissue that is attached to the wall of the uterus and acts as the life-support system for the fetus. It supplies oxygen, food, and antibodies and eliminates wastes—all by way of the mother's bloodstream.

Table 9.2 summarizes the major physical developments during the prenatal period.

Harmful Environmental Effects

People have long assumed that the behavior of a pregnant woman affects prenatal development. Medieval European doctors advised pregnant women that uplifting thoughts would help a baby develop into a good, happy person, while fear, despondency, and negative emotions might disrupt the pregnancy and possibly result in a sad or mean-spirited child. Research with animals shows that stress during pregnancy has effects on the later development of offspring (Pfister & Muir, 1992). Generalizing from such data, some pregnant women strap portable tape players around their abdomens and play soothing music to their unborn child, in the hope that the child will gain a benevolent perspective on the outside world.

While a fetus may not be affected by the mother's condition to the extent suggested by medieval doctors, the quality of the life support system provided by the mother does influence the embryo and fetus from conception until birth. Environmental factors such as diet, infection, radiation, and drugs affect both the mother *and* the baby. The developing child is especially vulnerable in certain *critical periods*, during which it is maturing rapidly and is particularly sensitive to the environment. During the first 2 years of life, nutrition is extremely important; research shows that breast feeding is beneficial compared to bottle feeding (Golding, Rogers, & Emmett, 1997). The brain is especially sensitive during these years; neuronal connections are undergoing many changes. Although the basic architecture of the brain is in place before birth, individual

Table 9.2 Major Developments during the Prenatal Period

	Age	Size	Characteristics
First trimester 1–12 weeks	1 week	150 cells	Zygote attaches to uterine lining.
	2 weeks	Several thousand cells	Placental circulation established.
	3 weeks	1/10 inch	Heart and blood vessels begin to develop. Basics of brain and central nervous system form.
	4 weeks	1/4 inch	Kidneys and digestive tract begin to form. Rudiments of ears, nose, and eyes are present.
	6 weeks	1/2 inch	Arms and legs develop. Jaws form around mouth.
	8 weeks	1 inch, 1/30 ounce	Bones begin to develop in limbs. Sex organs begin to form.
	12 weeks	3 inches, 1 ounce	Gender can be distinguished. Kidneys are functioning, and liver is manufacturing red blood cells. Fetal movements can be detected by a physician.
Second trimester 13–24 weeks	16 weeks	6 ½ inches, 4 ounces	Heartbeat can be detected by a physician. Bones begin to calcify.
	20 weeks	10 inches, 8 ounces	Mother feels fetal movements.
	24 weeks	12 inches, 1½ pounds	Vernix (white waxy substance) protects the body. Eyes open; eyebrows and eyelashes form; skin is wrinkled. Respiratory system is barely mature enough to support life.
Third trimester 25–38 weeks	28 weeks	15 inches, 2½ pounds	Fetus is fully developed but needs to gain in size, strength, and maturity of systems.
	32 weeks	17 inches, 4 pounds	A layer of fat forms beneath the skin to regulate body temperature.
	36 weeks	19 inches, 6 pounds	Fetus settles into position for birth.
	38 weeks	21 inches, 8 pounds	Fetus arrives at full term—266 days from conception.

connections between neurons are subject to considerable influence or damage in infancy.

Substances that can produce developmental malformations (birth defects) during the prenatal period are known as **teratogens.** In the United States, birth defects are the leading cause of death during the first year of life. Maternal drinking during pregnancy is the leading known cause of mental retardation in newborns. Studies show that many drugs affect prenatal development. High doses of aspirin, for example, may cause fetal bleeding, although the evidence is controversial (Werler, Mitchell, & Shapiro, 1989). Cigarette smoking constricts the oxygen supply to the fetus. Babies born to mothers who smoke cigarettes tend to be smaller and may be at increased risk for cleft palate and perhaps a slightly lower IQ. Certain drugs, including tranquilizers, can produce malformations of the head, face, and limbs as well as neurological disorders (Kopp & Kaler, 1989; Lester & Dreher, 1989). And, in recent years, hundreds of thousands of infants, such as the one in the photo, have been born addicted to crack and other drugs.

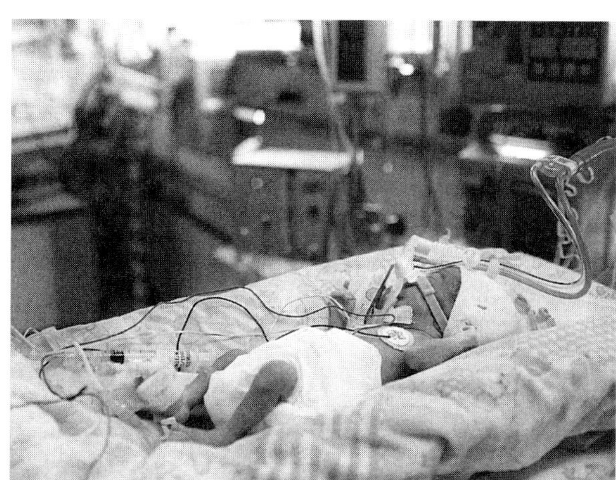

Newborns Come Well-Equipped

Newborns grow rapidly—seemingly almost overnight—and they are not nearly as helpless as many people believe. At birth, infants can hear, see, smell, and respond to the environment in adaptive ways; in other words, they have good sensory systems. They are also directly affected by experience. Psychologists try to find out exactly how experience affects infants' perceptual development. In doing so, they need to discover how infants think, what they perceive, and how they react to the world. Researchers want answers to various questions about newborns' perceptual world: What are a child's inborn abilities and reflexes? When do inborn abilities become evident? How does the environment affect inborn abilities?

Growth. An infant who weighs 7.5 pounds at birth may weigh as much as 20 or 25 pounds by 12 months. At 18 months, a child is usually walking and beginning to talk. For psychologists, infancy continues until the child begins to represent the world abstractly through language. Thus, *infancy* is the period from birth to about 18 months.

During the period of infancy and childhood (up through about age 13), the child grows physically from a being that requires constant care, attention, and assistance to a nearly full-size independent person. At the end of the first year of life, children can walk, climb, and manipulate their environment—skills that often lead to the need for a variety of safety features in the home. There is significant variability in the age at which children begin to walk or climb: Some do so early; others are slow to develop these abilities. The age at which these specific behaviors first occur seems unrelated to any other major developmental milestones.

Newborns' Reflexes. Touch the palm of a newborn baby, and you'll probably find one of your fingers held in the surprisingly firm grip of a tiny fist. The baby is exhibiting a reflexive reaction. Babies are born with innate *primary reflexes*—unlearned responses to stimuli. Some, such as the grasping reflex, no doubt helped ensure survival in humanity's primate ancestors; most of these reflexes disappear over the course of the first year of life. Physicians use the presence or absence of primary reflexes to assess neurological status at birth and to evaluate rate of development during infancy. Table 9.3 summarizes the primary reflexes and their duration. One primary reflex exhibited by infants is the **Babinski reflex**—a fanning out of the toes in response to a touch on the sole of the foot. Another is the **Moro reflex**—outstretching of the

Table 9.3 Newborns' Reflexes

Reflex	Initiated By	Response	Duration
Eye blink	Flashing a light in the infant's eyes	Closing both eyes	Continues throughout life
Babinski	Gently stroking the sole of the infant's foot	Flexing the big toe; fanning out the other toes	Usually disappears near the end of the first year
Withdrawal	Pricking the sole of the infant's foot	Flexing of the leg	Present during the first 10 days; present but less intense later
Plantar	Pressing a finger against the ball of the infant's foot	Curling all the toes under	Disappears between 8 and 12 months
Moro	Making a sudden loud sound	Extending the arms and legs; then bringing arms toward each other in convulsive manner; crying	Begins to decline in 3rd month; gone by 5th month
Rooting	Stroking the infant's cheek lightly with a finger or a nipple	Turning the head toward the finger, opening the mouth, and trying to suck	Disappears at approximately 3 to 4 months
Sucking	Placing a finger in the infant's mouth	Sucking rhythmically	Often less intense and less regular during the first 3 to 4 days of life but continues for several months

arms and legs and crying in response to a loud noise or an abrupt change in the environment. Newborns also exhibit the **rooting reflex**—turning the head toward a light touch (such as of a breast or hand) on their lips or cheek. They show the **sucking reflex** in response to a finger or nipple placed in their mouth and a vigorous **grasping reflex** in response to an object touching the palms of their hands or their fingers.

At first, an infant's abilities and reflexes are biologically determined by the human genetic code. Gradually, learned responses, such as reaching for desired objects, replace reflex reactions. The baby's experiences in the environment become more important in determining development. The complex interactions between nature and nurture follow a developmental timetable that continues throughout life.

Infant Perception: Fantz's Viewing Box. A mountain of research on infant perception shows that newborns have surprisingly well-developed perceptual systems. Robert Fantz (1961) did some of the earliest work on infant perception. Fantz designed a viewing box in which he placed an infant; he then had a hidden observer or camera record the infant's responses to stimuli.

The exciting part of Fantz's work was not so much that he asked interesting questions but that he was able to get "answers" from the infants. By showing infants various patterns and pictures of faces and recording their eye movements, he discovered their visual preferences. He recorded how long and how often the infants looked at each pattern or picture. Because the infants spent more time looking at pictures of faces than at patterns of random squiggles, Fantz concluded not only that they could see different patterns but that they preferred faces.

Other researchers confirm that infants prefer complex visual fields over simple ones, curved patterns over straight or angular ones, and normal human faces over random patterns or faces with mixed-up features (Wilson & Goldman-Rakic, 1994). Even in the first few months of life, babies can discriminate among facial features and prefer attractive faces to less attractive ones (Langlois et al., 1990, 1991). Newborns look at pictures of their parents more than at pictures of strangers (de Haan & Nelson, 1997). Babies as young as 3 months can discern a caregiver's shift of attention by observing the person's eyes and can then shift their own attention to the same object or event (Hood, Willen, & Driver, 1998). Babies sometimes respond to caregivers by imitating their facial expressions (pursed lips, stuck-out tongues)—although research in this area is controversial, and the findings are not always consistent (Abravanel & DeYong, 1997).

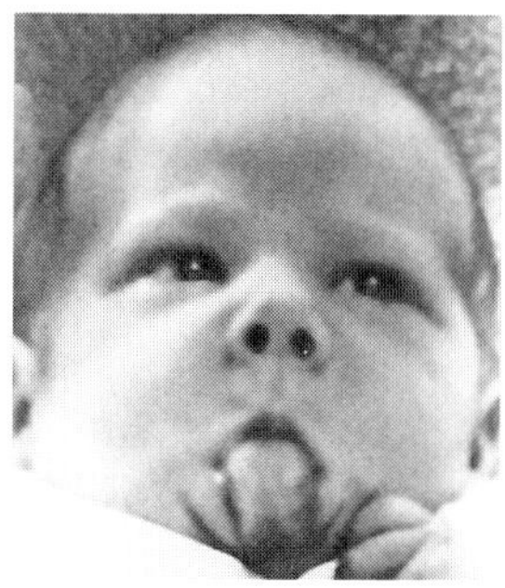

At about 4 to 8 weeks, an infant may sleep for 4 to 6 hours during the night, uninterrupted by the need to eat, a change that weary parents usually welcome. When awake, infants smile at the mother and listen attentively to human voices. Between 6 and 9 months, infants begin to crawl, giving them more freedom to seek out favorite people. The ability to crawl is accompanied by important changes in behavior; in fact, some researchers assert that crawling is what allows critical behavioral changes to occur (Bertenthal, Campos, & Kermoian, 1994).

By 7 months, infants can recognize happy faces and sounds and can discriminate among them. According to Arlene Walker-Andrews (1997), they recognize emotional expressions. Research suggests a timetable by which they develop the ability to discriminate among facial expressions.

Infant perception is quite good; it follows a maturational timetable, but there are discontinuities in perceptual development. At first, babies attend to the most prominent features in the world; as time passes, they attend to, recognize, and respond to the world based on their recognition of people and situations—they begin to make more cognitive-based perceptual decisions (Bhatt, 1997; Bronson, 1997). Cognitive development proceeds in a certain order and according to a rough timetable of events during infancy and early childhood. We consider these events next. (I)

Babinski reflex: Reflex in which a newborn fans out the toes when the sole of the foot is touched.

Moro reflex: Reflex in which a newborn stretches out the arms and legs and cries in response to a loud noise or an abrupt change in the environment.

Rooting reflex: Reflex that causes a newborn to turn the head toward a light touch on lips or cheek.

Sucking reflex: Reflex that causes a newborn to make sucking motions when a finger or nipple is placed in the mouth.

Grasping reflex: Reflex that causes a newborn to grasp vigorously any object touching the palm or fingers or placed in the hand.

Think Critically

- What survival value might each of the primary reflexes have had for humans' ancestors?
- What survival function might infants' preference for human faces have?

I Cognitive Development

Focus on issues and ideas

- Distinguishing between assimilation and accommodation
- Understanding Piaget's four stages of development
- The influence of Piaget and Vygotsky on developmental theory

Why do some parents insist on automobiles with childproof locks and windows? Why do they use gates to guard stairs and gadgets to keep kitchen cabinets closed? Why are young children's toys made so that small parts cannot come off? Because children are inquisitive and much more intelligent than many people give them credit for. Even 3-month-olds can learn the order of a list of items and, when given age-appropriate prompts, remember that information a day later (Gulya et al., 1998).

Infants' physical development is visible and dramatic; the cognitive changes that occur in young children are less visible, but no less dramatic. Children are continually developing, both physically and cognitively; they focus their attention on coping with an ever-expanding world. As they mature, they can determine causes of events. Much of this ability is cognitively based (Miller & Aloise, 1989).

Without question, the 20th century's leading researcher and theorist on the cognitive development of children and adults was Jean Piaget; his work laid the foundation for an understanding of the development of thought and still dominates the field of developmental psychology.

Scheme: In Piaget's view, a specific mental structure; an organized way of interacting with the environment and experiencing it.

Assimilation: According to Piaget, the process by which new ideas and experiences are absorbed and incorporated into existing mental structures and behaviors.

Accommodation: According to Piaget, the process by which existing mental structures and behaviors are modified to adapt to new experiences.

Sensorimotor stage: The first of Piaget's four stages of cognitive development (covering roughly the first 2 years of life), during which the child develops some motor coordination skills and a memory for past events.

Jean Piaget's Insights

Swiss psychologist Jean Piaget (1896–1980) came to believe that the fundamental development of all cognitive abilities takes place during the first 2 years of life; many psychologists and educators agree. Piaget devised ingenious procedures for examining the cognitive development of young children; he looked at what children did well, what mistakes they made, and when and how they gained insights into the world. Piaget's theory focuses on *how* people think instead of on *what* they think, making it applicable to people in all cultures. Perhaps Piaget's greatest strength, however, was his description of how a person's inherited capacities interact with the environment to produce cognitive functioning. Although psychologists were initially skeptical of Piaget's ideas and some criticisms persist, many researchers have shown that his assumptions are generally correct and can be applied cross-culturally. There are also dissenters (notably Russian psychologist Lev Vygotsky, whose theories we will consider a bit later), who stress society's role in shaping thought processes (Rogoff & Morelli, 1989). Piaget put more emphasis on biology, asserting that cognitive development depends on the interaction between biological changes that take place within a child and experiences and that it follows the same path in all social environments. What Piaget did best was focus on the details of children's cognitive life; he observed them in minute detail and noticed discontinuities in their abilities at various ages. Piaget's explanations of cognitive development focus, to a great extent, on its direction and development. He explains how a person changes from a self-centered infant to an independent thinker as an adolescent.

Piaget's Central Concepts. Piaget believed that what changes during development is the child's ability to make sense of experience. He called organized ways of interacting with the environment and experiencing the world **schemes,** sometimes referred to as *mental structures.* Initially, children develop schemes for motor behaviors, for example, realizing that reaching out and touching an object will cause it to move. Schemes develop because a child realizes that action brings results; those results, in turn, may affect the child's future behavior. So, a child reaches out, touches a mobile, the bells that are attached to the mobile make a sound, the mobile changes position—and the child observes that a specific action has influenced the world. This entire process is called *adap-*

tation. As adaptation continues, a child organizes his or her schemes into more complex mental representations, linking one scheme with another. Ultimately, children develop schemes about play, make-believe, and the permanence of objects. For a child to develop schemes and more complex mental structures, two important processes must occur: assimilation and accommodation.

Both children and adults use assimilation and accommodation to deal with new schemes. **Assimilation** is the process by which a person absorbs new ideas and experiences and incorporates them into existing mental structures and behaviors. **Accommodation** is the process of modifying previously developed mental structures and behaviors to adapt them to new experiences. A child who learns to grasp a ball demonstrates assimilation by later grasping other round objects. This assimilated behavior then serves as a foundation for accommodation. The child can learn new and more complex behaviors such as grasping forks, crayons, and sticks by modifying the earlier response—for example, by widening or narrowing the grasp. The two processes of assimilation and accommodation alternate in a never-ending cycle of cognitive growth, throughout the four stages of development that Piaget described. These stages and processes are part of an active construction of reality—babies and young children piece together their own view of the world, rather than just absorbing what adults teach them. Piaget asserts that children are active in their own cognitive development.

Without question, the 20th century's leading researcher and theorist on the cognitive development of children and adults was Jean Piaget.

Four stages of cognitive development are central to Piaget's theory. Piaget believed that just as standing must precede walking, some stages of cognitive development must precede others. For example, if a parent presents an idea that is too advanced, the child will not understand, and no real learning will take place. A 4-year-old who asks how babies are made will probably not understand a full, biologically accurate explanation and will not learn or remember it. If the same child asks the question a few years later, the more realistic and complex explanation will be more meaningful and more likely to be remembered. Piaget's stages are associated with approximate ages. The exact ages for each stage vary from person to person, but children in all cultures go through these same stages. Piaget acknowledged the complex interaction of environmental influences and genetic inheritances; nevertheless, he felt strongly that the order of stages was invariant. The four developmental stages he proposed are the sensorimotor stage, the preoperational stage, the concrete operational stage, and the formal operational stage.

The Sensorimotor Stage. Piaget considered the **sensorimotor stage**, which extends from birth to about age 2, to be the most significant, because the foundation for all cognitive development is established during this period. Consider the enormous changes that take place during the first 2 years of life. Newborns are totally dependent, reflexive organisms. Within a few weeks, infants learn some simple habits. They smile at their mothers or caregivers; they seek visual or auditory stimulation; they reach out and anticipate events in the environment, such as the mother's breast or a bottle. At 2 to 3 months, infants develop some motor coordination skills (Clifton et al., 1993; Thelen, 1994) and a memory for past events, and they are able to predict future visual events (Gulya et al., 1998; Haith & McCarty, 1990). According to Piaget, the acquisition of memory is a necessary foundation for further cognitive development.

By the age of 6 to 8 months, infants seek new and more interesting kinds of stimulation. They can sit up and crawl. No longer willing to merely watch what goes on around them, they begin to attempt to manipulate their environment. Piaget called this attempt "making interesting sights last"—that is, infants try to make interesting events recur. Karen Wynn (1992) suggests that even at this age infants have some very basic numerical reasoning abilities that lay the foundation for further development of arithmetic reasoning (Starkey, 1992). At about 8 months, infants have intentions, and they attempt to overcome obstacles in order to reach goals. They can crawl to the other side of a room to reach a cat or a toy or follow a parent into the next room.

From about 9 months on, babies develop *object permanence*—the realization that objects continue to exist even when they are out of sight. Prior to the development of object permanence, when the mother leaves the room and the baby can no longer see her, she no longer exists. After object permanence develops, the baby realizes that she is just out of view. Although the exact age at which object permanence becomes evident has not yet been established, Renée Baillargeon (1994, 1998) has shown the existence of object permanence for some tasks in 4-month-olds—earlier than Piaget believed possible. In general, Baillargeon (1998) asserts that infants have knowledge of the physical world and a specialized learning ability that guides their acquisition of such knowledge, with various aspects of object permanence evolving gradually throughout the sensorimotor stage.

In the second half of the sensorimotor stage (from about 12 to 24 months), children begin to walk, talk, and use simple forms of logic. Object permanence is more fully developed; a child can now follow a ball that rolls away and can search for her or his mother after she has left the room. Children also begin to use language to represent the world, an ability that takes them beyond the concrete world of visual imagery. By age 2, a child can talk about Grandma, Daddy, doggy, cookies, going bye-bye, and other people, objects, and events. No longer an uncoordinated, reflexive organism, the child has become a thinking, walking, talking human being. Simultaneously, children may become manipulative and difficult to deal with. Parents often describe this stage as the terrible twos; it is characterized by the use of the ever-popular "No!" The child's behavior may vacillate between charming and awful. This vacillation and the emergence of annoying new habits, such as being difficult to dress and bathe, are signs of normal development, marking the beginning of the stage of preoperational thought.

The Preoperational Stage. In the **preoperational stage,** which lasts from about age 2 to age 6 or 7, children begin to represent the world symbolically. As preschoolers, they play with objects in new ways and try to represent reality through symbolic thought, by playing "let's pretend." But they continue to think about specifics rather than in the abstract and cannot deal with thoughts that are not easily visually represented. They make few attempts to make their speech more intelligible if a listener does not understand or to justify their reasoning, and they may develop behavior problems such as inattentiveness, belligerence, and temper tantrums. During this stage, adults often begin trying to teach children how to interact with others, but major social changes will not become fully apparent until the next stage of development.

A key element of the preoperational stage—which affects a child's cognitive and emotional behavior—is egocentrism, or self-centeredness. Present in the sensorimotor stage, but especially apparent in the preoperational stage, **egocentrism** is the inability to perceive a situation or event except in relation to oneself. Children are unable to understand that the world does not exist solely to satisfy their interests and needs. They respond to questions such as "Why does it snow?" with answers such as "So I can play in it." Cognitive immaturity makes children in this stage continue to pester Mom even after she says she has a headache and wants to be left alone (Elkind, 1981a). Children still cannot put themselves in anyone else's position.

At the end of Piaget's preoperational stage, children are just beginning to understand the difference between their ideas, feelings, and interests and those of others. This process of **decentration**—the process of changing from a totally self-oriented point of view to one that recognizes other people's feelings, ideas, and viewpoints—continues for several years. The concepts of egocentrism and decentration are widely recognized as central to Piaget's theory. However, few contemporary researchers have incorporated these ideas into their conceptions of how development proceeds.

Piaget held that children's understanding of space and their construction of alternative visual perspectives are limited during the preoperational stage. Recent evidence, however, suggests that Piaget may have underestimated the spatial–perspective abilities of children. Researchers have found that even 5-year-olds can solve certain visual and spatial problems previously thought to be solvable only by children 9 to 10 years old or older (Newcombe & Huttenlocher, 1992). Also, 4-year-olds are able to represent and remember the past.

The Concrete Operational Stage. The **concrete operational stage** is Piaget's third stage of cognitive development, lasting from approximately age 6 or 7 to age 11 or 12; during this stage, a child develops the ability to understand constant factors in the environment, rules, and higher-order symbolic systems such as arithmetic and geography. Children in this stage attend school, have friends, can take care of dressing and feeding themselves, and may take on household responsibilities. They can look at a situation from more than one viewpoint. They have gained sufficient mental maturity to be able to distinguish between appearance and reality and to think ahead one or two moves in checkers or other games. During this stage, children discover constancy in the world; they learn rules and understand the reasons for them. For example, a child learns not to build a sandcastle right at the water's edge, because the rising tide will inevitably destroy it.

Cognitive and perceptual abilities continue to develop as children mature and, slowly and in different ways, begin to grasp ever more difficult concepts (Flavell, Green, & Flavell, 1989). For example, at around age 7, children come to realize the connectedness of their thoughts, and they become especially conscious of their inner mental life and its unpredictability at times (Flavell, Green, & Flavell, 1998).

The hallmark of this stage is an understanding of **conservation**—the ability to recognize that objects can be transformed in some way, visually or physically, yet still be the same in number, weight, substance, or volume. This concept has been the subject of considerable research. In a typical conservation task, a child is shown three beakers or glasses. Two are short and squat and contain the same amount of liquid (water or juice); the other is tall, narrow, and empty. The experimenter pours the liquid from one short, squat glass into the tall, narrow one and asks the child, "Which glass has more juice?" A child who does not understand the principle of conservation will claim that the taller glass contains more. A child who is able to conserve liquid quantity will recognize that the same amount of liquid is in both the tall and the short glasses. A child who masters the concept of conservation realizes that specific facts are true because they follow logically, not simply because they are observed. Thus, the child infers that the tall glass *must* contain the same amount of liquid as the short glass because no liquid was added or taken away when the contents of the short glass were poured into the tall one.

The Formal Operational Stage. The **formal operational stage** is Piaget's fourth and final stage of cognitive development (beginning at about age 12), during which the individual can think hypothetically, can consider future possibilities, and can use deductive logic. Unlike children in the concrete operational stage, whose thought is still tied to immediate situations, adolescents can engage in abstract thought. They can form hypotheses that allow them to think of different ways to represent situations, organizing them into various possible relationships and outcomes. The cognitive world of adolescents is full of informal theories of logic and ideas about life; they are able to undertake scientific experiments requiring the formation and testing of hypotheses.

By age 12, about the beginning of adolescence, the egocentrism of the sensorimotor and preoperational stages has for the most part disappeared, but another form of egocentrism has developed. According to Inhelder and Piaget (1958), "The adolescent goes through a phase in which he [or she] attributes an unlimited power to his [or her] own thoughts so that the dream of a glorious future or of transforming the world through ideas (even if this idealism takes a materialistic form) seems to be not only fantasy, but also an effective action which in itself modifies the empirical world" (pp. 345–346). The egocentrism and naive hopes of adolescents eventually decrease as they face and deal with the challenges of life.

Putting Piaget in Perspective. Parents, educators, and psychologists can enhance children's cognitive development by understanding how mental abilities develop. Piaget recognized that parental love and parent–child interactions are always important to a child's development, but he asserted that they are *essential* in the first 2 years of life. For a child to develop object permanence, to learn how to make interesting sights last, and to develop the rudiments of numerical reasoning, it is necessary for caregivers to provide abundant physical and cognitive stimuli, especially stimuli that move and change color, shape, and form. Research confirms that children and animals given sensory stimulation during their early months develop more quickly both cognitively and socially than those not given such stimulation. Parents and educators who agree with Piaget have devoted their efforts to ensuring that the first years of life are ones in which stimulation is plentiful, curiosity is encouraged, and opportunities for exploration are maximized. An enriched environment is one in which the child has the freedom to manipulate objects and see them from many vantage points; expensive toys are not necessary—variety is the key. From Piaget's point of view, stimulation and manipulation optimize children's potential. Although Piaget emphasized the first two years of life today researchers realize that brain development continues and must be considered a lifelong process (Bruer, 1999). *Experiencing Psychology* (on p. 244) shows that the psychologists who advised the federal government to begin Project Head Start in the 1960s agreed that an enriched preschool environment could help children develop cognitively.

Although Piaget's ideas have had an enormous influence on developmental psychology, some researchers have problems with his approach. Psychologist Rochel Gelman argues that Piaget tended to underestimate younger children's abilities. For example,

Preoperational stage: Piaget's second stage of cognitive development (lasting from about age 2 to age 6 or 7), during which the child begins to represent the world symbolically.

Egocentrism [ee-go-SENT-rism]: Inability to perceive a situation or event except in relation to oneself; also known as *self-centeredness.*

Decentration: Process of changing from a totally self-oriented point of view to one that recognizes other people's feelings, ideas, and viewpoints.

Concrete operational stage: Piaget's third stage of cognitive development (lasting from approximately age 6 or 7 to age 11 or 12), during which the child develops the ability to understand constant factors in the environment, rules, and higher-order symbolic systems.

Conservation: Ability to recognize that objects can be transformed in some way, visually or physically, yet still be the same in number, weight, substance, or volume.

Formal operational stage: Piaget's fourth and final stage of cognitive development (beginning at about age 12), during which the individual can think hypothetically, can consider future possibilities, and can use deductive logic.

EXPERIENCING PSYCHOLOGY

Project Head Start

Project Head Start was initiated in the 1960s in an effort to break the poverty cycle by raising the social and educational competency of disadvantaged preschool children. Today, Project Head Start enrolls about 750,000 children a year, most of them from the neediest families—mostly African American (65%) and from lower socioeconomic classes (Schnur, Brooks-Gunn, & Shipman, 1992). Head Start has received federal support for more than three decades, has served 13 million children, and is often referred to as a milestone in psychology. The multimillion-dollar project showed what can be done with remedial education, social support, and effective use of child development techniques.

Project Head Start gives preschool children an enriched environment. Children attend a school with a low teacher–student ratio and are provided nutritional and medical services. Children are given focused, individual attention; efforts are made to build their self-confidence and self-esteem. Basic skills that may lead to more complex learning strategies are taught. Helping preschoolers experience the joy of learning is emphasized. Parent involvement is central; parents work on school boards and in the classroom and also receive related social services such as family counseling. When parents are engaged, they respond more fully to their children's needs, and the children do better and feel better about themselves (Cronan et al., 1996; Mantzicopoulos, 1997).

Unfortunately, although they make significant gains in cognitive abilities, Head Start children still do not do as well as those from homes at higher socioeconomic levels. Why? One reason is that Head Start children tend to be especially disadvantaged, even when compared with other disadvantaged groups. Researchers suggest that a year of Head Start may not be enough to close the gap. Another reason is that about 47% of Head Start instructors earn low wages, only about $10,000 a year; the low pay scale is a serious obstacle to attracting good teachers. Other problems are lack of teacher training, substandard facilities, and short hours (most programs operate half-days or less). Ed Zigler, the architect of the original program, acknowledges that only about 40% of Head Start centers are of truly high quality (Zigler, 1994). He argues that the data pointing to the program's lack of success should be seen as a mandate for enhancing the program, suggesting that having children attend for a second year would be likely to magnify and solidify the Head Start advantage. Zigler (1987) wrote: "We simply cannot inoculate children in one year against the ravages of a life of deprivation" (p. 258). Clearly, disadvantaged children must be given an equal educational start in life. If Head Start is less than a complete success, its failures have more to do with its implementation than with its design (Zigler, 1994).

Well-designed Head Start programs can have lasting positive effects in a number of areas. Head Start makes sure that needy children get medical and dental care, helps their families gain access to social services, offers volunteer and paid jobs to family members, involves parents in governance of the program, serves children nutritious meals, and provides them with intellectual stimulation. Most important, it helps children develop the social competencies necessary to thrive in school (Zigler, 1999).

Research on programs like Head Start has led to important conclusions about early interventions and experiences and their effects on children's lives. Ramey and Ramey (1998) outline several important findings: Interventions need to begin early in development and continue for a long period of time; intensive programs (more hours per week) are better than nonintensive ones; direct intervention (rather than intervention through parental training) works best; programs that use multiple routes to enhance development are especially effective; individual differences must be emphasized, and so it is essential to find the right fit between children and programs; and environmental support at home and in the community is necessary for lasting and effective early intervention. Psychologists and educators know how to enhance Head Start and other similar programs; society just has to find the will and the resources to do it. ■

Shatz and Gelman (1973) found that 2-year-olds change the length of their sentences depending on whom they are talking to, using shorter sentences, for example, when speaking to younger children. The researchers point out that being decentered enough to make such a shift in point of view is a sign of cognitive maturity. Many other researchers claim that Piaget may have overestimated the degree of egocentrism in young children. Baillargeon asserts that Piaget also underestimated the spatial–perceptual abilities of infants. She holds that abilities such as understanding what actually happens to objects when they are hidden, which Piaget saw as developing at 18 months, can be seen at 6 months of age (Miller & Baillargeon, 1990). Most recently, Baillargeon (1998) has argued that infants are born with specialized learning mechanisms that allow for the acquisition of knowledge about the physical world—an interesting assertion that needs further research. And researchers such as Gopnik, Meltzoff, and Kuhl (1999) also agree that young babies know and are able to process far more than they have previously been given credit for.

Vygotsky's Sociocultural Theory: An Alternative to Piaget

Piaget saw the child as an organism that is self-motivated to understand the world. The child, he held, is a busy constructor of reality, making interesting sights last, inventing games, and learning abstract rules. But Lev Vygotsky (1896–1934) saw the child as not alone in this task but part of a social world filled with communication, with the self and with others. Vygotsky believed that children are constantly trying to extract meaning from the social world and to master higher-order concepts (Bruner, 1997). At first, children's mental life expresses itself in interactions with other people. Later, children engage in private speech (talking to themselves) to plan and guide their own behavior; when they use such speech, they do better in various tasks (Bivens & Berk, 1990). It is important to note that Piaget believed that private speech was egocentric and did not involve taking the perspective of others. Vygotsky suggested just the opposite: Private speech helps a child understand his or her world and that of other people. For Vygotsky (1934/1962), even the earliest speech is essentially social and useful; in fact, he asserts that social speech comes first, followed by private speech, then inner speech (thinking in words). Vygotsky wrote: "The most significant moment in the course of intellectual development . . . occurs . . . when speech and practical activity, two previously completely independent lines of development, converge" (Vygotsky, 1930/1978, p. 24).

To a great extent, Vygotsky's work focused on trying to understand what he called "culturally patterned dialogue." Vygotsky emphasized extracting meaning from the world, especially through verbal interchanges, and he was particularly interested in examining the culture and the situation—the context—through which meaning is extracted. Vygotsky's approach can be considered sociocultural (Bruner, 1997).

Vygotsky was especially concerned with how adults provide information about culture to children. From a Vygotskian perspective, skills and knowledge are culture-bound (Meadows, 1998). In Chapter 5, we considered the role of cooperative learning in education and saw that when students cooperate in teams they do better; Vygotsky's theory would predict such a result. He held that when children are presented tasks that are outside of their current abilities, they need the help of culture and society—usually parents—to accomplish them. When more skilled individuals help a child, the child then incorporates those new skills and ideas into his or her repertoire of behavior. In this interactive process, which Vygotsky called *scaffolding*, an adult sets up a structure for a child. As the child learns, the adult provides less help or makes the task slightly harder so that the child engages in more complex analysis and learning (Meadows, 1998; Stringer, 1998).

Theory of Mind

Piaget investigated how and when children develop intellectual abilities; Vygotsky extended the study of children's intellectual development by considering its social context. Recently, developmental theorists have been focusing on how and when children acquire theories about causation, including the causes of human behavior.

Adults use their knowledge of the world to construct informal and formal theories to explain behavior—other people's and their own. Adults are aware of their theories of human behavior and can articulate them: They say that people do what they do because of internal mental states, such as desires and beliefs. Joe climbed up on the kitchen counter because he "wanted" cookies; Jill looked for her glasses in the study because she "thought" she left them on her desk. Thus, adults possess and apply a **theory of mind**—an understanding of mental states such as feelings, desires, beliefs, and intentions and of the causal role they play in human behavior.

When do children first develop a theory of mind? Research indicates that children have little or no awareness of their own and other people's mental processes until about age 3 or 4. A typical research study in this area focuses on a situation like this: A child and two adults are in a room, with some object such as a ball in a box. One adult leaves the room, and the other moves the object, into a basket, for example.

Theory of mind: An understanding of mental states such as feelings, desires, beliefs, and intentions and of the causal role they play in human behavior.

The child is then asked where the person who left the room will expect the object to be when he or she returns. A child who has developed a theory of mind will correctly predict that the person will look for the object where it last was (in the box), because the person will believe that it should still be there, not knowing that it was moved. A younger child, who has not yet developed a theory of mind, will say that the person coming back into the room will look for the object in its new location (in the basket). Before the age of 3, children are not able to set aside their own knowledge of the situation and realize that the person who left the room does not know that the object was moved. Developmental researchers say that they don't yet have a theory of mind.

The concept of theory of mind has stimulated many lines of research, including studies of infant and child attention, infant desires, and the role of brain development in cognitive maturation. But, according to some researchers, acquisition of a theory of mind is not an automatic developmental process. Astington (1999) asserts that children do not acquire such an understanding on their own; rather, through participation in social activities, they come to share their culture's way of seeing and talking about people's relations to one another and to the world. How and when children develop a theory of mind is partly determined by their interactions with others—a key variable in the development of intelligence. Thus, the notion that social relationships play a crucial role in cognitive development—which, as we saw earlier, was first introduced by Vygotsky—continues to influence developmental theory and research. *(I)*

Think Critically

- Assuming that Piaget did in fact overestimate the extent of egocentrism in young children, what might be another explanation for apparently egocentric behavior in a child?
- What are the implications of Vygotsky's view that the most significant moment in intellectual development occurs when speech and practical activity converge?
- Describe how you might use scaffolding to teach a child a game.

Morality: A system of learned attitudes about social practices, institutions, and individual behavior used to evaluate situations and behavior as right or wrong, good or bad.

(I) Moral Reasoning

Focus on issues and ideas

- The role of justice in Kohlberg's theory of moral development
- How gender differences in morality might be affected by the mother–child relationship

Few children make it to adolescence without squabbling with a sibling over the "borrowing" of a sweater, a toy, or a couple of dollars. The adult in charge usually tells them to stop fighting and makes it clear that such behaviors and the resulting squabbles are unacceptable. As children grow, they develop the capacity to assess for themselves what is right or wrong, acceptable or unacceptable. From childhood on, individuals develop **morality**—a system of learned attitudes about social practices, institutions, and individual behavior used to evaluate situations and behavior as right or wrong, good or bad.

Children learn from their parents the behaviors, attitudes, and values considered appropriate and correct in their family and culture. Morality is also nurtured by teachers, by religious and community leaders, and by friends. As children mature, they acquire attitudes that accommodate an increasingly complex view of reality. Your moral views when you were a 10-year-old probably differ from your views today. The U.S. Supreme Court has restricted adolescents' rights to make important life decisions—in part because the court believes adolescents lack moral maturity (Gardner, Scherer, & Tester, 1989). But do they? Or is the reasoning and judgment of a child, a preteen, or an adolescent as sound as that of an adult?

Piaget and Kohlberg

Piaget examined children's ability to analyze questions of morality and found the results to be consistent with his ideas about cognitive development. Young children's ideas about morality are rigid and rule-bound; children expect justice to depend on particular actions. When playing a game, a young child will not allow the rules to be modified. Older children, on the other hand, recognize that rules are established by social convention and may need to be altered, depending on the situation. They have developed a sense of *moral relativity,* which allows them to recognize that situational factors affect the way things are perceived and that people may or may not receive their just reward or punishment (Piaget, 1932).

According to Piaget, as children mature, they move away from inflexibility and toward relativity in their moral judgments; they develop new cognitive structures and assimilate and accommodate new ideas. When young children are questioned about lying, for example, they respond that it is always bad, under any circumstances—a person should never lie. At some time between the ages of 5 and 12, however, children come to recognize that lying may be permissible in some circumstances—for example, lying to a bully so that he will not hurt a friend.

Piaget's theory of moral development was based on descriptions of how children respond to specific kinds of questions and the ages at which they switch and use other forms of answers. The research of Harvard psychologist Lawrence Kohlberg (1927–1987) grew out of Piaget's work. Kohlberg believed that moral development generally proceeds through three levels, each of which is divided into two stages. The central concept in Kohlberg's theory is that of justice. In his studies of moral reasoning, Kohlberg presented stories involving moral dilemmas to people of various ages and asked them to describe what the stories meant to them and how they felt about the stories (Kohlberg, 1969). Table 9.4 compares Piaget and Kohlberg's theories on moral development.

Table 9.4 A Comparison of Piaget and Kohlberg on Moral Development

Piaget	Kohlberg	
Sensorimotor and preoperational (birth–6 or 7 years)	*Level 1—Preconventional morality*	
	Stage 1:	Obedience and punishment orientation
	Stage 2:	Egocentric orientation
Concrete operational (7–11 or 12 years)	*Level 2—Conventional morality*	
	Stage 3:	Good-child orientation
	Stage 4:	Authority and social order orientation
Formal operations (12 years and beyond)	*Level 3—Postconventional morality*	
	Stage 5:	Contractual–legalistic orientation; societal needs considered
	Stage 6:	Conscience or principle orientation

Three Levels of Morality. In one of the stories used by Kohlberg, Heinz, a poor man, stole a drug for his wife, who would have died without it. Presented with the story of Heinz, children at level 1, *preconventional morality,* either condemn Heinz's behavior or justify it. They base their decisions about right and wrong on the likelihood of avoiding punishment and obtaining rewards. A child in this stage—still somewhat egocentric—would say it is "bad" to pull the cat's tail "because Mom will send me to my room." People at level 2, *conventional morality,* have internalized society's rules and say that Heinz broke the law by stealing and should go to jail. School-age children, who are at level 2, conform in order to avoid the disapproval of other people. At this stage, a 10-year-old might choose not to try cigarettes because his parents and friends disapprove of smoking. Considerations of the implications of a person's behavior also govern level 2 judgments: Why did the person do it? What will the consequences be for that person and for others? Does the act violate important laws and rules? Only people who have reached level 3, *postconventional morality,* can see that although Heinz's action was illegal, the ethical dilemma is complex. As individuals move toward level 3 they become better able to move beyond fixed rules and laws and focus on principles. In level 3 morality, people make judgments on the basis of their perception of the needs of society, with the goal of fulfilling social contracts and maintaining community welfare and order.

Only a minority of adults reach level 3. In advanced stages of level 3, people make judgments on the basis of personally constructed moral principles—rather than societal teachings. Conscientious objection to legally sanctioned behaviors is associated with this stage. For example, a person may be opposed to capital punishment, even though it is legal in some states. Postconventional morality allows a person to recognize some laws, such as those establishing segregation or apartheid, as unjust because they violate the basic principle of respect for the rights of all people. Research shows that such principled reasoning may incorporate a developed moral character and a sense of virtue and religiosity (Walker & Pitts, 1998). Broader ideas of postconventional morality such as the notion of pursuing moral excellence in everyday life go far beyond Kohlberg's initial views, but are receiving support (Hart, 1998).

Gender Differences: Gilligan's Work

Criticisms of Kohlberg's pioneering research came from Carol Gilligan (1982, 1995, 1997), who found that people look at more than justice when they analyze moral conflicts. She discovered that people are also concerned with caring, with relationships, and with connections with other people.

Though Kohlberg and his colleagues had not generally reported any gender differences, Gilligan did. *Gender differences* are, of course, differences between males and females in behavior or mental processes. Gilligan noted differences between girls and boys in their inclinations toward caring and justice. She found that girls are more concerned with care, relationships, and connections with other people—she hypothesized a feminine orientation to moral issues. As younger children, girls gravitate toward a morality of caring, whereas boys gravitate toward a morality of justice. Gilligan asserts that the difference between boys' and girls' approaches to morality is established by gender and by the child's relationship with the mother. Because of the gender difference between boys and their mothers, boys see that they are essentially different from other people, whereas girls develop a belief in their similarity (connectedness) to others. Gilligan asserts that the transition to adolescence is a crucial time, during which girls develop their own voice—a voice too often muted and suppressed (Brown, 1998; Gilligan, 1997). Gilligan shows that boys respond to Kohlberg's story of Heinz by indicating that sometimes people must act on their own to do the right thing. Like Kohlberg, Gilligan argues that the development of a morality of caring follows a time course: Initially, the child feels caring only toward herself, then later toward others as well, and ultimately (in some people) a more mature stage of caring for truth develops. Gilligan's work has influenced psychologists' evaluations of morality. Yet her approach fosters a continuation of gender stereotyping—women as nurturing, men as logical—and despite widespread acceptance of her view that Kohlberg's work is biased against women, surprisingly little research evidence supports that view (Lapsley, 1996; Lollis, Ross, & Leroux, 1996). Moreover, Gilligan's work has been limited to white, middle-class children and adults; it needs a broader, more multicultural basis (Woods, 1996). Nevertheless, Gilligan's work highlights an important element of moral reasoning: People think about other people in a caring, human way—not just in a legalistic manner, as Kohlberg suggested. Both men and women can and do emphasize caring when they face dilemmas involving relationships; similarly, both are likely to focus on justice when facing issues involving others' rights. (I)

Attachment: The strong emotional tie that a person feels toward special other persons in his or her life.

Think Critically

- What is a potential problem with using stories like Kohlberg's one about Heinz in research to study moral development?

(I) Emotional and Social Development

Focus on issues and ideas

- The short-term and long-term effects of attachment and separation
- How the reciprocal relationship between a child and parent can affect a child's temperament
- The impact of child care on children's emotional development
- The importance of having friendships

Anne Frank, the young Jewish girl who was hidden for a time from the Nazis during World War II, was eloquently thankful in the diary that survived her to the people who helped hide her and her family. She wrote extensively and beautifully about all her feelings—her hopes and fears, as well as her gratitude toward the people who were making sacrifices and putting their own lives at risk to help her family. For a teenage girl, Anne showed extraordinary emotional maturity. And what is even more amazing is that she attained this maturity while in hiding, where her connections with others were limited. Although emotional and social maturity may be revealed in one's teens, the process of maturing began long before. Emotional and social development begins shortly after birth with the attachments that infants form with caregivers.

Attachment: The Earliest Emotion

Attachment is the formal term psychologists use to describe the strong emotional tie that a person feels toward special other persons in his or her life. Attachment theory strongly influences psychologists' thinking about emotional development in children. The study of attachment and emotional expression and the bonds that form among people has a long history. Heavily influenced by some classic early work with monkeys done by Harry Harlow, this research was extended in the 1970s by work on bonding.

People's ability to express emotion and form attachments develops from birth through adulthood. Attachment behaviors encouraged in the early weeks and months of life are also nurtured during adolescence and adulthood, when people form close loving bonds with others. Most researchers consider these behaviors innate, even though they unfold slowly over the first year of life and are reinforced by caregivers. The reason is that emotional expressions—including attachment behaviors—not only appear in all cultures (see Chapter 8) but are found in deaf and blind people and in people without limbs, who have limited touch experiences (Izard & Saxton, 1988).

Classic Work: Attachment in Rhesus Monkeys. To find out how people develop attachment behaviors, Harry Harlow (1905–1981), a psychologist at the University of Wisconsin, studied the development of attachment in rhesus monkeys. Harlow's initial studies focused on early interactions among these monkeys. But he found that monkeys raised from birth in isolated bare-wire cages away from their mothers did not survive, even though they were well fed. Other monkeys, raised in the same conditions but with scraps of terry cloth in their cages, survived. Terry cloth hardly seems likely to be a critical variable in the growth and development of monkeys, yet its introduction into their cages did make a life-and-death difference in this case. Harlow inferred that the terry cloth provided some measure of security. That conclusion led him to attempt to discover whether infant monkeys had an inborn desire for love or warmth.

In a classic experiment, Harlow placed infant monkeys in cages along with two wire shapes resembling adult monkeys. One figure was covered with terry cloth; the other was left bare. Both could be fitted with bottles to provide milk. In some cases, the wire mother surrogate had the bottle of milk; in other cases, the terry-cloth mother surrogate had the bottle. Harlow found that the infant monkeys clung to the terry-cloth mother surrogates whether or not they provided milk. He concluded that the wire mother surrogate, even with a bottle of milk, could not provide the comfort that the terry-cloth mother surrogate did (Harlow & Zimmerman, 1958).

Another of Harlow's findings was that neither group of monkeys grew up to be totally normal. Harlow's monkeys were more aggressive and fearful than normally raised monkeys. They were also unable to engage in normal sexual relations. And some of the infants raised with wire mother surrogates exhibited self-destructive behaviors (Harlow, 1962).

Attachment in Infants. John Bowlby (1907–1990) was one of the first modern psychologists to study the close attachment between mothers and their newborns. Bowlby (1977) argued that the infant's emotional tie with the caregiver evolved because it promotes survival. Bowlby asserted that an infant's very early interactions with its parents are crucial to normal development. Some psychologists consider the establishment of a close and warm parent–child relationship one of the major accomplishments of the first year of life. Formation of attachment is considered a pivotal developmental event that helps an infant develop basic feelings of security.

By the age of 7 or 8 months, attachment to the mother may become so strong that her departure from the room causes a fear response, especially to strangers; this response is known as *separation anxiety* and reflects insecurity on the part of the infant. When infants fear that the principal caregiver, usually the mother, may not be consistently available, they become clingy and vigilant (Ainsworth, 1979; Bowlby, 1988; Cassidy & Berlin, 1994). In attempting to analyze attachment to parents, researchers have used a procedure called the *strange situation technique,* in which babies from 12 to 24 months old are observed with parents, separated from them briefly, and then reunited with them. Although attachment theory has been criticized for being largely based on behaviors observed during stressful situations that are somewhat artificial (Field, 1996), research with the strange situation technique shows that most babies (about 60%) are secure; they are distressed by a parent leaving but are easily comforted. Other babies (about 20%) are neither distressed by separations nor comforted by reunions—these babies are categorized as *avoidant* and are considered to have an insecure attachment. Still other babies (about 15%) are *resistant;* these babies seek closeness with the parent, become angry when separated from the parent, and then show mixed feelings when reunited. Last, some babies (about 5%) are characterized as *disoriented;* they show confused, contradictory attachment behaviors and may act angry, sad, or ambivalent at any time.

Researchers find that secure babies have mothers who are affectionate and especially responsive (Isabella, Belsky, & von Eye, 1989). According to some researchers, this mother–child relationship makes cognitive and emotional development smoother (Cassidy & Berlin, 1994; Hewlett et al., 1998). Not all researchers agree, and cross-cultural studies show significant variations among cultures (e.g., Tronick, Morelli, & Ivey, 1992). Children who have not formed warm, close attachments early in life lack a sense of security and become anxious and overly dependent. As 6-year-olds, they are perceived as more aggressive and less competent than their more secure counterparts (Cohn, 1990). Those who have close attachments require less discipline and are less easily distracted (Lewis & Feiring, 1989). When researchers examined relationships between older children and mothers, they found a positive correlation with ratings of attachment by the mothers.

Once established, early attachment is fairly stable. Babies are resilient (Kier & Lewis, 1997), and brief separations from parents, as in child-care centers, do not adversely affect attachment. Influential psychologist Mary Ainsworth (1979) asserts that early attachment affects the child's later friendships, relations with relatives, and enduring adult relationships; other research confirms that people's relationships as adults are related to the attachment styles they had as children (Brennan & Shaver, 1995). Can adoptive parents form the same type of secure, close attachment to the child as biological parents? In general, adoptive parents form supportive, healthy family relationships. A caretaking atmosphere that is warm, consistent, and governed by the infant's needs is the key. Both adoptive and biological parents can provide such an atmosphere, and both adoptive and biological children can form strong attachments to their parents (Singer et al., 1985).

Babies are resilient, and brief separations from parents, as in child-care centers, do not adversely affect attachment.

There is little doubt that attachment is important, but does it determine who we become? Human beings have an amazing ability to adapt, survive, and negotiate the future. Michael Lewis (1997, 1998) cautions that researchers often overestimate the long-term effects of attachment, and that separation anxiety at age 1 has little to do with adjustment at age 18, let alone at age 35. Lewis studied a group of individuals at age 1 and again at age 18 in terms of attachment to family and friends; he found that secure attachment did not protect children from later maladjustment, nor did insecure attachment predict later trouble. Thus, attachment probably doesn't determine adjustment as an adult, because too many life events, chance circumstances, and good and bad decisions can also affect the life course. As Kagan (1998) reminds researchers and parents, babies and children are amazingly resilient and adaptive, both emotionally and cognitively.

Emotional Exchanges. Verbal exchanges and other emotional interactions between infants and their caregivers increase significantly as infants mature. Dialogues in the form of gestures, smiles, and vocalizations become more common. Mothers and fathers initiate these interactions as often as the infants do. This early play is good for babies, as long as they are not overstimulated (Singer & Singer, 1990).

Verbal exchanges help establish ties, teach language, inform infants about the world, and socialize them. These exchanges seem to occur universally, between all infants and parents. In a cross-cultural study, parents in four countries—Argentina, France, Japan, and the United States—all used similar speech categories (Bornstein et al., 1992). There were some differences, too, of course. For example, Japanese mothers were more willing than mothers from the other countries to speak ungrammatically to their infants, using nonsense words, songs, and rhyme. But the similarities among cultures outweighed the differences. The researchers concluded: "[The] universal aspects of infancy . . . appear . . . to exert control over the content of maternal speech" (p. 601).

Several important variables influence the type and amount of interaction between parents and infants. One is the baby's physical attractiveness, or cuteness (Hildebrandt, 1983). People judge especially beautiful babies as more competent, more likeable, and healthier than average-looking or unattractive babies (Stephan & Langlois, 1984). Adults are more likely to play with, speak to, touch, jiggle, or smile at attractive children (Langlois et al., 1995). This is not surprising; psychologists know that people are biased by the attractiveness of others, whether children or adults (Ritter & Langlois, 1988). Further, mothers talk more to babies than fathers do (Leaper, Anderson, & Sanders, 1998). The baby's own behavior is also important. Clarke-Stewart (1973) found that the more often a child looked, smiled, or vocalized to the mother, the more affectionate and attached to the child she became and the more responsive to the child's distress. Tronick and Cohn (1989) found that infants and mothers both change their behavior in reaction to each other, and they argue that neither the baby nor the mother is a passive recipient of the other's emotions. Both are active participants in forming the attachment.

Temperament: Enduring Emotional Patterns

I get along very well with my sister; we both have fairly easygoing dispositions and have never had any real conflicts. But conflicts between siblings are common, and sometimes quite pronounced. The truth is that, because of temperamental differences, siblings often don't get along, and some parents can't or don't know how to smooth things over (Brody, 1998).

Temperament refers to early-emerging and long-lasting individual differences in disposition and in the intensity and especially the quality of emotional reactions. Some psychologists believe that each person is born with a specific temperament—easygoing, willful, outgoing, or shy, to name but a few. Newborns, infants, and children, like the adults they will eventually grow to be, are all different from one another. Generalizations from one child to all children are impossible, and even generalizations from a sample of children must be made with caution. So many variables can affect a child's growth and development that researchers painstakingly try to separate all the important ones. Thomas and Chess (1977), in their pioneering work in the New York Longitudinal Study, point out that temperament is not fixed and unchangeable. With these cautions in mind, let's look at some studies of temperament.

Data from the New York Longitudinal Study show that children tend to fall into four broad categories: easy (40% of children), difficult (10%), slow-to-warm-up (15%), and unique (35%). Easy children are happy-go-lucky and adapt easily to new situations; difficult children are resistant to environmental change and often react poorly to it; slow-to-warm-up children respond slowly, have low-intensity responses, and are often negative. Many children are unique, showing a varied blend of emotional reactions.

Many researchers contend that some specific initial temperamental characteristics may be biologically based. For example, Jerome Kagan and his colleagues found that 2- and 3-year-olds who were *extremely* inhibited—that is, cautious and shy—tended to remain that way for 4 more years. They also found physiological evidence (an increase in autonomic nervous system activity, for example) that these children may be more responsive to change and unfamiliarity (Kagan, 1997b; Kagan & Snidman, 1991). During the earliest months of life, some infants smile or reach out to a new face and readily accept being held or cuddled. Others are more inhibited. Still others exhibit extreme reticence, even distress, in the presence of strangers. Such xenophobic infants (those who fear strangers) may turn out to be inhibited, meek, and wavering as adults (Caspi, Elder, & Bem, 1988). Researchers know, however, that infant behaviors are not necessarily stable over time and may not be evident in later behavioral styles (except for very extreme cases—intense shyness or diffidence, for example). Further, what parents observe (social wariness with unfamiliar people) is different from the shyness that teachers observe (concern about social evaluation by peers), and so shyness—social inhibition and anxiety—varies in different situations (Eisenberg et al., 1998).

Daniels and Plomin (1985) found an important relationship between the shyness of 2-year-old adopted infants and the shyness of their biological mothers. These findings suggest that genetic factors play a role in shyness. Studies of identical twins on a range of emotional dimensions, especially temperament, also show support for a strong genetic component (Emde et al., 1992). Even maternal actions, such as time spent in daylight during pregnancy, may have an effect; Gortmaker and colleagues (1997) found that short exposure to daylight during pregnancy was associated with a higher likelihood of shy behavior in offspring. Further evidence for a biological predisposition comes from studies of basic physiological responsivity—infants' heart rates in response to a distracting stimulus are known to predict temperament (Huffman et al., 1998). However, shyness is somewhat culturally determined; in one cross-cultural study, researchers found that shyness among native Chinese students helps them gain acceptance from teachers; the opposite tends to be true for students in Western countries (Chen, Rubin, & Li, 1995).

In fact, shyness and other aspects of temperament can be changed; human behavior is the product of deliberative thought processes as well as biological forces. Imagine a child who is shy or diffident and not easy to coax into social situations. Researchers today suggest that such a disposition will affect parent–child discourse and parental discipline practices, and, ultimately, the child's socialization. Indeed, researchers assert that a child's conscience emerges because of these interactions and the growth of self-understanding (Kochanska & Thompson, 1997; Stilwell et al., 1998). Clearly, a child's temperament affects his or her interactions with parents in important ways and may determine in part how the parents treat the child—there is a reciprocal and mutually reinforcing influence. Parents recognize that they affect their child's temperament and personality; they assume that their child-rearing practices strongly influence development and that a child who might be categorized as difficult by Thomas and Chess (1977) may, if treated with patience, become easy as an adolescent.

Temperament: Early-emerging and long-lasting individual differences in disposition and in the intensity and especially the quality of emotional reactions.

Early Social Development and Child Rearing

Any bookstore has shelves lined with how-to books on child rearing written by physicians, parents, psychologists, and others. The variety of approaches and the number of experts show that ideas about child rearing are complicated and constantly changing. As society changes, so do beliefs and practices related to children's social development and ideas about how children form a sense of identity and self. As children move cognitively from being egocentric to a point perceiving themselves as different from the rest of the world, they also develop the ability to think about social relationships. As we will see, children develop socially in not one but many environments.

Regardless of culture, parents respond positively to good behaviors in children and negatively to bad ones. Although cultural differences exist (there is extensive scheduling of daytime childhood behaviors in France and noninterference and acceptance by Swedish parents, for example), parents worldwide respond to their children in similar ways (Honig & Chung, 1989). Although parents exert a powerful influence on children, theirs is not the sole influence. Despite vast differences in the way individual parents treat children, most children turn out all right. Some such as Harris (1998) assert that parents don't *determine* a child's destiny because a child has many environments, especially his or her play groups, which exert profound effects on social development.

Social development begins soon after birth, with the development of an attachment between parents and their newborn. The nature of a child's early interactions with parents is a crucial part of personality development. Infants have a great need to be hugged and cuddled, nurtured, and made to feel good. However, as psychoanalyst Bruno Bettelheim (1987) said, "Love is not enough." Eventually, the most important job for parents is teaching their children how to become independent and how to interact with others.

The First Months. In the first year of life, social interactions among children are limited; infants are largely egocentric and are basically unable to recognize any needs other than their own. By about the second half of the first year, children exhibit strong attachments to parents and other caregivers, along with fear of strangers.

As early as 9 months, infants show they like to play games by indicating their unhappiness when an adult stops playing with them (Ross & Lollis, 1987). They play by themselves; but as they grow older, especially after 2 years of age, they engage in more social play with other children (Howes, Unger, & Seidner, 1989).

By the end of their second year, children have begun to understand that they are separate from their parents—they are developing a sense of self. They begin to learn to interact with other people. They may play alongside other children, but they prefer to play with an adult rather than with another 2-year-old (Jennings, Curry, & Connors, 1986). Gradually, however, they begin to socialize with their peers.

Sharing. The noted pediatrician Benjamin Spock once said that the only two things children will share willingly are communicable diseases and their mother's age. Actually, from age 2 until they begin school, children vacillate between quiet conformity and happy sharing, on the one hand, and stubborn negative demands and egocentric behavior, on the other. Because sharing is a socially desirable behavior, learning to share becomes a top priority when children enter a day-care center, nursery school, or kindergarten. (*Experiencing Psychology* on pp. 254–255 discusses some developmental issues associated with day care.)

Very young children do not understand the concept of sharing—particularly the idea that if you share with another child, the other child is more likely to share with you. In a laboratory study of sharing, researchers observed pairs of children separated by a gate. Initially, one child was given toys and the other wasn't; then the situation was reversed. The researchers found that none of the children shared spontaneously; however, 65% shared a toy when their mothers asked them to. Moreover, a child who was deprived of a toy after having shared one often approached the child who now had the toy. One child even said, "I gave you a toy. Why don't you give me one?" Children do not initiate sharing at a young age; but once they share, they seem to exhibit knowledge about reciprocal arrangements (Levitt et al., 1985). Of course, sharing is more likely among children who are friends because they have had more frequent social interaction and make more attempts at conflict resolution (Newcomb & Bagwell, 1995).

Entry into kindergarten helps lead to a breakdown of egocentrism; however, many factors can either promote or retard this aspect of development. One variable is the type of toys children play with. Quilitch and Risley (1973) provided young children with two kinds of toys—those usually used by one child at a time (isolate toys) and those designed for use by two or more children at the same time (social toys). All the children played with both kinds of toys, but some were given social toys first and others were given isolate toys first. After the initial play period, more of the children who had been given social toys first chose to play with other children. The researchers concluded that the kinds of toys given to children altered the degree of egocentrism exhibited in their play.

Does Gender Make a Difference?

Women differ from men biologically, but the differences in height, weight, and strength, and even in behavior, are not necessarily deficits. Women *and* men are powerful, resourceful, sensitive, intuitive, and analytical. Yet, they exhibit those abilities in different circumstances (Hales, 1999). To an important extent, the study of gender differences in developmental psychology is an investigation of when, how, and why those abilities are revealed.

A generation ago, many parents tended to strongly encourage "masculine" traits such as athletic prowess in their sons and "feminine" traits such as popularity in their daughters. Parents often accepted and promoted gender-based social environments. Today, many parents deemphasize gender-based interests in their children, seeking to reduce or eliminate society's tendency to stereotype people on the basis of gender. This trend is also reflected in children's literature, which increasingly includes gender-neutral photographs and story lines. Such deemphasis of gender-specific behaviors and attitudes has led to a more even distribution of scores on various measures of cognitive ability (Feingold, 1993).

Gender differences are minimal when children are observed individually but become more evident in social situations.

Obviously, there are both similarities and differences between the genders. When young people are given equal schooling, measures of academic performance for boys and girls tend to be equal. Socially, both men and women value intelligence and a sense of humor in the opposite sex. But men and women differ in their biological makeup, and their experiences, biologically and environmentally, are not the same; for example, researchers find small but fairly consistent gender differences in domains closely related to sex and mating (Buss, 1995). Most researchers are aware that their preexisting ideas and sometimes their desires to be politically correct and to minimize differences may contaminate or obfuscate the truth. Alice Eagly (1995) argues that researchers must place gender differences within meaningful contexts in order to analyze them. This means looking at how parents treat children as a function of gender, how schools and religious institutions establish and reinforce gender-specific behaviors, and how society views the influence of gender on the daily life of children and young adults.

From the moment of birth, parents may begin treating their children differently on the basis of gender; from the beginning, girls and boys have different life experiences (Carli, 1997). Relatively few Americans have gender-neutral names such as Pat, Terry, Chris, or Lee (Van Fleet & Atwater, 1997). Moms and dads agonize over picking just the right name, one that will send the right signals and will be gender-appropriate. Some psychologists assert that the way parents talk to and treat boys and girls creates special problems. For example, Pollack (1998) argues that parents have such strong expectations about how boys should behave—independent, strong, and tough—that the pressure of these expectations puts boys at risk for various psychological problems. The truth is that many parents put similar, but different, pressure on girls—to be independent, strong, and feminine. Children today sometimes get mixed messages, and they certainly have high expectations placed on them, far more than when children were expected to be "seen but not heard" (Maccoby, 1998).

A **gender stereotype** is a fixed, overly simple, often wrong, and often negative idea about traits, attitudes, and behaviors of males or females. Gender stereotyping leads people to expect specific patterns of behavior based on gender. Young boys are given baseball gloves; young girls are given Barbie dolls. Boys wear blue; girls wear pink. And these distinctions have an impact at an early age (Leinbach, Hort, & Fagot, 1997). Is this a problem?

You may believe that most gender-stereotyped behavior results from parental influence—that boys and girls are treated differently in their formative years and for this reason develop differently. In fact, most of the differences in the way boys and girls are raised are small (Lytton & Romney, 1991). And these differences tend to result from many factors—many of which are subtle. For example, boys tend to be assigned chores that take them away from people (such as yard work and walking the dog), whereas girls tend to be assigned in-house activities. As a consequence, some researchers assert, girls interact more with people and may therefore become more nurturing, but they have fewer opportunities for inventive play. As a result of their experiences, boys may excel at manipulating objects and tools. And both girls and boys may receive approval and praise for their "gender-appropriate" behaviors, which reinforces those behaviors (Karniol & Aida, 1997). Not only is reinforcement important, but (as social learning theory shows)

Gender stereotype: A fixed, overly simple, often wrong, and often negative idea about traits, attitudes, and behaviors of males or females.

EXPERIENCING PSYCHOLOGY

Child Care

Psychologist Sandra Scarr (1998) put it truthfully, if bluntly: Child care exists so that maternal employment can exist. But child care can help in children's development and has been used throughout this century in intervention with disadvantaged children. Today, about 61% of mothers with children under the age of 6 are working or looking for work outside the home; the figure increases to 75% of women whose children are between 6 and 17. For families in which both parents have jobs, as well as for single-parent families, child care is a necessity. Child-care situations are becoming increasingly diverse as parents seek alternative arrangements for their children. While their mothers work, most preschool children are cared for in their own or other people's homes, often by babysitters, friends, fathers, grandparents, or other relatives. Child-care centers provide care for about 23% of preschool children whose mothers work.

Because of numerous variables, it isn't easy to determine the effects of child care. The variables include, among other things, the child's age at entry into a child-care program, the child's family background, the security of the child's attachment to parents, and the stability of the child-care arrangement (Belsky, 1990). Leaving an infant in someone else's care is stressful for parents; it is thus very important that child-care environments be supportive not only of the children but of their parents as well. If parents are overly anxious about child-care arrangements, this will affect their children (Harms, 1994). A child's home environment and socialization can, of course, moderate potential negative consequences of child care (Broberg et al., 1997). When there is harmony between the parents, parent–child relationships are enhanced, regardless of child-care arrangements (Erel & Burman, 1995; Willoughby & Glidden, 1995).

Some research has questioned current child-care practices, asserting that there is a basis for concern about the impact of child care on development (Bates et al., 1994; Kim, 1997). Some studies suggest that infants who receive more than 20 hours of child care per week display more avoidance of their mothers when they are reunited than do infants who spend only a couple of hours in child care (Belsky & Rovine, 1988). But more recent research (Caruso & Corsini, 1994) suggests that even when children enter child care at a young age, the impact of as much as 33 hours of child care a week is minimal.

Psychologists are especially interested in the relationship between child care and attachment, because they believe that a child's emotional security depends on a strong, loving bond with the mother or primary caretaker (Kagan, Kearsley, & Zelazo, 1980). Contrary to popular belief, studies of attachment behaviors find that nonparental care does not reduce a child's emotional attachment to the mother (Etaugh, 1980). Moreover, there is no firm evidence that temporary separations, such as those caused by child care for preschool children, create later psychological trauma (Bates et al., 1994).

Considerable evidence suggests that a stimulating, varied environment is necessary for optimal cognitive development and that high-quality child-care centers do provide a sufficiently stimulating environment. High-quality child care means an experienced, qualified, and well-paid staff, low staff-to-child ratio, and low staff turnover (Scarr, Eisenberg,

children learn gender-based ideas merely by watching the behavior of adults of their own gender (Luecke-Aleksa et al., 1995). Of course, television is also a source of endless hours of gender stereotypes—ideas that are often exaggerated, especially in children's cartoons (Olson & Douglas, 1997; Thompson & Zerbinos, 1997).

Some psychologists argue that women have a different way of knowing about the world; such a view argues that women learn, experience, and are taught differently (Goldberger, 1997). Yet, despite the fact that this view is widely held, surprisingly little research supports such differences (Brabeck & Larned, 1997). When differences exist, socioeconomic factors usually play a part (Luttrell, 1989). Some evidence suggests that there may be biological, especially hormonal, influences on gender differences; that is, children may have preexisting preferences for gender-based behaviors. Researchers know that 18-month-old boys and girls show greater involvement with toys conventionally associated with their own gender—boys like trucks and girls like dolls—even if parents have not promoted play with gender-stereotyped toys (Caldera, Huston, & O'Brien, 1989). This suggests a biological influence (Berenbaum & Snyder, 1995). Further, starting at age 3 and continuing for several years, children prefer same-gender playmates (Maccoby, 1998). According to Eleanor Maccoby (1998), this characteris-

& Deater-Deckard, 1994). In a study of middle-class children, Bates and his colleagues (1994) found no differences in intellectual functioning between children enrolled in high-quality child-care centers and children reared at home. In fact, high-quality child-care centers may increase children's positive social interactions with peers (Egeland & Hiester, 1995), may make children apparently happier (Vandell, Henderson, & Wilson, 1988), and may help prevent the declines in cognitive functioning that sometimes occur in children from low-income families who are not exposed to varied environments (Burchinal, Lee, & Ramey, 1989). Further, children in child-care centers typically share with other children more than they do at home, and child-care centers can produce other positive effects (Davis & Thornburg, 1994; Moorehouse, 1991). When parents are involved, even a little, in the day-care situation, parental satisfaction and the child's behavior are even better (Cronan, Walen, & Cruz, 1994; Fagan, 1994).

Typical of recent research is a longitudinal study conducted in Sweden by Anders Broberg and his colleagues (1997). The researchers studied 146 children, beginning when they were 16 months of age and concluding when they were 8. They measured an array of abilities, especially cognitive ability. Results showed that children who spent more time with caregivers, at home or in day care, scored better on tests of verbal ability. Involvement in small groups was correlated positively with mathematical ability. The researchers concluded, in looking at the same children over a long period of time, that being in day care did not place them at any disadvantage. Other research found virtually no difference in personality or attachment between children cared for at home and children who had received day care (NICHD Early Child Care Research Network, 1997; Schoelmerich et al., 1995; Wessels et al., 1997).

A comprehensive, multiyear study by Harvey (1999) assessed the cognitive, academic, behavioral, and emotional development of more than 6,000 children whose parents were both employed outside the home. The study tracked 12,600 mothers and their children, interviewing them each year starting in 1979, and it concluded that there were no permanent negative effects. In fact, there was even some support for the idea that early parental employment positively affected children's development by increasing family income. The large sample size and the longitudinal nature of the study make it an important piece of evidence that parental employment and child care do not have significant negative effects—if the care is of high quality.

Thus, with all factors considered, researchers generally assert that good-quality child care "is neither a benefit nor a detriment to the development of children from stable low-risk families" (Scarr & Eisenberg, 1993, p. 638). The impact of child care on children grown to adulthood so far seems negligible (Morrison, Ispa, & Thornburg, 1994). Scarr (1998, p. 95) concludes: "Widely varying qualities of child care have been shown to have only small effects on children's current development and no demonstrated long-term impact, except on disadvantaged children, whose homes put them at developmental risk." It is necessary to consider the facts about child care—the evidence—not just the hopes and fears of parents and psychologists (Scarr, Phillips, and McCartney, 1990). This means looking at studies that show "no difference" as well as those that show better or worse performance or attachment later in life. Further, and perhaps most important, young children's development must be studied within a context of multiple factors. From an ecological perspective, a child's development is unlikely to be determined by a single factor such as nonparental care (Bronfenbrenner, 1979), and psychologists must look at the joint influences of home, parent harmony, school, playground relationships and activities, grandparents, nutrition, and culture. ■

tic cuts across a variety of situations and is difficult to change. Gender segregation does not happen solely because children have been given "boy" toys or "girl" toys; nor does it result solely from inborn temperamental differences that lead to rough-and-tumble play for boys and more sedate play for girls (Berenbaum & Snyder, 1995). Rather, children know they are members of one gender or the other—and this knowledge provides a bond with other children of that gender. Children with widely different personalities are drawn together solely on the basis of their gender. Maccoby (1998) asserts that gender differences are minimal when children are observed individually but become more evident in social situations.

It is apparent that both biological and environmental influences are important in determining gender differences in children. However, gender differences in behavior are small and obvious only in certain situations, such as on the playground (Oliver & Hyde, 1993). Furthermore, gender differences are decreasing as people become more **androgynous**—exhibiting behaviors associated with both sexes—and endorse nontraditional roles for both men and women (Twenge, 1997). As parents consider the implications of re-

Androgynous: Exhibiting behavioral traits associated with both sexes.

search on gender differences, they must use critical thinking skills. They should foster, among other things, children's achievement, moral values, and self-esteem. None of these is gender-based; both boys and girls can and should be taught to reason and solve problems; all children should be taught basic human values and made to feel they are worthwhile.

Friendships: The Company We Keep

When you like someone who likes you, there is a good chance that you call yourselves friends. Although some people have many friends and others have few, most people, at one time or another, find someone with whom they share values, ideas, and thoughts. At its simplest, a friendship is a close emotional tie between two peers (Kerns, 1998). Children develop their first friendships around age 3. They develop more friends in elementary school, and most teenagers report having between three and five good friends. As much as 29% of adolescents' waking hours are spent with friends; among adults, for a whole range of reasons, the time spent interacting with friends drops to 7%. If you had lots of friends as a child, you are more likely to have lots of them as an adult, even if you don't spend a great deal of time with each one of them.

According to Hartup and Stevens (1997), there are some important developmental consequences of having or not having friends. Children and adolescents who have friends tend to be more socially competent than those who do not. Having friends provides someone to confide in, to be afraid with, and to grow with and sets the stage for intimacy with adults. Elementary school children tend to form same-gender friendships; cross-gender friendships are rare. Children also choose friends of the same ethnicity and age (Aboud & Mendelson, 1998). Friendship leads children to cooperate rather than compete with their friends, at least more so than with nonfriends (Hartup, 1989). Furthermore, when children have friends in the classroom, they do better in school (Ladd, 1990). Adolescent friendships can contribute to sharing and intimacy, although they can also be filled with conflict over social or political issues, drugs, gangs, and sexual behavior (Berndt, 1992). When friendships fall apart, a child's self-confidence is undermined (Keefe & Berndt, 1996).

Among adults, friendships between women differ from those between men; and both differ from a friendship between a man and a woman. In Western cultures, expectations for specific gender-based behaviors often control male–female interactions in friendship. Women talk more about family, personal matters, and doubts and fears than men do; men talk more about sports and work than do women. Women in general find friendships more satisfying than men do (Elkins & Peterson, 1993); nevertheless, men experience and seek intimacy and support in friendships (Botschner, 1996).

Many researchers report that intimacy and shared values are the key variables that define a friendship. Ideally, close friends participate as equals, enjoy each other's company, have mutual trust, provide mutual assistance, accept each other as they are, respect each other's judgment, feel free to be themselves with each other, understand each other in fundamental ways, and are intimate and share confidences (Davis & Todd, 1982).

From a developmental point of view, friends are an important resource cognitively and emotionally from childhood through old age (Hartup & Stevens, 1997). Friends help children in the socialization process on age-related tasks. But not all friendships are alike, and the meaning of a friendship is often buried below the surface conversation of shopping, school, or jobs.

Erik Erikson and the Search for Self

Developing an awareness of the self as different from others is an important step in early childhood social development. Self-perception begins when the child recognizes that he or she is separate from other people, particularly the mother; the self becomes more differentiated as a child develops an appreciation of his or her own inner mental world. Ideally, as children develop a concept of themselves, they develop self-esteem and significant attachments to others. Such cognitive, and then social, changes do not take place in isolation. They are influenced by the nature of a child's early attachments, by the cultural world surrounding the child, by the family's and society's child-rearing practices, and by how the child is taught to think about the causes of events in the world. The construction of an identity—a self—occurs slowly and gradually and is affected by myriad variables.

Perhaps no one studied the challenges of social development and self-understanding more closely than the psychoanalyst Erik H. Erikson (1902–1994). With sharp insight, a linguistic flair, and a logical, coherent approach to analyzing human behavior, Erikson, who studied with Freud in Austria, developed a theory of *psychosocial stages of development;* each of his stages contributes to the development of a unique self and helps define how a person develops a role, attitudes, and skills as a member of society. According to Erikson, a series of basic psychological conflicts determines the course of development. His theory is noted for its integration of individual disposition and environment with historical forces in the shaping of the self. Erikson's theory describes a continuum of stages, each involving a dilemma and a crisis, through which all individuals must pass. Each stage can have either a positive or a negative outcome. New dilemmas emerge as a person grows older and faces new responsibilities, tasks, and social relationships. A person may experience a dilemma as an opportunity and face it positively or may view the dilemma as a catastrophe and fail to cope with it effectively.

Table 9.5 lists the first four psychosocial stages in Erikson's theory, with their age ranges and the important events associated with them. These four stages cover birth through age 12. (We will look at Erikson's later stages, covering adolescence and adulthood, later.)

Stage 1 (birth to 12–18 months) involves the development of *basic trust versus basic mistrust*. During their first months, according to Erikson, infants make distinctions about the world and decide whether it is a comfortable, loving place in which they can feel basic trust. At this stage, they develop beliefs about people's essential trustworthiness. If their needs are adequately met, they learn that the world is a predictable and safe place. Infants whose needs are not met learn to distrust the world.

During stage 2 (18 months to 3 years), toddlers must resolve the crisis of *autonomy versus shame and doubt*. Success in toilet training and other tasks involving control leads to a sense of autonomy and more mature behavior. Difficulties dealing with control during this stage result in fears and a sense of shame and doubt.

Stage 3 of Erikson's theory (3 to 6 years) is that of *initiative versus guilt*, when children begin to exercise their own inventiveness, drive, and enthusiasm. During this stage, they either gain a sense of independence and good feelings about themselves or develop a sense of guilt, lack of acceptance, and negative feelings about themselves. If children learn to dress themselves, clean their rooms and accomplish other similar tasks, and develop friendships with other children, they can feel a sense of mastery; alternatively, they can be dependent or regretful.

During stage 4 (6 to 12 years), children must resolve the issue of *industry versus inferiority*. Children either develop feelings of competence and confidence in their abilities or experience inferiority, failure, and feelings of incompetence.

Erikson's theory asserts that children must go through each stage, resolving its crisis as best they can. Many factors have a bearing on the successful navigation of these stages. Of course, children grow older whether or not they are ready for the next stage. A person of any age may still have unresolved conflicts, opportunities, and dilemmas from previous stages. These can cause anxiety and discomfort and make resolution of advanced stages more difficult. Because adolescence is such a crucial stage for the formation of a firm identity, the environment surrounding an adolescent becomes especially important. We will turn to this topic in the next section. *I*

Table 9.5 Erikson's First Four Stages of Psychosocial Development

Stage	Approximate Age	Important Event	Description
1. Basic trust versus basic mistrust	Birth to 12–18 months	Feeding	The infant must form a loving, trusting relationship with the caregiver or develop a sense of mistrust.
2. Autonomy versus shame/doubt	18 months to 3 years	Toilet training	The child's energies are directed toward the development of physical skills, including walking and controlling the sphincter. The child learns control but may develop shame and doubt if not handled well.
3. Initiative versus guilt	3 to 6 years	Independence	The child continues to become more assertive and to take more initiative but may be chastised for being too forceful, which can lead to guilt feelings.
4. Industry versus inferiority	6 to 12 years	School	The child must deal with demands to learn new skills or risk a sense of inferiority, failure, and incompetence.

Think Critically

- Describe some ways in which physical and emotional development might interact.
- What are the implications for later emotional development of cross-cultural differences in responsiveness toward infants?
- Should employers provide day care for their employees' children? What might be the implications for workers and employers of doing so?

Ⓘ Adolescence: Bridging the Gap

Focus on issues and ideas

- The varied effects of physical development on the self-image of adolescents
- How the reemergence of egocentrism in adolescents affects behavior
- How the self-image of an adolescent changes from early adolescence to later adolescence
- The importance of gender identity in adolescence

Adulthood is the period in life when a person is relatively free of parental influence, especially financially, and accepts responsibility for himself or herself. In Western culture, the transition from childhood to adulthood brings dramatic cognitive, social, and emotional changes. Generally, this transition occurs between the ages of 12 and 20, a period known as *adolescence,* which bridges childhood and adulthood but is like neither of those states. **Adolescence** is the period extending from the onset of puberty to early adulthood. **Puberty** is the time when the reproductive system matures; it begins with an increase in the production of sex hormones, which signals the end of childhood. Although adolescents are in many ways like adults—they are nearly mature physically and mentally, and their moral development is fairly advanced—their emotional development may be far from complete and generally they have not yet become self-sufficient economically.

Adolescence [add-oh-LESS-sense]: The period extending from the onset of puberty to early adulthood.

Puberty [PEW-burr-tee]: The period during which the reproductive system matures; it begins with an increase in the production of sex hormones, which signals the end of childhood.

Secondary sex characteristics: The genetically determined physical features that differentiate the sexes but are not directly involved with reproduction.

Adolescence in Multiple Contexts

Adolescence is often referred to as a time of storm and stress brought on largely by raging hormones—and for some adolescents, like my daughter, this is the case. It is a popular stereotype that adolescents are in a state of conflict resulting in part from a lack of congruity among the various aspects—physical, cognitive, social, and emotional—of their development. There is some truth to this image. Most adolescents have normal conflicts, such as with parents, and some have atypical problems, such as poverty or parental alcoholism; what may compound these problems is that adolescents' coping mechanisms, or ways of dealing with such stressors, may not yet have evolved sufficiently. Consider alcohol abuse. Most adolescents know that underage drinking is illegal and that drinking is potentially deadly when combined with driving. Yet most are not mature enough to stand up to peer pressure and make a conscious decision not to drink.

Storm and stress do not give the whole picture of adolescence, however. Most adolescents go through this period of multiple changes without significant psychological difficulty (Larson & Ham, 1993). Although spurts of hormones do affect adolescents' reactions, nonbiological factors seem to be especially important in moderating the effects of hormones on adolescents' moods (Eccles et al., 1993). Adolescence may be a challenging life period, just as adulthood is, but fewer than 30% of adolescents have serious difficulties and most psychologists agree that adolescence is not typically marked by great psychological turmoil (Powers, Hauser, & Kilner, 1989). In fact, adolescents have no more psychological disturbances than the rest of the population (Hauser & Bowlds, 1990). This fact does not mean that adolescence is conflict-free or that parent–child relationships do not change during this period; what it does mean is that adolescence does not *have* to be a stressful time. Most adolescents experience healthy emotional and social development during these years, and the frequency and intensity of conflicts decrease as adolescents grow older (Laursen, Coy, & Collins, 1998).

While it is almost a cliché, for a teenager in the United States to feel that "no one understands me," it is difficult to imagine a teenager growing up in the jungles of New Guinea expressing the same sentiment; her focus during the teen years is not on self-expression but on learning specific skills. Thus, the problems of adolescence must be considered in a cultural context. Even when adolescents grow up in the same country, they experience life's joys and disappointments in different ways. Some American teenagers come from disadvantaged economic groups, perhaps from a Chicago ghetto or a Native American reservation. Some grow up in luxury, perhaps in a wealthy suburb of Los Angeles. Others are exposed to racial prejudice, alcohol and other drug abuse, nonsupportive families, or other stressors that lead them to feel a lack of control over their lives.

Unfortunately, most research on adolescence has been conducted on white, middle-class American teenagers. But researchers now understand that the life experiences of various ethnic and cultural groups are not alike. Each year, more studies compare the experiences of different groups and sensitize both professionals and the public to cultural differences among groups as well as to the diversity that exists within groups. Remember, there is often more diversity within a given group than between groups.

Physical Development in Adolescence

The words *adolescence* and *puberty* are often used interchangeably, but in fact they mean different things. As noted earlier, puberty is the period during which the reproductive system matures. The age when puberty begins varies widely; some girls begin to mature physically as early as age 8, and some boys at 9 or 10 (Marshall & Tanner, 1969). The average age at which individuals reach sexual maturity—the first menstruation for a girl, the first ejaculation for a boy—is 13, plus or minus a year or two (on average, girls enter puberty a year or two before boys). Just before the onset of sexual maturity, boys and girls experience significant *growth spurts,* gaining as much as 5 inches in height in a single year.

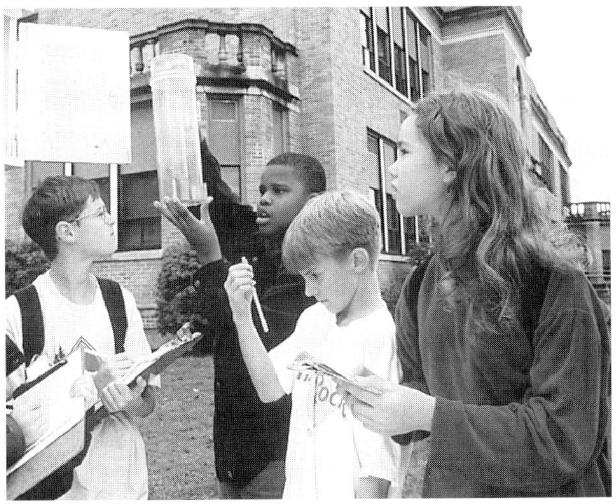

By the end of the first or second year of the growth spurt, changes have occurred in body proportions, fat distribution, bones and muscles, and physical strength and agility. In addition, the hormonal system has begun to trigger the development of secondary sex characteristics. **Secondary sex characteristics** are the genetically determined physical features that differentiate the sexes but are not directly involved with reproduction. These characteristics help distinguish men from women—for example, beards and chest hair in males, breasts in females. (Primary sex characteristics are the external genitalia and their associated internal structures, all of which are present at birth.) Boys experience an increase in body mass and a deepening of the voice, as well as the growth of pubic, underarm, and facial hair. Girls experience an increase in the size of the breasts, a widening of the hips, and the growth of underarm and pubic hair. Puberty ends with the maturation of the reproductive organs, at which time boys produce sperm and girls begin to menstruate. The first ejaculation for boys and the first menstrual cycle for girls (called *menarche*) are usually memorable events. The order and sequence of these physical changes is predictable, but, as noted earlier, the age at which puberty begins and the secondary sex characteristics emerge varies widely from person to person.

Puberty has received a good deal of research attention. For example, researchers have found that as boys pass through puberty, they feel more positive about their bodies, whereas girls are more likely to have negative feelings. Puberty itself does not create psychological maladjustment. However, adolescence means beginning to emerge as an adult, socially and sexually, and this requires significant adjustment. New forces affect the self-image of adolescents, and although these forces create new stresses, most adolescents perceive their new status as desirable. Physical maturation has implications for social development, because young people often gravitate to and choose environments and activities that complement their genetic tendencies.

Cognitive Development in Adolescence

As children mature physically, they also develop cognitively in rather complex ways. As you learned earlier in this chapter, Piaget and Vygotsky showed that children's cognitive development has both biological and social components. And cognitive development does not stop in adolescence. Most adolescents are in the formal operational stage. Because they can think about the world abstractly and develop hypotheses, they learn new cognitive strategies. Teenagers expand their vocabularies, seek out creative solutions, and make full use of their higher mental functions. Problem solving often becomes a focus for adolescent thought. Many adolescents become egocentric, idealistic, and critical of others. And, as *Diversity* points out, adolescents' cultural background may be another factor influencing their cognitive development.

DIVERSITY

Ethnic Differences in Achievement

Which group does best in school: Hispanic Americans, Asian Americans, or African Americans? It is widely believed that students of Asian American descent do better, thanks to cultural values that stress achievement. Researchers have found that this belief is accurate: Culture does affect achievement in direct and indirect ways. Students in Asian nations spend more classroom time on academic subjects than do students in the United States; it is not surprising that their math scores are higher (Stigler & Baranes, 1988). Further, families and teachers in Asian societies tend to treat all students as equal, emphasizing effort more than innate abilities—whereas in many Western cultures more attention is given to innate cognitive strengths. In addition, in Asian and other non-Western societies, success is often attributed to external factors and failure to internal factors such as ability; the reverse is true in Western societies (Kivilu & Rogers, 1998). Finally, Asian parents often expect more from their children in terms of academic success (Chen & Lan, 1998).

One research team set out to determine how a person's ethnic background and worldview (basic attitude toward life) might affect academic achievement. Steinberg, Dornbusch, and Brown (1992) administered a 30-page questionnaire to more than 15,000 students at nine U.S. high schools, which varied ethnically and socioeconomically. The questionnaire gathered information about the students' relationships, schooling, behavior problems, and potential maladjustment. The researchers focused on peer and family relationships and on such family variables as ethnicity, socioeconomic status, immigration history, and patterns of language use.

In the original study and in a follow-up study, the researchers found that parental behavior was important. Adolescents whose parents are *authoritative*—not rigidly authoritarian but accepting, warm, democratic, and firm—achieve more in school than their peers (Steinberg et al., 1992). But peer interactions also turn out to be important; strong peer support for academics can make up for a lack of positive parenting. Conversely, peer disdain for academics weakens a strong parental voice (Steinberg et al., 1993).

What about ethnic differences? Regardless of ethnic background, adolescents from authoritative homes functioned better socially than those from permissive or neglectful homes. In school performance, there was a slight difference among ethnic groups: Authoritative parenting seemed to make more of a difference to white teenagers than to African American or Asian American ones. Why would authoritativeness benefit African Americans and Asian Americans less in academic performance than in social development? The difference in academic versus social development may have to do with sharply differing worldviews. The researchers found that all of the students believed a good education would pay off, but Asian Americans in particular had been taught to fear the consequences of a poor education. In contrast, African American students were more likely to be optimistic and believe that life could have positive outcomes despite a poor education. Obviously, students who believe that they can succeed without doing well in school will devote far less energy to academic pursuits than will those who are more fearful of the negative consequences of school failure.

In a follow-up to their original study, Steinberg and his colleagues had students complete a battery of standardized tests to see if differences in achievement and adjustment were maintained over time. Results showed that the benefits of authoritative parenting were maintained and that "the deleterious effects of neglectful parenting continue to accumulate" (Steinberg et al., 1994, p. 754).

A child's worldview, taught by his or her parents and reinforced by peers, shapes future success (Chen & Lan, 1998). When it comes to school, distinctly different cultural views may alter motivation, performance, and later success in life and work. Steinberg, Dornbusch, and Brown (1992) and other researchers (Chen & Lan, 1998) have been careful in their conclusions; they realize that many factors interact to affect performance. Still, they assert that their research provides a foundation and an agenda for future studies. ■

Developing new cognitive abilities—moving into Piaget's stage of formal operations—is quite liberating for adolescents. But this newfound ability to understand the world and its subtleties is not always easy on adolescents, as they sometimes become argumentative and difficult—as my daughter Sarah did. Part of the problem, from Piaget's view, is that teenagers become wrapped up in themselves and in their own thoughts—in short, quite egocentric. This egocentrism leads to two cognitive distortions. The first is the **imaginary audience**—the feeling adolescents have that they are always "on stage," that there is an audience watching them. "Everyone will be watching," thinks a teenager, referring to his or her first date, dance, debate, or whatever else. The adolescent egocentrically believes the world is attending critically to her or his life, she or he will go to great lengths to avoid calling attention to herself or himself.

The adolescent egocentrically believes the world is attending critically to her or his life, she or he will go to great lengths to avoid calling attention to herself or himself.

Not only do adolescents believe that they are on stage, but they also develop an inflated sense of their own importance. This cognitive distortion is called the **personal fable**—the belief that they are so special and unique that other people cannot understand them and that risky behaviors, such as unsafe sex, that might harm other people will not harm them. The personal fable can lead to tragedy, such as when a teen thinks that he or she can drive after drinking. As we saw earlier in this chapter, according to Inhelder and Piaget (1958), adolescents go through a phase in which they attribute an unlimited power to their own thoughts.

The imaginary audience and the personal fable may not be so much a return to childhood egocentrism as a side effect of cognitive growth and the ability to think about thinking. Adolescent egocentrism may be a bridging mechanism that allows adolescents to take on new roles, break away from parents, and integrate new views of the self (Lapsley, 1993). Whatever its origins, it starts to disappear by late adolescence (Vartanian & Powlishta, 1996).

Cognitive differences between male and female adolescents are minimal. As we saw in Chapter 7, gender differences in verbal and mathematical abilities are exceedingly small. The cognitive differences found in recent research studies exist only in certain special populations—for example, among the very brightest mathematics students, boys continue to outscore girls. However, boys' scores are especially variable. There are some observed gender differences—for example, on certain tests (such as the SAT), males as a group outperform females in mathematics (Park, Bauer, & Sullivan, 1998). However, when certain socioeconomic and cultural variables are controlled, these gender differences are very small. And it's important to remember that they are overall group differences, having no bearing on any individual's achievements.

Researchers are still trying to determine whether there are basic differences in male and female intelligence and, if so, under what conditions. Biologically based mechanisms may account for some gender-based cognitive differences, but learning is far more potent in establishing and maintaining gender-role stereotypes and gender-specific attitudes (see Chapter 5).

Emotional and Social Development in Adolescence

Early childhood social interactions as well as advances in cognitive development profoundly affect adolescent social adjustment. Children whose early adjustment is poor are less likely to make good adolescent adjustments, social and otherwise. The trajectories of social development do not change much—troubled boys and girls tend to stay troubled, and happy and well-adjusted children are more likely to stay well adjusted. But, as mentioned earlier, regardless of their previous adjustment, teenagers' egocentrism—in the form of the imaginary audience and the personal fable—complicates their emotional and social adjustment.

Adolescents develop a self-image based on beliefs about themselves that are both cognitively and emotionally based, but other people also form expectations and beliefs about adolescents, which have an impact (Cairns & Cairns, 1994). So, an adolescent's personality and sense of self-esteem are affected by childhood experiences, events such as the timing of puberty and how peers and parents react to that timing, and stage of cognitive development. Parents and teachers can help troubled children and both

Imaginary audience: A cognitive distortion experienced by adolescents, in which they see themselves as always "on stage" with an audience watching.

Personal fable: A cognitive distortion experienced by adolescents, in which they believe they are so special and unique that other people cannot understand them and risky behaviors will not harm them.

early-maturing and late-maturing adolescents develop a stronger sense of self-esteem. For example, research shows that involvement in athletics can be a buffer against the initially negative feelings about body image that can sometimes arise during this period. For both girls and boys, increased time spent playing sports is associated with higher satisfaction with body image and higher self-ratings on strength and attractiveness. Physical activity is associated with higher achievement, weight reduction, improved muscle tone, and stress reduction, all of which foster a positive self-image (Kirshnit, Richards, & Ham, 1988).

There are sharp individual differences in the development of adolescent self-esteem. In contrast to middle or later adolescence, early adolescence is associated with lower self-esteem and with feelings of insecurity, inadequacy, and shyness. One of the sources of these differences is gender. In spite of the rapidly changing role of women in American culture, girls often develop low self-esteem by the time they reach high school, despite the fact that their early childhood ambitions and dreams may have been similar to those of boys. Television and the print media as well as school systems that still favor boys in many domains contribute to the disparity. Despite enormous gains, many attitudes and behaviors still need to change (Rhode, 1997).

Two important sources of influence on self-esteem and personality are parents and peers. Psychologists and parents disagree about the relative importance of peers versus parents (Harris, 1998), but most studies indicate that adolescents' attitudes fall somewhere between those of their parents and those of their peers (Paikoff & Brooks-Gunn, 1991). Some assert that the influence of peer groups is especially formidable—especially in the early years of adolescence when the impact of the imaginary audience is still great. *Peer groups* are people who identify with and compare themselves to one another. They often consist of people of the same age, gender, and ethnicity, although adolescents may change their peer group memberships and may belong to more than one group. As adolescents spend more time away from parents and home, they experience increasing pressure to conform to their peer groups' values regarding society, government, religion, music—and even fast-food restaurants. The desire for conformity especially affects same-sex peer relations (Bukowski et al., 1993). Peers constantly pressure one another to conform to behavioral standards, including standards for dress, social interaction, and even forms of rebellion, such as shoplifting and drug taking (Farrell & Danish, 1993). Most important, peers influence the adolescent's developing self-concept.

An adolescent's self-esteem and self-confidence are also undoubtedly affected by parents and their child-rearing style (Resnick et al., 1997). Are they authoritative, nurturing, and at the same time firm, or are they heavy-handed and dictatorial, or perhaps more interested in being their child's pal and thus too permissive? Both parents and peers set standards by which the adolescent judges his or her own behavior. These three sources of influence (parents, peers, and self-interpretation) can establish self-esteem and self-confidence and allow an individual to attain good social and emotional adjustment. Some of that social adjustment is gender-based, as we'll discover next.

Who Am I? The Search for Gender Identity

Gender matters. In fact, gender matters a great deal in both childhood and adulthood (Maccoby, 1998). Being a man or a woman in any culture carries with it certain roles. Men and women have different expectations for themselves and for members of the opposite sex, and those expectations often create gender inequality. It is widely held that women suffered serious discrimination "once upon a time," but that those days are over. The truth is that white males still dominate in the United States and many other Western societies (Rhode, 1997). Women still experience serious disparities in employment opportunities, pay, status, and access to leadership roles. This is a societal problem, which stems from society's definition of gender roles.

We saw in Chapter 7 that gender differences are differences between males and females in behavior or mental processes. Extensive research has revealed few important biologically determined behavioral or cognitive differences between the genders. Although girls often reach developmental milestones earlier than boys do, this difference between the genders usually disappears by late adolescence (Cohn, 1991). On the other hand, experience and learning—the way a person is raised and taught—have a profound impact on gender-based behaviors.

Gender Identity. As noted earlier, a key feature of adolescence is that it is a period of transition and change. Adolescents must develop their own identity, a sense of themselves as independent, mature individuals. One important aspect of identity is **gender identity**—a person's sense of being male or female. Children develop gender identity by age 3. By age 4 or 5, children realize that their gender identity is permanent; that is, they know that changing their hair, clothing, or behavior does not alter their gender. By this age, they typically segregate themselves in play groups according to gender (Maccoby, 1998).

Consider the experience that adolescents have when their bodies change in appearance very rapidly, sometimes in unpredictable ways. During the transition to adulthood, adolescents often try out various types of behaviors, including those relating to male–female relationships and dating. Some adolescents become extreme in their orientation toward maleness or femaleness. Boys, especially in groups, may become overtly aggressive; girls may act submissively and be especially concerned with their looks. This exaggeration of traditional male or female behaviors, called *gender intensification,* is often short-lived, and it may be related to the increased self-esteem that boys feel during adolescence and the decreased self-esteem that girls experience (Block & Robins, 1993).

Many psychologists believe that once gender identity is firmly established, children and adolescents attempt to bring their behavior and thoughts into conformity with generally accepted gender-specific roles. **Gender schema theory** asserts that children and adolescents use gender as an organizing theme to classify and interpret their perceptions about the world. (Recall from Chapter 6 that a *schema* is a conceptual framework that organizes information and makes sense of the world.) Young children decide which behaviors are appropriate and inappropriate gender behaviors by processing a wide array of social information. They develop shorthand concepts of what boys and girls are like; then they try to behave in ways that are consistent with those concepts. Thus, they show preferences for gender-related toys, activities, and vocations. In fact, children's and, later, adolescents' self-esteem and feelings of worth are often tied to their gender-based perceptions about themselves, many of which are determined by identification with the same-gender parent or by what they see as society's view of gender roles (Hudak, 1993).

Gender Roles. **Gender roles** are the full range of behaviors that are generally associated with one's gender and that help one establish who one is. However, in the course of establishing gender roles, people sometimes adopt **gender role stereotypes**—beliefs about which gender-based behaviors are appropriate and acceptable for each gender; such beliefs are strongly regulated and reinforced by society. Men, for example, may learn to hide their emotions; American society frowns on men who cry in public and reinforces men who appear strong and stoic when faced with sorrow or stress (Fischer & Good, 1998). In the workplace, gender role stereotypes still heavily influence wages and promotions. According to the U.S. Department of Labor (1998), on average, women in the United States earn about 76 cents for each dollar that men earn—this discrepancy is referred to as the *wage gap.* The wage gap exists largely because women still predominate in many lower-paid jobs.

Androgyny. Developing a gender identity in adolescence has always been part of the transition to adulthood. Today, this task is more complicated, especially for women. In earlier decades of this century, most educated American women were expected to pursue marriage and homemaking, which were considered full-time jobs. Today, women's plans often include a career outside the home, which may be interrupted for child rearing. In recent years, many women and men have developed new attitudes about gender roles—attitudes that encourage all people to cultivate both traditionally masculine and traditionally feminine traits. They have adopted behaviors that are *androgynous*—that represent a blend of stereotypically male and stereotypically female characteristics. Androgynous men and women may fix cars, pursue careers, do housework, and help care for children; they can be both assertive and emotionally sensitive. More than ever before, men today disparage violent toughness as part of the masculine role (Fischer & Good, 1998). Several studies have found that people who rate high in androgynous characteristics tend to feel more fulfilled and more competent when dealing with social and personal issues (Stake, 1997). As people become more androgynous in the United States, it will be interesting to see if this trend affects adolescents' friendships.

Sexual Behavior during Adolescence

Times have changed a great deal. For decades, up through the 1950s, remaining chaste until marriage was considered a virtue for most middle-class Americans; if sexual intimacy was engaged in, it was between

Gender identity: A person's sense of being male or female.

Gender schema theory: The theory that children and adolescents use gender as an organizing theme to classify and interpret their perceptions about the world.

Gender roles: The full range of behaviors that are generally associated with one's gender and help one establish who one is.

Gender role stereotypes: Beliefs about which gender-based behaviors are appropriate and acceptable for each gender; such beliefs are regulated and reinforced by society.

young adults who had committed themselves to one another. Today, sexual intimacy is seen as a rite of passage and a way of gaining adult status; about 50% of girls and boys aged 15 to 19 have engaged in sexual intercourse at least once. This is an important finding; sexually active teenagers are at greater risk for alcohol abuse, sexually transmitted diseases, and academic failure, among other negative outcomes. What initiated this change in adolescent sexual behavior?

In human beings, learned attitudes have a greater influence than biological factors on sexual behavior; and people first learn about such behavior at home. Children are profoundly influenced by parents' attitudes and behavior—the extent to which, for instance, parents hug and kiss openly, seem embarrassed by their bodies, or talk freely about sexual matters. The influence of parents on sexual behavior was shown in a study that examined how parents' discipline and control influence teenagers' sexual attitudes and behavior. Miller and colleagues (1986) surveyed more than 2,000 teenagers and their parents about parental discipline and teenage sexual behavior. The results showed that sexual permissiveness and intercourse were more frequent among adolescents who viewed their parents as not having rules or not being strict. Sexual behaviors, especially intercourse, were less frequent among teenagers who reported that their parents were strict. In addition, close relationships with parents and feelings of family support have been associated with later age at first intercourse (Brooks-Gunn & Furstenberg, 1989).

American adolescents view sexual intimacy as an important and normal part of growing up; premarital heterosexual activity has become increasingly common among adolescents, especially 13- to 17-year-olds. Three-fifths (60%) of white male teenagers have intercourse by age 18, and the same percentage of white female adolescents do so by just a year later, age 19. Among African Americans, 60% of males have intercourse by age 16, and 60% of females do so by age 18. There are great individual differences with regard to age at first intercourse and the subsequent frequency of intercourse. It is not uncommon for a teenager to have first intercourse at age 14 or 15 and then not to have sexual relations again for a year or two.

Dreyer (1982) suggests four reasons for the early expression of sexual behavior: First, adolescents are reaching sexual maturity at younger ages than in previous decades. Second, knowledge and use of contraception are becoming more widespread, thus reducing the fear of pregnancy. Third, adults' sexual attitudes and behaviors are changing. And, finally, adolescents consider sexual behavior normal in an intimate relationship.

More relaxed attitudes about adolescent sexual behavior have brought about increased awareness of the problems of teenage pregnancy. Each year in the United States, more than 500,000 unmarried teenage girls become pregnant. Adolescent pregnancy rates vary substantially with ethnicity; for example, whites have substantially lower rates than do Hispanics or African Americans (Coley & Chase-Lansdale, 1998). The more engaged students are with schooling, the less likely they are to become pregnant (Manlove, 1998). The consequences of child bearing for teenage mothers are serious. Teenage mothers are more likely to smoke and to have low-birthweight infants; they are also less likely to receive timely prenatal care. Furthermore, a young woman's chances of obtaining education and employment become more limited if she becomes a mother, and many young mothers are forced to rely on public assistance. Most studies indicate that women who bear children early in their lives will not achieve economic equality with women who postpone parenthood until they are adults (Furstenberg & Hughes, 1995); adolescent pregnancy is also associated with abuse of alcohol and other drugs and with depression (Martin, Hill, & Welsh, 1998).

Current studies show that, despite the threat of AIDS, high school and college students still engage in regular sexual activity, often without appropriate protection. Comprehensive school-based health-care programs that emphasize the complete picture of sexuality (attitudes, contraception, motivation, and behavior) reduce the risks of pregnancy in teenagers. But, for many parents and teenagers, such programs are controversial. *I*

Think Critically

- How do you think an increase in androgyny might affect adolescent friendships? How might it change the nature of courting? Of marriage?

I Adulthood: Years of Stability and Change

Focus on issues and ideas

- How a reinterpretation of Erikson's theory could transform the "mid-life crisis" into a mid-life transition

- ◆ The effects of physical and cognitive changes in adulthood
- ◆ The consequences of primary and secondary aging for longevity

American adults today have different life experiences than did adults of the 1950s, whose lives tended to follow more predictable and prescribed timetables. In the 1950s, many people married when they were in their late teens or early 20s and had children soon after. Wives frequently stayed at home to raise the children, while husbands worked to support the family. Today's adults tend to marry later, and some do not marry at all. Many people are postponing or rejecting parenting—of the 60 million American women aged 15 to 44 in 1995, 25 million were childless. Although some women choose to stay at home to raise children, many are concentrating on careers; in some cases, their husbands raise the children. Many grown children are returning home after college, and divorce has broken up numerous families. The 1950s stereotype of family structure has changed sharply, in a relatively short period of time.

The life experience of an American adult today is also different from that of adults in other cultures. Americans have some things in common with people from other Western cultures, but very few with people in Third World countries. These cultural differences have not been widely studied. In addition, until the 1970s, developmental psychologists in the United States concentrated largely on white middle-class infants and children.

Psychologists are now focusing on development across cultures and throughout the life span. They are recognizing that a person encounters new challenges in every stage of life. Researchers study adult development by looking at the factors that contribute to stability or change, to a sense of accomplishment or feelings of despair, and to physical well-being or diminished functioning. Think about the years after retirement, which can be a time of stability—bringing feelings of completion and well-being—or a difficult, unhappy time—full of physical and emotional troubles. Researchers also examine the differences between men and women, with emphasis on the unique experiences of women in American culture. Research studies and theories are recognizing and focusing on cultural diversity. And psychologists are now aware that a person's career is also a defining characteristic of adulthood. Adults spend an enormous amount of time and energy on their careers, and this aspect of adulthood has been examined relatively infrequently by psychologists.

The Search for Identity: Adult Stage Theories

Some people—perhaps the more poetic—think of life as a journey along a road from birth to death. The concept of a journey recalls Erik Erikson's stage theory, in which people move through a series of stages and must resolve a different dilemma in each stage in order to develop a healthy identity.

Erik Erikson Revisited. An important aspect of Erikson's stage theory is that people progress through well-defined stages from the beginning of life to the end—at each stage attempting to solve a particular dilemma. People move toward greater maturity as they pass from stage to stage. Stages 1–4 focus on childhood. Let's now consider the stages that begin with adolescence.

Erikson's stage 5, *identity versus role confusion,* marks the end of childhood and the beginning of adolescence. According to Erikson, the growth and turmoil of adolescence create an "identity crisis." The major task for adolescents is to resolve that crisis successfully by forming an *identity*—a sense of who they are, where they perceive themselves to be going, and what their place is in the world. Adolescents have to form a multifaceted identity that includes vocational choices, religious beliefs, gender roles, sexual behaviors, and ethnic customs. The task is quite daunting, which is one reason why adolescence is such a critical stage of development. From Erikson's view, the failure to form an identity leaves the adolescent confused about adult roles and unable to cope with the demands of adulthood, including the development of mature relationships with members of the opposite sex (Erikson, 1963, 1968). The special problems of adolescence—which sometimes include rebellion, suicidal feelings, and drug abuse—must also be dealt with at this stage.

Stage 6 (young adulthood) involves *intimacy versus isolation.* Young adults begin to select other people with whom they can form intimate, caring relationships. Ideally, they learn to relate emotionally to others and commit to a lasting relationship; the alternative is to become isolated.

In stage 7 (middle adulthood), *generativity versus stagnation,* people become more aware of their mortality and develop a concern for future generations. They now hope to convey information, love, and security to the next generation, particularly their own children. They do so through caring acts (Bradley & Marcia, 1998). As adults, they try to influence their family and the world; otherwise, they stagnate and become self-absorbed. Generativity is, of course, not

Table 9.6 Erikson's Last Four Stages of Psychosocial Development

Stage	Approximate Age	Important Event	Description
5. Identity versus role confusion	Adolescence	Peer relationships	The teenager must achieve a sense of identity that encompasses occupation, gender roles, sexual behavior, and religion.
6. Intimacy versus isolation	Young adulthood	Love relationships	The young adult must develop intimate relationships or suffer feelings of isolation.
7. Generativity versus stagnation	Middle adulthood	Parenting and work	Each adult must find some way to contribute to and support the next generation.
8. Ego integrity versus despair	Late adulthood	Reflection on and acceptance of one's life	Ideally, the person arrives at a sense of acceptance of oneself as one is and a sense of fulfillment.

limited to middle adulthood. Research shows that people in early adulthood also experience it (Stewart & Vandewater, 1998).

In stage 8 (late adulthood), *ego integrity versus despair,* people decide whether their existence is meaningful, happy, and cohesive or wasteful and unproductive. Many individuals never arrive at stage 8, and some who do are filled with regrets and a feeling that time is too short. Those who successfully resolve the conflict inherent in this stage feel fulfilled, with a sense that they understand, at least partly, what life is about.

Table 9.6 summarizes the last four stages of Erikson's theory.

Levinson's Life Structures. Another noted theorist, Daniel Levinson, has devised a different stage theory of adult development. He agrees that people go through stages and that they have similar experiences at key points in their lives. He also agrees that studying those shared experiences allows psychologists to help people manage their lives. Unlike Erikson, however, Levinson does not see life as a journey toward some specific goal such as ego integrity. Rather, he believes that a theory of development should lay out the eras during which individuals work out various developmental tasks. These tasks may not be the same for all individuals and do not lead to a specific end. In his words (Levinson, 1980, p. 289): "We change in different ways, according to different timetables. Yet, I believe that everyone lives through the same developmental periods in adulthood . . . though people go through them in their own ways."

Levinson (1978) suggests that as people grow older, they adapt to the demands and tasks of life. He describes four basic eras in the adult life cycle, each with distinctive qualities and different problems, tasks, and situations. Each era also brings with it different *life structures*—unique patterns of behavior and ways of interacting with the world. These are the "themes" of one's life at a given time, as reflected in two or three major areas of chosen commitment. Levinson's theory highlights periods of questioning and doubt alternating with periods of stability. The so-called midlife crisis is one of those major questioning periods. The four eras outlined by Levinson are adolescence, early adulthood, middle adulthood, and late adulthood.

During *adolescence* (ages 11–17), young people enter the adult world but are still immature and vulnerable. During *early adulthood* (ages 18–45), they make their first major life choices regarding family, occupation, and style of living. Throughout this period, adults move toward greater independence and senior positions in the community. They raise their children, launch them into the adult world, and strive to advance their own careers. Early adulthood is an era of striving for, gaining, and accepting responsibility. By the end of this era, at about age 45, most people are no longer caring for young children but may be increasingly involved in assisting aging parents.

The much-discussed midlife crisis occurs at the end of early adulthood. In fact, Levinson calls particular attention to it, asserting that most adults experience such a crisis in their early 40s. During this era, people often realize that their lives are half over—that if they are to change their lives, they must do so now. Some who are dissatisfied with the life they have made resign themselves to it; others decide to change and strive to achieve new goals. (This era is similar to Erikson's stage of generativity versus stagnation.)

Middle adulthood spans the years from 46 to 65. Adults who have gone through a midlife crisis learn to live with the decisions they made during early adulthood. Career and family are usually well established.

EXPERIENCING PSYCHOLOGY

Are Crises Unavoidable?

Most people go through transitions. At certain points, decisions must be made, and individuals must reassess who they are, where they are going, and how they want to get there. But does everyone go through a midlife crisis? The term *midlife crisis* may be a misnomer. Levinson himself (1980) suggested that the event should more properly be called a *midlife transition*—a change that may be more difficult for some individuals than others. The word *transition* suggests that a person has reached a time in life when old ways of coping are giving way to new ones and old tasks have been accomplished. A person in transition faces new challenges and responsibilities, which often require reassessment, reappraisal, and the development of new skills. A *crisis,* in contrast, occurs when old ways of coping become ineffective and a person is helpless—not knowing what to do and needing new, radically different coping strategies. Crises are often perceived as painful turning points in people's lives.

Not everyone experiences the infamous midlife crisis, but most people pass through at least one midlife transition. Some can experience two, three, or even more. A transition may occur at around age 30, during which careers and relationships begun in a person's 20s are reevaluated and sometimes rejected. In the transitions of early and middle adulthood—including the midlife transition at about age 40—people reorient their career and family choices. Sometimes parents experience another transition, called the *empty nest syndrome,* when their children leave home—although this transition is usually not too stressful and is less likely to be a problem for people who are engaged in paid employment outside the home (Adelmann et al., 1989). Transitions also occur at retirement, not only for the retiree but also for the person's spouse.

People who experience midlife transitions normally show no evidence of increased maladjustment or increased rates of suicide or alcoholism. For some people, however, midlife changes can be difficult. Midlife changes must be examined on a case-by-case basis; few generalizations apply to all individuals. Like adolescents, some adults grapple with the transitions in their lives, while others sail through them, not perceiving them as difficult or painful. Their attitudes depend on their unique personalities and ways of coping with the world. I like to think of midlife transitions as normative; most people experience them, and some people experience several. ■

People experience either a sense of satisfaction, self-worth, and accomplishment or a sense that much of their life has been wasted. During this period, many people reach their peak of creativity and achievement (Simonton, 1988). And most people report that the quality of their life is good; in general, they feel happy and more able to regulate their emotional life (Mroczek & Kolarz, 1998). Today, more than ever before, people in midlife tend to have a youthful, buoyant outlook. In the middle of this era, some people go through a crisis similar to that of early adulthood. Sometimes, this is a continuation of the earlier crisis; at other times, it is a new one (see *Experiencing Psychology*).

The years after age 50 are ones of mellowing. People approaching their 60s begin to prepare for late adulthood, making whatever major career and family decisions are necessary before retirement. People in their early 60s generally learn to assess their lives not in terms of money or day-to-day achievements but according to whether life has been meaningful, happy, and cohesive. At this time, people may stop blaming others for their problems and become less concerned about disputes with others. They often try to optimize and control their life, because they know that at least two-thirds of it has passed and they wish to make the most of their remaining years (Lachman & Weaver, 1998). Depending on how well people come to accept themselves at this stage, the next decade can be one of great fulfillment or great despair.

Levinson's fourth and final era, *late adulthood,* covers the years from age 65 on. During retirement, many people relax and enjoy the fruits of their labors. Children, grandchildren, and even great-grandchildren can become the focus of an older person's life.

Levinson's stage theory has a slightly more rigid timetable than does Erikson's, and it focuses on developmental tasks, or themes. Levinson realizes that not all adults succeed in every era, at every task, or achieve feelings of independence. Who does and under what conditions are not clear. Levinson's theory is an alternative to Erikson's, but both suffer from being hard to evaluate experimentally and difficult to apply in making predictions about future behavior.

Gender Differences in Adult Stages. Levinson's theory has received wide acclaim, but it has also been challenged. A major shortcoming is that the theory was based on information gathered from a small sample of middle-class men between the ages of 35 and 45. Levinson developed his theory by studying 40 men in detail over several years. He interviewed the men weekly for several months and again after 2 years. Spouses were interviewed, and extensive biographical data were collected. Levinson's original study did not consider gender differences.

Women apparently follow life stages similar to those of men. But, as children, women are taught different values, goals, and approaches to life, which are often reflected later in their choice of vocations, hobbies, and intellectual pursuits. Women have traditionally sought different careers, although this is changing. In the field of law, for example, women now comprise nearly half of all law school students. However, female attorneys often choose careers that do not follow the traditional associate–partnership ladder chosen by males. In a follow-up book, *The Seasons of a Woman's Life* (1996), Levinson points out the complexities of women's lives based on his interviews with a small sample of women. According to Levinson, women must deal with contradictory roles and responsibilities, which make their lives more complex and difficult to understand than men's. Career women and homemakers go through the same sequence of stages, but these stages differ in their details.

Women still face discrimination in the workplace, and society continues to be ambivalent in its expectations of women.

Some women tend to experience transitions and life events at later ages and in less orderly sequences than men do (Smart & Peterson, 1994). In addition, women experience events such as midlife transitions differently than men; whereas some men approach a midlife crisis at age 40 as a last chance to hold on to their youth, many women see it as a time to reassess, refocus, and revitalize their creative energies (Levinson, 1996). As they approach 50, many women become aware of aging as they notice physical changes in their bodies—especially declining fertility—and these changes create still another transition (Stewart & Ostrove, 1998). However, the idea that women over 50—postmenopausal women—have a tough time is simply not true. Most women of this age feel relief at having gone through menopause, and like their male counterparts, they have a sense of youthfulness, autonomy, and effectiveness in managing their world. Stewart and Ostrove (1998) suggest that midlife brings women an increased sense of personal identity, personal efficacy, and capacity for generativity—women of this age are doing well and feeling both vigorous and well-adjusted.

In a major study of women's transitions, Mercer, Nichols, and Doyle (1989) identified a developmental progression for women. They considered especially the role of motherhood and how it influences the life course of women. In the *launch into adulthood era* (ages 16 through 25), women break away from families to go to school, marry, and work. In the *leveling era* (ages 26 through 30), many women readjust their life course; this is often a time for marriage or separation and divorce. In the *liberation era* (ages 36 through 40), women focus their aspirations, grow personally, and may initiate or change careers. Mercer and colleagues did not find major transitions for women in the years from 40 through 60; they found greater flux and crises in earlier and later years. In the *regeneration/redirection era* (ages 61 through 65), women, like men, adjust to their life choices and prepare for retirement and a more leisurely lifestyle. These two latter stages (liberation and regeneration) are times of great empowerment for women, when growth is often reinforced and purpose redefined, resulting in a sense of true contentment. In the last stage of life, the *creativity/destructiveness era* (age 65 on), women are challenged to adapt to health changes and the loss of spouses and friends; this time may also be characterized by a surge of creativity or, sometimes, depression.

Women still face discrimination in the workplace, and society continues to be ambivalent in its expectations of women. They still have the primary burden of family responsibilities, especially child care; in the aftermath of a divorce, the woman usually gets physical custody of the children. Women often must juggle multiple roles, which place enormous burdens on them (Williams et al., 1991). The assumption of sole child-care responsibility after divorce has sharp economic consequences that alter a woman's lifestyle, mental health, and course of life stages. Further, the issues of women's transitions are often different from those of men's; women tend to focus more on intimacy and relationships than do men (Caffarella & Olson, 1993). Thus, obvious life-stage differences exist for men and women—whether they are upper, middle, or lower class—but even greater differences exist *within* groups of demographically similar men or women. Even popular accounts of life span development, such as Gail Sheehy's *New Passages* (1995) and *Understanding Men's Passages* (1998), recognize the enormous individual differences that exist in people's ability to customize and create their own life courses.

Physical Development in Adulthood

One hundred years ago, only about half of all Americans who reached age 20 lived beyond age 65. Today, most people live well into their 70s, but psychologists know relatively little about those middle years from 20 to 70. Psychologists study childhood physical development extensively, but in comparison pay little attention to adult physical development. Although physical development in adulthood is slower, less dramatic, and generally less visible than that in childhood and adolescence, it does occur.

It is important to distinguish between primary and secondary aging. *Primary aging* is the normal, inevitable change that occurs in every human being and is irreversible and progressive. Such aging happens despite good health, and it can make a person more vulnerable to American society's fast-paced and sometimes stressful lifestyle. *Secondary aging* is aging that is due to extrinsic factors such as disease, environmental pollution, and smoking. Lack of good nutrition is a secondary aging factor that is a principal cause of poor health and aging among the lower-income elderly in the United States.

Fitness Changes. Most of the adult years are years of health and fitness; the leading cause of death, for example, for people ages 25–44 is accidental injury—for example, from motor vehicle crashes. Psychologists often speak of *fitness* as involving both a psychological and a physical sense of well-being. Physically, human beings are at their peak of agility, speed, and strength between ages 18 and 30. From 30 to 40, there is some loss of agility and speed. And between 40 and 60, much greater losses occur. In general, strength, muscle tone, and overall fitness deteriorate gradually from age 30 on. People become more susceptible to disease. Respiratory, circulatory, and blood pressure problems are more apparent; lung capacity and physical strength are significantly reduced. Decreases in bone mass and strength occur, especially in women after menopause; the resulting condition is called *osteoporosis.* Immune system responsivity and the ability to fight disease diminish significantly among older adults.

Sensory Changes. In early adulthood, most sensory abilities remain fairly stable. As the years pass, however, adults must contend with almost inevitable sensory losses. Reaction time slows. Vision, hearing, taste, and smell require a higher level of stimulation than they did at a younger age. Older people, for example, usually are unable to make fine visual discriminations without the aid of glasses, have limited capacity for dark adaptation, and are at greater risk for glaucoma, cataracts, and retinal detachment. Older adults often have some degree of hearing loss, especially in the high-frequency ranges. By age 65, many people can no longer hear very high-frequency sounds, and some are unable to hear ordinary speech. The hearing loss is greater for men than for women.

Sexual Changes. In adults of both sexes, advancing years bring changes in sexual behavior and desire as well as physical changes related to sexuality. For example, in the child-rearing years, women's and men's sexual desires are sometimes moderated by the stresses of raising a family and juggling a work schedule. Women often experience an increase in sexual desire in their 30s and 40s, but men achieve erections less rapidly at that age. For women, midlife changes in hormones lead to the cessation of ovulation and menstruation at about 50, a process known as *menopause.* Menopause is generally seen as a transition, after which women no longer have to deal with birth control issues; some women, however, perceive it as the beginning of old age and an end to youthful femininity. At about the same age, men's testosterone levels decrease, their ejaculations are weaker and briefer, and their desire for sexual intercourse typically decreases from adolescent levels (Rowland et al., 1993). Nevertheless, older people continue to engage in sexual activities and to find them enjoyable, and a significant percentage find their sexual activities more satisfying than when they were younger (National Council on Aging, 1998). According to the National Council on Aging, sex remains a significant part of life for many older Americans. Nearly half of all Americans aged 60 or older engage in sexual activity at least once a month. If older people are not active sexually, it is usually because they lack a partner or have a disabling medical condition. As with their younger counterparts, however, there is considerable variation from person to person.

Cognitive Changes in Adulthood

Perhaps the most distressing change that may occur with aging is a decline in cognitive ability. Although many people believe that declines in intellectual functioning are drastic and universal, they are not. However, researchers do agree that certain cognitive abilities, especially in mathematics and memory functions, deteriorate with age in many people.

However, it is difficult to predict exactly how and to what extent intellectual functioning changes. A major problem is defining intellectual functioning itself.

Older people are likely to do poorly on standardized intelligence tests, not because their intelligence is low but because the tests require the manipulation of objects during a timed interval—and older people often have a slower reaction time or decreased manual dexterity (often because of arthritis). In addition, many older persons do not do well on intelligence tests because they are not as highly motivated as younger persons are. To overcome these disadvantages, researchers have devised new methodologies for studying intelligence in older people.

Although most research indicates that cognitive abilities and memory functions typically decrease with advancing age, many of the changes are of little importance for day-to-day functioning (Salthouse, 1999). For example, overall vocabulary decreases only slightly. Moreover, some of the changes observed in laboratory tasks (for example, reaction-time tasks) are small and can be forestalled or reversed through cognitive interventions. Yet there is no doubt that the brain encodes information differently in the young than in the old.

For more than 35 years, K. Warner Schaie has been following thousands of men and women and testing them at regular intervals on various cognitive tasks. He argues that there is extreme variability in both the types and causes of cognitive deficits. He suggests that changes in health and family situation may produce severe biological and psychological consequences that, in turn, affect intellectual functioning (Schaie, 1994). See Table 9.7 for a summary of age-related changes in intellectual skills through adulthood.

Whatever the causes, changes in intellectual functioning that occur with age may influence behavior but are seldom devastating. Up to the ages of 60 through 65, there is little decline in learning or memory; motivation, interest, and recent educational experience (or lack of it) are probably more important than age with regard to a person's ability to master complex knowledge.

Researchers generally acknowledge that some age-related decrements do occur (e.g., Salthouse, 1999); however, such effects are often less apparent in cognitively active individuals (Shimamura et al., 1995). Many researchers suggest a "use it and you are less likely to lose it" approach (Krampe & Ericsson, 1996). When deficits do occur, older individuals can compensate to optimize their performance. The truth is that most Americans are aging well and that with appropriate health care and social support systems, older individuals can do just fine, especially in everyday situations.

Remember that, despite evidence that old age takes a toll, remarkable examples of achievements by people 70 years old or older are everywhere. Golda Meir, for example, became Prime Minister of Israel at age 70. Benjamin Franklin invented bifocal eyeglasses at 74 and helped to frame the Constitution of the United States at 81. Arthur Rubinstein, the Polish-born American concert pianist, gave one of his greatest recitals at New York's Carnegie Hall at age 81. A list of the achievements of people who have lived a long life would be endless.

Personality Development in Adulthood

A basic tenet of most personality theories is that, regardless of day-to-day variations, an individual's personality remains stable over time. That is, despite deviations from normal patterns of development, the way a person copes with life tends to remain fairly

Table 9.7 Summary of Age-Related Changes in Intellectual Skills

Ages 20–40	Ages 40–65	Age 65 and Older
Peak intellectual ability between about 20 and 35	Maintenance of skill on measures of verbal intelligence; some decline of skill on measures of performance intelligence; decline usually not functionally significant till age 60 or older	Some loss of verbal intelligence; most noticeable in adults with poorer health, lower levels of activity, and less education
Optimal performance on memory tasks	Little change in performance on memory tasks, except perhaps some slowing later in this period	Slowing of retrieval processes and other memory processes; less skillful use of coding strategies for new memories
Peak performance on laboratory tests of problem solving	Peak performance on real-life problem-solving tasks and many verbal abilities	Decline in problem-solving performance on both laboratory and real-life tests

Source: Adapted from Bee (1987).

consistent throughout her or his lifetime. But research shows that personality may also be sensitive to the unique experiences of the individual, especially during the adult years. Major life events—for example, a child's tragic death, a highly stressful job situation, or a divorce—can, not surprisingly, alter an individual's personality.

The adult years are filled with great personal challenges and opportunities and therefore require people to be innovative, flexible, and adaptive. Positive changes during adulthood—the development of a sense of generativity, the fulfillment of yearnings for love and respect—usually depend on some degree of success during earlier life stages. Adults who continue to have an especially narrow outlook are less likely to experience personality growth in later life.

Women have undergone special scrutiny since the early 1970s. As we have seen, researchers now recognize that the profession of psychology was male-dominated in the 1950s and generated a host of personality theories based on studies of men. Not surprisingly, these failed to address women's unique personality and development issues. Personality researchers acknowledge that contemporary women face challenges in the work force and the home that were not conceived of three decades ago. These challenges have given rise to the "supermom" phenomenon—women trying to achieve home, family, career, and personal satisfaction, all within the same span of years. Serious research into the psychological life of women is just beginning to emerge.

Aspects of personality development are discussed in further detail in Chapter 10. 

Think Critically

- What do you think are the implications of the finding that women follow a different developmental progression than do men?

Late Adulthood: Limitations and Possibilities

Focus on issues and ideas

- Developing an awareness of the myths and stereotypes of the elderly and why a change is needed
- How Alzheimer's disease ravages both individual patients and their families
- Understanding how hospice care has aided both the dying individuals and their families

As we grow older, we age experientially as well as physically; that is, we gather experiences and usually expand our worldview. Nevertheless, in Western society, growing older is not always easy, especially because of the negative stereotypes associated with the aging process. Today, however, people are healthier than ever before, are approaching their later years with vigor, and often look forward to second and sometimes third careers. In general, being over age 65 brings with it new developmental tasks—retirement, coping with health issues, and maintenance of an adequate standard of living.

How older people view themselves depends in part on how society treats them. Many Asian and African cultures greatly respect the elderly for their wisdom and maturity; in such societies, gray hair is a mark of distinction, not an embarrassment. In contrast, the United States is a youth-oriented society in which people spend a fortune on everything from hair dyes to facelifts to make themselves look younger. However, because the average age of Americans is increasing, how the elderly are perceived by their fellow Americans and how they perceive themselves may be changing.

Approximately 12% of the U.S. population—or more than 33 million Americans—is 65 years old or older. According to the U.S. Bureau of the Census, the proportion of elderly people is expected to increase to between 20% and 25% of the total population by 2030, and the number of Americans over 65 will exceed 60 million by then and 78 million by 2050. At present, the average life expectancy at birth in the United States is about 76 years, and the oldest of the old—those over 85—are the most rapidly growing elderly age group. Life expectancy is different for men and women, however. Women live about 6 years longer than men, on average.

For many people, the years after age 60 are filled with new activities and interests. Both men and women enjoy doing things that they may have had to forgo earlier because of family commitments. Financially, two-thirds of American retirees are covered by pension plans provided by their employers, and virtually all receive Social Security checks. Socially, most older people maintain close friendships and stay in touch with family members. Some, however, have financial problems, and others experience loneliness and isolation because many of their friends and relatives have died or they have lost touch with their families. In the United States, there are now as many people over the age of 60 as there are under the age of 7, yet funding for programs to support the health and psychological well-being of older people is relatively limited.

Myths, Realities, and Stereotypes

There is a widely held myth that older people are less intelligent than younger people, less able to care for themselves, inflexible, and sickly. The reality is that many elderly people are as competent and capable as they were in their earlier adulthood. They work, play golf, run marathons, socialize, and stay politically aware and active. Most older adults maintain a regular and satisfying sex life (Bretschneider & McCoy, 1988) and good mental health. Some people conduct life's activities in a frail, disorganized manner, even when young; others, although chronologically old, are youthful and vigorous.

Ageism. Stereotypes about the elderly have given rise to **ageism**—prejudice against the elderly and the discrimination that follows from it. Ageism is prevalent in the job market, in which older people are not given the same opportunities as their younger coworkers, and in housing and health care. It is exceptionally prevalent in the media—on television and in newspapers and magazines—and in everyday language (Schaie, 1993). Schmidt and Boland (1986) examined everyday language to learn how people perceive older adults. They found interesting differences. For example, *elder statesman* implies that a person is experienced, wise, or perhaps conservative. However, *old statesman* might suggest that a person is past his prime, tired, or useless. The phrase *old people* may allude to positive traits of older adults—for example, being the perfect grandparent—or to negative qualities such as grouchiness or mental deficiencies. What does *old* mean?

Older people who are perceived as representing negative stereotypes are more likely to suffer discrimination than those who appear to represent more positive stereotypes. This means that an older person who appears healthy, bright, and alert is more likely to be treated with the same respect shown to younger people. By contrast, an older adult who appears less capable may not be given the same treatment. First impressions have a potent effect on people's behavior. This seems to be particularly true for older people. Ageism can be reduced if people recognize the diversity that exists among aging populations.

Brain Disorders. Aging was once seen as almost inevitably accompanied, sooner or later, by *senility*, a term used to describe cognitive changes that occur in older people. Today, these cognitive deficits are known to be caused by brain disorders, sometimes termed *dementias*, that occur only in *some* older people. **Dementias** are impairments of mental functioning and global cognitive abilities in otherwise alert individuals, causing memory loss and related symptoms, and typically having a progressive nature (that is, growing worse over time). Dementia usually involves a loss of function in at least two areas of behavior, including language, memory, visual and spatial abilities, and judgment, which significantly interferes with a person's daily activities. It is important to point out that dementia is not a normal part of the aging process. Dementias are caused by abnormal disease processes and can affect younger as well as older persons. Only 0.4% of people aged 60 to 65 suffer from dementias. The percentage increases to 3.6% of people aged 75 to 79 and to 23.8% of those aged 85 to 93 (Selkoe, 1992). Memory loss from dementia often occurs first for recent events and later for past events. Additional symptoms of dementias include loss of language skills, reduced capacity for abstract thinking, personality changes, and loss of a sense of time and place. Severe and disabling dementias affect about 1.5 million Americans. With the increasing number of elderly citizens, these statistics are on the rise.

More than 70 conditions cause dementias. Among them is AIDS; AIDS patients with failing immune systems cannot combat brain infections, which in turn can lead to dementia. To diagnose dementia, a complete medical and neuropsychological evaluation is usually required. Brain scans such as CT or MRI are an important part of the process. Much of the diagnostic procedure is an attempt to rule out treatable causes of dementia. Some conditions that cause dementia can be treated, and the treatment often halts (but does not necessarily reverse) the dementia. *Reversible dementias*, which can be caused by malnutrition, alcoholism, or toxins (poisons), usually affect younger people. *Irreversible dementias* are of two types: multiple infarct dementia and Alzheimer's disease. *Multiple infarct dementia* is usually caused by two or more small strokes (ruptures of small blood vessels in the brain); it results in a slow degeneration of the brain. **Alzheimer's disease** is a chronic and pro-

Ageism: Prejudice against the elderly and the discrimination that follows from it.

Dementia: Impairment of mental functioning and global cognitive abilities in otherwise alert individuals, causing memory loss and related symptoms and typically having a progressive nature.

Alzheimer's [ALTZ-hy-merz] disease: A chronic and progressive disorder of the brain that is the most common cause of degenerative dementia.

gressive disorder of the brain and the most common cause of degenerative dementia in the United States. Named after Dr. Alois Alzheimer, a German physician who first studied its symptoms, it could well be the most widespread neurological disorder of all time.

People of all kinds can be victims of Alzheimer's disease, and all confront an unkind fate. In addition to memory loss, language deterioration, poor visual/spatial skills, and indifferent attitudes characterize this disease. It accounts for about 50% of the cases of progressive memory loss in aging individuals. (Vascular dementia and other similar disease processes account for 10–20%, and depression for about 1–5%. The other causes are metabolic, infectious, traumatic, inflammatory, and mass lesion disorders.)

As the population grows older, the number of cases of Alzheimer's disease increases. Currently, there are about 4 million diagnosed Alzheimer's patients in the United States and nearly 20 million worldwide; in addition, there are an untold number of undiagnosed cases. One recent estimate suggests that the numbers may be greater than those usually cited: 1 in 10 people over 65 may have the disease, and almost half of those over 85 may have it (Evans et al., 1989). By the year 2040, the number of Americans with Alzheimer's disease may exceed 6 million. Alzheimer's disease affects women more than men, even after adjusting for the higher number of women who survive to old age. Because Alzheimer's is a degenerative disease, its progression cannot be stopped; it is irreversible and ultimately ends in death. To date, there is no fully effective method of prevention, treatment, or cure. What causes this disease? What are its psychological impacts? How does it affect families?

The impact of Alzheimer's disease on the patient is enormous; the disease severely damages the quality of life. At the beginning, patients are not necessarily stripped of their vigor or strength, but they slowly become confused and helpless. Initially, they may forget to do small things. Later, they may forget appointments, anniversaries, and the like. The forgetfulness is often overlooked at first. Jokes and other coping strategies cover up for memory lapses. The memory loss is not always apparent; some days are better than others. Ultimately, however, the disorder grows worse. Alzheimer's patients start to have trouble finding their way home and remembering their own names and the names of their spouses and children. At least initially, retrieval of episodic memories is affected more than retrieval of semantic memories, and short-term memory is more likely than long-term memory to be impaired (Backman & Lipinska, 1993). Patients' personalities also change. They may become abrupt, abusive, and hostile to family members. Within months, or sometimes years, they lose their speech and language functions. Eventually, they lose all control of memory and even of basic bodily functions.

What Causes Alzheimer's Disease? A definitive diagnosis of Alzheimer's disease can be made only by an examination of brain tissue after death; a tangled bundle of neurons is the typical finding. Brain scans usually confirm that the patient's neurons seem to be twisted, gnarled, and coated with *plaque* (fibrous tissue that impedes neural transmission). These tangled bundles of fibers are known as *neurofibrillary tangles.* Levels of neurotransmitters—specifically, acetylcholine—are usually low; there is usually a loss of functioning neurons.

Scientific findings about possible causes of the disease come from a wide variety of sources, and it is generally argued that there are multiple routes to the disease. Correlational research shows that Alzheimer's disease tends to run in families, which suggests a genetic basis for the disorder or at least for a predisposition to it. Some researchers posit a depletion of enzymes; others suggest an accumulation of toxins; still others focus on neurotransmitters, insensitivity of receptors, and metabolic patterns (Joseph, 1992). Genetic mutations have been implicated. Blood supply problems, immune system factors, head injuries, nutrition, and viruses—both latent viruses and newly introduced ones—have also been proposed as contributors to the disease.

In studying cell biology, researchers have found a highly orchestrated form of cell death that seems to be implicated in Alzheimer's—it is referred to as *apoptosis,* or programmed cell death. Some proteins found in the brain and body seem to drive cells to apoptosis under certain conditions (Barinaga, 1998). Proteins that accumulate in the brain of Alzheimer's patients seem to kill cells involved in memory unless they have another specific protein (called a *nerve growth factor,* or

NGF) bound to them (Rabizadeh et al., 1993). It is speculated that memory loss might be averted or stopped by treating cells with NGF or other drugs that mimic the action of NGF.

Not only do researchers not know the causes of Alzheimer's disease, no one has developed an effective treatment. Researchers are beginning to think that there are many types of Alzheimer's disease, some of which may be hereditary and some of which may be the consequence of early life events, such as head injuries. Research is showing that there may be specific genes on specific chromosomes that cause nearly all of the cases of early-onset familial Alzheimer's; such research may lead to an understanding of the biochemical causes of the disease (Sherrington et al., 1995). The discovery of these genes may lead to diagnostic tests that can be offered individuals who are at risk because of family history.

The expected increase in the elderly population means that the United States will see more and more Alzheimer's patients. The financial and emotional cost to patients and their families is astounding because the patients can live in a dependent, nonfunctional state for years. Nationally, the monetary cost of caring for individuals with Alzheimer's disease and related dementias is enormous; conservative estimates range between $38 and $42 billion per year. Caring for an Alzheimer's patient imposes immense physical, emotional, and financial hardships. The patient's loved ones "walk a tightrope between meeting the patient's needs and preserving their own well-being" (Heckler, 1985, p. 1241). Alzheimer's disease changes family life in irreversible ways; most patients are placed in nursing homes or hospitals after extensive and exhausting care at home. Brody, Lawton, and Liebowitz (1984, p. 1331) assert: "In the overwhelming majority of cases, nursing home placement occurs only after responsible family caregivers have endured prolonged, unrelenting caring (often for years) and no longer have the capacity to continue their caregiving efforts." Nursing home care for Alzheimer's patients in the United States is increasing at an unprecedented rate.

The financial and emotional cost to patients and their families is astounding because the patients can live in a dependent, nonfunctional state for years.

Death: The Final Transition

People's overall health deteriorates as they age. For men, the probability of dying doubles in each decade after midlife. In some people, blood pressure rises, cardiac output decreases, and the likelihood of stroke increases, often as a result of cardiovascular disease, which also affects intellectual functioning by decreasing blood flow to the brain. Some individuals experience what is known as *terminal drop*—a rapid decline in intellectual functioning in the year before death. However, although there is evidence for the terminal drop, no satisfactory method exists for predicting death on the basis of poor performance on intelligence or neuropsychological tests (Botwinick, 1984).

If you are young, perhaps an adolescent, you are more likely than older people to die from an auto accident or AIDS. But the majority of the population die at an older age, and the leading causes of death in the United States are heart disease, cancer, strokes, and accidents; in fact, 7 out of 10 older Americans die from one of the first three of these causes. The number of Americans who succumb to heart disease has decreased because of improved health, reduced smoking, and positive lifestyle changes. Rates of strokes are significantly lower among men and women who do not smoke, who manage their high blood pressure, and who regularly exercise. But cancer continues to increase; despite good cure rates, half of all cancers are found in men and women over the age of 65. A healthy lifestyle decreases the likelihood of disease, and research shows that older adults can achieve the fitness levels of younger adults (Danner & Edwards, 1992). Reducing risk factors can reduce early deaths, and this is best accomplished through health promotion and education (Becker, 1993).

Everyone recognizes that death is inevitable; but in the 20th century, few people actually witness death (Aiken, 1985). Before this century, most people died in bed at home, where other people were likely to be with them. Today, although about 8 million Americans experience the death of an immediate family member each year, nearly 80% of those people die in hospitals and nursing homes. In part because of the increasing age of the U.S. population, **thanatology,** the study of the psychological and medical aspects of death and dying, has become an interdisciplinary specialty. Researchers and theorists in several areas—including theology, law, history, psychology, sociology, and medicine—have come together to better understand death and dying. For psychologists, dealing with the process of dying is especially complicated because people do not like to talk or think about death. Nevertheless, considerable progress has been made toward understanding the psychology of dying.

Kübler-Ross's Stage Theory. Elisabeth Kübler-Ross has become famous for her studies of the way people respond psychologically to their impending death (Kübler-Ross, 1969, 1975). She believes that people in Western society fear death because it is unfamiliar, often hidden away in hospitals. She suggests that a way to reduce this fear is to involve members of a dying person's family more closely in what is, in fact, a very natural process. She contends that it is better for people to die at home than in an unfamiliar hospital room. In addition to imposing emotional stress on the terminally ill patient, impending death also causes stress for the patient's family. Kübler-Ross has drawn attention to the additional stress on family members created by interactions with doctors, especially in impersonal hospital settings. Like many other physicians and psychologists, she believes that a more homelike setting can help patients and their families deal better with death. One answer to the problem of death in institutional settings is the hospice, discussed below.

Kübler-Ross was one of the first researchers to use a stage theory to discuss people's reactions to their own death and that of loved ones. People who learn they are terminally ill, in Kübler-Ross's view, typically go through five stages: *denial,* which serves as a buffer against the shocking news; *anger,* directed against family, friends, or medical staff; *bargaining,* in which people try to gain more time by "making a deal" with God, themselves, or their doctors; *depression,* often caused by the pain of their illness and guilt over inconveniencing their family; and finally, *acceptance,* in which people stop fighting and accept death.

Kübler-Ross's theory has been subject to considerable criticism. Not all researchers find the same sequence of events in the dying process (Stephenson, 1985). Critics argue that the sequence outlined by Kübler-Ross does not apply to all people and that the stages are not necessarily experienced in the order she suggests. However, Kübler-Ross contends that her theory was intended to be an overall outline, not a strict set of steps.

Kübler-Ross has also been criticized for her research techniques. Her interviews were not very systematic, she offers few statistics, and some of her ideas rely more on intuition than on facts established through scientific methods. Specifically, her data-gathering techniques have been condemned as highly subjective. Schaie and Willis (1986) have suggested that the ideas put forth by Kübler-Ross should not be considered a theory but "an insightful discussion of some of the attitudes that are often displayed by people who are dying" (p. 483). Although Kübler-Ross's ideas about death and dying may not be universally valid, many practitioners find them useful in guiding new medical staff through the difficult task of helping the dying, especially those who are facing premature death because of illnesses such as cancer.

Whether or not one accepts Kübler-Ross's stages as typical, it is clear that, in general, people fear the process of dying and the accompanying pain, disability, and dependency that often precede death—although they are more fearful of death in middle age than at any other time in the life cycle. However, as in all areas of life, different people view death with different attitudes. Religious people fear death less than others, and financially stable people have less negative attitudes toward death than do poor people. Moreover, most psychologists believe that the ways in which people have dealt with previous times of stress in their lives largely predict how they will deal with dying.

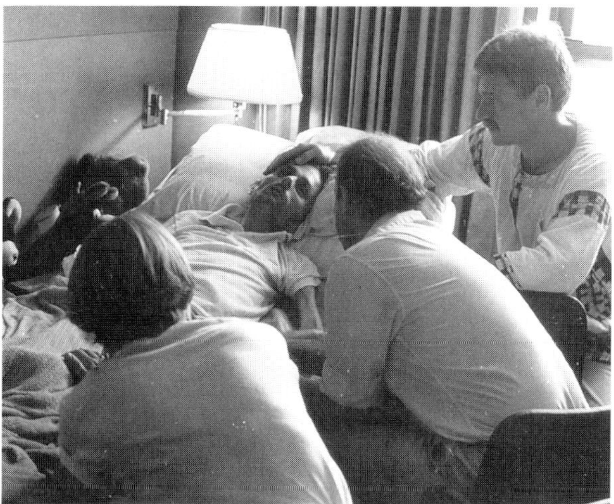

Hospice Care. *Hospices* were initially conceived of as special facilities established to provide efficient and humane care to terminally ill patients and their families. They were to address emotional, social, and spiritual needs in addition to physical ones and to combine humane treatment with sensitivity to the financial costs of patient care (Butterfield-Picard & Magno, 1982; Smyser, 1982). Today, in the United States, hospices are not merely places—they are agencies. A *hospice* is thus an alternative source of care that helps provide a variety of resources to terminally ill patients and their families. Hospice care takes psychological principles used in therapy and puts them to work in the day-to-day care of the terminally ill. Hospice care focuses on the psychological needs of the patient, while acknowledging that death is inevitable and imminent.

The hospice approach is not appropriate for every dying person. Using a hospice requires specific kinds of

Thanatology: The study of the psychological and medical aspects of death and dying.

commitment from the patient and family members. Therefore, before providing care, hospices evaluate both the patient and the family. Hospices and their staffs operate under a set of guidelines that differ from those used by hospitals and nursing homes that care for the terminally ill (Butterfield-Picard & Magno, 1982):

- Control of decisions concerning the patient's care rests with the patient and the family.
- Many aspects of traditional care, such as life-support procedures, are discontinued when the patient desires.
- Pain is kept to a minimum so that the patient can experience life as fully as possible until death.
- A team of professionals is available around the clock.
- Surroundings are homelike rather than clinical; often the patient is actually at home.
- When possible, family members and the hospice team are the caregivers.
- Family members receive counseling before and after the patient dies.

There are currently over 2000 hospices in the United States treating about 350,000 patients—in fact, hospice care is one of the fastest-growing segments of the health care delivery system. Family members who use hospices, as well as friends and practitioners, have to deal with ethical and practical questions about care and costs, life-support systems, and medications. To help these concerned individuals, researchers and applied psychologists are exploring such issues as how to determine exactly when death occurs, how the dying should be treated, and how families and friends can cope better with the dying process, with grief over their loss, and with guilt about their feelings of relief.

Think Critically

- How might the cognitive changes associated with aging influence the health and well-being of older adults?
- What special emotional problems might need to be addressed when a terminally ill person enters a hospice program?

www.abacon.com/leftononline

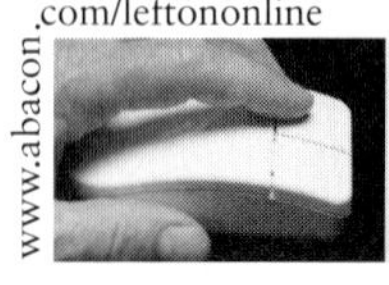

Your password-protected Website allows you access to the most comprehensive set of materials in The Psychology Place.

Summary and Review

Key Issues, Theories, and Research Designs

What is developmental psychology?

What are some issues in the study of human development and some methods of studying development?

KEY TERM
developmental psychology, p. 234

The First Ten Months

Distinguish between an embryo and a fetus.

How is a newborn equipped to deal with the world?

KEY TERMS
zygote, p. 235; embryo, p. 236; fetus, p. 236; placenta, p. 236; teratogen, p. 237; Babinski reflex, p. 238; Moro reflex, p. 238; rooting reflex, p. 239; sucking reflex, p. 239; grasping reflex, p. 239

Cognitive Development

What is the difference between Piaget's concepts of assimilation and accommodation?

Describe Piaget's stages of cognitive development.

KEY TERMS
scheme, p. 240; assimilation, p. 241; accommodation, p. 241; sensorimotor stage, p. 241; preoperational stage, p. 242; egocentrism, p. 242; decentration, p. 242; concrete operational stage, p. 242; conservation, p. 242; formal operational stage, p. 243; theory of mind, p. 245

Moral Reasoning

How do Piaget's and Kohlberg's views of the development of morality differ?

What was Gilligan's main criticism of Kohlberg's work?

KEY TERM
morality, p. 246

Emotional and Social Development

What is attachment, and why is it important?

How permanent is temperament?

When do children begin to develop a sense of self?

What are gender stereotypes?

What is friendship?

Describe Erikson's stage theory of psychosocial development.

KEY TERMS
attachment, p. 248; temperament, p. 251; gender stereotype, p. 253; androgynous, p. 255

Adolescence: Bridging the Gap

Distinguish between puberty and adolescence.

What are the major changes experienced by adolescents?

Describe some factors that influence cognitive and social development in adolescence, especially with respect to gender similarities and differences.

How have adolescent sexual behavior and attitudes changed in recent years?

KEY TERMS
adolescence, p. 258; puberty, p. 258; secondary sex characteristics, p. 259; imaginary audience, p. 261; personal fable, p. 261; gender identity, p. 262; gender schema theory, p. 263; gender role, p. 263; gender role stereotype, p. 263

Adulthood: Years of Stability and Change

Describe Erikson's last four stages of psychosocial development.

Describe Levinson's theory of adult development.

Differentiate between life transitions and crises.

Do women's life stages parallel men's?

Describe the effects of aging.

Late Adulthood: Limitations and Possibilities

Who are the aged, and how is life different in late adulthood?

What are the essential elements of Kübler-Ross's theory of dying?

How can hospices aid the dying and their families?

KEY TERMS
ageism, p. 272; dementia, p. 272; Alzheimer's disease, p. 272; thanatology, p. 274

Self-Test

1. A researcher tests the same group of children at ages 2, 4, and 6. What experimental design is being used?
   A. cross-sectional research design
   B. longitudinal research design
   C. trisectional research design
   D. continuous research design
2. Before a fertilized egg implants into the uterine wall, it is called a(n):
   A. zygote
   B. embryo
   C. fetus
   D. neonate
3. When a child realizes that a toy continues to exist when it is out of sight, that child has developed:
   A. conservation
   B. egocentrism
   C. decentration
   D. object permanence
4. Meghan knows her dad's name is John, and she is introduced to a family friend who is also named John. She knows that more than one person can have the same name. Meghan has
   A. adapted to roles
   B. conserved number
   C. assimilated the naming process
   D. accommodated to language
5. The only reason Leo does not take a fresh cookie off the plate is because his mother would yell at him. At which level of morality is Leo operating?
   A. preconventional morality
   B. postconventional morality
   C. midconventional morality
   D. conventional morality
6. Most babies have ____________ attachment; they become distressed when their principal caregiver leaves, but they are easily comforted.
   A. avoidant
   B. resistant
   C. secure
   D. disoriented
7. Children and adolescents who have many friendships benefit from all of the following except:
   A. competitiveness
   B. social competence
   C. providing confidant
   D. learning intimacy

8. At which of Erikson's stages are toilet training and mastery of physical skills important?
   A. initiative versus guilt
   B. autonomy versus shame and doubt
   C. trust versus mistrust
   D. industry versus inferiority

9. What percentage of adolescents experience serious difficulties and turmoil?
   A. 95%
   B. 75%
   C. 50%
   D. 30%

10. Which is an example of a primary sex characteristic?
    A. breasts
    B. facial hair
    C. testes
    D. increased body mass

11. Two important influences on an adolescent's self-esteem are:
    A. peers and friends
    B. peers and parents
    C. parents and family
    D. parents and teachers

12. Paul has been dating a lot, trying to decide whether to settle down and get married. Which of Erikson's stages is Paul most likely in?
    A. identity versus role confusion
    B. intimacy versus isolation
    C. generativity versus stagnation
    D. ego integrity versus despair

13. Sarah's dad, who is 44, recently bought a new Harley Davidson motorcycle. He had never ridden a motorcycle before but now drives his new one to work and around the neighborhood on weekends. According to Levinson, this way of coping should be called:
    A. midlife crisis
    B. midlife transition
    C. midlife trauma
    D. midlife generativity

14. Which type of dementia is characterized by plaques and neurofibrillary tangles?
    A. Alzheimer's disease
    B. multiple infarct dementia
    C. reversible dementias
    D. AIDS-related dementia

15. According to Kübler-Ross, terminally ill people go through a series of stages before death. The order of these stages are
    A. anger, denial, depression, bargaining, acceptance
    B. acceptance, bargaining, anger, depression, denial
    C. depression, denial, anger, bargaining, acceptance
    D. denial, anger, bargaining, depression, acceptance

Personality and Its Assessment

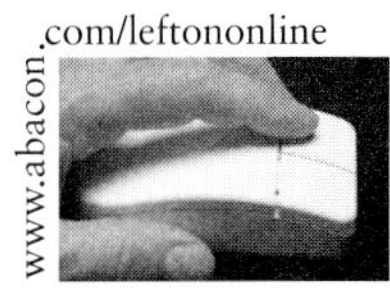

Go to your password-protected Website for full-color art, Weblinks, and more!

Who has had the greatest impact on who you are as a person? Choose the best answer.

1. My parents—I turned out pretty much the way they wanted me to.
2. My parents—but I turned out just the opposite of how they intended.
3. I did—I decided who I wanted to be and I've become that person.
4. I really can't remember ever deciding to be this way; I've always been just who I am.

If you asked a personality psychologist why you turned out the way you did, the answer would depend on his or her orientation to personality. A behaviorist would choose answer 1—your parents and the environment you grow up in shape your behavior, especially during the early years. A psychoanalytically oriented psychologist (a follower of Freud) would choose answer 2—your parents shape you, especially during the early years, and in reaction you choose opposite behaviors to disguise, repress, or modify your feelings of being directed. A humanist would choose answer 3, arguing that you decide who you will become because you are a free agent and are always trying to be your best. A biologically oriented psychologist would be most likely to choose answer 4 and assert that you have little choice, that much of your personality is laid down at conception by your genetic makeup.

The correct answer is probably "none of the above," because personality is a mixture of biological predisposition, learning, shaping, choice, and environment. The fact is that it is a complicated process to characterize people, and especially difficult to do so from a very small sample of the range of behaviors in which they engage. No other phenomenon is as resistant to easy definition and assessment as the human character. ■

For psychologists, **personality** is a set of relatively enduring behavioral characteristics (including thoughts) and internal predispositions that describe how a person reacts to the environment. Psychologists recognize that an individual's behavior is not consistent in every situation.

What causes people to have certain behavioral characteristics? To answer this question, some personality theorists focus on day-to-day behaviors that characterize people; others focus on the inner conflicts that shape personality. Some see human beings as individuals who react to the environment. Others emphasize the internal, even genetic, influences that impel people to act. Personality theorists must consider social psychological concepts such as attitudes, motivational concepts such as expectancies, and even biological theories that suggest that inherited predispositions determine such personality characteristics as shyness. The earliest personality theorists (for example, Freud) tended to think of personality as something stable within the individual. Later theorists began to recognize that personality depends on a host of environmental situations. Contemporary theorists, especially those with behavioral and cognitive orientations, tend to focus more on environmental determinants of personality than on internal predispositions.

Personality theories consist of interrelated ideas and facts put forward to explain and predict behavior and mental processes. Being able to predict and explain behavior enables psychologists to help people anticipate situations and express their feelings in manageable and reasonable ways. Personality theories focus on a few key questions:

- Does nature or nurture play a greater role in day-to-day behavior?
- Do unconscious processes direct behavior?
- Are human behavior patterns fixed?
- Does a person's behavior depend on the situation?
- What makes people behave consistently?

We begin by examining psychoanalytic theory—an approach to personality that focuses on how the unconscious mind directs day-to-day behavior. This approach is based on the well-known and widely disputed theory of Sigmund Freud. (I)

(I) Psychoanalytic Theory: Unconscious Drives and Defenses

Focus on issues and ideas

- The three key concepts of Freud's theory of personality
- The structure of consciousness in directing behavior
- How aspects of personality are established and maintained
- The key ideas of the neo-Freudians

Sigmund Freud (1856–1939) was an Austrian physician whose influence on psychology was so great that some of his basic concepts are taken for granted. Such terms as *ego, oral fixation, death wish, anal retentive, Freudian slip, unconscious motivation,* and *Oedipus complex* are part of people's everyday language. However, when Freud introduced his ideas, he was seen as strange and off-base. At the time, psychologists thought the proper subject matter of psychology was observable behavior and its measurement. Studying the unconscious and suggesting that children have sexual experiences, as Freud did, were, to say the least, out of the mainstream.

Freud used hypnosis and later a process known as *free association* to treat people with physical and emotional problems. (We will discuss free association in Chapter 14.) Most of his patients were from the middle and upper classes of Austrian society. Many were married women of wealth and position who, because they lived in a repressive society, had limited opportunities for the release of anxiety and tension. Freud noticed that many of them needed to discuss their problems and often felt better after having done so. From his studies of hypnosis and his work with these patients, he began to formulate a theory of behavior; many of his early conclusions focused on the role of sexual frustration in producing physical symptoms. Over time, Freud developed an elaborate theory of personality and an accompanying approach to therapy: The former came to be called *psychoanalytic theory,* and the latter, *psychoanalysis.*

Three Key Concepts

Many psychological theories are based on a pivotal concept around which they grow. Freud's theory has three such concepts: psychic determinism, unconscious motivation, and conflict. **Psychic determinism** is the psychoanalytic assumption that all feelings, thoughts, and actions have a purpose and are determined by past events. For example, people do not have accidental slips of the tongue or random changes of mood. Instead, past events cause all actions. Moreover, most of a person's thoughts and behavior are determined by unconscious motivation. **Unconscious motivation** is the psychoanalytic assumption that behavior is determined by desires, goals, and internal states of which an individual is unaware, because they are buried deep within the unconscious. By definition, people are unaware of the contents and workings of the unconscious.

Freud also theorized that people are constantly in conflict. They are energized to act the way they do because of two basic instinctual drives: the drive toward *life,* which is expressed through sex and sexual energy, and the drive toward *death,* which is expressed through aggression. These instincts are buried deep within the unconscious, and their expression is not always socially acceptable. Freud wrote little about aggression until late in his life; he focused mainly on sexual instincts, which he termed the **libido**—the instinctual (and sexual) life force that, working on the pleasure principle and seeking immediate gratification, energizes the id. (We'll look more closely at the id shortly.) In his later writings, Freud referred to the libido as "life energy." His critics claim that he was inordinately preoccupied with sexual matters.

When people exhibit socially unacceptable behaviors or have feelings they consider socially unacceptable, especially sexual feelings, they often experience self-punishment, guilt, and anxiety—all forms of inner conflict. Freud's theory thus describes a conflict between a person's instinctual (often unconscious) need for gratification and society's demand that each individual be socialized. In other words, it paints a picture of human beings caught in a conflict between basic sexual and aggressive desires and socialization. For Freud, a person's basic desire is to maximize instinctual gratification while minimizing punishment and guilt.

Structure of Consciousness and the Mind

In his theory, Freud considered the sources and consequences of conflict and how people deal with it. For Freud, the energy to deal with conflict is biologically determined and lies in the structure of consciousness.

Structure of Consciousness. According to Freud, consciousness consists of three levels of awareness. The first level, the **conscious,** consists of the thoughts, feelings, and actions of which people are

Personality: A set of relatively enduring behavioral characteristics and internal predispositions that describe how a person reacts to the environment.

Psychic [SYE-kick] determinism: The psychoanalytic assumption that all feelings, thoughts, and actions have a purpose and are determined by past events.

Unconscious motivation: The psychoanalytic assumption that behavior is determined by desires, goals, and internal states of which an individual is unaware, because they are buried deep within the unconscious.

Libido [lih-BEE-doe]: In Freud's theory, the instinctual (and sexual) life force that, working on the pleasure principle and seeking immediate gratification, energizes the id.

Conscious: Freud's first level of awareness, consisting of the thoughts, feelings, and actions of which people are aware.

aware. The second level, the **preconscious**, consists of mental activities of which people can become aware if they attend to them. The third level, the **unconscious**, consists of the mental activities beyond people's normal awareness. They become aware of these activities only through specific therapeutic techniques, such as dream analysis. Suppose a woman decides to become a psychotherapist for a *conscious* reason. She tells her family and friends that she wants to help people. Later, during an introspective moment, she realizes that her *preconscious* motivation for becoming a psychotherapist stems from a desire to resolve her own unhappiness. Finally, through psychoanalysis, she discovers that she hungers for love and intimacy, which her parents denied her. *Unconsciously,* she has been hoping that her patients will satisfy that hunger by making her feel needed.

According to Freud, the ego acts as a manager, adjusting cognitive and perceptual processes to balance the person's functioning, to control the id, and to keep the person in touch with reality.

Id, Ego, and Superego. According to Freud's theory, the primary structural elements of the mind and personality are three mental forces (not physical structures of the brain) that reside, fully or partially, in the unconscious: the id, the ego, and the superego. Each force accounts for a different aspect of functioning (see Table 10.1).

The **id** is the source of a person's instinctual energy, which, according to Freud, is either sexual or aggressive. The id works mainly by the *pleasure principle;* that is, it tries to maximize immediate gratification through the satisfaction of raw impulses. Residing deep within the unconscious, the demanding, irrational, and selfish id seeks pleasure—without regard for morals, society, or other people.

While the id seeks to maximize pleasure and obtain immediate gratification, the **ego** (which grows out of the id) is the part of the personality that seeks to satisfy the individual's instinctual needs in accordance with reality; that is, it works by the *reality principle.* According to Freud, the ego acts as a manager, adjusting cognitive and perceptual processes to balance the person's functioning, to control the id, and to keep the person in touch with reality. For example, a 4-year-old boy who is in a grocery store sees candy; his id says, "Take the candy." The ego may recognize that the boy could steal the candy, but it acknowledges that he is likely to be caught and punished. Working on the reality principle, the boy realizes that gratifying his id by stealing the candy is dangerous.

As a child grows, the superego develops. The **superego** in Freud's theory is the moral aspect of mental functioning, comprising the *ego ideal* (what a person would ideally like to be) and the *conscience* and taught by parents and society. The superego tells the id and the ego whether gratification in a particular instance is ethical. It attempts to control the id by internalizing parental authority through the process of socialization and by punishing transgressions with feelings of guilt and anxiety. Suppose an older child is sent to the store with $2 to buy a loaf of bread. Upon seeing the candy at the checkout, the child is tempted; his id says, "Steal it." The ego sees that it is possible that the boy may not get caught because the store is so busy—the ego may give in to the id a bit. Then, the superego is heard from: "Taking the candy would be morally wrong; it would be stealing. Shame would follow if Mom found out." The ego and superego thus

Table 10.1 Comparison of Freud's Three Systems of Personality

	Id	Ego	Superego
Nature	Represents biological aspect	Represents psychological aspect	Represents societal aspect
Level	Unconscious	Conscious and preconscious	Conscious, preconscious, and unconscious
Principle	Pleasure	Reality	Morality
Purpose	To seek pleasure and avoid pain	To adapt to reality	To represent right and wrong
Aim	Immediate gratification	Safety and compromise	Perfection

Table 10.2 Freud's Five Psychosexual Stages of Personality Development

Stage	Erogenous Zone	Conflicts/ Experiences	Adult Traits or Fixations Associated with Problems at a Stage
Oral (birth to 2 years)	Mouth	Infant achieves gratification through oral activities such as feeding, thumb sucking, and cooing.	Optimism, gullibility, passivity, hostility, substance abuse
Anal (2 to 3 years)	Anus	The child learns to respond to some parental demands (such as for bladder and bowel control).	Excessive cleanliness, orderliness, messiness, rebelliousness
Phallic (4 to 7 years)	Genitals	The child learns to realize the differences between males and females and becomes aware of sexuality.	Flirtatiousness, vanity, promiscuity, chastity, disorder in gender identity
Latency (7 to puberty)	None	The child continues developing but sexual urges are relatively quiet.	Not specified
Genital (puberty on)	Genitals	The growing adolescent shakes off old dependencies and learns to deal maturely with the opposite sex.	Not specified

attempt to moderate the demands of the id and direct it toward appropriate ways of behaving.

Development of Personality

Freud strongly believed that if people looked at their past, they could gain insight into their current behavior. This belief led him to create an elaborate psycho sexual stage theory of personality development. Freud believed that the core aspects of personality are established early, remain stable throughout life, and are changed only with great difficulty. He argued that all people pass through five critical stages of personality development: oral, anal, phallic, latency, and genital (see Table 10.2). At each of these stages, Freud asserted, people experience conflicts and issues associated with *erogenous zones*—areas of the body that give rise to erotic or sexual sensations when they are stimulated.

Oral Stage. The concept of the **oral stage** is based on the fact that the instincts of infants (from birth to about age 2) are focused on the mouth as the primary pleasure center. Infants receive oral gratification through feeding, thumb sucking, and cooing during the early months of life, when their basic feelings about the world are being established. Relying heavily on symbolism, Freud contended that adults who consider the world a bitter place (referring to the mouth and taste senses) probably had difficulty during the oral stage of development and may have traits associated with passivity and hostility. Their problems tend to focus on their need for nurturing, warmth, and love.

Anal Stage. The **anal stage** is Freud's second stage of personality development, from age 2 to about age 3, during which children learn to control the immediate gratification they obtain through defecation and to become responsive to the demands of society. At about age 2 or 3, children learn to respond to some of parents' and society's demands. One parental demand

Preconscious: Freud's second level of awareness, consisting of mental activities of which people can become aware by attending to them.

Unconscious: Freud's third level of awareness, consisting of mental activities beyond people's normal awareness.

Id: In Freud's theory, the source of a person's instinctual energy, which works mainly on the pleasure principle.

Ego: In Freud's theory, the part of personality that seeks to satisfy instinctual needs in accordance with reality.

Superego [sue-pur-EE-go]: In Freud's theory, the moral aspect of mental functioning, comprising the ego ideal (what a person would ideally like to be) and the conscience and taught by parents and society.

Oral stage: Freud's first stage of personality development, from birth to about age 2, during which the instincts of infants are focused on the mouth as the primary pleasure center.

Anal stage: Freud's second stage of personality development, from about age 2 to about age 3, during which children learn to control the immediate gratification they obtain through defecation and to become responsive to the demands of society.

is that children control their bodily functions of urination and defecation and become toilet-trained. Most 2- and 3-year-olds experience pleasure in moving their bowels. This stage therefore establishes the basis for conflict between the id and the ego—between the desire for immediate gratification of physical urges and the demand for controlled behavior. Freud claimed that during the anal stage, children develop certain lasting personality characteristics related to control, such as neatness and orderliness, that reflect their toilet training. Thus, adults who had difficulty in the anal stage tend to have problems that focus on orderliness (or lack of it) and also might be compulsive in many behaviors.

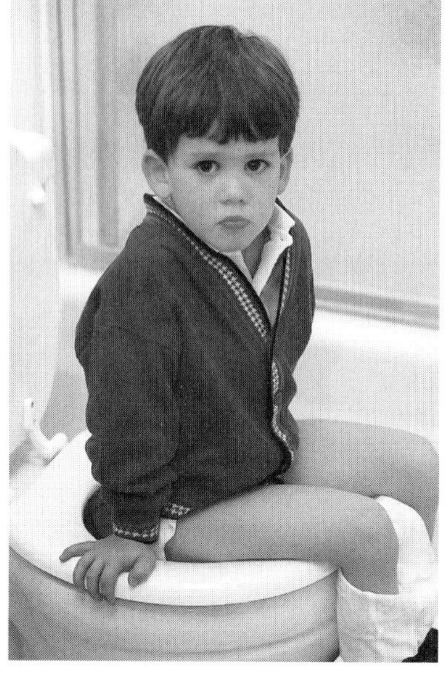

Phallic Stage. The **phallic stage** is Freud's third stage of personality development, from about age 4 through 7, during which children obtain gratification primarily from the genitals. At about age 4 or 5, children become aware of their sexuality. Freud claimed that numerous feelings are repressed so deeply during this stage that children (and later adults) are unaware of many of their sexual urges. Nonetheless, gender role development begins during this period.

During the phallic stage, children pass through what Freud termed the Oedipus (or Electra) complex. According to Freud, this complex is a group (or complex) of unconscious wishes to "possess" the opposite-sex parent and "remove" the same-sex parent. Freud derived the term *Oedipus complex* from the story of Oedipus as told by the Greek playwright Sophocles. Oedipus unknowingly killed his father and married his mother; Electra, in a slightly different plot twist, urged her brother to kill her father. Although Oedipus and Electra committed different dramatic sins, today, for convenience, both complexes are subsumed under the name *Oedipus complex*.

Phallic [FAL-ick] stage: Freud's third stage of personality development, from about age 4 through age 7, during which children obtain gratification primarily from the genitals.

Oedipus [ED-i-pus] complex: Feelings of rivalry with the parent of the same sex and love of the parent of the opposite sex, occurring during the phallic stage and ultimately resolved through identification with the parent of the same sex; in girls, the process is called the *Electra complex*.

Latency [LAY-ten-see] stage: Freud's fourth stage of personality development, from about age 7 until puberty, during which sexual urges are inactive.

The **Oedipus complex** involves feelings of rivalry with the parent of the same sex and love for the parent of the opposite sex and is ultimately resolved through identification with the parent of the same sex. The Oedipus complex thus refers to a boy's love for his mother, hostility toward his father, and consequent fear of castration by the father as punishment for the hostility and rivalry. In resolving the Oedipus complex, the boy eventually accepts his father's close relationship with his mother. Rather than feel excluded by it, he chooses to gratify his need for his mother's attention by identifying with his father. In this way, a young boy begins to model his behavior after that of his father. For females, Freud argued that the *Electra complex* follows a slightly different course. Freud held that when a young girl realizes that she has no penis, she develops what he called *penis envy*. He suggested that she could symbolically acquire a penis by attaching her love to her father. Thus, a young girl might ask her father to marry her so that they can raise a family together. When she realizes that this is unlikely, she may identify with her mother and copy her mother's behavior as a means of obtaining (or sharing in) her father's affection. Like the young boy, the young girl identifies with the parent of the same sex in the hope of obtaining affection from the parent of the opposite sex. For both boys and girls, the critical component in resolving the Oedipus or Electra complex is the development of identification with the parent of the same sex. Adult traits associated with problems at this stage usually involve sexuality and may include vanity, promiscuity, or excessive worry about chastity.

Whether the Oedipus complex explains behavior is controversial and widely debated, especially because many people find the idea sexist and degrading to women. There is no doubt about Freud's view of women; he saw them as weaker and less rational than men and believed they should be subservient to men. Most researchers now believe that Freud's notion of penis envy was imaginative but unconvincing, overdrawn, and lacking credibility (Stagner, 1988; Webster, 1995). Is it a good explanation of the dynamics of 4- and 5-year-olds with their parents? Again, most researchers think not.

Latency Stage. The **latency stage** lasts from about age 7 until puberty. During this period, children develop physically, but sexual urges are inactive (latent). Much of children's energy is channeled into social or intellectual activities. Some psychoanalysts believe that this stage has disappeared from the development of American children because of their rapid maturation into adolescence.

Genital Stage. Freud's last stage of personality development, the **genital stage,** begins at the onset of puberty and continues through adolescence into adulthood. When individuals reach this stage, the sexuality, fears, and repressed feelings of earlier stages are once again exhibited. Many repressed sexual feelings toward one's parents resurface at puberty. Over the course of the genital stage, the adolescent shakes off dependence on parents and learns to deal with members of the opposite sex in socially and sexually mature ways. Members of the opposite sex, who were ignored during the latency stage, are now seen as attractive. Many unresolved conflicts and repressed urges affect behavior during this stage. Ideally, if people have passed successfully through previous stages of development, they will develop conventional relations with members of the opposite sex. If not, they may continue to have unresolved conflicts within their unconscious throughout their adult life.

Unresolved Conflicts

As children proceed from one developmental stage to the next, they adjust their views of the world. Successfully passing through a stage requires resolution of that stage's principal conflict. Freud likened the process to military troops moving from battle to battle—a failure to successfully resolve one conflict weakens an army at its next. According to Freud, if children do not successfully pass through a stage and resolve its principal conflicts, they acquire a fixation and begin to use one or more defense mechanisms.

Fixations. A **fixation** is an excessive attachment to some person or object that was appropriate only at an earlier stage of development. A person who becomes fixated is said to be *arrested* at a particular stage of development. Fixation at one developmental stage does not prevent all further development, but it does mean that later stages cannot be fully mastered. For example, a child who does not successfully pass through the phallic stage probably has not resolved the Oedipus complex and may feel hostility toward the parent of the same sex. The child may suffer the consequences (often in the form of sexual problems) of this unresolved conflict throughout life.

Fixations or partial fixations usually occur because of frustration or overindulgence that hinders the expression of sexual or aggressive energy at a particular developmental stage. According to Freud, good personality adjustment generally involves a balance among competing forces. The child, and later the adult, should be neither too self-centered nor too moralistic. Parents who are restrictive, punitive, and overbearing or those who are indifferent, smothering, or overindulgent produce emotionally disturbed children who have a difficult time coping with life because of their resulting fixations. What happens when a person becomes fixated? According to Freud, the person becomes maladjusted and develops defense mechanisms.

Defense Mechanisms. A **defense mechanism** is an unconscious way of reducing anxiety by distorting perceptions of reality. Defense mechanisms allow the ego to deal with the uncomfortable feelings that anxiety produces. Everyone defends against anxiety from time to time, but individuals are typically unaware that they are using defense mechanisms. And people who use them to such an extent that reality is sharply distorted can become maladjusted.

Freud described many kinds of defense mechanisms, but he identified repression as the most important. In **repression,** anxiety-provoking thoughts and feelings are totally relegated to the unconscious. When people repress a feeling or desire, they become unaware of it. Thus, a young boy who was abused by a football coach may later become a father who inexplicably refuses to allow his son to try out for the team.

In addition to repression, Freud identified five other defense mechanisms:

- **Projection** is a defense mechanism by which people attribute their own undesirable traits to others. A friend who inexplicably asks "Are you mad at me?" may actually be mad at you but afraid to admit it to himself; instead, he sees *your* behavior as angry. Similarly, a woman with deep aggressive tendencies may see other people as acting in an excessively hostile way.
- **Denial** is the defense mechanism by which people refuse to accept reality or recognize the true

Genital [JEN-it-ul] stage: Freud's last stage of personality development, from the onset of puberty through adulthood, during which the sexual conflicts of childhood resurface (at puberty) and are often resolved (during adolescence).

Fixation: An excessive attachment to some person or object that was appropriate only at an earlier stage of development.

Defense mechanism: An unconscious way of reducing anxiety by distorting perceptions of reality.

Repression: Defense mechanism by which anxiety-provoking thoughts and feelings are totally relegated to the unconscious.

Projection: Defense mechanism by which people attribute their own undesirable traits to others.

Denial: Defense mechanism by which people refuse to accept reality or recognize the true source of their anxiety.

source of their anxiety. For example, someone with strong sexual urges may deny any interest in sex rather than deal with those urges. Or a student who is failing a mathematics course may unconcernedly tell friends that all is well academically.

- **Reaction formation** is the defense mechanism by which people behave in a way opposite to what their true but anxiety-provoking feelings would dictate. A classic example of reaction formation is the behavior of a person who has strong sexual urges but who becomes extremely chaste. Similarly, a student athlete who is extraordinarily competitive may choose to sit out a meet rather than put herself up for a potentially disheartening failure.
- **Sublimation** is the defense mechanism by which people redirect socially unacceptable impulses toward acceptable goals. Thus, a man who has sexual desire for someone he knows is off limits (perhaps a cousin) may channel that desire into working 14-hour days for his church. Similarly, a student who wants to drop out of school may throw himself into artistic endeavors or athletics.
- **Rationalization** is the defense mechanism by which people reinterpret undesirable feelings or behaviors in terms that make them seem acceptable. For example, a shoplifter may rationalize that no one will miss the things she steals or that she needs the things more than other people do. A student may cheat, asserting to himself that failing the course would hurt his parents far too much for them to bear.

Freud Today—Much Dissent

When Freud's psychosexual theory of development was first proposed, around 1900, it received a great deal of unfavorable attention. It was considered absurd to suggest that young children had sexual feelings toward their parents. Yet, if you watch how young children respond to and identify with their parents, you will see that there are elements of truth in Freud's conception of how personality development proceeds. Little girls do tend to idolize their fathers, and little boys often become strongly attached to their mothers. And it is widely accepted that individuals use projection and other defense mechanisms (Newman, Duff, & Baumeister, 1997).

Despite these observations, Freud's theories have been sharply criticized. Some psychologists object to Freud's basic conception of human nature—his emphasis on sexual urges toward parents and his idea that human behavior is so biologically determined. Others reject his predictions about psychosexual stages and fixations. Still others assert that his theory does not account for changing situations and differing cultures. Many people find Freud's ideas about women offensive. His case histories are seen by many today as "clinical romances" and intellectually contrived (Webster, 1995). At a minimum, Freud's ideas are controversial, and many, if not most, psychologists do not regard them as valid (Schatzman, 1992). Freud used poorly defined terms; he occasionally failed to distinguish between his observations and the inferences he made from them; he confused correlation with causation. Almost all agree that his theory is fuzzy. And because it can be stretched to account for any outcome, it makes predictions about an individual's behavior almost impossible to test. Freud's theory also has to be considered in a cultural context. The rigid standards of behavior of Austrian society at the start of the 20th century and the wealth and social position of Freud's patients biased him in ways that few theorists accept today.

At a minimum, Freud's ideas are controversial, and many, if not most, psychologists do not regard them as valid.

Regardless of whether Freud had the final word on human behavior, his influence on psychology and on Western culture exceeds that of any other personality theorist, present or past. His theory weaves together his clinical experiences with patients, his speculations about human nature, and his own complex and dark personality. In many ways, Freud's theory paved the way for other developmental stage theories, such as those of Piaget, Erikson, and Levinson, who made more specific predictions about specific behaviors.

Cultural Determinants of Personality. The fact that Freud's patients were primarily from a certain segment of Austrian society has wide implications. Freud developed a theory from dealing with a particular group of patients whose day-to-day behavior, personalities, and problems were shaped by the culture in which they lived. *Culture,* as we have seen, refers to the norms, ideals, values, rules, patterns of communication, and beliefs adopted by a group of people. Within a culture, there may be different social classes, but all of the people have the same basic set of norms.

Cultural differences between countries are still apparent. For example, people in England, Spain, France, Germany, and Turkey have distinctly different value systems, lifestyles, and personalities. Modes of dress and attitudes about work, family, and religion all differ. Culture is significant, because it shapes how people raise their children, what values they teach, and what family life is like.

Cultural values thus shape personality. Therefore, personality theories must be considered in a cultural context. Most Western societies value competitiveness, autonomy, and self-reliance; in addition, Western conceptions of personality focus on the individual. In contrast, many non-Western cultures value interdependence and cooperation; they also focus more on group dynamics in constructing conceptions of personality. For developing adolescents, one culture may value conformity to rules, strict adherence to religious values, and obedience to parental authority. Another culture may stress independence of thought, experimentation, and less reliance on parental authority. Even within American culture, there are significant variations in values and social norms among various ethnic and cultural groups.

Personality theories must be adjusted and refined to take into account ethnicity, gender, age, and class, as well as culture. Accordingly, every personality theory and concept must be evaluated from a multicultural perspective. This multicultural theme is relevant to the theory of Walter Mischel (which we examine later in this chapter). He argues that the context in which behavior occurs must be a focus of personality psychologists.

Neo-Freudians—Dissent and Revision. Despite Freud's enormous impact on psychological thought, modern personality theorists, including some of Freud's students, have found what they consider serious omissions, errors, and biases in Freudian theory. Many of these theorists have developed new ideas based loosely on Freud's original concepts, but usually attributing greater influence to cultural and interpersonal factors. These theorists have become known as **neo-Freudians.** Carl Jung is one of the best known of the neo-Freudians; we explore his influential theory next.

Jung's Analytical Psychology

Carl Gustav Jung (1875–1961) was a psychiatrist who became a close friend and follower of Freud. However, Jung, a brilliant thinker, ultimately broke with Freud over several key issues. Compared to Freud, Jung placed relatively little emphasis on sex. He focused instead on people's desire to conform their basic drives (including sex) with the demands of the real world. Thus, Jung saw people's behavior as less rigidly fixed and determined than Freud described. Jung also emphasized the search for meaning in life and focused on religiosity. By 1911, he and Freud were exchanging angry letters; in 1917, when Jung declared publicly his disagreements with Freud, the two severed their relationship—Freud was intolerant of followers who deviated too much from his positions.

Jung chose to differentiate his approach from Freud's by terming it an *analytic* approach rather than a *psychoanalytic* approach. Like Freud, Jung emphasized unconscious processes as determinants of behavior, and he believed that each person houses past events in the unconscious. Jung's version of the unconscious was slightly different from Freud's, however. Unlike Freud, Jung held that the unconscious anticipates the future and redirects an individual's behavior when he or she is leaning too much in one psychological direction. Thus, for example, if a person is using too many defense mechanisms, the unconscious can anticipate problems and help the person deal with anxiety rather than distort it.

In addition, as a central element of his approach, Jung developed a new concept—the collective unconscious. The **collective unconscious** is a shared storehouse of primitive ideas and images that reside in the unconscious and are inherited from one's ancestors. Called **archetypes,** these inherited ideas and images are emotionally charged and rich in meaning and symbolism.

Reaction formation: Defense mechanism by which people behave in a way opposite to what their true but anxiety-provoking feelings would dictate.

Sublimation [sub-li-MAY-shun]: Defense mechanism by which people redirect socially unacceptable impulses toward acceptable goals.

Rationalization: Defense mechanism by which people reinterpret undesirable feelings or behaviors in terms that make them appear acceptable.

Neo-Freudians: Personality theorists who have proposed variations on Freud's basic ideas, usually attributing a greater influence to cultural and interpersonal factors than Freud did.

Collective unconscious: In Jung's theory, a shared storehouse of primitive ideas and images that reside in the unconscious and are inherited from one's ancestors.

Archetypes [AR-ki-types]: In Jung's theory, the emotionally charged ideas and images that are rich in meaning and symbolism and exist within the collective unconscious.

The archetypes of the collective unconscious emerge in art, in religion, and especially in dreams. One especially important archetype is the *mandala,* a mystical symbol, generally circular in form, that in Jung's view represents a person's inward striving for unity. Jung pointed out that many religions have mandala-like symbols; indeed, Hinduism and Buddhism use such symbols as aids to meditation. Another archetype is the concept of mother; each individual is born with a predisposition to react to certain types of persons or entities as mother figures. Such figures are seen as warm, accepting, and nurturing; some examples are the Virgin Mary and Mother Earth. There are archetypes for wise older men and wizards, among dozens of others. Jung found rich symbolism in dreams and used archetypes such as the mandala and the mother to help people understand themselves.

Jung's ideas are widely known but not widely accepted by mainstream psychologists. Although their impact on psychoanalytic theory is important, Jung's ideas never achieved prominence in leading psychological thought because they cannot be verified. Some theorists even view them as mere poetic speculation. Soon to develop were theories that stress the idea that human beings are inherently good and strive to be better. We consider these humanistic theories next. *I*

Think Critically

- What is it about a society that can shape a personality theorist's point of view?
- Jung's view of how personality develops was radically different from Freud's. What implications did this difference have for Jung's theory of personality? In general, how do assumptions about human nature shape personality theories?

I Humanistic Approaches: Self-Fulfillment and Self-Actualization

Focus on issues and ideas

- The assumptions of humanistic approaches compared to those of Freud's theory
- The importance of self-concept in the development of personality

Dehumanizing was the term that many psychologists used to describe psychoanalytic theory; Freud characterized people as primitive, and his theory was viewed by many as too deterministic. Humanistic approaches developed in the 1950s in part as a backlash against Freud. These approaches attempted to humanize the study of personality by focusing on the unique qualities of human beings. Humanistic theorists are interested in people's conceptions of themselves and what they would like to become. In general, humanistic theories assume that people are motivated by internal forces to achieve personal goals. Humanistic psychology focuses not on maladjustment or abnormal behavior but on the well-adjusted individual.

Humanistic theories emphasize fulfillment and, as already suggested, were developed partly in response to Freud's theory, which stresses the conflict of inner forces. Whereas Freud believed that people are in constant inner conflict, warding off evil thoughts and desires with defense mechanisms, humanistic psychologists see people as basically decent (although some of their specific behaviors may not be). Moreover, humanistic theories enable theoreticians and practitioners to make predictions about specific behaviors.

Sometimes humanistic theories are called *phenomenological approaches,* because they focus on the individual's unique experiences with and ways of interpreting the things and people in the world (phenomena). These approaches are more likely to examine immediate experiences than past ones and are more likely to deal with an individual's perception of the world than with a therapist's perception of the individual. Finally, they focus on self-determination; the theories assert that people carve their own destinies, from their own vantage points, and in their own ways. Two well-known psychologists, Abraham Maslow and Carl Rogers, whose theories we examine next, embody the humanistic perspective.

Abraham Maslow

No single individual is more closely associated with humanistic psychology than Abraham Maslow (1908–1970). In Chapter 8, we examined Maslow's theory of motivation, which states that human needs are arranged in a pyramidal hierarchy. Lower needs—for food and water, for example—are powerful and drive people toward fulfilling them. In the middle of the pyramid are the needs for safety, belongingness, and self-esteem. At the top of the pyramid is the need for self-actualization. The higher a need is in the hierarchy, the more distinctly human it is.

As a humanist, Maslow believed human beings are born healthy and undamaged, and he had a strong bias toward studying well-adjusted people. Maslow spoke about personality in terms of human uniqueness and the human need for **self-actualization**—the process of growth and the realization of individual potential. He focused not on what was missing from one's personality or life but on what one might achieve in realizing one's full potential. Critics of Maslow find his notions too fuzzy and view his approach to psychology as romantic and not fully developed. Also, his theory is virtually untestable because he provided little explanation of the nature of self-actualizing tendencies. Carl Rogers formulated a more complete and scientific humanistic approach.

Rogers and Self Theory

Carl Rogers (1902–1987) began to formulate his personality theory during the first years of his practice as a clinician in Rochester, New York. He listened to thousands of patients and was among the first psychologists to tape-record and transcribe his interactions with patients. What Rogers's patients said about their experiences, their thoughts, and themselves led him to make three basic assumptions about behavior: (1) Behavior is goal-directed. (2) People are innately good, so they will almost always choose adaptive, enhancing, and self-actualizing behaviors. (3) How individuals see their world determines how they will behave.

Key Concepts. Rogers believed that personal experiences provide an individual with a unique and subjective internal frame of reference and worldview. He believed that **fulfillment**—an inborn tendency directing people toward actualizing their essential nature and thus attaining their potential—is the force that motivates personality development. Thus, people strive naturally to express their capabilities and talents. Rogers's approach is *unidirectional,* because it posits that personality development always moves in the direction of fulfillment. This does not mean that an individual's personality undergoes uninterrupted growth. During some periods, no growth is evident. However, for Rogers, a person's core tendency is to actualize her or his essential nature and to maintain and enhance life. Rogers compared the striving for fulfillment to the growth of a seed, which if watered grows into a strong, healthy plant.

Structure of Personality. Rogers's theory of personality is structured around the concept of the **self**—the perception an individual has of himself or herself and of his or her relationships to other people and to various aspects of life. The *self-concept* is how people see their own behavior and internal characteristics. As mentioned before, Rogers's theory assumes that individuals are constantly engaged in the process of fulfilling their potential—of actualizing themselves.

Rogers suggested that each person has a concept not only of self but also of an ideal self. The **ideal self** is the self a person would ideally like to be (such as a competent professional, a devoted mate, or a loving parent). According to Rogers, each person's happiness is measured by reference to the ideal self. A person is generally happy when there is agreement between the real (Rogers used the term *phenomenal*) self and the ideal self. Great discrepancies between real and ideal selves create unhappiness, dissatisfaction, and, in extreme cases, maladjustment.

Rogers's focus on the self led him to his basic principle—that people tend to maximize their self-concept through *self-actualization.* In Rogers's view of the self-actualization process, the self grows and becomes social. People are self-actualized when they have expanded their self-concept and developed their potential to approximate their ideal selves by attempting to minimize ill health, be fully functioning, have a clear perception of reality, and feel a strong sense of self-acceptance. When people's self-concepts are not what they would like them to be, they become anxious. Rogers saw anxiety as useful because it motivates people to try to actualize their best selves, to become all they are capable of being.

Development of Personality. Unlike Freud, Rogers suggested that personality development occurs gradually, not in discrete stages. He contended that development involves regular self-assessment in order to master the process of self-actualization—which takes a lifetime.

Rogers was particularly aware that children develop basic feelings about themselves early in life. This awareness led him to consider the role of social influences in the development of self-concepts. The self-assessments of children who are told that they are beautiful, intelligent, and good are radically different from

Self-actualization: The process of growth and the realization of individual potential; in the humanistic view, a final level of psychological development in which a person attempts to minimize ill health, be fully functioning, have a superior perception of reality, and feel a strong sense of self-acceptance.

Fulfillment: In Rogers's theory of personality, an inborn tendency directing people toward actualizing their essential nature and thus attaining their potential.

Self: In Rogers's theory of personality, the perception an individual has of himself or herself and of his or her relationships to other people and to various aspects of life.

Ideal self: In Rogers's theory of personality, the self a person would ideally like to be.

those of children who are told that they are bad, dirty, stupid, and a nuisance. Rogers did not claim that adults should never react negatively to children's behavior; rather, children should have a sense that they themselves are worthwhile and good, even though some specific behaviors they exhibit are unacceptable. Rogers suggested that children must grow up in an atmosphere in which they can experience life fully. This involves their recognizing both the good and the bad sides of their behavior.

Each person must evaluate her or his own situation using a personal (internal) frame of reference, not the external framework provided by society or others.

The Importance of Self-Concepts. People with rigid self-concepts guard themselves against potentially threatening feelings and experiences. Rogers suggested that such people become unhappy when they are unable to fit new types of behavior into their existing self-concepts. They then distort their perceptions of their behavior in order to make the perceptions compatible with the self-concept. A man whose self-concept includes high moral principles, rigid religious observance, and strict self-control, for example, might become anxious when he feels greed; such a feeling is inconsistent with his self-concept. To avoid anxiety, he denies or distorts what he is truly experiencing. He may deny that he feels greed, or he may insist that he is entitled to the object he covets.

A changing world may threaten a person's self-concept. The person may then repress or deny unacceptable ideas or thoughts; this reaction tends to create a narrow outlook, a limited conception of the world, and to restrict personal growth. But individuals can reduce or eliminate their fear by broadening their frame of reference and by considering alternative behaviors. People with healthy self-concepts can allow new experiences into their lives and can accept or reject them. Such people move in a positive direction. With each new experience, the self-concept becomes stronger and more defined, and the goal of self-actualization moves closer.

Individual Development. Rogers's concept of personality shows an abiding concern for individual development. Rogers stressed that each person must evaluate her or his own situation using a personal (internal) frame of reference, not the external framework provided by society or others.

Freud's and Rogers's theories of personality make fundamentally different assumptions about human nature and about how personality is expressed. Freud saw biologically driven individuals in conflict; Rogers saw people as inherently good and trying to be everything they could be. Freud was strongly deterministic; Rogers, a humanist, was strongly oriented toward free will. Humanists believe people can rise above biologically inherited traits and can use decision-making processes to guide behavior. The treatment procedures that developed out of the theories of Freud and Rogers—psychoanalysis and client-centered therapy (to be discussed in Chapter 14)—are fundamentally different.

Next, we examine an approach to personality development that focuses on traits and on the specific behavioral responses that individuals make throughout their lives.

Trait: Any readily identifiable stable quality that characterizes how an individual differs from other individuals.

Types: Personality categories in which broad collections of traits are loosely tied together and interrelated.

Trait and Type Theories: Stable Behavioral Dispositions

Focus on issues and ideas

- Understanding the relationship between trait theories and type theories
- The five broad trait categories accepted by many theorists
- The strengths and weaknesses of trait and type theories

Some early psychologists based their personality theories on people's openly exhibited traits, such as shyness, impulsiveness, and aggressiveness. And research shows that many of these easily observed characteristics do predict other behaviors. For example, extremely shy people are more likely than others to be anxious and lonely and to have low self-esteem, and adolescents with behavior problems often have low self-esteem. Theories based on these observations—trait and type theories of personality—make intuitive sense and thus have been very popular. They focus on broad, stable behavioral dispositions.

Trait theorists study specific traits. A **trait** is any readily identifiable stable quality that characterizes how an individual differs from other individuals. Someone might characterize one political figure as energetic and forward-looking and another as tough and patriotic, for example. Such characterizations present specific ideas about a person's *disposition*—the way a person is likely to behave across a wide range of circumstances and situations. Traits can be evaluated on a continuum, so a person can be extremely shy, very shy, shy, or mildly shy, for example. (The trait of shyness is investigated in more detail in *Experiencing Psychology.*) For some personality theorists, traits are the elements of which personality is made.

Type theorists group together traits common to specific personalities. **Types**, therefore, are personality categories in which broad collections of traits are loosely tied together and interrelated. Although the distinction between traits and types sometimes blurs, as Gordon Allport (1937, p. 295) explained, "A man

EXPERIENCING PSYCHOLOGY

Shyness

About 40% of adults report being shy, and for at least 2 million adults, shyness is a serious behavior problem that inhibits personal, social, and professional growth. Shy people show extreme anxiety in social situations; they are extremely reticent and often overly concerned with how others view them. They fear acting foolishly; as a consequence, they may develop clammy hands, dry mouth, excessive perspiration, trembling, nausea, blushing, and a need to go to the bathroom frequently. Shyness makes children and adults avoid social situations and makes them speak softly, when they speak at all (Schmidt et al., 1997); shy people also avoid approaching other people (Asendorpf, 1989). In contrast to bold children, shy children are more likely to have higher heart rates (Arcus, 1994). Most shy people report that they have always been shy, and half of all shy people feel they are shyer than other people in similar situations (Carducci & Stein, 1988). The causes of extreme shyness have been thought to be biological in origin (Kagan, Reznick, & Snidman, 1988), although the exact mechanism that might underlie it is still unknown. Genetic predispositions are suggested, and research shows that even a mother's exposure to daylight during pregnancy affects hormonal and other biological mechanisms that may determine her newborn's shyness (Gortmaker et al., 1997).

Personality researchers contend that certain personality traits, including shyness, are long-lasting. Jerome Kagan found that 2- and 3-year-olds who were extremely cautious and shy tended to remain that way for years (Kagan, 1997a; Schmidt et al., 1997). Daniels and Plomin (1985) also found an important relationship between adopted infants' shyness at 2 years of age and the shyness of their biological mothers. This finding also suggests that genetic factors play an important role in shyness (Hamer & Copeland, 1998; Lykken et al., 1992).

Although Kagan also suggests that extreme shyness may have a biological basis, he believes that shyness emerges because people develop distorted self-concepts—negative views about their competencies and a lack of self-esteem (Kagan, 1997a). Such individuals view themselves as having few social graces. These thoughts, combined with such actions as withdrawal and nervousness, set a person up for social failure. When negative events occur, the person then says, "See, I was right." A person's thoughts, bodily reactions, and social behaviors thus perpetuate his or her shyness (Bruch, Berko, & Haase, 1998). A parent's shyness and sociability can affect a child's behavior; the more sociable the parents, the less shy the children are (Chung & Doh, 1997). The consequences of being shy can be profound; shy children marry later in life and have children later (Kerr, Lambert, & Bem, 1996); such life-course decisions affect careers as well.

Treatment programs exist to help people overcome extreme shyness (Carducci & Stein, 1988). If you are shy, here are some things you can do:

- Rehearse what you want to say before speaking.
- Build your self-esteem by focusing on your good points.
- Accept who you are.
- Practice smiling and making eye contact.
- Observe the behavior of others whom you admire, and copy it.
- Think about how others feel; remember that about 40% of people feel the way you do.
- Begin some relaxation training, perhaps involving self-hypnosis, yoga, or even biofeedback.
- Think positively; having a positive attitude about yourself and other people can go a long way toward helping to overcome shyness. ■

can be said to *have* a trait; but he cannot be said to *have* a type. Rather, he fits a type."

We'll examine the trait and type theories of Gordon Allport, Raymond Cattell, and Hans Eysenck, as well as a newer model of traits—the Big Five.

Allport's Trait Theory and Cattell's Factor Theory

The distinguished psychologist Gordon Allport (1897–1967) was a leading trait theorist who suggested that each individual has a unique set of personality traits. According to Allport (1937), if a person's traits are known, it is possible to predict how the person will respond to various events in the environment. Allport quickly discovered that although thousands of traits characterize people's behavior, some are more dominant than others.

Allport decided that traits could be grouped into three categories: cardinal, central, and secondary. *Cardinal traits* are enduring characteristics that determine the direction of a person's life. A clergyman's cardinal trait may be belief in and devotion to God; a civil rights leader's, the desire to rectify social and political injustices. Allport noted that many people have no cardinal traits. The more common *central traits* are reasonably easy to identify; they are the qualities that characterize a person's daily interactions. The central traits—including self-control, apprehension, tension, self-assuredness, forthrightness, and practicality, among others—are the basic units of personality. Allport believed that central traits adequately describe many personalities. For example, tennis legend John McEnroe could be characterized as self-assured and lacking emotional control; Woody Allen's typical film persona could be described as tense and apprehensive. *Secondary traits* are characteristics that are exhibited in response to specific situations. For example, a person may have a secondary trait of xenophobia—a fear and intolerance of strangers or foreigners. Secondary traits are more easily modified than central traits and are not necessarily exhibited on a daily basis.

Everyone has different combinations of traits, which is why Allport claimed that each person is unique. To identify a person's traits, Allport recommended an in-depth study of that individual. Although such a study would be incredibly time-consuming and might never result in accurate predictions of the person's behavior, Allport and other psychologists such as Raymond B. Cattell have argued that it is possible to tell a great deal about a person by knowing only a few of his or her traits. Cattell (1965) used the technique of *factor analysis*—a statistical procedure in which psychologists analyze groups of variables (factors) to detect which are related—to show that groups of traits tend to cluster together. Thus, researchers find that people who describe themselves as warm and accepting also tend to rate themselves as high in nurturance and tenderness and low in aggression, suspiciousness, and apprehensiveness. Researchers also see patterns within professions: For example, artists may see themselves as creative, sensitive, and open; accountants may describe themselves as careful, serious, conservative, and thorough-minded. Cattell termed obvious, day-to-day traits *surface traits* and called higher-order, "deep" traits *source traits.*

Eysenck's Type Theory

Whereas Allport and Cattell focused on traits, Hans Eysenck (1916–1997) focused on higher levels of trait organization, or what he called *types*. Each type incorporates lower-level elements (traits), and each trait incorporates lower-order qualities (habits). Eysenck (1970) argued that all personality traits could be grouped under three basic dimensions: emotional stability, introversion or extroversion, and psychoticism.

Emotional stability is the extent to which people control their feelings. At one extreme of this dimension, people can be spontaneous, genuine, and warm; at the other, they can be controlled, calm, flat, unresponsive, and stilted. The dimension of introversion or extroversion has to do with the extent to which people are withdrawn or open. Introverts are socially withdrawn and shy; extroverts are socially outgoing and open and like to meet new people. Eysenck's third dimension, psychoticism, is sometimes called tough- or tender-mindedness. At one extreme, people are troublesome, impulsive, sensation-seeking, and insensitive; at the other, they are empathic, warm, gregarious, and able to control their impulses.

Eysenck argued that personality has a biological basis but emphasized that learning and experience also shape an individual's behavior. For example, he said that introverts and extroverts experience different

levels of arousal in the cortex of the brain. Accordingly, persons of each type seek the amount of stimulation necessary to achieve their preferred level of arousal. For example, a person who prefers a low level of arousal, in which stimulation is less intense, might become a librarian; a person who prefers a high level of arousal might become a racecar driver. Many people who prefer high levels of arousal might be characterized as sensation seekers; they climb mountains, ride dirt bikes, gamble, and take drugs. *Diversity* explores the question of whether people who are religious share a personality type.

DIVERSITY

Is There a Religious Personality Type?

When you picture a "religious" person, who comes to mind? Do you think of Mother Teresa? The pope? Your rabbi or minister? Does your image involve acts of kindness performed by a spiritual person, or do you envision someone repressed, rigid, and inflexible? Religiousness can be expressed in many ways—in worship services, community outreach, individual acts of kindness, or prayer. Religion plays a key role in many people's lives, but it does so in many ways, with seemingly endless variations (Levin & Taylor, 1997).

Some people have strong stereotyped views of those who are religious. But is religiousness a personality trait? Does one's personality determine whether one will be religious? Researchers have found, usually through questionnaires and surveys, a complicated picture of individual religious development. People who are religious—regardless of their tradition, ethnicity, or culture—don't tend to be one personality type (Stark, 1997). Yes, some religious people are indeed authoritarian individuals who adopt strict guidelines and use rigid punishments to raise their children. But a similar number of religious people are nonauthoritarian. When all the data are taken together, it turns out that authoritarianism is not correlated in any direct way with being religious. Similarly, the religious, across all groups, tend not to be any more or less suggestible to ideas than are other individuals, although greater suggestibility is seen within some religious denominations.

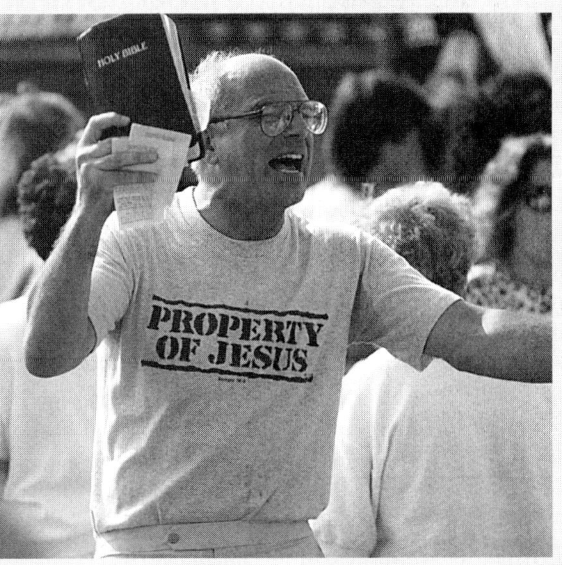

Religious individuals who are deeply committed to a life of faith report a sense of well-being. Researchers have tried to determine whether this sense of well-being comes from being religious or whether it emerges for other reasons. Paloutzian (1996) concludes that spiritual well-being is an overriding sense of the quality of daily life; but religion is only one aspect of a person's life that can create that sense of peace. For example, it turns out that spiritual well-being is positively correlated to people's feelings about their own health (Chamberlain & Zika, 1992).

Those who are religious aren't all upbeat; nor are they more reserved than other people. They aren't any more or less authoritarian or dogmatic than the nonreligious. Religious people feel better about themselves and their lives than the nonreligious do—their sense of well-being is greater. But remember that correlation is not equivalent to causation: Being religious does not necessarily *cause* one to feel better.

The role of religion in people's lives has just begun to be explored by psychologists, and research on it has yet to be integrated into mainstream psychology (Kirkpatrick, 1997). This is quite astonishing, given the large role religion plays in so many Americans' lives. Researchers have begun to ask whether and how religion shapes personality or whether personality helps shape religious experience. Some of the latest research efforts have looked at differences in religiousness from feminist (Neitz, 1995), developmental (Tamminen, 1994), and cross-cultural perspectives (Chia & Jih, 1994). ■

The idea of a biological component to traits is widely debated (Bullock & Gilliland, 1993; Heath & Martin, 1990), and the debate is not yet resolved. Most psychologists agree that some traits or perhaps a disposition to some traits may be passed on genetically—at least to some extent (e.g., Hamer & Copeland, 1998; Plomin, 1994a). Behavioral geneticists consider the environment to be a minimal influence; but most psychologists maintain that environmental influences are so strong that much of a person's personality is shaped by day-to-day interactions.

The Big Five

Because trait and type theories follow a commonsense approach, researchers today still find them attractive. However, rather than speaking of hundreds of traits or of a few types, many theorists agree that there are five broad trait categories. These categories have become known as the *Big Five* (McCrae & Costa, 1987):

- *Extroversion–introversion,* or the extent to which people are social or unsocial, talkative or quiet, affectionate or reserved
- *Agreeableness–antagonism,* or the extent to which people are good-natured or irritable, courteous or rude, flexible or stubborn, lenient or critical
- *Conscientiousness–undirectedness,* or the extent to which people are reliable or undependable, careful or careless, punctual or late, well organized or disorganized
- *Neuroticism–stability,* or the extent to which people are worried or calm, nervous or at ease, insecure or secure
- *Openness to experience,* or the extent to which people are open to experience or closed, independent or conforming, creative or uncreative, daring or timid

Although dozens of traits can describe people, researchers think of the Big Five categories as "supertraits," the important dimensions that characterize every personality (McCrea & Costa, 1990, 1994). Research has supported the idea of the Big Five (Busato et al., 1999) and shown the stability of the categories (Borkenau & Ostendorf, 1998); in addition, the Big Five hold up cross-culturally (McCrea et al., 1998). Some research suggests there may be genetic influences on the categories (Loehlin et al., 1998). Finally, the Big Five may help us understand children's personalities (Shiner, 1998), although little research has been conducted on children and personality development.

The Big Five are easily understood (Sneed, McCrae, & Funder, 1998), can be used by practitioners and theoreticians to make predictions about happiness (DeNeve & Cooper, 1998), and can be used in practical situations (Botwin, Buss, & Shackelford, 1997), to predict job performance (Mount, Barrick, & Stewart, 1998), and as part of psychological assessment. However, as good as the Big Five is at predicting behavior, it is still only a model that psychologists use as a way of understanding personality; it is not necessarily a final or complete description of personality (Bouchard, 1997). And not all researchers agree on the categories (Deniston & Ramanaiah, 1993). For example, researchers recently found evidence for two additional dimensions (*excellent–ordinary* and *evil–decent*); the Big Five may soon be considered the Big Seven (Benet-Martinez & Waller, 1997). Moreover, certain elements of personality are not well identified by the Big Five (Schinka, Dye, & Curtiss, 1997), especially in the area of health-related concerns (Marshall et al., 1994); more research is needed into the meaning of the factors.

Criticisms of Trait and Type Theories

Trait and type theories are appealing because they characterize people along important dimensions, providing simple explanations for how individuals behave. The idea of traits as accurate predictors of behavior has been supported by some research (Funder, 1995), but more often psychologists have criticized these theories on several fronts: First, they say trait theories are not actually personality *theories;* that is, they do not make good predictions about behaviors or explain why the behaviors occur, particularly since an individual's behavior often depends on the situation or context (Schmit & Ryan, 1993). Some psychologists contend that the failure of trait theories to account for situational differences is a crucial weakness. Others claim that trait theories are merely lists of behaviors arranged into a hierarchy. Second, most trait theories do not tell which personality characteristics last a lifetime and which are transient. Extraordinary events can alter traits and types. Third, trait theories do not account for changing cultural elements. If you test the same person at 10-year intervals, the person's traits are likely to be different. But society will also be different, as will people's values and ideas. Trait and type theories do not account for changing cultural norms. Fourth, not only does each culture change, but the differences between cultures are great, and trait theories do not account for them (Matsumoto, 1996). Finally, trait and type theories do not explain why people develop traits. Nor do they explain why traits change.

Trait and type theories continue to evolve, and debate about the number of stable traits continues.

However, psychologists want personality theories that (1) explain the development of personality, (2) predict maladjustment, and especially (3) explain why a person's behavior can be dramatically different in different situations. Theories that attempt to describe, explain, and predict behaviors with more precision tend to be behavioral ones, the next major group of theories we examine.

Think Critically

- What do you think is the most important way in which humanistic theory differs from Freudian theory?
- Many psychologists accept the basic idea of the Big Five but think the list should be the Big Six or Seven or the Big Four. What do you think of the inclusiveness of the Big Five? Are five dimensions too many or not enough to characterize individual differences in personality?

Behavioral Approaches: Learning Is Key

Focus on issues and ideas

- Why behavioral theories are often viewed as a reaction to the conceptual vagueness of traditional personality theories
- The role of learning and experiences in shaping personality

We often speculate about what goes on "inside" the minds of our favorite movie stars, athletes, or other famous figures; we try to guess what their personal and professional lives might be like and infer things about their personalities. But B. F. Skinner, a leader of American behaviorism, would have argued that such an exercise is a waste of time—you cannot see inside people's minds. He and behavioral colleagues would argue that speculating about private, unobservable behavior is fruitless. Skinner would further assert that inner drives, psychic urges, and the need for self-actualization are concepts that are impossible to define.

Behavioral theories tend to center on precisely defined elements, such as the relationship between stimuli and responses.

Behaviorists assert that concepts such as psychic urges are not the proper subject matter of personality study. Behavioral theorists are practical. They believe that people often need to change aspects of their lives quickly and efficiently and that many people do not have the time, money, or energy for lengthy psychotherapy.

Key Behavioral Concepts

Behaviorists look at personality very differently than do any of the theorists described so far. They generally do not look within the psyche; they look only at overt behavior. Behavioral approaches are often viewed as a reaction to the conceptual vagueness of traditional personality theories. Behavioral personality theorists assert that personality develops as people learn from their environments. The key word is *learn*. According to behaviorists, personality characteristics are not long-lasting and fixed; instead, they are subject to change. Thus, for behaviorists such as Skinner, personality is the sum of a person's learned tendencies.

Precisely Defined Elements. Behavioral theories tend to center on precisely defined elements, such as the relationship between stimuli and responses, the strength of stimuli, and the strength, duration, and timing of reinforcers. All of these can be tested in a laboratory or clinical setting. By focusing on stimuli and responses, behaviorists avoid trying to conceptualize human nature and concentrate instead on predicting behavior in specific circumstances. As a result, their assertions are more easily tested than are those of other theorists. Behaviorists see the development of personality as simply a change in response characteristics—a person learns new behaviors in response to new environments and stimuli.

Responses to Stimuli. For most behaviorists, the structural unit of personality is the response to stimuli. Any behavior, regardless of the situation, is seen as a response to a stimulus or a response in anticipation of reinforcement (or punishment). When an identifiable stimulus leads to an identifiable response, researchers predict that every time that stimulus occurs, so will the response. This stimulus–response relationship helps explain the constancy of personality. For example, whenever my wife has something unpleasant to discuss with me, she starts off the conversation in a really quiet voice, saying, "We need to talk about something." My response is often to tense up and become defensive. We have both learned through repetition over the years that my initial response is predictable: The stimulus of a quiet voice announcing that we have to talk leads to my initial response of defensiveness.

Behavior Patterns. Using behavioral analysis, psychologists can discover how people develop behavior patterns (such as procrastinating or overreacting to criticism) and why behavior is in constant flux. The behavioral approach suggests that learning is the process that shapes personality and that learning takes place through experience. Because new experiences happen all the time, a person is constantly learning about the world and changing her or his response patterns accordingly. Just as there are several learning principles involving stimuli, responses, and reinforcement (for a review, see Chapter 5), there are several behavioral personality theories. These theories are based on classical conditioning, operant conditioning, and observational learning.

Three Approaches to Learning

Classical Conditioning. Most people are fearful or anxious under certain circumstances. Some are fearful more often than not. How do people become fearful? What causes constant anxiety?

Many behavioral psychologists maintain that people develop fearfulness, anxiety, and timidity through classical conditioning, in which a neutral stimulus is paired with another stimulus that elicits some response. Eventually, the neutral stimulus can elicit the response on its own. For example, many people fear rats. Because rats are often encountered in dark cellars, a person may learn to fear dark cellars; that is, dark cellars become a feared stimulus. Later, the person may develop a generalized fear of dark places. If the first time the person sees a train, it's in a darkened station that looks like a cellar, the person may learn to fear trains. Classical conditioning thus allows researchers to explain the predictability of a person's day-to-day responses to specific stimuli. It describes the relationship between one stimulus and a person's expectation of another, as well as the predictable response the person makes (Rescorla, 1988).

Operant Conditioning. In operant conditioning, behavior is followed by a consequence, either reinforcement or punishment. According to behaviorists, personality can be explained as spontaneous behavior that is reinforced. For example, when a person is affectionate and that behavior is reinforced with smiles and hugs, the person is likely to continue to be affectionate.

Behavioral psychologists often use the operant learning principles of reinforcement and punishment to help children control themselves and shape aspects of their own personalities. For example, the time-out procedure is often used in learning situations in both classrooms and laboratories. As with any reinforcement or punishment procedure, the person learns that the time out is contingent on behavior

Observational Learning. Observational learning theories assume that people learn new behaviors by watching the behaviors of others. The theories contend that an observer will imitate the behaviors of a model and thus develop a specific set of behavioral tendencies. Personality is thus seen as developing through the process of observation and imitation.

Observational learning theories stress the importance of the relationship between the observer and the model in eliciting imitative behavior. When children view the behavior of a parent or other important person, their imitative behavior is significantly more extensive than when they observe the actions of someone less important to them. A son is more likely to adopt his father's tough-minded attitudes than his teacher's more relaxed attitudes, even if the boy spends roughly equal amounts of time in the presence of each.

People can learn abnormal as well as acceptable behaviors and personality characteristics through observation and imitation. In fact, the most notable negative behavior that people observe and then imitate may be violence. As we'll see in Chapter 11, children who observe a violent TV program are more willing to hurt others after watching the program. If children observe people who are reinforced for violent, aggressive behavior, they are more likely to imitate that behavior than more socially desirable behaviors.

Observational learning theories assume that learning a new response through imitation can occur without reinforcement, but that later reinforcement acts to maintain such learned behavior, and thus personality characteristics. Most people, for example, have observed aggressive, hostile behavior in others but choose different ways to express emotions. Together, the imitative aspects of observational learning theories and the reinforcement properties of conditioned learning can account for most behaviors. For example, a daughter may become logical and forthright by watching her lawyer mother prepare winning arguments for court cases.

Researchers who focus on observational learning recognize that people *choose* to behave certain ways and not others. Accordingly, some researchers focus on observational learning in combination with another element—thought (cognition). The cognitive approaches to personality, which we consider next, focus on the interaction between thoughts and behavior. I

(I) Cognitive Approaches: Dynamics of Personality

Focus on issues and ideas

- How cognitive approaches consider the thought processes of individuals and assume that individuals are decision makers, planners, and evaluators of their own behavior
- How one's self-perception of control can affect personality
- How one's beliefs can determine successful outcomes

Behaviorists, especially the early behaviorists, were single-minded in their belief that psychologists should study only observable, measurable behavior. But human beings clearly have an inner mental and psychic life; they think about things and react emotionally, and those thoughts and reactions are not always evident in observable behavior. In important ways, cognitive approaches to personality appeared as a reaction to strict behavioral models and added a new dimension to scientists' understanding of personality. The cognitive emphasis is on the interaction of thoughts and behavior. Cognitive approaches consider the uniqueness of human beings, especially of their thought processes, and assume that human beings are decision makers, planners, and evaluators of their own behavior. Rather than viewing people as having stable traits, cognitive approaches assume people are fluid and dynamic in their behavior and responses to the world.

Key Cognitive Concepts

From a cognitive point of view, the mere association of stimuli and responses is not enough for conditioning and learning to occur in human beings; thought processes also have to be involved. Thought and behavior affect one another. According to cognitive theory, whether a person exhibits learned behavior depends on the situation and personal needs at a particular time. If thought and behavior are closely intertwined, then when something affects the person's thoughts, it should also affect his or her behavior.

One of the key elements of the cognitive approach to personality is the idea that people develop self-schemata. As we saw in Chapter 6, a *schema* is a conceptual framework by which people make sense of the world. Self-schemata (*schemata* is the plural of *schema*) are collections of ideas and bits of self-knowledge that organize people's thoughts about themselves. They are often global themes that help individuals define themselves. A man's self-schemata may comprise one self-schema that involves exercise, another that concerns his wife, and still others that are about work, family, and religious feelings. Cognitive researchers assert that people's self-schemata help shape their day-to-day behavior. They may affect people's adjustment, maladjustment, and ability to regulate their own behavior. Thus, someone who has a self-schema for being in control of her emotions may find the death of a loved one a unique challenge to normal day-to-day coping mechanisms.

Over the years, a number of cognitive constructs and theories have been developed, dealing with how people perceive themselves and their relationship with the world. Like their behaviorist colleagues, cognitive psychologists have reacted against psychoanalytic and humanistic theories, which they deem difficult or impossible to verify scientifically. Cognitive theories attempt to account for specific behaviors in specific situations. Because cognitive concepts are far better defined, they are easier to test. We will consider three such concepts and theories next: Julian Rotter's concept of locus of control, Albert Bandura's concept of self-efficacy, and Walter Mischel's concept of cognitive social learning. Each helps clarify different aspects of personality.

Locus of Control

When patients seek the help of a therapist, it is often because they feel "a lack of control." And often the task of therapy is to help clients realize what forces are shaping events and what they can do to gain a sense of control. One widely studied cognitive–behavioral concept that therapists often make use of is locus of control, introduced in the 1950s and systematically developed by Julian Rotter and Herbert Lefcourt. *Locus of control* involves the extent to which individuals believe that a reinforcer or an outcome is contingent on their own behavior or personal characteristics rather than being a function of external events not under their control or simply unpredictable (Lefcourt, 1992; Rotter, 1990). Rotter focused on whether people place their locus of control inside themselves (internal) or in their environments (external). Locus of control influences how people view the world and how they identify the causes of success or failure in their lives. In an important way, locus of control reflects people's personalities—their views of the world and their reactions to it.

To examine locus of control, Rotter developed a test consisting of a series of statements about oneself and other people. To determine whether your locus of control is internal or external, ask yourself to what

Table 10.3 Statements Reflecting Internal versus External Locus of Control

Internal Locus of Control		External Locus of Control
People's misfortunes result from the mistakes they make.	*versus*	Many of the unhappy things in people's lives are partly due to bad luck.
With enough effort, we can wipe out political corruption.	*versus*	It is difficult to have much control over the things politicians do in office.
There is a direct connection between how hard I study and the grade I get.	*versus*	Sometimes I can't understand how teachers arrive at the grades they give.
What happens to me is my own doing.	*versus*	Sometimes I feel that I don't have enough control over the direction my life is taking.

extent you agree with the statements in Table 10.3. People with an internal locus of control (shown by their choice of statements) feel a need to control their environment. They are more likely to engage in proactive behavior, such as preventive health measures and dieting, than are people with an external locus of control. College students characterized as internal are more likely than others to profit from psychotherapy and to show high academic achievement (Lefcourt & Davidson-Katz, 1991). Similarly, hospital nurses characterized as having a strong internal locus of control are more likely to attempt to reform unjust situations (Parker, 1993). In contrast, people with an external locus of control believe they have little control over their lives. A college student characterized as external may attribute a poor grade to a lousy teacher, feeling there was nothing he or she could have done to get a good grade. Individuals who develop an internal locus of control, on the other hand, feel they can master any course they take because they believe that hard work will allow them to do well in any subject. In general, such people report less stress in their lives (Carton, Nowicki, & Balser, 1996).

Locus of control influences how people view the world and how they identify the causes of success or failure in their lives.

People develop expectations based on their beliefs about the sources of reinforcement in their environment. These expectations lead to the specific behaviors. Reinforcement of these behaviors in turn strengthens expectancy and leads to increased belief in internal or external control. Not surprisingly, in therapeutic situations where self-esteem is an issue, psychologists often seek to bolster a client's self-esteem by helping the person recognize the things she or he can control effectively.

Locus of control integrates personality theory, expectancy theories, and reinforcement theory. It describes several specific behaviors but is not comprehensive enough to explain all, or even most, of an individual's behavior. For example, people often develop disproportionately negative thoughts about themselves and acquire a poor sense of self-esteem. Sometimes this is shown in the behavior pattern known as *shyness* (which was discussed in *Experiencing Psychology* on p. 291). Bandura's theory, which we examine next, specifically addresses people's thoughts about their own effectiveness.

Self-Efficacy

Albert Bandura, who is a past president of the American Psychological Association, developed one of the most influential cognitive theories of personality. His conception of personality began with observational learning theory and the idea that human beings observe, think about, and imitate behavior (Bandura, 1977a). Bandura played a major role in reintroducing thought processes into learning and personality theory.

Bandura argued that people's expectations of attaining mastery and achievement and their convictions about their own effectiveness determine the types of behavior they will engage in and the amount of risk they will undertake (Bandura, 1977a, 1977b). He used the term **self-efficacy** to describe a person's belief about whether he or she can successfully engage in and execute a specific behavior. Judgments about self-efficacy determine how much effort people will expend and how long they will persist in the face of obstacles (Bandura, 1997).

A strong sense of self-efficacy allows people to feel free to influence and even create the circumstances of their own lives. Also, people's perceived self-efficacy in managing a situation heightens their sense that they can control it (Conyers, Enright, & Strauser, 1998). Thus, people who have a high level of self-efficacy are more likely than others to attribute success to variables within themselves rather than to chance factors and are more likely to pursue their own goals. Because people can think about their motivation, and even their own thoughts, they can effect changes in themselves, persevere during tough times (Sterrett, 1998), and do better at difficult tasks (Stajkovic & Luthans, 1998).

Bad luck or nonreinforcing experiences can damage a developing sense of self-efficacy. Observation of positive, prosocial models during the formative years, on the other hand, can help people to develop a strong sense of self-efficacy that will encourage them in directing their own lives. Bandura's theory allows individual flexibility in behavior. People are not locked into specific responses to specific stimuli, as some strict behaviorists might assert. According to Bandura, people choose the behaviors they will imitate, and they are free to adapt their behavior to any situation. Self-efficacy both determines and flows from feelings of self-worth. Thus, people's sense of self-efficacy may determine how they present themselves to other people. For example, a man whom others view as successful may not share that view, whereas a man who has received no public recognition may nevertheless consider himself a capable and worthy person; each of these men will present himself as he sees himself (as a failure or a worthy person), not as others see him.

Bandura's theory is optimistic. It is a long way from Freud's view, which argues that conflicting biologically based forces determine human behavior. It is also a long way from a strict behavioral theory, which suggests that environmental contingencies shape behavior. Bandura believes that human beings have choices, that they direct the course of their lives. He also believes that society, parents, experiences, and even luck help shape the life course.

Cognitive Social Learning

Like Bandura, Walter Mischel claims that thought is crucial in determining human behavior and that both past experiences and current reinforcement are important. But Mischel is an *interactionist*—he focuses on the interaction of people and their environment (Mischel, 1983). Mischel and other cognitive theorists argue that people respond flexibly to various situations. They change their responses on the basis of their past experiences and their current assessment of the present situation (Brown & Moskowitz, 1998). This process of adjustment is called *self-regulation.* For example, people make subtle adjustments in their tone of voice and overt behavior (aspects of their personality), depending on the context in which they find themselves. Those who tend to be warm, caring, and attentive, for example, can in certain situations become hostile and dismissive.

People's personalities, and particularly their responses to any given stimulus, are determined by several variables (Mischel, 1979): *competencies* (what people know and can do), *encoding strategies* (the way they process, attend to, and select information), *expectancies* (their anticipation of outcomes), *personal values* (the importance they attach to various aspects of life), and *self-regulatory systems* (the systems of rules they have established for themselves to guide their behavior).

Mischel has had a great impact on psychological thought, because he has challenged researchers to consider the idea that traits alone cannot predict behavior. The context of the situation must also be considered—not only the immediate situation but also the culture in which a person lives and was raised, as well as other variables such as the gender and age of the person whose behavior is being predicted. Day-to-day variations in behavior should not be seen as aberrations, but rather as meaningful responses to changing circumstances (Brown & Moskowitz, 1998).

Cognitive Theories Continue to Evolve

Cognitive personality theorists believe that reinforcement, past experiences, current feelings, future expectations, and subjective values all influence people's responses to their environments. Human beings have unique and characteristic ways of responding, but those ways—their personalities—change, depending on specific circumstances.

Cognitive theories of personality are well researched but do not, as yet, clearly explain the development of personality from childhood to adulthood. They are also not yet well integrated. Bandura, for example, has shifted his focus from observational learning to self-regulation to self-efficacy without tying together the threads of those research efforts. However, Bandura never claimed to have developed a complete theory of personality, and what this incompleteness signifies is that personality is an exceedingly complex phenomenon. Further research and new ideas are still needed to generate more complete, sophisticated theories.

Self-efficacy: A person's belief about whether he or she can successfully engage in and execute a specific behavior.

Personality theories are diverse, and their explanations of specific behaviors vary sharply; each one views the development of personality and maladjustment from a different vantage point.

Personality is often an issue for people who seek therapy. Many people want to understand and even change their personalities through therapy. When a therapist, regardless of orientation, meets a new client, the therapist may choose to assess the client's personality before the therapy begins. There are several ways the client can be evaluated. These techniques are the focus of personality assessment, the topic we consider next.

Think Critically

- What are some possible explanations a cognitive psychologist might offer for the constancy of personality?
- If an individual has an internal locus of control, under what conditions do you think he or she would be likely to develop maladjustment or extreme anxiety?

Personality Assessment

Focus on issues and ideas

- The purpose of personality assessment
- The uses of objective and projective personality tests
- The contributions of nature and nurture to the stability of personality

When you think to yourself that your neighbor is a fun-loving guy, that your mom is an affectionate person, or that your brother is politically skillful, you are making assessments of their personalities. We all do it from time to time, and psychologists do it systematically.

Assessment is the process of evaluating individual differences among human beings by means of tests, interviews, observations, and recordings of physiological processes. Psychologists who conduct personality assessments are seeking to evaluate personality in order to explain behavior, to diagnose and classify maladjusted people, and to develop treatment plans when necessary. Many individuals and organizations give tests—school systems often give IQ tests, for example—but these are not full-blown assessments. Businesses conduct assessments for personnel selection; assessments are also used to supplement psychological research on personality types.

Therapists sometimes conduct assessments of clients who may be in distress. In this forum, the type of assessment used is determined by the client's needs (Matarazzo, 1990). Often, more than one assessment procedure is needed to provide all the necessary information, and many psychologists administer a group, or *battery*, of tests. The goal of using a variety of available tests is to accumulate a wide range of information on which to base an intelligent, informed conclusion. As Kaufman (1990, p. 29) asserts, "Psychologists need to be shrewd detectives to uncover test interpretations that are truly 'individual' . . . and will ultimately help the person referred for evaluation."

A psychologist may assess personality with the Minnesota Multiphasic Personality Inventory–2nd Edition (MMPI–2) (discussed later in this section), intelligence with the WAIS-R (described in Chapter 7), or a specific skill (such as coordination) with some other specific test. More confidence can be placed in data gathered from several tests than in the data from a single test; as *Experiencing Psychology* shows, no single test can characterize a personality completely. Hundreds of personality tests exist; there are more than 100 tests just for measuring the various elements of anxiety. The purpose of the testing determines the type of tests administered.

Objective Personality Tests

Next to intelligence tests, the most widely given tests are *objective personality tests*. These tests, sometimes termed *personality inventories*, generally consist of true/false or multiple-choice questions. The aims of objective personality tests vary. Raymond Cattell developed a test called the 16PF (the name refers to 16 personality factors) to screen job applicants and to examine individuals who fall within a normal range of personality functioning. The California Psychological Inventory (CPI) is used primarily to identify and assess normal aspects of personality. Based on a large sample of normal subjects, it examines personality traits such as sociability, self-control, and responsibility. Well-constructed personality tests turn out to be valid predictors of performance in a wide array of jobs; this is true for people of various ethnicities and minority status groups (Hogan, Hogan, & Roberts, 1996).

One of the most widely used and best-researched personality tests is the Minnesota Multiphasic Personality Inventory–2nd Edition (the MMPI–2). The original MMPI was widely used, and the second edition, published in 1989, is considered a major revision. The MMPI–2 consists of 567 true/false statements that focus on the test taker's attitudes, feelings,

EXPERIENCING PSYCHOLOGY

The MBTI, A Single Personality Test?

The summer before my first year of college, I took a course called "How to Study." The instructor told us that having a better idea of our own personality style would make us better test takers. He argued that personality tests, along with interest and ability tests, were also useful in predicting vocational preferences. He then gave us a number of personality tests. One of the tests he used was developed in the 1960s by Peter Myers and Isabel Briggs.

The Myers-Briggs Type Indicator, often called the MBTI, is a test based on Jung's theory of personality. Jung proposed that each individual favors specific modalities, or ways of dealing with and learning about the world; the modalities you prefer define your personality type. The MBTI asks you to choose between pairs of statements that deal with your preferences or inclinations; for instance: "Do you think that having a daily routine is (a) an easy way to get things done, or (b) difficult even when necessary?"

The MBTI is scored so that the test taker is characterized as predominantly at one pole or another on four distinct dimensions: Extroversion–Introversion (E or I), Sensing–Intuition (S or N), Thinking–Feeling (T or F), and Judging–Perceptive (J or P). The various possible combinations thus yield 16 personality types. For example, an ENFP type is an individual whose principal modalities are extroversion, intuition, feeling, and perceptiveness. A person of this type feels a greater relatedness to the outer world of people than to the inner world of ideas (E), tends to look for possibilities rather than to work with what is known (N), makes decisions based on personal values rather than on logic (F), and shows a preference for a spontaneous way of life rather than an orderly existence (P).

Unfortunately, the MBTI has many problems. It can be scored in sophisticated ways, but often it is simply interpreted by unskilled examiners—like my precollege study skills instructor—for purposes of vocational counseling. The MBTI was normed for students in grades 4 through 12, so it is best used for individuals of those ages. Cultural vantage points are not taken into account. Further, the possibility of maladjustment is not considered.

In fairness, the MBTI is a quick and easy way to gather basic data about personality; when combined with other personality instruments such as the MMPI–2, the California Psychological Inventory, and the 16PF questionnaire, it can be useful in helping a skilled clinician evaluate important elements about an individual—for example, stress level (Ware, Rytting, & Jenkins, 1994). Research also shows that the MBTI can be used to assess the quality of therapeutic relationships and the extent to which people are able to perceive consumer messages, and that it can be helpful in designing techniques for classroom management (Carland et al., 1994; Claxton & McIntyre, 1994; Nelson & Stake, 1994). But, as we saw in Chapter 7, no single test score can reveal everything about an individual, even though some might claim it can. ■

motor disturbances, and bodily complaints. Typical statements on the MMPI–2 are as follows:

I tire easily.

I become very anxious before examinations.

I worry about sex matters.

I become bored easily.

A series of subscales examine different aspects of functioning and measure the truthfulness of the test taker's responses; these subscales, called the clinical and validity scales, are summarized in Table 10.4 (on p. 302). In 1992, a special version of the MMPI, called the MMPI-A, was developed for adolescents. Items on this test cover adolescent issues such as eating disorders, substance abuse, and family and school problems.

The MMPI–2 can be administered individually or to a group. The test takes 90 minutes to complete and can be scored in less than a half-hour. It provides a profile that lets psychologists assess an individual's current level of functioning and his or her characteristic way of dealing with the world; it also provides a description of some specific personality characteristics. The MMPI–2 also enables psychologists to make reasonable predictions about a person's ability to function in specific situations, such as working in a mental

Assessment: Process of evaluating individual differences among human beings by means of tests, interviews, observations, and recordings of physiological processes.

Table 10.4 The Clinical and Validity Scales of the MMPI–2

Scale Name	Interpretation
Clinical Scales	
1. Hypochondriasis (Hs)	High scorers reflect an exaggerated concern about their physical health.
2. Depression (D)	High scorers are usually depressed, despondent, and distressed.
3. Hysteria (Hy)	High scorers complain often about physical symptoms, which have no apparent organic cause.
4. Psychopathic deviate (Pd)	High scorers show a disregard for social and moral standards.
5. Masculinity/femininity (Mf)	Extreme scorers show "traditional" masculine or feminine attitudes and values.
6. Paranoia (Pa)	High scorers demonstrate extreme suspiciousness and feelings of persecution.
7. Psychasthenia (Pt)	High scorers tend to be highly anxious, rigid, tense, and worried.
8. Schizophrenia (Sc)	High scorers tend to be socially withdrawn and to engage in bizarre and unusual thinking.
9. Hypomania (Ma)	High scorers are emotionally excitable, energetic, and impulsive.
10. Social introversion (S)	High scorers tend to be modest, self-effacing, and shy.
Validity Scales	
1. Cannot say (?)	High scorers may be evasive in filling out the questionnaire.
2. Lie (L)	High scorers attempt to present themselves in a very favorable light and possibly tell lies to do so.
3. Infrequency (F)	High scorers are presenting themselves in a particularly bad way and may well be "faking bad."
4. Defensiveness (K)	High scorers may be very defensive in filling out the questionnaire.

hospital or as a security guard. Many businesses today require job applicants to take the MMPI as part of the screening process for certain jobs.

Generally, the MMPI–2 is used as a screening device for maladjustment. Its norms are based on the profiles of thousands of normal people and a smaller group of psychiatric patients. Each scale tells how most normal individuals score. In general, a score significantly above normal may be considered evidence of maladjustment. The test has built-in safeguards to prevent test takers from controlling the test's outcome. Interpretation of the MMPI–2 generally involves looking at patterns of scores, rather than at a person's score on a single scale.

Nearly 5,000 published studies examined the validity and reliability of the original MMPI. For the most part, these studies have concluded that it was a valid and useful predictive tool. The MMPI–2 was standardized using a much larger sample (2,600 people) of subjects, who were more representative of the overall population than were the initial group of subjects. The MMPI–2 includes questions that focus on eating disorders and drug abuse; older questions that had a gender bias were revised. Because many of the test's traditional features remain unchanged, the refinements and modifications should only improve its predictive validity (Butcher et al., 1990, 1998). Yet the MMPI–2 is by no means a perfect instrument for valid predictions about future behavior; it should only be used as part of a battery of tests (Helmes & Reddon, 1993).

Projective tests: Devices or instruments used to assess personality, in which examinees are shown a standard set of ambiguous stimuli and asked to respond to the stimuli in their own way.

Projective Tests

The fundamental idea underlying the use of projective assessment techniques is that a person's unconscious motives direct daily thoughts and behavior. To uncover a person's unconscious motives, psychologists have developed **projective tests**—devices or instruments used to assess personality by showing examinees a standard set of ambiguous stimuli and asking them to respond to the stimuli in their own way. The examinees are assumed to project their unconscious feelings, drives, and motives onto the ambiguous stimuli. Such tests help clinicians assess the deeper levels of an individual's personality structure and uncover motives of which the individual may not be aware. Projective tests are used when it is important to determine whether an examinee is trying to hide something. They tend to be used by psychologists with a psychoanalytic orientation. They do not have the rigorous development on standardized scoring procedures associated with IQ tests, and they are less reliable than objective personality tests—nevertheless, they help complete a picture of psychological functioning.

Projective tests have a poor reputation among many psychologists who are not psychoanalytically oriented.

Rorschach Inkblot Test. A classic projective test is the *Rorschach Inkblot Test.* The test taker is shown ten inkblots, one at a time. The blots are symmetrical, with a distinctive form; five are black and white, two also have some red ink, and three have various pastel colors. Examinees tell the clinician what they see in the design, and a detailed report of the response is made for later interpretation. Aiken (1988, p. 390) reports a typical response:

> My first impression was a big bug, a fly maybe. I see in the background two facelike figures pointing toward each other as if they're talking. It also has a resemblance to a skeleton—the pelvis area. I see a cute little bat right in the middle. The upper half looks like a mouse.

After the inkblots have been shown, the examiner elicits more information from the test taker with instructions or questions, such as these: "Describe the facelike figures." "What were the figures talking about?" Although norms are available for responses, skilled interpretation and good clinical judgment are necessary in order to place an individual's responses in a meaningful context. Long-term predictions can be formulated only with great caution because of a lack of substantive supporting research.

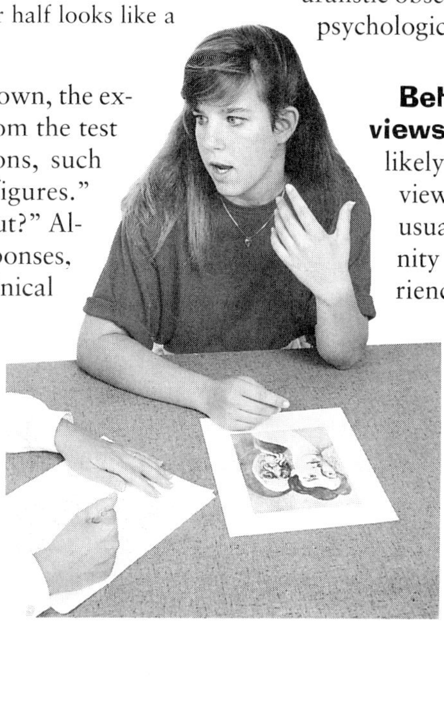

Thematic Apperception Test. The *Thematic Apperception Test* (TAT) is much more structured than the Rorschach. (The TAT was discussed in Chapter 8 as one way to assess a person's need for achievement.) It consists of black-and-white pictures, each depicting one or more people in an ambiguous situation; examinees are asked to tell a story describing the situation. Specifically, they are asked what led up to the situation, what will happen in the future, and what the people are thinking and feeling. The TAT is particularly useful as part of a battery of tests to assess a person's characteristic way of dealing with others and of interacting with the world.

To some extent, projective tests have a poor reputation among many psychologists who are not psychoanalytically oriented. Most argue that the interpretation of pictures is just too subjective and prone to error. Practicing clinicians, even those who use projective tests, often rely more heavily on behavioral assessment techniques, discussed next.

Behavioral Assessment Techniques

Traditionally, *behavioral assessment* focused on overt behaviors that could be examined directly. Today, practitioners and researchers examine cognitive activity as well. Their aim is to gather information in order to both diagnose maladjustment and prescribe treatment. Four popular and widely used behavioral assessment techniques are behavioral assessment interviews, naturalistic observation, self-monitoring, and neuropsychological assessment.

Behavioral Assessment Interviews. Any psychological assessment is likely to begin with an interview. Interviews are personal, giving the client (and usually the client's family) an opportunity to express feelings, facts, and experiences that might not be revealed by other assessment procedures. Interviews yield important information about the client's family situation, occupational stresses, and other events that affect the behavior being examined. They also allow psychologists to evaluate the client's motivations and to inform the client about the assessment process.

Behavioral assessment interviews tend to be systematic and structured, focusing on overt and current behaviors and paying attention to the situations in which these behaviors occur. The interviewer will ask the examinee about the events that led up to a specific response, how the examinee felt while making the response, and whether the same response might occur in other situations. Through this type of interview, the clinician has the opportunity to select the problems to be dealt with in therapy and to set treatment goals. Many clinicians consider their first interview with a client a key component in the assessment process. Interviews reveal only what the interviewee wishes to disclose, however, and are subject to bias on the part of the interviewer. Nonetheless, when followed up with other behavioral measures, interviews are a good starting point.

Naturalistic Observation. Naturalistic observation involves an observer's entering a person's natural environment and recording the occurrence of specified behaviors at predetermined intervals. (Ideally, there should be two observers to check for accuracy and reliability, but typically only one observer is available.) In a personality assessment, for example, psychologists might observe how often a child in a classroom jumps out of his seat or how often a hospitalized patient refers to her depressed state. The purpose of using naturalistic observation as a behavioral assessment technique is to learn about people's behavior without interfering with it. The strength of the approach is that it provides information that might otherwise be unavailable or difficult to piece together. For example, observation can help psychologists learn what sequences of events can lead up to an outburst of antisocial behaviors.

Naturalistic observation is not without its problems, however. How does a researcher record behavior in a home setting without being observed? Do behaviors observed in one setting accurately represent interactions in other settings? Does the observer have any biases, make inaccurate judgments, or collect inadequate data? Although naturalistic observation is not perfect, it is a powerful technique.

Self-Monitoring. Self-monitoring is an assessment procedure in which a person systematically counts and records the frequency and duration of his or her own specific behaviors. One person might record the number and duration of such symptoms as migraine headaches, backaches, or feelings of panic. Another person might self-monitor his or her eating or sleeping patterns, sexual behavior, or smoking. Self-monitoring is inexpensive, easy to do, and applicable to a variety of problems. It reveals information that might otherwise be inaccessible, and it enables practitioners to probe the events that preceded the monitored activity to see if they conform to some readily identifiable pattern. In addition, self-monitoring helps clients become more aware of their own behaviors and the situations in which they occur.

Self-monitoring: An assessment procedure in which a person systematically counts and records the frequency and duration of his or her own specific behaviors.

Neuropsychological Assessment. Some personality changes and some forms of maladjustment result from a brain disorder or a malfunction in the nervous system. Problems in brain functioning are sometimes evident in a neuropsychological examination. The newest way to detect brain–behavior disorders is neuropsychological assessment. (Neurologists are physicians who study the physiology of the brain and its disorders; neuropsychologists are psychologists who study the brain and its disorders as they relate to behavior.) Though neuropsychology is a traditional area in experimental psychology, the use of neuropsychological assessment techniques by practitioners is a relatively recent development.

The signs of neuropsychological disorders may become evident through the use of traditional assessment devices such as histories (a history of headaches, for example), intelligence tests (showing slow reaction times), or observation during a therapeutic session (atypical head motions or muscle spasms might be observed, for example). If a child who frequently and inappropriately makes obscene gestures or remarks accompanies them with facial tics, the practitioner may suspect the existence of the neurological disorder known as Tourette's disorder, in which such behaviors are often evident. Psychologists who see evidence of neuropsychological deficits often refer the client with the problem to a neuropsychologist or neurologist for further evaluation.

Personality: Only Half of the Story?

If personality is a set of relatively enduring predispositions that determine how a person reacts to the environment, then why do people sometimes behave unpredictably? Psychologists have long recognized that an individual's behavior is not consistent all the time. What makes the difference? Is a person's brain chemistry being altered? Or is it the varying context in which a person acts that results in the different behavior? This chapter has suggested that personality may be enduring, but there are a host of circumstances that alter how a person behaves. An outgrowth of personality studies and an attempt to understand the dynamics of human behavior is the field of social psychology, which examines how an individual's behavior is affected by other people. Social psychology is the topic of the next chapter.

Think Critically

- Do you think that projective tests such as the TAT and the Rorschach Inkblot Test can achieve their goal?
- What aspects of personality do you think a personality test might be unable to characterize?

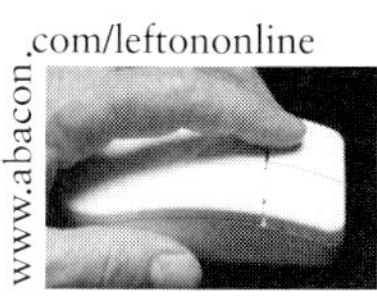

Your password-protected Website allows you access to the most comprehensive set of materials in The Psychology Place.

Summary and Review

How do psychologists define personality?

KEY TERM
personality, p. 280

Psychoanalytic Theory: Unconscious Drives and Defenses

What fundamental assumptions about human behavior and the mind underlie Freud's theory?

What is the fundamental function of all of Freud's defense mechanisms?

To which of Freud's fundamental assumptions did the neo-Freudians react?

KEY TERMS
psychic determinism, p. 281; unconscious motivation, p. 281; libido, p. 281; conscious, p. 281; preconscious, p. 282; unconscious, p. 282; id, p. 282; ego, p. 282; superego, p. 282; oral stage, p. 283; anal stage, p. 283; phallic stage, p. 284; Oedipus complex, p. 284; latency stage, p. 284; genital stage, p. 285; fixation, p. 285; defense mechanism, p. 285; repression, p. 285; projection, p. 285; denial, p. 285; reaction formation, p. 286; sublimation, p. 286; rationalization, p. 286; neo-Freudians, p. 287; collective unconscious, p. 287; archetypes, p. 287

Humanistic Approaches: Self-Fulfillment and Self-Actualization

What are the motivating forces of personality development, according to Maslow's and Rogers's theories?

KEY TERMS
self-actualization, p. 289; fulfillment, p. 289; self, p. 289; ideal self, p. 289

Trait and Type Theories: Stable Behavioral Dispositions

Distinguish between a trait and a type.

Describe the ideas of Allport, Cattell, and Eysenck regarding traits.

What are the Big Five?

KEY TERMS
trait, p. 290; types, p. 291

Behavioral Approaches: Learning Is Key

What are the important aspects of behavioral approaches to personality?

Describe how behavioral concepts are used to explain personality development.

Cognitive Approaches: Dynamics of Personality

What are the key ideas of the cognitive approach to personality?

KEY TERMS
self-efficacy, p. 298

Personality Assessment

Describe assessment.

What is the MMPI–2?

What is a projective test?

Identify the techniques of behavioral assessment.

KEY TERMS
assessment, p. 300; projective tests, p. 302; self-monitoring, p. 304

Self-Test

1. Freud's commitment to psychic determinism makes it clear that he rejected the concept of:
   A. conflict
   B. instinct
   C. free will
   D. fixation

2. The primary function of the ego is to:
   A. satisfy the desires of the id in a socially acceptable way
   B. deny and overpower the id
   C. shift energy from the id to the superego
   D. promote behavior that is unselfish and ethical

3. The Oedipus complex arises and must be resolved during the ____________ stage of psychosexual development.
   A. genital
   B. phallic
   C. anal
   D. oral

4. Self-determination is most prominently associated with which of the following personality theories?
   A. psychoanalytic
   B. trait
   C. humanistic
   D. behavioral

5. A stable defining feature of an individual's personality is a:
   A. factor
   B. self-concept
   C. type
   D. trait

6. That they fail to provide an account of the development of personality is a criticism made of ____________ theories.
   A. psychoanalytic
   B. trait
   C. humanistic
   D. behavioral

7. After seeing his father put on a tie, Jake tried to wear one as well. This is an example of:
   A. observational learning
   B. classical conditioning
   C. operant conditioning
   D. spontaneous behavior

8. Jonathan believes that forces beyond his control have resulted in his having a low-paying job and an unhappy marriage. Rotter might say that Jonathan has:
   A. low self-efficacy
   B. high self-efficacy
   C. external locus of control
   D. internal locus of control

9. Paula was asked to interpret a blob of ink, and a psychologist analyzed her answers. What type of personality test was Paula taking?
   A. Rorschach Inkblot Test
   B. Ink Blot Modeling Test
   C. Thematic Apperception Test
   D. MMPI–2

10. Which type of behavioral assessment technique involves having an individual keep a record of his or her own behaviors?
    A. behavioral assessment interview
    B. naturalistic observation
    C. self-monitoring
    D. neuropsychological assessment

Chapter 11

Social Psychology

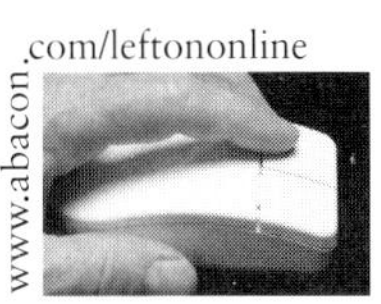

Go to your password-protected Website for full-color art, Weblinks, and more!

Littleton, Colorado. April 20, 1999. At Columbine High School, in a quiet, middle-class suburb, the lives of twelve students and one teacher were ended in a massacre that shook the nation. Stunned and grieving, parents, teachers, and schoolmates asked themselves "Why?" and "What went wrong?" Soon, media news analysts and editorial writers were probing the causes as well. No one will ever know for sure what went so terribly wrong in the lives of Eric Harris and Dylan Klebold, the two high school students who planned and executed the devastating massacre. While trying to help the traumatized families and friends of the victims, psychologists became aware, yet again, of how little we really know about one another, about how our actions and words influence others. If the two boys who gunned down their peers and then took their own lives had been treated differently, would it have averted the tragedy? Were there key events or interactions that shaped their attitudes and behaviors? Many questions like these will be asked again and again as the families and friends of the victims try to recover from their shock and grief.

Psychologists recognize that people's behavior is shaped by early experiences, by others in their lives, and by such daily influences as advertisements and school events. People examine each other's nonverbal messages—looking beyond the smiles—and resist (or give in to) attempts to change their attitudes or to gain their compliance. No person is an island, unaffected by other people's attitudes and behavior. ■

In this chapter, we examine the world of social interactions among individuals and within groups. We will see that people affect one another's attitudes, self-perceptions, and behavior. **Social psychology** is the scientific study of how people think about, interact with, influence, and are influenced by the thoughts, feelings, and behaviors of others. This chapter looks at some of the traditional concepts in social psychology: attitudes, social cognition, and social interactions. These concepts help psychologists form an understanding of behavior involving more than one person—that is, of social behavior. Let's look first at how individual attitudes are affected by other people. (I)

(I) Attitudes: Deeply Held Feelings and Beliefs

Focus on issues and ideas

- How our lasting feelings and beliefs serve key functions
- The relationship between attitudes and behavior
- How attitudes can be changed
- How cognitive conflict contributes to attitude change

Attitudes are long-lasting patterns of feelings and beliefs about other people, ideas, or objects, which are based in a person's past experiences and shape his or her future behavior. They are usually evaluative and serve certain functions, such as guiding new behaviors and helping a person interpret the world efficiently (Eagly & Chaiken, 1993). Attitudes are shaped by how a person perceives other people, how others perceive him or her, and how the person *thinks* others see him or her.

Social psychology: The scientific study of how people think about, interact with, influence, and are influenced by the thoughts, feelings, and behaviors of other people.

Attitudes: Long-lasting patterns of feelings and beliefs about other people, ideas, or objects, which are based in a person's past experiences, shape his or her future behavior, and are evaluative in nature.

Dimensions and Functions of Attitudes

Football fans are often fanatical in their attitudes: They know every possible statistic about the team's record, they are elated or down in the dumps after each game, and they often back up their feelings with visible support for the team. People's feelings and beliefs about football, or any other subject, are a crucial part of their attitudes. Attitudes have three dimensions—cognitive, emotional, and behavioral—each of which serves a specific function.

The *cognitive dimension* of an attitude consists of thoughts and beliefs. When someone forms an attitude about a group of people, a series of events, or a political philosophy, the cognitive dimension of the attitude functions to help the person categorize, process, and remember the people, events, or philosophy. The *emotional dimension* of an attitude involves evaluative feelings, such as liking or disliking. For example, some people like the improvisational abstractions of cool jazz; others prefer the down-to-earth sound of country and western music. The *behavioral dimension* of an attitude determines how the beliefs and evaluative feelings are demonstrated (Eagly, 1992), such as by voting in accordance with one's political beliefs or attending the concerts of a favorite group. Behaviorally, attitudes function to shape specific actions. Individuals do not always express their attitudes in behavior, of course, especially when the attitudes are not yet firmly established or when they hold two attitudes that are inconsistent with one another. For example, many more people cognitively and emotionally support a nuclear arms freeze than give their time, energy, or money to organizations supporting this cause (Gilbert, 1988). Similarly, your aunt might give you a gift that you think is hideous or frivolous, but in deference to your affection for her, you express gratitude for the "special" present—your real attitude is not expressed.

When people have strongly held attitudes about a specific topic, they are said to have a *conviction*. Once people form a conviction, they think about it and become identified with it (which makes convictions long-lasting and resistant to change). This is especially true of religious and political convictions (Abelson, 1988). For example, despite evidence to the contrary, many people still believe that President John F. Kennedy was assassinated by agents of the CIA in a plot to overthrow the government. Once people have formed a conviction, it functions to justify a wide range of behaviors and colors their interpretation of new information about events.

What variables play a role in determining how attitudes are formed, displayed, or changed? Why are some attitudes much harder to modify than others? We consider these questions in the following sections, beginning with attitude formation.

Forming Attitudes

Attitudes are formed through learning that begins early in life. Thus, psychologists rely on learning theories to explain how children form attitudes. Three learning theory concepts that help explain attitude formation are classical conditioning, operant conditioning, and observational learning (see Chapter 5 for a detailed explanation of these concepts).

The association of people, events, and ideologies with certain attitudes often goes unnoticed because it happens so effortlessly. However, such associations can shape children's views of and emotional responses to the world, thereby forming the basis of their future attitudes as adults. For example, suppose a parent never has a good word to say about Democrats ("bleeding-heart liberals," and so on). *Classical conditioning* pairs the formerly neutral stimulus (the Democrat) with an unconditioned stimulus (derogatory comments). Because derogatory comments naturally elicit negative feelings as a response, the resulting negative feelings can be considered an unconditioned response. If a child hears such remarks repeatedly, Democrats will eventually evoke a response of negative feelings (now a conditioned response) in the child.

A key principle of *operant conditioning* is that reinforced behaviors are likely to recur; this principle helps explain how attitudes are maintained over time. In socializing their children, parents express approval for and reinforce ideas and behaviors consistent with their own "correct" view of the world. Such approval and reinforcement lead children to adopt their parents' "correct" attitudes.

According to the concept of *observational learning*, people establish attitudes by watching the behavior of those they consider significant and then imitating that behavior. The new attitudes people learn eventually become their own. Suppose a young girl sees her father react angrily to a TV news commentator who contradicts a tenet of the family's religious faith. The next time the child hears a similar argument, she will be likely to mimic her father's attitude; doing so will partially shape her own attitude.

Do Attitudes Predict Behavior?

Social psychologists can assess people's attitudes, but whether those attitudes predict behavior depends on numerous variables. Some of these variables are attitude strength, vested interest, specificity of attitudes, and accessibility of attitudes.

Attitudes are better predictors of behavior when they are strong and there are few competing outside influences, such as conflicting advertising appeals or advice from friends. A person who believes strongly in the health hazards of cigarette smoking, even after being bombarded by Camel and Marlboro advertisements, may work actively for an antismoking campaign. Furthermore, attitudes people consider personally important (those in which they have a vested interest) are more likely to be shown in behavior and to stay intact, regardless of how situations change over time (Krosnick, 1988). If a parent believes strongly in improving her child's educational opportunities, she will be far more likely to attend PTA meetings. The extent to which a belief is tied up with a person's self-concept is also a good predictor of both the strength of the belief and the likelihood that the person will act on it (Pomerantz, Chaiken, & Tordesillas, 1995).

Attitudes are also more likely to foretell behavior when they are specific and the situation requiring a decision closely matches the situation to which the attitude applies. Global attitudes, and even stereotypes about groups of people, do not predict specific behaviors very well (Haddock, Zanna, & Esses, 1994). For example, a person may have broadly liberal political beliefs, but only a specific attitude about health care, welfare reform, or government waste will predict whether the person will vote for a specific candidate. Last, attitudes predict behavior best when they are accessible, that is, clearly stated and easily remembered. When people have sharply delineated ideas about a political position, they can easily decide how favorably they rate a new candidate. When they cannot easily remember or articulate their views, making such judgments is more time-consuming and less predictable.

Does Behavior Determine Attitudes?

Is it possible that your attitudes don't determine your behavior, but just the opposite—that your behavior shapes your attitudes? Mounting evidence argues that to a certain extent this is the case. People often develop positive attitudes toward a charity after making a contribution, however small. In weight control programs, alcohol abstinence programs, and many therapy groups, facilitators try to change behaviors (get people to abstain from alcohol, for example) with the idea that positive attitudes about a new life will *follow* changes in behavior.

A dramatic demonstration of attitudes resulting from behaviors occurred in the 1970s. In studies that came to be known as the Stanford Prison Experiment (Haney, Banks, & Zimbardo, 1973; Haney & Zimbardo, 1998), researchers asked normal well-adjusted college students to dress and act as either prisoners or guards. Guards were given uniforms, billy clubs, and whistles; prisoners were given prison jumpsuits and were locked in cells. Within a few days, "guards" were harassing and degrading "prisoners." Prisoners were caving in and becoming obedient, and many were suffering intense psychological pain. The experiment was aborted after a week. This research study, with its shocking result, would not be conducted today because of ethical considerations. The study showed that an individual could play a role—guard or prisoner—and quickly adapt to that role, develop attitudes that were consistent with it, and become actively committed to the attitudes associated with that role.

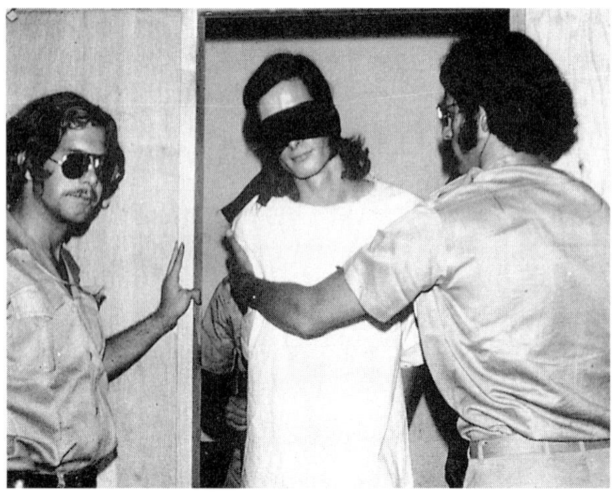

Persuasion: Changing Attitudes

Television is one of the prime means politicians and marketing executives use to try to change attitudes. They know that since attitudes are learned, they can be changed or replaced. Changed attitudes may impel a person to do almost anything—from voting Democratic, to trying a new brand of soap, to undergoing a religious conversion, to becoming a lover of jazz. In the 1950s, Carl Hovland was one of the first social psychologists to identify key components of attitude change: the communicator, the communication, the medium, and the audience.

The Communicator. To be persuasive, the communicator—the person trying to effect attitude change—must project integrity, credibility, and trustworthiness. If people don't respect, believe, or trust the communicator, they are unlikely to change their attitudes. Researchers have also found that the perceived power, prestige, celebrity, prominence, modesty, and attractiveness of the communicator are extremely important (Cialdini, 1994; Dabul et al., 1997). Information received from friends is considered more influential than information from the communications media.

The Communication. A clear, convincing, and logical argument is the most effective tool for changing attitudes—especially attitudes with a strong emotional dimension, such as those concerning capital punishment or school desegregation (Millar & Millar, 1990). This is especially true in Western culture, where appeals to logic and reason are more prevalent than in Japan, for example, where appeals to authority and tradition are common.

Research is beginning to show that negative information tends to influence people more strongly than positive information (Ito, Larsen, Smith, & Cacioppo, 1998). Researchers have also found that if people hear a persuasive message often enough, they begin to believe it, regardless of its validity. Repeated exposure to certain situations can also change attitudes. Similarly, a name that is heard often is more likely to be viewed positively than is one heard infrequently; this is called the *mere exposure effect* (Jacoby et al., 1989).

The Medium. The means by which a communication is presented—its medium—influences people's receptiveness to attitude change. Today, one of the most common avenues for attempts at attitude change is the mass media, particularly television. After all, the goal of TV commercials is either to change or to reinforce people's behavior. Commercials exhort viewers to drink Pepsi instead of Coke, to say no to

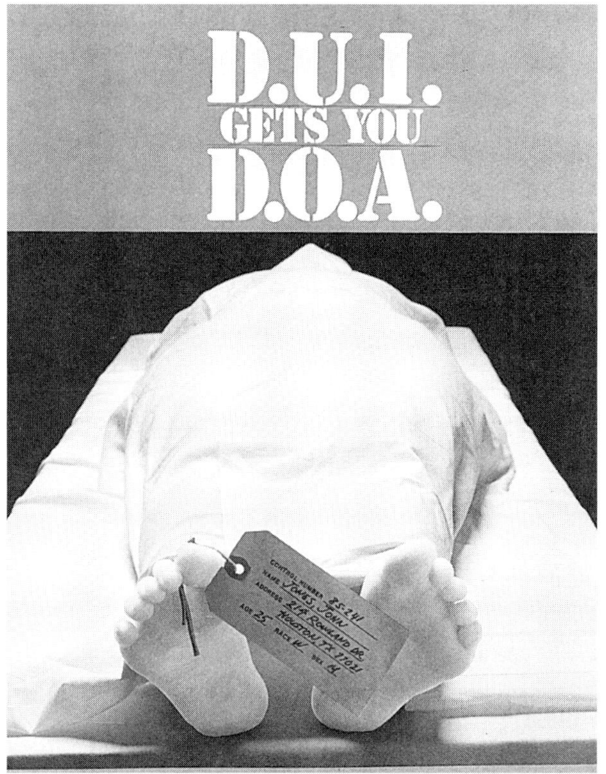

drugs, or to vote for a Democrat instead of a Republican. Research shows that TV advertising is one of the most influential media for changing attitudes in the Western world; this is not too surprising, given the fact that the television is on for more than 4 hours every day in the average American household.

Nevertheless, face-to-face communication often has more impact than communication through television or in writing. Thus, even though candidates for public office rely heavily on TV, radio, and printed ads, they also try to meet people face-to-face, sometimes taking bus or train tours to deliver their message directly to the people. This is important, because research shows that the impact of bursts of political advertising in the mass media is often overrated. Television advertising may serve only to strengthen preexisting ideas, except when a candidate uses massive (and expensive) campaigns and voters' preexisting attitudes are weak (Sears & Kosterman, 1994).

Changing people's attitudes, and ultimately their behavior, can be difficult if they have well-established habits.

The Audience. From time to time, people actually want to have their attitudes changed and seek out alternative views. At other times, they fold their arms and firmly announce, "It's going to take an act of Congress to change my mind" (Johnson & Eagly, 1989). Openness to attitude change is related in part to age and education. People are most susceptible to attitude change in their early adult years; this susceptibility drops off in later years (Krosnick & Alwin, 1989). People of high intelligence are less likely to have their opinions changed, and those who have high self-esteem tend to be similarly unyielding (Rhodes & Wood, 1992). A change is far more likely to occur if the person trying to change another's attitude is a friend (Cialdini, 1994).

Changing people's attitudes, and ultimately their behavior, can be difficult if they have well-established habits (which often come with advancing age) or are highly motivated in the direction opposite to the desired change. Consider attitudes toward smoking. Although most people generally believe in the serious health consequences of smoking, 25% of the people in the United States still smoke. Getting someone to stop smoking takes more than fostering positive attitudes about health; it also requires instilling a new habit and removing an old one. Education can be helpful, as can devices to help people remember not to smoke (such as warning buzzers or strings on fingers); nevertheless, because of its addictive properties, smoking is hard to stop.

Experiencing Psychology (on p. 312) describes some tried-and-true techniques that have been used for decades to influence attitudes, change behaviors, and obtain favors.

Cognitive Approaches to Attitude Change: The Elaboration Likelihood Model. Decades of research have identified the basic components of attitude change. But researchers have only recently begun to focus on what happens cognitively to individuals whose attitudes are being changed. Various theories attempt to understand such individuals' thought processes so as to be able to predict attitude change. One such theory, proposed by Richard Petty and John Cacioppo (1981, 1985), suggests that people generally want to have attitudes and beliefs that will prove helpful in the face of day-to-day challenges and problems (Petty et al., 1994). This theory is called the **elaboration likelihood model**—a view of attitude change suggesting that it can be accomplished via two routes: central and peripheral.

Elaboration likelihood model: Theory suggesting that there are two routes to attitude change: the central route, which focuses on thoughtful consideration of an argument for change, and the peripheral route, which focuses on less careful, more emotional, and even superficial evaluation.

EXPERIENCING PSYCHOLOGY

Techniques for Inducing Attitude Change

Change a person's attitudes and you can change his or her behavior—many practitioners believe this and use it in their therapeutic techniques. Many applied psychologists also use this idea to help people do better at work. How do people actually influence one another? What techniques promote attitude change? Bosses, salespeople, parents, and politicians all apply the principles of social psychology. They influence others regularly by using social psychological techniques such as the foot-in-the-door technique, the door-in-the-face technique, the ask-and-you-shall-be-given approach, lowballing, modeling, and incentives.

Foot-in-the-Door Technique. To get someone to change an attitude or grant a favor, begin by asking for a small attitude change or a small favor. In other words, get your foot in the door. Ask to borrow a quarter today, next week ask for a dollar, and next month ask for money for your tuition. The essence of the *foot-in-the-door technique* is that a person who grants a small request is likely to comply with a larger request later. It works, however, only if the person first grants the small favor, and it works best if there is some time between the first, small request and the later, larger one. A person who says no to the first favor may find it even easier to say no to subsequent ones. Although use of the foot-in-the-door technique is relatively common in U.S. society, cross-cultural studies show that it is not as effective in all cultures (Kilbourne, 1989).

Door-in-the-Face Technique. To use the *door-in-the-face technique,* first ask for something outrageous, and then ask for something much smaller and more reasonable. Ask a friend to lend you $100; after being turned down, ask to borrow $5. Your friend may be relieved to give you the smaller amount. The door-in-the-face technique assumes that a person may be more likely to grant a small request after turning down a larger one; it appears to work because people do not want to turn someone down twice, and it works best if there is little time between requests. To look good and maintain a positive self-image, people agree to the lesser of two requests.

Ask-and-You-Shall-Be-Given Technique. When people are asked for money for what they perceive as a good cause, whether the request is large or small, they usually will respond positively. If the person has given before, the request is even more likely to be granted (Doob & McLaughlin, 1989), especially if the person is in a good mood (Forgas, 1998). Fund raisers for universities, religious groups, and museums know that asking usually will get a positive response. Research indicates that asking in an unusual way can pique a person's interest, turn the donor aside from his or her well-rehearsed script of saying no, and increase the likelihood of giving (Santos, Leve, & Pratkanis, 1994).

Lowballing Technique. *Lowballing* is a technique by which a person is influenced to make a decision or commitment because of the low stakes associated with it. Once the decision is made, the stakes may increase; but the person is likely to stick with the original decision. For example, if a man agrees to buy a car for $14,000, he may still buy it even if several options are added on, increasing the price to $15,000. Lowballing works because people tend to stick to their commitments, even if the stakes are raised. Changing one's mind may suggest a lack of good judgment, may cause stress, and may make the person feel as if she or he were violating an (often imaginary) obligation.

Modeling. Modeling good behavior for someone increases the likelihood that the person will behave similarly. *Modeling,* which we examined in Chapter 5, is a powerful technique for influencing behaviors and attitudes by demonstrating those behaviors and expressing those attitudes. When well-known athletes exhibit generosity of spirit and act like good sports, they serve as models for youngsters.

Incentives Technique. Nothing succeeds better in eliciting a particular behavior than a desired incentive. Offering a 16-year-old unlimited use of the family car for setting the dinner table every day usually results in a neatly set dinner table. Offering a large monetary bonus to a sales agent for achieving higher-than-usual performance usually boosts sales figures. Offering incentives can bring about such behavior changes, but it usually doesn't produce attitude changes—the 16-year-old sets the table, but still hates doing so. ■

The *central route* emphasizes conscious, thoughtful consideration and elaboration of arguments concerning a given issue. Attitude change via this route depends on how effective, authoritative, and logical a communication is. Confronted with scientific evidence about the effects of secondhand smoke on people's health, especially concerning the prevalence of respiratory diseases, most people are convinced via the central route that secondhand smoke is in fact detrimental to health. That is, unless they are highly motivated to believe otherwise, they conclude that the scientific arguments on this topic are too strong to refute.

The *peripheral route* emphasizes less careful and more emotional, even superficial, evaluation of the message. This route has an indirect but nevertheless powerful effect, especially when there are no logical arguments that can force the use of the central route. This is what happens frequently with political messages (DeBono, 1992; Petty et al., 1993). Ross Perot tried to sell his brand of no-nonsense politics by appealing in emotion-laden terms to what he considered voters' common sense. Whether a person accepts a message delivered via this route depends on how the person perceives its pleasantness, its similarity to well-established personal attitudes, and the communicator. Think of an "infomercial" you may have seen on television that attempts to sell exercise equipment. Such commercials often make their pitch while featuring attractive models and an upbeat, eager (and trim) audience. You may believe the evidence presented only because a respected, convincing, and seemingly honest person has expressed the ideas. The attitude change that you may show—desire to buy the product—often stems largely from emotional or personal rather than logical arguments and therefore may not be long-lasting (Petty et al., 1993).

When people experience conflict among their attitudes or between their attitudes and their behavior, they are motivated to change either their attitudes or their behavior.

The key idea of the elaboration likelihood model is that people can form or change attitudes because of thoughtful conscious decisions (central route) or because of quick, emotional choices (peripheral route). The central route is used when people have the ability, time, and energy to think through arguments carefully; the peripheral route is more likely to be used when motivation is low, time is short, or ability to think through arguments is impaired (Petty et al., 1994).

Searching for Cognitive Consistency

People often try to maintain consistency among their various attitudes and between their attitudes and their behavior. *Consistency* refers to a high degree of coherence among elements of behavior and mental processes; such coherence makes day-to-day life go a bit smoother and enables people to make decisions about their future behavior without having to filter out numerous alternatives.

Cognitive Dissonance. Imagine the dilemma faced by a scientist who smokes cigarettes and who finds through her research that cigarettes do indeed cause cancer. As a scientist, she must find the research evidence compelling; as a smoker, she can't help pointing out that she feels fine after smoking for years and that her 92-year-old grandmother still smokes. How does she reconcile these opposing facts? Moreover, what further confusion would she suffer if she learned that a chest X-ray showed her grandmother's lungs to be totally clear?

Whenever people's attitudes conflict with one another or with their behavior, they feel uncomfortable. Leon Festinger (1919–1989) termed this feeling **cognitive dissonance**—a state of mental discomfort that arises from a discrepancy between two or more of a person's beliefs or between a person's beliefs and overt behavior. Based on the premise that people seek to reduce such dissonance, Festinger (1957) proposed a *cognitive dissonance theory*. According to the theory, when people experience conflict among their attitudes or between their attitudes and their behavior, they are motivated to change either their attitudes or their behavior. Most psychologists consider cognitive dissonance theory to be a type of motivation theory, because it suggests that people become energized by their cognitive dissonance to do something (Elliot & Devine, 1994). As an example of behavior attitude conflict, suppose you are a strong proponent of animal rights. You support the American Society for the Prevention of Cruelty to Animals (ASPCA) and Greenpeace, refrain from eating meat, and are repulsed by fur coats. Then you win a raffle and are awarded a stylish black leather coat. Wearing the coat goes against your beliefs; but you know it looks great on you, and all your friends admire it. According to cognitive dissonance theory, you are experiencing conflict between your attitudes (belief in animal rights) and your behavior (wearing the coat). To relieve the conflict, you either stop wearing the coat or modify your attitude (leather becomes an acceptable choice). People generally choose the most direct method to reduce dissonance (Stone et al., 1997). Psychologists have devised measures of a person's preference for consistency (Cialdini, Trost, & Newsom, 1995); but

Cognitive dissonance [COG-nih-tiv DIS-uh-nents]: A state of mental discomfort arising from a discrepancy between two or more of a person's beliefs or between a person's beliefs and overt behavior.

not all people are consistent, nor do all psychologists suggest that consistency is important.

Self-Perception Theory. Social psychologist Daryl Bem (1972) claims that people do not change their attitudes because of internal states such as dissonance. He has proposed **self-perception theory**—an approach to attitude formation that assumes that people infer their attitudes and emotional states from their behavior. Bem holds that people don't know what their attitudes are until they stop and examine their behavior. First, they search for an external explanation, such as "someone forced me to do this." If no such explanation is available, they turn to an internal one. That is, people look at their behavior and say, "I must have felt like this if I behaved that way."

Bem's research is supported to some extent by the cognitive work of Stanley Schachter (which was reviewed in Chapter 8). Schachter showed that research participants inferred aspects of their emotional states from both their physical states and the situations in which they found themselves. Thus, a person who is physically aroused and is surrounded by happy people reports feeling happy. A person who is physically aroused and is in a tense situation reports feeling angry.

Reactance Theory. Our attitudes—and even our deepest beliefs—are often challenged by the behaviors of others. How do we respond to such challenges? Have you ever been ordered (perhaps by a parent) to do something and realized that you wanted to do the exact opposite? According to social psychologist Jack Brehm (1966), whenever people feel their freedom of choice is being unjustly restricted, they are motivated to reestablish it. Brehm terms this form of negative influence *reactance*. **Reactance** is the negative response evoked when there is an inconsistency between a person's self-image as being free to choose and the person's realization that someone is trying to force him or her to choose a particular alternative.

Reactance theory focuses on how people reestablish a feeling that they have freedom of choice. Often, forbidden activities become attractive; choosing the "forbidden fruit" may boost an individual's sense of autonomy. For example, an adolescent who is told he cannot be friends with a member of a minority group may seek out members of that group more often. When coercion is used, resistance follows. According to reactance theory, the extent of reactance is directly related to the extent of the restriction on freedom of choice. If a person does not consider the choice very important and if the restriction is slight, little reactance develops. The wording or delivery of the restriction also affects the extent of reactance. People who are told they *must* respond in a certain way are more likely to react negatively than if they merely receive a suggestion or are given a relatively free choice. *I*

Think Critically

- Under what conditions are attitudes most likely to predict behaviors? Can you think of any examples of attitudes that do not predict future behaviors?

I Social Cognition: The Impact of Thought

Focus on issues and ideas

- How people seek to be "cognitive misers" by processing information superficially
- The major forms of nonverbal communication: facial expressions, body language, and eye contact
- How people infer the motives of others from their behavior and how we err in this process
- How discrimination can be prevented by understanding prejudice and stereotyping

On meeting someone for the first time, you might say, "I really like him!" or "I can't put my finger on why, but she irritates me." Often, first impressions are based on nothing more than someone's appearance, body language, and speech patterns. Yet these impressions can have lasting effects. Such individual impressions form one aspect of social cognition—one's view of the entire social milieu.

Social cognition is the process of analyzing and interpreting events, other people, oneself, and the world in general. It focuses on social information in memory, which affects judgments, choices, evaluations, and, ultimately, behavior (Fiske, 1992). Social cognition is a useful and pragmatic process in which people often use mental shortcuts to help them make sense of the world. The process often begins with attempts to form impressions of other people and understand their communications, which can be verbal (words) or nonverbal (looks, gestures, and other means of expression). The process by which people use the behavior and appearance of others to form attitudes about them is known as **impression formation**; sometimes the impressions are accurate, but certainly not always. We'll look at impression formation in more depth later in this section, when we study attribution.

Organizing the World Using Mental Shortcuts

You saw earlier that people use their attitudes to help them make decisions and organize their lives. In a related way, using mental shortcuts helps people process information and avoid or reduce information overload. People seek to be "cognitive misers," processing information superficially unless they are motivated to do otherwise. According to Susan Fiske (1992, p. 879), "Social cognition operates in the service of practical consequences." To help themselves make decisions, people develop pragmatic (results-oriented) rules of thumb.

One rule of thumb is *representativeness;* individuals or events that appear to be representative of other members of a group are quickly classified as such, often despite a complete lack of evidence. If you see a 6-foot-6-inch young man, you are likely to assume that he plays basketball—without knowing anything else about him, let alone his interests or abilities. Another rule of thumb is *availability;* the easier it is to bring to mind instances of a category, type, or idea, the more likely it is that the category, type, or idea will be used to describe an event. Politicians count on the availability principle when they associate memorable images and ideas with themselves or their opponents. The more vivid the image, the more likely it will remain available in constituents' memories. Still another rule of thumb is the *false consensus effect;* people tend to think that others believe what they do. Finally, *framing,* the way in which information is presented to people, helps determine how easily they accept it. Consider the different impact of two versions of a public health warning: "95% of the population will not be affected by the disease, and only 5% will be seriously ill" versus "5% of the population will become seriously ill; the rest of the public will be unaffected."

When other people's behavior fits neatly into your conceptions of the world, you do not need to expend much effort to make judgments about it. One of the most powerful ways of sending easily interpreted signals is nonverbal communication.

Assessing the World Using Nonverbal Communication

Impression formation often begins with **nonverbal communication,** the communication of information by physical cues or actions that include gestures, tone of voice, vocal inflections, and facial expressions. When a person irritates you, it may be a shrill laugh, a grimace, or an averting of the eyes that generates your bad feelings—not the words the person uses (Ambady & Rosenthal, 1993). Nonverbal communication is difficult to suppress and is easily accessible to observers (DePaulo, 1992). Three major forms of nonverbal communication are facial expressions, body language, and eye contact.

Facial Expressions. Many of the conclusions we draw about other people are based on their facial expressions. Most people, across cultures, can distinguish six basic emotions in the facial expressions of other people: happy, sad, angry, fearful, surprised, and disgusted. A simple expression such as a smile, for example, gives others a powerful cue about a person's truthfulness. Research shows that when a person smiles, both the smile and the muscular activity around the eyes help determine if the person is telling the truth or is smiling to mask another emotion (Ekman & Keltner, 1997).

Body Language. People also convey information about their moods and attitudes through body positions and gestures—**body language.** Such movements as crossing the arms, lowering the head, and standing rigidly can communicate negative attitudes. On the other hand, when a server in a restaurant moves close to the table and makes direct eye contact, tips increase (Lynn & Mynier, 1993). Aspects of body language differ with culture and gender. For example, in the United States, the energetic and forceful way younger people walk makes them appear sexier, more carefree, and happier than older people (Montepare & Zebrowitz-McArthur, 1988). A pensive, reflective posture or a deferential movement or head position might signal composure, confidence, and status in Japan (Matsumoto & Kudoh, 1993). Gestures also have different meanings in different societies. For example, the American A-OK sign (a circle formed with the

Self-perception theory: Approach to attitude formation that assumes that people infer their attitudes and emotional states from their behavior.

Reactance: The negative response evoked when there is an inconsistency between a person's self-image as being free to choose and the person's realization that someone is trying to force him or her to choose a particular alternative.

Social cognition: The process of analyzing and interpreting events, other people, oneself, and the world in general.

Impression formation: The process by which a person uses the behavior and appearance of others to form attitudes about them.

Nonverbal communication: The communication of information by cues or actions that include gestures, tone of voice, vocal inflections, and facial expressions.

Body language: Communication of information through body positions and gestures.

thumb and forefinger) is a rude gesture referring to sexual acts in many cultures. Research also shows that in Western cultures, women are often better than men at communicating and interpreting nonverbal messages, especially facial expressions. Women are more likely to send nonverbal facial messages but are also more cautious in interpreting nonverbal messages sent to them by men.

Eye Contact. Another form of nonverbal communication is *eye contact.* The eyes convey a surprising amount of information about feelings. A person who is looking at you may glance briefly or stare; you may glance or stare back. You would probably gaze tenderly at someone you were fond of but avoid eye contact with someone you did not trust or like or did not know well (Teske, 1988). Frequent eye contact between two people may indicate that they are sexually attracted to each other.

People tend to judge others based on the eye contact they engage in, making inferences (attributions) about others' internal dispositions from the degree of eye contact. Americans generally prefer modest amounts of eye contact rather than constant eye contact or none at all. Job applicants, for example, are rated more favorably when they make moderate amounts of eye contact; speakers who make more rather than less eye contact are preferred; and witnesses testifying in a court trial are perceived as more credible when they make eye contact with the attorney (DePaulo, 1992). However, all this is true only in Western cultures, which foster an individualistic stance; in some non-Western cultures—for example, Japan—making direct eye contact may be a sign of disrespect, arrogance, or even a challenge.

Inferring the Causes of Behavior: Attribution

If you see people standing in line at a bus stop, you can be fairly certain that they are waiting for a bus. Similarly, if you saw a man at the bus stop reading the Muslim holy book, the Koran, you might infer that he is a devout Muslim. In getting to know others, people often infer the causes of their behavior. When they do, they are making attributions. **Attribution** is the process by which a person infers other people's motives or intentions by observing their behavior. Through attribution, people decide how they will react toward others, in an attempt to evaluate and to make sense of their social world. Attribution may seem like a fairly straightforward process based on common sense. However, it must take into account internal as well as external causes of behavior. Someone making an *internal attribution* thinks the behavior being observed comes from within the person, that it arises somehow from the individual's personality. Someone making an *external attribution* believes that the person's behavior is caused by outside events, such as the weather or luck.

People can be mistaken when they infer the causes of another person's behavior. Suppose that the man you saw reading the Koran is actually a Catholic taking a class in world religions that uses the book as a text. In that case, your original attribution (that he is a Muslim) is wrong. It is also easy to see that culture shapes attributions; Morris and Peng (1994) found that accounts of certain crimes in English-language newspapers were dispositional in tone, but that Chinese newspapers were more situational in their explanations of the same crimes.

To learn more about attribution, researchers have attempted to conceptualize the process. Harold Kelley's (1972, 1973) theory of attribution suggests that people decide whether the causes of a behavior are internal or external based on three criteria: *consensus, consistency,* and *distinctiveness.* According to Kelley, to infer that someone's behavior is caused by internal characteristics, you must believe that (1) few other people in the same situation would act in the same way (low consensus), (2) the person has acted in the same way in similar situations in the past (high consistency), and (3) the person acts in the same way in different situations (low distinctiveness). To infer that a person's behavior is caused by external factors, you must believe that (1) most people would act that way in that sort of situation (high consensus); (2) the person has acted that way in similar situations in the past (high consistency); and (3) the person acts differently in other situations (high distinctiveness).

To see how Kelley's theory works, suppose that a man in an office gets into an argument with his supervisor, but other people in the same office do not enter into the discussion (low consensus). Also, suppose that the man has argued about the same issue on other occasions (high consistency). Finally, assume that he argues with everybody (low distinctiveness). In such a case, people will no doubt attribute the argument with the supervisor to the man's personality; he is simply argumentative. Now, suppose that many of the man's coworkers join in and support him in the debate (high consensus), that the man has argued about the same issue in the past (high consistency), but that he does not argue in other situations (high distinctiveness). People will be more likely in this case to attribute the argument with the supervisor to situational factors, such as the supervisor's incompetence.

Why People Make Attributions. Why do people make attributions? What motivates a person to want to know the causes of other people's behavior? The accepted explanation is that people use the process of attribution to maintain a sense of control over their environment. Attribution helps people feel competent and masterful, because they think that knowledge about the causes of behavior will help them control and predict similar events in the future (Burger & Hemans, 1988). People also make attributions in order to make sense of the world quickly. If a person's behavior fits in with a pattern you have seen before, why analyze it in depth? People are quick to make causal attributions if the behavior being observed is not unusual.

Errors in Attribution. The residents of Lake Wobegon are strong women, good-looking men, and above-average children. Like the fictional characters of Garrison Keillor, most of us tend to see ourselves in flattering ways—we often have unrealistic and positive perceptions of our abilities and of our control of our world. Like Lake Wobegoners, we tend to see ourselves and the rest of our peer group as above average (Klar & Giladi, 1997). These perceptions are self-enhancing and even egocentric (Farwell & Wohlwend-Lloyd, 1998). Social psychologists have found that people can be especially error-prone or biased in their attributions concerning the behaviors of others. Sometimes they make errors because they use mental shortcuts that are not accurate. Two of the most common attribution errors are the fundamental attribution error and the actor–observer effect.

People generally perceive themselves as having more positive traits than others do and as being more flexible and adaptable.

When people commit the **fundamental attribution error,** they assume that other people's behavior is caused by their internal dispositions and underestimate situational influences. A man in a restaurant loses his temper, for example, and you assume he is "hot tempered"; but the truth is he was kept waiting for his table, treated rudely by the staff, served the wrong entree, and then overcharged for his meal. We often observe a behavior and tend to discount or not pay attention to the circumstances.

The **actor–observer effect** is the tendency to attribute the behavior (especially the failings) of others to dispositional causes but to attribute one's own behavior to situational causes. Individuals know themselves and know that their own day-to-day behavior varies; as observers, on the other hand, they have less information to go on and are more likely to make dispositional attributions. A young child who falls off his bike may say, "The sidewalk was bumpy." When a friend does the same thing, however, the same child may say, "You're clumsy."

Errors in attribution are often judgments made in a limited context, with limited knowledge. Often, they do not help people cope any better—they simply assign blame. Errors in attribution cause people to blame rape victims rather than rapists, for example (Bell, Kuriloff, & Lottes, 1994). Some errors in attribution come from the fact that people generally perceive themselves as having more positive traits than others do and as being more flexible and adaptable. This tendency has been seen cross-culturally, but it does not exist to the same extent or have the same meaning in every culture (Matsumoto, 1994). This has important implications in business relationships, where good will and trust are important. If a businessperson tends to see others as less (or more) flexible than the people in his or her company, this attribution error may affect a negotiation in a fundamental way.

Self-Serving Bias. The **self-serving bias** is people's tendency to ascribe their positive behaviors to their own internal traits and characteristics but to blame their failures and shortcomings on external, situational factors. People may develop a self-serving bias because it helps meet their need for self-esteem. This bias can be seen as an adaptive response that helps people deal with their limitations and gives them the courage to venture into areas they normally might not explore. People also develop this bias to help maintain a sense of balance by resolving inconsistencies between old and new information about themselves (Snyder & Higgins, 1988). Often, a person who makes an excuse about some negative personal behavior mentally shifts the cause of the behavior to a less central element of personality or to situational factors. This results in an enhanced self-image and a sense of control. Furthermore, a self-serving bias allows people to present

Attribution: The process by which a person infers other people's motives or intentions by observing their behavior.

Fundamental attribution error: The tendency to attribute other people's behavior to dispositional (internal) causes rather than situational (external) causes.

Actor–observer effect: The tendency to attribute the behavior of others to dispositional causes but to attribute one's own behavior to situational causes.

Self-serving bias: People's tendency to ascribe their positive behaviors to their own internal traits, but their failures and shortcomings to external, situational factors.

themselves to others in a positive light (Celuch & Slama, 1995). The self-serving bias is more common in men than in women, and in Western than in non-Western cultures (Cross & Madson, 1997).

Errors in attribution contribute to the self-serving bias. People tend to take credit for their successes but to blame others for their failures; that is, people assume that good things happen to them because they deserve them and that bad things happen to them because they have bad luck. The combination of attribution errors and self-serving bias helps *some* people maintain self-esteem and appear competent. Such an attitude, however, may inhibit people from having realistic goals, thus setting them up for disappointment.

The truth is that people are concerned about how they appear to others. And this is especially true if they are somewhat different from other people. For example, Claude Steele has asserted that whenever members of minority groups concentrate on scholastic tasks, they worry about the risk of confirming negative stereotypes about their group (Aronson, Quinn, & Spencer, 1998; Steele, 1997). This burden may drag down their performance, through what Steele calls *stereotype threat.* Stereotype threat probably occurs in part because situational, academic pressure threatens self-esteem; people fear being reduced to a stereotype, so they stop trying and ultimately do worse because of the fear. This behavior (no longer trying) is referred to as *disidentification;* it suggests that there was once a relationship between academic success and self-esteem, but it no longer exists. It turns out that African Americans boys are especially affected by stereotype threat—they stop trying (they disidentify) because they are no longer uplifted by academic success (Osborne, 1997). Unless minorities (African Americans, older adults, gang members) are resilient to stereotype threat, their performance is likely to suffer (Steele, 1997). The flip-side of stereotype threat is positive stereotyping. When people are stereotyped positively—for example, Asian Americans as having superior math skills—their individual performance is enhanced. Shih, Pittinsky, and Ambady (1999) assert that the stereotype itself positively influences performance.

Prejudice: Negative evaluation of an entire group of people, typically based on unfavorable (and often wrong) stereotypes about the group.

Stereotypes: Fixed, overly simple, and often erroneous ideas about traits, attitudes, and behaviors of groups of people; stereotypes assume that all members of a given group are alike.

Discrimination: Behavior targeted at individuals or groups and intended to hold them apart and treat them differently.

People constantly assess the reasons for other people's behavior in order to make judgments about them. Most people also regularly reflect on their own behavior and in doing so form self-perceptions. Of course, not everyone forms attributions in the same way, and some people, especially in some cultures, are more likely to be sensitive to situational causes of behavior. For example, people in East Asian cultures are less likely to attach traits to an individual and thus consider situational variables more than people in Western cultures do (Choi, Nisbett, & Norenzayan, 1999). *Diversity* examines the influence of ethnicity on self-perception.

Prejudice: The Darker Side of Attitudes

People's ideas about themselves and others help define who they are, how they view the world, and ultimately how they behave. But what happens when the ideas, values, or activities of another person or another group of people are different from yours? What happens when you do not know the other group of people well, or at all? Why do some people form negative evaluations of certain groups, such as African Americans, Asians, Jews, or lesbians and gay men? In this section, we explore prejudice—the darker side of attitudes and attributions about others—and how it can be prevented.

Prejudice is a negative evaluation of an entire group of people that is typically based on unfavorable (and often wrong) stereotypes about the group. It is usually based on a small sample of experience with an individual from the group being evaluated, or even on no experience. **Stereotypes** are fixed, overly simple, and often erroneous ideas about traits, attitudes, and behaviors of groups of people; stereotypes assume that all members of a given group are alike. Stereotypes exist about Native Americans, Catholics, women, and mountain folk, among others; such stereotypes, often shared by many people, can lead to prejudice.

Prejudice, as an attitude, is composed of a cognitive belief (all Xs are stupid), an emotional element (I hate those Xs), and often a behavior (I am doing everything I can to keep those Xs out of my neighborhood). When prejudice is translated into behavior, it is called **discrimination**—behavior targeted at individuals or groups and intended to hold them apart and treat them differently. Stereotyping promotes prejudice, and prejudice promotes discrimination. You can think of discrimination as prejudice in action. One common type of discrimination is *sexism* (arising from prejudice based on gender), which involves accepting the strong and widely held beliefs of rigid gender role

DIVERSITY

Self-Perceptions of African American Women

Psychologists know that men and women perceive themselves differently. So do teenagers and people over age 65, people from the North and those from the South, and African Americans and white Americans.

Victoria Binion (1990) undertook a study of self-perception in a sample of African American and white women. Among other things, she was interested in the relationship between ethnicity and gender identity. Binion interviewed more than 175 women in a low-income community close to downtown Detroit. She asked the participants about their gender identity, gender role attitudes, and self-perceptions. The participants either agreed or disagreed (on a scale of 1 to 5) with statements such as "The only way for women to survive is to have men protect them" and "Women can handle a lot more hurt than men can." The women were young (about 26 years old) and were all high school graduates.

The African American women in the study characterized themselves as androgynous (37%), masculine (24%), feminine (18%), or undifferentiated (none of the above) (almost 22%). Women who saw themselves as masculine showed traits such as independence and courage. Women who saw themselves as feminine tended to view themselves as weak and needing help. Women self-described as androgynous showed traits and agreed with statements that were both masculine and feminine.

There is a strong cultural influence on self-perception and gender identity. The African American women in Binion's study were more than twice as likely as the white women (37% compared to 16%) to characterize themselves as androgynous, and they were less likely than the white women were (18% compared to 22%) to characterize themselves as feminine. Further, the responses of the African American women indicated that they were less flexible than the white women about the female role in the family: They identified a narrower role for wives and mothers and expressed less flexible gender role attitudes than did the white women. Paradoxically, although the African American women tended to report more traditional gender role attitudes (women as weaker and dependent), many identified themselves as androgynous.

The relationships among culture, gender identity, and self-perceptions are complex. For example, women who are college graduates have more flexible views about the female role regardless of their ethnic background. A woman's relationship with her parents is linked to her self-report of masculinity or femininity; for example, women who were brought up with a father in the home tended to have more flexible views about the woman's role in the family than women who were raised by their mother alone.

There is enormous diversity among individual women and individual families, within any community. Parenting, education, and ethnicity affect each person's self-perception. When social psychologists develop theories of self-perception, ethnicity is one variable they are going to have to take into account. People are diverse, and the data show that culture affects how they perceive themselves. ■

stereotyping. We examined gender role stereotyping in Chapter 9. Overt discrimination based on gender is illegal, but it still exists, and many people's expectations for women are still based on old stereotypes about gender (Glick & Fiske, 1997).

Sometimes people are prejudiced but do not show that attitude in their behavior; that is, they do not discriminate. Merton (1949) referred to such people as *cautious bigots* (unlike true bigots, who *do* discriminate). Also, people sometimes show *reverse discrimination*, bending over backward to show favoritism to someone from a group that is otherwise discriminated against, in order to counter preexisting biases or stereotypes that are common in society (Chidester, 1986). That is, someone who deplores prejudice toward African Americans may treat an African American per-

Table 11.1 Prejudice and Discrimination

Prejudice and discrimination interact in such a way that one can be evident without the other.

	Presence of Prejudice	Absence of Prejudice
Presence of Discrimination	An employer believes that nonwhites cannot do quality work and does not promote them, regardless of their performance.	An employer believes that all people can do quality work but does not promote minorities because of long-held company policies.
Absence of Discrimination	An employer believes that nonwhites cannot do quality work but promotes them on the basis of their performance rather than following preconceived ideas.	An employer believes that all people can do quality work and promotes people on the basis of their performance on the job.

son oversolicitously and may evaluate the person favorably on the basis of standards different from those used for others. This, too, is discrimination. (Table 11.1 outlines the interactions between prejudice and discrimination.)

A related behavior is *tokenism,* in which the actions of prejudiced people toward members of a group they dislike are only superficially positive. A male executive may make a token gesture toward a woman on his staff by assigning her to coordinate a project that is of no importance; a manager may hire one token Hispanic American so as to appear not to discriminate against that group. By engaging in tokenism, a person often attempts to avoid taking more important actions, such as changing overall personnel or hiring practices. The trivial behavior signifies that he or she has done something for the disliked group. Tokenism has negative consequences for the self-esteem of the person it is applied to, and it perpetuates discrimination.

What Causes Prejudice? The causes of prejudice cannot be summarized with a single explanation. Like so many other human behaviors, prejudice is a cross-cultural phenomenon (Pettigrew et al., 1998); it has multiple causes and can be examined within an individual, between individuals, within a group, or within society (Duckitt, 1992). We'll consider four theories to explain prejudice: social learning theory, motivational theory, cognitive theory, and personality theory.

According to *social learning theory,* children *learn* to be prejudiced: They watch parents, other relatives, and neighbors engaged in acts of discrimination, which often include stereotyped judgments and racial slurs; they then incorporate those ideas into their own behavioral repertoire. After children have observed such behaviors, they are reinforced (operant conditioning) for exhibiting similar behaviors. Thus, through imitation and reinforcement, a prejudiced view is transmitted from one generation to the next.

We saw in Chapter 8 that people are motivated to succeed, to get ahead, and to provide for basic as well as high-level emotional needs. If people are raised to compete against others for scarce resources, the competition can foster negative feelings about those competitors. *Motivational theory* asserts that individuals learn to dislike specific individuals (competitors) and then generalize that dislike to whole classes of similar individuals (races, religions, or cultures). Gordon Allport claimed that the arousal of competition followed by erroneous generalizations creates specific prejudice toward minority groups (Allport, 1954/1979). This helps make minorities that are seen as economic competitors into scapegoats—for example, every new wave of immigrants that has come to the United States (the Italians, Chinese, and Irish in the early part of the 20th century and Mexicans and people from Central America today). Research with children, adolescents, and adults shows that people who are initially seen as friends or as neutral are sometimes treated badly if they become competitors. Competition for jobs among immigrants can also create prejudice, particularly in times of economic hardship.

Cognitive theorists assert that people think about individuals and their groups of origin as a way of organizing the world. Cialdini (1993) argues that there are so many events, circumstances, and changing variables in their lives that people cannot easily analyze all the relevant data about any one thing. People thus devise mental shortcuts to help them make decisions. One of those shortcuts is to stereotype individuals and the groups they belong to—for example, all Hispanics, all homeless people, all men, all lawyers. By devising such shortcuts in thinking, people develop ideas about who is in an *in group*—that is, who is a member of a group to which they belong or want to belong. The division of the world into groups labeled "in" ver-

Social categorization: The process of dividing the world into "in" groups and "out" groups.

sus "out" or "us" versus "them" is known as **social categorization.** Not only do people divide the world into in groups and out groups, but they tend to see themselves and other members of an in group in a favorable light; doing so bolsters their self-esteem and occurs almost automatically (Fiske, 1998).

The division of the world into groups labeled "in" versus "out" or "us" versus "them" is known as social categorization.

Researchers such as Susan Fiske (1998) assert that when people develop stereotypes about groups—who's in and who's out—the stereotype and the prejudice that follows from it are more complex than previously thought. For example, a person may like but not respect a member of a certain group, or vice versa. A traditional housewife may be liked, but not respected; similarly, a militant feminist may be respected, but not liked. This duality of liking/respecting may translate into complex social behaviors such as sexism and racism in which individual members of a given group are treated benevolently while the group as a whole is treated with hostility (Glick & Fiske, 1997).

Personality psychologists assert that a person who develops prejudices has a "prejudice-prone personality." In fact, some personality tests examine the extent to which people are likely to be prejudiced. Ideas about the relationship between personality and prejudice have roots in psychoanalytic theory and are hotly debated.

Subtle Prejudice for Modern Times. In the late 1970s and 1980s, researchers began to look at *symbolic racism*—the expression by whites, in terms of day-to-day behaviors, of the feeling that blacks violate certain cherished American values (McConahay & Hough, 1976). Kinder and Sanders (1996) argue that whites adopt a socially acceptable and ostensibly nonprejudicial reason to reject minorities—blacks have supposedly violated the cherished American value of being independent and self-sufficient by accepting welfare payments. This less blatant but still overt form of racism is expressed by voting against all black candidates and opposing busing, integration, and affirmative action. Today, proponents of this idea, especially Donald Kinder (Kinder & Sanders, 1996), call it *racial resentment* and assert that it features indignation as a central emotional theme, provoked by the idea that minorities—in this case, African Americans—are getting more than their fair share economically. Racial resentment is thought to be at the heart of white American feelings toward blacks. Although not all researchers agree, Kinder argues that racial resentment colors whites' views of blacks and fuels their prejudiced and discriminatory behaviors.

How to Reduce and Eliminate Prejudice. To reduce and eliminate prejudice, people can teach rational thinking, try to judge others based on their behavior, promote equality, and avoid labels that perpetuate stereotypes (Jussim et al., 1995). Changing behaviors, and then letting attitudes follow in due course, can reduce prejudice. Research shows that once people have worked on a community project with a member of a different culture, lived with a person of another race, or prayed with members of a different church, their emotional views of them as individuals change (Pettigrew, 1997).

A society can pass laws that mandate equal treatment for all people—for example, laws that forbid discrimination in the workplace or in the housing market. Such laws generally reflect changing beliefs (Bobo & Kluegel, 1997). Voters can elect officials on the basis of their competence, throw them out on the basis of their incompetence, and make gender-neutral judgments of performance. Margaret Thatcher, former prime minister of Great Britain, and U.S. Secretary of State Madeleine Albright have been judged by their performance, not by their gender. And General Colin Powell, who is widely perceived to have integrity and a strong character, has the ability to transform people's views of the role of African Americans in U.S. society (Sigelman, 1997).

Psychologists—and students of psychology—must be especially sensitive to the need to think about *individuals* rather than about groups. Through examination of individuals, psychologists become sensitive to the wide diversity of human behavior. Although it is tempting to make broad generalizations about behavior and about the causes of behavior, researchers must focus on individuals. When they focus on individuals, they see that human beings are engaged in and are affected by a whole array of behaviors. *I*

Think Critically

- Can you describe any useful functions that errors in attribution have served for you or a friend in the last few months? Have such errors helped someone feel more intelligent, more worthwhile, or less at fault?
- In the United States, prejudice has led to unfair treatment of African Americans, women, the aged, gays, and many minority groups. What are some effective techniques (not necessarily governmental policies) that can be used to help eliminate prejudice, right previous injustices, and make for a more tolerant society?

Social Interactions: The Power of People and Situations

Focus on issues and ideas

- How social interactions affect individual behavior
- How ordinary people are remarkably willing to comply with the wishes of others, especially if they see the others as legitimate authority figures
- How group membership influences individual behavior
- The behavioral effects on children of viewing violence on television
- What conditions contribute to our willingness to help others
- Why people are attracted to others and form interpersonal relationships

How to initiate a conversation with someone you haven't met before is a problem you have no doubt had to face. When people interact, new realms of possible behaviors open up. From obeying authority to helping a person in distress, day-to-day social interactions can be exceedingly complex, affected by many variables.

Social Influence

Parents try to instill specific values in their children. An adolescent admires the hairstyle or mannerisms of an attractive peer and decides to adopt them. Adoring fans emulate the behavior or appearance of a rock star or top athlete. Religious leaders exhort their followers to live in certain ways. Social interactions affect individual behavior in profound ways; when people are members of a group, their social interactions are often even more noticeable than their individual behavior.

Social influence refers to the ways people alter the attitudes or behaviors of others, either directly or indirectly. Two important topics studied by researchers on social influence are conformity and obedience.

Conformity. When someone changes her or his attitudes or behaviors so that they are consistent with those of other people or with social norms, the person is exhibiting **conformity,** or trying to fit in. An individual may adopt positive, prosocial behaviors such as wearing seatbelts, volunteering time and money to a charity, or buying only products that are safe for the environment. Sometimes, however, conformity leads to counterproductive, antisocial behaviors, such as drug abuse, fraternity hazing, or mob action.

People conform to the behaviors and attitudes of their peer or family groups. A young executive may wear conservative dark suits and drive a BMW in order to fit in with office colleagues. Similarly, the desire to conform can induce people to do things they might not do otherwise. An infamous example is the My Lai massacre, in which American soldiers slaughtered Vietnamese civilians during the Vietnam War. Although several factors account for the soldiers' behavior (including combat stress, hostility toward the Vietnamese, and obedience to authority), the soldiers also yielded to extreme group pressure. The few soldiers who refused to kill civilians hid that fact from their comrades. One soldier even shot himself in the foot to avoid taking part in the slaughter.

Groups strongly influence conformity. Solomon Asch (1907–1996) found that people in a group adopt its standards. Examples of conformity to group standards range from an individual's refraining from speaking during a public address to a whole nation's discriminating against a particular ethnic group. Studies also show that individuals conform to group norms even when they are not pressured to do so. Consider what happens when an instructor asks a class of 250 students to answer a relatively simple question, but no one volunteers. When asked, most of the students will report that they did not raise their hand because no one else did. Asch (1955, p. 6) stated: "The tendency to conformity in our society [is] so strong that reasonably intelligent and well-meaning young people [being] willing to call white black is a matter of concern. It raises questions about our ways of education and about the values that guide our conduct."

Suppose you have agreed to participate in an experiment. You are seated at a table with four other students. The experimenter holds up a card with two straight lines printed on it and asks each of you to pick which of the two lines is longer, A or B. You quickly discover that the task is simple. The experimenter holds up successive cards showing pairs of lines; in each case, every participant correctly identifies the longer line. Suddenly, after several rounds, you notice that the first person has chosen line A instead of line B, though B is obviously longer. You are surprised when the second person also chooses line A, then the third, then the fourth. Your turn is next. You are sure that line B is longer. What do you do?

In 1951, Asch performed an experiment like this to explore conformity. Seven to nine people were brought together and asked to judge which of three lines matched a standard line. However, only one group member—the naive participant—was unaware of the purpose of the study. The others were confederates of the researcher, and they deliberately gave false answers to try to influence the naive participant. Asch found that some naive participants would go along with the group, even though the majority answer was obviously wrong and even though the group exerted no explicit pressure to conform.

It turns out that the number of confederates a researcher uses is a critical variable. When 1 or 2 individuals collaborate with the researcher, the naive participant shows considerably less tendency to conform than when 10 do. Another important variable is the existence of dissenting votes. If even 1 of 15 people disagrees with the other collaborating participants, the naive participant is more likely to choose the correct line.

How do groups influence individuals to conform? One conformity variable is the *amount of information* provided when a decision is to be made. When people are uncertain of how to behave in ambiguous situations, they seek the opinions of others. For example, people who are unsure of how they should vote in an election will often ask trusted friends for advice.

Another important variable that affects the degree of conformity is the *relative competence* of the group. People are more likely to conform to the decision of a group if they perceive its members as being more competent than they are. This pressure becomes stronger as group size increases. A first-year student in a large class, for example, may not answer even a simple question if no one else speaks up, because he assumes that his classmates are more competent than he is.

Position within a group also affects individual behavior. A person who confidently believes that a group holds her in high esteem will respond independently. If she feels insecure about her status, she may respond as the group does in order not to worsen her position within the group.

The *public nature of behavior* also determines people's responses. Individuals are more willing to make decisions that are inconsistent with those of a group when the behavior is private. In a democracy, for example, citizens vote privately so as to minimize group pressure on how individuals vote.

Why do people tend to conform? Several theories have attempted to explain this phenomenon. The *social conformity approach* states that people conform to avoid the stigma of being wrong, deviant, or different from others. According to this view, people want to do the right thing, and they define "right" as whatever is generally accepted (Festinger, 1954). Another explanation for why individuals in a group conform—or don't conform—is *attribution*. When a person can identify causes for the behavior of others in a group and strongly disagrees with those causes, conformity disappears (Ross, Bierbrauer, & Hoffman, 1976). The issue of *independence* also helps explain conformity (or the lack of it). Although most people would like to be independent, independence is risky. People in a group may have to face the consequences of their independence, such as serious disapproval, peer pressure to conform, being seen as deviant, becoming less powerful, or simply being left out. Last, conformity is partly a matter of *expediency;* conforming conserves mental energy. Recall Cialdini's (1993) argument that people face too many events, circumstances, and changing variables to be able to analyze all the relevant data. People therefore need shortcuts to help them make decisions. It is efficient and easy for people to go along with others whom they trust and respect, especially if the basic elements of a situation fit in with their views.

It is important to recognize that not everyone conforms to group pressures all the time. Both everyday experience and research show that *dissenting opinions* help counteract group influence and conformity. Even one or two people in a large group can seriously influence decision making. Moreover, when group decision making occurs, a consistent opposing voice (think of South African leader Nelson Mandela) can exert substantial influence and foster a sense of liberation, even when the opposition has little power or status (Kitayama & Burnstein, 1994). Not surprisingly, analysis of cross-cultural studies shows that people in countries with collectivist cultures exhibit more conformity than do people in countries with individualistic cultures (Bond & Smith, 1996).

Obedience and Milgram's Study. Obedience is compliance with the orders of another person or group of people. The studies on obedience by Stanley Milgram (1933–1984) are classic, and his results and interpretations still generate debate. Milgram's work focused on the extent to which an individual will obey a significant person. His studies showed that ordinary people were remarkably willing to comply with the wishes of others, especially if they saw the others as legitimate authority figures.

Imagine that you are one of the participants in Milgram's 1963 study at Yale University. You and a man you do not know are brought into a laboratory

Social influence: The ways people alter the attitudes or behaviors of others, either directly or indirectly.

Conformity: People's tendency to change attitudes or behaviors so that they are consistent with those of other people or with social norms.

Obedience: Compliance with the orders of another person or group of people.

and are told that you will be participating in an experiment on paired-associate learning. You draw lots to determine who will be the teacher and who will be the learner. The drawing is actually rigged so that you will be the teacher and the man, who is collaborating with the experimenter, will be the learner.

The learner/collaborator is taken to an adjoining room. You are shown a shock-generating box containing 30 switches, with labels that range from "Slight Shock" to "Danger: Severe Shock." You are told that the shock-generating equipment is connected to the learner in the other room. The learner will be given a test, and you will listen to his answers. Your job is to shock the learner by flipping one of the switches every time he makes an error on the test.

As the test continues, the experimenter and an assistant, both wearing white lab coats, encourage you to increase the shock voltage by one level each time the learner makes a mistake. As the shock level rises, the learner/collaborator screams as if he is suffering increasing pain. When the shocks reach a certain intensity, the learner stops responding vocally and instead pounds on the walls of the booth. The experimenter tells you to treat the learner's lack of vocal response as an error and to continue increasing the levels of shock. What would you do?

This was the basic scenario of the Milgram study. As you may have guessed by now, the learner/collaborators were not actually receiving shocks; they were only pretending to be in pain. Sixty-five percent of the participants in the study continued to shock the learner until they had delivered shocks at all levels. However, not all of Milgram's participants were obedient. Moreover, in a follow-up study, the presence of another "teacher" who refused to participate reduced the probability of obedience to as little as 10% (Milgram, 1965; Powers & Geen, 1972). These data suggest that obedience is sensitive to both authority and peer behavior. The fact that an individual's ability to resist coercion improves in the presence of an ally who also resists indicates the importance of other social influences on behavior.

Did conducting the study at the prestigious Yale University influence the participants? Milgram (1965) suggested that his experiment might have involved a particular type of experimental bias—*background authority.* To investigate the issue, Milgram conducted a second study in an office building in Bridgeport, Connecticut. Participants were contacted by mail and had no knowledge that Milgram or his associates were from Yale. In this second study, 48% of the participants delivered the maximum level of shock, as compared with the 65% of those who participated at Yale. Although this was not a big difference, Milgram inferred that the perceived authority of an institution could induce obedience in participants. Moreover, an institution's qualitative position within a category (for example, a prestigious university versus a little-known one) may be less important than the simple fact that it is some type of institution (for example, a university rather than an office building).

Explaining Milgram's Results. Why did so many participants in Milgram's experiments obey the wishes of the authority figure? One reason is that they were volunteers. Volunteers often bring undetected biases to an experimental situation, and one such bias is a willingness to go along with authority. When instructed to shock, Milgram's participants did what they were told. Another explanation derives from learning theories. Children learn that authority figures, such as teachers and parents, know more than they do and that taking their advice generally proves beneficial. As adults, they maintain those beliefs and apply them to authority figures such as employers, judges, government leaders, and so on. Cialdini (1993) also notes that obedience has practical advantages, such as helping people make decisions quickly: "It is easy to allow ourselves the convenience of automatic obedience. . . . We don't have to think, therefore we don't" (p. 178).

Other researchers repeated Milgram's methods, and the results of one study suggest that obedience to authority is not specific to Western cultures (Shanab & Yahya, 1978). People tend to obey those in authority, and such obedience is even more highly valued in many non-Western cultures. Students at the University of Jordan participated in a study similar to Milgram's; as in the original Milgram study, about 65% were willing to give high levels of shock to other students. Milgram's findings apply to men and women, old and young; they show that people's interactions within the social world are strongly affected by others.

Whenever they study social influence, researchers worry about ethical issues, and Milgram's experimental methods certainly raised such issues. The primary issue was deception; another involved potential harm to those who participated. Obtaining unbiased responses in psychological research often requires deceiving naive participants. To ensure that participants do not have any lasting ill effects, researchers debrief them after the experiment. **Debriefing** means informing participants about the true nature of an experiment after its completion, including an explanation of hypotheses, methods, and expected or potential results. Debriefing *after* the experiment preserves the validity of the responses while taking ethical considerations into account. Of course, debriefing must be done clearly and with sensitivity, especially in studies like Milgram's, which could affect a participant's self-esteem.

Milgram's participants were fully debriefed and shown that they had not actually harmed the other person. Nevertheless, critics argued, the participants came to realize that they were capable of inflicting severe pain on other people. Milgram therefore had a psychiatrist interview a sample of his obedient participants a year after the study. No evidence of psychological trauma or injury was found. Moreover, one study reported that participants viewed participation in the obedience experiment as a positive experience. They did not regret having participated; nor did they report any short-term negative psychological effects (Ring, Wallston, & Corey, 1970). Today, because more stringent ethical constraints are now in place, Milgram's study and its variations would not be allowed in research laboratories.

Studies of social influence, especially conformity and obedience studies, show that people exert powerful influences on others and those influences are even greater when they are exerted by a group. Let's look next at the effects of groups on individual behavior and how individuals behave within groups.

Groups: Sharing Common Goals

Membership in a group does confer certain advantages, which is why people belong to all kinds of groups. There are formal groups, such as the American Association of University Students, and informal ones, such as a lunch group of coworkers. A **group** can be any number of people who are working with a common purpose or have some common goals, characteristics, or interests. By joining a group, people indicate that they agree with or have a serious interest in its purpose. For example, a major function of the American Cancer Society is to raise money for cancer research, and a person's membership indicates an interest in finding a cure for cancer. It has generally been thought that groups enhance individual performance; research shows, however, that this effect is modest and that the larger effect that emanates from a group is a sense of cohesion, solidarity, and commitment to a task (Mullen & Copper, 1994).

Social Facilitation. Individual behavior is affected not only by membership in a group but also by the mere presence of a group. **Social facilitation** is a change in behavior that occurs when people believe they are in the presence of other people. For example, an accomplished person who is playing a sport may do even better when other people are watching. A person who is less accomplished, however, may do worse when other people are around. Research studies that examine people's performance at various tasks—for example, keyboard data entry—show this effect (Aiello & Kolb, 1995).

According to Zajonc, the presence of others produces heightened arousal, which leads to a greater likelihood that an individual will exhibit a particular response (Jackson & Latané, 1981; Zajonc, 1965). But just what is the nature of the heightened arousal? This is a source of some debate. One theory of social facilitation suggests that fear of evaluation—not the mere presence of people—is what brings about changes in performance (Innes & Young, 1975). If an auto mechanic knows that a customer is watching him repair an engine, he is likely to increase his work speed to demonstrate his efficiency and professionalism. Bond and Titus (1983) suggest that the effects of social facilitation are often overestimated and the effects of believing oneself to be observed are often underestimated. They caution that studies of social facilitation must take into account the actual and believed presence of observers, as well as the perceived importance of the evaluation by the observers. Being evaluated by a friend has a different effect than being evaluated by a stranger (Buck et al., 1992).

A decrease in an individual's effort and productivity as a result of working in a group is known as **social loafing.** Suppose you and your friends join forces to help clean up and paint the recreation rooms of a community center. Do you expend as much effort as a member of the group as you would have expended if you had to do the job by yourself? Research confirms the social loafing effect. In an experiment in which participants were instructed to clap their hands and cheer, they clapped and cheered less loudly when they were part of a group (Latané, Williams, & Harkins, 1979).

Most psychologists claim that social loafing occurs when individual performance within a group cannot be evaluated—that is, when poor performance may go undetected and exceptional performance may go unrecognized. Consequently, people feel less pressure to work hard or efficiently. One study showed that as group size increased, individual members believed their efforts were more dispensable—the

Debriefing: Informing participants about the true nature of an experiment after its completion.

Group: Two or more individuals who are working with a common purpose or have some common goals, characteristics, or interests.

Social facilitation: Change in behavior that occurs when people believe they are in the presence of other people.

Social loafing: Decrease in effort and productivity that occurs when an individual works in a group instead of alone.

group could function without their help. "Let George do it" became the prevailing attitude (Kerr & Bruun, 1983). Such findings are evident cross-culturally; for example, Jordanian students, who come from a society that stresses cohesion and group cooperation, worked less hard when they were working together than when working alone (Atoum & Farah, 1993).

Social loafing is minimized when the task is attractive and rewarding and when the group is cohesive and committed to task performance (Karau & Williams, 1997). It is also less apparent when the group is small, when the members know one another well, and when a group leader calls on individuals by name or lets it be known that individual performance may be evaluated (Williams, Harkins, & Latané, 1981). Some researchers have observed decreases in social loafing when individuals have the opportunity to assess their own performance relative to an objective standard or relative to other people's performance, even though no one else is evaluating them (Harkins & Szymanski, 1988; Szymanski & Harkins, 1993). As with so many other social phenomena, a wide array of variables can alter the extent of social loafing; yet researchers conclude that it occurs across a wide variety of tasks and situations (Karau & Williams, 1997).

Group Polarization. People in groups may be willing to adopt behaviors slightly more extreme than their individual behavioral tendencies. They may be willing to make decisions that are risky or even daring. Some early research on group decision making focused on the willingness of individuals to accept more risky alternatives when other members of the group did so; this research described such individuals as making a *risky shift* in decisions.

In a group, individuals initially perceive themselves as being more extreme than the other members of the group. They also believe they are more fair, more right-minded, more liberal, and so on. When they discover that their positions are not very different from those of others in the group, they shift, or become *polarized,* to show that they are even more right-minded, fairer, or more liberal. They also may become more assertive in expressing their views. Shifts or exaggerations in group members' attitudes or behavior that take place after group discussion are referred to as **group polarization;** in an individual, such a shift is known as a *choice shift* (Zuber, Crott, & Werner, 1992).

Another explanation of the polarization phenomenon, *persuasive argument,* asserts that people tend to become more extreme after hearing views similar to their own. A person who is mildly liberal on an issue becomes even more liberal, more polarized. This explanation suggests that people in a group often become more wedded to their initial views instead of becoming more moderate. If other people in the group hold similar views, that may polarize individual members even more. The effects of group polarization are particularly evident among juries. After group discussion, jury members are likely to return to their initial views and argue for them more strongly. Thus, individual jury members who initially have doubts about a witness will have even deeper doubts after group discussion.

Another explanation for group polarization is *diffusion of responsibility*—the feeling of individual members of a group that they cannot be held responsible for the group's actions. If a group makes a decision to invest money, for example, no single individual is responsible. Diffusion of responsibility may allow the members to make far more extreme investment decisions as a group than they would individually.

Social comparison may also play a role in group polarization. People compare their views with the ideas of others whom they respect and who may hold more extreme attitudes than theirs. Feeling as right-minded as their colleagues, they become at least as liberal or as conservative as their peer group—they polarize their views.

Groupthink. Studies of decision making in government have often focused on **groupthink**—the tendency of people in a group to seek concurrence with one another when reaching a decision, rather than effectively evaluating the options. Groupthink occurs when group members reinforce shared beliefs in the interest of getting along. The group does not allow its members to disagree, to accept dissenting opinions, or to evaluate options realistically (Janis, 1983). Groupthink discredits or ignores information not held in common, and thus cohesive groups are more likely to exhibit it (Mullen et al., 1994).

Social psychologist Ivan Steiner (1982) suggests that groupthink occurs when members' overriding concern is to maintain group cohesiveness and harmony. Cohesiveness helps individuals believe that the group cannot make mistakes. In addition, strong lead-

Group polarization: Shifts or exaggeration in group members' attitudes or behavior as a result of group discussion.

Groupthink: The tendency of people in a group to seek concurrence with one another when reaching a decision, rather than effectively evaluating the options.

Deindividuation: The process by which individuals lose their self-awareness and distinctive personality in the context of a group, which may lead them to engage in antinormative behavior.

Aggression: Any behavior intended to harm another person or thing.

ers often insulate a group from outside information to keep the group thinking along the same line (McCauley, 1989).

Despite the intuitive appeal of the groupthink concept, however, research support for it is minimal. Nevertheless, Aldag and Fuller (1993) assert that despite its lack of empirical support, groupthink *can* happen. They maintain that it is a defective process that people should guard against, and they argue that research on leaders, committees, and technology needs to focus on the variables that may create groupthink, as well as factors that help defend against it (Miranda, 1994).

Unrestrained Group Behavior. The presence of other people can arouse people (social facilitation), can make them less active (social loafing), can cause them to take extreme views (group polarization), or can lead to poor decisions (groupthink). When placed in a group, normally thoughtful people have been known to make bad decisions and even to exhibit irrational behaviors. Consider mob violence. When people engage in a riot, looting, or other violent behavior, individuals explain their participation not in terms of individual responsibility but as a group decision.

A key component of unrestrained behavior such as mob violence is *anonymity.* Anonymity produces a lack of self-awareness and self-perception that leads to decreased concern with social evaluation. When people have fewer concerns about being evaluated, they are more willing to engage in inappropriate or irrational behaviors. When there is violence or illegal drug use among a crowd at a rock concert, for example, people feel less responsible. The view that no single individual can be held responsible for the behavior of a group arises out of **deindividuation**—the process by which individuals lose their self-awareness and distinctive personality in the context of a group, which may lead them to engage in antinormative behavior (Diener et al., 1980). Deindividuation (and its accompanying arousal) can lead to shifts in people's perceptions of how their behavior will be viewed—and thus to less controlled, less self-conscious, or less careful decisions about behavior. With deindividuation, people alter their thoughts about decisions.

Groups such as the military, prisons, and cults use deindividuation to encourage their members to conform. With their unique personality stripped away, they are no longer treated as individuals and are made to behave as members of the larger group. In boot camp, military recruits are made to feel that they are there to serve the group, not their conscience. In prisons, inmates are made to wear uniforms and are assigned numbers. A cult persuades members to go along with group beliefs and acquire a sense of obligation to the group by asking individual members

to perform increasingly difficult acts on the group's behalf. In the end, an individual's behavior in a group often becomes distorted, more extreme, and less rational; the group makes members feel less accountable for their own actions. Initial research on deindividuation appeared to confirm the phenomenon (Prentice-Dunn, 1991), but more recent research is yielding inconsistent results (Postmes & Spears, 1998)—so this seemingly useful concept, like many theories in psychology, is being evaluated and reevaluated to assess its durability.

Aggression and Violence: The Dark Side of Human Behavior

The two teenagers responsible for the 1999 Columbine High School massacre made the pipe bombs more than a year before they used them. Although their schoolmates saw the two as outsiders—part of the out group—no one seemed to be fully aware of the dark path the boys' thoughts were taking. Social interactions are sometimes quite inconsequential—briefly saying hello to others we pass in school or on the street, for example. Other social interactions affect important relationships—such as when your teacher or boss makes a point to commend your good work. But social interactions also include the dark side of people's behaviors, including aggressive and violent acts—children, adolescents, and adults terrorize, hurt, and even kill each other. Often, the cause is not apparent or does not justify the act. As you will see in the following pages, aggressive or violent social interactions are shaped by a wide array of events in people's lives.

When people feel unable to control situations that affect their lives, they may become frustrated, angry, and aggressive. Social psychologists define **aggression** as any behavior intended to harm another person or thing. An aggressive person may attempt to harm others physically through force, verbally through rumors or irritating comments, or emotionally by withholding attention or love. On a larger scale, whole countries attempt to harm others by acts of war. Three major theoretical explanations for aggressive behavior focus on instincts, acquired drives, and cognitive psychology.

Instincts. Some psychologists believe that many aspects of behavior, including aggression, are inborn (DiLalla & Gottesman, 1991). Those who believe that people are genetically predisposed toward aggression are termed *nativists.* Freud was an early nativist as was the ethologist and Nobel laureate Konrad Lorenz (1903–1989). According to Lorenz (1964), aggression is instinctive and spontaneous; the aggressive instinct allows animal populations to make optimal use of food, space, and resources. Lorenz stressed the social implications of aggressive instincts in humans, focusing on the adaptive value of such instincts.

Both animals and human beings can be aggressive, and there is evidence that some people may have a biological predisposition to aggressiveness (Niehoff, 1999). Whether aggression is inhibited or expressed depends on the organism's previous experiences and current social context—for example, whether it has been raised in a hostile environment or is currently being provoked.

Acquired Drives. Another explanation for aggressive behavior is that it results when goal-directed behavior has been frustrated—this is the *frustration–aggression hypothesis,* initially proposed by Dollard and colleagues (1939). This theory relies on observations demonstrating that people involved in everyday goal-oriented tasks often become aggressive or angry when frustrated. For example, ordinarily, you may be unlikely to become upset if another car pulls out into traffic in front of you. However, if you are late for work, you might honk or mutter angrily at the other driver. On a larger scale, the violence between Catholics and Protestants in Northern Ireland is fueled in part by intense competition for decent jobs in a depressed economy.

Berkowitz (1964) examined the evidence for the frustration–aggression hypothesis and proposed a modified version of it. He suggested that frustration creates a *readiness* for aggressive acts rather than producing actual aggression. He showed that, even when frustration is present, certain events must occur or certain conditions must exist before aggression results; for example, someone embroiled in a heated argument might be more likely to become aggressive if there is a weapon lying on a nearby table. In a later reformulation, Berkowitz (1989) suggested that frustrations generate aggressive inclinations to the extent that they arouse negative feelings in the frustrated individual (Berkowitz, 1990). Berkowitz's conception accounts for the instances when frustrated people don't become aggressive. Although many psychologists find the frustration–aggression hypothesis too simplistic, it is useful, in part because it has led to other research that helps describe behavior—for example, cognitive theory.

Cognitive Psychology. Theories are perishable; they eventually become outdated and are replaced. This has been especially true in the study of aggression. Old ideas about aggression being inborn and people having inherited tendencies to violence have come to be considered wrong; see Table 11.2. Early research on aggression was based on learning theory explanations of how children learn aggressive behavior, which were popular in the 1950s and 1960s. Later, with the increasing influence of Skinner's behaviorism, researchers focused on more refined interpretations of aggression based on operant conditioning. They studied the effects of punishing children for aggressive behavior and rewarding them for nonaggressive behavior. A shift toward observational (social) learning theory occurred in the 1970s, and the effects of TV viewing were a prime focus (see *Experiencing Psychology*). In the 1980s, cognitive explanations of aggression became prevalent, and researchers began to speak in terms of thought, interpretations, and expectations.

Table 11.2 A Tendency to Violence Is Not Inherited

Scientific groups, including the American Psychological Association, have adopted a statement called the Seville Statement on Violence, which asserts that the use of scientific data to support war is wrong and is based on erroneous assumptions.

The following statements are scientifically incorrect:

We have inherited a tendency to make war from our animal ancestors.

War or any other violent behavior is programmed into our human nature.

Through the course of human evolution, aggression more than any other characteristic has been programmed into human behavior.

Humans have a violent brain.

War is caused by instinct or any other specific inborn motivation.

Source: Adapted from the Seville Statement on Violence (APA, 1994).

EXPERIENCING PSYCHOLOGY

Exposure to Violence

Exposure to violence in its many forms has been likened to a public health epidemic; violence is seen on city streets, in rural communities, and on the worldwide stage. Violence is almost commonplace, and its impact on childhood development grows daily (Osofsky, 1995). Nowhere are violence and aggression, especially sexual aggression, more prevalent than on television (MacKay & Covell, 1997). And most children aged 2–11 spend more hours watching television (an average of almost 22 hours a week) than in any other activity except sleep; they are also often indiscriminate viewers (Huston et al., 1992; Kubey & Csikszentmihalyi, 1990). Television thus serves as a major source of behavior for children to imitate. For example, watching television has been shown to affect children's career aspirations. Furthermore, it may alter their aggressive thoughts and their overall views of life and may decrease their creativity (Valkenberg & van der Voort, 1994).

The fact that television portrays so much aggressive behavior concerns parents and educators as well as social psychologists. Half of all prime-time TV characters are involved in violent activity of some kind; about one-tenth kill or are killed; the perpetrators of these crimes go unpunished in nearly three-quarters of violent scenes. Sixty-one percent of television programs contain violence—and that violence is often glamorized (Smith et al., 1998). Moreover, about 20% of males appearing on TV shows are employed in law enforcement, whereas less than 1% of adult men are so employed in the real world. Although the overall amount of violence on television is staggering, some programs account for a disproportionate number of violent acts (Gunter & Harrison, 1998).

Research generally supports the contention that viewers who frequently watch violent programs on television are more likely to be aggressive than are viewers who see less TV violence (Hogben, 1998). Further, children exposed to large doses of TV violence are less likely to help a real-life victim of violence, and viewers of violence are less sympathetic to victims than are nonviewers (Huston et al., 1992). Viewers of violence also are more fearful of becoming victims of violent acts. One study found that the viewing of TV violence at age 8 predicted aggressive behavior at age 19 (Eron & Huesmann, 1980). Children who play violent video games also seem to act more aggressively at later ages (Schutte et al., 1988), and even infants can become fearful from watching television (Meltzoff, 1988). According to Stacy Smith and her colleagues (1998), who conducted the National Television Violence Study, violence on television hasn't changed appreciably in decades—neither its overall prevalence nor how it is presented have changed much. How does watching violence on television affect viewers? Smith and her colleagues describe some of the key effects of viewing violence on television:

- It weakens viewers' inhibitions.
- It may suggest new ideas and techniques to the uninitiated.
- It may activate or stimulate existing aggressive ideas and behaviors.
- It desensitizes people, reducing their overall emotional sensitivity to violence.
- It introduces a fear of being a victim of violence.

Of course, television can also have positive effects on children. In one study, children exposed to shows such as *Sesame Street* and *Mister Rogers' Neighborhood,* which focus on topics such as sharing and caring, were more likely to engage in prosocial behavior with other children than were children in a control group who did not watch those shows (Coates, Pusser, & Goodman, 1976). However, watching too much television has a deleterious impact on children's reading comprehension skills (Koolstra, van der Voort, & van der Kamp, 1997).

Research on the effects of television and other media is tricky. Often the effects are subtle because potential influences—violence, sex, and education—are sometimes combined in one program. Some assert that children are "protected" from the effects of violence by knowledge that what they see is not real (Davies, 1997); if this is the case, at what age does such "preventive knowledge" appear? In the end, the data are fairly clear: TV programming, for better or worse, can affect children. So, how, when, and how often information is conveyed to children ultimately has important social implications (Calvert, 1998). Social psychologists interested in public policy are suggesting requiring every TV station to broadcast at least a certain amount of educational programming for children and establishing controls to protect children from advertising that exploits their special vulnerability (Smith et al., 1998). ■

Researchers today are examining how stimuli in an individual's environment may elicit thoughts and emotional responses that lead to aggressive behavior (Bushman & Geen, 1990). Stimuli that have been examined include difficult personal situations and frustrating social conditions (Staub, 1996). Such views have led researchers to believe that harsh, punitive parenting leads to aggressiveness and negativity. Aggressive children see others as hostile to them, and they respond in kind. But not all theorists agree; some researchers assert that a key cognitive variable that may predispose people to aggression is self-esteem.

The conventional wisdom has held that people with low self-esteem—unfavorable global impressions of themselves—are more likely to be violent and aggressive. But a review of research shows that crime, violence, and aggression are not *caused by* low self-esteem (or, for that matter, by high self-esteem). According to Roy Baumeister (Bushman & Baumeister, 1998), aggression is caused by *threats* to a person's level of self-esteem. When their views of themselves (however high or low) are threatened or contradicted, people become aggressive. This view suggests that those who fail to adjust their self-appraisal—despite evidence of the correctness of the new view—may become aggressive. There are some strong direct implications of such an idea. Western society places a strong emphasis on helping develop individuals' self-esteem. But development of self-esteem doesn't protect individuals from threats to it. Baumeister suggests that societal pursuit of high self-esteem for everyone may end up doing considerable harm, given the fact that it is impossible to insulate everyone from threats to self-esteem! As yet there is little research on how threats to self-esteem affect aggression, but the idea has considerable interest.

Gender Differences in Aggression. Many people believe that men are naturally more aggressive than women. They refer to aggressive contact sports such as football and boxing, the aggressive behavior of men in business, the overwhelming number of violent crimes committed by men, and the traditional view that men are more likely than women to be ruthless and unsympathetic. It is also generally accepted that "more masculine" people (whether men or women) are more aggressive (Kogut, Langley, & O'Neal, 1992), and this is reflected in children's toys (Dietz, 1998) and on television (Browne, 1998). But are men really more aggressive than women?

Eagly and Steffen (1986) confirmed what people had already observed—men are more *physically* aggressive than women—a finding supported by others (Harris & Knight-Bohnhoff, 1996). But they also found that both men and women use *psychological* aggression such as verbal abuse and angry gestures. Their interpretation of the findings suggests that the differences in aggression that appear between men and women are directly related to the perceived consequences of the aggression. Women in many cultures have been raised with values that make them feel especially guilty if they cause physical pain; men have not been raised with those values, at least not to the same extent. However, gender roles in American society are changing, and perhaps gender differences in willingness to cause pain—and act aggressively—will diminish in the future.

The differences in aggression that appear between men and women are directly related to the perceived consequences of the aggression.

The research picture is complicated, and some important and subtle effects occur. For example, research shows that the age at which aggression occurs varies in men and women; girls develop aggressive behaviors in adolescence, while boys do so earlier. Furthermore, early maturing girls are at higher risk for psychological problems and aggressive behaviors (Loeber & Stouthamer-Loeber, 1998). Some social behaviors may be genetically programmed and may have an evolutionary basis, but the weight of the evidence leans toward socialization by society (Archer, 1996). Psychologists are just beginning to assess the important

Prosocial behavior: Behavior that benefits someone else or society but that generally offers no obvious benefit to the person performing it and may even involve some personal risk or sacrifice.

Altruism [AL-true-ism]: Behaviors that benefit other people and for which there is no discernible extrinsic reward, recognition, or appreciation.

issues involving gender and the developmental course of aggression.

Think Critically

- Consider some famous dissenters in history. How did their refusal to conform to group pressure affect their lives? How did their dissent influence society?
- How might it be possible to shape a society to make it less aggressive?

Prosocial Behavior

Are small-town people more helpful than city people? It turns out that they are, and that this is true all over the world (Yousif & Korte, 1995). What factors are at work? Under what conditions are people helpful? For example, if you are walking down the street with a bag of groceries and you drop them, what is the likelihood that someone will help you pick them up? Will a bystander who observes a serious accident or a crime help the victim? What attributions will the bystander make about the causes of an incident? What attitudes about helping behavior or about people being victims will the bystander bring to the incident? Psychologists trying to find out when, and under what conditions, someone will help a stranger are examining the likelihood of **prosocial behavior**—behavior that benefits someone else or society but that generally offers no obvious benefit to the person performing it and may even involve some personal risk or sacrifice.

Altruism: Helping without Rewards. Why does Peter Beneson, the founder of Amnesty International, devote so much time and effort to helping "prisoners of conscience" around the world? What compelled Mother Teresa to wander Calcutta's streets and attend to the wounds and diseases of people no one else would touch? Why did Oskar Schindler risk his life to save 1,100 Jews from the Nazi death camps during World War II?

Altruism consists of behaviors that benefit other people and for which there is no discernible extrinsic reward, recognition, or appreciation (Quigley, Gaes, & Tedeschi, 1989). The key is that rewards are not part of the altruism equation. Although many prosocial behaviors involve rewards and altruistic behaviors are prosocial, altruistic behaviors are done without any expectation of reward. But isn't the feeling of well-being after performing an altruistic act a type of reward?

Many behaviorists contend that some element of personality directs people to seek social approval by helping. According to this view, people with a high need for achievement are more likely than others to be helpful, and people may continue to be helpful because the positive consequences of their actions are self-reinforcing (Batson et al., 1991; Puffer, 1987). From a behavioral view, intrinsically rewarding activities become powerful behavior initiators; thus, for example, when you have a relationship with a person, the person's affection and approval make you more likely to be caring and helpful (Batson, 1990). Further, once kindness and helpfulness become well established and even routine, individuals are more likely to help others, such as the homeless, disadvantaged senior citizens, and orphans.

Other theorists argue that biological drives underlie altruistic behavior. Consider the following scenario: An infant crawls into a busy street as a truck is approaching. The mother darts in front of the oncoming vehicle and carries her child to safety. Most people would say that love impels the mother to risk her life to save the child. Sociobiologists would argue that the mother commits her brave deed so that her genes will be passed on to another generation.

The idea that people are genetically predisposed toward certain behaviors was described by Edward Wilson, a Harvard University zoologist, in his book *Sociobiology: A New Synthesis* (1975).Wilson argued that genetic factors underlie all behavior. But he went one step further. He founded a new field, **sociobiology,** based on the premise that even day-to-day behaviors are determined by the process of natural selection—that social behaviors that contribute to the survival of a species are passed on via the genes from one generation to the next. Natural selection accounts for the mechanisms that have evolved to produce altruistic behaviors (Crawford & Anderson, 1989). For the sociobiologist, genetics is the key to daily behavior.

Psychologists hotly debate sociobiological theory, because it places genetics in a position of primary importance and minimizes the role of learning. Most psychologists feel strongly that learning plays a key role in the day-to-day activities of human beings. People *learn* to love, to become angry, to help or hurt others, and to develop relationships with others. But although sociobiology is too fixed and rigid for most psychologists, it does raise interesting questions about the role of biology and genetics in social behavior.

Behavioral theories and sociobiology are two ways of explaining why people help others. People

Sociobiology: A discipline based on the premise that even day-to-day behaviors are determined by the process of natural selection—that social behaviors that contribute to the survival of a species are passed on via the genes from one generation to the next.

don't always help, however. One important area of research seeks to explain why.

Bystander Apathy: Failing to Help. The study of helping behavior has taken some interesting twists and turns. For example, psychologists have found that in large cities, where potentially lethal emergencies (accidents, thefts, stabbings, rapes, and murders) occur frequently, people often exhibit bystander apathy—they watch but do not help. **Bystander apathy** is the unwillingness of witnesses to an event to help; this unwillingness increases with the number of observers, a fact that has been termed the *bystander effect.* In a well-known incident in New York City in 1964, Kitty Genovese was walking home when a man approached her with a knife. A chase ensued, during which she screamed for help. He stabbed her, and she continued screaming. When lights came on in nearby buildings, the attacker fled. But when he saw that no one was coming to his victim's aid, he returned and stabbed her again. The assault lasted more than 30 minutes and was heard by dozens of neighbors; yet no one came to the victim's aid. This is a classic case of bystander apathy.

Bibb Latané and John Darley (1970) investigated bystander apathy in a long series of studies. They found that people must decide whether to introduce themselves into a problematic situation, especially when there are other bystanders. But first they have to decide what is going on (whether or not there is an emergency), and they are often misled by the *apparent* lack of concern among other bystanders to conclude that nothing really bad is going on after all—so they don't help. Latané and Darley reasoned that when people are aware of other bystanders in an emergency situation, they may also be less likely to help because they experience *diffusion of responsibility* (the feeling that they cannot be held responsible). To test their hypothesis, the researchers brought college students to a laboratory and told them they were going to be involved in a study of people who were interested in discussing college life in New York City. The researchers explained that, in the interest of preserving people's anonymity, a group discussion would be held over an intercom system rather than face-to-face, and that each person in the group would talk in turn. In fact, there was only one actual participant in each experimental session. Assistants who worked for the researchers prerecorded all the other conversations.

Bystander apathy: Unwillingness to help exhibited by witnesses to an event, which increases when there are more observers.

Interpersonal attraction: The tendency of one person to evaluate another person (or a symbol or image of another person) in a positive way.

The independent variable was the number of people the naive participant thought were in the discussion group. The dependent variable was whether and how fast the naive participant reported as an emergency an apparently serious seizure affecting one of the other "participants." The future "seizure victim" spoke first; he talked about his difficulties getting adjusted to New York and mentioned that he was prone to seizures, particularly when studying hard. Next, the naive participant spoke. Then came the prerecorded discussions by assistants. Then the "seizure victim" talked again. After a few relatively calm remarks, his speech became increasingly loud and incoherent; he stuttered and indicated that he needed help. At this point, the experimenters began timing the speed of the naive participant's response.

Each naive participant was led to believe that his or her discussion group contained either two, three, or six people. That is, participants in the two-person group believed they were the only bystanders when the "victim" suffered his seizure; participants in the three-person group thought there was one other bystander. Eighty-five percent of participants who thought they were the only bystanders responded before the end of the seizure; 62% of the participants who thought there was only one other bystander responded by the end of the seizure. When participants thought there were four additional bystanders, only 31% responded by the end of the seizure.

In general, research has shown that bystanders will help under some conditions. For one thing, people's self-concepts and previous experiences affect their willingness to intercede. Bystanders who see themselves as being especially competent in emergencies (for example, doctors and nurses) are likely to help a victim regardless of the number of people present (Pantin & Carver, 1982). If the person who needs help has a relationship with the person who can offer help, help is more likely to be given (Batson, 1990). Research in cities of various sizes shows that people who live in smaller communities are more likely to help (Levine et al., 1994). Also, personality characteristics of the individual involved in a bystander situation are important. Men respond more often than women (Salminen & Glad, 1992). Tice and Baumeister (1985) found, however, that participants with a high degree of masculinity were less likely to respond. They contended that highly masculine subjects might be especially fearful of embarrassment. In U.S. society, the ideal personality characteristics for men, in general, emphasize strength and aggression rather than sensitivity and nurturing. This finding is supported by work showing that women are more likely than men to help friends, and that when women do so, they do it in a nurturing rather than a problem-solving way (Belansky & Boggiano, 1994).

Relationships and Attraction

Some people feel that life is predetermined and that their relationships with others—especially love relationships—are a part of their personal destiny. It turns out that people who believe in romantic destiny—that members of a couple are meant for each other—tend to have long relationships, if they let a relationship get started in the first place (Knee, 1998). But relationships with friends, lovers, and spouses are intricate. What is it about people that attracts you and makes you want to maintain a relationship with them in the first place? We saw in Chapter 9 that people develop relationships to fulfill their needs for warmth, understanding, and emotional security. Social psychologists also know that people are attracted to those who live or work near them, whom they consider good-looking, who share their attitudes, and with whom they spend time. These factors are related to **interpersonal attraction,** the tendency of one person to evaluate another person (or a symbol or image of another person) in a positive way.

Proximity. People are more likely to develop a relationship with a neighbor than with someone who lives several blocks or miles away. Three decades of research show that the closer people are geographically, the more likely they are to become attracted. A simple explanation is that they are likely to see each other more often, and repeated exposure leads to familiarity, which leads to attraction. Another reason is that attraction is facilitated by the anticipation of a relationship with someone one encounters frequently. In addition, people who are members of the same group, such as a club, a volunteer organization, or a class, perceive themselves as sharing the same feelings, attitudes, and values as others in the group. That perception leads to attraction.

People judge an attractive individual to have more positive traits and characteristics than an unattractive one.

Physical Attractiveness. Within seconds of seeing a person, you are able to decide if they are attractive to you (Locher et al., 1993). Attractiveness is affected by subtle but powerful variables. For example, in a recent study, both men and women were shown images of the faces of Caucasian and Japanese females and males like those in the photo; the shapes of the faces had been "feminized" or "masculinized" using a computer (Perrett et al., 1998). Both Caucasian and Japanese participants preferred and rated as most attractive the faces that were feminized. Interestingly, both men and women tend to find more appealing men who are more feminine looking than rugged. The researchers suggested that computer alteration of men's faces to make them slightly feminine makes them appear less menacing and softens other features that are associated with negative traits. The researchers assert that more feminine faces appear younger and that people's preferences for young faces are correlated with their preferences for feminized faces. Such results are probably no surprise to Leonardo DiCaprio's agent.

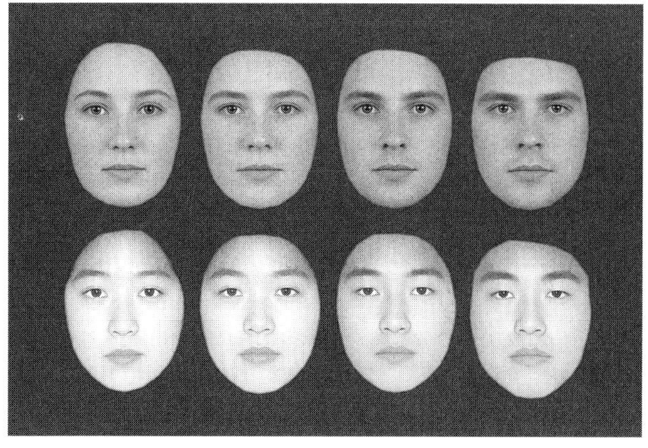

Volumes of research show that people are attracted romantically, at least at first, to those whom they find physically attractive. People judge an attractive individual to have more positive traits and characteristics than an unattractive one, especially when appearance is the first information provided (DeSantis & Kayson, 1997). People feel more personal regard for and ascribe more power, status, and com petence to individuals they find physically attractive than to those they don't; this affects who can best change people's attitudes (Feingold, 1992a, 1992b). Attractive people are granted more freedom and are perceived as being fairer and more healthy than unattractive people (Kalick et al., 1998). For example, attractive college professors are seen as better teachers and are less likely to be blamed by a student who receives a failing grade in a course (Romano & Bordieri, 1989). But such findings about attractiveness are a distinctly Western phenomenon; ideas about attractiveness differ cross-culturally (Matsumoto & Kudoh, 1993).

How important is physical attractiveness when it comes to dating? Do people always select the best-looking person to date? Research shows that people prefer attractive dates, and some studies show that people seek out those of their own level of attractiveness. But other variables also seem to play an important role; educational level, intelligence, socioeconomic status, and similarity of previous experiences all weigh heavily in the choice of whom to date or marry (Feingold, 1988). Although physical attractiveness and youthfulness are initially important in the selection of dates and mates (especially among men), appearance is just one variable among many (Sprecher, Sullivan, & Hatfield, 1994).

Liking Those Who Share the Feeling and Who Hold Similar Attitudes. Learning theorists contend that people are attracted to and form relationships with those who give them positive reinforcement and that they dislike those who punish them. The basic idea is simple: You like the people who like you. Moreover, if you like someone, you tend to assume (sometimes incorrectly) that the other person likes you in return and that the two of you share similar qualities. This tendency is especially prevalent in people who need social approval—for example, people with low self-esteem (Jacobs, Berscheid, & Walster, 1971).

Another attribute that affects the development of relationships is real or perceived similarity in attitudes and opinions. If you perceive someone's attitudes as being similar to your own, this perception increases the probability that you will like that person. Having similar values, interests, and backgrounds is a good predictor of a friendship (Miller, 1990). Similarly, voters who agree with the views of a particular candidate tend to rate that person as more honest, friendly, and persuasive than the candidates with whom they disagree. Researchers have also found that, conversely, if you already like someone, you will perceive that person's attitudes as being similar to your own. For example, voters who like a particular candidate, perhaps because they perceive the candidate as warm-hearted or physically attractive, will tend to minimize their attitudinal differences.

That you like those who like you is explained by cognitive consistency theory, which suggests that sharing similar attitudes reduces cognitive dissonance (a phenomenon we examined earlier). Given a natural inclination to avoid dissonance, you feel attracted to those you believe share similar attitudes; shared attitudes in turn lead to attraction and liking. Learning theories also suggest that you like people with similar attitudes because similar attitudes are reinforcing to you.

Friendships and the Role of Equity. Laverne and Shirley, Richie and Potsy, Lucy and Ethel—liking each other and sharing ideas and values has been the basis of many friendships. *Friendship* is a special two-way relationship between people. According to one influential group of researchers, if two people's behaviors, emotions, and thoughts are similar, and the people are dependent on one another, a close relationship exists (Kelley et al., 1983). Closeness is reported by many researchers as the key variable that defines a friendship, although *close* must be defined so that all researchers mean the same thing when they use the word (Berscheid, Snyder, & Omoto, 1989).

As we discussed in Chapter 9 (p. 256), ideally, friends participate as equals, are intimate, and share confidences (Davis & Todd, 1982). Reciprocity and commitment are essential to friendship (Hartup, 1989). Close friends interact frequently across a wider range of settings, are more exclusive, and offer each other more benefits (Hays, 1989). Elementary school children tend to form same-gender friendships; cross-gender friendships are rare. With youngsters, friendships lead to cooperation rather than competition, at least more than with nonfriends (Hartup, 1989). Furthermore, children who have friends in the classroom do better in school (Ladd, 1990). Adolescent friendships sometimes provide an arena for sharing and intimacy, although they can also be filled with conflict over social or political issues, drugs, gangs, and sexual behavior (Berndt, 1992). Western cultural expectations for specific gender-based behaviors often control male–female interactions in friendship. Women talk more about family, personal matters, and doubts and fears than men do; men talk more than women about sports and work.

Equity plays an important role in close relationships. **Equity theory** states that people attempt to maintain stable, consistent interpersonal relationships in which the ratio of members' contributions is balanced. People in a close relationship usually feel a sense of balance in the relationship and believe it will last for a long time (Clark & Reis, 1988).

According to equity theory, one way people maintain a balanced relationship is to make restitution when it is demanded. Apologies help restore a sense of autonomy and fairness in an injured individual. Similarly, people who do favors expect favors in return, often using the principle of equity unconsciously in day-to-day life. If a friend helps you move into your new apartment, you may be expected to lend her a hand when she has to take an old refrigerator to the dump. Research shows that when a person senses inequity in a situation, this affects her or his feelings about the other person (Griffeth, Vecchio, & Logan, 1989).

Intimate Relationships and Love. People involved in a close relationship may be intimate with one another. **Intimacy** is a state of being or feeling in

Equity theory: Social psychological theory that states that people attempt to maintain stable, consistent interpersonal relationships in which the ratio of members' contributions is balanced.

Intimacy: A state of being or feeling in which each person in a relationship is willing to self-disclose and to express important feelings and information to the other person.

which each person in a relationship is willing to self-disclose and to express important feelings and information to the other person; in response, the other person usually acknowledges the first person's feelings, a process that makes each feel valued and cared for (Reis & Shaver, 1988). Research shows that self-disclosure tends to be reciprocal; people who disclose themselves to others are usually recipients of intimate information (Collins & Miller, 1994). When people self-disclose, they validate each other; that is, they accept each other's positive and negative attributes.

Unfortunately, there is little research on intimate relationships outside of marriage. Communication, affection, consideration, and self-disclosure between friends have been studied relatively little. However, important individual and gender differences in friendships have been identified. For example, women, more than men, incorporate close relationships into their view of themselves and let those views affect their thoughts and behaviors (Cross & Madson, 1997). Women also evaluate same-sex friendships more positively than men do (Veniegas & Peplau, 1997). Furthermore, in general, men are less likely to be self-disclosing and intimate than are women (Dindia & Allen, 1992), but men are more self-disclosing with a woman than they are with another man. On the whole, however, psychologists know much more about intimate relationships that involve sex, love, and marriage (Miller, 1990).

Love, emotional commitment, and sex are the parts of relationships that most people think of when they hear the word *intimacy.* People in love relationships often express feelings in unique ways—they give flowers, take moonlit walks, write lengthy letters, and have romantic dinners. According to psychologists, love has psychological, emotional, biochemical, and social factors.

Many classifications of love have been suggested, and all have some overlapping components. One influential view is that of Sternberg (1986b), which sees love as having three components: intimacy, commitment, and passion. *Intimacy* is a sense of emotional closeness. *Commitment* is the extent to which a relationship is permanent and long-lasting. *Passion* is arousal, partly sexual, partly intellectual, and partly inspirational. When all three components are present, the highest type of love—*consummate love*—results. Another view of love (Hendrick & Hendrick, 1986) identifies six distinct varieties: passionate, game-playing, friendship, logical, possessive, and selfless. Table 11.3 shows a series of statements that are used on a test to measure the way people relate in a love relationship.

Different as all of the classifications may be, researchers have nonetheless identified some common elements in love relationships. Love usually involves the idealization of another person; people see their loved ones in a positive light. It also involves caring for

Table 11.3 Six Varieties of Love

Variety of Love	Sample Items
Passionate love	My lover and I were attracted to each other immediately after we first met.
	My lover and I became emotionally involved rather quickly.
Game-playing love	I have sometimes had to keep two of my lovers from finding out about each other.
	I can get over love affairs pretty easily and quickly.
Friendship love	The best kind of love grows out of a long friendship.
	Love is really a deep friendship, not a mysterious, mystical emotion.
Logical love	It is best to love someone with a similar background.
	An important factor in choosing a partner is whether or not he (she) will be a good parent.
Possessive love	When my lover doesn't pay attention to me, I feel sick all over.
	I cannot relax if I suspect that my lover is with someone else.
Selfless love	I would rather suffer myself than let my lover suffer.
	Whatever I own is my lover's to use as he (she) chooses.

Source: From Hendrick and Hendrick (1986).

another person and being fascinated with that person. Love includes trust, respect, liking, honesty, companionship, and (sometimes) sexual attraction. A central element is commitment; however, researchers disagree as to whether love and commitment can be separated, because one usually follows from, or is part of, the other (Fehr & Russell, 1991).

For couples that stay together, love grows over time (Sprecher, 1999). But what happens when love disappears? People in a close emotional relationship, whether married or not, experience emotional distress when they break up. Sadness, anger, loss, and despair are among the emotions experienced by people at the end of a close relationship. However, research shows that the extent of those feelings is determined by an individual's level of security. If you lose a lover or spouse, your reaction will be determined not only by the loss of the relationship but also by your own basic feelings of security, attachment, and anxiety (Simpson, 1990).

Love is a state, but it is also a series of behaviors. Thus, although a person may be in love, most psychologists think of love in terms of the behaviors that demonstrate it, including remaining faithful sexually and showing caring (Buss, 1988). Yet researchers also wish to know whether love has a biological basis.

Love is expressed differently in every culture, and there are enormous variations in its expression even within a single culture. Cultural differences in love relationships arise in part because of the nature of marriage. In cultures where marriages are arranged by parents, love comes about slowly over time. In cultures where passionate love is equated with happiness, such as in the United States, love is often seen to wane over time; in cultures where romantic, passionate love is valued less, the depth of relationships and the waning of passion are viewed differently and have a different time course. Even within American culture, there are differences in decisions to marry among ethnic groups; for example, African American women are more likely than white women to insist on having economic supports, such as a steady job, in place before marriage (Bulcroft & Bulcroft, 1993). Psychologists know far too little about love relationships in various cultures; yet love is a basic human emotion that is nurtured from birth to death and is seen in every culture. As psychologists discern the key elements of friendship, they will be better prepared to tackle the even more complicated subject of love. (I)

Think Critically

- Provide a psychological explanation of why you probably will like someone whose attitudes you perceive as similar to your own. Why might that person be able to influence you to do things that you might otherwise not do?
- Psychologists know that people like those who are like themselves. What psychological principles could you call on to increase the likelihood that you will get a job or be promoted in the job you are in?

www.abacon.com/leftononline

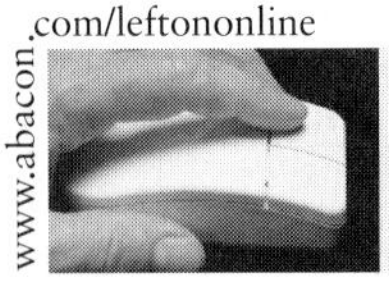

Your password-protected Website allows you access to the most comprehensive set of materials in The Psychology Place.

(I) Summary and Review

What is social psychology?

KEY TERM
social psychology, p. 308

Attitudes: Deeply Held Feelings and Beliefs

What is the relationship between attitudes and behavior?

What are the key components of attitude change?

KEY TERMS
attitudes, p. 308; elaboration likelihood model, p. 311; cognitive dissonance, p. 313; self-perception theory, p. 314; reactance, p. 314

Social Cognition: The Impact of Thought

What is social cognition?

What are nonverbal communication and attribution theory?

Describe the most common attribution errors.

Define prejudice and identify the theories that explain it.

KEY TERMS
social cognition, p. 314; impression formation, p. 314; nonverbal communication, p. 315; body language, p. 315; attribution, p. 316; fundamental attribution error, p. 317; actor–observer effect, p. 317; self-serving bias, p. 317;

prejudice, p. 318; stereotypes, p. 318; discrimination, p. 318; social categorization, p. 321

Social Interactions: The Power of People and Situations

Explain social influence and conformity.

What is obedience, and what did Milgram's studies of obedience demonstrate?

What are social facilitation and social loafing?

Identify three processes that may occur in group decision making and may or may not be helpful.

Describe aggression, prosocial behavior, and bystander apathy.

Define interpersonal attraction.

Define friendship and love and distinguish between them.

KEY TERMS

social influence, p. 322; conformity, p. 322; obedience, p. 323; debriefing, p. 324; group, p. 325; social facilitation, p. 325; social loafing, p. 325; group polarization, p. 326; groupthink, p. 326; deindividuation, p. 327; aggression, p. 327; prosocial behavior, p. 331; altruism, p. 331; sociobiology, p. 331; bystander apathy, p. 332; interpersonal attraction, p. 333; equity theory, p. 334; intimacy, p. 334

Self-Test

1. A person who is most likely to be susceptible to attitude change is:
   A. older
   B. younger
   C. highly educated
   D. high in self-esteem
2. A person has a strong liking for country music and refuses to listen to rock and roll. Which dimension of an attitude does this illustrate?
   A. cognitive
   B. emotional
   C. physical
   D. theoretical
3. Which attitude-changing technique starts with asking for a small favor and then goes on to ask for a larger favor?
   A. door-in-the-face technique
   B. lowballing technique
   C. foot-in-the-door technique
   D. incentives technique
4. Little Alex was given a toy that he was originally uninterested in. When his parents gave the unused toy to Alex's brother, Alex decided that the toy was now his favorite toy. Which of the following theories can explain his attitude change?
   A. cognitive dissonance
   B. self-perception theory
   C. reactance theory
   D. elaboration likelihood model
5. When a person believes that everyone feels the same way that he or she does about an issue, what type of mental shortcut is he or she using?
   A. representativeness
   B. availability
   C. framing
   D. false consensus effect
6. Last night John was asking his father for permission to go to the beach for the weekend with some school friends. His father did not respond or make eye contact. John's father was saying no to the request by using a form of communication known as:
   A. facial expressions
   B. body language
   C. cognitive dissonance
   D. attribution
7. A woman backs out of her parking space and almost runs into your car. You will attribute her action to the situation rather than to her poor driving skills if you believe that:
   A. few other people would act this way in the same situation
   B. this person drives like this all the time
   C. this person acts carelessly all the time
   D. others would be distracted in this situation as well
8. When Liza does something well, she attributes her success to her own skill. However, when she does something poorly, she attributes her failure

to the situation. This phenomenon can be described as:

A. self-serving bias
B. fundamental attribution error
C. actor–observer effect
D. disidentification

9. When ______________ is(are) translated into behavior, the behavior is called ______________.
   A. stereotypes; prejudice
   B. discrimination; hate
   C. prejudice; hate
   D. prejudice; discrimination

10. Which situation will decrease the likelihood that an individual will conform to the behavior of a group?
    A. ambiguous situation
    B. large group size
    C. a public response
    D. the presence of a dissenter

11. People in groups may be willing to adopt behaviors slightly more extreme than their usual behavioral tendencies. This result can be described as:
    A. social facilitation
    B. social loafing
    C. group polarization
    D. groupthink

12. You are late for a meeting and someone has just taken the last spot in the company parking lot. Although you don't normally get angry, you honk and yell at the other driver. Which explanation of your behavior fits best?
    A. frustration–aggression hypothesis
    B. nativist hypothesis
    C. situation–aggression hypothesis
    D. social–aggression hypothesis

13. Every member of Chuck's company was asked to contribute to the local charity for the homeless. The number of contributions was extremely low. When Chuck was asked why he did not participate, he responded, "No one else gave, so why should I?" This type of behavior is an example of:
    A. social loafing
    B. social facilitation
    C. conformity
    D. obedience

14. The CEO of Internet World (an AHR corporation) decided to donate a substantial percentage of his revenues anonymously to charity. He could be said to be:
    A. altruistic
    B. insane
    C. apathetic
    D. socially responsible

15. According to Sternberg, love has three components. These are:
    A. permanency, devotion, and attraction
    B. friendship, selflessness, and intimacy
    C. passion, intimacy, and commitment
    D. devotion, passion, and selflessness

Chapter 12

It's InterActive!

Stress and Health Psychology

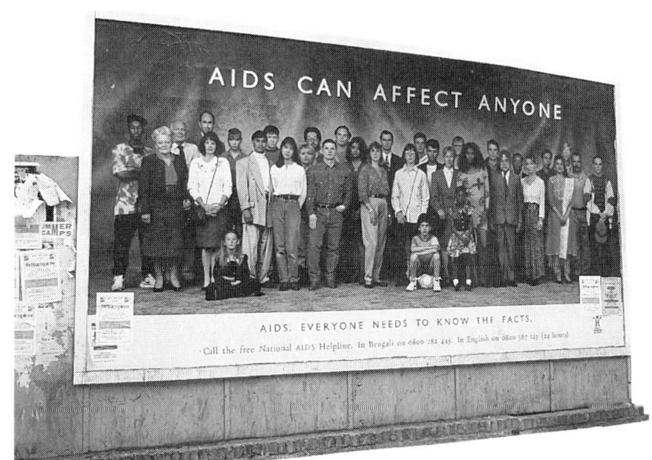
AIDS CAN AFFECT ANYONE
AIDS. EVERYONE NEEDS TO KNOW THE FACTS.

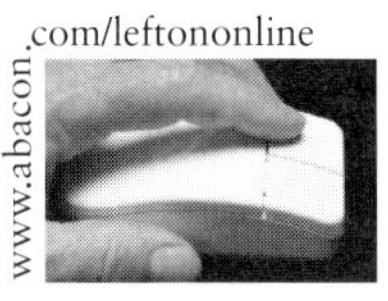
www.abacon.com/leftononline

Go to your password-protected Website for full-color art, Weblinks, and more!

Going out for a drive on Sunday afternoon is part of American popular culture—dad and mom ensconced in the front seat, son and daughter squabbling in the back. Although some people still find it relaxing to take a leisurely ride on a country road, the reality on most U.S. highways is traffic tie-ups and frustration. There are too many cars and trucks, and not enough time to get wherever we want to go.

For most commuters—and even for people on Sunday outings—traveling by car means tailgating, congestion, fumes, and occasionally an out-of-control driver. "Road rage" has become the popular term for this well-known phenomenon—people losing control of their emotions and responding violently to others on the highway. In reaction to traffic situations, some people have slammed into other cars, run over bicyclists, or drawn guns and shot drivers who were in their way. Cars have become weapons for letting out frustration, anger, and stress.

Experts say that aggressive driving behaviors are triggered by a variety of stimuli. Some are provoked by the actions of another driver; others are set off by roadway congestion. But most are caused by the drivers' own moods and reactions when they get behind the wheel. Drivers of all ages and ethnic groups, any socioeconomic status, and both genders display aggressive behaviors. Even usually mild-mannered people may blow their tops behind the wheel, exclaiming that the slow driver in front of them is an idiot or that the speedster who shoots past them and cuts them off is a moron. Individuals who are characteristically cynical, rude, angry, or aggressive are prone to get angry more often. These people "rage" at home, at work, *and* on the road. Testimony given before the U.S. House of Representatives (1997) revealed that aggressive driving—tailgating, speeding, running red lights, giving other drivers dirty looks or obscene gestures—had increased 51% over the preceding 5 years. Between 1990 and 1996, there were at least 10,037 incidents of road rage that resulted in 218 deaths and 12,000 injuries. And the problem shows no signs of lessening. ■

Of course, everybody experiences bad moods, anger, and stress from time to time. As a student, you face a variety of stressors: studying for multiple exams in the same week, juggling studies and a part-time job, getting along with a difficult roommate in cramped quarters. Stressors, from the hassles of filing tax returns to the traumas of war, are a reality for everyone. Some people suffer from stress-related health problems, such as high blood pressure and insomnia. Others try to escape stress by turning to alcohol or other drugs. People can deal with stressors in either positive or negative ways; unfortunately, many don't cope effectively, and some take their frustrations out on others.

In this chapter, we examine the nature of stress, discuss how to cope with it, and look at the interrelationship of health and stress. We also look into how learned skills and personality work together to influence the ability to cope with stress in day-to-day life. (I)

(I) Stress

Focus on issues and ideas

- What constitutes a stressful event
- Recognizing the sources of stress in your environment
- The intensity of some stress responses and the body's physiological reaction to stressors
- The health consequences of stress

Popping antacid tablets like candy, launching into tirades at coworkers or friends, pounding their fists on a table, and downing cocktails each night are a way of life for many people who succumb to stress caused by their jobs, families, or financial burdens. One person may have a high-pressure job that affects her social life and causes regular migraines. A coworker may manage the same amount of stress in more positive ways, without suffering negative health consequences. Such examples illustrate an important point: Different people evaluate and handle stress in different ways.

What Is Stress?

A **stressor** is an environmental stimulus that affects an organism in physically or psychologically injurious ways, usually producing anxiety, tension, and physiological arousal. **Anxiety** is a generalized feeling of fear and apprehension that may be related to a particular event or object and is often accompanied by increased physiological arousal. Physiological arousal, often the first change that appears when a person responds to a stressor, is indicated by changes in the autonomic nervous system, including increased heart rate, faster breathing, higher blood pressure, sweating palms, and dilation of the pupils.

Whenever something affects someone negatively, whether physically or psychologically, the person may experience the effect as stress. **Stress** is a nonspecific response to real or imagined challenges or threats; it is a result of a cognitive appraisal. The key is that not all people view a situation in the same way; *a person must appraise a situation as stressful for it to be stress-*

ful. This broad definition recognizes that everyone experiences stress at times, but also that stress is an interpreted state; it is a response by an individual. Richard Lazarus (1993), a leader in the study of emotion and stress, asserts that people *actively negotiate* between the demands of the environment (stressors) and personal beliefs and behaviors. Cognitive researchers refer to this active negotiation as *cognitive appraisal.* Sometimes the arousal that stressors bring about initiates positive actions; sometimes its effects are detrimental. Thinking "I can't possibly handle this!" is likely to lead to a less positive response than is thinking "This is my chance to really show my stuff!" (Lyubomirsky & Tucker, 1998).

Not all people view a situation in the same way; a person must appraise a situation as stressful for it to be stressful.

What, in addition to an individual's cognitive appraisal, determines whether a particular event will be stressful? The answer lies in the extent to which the person is familiar with the event, how much she or he has anticipated the event, and how much control she or he has over the event and the response to it. For example, the first day of a new course brings excitement and some apprehension about the instructor's expectations and whether the time commitments for the course will be burdensome; the second or third time the class meets is usually much less worrisome. When people can predict events and are familiar with them, they feel more in control, more confident that they can have some impact on the future.

It is important to recognize that stress is both a psychological and a physiological response. Thus, we can think of it as a complex *psychobiological process.* Some researchers have focused on studying the stimuli that bring about stress, others have investigated the psychological processes involved in establishing and maintaining stress responses, and still others have explored the physiological processes. Let's explore the sources of stress in our lives: frustration, conflict, and pressure.

Sources of Stress

Frustration. When people are hindered from reaching their goals, they often feel frustrated. **Frustration** is the emotional state or condition that results when a goal—work, family, or personal—is thwarted or blocked or when a situation is perceived to be beyond one's control. When you are unable to obtain a summer job because of a lack of experience, you may experience feelings of frustration. When a grandparent becomes ill, you may feel helpless; this can cause frustration. When there is an environmental threat over which people have no control, frustration is often the result (Hallman & Wandersman, 1992).

Some frustration people experience has discernible causes; examples are your lack of experience for a specific job or your grandparent's illness. Specific people can also cause frustration: Your boss may be unfair in his appraisal of you, or your roommate may disturb you by watching television too late at night. You can sometimes alleviate the frustration of dealing with other people by taking some action; deciding on an appropriate action, however, may place you in conflict—another type of stress.

Conflict. When people must make difficult decisions, they may experience a state of conflict. **Conflict** is the emotional state or condition that arises when a person must make a difficult decision about two or more competing motives, behaviors, or impulses. Consider the difficult decision facing American draftees who did not want to fight in the Vietnam War but also did not want to flee to Canada or go to prison. Another example of a situation resulting in conflict is when a student must choose between two equally desirable academic courses, both of which will advance the student's career plans but which meet at the same time.

One of the first psychologists to describe and quantify such conflict situations was Neal Miller (1944, 1959). Miller developed hypotheses about how animals and human beings behave in situations that have both positive and negative aspects. In general, he described three types of conflicts that result when situations involve competing goals or demands: approach–approach conflict, avoidance–avoidance conflict, and approach–avoidance conflict.

Stressor: An environmental stimulus that affects an organism in physically or psychologically injurious ways, usually producing anxiety, tension, and physiological arousal.

Anxiety: Generalized feeling of fear and apprehension that may be related to a particular event or object and is often accompanied by increased physiological arousal.

Stress: A nonspecific emotional response to real or imagined challenges or threats; it is a result of a cognitive appraisal by the individual.

Frustration: The emotional state or condition that results when a goal—work, family, or personal—is thwarted or blocked or when a situation is perceived to be beyond one's control.

Conflict: The emotional state or condition that arises when a person must make a difficult decision about two or more competing motives, behaviors, or impulses.

Approach–approach conflict is conflict that results when a person must choose between two equally attractive alternatives (for example, two wonderful jobs). Approach–approach conflict generates discomfort and a stress response; however, people can usually tolerate it because either alternative is pleasant. **Avoidance–avoidance conflict** is conflict that results from having to choose between two equally distasteful alternatives (for example, mowing the lawn or cleaning the garage). **Approach–avoidance conflict** is conflict that results from having to choose an alternative that has both attractive and repellent aspects. Whether to study for an exam, which can lead to good grades but is difficult and time-consuming, is an approach–avoidance conflict. The three types of conflict situations lead to different degrees of stress. Miller developed principles to predict behavior in conflict situations, particularly in approach–avoidance conflicts: (1) The closer a person is to achieving a goal, the stronger the tendency is to approach the goal. (2) When two incompatible responses are available, the stronger one will be expressed. (3) The strength of the tendency to approach or avoid is correlated with the strength of the motivating drive. (Thus, someone on a diet who is considering ordering a hot fudge sundae may yield to temptation if the desire for the sundae is stronger than the desire to lose weight.) People regularly face conflict situations that may cause them to become anxious. Moreover, if conflicts affect day-to-day behavior, people may exhibit symptoms of maladjustment.

Those with few social ties and lack of social support are more likely to be stressed, depressed, and physically ill.

Pressure from Work, Insufficient Time, and Life Events. Arousal and stress may occur when people feel **pressure**—the emotional state or condition created by the real or imagined expectations of other people concerning certain behaviors or results. Although individual situations differ, almost everyone feels pressure. Much of it is due to work, a lack of time, or life events.

Approach–approach conflict: Conflict that results from having to choose between two equally attractive alternatives.

Avoidance–avoidance conflict: Conflict that results from having to choose between two equally distasteful alternatives.

Approach–avoidance conflict: Conflict that results from having to choose an alternative that has both attractive and repellent aspects.

Pressure: Emotional state or condition created by others' expectations concerning specific behaviors or results.

Work that is either overstimulating or understimulating can cause stress. Work-related stress also can come from fear of retirement, of being passed over for promotion, or of organizational changes. In addition, the physical work setting may be too noisy or crowded or isolated. Work-related pressure from deadlines, competition, or on-the-job relationships (to name just a few possibilities) can cause a variety of physical problems. People suffering from work stress may experience migraines, sleeplessness, a desire for sweets, overeating, and/or intestinal distress. Stress at work often impairs the functioning of the immune system, which in turn leads to illness, resulting in lost efficiency and absenteeism (Levi, 1990). Stress at work can also spill over to the nonwork hours and lead to other problems, such as alcoholism (Grunberg, Moore, & Greenberg, 1998).

Individuals with high-stress jobs, particularly those in which the stress is constant and the stressors are beyond the individual's control, show the effects most dramatically. Surgeons, for example, are responsible for the lives of other people every day and must be alert and efficient at all times. If they work too many hours without relief, they may even make a fatal mistake. Others with high-stress jobs include inner-city high school teachers, customer service agents, waiters and waitresses, and emergency workers.

Lack of time is another common source of stress. Everyone faces deadlines: Students must complete tests before class ends, auto workers must keep pace with the assembly line, and taxpayers must file their returns by April 15. People have only a limited number of hours each day in which to accomplish tasks; therefore, many people carefully allocate their time. They may establish routines, make lists, set schedules, leave optional meetings early, and set aside leisure time in which to rid themselves of stressful feelings. If people do not handle time pressure successfully, they may begin to feel overloaded and stressed.

A third common source of stress is life events, which don't have to be negative to be stressful. Consider marriage. Marriage is celebrated as a positive event in Western culture. Nonetheless, adjusting to married life means becoming familiar with new experiences, responding in new ways, and having less control over many aspects of day-to-day life—all of which can be stressful. Also, at times, marriage involves interpersonal conflict. One partner may not be fulfilling obligations or may be preoccupied in some way, causing the spouse to feel left out; both possibilities may bring about stress and even health problems (Tesser & Beach, 1998).

Stress affects children as well as adults. Children are much less able to change or control the circumstances in which they find themselves. They often experience stress in school; Japanese students, for example, are under considerable pressure to perform academically, and test time is considered especially stressful. A child's stress can also be caused by an abusive parent, by parents' divorce, or by peer pressure. Like adults, children often show their stress response in physical symptoms. In fact, physical symptoms are the most common evidence of stress in children. Also, like adults, children's appraisal of a situation is what determines whether it is stressful, and some children are more vulnerable than others.

We will examine stressful life events in more detail later in this chapter. Even routine life events can cause stress. Table 12.1 presents the 10 daily hassles most frequently cited as sources of stress. These daily hassles are correlated with symptoms such as headaches.

Table 12.1 Life's Little Hassles—The Top Ten

1. Concerns about weight
2. Health of a family member
3. Rising prices of common goods
4. Home maintenance
5. Too many things to do
6. Misplacing or losing things
7. Yard work or outside home maintenance
8. Property, investments, or taxes
9. Crime
10. Physical appearance

Source: Kanner et al., 1981.

Unhealthy Environments and Stress

Some environments may be hazardous to people's health. A neighborhood or work environment may contain toxins that cause health risks (Taylor, Repetti, & Seeman, 1997). A stressful neighborhood or work environment may also cause mental distress, depression, anxiety, or hostility—and these are related to heart attacks and other health problems (Frasure-Smith et al., 1995). Of course, some environments are better than others in allowing people to cope with stressors—either by better managing the stress and conflict or by developing social support and relationships. And not all individuals in the same environment will be affected in the same way; among individuals in the same high-risk environment, some will suffer the ill effects more than others.

What are some of the key variables determining environmental stressfulness? People who live in impoverished homes, have low education levels and menial occupations—those in *low socioeconomic groups*—are at higher risk for stress, anxiety, and associated health consequences. Some *communities* have especially high levels of stress—poor, overcrowded neighborhoods and areas with high levels of noise, crime, and violence put people at higher risk. The *family environment* is key. A family in which children experience sexual or physical abuse, parental alcoholism, or few opportunities for warmth and affection puts them at risk for stress and health consequences. The *peer environment* can place children at increased risk—schools may be ill-equipped to deal with problem children, whose behavior may therefore have adverse effects on the academic and social habits of their classmates. The *social environment* is also important; research shows that those with few social ties and lack of social support are more likely to be stressed, depressed, and physically ill. Finally, the *work environment* is crucial—people who have meaningful employment report a higher quality of life than people who don't work. But, if the work environment is stressful and lacks incentives, if people think their contributions are unimportant and the effort required of them is excessive, they are more likely to be unhappy and to develop health problems.

As Taylor, Repetti, and Seeman (1997) argue, any of these environments can have detrimental effects when safety is threatened, when social ties are few, and when conflict abounds. Any or all of them can affect physiology and health—either positively or negatively—across the entire lifespan.

Catastrophes and Stress

Throughout history, there have been many *catastrophes*—stressors of massive proportion like earthquakes and floods—that have affected people and communities profoundly. How do people respond to catastrophes? How do they cope? It turns out that people are amazingly resilient (a topic we'll consider later), but the impact of a catastrophe—of a natural disaster, war, or traumatic event—can be long-lasting. Mental health practitioners see many clients who continue to suffer long after an event that has changed their lives. Many report being haunted for years by nightmares. A severe stress-related disorder is termed a **posttraumatic stress disorder (PTSD)**—a psychological disorder that may become evident after a person has undergone severe stress caused by some type of disaster.

Origins and Symptoms. Victims of rape, natural disasters (tornadoes, earthquakes, hurricanes, floods), or disasters caused by human beings (wars, train wrecks, toxic chemical spills) often suffer from PTSD. Many survivors of the 1989 San Francisco earthquake still fear the double-decker freeways, whose collapse during the quake took several lives. PTSD is also still evident in those who lived through the 1980 volcanic eruption of Mt. St. Helens (Shore, Vollmer, & Tatum, 1989). The terrorist bombing at New York City's World Trade Center in 1993 affected hundreds of people who were trapped and many others who witnessed the event. The 1993 floods along the Missouri and Mississippi rivers left in their wake many people suffering from PTSD. And divers trying to recover the wreckage and victims of TWA flight 800 in 1997 suffered PTSD (Leffler & Dembert, 1998). The likelihood that a person will experience PTSD at some time during his or her life is about 8% (Kessler et al., 1995).

Common symptoms of PTSD are vivid, intrusive recollections or reexperiences of the traumatic event and occasional lapses of normal consciousness (Morgan et al., 1998; Wood et al., 1992). People may develop anxiety, depression, or exceptionally aggressive behavior; they may avoid situations that resemble the traumatizing events. Such behaviors may eventually interfere with daily functioning, family interactions, and health. Research on PTSD is attempting to identify a possible genetic predisposition (True et al., 1993), a physiological explanation (Tryon, 1998), and psychological causes such as motivated forgetting of difficult circumstances (Karon & Widener, 1998). An increasing number of studies are focusing on the psychological aftermath of natural disasters such as earthquakes, tornadoes, and floods, as well as the impact on survivors of traumatic events such as the Holocaust of World War II (Yehuda et al., 1998) and the displacement of refugee children (Ajdukovic & Ajdukovic, 1998). Many more studies have focused on military personnel, especially Vietnam veterans and those exposed to sudden death (Keane, 1998; Rosebush, 1998).

Posttraumatic stress disorder (PTSD): Psychological disorder that may become evident after a person has undergone extreme stress caused by some type of disaster; common symptoms include vivid, intrusive recollections or reexperiences of the traumatic event and occasional lapses of normal consciousness.

Burnout: State of emotional and physical exhaustion, lowered productivity, and feelings of isolation, often caused by work-related pressures.

Responses to Stress

People respond to stress in a wide variety of ways. Some individuals show modest increases in physiological arousal; others exhibit significant physical symptoms. In extreme cases, people become so aroused, anxious, and disorganized that their behavior becomes maladaptive or maladjusted. The basic idea underlying the work of many researchers is that stress activates a biological predisposition toward maladjustment.

Emotion, Physiology, and Behavior. Psychologists who study stress typically divide the stress reaction into emotional, physiological, and behavioral components. *Emotionally,* people's reactions often depend on their level of frustration, the pressures they perceive themselves facing, and the conflicts they must resolve. When frustrated, people become angry or annoyed; when pressured, they become aroused and anxious; when placed in situations of conflict, they may vacillate or become irritable and hostile. *Physiologically,* the stress response is characterized by arousal. As mentioned before, when psychologists refer to arousal, they usually mean changes in the autonomic nervous system, including increased heart rate, faster breathing, higher blood pressure, sweating palms, and dilation of the pupils. Arousal is often the first change that occurs when a person feels stressed. *Behaviorally,* stress and arousal are related. Psychologist Donald Hebb (1972) has argued that effective behavior depends on a person's state of arousal. When people are moderately aroused, they behave with optimal effectiveness. When they are underaroused, they lack the stimulation to behave effectively. Overarousal tends to produce disorganized and ineffective behavior, particularly if the tasks people undertake are complex.

A moderate level of stress and the arousal that accompanies it may be unavoidable. Arousal keeps people active and involved. It impels students to study, athletes to excel during competition, and workers to perform better on the job. In short, stress and arousal can help people achieve their potential.

Stress affects the immune system, making people more vulnerable to disease.

Burnout. A reaction to stress that is especially common in people with high standards is burnout. **Burnout** is a state of emotional and physical exhaustion, lowered productivity, and feelings of isolation, often caused by work-related pressures (Kalimo & Mejman, 1987). People who face high-pressure situations daily often feel debilitated, hopeless, and emotionally drained and may eventually stop trying to cope. Although burnout is most often work-related, pressures caused by family, financial, or social situations can create the same feelings. Burnout victims develop negative self-concepts because they are unable to maintain the high standards they have set for themselves. They often cease to be concerned about others, and they may experience physical as well as social problems.

Health Consequences of Stress. A research study found that stress contributes to susceptibility to the common cold (Cohen, Tyrrell, & Smith, 1993). Mothers and self-help books have long advised people to reduce their levels of stress to keep from getting sick, and research now supports their advice. Stress does not cause disease directly. However, it contributes to many diseases, including the five major causes of death in the United States: heart disease, cancer, stroke, lung ailments, and accidental injuries. In general, stress affects the immune system, making people more vulnerable to disease (Cohen, Tyrrell, & Smith, 1991; Sher, 1998). More specifically, when stress responses are unexpressed, people show increased levels of autonomic nervous system activity (Hughes, Uhlmann, & Pennebaker, 1994). This, in turn, can lead to higher blood pressure, which has been linked to heart disease and other problems. Stress may also lead to headaches, backaches, decreased productivity, and family health problems. Stress is often correlated with flareups of peptic ulcers (Levenstein et al., 1996). Extreme stress has been implicated in sudden heart attacks (Bosma et al., 1998). At a minimum, stress-related illnesses cause an increase in medical costs for both individuals and employers.

Studying Stress: A Focus on Physiology

Although stress was recognized as a medical issue in ancient Greece, the modern study of stress responses did not begin in earnest until the 1920s. Researchers such as James, Lange, Cannon, and Bard (whom we discussed in Chapter 8) studied emotions, focusing on when an emotion was felt in response to a stressful incident—during or after the actual event. Psychologists have also asked how lifestyles and life events affect people's physical and psychological well-being. For example, does intense competition make business-people more susceptible to heart attacks? How can psychologists help people cope with life stressors, such as having a baby? How can therapists help veterans who are traumatized by war? Such questions have helped researchers develop theories of stressors. One of the best-known and most influential of these theories is Hans Selye's general adaptation syndrome.

Selye's General Adaptation Syndrome. In the 1930s, Canadian Hans Selye (1907–1982) began a systematic study of stressors and stress. He investigated the physiological changes in people who were experiencing various amounts of stress. Selye conceptualized people's responses to stress in terms of a *general adaptation syndrome* (1956, 1976). (A *syndrome* is a set of responses; in the case of stress, it is a set of behaviors and physical symptoms.) Selye's work initiated thousands of studies on stress and stress reactions, and Selye himself published more than 1,600 articles on the topic.

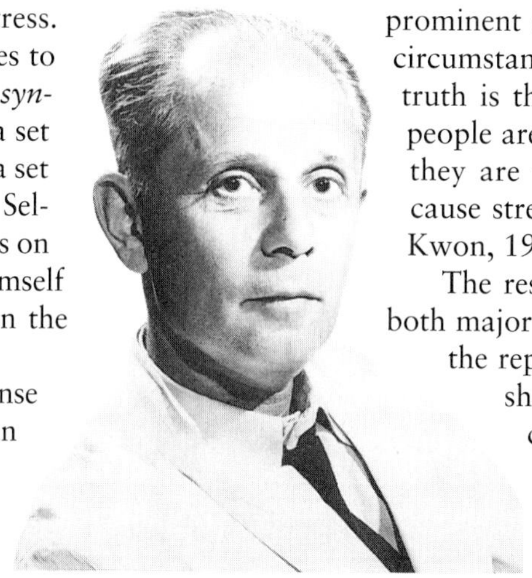

According to Selye, people's response to a stressor occurs in three stages: (1) an initial short-term stage of alarm, (2) a longer period of resistance, and (3) a final stage of exhaustion. During the *alarm stage,* people experience increased physiological arousal. They become excited, anxious, or frightened. Bodily resources are mobilized. Metabolism speeds up dramatically, and blood is diverted from the skin to the brain, resulting in a pale appearance. (The response is much like the fight-or-flight syndrome, in which the sympathetic nervous system is activated; see Chapter 2.) Later on in the stress response, people may also experience loss of appetite, sleeplessness, headaches, ulcers, or hormone imbalances.

Because people cannot remain highly aroused for very long, the initial alarm response usually leads to *resistance.* During this stage, physiological and behavioral responses become more moderate and sustained. People in the resistance stage are often irritable, impatient, and angry; they may be constantly tired. This stage can persist for a few hours, several days, or even years, although eventually resistance begins to decline. Couples who suffer traumatic divorces sometimes exhibit anger and emotional fatigue years after the conflict has been resolved in court.

The final stage is *exhaustion.* Stress saps psychological and physical energy; adaptability is depleted. If people don't reduce their level of stress, they can become so exhausted physically, mentally, and emotionally that they can't adapt. At that point, they again become extremely alarmed; they finally give up. The air traffic controller or surgeon who takes no vacations, works long shifts, and is expected to do more with less help may show the symptoms of maladjustment or withdrawal. In extreme cases of constant stress, as in war, serious illness and death may occur. Of course, not everyone shows the same behaviors in each stage.

Holmes–Rahe. Among the many researchers inspired by Selye to study stressors and refine the theory are Thomas Holmes and Richard Rahe. Their basic assumption is that stressful life events, especially occurring in combination, will damage health (Holmes & Rahe, 1967; Rahe, 1989). *Stressful life events* are prominent events in a person's day-to-day circumstances that necessitate change. The truth is that the stressors faced by most people are seldom major events or crises; they are the day-to-day irritations that cause stress over the years (Whisman & Kwon, 1993).

The results of a study of the effect of both major life events and daily hassles on the reported health of elderly subjects showed that hassles are more closely related to psychological and physical ill health than are major life events (Chamberlain & Zika, 1990). Other studies found that flu, headaches, sore throats, and backaches were correlated with daily hassles (DeLongis, Folkman, & Lazarus, 1988). Further, stressful life events affect the quality of intimate relationships (Tesser & Beach, 1998), and there may be a genetic predisposition to high levels of autonomic nervous system activity in response to stressful life events (Kendler, Neale, MacLean, et al., 1993). It is not surprising that people with an external locus of control (see Chapter 10, pp. 297–298), little social support (to be discussed in a later section), and high levels of stress see life as much more difficult than others do (Jorgensen & Johnson, 1990). *Diversity* examines the influence of culture on the ways people perceive and handle stressors.

Heart Disease and Stress

It wasn't long after researchers began to study stress reactions that they discovered a link—or at least a correlation—between stress and various illnesses, especially heart disease. Heart disease is the number one killer of both men and women in the United States. Each year, more than 500,000 Americans die of heart attacks, caused by coronary heart disease, whose major symptom is a thickening of the inside walls of the coronary arteries. Physicians and psychologists view coronary heart disease as a disorder of lifestyle. Three components of day-to-day life that are being studied in connection to this disease are work-site stress, Type A behavior, and physiological reactivity. Intense research on these biobehavioral factors has altered treatment for heart patients, because it is becoming clear that all three are related and interact in complex ways (Jorgensen et al., 1996).

Work-Site Stress. Work-site stress increases the prevalence of heart attacks (Levi, 1990). Researchers theorize that this may happen because physiological components of the stress response place extra burdens

DIVERSITY

Hispanic Americans' Stress

Research shows that Hispanic Americans are more likely to be depressed than people of similar age who are white, African American, or Asian American (Siegel et al., 1998). Furthermore, high-school-age students who are Mexican Americans or new Hispanic immigrants who are trying to fit in are at greater risk for depression and suicidal thoughts (Hovey, 1998; Sanchez & Fernandez, 1993). Stress seems to be a key factor—especially the stress of trying to adjust to American society.

If you're not like other people in your school, neighborhood, or community, the impact of acculturation—trying to adapt to and adopt the cultural traits of a society—can be profound, and usually stressful. Researchers have long known that stress depletes people's psychological resources. One aspect of stress that has remained relatively unexplored has been how different cultural groups in the U.S. population experience and cope with stressors, especially those due to acculturation. For example, are Hispanic Americans more vulnerable to stress than non-Hispanic whites? Three California researchers, Jacqueline Golding, Marilyn Potts, and Carol Aneshensel, investigated this question.

Question and Method. Golding, Potts, and Aneshensel (1991) questioned whether Hispanic Americans are more at risk for stress than non-Hispanic whites. They examined the data from a large epidemiological study by the National Institute of Mental Health, which estimated the prevalence of mental disorders in the general population. More than 2,300 individuals responded to a set of questions about psychiatric disorders, use of health services, and demographic characteristics. The study was conducted in Los Angeles County, California, and it included 1,244 respondents who were Hispanic (538 of whom were born in the United States and 706 of whom were born in Mexico and immigrated to the United States). In addition, there were 1,149 non-Hispanic white respondents.

Measures. Respondents indicated whether they had experienced stress from life events in the past 6 months—including family or relationship events (such as divorce), work- or money-related events (such as being fired or getting into financial trouble), legal events (such as being arrested), crime victimization (such as being burglarized), housing changes (moving), medical or psychological problems (a physical illness or drug problem), and death in the family. In addition to questions about psychological stress, the researchers investigated the level of economic strain among respondents, by asking about any difficulty affording clothes, food, or medical care or paying bills.

To make appropriate comparisons, the researchers had to ensure that they studied equivalent participants. They did not want to compare more wealthy Hispanic American participants with poor ones, for example; thus, they used a variety of statistical and sampling techniques to ensure comparable groups of participants.

Results. Golding, Potts, and Aneshensel (1991) found that rates of stressful life events were fairly similar among Hispanic and non-Hispanic white participants. Among both Hispanic Americans and non-Hispanic white Americans, the uneducated were more likely to be burglarized, to suffer from unemployment, and to have marital problems. The only important differences were related to economic strain. Hispanic participants, especially those who were immigrants, reported more economic strain than did whites. Being female and coming from a large household were also associated with greater economic strain.

Conclusions. There are few differences between Hispanic Americans and non-Hispanic white Americans in terms of stressful life events (Golding, Potts, and Aneshensel, 1991). The stressors of divorce, unemployment, moving, and acculturation were equally common in comparable groups. But economic strain and the day-to-day hassles of being economically disadvantaged and unable to afford life's necessities seemed to affect the Hispanic participants, especially the immigrants trying to fit in, more than the non-Hispanic whites (see also Knight et al., 1994). The researchers point out that stresses resulting from adverse life events and economic strain are difficult to separate because these stressors invariably occur together. Complicating the situation is alcoholism, which makes the stressors worse (Barrera, Li, & Chassin, 1993). Different patterns of stressors lead to different outcomes for both groups, but one thing is certain: Being an immigrant and trying to make a successful adjustment to life in the United States brings with it a significant number of stressors (Guarnaccia, 1997; Prelow & Guarnaccia, 1997). Everyone, regardless of ethnicity, is adversely affected by life's difficulties. ■

on the heart over many years. The likelihood of a heart attack increases significantly for surgeons, for example, because their job is fraught with potential stressors. Other jobs may cause stress by demanding too little or too much of a worker. Stress is also affected by a person's degree of *autonomy*—the extent to which the person controls the speed, flow, and level of work. A position with high demands and low control brings higher levels of stress. A factory worker, for example, usually has little control over the work and may therefore experience stress.

People who are extremely anxious, depressed, angry, and unhappy have a higher rate of heart disease than do normally adjusted people.

Men are more likely than women to develop heart disease related to work-site stress. However, in recent years, the work and home situations of men and women have become much more parallel. Men and women in similar situations seem to have similar rates of heart disease (Hamilton & Fagot, 1988).

Type A Behavior. In the late 1950s, physicians Meyer Friedman and Ray Rosenman identified a pattern of behavior that they believe contributes to heart disease; they called it Type A behavior (Friedman & Rosenman, 1974). **Type A behavior** is the behavior pattern of individuals who are competitive, impatient, hostile, and always striving to do more in less time. **Type B behavior** is the pattern exhibited by people who are calmer, more patient, and less hurried.

Early studies of Type A behavior showed a positive association with heart disease; that is, Type A individuals were more likely than Type B individuals to have heart attacks. More recent research, however, suggests that only some elements of Type A behavior are related to heart disease (Johnsen, Espnes, & Gillard, 1998; Lilla et al., 1998), but the overall Type A behavior pattern is not. For example, hostility and anger have been related to heart disease (Morren, 1998), as have suspiciousness and mistrust (Weidner et al., 1989). Culture plays a role: Some consider Type A behavior and its relationship to heart disease a Western phenomenon, mainly involving middle-aged, North American businessmen (Helman, 1992). One important research finding is that expressing the emotions associated with stress verbally or in writing decreases the risk of health problems (Berry & Pennebaker, 1993; Friedman, 1996). Another is that women experience distress more frequently than men do but are less likely to stay distressed (Almeida & Kessler, 1998). People who are extremely anxious, depressed, angry, and unhappy have a higher rate of heart disease than do normally adjusted people (Miller et al., 1991), although the physiological mechanism underlying this finding is unclear (Suls & Wan, 1993). In sum, the Type A behavior pattern exists; however, its relationship to heart disease, or other disorders for that matter, is indirect or nonexistent (Koehler, Kuhnt, & Richter, 1998; Matthews, 1988).

Type A behavior: Behavior pattern characterized by competitiveness, impatience, hostility, and constant efforts to do more in less time.

Type B behavior: Behavior pattern exhibited by people who are calmer, more patient, and less hurried than Type A individuals.

Physiological Reactivity. A third factor possibly relating stress to heart disease is how the body reacts to stressors—its *reactivity,* or *physiological reactivity.* A situation interpreted as stressful may cause physiological reactions, triggering bodily processes that lead to heart disease (Sher, 1998). Research shows that the Type A behavior pattern is associated with increased physiological reactivity (Contrada, 1989), long-lasting emotional distress (Suls & Wan, 1989a, 1989b), and feelings of anger and hostility (Suarez & Williams, 1989). But it is still not clear whether the reactivity predisposes people to high blood pressure and heart disease or whether those predisposed to such physical problems show increased reactivity. People who are physically fit react better physiologically to stressful situations than those who are not fit.

Thus, work-site stress, aspects of the Type A behavior pattern, and physiological reactivity may be individually linked to heart disease. But research suggests that these factors are interactive; that is, they affect one another (Krantz et al., 1988). More research is needed on how an individual's culture and worldview affect work-site stress, Type A behavior, and physiological reactivity. For example, some research shows that Japanese Americans with more traditional Japanese cultural views (collectivistic, for example) had a lower incidence of heart disease when compared with Japanese Americans with less traditional Japanese values (Matsumoto, 1996). Thus, culture does, in part, determine people's level of stress. Another factor affecting stress levels is one's approach to getting tasks done in a timely manner, as discussed next.

Procrastination and Stress

Why do now what you can put off until tomorrow? The answer is that if you habitually put things off, your work will suffer and so may your health.

Getting work done on time is considered proper, rational adult behavior, especially in Western culture. But an awful lot of us procrastinate occasionally, and some people put off, delay, and make excuses for lateness very often. Critics of procrastinators call them lazy or self-indulgent and argue that their work performance suffers from the high stress levels they experience. Defenders—and many procrastinators themselves—assert that work performance is the same, sometimes better, because of heightened pressure to get the job done. They'll argue, "I do my best work under pressure." But do they?

Diana Tice and Roy Baumeister (1997) investigated the effects of procrastination on performance, stress, and illness. Students were given an assignment with a deadline. Procrastinators were identified using a standard scale. The students' well-being was assessed with self-reports of stress and illness. Finally, task performance was checked by ascertaining whether students turned in assignments early, on time, or late.

The researchers hypothesized that procrastinators might show poorer performance and health and higher stress levels. Alternatively, they acknowledged that there might indeed be benefits from intense, last-minute efforts.

Participants and Method. The participants were volunteers from a class of students taking a health psychology course. They were assigned a term paper and were told that if they could not turn the paper in on the due date they would automatically be given an extension. Researchers recorded when students turned in their papers and then asked them to fill out questionnaires about health and stress. The instructor who graded the papers did not know who turned in which paper and when; the research design was thus blind.

Results. As expected, procrastinators (as identified at the beginning of the study) turned in their papers late; procrastinators also received lower grades than the nonprocrastinators. Interestingly, procrastinators' scores were negatively correlated with stress and reporting of symptoms—that is, the more of a procrastinator a student was, the fewer stress and wellness problems he or she reported. The procrastinators thus reported feeling better but had poorer grades.

Discussion. It appears that procrastination brings short-term health benefits. Procrastinators benefit from the carefree, casual situation they create for themselves—stress is lowered and illness is reduced. But when Tice and Baumeister did another study to assess whether these effects were the same at all points in the semester, they found that the procrastinators experienced much more stress late in the semester than the nonprocrastinators did. In fact, when the impact of procrastination is considered relative to the time (early or late in the semester), the effects are negative—total stress and illness are higher for procrastinators. As the researchers put it, the early benefits of tardiness were outweighed by the later costs of stress and ill health. Especially important is the finding that procrastinators wound up with inferior work—postponing work seemed to lead to compromises and sacrifices in quality.

The researchers acknowledge that this study was not perfect. Participants were not randomly assigned. That stress, illness, and procrastination are related does not prove a causal effect. Further, some people wind up doing their work late for reasons other than procrastination, such as family emergencies. And, of course, university students are not representative of the general population.

Implications. The study suggests that procrastination should be considered a self-defeating behavior because it leads to stress, illness, and inferior performance. The tendency to prefer a short-term benefit *may* identify people who make other self-defeating mistakes such as abusing alcohol or drugs or committing other impulsive acts. Of course, some procrastinators mistakenly believe that they can improve performance by postponement, but the evidence to support this view is scant. In the end, procrastination is not adaptive—procrastinators end up suffering more and performing worse than other people. Procrastinators of the world, organize now! *I*

Think Critically

- What do you think defines a catastrophe?
- Do you see yourself as a Type A person or a Type B person? If you know any Type A people, does their health seem to be affected by their behavior?

I Coping

Focus on issues and ideas

- Developing appropriate coping skills
- Understanding that stress management—coping with stress—is becoming increasingly important in today's fast-paced society
- The impact of stress on the human immune system

Everyone needs a way to cope with anxiety and with the physical ailments produced by stress, but most people just muddle through any way they can—

venting their frustrations to sympathetic friends or family members or perhaps taking the occasional sick day. Some people go further and seek medical or psychological help; others turn to alcohol or other drugs. Obviously, coping strategies need to be tailored to the individual and the situation—and it's equally obvious that some strategies are better than others.

What Is Coping?

In general, *coping* means dealing with a situation. However, for a psychologist, **coping** is the process by which a person takes some action to manage, master, tolerate, or reduce environmental and internal demands that cause or might cause stress and that will tax the individual's inner resources. This definition of coping involves five important assumptions. First, coping is constantly changing and being evaluated and is therefore a process or a strategy. Second, coping involves managing situations, not necessarily bringing them under complete control. Third, coping is effortful; it does not happen automatically. Fourth, coping aims to manage cognitive as well as behavioral events. Finally, coping is learned.

There are many types of coping strategies; a person may use a few or many of them. Coping begins at the physiological level. People's bodies respond to stress with specific reactions, including changes in hormone levels, in autonomic nervous system activity, and in the levels of neurotransmitters in the brain. Effective coping strategies are developed when people learn new ways of dealing with their vulnerabilities.

Resilience, Coping Skills, and Social Support

Resilience is the extent to which people are flexible and respond adaptively to external or internal demands. A person who is resilient is said to be less vulnerable to stressors (Zuckerman, 1999). Resilience depends on **coping skills**—the techniques people use to deal with changing situations and stress. People who have effective coping skills are better prepared to deal with stress-related situations and are thus less vulnerable (Wiebe, 1991). People with poor or less well-developed coping skills may be extremely vulnerable and incapable of dealing with stress. Hilsman and Garber (1995) showed that this is especially true for children, who, because they are young, are less likely to have well-developed coping skills. In some cases, children may even develop a sense of learned helplessness; finding that rewards and punishments are not contingent on their behavior, they learn not to try to cope, thereby remaining helpless (Job & Barnes, 1995). Faced with poor coping skills and a loss of control, some adults, too, stop responding. (We examined learned helplessness in Chapter 5.)

The level of social support available to them affects people's resilience and vulnerability. **Social support** consists of the comfort, recognition, approval, and encouragement available from other people, including friends, family members, and coworkers. Even animals can provide social support (Siegel, 1990). When people feel supported by others' emotional concern and displays of caring, they can cope better with extraordinary pressure. The support is especially valuable when it is offered by someone who is important to the vulnerable person. In addition to (and sometimes in place of) friends and family, group therapy (to be examined in Chapter 14) can be especially effective in alleviating anxiety. In group therapy, other people who are in a similar situation can offer concern and emotional support.

In addition to being more resilient than others are, some people may also be hardier. Psychologists say that people are hardy, or exhibit *hardiness,* when they cope with disruptive changes and conflicts in effective ways. People who exhibit hardiness tend to appraise situations as less threatening than others do. In some ways, the characteristic of hardiness suggests an optimistic outlook. Hardy individuals expect positive outcomes and take actions to increase the likelihood that those outcomes will in fact occur. These actions, often referred to as *coping strategies,* are considered next.

Coping: Process by which a person takes some action to manage, master, tolerate, or reduce environmental or internal demands that cause or might cause stress and that tax the individual's inner resources.

Resilience: The extent to which people are flexible and respond adaptively to external or internal demands.

Coping skills: Techniques people use to deal with changing situations and stress.

Social support: The comfort, recognition, approval, and encouragement available from other people, including friends, family members, and coworkers.

Stress inoculation [in-OK-you-LAY-shun]: Procedure of giving people realistic warnings, recommendations, and reassurances to help them prepare for and cope with impending threats or losses.

Defense-Oriented and Task-Oriented Coping Strategies

Stress management—coping with stress—is becoming increasingly important to highly stressed individuals. Counselors commonly treat stress by first identifying the stressor and then helping the client untangle her or his feelings about the stressful situation and modify behavior to cope with it. Students about to enter college, for example, often show signs of stress. They're worried about academic pressures, social life, and overall adjustment. At some schools, incoming college students can receive counseling to learn how to deal with their stress. Similarly, stress management seminars, in which psychologists help business executives deal with stress in the corporate world, are becoming popular. The aim of both the counseling and the seminars is the same—to modify people's responses to stressors by replacing maladaptive responses with more useful ones.

According to psychologist Richard S. Lazarus (1982), people faced with constant stress use either defense- or task-oriented coping strategies. *Defense-oriented coping strategies* do not reduce stressors; however, they help people protect themselves from the effects of those stressors. These strategies ease stress, thereby enabling people to tolerate and deal with disturbances. As we saw in Chapter 10, people may use defense mechanisms to distort reality in order to defend themselves against life's difficulties. One such mechanism is *rationalization,* a reinterpretation of reality to make it more palatable. If your boyfriend or girlfriend dumps you, you may cope by telling your friends that you "never really liked him/her that much anyway." Similarly, a person who is turned down for a job may rationalize that he didn't want to work for that company after all. Another defense mechanism is *reaction formation.* A woman who dreads her tedious work but is especially cheerful at the office has developed a reaction formation—she is expressing a feeling that is the opposite of her true one.

Most psychologists, and especially behavioral psychologists, recommend *task-oriented coping strategies* for managing stress. The strategies usually involve several tasks, or steps. Essentially, these steps are (1) identifying the stressor, (2) choosing an appropriate course of action for stress reduction, (3) implementing the plan, and (4) evaluating its success. A person's biases, attitudes, value systems, and previous environmental stressors affect each of these steps (which are not always undertaken in this order).

Identifying the Stressor. Since many people are exposed to multiple stress-producing situations simultaneously, identifying the stressor is often difficult. A woman may be experiencing problems with her workload, her finances, her social life, and her roommate. She must decide what is causing her the most stress and whether her problems with her social life, for example, are in some way tied to her work situation. Older people seem to have as much difficulty as younger people in identifying and controlling the sources of stress (Lazarus & DeLongis, 1983).

Choosing the Action. Once the stressor is found, people need to choose among several coping strategies. For example, they can withdraw from a stress-inducing situation—by quitting work, leaving a spouse, or declaring bankruptcy. More often, they turn to other people or other methods of coping.

Because arousal and excitement usually accompany stress, people may cope by using *relaxation techniques.* These techniques include biofeedback, hypnosis, and meditation, all of which help people refocus their energies. Aerobic exercise is another effective way to relax, relieve stress, and improve one's mood (Aganoff & Boyle, 1994; Steptoe, Kimbell, & Basford, 1998).

Many people manage stress and anxiety with *cognitive coping strategies;* that is, they prepare themselves to handle pressure through gradual exposure to increasingly intense stressors (Janis, 1985). A major goal of current research on stress is helping people learn to react in constructive ways to early warning signs of stress. Research shows that people can help minimize stress by talking to themselves and using imagery (Ilacqua, 1994). The self-talk procedure, which is used widely, is effective in helping people confront stressors and cope with pain and the feeling of being overwhelmed (Turk, Meichenbaum, & Genest, 1983). By talking to themselves, people gain control over their emotions, state of arousal, and stress reactions; this technique is especially useful for people who must undergo unpleasant medical procedures such as chemotherapy (Ludwick-Rosenthal & Neufeld, 1988).

Implementing the Plan. Stress management counselors help people prepare for stressful situations by providing them with new ideas. **Stress inoculation** is the procedure of giving people realistic warnings, recommendations, and reassurances to help them prepare for and cope with impending threats or losses. Stress inoculation may involve a single technique, such as breathing deeply and regularly. Or it can be more elaborate, involving graded exposure to various levels of threats or detailed information about a forthcoming procedure (Janis, 1985). Janis likens stress inoculation to an antibiotic given to ward off disease. It helps people defend themselves and cope with stressors when they occur. Essentially, stress inoculation does the following:

- Increases the predictability of stressful events
- Fosters coping skills
- Generates self-talking
- Encourages confidence about successful outcomes

- Builds a commitment to personal action and responsibility for an adaptive course of action

Evaluating the Success of the Plan. A well-designed coping plan includes evaluation of the degree of success. Have the techniques been effective? Is there still more to do? Are new or further actions needed? All of these questions need to be answered as part of a task-oriented coping strategy.

To cope well both at home and at work, people should be task-oriented, self-monitoring, realistic, open to supportive relationships, and patient (Sarason & Sarason, 1987). They also need to eat sensibly, get enough sleep, stand up to the boss from time to time, find a hobby, and take refuge in family and friends. Most important, people have to believe in themselves and in their ability to cope well with stress (Bandura et al., 1988). It can sometimes be very helpful to anticipate events that may cause stress—that is, to engage in **proactive coping,** or taking action in advance of a potentially stressful situation to prevent it, modify it, or prepare for it before it occurs. Proactive coping precedes the stressful situation and requires different skills than does coping with an immediate stressor (Aspinwall and Taylor, 1997). *Experiencing Psychology* examines this strategy in more detail.

Taking a positive approach and believing in one's own abilities helps ward off stress.

Coping, Health, and a Positive Attitude

Physicians and psychologists know that some people have stress-related physical illnesses. Increase a person's stress level and he or she responds with headaches, for example. But such psychophysiological responses can be averted. Applied psychologists claim that simply maintaining a positive attitude can help a person cope with stress and can even reduce its physical symptoms. People who believe they have control over their lives, health, and well-being are more relaxed and happier than those who do not (Thompson et al., 1993). An upbeat mood, a positive sense of personal control, and even a self-serving bias can facilitate such worthwhile behaviors as helping others and evaluating people favorably (Diener et al., 1999). Applied psychologists suggest that people who have positive attitudes may even live longer.

Sometimes, reframing a situation helps make it easier to accept and thus less anxiety-provoking. One

EXPERIENCING PSYCHOLOGY

A Stitch in Time—Proactive Coping

If you know that you are going to have a challenging semester next fall, you might try to get a full-time job over the summer so that you'll only need to work part-time when school starts. By doing so (whether you think of it that way or not), you are already coping with your tough fall semester.

Psychologists have spent decades examining how people cope when stressors occur—how they marshal friends, social support, and emotional strength and take specific actions. But little research has been conducted on how people prepare in advance to face stress. Anticipating a lonely holiday season, a student in a foreign country, far from home, may plan a skiing expedition. Recognizing that job opportunities seem to be shrinking in her chosen profession, a person might choose to take courses to expand her qualifications.

Lisa Aspinwall and Shelley Taylor (1997) have asserted that proactive coping is really a five-stage process: First, we *accumulate resources,* mustering time, money, and social support and managing current situations. Next, we *recognize* that a stressful event is coming. Third, we *appraise* the event for its difficulty and its potential impact. Fourth, we *engage in preliminary coping,* to see what we can do now to prevent or minimize a threat. And last, we *elicit and use feedback* to assess whether or not we have averted a future stressor.

The truth is that many stressors in life can be avoided. If we understand what we can do, in advance, to avoid them, our lives will be better. This is proactive coping—an active process that requires people to be practical and take action, not simply seek emotional support after the fact. In the view of Aspinwall and Taylor, we can lead happier lives if we think ahead and act now. ■

study showed that people who engage in attempts to reframe events to make them less anxiety-provoking may be healthier than people who focus on their anxiety. In an unpublished study that ran from 1946 through 1988, Peterson, Seligman, and Vaillant (reported in DeAngelis, 1988) found that people who looked at the bright side of negative events in 1946 had better health in 1988. Such results indicate that people who emphasize the downside of life may develop learned helplessness. They may then choose inaction because they believe themselves to be powerless to control events. Taking a positive approach and believing in one's own abilities helps ward off stress and avoid the fear and arousal that come from feelings of despair and low self-esteem (Bandura et al., 1988). Seligman (1988) argues that optimism helps people achieve goals and cope more effectively; for example, optimistic salespeople substantially outsell their pessimistic colleagues. Maintaining an optimistic attitude is likely to help people engage in self-protective behaviors that will foster change for the better (Scheier & Carver, 1993).

Taking responsibility for preventive behaviors can be an important step toward better physical and mental health (Ewart, 1991). There are a number of steps you can take to cope, manage stress, and stay healthy:

- *Increase exercise.* People are able to cope better when they improve their physical fitness. In addition, increased exercise will lower blood pressure and reduce the risk of heart disease.
- *Eat well.* People feel better and cope better when they eat well and have a balanced diet. This also helps prevent being overweight.
- *Sleep well.* People react better to life when they have had a good night's sleep; being well-rested improves both reaction time and judgment.
- *Be flexible.* Life is unpredictable. Accept that fact, and day-to-day changes and surprises will be easier to handle.
- *Leave stress at school or the office.* Work-related stressors should be kept in the work environment. Bringing stressors home will only make stress worse. People are more likely to fall prey to substance abuse or domestic violence when they bring stressors home with them.
- *Communicate.* Share your ideas, feelings, and thoughts with the significant people in your life. This will decrease misunderstanding, mistrust, and stress.
- *Learn to relax.* In this fast-paced society, people seldom take the time to relax and get rid of uncomfortable ideas and feelings. Learn meditation, yoga, or deep breathing. Schedule some time each day for yourself.
- *Seek support.* Social support from family, friends, and self-help groups helps you appraise situations differently. Remember, you have to appraise a situation as stressful for it to be stressful. Social support helps you keep stressful situations in perspective.

The Immune Response and Stress

The *immune system* is a complex network of specialized cells and organs that has evolved to defend the body against attacks by "foreign invaders"—bacteria and viruses. Physicians have long known that people who contract certain diseases generally do not catch these illnesses again. The protection acquired by experiencing the infection once is specific for that infection—it is due to a specific acquired immunity. There are some infectious conditions such as the common cold, influenza, and pneumonia that can be experienced again and again. The reason why these illnesses can recur is that they are due to different infectious agents that produce similar symptoms. But why is it that some people who are exposed to a specific bacteria or virus get sick, and others don't? Is it possible that people who are under stress are more likely to become sick?

The human immune system displays several extraordinary characteristics: It can distinguish between "self" and "non-self." And it is able to "remember" previous experiences and react accordingly. For example, a child who has come down with measles becomes immune to the measles virus for life. If the person is exposed to this specific virus later in life, the immune system is able to recognize it and respond to prevent reinfection. The immune system has at its command an efficient and effective array of weapons. Its success in defending the body against infectious attacks relies on an incredibly complicated communication system that produces an immune response. But when people are stressed, the immune system responds less efficiently. Research shows that chronic stress impairs immune system functioning (Schedlowski et al., 1995). Patients under stress show more acute symptoms and more infections than those who are not under stress; in contrast, patients who are optimistic have a more effective immune system response (Leserman et al., 1997; Segerstrom et al., 1998).

Proactive coping: Taking action in advance of a potentially stressful situation to prevent it, modify it, or prepare for it before it occurs

Positive Attitudes and the Immune System

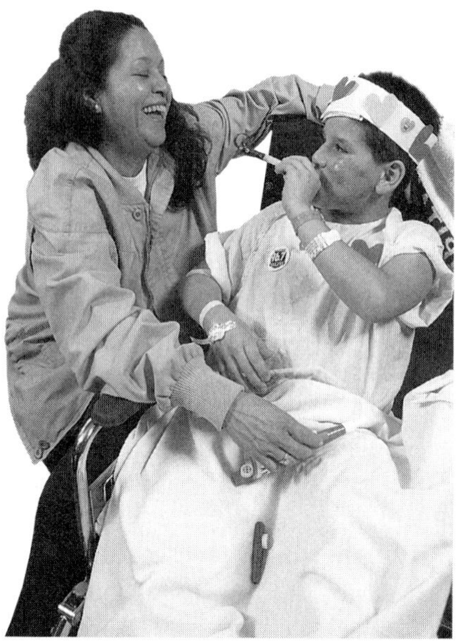

Can someone's thoughts affect his or her body's natural defense system? Today, some psychologists think they can, and the evidence is mounting. Research in psychoneuroimmunology (PNI) shows that the immune system (which fights disease) responds to a person's moods, stress level, and basic attitudes about life (Kiecolt-Glaser et al., 1998). **Psychoneuroimmunology (PNI)** is the study of how psychological processes and the nervous system affect and, in turn, are affected by the body's natural defense system—the immune system. According to PNI researchers, the brain provides information to the immune system about how and when to respond (Altman, 1998; Miller, 1998). The nervous and immune systems seem to be linked, each producing substances that alter the functions of the other (Maier & Watkins, 1998). The brain—especially after activation of the sympathetic nervous system—sends signals to the immune system that trigger its disease-fighting ability, including the production of white blood cells and other types of disease-fighting cells (Overmier & Gahtan, 1998). The immune system sends signals to the brain that alter its functioning (Maier, Watkins, & Fleshner, 1994). Research has shown that the immune system of a person with a positive, upbeat attitude responds better and faster than does that of a person who is depressed and lethargic (Segerstrom et al., 1998). Consider people whose loved ones have recently died; they consistently show higher rates of illness and depression (Schleifer, Keller, & Stein, 1987). Today, many AIDS patients are provided with counseling designed to bolster their immune systems by improving their attitudes; this may help them live longer.

Not all researchers agree about the role of positive thoughts, but most psychologists agree that thoughts and ideas play an important role both in preventing illness and in determining how people respond to becoming sick (Biondi & Zannino, 1997). Some psychologists still find it difficult to accept the idea that the immune system responds to mental attitudes. Researchers, however, are beginning to realize the power of positive thinking on certain bodily processes (Herbert & Cohen, 1993).

Of course, even though positive attitudes and thoughts can be beneficial, they can go only so far in helping to alleviate illness, and only with some people (Manuck et al., 1991). Sometimes having a positive attitude and practicing meditation, exercise, or other traditional coping techniques fail to reduce stress. This failure sometimes occurs because attempts have been half-hearted; at other times, the problem is a lack of expertise. More often, though, people just lack coping skills or even the knowledge that such skills exist. Wearing rose-colored glasses from time to time can be beneficial; however, continuous self-deception can lead to maladjustment, lies, and a badly distorted view of reality. (I)

Think Critically

- From your own experience, what coping techniques are more effective than others?
- Do you think that undergoing stress inoculation might allow people to build an immunity to stress?

(I) Health Psychology

Focus on issues and ideas

- The five variables health researchers have found to correlate strongly with health and illness: personality, cognitions, social environment, gender, and sociocultural variables
- How health psychology has developed as an action-oriented discipline
- The applications of health psychology in daily life

At least half of all the premature deaths in the United States are the result of unhealthy lifestyles. In the past, most people died from causes beyond their control—influenza, tuberculosis, and pneumonia, for example. Today, the leading causes of death in the United States—heart disease, cancer, stroke, and accidents—can be controlled to some extent by modifying environmental and behavioral variables. Psychologists believe that there is a direct relationship between people's health and their behavior. **Health psychology** is the subfield concerned with the use of psychological ideas and principles to enhance health, prevent illness, diagnose and treat disease, and improve rehabilitation. It is an action-oriented discipline that assumes that people's ideas and behaviors contribute to the onset and prevention of illness. A closely related field, *behavioral medicine,* integrates behavioral science with biomedical knowledge and techniques; it is narrower in focus than health psychology. Of growing interest is the relationship of genetics to health; researchers are asking whether some aspects of health may be preprogrammed. What if some people have predispositions to develop certain diseases or disorders? How can psychologists help promote a healthy lifestyle to forestall, delay, or lessen the impact of disease processes?

Traditionally, physicians have considered health to be the absence of disease. A person who was not experiencing adverse effects from an infection, injury, or abnormal condition of some kind was considered healthy. Now, however, physicians and psychologists acknowledge that health is not just the absence of disease but a person's total social, physical, and mental well-being. This new orientation gives health psychology a focus on the positive—health promotion. Health and wellness are seen as conditions people can actively pursue by eating well, exercising regularly, and managing stress effectively (Cowen, 1991). Unlike medicine, which focuses on specific diseases, health psychology looks at the broad effects of thoughts and behaviors on fundamental psychosocial mechanisms. Today, researchers are focusing on the positive effects of health-promoting behaviors (Millar & Millar, 1995).

Educating people about prevention and wellness and discovering the variables that affect health are central objectives of health psychologists. And many health psychologists focus on disease prevention—for example, preventing the spread of AIDS (acquired immune deficiency syndrome), which is killing thousands each year in the United States and worldwide. One in 250 persons in the United States is infected with the human immunodeficiency virus (HIV), the virus that causes AIDS. Reports from the Centers for Disease Control and Prevention and the United Nations show that more than 390,000 deaths from AIDS have occurred so far in the United States, and an estimated 650,000 Americans are infected with HIV. Worldwide, 34 million persons are infected. Most people who have AIDS are between 20 and 49 years of age. Although some states (notably New York and California) currently have a higher percentage of cases than others, most experts believe that the infection rate by state will become similar over time. *Experiencing Psychology* (on p. 356) discusses AIDS in more detail.

Variables That Affect Health and Illness

We can set a positive tone for our lives, enhance feelings of belonging, and see the bright side of things. We can laugh at things and wear "rose-colored glasses" to help ward off the impact of negative or difficult life events (Kuiper & Martin, 1998). Our attitudes, behavior, and outlook affect health and illness—but they in turn are affected by complex interrelationships among many events (Cohen, 1996; Lefcourt & Thomas, 1998). Thus, health researchers have explored five variables that correlate strongly with health and illness: personality, cognitions, social environment, gender, and sociocultural variables (Rodin & Salovey, 1989).

Personality. Do certain personality variables predispose people to illness? Or does illness predispose a person to a specific personality type? Some evidence suggests that angry, hostile people are more prone to illness than are optimists. But which comes first? Perhaps the lack of illness causes optimism, or at least a positive lifestyle. The role of personality as variable affecting health and illness is still unclear, and much more research is needed (as we saw when we examined the role of Type A behavior in heart disease, on p. 348).

Cognitions. People's thoughts and beliefs about themselves, other people, and situations affect health-related behaviors. For example, one important variable is the extent to which people believe they control their lives, including health and illness. People with an internal locus of control (examined in Chapter 10) are more likely to take charge when they are ill and attempt to get better than are people with an external locus of control. When people sense that they can control their own health, they are more likely to engage in health-conscious behaviors, such as eating better and exercising more. But when people fear that something will happen that will damage their health, they tend to be at higher risk for stress-related symptoms, including high blood pressure. Researchers have long known that stress lowers resistance to colds and

Psychoneuroimmunology (PNI) [SYE-ko-NEW-ro-IM-you-NOLL-oh-gee]: The study of how psychological processes and the nervous system affect and, in turn, are affected by the body's natural defense system—the immune system.

Health psychology: Subfield concerned with the use of psychological ideas and principles to enhance health, prevent illness, diagnose and treat disease, and improve rehabilitation.

EXPERIENCING PSYCHOLOGY

AIDS—Education and Prevention

People who are infected with HIV can harbor the virus for many years without developing a full-blown case of AIDS. A great deal is known about this disease, but at present there are no preventive vaccines or cures, although "cocktails" of several drugs significantly slow the virus's destructive course in many people. Some people, fearing contamination, still shun AIDS patients. Also, because most of those who have AIDS were infected through sexual contact or intravenous drug use, some people attach a moral stigma to the disease. For all these reasons, AIDS is accompanied by devastating psychological consequences.

Few other diseases are accompanied by so many losses. AIDS patients face the loss of physical strength, mental acuity, ability to work and care for themselves or their families, self-sufficiency, social roles, income and savings, housing, the emotional support of friends and loved ones, and ultimately life itself. Some schools have prohibited children with AIDS, or even those who have family members with AIDS, from attending classes. People with AIDS have been fired, and coworkers have quit their jobs to avoid them. For many people with AIDS, self-esteem fades rapidly as they blame themselves for having contracted the disease. This self-blame leads to depression, anxiety, anger at oneself or guilt, and a negative outlook on life. Families and friends become similarly affected as they cope with a dying loved one and face their own inability to reverse the disease. Those who have lived with AIDS and AIDS-related diseases for a decade or more may have had to cope with the deaths of friends and may have been economically devastated.

There is some good news. Because better treatments that slow the natural course of HIV infection are being used, the incidence of new cases of full-blown AIDS has dropped significantly in the United States; furthermore, death among people with AIDS has declined from its all-time high in 1994 by as much as 50%. But as the number of deaths declines, the number of people living with HIV and AIDS continues to rise. Many people with HIV and AIDS now feel healthy again (although not cured). But they have to figure out how to live again as a relatively healthy person; like their ill counterparts, some feel guilty and others depressed, but some welcome and make the best of their newfound lease on life.

In their AIDS-prevention efforts, psychologists pay particular attention to high-risk behaviors so as to help individuals avoid risky situations. High-risk behaviors are those that directly expose a person to the blood or semen of others who are likely to have been exposed to the virus—in other words, to others who are likely to have engaged in high-risk behaviors. Individuals who have engaged in high-risk behaviors are often sexually promiscuous men and women, homosexual or bisexual men, or present or past intravenous drug abusers. Heterosexuals who have had sexual contact with carriers of AIDS are at significant risk. In the United States, about 18% of known cases of AIDS occur from heterosexual sex. But, according to the Centers for Disease Control and Prevention, heterosexual sex accounts for 75% of reported AIDS cases in other parts of the world. Everywhere, adolescents are at especially high risk because they, more than adults, are likely to engage in unprotected sexual activity, and they have some of the highest rates of sexually transmitted diseases, including HIV.

AIDS education aimed at young people is critically important, because education can be effective in changing behavior. However, in the case of AIDS, the relationship often does not hold up—people who know about AIDS, its transmission routes, and its prevention still engage in risky behaviors (Helweg-Larsen & Collins, 1997). For example, among sexually active high school students, only 54% reported using a condom the last time they had intercourse (Centers for Disease Control and Prevention, 1996). AIDS education, and research in general, has ignored gender as a crucial variable; but analyses show that women often respond better than men do to education about high-risk behaviors (Amaro, 1995). Further, when men and women engaging in sexual behaviors communicate better, they are more likely to minimize the risks of transmission (Dolcini et al., 1995). Research shows that the most effective way to get men and women to use condoms is not through fear but through engendering positive attitudes about condoms—that others will accept and like condoms and that carrying and using condoms is a positive and rewarding behavior (Sheeran, Abraham, & Orbell, 1999). ■

other infectious diseases—although they do not know how or why (Cohen et al., 1998).

Social Environment. Family, close friends, and work can be sources of social support—a key element in helping a person maintain health and recover from illness. Greater self-esteem, positive feelings about the future, and a sense of control are characteristic of people with strong social support. Adults in stable long-term relationships, including marriage, are less likely to be ill than are people without strong social support networks (Cohen, Tyrrell, & Smith, 1997; Lorenz, Simons, & Conger, 1997); in addition, the children of stable marriages are likely to be healthier (Gottman & Katz, 1989). Support from coworkers and supervisors in the work environment may also improve health (Repetti, Matthews, & Waldron, 1989). Individuals with social support are more likely to engage in preventive dental care, proper eating habits, and safety practices that extend life, such as wearing seat belts.

Gender. Some health concerns apply only to women (those related to child bearing and menopause, for example), and some health conditions affect women disproportionately (for example, eating disorders). Women are prescribed medication twice as often as men are (Prather & Minkow, 1991). Although women tend to visit physicians more often than men, in some cultures (including that of the United States), they often do not receive the same quality of treatment as is given men. While women have enjoyed an advantage with respect to longevity, the gap in average life span between men and women has been decreasing. Women's changing lifestyles and work patterns are highly correlated with increased medical problems and decreased average life span.

Adults in stable long-term relationships, including marriage, are less likely to be ill than are people without strong social support networks.

Sociocultural Variables. Cultural or ethnic background, age, and socioeconomic class are other important variables that affect health. Further, people from lower socioeconomic groups may lack knowledge, funds, or access to preventive care. Health is strongly correlated with behaviors such as eating well and exercising; when age, education, and income are taken into account, there are no strong ethnic differences (Kim et al., 1998). Adolescents present a complex picture: African American teenagers are more likely to experience stress compared to whites, but both African-American and white females report high rates of illness (Baldwin, Harris, & Chambliss, 1997).

With advancing age, people are more likely to become ill or depressed (although there is much individual variation). Often, the problem of illness among the elderly is compounded by other variables, such as loneliness and isolation from family. In addition, older, less educated, and less affluent individuals are far less likely to engage in exercise, which helps to prevent illness.

The Psychology of Being Sick

When a person has an illness that impairs day-to-day functioning, the effects can be devastating and profound, both psychologically and economically. Illness also seriously affects the sick person's family members. Health psychologists are concerned not only with the links between stress and illness, but with how people cope with illness when it occurs.

Seeking Medical Care. When do people seek medical care? What are the variables that prompt a person to try to get help to become well again? Most people avoid medical care and advice except when it becomes absolutely necessary. Usually, when people have visible symptoms (rashes, cuts, swellings, or fever) and the symptoms appear threatening or are painful and persistent, people seek professional help. They are more likely to seek such help when they are sure the problem is physical rather than psychological and when they think medical attention will provide a cure. If they think medical attention will be a waste of time or if they dread a diagnosis, they often delay seeking help.

There are gender differences in people's willingness to seek medical attention. Women seek medical help more than men do and take more prescription medication. Men have a shorter life span than do women and have higher rates of ulcers, heart disease, and stroke—perhaps in part because men may be less willing to seek medical attention, perceiving it as a weakness in character. Because some women are not in the work force, they may have more time to think about their symptoms or to visit a doctor. In addition, women often seek a doctor's care for normal, nonpathological conditions (conditions not caused by disease) such as pregnancy, childbirth, and menopause.

Major cultural differences also exist in health-care seeking; a country's technological and political systems shape health-care delivery, as does its level of economic development. These factors, in turn, affect individuals' willingness to seek health care and to trust health-care providers. Matsumoto (1996) describes research showing that even though Japanese women trust their physicians less than American women do, they are more likely to comply with a physician's advice recommending an invasive medical procedure. Power relationships and trust, two culturally determined variables, greatly affect health-care seeking.

The Sick Role. When people do what they think will help them get well, they are adopting a *sick role*. For most people, this means taking specific steps to get well, relieving themselves of normal responsibilities, and realizing that they are not at fault for their illness. When they are in the hospital, they give the responsibility for their care to physicians and nurses. Of course, a person can also adopt behaviors associated with illness when in fact there is no pathology.

Although American culture fosters an attitude that says people should be cheerful when sick, it is normal for sick people to be slightly depressed or even angry, especially when hospitalized. Because sickness is generally seen as a temporary state, people are expected to work toward getting well—taking medication, sleeping, and, especially, complying with medical advice. An unfortunate extension of this view is that many people blame the ailing person for being sick, even though the illness may be unrelated to any preventive measures a person might have taken.

Compliance with Medical Advice. Getting people to adhere to health regimens or to follow their physicians' advice has long been a focus of health psychologists. People will comply with specific recommendations for a particular health problem, such as "Take three tablets a day for 10 days." However, they are less likely to adhere to general recommendations aimed at improving overall health conditions, such as quitting smoking or getting more exercise. For example, cigarette smoking is one of the largest health concerns today, causing about a half million deaths annually in the United States alone. Yet about 48 million American adults, 25% of the population, continue to smoke (Wetter et al., 1998). When long-term exercise is the prescribed treatment, most people drop out of a program within 6 months.

Compliance with medical advice depends on the severity of the problem. If an illness causes pain or discomfort, people are more likely to comply with a regimen of treatment to alleviate the discomfort. People are more receptive to medical treatment when it is specific, simple, and easy to do, when it has minimal side effects, and when it brings immediate relief (Klonoff, Annechild, & Landrine, 1994). Even when the impact of not taking a preventive medication is serious, people are not particularly compliant; this is especially true for lengthy or difficult treatments, such as four-times-daily insulin injections (Hanson et al., 1989).

Compliance with a health-care regimen is increased when the regimen is tailored to the person's lifestyle and habits. And written agreements between practitioners and clients can be helpful. Health psychologists have found clients more likely to adhere to treatments when a physician's influence and the family support systems are substantial. Social support from family and friends turns out to be especially effective in getting even very sick people to comply with guidelines for treatment (DiMatteo & DiNicola, 1982). Helping people to build resourcefulness, to manage stress, and to understand the implications of their medical regimen is key to improved compliance (Aikens et al., 1992).

Health Psychology and Adaptive Behavior

Health psychologists focus on adaptive behaviors that will improve people's day-to-day lives. They recommend preventive programs in the workplace to educate people about ways to manage stress and about other positive behaviors that can enhance and prolong life. They frequently conduct stress management workshops to help managers and workers cope with increasing pressures and heavy workloads; they are also involved in helping people quit smoking, control their alcohol intake, follow exercise programs, and practice good nutrition.

Health psychology is an action-oriented discipline, and as people seek healthier lifestyles, psychologists are playing an instrumental role in their quest. Today, health psychologists attempt to change people's behavior before it gets out of hand. However, they also help people deal with existing problems such as obesity, diabetes, and high stress levels. Let's examine three ways of dealing with health problems: behavioral interventions, pain management, and stress management.

Behavioral Interventions. To manage existing health problems and help prevent disease, behavioral interventions are necessary and important. Health psychologists know that many problem behaviors can be modified through therapy; these include smoking, excessive drinking, drug abuse, and overeating.

Pain Management. People with crippling arthritis or bone cancer must live with a great deal of pain. Psychologists work to help such individuals manage this pain. Some types of chronic pain can be treated with drugs, surgery, or other medical interventions; other types may call for nontraditional psychological techniques.

Pain management programs usually work on two fronts: They try to reduce *psychological* suffering while using drugs to reduce the *physical* aspects of pain. Two nontraditional techniques for pain management are hypnosis and biofeedback (examined in Chapter 4). Others are behavior modification and cognitive therapy. Behavior modification uses learning principles (see Chapter 5) to teach people new effective behaviors and to help them unlearn maladaptive behaviors.

Stress Management. The task of managing stress in daily life is becoming greater each day. Because everyone is affected by stressors—whether school exams, family or relationship problems, natural disasters, illness, or financial difficulties—many health psychologists focus on stress management. With the help of health psychologists, employers are sponsoring programs for managing stress in the workplace (Glasgow & Terborg, 1988). The programs usually involve education, exercise, nutrition, and counseling. The results are fewer workdays lost to illness and lower health-care costs.

Stress and Health Psychology: The Future

At the beginning of this chapter, we considered the idea that stress is a psychobiological phenomenon involving both physiological and cognitive factors. Health is also considered to be a psychobiological phenomenon, and a number of social factors are especially important. These include social support, education, proper nutrition, and good medical care. Biological, behavioral, and social factors all intersect to determine each person's state of wellness.

Whether studying stress and its causes and treatment or looking at ways to improve health, psychologists are taking a prosocial, action-oriented approach. In many ways, the study of stress and health can be considered the future of the discipline. If people can learn to manage their stressors, they may be able to avoid many psychological and physical problems and optimize the various aspects of their daily lives. Stress and health psychology are thus applied disciplines that are rooted in basic research into human personality, motivation, learning, and biology but that help people develop and maintain fulfilling and productive lifestyles. (I)

> **Think Critically**
>
> ◆ What are the implications of the finding that women seem to respond better than men to education about high-risk behaviors that may lead to AIDS?

www.abacon.com/leftononline

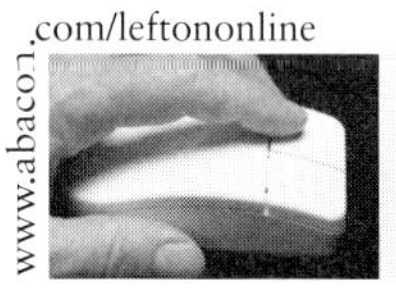

Your password-protected Website allows you access to the most comprehensive set of materials in The Psychology Place.

(I) Summary and Review

Stress

Why is appraisal a key component of stress?

What kinds of conflicts result in stress?

Describe three stages of Selye's general adaptation syndrome.

Characterize Type A behavior.

What is the link between stress and ill health?

KEY TERMS
stressor, p. 340; anxiety, p. 340; stress, p. 340; frustration, p. 341; conflict, p. 341; approach–approach conflict, p. 342; avoidance–avoidance conflict, p. 342; approach–avoidance conflict, p. 342; pressure, p. 342; posttraumatic stress disorder (PTSD), p. 344; burnout, p. 345; Type A behavior, p. 348; Type B behavior, p. 348

Coping

Distinguish various forms of coping.

KEY TERMS
coping, p. 350; resilience, p. 350; coping skills, p. 350; social support, p. 350; stress inoculation, p. 351; proactive coping, p. 352; psychoneuroimmunology (PNI), p. 354

Health Psychology

What is the role of health psychology?

Under what conditions do people comply with medical advice?

KEY TERM
health psychology, p. 354

Self-Test

1. Environmental stimuli that may lead to physical or psychological injury to an organism are:
   A. frustrations
   B. pressures
   C. toxins
   D. stressors

2. A generalized feeling of fear or apprehension that may be associated with a particular object is:
   A. stress
   B. conflict
   C. anxiety
   D. physiological arousal

3. The most important component in determining whether an event is stressful is:
   A. cultural background
   B. appraisal
   C. frequency of the event
   D. emotional stability

4. When Meghan's parents caught her teasing her sister, she was given the option of two consequences, loss of a privilege or 1 hour of quiet time in her room. Meghan was faced with an:
   A. approach–avoidance conflict
   B. approach–approach conflict
   C. avoidance-approach conflict
   D. avoidance–avoidance conflict

5. Caitlin has a test tomorrow and her computer is not working. She has lost her notes. She is most likely experiencing:
   A. depression
   B. frustration
   C. hard drive anxiety
   D. loss of control

6. An environment is most likely to be stressful if it:
   A. threatens safety
   B. provides conflict
   C. has limited social ties
   D. all of the above

7. When a person has psychological problems as a consequence of some type of disaster, he or she is suffering from:
   A. psychogenic stress disorder
   B. delusional behavior
   C. catastrophic stress
   D. posttraumatic stress disorder

8. The stress response can be divided into three major components. They are:
   A. frustration, pressure, conflict
   B. emotional, physiological, behavioral
   C. time, goals, conflicts
   D. perceptions, appraisals, cognitions

9. In Selye's general adaptation syndrome, the focus is on ______________ responses.
   A. physiological
   B. behavioral
   C. cognitive
   D. emotional

10. Early research by Holmes and Rahe suggested that:
    A. only major events cause stress
    B. minor events cause more stress
    C. perception of stress causes stress
    D. combinations of life events cause stress

11. Heart disease has been correlated with three day-to-day life components. They are:
    A. work-site stress, Type A behavior, physiological reactivity
    B. autonomy, gender, Type B behavior
    C. competitiveness, emotional reactivity, resilience
    D. procrastination, heredity, coping skills

12. Stress management is a key part of the ______________ process individuals use to deal with the challenges that arise in their lives.
    A. time management
    B. resilience
    C. defense
    D. coping

13. Having a positive attitude about life may reduce stress because:
    A. it makes a person more easily satisfied
    B. it can shorten a person's life
    C. it helps a person cope better
    D. it produces lower arousal

14. Health researchers are exploring five variables that correlate with good health. These are:
    A. personality, cognitions, social environment, gender, sociocultural variables
    B. attitudes, intelligence, heredity, exercise, adaptive behavior
    C. attitudes, intelligence, heredity, nutrition, adaptive behavior
    D. personality, social crowding, gender identification, sociocultural variables, cognitions

15. Women are more likely than men to seek medical care because women are:
    A. more likely to be sick
    B. more sensitive to their symptoms
    C. smarter than men
    D. more accustomed to seeing a physician

Psychological Disorders

www.abacon.com/leftononline

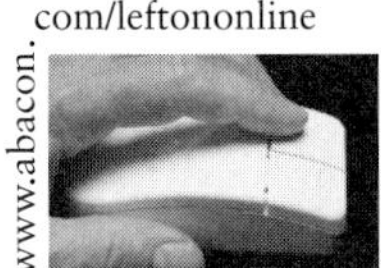

Go to your password-protected Website for full-color art, Weblinks, and more!

Calista Flockhart, star of the TV show *Ally McBeal,* has been the subject of considerable speculation because of her extreme thinness. Flockhart claims she is just thin, but many critics and psychologists assert that she has an eating disorder. This issue grabbed the public's attention because nearly 1 in 150 girls have the eating disorder anorexia nervosa (which we discussed in Chapter 8). Flockhart's weight and her eating behavior are between her and her doctor, but they raise questions about mental illness: When has someone gone over the line? How different must a person's behavior be to qualify as abnormal? Are Flockhart's eating habits any stranger than the behavior of an old man who leaves a multimillion-dollar fortune to his cats? Is becoming extremely thin and avoiding food any stranger than taking a midwinter dip in an ice-covered lake, as members of the Polar Bear Club do, or than undergoing extensive cosmetic surgery to obtain a "perfect" face? In this chapter, we will consider these and related questions. ■

(I) What Is Abnormal Behavior?

Focus on issues and ideas

- How different models of abnormality are used to predict and explain behavior
- The purpose of a multiaxial diagnostic system

Visiting New York City, I was shocked at how many homeless people there were. On the steps of a great cathedral, a number of people were bedding down for the night in large boxes. Such scenes are common in the United States. Starting in the 1970s, many people who were diagnosed as mentally ill were deinstitutionalized (released from hospitals). Lacking resources and coping mechanisms, they became the core of a homeless population. With their organized shopping carts in tow, these people seem to live their own lifestyle. Of course, not all homeless people have mental illnesses or display bizarre behavior. But if a homeless person talks to himself or herself, isn't that behavior abnormal? To some extent, the answer depends on the culture; every society has its own definition of abnormal behavior. In Russia, for example, people were once regularly placed in mental institutions for engaging in political dissent. Generally, however, behavior classified by psychologists as abnormal is more than odd. In any single month, about 15% of adults in the U.S. population meet the criteria for having a mental disorder; that is, they exhibit symptoms of abnormality (Reiger et al., 1988).

A Definition

Abnormal behavior is behavior characterized as (1) atypical, (2) socially unacceptable, (3) distressing to the person who exhibits it or to the person's friends and family, (4) maladaptive, and/or (5) the result of distorted cognitions. Let's consider these five distinguishing characteristics in turn.

First, abnormal behavior is *atypical.* Many behaviors are unusual; however, abnormal behaviors tend to be so unusual as to be statistically rare. For example, ear or body piercing cannot be considered abnormal, because the practice is fairly common among teenagers today. However, washing one's hands every few minutes during the day until the skin is raw is abnormal. Of course, not all atypical behavior is necessarily abnormal. Michael Jordan's athleticism and grace are statistically uncommon but not abnormal.

Second, abnormal behavior is also often *socially unacceptable.* To some degree, ideas about what is normal and abnormal vary according to cultural values. What is acceptable in one culture may be labeled unacceptable in another. Similarly, behavior that was considered unacceptable 25 years ago, such as a woman calling a man for a date, may be considered acceptable today. A behavior that is judged abnormal, however, is one that is unacceptable to society in general.

Third, a person's abnormal behavior often causes *distress* to the person or to those around the person. While feelings of anxiety or distress are normal in many situations, prolonged anxiety (distress) may result from abnormal behavior. You may feel anxious while you are preparing to speak in front of a group; but constant, unrelenting anxiety, the avoidance of any situation that might require public speaking, and fear of people in general suggest a problem.

Fourth, abnormal behavior is usually *maladaptive,* or self-defeating to the person exhibiting it. Maladaptive

Abnormal behavior: Behavior characterized as atypical, socially unacceptable, distressing to the individual or others, maladaptive, and/or the result of distorted cognitions.

behavior, such as drug abuse, is harmful and nonproductive. It often leads to misery and prevents people from making positive changes in their lives.

Last, abnormal behavior is often the result of *distorted cognitions* (thoughts). For example, a young man with distorted cognitions may falsely believe that people are out to get him. A woman suffering from major depression may believe that she is worthless, stupid, and unlovable.

The suffering that occurs when people are depressed, schizophrenic, or phobic is too great to be faked or purposely self-imposed.

In recent years, psychologists have begun to describe behavior in terms of *maladjustment* rather than *abnormality.* The distinction is important because it implies that maladaptive behavior can, with treatment, be adjusted—and become adaptive and productive. The term *maladjustment* also emphasizes specific behaviors rather than labeling the entire person.

Using the sociocultural approach (described on p. 365), researchers such as Thomas Szasz go so far as to say that maladjustment and mental illness are socially constructed and defined. Szasz argues that there is, in fact, a myth of mental illness; according to Szasz, once a practitioner labels a person as "abnormal," the person starts to act that way (Szasz, 1984, 1987). The patient confirms the therapist's expectations about his or her abnormality, even when the expectations may not reflect the patient's real condition. In Szasz's view, a patient in therapy creates situations that lead to behaviors that the therapist has predicted; in Chapter 1, this phenomenon was introduced in the context of researcher–participant interactions as the *self-fulfilling prophecy* (see p. 8). Because of the phenomenon of the self-fulfilling prophecy, it is important for a therapist to label people as little as possible. Giving a person or the person's behavior a label or tag rarely helps; in Szasz's view, "mental illness" is a label that serves no good purpose. The truth is, however, that people *do* suffer from mental illness, and although labels rarely help, to throw "mental illness" out because it is merely a social construction, a myth, is a mistake. The suffering that occurs when people are depressed, schizophrenic, or phobic is too great to be faked or purposely self-imposed; to think that a person would "choose" to adopt behaviors typical of the schizophrenic is to romanticize or even make light of a serious, debilitating illness. Last, labels help researchers and practitioners communicate effectively with one another. They help provide consistency in research and practice and allow practitioners to anticipate likely symptoms and treat them in a timely fashion.

Perspectives on Abnormality

In 1999, 15-year-old honor student Kip Kinkel (shown in the photo) killed his parents and two classmates and injured several others. He showed no clear signs of maladjustment prior to the shootings. What could have brought on his abnormal behavior? Mental health practitioners want to know why a person is maladjusted, because establishing the cause of a disorder can sometimes help in defining a treatment plan. Therefore, practitioners often turn to theories and models that attempt to explain the causes of abnormality. A **model** is an analogy or a perspective that helps scientists discover relationships among data; it uses a structure from one field to help describe data in another. Psychologists use models to make predictions about behavior. Models of maladjustment help form the basis of **abnormal psychology,** the field of psychology concerned with the assessment, treatment, and prevention of maladaptive behavior. Several models help explain abnormal behavior: medical–biological, psychodynamic, humanistic, behavioral, cognitive, sociocultural, legal, and interactionist.

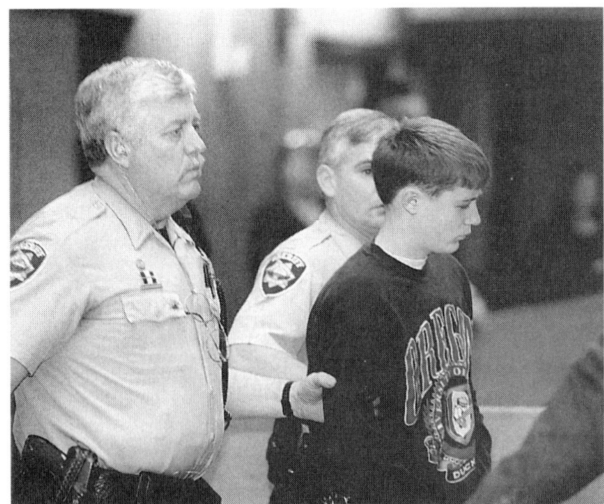

Medical-Biological Model. The *medical–biological model* of abnormal behavior focuses on the physiological conditions that initiate abnormal behaviors. This model adequately deals with a range of mental ailments, such as those caused by mercury poisoning or viral infections. It focuses on genetic abnormalities, problems in the central nervous system, and hormonal changes. It also helps explain and treat substance abuse problems and schizophrenia, two disorders that may have a strong biological component. Proponents of the medical–biological model might explain a homeless person's ramblings as the result of a chemical or hormonal imbalance that alters judgment.

Many of the terms and concepts used in psychology and psychiatry are borrowed from medicine—among them *treatment, case, symptom,* and *syndrome,* as well as *mental illness.* The medical model assumes that abnormal behavior, like other illnesses, can be diagnosed, treated, and often cured. This approach has not gone unchallenged, however. Its critics say that it does not take advantage of modern psychological insights, such as those of learning theory. A major—but not surprising—disadvantage of the medical model is that it emphasizes hospitalization and drug treatment rather than psychological insights into mental problems. Use of the medical model has also fostered the incorrect notion that abnormal behavior can be infectious, much like a disease.

Psychodynamic Model. The *psychodynamic model* of abnormal behavior is loosely rooted in Freud's theory of personality (discussed in Chapter 10). This model assumes that psychological disorders result from anxiety produced by unresolved conflicts and forces of which a person may be unaware. It asserts that maladjustment occurs when a person relies on too many defense mechanisms or when defense mechanisms fail. A homeless person's talking to himself might be explained as loneliness, despair, or anger turned inward. Although many homeless people are bright and capable, being homeless might be seen as a reaction to fear of competing caused by low self-esteem that was initiated in childhood. Treatments of disorders based on the psychodynamic model usually involve helping patients become aware of motivations and conflicts so that they can have a healthier lifestyle. We will explore psychodynamic approaches to treatment in more detail in Chapter 14.

Humanistic Model. Like the psychodynamic model, the *humanistic model* of abnormal behavior assumes that inner psychic forces are important in establishing and maintaining a normal lifestyle. Unlike psychodynamic theorists, however, humanists believe that people have a good deal of control over their lives. The humanistic model focuses on individual uniqueness and decision making. It contends that people become maladjusted when their expectations far exceed their achievements. In the case of a homeless person who exhibits disorganized behavior, a humanist might focus on her dignity and self-respect as vehicles to help her lead a more structured life. Humanistic treatment usually involves helping maladjusted people to discover and accept their true selves, formulate more realistic self-concepts and expectations, and become more like their ideal selves.

Behavioral Model. The *behavioral model* of abnormal behavior states that such behavior is caused by faulty or ineffective learning and conditioning patterns. Two fundamental assumptions of behavioral (learning) theorists are that disordered behavior can be reshaped and that more appropriate, worthwhile behaviors can be substituted through traditional learning techniques (see Chapter 5). Behavioral theorists assume that events in a person's environment selectively reinforce or punish various behaviors and, in doing so, shape personality and may create maladjustment.

Cognitive Model. The *cognitive model* of abnormal behavior asserts that human beings engage in both prosocial and maladjusted behaviors because of their thoughts. As thinking organisms, people decide how to behave; abnormal behavior is based on false assumptions or unrealistic coping strategies. Practitioners with a cognitive perspective treat people with psychological disorders by helping them develop new thought processes that instill new values. A cognitive theorist might assume that maladjusted people have developed wrong ideas about the world, which have led to maladaptive behaviors.

Sociocultural Model. According to the *sociocultural model* of abnormal behavior, people develop abnormalities within and because of a context—the context of the family, the community, and the society. Cross-cultural researchers have shown that personality development and psychological disorders reflect the culture, and the stressors in the society. Relying heavily on the learning and cognitive frameworks, the sociocultural model focuses on cultural variables as key determinants of maladjustment.

As researchers examine the frequency and types of disorders that occur in different societies, they also note some sharp differences between societies. In China, for example, depression is relatively uncommon, but stress reactions manifested in the form of physical ailments are frequent. Americans and Europeans report guilt and shame when they are depressed; depressed individuals in Africa, on the other hand, are less likely to report these symptoms but more likely to report somatic (physical) complaints. Certain disorders seem

Model: An analogy or a perspective that uses a structure from one field to help scientists describe data in another field.

Abnormal psychology: The field of psychology concerned with the assessment, treatment, and prevention of maladaptive behavior.

highly culture-specific; for example, *amok* (as in "running amok") is a disorder that is characterized by sudden rage and homicidal aggression and is seen in some Asian countries, such as Malaysia and Thailand. Brought on by stress, sleep deprivation, and alcohol consumption, the behavior can be broken down into a series of stages. Similarly, anorexia nervosa, discussed in Chapter 8, is a disorder primarily confined to the West. Researchers now recognize that some disorders are *culturally indigenous*; that is, specific to a culture.

Legal Model. The *legal model* of abnormal behavior defines such behavior strictly in terms of guilt, innocence, and sanity. For example, a jury declared John W. Hinckley Jr., the man who attempted to assassinate President Ronald Reagan, "not guilty by reason of insanity," and he was acquitted of attempted murder charges. Most people overestimate how often such pleas are made. The truth is that only about 1% of all felony defendants use an insanity defense—and the plea is successful only about one-quarter of the time (Perlin, 1996).

The term *insane* is a legal term, not a psychological one. *Insanity* refers to a condition that excuses people from responsibility and protects them from punishment. From the legal point of view, a person cannot be held responsible for a crime if, at the time of the crime, the person lacked the capacity to distinguish right from wrong or to obey the law.

Although perhaps useful for judicial purposes, the legal definition of abnormal behavior is not useful in treating clients. The legal system tends to mix mental illness, sin, law, theology, and people's needs for retribution and forgiveness.

Interactionist Model. No single model can explain every kind of abnormal behavior; despite their philosophical incompatibilities, however, each model has value. For some disorders (such as phobias), learning theory explains the cause and prescribes an effective course of treatment. For other disorders (such as schizophrenia), medical–biological theory clarifies a significant part of the problem. Consequently, many psychologists use an *interactionist model* (sometimes termed an *eclectic model*) of abnormal behavior, one that draws on all these perspectives. Such practitioners use the best features of two or more models.

Next, we consider a system that has been developed to help practitioners make diagnoses. The system is presented in the *Diagnostic and Statistical Manual of Mental Disorders.*

Prevalence: The percentage of a population displaying a disorder during any specified period.

Diagnosing Maladjustment: The DSM-IV

Ask psychologists and psychiatrists to explain homeless people and they are likely to say that those individuals may be odd but not necessarily abnormal. This controversy underscores the fact that diagnosing maladjusted behavior is a complicated process.

Diagnostic and Statistical Manual of Mental Disorders. The American Psychiatric Association has devised a system for diagnosing maladjusted behavior—the *Diagnostic and Statistical Manual of Mental Disorders,* usually called the *DSM*. The current edition of the manual is the fourth, or the *DSM–IV,* published in 1994. The goals of the *DSM* are to improve the reliability of diagnoses by categorizing disorders according to observable behaviors and to make sure that diagnoses are consistent with research evidence and practical experience (Widiger et al., 1991). The *DSM* designates 16 major categories of maladjustment and more than 200 subcategories. (Table 13.1 lists some of the major classifications.)

Table 13.1 Major Classifications of the *Diagnostic and Statistical Manual of Mental Disorders,* Fourth Edition

Disorders First Diagnosed in Infancy, Childhood, and Adolescence
Delirium, Dementia, and Other Cognitive Disorders
Substance-Related Disorders
Schizophrenia and Other Psychotic Disorders
Mood Disorders
Anxiety Disorders
Somatoform Disorders
Factitious Disorders
Dissociative Disorders
Sexual and Gender Identity Disorders
Eating Disorders
Sleep Disorders
Impulse Control Disorders

Note: Each classification is further broken down into subtypes.

Table 13.1 also cites the **prevalence** of each disorder—the percentage of the population displaying the disorder during any specified period. For most psychological disorders, the *DSM* also indicates the lifetime prevalence—the statistical likelihood that a person will develop the disorder during his or her lifetime. So, a typical *DSM* statement might read, "The lifetime prevalence for this disorder in young adult females is approximately 1%–3%; the rate of occurrence of this disorder in males is approximately one-tenth of that in females" (American Psychiatric Association, 1994, p. 548). (The disorder being referred to is bulimia nervosa.) Although the names of the various disorders that are described in the DSM have been imposed by researchers, psychologists didn't suddenly discover depression, schizophrenia, or attention deficit hyperactivity disorder. The behaviors associated with each disorder have been around for years—but only recently have they been systematically classified and named by psychologists.

The prevalence rate of a specific disorder in a particular country probably reflects ethnic, religious, and cultural biases; it especially reflects the specific culture-bound behavior patterns that a society considers normal.

An important feature of the *DSM* is that diagnostic information for any disorder is laid out on five different dimensions. The *DSM* refers to these dimensions as *axes*; the manual thus uses what is called a *multiaxial system,* in order to be as informative, precise, reliable, and valid as possible about an individual's condition. Axis I describes the *major disorders* themselves. Axis II describes *personality disorders and prominent maladaptive personality features,* as well as defense mechanisms—for example, inflexible thinking strategies. Axis III describes *current medical conditions* that might be pertinent to understanding or managing the individual's mental disorder—diabetes may affect eating behavior, for instance, which is a relevant factor in anorexia nervosa. Other relevant medical conditions include diseases of the circulatory, digestive, and respiratory systems. Axis IV, *psychosocial or environmental problems,* refers to life stresses (including economic or educational problems) and familial support systems that may or may not facilitate a person's treatment or recovery. Finally, Axis V comprises a *global assessment of functioning,* which reports the clinician's overall assessment of the person's functioning in the psychological, social, and occupational domains. For example, a client might be said to have some mild symptoms such as insomnia and occasional truancy from school but to be generally functioning pretty well, with some meaningful personal relationships. These five axes, when viewed together, help a clinician fully describe the nature of a person's maladjustment. It is important to note that a clinician might not assess a client on a particular axis. So, for example, there may be no medical condition to report on Axis III. Table 13.2 describes the axes of the *DSM–IV.*

You might think that such a diagnostic manual would be straightforward, like an encyclopedia of mental disorders. However, because it was written by committees, the *DSM* represents various compromises; therefore, it has met with resistance and engendered controversy. Some take issue with the way the *DSM* groups disorders based on symptoms rather than causes. Others argue that it is too precise and complicated—but some assert that, despite its rigor, it is still not precise enough. Some have concerns about potential gender bias against women (e.g., Hartung & Widiger, 1998). Still others believe the *DSM* should go beyond its descriptive approach and include problem-oriented and problem-solving information rather than just symptoms. Many psychologists are

Table 13.2 The Axes of the *DSM–IV*

Axis	Description
Axis I	Symptoms that cause distress or significantly impair social or occupational functioning
Axis II	Personality disorders—personality patterns that are so pervasive, inflexible, and maladaptive that they impair interpersonal or occupational functioning
Axis III	Medical conditions that may be relevant to the understanding or treatment of a psychological disorder
Axis IV	Psychosocial and environmental problems (such as negative life events and interpersonal stressors) that may affect the diagnosis, treatment, and prognosis of psychological disorders
Axis V	Global assessment of functioning—the individual's overall level of functioning in social, occupational, and leisure activities

Source: Adapted from *Diagnostic and Statistical Manual of Mental Disorders,* Fourth Edition, American Psychiatric Association, 1994.

unhappy with the use of psychiatric terms that perpetuate a medical rather than a behavioral model. Finally, a few psychologists maintain that the *DSM* pathologizes everyday behaviors and allows some practitioners to take advantage of its legitimization of the psychiatric terms for political and monetary gain (Kutchins & Kirk, 1997).

The *DSM* is continually being evaluated and revised to reflect the latest scientific knowledge and is thus an evolving system of classification (Clark, Watson, & Reynolds, 1995). *Experiencing Psychology* illustrates the process by asking, "Is there such a thing as chronic fatigue syndrome? And is it a disorder?"

Diversity and Diagnoses. The *DSM* is by no means the final word in diagnosing maladjustment; as was noted above, it is a developing system of classification. Some psychologists applaud its recognition of social and environmental influences on behavior; others insist that it needs to become more sensitive to issues of diversity.

EXPERIENCING PSYCHOLOGY

The Emergence of a New Disorder?

Is there such a thing as a "new" disorder? Or do psychologists just relabel a disorder that has been around for a long time. There are some politics involved in classifying mental disorders, and some science. Chronic fatigue syndrome is a case in point.

Chronic fatigue syndrome, often referred to as CFS, has emerged as a diagnostic category only in the last decade—and it is not yet part of the *DSM*. Interestingly, the symptoms of CFS have been around for a long time—it is probably the same disorder or syndrome that was known as "neurasthenia" in the 19th century. The most significant symptom of CFS is debilitating fatigue, but other symptoms include sore throat, muscle pain, and sleep problems. The entertainer and singer Cher is one of the current sufferers from CFS—does she have a medical problem or a mental disorder? In the past, most researchers assumed that CFS was a relatively rare disorder that accompanied other psychological disorders such as depression. Many practitioners minimized the seriousness and prevalence of CFS. Many considered it a strictly physical disorder, not psychological at all. However, over the last decade, practitioners and researchers alike have reevaluated their positions.

CFS is a poorly understood, threatening affliction that can severely stress a person's individual coping mechanisms and thus affect social and occupational relationships. Thus, a practitioner must assess the impact of the illness in the context of the patient's life and must be alert to signs of overpowering distress. Such signs could include heightened interpersonal difficulties, substance abuse, unnecessary avoidance of people and activities, extreme helplessness, difficulty tolerating dependency, panic, misplaced anger, self-blame and guilt, and hopelessness.

CFS seems to have a fairly high prevalence. But the rate depends partly on how the disorder is defined. Some definitions require a definite onset and substantial reductions in occupational, social, and personal activities. Some require that a patient exhibit as many as eight symptoms; others require only four. Thus, the definition used to diagnose an individual as having the disorder determines its relative frequency in the population. Furthermore, family doctors are often the ones who make a referral to a psychologist or psychiatrist when they suspect a patient of having CFS. So, a physician's preconceived notion of whether CFS is a medical condition or a psychological one is important. A great deal of controversy and speculation surrounds CFS. Is it a psychological disorder or a medical condition? What is its relationship to infections, the immune system, and mood disturbances?

In reviewing the history, politics, and science of CFS, Leonard Jason and his colleagues (Jason et al., 1997) argued that psychologists, through research and careful evaluation, have to decide what the diagnostic criteria are. Only then can true estimates of prevalence be established. After these two goals are reached, researchers will be better able to establish effective treatment plans (Friedberg & Jason, 1998).

Does CFS exist? The answer is probably yes. Is it often mixed up with other disorders? Again, the answer is probably yes. More research is necessary to differentiate CFS from other disorders that share some of its symptoms. A biopsychological model that explains the disorder with reference to both medical and psychological aspects may be the most constructive way to approach the problem (Johnson, 1998). ■

Not all ethnic groups exhibit symptoms of every disorder; nor do all members of one ethnic group have an equal likelihood of exhibiting specific symptoms. However, research shows that the likelihood of a specific diagnosis is indeed related to ethnicity. For example, Asian Americans and African Americans receive more diagnoses of schizophrenia than do whites, despite the fact that Asians in general do not seek mental health services as often as whites do (Uba, 1994). Hispanic Americans receive fewer diagnoses of schizophrenia than do whites (Flaskerud & Hu, 1992). Similarly, Koreans are more likely to be diagnosed as depressed than are Taiwanese, Filipinos, or Americans (Crittenden et al., 1992). The prevalence rate of a specific disorder in a particular country probably reflects ethnic, religious, and cultural biases; it especially reflects the specific culture-bound behavior patterns that a society considers normal. As suggested earlier, various cultures allow for, and perhaps encourage, specific symptomatology. The effect of culture on clinical diagnosis and treatment plans is underresearched and constitutes an important area of concern for practicing psychologists. The American Psychological Association (1993) suggests that practitioners should do several things:

- Recognize cultural diversity
- Understand the role of culture and ethnicity in development
- Help clients to a fuller awareness of their own ethnic and cultural identification
- Understand how culture, race, gender, and sexual orientation interact to affect behavior

The remainder of this chapter explores some of the most common disorders described in *DSM–IV* and their consequences. We begin with anxiety disorders. (I)

Think Critically

- Do you think there are any behaviors that are perceived as abnormal in all cultures? Explain.
- A medical model assumes that people who suffer from a psychological disorder have no more control over their problem than do people who suffer from cancer. What do you think are the implications of such an assumption for the diagnosis and treatment of mental illnesses?
- If you had a say in what the next edition of the DSM would include, what would you add to make it more useful?

(I) Anxiety, Somatoform, and Dissociative Disorders

Focus on issues and ideas

- What the terms anxiety and free-floating anxiety mean
- How the abnormal behavior associated with anxiety, somatoform, and dissociative disorders is characterized

Everyone experiences anxiety. Most people feel anxious in specific situations, such as before taking an examination, competing in a swim meet, or delivering a speech. Although anxiety can be a positive, motivating force, its effects can also be debilitating; left untreated, chronic anxiety may eventually impair a person's health. Those who have had anxiety problems serious enough to cause them to be hospitalized are at increased risk for suicide (Allgulander, 1994). Anxiety disorders as a whole are common in the general population, although research into them is not extensive.

Defining Anxiety

Anxiety is a generalized feeling of fear and apprehension that may be related to a particular situation or object and is often accompanied by increased physiological arousal. Horney considered it a motivating force, an intrapsychic urge, and a signal of distress. Psychologists recognize that anxiety is a key symptom of maladjustment—not necessarily the cause of maladjustment. Thoughts, environmental stimuli, or perhaps some long-standing and as yet unresolved conflict causes apprehension, fear, and its accompanying autonomic nervous system arousal. Feelings of not being able to control a situation are common to both children's and adults' anxiety; some researchers speculate that childhood anxiety and a perceived sense of lack of control may lead to similar, if not identical, feelings in adulthood, which may result in a disorder (Chorpita & Barlow, 1998). This may be the case with generalized anxiety disorder, considered next.

Anxiety: A generalized feeling of fear and apprehension that may be related to a particular situation or object and is often accompanied by increased physiological arousal.

Generalized Anxiety Disorder

Every anxiety disorder represents a different pattern of behavior and maladjustment, and the *DSM–IV* classifies these disorders under several categories. That in which anxiety is the most prominent feature is designated as generalized anxiety disorder. **Generalized anxiety disorder** is an anxiety disorder characterized by persistent anxiety occurring on more days than not for at least 6 months, sometimes with autonomic hyperactivity, apprehension, excessive muscle tension, and difficulty in concentrating. People with generalized anxiety disorder feel anxious almost constantly, even though nothing seems to provoke their anxiety. Expressed fears often revolve around health, money, family, or work. Unable to relax, they have trouble falling asleep; they tend to feel tired and have trouble concentrating. They often report excessive sweating, headaches, and insomnia. They are tense and irritable, have difficulty making decisions, and may hyperventilate (Kendall, Krain, & Treadwell, 1999).

The *DSM–IV* states that a person must show persistent anxiety to be diagnosed with generalized anxiety disorder. When such chronic anxiety has no obvious source, it is called *free-floating anxiety.* **Free-floating anxiety** is persistent anxiety not clearly related to any specific object or situation and accompanied by a sense of impending doom. Of course, the original source of such extreme anxiety may have been a specific stressor, such as having been a prisoner of war.

People with generalized anxiety disorder show impairment in three areas of functioning. One area is *motor tension*—the person is unable to relax and exhibits jumpiness, restlessness, and tension. The second area is *autonomic hyperactivity*—the person sweats, has a dry mouth, has a high resting pulse rate, urinates frequently, and may complain of a lump in the throat. The third area is *vigilance*—the person has difficulty concentrating and is irritable and impatient.

Generalized anxiety disorder: Anxiety disorder characterized by persistent anxiety that lasts for at least 6 months, sometimes with autonomic hyperactivity, apprehension, excessive muscle tension, and concentration.

Free-floating anxiety: Persistent anxiety not clearly related to any specific object or situation and accompanied by a sense of impending doom.

Phobic disorders: Anxiety disorders characterized by excessive and irrational fear of, and consequent attempted avoidance of, specific objects or situations.

Agoraphobia [AG-or-uh-FOE-bee-uh]: Anxiety disorder characterized by marked fear and avoidance of being alone in a place from which escape might be difficult or embarrassing.

Social phobia [FOE-bee-uh]: Anxiety disorder characterized by fear of, and desire to avoid, situations in which the person might be exposed to scrutiny by others and might behave in an embarrassing or humiliating way.

Specific phobia: Anxiety disorder characterized by irrational and persistent fear of a particular object or situation, along with a compelling desire to avoid it.

Obsessive–compulsive disorder: Anxiety disorder characterized by persistent and uncontrollable thoughts and irrational beliefs that cause the performance of compulsive rituals that interfere with daily life.

Phobic Disorders

Do you know someone who is petrified at the thought of flying in a plane, who avoids crowds at all cost, or who shudders at the sight of a harmless garden snake? That person may suffer from a **phobic disorder**—an anxiety disorder involving excessive irrational fear of, and consequent avoidance of, specific objects or situations. Unlike people who feel anxious almost constantly, the anxiety of those who suffer from phobic disorders is far more focused. People with a phobic disorder exhibit avoidance and escape behaviors, show increased heart rate and irregular breathing patterns, and report thoughts of disaster and severe embarrassment. Many psychologists agree that, once a phobia is established, it is maintained by the relief a person derives from escaping or avoiding the feared situation.

One key to diagnosing phobic disorders is that the fear must be excessive and disproportionate to the situation, enough to induce a person to avoid the situation altogether. Most people who fear heights would not avoid visiting a friend who lived on the top floor of a tall building; a person with a phobia of heights would, however. Fear alone does not distinguish a phobia; both fear and avoidance must be evident.

Mild phobic disorders occur in about 7.5% of the U.S. population. They are, in fact, relatively common in well-adjusted people. Severe, disabling phobias occur in less than 0.05% of the population, typically in patients with other disorders (Seif & Atkins, 1979). Phobias occur most frequently between the ages of 30 and 60 and affect men and women about equally (Marks, 1977). An almost infinite number of objects and situations inspire fear in people. Because of the diversity and number of phobias, the *DSM* classifies three basic kinds: agoraphobia, social phobia, and specific phobia. We consider these next.

Agoraphobia. **Agoraphobia** is an anxiety disorder characterized by marked fear and avoidance of being alone in a place from which escape might be difficult or embarrassing. This phobia is accompanied by avoidance behaviors that may eventually interfere with normal activities. It can become so debilitating that it prevents the individual from going into a space from which escape might be difficult or awkward (for example, airplanes or tunnels) or from being in crowds. People with severe cases may decide never to leave their homes, fearing that they will lose control, panic, or cause a scene in a public place. An episode of agoraphobia is often brought on by stress, particularly interpersonal stress. It is far more common in women than in men, and it is often accompanied by other disorders.

Symptoms of agoraphobia are hyperventilation, extreme tension, and even cognitive disorganization (Zitrin, 1981). Agoraphobics are also often seriously depressed. They often feel weak and dizzy and often suffer from severe panic attacks. *Panic attacks* are characterized as acute anxiety, accompanied by sharp increases in autonomic nervous system arousal, that is not triggered by a specific event; persons who experience such attacks often avoid the situations that are associated with them, thus perpetuating the agoraphobia (McNally, 1994). Some cognitive psychologists think of a panic attack as a "fear of fear"; attempting to avoid anxiety because they are so sensitive to it and its symptoms, people may panic while trying to avoid the symptoms of being fearful (McNally et al., 1997). Despite much research, no simple cause for the disorder has been found.

Social Phobia. A person with a social phobia tends to avoid situations involving possible exposure to the scrutiny of other people. A **social phobia** is an anxiety disorder characterized by fear of, and desire to avoid, situations in which one might be exposed to scrutiny by others and might behave in an embarrassing or humiliating way. A person with a social phobia avoids eating in public, for example, or speaking before other people. Such a person also avoids evaluation by refusing to enter into situations in which evaluation and a lowering of self-esteem might occur (Williams, Kinney, & Falbo, 1989). The most common social phobia is a fear of speaking in public, although going to parties where many unknown people will be is also associated with a high level of anxiety. Social phobia is more than being shy; shy individuals don't actually avoid circumstances that make them uncomfortable or self-conscious. Social phobia disrupts normal living and social relationships. The dread of speaking to a group or attending a social function can begin weeks in advance and lead to debilitating symptoms.

Specific Phobia. A **specific phobia** is an anxiety disorder characterized by irrational and persistent fear of a particular object or situation, along with a compelling desire to avoid it. Most people are familiar with specific phobias; see Table 13.3 for some examples. Among specific phobias are *claustrophobia* (fear of closed spaces), *hematophobia* (fear of blood), and *acrophobia* (fear of heights). Many specific phobias develop in childhood, adolescence, or early adulthood. Most people who have fears of heights, small spaces, water, doctors, or flying can calm themselves and deal with their fears; but those who cannot—true phobics—often seek the help of a psychotherapist when the phobia interferes with their health or with day-to-day functioning. Treatment using behavior therapy is typically effective.

Diversity (on p. 372) examines the prevalence of anxiety disorders among ethnic minorities.

Obsessive–Compulsive Disorder

Being orderly and organized is usually an asset, especially in today's fast-paced, complex society. However, when orderliness becomes an overriding concern, a person may be suffering from obsessive–compulsive disorder. **Obsessive–compulsive disorder** is an anxiety disorder characterized by persistent and uncontrollable

Table 13.3 Some Common Specific Phobias

Acrophobia (fear of high places)	Hematophobia (fear of blood)
Ailurophobia (fear of cats)	Mysophobia (fear of contamination)
Algophobia (fear of pain)	Nyctophobia (fear of darkness)
Anthropophobia (fear of men)	Pathophobia (fear of disease)
Aquaphobia (fear of water)	Pyrophobia (fear of fire)
Astraphobia (fear of storms, thunder, and lightning)	Thanatophobia (fear of death)
Claustrophobia (fear of closed places)	Xenophobia (fear of strangers)
Cynophobia (fear of dogs)	Zoophobia (fear of animals)

DIVERSITY

Anxiety Disorders among Ethnic Minorities

In the United States, members of ethnic minorities are more likely than nonminority individuals to suffer from an anxiety disorder. Relatively little research attention has been given to anxiety disorders among ethnic minorities. Neal and Turner (1991) found that African Americans had a higher prevalence of agoraphobia and specific phobias than any other ethnic group. The percentage of African Americans who are diagnosed as agoraphobic is 1.5 times that of whites. African Americans are also more likely than whites to report social phobias (Last & Perrin, 1993). Further, the percentage of African American Vietnam veterans who suffer from posttraumatic stress disorder is higher than the percentage of white veterans. And childhood anxiety disorders are less likely among white adolescents than among African American adolescents (Beidel, Turner, & Trager, 1994).

Neither Neal and Turner (1991) nor Last and Perrin (1993) are sure why these problematic differences exist. Further research on the topic is made especially difficult by certain facts. First, within the African American community, research does not have an honorable reputation, because of abuses that occurred in the past. As a consequence, few individuals are willing to participate in research studies. Second, at times of emotional distress, African Americans are more likely to seek help from an emergency room physician or a minister than from a mental health professional (Kirmayer, Young, & Hayton, 1995); again, this situation results in few participants for research (Paradis, Hatch, & Friedman, 1994). Finally, the number of African Americans who are themselves engaged in clinical research is exceptionally small.

Today, community mental health professionals often know the appropriate questions to ask; however, they usually lack the personnel and the resources to fully implement their research ideas. There is a high frequency of mental disorders among ethnic minorities in general and of anxiety disorders among African Americans in particular, and complicated social and cultural factors may underlie these higher rates. These factors are only now being recognized as important areas for research. ■

thoughts and irrational beliefs that cause the performance of compulsive rituals that interfere with daily life. The unwanted thoughts, urges, and actions of people with obsessive–compulsive disorder focus on maintaining order and control. About 2% of the U.S. population suffers from obsessive–compulsive disorder. Of those with the disorder, about 20% have only obsessions or compulsions; about 80% have both.

People with obsessive–compulsive disorder combat anxiety by carrying out ritual behaviors that reduce tension; they feel they have to *do* something. Their thoughts have extraordinary power to control actions. For example, a man obsessed with avoiding germs may wash his hands a hundred times a day and may wear white gloves to avoid touching contaminated objects. If he does not perform these compulsive acts, he may develop severe anxiety. A woman obsessed with punctuality may become extremely anxious if she might arrive late for a dinner date. Adolescents with obsessive–compulsive disorder tend to wash and rewash, check, count, touch, and straighten items in their environment (March, Leonard, & Swedo, 1995). A person may compulsively write notes about every detail of every task before permitting herself or himself to take any action.

Freud and other psychodynamic theorists believed that obsessive–compulsive disorder stems largely from difficulties during the anal stage of development, when orderliness and cleanliness are often stressed. Learning theorists argue that bringing order to the environment reduces uncertainty and risk and thus is reinforcing. Because reinforced behaviors tend to recur, these behaviors become exaggerated during times of stress. Neuroscience-oriented theorists now believe strongly that such factors as dysfunction in the basal ganglia, chronic elevated levels of arousal, a genetic link, and brain trauma explain obsessive–compulsive disorder (Last et al., 1991). Research on the neuroanatomy that may underlie such a disorder has proceeded at a fast pace, although with varying conclusions—it turns out that results are hard to replicate. It may be that obsessive symptoms and compulsive symptoms have a different anatomical locus; patients who are medicated (who may otherwise be good participants) are often excluded from studies. So, although scientists are making headway in formulating neuroscientific explanations of obsessive–compulsive disorder, there is still much to understand (K. D. Wilson, 1998).

Practitioners report that full-blown cases of obsessive–compulsive disorder are relatively rare. Treatment often includes drugs (such as Anafrinil, Prozac, or Zoloft; see Chapter 14) combined with relaxation exercises (March, Leonard, & Swedo, 1995) and cognitive behavior therapy (Abramowitz, 1998). Such treatment helps change ideas about stress and the consequences of anxiety. Family support and family psychotherapy are also helpful; families are taught that they should neither encourage the behaviors nor participate in the person's rituals. Today, self-help groups are also part of successful treatments. People who develop obsessive–compulsive disorder before age 20 are less likely to improve over time; most people improve, even without treatment, over a period of five years or more (Skoog & Skoog, 1999). Somatoform and dissociative disorders, discussed next, are harder to understand and treat.

Somatoform Disorders

If you were a writer for a daytime TV drama or a miniseries, you might have on your desk a copy of the *DSM–IV*, with the page turned down at somatoform and dissociative disorders. These disorders are relatively rare and are studied less than other disorders; however, they are fascinating to read about (and riveting as part of TV plots!).

Somatoform disorders comprise a broad class of psychological disorders that are characterized by real physical symptoms that are not under voluntary control and for which no apparent physical cause exists. Evidence suggests that the causes are psychological. Three types of somatoform disorders are somatization disorder, conversion disorder, and hypochondriasis. Many people suffering from these disorders are also diagnosed as having personality disorders, which we'll discuss later (Bass & Murphy, 1995).

Somatization Disorder. **Somatization disorder** is a somatoform disorder characterized by recurrent and multiple physical complaints of several years' duration for which medical attention has been ineffective. Despite physicians' inability to help, those with the disorder tend to seek medical attention at least once a year. The disorder typically appears before age 30. It is diagnosed in only about 1% of females and is even rarer in males.

Patients with this disorder feel sickly for much of their lives and may report muscle weakness, double vision, memory loss, and hallucinations. Other commonly reported symptoms include gastrointestinal problems, painful menstrual periods with excessive bleeding, sexual indifference, and pains in the back, chest, and genitals. Anxiety and depression often beset patients.

Individuals with somatization disorder often have a host of emotional problems that cause their physical complaints. However, like everyone else, they experience physical problems that are not psychologically caused, and physicians must be especially careful to address conditions that need medical treatment and not to dismiss all of a patient's problems as psychological.

Conversion Disorder. **Conversion disorder** is a somatoform disorder characterized by the loss or alteration of physical functioning for no apparent physiological reason. People suffering from conversion disorder often lose the use of their arms, hands, or legs or their vision or another sense. They may develop a combination of ailments. For example, a patient may become not only blind but also deaf, mute, or totally paralyzed. Although patients may be unaware of the relationship, conversion disorder is generally considered to be a way to escape from or avoid upsetting situations. Also, the attention and support patients sometimes receive because of the symptoms may cause them to maintain the disorder. Conversion disorder is often associated with a history of psychosomatic illness. Men and women are equally likely to develop conversion disorder, which, like somatization disorder, is rare. Interestingly, those suffering from conversion disorder often do not seem especially concerned about their loss of functioning—this is in contrast with hypochondriasis, considered next.

Hypochondriasis. When a person spends a lot of time going to physicians with all types of bodily complaints for which the physicians can find no cause, psychologists suspect hypochondriasis. **Hypochondriasis** is a somatoform disorder characterized by an inordinate preoccupation with health and illness, coupled with excessive anxiety about disease. Hypochondriacs believe, erroneously, that they have grave afflictions that might be fatal. They become preoccupied with minor aches and pains and often miss work and create alarm among family members. Every ache, every minor symptom is examined, interpreted, and feared.

Somatoform [so-MAT-oh-form] disorders: Psychological disorders characterized by real physical symptoms that are not under voluntary control and for which no apparent physical cause exists.

Somatization disorder: Somatoform disorder characterized by recurrent and multiple physical complaints of several years' duration for which medical attention has been ineffective.

Conversion disorder: Somatoform disorder characterized by the loss or alteration of physical functioning for no apparent physiological reason.

Hypochondriasis [hy-po-kon-DRY-a-sis]: Somatoform disorder characterized by an inordinate preoccupation with health and illness, coupled with excessive anxiety about disease.

Psychodynamic views of hypochondriasis focus on how the symptoms of the illness keep the person from dealing with some other painful source of stress. Behavioral psychologists focus on how the illness can be reinforcing: People are given extra attention and care, and the illness diverts attention from tasks at which the individual may not be succeeding. By focusing on illness, a person may avoid dealing with marital problems, financial affairs, or educational goals. Of course, to the hypochondriac, the fears and anxiety are real. Only through psychotherapy can their true causes be addressed.

Dissociative Disorders

Dissociative disorders are psychological disorders characterized by a sudden but temporary alteration in consciousness, identity, sensory/motor behavior, or memory. Although relatively rare, these disorders are easily identifiable. They include dissociative amnesia and dissociative identity disorder.

Dissociative Amnesia. Dissociative amnesia (formerly called *psychogenic amnesia*) is a dissociative disorder characterized by the sudden and extensive inability to recall important personal information, usually information of a traumatic or stressful nature. The memory loss is too extensive to be explained as ordinary forgetfulness. Dissociative amnesia is not the same as amnesia due to head trauma—in that case, there is an organic cause for the problem. Often, dissociative amnesia is brought on by a traumatic incident involving the threat of physical injury or death. The condition, which is relatively rare, occurs most often during wars or natural disasters.

Despite the impression given by popular movies and books, dissociative identity disorder is an extremely rare disorder.

Dissociative Identity Disorder: Multiple Personality. Another form of dissociative disorder, often associated with dissociative amnesia but presenting a dramatically different kind of behavior, is **dissociative identity disorder,** more commonly known as *multiple personality.* Dissociative identity disorder is characterized by the existence within an individual of two or more distinct personalities, each of which is dominant at different times and directs the individual's behavior at those times. The person with the disorder often gives the various personalities different names, and their identities may differ quite sharply from the person's principal identity. A person with dissociative identity disorder usually cannot recall what occurs when one of the alternate personalities is controlling the person's behavior. Each personality has unique traits, memories, and behavioral patterns. For example, one personality may be adaptive and efficient at coping with life, while another may exhibit maladaptive behavior. Some people's alternate personalities are of the opposite sex. Each of the alternate personalities is sometimes aware of the other ones (Putnam & Carlson, 1998; Schacter et al., 1989; Steinberg, 1995). Each personality, when active, acknowledges that time has gone by but cannot account for it. The switch from one personality to another is usually brought on by stress.

Despite the impression given by popular movies and books, dissociative identity disorder is an extremely rare disorder, with only a few hundred well-documented cases on record. Many people confuse multiple personality with schizophrenia, a much more common disorder that we'll examine later in this chapter (Steinberg et al., 1994).

Psychologists have little data on the causes of dissociative identity disorder and debate about how best to classify it (Gleaves, 1996). Some doubt whether multiple personality actually exists; some assert that it exists but that practitioners don't recognize it (Huapaya, 1994; Lowenstein, 1993). Other psychologists assert that it can nearly always be traced back to severe, prolonged child abuse. Some psychologists think that people invent multiple personalities to avoid taking responsibility for their own behavior, especially when they have committed criminal acts. Others think that some therapists subtly encourage patients to show symptoms of this disorder so that the therapists can

Dissociative disorders: Psychological disorders characterized by a sudden but temporary alteration in consciousness, identity, sensory/motor behavior, or memory.

Dissociative amnesia: Dissociative disorder characterized by the sudden and extensive inability to recall important personal information, usually of a traumatic or stressful nature.

Dissociative identity disorder: Dissociative disorder characterized by the existence within an individual of two or more distinct personalities, each of which is dominant at different times and directs the individual's behavior at those times; commonly known as *multiple personality.*

Personality disorders: Psychological disorders characterized by inflexible and long-standing maladaptive behaviors that typically cause stress and/or social or occupational problems.

Antisocial personality disorder: Personality disorder characterized by egocentricity, behavior that is irresponsible and that violates the rights of other people, a lack of guilt feelings, an inability to understand other people, and a lack of fear of punishment.

achieve recognition. In any case, dissociative identity disorder is vivid and interesting, and much more research is needed before comprehensive theories and effective treatments will become available. (I)

Think Critically

- What are the implications of dissociative identity disorder for traditional theories of personality?

(I) Personality Disorders

Focus on issues and ideas

- The three broad classes of personality disorders based on people's behavior
- Understanding why antisocial personality disorder is so difficult to treat

People who exhibit inflexible and long-standing maladaptive behaviors that typically cause stress and/or social or occupational difficulties may have one of the **personality disorders.** Often, these disorders begin in childhood or adolescence and persist throughout adulthood. People with personality disorders are easy to spot but difficult to treat.

People with personality disorders are divided into three broad classes: (1) those whose behavior appears odd or eccentric, (2) those whose behavior is dramatic, emotional, and erratic, and (3) those who are fearful or anxious. We'll consider six specific personality disorders: paranoid, borderline, histrionic, narcissistic, antisocial, and dependent. In considering personality disorders, it is important to realize that the line separating normal from abnormal behavior—as well as the characteristics of each class of disorder sometimes can be blurry. Furthermore, a person with a personality disorder is often at high risk for other disorders; thus it is not uncommon for an individual to exhibit symptoms of two disorders simultaneously.

Paranoid Personality Disorder. Fitting into the first class, by showing odd or eccentric behavior, are people suffering from *paranoid personality disorder,* who have unwarranted feelings of persecution and who mistrust almost everyone. They are hypersensitive to criticism and have a restricted range of emotional responses. They have strong fears of being exploited and of losing control and independence. Sometimes they appear cold, humorless, and even scheming. As you might expect, people with paranoid personality disorder are suspicious and seldom able to form close, intimate relationships with others.

Borderline Personality Disorder. Fitting into the second behavior classification, individuals with *borderline personality disorder* have trouble with relationships; they show a pattern of instability in interpersonal relationships, self-image, and affect. In addition, they are often impulsive. They are sometimes suicidal; they report feelings of emptiness and are sometimes inappropriately angry. Easily bored and distracted, such individuals fear abandonment. Individuals with borderline personality disorder often sabotage or undermine themselves just before a goal is to be reached—for example, by dropping out of school just before graduation.

Histrionic Personality Disorder. Fitting into the second broad class, because of their dramatic, emotional, and erratic behaviors, are those people with *histrionic personality disorder.* Individuals with this disorder seek attention by exaggerating situations in their lives. They have stormy personal relationships, are excessively emotional, and demand constant reassurance and praise.

Narcissistic Personality Disorder. Closely related to histrionic personality disorder, and also classified in the second class, is *narcissistic personality disorder.* People with this disorder have an extremely exaggerated sense of self-importance, expect favors, and need constant admiration and attention. They show little concern for others, and they react to criticism with rage, shame, or humiliation.

Antisocial Personality Disorder. Perhaps the most widely recognized personality disorder in the second class is antisocial personality disorder. **Antisocial personality disorder** is characterized by egocentricity, behavior that is irresponsible and that violates the rights of other people (such as lying, theft, cheating, and other violations of social rules), a lack of guilt feelings, an inability to understand other people, and a lack of fear of punishment. Individuals with this disorder may be superficially charming, but their behavior is destructive and often reckless. To be diagnosed as having antisocial personality, a person must be at least 18 years old, and there must be evidence that a conduct disorder existed before age 13. A conduct disorder involves behavior violating the rights of other people, including aggression toward people or animals, deceitfulness, theft, and serious violations of rules (truancy or running away).

A person who frequently changes jobs, does not take proper care of his or her children, is arrested often, fails to pay bills, and lies constantly displays behaviors typical of antisocial personality disorder. Such individuals are relatively unsocialized; they are unwilling to conform to and live by society's rules, and their behavior often brings them into conflict with society. People with antisocial personality disorder consistently blame others for their behavior. They seldom feel guilt or learn from experience or punishment. The disorder occurs six times more often in men than in women. Cold-blooded killers, such as Charles Manson and Ted Bundy, display this disorder, although most people exhibit the disorder through less deadly and sensational behaviors. As many as 3% of all individuals may be diagnosed with antisocial personality disorder. But understanding of the disorder is incomplete because psychologists have mostly been able to study only the most extreme cases—those who have been convicted of serious crimes and are in prison.

Adopted children separated at birth from antisocial biological parents are likely to show antisocial behavior later in life; this and other evidence suggest a genetic (nature) contribution to the disorder (Lyons et al., 1995; Nigg & Goldsmith, 1994). Another fact that suggests a genetic contribution is that the nervous systems of people diagnosed with antisocial personality disorder seem to be different from those of normal people. When normal people do something wrong, their autonomic nervous systems react with symptoms of anxiety, such as fear, heart palpitations, and sweating. Evidence suggests that *decreased* autonomic arousal is characteristic of people with antisocial personality disorder (Patrick, 1994). These people do not function at sufficiently high levels of autonomic nervous system arousal, do not experience the physiological symptoms of anxiety, and thus do not learn to associate those symptoms with antisocial behavior.

On the environmental (nurture) side, some psychologists believe that poor child-rearing practices and unstable family situations render individuals with antisocial personality disorder unable to learn to feel fear and guilt and to avoid punishment. Such people seem to have learned maladaptive functioning from their family situations and consequently to have developed inappropriate behaviors. Also, the symptoms of antisocial personality disorder are often seen first in a person's interactions with family members (Ge et al., 1996). Family relationships become strained, and some people suffering with the disorder may become involved in domestic violence—including child abuse. Ge and his colleagues (1996) found that adopting children with negative behavioral characteristics, some of which may be biologically based, changes the way the adoptive family interacts—often not for the better. If the environmental viewpoint is correct, antisocial personality disorder may be a learned behavior.

The biological roots of antisocial personality disorder may derive from any of several sources: genetics, hormonal imbalances, serotonin depletion, or brain injury, for example. Further, abuse, neglect, domestic violence, or poverty may exacerbate any of the biological problems. As Black and Larson (1999) argue, biological forces may conspire with social forces to cause someone to develop antisocial personality disorder, but that person is not necessarily doomed to suffer it forever. Some people with the disorder do get better and lead more satisfying and productive lives—not all bad boys become bad men.

Dependent Personality Disorder. Fitting into the third behavioral classification, by acting fearful or anxious, are individuals with *dependent personality disorder.* Such people are submissive and clinging; they let others make all the important decisions in their lives. They try to appear pleasant and agreeable at all times. They act meek, humble, and affectionate in order to keep their protectors. Battered wives often suffer from the dependent personality disorder, which may be the result of the mistreatment they receive. Overprotective, authoritarian parenting seems to be a major initiating cause of dependency (Bornstein, 1992). *I*

Think Critically

- Do you think the autonomic nervous system might be trained in some way and thus help people with antisocial personality disorder?

I Mood Disorders

Focus on issues and ideas

- Distinguishing between bipolar disorder and major depression
- The prevalance and symptoms of major depression
- The biological and psychological causes of mood disorders
- How depressed individuals are at significantly greater risk for suicide than nondepressed individuals

Everyone experiences dark moods at one time or another. Ending a long-term intimate relationship, feeling overwhelmed during final exams, mourning the death of a close friend, and experiencing serious financial problems can all be sources of depression. We often

Table 13.4 Bipolar Disorder Involves Cycles of Mania and Depression

	Manic Behavior	Depressive Behavior
Emotional characteristics	Elation, euphoria Extreme sociability, expansiveness Impatience Distractibility Inflated self-esteem	Gloominess, hopelessness Social withdrawal Irritability
Cognitive characteristics	Desire for action Impulsiveness Talkativeness Grandiosity	Indecisiveness Slowness of thought Obsessive worrying about death Negative self-image Delusions of guilt Difficulty in concentrating
Motor characteristics	Hyperactivity Decreased need for sleep Sexual indiscretion Increased appetite	Fatigue Difficulty in sleeping Decreased sex drive Decreased appetite Decreased motor activity

refer to *depression* in a colloquial sense. But when people become so depressed or sad that a change occurs in their outlook and overt behavior, they may be suffering from *clinical depression*, a term that has a specific meaning for psychologists. Depression is considered to be a type of mood disorder. Mood disorders, which include bipolar disorder and depressive disorders, may sometimes be precipitated by a specific event, although for many individuals the symptoms develop gradually.

Bipolar Disorder

People who suffer from bipolar disorder feel that they have become a different person—an unhappier one. They experience a zest for living *and* a sense of despair. These feelings often alternate and, for some individuals, may do so in the course of a single hour. **Bipolar disorder,** which was originally known as *manic–depressive disorder,* gets its name from the fact that patients' behavior vacillates between two extremes: mania and depression. The *manic phase* is characterized by rapid speech, inflated self-esteem, impulsiveness, euphoria, and decreased need for sleep. People in the manic phase are easily distracted, get angry when things do not go their way, and seem to have boundless energy. A person in the *depressed phase,* which often follows the manic phase, is moody and sad, with feelings of hopelessness.

About 2 million Americans suffer from bipolar disorder; men and women are equally likely to be affected. People who suffer from bipolar disorder are often in their late 20s before they begin to manifest the symptoms overtly, and the disorder often continues throughout life. Bipolar disorder may go unrecognized and be underdiagnosed in children and adolescents (Bowring & Kovacs, 1992).

Patients with bipolar disorder can be relatively normal for a few days, weeks, or months between episodes of excitement and depression, or they can rapidly vacillate between the two moods. The key component of bipolar disorder is the shift from excited states to depressive states of sadness and hopelessness. The disorder seems to have a biological basis, and patients often respond fairly well to drug treatment, especially to lithium and other drugs that are considered second- and third-generation drugs (which we'll discuss in Chapter 14) (Barondes, 1998). Although those who take the appropriate medications for the disorder respond fairly well, many refuse to medicate themselves because it means forgoing the "highs" of the manic episodes. As many as 50% of individuals who suffer from bipolar disorder also exhibit maladaptive personality traits, such as obsessions and compulsions or extreme dependence or narcissism (Peselow, Sanfilipo, & Fieve, 1995). Table 13.4 lists the signs and symptoms of mania and depression in bipolar disorder.

Depressive Disorders

Bonnie Strickland, former president of the American Psychological Association, said during the 1988 APA annual meeting, "Depression has been called the

Bipolar disorder: Mood disorder originally known as manic–depressive disorder because it is characterized by behavior that vacillates between two extremes: mania and depression.

common cold of psychological disturbances . . . which underscores its prevalence but trivializes its impact." Strickland noted that at any time, about 14 million people are suffering from this disabling disorder. And many of those people are misdiagnosed or undiagnosed and are not receiving treatment, despite its availability (Hirschfeld et al., 1997).

"Depression has been called the common cold of psychological disturbances . . . which underscores its prevalence but trivializes its impact."

Depressed people are more than simply blue or sad. Depression is debilitating, dangerous, and overwhelming. **Depressive disorders** are mood disorders in which people show on a day-to-day basis extreme and persistent sadness, despair, and loss of interest in life's usual activities. The main difference between depressive disorders and bipolar disorder is that people with depressive disorders do not vacillate between excitement and depression; they tend to be depressed more often than not. One type of depressive disorder, major depressive disorder, is eight times more common than bipolar disorder.

Major depressive disorder, one of several depressive disorders, is characterized by loss of interest in almost all of life's usual activities; a sad, hopeless, or discouraged mood; sleep disturbance; loss of appetite; loss of energy; and feelings of unworthiness and guilt. Someone experiencing major depressive disorder is not merely experiencing fleeting anxiety or sadness, although this disorder may be triggered by a specific event, such as the loss of a loved one, a job, or a home. Sufferers show at least some impairment of social and occupational functioning, although their behavior is not necessarily bizarre.

Symptoms. The symptoms of major depressive disorder include poor appetite, insomnia, weight loss, loss of energy, feelings of worthlessness and intense guilt, inability to concentrate, and sometimes thoughts of death and suicide (Buchwald & Rudick-Davis, 1993). Depressed patients have a gloomy outlook on life, an extremely distorted view of their problems, a tendency to blame themselves, and low self-esteem (Maddux & Meier, 1995). They often withdraw from social and physical contact with others. Every task seems to require a great effort, thought is slow and unfocused, and problem-solving abilities are impaired. Individuals may display certain physical problems as well; for example, decrease in bone density and heightened risk of osteoporosis occur in those who suffer from depression, and depression is associated with abnormal brain activity in the frontal lobes and with immune system problems (George, Ketter, & Post, 1993; Herbert & Cohen, 1993; Schweiger et al., 1994).

Depressed people may also have **delusions**—false beliefs that are inconsistent with reality but are held in spite of evidence that disproves them. Delusions may induce feelings of guilt, shame, and persecution. Seriously disturbed patients show even greater disruptions in thought and motor processes and a total lack of spontaneity and motivation. Such patients typically report that they have no hope for themselves or the world; nothing seems to interest them. They are often extremely self-critical (Blatt, 1995). Some feel responsible for serious world problems such as economic depression, disease, or hunger. They report strange diseases and may insist that their body is disintegrating or that their brain is being eaten from the inside out. Most people who exhibit symptoms of major depressive disorder can describe their reasons for feeling sad and dejected; however, they may be unable to explain why their response is so deep and so prolonged.

Psychologists say that many people suffering from major depressive disorder are poor at reality testing. *Reality testing* is a person's ability to judge the demands of the environment accurately and to deal with those demands. People who are poor at reality testing are unable to cope with the demands of life in rational ways because their reasoning ability is grossly impaired.

Onset and Duration. A major depressive episode can occur at any age, although people who experience these episodes usually undergo the first one before age 40. Symptoms are readily apparent and last for a few days, weeks, or months. Because so many different circumstances can be involved, the extent of depression varies dramatically from individual to individual. Episodes may occur once or many times. Sometimes a depressive episode may be followed by years of normal functioning—followed by two or three brief incidents of depression a few weeks apart. Stressful life events are sometimes predictors of depression (Monroe, Simons, & Thase, 1991). Major depressive disorder is not exclusively an adult disorder; researchers find evidence of it in children and adolescents

Depressive disorders: General category of mood disorders in which people show extreme and persistent sadness, despair, and loss of interest in life's usual activities.

Major depressive disorder: Depressive disorder characterized by loss of interest in almost all of life's usual activities; a sad, hopeless, or discouraged mood; sleep disturbance; loss of appetite; loss of energy; and feelings of unworthiness and guilt.

Delusions: False beliefs that are inconsistent with reality but are held in spite of evidence that disproves them.

(Lewinsohn et al., 1999). When children suffer from depression, they often have other symptoms, especially anxiety and loneliness. Treatment plans must be flexible and must take into account the wide array of family situations in which children find themselves—situations that might include divorce or foster care, parental alcoholism, or child abuse, for example.

Prevalence. According to the National Institutes of Mental Health, major depressive disorder strikes about 14 to 15 million Americans each year. Women are two to three times as likely as men to be diagnosed as depressed and are more likely to express feelings of depression openly (Culbertson, 1997). In the United States, about 19–23% of women and 8–11% of men have experienced a major depressive episode at some time. About 6% of women and 3% of men have experienced episodes severe enough to require hospitalization. It is unclear why women experience depression more often than men do; research on gender differences in both causes and treatment is limited. However, girls may exhibit more passive and ruminating coping styles, which may be associated with longer and more severe depressive symptoms. Furthermore, girls may face more negative life events and social conditions, such as sexual abuse, and more complicated parental expectations than do boys (Nolen-Hoeksema, 1994).

According to several studies, Americans born since 1960 suffer up to ten times as many episodes of major depressive disorder as did their grandparents or great-grandparents (Lewinsohn et al., 1993). This may be due to changes in diagnosis or reporting frequency or perhaps to an increase in the stressors in society; the answer is not yet clear. In addition, people in developing cultures are far less likely to develop the passivity, feelings of hopelessness, diminished self-esteem, and suicidal tendencies that typify Westerners afflicted by major depressive disorder. Martin Seligman (1988) suggests that the increased incidence of depression in the United States stems from too much emphasis on the individual, coupled with a loss of faith in such supportive institutions as family, country, and religion.

Causes of Major Depressive Disorder

Most psychologists believe that major depressive disorder is caused by a combination of biological, learning, and cognitive factors. Biological theories suggest that chemical and genetic processes account for depression. Learning theories suggest that people develop faulty behaviors. Cognitive theories suggest that irrational ideas guide behavior. Those based on the concept of learned helplessness suggest that people may choose not to respond to life's multiple stresses, over which they feel they have little control, and instead give up. Let's look at each explanation in more detail.

Genetic Vulnerability and the Neurochemistry of Depression. Hundreds of thousands of people in the United States are taking medication daily for depression; Prozac, Zoloft, and Elavil have become household names. Researchers and clinicians have found that giving these medications to people who exhibit symptoms of depression lifts their depressed mood within a few weeks. People can get on with their lives, and at this point, they often initiate talking therapy. Practitioners who prescribe such medication make a fundamental assumption: Depression is caused by an imbalance of various substances in the brain. The causes of the imbalance are in dispute, but the practitioners know that in the great majority of cases, medications that alter the levels of certain neurotransmitters affect depression.

In the great majority of cases, medications that alter the levels of certain neurotransmitters affect depression.

If depression is biologically based, are some people born with a predisposition to it? It appears that depression may be genetically based, especially its most severe forms (Lyons et al., 1998). Children of depressed parents are more likely than other children to be depressed; further, twin studies indicate that genetic factors play a substantial role in depression (Barondes, 1998; Kendler et al., 1992; Kendler, Neale, Kessler et al., 1993). But most current research is focusing on the idea that, for whatever reason, depression is caused by an insufficient amount of some neurotransmitter in the brain. Research shows that if the level of key neurotransmitters at receptor sites in the brain is increased, depression is alleviated. Because traumatic events decrease such neurotransmitter levels, being in a stressful situation could bring about depression.

Knowledge of how drugs work to alleviate depression comes partly from researchers' understanding of how neurotransmitters move from one neuron to the next. Neurotransmitters held within synaptic vesicles in one neuron are released, move across the synapse, and bind to receptor sites on an adjacent neuron. (See Chapter 2, pp. 35–36.) The receptors have binding sites for particular neurotransmitters. This is an important point, because a specific neurotransmitter can and will influence only those cells that have receptors for it. Four of the key neurotransmitters in the brain are dopamine, norepinephrine,

epinephrine, and serotonin, all of which are categorized chemically as *monoamines.*

When monoamines are released but do not bind to the next neuron, researchers find that patients report feeling depressed. What happens is that the neurotransmitter is then either neutralized or taken back up by the neuron that released it, in a process called *reuptake.* (Again, see Chapter 2 for a review of this process.) When a person is given drugs that do not allow the neurotransmitters to be neutralized or restored to the releasing cell, the neurotransmitter is more likely to bind, and depression is averted.

With each passing month, there is new support for what researchers generally call the *monoamine theory of depression,* which suggests that major depression results from a deficiency of monoamines or inefficient monoamine receptors (Mann et al., 1996; Soares & Mann, 1997). The monoamine theory of depression is based on the finding that three classes of drugs—monoamine inhibitors, tricyclics, and serotonin-reuptake inhibitors—block the reuptake of monoamines (especially serotonin and norepinephrine). The evidence in support of this theory comes from genetic studies, studies of the effectiveness of selective serotonin-reuptake inhibitors, and studies of reduced levels of serotonin.

Remember that the brain has about 10 billion receptors, so the process is anything but simple. For example, the monoamine neurotransmitter serotonin plays a complicated role, and there are at least seven families of closely chemically related neurotransmitters. Thus, there are many drug variations that can be devised to block reuptake. One of those drugs, Prozac, has received a great deal of media attention because it is prescribed so widely and has helped so many people. Research continues on a wide variety of substances. For example, substance P, which has been used as a pain reliever, has recently been found to have antidepressant qualities (Kramer et al., 1998). It is likely that this drug, along with others yet to be discovered, will drastically change the pharmacological treatment of depression in the next few years.

Even though monoamines and other drugs seem to affect depression, it is not clear how they work. For example, in a patient who takes a serotonin-reuptake inhibitor, alleviation of depression takes weeks to occur, but changes in blood levels of neurotransmitters happen in days; this inconsistency is hard to understand. In addition, some other drugs that also block monoamine reuptake do not have antidepressant effects. Further, despite the availability of dozens of approved antidepressant drugs, relief for many patients remains elusive. Widely respected researchers such as Elliot Valenstein (1998) have questioned brain chemistry explanations of depression and argue that a quick fix via the use of pills is not the whole answer. Others agree. The next decade of research should prove illuminating because, as we will see in Chapter 14, some researchers assert that a talking therapy is as effective or more effective than drug therapy (Antonuccio, Danton, & DeNelsky, 1995).

Learned helplessness: The behavior of giving up or not responding, exhibited by people and animals exposed to negative consequences or punishment over which they feel they have no control.

Vulnerability: A person's diminished ability to deal with demanding life events.

Learning and Cognitive Theories. Learning and cognitive theorists argue that people learn depressive behaviors and thoughts. People with poor social skills who never learn to express prosocial behaviors and who are punished for the behaviors they do exhibit experience the world as aversive and depressing. In support of this idea is the finding that children of depressed parents, having been exposed to so many depressive behaviors, are more likely than other children to be depressed (Downey & Coyne, 1990). (A problem with this argument, of course, is that children of depressed parents are biologically related to them—so it is hard to separate nurture from nature.) In addition, Peter Lewinsohn (1974) believes that people who have few positive reinforcements in their lives (often the old, the sickly, and the poor) become depressed. Other people find them unpleasant to be with and avoid them, thus creating a nonreinforcing environment (Lewinsohn & Talkington, 1979). Lewinsohn stresses that depressed people often lack the social skills needed to obtain reinforcement, such as asking a neighbor or friend for help with a problem.

Psychiatrist Aaron Beck proposed another influential learning theory. Beck (1967) suggested that depressed people already have negative views of themselves, the environment, and the future, and these views cause them to magnify their errors. They compare themselves to other people, usually unfairly; when they come up short, they see the difference as disastrous. They see the human condition as universally wretched and view the world as a place that defeats positive behavior. Their poor self-concept and negative expectations about the world lead to depression. All of this is magnified in adolescents, who are going through many bodily changes that may heighten their risk of depression (Allgood-Merten, Lewinsohn, & Hops, 1990).

Beck (1967, 1972, 1976) theorized that depression does not cause negative feelings but that negative feelings and expectations cause depression. Research supports Beck's theory. Depressed people are harsher on themselves than nondepressed people are, and they have particularly low self-expectations and self-esteem

(Maddux, 1995). They make judgments based on insufficient data, they overgeneralize, and they exaggerate the negative outcomes in their lives. According to Beck, being depressed causes poor judgments and thus affects people's cognitions. Beck's theory is influential among psychologists for two reasons: First, it is consistent with the notion that depression stems from a lack of appropriate positive reinforcements in the environment. Second, it acknowledges both cognitive and environmental variables such as family interactions.

Learned Helplessness. What would you do if you failed every exam you took, regardless of your efforts? What happens when a person's hopes and dreams are constantly thwarted, regardless of her or his behavior? The result may be **learned helplessness**—the behavior of giving up or not responding, exhibited by people and animals exposed to negative consequences or punishment over which they feel they have no control.

Seligman (1976) has suggested that people's beliefs about the causes of their failures determine whether they will become depressed. When they attribute their failures to unalterable conditions within themselves ("my own weakness, which is unlikely to change"), their self-esteem is diminished (Maddux & Meier, 1995). People who develop learned helplessness feel that they cannot change highly aversive life events (Abramson, Metalsky, and Alloy, 1989). That is, when people come to believe that outcomes are unrelated to anything under their control, they develop learned helplessness and become pessimistic rather than optimistic. For example, a man who comes to believe that his effort to meet new people by being outgoing and friendly never works may stop trying. Eventually, he will choose not to respond to the environment, because he has learned that his behavior makes no difference (Peterson & Seligman, 1984). According to Seligman, the major cause of learned helplessness is a person's or animal's belief that its response will not affect what happens to it in the future. The result of this belief is anxiety, depression, and, eventually, nonresponsiveness. The opposite of learned helplessness is *learned optimism*—a sense that the world has positive outcomes, which leads people to see happy things in their lives (Seligman, 1991). Seligman asserts that *learning* is key to developing a sense of doom or optimism. Seligman (1988) argues that the environment, not genetics, is the cause of pessimism, depression, and helplessness, especially when people believe that they are responsible for long-standing failures in many areas of their lives.

The idea that learned helplessness is a key factor in depression has received research support, although how it operates is not yet fully understood (Joiner & Wagner, 1995; Overmier & Gahtan, 1998). The effects of learned helplessness are poignant and painful. They influence a person's day-to-day life, work environment, and family roles. People who develop learned helplessness assume that their depression will last forever and blame themselves most of the time. Such self-blame is a typically Western idea, in that people assume personal responsibility for their acts; in non-Western cultures, in contrast, cooperative efforts are stressed more.

A Vicious Cycle. Many variables determine whether an individual will develop depression, or any other disorder, for that matter. Some people—because of family environment, genetic history, or brain chemistry—are more vulnerable than others. **Vulnerability** is a person's diminished ability to deal with demanding life events. The more vulnerable a person is, the less necessary environmental stress or other factors (such as anxiety) are to the initiation of depression. This is the vulnerability–stress hypothesis, sometimes termed the *diathesis–stress model.*

The more vulnerable a person is, the less necessary environmental stress or other factors (such as anxiety) are to the initiation of depression.

Some people lack good social skills, and this puts them at a disadvantage. They say the wrong things, behave awkwardly, and find few reinforcers in their lives. Needless to say, this leads to negative thinking. To a substantial extent, these thoughts affect, even determine, depression. At the same time, depression determines thoughts. Adding one or more stressful life experiences and a sense of learned helplessness to the mix creates a vicious cycle of events that keep a person feeling depressed. And when depressed, people are often irritable and pessimistic, and they tend to annoy people around them—they're sort of depressing. The consequence is that people avoid them—which gives yet another cause to feel bad. This "common cold" of psychiatric disturbances affects millions, leaves them feeling as if they were in a dark, lonely place, struggling, feeling deficient and incapable of moving ahead. Unmanaged, this vicious cycle leads to self-blame, further isolation, loneliness—and sometimes to suicide.

Suicide

Depressed individuals are at greater risk for suicide than nondepressed individuals. Fortunately, most

people who think about suicide do not actually commit the act. But when people become depressed and feel hopeless, the likelihood that they will commit suicide increases sharply, especially among older white males (Rifai et al., 1994). Each day, about 80 people in the United States commit suicide; that's almost 30,000 people each year. People who commit suicide believe things cannot and will not get better, and that suicide is their best resolution. They are unable to see their other options because they are so distressed.

A distinction must be drawn between attempters and completers. *Attempters* try to commit suicide but are unsuccessful. They tend to be young, impulsive, more often women than men, and more likely to make nonfatal attempts such as making only shallow cuts on the wrists. *Completers* succeed in taking their lives. They tend to be white, male, and older, and they use highly lethal techniques of self-destruction, such as handguns. Although estimates vary with age and gender, there are an estimated 10–25 attempted suicides for every completion.

Who commits suicide? More than four times as many men as women actually succeed in ending their lives, although twice as many women as men attempt (but fail) to do so (Weissman et al., 1999). Among adolescents, suicide is the second leading cause of death (after accidents); for adults, it is the ninth leading cause of death. Each year, 1 out of every 1,000 adolescents attempts suicide, and nearly 5,000 young people between the ages of 15 and 24 are successful (Garland & Zigler, 1993). The elderly, the divorced, and those previously treated for psychological disorders have a higher likelihood than others of attempting and committing suicide. In fact, the elderly make up 23% of those who commit suicide. Alcoholics have a high rate of suicide, as do Native Americans, partly because alcoholism is a common problem for them (Murphy et al., 1992; Young & French, 1993). People who have been suffering from major depression are more likely to attempt suicide while they are recovering, when their energy level is higher, than at the depths of depression; during the worst of a depressive episode, a person is usually too distracted and lacking in energy to commit suicide. Although only 15% of depressed people are suicidal, most suicide-prone individuals are depressed.

Are there warning signs of suicide? Research shows that predicting suicide is difficult, but not impossible (Shneidman, 1994). There are several indicators: changes in personal appearance, a dramatic drop in quality of school or job performance, changes in drug abuse patterns, decreased appetite, and the giving away of prized possessions. Most important, nearly everyone who is suicidal exhibits depression, shown by changes in sleeping patterns (especially insomnia), a diminished ability to concentrate, fatigue, feelings of worthlessness, and decreased problem-solving abilities (Hughes & Neimeyer, 1993). In addition, 86% of those who are successful have attempted suicide before. Clearly, suicide attempters may become suicide completers if no one intervenes.

Causes. For some individuals who take their own lives, societal pressures serve as a catalyst for suicide. For others, the catalyst may be the responsibility of caring for aging parents, substance abuse that impairs judgment, or some traumatic event. For still other people, a long-standing series of psychological disorders may predispose them to suicide. The psychological antecedents of suicide are about the same in non-Western as in Western cultures (Cheng, 1995). Table 13.5 presents some of the many myths about suicide and counters them with facts.

Psychologists cite a broad array of factors that may influence a suicide attempt. *Biological psychologists* assert that genetics plays a role (Roy et al., 1999) and that certain neurotransmitters, especially serotonin, have been linked to disorders that predispose individuals to suicide; for example, research shows that there are alterations in the serotonin system of those who attempt and complete suicide (Mann et al., 1999). *Behavioral psychologists* suggest that past experiences with suicide reinforce people's attempts to commit suicide—other people who have taken their lives may serve as models for suicidal behavior. *Psychodynamically oriented psychologists* suggest that the suicidal person is turning hostility and anger inward. Freud might argue that the act of suicide is the ultimate release of the aggressive instinct. *Cognitive psychologists* assert that suicide is the failure of a person's problem-solving abilities in response to stress or,

Table 13.5 Myths and Facts about Suicide

Myth	Fact
1. Suicide happens without warning.	1. Suicidal individuals give many clues; 80% have to some degree discussed with others their intent to commit suicide.
2. Once people become suicidal, they remain so.	2. Suicidal persons remain so for limited periods—thus the value of restraint.
3. Suicide occurs almost exclusively among affluent or very poor individuals.	3. Suicide tends to occur in the same proportion at all economic levels of society.
4. Virtually all suicidal individuals are mentally ill.	4. This is not so, although most are depressed to some degree.
5. Suicidal tendencies are inherited or run in families.	5. There is no evidence for a direct genetic factor.
6. Suicide does not occur in primitive cultures.	6. Suicide occurs in almost all societies and cultures.
7. In Japan, ritual suicide is common.	7. In modern Japan, ritual suicide is rare; the most common method is barbiturate overdose.
8. Writers and artists have the highest suicide rates because they are "a bit crazy to begin with."	8. Physicians and police officers have the highest suicide rates; they have access to the most lethal means, and their work involves a high level of frustration.
9. Once a person starts to come out of a depression, the risk of suicide dissipates.	9. The risk of suicide is highest in the initial phase of an upswing from the depth of depression.
10. People who attempt suicide fully intend to die.	10. People who attempt suicide have diverse motives.

Source: Meyer & Salmon, 1988.

alternatively, that the person's cognitive assessment is that the future is hopeless. *Humanistic psychologists* see suicide as the end result of a feeling that life offers nothing of value, and they attempt to help suicidal patients focus on what is meaningful in their lives so that they can fulfill rather than destroy themselves. Many theorists, regardless of orientation, focus on a person's attempt to avoid self-awareness (Baumeister, 1990).

Adolescent suicide has received a great deal of attention because it is increasingly prevalent. The suicide rate among teenage males is six times higher than that among teenage females (O'Donnell, 1995), and 60% of all youths aged 15 to 19 who commit suicide use a gun. Adolescents who attempt suicide often see a wide discrepancy between their high personal ambitions and actual outcomes. The causes of adolescent suicide are not fully understood, but the increasing pressures and stress encountered by adolescents in the United States today certainly contribute to the rising number of suicides. Adolescents face an extremely competitive work force, alternating pressures to conform and to be an individual, and a social situation teeming with violence, crime, and drugs. Often, angry and frustrated adolescents exhibit self-destructive behaviors, such as drug use, in addition to feeling hopelessness and low self-esteem (Kashani, Reid, & Rosenberg, 1989). Prevention efforts must focus on counseling, education, and reduction of the risk factors that lead to suicide.

Prevention. Most individuals who attempt suicide really want to live. However, their sense of helplessness about the future tells them that death is the only way out. Some people are helped by crisis intervention and by counselors on suicide hotlines. But a primary goal should be to help eliminate conditions that lead to and foster suicide, including alcoholism, drug abuse, emotional isolation, and the ready availability of guns (Maris & Silverman, 1995).

When a person makes a suicide threat, take it seriously. Most people who commit suicide leave clues to their intentions ahead of time. Statements such as "I don't want to go on" or "I'm a burden to everyone, so maybe I should end it all" should be taken as warning signs. When people begin to give things away or to write letters with ominous overtones to relatives and friends, these are signs, too.

If you know someone you think may be contemplating suicide, here are some steps you can take (Curran, 1987):

- Talk about stressors with the person who is at risk. The more a suicidal individual talks, the better. Don't be afraid to talk about suicide; it will not influence your friend or relative in favor of that act.
- Help the person who is contemplating suicide to seek out a psychologist, psychiatrist, counselor, or parent. A person thinking of suicide needs counseling.
- Do not keep a contemplated suicide a secret. Resist the person's attempts to force you to remain quiet about his or her confidences. Tell the person's spouse, parent, guardian, or counselor.

Bipolar and depressive disorders leave people unable to cope effectively on a day-to-day basis. An even more disabling disorder is schizophrenia, which we examine next.

Think Critically

- What are the implications of the finding that many people who experience manic episodes also suffer from personality disorders?
- How might Szasz (who claimed mental illness is just a label) explain the behavior of a person showing depressive symptoms?
- If you have known someone who committed suicide, do the psychological theories you've just studied seem to apply to that person? Why or why not?

Schizophrenia

Focus on issues and ideas

- The key symptoms of schizophrenia
- Identifying the five types of schizophrenia
- The role of nature versus nurture in schizophrenia

Schizophrenic [SKIT-soh-FREN-ick] disorders: A group of psychological disorders characterized by a lack of reality testing and by deterioration of social and intellectual functioning and personality, beginning before age 45 and lasting at least 6 months.

Psychotic [sye-KOT-ick]: Suffering from a gross impairment in reality testing that interferes with the ability to meet the ordinary demands of life.

Schizophrenia is considered the most devastating, puzzling, and frustrating of all mental disorders; people with this disorder lose touch with reality and are often unable to function in a world that makes no sense to them. The word *schizophrenia* comes from two Greek words that together mean "split mind," and the split refers to the fragmentation of thought processes. In 1911, when one of the most influential psychiatrists of the time, Eugen Bleuler, coined the term, he recognized that people suffer from schizophrenia when they have seriously disorganized thinking, perceptions, emotions, and actions. (A caution—schizophrenia is not split personality. People sometimes confuse the notion of a "split mind" with dissociative identity disorder, which is characterized by the existence within one person of two or more distinct personalities; that disorder was covered earlier in this chapter, on p. 374.)

A person with schizophrenia is said to have a schizophrenic disorder; this is because schizophrenia is really a range of disorders. **Schizophrenic disorders** are a group of disorders characterized by a lack of reality testing and by deterioration of social and intellectual functioning, beginning before age 45 and lasting at least 6 months. People diagnosed as having a schizophrenic disorder often show serious personality disintegration. They may be **psychotic**—suffering from a gross impairment in reality testing that is wide-ranging and interferes with their ability to meet the ordinary demands of life.

Schizophrenia begins slowly, with more symptoms developing as time passes. It affects 1 out of every 100 people in the United States and accounts for almost 25% of all mental hospital admissions each year. There are about 100,000 schizophrenic patients in public mental hospitals. The diagnosis is applied more frequently to those in lower socioeconomic groups, to nonwhites, and to younger people (Lindsey & Paul, 1989). African Americans are more likely than whites to be diagnosed as schizophrenic. Cultural biases against poor people and nonwhites, as well as these groups' higher stress levels, may account for these higher diagnosis rates.

Essential Characteristics of Schizophrenic Disorders

People with schizophrenic disorders display sudden significant changes in thought, perception, mood, and overall behavior. How they think about themselves, social situations, and other people—their social cognition—becomes seriously distorted (Penn et al., 1997). Those changes are often accompanied by distortions of reality and an inability to respond with appropriate thoughts, perceptions, or emotions. Some symptoms are *positive symptoms*, exhibited by their presence—for example, delusions or hallucinations. Some symptoms are *negative symptoms*, exhibited by their absence—for example, an inability to experience pleasure. Not all of the symptoms of a schizophrenic disorder are necessarily present in any given patient, although many are often seen together.

Thought Disorders. One of the first signs of schizophrenia is difficulty maintaining logical thought and coherent conversation. People with schizophrenic disorders show disordered thinking and impaired memory (Sengel & Lovallo, 1983). They may also suffer from *delusions*. Many have delusions of persecution and believe that the world is a hostile place. These delusions are often accompanied by delusions of grandeur, which cause the patient to believe that he or she is a particularly important person. This importance becomes the reason for the persecution. Some patients take on the role of an important character in history—for example, Jesus Christ or the Queen of England—and imagine that people are conspiring to harm them. Delusional thought is often apparent in schizophrenics' speech, in which sentence structure, words, and ideas become jumbled and disordered, creating a "word salad" of thoughts.

Perceptual Disorders. Another sign of schizophrenic disorders is the presence of *hallucinations*—compelling perceptual (visual, tactile, olfactory, or auditory) experiences that occur without any actual physical stimulus. Auditory hallucinations are the most common. The patient reports hearing voices originating outside his or her head. The voices may comment on the patient's behavior or direct the patient to behave in certain ways (Bentall, 1990). Hallucinations have a biological basis; they are caused by abnormal brain responses (Asaad & Shapiro, 1986).

Emotional Disorders. One of the most striking characteristics of schizophrenia is the display of *inappropriate affect*—emotional responses that do not fit the circumstances. A patient with schizophrenia may become depressed and cry when her favorite food falls on the floor, yet laugh hysterically at the death of a close friend or relative. Some patients display no emotion (either appropriate or inappropriate) and seem incapable of experiencing a normal range of feeling. Their affect is constricted, or *flat*. Their faces are blank and expressionless, even when they are presented with a deliberately provocative remark or situation. Other patients exhibit *ambivalent* affect. They go through a wide range of emotional behaviors in a brief period, seeming happy one moment and dejected the next.

Types of Schizophrenia

The term *schizophrenia* is a catchall for patients displaying many symptoms; however, there are actually five types of schizophrenia: disorganized, paranoid, catatonic, residual, and undifferentiated. Each of these has different symptoms, diagnostic criteria, and causes (see Table 13.6). Regardless of the type, a diagnosis of schizophrenia requires the presence of the following features:

- Lack of reality testing
- Involvement of more than one area of psychological functioning
- Deterioration in social and intellectual functioning
- Onset generally occurring before age 45
- Duration of at least 6 months

Table 13.6 Types and Symptoms of Schizophrenia

Type	Symptoms
Disorganized	Frequent incoherence; disorganized behavior; blunted, inappropriate, or silly affect
Paranoid	Delusions and hallucinations of persecution or grandeur (or both) and sometimes irrational jealousy
Catatonic	Stupor in which there is a negative attitude and marked decrease in reactivity to the environment, or an excited phase in which there is agitated motor activity not influenced by external stimuli and which may appear or disappear suddenly
Residual	History of at least one previous episode of schizophrenia with prominent psychotic symptoms but at present a clinical picture without any prominent psychotic symptoms; continuing evidence of the illness, such as inappropriate affect, illogical thinking, social withdrawal, or eccentric behavior
Undifferentiated	Prominent delusions, hallucinations, incoherence, or grossly disorganized behavior, which do not meet the criteria for any other types or which meet the criteria for more than one type

Disorganized Type. The **disorganized type of schizophrenia** is characterized by severely disturbed thought processes, frequent incoherence, disorganized behavior, and inappropriate affect. Patients may exhibit bizarre emotions, with periods of giggling, crying, or irritability for no apparent reason. Their behavior can be silly or even obscene. They show a severe disintegration of normal personality, a total lack of reality testing, and often poor personal hygiene. Their chances for recovery are poor. Ted Kaczynski, known as the Unabomber, refused to allow prosecution psychiatrists to examine him, although he exhibited a mental deterioration that convinced many that his crimes were the product of schizophrenia.

Paranoid Type. The paranoid type of schizophrenia is one of the most difficult to identify and study, because outward behavior often seems appropriate to the situation. The **paranoid type of schizophrenia** is characterized by hallucinations and delusions of persecution or grandeur (or both), and sometimes irrational jealousy. Paranoid schizophrenics may actively seek out other people rather than withdrawing from social interaction. Their degree of disturbance varies over time. (The paranoid type of schizophrenia is different from the paranoid personality disorder, which was discussed on p. 375 and which is less likely to have a biological cause.)

Paranoid schizophrenics may be alert, intelligent, and responsive. However, their delusions and hallucinations impair their ability to deal with reality, and their behavior is often unpredictable and sometimes hostile. They may see bizarre images and are likely to have auditory hallucinations. They may think they are being chased by ghosts or by intruders from another planet. They may believe certain world events are particularly significant to them. If, for example, the president of the United States makes a speech deploring crime, a paranoid schizophrenic patient may believe that the president is referring specifically to his or her own behavior. Patients with the paranoid type of schizophrenia have a better chance of recovery than do patients with other types of schizophrenia.

Catatonic Type. The **catatonic type of schizophrenia** is characterized either by displays of excited or violent motor activity or by stupor. That is, there are actually two subtypes of the catatonic type of schizophrenia—excited and withdrawn. Both of these involve extreme overt behavior. *Excited* catatonic patients show excessive activity. They may talk and shout continuously and engage in seemingly uninhibited, agitated, and aggressive motor activity. These episodes usually appear and disappear suddenly. *Withdrawn* catatonic patients tend to appear stuporous—mute and basically unresponsive. Although they occasionally exhibit some signs of the excited type, they usually show a high degree of muscular rigidity. They are not immobile, but they speak, move, and respond very little, although they are usually aware of events around them. Withdrawn catatonic patients may use immobility and unresponsiveness to maintain control over their environment; their behavior relieves them of the responsibility of responding to external stimuli.

Residual and Undifferentiated Type. People who show symptoms attributable to schizophrenia but who remain in touch with reality are said to have the **residual type of schizophrenia.** Such patients show inappropriate affect, illogical thinking, and/or eccentric behavior. They have a history of at least one previous schizophrenic episode.

Sometimes it is difficult to determine which category a specific patient best fits into (Gift et al., 1980). Some patients exhibit all the essential features of schizophrenia—prominent delusions, hallucinations, incoherence, and grossly disorganized behavior—but do not fit neatly into the category of disorganized, catatonic, paranoid, or residual. Individuals with these characteristics are said to have the **undifferentiated type of schizophrenia.**

Causes of Schizophrenia

What causes schizophrenics to lose their grasp on reality with such devastating results? Are people born with schizophrenia, or do they develop it as a result of painful childhood experiences? Researchers take markedly different positions on the origins of schizophrenia. Biologically oriented psychologists focus on chemicals in the brain and a person's genetic heritage; their basic argument is that schizophrenia is a brain disease. Learning theorists argue that a person's environment and early experiences cause schizophrenia. The arguments for each approach are compelling, but most theorists adopt a *diathesis–stress model,* asserting that people with an underlying genetic predisposition or vulnerability develop a schizophrenic disorder when they are beset with a stressful life situation. Let's look at the data.

Biological Causes. Substantial evidence suggests the presence of some kind of biological determinant of, or predisposition to, schizophrenia. People born with that predisposition have a greater probability of developing schizophrenia than do other people. In the early or middle stages of fetal development, brain connections may go awry and result in later cerebral malfunctioning (Waddington, 1993). This may occur because key RNA molecules may be missing when the major neurotransmitters, such as GABA (discussed in Chapter 2), are forming (Akbarian et al., 1995). Using this evidence, researchers assert that schizophrenia is caused by brain chemistry and perhaps an impaired autonomic nervous system response (Hollister et al., 1994).

About 1% of the U.S. population is schizophrenic. When one parent has schizophrenia, the probability that an offspring will develop the disorder is between 3% and 14%. If both parents have schizophrenia, their children have about a 35% probability of developing it. It is now generally accepted that schizophrenia runs in families; the children and siblings of schizophrenic patients are more likely to exhibit maladjustment and schizophrenic symptoms than are other people (Kety et al., 1994). Researchers have been looking for a gene that might carry specific traits associated with schizophrenia, although such efforts have had only limited success (Markow, 1992).

Researchers are aware that the family environment of children of schizophrenics is unusual. Thus, they acknowledge that the genetic evidence is only suggestive and that environment is also likely to play a role in the development of the disorder. If schizophrenia were totally genetic, the likelihood that identical (monozygotic) twins, who have identical genes, would both show the disorder if one did would be 100%. This kind of estimate of the degree to which a condition or trait is shared by two or more individuals or groups is referred to as a **concordance rate.** But studies of schizophrenia in identical twins show concordance rates that range from 15% to 86% (DiLalla & Gottesman, 1995), suggesting that other factors are involved. In one important study, analysis of brain structures showed subtle but important brain abnormalities in a schizophrenic individual whose identical twin did not show the abnormality. Such studies support the hypothesis that nongenetic factors must exert an important influence on schizophrenia and are critical in its development (DiLalla & Gottesman, 1995). Nevertheless, most researchers agree that genetic background is a fundamental factor in the disorder. The concordance rate for schizophrenia in identical twins is almost five times that in fraternal twins. Moreover, identical twins reared apart from their natural parents and from each other show a higher concordance rate than do fraternal twins or controls (Stone, 1980).

Support for a biological basis for schizophrenia comes from other sources as well, notably studies of biochemical processes and drugs. Like many discoveries in science, the discovery of the first antischizophrenia drug—chlorpromazine—happened by accident in the 1950s. First used as an antihistamine, the drug was found to have calming effects on patients, including agitated schizophrenic patients. This drug was followed by others, such as reserpine, leading to further breakthroughs in drug treatment for schizophrenia, all of which contributed to a better understanding of the biochemistry of the disorder.

Researchers today readily acknowledge that neurotransmitters and their actions contribute to the development of schizophrenia; this understanding initially led to the *dopamine theory of schizophrenia.* This theory asserts that too much dopamine or too much activity at dopamine receptors causes schizophrenia and that using antischizophrenia drugs, which decrease levels of dopamine activity, can avert schizophrenic symptoms. Dopamine receptors are considered to be major sites of biochemical disturbances in the brain (Fang, 1996; Masotto & Racagni, 1995). A class of drugs known as phenothiazines appears to block these sites. When patients with schizophrenia

Disorganized type of schizophrenia: Type of schizophrenia characterized by severely disturbed thought processes; frequent incoherence; disorganized behavior; and inappropriate affect.

Paranoid [PAIR-uh-noid] type of schizophrenia: Type of schizophrenia characterized by hallucinations and delusions of persecution or grandeur (or both), and sometimes irrational jealousy.

Catatonic [CAT-uh-TONN-ick] type of schizophrenia: Type of schizophrenia characterized either by displays of excited or violent motor activity or by stupor.

Residual type of schizophrenia: A schizophrenic disorder in which the patient exhibits inappropriate affect, illogical thinking, and/or eccentric behavior but seems generally in touch with reality.

Undifferentiated type of schizophrenia: A schizophrenic disorder that is characterized by a mixture of symptoms and does not meet the diagnostic criteria of any one type.

Concordance rate: The degree to which a condition or trait is shared by two or more individuals or groups.

are given phenothiazines, many of their disturbed thought processes and hallucinations disappear. Conversely, drugs that stimulate the dopamine system and increase brain dopamine levels (such as amphetamines) aggravate existing schizophrenic disorders. Researchers have also found that there are subtypes of dopamine receptors, and that some drugs—*neuroleptics*—bind to the specific receptors that most likely inhibit schizophrenic symptoms, especially positive symptoms (O'Connor, 1998).

Of course, new evidence on biological causes of schizophrenia emerges each year. The latest focuses on glutamate. GABA and glutamate, the most common neurotransmitters in the brain, are examples of amino acids that act as neurotransmitters. An increasing body of evidence suggests that glutamate pathways play a key role in schizophrenia. Neuroleptics, in addition to their immediate effects on dopamine pathways, have been shown to have slowly emerging effects on glutamate pathways. This property of the drugs may explain why it generally takes several weeks before those taking them experience a significant improvement in their symptoms. Further, compounds that block the activity of glutamate-sensitive neurons produce symptoms that closely mimic schizophrenic ones in healthy people and strongly worsen existing symptoms among schizophrenic patients. Thus, the dopamine hypothesis has been revised to incorporate the notion that schizophrenia is associated with too little activity in certain glutamate pathways. Leading schizophrenia researchers now refer to a *dopamine–glutamate imbalance*.

Biochemistry is not the whole story—if it were, patients with schizophrenia could be cured. Certain portions of the brains of schizophrenic patients and their relatives exhibit abnormalities, although it is not yet clear whether schizophrenia causes the abnormalities or the abnormalities cause schizophrenia (Cannon & Marco, 1994). For example, the *ventricles* (hollow areas in the brain that are normally filled with fluid) are enlarged in some schizophrenic patients (Raz & Raz, 1990; Suddath et al., 1990). Furthermore, some brain structures, notably the frontal lobes, show reduced blood flow and functioning in schizophrenics (Resnick, 1992). The prefrontal cortex in a schizophrenic patient contains a different number of binding sites for serotonin than the cortex of a normal person (Burnet, Eastwood, & Harrison, 1996; Kahn, Davidson, & Davis, 1996). When Buchsbaum and Hazlett (1997) examined the literature on brain-imaging studies of schizophrenic patients compared with normal individuals, they found that schizophrenic patients showed anatomical structures that looked like those of older normal participants; these researchers

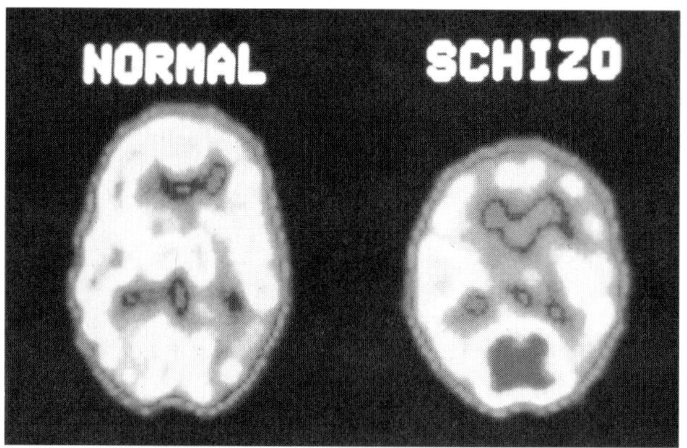

suggest that in some patients, schizophrenia may resemble a rapid aging process that prematurely affects the brain.

In sum, researchers now assert that genetic and biochemical factors and brain abnormalities are all associated with schizophrenia. While many stress factors (which are the focus of environmental researchers) may contribute to schizophrenia, a genetic component seems to be essential.

Environmental Factors. Some psychologists believe that, in addition to genetic factors, environmental interactions determine the onset and development of schizophrenia. Freudian psychologists, for example, suggest that early childhood relationships can cause a person to become fixated at the oral stage and develop a disorder such as schizophrenia. Such a person does not have a fully developed ego and will make judgments based on the id's pleasure principle. Lacking a functioning ego, which uses the reality principle in making judgments, the individual will seek immediate gratification and thus be unable to deal effectively with reality. Freudian psychologists assert that a person who has successfully passed through the oral stage and has developed a strong ego is unlikely to suffer from schizophrenia. There is a lack of rigorous scientific evidence to support this assertion, however.

Behavioral explanations of schizophrenia are based on traditional learning principles (explored in Chapter 5). The behavioral approach argues that faulty reinforcement and extinction procedures, as well as social learning processes, can account for schizophrenia. Imagine a child brought up in a family where the parents constantly argue, where the father or the mother is an alcoholic, and where neither parent shows much affection for the other parent or for anyone else. Such a child, receiving no reinforcement for showing interest in events, people, and objects in the outside world, may become withdrawn and begin to exhibit schizophrenic behavior. Lidz (1973) argues that children who grow up in such homes adopt the family's faulty view of the world and of relationships and thus are likely to expect reinforcement for abnormal behaviors. Growing up in such an emotionally fragmented environment may predispose individuals to emotional disorders and eventually schizophrenia (Miklowitz, 1994; Walker et al., 1983). In addition, if the parents themselves are schizophrenic and they mistreat the child, the likelihood of problems such as schizophrenia in the child's future increases.

Even in families in which there is no marital conflict, parents sometimes confuse their children or have difficulty communicating effectively with them. Researchers have found that families affect the developmental course and severity of a member's schizophrenia. When families have an interaction style characterized by hostility, criticism, emotional overinvolvement, and a lack of boundaries (overintrusiveness), their level of *expressed emotions* is said to be high. Patients who return to families in which there are high levels of expressed emotion have a higher relapse rate than that of patients from families with low levels of expressed emotion. In addition, parents can place their children in a situation that offers inconsistent messages, a **double bind.** Initially described by Bateson as an explanation for the causes of schizophrenia (Bateson et al., 1956), double bind usually occurs between individuals with a strong emotional attachment, such as a child and a parent (Mishler & Waxler, 1968). For example, a parent may present a gift and teasingly say, "No, you may not have this," while smiling and giving other nonverbal assurances that the individual may have the gift. Most children understand that the parent is teasing. However, not all children will understand this, and not all situations are so clearly cued. And research shows that schizophrenic patients are less accurate at interpreting emotional communications than are control participants (Fagan & Silverthorn, 1998). Games and ineffective communication of this kind, if occurring frequently, may shape an environment of confusion conducive to the development and maintenance of schizophrenia. However, what Bateson saw as a cause of schizophrenia may be more a pattern of a lack of communication skills, especially during stressful periods (Docherty, Hall, & Gordinier, 1998).

A connection exists between heredity and schizophrenia, although genetic factors alone cannot account for its development.

According to learning theory, a person who receives a great deal of attention for behaviors that other people see as bizarre is likely to continue those behaviors. People who fail to develop effective social skills are more at risk for bizarre behaviors (Mueser et al., 1990). Other learning theories suggest that bizarre behavior and thoughts are themselves reinforcing, because they allow the person to escape from both acute anxiety and an overactive autonomic nervous system.

Nature and Nurture. Many variables determine whether an individual will develop schizophrenia. Some people, because of family environment, genetic history, or brain chemistry, are more vulnerable than others. As with mood disorders, *vulnerability* is a person's diminished ability to deal with demanding life events. The more vulnerable a person is, the less necessary environmental stress or other disorders (such as anxiety) are to the initiation of a schizophrenic episode. To summarize, although the exact causes of schizophrenia are still unknown, research suggests the following:

- A connection exists between heredity and schizophrenia, although genetic factors alone cannot account for its development.
- The production and activity of specific types of chemical substances in the brain are associated with schizophrenia.
- Environmental factors (such as marital conflict and a double bind) contribute to the development of schizophrenia. Among these factors, early childhood relationships may be especially important.
- The most likely cause of schizophrenia is a biological predisposition in the individual, which is aggravated by a climate of emotional immaturity, lack of effective communication, and emotional instability.

I

Think Critically

- How likely would it be for a homeless person to be diagnosed as schizophrenic? Explain.
- Why do researchers place more emphasis on longitudinal research than on cross-sectional research in studying schizophrenia?

Double bind: A situation in which an individual is given two different and inconsistent messages.

Summary and Review

What Is Abnormal Behavior?

Define abnormal behavior, and describe the major perspectives that try to explain it.

What are the goals of the *DSM*, and what are its advantages and disadvantages?

What are the essential characteristics of chronic fatigue syndrome?

KEY TERMS
abnormal behavior, 363; model, 364; abnormal psychology, 364; prevalence, 367

Anxiety, Somatoform, and Dissociative Disorders

What are the chief characteristics of anxiety, somatoform, and dissociative disorders?

KEY TERMS
anxiety, p. 369; generalized anxiety disorder, p. 370; free-floating anxiety, p. 370; phobic disorders, p. 370; agoraphobia, p. 370; social phobia, p. 371; specific phobia, p. 371; obsessive–compulsive disorder, p. 371; somatoform disorders, p. 373; somatization disorder, p. 373; conversion disorder, p. 373; hypochondriasis, p. 373; dissociative disorders, p. 374; dissociative amnesia, p. 374; dissociative identity disorder, p. 374

Personality Disorders

What are the chief characteristics of six key personality disorders?

KEY TERMS
personality disorders, p. 375; antisocial personality disorder, p. 375

Mood Disorders

What are the characteristics of the major mood disorders, and what theories account for these disorders?

Who attempts suicide?

KEY TERMS
bipolar disorder, p. 377; depressive disorders, p. 378; major depressive disorder, p. 378; delusions, p. 378; learned helplessness, p. 381; vulnerability, p. 381

Schizophrenia

Identify the essential characteristics of the five major types of schizophrenia.

What has research revealed about the causes of schizophrenia?

KEY TERMS
schizophrenic disorders, p. 384; psychotic, p. 384; disorganized type of schizophrenia, p. 386; paranoid type of schizophrenia, p. 386; catatonic type of schizophrenia, p. 386; residual type of schizophrenia, p. 386; undifferentiated type of schizophrenia, p. 386; concordance rate, p. 387; double bind, p. 389

Self-Test

1. Which of the following is not a characteristic of abnormal behavior?
   A. maladaptive
   B. socially unacceptable
   C. disturbing to others
   D. resulting from distorted cognitions

2. Which model of abnormal behavior emphasizes hospitalization and drug treatment programs?
   A. humanistic model
   B. medical–biological model
   C. psychodynamic model
   D. sociocultural model

3. An important feature of the *DSM–IV* is:
   A. prevalence rates
   B. specific treatment plans
   C. drug intervention options
   D. probabilities of achieving a cure

4. Karen has a persistent feeling of anxiety and an impending sense of doom, but her anxiety is not related to any specific object or situation. She is suffering from:
   A. agoraphobia
   B. free-floating anxiety
   C. social phobia
   D. obsessive–compulsive disorder

5. John's roommate keeps his room immaculate and washes his hands all the time. He claims he is just trying to avoid getting germs and becoming contaminated. He may be suffering from:
   A. somatoform disorder
   B. germaphobia
   C. psychogenic trauma
   D. obsessive–compulsive disorder

6. A disorder that involves unwarranted fear and feelings of persecution and mistrust is:
   A. histrionic personality disorder
   B. paranoid personality disorder
   C. inadequate personality disorder
   D. dependent personality disorder

7. Missy is constantly complaining about her boyfriend and telling wild, exaggerated stories about how he treats her. She might be diagnosed with:
   A. borderline personality disorder
   B. narcissistic personality disorder
   C. conversion disorder
   D. histrionic personality disorder

8. Beth is one of the most active parents in Meghan's school. She is involved in numerous school projects and likes to be in charge. Occasionally, she will be absent for several days at a time and neglect important responsibilities. She may be showing symptoms of:
   A. bipolar disorder
   B. dependent personality disorder
   C. narcissistic personality disorder
   D. major depression

9. According to the learning and cognitive theories of depression:
   A. people are born with a predisposition to become depressed
   B. people who fail become addicted to failure
   C. people learn from their environment
   D. people have chemical imbalances leading to depression

10. Suicide is most highly correlated with:
    A. personality disorders
    B. somataform disorders
    C. dissociative disorders
    D. depression

11. Cognitive psychologists would assert that suicide attempts are a result of:
    A. loss of serotonin
    B. learned helplessness
    C. failure of problem-solving abilities
    D. hostile feelings toward oneself

12. Andy claims that he knows about the government's plan to influence people's minds via the Internet. He fears that if he tells anyone the government will have him assassinated. Andy may be diagnosed as having:
    A. paranoid schizophrenia
    B. delusions of grandeur
    C. disorganized schizophrenia
    D. rational thoughts

Chapter 14

Therapy

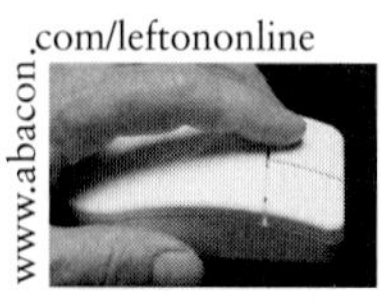

Go to your password-protected Website for full-color art, Weblinks, and more!

It was a cold, dark Sunday morning when Rob Terman finally began to admit that his life was changing—for the worse. He'd slept badly the night before; in fact, he'd awakened in the middle of the night, drenched in a cold sweat. Rob was slowly slipping into a depressed state. At first, he'd become moody, unable to concentrate at work; later, he began to withdraw from his friends. He chalked it up to an early midlife crisis and decided that he needed a new girlfriend. But things got worse—over a period of 2 months, he lost weight, had great difficulty sleeping, developed an array of physical complaints, and lost interest in his usual activities and friends. Feeling angry or exasperated by the smallest things and either anxious or despondent most of the time, losing sleep, losing weight, and abusing alcohol on the weekends, Rob finally realized he needed help. That help came from his company's staff nurse, who referred him to a psychologist who was part of his health maintenance organization (HMO). The psychologist first had Rob undergo a physical check-up; after consulting together, the psychologist and the physician agreed that an antidepressant to combat Rob's depression was in order for a short time. Prozac was prescribed—and it helped a great deal. In fact, within 10 days Rob's mood started to lift, which made his weekly session with his therapist much easier. Problems came into sharper focus; his energy increased. Rob even started to mend his strained relationship with his father and brother. The struggle up from the depths of despair to recovery was long and tough, though. It involved months of therapy dealing with diverse issues, including self-esteem, distorted ideas about work demands, and his family relationships. ■

Was it the psychological therapy that helped Rob, or was it the drug? The truth is that it was probably a combination of the two that helped him move ahead. Would one have worked without the other? Perhaps—but the combination turned out to be extremely effective. Many researchers think that combining medication and talking is the key to effective therapy; others insist on approaches involving only talking therapies or only drug therapies. A great deal depends on the type of problem a client is having.

In some important ways, therapy is changing; people are relying more and more on drugs for the treatment of anxiety and depression. But many psychologists think there is a tendency to overdiagnose people's problems (Kutchins & Kirk, 1997) and then to overmedicate patients (Valenstein, 1998). The fact is that the causes of people's disorders—the initiators of psychological distress—are not usually biological. When people have marital problems, workplace stress or conflicts, or other psychological difficulties, help from a therapist—not a drug—is usually the order of the day. Today, mental health and therapy efforts are complicated by two facts: First, HMOs are putting pressure on practitioners to find fast, efficient cures that are less costly; second, some disorders, especially disorders like depression, are often undiagnosed and untreated, which leads to greater problems later on (Hirschfeld et al., 1997). Let's look at the available therapies to try to determine what works best, and when. (I)

Psychotherapy [SYE-ko-THER-uh-pee]: The treatment of emotional or behavioral problems through psychological techniques.

(I) Therapy Comes in Many Forms

Focus on issues and ideas

- The many types of therapists and therapy available to assist people
- Developing an informed opinion on which type of therapist and therapy is effective

Many sources and types of treatment are available to people who are having difficulty coping with their problem. When a person seeks help from a physician, mental health counseling center, or drug treatment center, an initial working diagnosis is necessary. Does the person have medical problems? Should the person be hospitalized? Is the person dangerous? If talking therapy is in order, what type of practitioner is best suited for the person? There are two broad types of therapy: biologically based therapy and psychotherapy.

Biologically based therapy has traditionally been called *somatic therapy;* this term refers to treating psychological disorders by treating the body, often using therapy that affects hormone levels and the brain. For example, severely depressed individuals may need antidepressants; those diagnosed with schizophrenia may need antipsychotic drugs; those with less severe disorders may be advised to change their diet and exercise more, because exercise has mood-enhancing effects (Byrne & Byrne, 1993). We'll examine some biological therapies later in this chapter, after we explore the broad array of psychological therapies that are available for people suffering from life problems or maladjustment.

Psychotherapy is the treatment of emotional or behavioral problems through psychological techniques. It is a change-oriented process, and sometimes a fairly emotional one, whose goal is to help individuals cope better with their problems and achieve more emotionally satisfying lives. Psychotherapy accomplishes its goal by teaching people how to relieve stress, improve interpersonal communication, understand previous events in their lives, and/or modify their faulty ideas about the world. Psychotherapy helps people improve their self-image and adapt to new and challenging situations.

The effectiveness of therapy and the client's speed of response vary with the type of problem.

Of course, different cultures perceive different outcomes as optimal. Thus, in the United States, enhancing a client's self-esteem through some personal accomplishment may be seen as an optimal goal of psychotherapy. In Asia, a desired outcome may be improving family harmony, which may enhance self-esteem but involves working for a collective rather than a client's personal good. This difference in goals is highlighted in *Diversity;* it is also recognized by professional organizations such as the American Psychological Association (1993) and the American Psychiatric Association (1995).

Is Psychotherapy Necessary and Effective?

The images presented to the public by the mass media often shape the public's perception of psychotherapy. Talk-show psychologist Frasier Crane of the TV series *Frasier* bumbles through his own life; Barbra Streisand, in her role as a psychiatrist in the film *Prince of Tides,* stretched the ethical boundaries by sleeping with her client's brother. These images, as well as talk-show pop psychology, make many ask, "Is psychotherapy really necessary or effective?" Some researchers note that many clients could outgrow or otherwise find relief from their symptoms without psychotherapy. Others assert that psychotherapy is more art than science. Still others believe psychotherapy provides only temporary relief. Let's consider some of the arguments.

Placebo Effects. A placebo effect is a nonspecific improvement that occurs as a result of a person's expectations of change rather than as a result of any specific therapeutic treatment. Is the benefit of psychotherapy largely a placebo effect? Physicians report that sometimes people experience relief from their symptoms when they are given sugar pills and are told that the pills are medicine. Similarly, some patients in psychotherapy may show relief from their symptoms simply because they have entered therapy and expect change. For some people, just the attention of a therapist and the chance to express their feelings can be therapeutic. One research study even showed that clients who paid for therapy had a better therapeutic outcome than clients who did not pay (Roberts et al., 1993).

But any placebo effect in psychotherapy is likely to be temporary. Long-lasting therapeutic benefits generally require the client's and therapist's combined efforts. Research studies that compare traditional psychotherapies with placebo treatment show that the therapies are consistently more effective (Lipsey & Wilson, 1993).

Placebo [pluh-SEE-bo] effect: A nonspecific improvement that occurs as a result of a person's expectations of change rather than as a direct result of any specific therapeutic treatment.

Research on Psychotherapy. In 1952, an important paper by Hans Eysenck challenged the effectiveness of psychotherapy, claiming that it produces no greater change in maladjusted individuals than do naturally occurring life experiences. Thousands of studies attempting to investigate the effectiveness of therapy followed. These studies showed what clients and therapists have known for decades: Eysenck was wrong. Analyses of large amounts of data using sophisticated statistical techniques found psychotherapy effective (Bachar, 1998; Lipsey & Wilson, 1993). Although some psychologists challenge the data, techniques, and conclusions of these analyses, most are still convinced that psychotherapy is effective with a wide array of clients (e.g., Seligman, 1995). The effectiveness of therapy and the client's speed of response vary with the type of problem—anxiety and depression respond more rapidly to psychotherapy than do personality disorders, for example (Kopta et al., 1994). Table 14.1 (on p. 396) presents some generally recognized signs of good progress in therapy.

Is one type of therapy more effective than another? Many researchers contend that most psychotherapies are equally effective; that is, regardless of the approach a therapist uses, the results are often the same (Wampold et al., 1997). Some newer and trendier approaches—the kinds that often appear in popular magazines—tend to be less reliable and to reflect a culture that is fascinated with novelty. Critics such as Robyn Dawes (1994) assert that many therapists do not pay attention to known data and that some therapists—often those with little training—do their cli-

DIVERSITY

Asian Americans and Mental Health

Asian Americans are as difficult as African Americans or Protestants to characterize as a group. That is, there are considerable differences within each group, including diversity in language, education, traditions, and socioeconomic levels. Like any other ethnic experience, the Asian American experience must be seen from a unique perspective—a perspective that requires a sensitivity to and an understanding of the Asian American cultural heritage. Although the overall prevalence of mental disorders among Asian Americans is quite comparable to that among other groups of Americans (Yamamoto, Rhee, & Chang, 1994) and although Asian Americans do seek counseling, they are more likely to report a bodily ailment as an initial complaint to a therapist (Lippincott & Mierzwa, 1995). To improve the mental health of Asian Americans, psychologists must understand what *healing* and *family* mean to them and the role of spirituality in their cultural traditions—as well as the relationship of these variables to therapy (Gerber, 1994; Tempo & Saito, 1996). As Tsai and Uemura (1988) assert, one must understand at least three core cultural values that shape the responses of Asian Americans to stress and to the world: family, harmony, and stoicism.

In traditional Asian cultures, the *family* is the primary source of emotional support. The most important family relationship is not the husband–wife–children relationship but rather the parent–child relationship. A person is defined by her or his roles in the family, including parent roles, grandparent roles, and child roles. Children of any age—including adult children—are expected to maintain a deferential and respectful relationship to their elders. These roles and the consequent responsibilities provide emotional support for individual family members.

Harmony results from minimizing shame and keeping dignity intact. Harmony is essential if an Asian American is to have a good relationship with his or her family and thus high self-esteem. If everyone preserves dignity, or "face," interpersonal harmony is optimized.

Asian Americans also rely on personal strength and a sense of *stoicism;* that is, restraint is valued, and emotional maturity means suffering silently and suppressing emotions. The open expression of emotion is discouraged.

These three values—family, harmony, and stoicism—tend to keep Asian Americans from utilizing mental health services provided in the community (Tsai & Uemura, 1988). Asian Americans may subject themselves to extremely high levels of stress before seeking outside help; they tend, as a group, to seek such help only in real crises. They are far more likely to ask for help from family, thus maintaining harmony and saving face by being stoic toward the outside world. For example, Asian Americans were ordered by the U.S. government to be held in camps isolated from the rest of the population during World War II. Those who were confined at the Manzanar camp in California and at other, similar camps suffered many emotional problems with great dignity and stoicism; to this day, however, survivors of the camps still bear emotional scars.

A challenge for psychologists is to reach out to the Asian American community by making psychological services available in a way that minimizes shame, improves family unity, and respects cultural differences. The therapeutic alliance must respect the family, its life cycle, and its traditions and recognize the types of problems presented to practitioners (Tempo & Saito, 1996). Often, emphasizing family bonds—perhaps through family therapy—is an effective technique, as is relying on traditional and familiar Asian American philosophical traditions. Not all Americans have the same needs. ■

ents a disservice by ignoring the facts and looking for the exotic or easy way out. But if most of the traditional therapies are effective, there must be some common underlying component that makes them successful. The American Psychological Association and many individual researchers are seeking to systematize research strategies so as to investigate the effectiveness of therapies; this research will lead to a clearer picture

Table 14.1 Signs of Good Progress in Therapy

The client is providing personally revealing and significant material.
The client is exploring the meanings of feelings and occurrences.
The client is exploring material avoided earlier in therapy.
The client is expressing significant insight into personal behavior.
The client's method of communicating is active, alive, and energetic.
There is a valued client–therapist working relationship.
The client feels free to express strong feelings toward the therapist—either positive or negative.
The client is expressing strong feelings outside of therapy.
The client is moving toward a different set of personality characteristics.
The client is showing improved functioning outside of therapy.
The client indicates a general state of well-being, good feelings, and positive attitudes.

Source: Mahrer & Nadler, 1986.

of which approaches are best for certain disorders and for clients of various ages and different ethnic groups (Chambless & Hollon, 1998; Kazdin & Weisz, 1998). Furthermore, researchers are suggesting ways to validate therapy findings in the laboratory and in the real world (Goldfried & Wolfe, 1998).

Which Therapy, Which Therapist?

Before 1950, there were about 15 types of psychotherapy; today, there are hundreds. Some focus on individuals, some on groups of individuals (group therapy), and others on families (family therapy). Some psychologists even deal with whole communities; these *community psychologists* focus on helping members of communities develop more action-oriented approaches to individual and social problems. A therapist's training usually determines the type of treatment approach he or she takes. Rather than using just one type of psychotherapy, many therapists take an *eclectic approach*—that is, they combine several different techniques when treating clients.

A number of systematic psychotherapeutic approaches are in use today. Each can be applied in several formats—with individuals, couples, or groups—and each will be defined and examined in greater detail in later sections of this chapter. Some practitioners use *psychodynamically based approaches,* which follow Freud's basic ideas to varying degrees. These therapists' aim is to help patients understand the motivations underlying their behavior. They assume that maladjustment and abnormal behavior occur when people do not understand themselves adequately. Practitioners of *humanistic therapy* assume that people are essentially good—that they have an innate disposition to develop their potential and to seek beauty, truth, and goodness. This type of therapy tries to help people realize their full potential and find meaning in life. In contrast, *behavior therapy* is based on the assumption that most behaviors, whether normal or abnormal, are learned. Behavior therapists encourage their clients to learn new adaptive behaviors. Growing out of behavior therapy and cognitive psychology is *cognitive therapy,* which focuses on changing a client's behavior by changing her or his thoughts and perceptions.

In most of the therapy approaches we will discuss, practitioners adopt a point of view that guides both research and practice. A clear example is psychoanalysis, which prescribes a strict set of guidelines for therapy. But a new approach, called *psychotherapy integration,* is emerging. Psychotherapy integration is not a single-school approach, but rather is open to using diverse theories and techniques. Psychotherapy integration is more than an eclectic approach because the goal is to integrate theories into a new approach to solve problems. Research on psychotherapy integration is relatively scarce, however, because it is difficult to generate testable hypotheses from the new points of view that are created by integrating theories. Arkowitz (1997) argues that psychotherapy integration does not try to develop one, overarching view of therapy; he suggests that it is a way of thinking about and doing psychotherapy that reflects an openness to points of view other than the one with which a therapist is most familiar. In some important ways, psychotherapy integration is an ongoing process that may help define the future of psychotherapy. Another ongoing development that may prove a better avenue to explore is research on prevention of disorders.

Let's return for a moment to Rob Terman, whose problems were outlined in the beginning of the chap-

Psychoanalysis [SYE-ko-uh-NAL-uh-sis]: A lengthy insight therapy that was developed by Freud and aims at uncovering conflicts and unconscious impulses through special techniques, including free association, dream analysis, and transference.

ter. What type of therapy would best suit his situation? As mentioned before, the effectiveness of the different kinds of therapy varies with the type of disorder being treated and the goals of the client. Research to discover the best treatment method often focuses on specific disorders, such as depression. Results from such studies usually limit their conclusions to recommending a specific method as being effective for a specific problem. For example, cognitive behavior therapy has a good success rate for people with phobias, but it is less successful for those with schizophrenia. Long-term group therapy is more effective than short-term individual therapy for people with personality disorders. Behavior therapy is usually the most effective approach with children, regardless of the disorder.

Rob could therefore receive effective treatment from a variety of therapists (Wampold et al., 1997). One therapist might focus on the root causes of his maladjustment. Another might concentrate on eliminating his symptoms: sadness, anxiety, and alcohol abuse. Besides the therapeutic approaches, some characteristics of the therapists themselves affect the treatment; among these characteristics are ethnicity, personality, level of experience, and degree of empathy. Zlotnick, Elkin, and Shea (1998) found that the gender of the therapist was not a crucial variable with regard to the success of therapy. Garfield (1998) suggests that not enough research is being done on which variables are the most important to therapeutic change, which is unfortunate, because certain combinations of variables might lead to preferred outcomes in some cases.

Although there are differences among the various psychotherapies and therapists, there are also some commonalties. No matter which therapy they experience, clients usually expect a positive outcome, which helps them strive for change. In addition, clients receive attention, which helps them maintain a positive attitude. Moreover, no matter what type of therapy is involved, certain characteristics must be present in both therapist and client for therapeutic changes to occur. For example, good therapists communicate interest, understanding, respect, tact, maturity, and ability to help. They respect clients' ability to cope with their troubles (Fischer, 1991). They use suggestion, encouragement, interpretation, examples, and perhaps rewards to help clients change or rethink their situations. But clients must be willing to make some changes in their lifestyle and ideas. A knowledgeable, accepting, and objective therapist can facilitate behavior changes, but the client is the one who must make the changes (Lafferty, Beutler, & Crago, 1989).

Variables such as the client's social class, gender, age, level of education, expectations for the therapy, and level of anxiety are also important. For example, therapists need to understand the unique life stresses experienced by women. Similarly, they must address the special obstacles facing clients of various ethnic and minority groups (Sue, 1988). In general, the therapist and client must form an alliance to work together purposefully (Luborsky, Barber, & Crits-Christoph, 1990); such alliances are formed more readily if the therapist and client share some values (Kelly & Strupp, 1992). Because psychoanalysis is based on the development of a unique relationship between the therapist and the patient, compatibility is especially critical to the success of that type of therapy.

Table 14.2 (on p. 398) presents an overview of the major types of psychotherapeutic practitioners, including the degrees they most likely have earned and their activities. The table lists some practitioners who do not have as much training in psychotherapy as do psychologists—for example, psychiatric nurses and social workers. These types of practitioners often work along with a clinical psychologist or a psychiatrist, as part of a team that delivers mental health services to clients.

To clarify the main issues involved in psychotherapy, the next sections will look more closely at the four major psychotherapeutic approaches: psychodynamic, humanistic, behavior, and cognitive therapies. Then we will examine the biologically based approaches. (I)

Think Critically

- Imagine that you are undergoing treatment for anxiety or depression. What would you expect to gain, lose, or change during therapy?
- Why do you think some disorders respond to therapy more quickly than others?
- What are the implications of the fact that the rich and the poor have access to dramatically different mental health services?

(I) Psychoanalysis and Psychodynamic Therapies

Focus on issues and ideas

- The goals of psychoanalysis
- The techniques that traditional psychoanalysts consider useful and essential

Psychoanalysis is a lengthy insight therapy that was developed by Freud and aims at uncovering conflicts

Table 14.2 Psychotherapy Practitioners and Their Activities

Type of Practitioner	Degree	Years of Education beyond Undergraduate Degree	Activities
Clinical or counseling psychologist	PhD (Doctor of Philosophy) or PsyD (Doctor of Psychology)	5–8	Diagnosis, testing, and treatment using a wide array of techniques, including insight and behavior therapy
Psychiatrist	MD (Doctor of Medicine)	8	Biomedical therapy, diagnosis, and treatment, often with a psychoanalytic emphasis
Social worker	MSW (Master of Social Work)	2	Family therapy or behavior therapy, often in community-based settings such as hospitals
Psychiatric nurse	BSN (Bachelor of Science in Nursing) or MA (Master of Arts)	0–2	Inpatient psychiatric care, supportive therapy of various types
Counselor	MA (Master of Arts, often in counseling)	2	Supportive therapy, family therapy, vocational readjustment, alcoholism and drug abuse counseling

and unconscious impulses through special techniques, including free association, dream analysis, and transference. There are about 3,300 practicing psychoanalysts in the United States. Many other psychologists use some kind of therapy loosely connected to or rooted in Freudian theory. These psychologists refer to their therapies as **psychodynamically based therapies**—therapies that use approaches or techniques derived from Freud, but that reject or modify some elements of Freud's theory.

Sigmund Freud believed that the exchange of words in psychoanalysis causes therapeutic change. According to Freud (1966/1920):

> The patient talks, tells of his past experiences and present impressions, complains, and expresses his wishes and his emotions. The physician listens, attempts to direct the patient's thought-processes, reminds him, forces his attention in certain directions, gives him explanations and observes the reactions of understanding or denial thus evoked. (p. 21)

Freud's therapy is an **insight therapy**—a therapy that attempts to discover relationships between unconscious motivations and current abnormal behavior. Any insight therapy is based on two basic assumptions: (1) that becoming aware of one's motivations helps one change and become more adaptable, and (2) that the causes of maladjustment are unresolved conflicts that the person was unaware of and therefore unable to deal with. The goal of insight therapy is to treat the causes of abnormal behaviors rather than the behaviors themselves. In general, insight therapists try to help people see life from a different perspective so that they can choose more adaptive behaviors.

Goals of Psychoanalysis

Many individuals who seek psychotherapy are unhappy with their behavior but are unable to change it. As we saw in the discussion of Freud's theory of personality (Chapter 10), Freud believed that conflicts among a person's unconscious thoughts produce maladjusted behavior. The general goal of psychoanalysis is to help patients understand the unconscious motivations that direct their behavior. Only when they become aware of those motivations can they begin to choose behaviors that lead to more fulfilling lives. In psychoanalysis, patients are encouraged to express healthy impulses, to strengthen day-to-day functioning based on reality, and to perceive the world as a positive rather than a punishing place.

To illustrate the psychoanalytic approach, suppose that Rob Terman seeks the help of a psychologist who uses a psychodynamically based therapy. The psychologist might attempt to discover the source of Rob's problems by asking him to describe how he relates to his parents—especially to his father. Rob realizes that he has sought his father's love all his life, but has always felt that his father preferred his brother. Through therapy, he realizes he is torn between love for his father and rage toward him. Rob discovers that he has been incapable of expressing his anger appropriately to his father. Frustrated and hostile, he has lost interest in work, lost his self-esteem, and become depressed.

Techniques of Psychoanalysis

In general, psychoanalytic techniques are geared toward the exploration of early experiences. In traditional psychoanalysis, the patient lies on a couch and the therapist sits in a chair out of the patient's view. Freud used this arrangement in his office in Vienna, because he believed it would allow the patient to be more relaxed and feel less threatened than if the therapist was in view. Today, however, many followers of Freud prefer face-to-face interactions with patients.

In free association, the patient is asked to report whatever comes to mind, regardless of how disorganized it might be, how trivial it might seem, or how disagreeable it might sound.

Two major techniques used in psychoanalysis are free association and dream analysis. In **free association,** the patient is asked to report whatever comes to mind, regardless of how disorganized it might be, how trivial it might seem, or how disagreeable it might sound. A therapist might say, "I can help you best if you say whatever thoughts and feelings come to your mind, even if they seem irrelevant, immaterial, foolish, embarrassing, upsetting, or even if they're about me, even very personally, just as they come, without censoring or editing" (Lewin, 1970, p. 67). The purpose of free association is to help patients learn to recognize connections and patterns among their thoughts and to allow the unconscious to express itself freely.

In **dream analysis,** patients are asked to describe their dreams in detail; the dreams are interpreted so as to provide insight into unconscious motivations. Sometimes lifelike, sometimes chaotic, sometimes incoherent, dreams may at times replay a person's life history and at other times venture into the person's current problems. Freud believed that dreams represent some element of the unconscious seeking expression. Psychodynamically oriented therapists believe that dreams are full of symbolism; they assert that the content of a dream hides its true meaning. The goal of dream analysis is to help therapists reveal patients' unconscious desires and motivations by discovering the meaning of their dreams.

Both free association and dream analysis involve the therapist's interpretation. **Interpretation,** in Freud's theory, is the technique of providing a context, meaning, or cause for a specific idea, feeling, or set of behaviors; it is the process of tying a set of behaviors to its unconscious determinant. With this technique, the therapist tries to find common threads in a patient's behavior and thoughts. Patients' use of *defense mechanisms* (ways of reducing anxiety by distorting reality, described in Chapter 10) is often a sign pointing to an area that may need to be explored. For example, if a male patient avoids the subject of women, invariably deflecting the topic with an offhand remark or a joke, the therapist may wonder if the man is experiencing some kind of denial. The therapist may then encourage the patient to explore his attitudes and feelings about women in general and about his mother in particular.

Two processes are central to psychoanalysis: resistance and transference. **Resistance** is an unwillingness to cooperate, which a patient signals by showing a reluctance to provide the therapist with information or to help the therapist understand or interpret a situation. Resistance can sometimes reach the point of belligerence. For example, a patient disturbed by her analyst's unsettling interpretations might become angry and start resisting treatment by missing appointments or failing to pay for therapy. Analysts usually interpret resistance as meaning either that the patient wishes to avoid discussing a particular subject or that an especially difficult stage in psychotherapy has been reached. To minimize resistance, analysts try to accept patients' behavior. When a therapist does not

Psychodynamically [SYE-ko-dye-NAM-ick-lee] based therapies: Therapies that use approaches or techniques derived from Freud, but that reject or modify some elements of Freud's theory.

Insight therapy: Any therapy that attempts to discover relationships between unconscious motivations and current abnormal behavior.

Free association: Psychoanalytic technique in which a person is asked to report to the therapist his or her thoughts and feelings as they occur, regardless of how trivial, illogical, or objectionable their content may appear.

Dream analysis: Psychoanalytic technique in which a patient's dreams are described in detail and interpreted so as to provide insight into the individual's unconscious motivations.

Interpretation: In Freud's theory, the technique of providing a context, meaning, or cause for a specific idea, feeling, or set of behaviors; the process of tying a set of behaviors to its unconscious determinant.

Resistance: In psychoanalysis, an unwillingness to cooperate, which a patient signals by showing a reluctance to provide the therapist with information or to help the therapist understand or interpret a situation.

judge but merely listens, a patient is more likely to describe feelings thoroughly.

Transference is a psychoanalytic phenomenon in which a therapist becomes the object of a patient's emotional attitudes about an important person in the patient's life, such as a parent. For example, if Rob Terman's therapist is a man, and Rob becomes hostile toward him, a psychoanalyst would say that Rob is acting as though the therapist were his father; that is, he is directing attitudes and emotional reactions from that earlier relationship toward the therapist (Butler & Strupp, 1991). The importance of transference is that the psychotherapist will respond differently to Rob than Rob's father might have, so Rob can experience the conflict differently, which will lead him to a better understanding of the issue. By permitting transference, a therapist gives patients a new opportunity to understand their feelings and can guide them in the exploration of repressed or difficult material. The examination of thoughts or feelings that were previously considered unacceptable (and therefore were often repressed) helps patients understand and identify the underlying conflicts that direct their behavior.

An ego analyst asserts that the ego is independent of the id, controls memory and perception, and is not in constant conflict with the id.

Psychoanalysis, with its slowly gained insights into the unconscious, is a gradual and continual process. Through their insights, patients learn new ways of coping with instinctual urges and develop more mature means of dealing with anxiety and guilt. The cycle of interpretation, resistance to interpretation, and transference occurs repeatedly in the process of psychoanalysis and is sometimes referred to as **working through.**

Transference: Psychoanalytic phenomenon in which a therapist becomes the object of a patient's emotional attitudes about an important person in the patient's life, such as a parent.

Working through: In psychoanalysis, the repetitive cycle of interpretation, resistance to interpretation, and transference.

Client-centered therapy: An insight therapy, developed by Carl Rogers, that seeks to help people evaluate the world and themselves from their own perspective by providing them with a nondirective environment and unconditional positive regard; also known as *person-centered therapy.*

Nondirective therapy: Any form of therapy in which the client determines the direction while the therapist remains permissive and almost passive and totally accepts the client's feelings and behavior.

Criticisms of Psychoanalysis

Freud's theory has not been universally accepted; even his followers have often disagreed with him. One group of psychoanalysts, referred to as *ego analysts,* or *ego psychologists,* have modified some of Freud's basic ideas. *Ego analysts* are psychoanalytic practitioners who assume that the ego has greater control over behavior than Freud suggested and who focus more on a patient's reality testing and control over the environment than on unconscious motivations and processes. Like Freud, ego analysts believe that psychoanalysis is the appropriate method for treating patients with emotional problems. Unlike Freud, however, they assume that people have voluntary control over whether, when, and in what ways their biological urges will be expressed.

A major disagreement between ego analysts and traditional psychoanalysts has to do with the role of the id and the ego. (Recall from Chapter 10 that the id operates on the pleasure principle, while the ego operates on the reality principle and tries to control the id's impulsivity.) A traditional Freudian asserts that the ego grows out of the id and controls it—but an ego analyst asserts that the ego is independent of the id, controls memory and perception, and is not in constant conflict with the id. Whereas traditional psychoanalysts begin by focusing on unconscious material in the id and only later try to increase the patient's ego control, ego analysts begin by helping clients develop stronger egos. They may ask a client to be assertive and take control of a situation—to let reason, rather than feeling, guide a specific behavior pattern. From an ego analyst's point of view, a weak ego may cause maladjustment through its failure to perceive, understand, and control the id. Thus, by learning to master and develop their egos—including moral reasoning and judgment—people gain greater control over their lives.

Critics of psychoanalysis contend that the approach is unscientific, imprecise, and subjective; they assert that psychoanalytic concepts such as id, ego, and superego are not linked to reality or to day-to-day behavior. Other critics object to Freud's biologically oriented approach, which suggests that a human being is a mere bundle of energy caught in conflict and driven toward some hedonistic goal. These critics ask: Where does human free will enter the picture? Also, elements of Freud's theory are untestable, and some are sexist. Freud conceived of men and women in prescribed roles; most practitioners today find this idea objectionable.

Aside from these criticisms, the effectiveness of psychoanalysis is open to question. Research shows that psychoanalysis is more effective for some people than for others. It is more effective, for example, for people with anxiety disorders than for those diagnosed as schizophrenic. In addition, younger patients improve more than older ones. In general, studies show that psychoanalysis can be as effective as other therapies, but no more so (Garfield & Bergin, 1986). Psychoanalysis does have certain inherent disadvantages. The problems it addresses are difficult, and a patient must be highly motivated and articulate to grasp the complicated and subtle relationships being explored. Further, because traditional psychoanalysis involves meeting with the analyst for an hour at a time, 5 days a week, for approximately 5 years, psychoanalysis is typically extremely expensive. Many people who seek therapy cannot afford the money or the time for this type of treatment, nor will most insurance companies foot the bill. Humanistic therapies, which we'll examine next, are neither as time-consuming nor as comprehensive in their goals as psychoanalysis. (I)

Think Critically

- Why do you think most practitioners feel that psychoanalysis is not the most appropriate treatment for marital problems?

(I) Humanistic Therapies

Focus on issues and ideas

- The assumptions humanistic therapists make about individuals
- The techniques of humanistic therapies

Humanistic therapies, unlike psychoanalytic therapies, emphasize the uniqueness of the human experience, the human ability to reflect on conscious experience, and the idea that human beings have free will to determine their destinies. Humanistic psychologists tend to focus on the present and the future rather than on the past, and they assert that human beings are creative and born with an innate desire to fulfill themselves. To some extent, humanistic approaches, being insight-oriented, are an outgrowth of psychodynamically based insight therapies: Humanistic therapies focus on helping basically healthy people understand the causes of their behavior—both normal and maladjusted—and helping them take responsibility for their future by promoting growth and fulfillment. Client-centered therapy and Gestalt therapy are two humanistic therapies that center on self-determination.

Client-Centered Therapy

Client-centered therapy, or *person-centered therapy*, is an insight therapy that seeks to help people evaluate the world and themselves from their own perspective by providing them with a nondirective environment and unconditional positive regard (which we'll soon discuss in more detail). Carl Rogers (1902–1987) first developed client-centered therapy. He was a quiet, caring man who turned the psychoanalytic world upside-down when he introduced his approach. He focused on the person, listening intently to his clients and encouraging them to define their own "cures." Rogers saw people as basically good, competent, social beings who move forward and grow. He believed that people move toward their ideal selves throughout life, maturing into fulfilled individuals through the process of self-actualization.

Rogerian therapists hold that problem behaviors occur when the environment prevents a person from developing his or her own innate potential. If children are given love and reinforcement only for their achievements, for example, then, as adults, they may see themselves and others almost solely in terms of achievement. Rogerian treatment involves helping people improve their self-regard. To this end, a Rogerian therapist might treat Rob Terman by first encouraging him to explore his past goals, current desires, and expectations for the future. This places his current behavior in a framework. It also allows the therapist to then ask Rob whether he can achieve what he wants through a new relationship with a woman or even at work. Table 14.3 (on p. 402) presents the basic assumptions underlying Rogers's approach to treatment.

Techniques of Client-Centered Therapy. Because its goal is to help clients discover and actualize their as-yet-undiscovered ideal selves, client-centered therapy is nondirective. **Nondirective therapy** is any form of therapy in which the client determines the direction of therapy while the therapist remains permissive and almost passive and totally accepts the client's feelings and behavior. In nondirective therapy, the therapist does not dominate the client but instead encourages the client's search for growth and self-discovery.

The use of the word *client* rather than *patient* is a key aspect of Rogers's approach to therapy (*patient* connotes a medical model). In psychoanalysis, the

Table 14.3 Rogers's Assumptions about Human Beings

1. People are innately good and are effective in dealing with their environments.
2. Behavior is purposeful and goal-directed.
3. Healthy people are aware of all their behavior; they choose their behavior patterns.
4. A client's behavior can be understood only from the client's point of view. Even if a client has misconstrued events in the world, the therapist must understand how the client sees those events.
5. Effective therapy occurs only when a client modifies his or her behavior, not when the therapist manipulates it.

therapist *directs* the "cure" and helps patients understand their behavior; in client-centered therapy, the therapist *guides* clients and helps them realize what they feel is right for themselves. Clients are viewed as the experts concerning their own experience. The clients direct the conversation, and the therapist helps them organize their thoughts and ideas simply by asking the right questions, by giving neutral responses to encourage the client to continue, and by reflecting back the clients' feelings. (That is, the therapist may *paraphrase* a client's ideas, ask the client to clarify and *restate* his or her ideas and feelings in other words, or *reflect* back what the client has just said so that the person can hear his or her own words again.) Even a small physical movement, such as a nod or gesture, can help clients stay on the right track. The client learns to evaluate the world from a personal vantage point, with little interpretation by the therapist.

A basic tenet of client-centered therapy is that the therapist must be a warm, accepting person who projects positive feelings toward clients. To counteract clients' negative experiences with people who were unaccepting, and who thus have taught them to think they are bad or unlikable, client-centered therapists accept clients as they are, with good and bad points; they respect them as individuals and show them *unconditional positive regard. Empathic understanding,* whereby therapists communicate acceptance and recognition of clients' emotions and encourage clients to discuss whatever feelings they have, is an important part of the therapeutic relationship.

Client-centered therapy can be viewed as a consciousness-raising process that helps people expand their awareness so as to construct new meanings. Initially, clients tend to express the attitudes and ideas they have adopted from other people. Thus, Rob Terman might say, "I should be making top sales figures," implying "because my father expects me to be a success." As therapy progresses and he experiences the empathic understanding of the therapist, Rob will begin to use his own ideas and standards when evaluating himself (Rogers, 1951). As a result, he may begin to talk about himself in more positive ways and try to please himself rather than others, part of the process of constructing new meanings. He may say, "I'm satisfied with my sales efforts," reflecting a more positive, more accepting attitude about himself. As he begins to feel better about himself, he will eventually suggest to the therapist that he feels ready to deal with the world and may be ready to leave therapy.

Client-centered therapists accept clients as they are, with good and bad points; they respect them as individuals and show them unconditional positive regard.

Criticisms of Client-Centered Therapy. Client-centered therapy is acclaimed for its focus on the therapeutic relationship. No other therapy makes clients feel so warm, accepted, and safe. These are important characteristics of any type of therapy, but critics argue that they may not be enough to bring about long-lasting change. And some critics assert that lengthy discussions about past problems do not necessarily help people with their present difficulties. They believe that this therapy may be making therapeutic promises that cannot be fulfilled and that it focuses on concepts that are hard to define, such as self-actualization.

Gestalt Therapy

With its aim of creating an awareness of a person's whole self, Gestalt therapy differs significantly from psychoanalysis. **Gestalt therapy** is an insight therapy that emphasizes the importance of a person's being aware of current feelings and situations. It assumes that human beings are responsible for themselves and their lives and that they need to focus not on the past but on the present, the "here and now." Gestalt ther-

Gestalt [Gesh-TALT] therapy: An insight therapy that emphasizes the importance of a person's being aware of current feelings and situations.

Behavior therapy: A therapy that is based on the application of learning principles to human behavior and that focuses on changing overt behaviors rather than on understanding subjective feelings, unconscious processes, or motivations; also known as *behavior modification.*

apy is the representation of current feelings and behaviors as a meaningful, coherent whole.

Frederick S. ("Fritz") Perls (1893–1970), a physician and psychoanalyst trained in Europe, was the founder and the principal proponent of Gestalt therapy. He was a dynamic and charismatic therapist, and many psychologists followed him and his ideas closely. Perls assumed that the best way to help clients cope with anxiety and other unpleasant feelings is to focus on their current understanding and awareness of the world, not on past situations and experiences.

Gestalt psychologists help people deal with feelings left over from what Perls termed *incomplete Gestalts*—that is, unfinished business or unresolved conflicts that affect current behavior, such as previously unrecognized feelings of anger toward a spouse or envy of a brother or sister. Only when people become aware of the here and now can they become sensitive to the tension and repression that made their behavior maladaptive. Thus, a major goal of Gestalt therapy is to get people in touch with their feelings so that they can construct an accurate picture of their psychological world. Usually, the therapist asks the client to concentrate on current feelings about a difficult past experience—for example, to relive a situation and discuss it as if it were happening in the present.

Another Gestalt technique is to have clients change the way they talk; a client who has trouble being assertive might be asked to speak assertively to each member of a group. Still another technique is to ask clients to behave in a manner opposite to the way they feel; a man who feels hostile or angry toward his parents because of their indifference when he was a child, for example, might be asked to behave as though their relationship were warm and affectionate. The underlying assumption is that expressed feelings can be understood and dealt with more easily than can remembered feelings. In addition, it is sometimes easier and less painful to express feelings that are not so direct and immediate—and so expressing *opposite* feelings allows a client to place feelings in an immediate context for consideration and reflection. For these reasons, Gestalt therapy is considered an experiential therapy.

Some critics believe Perls was too focused on individuals' happiness and growth, that he encouraged the attainment of these goals at the expense of others. Critics also assert that Gestalt therapy focuses too much on feelings and not enough on thought and decision making. Last, critics point out that Gestalt therapy may work well for healthy people who want to grow, but that it may not be as successful for severely maladjusted people who cannot make it through the day. *(I)*

Think Critically

- What are the implications for a theory of therapy of assuming that people are inherently good, as Rogers did?
- How might psychodynamic and humanistic therapists use hypnosis differently?

(I) Behavior Therapy

Focus on issues and ideas

- The learning principles that underlie behavioral therapy
- Why behaviorists are dissatisfied with psychodynamic and humanistic therapies
- How operant conditioning procedures are used in therapy
- The procedures of systematic desensitization

Behavior therapy has assumptions and goals that differ from those of psychodynamic and humanistic therapies. It has become especially popular in the last three decades for three principal reasons. First, people sometimes have problems that may not warrant an in-depth discussion of early childhood experiences, an exploration of unconscious motivations, a lengthy discussion about current feelings, or a resolution of inner conflicts. Examples of such problems are fear of heights, anxiety about public speaking, marital conflicts, and sexual dysfunction. In these cases, behavior therapy may be more appropriate than psychodynamically based or humanistic therapies. Second, behavior therapy has become popular because HMOs and other insurance organizations are seeking quicker, less expensive solutions to everyday problems. Last, behavior therapy can be very effective. As you will see, this type of therapy is very focused on changing current behavior and on designing solutions to problems.

Goals of Behavior Therapy

Behavior therapy is a therapy based on the application of learning principles to human behavior. Also called *behavior modification,* it focuses on changing overt behaviors rather than on understanding subjective feelings, unconscious processes, or motivations. It uses learning principles to help people replace maladaptive behaviors with more effective ones. Behavior therapists assume that changes in people's environment affect the way they respond to that environment and the way they interact with other people—their behavior. Unlike psychodynamically based therapies, behavior therapy does not aim to discover the origins of a behavior; it works only to alter it. For a person with a nervous twitch, for example, the goal would be to eliminate the twitch. Thus, behavior therapists treat people by having them first unlearn faulty behaviors and then learn more acceptable or effective ones.

Behavior therapists do not always focus on the problem that caused the client to seek therapy. If they see that the client's problem is associated with some other situation, they may focus on changing that situation. For example, a man may seek therapy because of a faltering marriage. However, the therapist may discover that the marriage is suffering because of the client's frequent and acrimonious arguments with his wife, each of which is followed by a period of heavy drinking. The therapist may then discover that both the arguments and the drinking are brought on by stress at work, aggravated by the client's unrealistic expectations regarding his performance. In this situation, the therapist may focus on helping the client develop standards that will ease the original cause of the problem—the tension experienced at work—and that will be consistent with the client's capabilities, past performance, and realistic likelihood of future performance.

Research shows that behavior therapy is at least as effective as insight therapy and in some cases more effective.

Unlike psychodynamic and humanistic therapies, behavior therapy does not encourage clients to interpret past events to find their meaning. Although a behavior therapist may uncover a chain of events leading to a specific behavior, that discovery will not generally prompt a close examination of the client's early experiences.

When people enter behavior therapy, many aspects of their behavior may change, not just those specifically being treated. Thus, a woman being treated for extreme shyness may find not only that the shyness decreases, but also that she can engage more easily in discussions about emotional topics and can perform better on the job. Behaviorists argue that once a person's behavior has changed, it may be easier for the person to manage attitudes, fears, and conflicts.

Behaviorists are dissatisfied with psychodynamic and humanistic therapies for three basic reasons: (1) Those therapies use concepts that are almost impossible to define and measure (such as the id and self-actualization). (2) Some studies show that patients who do not receive psychodynamic and humanistic therapies improve anyway. (3) Once a therapist has labeled a person as abnormal, the label itself may lead to maladaptive behavior. (Although this is true of any type of therapy, psychodynamic therapy tends to use labels more than behavior therapy does.) Behavior therapists assume that people display maladaptive behaviors not because they are abnormal but because they are having trouble adjusting to their environment; if they are taught new ways of coping, the maladjustment will disappear. A great strength of behavior therapy is that it provides a coherent conceptual framework.

However, behavior therapy is not without its critics. Most insight therapists, especially those who are psychodynamically based, believe that if only overt behavior is treated, symptom substitution may occur. **Symptom substitution** is the appearance of one overt symptom to replace another that has been eliminated by treatment. Thus, insight therapists argue that if a therapist eliminates a nervous twitch without examining its underlying causes, the client will express the underlying disorder by developing some other symptom, such as a speech impediment. Behavior therapists, on the other hand, contend that symptom substitution does not occur if the treatment makes proper use of behavioral principles. Research shows that behavior therapy is at least as effective as insight therapy and in some cases more effective (Jacobson, 1991; McGlynn, 1990).

Techniques of Behavior Therapy

Behavior therapists use an array of techniques, often in combination, to help people change their behavior; chief among these techniques are operant conditioning, counterconditioning, and modeling. A good therapist will use whatever combination of techniques will help a client most efficiently and effectively—so, in addition to using several behavioral techniques, a behavior therapist may use some insight techniques. The more complicated the disorder being treated, the more likely it is that a practitioner will use a mix of therapeutic approaches.

Behavior therapy usually involves three general procedures: (1) identifying the problem behavior and its frequency by examining what people actually do; (2) treating a client with treatment strategies that are individually tailored to the client, perhaps by reeducation, communication training, or some type of counterconditioning; and (3) continually assessing whether there is a behavior change. If the client exhibits a new behavior for several weeks or months, the therapist concludes that treatment was effective. Let's now explore the three major behavior therapy techniques: operant conditioning, counterconditioning, and modeling.

Operant Conditioning

Operant conditioning procedures are used with various people in different settings to achieve a wide range of desirable behaviors, including increased reading speed, improved classroom behavior, and the maintenance of personal hygiene. As we saw in Chapter 5, operant conditioning to establish new behaviors often depends on a *reinforcer*—an event or circumstance that increases the probability that a particular response will recur. Rob Terman could employ operant conditioning to help himself adopt more positive responses toward himself. For example, he could ask his girlfriend to acknowledge his effort every time he tries to express his feelings openly.

One of the most effective uses of operant conditioning is with children who are antisocial, slow to learn, or in some way maladjusted. Operant conditioning is also effective with patients in mental hospitals. Ayllon and Haughton (1964), for example, instructed hospital staff members to reinforce patients for psychotic, bizarre, or meaningless verbalizations during one period and for neutral verbalizations (such as comments about the weather) during another. As expected, the relative frequency of each type of verbalization increased when it was reinforced and decreased when it was not reinforced.

Token Economies. One way of rewarding adaptive behavior is with a **token economy**—an operant conditioning procedure in which individuals who display appropriate behavior receive tokens that they can exchange for desirable items or activities. In a hospital setting, for example, some rewards might be candy, new clothes, games, or time with important people in the patients' lives; the more tokens individuals earn, the more items or activities they can obtain. Token economies have also been effective in school settings. Teachers who use a token economy often keep track of tokens publicly and reward students with some fanfare.

Token economies are used to modify behavior in social settings; they aim to strengthen behaviors that are compatible with social norms. For example, a patient in a mental hospital might receive tokens for cleaning tables, helping in the hospital laundry, or maintaining certain standards of personal hygiene and appearance. The level of difficulty of the behavior or task determines the number of tokens earned. Thus, patients might receive 3 tokens for brushing their teeth but 40 tokens for engaging in helping behaviors.

Ayllon and Azrin (1965) monitored the performance of a group of hospitalized patients who were involved in doing simple tasks for 45 days. They found that when tokens (reinforcement) were contingent on performance, the patients worked about four times as long each day as when tokens were not delivered. Token economies become especially effective when combined with other behavioral techniques (Miller, Cosgrove, & Doke, 1990). We examine three of these techniques next—extinction, punishment, and time-out.

Extinction. As we saw in Chapter 5, if reinforcers are withheld, extinction of a behavior will occur. Suppose a 6-year-old girl refuses to go to bed at the designated time. When she is taken to her bedroom, she cries and screams violently. If the parents give in and allow her to stay up, they are reinforcing the crying behavior: The child cries; the parents give in. A therapist might suggest that the parents stop reinforcing the crying behavior by insisting that their daughter go to bed and stay there. Chances are that the child will cry loudly and violently for two or three nights, but the behavior will eventually be extinguished (Williams, 1959).

Punishment. Another way to decrease the frequency of an undesired behavior is to punish it. Punishment often involves the presentation of an aversive stimulus. In the laboratory, researchers might use slight electric shocks to get adult participants to stop performing a specific behavior. As we saw in Chapter 5, a serious limitation of punishment as a behavior-shaping device is that it only suppresses existing behaviors; it cannot be used to establish new, desired behaviors. Thus, punishment for undesired behaviors is usually combined with positive reinforcement for desired behaviors.

Research also shows that people, especially young people, imitate aggression. Thus, a child (or institutionalized person) in therapy may strike out at the therapist who administers punishment in an attempt to eliminate the source of punishment, sometimes inflicting serious injury. Punishment can also bring about generalized aggression. This is especially true for prison inmates, whose hostility is well recognized, and for class bullies, who are often the children most strictly disciplined by their parents or teachers. Skinner

Symptom substitution: The appearance of one overt symptom to replace another that has been eliminated by treatment.

Token economy: An operant conditioning procedure in which individuals who display appropriate behavior receive tokens that they can exchange for desirable items or activities.

(1988) believed that punishment is harmful; he advocated nonpunitive therapeutic techniques, which might involve developing strong bonds between clients and therapists and reinforcing specific prosocial activities. In general, procedures that lead to a perception of control on the part of a client are much more likely to lead to the extinction of undesired behavior.

Time-Out. As we saw in Chapter 5, one effective operant conditioning procedure is **time-out**—the physical removal of a person from sources of reinforcement in order to decrease the occurrence of undesired behaviors. Suppose a boy regularly throws a temper tantrum each time he wants a piece of candy, an ice-cream cone, or his little brother's toys. With the time-out procedure, whenever the child misbehaves, he is taken to a restricted area (such as a chair or a room) away from the rest of the family, without sweets, toys, or other people, or any type of reinforcer. He is made to stay in the restricted area for a short period, say, 5 or 10 minutes; if he leaves, more time is added. The procedure ensures that the child not only does not get what he wants, but that he is also removed from any potential source of reinforcement. Time-out is principally used with children; it is especially effective when it is combined with positive reinforcers for appropriate behavior and is administered by a knowledgeable parent or child-care specialist (Crespi, 1988).

Counterconditioning

A second major technique of behavior therapy is **counterconditioning**—a process of reconditioning in which a person is taught a new, more adaptive response to a familiar stimulus. For example, anxiety in response to any of a number of stimuli is one of the main reasons people seek therapy. If a therapist can condition a person to respond to a stimulus with something other than anxiety—that is, if the therapist can *countercondition* the person—a real breakthrough will be achieved, and the person's anxiety will be reduced.

Joseph Wolpe (1915–1997) was one of the initial proponents of counterconditioning. His work in classical conditioning, especially in situations in which animals show conditioned anxiety responses, led him to attempt to inhibit or decrease anxiety as a response in human beings. His therapeutic goal was to replace anxiety with some other response, such as relaxation, amusement, or pleasure.

Behavior therapy using counterconditioning begins with a specific stimulus (S1), which elicits a specific response (R1). After the person undergoes counterconditioning, the same stimulus (S1) should elicit a new response (R2) (Wolpe, 1958). There are two basic approaches to counterconditioning: systematic desensitization and aversive counterconditioning.

Systematic Desensitization. **Systematic desensitization** is a three-stage counterconditioning procedure in which people are taught to relax when confronting stimuli that formerly elicited anxiety. The client first learns how to relax, then describes the specific situations that arouse anxiety, and finally, while deeply relaxed, imagines increasingly vivid scenes of the situations that elicit anxiety. In this way, the client is gradually, step by step, exposed to the source of anxiety, usually by imagining (while relaxed) a series of progressively more fear- or anxiety-provoking situations. With each successive experience, the client learns relaxation rather than fear as a response. Eventually, the client confronts the real-life situation.

Flying in an airplane, for example, is a stimulus situation (S1) that can bring about a fear response (R1). With systematic desensitization therapy, the idea of flying (S1) can eventually elicit a response of curiosity or even relaxation (R2). The therapist might first ask the relaxed client to imagine sitting in an airplane on the ground, then to imagine the airplane taxiing down a runway, and eventually to imagine flying though the billowing clouds. As the client practices relaxation while imagining the scene, he or she becomes able to tolerate more stressful imagery and may eventually be able to perform the behavior that previously elicited anxiety—in this case, flying in an airplane. Eventually, practicing and becoming desensitized in real-world situations produce the most lasting effects (Hoffart, 1996). If systematic desensitization is combined with efforts to change a person's ideas about the world—cognitive therapy, which we examine in the next section—the person can cope better. Through systematic desensitization and cognitive therapy, people can lose their fear of flying—which is a major problem for 25 million Americans.

Time-out: An operant conditioning procedure in which a person is physically removed from sources of reinforcement to decrease the occurrence of undesired behaviors.

Counterconditioning: A process of reconditioning in which a person is taught a new, more adaptive response to a familiar stimulus.

Systematic desensitization: A three-stage counterconditioning procedure in which people are taught to relax when confronting stimuli that formerly elicited anxiety.

Aversive counterconditioning: A counterconditioning technique in which an aversive or noxious stimulus is paired with a stimulus that elicits an undesirable behavior so that the person will cease responding to the familiar stimulus with the undesirable behavior.

Systematic desensitization is most successful for people who have problems such as impulse control or who exhibit particular forms of anxiety such as phobias. It is not especially effective for people who exhibit serious psychotic symptoms; nor is it the best treatment for situations involving interpersonal conflict.

Aversive Counterconditioning. Clients often have problems because they do not avoid a stimulus that prompts inappropriate behavior. This is where aversive counterconditioning can be used. **Aversive counterconditioning** is a counterconditioning technique in which an aversive or noxious stimulus is paired with a stimulus that elicits an undesirable behavior so that the person will cease responding to the familiar stimulus with the undesirable behavior. As with systematic desensitization, the objective is to teach a new response to the original stimulus. A behavior therapist might use aversive counterconditioning to teach an alcoholic client to avoid alcohol. The first step might be to teach the person to associate alcohol (the original stimulus) with the sensation of nausea (a noxious stimulus). If having the client simply imagine the association is not enough, the therapist might administer a drug that causes the client to feel nauseous whenever he or she consumes alcohol. The goal is to make drinking alcohol unpleasant. Eventually, the treatment will make the client experience nausea just at the *thought* of consuming alcohol, thus causing the client to avoid alcohol.

Modeling

Both children and adults learn behaviors by watching and imitating other people—in other words, by observing models. Children learn a whole host of behaviors—from table manners to toileting behavior to appropriate responses to animals—by observing and imitating their parents and other models. Similarly, the music you listen to, the clothing styles you wear, and the social or political causes you support are determined, in part, by the people around you.

According to Albert Bandura (1977a), modeling is a behavior therapy technique that is most effective for (1) teaching new behavior, (2) helping to eliminate fears, especially phobias, and (3) enhancing already existing behavior. By watching the behavior of others, people learn to exhibit more adaptive and appropriate behavior. Bandura, Blanchard, and Ritter (1969), for example, asked people with snake phobia to watch other people handling snakes. Afterward, the watchers' fear of snakes was reduced.

One problem with modeling is that people may observe and imitate the behavior of inappropriate models. As we saw in Chapter 11, people imitate violent behaviors they have observed on television and in movies. Further, many adolescents abuse alcohol and other drugs because they imitate their peers. Such imitation often occurs because of faulty thinking about situations, people, or goals.

Behavior Therapy in a Contemporary Context

Behavior therapy, along with cognitive therapy (to be considered next), with which it is closely allied, have been heavily influenced by HMOs and managed care. A managed care organization usually controls the reimbursement of therapists and thus intervenes between a client and a therapist to make rulings about various questions: Does this problem qualify for reimbursement? What technique should be used to treat this client? Is this clinician the appropriate therapist for this client? Many psychologists see managed care as a crisis, a nightmare, and the downfall of psychotherapy (Fishman & Franks, 1997). Behavior therapists, however, more than other therapists, have become allies of managed care organizations because of the close alignment of their shared goals, especially the goal of efficiency. *I*

Think Critically

- How would a behavior therapist's approach to assisting a person suffering from low self-esteem differ from the approach of a Gestalt therapist?
- Why do you think modeling is especially effective in the treatment of phobias?
- Do you think that HMOs should be permitted to determine the best therapy for a client?

Ⓘ Cognitive Therapy

Focus on issues and ideas

- The assertion of cognitive therapists that wrong, distorted, or underdeveloped ideas and thoughts often prevent a person from coping well
- The numerous problems that can be treated using cognitive therapy
- The impact of managed care on psychotherapy

According to cognitive therapists, wrong, distorted, or underdeveloped ideas and thoughts often prevent a person from establishing effective coping strategies. Growing out of behavior therapy and the developing study of cognitive psychology, *cognitive therapy* focuses on changing a client's behavior by changing his or her thoughts and perceptions. Cognitive therapy is derived from three basic propositions: (1) Cognitive activity affects behavior. (2) Cognitive activity can be monitored. (3) Behavior changes can be effected through cognitive changes. Cognitive psychologists have had a profound impact in many areas of psychology, especially in therapy. In the past, behavior therapists were concerned only with overt behavior; today, many incorporate thought processes into their treatments. For this reason, their work is often called *cognitive behavior therapy.* Researchers now suggest that thought processes may hold the key to managing many forms of maladjustment, including disorders such as obsessive–compulsive disorder (Abramowitz, 1998).

Therapists who use *cognitive restructuring* (cognitive therapy) are interested in modifying the faulty thought patterns of disturbed people (Mahoney, 1977). This type of therapy is effective for people who have attached overly narrow or otherwise inappropriate labels to certain behaviors or situations; for example, such a person may believe that sex is dirty or that assertiveness is unwomanly. Whenever presented with a situation that involves sex or assertiveness, the person will respond in a way that is determined by his or her thoughts about the situation rather than by the facts of the situation.

Cognitive therapy typically focuses on current behavior and current thoughts. It is not especially concerned with uncovering forgotten childhood experiences, although it can be used to alter thoughts about those experiences. It has been used effectively to assist in weight loss and to treat depression, bulimia, excessive anger, and adolescent behavior problems (Kendall, 1993; Shapiro et al., 1994). When cognitive restructuring is combined with other psychological techniques, such as reinforcement, which help a person make behavioral changes, results are even more impressive (Kirsch, Montgomery, & Sapirstein, 1995). Cognitive therapy has gone through three decades of development, and its future looks promising (Beck et al., 1994).

Rational–emotive therapy: A cognitive behavior therapy that emphasizes the importance of logical, rational thought processes.

Rational-Emotive Therapy

The best-known of the cognitive therapies is **rational–emotive therapy**—a cognitive behavior therapy that emphasizes the importance of logical, rational thought processes. Researcher Albert Ellis developed this therapy more than 30 years ago. Most behavior therapists assume that abnormal behavior is caused by faulty and irrational *behavior* patterns. Ellis and his colleagues, however, assume that it is caused by faulty and irrational *thinking* patterns (Ellis, 1970; Ellis & Harper, 1961). They believe that if faulty thought processes can be replaced with rational ones, maladjustment and abnormal behavior will disappear.

According to Ellis, psychological disturbance is a result of events in a person's life that give rise to irrational beliefs leading to negative emotions and behaviors. Moreover, these beliefs are a breeding ground for further irrational ideas (Dryden & Ellis, 1988). Ellis (1988) argues that people make demands on themselves and on other people, and they rigidly hold onto them no matter how unrealistic and illogical they are.

Thus, a major goal of rational–emotive therapy is to help people examine the past events that produced the irrational beliefs. Ellis, for example, tries to focus on a client's basic philosophy of life and determine whether it is self-defeating. He thus tries to uncover the client's thought patterns and help the client recognize that the underlying beliefs are faulty. Table 14.4 lists ten irrational assumptions that, according to Ellis, cause emotional problems and maladaptive behaviors. They are based on people's needs to be liked, to be competent, to be loved, and to feel secure. When people assign irrational or exaggerated value to fulfilling these needs, the needs become maladaptive and lead to emotional disturbance, anxiety, and abnormal behavior. If rational–emotive therapy is successful, the client adopts different behaviors based on more rational thought processes. Research supports the effectiveness of the approach (Abrams & Ellis, 1994; Haaga & Davison, 1993), and Ellis (1993) asserts that rational–emotive therapy has broad applications in both therapeutic and classroom settings.

Beck's Approach

Another cognitive therapy that focuses on irrational ideas is that of Aaron Beck (1963). As we saw in

Table 14.4 Ellis's Outline of Ten Irrational Assumptions

1. It is a necessity for an adult to be loved and approved of by almost everyone for virtually everything.
2. A person must be thoroughly competent, adequate, and successful in all respects.
3. Certain people are bad, wicked, or villainous and should be punished for their sins.
4. It is catastrophic when things are not going the way one would like.
5. Human unhappiness is externally caused. People have little or no ability to control their sorrows or to rid themselves of negative feelings.
6. It is right to be terribly preoccupied with and upset about something that may be dangerous or fearsome.
7. It is easier to avoid facing many of life's difficulties and responsibilities than it is to undertake more rewarding forms of self-discipline.
8. The past is all-important. Because something once strongly affected someone's life, it should continue to do so indefinitely.
9. People and things should be different from the way they are. It is catastrophic if perfect solutions to the grim realities of life are not immediately found.
10. Maximal human happiness can be achieved by inertia and inaction or by passively and without commitment "enjoying oneself."

Source: Ellis & Harper, 1961.

Chapter 13, Beck's theory assumes that depression is caused by people's distorted thoughts about reality, which lead to negative views about the world, themselves, and the future, and often to gross overgeneralizations. For example, people who think they have no future—that all of their options are blocked—and who undervalue their intelligence are likely to be depressed. Such individuals form appraisals of situations that are distorted and based on insufficient (and sometimes wrong) data. The goal of therapy, therefore, is to help them to develop realistic appraisals of the situations they encounter and to solve their problems (Beck, 1991). The therapist acts as a trainer and coinvestigator, providing data to be examined and guidance in understanding how cognitions influence behavior (Beck & Weishaar, 1989).

According to Beck (1976), a successful client passes through four stages in the course of correcting faulty views and moving toward improved mental health: "First, he has to become aware of what he is thinking. Second, he needs to recognize what thoughts are awry. Then he has to substitute accurate for inaccurate judgments. Finally, he needs feedback to inform him whether his changes are correct" (p. 217).

Meichenbaum's Approach

Some researchers, among them Donald Meichenbaum, believe that what people say to themselves determines what they will do. Therefore, a key goal of therapy is to change the things people say to themselves. According to Meichenbaum, the therapist has to change the client's appraisal of stressful events and the client's use of self-instructions, thus normalizing her or his reactions (Meichenbaum, 1993).

A strength of Meichenbaum's theory is that self-instruction can be used in many settings for many kinds of problems. It can help people who are shy or impulsive, people with speech impediments, and even those who are schizophrenic (Meichenbaum, 1974; Meichenbaum & Cameron, 1973). Rather than attempting to change their irrational beliefs, clients learn a repertoire of activities they can use to make their behavior more adaptive. For example, they may learn to conduct a private monologue in which they work out adaptive ways of coping with situations. They can then discuss with a therapist the quality and usefulness of these self-instructional statements. They may learn to organize their responses to specific situations in an orderly set of steps that can be easily carried out.

Cognitive therapy in its many forms has been used with adults and children and with groups having particular characteristics, such as women and the elderly (Davis & Padesky, 1989). It can be applied to such problems as anxiety disorders, marital difficulties, chronic pain, and (as is evident from Beck's work) depression. Cognitive therapy continues to make enormous strides. It is influencing an increasing number of theorists and practitioners who conduct both long-term therapy and brief therapy (which is considered in *Experiencing Psychology*, on p. 410). (I)

(I) Group Therapy

Focus on issues and ideas

- Why group therapy can be more effective than individual therapy and why the formation of the group is important in such therapy
- The format and techniques of traditional group therapy
- The eclectic approach of family therapy

EXPERIENCING PSYCHOLOGY

The Impact of Managed Care—Brief Therapy

Whether psychologists like it or not, there is a new model of psychotherapy in town. The advent of managed care and control by HMOs of the extent and cost of patients' medical and psychological care has forced professionals and patients to accept a model of therapy that is often short, for economic reasons, but is focused—and sometimes especially effective (Cummings, Budman, & Thomas, 1998). The model rejects many of the ideas of the various traditional therapies discussed so far in this chapter. Its proponents reject the idea that any single therapeutic approach can help all people with any behavioral or emotional problem. It rejects the belief that a person must understand her or his unconscious motivations or life history fully before therapy can end. Last, it disavows the idea that the therapist and the client have to resolve past or future psychological problems during psychotherapy sessions.

Sometimes termed *brief therapy*, this therapeutic approach is based on a blend of psychotherapeutic orientations and skills (Cummings, 1986). A basic goal is to give clients what they need; the therapy therefore focuses on treating clients' problems efficiently and getting them back on their own as quickly as possible. The time frame varies from therapist to therapist, client to client, and HMO to HMO, but 6 weeks is common; anything more than 16 weeks is considered lengthy. One of the objectives is to save clients time and money. Although HMOs or insurance companies may place limits on the number of sessions, clients may remain in therapy longer if they feel the need and are willing and able to continue to pay. They can also return if they need help in the future. The primary effect of this approach to therapy is that more and more therapists are thinking in terms of *planned* short-term treatments (Messer & Wachtel, 1997).

The therapist makes sure that treatment begins in the first session of brief therapy. He or she strives to perform an *operational diagnosis* that answers this question: Why is the client here today instead of last week, last month, last year, or next year? The answer helps the therapist pinpoint the specific problem for which the client is seeking help. Also, in the first session, "every client makes a therapeutic contract with every therapist" (Cummings, 1986, p. 430; Goulding, 1990). The goals of therapy are established and agreed on by the client and the therapist, and the therapy is precise, active, and directive, with no unnecessary steps (Clarkin & Hull, 1991; Lazarus & Fay, 1990).

Published research on brief therapy is encouraging, suggesting that the therapy is effective and that the effects are long-lasting (Barber & Ellman, 1996). Research has been limited to relatively few clients with a narrow range of problems. Nonetheless, researchers have found brief therapy to be effective when treatment goals and procedures are tailored to the client's needs and the time. It can be especially effective with couples (Donovan, 1998) and when combined with cognitive restructuring (Ellis, 1990).

Brief therapy is not a cure-all. Like all therapies, its aim is to help relieve clients' suffering, and it is effective with some clients and with some problems some of the time (Franko & Erb, 1998). Further research on brief therapy is being conducted, and its future will depend on the results of that research. ■

When several people meet as a group to receive psychological help from a therapist, the treatment is referred to as **group therapy.** This technique was introduced in the early 1900s and has become increasingly popular since World War II. One reason for its popularity is that in the United States the demand for therapists exceeds the number available. Individually, a therapist can generally see up to 40 clients a week for 1 hour each. But in a group, the same therapist might see 8 to 10 clients in just 1 hour. Another reason for the popularity is that the therapist's fee is shared among the members of the group, making group therapy less expensive than individual therapy.

Group therapy can also be more effective than individual therapy (McRoberts, Burlingame, & Hoag, 1998), because the social pressures that operate in a group can help shape the members' behavior. In addition, group members can be useful models of behavior for one another, and they can provide mutual reinforcement and support.

Techniques and Formats

The techniques used in group therapy are determined largely by the nature of the group and by the orientation of the therapist—psychoanalytic, client-centered, Gestalt, behavioral, or other. No two groups are alike, and no two therapists deal with individual group members in the same way.

In traditional group therapy, 6 to 12 clients meet regularly (usually once a week) with a therapist in a clinic, hospital, or the therapist's office. Generally, the therapist selects members on the basis of what they can gain from and offer to the group. The goal is to construct a group whose members are compatible (though not necessarily the same) in terms of age, needs, and problems. The duration of group therapy varies; it usually takes longer than 6 months, but there are a growing number of short-term groups that meet for fewer than 12 weeks (Rose, 1991). The format of traditional group therapy varies, but generally each member describes her or his problems to the other members, who in turn relate their experiences with similar problems and how they coped with them. This gives individuals a chance to express their fears and anxieties to people who are accepting; each member eventually realizes that everyone has emotional problems. Group members also have opportunities to role play (try out) new behaviors in a safe environment. In a mental health center, for example, a therapist might help group members relive past traumas and cope with their continuing fears. Sometimes, the therapist is directive in helping the group address a problem. At other times, the therapist allows the group to resolve a problem independently. Members can also exert pressure on an individual to behave in more appropriate ways.

Nontraditional Group Therapy Techniques

Two nontraditional techniques sometimes used in group therapy are psychodrama and encounter groups. **Psychodrama** is a group therapy technique in which members act out their situations, feelings, and roles. It stems from the work of J. L. Moreno, a Viennese psychiatrist who used it in the 1920s and 1930s. Those who participate can practice expressing their feelings and responding to the feelings of others. Even those who do not participate can see how others respond to different emotions and situations. Psychodrama can help open the floodgates of emotion and can be used to refine social skills and define problem areas that need to be worked on (Naar, 1990).

People come together in all kinds of groups to learn more about their feelings, behavior, and interactions. In the 1960s and 1970s, such groups were termed **encounter groups;** today, they often take on more specific names such as "The Special Awareness Group" or the "Mediation as a Way of Life Group." These groups are usually not primarily problem-oriented; rather, they are designed to offer people experiences that will help them become self-actualized and develop better interpersonal relationships and a sense of authenticity or genuineness. (Self-actualization, which we examined in Chapters 8 and 10, is the process by which people move toward fulfilling their potential.) These special groups also enable their members to work on resolving their own problems and perceiving—and ultimately minimizing—the effects of their problems on others. Each kind of encounter group is unique. Some are like traditional therapy groups; in others, the therapist participates minimally, if at all. Some researchers believe that encounter groups made up of specific types of people—such as female athletes, drug addicts, alcoholics, homosexuals, or single people—can be especially helpful to their members.

Family Therapy

Family therapy is a special form of group therapy in which two or more people who are committed to each other's well-being are treated together in an effort to change the ways they interact. (Marital, or couples, therapy is thus a subcategory of family therapy.) A *family* is defined as any group of people who are committed to one another's well-being, preferably for life (Bronfenbrenner, 1989). Today's therapists recognize that families are often nontraditional; blended families and single-parent families are very common, for example. Different kinds of families are shaping the way people respond to the world and must be considered as part of the cultural context in which psychologists view behavior. And even for traditional families, life has grown more complicated by the increasing need to juggle work and family responsibilities and cope with societal problems.

With families facing new kinds of problems, family therapy is now used by a large number of practitioners, especially social workers. In today's world of managed care and HMOs, brief family therapy is the order of the day, and symptom relief is usually the first, but certainly not the only, goal. From a family therapist's point of view, the real focus of family therapy is the family's structure and organization. While family members may identify one person—perhaps a

Group therapy: Psychotherapeutic process in which several people meet as a group with a therapist to receive psychological help.

Psychodrama [SYE-ko-drama]: A group therapy technique in which members act out their situations, feelings, and roles.

Encounter group: Group of people who meet to learn more about their feelings, behavior, and interactions.

Family therapy: A type of therapy in which two or more people who are committed to one another's well-being are treated at once, in an effort to change the ways they interact.

delinquent child—as the problem, family therapists believe that in many cases, that person may simply be a scapegoat. The so-called problem member diverts the family's attention from structural problems that are difficult to confront. Any clinician who works with a person who has some type of adjustment problem must also consider the impact of this problem on the people that individual interacts with.

Sometimes family therapy is called *relationship therapy,* because relationships are often the focus of the intervention, especially with couples (Jacobson & Addis, 1993). Research indicates that, like other forms of therapy, family therapy and marital (couples) therapy are effective (Pinsof, Wynne, & Hambright, 1996). However, because of the myriad of variables operating within families, such research is complicated, to say the least (Lebow & Gurman, 1995).

Family therapists often attempt to change *family systems.* This means that treatment takes place within the dynamic social system of the marriage or the family (Fruzzetti & Jacobson, 1991). Therapists assume that there are multiple sources of psychological influence: Individuals within a family affect family interactions, and family interactions affect individuals; the family is thus an interactive system (Sturges, 1994). For example, when a mother labels a son "lazy" because he doesn't have a job, the son may feel shame, but he may act out his feeling as anger. He may lash out at his father's poor work habits and lack of success. This reaction may be followed by a squabble over who "brings home the bacon," and so forth. The mother's attitude thus leads to a clash among all the individuals within the family system. The family systems approach has become especially popular in colleges of social work, in departments of psychology, and even in colleges of medicine, where patients are often seen in a family setting. A useful technique in family therapy is to *restructure* the family's interactions. If a son is responding passively to his domineering mother, for example, the therapist may suggest that the son be assigned chores only by his father.

An issue that often emerges in family therapy is how all members of the family can become enmeshed in one member's problem—for example, depression, alcoholism, drug abuse, or anxiety disorder. Such involvement often becomes devastating for the whole family. This problem is termed *codependence.* Practitioners often see patients with alcoholism or cocaine addiction whose friends or family members are codependent. Codependence is not a disorder in the *DSM–IV.* In fact, the families of people with problems such as substance abuse have gone relatively unnoticed. But practitioners who treat whole families, not just the person suffering from maladjustment, view codependence as an additional type of adjustment problem—not for the patient but for the patient's family and friends.

The codependents—the patient's family members or friends—are often plagued by intense feelings of shame, fear, anger, and pain; they cannot express those feelings, however, because they feel obligated to care for the person suffering from the disorder or addiction. Codependent children may believe their job is to take care of their maladjusted parents. Codependent adults may strive to help their maladjusted spouses, relatives, or friends with their problems. They often think that if they were perfect, they could help the maladjusted individual. In some cases, people actually *need* the person to stay disordered; family members sometimes subconsciously want a member with a problem to remain dependent on them so that they can remain in a controlling position.

In today's world of managed care and HMOs, brief family therapy is the order of the day.

Some researchers believe the family systems approach to be as effective as individual therapy—and more effective in some situations (Ford et al., 1998). Not all families profit equally from such interventions, however. Family therapy is difficult with families that are disorganized. Younger couples and families seem to have better outcomes. When depression is evident, outcomes are not as good (Lebow & Gurman, 1995). In addition, some family members may refuse to participate or drop out of therapy; this almost always has negative consequences (Prinz & Miller, 1994).

Family therapy is eclectic, borrowing from many schools of therapy and treating a broad range of families and problems (Guerin & Chabot, 1997). Family therapists join with families in helping them change because they acknowledge and recognize that change of one sort or another is inevitable in a dynamic system. They further assert that only a small change for the better is necessary to make a big difference. Most family therapists assert that clients have the strength and resources to change and that people don't need to understand the origins of a problem to solve it. Last, there is no *one* solution to family problems—especially given today's complicated families (Selekman, 1993). (I)

Psychosurgery: Brain surgery used in the past to alleviate symptoms of serious mental disorders.

Electroconvulsive [ee-LECK-tro-con-VUL-siv] therapy (ECT): A treatment for severe mental illness in which an electric current is briefly applied to the head in order to produce a generalized seizure; also known as *shock treatment.*

Think Critically

- Why do you think that having several people in treatment together makes such a difference? Isn't getting a great deal of one-on-one attention—individual therapy—likely to produce superior results?

I Biologically Based Therapies

Focus on issues and ideas

- When a biologically based therapy is recommended
- The limited uses of psychosurgery and ECT
- The different classes of drugs used in drug therapy
- The mechanism of action of selective serotonin reuptake inhibitors (SSRIs)

When a person seeks a therapist for help with a psychological problem, the usual approach involves some form of talking therapy that may be based on psychodynamic, humanistic, behavioral, or cognitive theories. For some patients, however, talking therapy is not enough. Some may be too profoundly depressed; others may be exhibiting symptoms of bipolar disorders (manic depression) or schizophrenia; still others may need hospitalization because they are suicidal. This is where biologically based therapies enter the picture. These therapies often involve medication, hospitalization, and physicians. They are generally used in combination with traditional forms of psychotherapy. Biologically based therapies fall into three broad classes: psychosurgery (rarely used), electroconvulsive therapy (occasionally used), and drug therapy (often used).

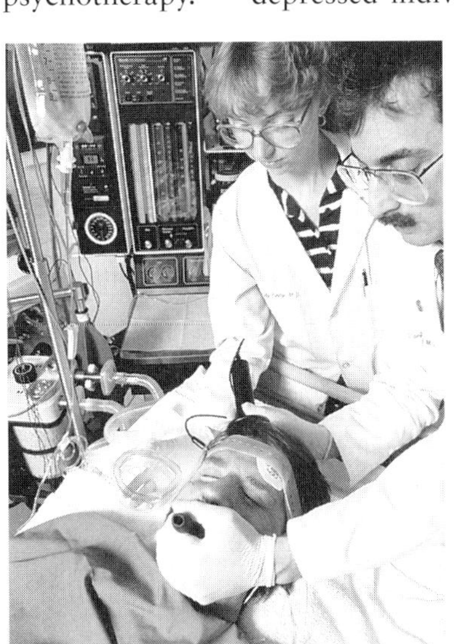

Psychosurgery and Electroconvulsive Therapy

Psychosurgery is brain surgery; it was used in the past to alleviate symptoms of serious mental disorders. A particular type of psychosurgery commonly performed in the 1940s and 1950s was the *prefrontal lobotomy,* in which the surgeon would sever parts of the brain's frontal lobes from the rest of the brain. The frontal lobes were thought to control emotions; their removal destroyed connections within the brain, making patients docile. Patients lost the symptoms of their mental disorders, but they also became unnaturally calm and completely unemotional. Some became unable to control their impulses, and an estimated 1–4% of patients died from the operation.

Today, despite advances in technology and in the precision of the operation, psychosurgery is rarely used, for three reasons: First, drug therapy has proved more effective than surgical procedures. Second, the long-term effects of psychosurgery are questionable. Third, and most important, the procedure is irreversible and therefore morally objectionable to most practitioners and to patients and their families. Its widespread use during the 1940s and 1950s is considered by many to have been a serious mistake.

Electroconvulsive therapy (ECT), or *shock treatment,* once widely employed with depressed individuals, is a treatment for severe mental illness in which an electric current is briefly applied to the head in order to produce a generalized seizure (convulsion). The duration of the shock is less than a second, and patients are treated in 3 to 12 sessions over several weeks. In the 1940s and 1950s, ECT was routinely given to severely disturbed patients in mental hospitals. Unfortunately, it was often used on patients (mostly women) who did not need it or by overzealous physicians who wished to control unruly patients. Today, ECT is not a common treatment. According to the National Institutes of Health, fewer than 2.5% of all psychiatric hospital patients are treated with ECT.

Is ECT at all effective? Could drug therapy or traditional psychotherapy be used in its place? ECT is effective in the short-term management of severely depressed individuals, those suffering from extreme episodes of mania, and people with psychotic depression (Flint & Rifat, 1998); it is sometimes used when a particular patient is at risk of suicide (Cohen, Tyrrell, & Smith, 1997). However, its effects are only temporary if it is not followed by drug therapy and psychotherapy (Parker et al., 1992). Generally speaking, ECT should be used as a last resort, when other forms of treatment have been ineffective and when a patient is not responsive to medications (Prudic, Sackheim, & Devanand, 1990). ECT is not appropriate for treating schizophrenia or for managing unruly behaviors associated with other psychological disorders.

The risk of death during the administration of ECT is low (Coffey et al., 1991). However, there is a potential for temporary memory loss and for a decreased ability to learn and retain new information that may endure for several weeks (Prudic, Sackheim, & Devanand, 1990). In addition, ECT may frighten patients and can leave them feeling ashamed and stigmatized (Fink, 1997). If practitioners determine that ECT is warranted, the law requires (and medical ethics demand) that the patient be given the option to accept or reject the treatment—as is true for *any* treatment.

Drug Therapy

In this fast-paced society, people seem to want quick fixes. Every few years, politicians promise a new plan to eliminate poverty or a simple solution to racial tension. Similarly, people often want to take drugs to alleviate emotional problems. Drug therapy is an important form of treatment, especially for anxiety, depression, and schizophrenia. It is the most widely used biologically based therapy, and it is effective when used correctly and carefully. Drug therapy is sometimes used in combination with traditional talking therapy (see *Experiencing Psychology*). However, clinicians are often reluctant to turn to drug therapy until after traditional forms of psychotherapy have failed—which may cause a delay in the patient's healing. Clinicians who recommend drug therapy must be aware of several key issues. Dosages are especially important and must be monitored; too much or too little of certain drugs is dangerous. Long-term use of many drugs is ill advised. Further, no drug will permanently cure the maladjustment of people who are not coping well. Last, physicians and psychiatrists must be sensitive to the issues of overmedication and long-term dependence on drugs.

In the last decade, clinical psychologists have been lobbying for the legal right to write prescriptions for a limited class of drugs. The argument is that patients would benefit by the better integration of medications and psychological techniques (Hines, 1997; Tuckman, 1996)—but this is a controversial proposition even among psychologists (Gutierrez & Silk, 1998; Plante, Boccaccini, & Andersen, 1998). Those who do support the idea recognize that additional training would be necessary and licensing authority would need to be instituted (Klusman, 1998). This debate continues among physicians and psychologists as well as state licensing boards.

When physicians (often psychiatrists) do administer drugs, people may experience relief from symptoms of anxiety, mania, depression, and schizophrenia. Drugs for the relief of mental problems are sometimes called *psychotropic drugs;* they are usually grouped into four classes: antianxiety drugs, antidepressant drugs, antimania drugs, and antipsychotic drugs.

Antianxiety Drugs. Antianxiety drugs, or tranquilizers (technically, *anxiolytics*) are mood-altering substances. Librium, Xanax, and Valium are trade names of the most widely prescribed antianxiety drugs. Widely used in the United States (and probably overprescribed), these drugs reduce stressful feelings, calm patients, and lower excitability. When taken occasionally to help a person through a stressful situation, such drugs are useful. They can also help moderate anxiety in a person who is extremely anxious, particularly when the person is also receiving some form of psychotherapy. However, long-term use of antianxiety drugs without some adjunct therapy is usually ill advised. Today, physicians are wary of patients who seek antianxiety drugs for management of daily stress; they worry about substance abuse and an overreliance on drugs to get through the day.

Antidepressant Drugs. As their name suggests, antidepressants (technically, *thymoleptics*) are sometimes considered mood elevators. They work by altering the level of neurotransmitters in the brain. With the wide availability of antidepressants, it is surprising that half of those who have been depressed for more than 20 years have never taken an antidepressant (Hirschfeld et al., 1997). Depression often goes undiagnosed and is definitely undertreated.

One kind of antidepressant, selective serotonin reuptake inhibitors (SSRIs), or simply serotonin reuptake inhibitors, blocks the reuptake of serotonin. SSRIs work by prolonging the time that serotonin stays in a synapse. According to researchers, when a key neurotransmitter like serotonin is released in order to bind to the next cell but doesn't, the person experiences melancholy. What happens is the neurotransmitter is either neutralized in the synapse or taken back up by the neuron that released it, in the process called *reuptake.* Drugs like Prozac do not allow the neurotransmitter to be neutralized or restored to the releasing cell; thus, it stays in the synapse longer, where it is more likely to bind and depression is averted.

Drugs such as Prozac, Zoloft, and Paxil are SSRIs. These drugs account for 60% of antidepressant sales in the United States. The next section discusses the success of Prozac. Extremely depressed people who take such antidepressants often become more optimistic and redevelop a sense of purpose in their lives. These medications allow many people to function outside a hospital setting. The drugs can take as long as 4 weeks to reach their full effectiveness, and daily doses are necessary.

EXPERIENCING PSYCHOLOGY

Talking Therapy, Drug Therapy, and Depression

Depression is the most common disorder seen by the medical, psychiatric, and psychological communities. Women are twice as likely as men to be diagnosed as depressed; the aged are especially likely to be depressed, as are widows and people with lower incomes (Lepine & Bouchez, 1998; Umberson, Wortman, & Kessler, 1992).

Treatment for depression has traditionally involved insight therapy, drug therapy, or a combination of the two. Insight therapy has been used to help patients gain an understanding of the causes of their feelings of sadness. Drug therapy has proved especially effective in altering brain activity to alleviate depressive symptoms. Prozac and Zoloft are two popular and effective drugs. Most practitioners and theoreticians believe that the most effective treatment is drugs in combination with psychotherapy.

New research is challenging this belief, however. In the last decade, psychologists have found that (1) psychotherapy is especially effective for depression, (2) the benefits of psychotherapy for depression are long-lasting, and (3) most important, combinations of psychotherapy and drug therapy are *not* necessarily more effective than either of the treatments alone (Persons, Thase, & Crits-Christoph, 1996). In important reviews of the research literature on the treatment of depression, Muñoz and colleagues (1994) argued that psychotherapy is more effective than drugs for depression; Antonuccio, Danton, and DeNelsky (1995) came to the same conclusion. Earlier, Robinson, Berman, and Neimeyer (1990) argued that drug therapy alone *or* traditional psychotherapy alone is equally effective for patients suffering from depression. These researchers' findings startled some members of the psychological community, because they challenged the long-held idea that combination treatments are the most effective. The researchers acknowledge that drug therapy plus psychotherapy may be the most effective treatment for some other disorders. And research shows that for anxiety disorders in adolescents (Kearney & Silverman, 1998) and depression in the elderly (Reynolds et al., 1999), a combination of drug therapy and behavior therapy is especially effective. However, for the types of drugs examined by Robinson and his colleagues and for patients suffering from clinical depression, the result was clear: The combination treatment provided no additional benefit over drug therapy alone or psychotherapy alone.

The work of these researchers raises a question: How many widows, other women, and people from lower socioeconomic levels are being given drugs when they don't need them? Obviously, it's impossible to know; but with each passing month, new research on various disorders and on the role of psychotherapy and drug therapy is emerging (Southwick & Yehuda, 1993). For example, Wexler and Cicchetti (1992), like Muñoz and colleagues (1994), argue that psychotherapy alone has the advantage. These studies led Antonuccio (1995) to assert that "when treating depression, there is no stronger medicine than psychotherapy" (p. 451). In their review of studies on psychotherapy and depression, Antonuccio, Danton, and DeNelsky (1995, p. 582) wrote: "There is a tendency to underestimate the power and cost-effectiveness of a caring, confidential psychotherapeutic relationship in the treatment of depression. . . . For those who do not respond to psychotherapy, the costs and benefits of drug treatments or combined treatments can then be carefully weighed." Today, most therapists are practical and suggest to clients that an initial treatment with psychotherapy alone might perhaps be followed by combination treatment. There are likely to be further studies showing which types of depressive disorders can best benefit from drug therapy, which from insight therapy, which from cognitive therapy, and which from combinations of drug therapy and traditional talking therapies. ■

A Best-Selling Medication—Prozac

Since its introduction in 1987, about 28 million people have taken the drug Prozac. Along with two other drugs, Zoloft and Paxil, which are similar to Prozac in chemical make-up, this "wonder drug" is so popular that pharmacies need whole shelves to stock the supply necessary for a week. Yearly sales of such drugs bring in more than $4 billion.

Many people who take Prozac and its sister medications feel better—symptoms of depression lift, appetite returns, and the outlook seems less bleak. People who take the drug feel so much better that they do better in their work and their relationships, and life seems to turn around. The drugs decrease the likelihood of new episodes of depression (Montgomery & Kasper, 1998) and work well for older adults (Mittmann et al., 1997; Salzman, 1997) and even for children (Ryan & Varma, 1998).

The number of side effects from drugs like Prozac is small compared to drugs used earlier. Those drugs had potent side effects—increased heart rate, increased blood pressure, nausea, and sleepiness, to name a few. So one reason why Prozac has been so successful is that it is relatively free of serious side effects. But it is not totally without them.

Researchers have long known that drugs that affect the reuptake of monoamines (serotonin, dopamine, norepinephrine, and epinephrine) can lighten some depressive symptoms. But the runaway success of Prozac has startled practitioners and researchers alike. They are also puzzled because not everyone who takes Prozac feels better. Furthermore, Prozac does have side effects, including a diminution of sexual appetite. Originally intended to be taken for shorter durations—6 months or so—Prozac is now being taken for years on end. Are people staying on the drug too long? Researchers are wondering if the drug (like many others) is being overprescribed (Messer & Wachtel, 1997). How many people who take the drug actually need it? How many were not properly diagnosed?

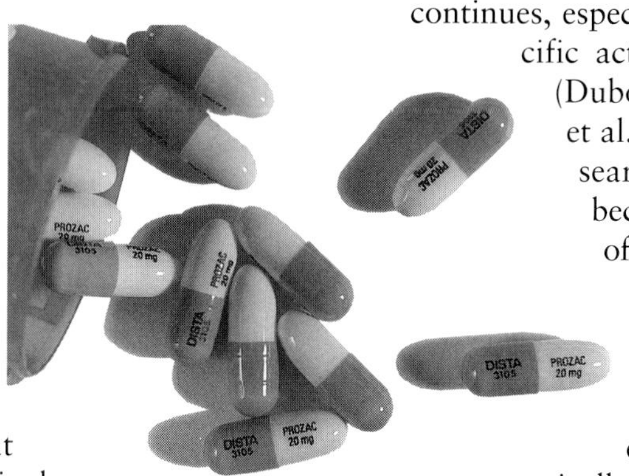

The effects of this class of drugs are so quickly evident, and the side effects so few, that psychologists worry that the original problems—low self-esteem or depression over a bad relationship, for example—may not get the attention they deserve. SSRIs have an important place in the treatment of people with various disorders—but most psychologists feel they should be part of a full treatment program that also involves short-term or perhaps even long-term psychotherapy.

Some researchers have questioned whether depression, schizophrenia, and a host of other disorders can be explained solely on the basis of brain chemistry (Valenstein, 1998). They argue that easy explanations and quick fixes with drugs are rarely the complete answer to psychological problems. Will new drugs evolve that will be better, more refined, and more potent than today's SSRIs? The answer is undoubtedly yes. Will drugs alone solve people's psychological problems? The answer is surely no. Are they part of a solution for some people? The answer is unquestionably yes.

Antidepressants also include two other major categories of drugs: tricyclics and monoamine oxidase (MAO) inhibitors. Both types of drugs are potent. The tricyclics (named for their chemical structure) act like SSRIs to block reuptake, but MAO inhibitors work by breaking down monoamine oxidase, an enzyme that destroys the neurotransmitters. Tricyclics are prescribed much more often than MAO inhibitors because they pose less danger of medical complications. (Patients on MAO inhibitors have to adhere to special diets and some other restrictions to prevent adverse physical reactions to the drugs.) To help a patient suffering from a severe bout of depression, a physician might prescribe a commonly used tricyclic such as imipramine (Tofranil) or amitriptyline (Elavil), which has fewer serious side effects and can alleviate symptoms in the majority of people with depressive problems.

Research on the effectiveness of antidepressant drugs is contradictory. Some researchers assert that these drugs have strong effects; others report only modest help from the drugs (Greenberg et al., 1992; Schulberg & Rush, 1994). Research using double-blind procedures and carefully controlled conditions continues, especially with drugs that have specific actions on depressive behaviors (Dubovsky & Thomas, 1995; Roose et al., 1994). The impact of new research findings will be profound, because there are a great number of people with depressive disorders.

Antimania Drugs. Lithium carbonate has long been used as an effective antimania drug (like antidepressants, technically, a *thymoleptic*) and has come into wide use for patients with bipolar (manic–depressive) disorder because it relieves the manic symptoms. Psychiatrists find that when clients take a daily maintenance dose, lithium is especially helpful in warding off episodes of mania. The dosage of any drug is important, but in the case of lithium it is vital. Too much produces noxious side effects; too little has no effect. No drug will cure all individuals with bipolar disorder of all their symptoms and solve all their problems (for example, lithium is less effective with young patients); in general, however, lithium allows some patients to cope better, to control their symptoms, and to seek other therapies that allow them to manage their lives in the most productive way possible (Moncrieff, 1997). The same is true of other drugs in this class, including valproic acid, or valproate.

Antipsychotic Drugs. Antipsychotic drugs (technically, *neuroleptics*) are used mainly for people who suffer from the disabling disorder schizophrenia. These drugs reduce hostility and aggression in violent

Table 14.5 Drugs Commonly Used to Treat Psychiatric Disorders

Effect Group	Chemical Group	Generic Name	Trade Name
Antianxiety (anxiolytic)	Benzodiazepines	Diazepam Chlordiazepoxide Alprazolam Clonazepam	Valium Librium Xanax Klonapin
	Nonbenzodiazepine	Buspirone	Buspar
Antidepressant (thymoleptic)	Tricylics	Amitriptyline Imipramine Nortriptyline Desipramine Doxepin Clomipramine	Elavil Tofranil Pamelor Norpramin Sinequan Anafranil
	Monoamine oxidase inhibitors	Phenelzine Tranylcypromine	Nardil Parnate
	Serotonin reuptake inhibitors	Fluoxetine Sertraline Paroxetine Fluvoxamine	Prozac Zoloft Paxil Luvox
Antimanic (thymoleptic)	Lithium carbonate	Lithium	Eskalith Lithonate Lithobid
	GABA agonist	Valproic acid	Depakene
Antipsychotic (neuroleptic)	Phenothiazines	Chlorpromazine Trifluoperazine Fluphenazine Thioridazine	Thorazine Stelazine Prolixin Mellaril
	Atypical antipsychotic	Clozapine Risperidone	Clozaril Risperdal

patients. They also reduce delusions and allow some patients to manage life outside a hospital setting.

Most of the antipsychotic drugs prescribed are phenothiazines, of which one of the most common is chlorpromazine (Thorazine). However, a number of other antipsychotic drugs (sometimes called "atypical antipsychotics") have been introduced in the last decade. One of these, clozapine (Clozaril), has been shown to be especially effective but can have severe side effects. Even newer antipsychotic drugs, such as risperidone (Risperdal), are safer than either chlorproazine or clozapine, and they also may be tolerated better.

Antipsychotic drugs are often very effective in treating certain symptoms of schizophrenia, particularly hallucinations and delusions; unfortunately, they may not be as effective for other symptoms, such as reduced motivation and emotional expressiveness. As with antidepressants, dosages of antipsychotic drugs are crucial. Further, if patients are maintained on antipsychotic drugs for too long, other problems can emerge. One such problem is *tardive dyskinesia*—a central nervous system disorder characterized by involuntary, spasmodic movements of the upper body, especially the face and fingers, and including leg jiggling and tongue protrusions, facial tics, and involuntary movements of the mouth and shoulders. See Table 14.5 for a detailed listing of some common drugs used to treat psychiatric disorders. (I)

Think Critically

- What is the implication of the lag time that occurs before some drug treatments have an effect?
- If drug therapy is so effective, why aren't more people being treated in this way?
- What is the solution to the problem of the overprescription of some medications, especially antidepressants?

www.abacon.com/leftononline

Your password-protected Website allows you access to the most comprehensive set of materials in The Psychology Place.

Summary and Review

Therapy Comes in Many Forms

What is the essential difference between biologically based therapy and psychotherapy?

What is the placebo effect in therapy?

KEY TERMS
psychotherapy, p. 393; placebo effect, p. 394

Psychoanalysis and Psychodynamic Therapies

According to psychoanalytic theory, what causes maladjustment and what processes are involved in treatment?

What are the basic criticisms of psychoanalysis?

KEY TERMS
psychoanalysis, p. 397; psychodynamically based therapies, p. 398; insight therapy, p. 398; free association, p. 399; dream analysis, p. 399; interpretation, p. 399; resistance, p. 399; transference, p. 400; working through, p. 400

Humanistic Therapies

Briefly describe the focus of client-centered therapy and of Gestalt therapy.

KEY TERMS
client-centered therapy, p. 401; nondirective therapy, p. 401; Gestalt therapy, p. 402

Behavior Therapy

Identify the basic assumptions and techniques of behavior therapy.

KEY TERMS
behavior therapy, p. 403; symptom substitution, p. 404; token economy, p. 405; time-out, p. 406; counterconditioning, p. 406; systematic desensitization, p. 406; aversive counterconditioning, p. 407

Cognitive Therapy

What are the basic propositions that guide cognitive therapy?

KEY TERM
rational–emotive therapy, p. 408

Group Therapy

What is group therapy, and what is the function of family therapy?

KEY TERMS
group therapy, p. 410; psychodrama, p. 411; encounter group, p. 411; family therapy, p. 411

Biologically Based Therapies

What are the major types of biologically based therapies and the major classes of psychotropic drugs?

KEY TERM
psychosurgery, p. 413; electroconvulsive therapy (ECT), p. 413

Self-Test

1. The goal of psychotherapy is to help people:
   A. cope with their problems and achieve more emotionally satisfying lives
   B. learn about themselves and discover their strengths and weaknesses
   C. grow by treating the body and mind together
   D. understand the importance of family relationships

2. The approach to therapy that combines diverse theories and techniques in order to solve problems is called:
   A. cognitive therapy
   B. psychotherapy integration
   C. eclectic therapy
   D. psychodynamic therapy

3. In psychoanalysis two techniques that are considered central to success are:
   A. free association, dream analysis
   B. dream analysis, resistance
   C. resistance, free association
   D. resistance, transference
4. Mary got into a heated argument with her therapist, who was trying to help her with difficulties between her and her father. She is thought to have experienced:
   A. resistible anxiety
   B. secondary trauma
   C. transference
   D. association
5. Facilitating the process of self-actualization is a key goal of:
   A. psychodynamic therapy
   B. cognitive therapy
   C. Gestalt therapy
   D. humanistic therapy
6. The assumption underlying behavior therapy is that psychological disorders are the consequence of:
   A. illogical thinking
   B. faulty learning
   C. inadequate behavior
   D. symptom substitution
7. Jessie was throwing a temper tantrum in the mall, and her mother placed her on a bench and ignored her until she became quiet. Jessie's mother was using the behavioral technique called:
   A. negative reinforcement
   B. positive reinforcement
   C. punishment
   D. time-out
8. Systematic desensitization is often ideal for treating:
   A. depression
   B. fears and phobias
   C. anxiety and repression
   D. eating disorders
9. According to cognitive therapists, disorders are caused by:
   A. faulty learning
   B. faulty thought processes
   C. unconscious conflict
   D. chemical imbalance
10. In many families participating in family therapy, the members become enmeshed in the problems of one family member. This problem is called:
    A. restructuring
    B. codependence
    C. relationship therapy
    D. family systems
11. Which drug is especially effective in treating bipolar disorder?
    A. Prozac
    B. tranquilizers
    C. Xanax
    D. lithium
12. Librium, Xanax, and Valium are mood-altering drugs that are especially effective in treating:
    A. mood disorders
    B. depression
    C. anxiety disorders
    D. psychosis

References

Abbott, L. F., Varela, J. A., Sen, K., & Nelson, S. B. (1997). Synaptic depression and cortical gain control. *Science, 275,* 220–224.

Abdullaev, Y. G., & Posner, M. I. (1998). Event-related brain potential imaging of semantic encoding during processing single words. *Neuroimage, 7*(1), 1–13.

Abed, F. (1991). Cultural influences on visual scanning patterns. *Journal of Cross-Cultural Psychology, 22,* 525–534.

Abel, T., Martin, K. C., Bartsch, D., & Kandel, E. R. (1998). Memory suppressor genes: Inhibitory constraints on the storage of long-term memory. *Science, 279,* 338–341.

Abelson, R. P. (1988). Conviction. *American Psychologist, 43,* 267–276.

Aboud, R. E., & Mendelson, M. J. (1998). Determinants of friendship selection and quality: Developmental perspectives. In W. M. Bukowski et al. (Eds.), *The company they keep: Friendship in childhood and adolescence.* New York: Cambridge University Press.

Abramowitz, J. S. (1998). Does cognitive-behavioral therapy cure obsessive-compulsive disorder? A meta-analytic evaluation of clinical significance. *Behavior Therapy, 29,* 339–355.

Abrams, M., & Ellis, A. (1994). Stress management and counselling: Rational emotive behaviour therapy in the treatment of stress. *British Journal of Guidance and Counselling, 22,* 39–50.

Abramson, L. Y., Metalsky, G. I., & Alloy, L. B. (1989). Hopelessness depression: A theory-based subtype of depression. *Psychological Review, 96,* 358–372.

Abravanel, E., & DeYong, N. G. (1997). Exploring the roles of peer and adult video models for infant imitations. *Journal of Genetic Psychology, 158*(2), 133–150.

Acker, J. R. (1993). A different agenda: The Supreme Court, empirical research evidence, and capital punishment decisions, 1986–1989. *Law & Society Review, 27*(1), 65–88.

Adelmann, P. K., Antonucci, T. C., Crohan, S. E., & Coleman, L. M. (1989). Empty nest, cohort, and employment in the well-being of midlife women. *Sex Roles, 20,* 173–180.

Ader, R., & Cohen, N. (1985). CNS-immune system interactions: Conditioning phenomena. *Behavioral and Brain Sciences, 8*(3), 379–426.

Ader, R., & Cohen, N. (1993). Psychoneuroimmunology: Conditioning and stress. *Annual Review of Psychology, 44,* 53–85.

Adler, A. (1969). *The science of living.* Garden City, NY: Anchor Books. (Original work published 1929.)

Adorno, T., Frenkel-Brunswick, E., Levinson, D., & Sanford, R. (1950). *The authoritarian personality.* New York: Harper & Row.

Aganoff, J. A., & Boyle, G. J. (1994). Aerobic exercise, mood states and menstrual cycle symptoms. *Journal of Psychosomatic Research, 38,* 183–192.

Agne, K. J. (1999). Caring: The way of the master teacher. In R. P. Lipka, T. M. Brinthaupt, et al. (Eds.), *The role of self in teacher development. SUNY series, studying the self* (pp. 165–188). Albany: State University of New York Press.

Agnew, H. W., Jr., & Webb, W. B. (1973). The influence of time course variable on REM sleep. *Bulletin of the Psychonomic Society, 2,* 131–133.

Agras, W. S. (1992). Some structural changes that might facilitate the development of behavioral medicine. *Journal of Consulting and Clinical Psychology, 4,* 499–509.

Aiello, J. R., & Kolb, K. J. (1995). Electronic performance monitoring and social context: Impact on productivity and stress. *Journal of Applied Psychology, 80,* 339–353.

Aiken, L. R. (1985). *Dying, death, and bereavement.* Boston: Allyn & Bacon.

Aiken, L. R. (1988). *Psychological testing and assessment* (6th ed). Boston: Allyn & Bacon.

Aikens, J. E., Wallander, J. L., Bell, D. S. H., & Cole, J. A. (1992). Daily stress variability, learned resourcefulness, regimen adherence, and metabolic control in type I diabetes mellitus: Evaluation of a path model. *Journal of Consulting and Clinical Psychology, 60,* 113–118.

Ainsworth, M. D. S. (1979). Infant–mother attachment. *American Psychologist, 34,* 932–937.

Ajdukovic, M., & Ajdukovic, D. (1998). Impact of displacement on the psychological well-being of refugee children. *International Review of Psychiatry, 10*(3), 186–195.

Akbarian, S., Kim, J. J., Potkin, S. G., Hagman, J. O., Tafazzoli, A., Bunney, W. E., Jr., & Jones, E. G. (1995). Gene expression for glutamic acid decarboxylase is reduced without loss of neurons in prefrontal cortex of schizophrenics. *Archives of General Psychiatry, 52,* 258–266.

Aldag, R. J., & Fuller, S. R. (1993). Beyond fiasco: A reappraisal of the groupthink phenomenon and a new model of group decision processes. *Psychological Bulletin, 113,* 533–552.

Algera, J. A. (1990). The job characteristics model of work motivation revisited. In U. Kleinbeck, H. Quast, H. Thierry, & H. Hacker (Eds.), *Work motivation.* Hillsdale, NJ: Erlbaum.

Alivisatos, B., & Petrides, M. (1997). Functional activation of the human brain during mental rotation. *Neuropsychologia, 35*(2), 111–118.

Alkon, D. L. (1989, July). Memory storage and neural systems. *Scientific American,* 42–50.

Allen, B. P. (1995). Gender stereotypes are not accurate: A replication of Martin (1987) using diagnostic vs. self-report and behavioral criteria. *Sex Roles, 32*(9/10), 583–586.

Allen, G. L. (1981). A developmental perspective on the effects of "subdividing" macrospatial experience. *Journal of Experimental Psychology: Human Learning and Memory, 7,* 120–132.

Allen, G. L. (1987). Cognitive influences on the acquisition of route knowledge in children and adults. In P. Ellen & C. Thinus-Blanc (Eds.), *Cognitive processes and spatial orientation in animal and man: Vol. 2.* Neurophysiology and developmental aspects. Boston: Martinus Nijhoff.

Allen, K. E., Turner, K. D., & Everett, P. M. (1970). A behavior modification classroom for Head Start children with problem behaviors. *Exceptional Children, 37,* 119–127.

Allgood-Merten, B., Lewinsohn, P. M., & Hops, H. (1990). Sex differences and adolescent depression. *Journal of Abnormal Psychology, 99,* 55–63.

Allgulander, C. (1994). Suicide and mortality patterns in anxiety neurosis and depressive neurosis. *Archives of General Psychiatry, 51,* 708–712.

Allgulander, C., Nowak, J., & Rice, J. P. (1990). Psychopathology and treatment of 30,344 twins in Sweden: I. The appropriateness of psychoactive drug treatment. *Acta Psychiatrica Scandinavica, 82*(6), 420–426.

Allington, R. L. (1981). Sensitivity to orthographic structure in educable mentally retarded children. *Contemporary Educational Psychology, 6,* 135–139.

Allison, T., Ginter, H., McCarthy, G., Nobre, A. C., Puce, A., Luby, M., & Spencer, D. D. (1994). Face recognition in human extrastriate cortex. *Journal of Neurophysiology, 71,* 821–825.

Allport, G. W. (1937). *Personality: A psychological interpretation.* New York: Holt.

Allport, G. W. (1979). *The nature of prejudice.* Cambridge, MA: Addison-Wesley. (Original work published in 1954.)

Almagor, M., Tellegen, A., & Waller, N. G. (1995). The big seven model: A cross-cultural replication and further exploration of the basic dimensions of natural language trait descriptors. *Journal of Personality and Social Psychology, 69,* 300–307.

Almeida, D. M., & Kessler, R. C. (1998). Everyday stressors and gender differences in daily distress. *Journal of Personality & Social Psychology, 75*(3), 670–680.

Altman, F. (1998). Where is the "neuro" in psychoneuroimmunology? *Brain, Behavior, and Immunity, 11*(1), 1–8.

Altman, I. (1975). *The environment and social behavior.* Monterey, CA: Brooks/Cole.

Altman, I., & Vinsel, A. M. (1977). Personal space: An analysis of E. T. Hall's proxemics framework. In I. Altman, A. Rapoport, & J. F. Wohlwill (Eds.), *Human behavior and environment: Vol. 2. Advances in theory and research.* New York: Plenum.

Amaro, H. (1995). Love, sex, and power: Considering women's realities in HIV prevention. *American Psychologist, 50,* 437–447.

Ambady, N., & Rosenthal, R. (1993). Half a minute: Predicting teacher evaluations from thin slices of nonverbal behavior and physical attractiveness. *Journal of Personality and Social Psychology, 64,* 431–441.

American Association of University Women Educational Foundation. (1998). *Gender gaps: Where schools still fail our children.* (Special Report). Washington, DC: Author.

American Association on Mental Retardation (1992). *Mental retardation.* Washington, DC: Author.

American Psychiatric Association (1994). *Diagnostic and statistical manual of mental disorders* (4th ed.) *(DSM—IV).* Washington, DC: Author.

American Psychiatric Association (1995). Practice guideline for psychiatric evaluation of adults. *American Journal of Psychiatry, 152,* 67–80.

American Psychological Association (1992). Ethical principles of psychologists and code of conduct. *American Psychologist, 47,* 1597–1611.

American Psychological Association (1993). Guidelines for providers of psychological services to ethnic, linguistic, and culturally diverse populations. *American Psychologist, 48,* 45–48.

American Psychological Association (1994). The Seville statement on violence. *American Psychologist, 49,* 845–846.

American Psychological Association (1995). *Demographic characteristics of APA members by membership status, 1993.* Washington, DC: Office of Demographic, Employment, and Educational Research, APA Education Directorate.

Anderson, C. A. (1989). Temperature and aggression: Ubiquitous effects of heat on occurrence of human violence. *Psychological Bulletin, 106,* 74–96.

Anderson, C. A., & Anderson, K. B. (1998). Temperature and aggression: Paradox, controversy, and a (fairly) clear picture. In R. G. Geen, E. Donnerstein, et al. (Eds.), *Human aggression: Theories, research, and implications for social policy* (pp. 247–298). San Diego, CA: Academic Press, Inc.

Anderson, C. A., Anderson, K. B., & Deuser, W. E. (1996). Examining an affective aggression framework: Weapon and temperature effects on aggressive thoughts, affect, and attitudes. *Personality and Social Psychology Bulletin, 22*(4), 366–376.

Anderson, C. A., & DeNeve, K. M. (1992). Temperature, aggression, and the negative affect escape model. *Psychological Bulletin, 111,* 347–351.

Andreasen, N. C. (1997). Neuroimaging techniques in the investigation of schizophrenia. *Journal of Clinical Psychiatry Monograph Series, 15*(3), 16–19.

Angoff, W. H. (1988). The nature–nuture debate, aptitudes, and group differences. *American Psychologist, 43,* 713–720.

Antonuccio, D. O., Danton, W. G., & DeNelsky, G. Y. (1995). Psychotherapy versus medication for depression: Challenging the conventional wisdom with data. *Professional Psychology: Research and Practice, 26,* 574–585.

Apter, A., Galatzer, A., Beth-Halachmi, N., & Laron, Z. (1981). Self-image in adolescents with delayed puberty and growth retardation. *Journal of Youth and Adolescence, 10,* 501–505.

Apter, T. (1995). *Secret paths: Women in the new midlife.* New York: Norton.

Arango, V., Underwood, M. D., & Mann, J. J. (1992). Alterations in monoamine receptors in the brain of suicide victims. *Journal of Clinical Psychopharmacology, 12,* 8S—12S.

Arceneaux, M. C., & Murdock, J. Y. (1997). Peer prompting reduces disruptive vocalizations of a student with developmental disabilities in a general eighth-grade classroom. *Focus on Autism and Other Developmental Disabilities, 12*(3), 182–186.

Archer, J. (1996). Sex differences in social behavior: Are the social role and evolutionary explanations compatible? *American Psychologist, 51*(9), 909–917.

Arcus, D. (1994). Biological mechanisms and personality: Evidence from shy children. *Advances, 10*(4), 40–50.

Ariel, M., & Giora, R. (1992). Gender versus group-relation analysis of impositive speech acts. In K. Hall et al. (Eds.), *Locating power: Proceedings of the second Berkeley Women and Language Conference.* Berkeley: University of California Press.

Arkowitz, H. (1997). Integrative theories of therapy. In P. L. Wachtel & S. B. Messer (Eds.), *Theories of psychotherapy: Origins and evolution* (pp. 227–288). Washington, DC: American Psychological Association.

Arnon, R., & Kreitler, S. (1984). Effects of meaning training on overcoming functional fixedness. *Current Psychological Research and Reviews, 3*(4), 11–24.

Aron, A., & Aron, E. N. (1997). Self-expansion motivation and including other in the self. In S. Duck (Ed.), *Handbook of personal relationships: Theory, research and interventions.* Chichester, England: John Wiley & Sons, Inc.

Aronson, J., Quinn, D. M., & Spencer, S. J. (1998). Stereotype threat and the academic underperformance of minorities and women. In J. K. Swim, C. Stangor, et al. (Eds.). *Prejudice: The target's perspective* (pp. 83–103). San Diego, CA: Academic Press.

Arvey, R. D., & Campion, J. E. (1982). The employment interview: A summary and review of recent research. *Personnel Psychology, 35,* 281–322.

Asaad, G., & Shapiro, B. (1986). Hallucinations: Theoretical and clinical overview. *American Journal of Psychiatry, 143,* 1088–1097.

Asch, S. E. (1955, November). Opinions and social pressure. *Scientific American,* 31–35.

Asendorpf, J. B. (1989). Shyness as a final common pathway for two different kinds of inhibition. *Journal of Personality and Social Psychology, 57,* 481–492.

Ashcraft, M. H. (1989). *Human memory and cognition,* Glenview, IL: Scott, Foresman.

Aspinwall, L. G., & Taylor, S. E. (1997). A stitch in time: Self-regulation and proactive coping. *Psychological Bulletin, 121*(3), 417–436.

Asthana, H. S., & Mandal, M. K. (1997). Hemiregional variations in facial expression of emotions. *British Journal of Psychology, 88,* 519–525.

Astington, J. (1999). What is theoretical about the child's theory of mind? A Vygotskian view of its development. In P. Lloyd, C. Fernhough, et al. (Eds.), *Lev Vygotsky: Critical assessments, future directions,* Vol. IV (pp. 401–418). New York: Routledge.

Atoum, A. O., & Farah, A. M. (1993). Social loafing and personal involvement among Jordanian college students. *Journal of Social Psychology, 133,* 785–789.

Attie, I., & Brooks-Gunn, J. (1989). Development of eating problems in adolescent girls: A longitudinal study. *Developmental Psychology, 25,* 70–79.

Audia, G., Kristof-Brown, K. G., & Locke, E. A. (1996). Relationship of goals and micro-level work processes to performance on a multi-path manual task. *Journal of Applied Psychology, 81*(5), 483–497.

Ayllon, T., & Azrin, N. H. (1965). The measurement and reinforcement behavior of psychotics. *Journal of the Experimental Analysis of Behavior, 8,* 357–383.

Ayllon, T., & Haughton, E. (1964). Modification of symptomatic verbal behavior of mental patients. *Behavior Research and Therapy, 2,* 87–97.

Azrin, N. H., & Holtz, W. C. (1966). Punishment. In W. K. Honig (Ed.), *Operant behavior: Areas of research and application.* New York: Appleton-Century-Crofts.

Bachar, E. (1998). Psychotherapy—an active agent: Assessing the effectiveness of psychotherapy and its curative factors. *Israel Journal of Psychiatry and Related Sciences, 35*(2), 128–135.

Backman, L., & Lipinska, B. (1993). Monitoring of general knowledge: Evidence for preservation in early Alzheimer's disease. *Neuropsychologia, 31,* 335–345.

Backman, L., & Nilsson, L. G. (1996). Semantic memory functioning across the adult life span. *European Psychologist, 1*(1), 27–33.

Baddeley, A. (1994). The magical number seven: Still magic after all these years? *Psychological Review, 101,* 353–356.

Baddeley, A. D., & Hitch, G. (1974). Working memory. In G. Bower (Ed.), *Recent advances in learning and motivating* (Vol.8). New York: Academic.

Baddeley, A. D., & Hitch, G. J. (1994). Developments in the concept of working memory. *Neuropsychology, 6,* 485–493.

Baddeley, A. D., & Longman, D. J. (1978). The influence of length and frequency of training session on the rate of learning to type. *Ergonomics, 21*(8), 627–635.

Bailey, W. C., & Perterson, R. D. (1999). Capital punishment, homicide, and deterrence: An assessment of the evidence and extension to female homicide. In M. D. Smith, M. Zahn, et al. (Eds.), *Homicide: A sourcebook of social research* (pp. 257–276). Thousand Oaks, CA: Sage Publications, Inc.

Baillargeon, R. (1994). How do infants learn about the physical world? *Current Directions in Psychological Science, 3,* 133–140.

Baillargeon, R. (1998). Infants' understanding of the physical world. In M. Sabourin, F. Craik, et al. (Eds.), *Advances in psychological science, Vol. II: Biological and cognitive aspects* (pp. 503–529). Hove, England: Psychology Press/Erlbaum, Taylor & Francis.

Baird, J. C., Wagner, M., & Fuld, K. (1990). A simple but powerful theory of the moon illusion. *Journal of Experimental Psychology: Human Perception and Performance, 16,* 675–677.

Baischer, W. (1995). Acupuncture in migraine: Long-term outcome and predicting factors. *Headache, 35*(8), 472–474.

Bak, M., Girvin, J. P., Hambrecht, F. T., Kufta, C. V., Loeb, G. E., & Schmidt, E. M. (1990). Visual sensations produced by intracortical microstimulation of the human occipital cortex. *Medical and Biological Engineering and Computing, 28,* 257–259.

Balay, J., & Shevrin, H. (1988). The subliminal psychodynamic activation method. *American Psychologist, 3,* 161–174.

Baldwin, D. R., Harris, S. M., & Chambliss, L. N. (1997). Stress and illness in adolescence: Issues of race and gender. *Adolescence, 32*(128), 839–853.

Baldwin, E. (1993). The case for animal research in psychology. *Journal of Social Issues, 49,* 121–131.

Ballen, W. (1997). Freud's views and the contemporary application of hypnosis: Enhancing therapy within a psychoanalytic framework. *Journal of Contemporary Psychotherapy, 27*(3), 201–214.

Baltes, P. B. (1987). Theoretical propositions of life-span developmental psychology: On the dynamics between growth and decline. *Developmental Psychology, 23,* 611–626.

Baltes, P. B. (1993). The aging mind: Potential and limits. *Gerontologist, 33*(5), 580–594.

Band, E. B., & Weisz, J. R. (1988). How to feel better when it feels bad: Children's perspectives on coping with everyday stress. *Developmental Psychology, 24,* 247–253.

Bandura, A. (1969). *Principles of behavior modification.* New York: Holt, Rinehart & Winston.

Bandura, A. (1977a). Self-efficacy: Toward a unifying theory of behavioral change. *Psychological Review, 84,* 191–215.

Bandura, A. (1977b). *Social learning theory.* Englewood Cliffs, NJ: Prentice-Hall.

Bandura, A. (1988). Self-regulation of motivation and action through goal systems. In V. Hamilton, G. H. Bower, & N. H. Frijda (Eds.), *Cognitive perspectives on emotion and motivation* (pp. 37–61). Dordrecht, Netherlands: Kluwer Academic.

Bandura, A. (1997). *Self-efficacy: The exercise of control.* New York: W. H. Freeman & Co.

Bandura, A., Blanchard, E. B., & Ritter, B. (1969). Relative efficacy of desensitization and modeling approaches for inducing behavioral, affective, and attitudinal changes. *Journal of Personality and Social Psychology, 13,* 173–199.

Bandura, A., Cioffi, D., Taylor, B., & Brouillard, M. E. (1988). Perceived self-efficacy in coping with cognitive stressors and opioid activation. *Journal of Personality and Social Psychology, 55,* 479–488.

Bandura, A., & Menlove, F. L. (1968). Factors determining vicarious extinction of avoidance through symbolic modeling. *Journal of Personality and Social Psychology, 8,* 99–108.

Bandura, A., Ross, D., & Ross, S. A. (1963). Imitation of film-mediated aggressive models. *Journal of Abnormal and Social Psychology, 66,* 3–11.

Bandura, A., & Walters, R. (1963). *Social learning and personality development.* New York: Holt, Rinehart & Winston.

Barbaree, H. E., & Marshall, W. L. (1991). The role of male sexual arousal in rape: Six models. *Journal of Consulting and Clinical Psychology, 59,* 621–630.

Barbato, G., Barker, C., Bender, C., Giesen, H. A., & Wehr, T. A. (1994). Extended sleep in humans in 14 hour nights (LD 10:14): Relationship between REM density and spontaneous awakening. *Electroencephalography and Clinical Neurophysiology, 90,* 291–297.

Barber, J. P., & Ellman, J. (1996). Advances in short-term dynamic psychotherapy. *Current Opinion in Psychiatry, 9,* 188–192.

Barber, T. X. (1991). The locksmith model: Accessing hypnotic responsiveness. In S. J. Lynn & J. W. Rhue (Eds.), *Theories of hypnosis: Current models and perspectives* (pp. 241–274). New York: Guilford Press.

Barber, T. X., Spanos, N. P., & Chaves, J. F. (1974). *Hypnosis, imagination, and human potentialities.* New York: Pergamon.

Barbuto, J. E., Jr. (1997). Taking the charisma out of transformational leadership. *Journal of Social Behavior and Personality, 12*(3), 689–697.

Bard, P. (1934). Emotion: The neuro-humoral basis of emotional reactions. In C. Murchison (Ed.), *Handbook of general experimental psychology.* Worcester, MA: Clark University Press.

Bardon, J. I. (1983). Psychology applied to education: A specialty in search of an identity. *American Psychologist, 38,* 185–196.

Barinaga, M. (1998). Is apoptosis key in Alzheimer's disease? *Science, 281,* 1303–1304.

Baron, R. A. (1993). Interviewers' moods and evaluations of job applicants: The role of applicant qualifications. *Journal of Applied Social Psychology, 23,* 253–271.

Barondes, S. H. (1998). *Mood genes: Hunting for origins of mania and depression.* New York: W. H. Freeman.

Bar-Or, O., Foreyt, J., Bouchard, C., Brownell, K. D., Dietz, W. H., Ravussin, E., Salbe, A. D., Schwenger, S., St. Jeor, S., & Torun, B. (1998). Physical activity, genetic, and nutritional considerations in childhood weight management. *Medicine and Science in Sports and Exercise, 30*(1), 2–10.

Barrera, M., Li, S. A., & Chassin, L. (1993). Ethnic group differences in vulnerability to parental alcoholism and life stress: A study of Hispanic and non-Hispanic Caucasian adolescents. *American Journal of Community Psychology, 21*(1), 15–35.

Barrett, G. V., & Depinet, R. L. (1991). A reconsideration of testing for competence rather than for intelligence. *American Psychologist, 46,* 1012–1024.

Bartlett, F. C. (1932). *Remembering: A study in experimental and social psychology.* New York: Macmillan.

Bartoshuk, L. M., Duffy, V. B., & Miller, I. J. (1994, December). PTC/PROP taste: Anatomy, psychophysics, and sex effects. Paper presented at the Kirin International Symposium on Bitter Taste. *Physiology and Behavior, 56*(6), 1165–1171.

Bartoshuk, L. M., Duffy, V. B., Reed, D., & Williams, A. (1996). Supertasting, earaches and head injury: Genetics and pathology alter our taste worlds. *Neuroscience and Biobehavioral Reviews, 20*(1), 79–87.

Bashore, T. R., & Rapp, R. E. (1993). Are there alternatives to traditional polygraph procedures? *Psychological Bulletin, 113,* 3–22.

Bass, B. M. (1985). *Leadership and performance beyond expectations.* New York: Free Press.

Bass, B. M. (1990). From transactional to transformational leadership: Learning to share the vision. *Organizational Dynamics, 18,* 19–31.

Bass, B. M. (1997). Does the transactional–transformational leadership paradigm transcend organizational and national boundaries? *American Psychologist, 52*(2), 130–139.

Bass, B. M. (1998). *Transformational leadership: Industrial, military, and educational impact.* Mahwah, NJ: Lawrence Erlbaum Associates, Inc.

Bass, C., & Murphy, M. (1995). Somatoform and personality disorders: Syndromal comorbidity and overlapping developmental pathways. *Journal of Psychosomatic Research, 39,* 403–427.

Bates, E., & Elman, J. (1996). Learning rediscovered. *Science, 274,* 1849–1850.

Bates, J. E., Marvinney, D., Kelly, T., Dodge, K. A., Bennett, D. S., & Pettit, G. S. (1994). Child-care history and kindergarten adjustment. *Developmental Psychology, 30,* 690–700.

Bateson, G., Jackson, D. D., Haley, J., & Weakland, J. (1956). Toward a theory of schizophrenia. *Behavioral Science, 1,* 251–264.

Batson, C. D. (1990). How social an animal? *American Psychologist, 45,* 336–346.

Batson, C. D., Batson, J. G., Slingsby, J. K., Harrell, K. L., Peekna, H. M., & Todd, R. M. (1991). Empathic joy and the empathy–altruism hypothesis. *Journal of Personality and Social Psychology, 61,* 413–426.

Baum, A. (1987). Crowding. In D. Stokols & I. Altman (Eds.), *Handbook of environmental psychology.* New York: Wiley.

Baum, A., Grunberg, N. E., & Singer, J. E. (1992). Biochemical measurements in the study of emotion. *Psychological Science, 3,* 56–62.

Baumeister, R. F. (1990). Suicide as escape from self. *Psychological Review, 97,* 90–113.

Baumeister, R. F., Smart, L., & Boden, J. (1996). Relation of threatened egotism to violence and aggression: The dark side of high self-esteem. *Psychological Review, 103*(1), 5–33.

Baumeister, R. F., & Tice, D. M. (1985). Self-esteem and responses to success and failure: Subsequent performance and intrinsic motivation. *Journal of Personality, 53,* 450–467.

Bayley, N. (1969). Consistency and variability in the growth of intelligence from birth to eighteen years. *Journal of Genetic Psychology, 25,* 165–196.

Baynes, K., Eliassen, J. C., Lutsep, H. L., & Gazzaniga, M. S. (1998). Modular organization of cognitive systems masked by interhemispheric integration. *Science, 280,* 902–905.

Beaulieu, C., & Colonnier, M. (1988). Richness of environment affects the number of contacts formed by boutons containing flat vesicles but does not alter the number of these boutons per neuron. *Journal of Comparative Neurology, 274*(3), 347–356.

Beaulieu, C., & Colonnier, M. (1989). Number and size of neurons and synapses in the motor cortex of cats raised in different environmental complexities. *Journal of Comparative Neurology, 289*(1), 178–181.

Bechara, A., Tranel, D., Damasio, H., Adolphs, R., Rockland, C., & Damasio, A. R. (1995). Double dissociation of conditioning and declarative knowledge relative to the amygdala and hippocampus in humans. *Science, 269,* 1115–1118.

Beck, A. T. (1963). Thinking and depression: 1. Idiosyncratic content in cognitive distortions. *Archives of General Psychiatry, 9,* 324–333.

Beck, A. T. (1967). *Depression: Clinical, experimental, and theoretical aspects.* New York: Hober.

Beck, A. T. (1972). *Depression: Causes and treatment.* Philadelphia: University of Pennsylvania Press.

Beck, A. T. (1976). *Cognitive therapy and emotional disorders.* New York: International Universities Press.

Beck, A. T. (1991). Cognitive therapy. *American Psychologist, 46,* 368–375.

Beck, A. T., & Weishaar, M. (1989). Cognitive therapy. In A. Freeman, K. M. Simon, L. E. Beutler, & H. Arkowitz (Eds.), *Comprehensive handbook of cognitive therapy.* New York: Plenum.

Beck, J. (1966). Effects of orientation and of shape similarity on perceptual grouping. *Perception and Psychophysics, 1,* 311–312.

Beck, J. G., Stanley, M. A., Baldwin, L. E., Deagle, E. A., III, & Averill, P. M. (1994). Comparison of cognitive therapy and relaxation training for panic disorder. *Journal of Consulting and Clinical Psychology, 62,* 818–826.

Becker, M. H. (1993). A medical sociologist looks at health promotion. *Journal of Health and Social Behavior, 34,* 1–6.

Bee, H. L. (1987). *The journey of adulthood.* New York: Macmillan.

Begg, I. M., Needham, D. R., & Bookbinder, M. (1993). Do backward messages unconsciously affect listeners? No. *Canadian Journal of Experimental Psychology, 47,* 1–14.

Beidel, D. C., Turner, M. W., & Trager, K. N. (1994). Test anxiety and childhood anxiety disorders in African-American and white school children. *Journal of Anxiety Disorders, 8,* 169–179.

Beisteiner, R., Altenmuller, E., Lang, W., & Lindinger, G. (1994). Musicians processing music: Measurement of brain potentials with EEG. *European Journal of Cognitive Psychology, 6*(3), 311–327.

Beitel, A. H., & Parke, R. D. (1998). Paternal involvement in infancy: The role of maternal and paternal attitudes. *Journal of Family Psychology, 12*(2), 268–288.

Bekerian, D. A., & Bowers, J. M. (1983). Eyewitness testimony: Were we misled? *Journal of Experimental Psychology: Learning, Memory, and Cognition, 9,* 139–145.

Bekhtereva, N. P., Gilerovich, E. G., Gurchin, F. A., Lukin, V. A., et al. (1990). The first results of the use of embryonal nervous tissue transplantation for the treatment of Parkinsonism. *Ahurnal Nevropatologii i Psikhiatrii Imeni S-S-Korsakova, 90*(11), 10–13.

Belansky, E. S., & Boggiano, A. K. (1994). Predicting helping behaviors: The role of gender and instrumental/expressive self-schemata. *Sex Roles, 30,* 647–662.

Bell, B. E., & Loftus, E. F. (1989). Trivial persuasion in the courtroom: The power of (a few) minor details. *Journal of Personality and Social Psychology, 56,* 669–679.

Bell, S. T., Kuriloff, P. J., & Lottes, I. (1994). Understanding attributions of blame in stranger rape and date rape situations: An examination of gender, race, identification, and students' social perceptions of rape victims. *Journal of Applied Social Psychology, 24*(19), 1719–1734.

Belsky, J. (1990). Parental and nonparental child care and children's socioemotional development: A decade in review. *Journal of Marriage and the Family, 52,* 885–903.

Belsky, J. (1993). Etiology of child maltreatment: A developmental–ecological analysis. *Psychological Bulletin, 114,* 413–434.

Belsky, J., & Rovine, M. J. (1988). Nonmaternal care in the first year of life and the security of infant–parent attachment. *Child Development, 59,* 157–167.

Bem, D. J. (1972). Self-perception theory. In L. Berkowitz (Ed.), *Advances in experimental social psychology.* New York: Academic.

Bem, D. J. (1996). Exotic becomes erotic: A developmental theory of sexual orientation. *Psychological Review, 103*(2), 320–335.

Bem, S. L. (1985). Androgyny and gender schema theory: A conceptual and empirical integration. In T. B. Sonderegger (Ed.), *Nebraska symposium on motivation.* Lincoln: University of Nebraska Press.

Bem, S. L. (1993). *The lenses of gender.* New Haven, CT: Yale University Press.

Benet-Martinez, V., & Waller, N. G. (1997). Further evidence for the cross-cultural generality of the Big Seven Factor model: Indigenous and imported Spanish personality constructs. *Journal of Personality, 65*(3), 567–598.

Benjamin, L. T., Jr., Durkin, M., Link, M., Vestal, M., & Acord, J. (1992). Wundt's American doctoral students. *American Psychologist, 47,* 123–131.

Bentall, R. P. (1990). The illusion of reality: A review and integration of psychological research on hallucinations. *Psychological Bulletin, 107,* 82–95.

Berenbaum, S. A., & Snyder, E. (1995). Early hormonal influences on childhood sex-typed activity and playmate preferences: Implications for the development of sexual orientation. *Developmental Psychology, 3,* 31–42.

Berg, T. R. (1991). The importance of equity perception and job satisfaction in predicting employee intent to stay at television stations. *Group and Organizational Studies, 16,* 268–284.

Berhardt, P. C. (1997). Influences of serotonin and testosterone in aggression and dominance: Convergence with social psychology. *American Psychological Society, 6*(2), 44–48.

Berk, L. E. (1994). *Child development* (3rd. ed.). Boston: Allyn & Bacon.

Berkley, K. J. (1997). Sex differences in pain. *Behavioral and Brain Sciences, 20*(3), 371–380.

Berkowitz, L. (1964). *The effects of observing violence.* San Francisco: Freeman.

Berkowitz, L. (1989). Frustration–aggression hypothesis: Examination and reformulation. *Psychological Bulletin, 106,* 59–73.

Berkowitz, L. (1990). On the formation and regulation of anger and aggression. *American Psychologist, 45,* 494–503.

Berkowitz, L. (1993). Pain and aggression: Some findings and implications. *Motivation and Emotion, 17,* 277–294.

Berlin, B., & Kay, P. (1969). *Basic color terms: Their universality and evolution.* Berkeley: University of California Press.

Berman, F. E., & Miner, J. B. (1985). Motivation to manage at the top executive level: A test of the hierarchic role-motivation theory. *Personnel Psychology, 38,* 377–391.

Bernal, G., & Berger, S. M. (1976). Vicarious eyelid conditioning. *Journal of Personality and Social Psychology, 34,* 62–68.

Berndt, T. J. (1992). Friendship and friends' influence in adolescence. *Psychological Science, 1,* 156–159.

Bernstein, D., & Ebbesen, E. (1978). Reinforcement and substitution in humans: A multiple-response analysis. *Journal of the Experimental Analysis of Behavior, 30,* 243–253.

Bernstein, I. L. (1988, September). *What does learning have to do with weight loss and cancer?* Paper presented at a science and public policy seminar sponsored by the Federation of Behavioral, Psychological, and Cognitive Sciences, Washington, DC.

Bernstein, I. L. (1991). Aversion conditioning in response to cancer and cancer treatment. *Clinical Psychology Review, 11*(2), 185–191.

Berridge, K. C., & Robinson, T. E. (1995). The mind of an addicted brain: Neural sensitization of wanting versus liking. *Current Directions in Psychological Science, 4,* 71–76.

Berry, D. S., & Landry, J. C. (1997). Facial maturity and daily social interaction. *Journal of Personality and Social Psychology, 72*(3), 570–580.

Berry, D. S., & Pennebaker, J. W. (1993). Nonverbal and verbal emotional expression and health. *Psychotherapy and Psychosomatics, 59,* 11–19.

Berscheid, E., Snyder, M., & Omoto, A. M. (1989). The relationship closeness inventory: Assessing the closeness of interpersonal relationships. *Journal of Personality and Social Psychology, 57,* 792–807.

Bertenthal, B. I., Campos, J. J., & Kermoian, R. (1994). An epigenetic perspective on the development of self-produced locomotion and its consequences. *Current Directions in Psychological Science, 3,* 140–145.

Best, C. T., & Queen, H. F. (1989). Baby, it's in your smile: Right hemiface bias in infant emotional expressions. *Developmental Psychology, 25,* 264–276.

Bettelheim, B. (1987). *A good enough parent: A book on child-rearing.* New York: Knopf.

Betz, N. E. (1992). Counseling uses of career self-efficacy theory. *Career Development Quarterly, 41*(1), 22–26.

Beutler, L. E., Williams, R. E., Wakefield, P. J., & Entwistle, S. R. (1995). Bridging scientist and practitioner perspectives in clinical psychology. *American Psychologist, 50,* 984–994.

Bexton, W. H., Heron, W., & Scott, T. H. (1954). Effects of decreased variation in the sensory environment. *Canadian Journal of Psychology, 8,* 70–76.

Bhatt, R. S. (1997). The interface between perception and cognition: Feature detection, visual pop-out effects, feature integration, and long-term memory in infancy. In C. Rovee-Collier & L. P. Lipsitt (Eds.), *Advances in infancy research.* Greenwich, CT: Ablex Publishing Corporation.

Bickerton, D. (1995). *Language and human behavior.* Seattle: University of Washington Press.

Bickman, L., Teger, A., Gabriele, T., McLaughlin, C., Berger, M., & Sunaday, E. (1973). Dormitory density and helping behavior. *Environment and Behavior, 5,* 465–466.

Binion, V. J. (1990). Psychological androgyny: A black female perspective. *Sex Roles, 22,* 487–507.

Biondi, M., & Zannino, L. G. (1997). Psychological stress, neuroimmunomodulation, and susceptibility to infectious diseases in animals and man: A review. *Psychotherapy and Psychosomatics, 66*(1), 3–26.

Bivens, J. A., & Berk, L. E. (1990). A longitudinal study of the development of elementary school children's private speech. *Merrill-Palmer Quarterly, 36,* 443–463.

Black, D. W., & Larson, C. L. (1999). *Bad boys, bad men: Confronting antisocial personality disorder.* New York: Oxford University Press.

Blagrove, M. (1996). Problems with the cognitive psychological modeling of dreaming. *Journal of Mind and Behavior, 17,* 99–134.

Blakemore, C., & Cooper, G. F. (1970). Development of the brain depends on the visual environment. *Nature, 228,* 477–478.

Blanc-Garin, J., Fauré, S., & Sabio, P. (1993). Right hemisphere performance and competence in processing mental images in a case of partial interhemispheric disconnection. *Brain and Cognition, 22,* 118–133.

Blanchard, E. B., Appelbaum, K. A., Radnitz, C. L., Michultka, D., Morrill, B., Kirsch, C., Hillhouse, J., Evans, D. D., Guarnieri, P., Attanasio, V., Andrasik, F., Jaccard, J., & Dentinger, M. P. (1990). Placebo-controlled evaluation of abbreviated progressive muscle relaxation and of relaxation combined with cognitive therapy in the treatment of tension headache. *Journal of Consulting and Clinical Psychology, 58,* 210–215.

Blatt, S. J. (1995). The destructiveness of perfectionism. *American Psychologist, 50,* 1003–1020.

Block, J., & Robins, R. W. (1993). A longitudinal study of consistency and change in self-esteem from early adolescence to early adulthood. *Child Development, 64,* 909–923.

Bloom, F. E. (1981, October). Neuropeptides. *Scientific American,* 148–168.

Bobo, L., & Kluegel, J. R. (1997). Status, ideology, and dimensions of whites' racial beliefs and attitudes: Progress and stagnation. In S. A. Tuch & J. K. Martin (Eds.), *Racial attitudes in the 1990s: Continuity and change.* Westport, CT: Praeger.

Bohannon, J. N., III (1988). Flashbulb memories for the space shuttle disaster: A tale of two theories. *Cognition, 29,* 179–196.

Boivin, D. B., Duffy, J. F., Kronauer, R. E., & Czeisler, C. A. (1996). Dose-response relationships for resetting of human circadian clock by light. *Nature, 379,* 540–542.

Bond, C. F., Jr., & Titus, L. J. (1983). Social facilitation: A meta-analysis of 241 studies. *Psychological Bulletin, 94,* 265–292.

Bond, R., & Smith, P. B. (1996). Culture and conformity: A meta-analysis of studies using Asch's (1952b, 1956) line judgement task. *Psychological Bulletin, 119,* 111–137.

Boninger, D. S., Brock, T. C., Cook, T. D., Gruder, C. L., & Romer, D. (1990). Discovery of reliable attitude change persistence resulting from a transmitter tuning set. *Psychological Science, 1,* 268–271.

Bonnet, M. H. (1980). Sleep, performance, and mood after the energy-expenditure equivalent of 40 hours of sleep deprivation. *Psychophysiology, 17,* 56–63.

Borg, E., & Counter, S. A. (1989, August). The middle-ear muscles. *Scientific American,* 74–80.

Borkenau, P., & Ostendorf, F. (1998). The Big Five as states: How useful is the five-factor model to describe intraindividual variations over time? *Journal of Research in Personality, 32*(2), 202–221.

Bornstein, M. H., Tal, J., Rahn, C., Galperin, C. Z., Pecheux, M. G., Lamour, M., Toda, S., Azuma, H., Ogino, M., & Tamis-Lemonda, C. S. (1992). Functional analysis of the contents of maternal speech to infants of 5 and 13 months in four cultures: Argentina, France, Japan, and the United States. *Developmental Psychology, 28,* 593–603.

Bornstein, R. F. (1989). Exposure and affect: Overview and meta-analysis of research, 1968–1987. *Psychological Bulletin, 106,* 265–289.

Bornstein, R. F. (1992). The dependent personality: Developmental, social, and clinical perspectives. *Psychological Bulletin, 112,* 3–23.

Boronat, C. B., & Logan, G. D. (1997). The role of attention in automatization: Does attention operate at encoding, or retrieval, or both? *Memory and Cognition, 25*(1), 36–46.

Borrie, R. A. (1991). The use of restricted environmental stimulation therapy in treating addictive behaviors. *International Journal of the Addictions, 25,* 995–1015.

Bosma, H., Richard, P., Siegrist, J., & Marmot, M. (1998). Two alternative job stress models and the risk of coronary heart disease. *American Journal of Public Health, 88*(1), 68–74.

Botschner, J. V. (1996). Reconsidering male friendships: A social-development perspective. In C. W. Tolman et al. (Eds.), *Problems of theoretical psychology.* North York, Ontario: Captus Press.

Botwin, M. D., Buss, D. M., & Shackelford, T. K. (1997). Personality and mate preferences: Five factors in mate selection and marital satisfaction. *Journal of Personality, 65*(1), 107–136.

Botwinick, J. (1984). *Aging and behavior: A comprehensive integration of research findings* (3rd ed.). New York: Springer-Verlag.

Bouchard, T. J., Jr., (1997). The genetics of personality. In K. Blum et al. (Eds.), *Handbook of psychiatric genetics.* Boca Raton, FL: CRC Press.

Bouchard, T. J., Jr., & Hur, Y. (1998). Genetic and environmental influences on the continuous scales of the Myers–Briggs Type Indicator: An analysis based on twins reared apart. *Journal of Personality, 66*(2), 135–147.

Bouchard, T. J., Jr., Lykken, D. T., McGue, M., Segal, N. L., & Tellegen, A. (1990). Sources of human psychological differences: The Minnesota study of twins reared apart. *Science, 250,* 223–228.

Bouchard, T. J., Jr., & McGue, M. (1981). Familial studies of intelligence: A review. *Science, 212,* 1055–1058.

Bourque, L. B. (1989). *Defining rape.* Durham, NC: Duke University Press.

Bourtchuladze, R., Frenguelli, B., Blendy, J., Cioffi, D., Schutz, G., & Silva, A. J. (1994). Deficient long-term memory in mice with a targeted mutation of the camp-responsive element-binding protein. *Cell, 79,* 59–68.

Boutcher, S. H. (1992). Attention and athletic performance: An integrated approach. In T. S. Horn (Ed.), *Advances in sport psychology* (pp. 251–265). Champaign, IL: Human Kinetics.

Bouton, M. E. (1994). Conditioning, remembering, and forgetting. *Journal of Experimental Psychology: Animal Behavior Processes, 20,* 219–231.

Bovbjerg, D. H., Redd, W. H., Jacobsen, P. B., Manne, S. L., Taylor, K. L., Surbone, A., Crown, J. P., Norton, L., Gilewski, T. A., Hudis, C. F., Reichman, B. S., Kaufman, R. J., Currie, V. E., & Hakes, T. B. (1992). An experimental analysis of classically conditioned nausea during cancer chemotherapy. *Psychosomatic Medicine, 54,* 623–637.

Bowden, E. M., & Beeman, M. J. (1998). Getting the right idea: Semantic activation in the right hemisphere may help solve insight problems. *American Psychological Society,* 9(6), 435–440.

Bower, G. H. (1981). Mood and memory. *American Psychologist, 36,* 126–148.

Bower, T. G. R. (1966, December). The visual world of infants. *Scientific American,* 80–92.

Bowers, K. S. (1979). Time distortion and hypnotic ability: Underestimating the duration of hypnosis. *Journal of Abnormal Psychology, 88,* 435–439.

Bowers, K. S. (1992). Imagination and dissociation in hypnotic responding. *International Journal of Clinical and Experimental Hypnosis, 40,* 253–275.

Bowers, K. S., Regehr, G., Balthazard, C., & Parker, K. (1990). Intuition in the context of discovery. *Cognitive Psychology, 22,* 72–110.

Bowlby, J. (1977). The making and breaking of affectional bonds: Etiology and psychopathology in the light of attachment theory. *British Journal of Psychiatry, 130,* 201–210.

Bowlby, J. (1988). *A secure base.* New York: Basic Books.

Bowring, M. A., & Kovacs, M. (1992). Difficulties in diagnosing manic disorders among children and adolescents. *Journal of the American Academy of Child and Adolescent Psychiatry, 31*(4), 611–614.

Boyd, B., & Wandersman, A. (1991). Predicting undergraduate condom use with the Fishbein and Ajzen and the Triandis attitude–behavior models: Implications for public health interventions. *Journal of Applied Social Psychology, 21,* 1810–1830.

Boynton, R. M. (1988). Color vision. *Annual Review of Psychology, 39,* 69–101.

Boysen, S. T., & Berntson, G. G. (1989). Numerical competence in a chimpanzee (Pan troglodytes). *Journal of Comparative Psychology, 103,* 23–31.

Boyum, L. A., & Parke, R. D. (1995). The role of family emotional expressiveness in the development of children's social competence. *Journal of Marriage and the Family, 57*(3), 593–608.

Brabeck, M. M., & Larned, A. G. (1997). What we do not know about women's ways of knowing. In M. R. Walsh (Ed.), *Women, men, and gender: Ongoing debates.* New Haven, CT: Yale University Press.

Bradley, B. P. (1990). Behavioural addictions: Common features and treatment implications. *British Journal of Addiction, 85,* 1417–1419.

Bradley, C. L., & Marcia, J. E. (1998). Generativity-stagnation: A five-category model. *Journal of Personality, 66*(1), 39–44.

Brainerd, C. J., Reyna, V. F., & Brandse, E. (1995). Are children's false memories more persistent than their true memories? *Psychological Science, 6,* 359–364.

Branden, N. (1980). *The psychology of romantic love.* Los Angeles: Tarcher.

Brannon, E. M., & Terrace, H. S. (1998). Ordering of the numerosities 1 to 9 by monkeys. *Science, 282,* 746–750.

Braun, A. R., Balkin, T. J., Wesensten, N. J., Gwadry, F., Carson, R. E., Varga, M., Baldwin, P., Belenky, G., & Herscovitch, P. (1998). Dissociated pattern of activity in visual cortices and their projections during human rapid eye movement sleep. *Science, 279,* 91–96.

Breedlove, S. M. (1997). Sex on the brain. *Nature, 389,* 801.

Brehm, J. W. (1966). *A theory of psychological reactance.* New York: Academic.

Brennen, K. A., & Shaver, P. R. (1995). Dimensions of adult attachment, affect regulation, and romantic relationship functioning. *Personality and Social Psychology Bulletin, 21,* 267–283.

Bretschneider, J. G., & McCoy, N. L. (1988). Sexual interest and behavior in healthy 80- to 102-year-olds. *Archives of Sexual Behavior, 17,* 109–129.

Brewer, J. B., Zhao, Z., Desmond, J. E., Glover, G. H., & Gabrieli, J. D. (1998). Making memories: Brain activity that predicts how well visual experience will be remembered. *Science, 281,* 1185–1188.

Bridges, K. M. B. (1932). Emotional development in early infancy. *Child Development, 3,* 324–341.

Broadbent, D. E. (1958). *Perception and communication.* London: Pergamon.

Broberg, A. G., Wessels, H., Lamb, M. E., & Hwang, C. P. (1997). Effects of day care on the development of cognitive abilities in 8-year-olds: A longitudinal study. *Developmental Psychology, 33*(1), 62–69.

Brodsky, A. E. (1996). Resilient single mothers in risky neighborhoods: Negative psychological sense of community. *Journal of Community Psychology, 24*(4), 347–363.

Brody, E. M., Lawton, M. P., and Liebowitz, B. (1984). Senile dementia: Public policy and adequate institutional care. *American Journal of Public Health, 74,* 1381–1383.

Brody, G. H. (1998). Sibling relationship quality: Its causes and consequences. *Annual Review in Psychology, 49,* 1–24.

Brody, L. R. (1997). Gender and emotion: Beyond stereotypes. *Journal of Social Issues, 53*(2), 369–392.

Bronfenbrenner, U. (1979). *The ecology of human development.* Cambridge, MA: Harvard University Press.

Bronfenbrenner, U. (1989, September). *Who cares for children?* Invited address, UNESCO, Paris.

Bronson, G. W. (1997). The growth of visual capacity: Evidence from infant scanning patterns. In C. Rovee-Collier & L. P. Lipsitt (Eds.), *Advances in infancy research.* Greenwich, CT: Ablex Publishing.

Brooks-Gunn, J., & Furstenberg, F. F., Jr. (1989). Adolescent sexual behavior. *American Psychologist, 44,* 249–257.

Broughton, R. J. (1991). Field studies of sleep/wake patterns and performance: A laboratory experience. *Canadian Journal of Psychology, 45,* 240–253.

Brown, A. S. (1989). *How to increase your memory power.* Glenview, IL: Scott, Foresman.

Brown, G. M. (1994). Light, melatonin and the sleep–wake cycle. *Journal of Psychiatry & Neuroscience, 19,* 345–353.

Brown, K. W., & Moskowitz, D. S. (1998). Dynamic stability of behavior: The rhythms of our interpersonal lives. *Journal of Personality, 66*(1), 105–108.

Brown, L. M. (1998). *Raising their voices: The politics of girls' anger.* Cambridge, MA: Harvard University Press.

Brown, R. (1970). The first sentences of child and chimpanzee. In R. Brown (Ed.), *Psycholinguistics: Selected papers.* New York: Free Press.

Brown, R., & Kulik, J. (1977). Flashbulb memories. *Cognition, 5,* 73–99.

Brown, T. A., & Barlow, D. H. (1995). Long-term outcome in cognitive-behavioral treatment of panic disorder: Clinical predictors and alternative strategies for assessment. *Journal of Consulting and Clinical Psychology, 63,* 754–765.

Browne, B. A. (1998). Gender stereotypes in advertising on children's television in the 1990s: A cross-national analysis. *Journal of Advertising, 27*(1), 83–96.

Bruch, M. A., Berko, E. H., & Haase, R. F. (1998). Shyness, masculine ideology, physical attractiveness, and emotional inexpressiveness: Testing a mediational model of men's interpersonal competence. *Journal of Counseling Psychology, 45*(1), 84–97.

Bruer, J. T. (1999). *The myth of the first three years.* New York: Free Press.

Bruner, J. (1990). *Acts of meaning.* Cambridge, MA: Harvard University Press.

Bruner, J. (1997). Celebrating divergence: Piaget and Vygotsky. *Human Development, 40,* 63–73.

Bryant, R. A., & McConkey, K. M. (1989). Hypnotic blindness: A behavioral and experiential analysis. *Journal of Abnormal Psychology, 98,* 71–77.

Buchanan, C. M., Eccles, J. S., & Becker, J. B. (1992). Are adolescents the victims of raging hormones? Evidence for activational effects of hormones on moods and behavior at adolescence. *Psychological Bulletin, 111,* 62–107.

Buchsbaum, M. S., & Hazlett, E. A. (1997). Functional brain imaging and aging in schizophrenia. *Schizophrenia Research, 27*(2/3), 129–141.

Buchwald, A. M., & Rudick-Davis, D. (1993). The symptoms of major depression. *Journal of Abnormal Psychology, 102,* 197–205.

Buck, R., Losow, J. I., Murphy, M. M., & Costanzo, P. (1992). Social facilitation and inhibition of emotional expression and communication. *Journal of Personality and Social Psychology, 6,* 962–968.

Bukowski, W. M., Gauze, C., Hoza, B., & Newcomb, A. F. (1993). Differences and consistency between same-sex and other-sex peer relationships during early adolescence. *Developmental Psychology, 29,* 255–263.

Bulcroft, R. A., & Bulcroft, K. A. (1993). Race differences in attitudinal and motivational factors in the decision to marry. *Journal of Marriage and the Family, 55,* 338–355.

Bullock, W. A., & Gilliland, K. (1993). Eysenck's arousal theory of introversion–extraversion: A converging measures investigation. *Journal of Personality and Social Psychology, 64,* 113–123.

Burchinal, M., Lee, M., & Ramey, C. (1989). Type of daycare and preschool intellectual development in disadvantaged children. *Child Development, 60,* 128–137.

Burg, B., & Belmont, I. (1990). Mental abilities of children from different cultural backgrounds in Israel. *Journal of Cross-Cultural Psychology, 21,* 90–108.

Burger, J. M., & Hemans, L. T. (1988). Desire for control and the use of attribution processes. *Journal of Personality, 56,* 531–546.

Burman, B., Mednick, S. A., Machon, R. A., Parnas, J., & Schulsinger, F. (1987). Children at high risk for schizophrenia: Parent and offspring perceptions of family relationships. *Journal of Abnormal Psychology, 96,* 364–366.

Burn, S. M. (1991). Social psychology and the stimulation of recycling behaviors: The block leader approach. *Journal of Applied Social Psychology, 21,* 611–629.

Burnet, P. W., Eastwood, S. L., & Harrison, P. J. (1996). 5-HT-sub(1A) and 5-HT-sub(2A) receptor mRNAs and binding site densities are differentially altered in schizophrenia. *Neuropsychopharmacology, 15*(5), 442–455.

Busato, V. V., Prins, F. J., Elshout, J. J., & Hamaker, C. (1999). The relation between learning styles, the Big Five personality traits and achievement motivation in higher education. *Personality & Individual Differences, 26*(1), 129–140.

Bushman, B. J., & Baumeister, R. F. (1998). Threatened egotism, narcissism, self-esteem, and direct and displaced aggression: Does self-love or self-hate lead to violence? *Journal of Personality & Social Psychology, 75*(1), 219–229.

Bushman, B. J., & Geen, R. G. (1990). Role of cognitive–emotional mediators and individual differences in the effects of media violence on aggression. *Journal of Personality and Social Psychology, 58,* 156–163.

Buss, D. M. (1988). Love acts: The evolutionary biology of love. In R. J. Sternberg & M. L. Barnes (Eds.), *The psychology of love.* New Haven, CT: Yale University Press.

Buss, D. M. (1995). Psychological sex differences: Origins through sexual selection. *American Psychologist, 50,* 164–168.

Buss, D. M., Haselton, M. G., Shackelford, T. K., Bleske, A. L., & Wakefield, J. C. (1998). Adaptations, exaptations, and spandrels. *American Psychologist, 53*(5), 533–548.

Butcher, J. N., Graham, J. R., Dahlstrom, W. G., & Bowman, E. (1990). The MMPI-2 with college students. *Journal of Personality Assessment, 54,* 1–15.

Butcher, J. N., Lim, J., & Nezami, E. (1998). Objective study of abnormal personality in cross-cultural settings: The Minnesota Multiphasic Personality Inventory (MMPI-2). *Journal of Cross-Cultural Psychology, 29*(1), 189–211.

Butler, S. F., & Strupp, H. H. (1991). Psychodynamic psychotherapy. In M. Hersen, A. E. Kazdin, & A. S. Bellack (Eds.), *The clinical psychology handbook* (2nd ed.). New York: Pergamon.

Butterfield-Picard, H., & Magno, J. B. (1982). Hospice the adjective, not the noun: The future of a national priority. *American Psychologist, 37,* 1254–1259.

Byne, W. (1994, May). The biological evidence challenged. *Scientific American,* 50–55.

Byrne, A., & Byrne, D. G. (1993). The effect of exercise on depression, anxiety, and other mood states. *Journal of Psychosomatic Research, 37,* 565–574.

Cabeza, R., Kapur, S., Craik, F. I., McIntosh, A. R., Houle, S., & Tulving, E. (1997). Functional neuroanatomy of recall and recognition: A PET study of episodic memory. *Journal of Cognitive Neuroscience, 9*(2), 254–265.

Cabeza, R., & Nyberg, L. (1997). Imaging cognition: An empirical review of PET studies with normal subjects. *Journal of Cognitive Neuroscience, 9*(1), 1–26.

Cacioppo, J. T., Petty, R. E., Feinstein, J. A., & Jarvis, W. B. G. (1996). Dispositional differences in cognitive motivation: The life and times of individuals varying in need for cognition. *Psychological Bulletin, 119,* 197–253.

Cadoret, R. J., Yates, W. R., Troughton, E., Woodworth, G., & Stewart, M. A. (1995). Genetic-environmental interaction in the genesis of aggressivity and conduct disorders. *Archives of General Psychiatry, 52,* 916–924.

Caffarella, R. S., & Olson, S. K. (1993). Psychosocial development of women: A critical review of the literature. *Adult Education Quarterly, 43,* 125–151.

Cairns, R. B., & Cairns, B. D. (1994). *Lifelines and risks: Pathways of youth in our time.* Cambridge, England: Cambridge University Press.

Caldera, Y. M., Huston, A. C., & O'Brien, M. (1989). Social interactions and play patterns of parents and toddlers with feminine, masculine, and neutral toys. *Child Development, 109,* 70–76.

Call, V., Sprecher, S., & Schwartz, P. (1995). The incidence and frequency of marital sex in a national sample. *Journal of Marriage and the Family, 57*(3), 639–652.

Calvert, S. L. (1998). *Children's journeys through the information age.* New York: McGraw-Hill.

Calvin, W. H. (1996). *The cerebral code: Thinking a thought in the mosaics of the mind.* Cambridge, MA: MIT Press.

Camara, W. J., & Schneider, D. L. (1994). Integrity tests: Facts and unresolved issues. *American Psychologist, 49,* 112–119.

Cameron, P., & Cameron, K. (1998). "Definitive" University of Chicago sex survey overestimated prevalence of homosexual identity. *Psychological Reports, 82*(3, Pt. 1), 861–862.

Campbell, S. S., & Murphy, P. J. (1998). Extraocular circadian phototransduction in humans. *Science, 279,* 396–399.

Campfield, L. A., Smith, F. J., & Burn, P. (1998). Strategies and potential molecular targets for obesity treatment. *Science, 280,* 1383–1387.

Campion, M. A., Palmer, D. K., & Campion, J. E. (1998). Structuring employment interviews to improve reliability, validity, and users' reactions. *Current Directions in Psychological Science, 7*(3), 77–82.

Campis, L. B., Hebden-Curtis, C. J., & DeMaso, D. R. (1993). Developmental differences in detection and disclosure of sexual abuse. *Journal of the American Academy of Child and Adolescent Psychiatry, 32,* 920–924.

Camras, L. A., Oster, H., Campos, J. J., Miyake, K., & Bradshaw, D. (1992). Japanese and American infants' responses to arm restraint. *Developmental Psychology, 28,* 578–583.

Canavan-Gumpert, D. (1977). Generating reward and cost orientations through praise and criticism. *Journal of Personality and Social Psychology, 35,* 501–513.

Cannon, T. D., & Marco, E. (1994). Structural brain abnormalities as indicators of vulnerability to schizophrenia. *Schizophrenia Bulletin, 20,* 89–102.

Cannon, T. D., Mednick, S. A., & Parnas, J. (1990). Antecedents of predominantly negative- and predominantly positive-symptom schizophrenia in a high-risk population. *Archives of General Psychiatry, 47*(7), 622–632.

Cannon, W. B. (1927). The James–Lange theory of emotion: A critical examination and an alternative theory. *American Journal of Psychology, 39,* 106–124.

Cannon-Bowers, J. A., & Salas, E. (1998). Team performance and training in complex environments: Recent findings from applied research. *American Psychological Society, 7*(3), 83–87.

Capaldi, D. M., Crosby, L., & Stoolmiller, M. (1996). Predicting the timing of first sexual intercourse for at-risk adolescent males. *Child Development, 67,* 344–359.

Carducci, B. J., & Stein, N. D. (1988, April). *The personal and situational pervasiveness of shyness in college students: A nine-year comparison.* Paper presented at the meeting of the Southeastern Psychological Association, New Orleans.

Carland, J. C., Carland, J. W., Ensley, M. D., & Stewart, H. W. (1994). The implications of cognition and learning styles for management education. *Management Learning, 25,* 413–431.

Carless, S. A. (1998). Gender differences in transformational leadership: An examination of superior, leader, and subordinate perspectives. *Sex Roles, 39*(11/12), 887–902.

Carli, L. L. (1997). Biology does not create gender differences in personality. In M. R. Walsh (Ed.), *Women, men, and gender: Ongoing debates.* New Haven, CT: Yale University Press.

Carlson, C. R., Gantz, F. P., & Masters, J. C. (1983). Adults' emotional states and recognition of emotion in young children. *Motivation and Emotion, 7,* 81–102.

Carpenter, P. A., Just, M. A., & Shell, P. (1990). What one intelligence test measures: A theoretical account of the processing in the Raven Progressive Matrices Test. *Psychological Review, 97*(3), 404–431.

Carr, M., Borkowski, J. G., & Maxwell, S. E. (1991). Motivational components of underachievement. *Developmental Psychology, 27,* 108–118.

Carton, J. S., & Nowicki, S. (1994). Antecedents of individual differences in locus of control of reinforcement: A critical review. *Genetic, Social, and General Psychology Monographs, 120*(1), 31–81.

Carton, J. S., Nowicki, S., & Balser, G. M. (1996). An observational study of antecedents of locus of control of reinforcement. *International Journal of Behavioral Development, 19*(1), 161–175.

Caruso, G. A. L., & Corsini, D. A. (1994). The prevalence of behavior problems among toddlers in child care. *Early Education and Development, 5,* 27–40.

Carver, C. S., & Scheier, M. F. (1990). Origins and functions of positive and negative affect: A control-process view. *Psychological Review, 97,* 19–35.

Casagrande, M., Violani, C., Lucidi, F., & Buttinelli, E. (1996). Variations in sleep mentation as a function of time of night. *International Journal of Neuroscience, 85*(1/2), 19–30.

Cascio, W. F. (1995). Whither industrial and organizational psychology in a changing world of work? *American Psychologist, 50,* 928–939.

Caspi, A., Elder, G. H., & Bem, D. J. (1988). Moving away from the world: Life-course patterns of shy children. *Developmental Psychology, 24,* 824–831.

Cassidy, J., & Berlin, L. J. (1994). The insecure/ambivalent pattern of attachment: Theory and research. *Child Development, 65,* 971–991.

Cattell, R. B. (1965). *The scientific analysis of personality.* Baltimore: Penguin.

Cavalier, A. R., Ferretti, R. P., & Hodges, A. E. (1997). Self-management within a classroom token economy for students with learning disabilities. *Research in Development Disabilities, 18*(3), 167–178.

Cavanagh, P., & Leclerc, Y. G. (1989). Shape from shadows. *Journal of Experimental Psychology: Human Perception and Performance, 15,* 3–27.

Ceci, S. J. (1991). How much does schooling influence general intelligence and its cognitive components? A reassessment of the evidence. *Developmental Psychology, 27,* 703–722.

Ceci, S. J., & Bruck, M. (1993). Suggestibility of the child witness: A historical review and synthesis. *Psychological Bulletin, 113,* 403–439.

Ceci, S. J., Rosenblum, T. B., & Kumpf, M. (1998). The shrinking gap between high- and low-scoring groups: Current trends and possible causes. In U. Neisser (Ed.), *The rising curve: Long-term gains in IQ and related measures* (pp. 287–302). Washington, DC: American Psychological Association.

Ceci, S. J., & Williams, W. M. (1997). Schooling, intelligence, and income. *American Psychologist, 52*(10), 1051–1058.

Celuch, K., & Slama, M. (1995). Getting along and getting ahead as motives for self-presentation: Their impact on advertising effectiveness. *Journal of Applied Social Psychology, 25,* 1700–1713.

Centers for Disease Control and Prevention. (1996, September 27). CDS surveillance summaries. *Morbidity and Mortality Weekly Report, 45* (No. SS-4).

Cermak, L. S. (1975). *Improving your memory.* New York: Norton.

Chaiken, S., & Eagly, A. H. (1983). Communication modality as a determinant of persuasion: The role of communicator salience. *Journal of Personality and Social Psychology, 45,* 241–256.

Chalmers, D. J. (1996). *Conscious mind: In search of a fundamental theory.* New York: Oxford University Press.

Chamberlain, K., & Zika, S. (1990). The minor events approach to stress: Support for the use of daily hassles. *British Journal of Psychology, 81,* 469–481.

Chamberlain, K., & Zika, S. (1992). Religiosity, meaning in life, and psychological well-being. In J. F. Schumaker (Ed.), *Religion and mental health.* New York: Oxford University Press.

Chambless, D. L., & Hollon, S. D. (1998). Defining empirically supported therapies. *Journal of Consulting and Clinical Psychology, 66*(1), 7–18.

Chamizo, V. D., & Mackintosh, N. J. (1989). Latent learning and latent inhibition in maze discriminations. *Quarterly Journal of Experimental Psychology, 41B,* 21–31.

Chang, F. I. F., Isaacs, K. R., & Greenough, W. T. (1991). Synapse formation occurs in association with the induction of long-term potentiation in two-year-old rat hippocampus in vitro. *Neurobiology of Aging, 12,* 517–522.

Charles, C. M. (1985). *Building classroom discipline: From models to practice* (2nd ed.). New York: Longman.

Chassin, L., Pillow, D. R., Curran, P. J., Molina, B. S. G., & Barrera, M., Jr. (1993). Relation of parental alcoholism to early adolescent substance use: A test of three mediating mechanisms. *Journal of Abnormal Psychology, 102,* 3–19.

Chaves, J. F., & Dworkin, S. F. (1997). Hypnotic control of pain: Historical perspectives and future prospects. *International Journal of Clinical and Experimental Hypnosis, 45*(4), 356–376.

Chen, H., & Lan, W. (1998). Adolescents' perception of their parents' academic expectations: Comparison of American, Chinese-American, and Chinese high school students. *Adolescence, 33*(130), 385.

Chen, X., Rubin, K. H., & Li, Z. (1995). Social functioning and adjustment in Chinese children: A longitudinal study. *Developmental Psychology, 31,* 531–539.

Cheng, A. T. A. (1995). Mental illness and suicide: A case-control study in East Taiwan. *Archives of General Psychiatry, 52,* 594–603.

Cherulnik, P. D., Turns, L. C., & Wilderman, S. K. (1990). Physical appearance and leadership: Exploring the role of appearance-based attribution in leader emergence. *Journal of Applied Social Psychology, 20,* 1530–1539.

Chia, E. K. F., & Jih, C. S. (1994). The effects of stereotyping on impression formation: Cross-cultural perspectives on viewing religious persons. *Journal of Psychology, 128*(5), 559–565.

Chidester, T. R. (1986). Problems in the study of interracial interaction: Pseudo-interracial dyad paradigm. *Journal of Personality and Social Psychology, 50,* 74–79.

Choi, I., Nisbett, R. E., & Norenzayan, A. (1999). Causal attribution across cultures: Variation and universality. *Psychological Bulletin, 125*(1), 47–63.

Chomsky, N. (1957). *Syntactic structures.* The Hague, Netherlands: Mouton.

Chomsky, N. (1986). *Knowledge of language: Its nature, origin, and use.* New York: Praeger.

Chomsky, N. (1990). On the nature, use and acquisition of language. In W. G. Lycan (Ed.), *Mind and cognition* (pp. 627–646). Oxford, England: Blackwell.

Chorney, M. J., Chorney, K., Seese, N., Owen, M. J., Daniels, J., McGuffin, P., Thompson, L. A., Detterman, D. K., Benbow, C., Lubinski, D., Eley, T., & Plomin, R. (1998). A quantitative trait locus associated with cognitive ability in children. *Psychological Science, 9*(3), 159–166.

Chorpita, B. F., & Barlow, D. H. (1998). The development of anxiety: The role of control in the early environment. *Psychological Bulletin, 124*(1), 3–21.

Christenfeld, N., Gerin, W., Linden, W., & Sanders, M. (1997). Social support effects on cardiovascular reactivity: Is a stranger as effective as a friend? *Psychosomatic Medicine, 59*(4), 388–398.

Chung, S. W., & Doh, H. S. (1997). Parental sociability, parenting behaviors, and shyness in children. [Korean]. *Korean Journal of Child Studies, 18*(2), 149–161.

Cialdini, R. B. (1993). *Influence* (3rd ed.). New York: HarperCollins.

Cialdini, R. B. (1994). Interpersonal influence. In S. Shavitt & T. C. Brock (Eds.), *Persuasion: Psychological insights and perspectives* (pp. 195–218). Boston: Allyn & Bacon.

Cialdini, R. B., Eisenberg, N., Green, B. L., Rhoads, K., & Bator, R. (1998). Undermining the undermining effect of reward on sustained interest. *Journal of Applied Social Psychology, 28*(3), 249–263.

Cialdini, R. B., Trost, M. R., & Newsom, J. T. (1995). Preference for consistency: The development of a valid measure and the discovery of surprising behavioral implications. *Journal of Personality and Social Psychology, 69,* 318–328.

Cicero, T. J. (1994). Effects of paternal exposure to alcohol on offspring development. *Alcohol Health and Research World, 18,* 37–41.

Clark, H. H. (1996). *Using language.* Cambridge, England: Cambridge University Press.

Clark, L. A., Watson, D., & Reynolds, S. (1995). Diagnosis and classification of psychopathology: Challenges to the current system and future directions. *Annual Review of Psychology, 46,* 121–153.

Clark, M. S., & Reis, H. T. (1988). Interpersonal processes in close relationships. *Annual Review of Psychology, 39,* 609–672.

Clarke-Stewart, A. (1973). Interactions between mothers and their young children: Characteristics and consequences. *Monographs of the Society for Research in Child Development,* 38.

Clarke-Stewart, A., Friedman, S., & Koch, J. B. (1985). *Child development: A topical approach.* New York: Wiley.

Clarkin, J. F., & Hull, J. W. (1991). The brief psychotherapies. In M. Hersen, A. E. Kazdin, & A. S. Bellack (Eds.), *The clinical psychology handbook* (2nd ed.). New York: Pergamon.

Claxon, G. (1975). Why can't we tickle ourselves. *Perceptual and Motor Skills, 41*(1), 335–338.

Claxton, R. P., & McIntyre, R. P. (1994). Empirical relationships between need for cognition and cognitive style: Implications for consumer psychology. *Psychological Reports, 74,* 723–732.

Clifton, R. K., Muir, D. W., Ashmead, D. H., & Clarkson, M. G. (1993). Is visually guided reaching in early infancy a myth? *Child Development, 64,* 1099–1110.

Coates, B., Pusser, H. E., & Goodman, I. (1976). The influence of "Sesame Street" and "Mister Rogers' Neighborhood" on children's social behavior in the preschool. *Child Development, 47,* 138–144.

Coffey, C. W., Weiner, R. D., Djang, W. T., Figiel, G. S., Soady, S. A. R., Patterson, L. J., Holt, P. D., Spritzer, C. E., & Wilinson, W. E. (1991). Brain anatomic effects of electroconvulsive therapy. *Archives of General Psychiatry, 48,* 1013–1021.

Cogan, J. C., Bhalla, S. K., Sefa-Dedeh, A., & Rothblum, E. D. (1996). A comparison study of United States and African students on perceptions of obesity and thinness. *Journal of Cross-Cultural Psychology, 27*(1), 98–113.

Cohen, R. J., Montague, P., Nathanson, L. S., & Swerdlik, M. E. (1988). *Psychological testing.* Mountain View, CA: Mayfield.

Cohen, S. (1996). Psychological stress, immunity, and upper respiratory infections. *Current Directions in Psychological Science, 5*(3), 86–90.

Cohen, S., Frank, E., Doyle, W. J., Skoner, D. P., Rabin, B. S., & Gwaltney, J. M., Jr. (1998). Types of stressors that increase susceptibility to the common cold in healthy adults. *Health Psychology, 17*(3), 214–223.

Cohen, S., Tyrrell, D. A. J., & Smith, A. P. (1991). Psychological stress and susceptibility to the common cold. *New England Journal of Medicine, 325,* 606–612.

Cohen, S., Tyrrell, D. A. J., & Smith, A. P. (1993). Negative life events, perceived stress, negative affect, and susceptibility to the common cold. *Journal of Personality and Social Psychology, 64,* 131–140.

Cohen, S., Tyrrell, D. A. J., & Smith, A. P. (1997). Psychological stress in humans and susceptibility to the common cold. In T. W. Miller et al. (Eds.), *Clinical disorders and stressful life events* (pp. 217–235). Madison, CT: International Universities Press, Inc.

Cohen, S., & Williamson, G. M. (1991). Stress and infectious disease in humans. *Psychological Bulletin, 109,* 5–24.

Cohn, D. A. (1990). Child–mother attachment of six-year-olds and social competence at school. *Child Development, 61,* 152–162.

Cohn, J. F., & Tronick, E. Z. (1983). Three-month-old infants' reaction to simulated maternal depression. *Child Development, 54,* 185–193.

Cohn, L. (1991). Sex differences in the course of personality development: A meta-analysis. *Psychological Bulletin, 109,* 252–266.

Cole, D. A. (1989). Psychopathology of adolescent suicide: Hopelessness, coping beliefs, and depression. *Journal of Abnormal Psychology, 98,* 248–255.

Coley, R. L., & Chase-Landsdale, P. L. (1998). Adolescent pregnancy and parenthood: Recent evidence and future directions. *American Psychologist, 53*(2), 152–166.

Collins, N. L., & Miller, L. C. (1994). Self-disclosure and liking: A meta-analytic review. *Psychological Bulletin, 116,* 457–475.

Colman, H., Nabekura, J., & Lichtman, J. W. (1997). Alterations in synaptic strength preceding axon withdrawal. *Science, 275,* 356–361.

Colvin, C. R., & Block, J. (1994). Do positive illusions foster mental health? An examination of the Taylor and Brown formulation. *Psychological Bulletin, 116,* 3–20.

Comer, J. P. (1988, November). Educating poor minority children. *Scientific American,* 42–51.

Comuzzie, A. G., &Allison, D. B. (1998). The search for human obesity genes. *Science, 280,* 1374–1377.

Contrada, R. J. (1989). Type A behavior, personality hardiness, and cardiovascular responses to stress. *Journal of Personality and Social Psychology, 57,* 895–903.

Conway, M. A. (1991). In defense of everyday memory. *American Psychologist, 46,* 19–26.

Conway, M. A., Anderson, S. J., Larsen, S. F., Donnelly, C. M., McDaniel, M. A., McClelland, A. G. R., Rawles, R. E., & Logie, R. H. (1994). The formation of flashbulb memories. *Memory & Cognition, 22,* 326–343.

Conyers, L. M., Enright, M. S., & Strauser, D. R. (1998). Applying self-efficacy theory to counseling college students with disabilities. *Journal of Applied Rehabilitation Counseling, 29*(1), 25–30.

Coppola, D. M., & O'Connell, R. J. (1988). Behavioral responses of peripubertal female mice towards puberty-accelerating and puberty-delaying chemical signals. *Chemical Senses, 13,* 407–424.

Corbetta, M., Shulman, G. L., Miezin, F. M., & Petersen, S. E. (1995). Superior parietal cortex activation during spatial attention shifts and visual feature conjunction. *Science, 270,* 802–805.

Cordova, D. I., & Lepper, M. R. (1996). Intrinsic motivation and the process of learning: Beneficial effects of contextualization, personalization, and choice. *Journal of Educational Psychology, 88*(4), 715–730.

Coren, S. (1996). *Sleep thieves: An eye-opening exploration into the science and mysteries of sleep.* New York: The Free Press.

Coren, S., & Aks, D. J. (1990). Moon illusion in pictures: A multimechanism approach. *Journal of Experimental Psychology: Human Perception and Performance, 16,* 365–380.

Coren, S., & Porac, C. (1977). Fifty centuries of right-handedness: The historic record. *Science, 198,* 631–632.

Corina, D. P., Vaid, J., & Bellugi, U. (1992). The linguistic basis of left hemisphere specialization. *Science, 255,* 1258–1260.

Coryell, W., Endicott, J., & Keller, M. (1992). Major depression in a nonclinical sample. *Archives of General Psychiatry, 49,* 117–125.

Costa, P. T., Jr., & McCrae, R. R. (1998). Trait theories of personality. In D. F. Barone, M. Hersen, et al. (Eds.), *Advanced personality. The Plenum series in social/clinical psychology* (pp. 103–121). New York: Plenum Press.

Costanza, D. P., Fleishman, E. A., & Marshall-Mies, J. (1999). Knowledges. In N. G. Peterson, M. D. Mumford, et al. (Eds.), *An occupational information system for the 21st century: The development of O*NET* (pp. 71–90). Washington, DC: American Psychological Association.

Costanzo, M. (1997). *Just revenge.* New York: St. Martin's Press.

Costanzo, M., Archer, D., Aronson, E., & Pettigrew, T. (1986). Energy conservation behavior: The difficult path from information to action. *American Psychologist, 41,* 521–528.

Costanzo, M., & Costanzo, S. (1994). The death penalty: Public opinions, legal decisions, and juror perspectives. In M. Costanzo, S. Oskamp, et al. (Eds.), *Violence and the law. Claremont symposium on applied psychology, 7* (pp. 246–272). Thousand Oaks, CA: Sage Publications.

Courtney, S. M., Petit, L., Maisog, J. M., Ungerleider, L. G., & Haxby J. V. (1998). An area specialized for spatial working memory in human frontal cortex. *Science, 279,* 1347–1351.

Cowen, E. L. (1991). In pursuit of wellness. *American Psychologist, 46,* 404–408.

Cox, R. H., Qiu, Y., & Liu, Z. (1993). Overview of sport psychology. In R. N. Singer, M. Murphey, & L. K. Tennant (Eds.), *Handbook of research on sport psychology* (pp. 3–31). New York: Macmillan.

Craft, M. A., Alber, S. R., & Heward, W. L. (1998). Teaching elementary students with developmental disabilities to recruit teacher attention in a general education classroom:

Effects on teacher praise and academic productivity. *Journal of Applied Behavior Analysis, 31*(3), 399–415.

Craik, F. I. (1994). Memory changes in normal aging. *Current Directions in Psychological Science, 3*, 155–158.

Craik, F. I. M., & Lockhart, R. S. (1972). Levels of processing: A framework for memory research. *Journal of Verbal Learning and Verbal Behavior, 11*, 671–784.

Craik, F. I. M., Moroz, T. M., Moscovitch, M., Stuss, D. T., Winocur, G., Tulving, E., & Kapur, S. (1999). In search of the self: A positron emission tomography study. *American Psychological Society, 10*(1), 26–34.

Crair, M. C., Gillespie, D. C., & Stryker, M. P. (1998). The role of visual experience in the development of columns in cat visual cortex. *Science, 279*, 565–570.

Crandall, C. S. (1994). Prejudice against fat people: Ideology and self-interest. *Journal of Personality and Social Psychology, 66*(5), 882–894.

Crandall, C. S., & Martinez, R. (1996). Culture, ideology, and anti-fat attitudes. *Personality and Social Psychology Bulletin, 22*(11), 1165–1176.

Crane, J. (1994). Exploding the myth of scientific support for the theory of black intellectual inferiority. *Journal of Black Psychology, 20*, 189–209.

Crawford, C. B., & Anderson, J. L. (1989). Sociobiology. *American Psychologist, 44*, 1449–1459.

Crawford, H. J. (1994). Brain dynamics and hypnosis: Attentional and disattentional processes. *The International Journal of Clinical and Experimental Hypnosis, 42*, 204–232.

Crawford, M., & MacLeod, M. (1990). Gender in the college classroom: An assessment of the "chilly climate" for women. *Sex Roles, 23*, 101–122.

Crespi, T. D. (1988). Effectiveness of time-out: A comparison of psychiatric, correctional and day-treatment programs. *Adolescence, 23*, 805–811.

Crick, F., & Koch, C. (1998). Contraints on cortical and thalamic projections: The no-strong-loops hypothesis. *Nature, 391*(15), 245–250.

Crittenden, K. S., Fugita, S. S., Bae, H., Lamug, C. B., & Lin, C. (1992). A cross-cultural study of self-report depressive symptoms among college students. *Journal of Cross-Cultural Psychology, 23*, 163–178.

Cronan, T. A., Cruz, S. G., Arriaga, R. I., & Sarkin, A. J. (1996). The effects of a community-based literacy program on young children's language and conceptual development. *American Journal of Community Psychology, 24*(2), 251–272.

Cronan, T. A., Walen, H. R., & Cruz, S. G. (1994). The effects of community-based literacy training on Head Start parents. *Journal of Community Psychology, 22*, 248–258.

Cross, S. E., & Madson, L. (1997a). Elaboration of models of the self: Reply to Baumeister and Sommer (1997) and Martin and Ruble (1997). *Psychological Bulletin, 122*(1), 51–55.

Cross, S. E., & Madson, L. (1997b). Models of the self: Self-construals and gender. *Psychological Bulletin, 122*(1), 5–37.

Crowl, R. K., & MacGinitie, W. H. (1974). The influence of students' speech characteristics on teachers' evaluations of oral answers. *Journal of Educational Psychology, 66*, 304–308.

Crystal, D. S., Chen, C., Fuligni, A. J., Stevenson, H. W., Hsu, C., Ko, H., Kitamura, S., & Kimura, S. (1994). Psychological maladjustment and academic achievement: A cross-cultural study of Japanese, Chinese, and American high school students. *Child Development, 65*, 738–753.

Csikszentmihalyi, M. (1996). *Creativity: Flow and the psychology of discovery and invention*. New York: HarperCollins.

Csikszentmihalyi, M. (1997). *Finding flow: The psychology of engagement with everyday life*. New York: Basic Books.

Culbertson, F. M. (1997). Depression and gender: An international review. *American Psychologist, 52*(1), 25–31.

Cummings, N. A. (1986). The dismantling of our health system: Strategies for the survival of psychological practice. *American Psychologist, 41*, 426–431.

Cummings, N. A., Budman, S. H., & Thomas, J. L. (1998). Efficient psychotherapy as a viable response to scarce resources and rationing of treatment. *Professional Psychology: Research and Practice, 29*(5), 460–469.

Cunningham, M. R., Barbee, A. P., & Pike, C. L. (1990). What do women want? Facialmetric assessment of multiple motives in the perception of male facial physical attractiveness. *Journal of Personality and Social Psychology, 59*, 61–72.

Curran, D. K. (1987). *Adolescent suicidal behavior*. Washington, DC: Hemisphere.

Czeisler, C. A., Johnson, M. P., Duffy, J. F., Brown, E. N., Ronda, J. M., & Kronauer, R. E. (1990). Exposure to bright light and darkness to treat physiologic maladaptation to night work. *New England Journal of Medicine, 322*, 1253–1259.

Dabul, A. J., Wosinska, W., Cialdini, R. B., Mandal, E., & Dion, R. W. (1997). Self-presentational modesty across cultures: The effects of gender and social context in the workplace. *Polish Psychological Bulletin, 28*(4), 295–306.

Dadds, M. R., Bovbjerg, D. H., Redd, W. H., & Cutmore, T. R. (1997). Imagery in human classical conditioning. *Psychological Bulletin, 122*(1), 89–103.

Dakof, G. A., & Taylor, S. E. (1990). Victims' perceptions of social support: What is helpful from whom? *Journal of Personality and Social Psychology, 58*, 80–89.

Damasio, A. R. (1994). *Descartes' error: Emotion, reason, and the human brain*. New York: Putnam.

Damasio, A. R. (1997). Towards a neuropathology of emotion and mood. *Nature, 386*(6627), 769–770.

Damasio, A. (1999) *The feeling of what happens*. New York: Harcourt, Brace.

Damasio, A. R., & Damasio, H. (1992, September). Brain and language. *Scientific American*, 89–95.

Damasio, A. R., Tranel, D., & Damasio, H. (1990). Face agnosia and the neural substrates of memory. *Annual Review of Neuroscience, 13*, 89–109.

Daniel, M. H. (1997). Intelligence testing. *American Psychologist, 52*(10), 1038–1045.

Daniels, D., & Plomin, R. (1985). Origins of individual differences in infant shyness. *Developmental Psychology, 21,* 118–121.

Danner, R., & Edwards, D. (1992). Life is movement: Exercise for the older adult. *Activities, Adaptation & Aging, 17,* 15–26.

Daum, I., Ackermann, H., Schugens, M. M., Reimold, C., Dichgans, J., & Birbaumer, N. (1993). The cerebellum and cognitive functions in humans. *Behavioral Neuroscience, 107,* 411–419.

Davidson, R. J. (1992). Emotion and affective style: Hemispheric substrates. *Psychological Science, 3,* 39–43.

Davies, M. M. (1997). *Fake, fact, and fantasy: Children's interpretations of television reality.* Mahwah, NJ: Lawrence Erlbaum Associates, Inc.

Davies, M., Stankov, L., & Roberts, R. D. (1998). Emotional intelligence: In search of an elusive construct. *Journal of Personality and Social Psychology, 75*(4), 989–1015.

Davis, D., & Padesky, C. (1989). Enhancing cognitive therapy with women. In A. Freeman, K. M. Simon, L. E. Beutler, & H. Arkowitz (Eds.), *Comprehensive handbook of cognitive therapy.* New York: Plenum.

Davis, K. E., & Todd, M. J. (1982). Friendship and love relationships. In K. E. Davis & T. Mitchell (Eds.), *Advances in descriptive psychology* (Vol. 2). Greenwich, CT: JAI.

Davis, N. S., & Thornburg, K. R. (1994). Child care: A synthesis of research. *Early Child Development and Care, 98,* 39–45.

Dawes, R. M. (1994). *House of cards: Psychology and psychotherapy built on myth.* New York: Free Press.

DeAngelis, T. (1988). In praise of rose-colored specs. *APA Monitor, 19,* 11.

Dearwater, S. R., Coben, J. H., Campbell, J. C., Nah, G., Glass, N., McLoughlin, E., & Bekemeier, B. (1998). Prevalence of intimate partner abuse in women treated at community hospital emergency departments. *Journal of the American Medical Association, 280*(5), 433–438.

DeBono, K. G. (1992). Pleasant scents and persuasion: An information processing approach. *Journal of Applied Social Psychology, 22,* 910–919.

DeCharms, R. C., Blake, D. T., & Merzenich, M. M. (1998). Optimizing sound features for cortical neurons. *Science, 280,* 1439–1443.

Deci, E. L. (1972). Effects of contingent and non-contingent rewards and controls on intrinsic motivation. *Organizational Behavior and Human Performance, 8,* 217–229.

Deci, E. L. (1975). *Intrinsic motivation.* New York: Plenum.

Decker, S. H., & Kohfeld, C. W. (1984). A deterrence study of the death penalty in Illinois, 1933–1980. *Journal of Criminal Justice, 12*(4), 367–377.

de Haan, M., & Nelson, C. A. (1997). Recognition of the mother's face by six-month-old infants: A neurobehavioral study. *Child Development, 68*(2), 187–210.

De Jongh, A., Muris, P., Ter Horst, G., & Duyx, M. P. M. A. (1995). Acquisition and maintenance of dental anxiety: The role of conditioning experiences and cognitive factors. *Behavior Research Theory, 33*(2), 205–210.

DeLongis, A., Folkman, S., & Lazarus, R. S. (1988). The impact of daily stress on health and mood: Psychological and social resources as mediators. *Journal of Personality and Social Psychology, 54,* 486–495.

Dement, W. C., Greenberg, S., & Klein, R. (1966). The effect of partial REM sleep deprivation and delayed recovery. *Journal of Psychiatric Research, 4,* 141–152.

Dement, W. C., & Wolpert, E. A. (1958). The relation of eye movements, body motility, and external stimuli to dream content. *Journal of Experimental Psychology, 55,* 543–553.

DeNeve, K. M., & Cooper, H. (1998). The happy personality: A meta-analysis of 137 personality traits and subjective well-being. *Psychological Bulletin, 124*(2), 197–229.

Deniston, W. M., & Ramanaiah, N. V. (1993). California Psychological Inventory and the five-factor model of personality. *Psychological Reports, 73,* 491–496.

Denmark, F. I. (1994). Engendering psychology. *American Psychologist, 49,* 329–334.

Dennett, D. C. (1991). *Consciousness explained.* Boston: Little, Brown.

Dennett, D. C. (1996). *Kinds of minds: Toward an understanding of consciousness.* New York: Basic Books.

Dentan, R. K. (1968). *The Semai: A nonviolent people of Malaya.* New York: Holt, Rinehart & Winston.

DePaulo, B. M. (1992). Nonverbal behavior and self-presentation. *Psychological Bulletin, 111,* 230–243.

DePaulo, B. M., Dull, W. R., Greenberg, J. M., & Swaim, G. W. (1989). Are shy people reluctant to ask for help? *Journal of Personality and Social Psychology, 56,* 834–844.

DePaulo, P. J., & DePaulo, B. M. (1989). Can deception by salespersons and customers be detected through nonverbal behavioral cues? *Journal of Applied Social Psychology, 19,* 1552–1577.

Deregowski, J. B. (1980). Perception. In H. C. Triandis & J. W. Berry (Eds.), *Handbook of cross-cultural psychology: Vol. 3. Basic processes.* Boston: Allyn & Bacon.

Dershowitz, A. M. (1986). *Reversal of fortune: Inside the von Bulow case.* New York: Random House.

DeSantis, A., & Kayson, W. A. (1997). Defendants' characteristics of attractiveness, race, and sex and sentencing decisions. *Psychological Reports, 81,* 679–683.

D'Esposito, M., Zarahn, E., & Aguirre, G. K. (1999). Event-related functional MRI: Implications for cognitive psychology. *Psychological Bulletin, 125*(1), 155–164.

Detterman, D. K., & Thompson, L. A. (1997). What is so special about special education? *American Psychologist, 52*(10), 1082–1090.

DeValois, R. L., & Jacobs, G. H. (1968). Primate color vision, *Science, 162,* 533–540.

Devine, P. G. (1989). Stereotypes and prejudice: Their automatic and controlled components. *Journal of Personality and Social Psychology, 56*(1), 5–18.

Diehl, M., Willis, S. L., & Schaie, K. W. (1995). Everyday problem solving in older adults: Observational assessment and cognitive correlates. *Psychology and Aging, 10*(3), 478–491.

Diener, E. (1998). Subjective well-being and personality. In D. Barone (Ed.), *Advanced personality. The Plenum series in social/clinical psychology.* New York: Plenum Press.

Diener, E., & Diener, C. (1996). Most people are happy. *American Psychological Society, 7*(3), 181–185.

Diener, E., Lusk, R., DeFour, D., & Flax, R. (1980). Deindividuation: Effects of group size, density, number of observers, and group member similarity on self-consciousness and disinhibited behavior. *Journal of Personality and Social Psychology, 39,* 449–459.

Diener, E., Suh, E. M., Lucas, R. E., & Smith, H. L. (1999). Subjective well-being: Three decades of progress. *Psychological Bulletin, 125*(2), 276–302.

Dietvorst, T. F. (1978). Biofeedback assisted relaxation training with patients recovering from myocardial infarction. *Dissertation Abstracts International, 38,* 3389.

Dietz, T. L. (1998). An examination of violence and gender role portrayals in video games: Implications for gender socialization and aggressive behavior. *Sex Roles, 38*(5/6), 425–428.

DiGiuseppe, R. (1989). Cognitive therapy with children. In A. Freeman, K. M. Simon, L. E. Beutler, & H. Arkowitz (Eds.), *Comprehensive handbook of cognitive therapy*. New York: Plenum Press.

DiLalla, D. L., & Gottesman, I. I. (1995). Normal personality characteristics in identical twins discordant for schizophrenia. *Journal of Abnormal Psychology, 104,* 490–499.

DiLalla, L. F., & Gottesman, I. I. (1991). Biological and genetic contributors to violence: Wisdom's untold tale. *Psychological Bulletin, 109*(1), 125–129.

DiLalla, L. F., Thompson, L. A., Plomin, R., Phillips, K., Fagan, J. F., III, Haith, M. M., Cyphers, L. H., & Fulker, D. W. (1990). Infant predictors of preschool and adult IQ: A study of infant twins and their parents. *Development Psychology, 26,* 759–769.

DiMatteo, M. R., & DiNicola, D. D. (1982). *Achieving patient compliance: The psychology of the medical practitioner's role.* New York: Pergamon.

Dindia, K., & Allen, M. (1992). Sex differences in self-disclosure: A meta-analysis. *Psychological Bulletin, 112,* 106–124.

Dinges, N. G., & Hull, P. V. (1993). Personality, culture, and international studies. In D. Lieberman (Ed.), *Revealing the world: An interdisciplinary reader for international studies.* Dubuque, IA: Kendall-Hunt.

Dion, K. K., Pak, A. W., & Dion, K. L. (1990). Stereotyping physical attractiveness. *Journal of Cross-Cultural Psychology, 21,* 158–179.

Dobson, K. S., & Block L. (1988). Historical and philosophical bases of the cognitive–behavioral therapies. In K. S. Dobson (Ed.), *Handbook of cognitive–behavioral therapies.* New York: Guilford.

Docherty, N. M., Hall, M. J., & Gordinier, S. W. (1998). Affective reactivity of speech in schizophrenia patients and their nonschizophrenic relatives. *Journal of Abnormal Psychology, 107*(3), 461–467.

Dohrenwend, B. P., & Shrout, P. E. (1985). "Hassles" in the conceptualization and measurement of life stress variables. *American Psychologist, 40,* 780–785.

Dolcini, M. M., Coates, T. J., Catania, J. A., Kegeles, S. M., & Hauck, W. W. (1995). Multiple sexual partners and their psychosocial correlates: The population-based AIDS in multiethnic neighborhoods (AMEN) study. *Health Psychology, 14,* 22–31.

Dollard, J., Doob, L. W., Miller, N. E., Mowrer, O. H., & Sears, R. R. (1939). *Frustration and aggression.* New Haven, CT: Yale University Press.

Dollins, A. B., Lynch, H. J., Wurtman, R. J., Deng, M. H., et al. (1993). Effects of illumination on human nocturnal serum melatonin levels and performance. *Physiology and Behavior, 53,* 153–160.

Donnelly, C. M., & McDaniel, M. A. (1993). Use of analogy in learning scientific concepts. *Journal of Experimental Psychology: Learning, Memory, and Cognition, 19,* 975–987.

Donovan, J. M. (1998). Brief couples therapy: Lessons from the history of brief individual treatment. *Psychotherapy: Theory, Research and Practice, 35*(1), 116–129.

Donson, N. (1999). Caring for day care: Models for early intervention and primary prevention. In T. B. Cohen, M. H. Etezady, et al. (Eds.), *The vulnerable child, Vol. 3* (pp. 181–212). Madison, CT: International Universities Press.

Doob, A. N., & McLaughlin, D. S. (1989). Ask and you shall be given: Request size and donations to a good cause. *Journal of Applied Social Psychology, 19,* 1049–1056.

Downey, G., & Coyne, J. C. (1990). Children of depressed parents: An integrative review. *Psychological Bulletin, 108,* 50–76.

Downey, V. W., & Landry, R. G. (1997). Self-reported sexual behaviours of high school juniors and seniors in North Dakota. *Psychological Reports, 80*(3, Pt. 2), 1357–1358.

Drennen, W. T., & Holden, E. W. (1984). Trait/set interactions in EMG biofeedback. *Psychological Reports, 54,* 843–849.

Dreyer, P. H. (1982). Sexuality during adolescence. In B. B. Wolman (Ed.), *Handbook of developmental psychology.* Englewood Cliffs, NJ: Prentice-Hall.

Dromi, E. (1997). Early lexical development. In M. Barerett (Ed.), *The development of language.* London: UCL.

Dryden, W., & Ellis, A. (1988). Rational–emotive therapy. In K. S. Dobson (Ed.), *Handbook of cognitive–behavioral therapies.* New York: Guilford.

Dubovsky, S. L., & Thomas, M. (1995). Beyond specificity: Effects of serotonin and serotonergic treatments on psychobiological dysfunction. *Journal of Psychosomatic Research, 39,* 429–444.

Duckitt, J. (1992). Psychology and prejudice. *American Psychologist, 47,* 1182–1193.

Duffy, R. D., Kalsher, M. J., & Wogalter, M. S. (1993). The effectiveness of an interactive warning in a realistic product-use situation. *Proceedings of the Human Factors and Ergonomics Society, 37th Annual Meeting,* 935–939.

Dunant, Y., & Israel, M. (1985, April). The release of acetylcholine. *Scientific American,* 58–83.

Dunlosky, J., & Connor, L. T. (1997). Age differences in the allocation of study time account for age differences in memory performance. *Memory and Cognition, 25*(5), 691–700.

Dura, J. R., Stukenberg, K. W., & Kiecolt-Glaser, J. K. (1990). Chronic stress and depressive disorders in older adults. *Journal of Abnormal Psychology, 99,* 284–290.

Dutton, D. G. (1998). *The abusive personality: Violence and control in intimate relationships.* New York: The Guilford Press.

Dweck, C. S. (1986). Motivational processes affecting learning: Special issue. Psychological science and education. *American Psychologist, 41,* 1040–1048.

Dweck, C. S., & Leggett, E. L. (1988). A socio-cognitive approach to motivation and personality. *Psychological Review, 95,* 256–273.

Dwyer, W. O., Leeming, F. C., Cobern, M. K., Porter, B. E., & Jackson, J. M. (1993). Critical review of behavioral interventions to preserve the environment: Research since 1980. *Environment and Behavior, 25,* 275–321.

Eacott, M. J., & Crawley, R. A. (1998). The offset of childhood amnesia: Memory for events that occurred before age 3. *Journal of Experimental Psychology: General, 127*(1), 22–33.

Eagly, A. H. (1992). Uneven progress: Social psychology and the study of attitudes. *Journal of Personality and Social Psychology, 63,* 693–710.

Eagly, A. H. (1995). The science and politics of comparing women and men. *American Psychologist, 50,* 145–158.

Eagly, A. H., Ashmore, R. D., Makhijani, M. G., & Longo, L. C. (1991). What is beautiful is good, but . . . : A meta-analytic review of research on the physical attractiveness stereotype. *Psychological Bulletin, 110,* 109–128.

Eagly, A. H., & Chaiken, S. (1993). *The psychology of attitudes.* Fort Worth, TX: Harcourt Brace Jovanovich.

Eagly, A. H., & Johnson, B. T. (1990). Gender and leadership style: A meta-analysis. *Psychological Bulletin, 108,* 233–256.

Eagly, A. H., Makhijani, M. G., & Klonsky, B. G. (1992). Gender and the evaluation of leaders: A meta-analysis. *Psychological Bulletin, 111*(1), 3–22.

Eagly, A. H., & Steffen, V. J. (1986). Gender and aggressive behavior: A meta-analytic review of the social psychological literature. *Psychological Bulletin, 100,* 309–330.

Eaton, M. J., & Dembo, M. H. (1997). Differences in the motivational beliefs of Asian American and non-Asian students. *Journal of Educational Psychology, 89*(3), 433–440.

Eccles, J. S., Wigfield, A., Midgley, C., Reuman, D., Buchanan, C. M., Flanagan, C., & MacIver, D. (1993). Development during adolescence: The impact of stage–environment fit on young adolescents' experiences in schools and families. *American Psychologist, 48,* 90–101.

Edwards, D. C. (1999). *Motivation and emotion: Evolutionary, physiological, cognitive, and social influences.* London: Sage Publications.

Edwards, K. (1998). The face of time: Temporal cues in facial expressions of emotion. *American Psychological Society,* 9(4), 270–276.

Egeland, B., & Heister, M. (1995). The long-term consequences of infant day-care and mother–infant attachment. *Child Development, 66,* 474–485.

Egeland, B., Jacobvitz, D., & Sroufe, L. A. (1988). Breaking the cycle of abuse. *Child Development, 59,* 1080–1088.

Eich, E. (1995). Searching for mood dependent memory. *Psychological Science, 6,* 67–75.

Eichenbaum, H. (1997). How does the brain organize memories? *Science, 277,* 330–332.

Eisenberg, N., Shepard, S. A., Faves, R. A., Murphy, B. C., & Guthrie, I. K. (1998). Shyness and children's emotionality, regulation, and coping: Contemporaneous, longitudinal, and across-context relations. *Child Development,* 69(3), 767–790.

Eisenberger, R., & Cameron, J. (1996). Detrimental effects of reward. *American Psychologist, 51*(11), 1153–1166.

Eisenman, R. (1993). Professor Anita Hill versus Judge Clarence Thomas: The view of students at a Southern university. *Bulletin of the Psychonomic Society, 31,* 179–180.

Ekman, P. (1992). Facial expressions of emotion: New findings, new questions. *Psychological Science, 3,* 34–38.

Ekman, P. (1993). Facial expression and emotion. *American Psychologist, 48,* 384–392.

Ekman, P. (1994). Strong evidence for universals in facial expressions: A reply to Russell's mistaken critique. *Psychological Bulletin, 115,* 268–287.

Ekman, P., Friesen, W. V., & O'Sullivan, M. (1988). Smiles when lying. *Journal of Personality and Social Psychology, 54,* 414–420.

Ekman, P., & Keltner, D. (1997). Universal facial expressions of emotion: An old controversy and new findings. In U. C. Segerstrale, P. Molnar, et al. (Eds.), *Noverbal communication: Where nature meets culture* (pp. 27–46). Mahwah, NJ: Lawrence Erlbaum Associates, Inc.

Elbert, T., Pantev, C., Wienbruch, C., Rockstroh, B., & Taub, E. (1995). Increased cortical representation of the fingers of the left hand in string players. *Science, 270,* 305–307.

Eley, T. C. (1997). General genes: A new theme in developmental psychopathology. *American Psychological Society,* 6(4), 90–95.

Elkind, D. (1981a). Giant in the nursery—Jean Piaget. In E. M. Hetherington & R. D. Parke (Eds.), *Contemporary readings in child psychology* (2nd ed.). New York: McGraw-Hill.

Elkins, L. E., & Peterson, C. (1993). Gender differences in best friendships. *Sex Roles, 29,* 497–508.

Elliot, A., & Devine, P. G. (1994). On the motivational nature of cognitive dissonance: Dissonance as psychological discomfort. *Journal of Personality and Social Psychology, 67*(3), 382–394.

Elliott, E. S., & Dweck, C. S. (1988). Goals: An approach to motivation and achievement. *Journal of Personality and Social Psychology, 54,* 5–12.

Elliott, R. (1987). *Litigating intelligence: IQ tests, special education, and social science in the courtroom.* Dover, MS: Auburn House.

Ellis, A. (1970). *The essence of rational psychotherapy: A comprehensive approach to treatment.* New York: Institute for Rational Living.

Ellis, A. (1988, August). *The philosophical basis of rational–emotive therapy (RET).* Paper presented at the 96th Annual Convention of the American Psychological Association, Atlanta.

Ellis, A. (1990). How can psychological treatment aim to be briefer and better? The rational–emotive approach to brief therapy. In J. K. Zeig & S. G. Gilligan (Eds.), *Brief therapy myths, methods, and metaphors,* New York: Brunner/Mazel.

Ellis, A. (1993). Reflections on rational–emotive therapy. *Journal of Consulting and Clinical Psychology, 61,* 199–201.

Ellis, A., & Harper, R. A. (1961). *A guide to rational living.* North Hollywood, CA: Wilshire.

Ellis, G. M. (1994). Acquaintance rape. *Perspectives in Psychiatric Care, 30,* 11–16.

Ellis, L. (1991). A synthesized (biosocial) theory of rape. *Journal of Consulting and Clinical Psychology, 59,* 631–642.

Ellis, R. J., & Oscar-Berman, M. (1989). Alcoholism, aging, and functional cerebral asymmetries. *Psychological Bulletin, 106,* 128–147.

Emde, R. N., Plomin, R., Robinson, J., Corley, R., DeFries, J., Fulker, D. W., Reznick, J. S., Campos, J., Kagan, J., & Zahn-Waxler, C. (1992). Temperament, emotion, and cognition at fourteen months: The MacArthur longitudinal twin study. *Child Development, 63,* 1437–1455.

Emery, R. E. (1989a). Family violence. *American Psychologist, 44,* 321–328.

Emery, R. E. (1989b, September 15). *Family violence: Has science met its match?* Edited transcript of a science and public policy seminar presented by the Federation of Behavioral, Psychological, and Cognitive Sciences in the Rayburn House Office Building, Washington, DC.

Erber, J. T., Caiola, M. A., Williams, M., & Prager, I. G. (1997). Age and forgetfulness: The effect of implicit priming. *Experimental Aging Research, 23*(1), 1–12.

Erel, O., & Burman, B. (1995). Interrelatedness of marital relations and parent–child relations: A meta-analytic review. *Psychological Bulletin, 118,* 108–132.

Ericsson, K. A., & Charness, N. (1994). Expert performance: Its structure and acquisition. *American Psychologist, 49,* 725–747.

Ericsson, K. A., Chase, W. G., & Faloon, S. (1980). Acquisition of a memory skill. *Science, 208,* 1181–1182.

Ericsson, K. A., Krampe, R. T., & Tesch-Römer, C. (1993). The role of deliberate practice in the acquisition of expert performance. *Psychological Review, 100,* 363–406.

Erikson, E. H. (1963). *Childhood and society* (2nd ed.). New York: Norton.

Erikson, E. H. (1968). *Identity: Youth and crisis.* New York: Norton.

Erlenmeyer-Kimling, L., & Jarvik, L. F. (1963). Genetics and intelligence: A review. *Science, 142,* 1477–1479.

Erngrund, K., Mantyla, T., & Nilsson, L. G. (1996). Adult age differences in source recall: A population-based study. *Journals of Gerontology Series B Psychological Sciences and Social Sciences, 51B*(6), 335–345.

Eron, L. D. (1987). The development of aggressive behavior from the perspective of a developing behaviorism. *American Psychologist, 42,* 435–442.

Eron, L. D., & Huesmann, L. R. (1980). Adolescent aggression and television. *Annals of the New York Academy of Sciences, 347,* 319–331.

Eslinger, P. J., Grattan, L. M., Damasio, H., & Damasio, A. R. (1992). Developmental consequences of childhood frontal lobe damage. *Archives of Neurology, 49,* 764–769.

Esses, V. M., & Webster, C. D. (1988). Physical attractiveness, dangerousness, and the Canadian criminal code. *Journal of Applied Social Psychology, 18,* 1017–1031.

Estes, D. (1998). Young children's awareness of their mental activity: The case of mental rotation. *Child Development, 69*(5), 1345–1360.

Etaugh, C. (1980). Effects of nonmaternal care on children. *American Psychologist, 35,* 309–319.

Evans, D. A., Funkenstein, H. H., Albert, M. S., Scherr, P. A., Cook, N. R., Chown, M. J., Hebert, L. E., Hennekens, C. H., & Taylor, J. O. (1989). Prevalence of Alzheimer's disease in a community population of older persons. *Journal of the American Medical Association, 262,* 2551–2556.

Evans, G. W., Hygge, S., & Bullinger, M. (1995). Chronic noise and psychological stress. *Psychological Science, 6,* 333–338.

Evans, G. W., Lepore, S. J., Shejwal, B. R., & Palsane, M. N. (1998). Chronic residential crowding and children's well-being: An ecological perspective. *Child Development, 69*(6), 1514–1523.

Ewart, C. K. (1991). Social action theory for a public health psychology. *American Psychologist, 46,* 931–946.

Exner, J. E., Jr., Thomas, E. A., & Mason, B. (1985). Children's Rorschachs: Description and prediction. *Journal of Personality Assessment, 49,* 13–14.

Eyer, D. E. (1992). *Mother–infant bonding: A scientific fiction.* New Haven, CT: Yale University Press.

Eysenck, H. J. (1970). *The structure of human personality* (3rd ed.). London: Methuen.

Eysenck, H. J. (1995). *Genius: The natural history of creativity.* Cambridge, England: Cambridge University Press.

Eysenck, H. J. (1998). *A new look at intelligence.* London: Transaction Publishers.

Fagan, J. (1994). Correlates of maternal involvement in on-site and off-site day care centers. *Child and Youth Care Forum, 23,* 275–290.

Fagan, J. (1996). A preliminary study of low-income African American fathers' play interactions with their preschool-age children. *Journal of Black Psychology, 22*(1), 7–19.

Fagan, J. (1997). Patterns of mother and father involvement in day care. *Child and Youth Care Forum, 26*(2), 113–126.

Fagan, J., & Silverthorn, A. S. (1998). Research on communication by touch. In E. W. Smith (Ed.), *Touch in psychotherapy: Theory, research, and practice* (pp. 59–73). New York: The Guildford Press.

Fan, X., Chen, M., & Matsumoto, A. R. (1997). Gender differences in mathematics achievement: Findings from the

National Longitudinal Study of 1988. *Journal of Experimental Education, 65*(3), 229–242.

Fang, H. (1996). Dopamine receptor studies in human postmortem brain by radioreceptor binding. *International Medical Journal, 3*(4), 265–272.

Fantz, R. L. (1961, May). The origin of form perception. *Scientific American*, 66–72.

Farah, M. J. (1990). *Visual agnosia: Disorders of object recognition and what they tell us about normal vision.* Cambridge, MA: MIT Press.

Farah, M. J., Levinson, K. L., & Klein, K. (1995). Face perception and within-category discrimination in prosopagnosia. *Neuropsychologia, 33*(6), 661–674.

Farah, M. J., O'Reilly, R. C., & Vecera, S. P. (1993). Dissociated overt and covert recognition as an emergent property of a lesioned neural network. *Psychological Review, 100*(4), 571–588.

Farah, M. J., Wilson, K. D., Drain, M., & Tanaka, J. N. (1998). What is special about face perception? *Psychological Review, 105*(3), 482–498.

Farrell, A. D., & Danish, S. J. (1993). Peer drug associations and emotional restraint: Causes or consequences of adolescents' drug use? *Journal of Consulting and Clinical Psychology, 61,* 327–334.

Farwell, L., & Wohlwend-Lloyd, R. (1998). Narcissistic processes: Optimistic expectations, favorable self-evaluations, and self-enhancing attributions. *Journal of Personality, 66*(1), 65–67.

Fazio, R. H. (1990). Multiple processes by which attitudes guide behavior: The MODE model as an integrative framework. In M. P. Zanna (Ed.), *Advances in experimental social psychology* (Vol. 23, pp. 75–109). San Diego: Academic.

Feeney, D. M. (1987). Human rights and animal welfare. *American Psychologist, 42,* 593–599.

Fehr, B., & Russell, J. A. (1991). The concept of love viewed from a prototype perspective. *Journal of Personality and Social Psychology, 60,* 425–438.

Feingold, A. (1988). Matching for attractiveness in romantic partners and same-sex friends: A meta-analysis and theoretical critique. *Psychological Bulletin, 104,* 226–235.

Feingold, A. (1992a). Gender differences in mate selection preferences: A test of the parental investment model. *Psychological Bulletin, 112,* 125–139.

Feingold, A. (1992b). Good-looking people are not what we think. *Psychological Bulletin, 111,* 304–341.

Feingold, A. (1993). Cognitive gender differences: A developmental perspective. *Sex Roles, 29,* 91–111.

Feingold, A. (1994). Gender differences in personality: A meta-analysis. *Psychological Bulletin, 116,* 429–456.

Feldman, L., Holowaty, P., Harvey, B., Rannie, K., Shortt, L., & Jamal, A. (1997). A comparison of the demographic, lifestyle, and sexual behaviour characteristics of virgin and non-virgin adolescents. *The Canadian Journal of Human Sexuality, 6*(3), 197–209.

Fenwick, D. T. (1998). Managing space, energy and self: Junior high teachers' experiences of classroom management. *Teaching & Teacher Education, 14*(6), 619–631.

Fenwick, P., Donaldson, S., Gillies, L., Bushman, J., Fenton, G., Perry, I., Tilsley, C., & Serafinowicz, H. (1977). Metabolic and EEG changes during transcendental meditation. *Biological Psychology, 5,* 101–118.

Fernandez, E., & Sheffield, J. (1996). Relative contributions of life events versus daily hassles to the frequency and intensity of headaches. *Headache, 36*(10), 595–602.

Fernandez, E., & Turk, D. C. (1992). Sensory and affective components of pain: Separation and synthesis. *Psychological Bulletin, 112,* 205–217.

Festinger, L. (1954). A theory of social comparison processes. *Human Relations, 7,* 117–140.

Festinger, L. (1957). *A theory of cognitive dissonance.* Evanston, IL: Row, Petersen.

Fiedler, F. E. (1964). A contingency model of leadership effectiveness. In L. Berkowitz (Ed.), *Advances in experimental social psychology* (Vol. 1). New York: Academic.

Fiedler, F. E. (1974). Personality, motivational systems, and behavior of high and low LPC persons. *Human Relations, 25,* 391–412.

Field, T. (1996). Attachment and separation in young children. *Annual Review of Psychology, 47,* 541–561.

Fine, A. (1986, August). Transplantation in the central nervous system. *Scientific American,* 52–67.

Fink, M. (1997). Prejudice against ECT: Competition with psychological philosophies as a contribution to its stigma. *Convulsive Therapy, 13*(4), 253–265.

Fischer, A. R., & Good, G. E. (1998). New directions for the study of gender role attitudes. *Psychology of Women Quarterly, 22,* 371–384.

Fischer, C. T. (1991). Phenomenological–existential psychotherapy. In M. Hersen, A. E. Kazdin, & A. S. Bellack (Eds.), *The clinical psychology handbook* (2nd ed.). New York: Pergamon.

Fischer, J., & Gochros, H. L. (1975). *Planned behavior change: Behavior modification in social work.* New York: Free Press.

Fisher, C. B., & Fyrberg, D. (1994). Participant partners: College students weigh the costs and benefits of deceptive research. *American Psychologist, 49,* 417–427.

Fisher, S. E., Vargha-Khadem, F., Watkins, K. E., Monaco, A. P., & Pembrey, M. E. (1998). Localisation of a gene implicated in severe speech and language disorder. *Nature Genetics, 18,* 168–170.

Fishman, D. B., & Franks, C. M. (1997). The conceptual evolution of behavior therapy. In P. L. Wachtel & S. B. Messer (Eds.), *Theories of psychotherapy: Origins and evolution* (pp. 131–180). Washington, DC: American Psychological Association.

Fiske, S. T. (1992). Thinking is for doing: Portraits of social cognition from daguerreotype to laserphoto. *Journal of Personality and Social Psychology, 63,* 877–889.

Fiske, S. T. (1998). Stereotyping, prejudice, and discrimination. In D. T. Gilbert et al. (Eds.), *The handbook of social psychology* (pp. 357–411). New York: McGraw-Hill.

Fitzgerald, L. F., & Osipow, S. H. (1986). An occupational analysis of counseling psychology. *American Psychologist, 41,* 535–544.

Flaskerud, J. H., & Hu, L. T. (1992). Relationship of ethnicity to psychiatric diagnosis. *Journal of Nervous and Mental Disease, 180,* 296–303.

Flavell, J. H. (1996). Piaget's legacy. *American Psychological Society,* 7(4), 200–203.

Flavell, J. H., Green, F. L., & Flavell, E. R. (1993). Children's understanding of the stream of consciousness. *Child Development, 64,* 387–398.

Flavell, J. H., Green, F. L., & Flavell, E. R. (1998). The mind has a mind of its own: Developing knowledge about mental uncontrollability. *Cognitive Development, 13,* 127–138.

Fleischman, D. A., Vaidya, C. J., Lange, K. L., & Gabrieli, J. D. E. (1997). A dissociation between perceptual explicit and implicit memory processes. *Brain & Cognition, 35*(1), 42–57.

Fleming, I., Baum, A., & Weiss, L. (1987). Social density and perceived control as mediators of crowding stress in high-density residential neighborhoods. *Journal of Personality and Social Psychology, 52,* 899–906.

Fleming, J. D. (1974, July). Field report: The state of the apes. *Psychology Today,* 31–46.

Flint, A. J., & Rifat, S. L. (1998). The treatment of psychotic depression in later life: A comparison of pharmacotherapy and ECT. *International Journal of Geriatric Psychiatry, 13*(1), 23–28.

Florence, S. L., Taub, H. B., & Kaas, J. H. (1998). Large-scale sprouting of cortical connections after peripheral injury in adult macaque monkeys. *Science, 282,* 1117–1120.

Flynn, J. R. (1987). Massive gains in 14 nations: What IQ tests really measure. *Psychological Bulletin, 101,* 171–191.

Flynn, J. R. (1998). IQ gains over time: Toward finding the causes. In U. Neisser (Ed.), *The rising curve: Long-term gains in IQ and related measures* (pp. 25–65). Washington, DC: American Psychological Association.

Flynn, J. R. (1999). Searching for justice: The discovery of IQ gains over time. *American Psychologist, 54*(1), 5–20.

Foa, E. B., & Riggs, D. S. (1995). Posttraumatic stress disorder following assault: Theoretical considerations and empirical findings. *Current Directions in Psychological Science, 4,* 61–65.

Ford, J. D., Chandler, P., Thacker, B., Greaves, D., Shaw, D., Sennhauser, S., & Schwartz, L. (1998). Family systems therapy after operation Desert Storm with European-theater veterans. *Journal of Marital and Family Therapy, 24*(2), 243–250.

Forgas, J. P. (1998). Asking nicely? The effects of mood on responding to more or less polite requests. *Personality and Social Psychology Bulletin, 24*(2), 173–185.

Forsythe, S. M. (1990). Effect of applicant's clothing on interviewer's decision to hire. *Journal of Applied Social Psychology, 20,* 1579–1595.

Fosshage, J. L. (1997). The organizing functions of dream mentation. *Contemporary Psychoanalysis, 33*(3), 429–458.

Foster, R. G. (1993). Photoreceptors and circadian systems. *Current Directions in Psychological Science, 2,* 34–39.

Foulkes, D. (1985). *Dreaming: A cognitive-psychological analysis.* Hillsdale, NJ: Lawrence Erlbaum.

Foulkes, D. (1990). Dreaming and consciousness. *European Journal of Cognitive Psychology, 2*(1), 39–55.

Foulkes, D. (1996). Dream research. *Sleep, 19*(8), 609–624.

Foulkes, D., & Kerr, N. H. (1994). Point of view in nocturnal dreaming. *Perceptual and Motor Skills, 78*(2), 690.

Foulkes, D., Meier, B., Strauch, I., & Kerr, N. H. (1993). Linguistic phenomena and language selection in the REM dreams of German-English bilinguals. *International Journal of Psychology, 28*(6), 871–891.

Fox, M. (1993). *Psychological perspectives in education.* New York: Cassell Educational.

Frable, D. E. (1989). Sex typing and gender ideology: Two facets of the individual's gender psychology that go together. *Journal of Personality and Social Psychology, 56,* 95–108.

Frank, M. G., & Ekman, P. (1997). The ability to detect deceit generalizes across different types of high-stake lies. *Journal of Personality and Social Psychology, 72*(6), 1429–1439.

Frank, M. G., Ekman, P., & Friesen, W. V. (1997). Behavioral markers and recognizability of the smile of enjoyment. In P. Ekman & E. L. Rosenberg (Eds.), *What the face reveals: Basic and applied studies of spontaneous expression using the Facial Action Coding System (FACS)* (pp. 217–242). New York: Oxford University Press.

Franko, D. L., & Erb, J. (1998). Managed care or mangled care? Treating eating disorders in the current healthcare climate. *Psychotherapy: Theory, Research and Practice, 35*(1), 43–53.

Frasure-Smith, N., Lesperance, F., & Talajic, M. (1993). Depression following myocardial infarction: Impact on 6-month survival. *Journal of the American Medical Association, 270,* 1819–1825.

Frasure-Smith N., Lesperance, F., & Talajic, M. (1995). The impact of negative emotions on prognosis following myocardial infarction: Is it more than depression? *Health Psychology, 14,* 388–398.

Frasure-Smith, N., & Prince, R. (1989). Long-term follow-up of the ischemic heart disease life stress monitoring program. *Psychosomatic Medicine, 51,* 485–513.

Frederiksen, N. (1986). Toward a broader conception of human intelligence. *American Psychologist, 41,* 445–452.

French, K. E., Spurgeon, J. H., & Nevett, M. E. (1995). Expert–novice differences in cognitive and skill execution components of youth baseball performance. *Research Quarterly for Exercise and Sport, 66,* 194–201.

Freud, S. (1933). *New introductory lectures on psychoanalysis.* New York: Norton.

Freud, S. (1953). The interpretation of dreams. In J. Stachey (Ed.), *The standard edition of the complete psychological works of Sigmund Freud* (Vols. 4 and 5). London: Hogarth. (Original work published 1900.)

Freud, S. (1966). *A general introduction to psychoanalysis* (J. Riviere, Trans.). New York: Washington Square. (Original work published 1920.)

Frezza, M., di Padova, C., Pozzato, G., Terpin, M., Baraona, E., & Lieber, C. S. (1990). High blood alcohol levels in women. *New England Journal of Medicine, 322,* 95–99.

Friedberg, F., & Jason, L. A. (1998). Understanding chronic fatigue syndrome: An empirical guide to assessment and treatment. *American Psychological Association, 17,* 266.

Friedman, M. (1996). *Type A behavior: Its diagnosis and treatment.* New York: Plenum Press.

Friedman, M., & Rosenman, R. H. (1974). *Type A behavior and your heart.* Greenwich, CT: Fawcett.

Friedman, S., Paradis, C. M., & Hatch, M. (1994). Characteristics of African-American and white patients with panic disorder and agoraphobia. *Hospital and Community Psychiatry, 45,* 798–803.

Friedman, W. J. (1993). Memory for the time of past events. *Psychological Bulletin, 113,* 44–66.

Frieze, I. H., Olson, J. E., & Russell, J. (1991). Attractiveness and income for men and women in management. *Journal of Applied Social Psychology, 21,* 1039–1057.

Fromm, E. (1956). *The art of loving.* New York: Harper & Row.

Fromme, K., Marlatt, G. A., Baer, J. S., & Kivlahan, D. R. (1994). The alcohol skills training program: A group intervention for young adult drinkers. *Journal of Substance Abuse Treatment, 11,* 143–154.

Fruzzetti, A. E., & Jacobson, N. S. (1991). Marital and family therapy. In M. Hersen, A. E. Kazdin, & A. S. Bellack (Eds.), *The clinical psychology handbook* (2nd ed.). New York: Pergamon.

Fuller, T. D., Edwards, J. N., Vorakitphokatorn, S., & Sermsri, S. (1996). Chronic stress and psychological wellbeing: Evidence from Thailand on household crowding. *Social Science and Medicine, 42*(2), 265–280.

Funder, D. C. (1995). On the accuracy of personality judgment: A realistic approach. *Psychological Review, 102,* 652–670.

Furby, L., Weinrott, M. R., & Blackshaw, L. (1989). Sex offender recidivism: A review. *Psychological Bulletin, 105,* 3–30.

Furstenberg, F. F., Jr., Brooks-Gunn, J., & Chase-Lansdale, L. (1989). Teenaged pregnancy and childbearing. *American Psychologist, 44,* 313–320.

Furstenberg, F. F., Jr., & Hughes, M. E. (1995). Social capital and successful development among at-risk youth. *Journal of Marriage and the Family, 57*(3), 580–592.

Gabrieli, J. D. E., Brewer, J. B, Desmond, J. E., & Glover, G. H. (1997). Separate neural bases of two fundamental memory processes in the human medial temporal lobe. *Science, 276,* 264–266.

Gaffan, E. A., Tsaousis, J., & Kemp-Wheeler, S. M. (1995). Researcher allegiance and meta-analysis: The case of cognitive therapy for depression. *Journal of Consulting and Clinical Psychology, 63,* 960–980.

Gaines, S. O., Jr., & Reed, E. S. (1995). Prejudice: From Allport to DuBois. *American Psychologist, 50,* 96–103.

Galambos, N. L. (1992). Parent–adolescent relations. *Current Directions, 1,* 146–149.

Galin, D. (1974). Implications for psychiatry of left and right cerebral specialization: A neurophysiological context for unconscious processes. *Archives of General Psychiatry, 31,* 572–583.

Gallup, G. G., Jr., & Suarez, S. D. (1985). Alternatives to the use of animals in psychological research. *American Psychologist, 40,* 1104–1111.

Gallwey, W. T. (1974). *The inner game of tennis.* New York: Random House.

Galotti, K. M. (1989). Approaches to studying formal and everyday reasoning. *Psychological Bulletin, 105,* 331–351.

Gannon, P. J., Holloway, R. L., Broadfield, D. C., & Braun, A. R. (1998). Asymmetry of chimpanzee planum temporale: Humanlike pattern of Wernicke's brain language area homolog. *Science, 279,* 220–222.

Garb, H. N., Florio, C. M., & Grove, W. M. (1998). The validity of the Rorschach and the Minnesota Multiphasic Personality Inventory: Results from meta-analyses. *American Psychological Society, 9*(5), 402–404.

Garcia, J., Gustavson, C. R., Kelly, D. J., & Sweeney, M. (1976). Preynlithium aversions: I. Coyotes and wolves. *Behavioral Biology, 16,* 61–72.

Garcia, J., & Koelling, R. A., (1971). The use of ionizing rays as a mammalian olfactory stimulus. In H. Autrum, R. Jung, W. R. Loewenstein, D. M. MacKay, & H. L. Teuber (Eds.), *Handbook of sensory physiology: Vol. 4. Chemical senses* (Pt. 1). New York: Springer-Verlag.

Gardner, H. (1983/1993). *Frames of mind: The theory of multiple intelligences.* New York: Basic Books.

Gardner, H. (1995). Multiple intelligences as a catalyst. *English Journal, 84*(8), 16–18.

Gardner, H. (1996). Personal communication.

Gardner, H., & Hatch, T. (1989). Multiple intelligences go to school: Educational implications of the theory of multiple intelligences. *Educational Researcher, 18,* 6.

Gardner, R. A., & Gardner, B. T. (1969). Teaching sign language to a chimp. *Science, 165,* 664–672.

Gardner, W., Scherer, D., & Tester, M. (1989). Asserting scientific authority: Cognitive development and adolescent legal rights. *American Psychologist, 6,* 895–902.

Gardner, W. L., & Avolio, B. J. (1998). The charismatic relationship: A dramaturgical perspective. *Academy of Management Review, 23*(1), 32–58.

Garfield, S. L. (1998). Some comments on empirically supported treatments. *Journal of Consulting and Clinical Psychology, 66*(1), 121–125.

Garfield, S. L., & Bergin, A. E. (1986). *Handbook of psychotherapy and behavior change* (3rd ed.). New York: Wiley.

Garfinkel, P. E., Lin, E., Goering, P., Spegg, C., et al. (1996). Purging and nonpurging forms of bulimia nervosa in a community sample. *International Journal of Eating Disorders, 20*(3), 231–238.

Garland, A. F., & Zigler, E. (1993). Adolescent suicide prevention. *American Psychologist, 48,* 169–182.

Garry, M. & Loftus, E. F. (1994). Pseudomemories without hypnosis. *The International Journal of Clinical and Experimental Hypnosis, 42,* 363–378.

Gazzaniga, M. S. (1983). Right hemisphere language following brain bisection: A 20-year perspective. *American Psychologist, 38,* 525–537.

Gazzaniga, M. S. (1989). Organization of the human brain. *Science, 245,* 947–952.

Ge, X., Conger, R. D., Cadoret, R. J., Neiderhiser, J. M., Yates, W., Troughton, E., et al. (1996). The developmental interface between nature and nurture: A mutual influence model of child antisocial behavior and parent behaviors. *Developmental Psychology, 32*(4), 574–589.

Ge, X., Conger, R. D., & Elder, G. H., Jr. (1996). Coming of age too early: Pubertal influences on girls' vulnerability to psychological distress. *Child Development, 67*(6), 3386–3400.

Geary, D. C. (1996). Biology, culture, and cross-national differences in mathematical ability. In R. J. Sternberg, T. Ben-Zeev, et al. (Eds.), *The nature of mathematical thinking. The studies in mathematical thinking and learning series* (pp. 145–171). Mahwah, NJ: Lawrence Erlbaum Associates, Inc.

Gebhardt, D. L., & Crump, C. E. (1990). Employee fitness and wellness programs in the workplace. *American Psychologist, 45,* 262–272.

Gedda, L. (1961). *Twins in history and science.* Springfield, IL: Charles C. Thomas.

Geen, R. G. (1991). Social motivation. *Annual Review of Psychology, 42,* 377–399.

Geller, E. S. (1975). Increasing desired waste disposals with instructions. *Man–Environment Systems, 5,* 125–128.

Geller, E. S. (1989). Applied behavior analysis and social marketing: An integration for environmental preservation. *Journal of Social Issues, 45,* 17–36.

Geller, E. S. (1992). It takes more than information to save energy. *American Psychologist, 47,* 814–815.

Geller, E. S. (1995). Integrating behaviorism and humanism for environmental protection. *Journal of Social Issues, 51*(4), 179–195.

Geller, E. S., Kalsher, M. J., Rudd, J. R., & Lehman, G. R. (1989). Promoting safety belt use on a university campus: An integration of commitment and incentive strategies. *Journal of Applied Social Psychology, 19*(1), 3–19.

Geller, E. S., Witmer, J. F., & Tuso, M. E. (1977). Environmental intervention for litter control. *Journal of Applied Psychology, 62,* 344–351.

George, J. M., & Brief, A. P. (1992). Feeling good—doing good: A conceptual analysis of the mood at work–organizational spontaneity relationship. *Psychological Bulletin, 112,* 310–329.

George, M. S., Ketter, T. A., & Post, R. M. (1993). SPECT and PET imaging in mood disorders. *Journal of Clinical Psychiatry, 54,* 6–13.

Gerber, L. (1994). Psychotherapy with southeast Asian refugees: Implications for treatment of Western patients. *American Journal of Psychotherapy, 48,* 280–293.

German, D. (1983). Analysis of word-finding disorders on the Kaufman Assessment Battery for Children (K-ABC). *Journal of Psychoeducational Assessment, 1,* 121–134.

Geschwind, N. (1972, April). Language and the brain. *Scientific American,* 76–83.

Gibson, E. J. (1992). How to think about perceptual learning: Twenty-five years later. In H. L. Pick, Jr., P. van den Broek, & D. C. Knill (Eds.), *Cognition: Conceptual and methodological issues* (pp. 215–238). Washington, DC: American Psychological Association.

Gibson, J. A. P., & Range, L. M. (1991). Are written reports of suicide and seeking help contagious? High schoolers' perceptions. *Journal of Applied Social Psychology, 21,* 1517–1523.

Gift, T. E., Strauss, J. S., Ritzler, B. A., Kokes, R. F., & Harder, D. W. (1980). How diagnostic concepts of schizophrenia differ. *Journal of Nervous and Mental Disease, 168,* 3–8.

Gilbert, R. K. (1988). The dynamics of inaction. *American Psychologist, 43,* 755–764.

Gillies, R. M., & Ashman, A. F. (1996). Teaching collaborative skills to primary school children in classroom-based work groups. *Learning and Instruction, 6*(3), 187–200.

Gilligan, C. (1982). *In a different voice: Psychological theory and women's development.* Cambridge, MA: Harvard University Press.

Gilligan, C. (1995). In a different voice: Women's conceptions of self and of morality. In B. Puka et al. (Eds.), *Caring voices and women's moral frames: Gilligan's view.* New York: Garland Publishing, Inc.

Gilligan, C. (1997). Remembering Iphigenia: Voice, resonance, and a talking cure. In B. Mark (Ed.), *The handbook of infant, child, and adolescent psychotherapy.* Northvale, NJ: Jason Aronson.

Glantz, M. D. (1989). Cognitive therapy with the elderly. In A. Freeman, K. M. Simon, L. E. Beutler, & H. Arkowitz (Eds.), *Comprehensive handbook of cognitive therapy.* New York: Plenum.

Glasgow, R. E., & Terborg, J. R. (1988). Occupational health promotion programs to reduce cardiovascular risk. *Journal of Consulting and Clinical Psychology, 56,* 365–373.

Gleaves, D. H. (1996). The sociocognitive model of dissociative identity disorder: A reexamination of the evidence. *Psychological Bulletin, 120,* 42–59.

Glick, P., Diebold, J., Bailey-Wexner, B., & Zhu, L. (1997). The two faces of Adam: Ambivalent sexism and polarized attitudes toward women. *Personality and Social Psychology Bulletin, 23*(12), 1323–1334.

Glick, P., & Fiske, S. T. (1997). Hostile and benevolent sexism: Measuring ambivalent sexism toward women. *Psychology of Women Quarterly, 21*(1), 119–135.

Goldberger, N. (1997). Ways of knowing: Does gender matter? In M. R. Walsh (Ed.), *Women, men, and gender: Ongoing debates.* New Haven, CT: Yale University Press.

Goldfried, M. R., & Wolfe, B. E. (1996). Psychotherapy practice and research: Repairing a strained alliance. *American Psychologist, 51*(10), 1007–1016.

Goldfried, M. R., & Wolfe, B. E. (1998). Toward a more clinically valid approach to therapy research. *Journal of Consulting and Clinical Psychology, 66*(1), 143–150.

Golding, J. M., Potts, M. K., & Aneshensel, C. S. (1991). Stress exposure among Mexican Americans and non-Hispanic whites. *Journal of Community Psychology, 19,* 37–59.

Golding, J., Rogers, I. S., & Emmett, P. M. (1997). Association between breast feeding, child development and behaviour. *Early Human Development, 49,* 175–184.

Goldman, M. S., Brown, S. A., Christiansen, B. A., & Smith, G. T. (1991). Alcoholism and memory: Broadening the scope of alcohol-expectancy research. *Psychological Bulletin, 110,* 137–146.

Goleman, D. (1995). *Emotional intelligence.* New York: Bantam.

Gonzales, L. R., Hays, R. B., Bond, M. A., & Kelly, J. G. (1983). Community mental health. In M. Hersen, A. E. Kazdin, & A. S. Bellack (Eds.), *The clinical psychology handbook.* New York: Pergamon.

Gonzales, R. R., & Roll, S. (1985). Relationship between acculturation, cognitive style, and intelligence. *Journal of Cross-Cultural Psychology, 16,* 190–205.

Goodwin, R., & Tang, D. (1991). Preferences for friends and close relationship partners: A cross-cultural comparison. *Journal of Social Psychology, 131,* 579–581.

Gopnik, A., Meltzoff, A. N., & Kuhl, P. K. (1999) *The scientist in the crib.* New York: Morrow.

Gortmaker, S. L., Kagan, J., Caspi, A., & Silva, P. A. (1997). Daylength during pregnancy and shyness in children: Results from Northern and Southern hemispheres. *Developmental Psychobiology, 31*(2), 107–114.

Gostin, L. O. (1997). The legal regulation of smoking (and smokers): Public health or secular morality? In A. Brandt, P. Rozin, et al. (Eds.), *Morality and health* (pp. 331–357). New York: Routledge.

Gothard, K. M., Skaggs, W. E., Moore, K. M., & McNaughton, B. L. (1996). Binding of hippocampal CA1 neural activity to multiple reference frames in a landmark-based navigation task. *Journal of Neuroscience, 16*(2), 823–835.

Gottman, J. M., & Katz, L. F. (1989). Effects of marital discord on young children's peer interaction and health. *Developmental Psychology, 25,* 373–381.

Goulding, M. M. (1990). Getting the important work done fast: Contract plus redecision. In J. K. Zeig & S. G. Gilligan (Eds.), *Brief therapy myths, methods, and metaphors.* New York: Brunner/ Mazel.

Graber, J. A., Lewinsohn, P. M., Seeley, J. R., & Brooks-Gunn, J. (1997). Is psychopathology associated with the timing of pubertal development? *Journal of the American Academy of Child and Adolescent Psychiatry, 36*(12), 1768–1776.

Grady, C. L., McIntosh, A. R., Horwitz, B., Maisog, J. M., Ungerleider, L. G., Mentis, M. J., Pietrini, P., Schapiro, M. B., & Haxby, J. V. (1995). Age-related reductions in human recognition memory due to impaired encoding. *Science, 269,* 218–220.

Graham, C. J., & Cleveland, E. (1995). Left-handedness as an injury risk factor in adolescents. *Journal of Adolescent Health, 16*(1), 50–52.

Graziano, M. S. A., & Gross, C. G. (1994). Mapping space with neurons. *Current Directions in Psychological Science, 3,* 164–167.

Graziano, M. S., Hu, X. T., & Gross, C. G. (1997). Coding the locations of objects in the dark. *Science, 277,* 239–240.

Greenberg, J. (1990). Employee theft as a reaction to underpayment inequity: The hidden cost of pay cuts. *Journal of Applied Psychology, 75,* 561–568.

Greenberg, J. (1998). Equity and workplace status: A field experiment. In S. Steven, S. Spencer, et al. (Eds.), *Readings in social psychology: The art and science of research* (p. 180). Boston: Houghton Mifflin.

Greenberg, R. P., Bornstein, R. F., Greenberg, M. D., Fisher, S., & Seymour, F. (1992). A meta-analysis of antidepressant outcome under "blinder" conditions. *Journal of Consulting and Clinical Psychology, 60,* 664–669.

Greene, K., & Rubin, D. L. (1991). Effects of gender inclusive/exclusive language in religious discourse. *Journal of Language and Social Psychology, 10*(2), 81–98.

Greenfield, P. M. (1997). You can't take it with you: Why ability assessments don't cross cultures. *American Psychologist, 52*(10), 1115–1124.

Greeno, C. G., & Wing, R. R. (1994). Stress-induced eating. *Psychological Bulletin, 115,* 444–464.

Greeno, J. G. (1989). A perspective on thinking. *American Psychologist, 44,* 134–141.

Greeno, J. G., and the Middle School Mathematics Through Applications Project Group. (1998). The situativity of knowing, learning, and research. *American Psychologist, 53*(1), 5–26.

Greenwald, A. G., Klinger, M. R., & Schuh, E. S. (1995). Activation by marginally perceptible ("subliminal") stimuli: Dissociation of unconscious from conscious cognition. *Journal of Experimental Psychology: General, 124*(1), 22–42.

Greer, S., & Brady, M. (1988). Natural killer cells: One possible link between cancer and the mind. *Stress Medicine, 4*(2), 105–111.

Griffeth, R. W., Vecchio, R. P., & Logan, J. W., Jr. (1989). Equity theory and interpersonal attraction. *Journal of Applied Psychology, 74,* 394–401.

Grilo, C. M., & Shiffman, S. (1994). Longitudinal investigation of the abstinence violation effect in binge eaters. *Journal of Consulting and Clinical Psychology, 62,* 611–619.

Gross, J. J., Fredrickson, B. L., & Levenson, R. W. (1994). The psychophysiology of crying. *Psychophysiology, 31,* 460–463.

Grossberg, S. (1995). The attentive brain. *American Scientist, 83,* 438–449.

Grossman, F. K., Pollack, W. S., & Golding, E. (1988). Fathers and children: Predicting the quality and quantity of fathering. *Developmental Psychology, 1,* 91–92.

Grunberg, L., Moore, S., & Greenberg, E. S. (1998). Work stress and problem alcohol behavior: A test of the spillover model. *Journal of Organizational Behavior, 19*(5), 487–502.

Guarnaccia, P. J. (1997). Social stress and psychological distress among Latinos in the United States. In I. Al-Ihsan et al. (Eds.), *Ethnicity, immigration, and psychopathology. The Plenum Series on stress and coping* (pp. 71–94). New York: Plenum Press.

Guerin, P. J., Jr., & Chabot, D. R. (1997). Development of family systems theory. In P. L. Wachtel & S. B. Messer (Eds.), *Theories of psychotherapy: Origins and evolution* (pp. 181–226). Washington, DC: American Psychological Association.

Guilford, J. P. (1967). *The nature of human intelligence.* New York: McGraw-Hill.

Gulevich, G., Dement, W., & Johnson, L. (1966). Psychiatric and EEG observations on a case of prolonged (264 hours) wakefulness. *Archives of General Psychiatry, 15,* 29–35.

Gulya, M., Rovee-Collier, C., Galluccio, L., & Wilk, A. (1998). Memory processing of a serial list by young infants. *American Psychological Society, 9*(4), 303–307.

Gunter, B., & Harrison, J. (1998). *Violence on television: An analysis of amount, nature, location and origin of violence in British programmes.* London: Routledge.

Gutierrez, P. M., & Silk, K. R. (1998). Prescription privileges for psychologists: A review of the psychological literature. *Professional Psychology: Research and Practice, 29*(3), 213–222.

Haaga, D. A. F., & Davison, G. C. (1993). An appraisal of rational–emotive therapy. *Journal of Consulting and Clinical Psychology, 61,* 215–220.

Haan, N., Millsap, R., & Hartka, E. (1986). As time goes by: Change and stability in personality over fifty years. *Psychology and Aging, 1,* 220–232.

Haber, R. N. (1979). Twenty years of haunting eidetic imagery: Where's the ghost? *Behavioral and Brain Sciences, 2,* 583–629.

Hackman, M. Z., Furniss, A. H., Hills, M. J., & Paterson, T. J. (1992). Perceptions of gender-role characteristics and transformational and transactional leadership behaviors. *Perceptual and Motor Skills, 75,* 311–319.

Hackman, M. Z., & Johnson, C. E. (1991). *Leadership: A communication perspective.* Prospect Heights, IL: Waveland.

Haddock, G., Zanna, M. P., & Esses, V. M. (1994). The (limited) role of trait-laden stereotypes in predicting attitudes toward native peoples. *British Journal of Social Psychology, 33,* 83–106.

Haith, M. M., & McCarty, M. E. (1990). Stability of visual expectations at 3.0 months of age. *Developmental Psychology, 26,* 68–74.

Hajek, P., & Belcher, M. (1991). Dreams of absent-minded transgression: An empirical study of a cognitive withdrawal symptom. *Journal of Abnormal Psychology, 100,* 487–491.

Hales, D. (1999). *Just like a woman: How gender science is redefining what makes us female.* New York: Bantam Books.

Halgren, E., Walter, R. D., Cherlow, A. G., & Crandall, P. H. (1978). Mental phenomena evoked by electrical stimulation of the human hippocampal formation and amygdala. *Brain, 101,* 83–117.

Hall, C. C. (1997). Cultural malpractice: The growing obsolescence of psychology with the changing U.S. population. *American Psychologist, 52*(6), 642–651.

Hall, E. T. (1966). *The hidden dimension.* Garden City, NY: Doubleday.

Hall, J. (1984). *Nonverbal sex differences: Communication accuracy and expressive style.* Baltimore: Johns Hopkins University Press.

Hall, S. M., Havassy, B. E., & Wasserman, D. A. (1991). Effects of commitment to abstinence, positive moods, stress, and coping on relapse to cocaine use. *Journal of Consulting and Clinical Psychology, 59,* 526–532.

Hallman, W. K., & Wandersman, A. H. (1992). Attribution of responsibility and individual and collective coping with environmental threats. *Journal of Social Issues, 48,* 101–118.

Halpern, D. F. (1986). *Sex differences in cognitive abilities.* Hillsdale, NJ: Erlbaum.

Halpern, D. F. (1997). Sex difference in intelligence. *American Psychologist, 52*(10), 1091–1102.

Halpern, D. F., & Coren, S. (1991). Handedness and life span. (Letter to the editor). *New England Journal of Medicine, 324,* 998.

Halpern, D. F., & Coren, S. (1993). Left-handedness and life span: A reply to Harris. *Psychological Bulletin, 114*(2), 235–241.

Hamann, S. B., & Squire, L. R. (1995). On the acquisition of new declarative knowledge in amnesia. *Behavioral Neuroscience, 109,* 1027–1044.

Hamer, D., & Copeland, P. (1998). *Living with our genes: Why they matter more than you think.* New York: Doubleday.

Hamer, D. H., Hu, S., Magnuson, V. L., Hu, N., & Pattatucci, A. M. L. (1993). A linkage between DNA markers on the X chromosome and male sexual orientation. *Science, 261,* 321–327.

Hamilton, S., & Fagot, B. I. (1988). Chronic stress and coping styles: A comparison of male and female undergraduates. *Journal of Personality and Social Psychology, 5,* 819–823.

Hammond, D. L. (1980). The responding of normals, alcoholics, and psychopaths in a laboratory lie-detection experiment. Doctoral dissertation presented to the faculty of the California School of Professional Psychology.

Haney, C., Banks, W., & Zimbardo, P. (1973). Interpersonal dynamics in a simulated prison. *International Journal of Criminology and Penology, 1,* 69–97.

Haney, C., & Zimbardo, P. (1998). The past and future of U.S. prison policy: Twenty-five years after the Stanford Prison experiment. *American Psychologist, 53*(7), 709–727.

Hanson, C. L., Cigrang, J. A., Harris, M. A., Carle, D. L., Relyea, G., & Burghen, G. A. (1989). Coping styles in youths with insulin-dependent diabetes mellitus. *Journal of Consulting and Clinical Psychology, 57,* 644–651.

Hardy, P. A. J. (1995). Pain management in old age. *Reviews in Clinical Gerontology, 5*(3), 259–273.

Harkins, S. G., & Szymanski, K. (1988). Social loafing and self-evaluation with an objective standard. *Journal of Experimental Social Psychology, 24,* 354–365.

Harlow, H. F. (1962). The heterosexual affectional system in monkeys. *American Psychologist, 17,* 1–9.

Harlow, H. F., & Zimmerman, R. R. (1958). The development of affectional responses in infant monkeys. *Proceedings of the American Philosophic Society, 102,* 501–509.

Harms, T. (1994). Humanizing infant environments for group care. *Children's Environments, 11,* 155–167.

Harper, J. F., & Marshall, E. (1991). Adolescents' problems and their relationship to self-esteem. *Adolescence, 26,* 799–803.

Harris, C. R., & Christenfeld, N. (1997). Humor, tickle, and the Darwin-Hecker hypothesis. *Cognition and Emotion, 11*(1), 103–110.

Harris, J. R. (1995). Where is the child's environment? A group socialization theory of development. *Psychological Review, 102,* 458–489.

Harris, J. R. (1998). *The nurture assumption: Why children turn out the way they do.* New York: The Free Press.

Harris, K. M., & Morgan, S. P. (1991). Fathers, sons, and daughters: Differential paternal involvement in parenting. *Journal of Marriage and the Family, 53,* 531–544.

Harris, M. B. (1994). Gender of subject and target as mediators of aggression. *Journal of Applied Social Psychology, 24,* 453–471.

Harris, M. B. (1996). Aggressive experiences and aggressiveness: Relationship to ethnicity, gender, and age. *Journal of Applied Social Psychology, 26*(10), 843–870.

Harris, M. B., & Knight-Bohnhoff, K. (1996). Gender and aggression: Personal aggressiveness. *Sex Roles, 35*(1/2), 27–42.

Harris, M. M., Gilbreath, B., & Sunday, J. A. (1998). A longitudinal examination of a merit pay system: Relationships among performance ratings, merit increases, and total pay increases. *Journal of Applied Psychology, 83*(5), 825–831.

Harris, V. A., & Katkin, E. S. (1975). Primary and secondary emotional behaviour: An analysis of the role of autonomic feedback on affect, arousal, and attribution. *Psychological Bulletin, 82,* 904–916.

Harrison, J. R., & Barabasz, A. F. (1991). Effects of restricted environmental stimulation therapy on the behavior of children with autism. *Child Study Journal, 21,* 153–166.

Harrison, Y., & Horne, J. A. (1996). Long-term extension to sleep—are we really chronically sleep deprived? *Psychophysiology, 33,* 22–30.

Hart, D. (1998). Can prototypes inform moral developmental theory? *Developmental Psychology, 34*(3), 420–423.

Hart, K. E. (1997). A moratorium on research using the Jenkins Activity Survey for Type A behavior? *Journal of Clinical Psychology, 53*(8), 905–907.

Hartmann, E. (1995). Making connections in a safe place: Is dreaming psychotherapy? *Dreaming, 5,* 213–228.

Hartmann, E. (1996). Outline for a theory on the nature and functions of dreaming. *Dreaming, 6,* 147–170.

Hartung, C. M., & Widiger, T. A. (1998). Gender differences in the diagnosis of mental disorders: Conclusions and controversies of the *DSM-IV. Psychological Bulletin, 123*(3), 260–278.

Hartup, W. W. (1989). Social relationships and their developmental significance. *American Psychologist, 44,* 120–126.

Hartup, W. W., & Stevens, N. (1997). Friendships and adaptation in the life course. *Psychological Bulletin, 121*(3), 355–370.

Harvey, E. (1999). Short-term and long-term effects of early parental employment on children of the National Longitudinal Survey of Youth. *Developmental Psychology, 35*(2), 445–459.

Harvey, M. L., Loomis, R. J., Bell, P. A., & Marino, M. (1998). The influence of museum exhibit design on immersion and psychological flow. *Environment and Behavior, 30*(5), 601–627.

Haslam, N. (1997). Evidence that male sexual orientation is a matter of degree. *Journal of Personality and Social Psychology, 73*(4), 862–870.

Hauser, S. T., & Bowlds, M. K. (1990). Stress, coping, and adaptation. In S. S. Feldman & G. R. Elliott (Eds.), *At the threshold.* Cambridge, MA: Harvard University Press.

Hawkins, J. D., Catalano, R. F., & Miller, J. Y. (1992). Risk and protective factors for alcohol and other drug problems in adolescence and early adulthood: Implications for substance abuse prevention. *Psychological Bulletin, 112,* 64–105.

Hayflick, L. (1994). *How and why we age.* New York: Ballantine.

Hays, R. B. (1989). The day-to-day functioning of close versus casual friendships. *Journal of Social and Personal Relationships, 6,* 21–37.

Heath, A. C., & Martin, N. G. (1990). Psychoticism as a dimension of personality: A multivariate genetic test of Eysenck and Eysenck's psychoticism construct. *Journal of Personality and Social Psychology, 58,* 111–121.

Heatherton, T. F., & Baumeister, R. F. (1991). Binge eating as escape from self-awareness. *Psychological Bulletin, 100,* 86–108.

Hebb, D. O. (1949). *Organization of behavior.* New York: Wiley.

Hebb, D. O. (1955). Drives and the C. N. S. (conceptual nervous system). *Psychological Review, 62,* 243–254.

Hebb, D. O. (1972). *Textbook of psychology* (3rd ed.). Philadelphia: Saunders.

Heckler, M. M. (1985). Psychology in the public forum: The fight against Alzheimer's disease. *American Psychologist, 40,* 1240–1244.

Hedges, L. V., & Nowell, A. (1995). Sex differences in mental test scores, variability, and numbers of high-scoring individuals. *Science, 269,* 41–45.

Heeger, D. J. (1994). The representation of visual stimuli in the primary visual cortex. *Current Directions in Psychological Science, 3,* 159–163.

Heider, E. R. (1971). "Focal" color areas and the development of color names. *Developmental Psychology, 4,* 447–455.

Heider, E. R. (1972). Universals in color naming and memory. *Journal of Experimental Psychology, 93,* 10–21.

Heider, E. R., & Olivier, D. C. (1972). The structure of the color space in naming and memory for two languages. *Cognitive Psychology, 3,* 337–354.

Heider, K. G. (1991). *Landscapes of emotion: Lexical maps and scenarios of emotion terms in Indonesia.* Cambridge, England: Cambridge University Press.

Heider, K. G. (1994, March). *An anthropologist discovers emotion in the New Guinea Highlands.* Paper presented at the University of South Carolina Educational Foundation

Research Award in Humanities and Social Sciences Lecture, Columbia, South Carolina.

Heilbrun, A. B., Jr., Wydra, D., & Friedberg, L. (1989). Parent identification and gender schema development. *Journal of Genetic Psychology, 150,* 293–299.

Heinlein, R. (1961). *Stranger in a strange land.* New York: Putnam.

Hellriegel, D., & Slocum, J. (1992). *Management* (6th ed). Reading, MA: Addison-Wesley.

Hellstedt, J. C. (1995). Invisible players: A family systems model. In S. M. Murphy (Ed.), *Sport psychology interventions* (pp. 117–146). Champaign, IL: Human Kinetics.

Helman, C. (1992). Heart disease and the cultural construction of time. In R. Frankenberg et al. (Eds.), *Time, health and medicine* (pp. 31–55). London: Sage Publications, Inc.

Helmes, E., & Reddon, J. R. (1993). A perspective on developments in assessing psychopathology: A critical review of the MMPI and MMPI-2. *Psychological Bulletin, 113,* 453–471.

Helms, J. E. (1992). Why is there no study of cultural equivalence in standardized cognitive ability testing? *American Psychologist, 47,* 1083–1101.

Helson, R., & Moane, G. (1987). Personality change in women from college to midlife. *Journal of Personality and Social Psychology, 53,* 176–186.

Helson, R., & Picano, J. (1990). Is the traditional role bad for women? *Journal of Personality and Social Psychology, 59,* 311–320.

Helson, R., Stewart, A. J., & Ostrove, J. (1995). Identity in three cohorts of midlife women. *Journal of Personality and Social Psychology, 69,* 544–557.

Helweg-Larsen, M., & Collins, B. E. (1997). A social psychological perspective on the role of knowledge about AIDS in AIDS prevention. *American Psychological Society, 6*(2), 23–26.

Hendrick, C., & Hendrick, S. S. (1986). A theory and method of love. *Journal of Personality and Social Psychology, 50,* 392–402.

Herbert, T. B., & Cohen, S. (1993). Depression and immunity: A meta-analytic review. *Psychological Bulletin, 113,* 472–486.

Herbert, T. B., Cohen, S., Marsland, A. L., Bachen, E. A., et al. (1994). Cardiovascular reactivity and the course of immune response to an acute psychological stressor. *Psychosomatic Medicine, 56,* 337–344.

Herman, L. M., Kuczaj, S. A., & Holder, M. D. (1993). Responses to anomalous gestural sequences by a language-trained dolphin: Evidence for processing of semantic relations and syntactic information. *Journal of Experimental Psychology: General, 122*(2), 184–194.

Hermans, H. J. M., & Kempen, H. J. G. (1998). Moving cultures: The perilous problems of cultural dichotomies in a globalizing society. *American Psychologist, 53*(10), 1111–1120.

Herrnstein, R. J., & Murray, C. (1994). *The bell curve: Intelligence and class structure in American life.* New York: Free Press.

Herz, R. S., & Engen, T. (1996). Odor memory: Review and analysis. *Psychonomic Bulletin & Review, 3*(3), 300–313.

Hewlett, B. S., Lamb, M. E., Shannon, D., Leyendecker, B., & Schoelmerich, A. (1998). Culture and early infancy among central African foragers and farmers. *Developmental Psychology, 34*(4), 653–661.

Hewlett, S. A., & West, C. (1998). *The war against parents: What we can do for America's beleaguered moms and dads.* Boston: Houghton Mifflin.

Hildebrandt, K. A. (1983). Effect of facial expression variations on ratings of infant's physical attractiveness. *Developmental Psychology, 29,* 414–417.

Hilgard, E. R. (1965). *Hypnotic susceptibility.* New York: Harcourt, Brace & World.

Hilgard, E. R. (1994). Neodissociation theory. In S. J. Lynn, J. W. Rhue, et al. (Eds.), *Dissociation: Clinical and theoretical perspectives.* New York: Guilford Press.

Hill, J. O., & Peters, J. C. (1998). Environmental contributions to the obesity epidemic. *Science, 280,* 1371–1374.

Hilsman, R., & Garber, J. (1995). A test of the cognitive diathesis–stress model of depression in children: Academic stressors, attributional style, perceived competence, and control. *Journal of Personality and Social Psychology, 69,* 370–380.

Hines, D. (1997). Arguments for prescription privileges for psychologists. *American Psychologist, 52*(3), 270–271.

Hinton, G. (1992, September). How neural networks learn from experience. *Scientific American,* 145–151.

Hinton, G., Plaut, D. C., & Shallice, T. (1993, April). Simulating brain damage. *Scientific American,* 76–83.

Hirsch, H. V. B., & Spinelli, D. N. (1971). Modification of the distribution of receptive field orientation in cats by selective exposure during development. *Experimental Brain Research, 13,* 509–527.

Hirschfeld, R. M. A., Keller, M. B., Panico, S., Arons, B. S., Barlow, D., Davidoff, F., Endicott, J., Froom, J., Goldstein, M., Gorman, J. M., Guthrie, D., Marek, R. G., Maurer, T. A., Meyer, R., Phillips, K., Ross, J., Schwenk, T. L., Sharfstein, S. S., Thase, M. E., & Wyatt, R. J. (1997). The National Depressive and Manic Depressive Association consensus statement on the undertreatment of depression. *Journal of the American Medical Association, 277*(4), 333–340.

Hobfoll, S. E. (1989). Conservation of resources: A new attempt at conceptualizing stress. *American Psychologist, 44,* 513–524.

Hobfoll, S. E., Spielberg, C. D., Breznitz, S., Figley, C., Folkman, S., Lepper-Green, B., Meichenbaum, D., Milgram, N. A., Sandler, I., Sarason, I., & Van der Kolk, B. (1991). War-related stress. *American Psychologist, 46,* 848–855.

Hobson, J. A. (1989). *Sleep.* New York: Freeman.

Hobson, J. A. (1994). *The chemistry of conscious states: How the brain changes its mind.* Boston: Little, Brown.

Hobson, J. A. (1996). *The chemistry of conscious states: Toward a unified model of the brain and the mind.* Boston: Little, Brown and Co.

Hobson, J. A., & McCarley, R. W. (1977). The brain as a dream state generator: An activation-synthesis of the dream process. *American Journal of Psychiatry, 134,* 1335–1348.

Hoffart, A. (1996). In vivo cognitive therapy of panic attacks. *Journal of Cognitive Psychotherapy, 10*(4), 281–289.

Hoffman, D. D. (1999). *Visual intelligence.* New York: Norton.

Hoffman, C., & Hurst, N. (1990). Gender stereotypes: Perception or rationalization? *Journal of Personality and Social Psychology, 58,* 197–208.

Hofstede, G. (1983). National cultures revisited. *Behavior Science Research, 18,* 285–305.

Hogan, R., Curphy, G. J., & Hogan, J. (1994). What we know about leadership: Effectiveness and personality. *American Psychologist, 49,* 493–504.

Hogan, R., Hogan, J., & Roberts, B. W. (1996). Personality measurement and employment decisions. *American Psychologist, 51*(5), 469–477.

Hogben, M. (1998). Factors moderating the effect of televised aggression on viewers. *Communication Research, 25*(2), 220–247.

Holder, M. D., Yirmiya, R., Garcia, J., & Raizer, J. (1989). Conditioned taste aversions are not readily disrupted by external excitation. *Behavioral Neuroscience, 103,* 605–611.

Holland, M. K. (1975). Using psychology: *Principles of behavior and your life.* Boston: Little, Brown.

Hollis, K. L. (1997). Contemporary research on Pavlovian conditioning: A "new" functional analysis. *American Psychologist, 52*(9), 956–965.

Hollister, J. M., Mednick, S. A., Brennan, P. A., & Cannon, T. D. (1994). Impaired autonomic nervous system habituation in those at genetic risk for schizophrenia. *Archives of General Psychiatry, 51,* 552–558.

Holloway, F. A. (1977). State-dependent retrieval based on time of day. In B. Ho, D. Chute, & D. Richards (Eds.), *Drug discrimination and state-dependent learning.* New York: Academic.

Holmes, D. S. (1984). Mediation and somatic arousal reduction. *American Psychologist, 39,* 1–10.

Holmes, T. H., & Rahe, R. H. (1967). The Social Readjustment Rating Scale. *Journal of Psychosomatic Research, 11,* 213–218.

Hom, H. L., Jr., & Arbuckle, B. (1988). Mood induction effects upon goal setting and performance in young children. *Motivation and Emotion, 12,* 113–122.

Honig, A. S., & Chung, M. (1989). Child-rearing practices of urban poor mothers of infants and three-year-olds in five cultures. *Child Development and Care, 50,* 75–97.

Honts, C. R. (1994). Psychophysiological detection of deception. *Current Directions in Psychological Science, 3,* 77–82.

Honts, C. R. (1996). Criterion development and validity of the CQT in field application. *Journal of General Psychology, 123,* 309–324.

Hood, B. M., Willen, J. D., & Driver, J. (1998). Adult's eyes trigger shifts of visual attention in human infants. *American Psychological Society, 9*(2), 131–134.

Hoosain, Z., & Roopnarine, J. L. (1994). African-American fathers' involvement with infants: Relationship to their functioning style, support, education, and income. *Infant Behavior and Development, 17,* 175–184.

Hopkins, W. D. (1997). Hemispheric specialization for local and global processing of hierarchical visual stimuli in chimpanzees (Pan troglodytes). *Neuropsychologia, 35*(3), 343–348.

Horne, J. (1988). *Why we sleep.* New York: Oxford University Press.

Horne, S. (1999). Domestic violence in Russia. *American Psychologist, 54*(1), 55–61.

Horney, K. (1937). *The neurotic personality of our time.* New York: Norton.

Hornstein, G. A. (1992). The return of the repressed. *American Psychologist, 47,* 254–263.

Hotamisligil, G. S., Johnson, R. S., Distel, R. J., Ellis, R., Papaioannou, V. E., & Spiegelman, B. M. (1996). Uncoupling of obesity from insulin resistance through a targeted mutation in aP2, the adipocyte fatty acid binding protein. *Science, 274,* 1377–1380.

Houde, J. F., & Jordan, M. I. (1998). Sensorimotor adaptation in speech production. *Science, 279,* 1213–1216.

Hovey, J. D. (1998). Acculturative stress, depression and suicidal ideation among Mexican-American adolescents: Implications for the development of suicide prevention programs in schools. *Psychological Reports, 83*(1), 249–250.

Howard, K. I., Kopta, S. M., Krause, M. S., & Orlinsky, D. E. (1986). The dose–effect relationships in psychotherapy. *American Psychologist, 41,* 159–164.

Howe, M. J. A., & Smith, J. (1988). Calendar calculating in "idiots savants": How do they do it? *British Journal of Psychology, 79,* 371–386.

Howell, J. M., & Avolio, B. J. (1993). Transformational leadership, transactional leadership, locus of control, and support for innovation: Key predictors of consolidated-business-unit performance. *Journal of Applied Psychology, 78,* 891–902.

Howell, W. C. (1993). Engineering psychology in a changing world. *Annual Review of Psychology, 44,* 231–263.

Howes, C., Hamilton, C. E., & Philipsen, L. C. (1998). Stability and continuity of child-caregiver and child-peer relationships. *Child Development, 69*(2), 418–426.

Howes, C., Unger, O., & Seidner, L. B. (1989). Social pretend play in toddlers: Parallels with social play and with solitary pretend. *Child Development, 60,* 77–84.

Hoyt, I. P., Nadon, R., Register, P. A., Chorny, J., Fleeson, W., Grigorian, E. M., & Otto, L. (1989). Daydreaming, absorption, and hypnotizability. *The International Journal of Clinical and Experimental Hypnosis, 37,* 332–342.

Huapaya, L. V. M. (1994). Four cases of supposed multiple personality disorder: Evidence of unjustified diagnoses. *Canadian Journal of Psychiatry, 39,* 247.

Hubel, D. H., & Wiesel, T. N. (1962). Receptive fields, binocular interaction, and functional architecture in the cat's visual cortex. *Journal of Physiology, 160,* 106–164.

Hudak, M. A. (1993). Gender schema theory revisited: Men's stereotypes of American women. *Sex Roles, 28,* 279–293.

Hudspeth, A. J. (1983, January). The hair cells of the inner ear. *Scientific American,* 54–73.

Huffcutt, A. I., & Roth, P. L. (1998). Racial group differences in employment interview evaluations. *Journal of Applied Psychology, 83*(2), 179–189.

Huffman, L. C., Bryan, Y. E., del Carmen, R., Pedersen, F. A., Doussard-Roosevelt, J. A., & Porgess, S. W. (1998). Infant temperament and cardiac vagal tone: Assessments at twelve weeks of age. *Child Development, 69*(3), 624–635.

Hughes, C. F., Uhlmann, C., & Pennebaker, J. W. (1994). The body's response to processing emotional trauma: Linking verbal text with autonomic activity. *Journal of Personality, 62,* 564–585.

Hughes, S. L., & Neimeyer, R. A. (1993). Cognitive predictors of suicide risk among hospitalized psychiatric patients: A prospective study. *Death Studies, 17,* 103–124.

Humphreys, K. (1996). Clinical psychologists as psychotherapists: History, future, and alternatives. *American Psychologist, 51,* 190–197.

Hunt, E. B., & Agnoli, F. (1991). The Whorfian hypothesis: A cognitive psychology perspective. *Psychological Review, 98,* 377–389.

Hunt, M. (1974). *Sexual behavior in the 1970s.* New York: Dell.

Hurvich, L., & Jameson, D. (1974). Opponent processes as a model of neural organization. *American Psychologist, 30,* 88–102.

Huston, A. C., Donnerstein, E., Fairchild, H., Feshback, N. D., Katz, P. A., Murray, J. P., Rubinstein, E. A., Wilcox, B. L., & Zuckerman, D. (1992). *Big world, small screen.* Lincoln: University of Nebraska Press.

Hyde, J. S., Fennema, E., & Lamon, S. J. (1990). Gender differences in mathematics performance: A meta-analysis. *Psychological Bulletin, 107,* 139–155.

Hyde, J. S., & Linn, M. C. (1988). Gender differences in verbal ability: A meta-analysis. *Psychological Bulletin, 104,* 53–69.

Idehen, E. E. (1997). The influence of gender and space sharing history on the conceptions of privacy by undergraduates. *Ife Psychologia: An International Journal, 5*(1), 59–75.

Ilacqua, G. E. (1994). Migraine headaches: Coping efficacy of guided imagery training. *Headache, 34,* 99–102.

Ilgen, D. R. (1990). Health issues at work: Opportunities for industrial/organizational psychology. *American Psychologist, 45,* 273–283.

Ilgen, D. R. (1999). Teams embedded in organizations: Some implications. *American Psychologist, 54*(2), 129–139.

Ingbar, D. H., & Gee, J. B. L. (1985). Pathophysiology and treatment of sleep apnea. *Annual Review of Medicine, 36,* 369–395.

Ingraham, L. J., Kugelmass, S., Frenkel, E., Nathan, M., et al. (1995). Twenty-five-year followup of the Israeli High-Risk Study. *Schizophrenia Bulletin, 21*(2), 183–192.

Inhelder, B., & Piaget, J. (1958). *The growth of logical thinking from childhood to adolescence.* New York: Basic Books.

Inhoff, A. W., Morris, R., & Calabrese, J. (1986). Eye movements in skilled transcription typing. *Bulletin of the Psychonomic Society, 2,* 113–114.

Innes, J. M., & Young, R. F. (1975). The effect of presence of an audience, evaluation apprehension, and objective self-awareness on learning. *Journal of Experimental Social Psychology, 11,* 35–42.

Intraub, H. (1980). Presentation rate and the representation of briefly glimpsed pictures in memory. *Journal of Experimental Psychology: Human Learning and Memory, 6,* 1–12.

Intraub, H., Gottesman, C. V., & Bills, A. J. (1998). Effects of perceiving and imagining scenes on memory for pictures. *Journal of Experimental Psychology: Learning, Memory, and Cognition, 24*(1), 186–201.

Irwin, M., Smith, T. L., & Gillin, J. C. (1992). Electroencephalographic sleep and natural killer activity in depressed patients and control subjects. *Psychosomatic Medicine, 54,* 10–21.

Isaac, R. J., & Armat, V. C. (1990). *Madness in the streets: How psychiatry and the law abandoned the mentally ill.* New York: Free Press.

Isabella, R. A., Belsky, J., & von Eye, A. (1989). Origins of infant–mother attachment: An examination of interactional synchrony during the infant's first year. *Developmental Psychology, 25,* 12–21.

Ito, T. A., Larsen, J. T., Smith, N. K., & Cacioppo, J. T. (1998). Negative information weighs more heavily on the brain: The negativity bias in evaluative categorizations. *Journal of Personality and Social Psychology, 75*(4), 887–900.

Ito, T. A., Miller, N., & Pollock, V. E. (1996). Alcohol and aggression: A meta-analysis on the moderation effects of inhibitory cues, triggering events, and self-focused attention. *Psychological Bulletin, 120*(1), 60–82.

Iwata, B. A., Pace, G. M., Cowdery, G. E., & Miltenberger, R. G. (1994). What makes extinction work: An analysis of procedural form and function. *Journal of Applied Behavior Analysis, 27,* 131–144.

Izard, C. E. (1990). Facial expressions and the regulation of emotions. *Journal of Personality and Social Psychology, 58*(3), 487–498.

Izard, C. E. (1994). Innate and universal facial expressions: Evidence from developmental and cross-cultural research. *Psychological Bulletin, 115,* 288–299.

Izard, C. E. (1997). Emotions and facial expressions: A perspective from differential emotions theory. In J. A. Russell, J. M. Fernandez-Dols, et al. (Eds.), *The psychology of facial expression. Studies in emotion and social interaction, 2nd series* (pp. 57–77). New York: Cambridge University Press.

Izard, C. E., & Saxton, P. M. (1988). Emotions. In R. C. Atkinson, R. J. Herrnstein, G. Lindzey, & R. D. Luce (Eds.), *Stevens handbook of experimental psychology: Vol. 1. Perception and motivation.* New York: Wiley.

Izquierdo, I., & Medina, J. H. (1997). The biochemistry of memory formation and its regulation by hormones and neuromodulators. *Psychobiology, 25*(1), 1–9.

Jaccard, J., Helbig, D. W., Wan, C. K., Gutman, M. A., & Kritz-Silverstein, D. C. (1990). Individual differences in attitude–behavior consistency: The prediction of contraceptive behavior. *Journal of Applied Social Psychology, 20,* 575–617.

Jackson, J. M., & Latané, B. (1981). All alone in front of all those people: Stage fright as a function of number and type of co-performers and audience. *Journal of Personality and Social Psychology, 40,* 73–85.

Jackson, S. E., & Schuler, R. S. (1990). Human resource planning: Challenges for industrial/organizational psychologists. *American Psychologist, 45,* 223–239.

Jackson, S. E., & Schuler, R. S. (1995). Understanding human resource management in the context of organizations and their environments. *Annual Review of Psychology, 46,* 237–264.

Jacobs, B., Schall, M., & Scheibel, A. B. (1993). A quantitative dendritic analysis of Wernicke's area. II. Gender, hemispheric, and environmental factors. *Journal of Comprehensive Neurology, 237,* 97–111.

Jacobs, L., Berscheid, E., & Walster, E. (1971). Self-esteem and attraction. *Journal of Personality and Social Psychology, 17,* 84–91.

Jacobs, R. A. (1997). Nature, nurture, and the development of functional specializations: A computational approach. *Psychonomic Bulletin and Review, 4*(3), 299–309.

Jacobs, R. A., & Kosslyn, S. M. (1994). Encoding shape and spatial relations: The role of receptive field size in coordinating complementary representations. *Cognitive Science, 18,* 361–386.

Jacobson, N. S. (1991). Behavioral versus insight-oriented marital therapy: Labels can be misleading. *Journal of Consulting and Clinical Psychology, 59,* 142–145.

Jacobson, N. S., & Addis, M. E. (1993). Research on couples and couple therapy: What do we know? Where are we going? *Journal of Consulting and Clinical Psychology, 61,* 85–93.

Jacoby, L. L., Kelley, C., Brown, J., & Jasechko, J. (1989). Becoming famous overnight: Limits on the ability to avoid unconscious influences of the past. *Journal of Personality and Social Psychology, 56,* 326–338.

James, W. (1884). What is an emotion? *Mind, 9,* 188–205.

James, W. (1890). *Principles of psychology.* New York: Dover.

James, W. (1910). *The will to believe and other essays in popular philosophy.* London: Longmans, Green, and Co.

Jan, J. E., Espezel, H., & Appleton, R. E. (1994). The treatment of sleep disorders with melatonin. *Developmental Medicine and Child Neurology, 36,* 97–107.

Janis, I. L. (1982). *Groupthink* (2nd ed.). Boston: Houghton Mifflin.

Janis, I. L. (1983). The role of social support in adherence to stressful decisions. *American Psychologist, 38,* 142–160.

Janis, I. L. (1985). Stress inoculation in health care: Theory and research. In A. Monat & R. S. Lazarus (Eds.), *Stress and coping* (2nd ed.). New York: Columbia University Press.

Jansen, A. S. P., Nguyen, X. V., Karpitskiy, V., Mettenleiter, T. C., & Loewy, A. D. (1995). Central command neurons of the sympathetic nervous system: Basis of the fight-or-flight response. *Science, 270,* 644–646.

Jarrett, M. E., & Lethbridge, D. J. (1994). Looking forward, looking back: Women's experience with waning fertility during midlife. *Qualitative Health Research, 4,* 370–384.

Jason, L. A., Richman, J. A., Friedberg, F., Wagner, L., Taylor, R., & Jordan, K. M. (1997). Politics, science, and the emergence of a new disease: The case of chronic fatigue syndrome. *American Psychologist, 52*(9), 973–983.

Jaynes, J. (1976). *The origin of consciousness in the breakdown of the bicameral mind.* Boston: Houghton Mifflin.

Jazwinski, S. M. (1996). Longevity, genes, and aging. *Science, 273,* 54–59.

Jeanneret, R. P. (1992). Applications of job component/synthetic validity to construct validity. *Human Performance, 5*(1/2), 81–96.

Jenkins, G. D., Jr., Mitra, A., Gupta, N., & Shaw, J. D. (1998). Are financial incentives related to performance? A meta-analytic review of empirical research. *Journal of Applied Psychology, 83*(5), 777–787.

Jenkins, H. M., & Harrison, R. H. (1960). Effect of discrimination training on auditory generalization. *Journal of Experimental Psychology, 59,* 244–253.

Jennings, K. D., Curry, N. E., & Connors, R. (1986). Toddlers' social behaviors in dyads and groups. *Journal of Genetic Psychology, 147,* 515–528.

Jensen, A. R. (1969). How much can we boost IQ and scholastic achievement? *Harvard Educational Review, 39,* 1–123.

Jensen, A. R. (1970). Can we and should we study race differences? In J. Hellmuth (Ed.), *Disadvantaged child* (Vol. 3). New York: Brunner/Mazel.

Jensen, A. R. (1987). Psychometric g as a focus on concerted research effort. *Intelligence, 11,* 193–198.

Jensen, A. R., & Weng, L. J. (1994). What is a good g? *Intelligence, 18,* 231–258.

Job, R. F. S., & Barnes, B. W. (1995). Stress and consumption: Inescapable shock, neophobia, and quinine finickiness in rats. *Behavioral Neuroscience, 109,* 106–116.

John, E. R., Chesler, P., Bartlett, F., & Victor, I. (1968). Observational learning in cats. *Science, 159,* 1489–1491.

Johnsen, K., Espnes, G. A., & Gillard, S. (1998). The associations between Type A/B behavioural dimension and Type 2/4 personality patterns. *Personality and Individual Differences, 25*(5), 937–945.

Johnson, B. T., & Eagly, A. H. (1989). Effects of involvement on persuasion: A meta-analysis. *Psychological Bulletin, 106,* 290–314.

Johnson, D. L. (1997). Weight loss for women: Studies of smokers and nonsmokers using hypnosis and multi-component treatments with and without overt aversion. *Psychological Reports, 80*(3, Pt. 1), 931–933.

Johnson, F. W. (1991). Biological factors and psychometric intelligence: A review. *Genetic, Social, and General Psychology Monographs, 117,* 315–357.

Johnson, L. C., Slye, E. S., & Dement, W. (1965). Electroencephalographic and autonomic activity during and after prolonged sleep deprivation. *Psychosomatic Medicine, 27,* 415–423.

Johnson, S. H. (1998). Cerebral organization of motor imagery: Contralateral control of grip selection in mentally represented prehension. *American Psychological Society, 9*(3), 219–222.

Johnson, S. K. (1998). The biopsychosocial model and chronic fatigue syndrome. *American Psychologist, 53*(9), 1080–1081.

Johnson, T. F. (1995). Aging well in contemporary society. *American Behavioral Scientist, 39*(2), 120–130.

Joiner, T. E., & Wagner, K. D. (1995). Attribution style and depression in children and adolescents: A meta-analytic review. *Clinical Psychology Review, 15*(8), 777–798.

Jones, E. G., & Pons, T. P. (1998). Thalamic and brainstem contributions to large-scale plasticity of primate somatosensory cortex. *Science, 282,* 1121–1125.

Jones, S. S., & Raag, T. (1989). Smile production in older infants: The importance of a social recipient for the facial signal. *Child Development, 60,* 811–818.

Jonides, J., Schumacher, E. H., Smith, E. E., & Lauber, E. J. (1997). Verbal working memory load affects regional brain activation as measured by PET. *Journal of Cognitive Neuroscience, 9*(4), 462–475.

Jorgensen, R. S., & Johnson, J. H. (1990). Contributors to the appraisal of major life changes: Gender, perceived controllability, sensation seeking, strain, and social support. *Journal of Applied Social Psychology, 20,* 1123–1138.

Jorgensen, R. S., Johnson, B. T., Kolodziej, M. E., & Schreer G. E. (1996). Elevated blood pressure and personality: A meta-analytic review. *Psychological Bulletin, 120*(2), 293–320.

Joseph, J. A. (1992). The putative role of free radicals in the loss of neuronal functioning in senescence. *Integrative Physiological and Behavioral Science, 27*(3), 216–227.

Josephs, R. A., Markus, H. R., & Tafarodi, R. W. (1992). Gender and self-esteem. *Journal of Personality and Social Psychology, 63,* 391–402.

Judge, T. A., Locke, E. A., Durham, C. C., & Kluger, A. N. (1998). Dispositional effects on job and life satisfaction: The role of core evaluations. *Journal of Applied Psychology, 83*(1), 17–34.

Jussim, L., Nelson, T. E., Manis, M., & Soffin, S. (1995). Prejudice, stereotypes, and labeling effects: Sources of bias in person perception. *Journal of Personality and Social Psychology, 68,* 228–246.

Just, M. A., Carpenter, P. A., Keller, T. A., Eddy, W. F., & Thulborn, K. R. (1996). Brain activation modulated by sentence comprehension. *Science, 274,* 114–116.

Kagan, B. L., Leskin, G., Haas, B., Wilkins, J., & Foy, D. (1999). Elevated lipid levels in Vietnam veterans with chronic posttraumatic stress disorders. *Biological Psychiatry, 45*(3), 374–377.

Kagan, J. (1997a). In the beginning: The contribution of temperament to personality development. *Modern Psychoanalysis, 22*(2), 145–155.

Kagan, J. (1997b). Temperament and the reactions to unfamiliarity. *Child Development, 68*(1), 139–143.

Kagan, J. (1998). *Three seductive ideas.* Cambridge, MA: Harvard University Press.

Kagan, J., Kearsley, R. B., & Zelazo, P. R. (1980). *Infancy: Its place in human development.* Cambridge, MA: Harvard University Press.

Kagan, J., Reznick, J. S., & Snidman, N. (1988). Biological bases of childhood shyness. *Science, 240,* 167–171.

Kagan, J., & Snidman, N. (1991). Infant predictors of inhibited and uninhibited profiles. *Psychological Science, 2,* 40–44.

Kahn, R. S., Davidson, M., & Davis, K. L. (1996). Dopamine and schizophrenia revisited. In S. J. Stanley et al. (Eds.), *Biology of schizophrenia and affective disease* (pp. 369–391). Washington, DC: American Psychiatric Press.

Kaitz, M., Lapidot, P., Bronner, R., & Eidelman, A. I. (1992). Parturient women can recognize their infants by touch. *Developmental Psychology, 28,* 35–39.

Kales, A., Tan, T. L., Kollar, E. J., Naithoh, P., Preson, T. A., & Malmstrom, E. J. (1970). Sleep patterns following 205 hours of sleep deprivation. *Psychosomatic Medicine, 32,* 189–200.

Kalichman, S. C., & Craig, M. E. (1991). Professional psychologists' decisions to report suspected child abuse: Clinician and situation influences. *Professional Psychology: Research and Practice, 22,* 84–89.

Kalichman, S. C., Szymanowski, D., McKee, G., Taylor, J., & Craig, M. E. (1989). Cluster analytically derived MMPI profile subgroups of incarcerated adult rapists. *Journal of Clinical Psychology, 45,* 149–155.

Kalick, S. M., Zebrowitz, L. A., Langlois, J. H., & Johnson, R. M. (1998). Does human facial attractiveness honestly advertise health? Longitudinal data on an evolutionary question. *Psychological Science, 9*(1), 8–13.

Kalimo, R., & Mejman, T. (1987). Psychological and behavioural responses to stress at work. In R. Kalimo, M. A. El-Batawi, & C. L. Cooper (Eds.), *Psychosocial factors at work and their relation to health.* Geneva: World Health Organization.

Kamarck, T., & Jennings, J. R. (1991). Biobehavioral factors in sudden cardiac death. *Psychological Bulletin, 109,* 42–75.

Kandel, E., & Abel, T. (1995). Neuropeptides, adenyl cyclase, and memory storage. *Science, 268,* 825–826.

Kanekar, S., Shaherwalla, A., Franco, B., Kunju, T., & Pinto, A. J. (1991). The acquaintance predicament of a rape victim. *Journal of Applied Social Psychology, 21,* 1524–1544.

Kanner, A. D., Coyne, J. C., Schaefer, C., & Lazarus, R. S. (1981). Comparison of two modes of stress measurement: Daily hassles and uplifts versus major life events. *Journal of Behavioral Medicine, 4,* 1–39.

Kaplan, C. A., & Simon, H. A. (1990). In search of insight. *Cognitive Psychology, 22,* 374–419.

Karabenick, S. A., & Collins, E. J. (1997). Relation of perceived instructional goals and incentives to college students' use of learning strategies. *Journal of Experimental Education, 65*(4), 331–341.

Karau, S. J., & Williams, K. D. (1997). The effects of group cohesiveness on social loafing and social compensation. *Group Dynamics, 1*(2), 156–168.

Karniol, R., & Aida, A. (1997). Judging toy breakers: Gender stereotypes have devious effects on children. *Sex Roles, 36*(¾), 195–205.

Karon, B. P., & Widener, A. (1998). Repressed memories: The real story. *Professional Psychology: Research and Practice, 29*(5), 482–487.

Karweit, N., & Slavin, R. E. (1981). Measurement and modeling choices in studies of time and learning. *American Educational Research Journal, 18,* 157–171.

Kashani, J. H., Reid, J. C., & Rosenberg, T. K. (1989). Levels of hopelessness in children and adolescents: A developmental perspective. *Journal of Consulting and Clinical Psychology, 57,* 496–499.

Kastner, S., De Weered, P., Desimone, R., & Ungerleider, L. G. (1998). Mechanisms of directed attention in the human extrastriate cortex as revealed by functional MRI. *Science, 282,* 108–111.

Katsuki, Y. (1961). Neutral mechanisms of auditory sensation in cats. In W. A. Rosenblith (Ed.), *Sensory communication.* Cambridge, MA: MIT Press.

Kaufman, A. S. (1983). Some questions and answers about the Kaufman Assessment Battery for Children (K—ABC). *Journal of Psychoeducational Assessment, 1,* 205–218.

Kaufman, A. S. (1990). *Assessing adolescent and adult intelligence.* Boston: Allyn & Bacon.

Kazdin, A. E. (1991). Treatment research: The investigation and evaluation of psychotherapy. In M. Hersen, A. E. Kazdin, & A. S. Bellack (Eds.), *The clinical psychology handbook* (2nd ed.). New York: Pergamon.

Kazdin, A. E., & Weisz, J. R. (1998). Identifying and developing empirically supported child and adolescent treatments. *Journal of Consulting and Clinical Psychology, 66*(1), 19–36.

Keane, T. M. (1998). Psychological effects of military combat. In B. P. Dohrenwend et al. (Eds.), *Adversity, stress, and psychopathology* (pp. 52–65). New York: Oxford University Press.

Kearney, C. A., & Silverman, W. K. (1998). A critical review of pharmacotherapy for youth with anxiety disorders: Things are not as they seem. *Journal of Anxiety Disorders, 12*(2), 83–102.

Kecklund, G., Akerstedt, T., & Lowden, A. (1997). Morning work: Effects of early rising on sleep and alertness. *Sleep, 20*(3), 215–223.

Keefe, K., & Berndt, T. J. (1996). Relations of friendship quality to self-esteem in early adolescence. *Journal of Early Adolescence, 16*(1), 110–129.

Keller, H. (1997). Evolutionary approaches. In J. W. Berry (Ed.), *Handbook of cross-cultural psychology, Vol. 1: Theory and method.* Boston: Allyn and Bacon.

Kelley, H. H. (1972). Attribution in social interaction. In E. E. Jones et al. (Eds.), *Attribution: Perceiving the causes of behavior.* Morristown, NJ: General Learning Press.

Kelley, H. H. (1973). Process of causal attribution. *American Psychologist, 28,* 107–128.

Kelley, H. H., Berscheid, E., Christensen, A., Harvey, J. H., Huston, T. L., et al. (1983). *Close relationships.* New York: Freeman.

Kelly, A. E., & McKillop, K. J. (1996). Consequences of revealing personal secrets. *Psychological Bulletin, 120*(3), 450–465.

Kelly, G. (1955). *The psychology of personal constructs.* New York: W. W. Norton.

Kelly, T. A., & Strupp, H. H. (1992). Patient and therapist values in psychotherapy: Perceived changes, assimilation, similarity, and outcome. *Journal of Consulting and Clinical Psychology, 60,* 34–40.

Keltner, D., & Buswell, B. N. (1997). Embarrassment: Its distinct form and appeasement functions. *Psychological Bulletin, 122*(3), 250–270.

Kempermann, G., Kuhn, H. G., & Gage, F. H. (1998). Experience-induced neurogenesis in the senescent dentate gyrus. *Journal of Neuroscience, 18*(9), 3206–3212.

Kendall, P. C. (1993). Cognitive–behavioral therapies with youth: Guiding theory, current status, and emerging developments. *Journal of Consulting and Clinical Psychology, 61,* 235–247.

Kendall, P. C., Krain, A., & Treadwell, K. R. H. (1999). Generalized anxiety disorder. In R. T. Ammerman, M. Hersen, et al. (Eds.), *Handbook of prescriptive treatments for children and adolescents* (2nd ed.) (pp. 155–171). Boston: Allyn & Bacon.

Kendler, K. S., Neale, M. C., Heath, A. C., Phil, D., et al. (1994). A twin-family study of alcoholism in women. *American Journal of Psychiatry, 151,* 707–715.

Kendler, K. S., Neale, M., Kessler, R., Heath, A., & Eaves, L. (1992). A population-based twin study of major depression in women. *Archives of General Psychiatry, 49,* 257–266.

Kendler, K. S., Neale, M., Kessler, R., Heath, A., & Eaves, L. (1993). A twin study of recent life events and difficulties. *Archives of General Psychiatry, 50,* 789–796.

Kendler, K. S., Neale, M., MacLean, C. J., Heath, A., Eaves, L., & Kessler, R. (1993). Smoking and major depression. *Archives of General Psychiatry, 50,* 36–43.

Kennell, J. H., Voos, D. K., & Klaus, M. H. (1979). Parent–infant bonding. In J. D. Osofsky (Ed.), *Handbook of infant development.* New York: Wiley.

Kerns, K. A. (1998). Individual differences in friendship quality: Links to child–mother attachment. In W. M. Bukowski et al. (Eds.), *The company they keep: Friendship in childhood and adolescence.* New York: Cambridge University Press.

Kerr, M., Lambert, W. W., & Bem, D. J. (1996). Life course sequelae of childhood shyness in Sweden: Comparison with the United States. *Developmental Psychology, 32*(6), 1100–1105.

Kerr, N., & Bruun, S. E. (1983). Dispensability of member effort and group motivation losses: Free-rider effects. *Journal of Personality and Social Psychology, 44,* 78–94.

Kessler, R. C., Kendler, K. S., Heath, A. C., Neale, M. C., & Eaves, L. J. (1992). Social support, depressed mood, and adjustment to stress: A genetic epidemiologic investigation. *Journal of Personality and Social Psychology, 62,* 257–272.

Kessler, R. C., Sonnega, A., Bromet, E., Hughes, M., & Nelson, C. B. (1995). Posttraumatic stress disorder in the National Comorbidity Survey. *Archives of General Psychiatry, 52,* 1048–1060.

Kety, S. S., Wender, P. H., Jacobsen, B., Ingraham, L. J., Jansson, L., Faber, B., & Kinney, D. K. (1994). Mental illness in the biological and adoptive relatives of schizophrenic adoptees: Replication of the Copenhagen study in the rest of Denmark. *Archives of General Psychiatry, 51,* 442–455.

Kiecolt-Glaser, J. K., Page, G. G., Marucha, P. T., MacCallum, R. C., & Glaser, R. (1998). Psychological influences on surgical recovery: Perspectives from psychoneuroimmunology. *American Psychologist, 53*(11), 1209–1218.

Kier, C., & Lewis, C. (1997). Infant–mother attachment in separated and married families. *Journal of Divorce and Remarriage, 26*(3/4), 185–194.

Kihlstrom, J. F. (1998). Dissociations and dissociation theory in hypnosis: Comment on Kirsch and Lynn. *Psychological Bulletin, 123*(2), 186–191.

Kihlstrom, J. F., Barnhardt, T. M., & Tataryn, D. J. (1992). The psychological unconscious. *American Psychologist, 47,* 788–791.

Kikoski, J. F. (1998). Effective communication in the performance appraisal interview: Face-to-face communication for public managers in the culturally diverse workplace. *Public Personnel Management, 27*(4), 491–513.

Kilbourne, B. K. (1989). A cross-cultural investigation of the foot-in-the-door compliance induction procedure. *Journal of Cross-Cultural Psychology, 20,* 3–38.

Kilgard, M. P., & Merzenich, M. M. (1998). Cortical map reorganization enabled by nucleus basalis activity. *Science, 279,* 1714–1718.

Kim, J. J., & Fanselow, M. S. (1992). Modality-specific retrograde amnesia of fear. *Science, 256,* 675–677.

Kim, J. S., Bramlett, M. H., Wright, L. K., & Poon, L. W. (1998). Racial differences in health status and health behaviors of older adults. *Nursing Research, 47*(4), 243–250.

Kim, S. R. (1997). Relationships between young children's day care experience and their attachment relationships with parents and socioemotional behavior problems. *Korean Journal of Child Studies, 18*(2), 5–18.

Kimberg, D. Y., D'Esposito, M., & Farah, M. J. (1997). Cognitive functions in the prefrontal cortex—working memory and executive control. *Current Directions in Psychological Science, 6*(6), 185–192.

Kimmel, D. C. (1980). *Adulthood and aging: An interdisciplinary view* (2nd ed.). New York: Wiley.

Kimura, D. (1992, September). Sex difference in the brain. *Scientific American,* 119–125.

Kinder, D. R., & Sanders, L. M. (1996). *Divided by color: Racial politics and democratic ideals.* Chicago: The University of Chicago Press.

Kingstone, A., Enns, J. T., Mangun, G. R., & Gazzaniga, M. S. (1995). Guided visual search is a left-hemisphere process in split-brain patients. *American Psychological Society, 6,* 118–121.

Kinnunen, T., & Zamansky, H. S. (1996). Hypnotic amnesia and learning: A dissociation interpretation. *American Journal of Clinical Hypnosis, 38*(4), 247–253.

Kinsbourne, M. (1975). The ontogeny of cerebral dominance. In D. Aaronson & R. W. Rieber (Eds.), *Developmental Psycholinguistics and Communication Disorders. Annals of the New York Academy of Science, 263,* 244–250.

Kinsey, A. C., Pomeroy, W. B., & Martin, C. E. (1948). *Sexual behavior in the human male.* Philadelphia: W. B. Saunders.

Kinsey, A. C., Pomeroy, W. B., Martin, C. E., & Gebhard, P. H. (1953). *Sexual behavior in the human female.* Philadelphia: W. B. Saunders.

Kirkpatrick, K., & Wasserman, E. A. (1997). The what and the where of the pigeon's processing of complex visual stimuli. *Journal of Experimental Psychology: Animal Behavior Processes, 22*(1), 60–67.

Kirkpatrick. L. A. (1997). An attachment-theory approach to the psychology of religion. In B. Spilka et al. (Eds.), *The psychology of religion: Theoretical approaches.* Boulder, CO: Westview Press.

Kirmayer, L. J., Young, A., & Hayton, B. C. (1995). The cultural context of anxiety disorders. *Psychiatric Clinics of North America, 18*(3), 503–521.

Kirsch, I., & Lynn, S. J. (1995). The altered state of hypnosis: Changes in the theoretical landscape. *American Psychologist, 50*(10), 846–858.

Kirsch, I., & Lynn, S. J. (1998a). Dissociating the wheat from the chaff in theories of hypnosis: Reply to Kihlstrom and Woody and Sadler. *Psychological Bulletin, 123*(2), 198–202.

Kirsch, I., & Lynn, S. J. (1998b). Dissociation theories of hypnosis. *Psychological Bulletin, 123*(1), 100–115.

Kirsch, I., Montgomery, G., & Sapirstein, G. (1995). Hypnosis as an adjunct to cognitive–behavioral psychotherapy: A meta-analysis. *Journal of Consulting and Clinical Psychology, 63,* 214–220.

Kirsch, I., Silva, C. E., Comey, G., & Reed, S. (1995). A spectral analysis of cognitive and personality variables in hypnosis: Empirical disconfirmation of the two-factor model of hypnotic responding. *Journal of Personality and Social Psychology, 69,* 167–175.

Kirshnit, C. E., Richards, M. H., & Ham, M. (1988, August). *Athletic participation and body-image during early adolescence.* Paper presented at the 96th Annual Convention of the American Psychological Association, Atlanta.

Kitayama, S., & Burnstein, E. (1994). Social influence, persuasion, and group decision making. In S. Shavitt & T. C. Brock (Eds.), *Persuasion: Psychological insights and perspectives* (pp. 175–194). Boston: Allyn & Bacon.

Kitwood, T. (1990). *Concern for others.* New York: Routledge.

Kivilu, J. M., & Rogers, W. T. (1998). A multi-level analysis of cultural experience and gender influences on causal attributions to perceived performance in mathematics. *British Journal of Educational Psychology, 68*(1), 25–37.

Klar, A. J. S. (1996). A single locus, RGHT, specifies preference for hand utilization in humans. *Cold Spring Harbor Symposium for Quantitative Biology, 61,* 59–65.

Klar, Y., & Giladi, E. E. (1997). No one in my group can be below the group's average: A robust positivity bias in favor of anonymous peers. *Journal of Personality and Social Psychology, 73*(5), 885–901.

Klaus, M. H., & Kennell, J. H. (1983). *Bonding: The beginnings of parent–infant attachment* (Rev. ed.). New York: New American Library.

Kleinke, C. L., Peterson, T. R., & Rutledge, T. R. (1998). Effects of self-generated facial expressions on mood. *Journal of Personality and Social Psychology, 74*(1), 272–279.

Kleinmuntz, B., & Szucko, J. J. (1984). Lie detection in ancient and modern times: A call for contemporary scientific study. *American Psychologist, 39*, 766–776.

Klesges, R. C., Isbell, T. R., & Klesges, L. M. (1992). Relationship between dietary restraint, energy intake, physical activity, and body weight: A prospective analysis. *Journal of Abnormal Psychology, 101*, 668–674.

Klingenspor, B. (1994). Gender identity and bulimic eating behavior. *Sex Roles, 31*, 407–432.

Klinger, M. R., & Greenwald, A. G. (1995). Unconscious priming of association judgments. *Journal of Experimental Psychology: Learning, Memory, and Cognition, 21*(3), 569–581.

Klonoff, E. A., Annechild, A., & Landrine, H. (1994). Predicting exercise adherence in women: The role of psychological and physiological factors. *Preventive Medicine, 23*, 257–262.

Klusman, L. E. (1998). Military health care providers' views on prescribing privileges for psychologists. *Professional Psychology: Research and Practice, 29*(3), 223–229.

Knee, C. R. (1998). Implicit theories of relationships: Assessment and prediction of romantic relationship initiation, coping, and longevity. *Journal of Personality and Social Psychology, 74*(2), 360–368.

Knight, G. P., Virdin, L. M., Ocampo, K. A., & Roosa, M. (1994). An examination of the cross-ethnic equivalence of measures of negative life events and mental health among Hispanic and Anglo-American children. *American Journal of Community Psychology, 22*(6), 767–783.

Knutson, J. F. (1995). Psychological characteristics of maltreated children: Putative risk factors and consequences. *Annual Review of Psychology, 46*, 401–431.

Knutson, J. F., & Selner, M. B. (1994). Punitive childhood experiences reported by young adults over a 10-year period. *Child Abuse and Neglect, 18*, 155–166.

Kochanska, G., & Thompson, R. A. (1997). The emergence and development of conscience in toddlerhood and early childhood. In J. E. Grusec, L. Kuczynski, et al. (Eds.), *Parenting and children's internalization of values: A handbook of contemporary theory* (pp. 53–77). New York: John Wiley and Sons.

Koehler, T., Kuhnt, K., & Richter, R. (1998). The role of life event stress in the pathogenesis of duodenal ulcer. *Stress Medicine, 14*(2), 121–124.

Kogut, D., Langley, T., & O'Neal, E. C. (1992). Gender role masculinity and angry aggression in women. *Sex Roles, 26*, 355–365.

Kohlberg, L. (1969). The cognitive-developmental approach to socialization. In D. A. Goslin (Ed.), *Handbook of socialization theory and research*. Chicago: Rand McNally.

Köhler, W. (1973). *The mentality of apes* (2nd ed.). New York: Liveright. (Original work published 1927.)

Kohn, A. (1992). *No contest: The case against competition.* Boston: Houghton Mifflin.

Kohn, A. (1993). *Punished by rewards: The trouble with gold stars, incentive plans, A's, praise, and other bribes.* Boston: Houghton Mifflin.

Kohout, J., Wicherski, M., & Cooney, B. (1992). *Characteristics of graduate departments of psychology: 1989–1990.* Washington, DC: Office of Demographic, Employment, and Educational Research, American Psychological Association.

Kolb, B. (1989). Brain development, plasticity, and behavior. *American Psychologist, 44*, 1203–1212.

Koolstra, C. M., van der Voort, T. H., & van der Kamp, L. J. (1997). Television's impact on children's reading comprehension and decoding skills: A 3-year panel study. *Reading Research Quarterly, 32*(2), 128–152.

Kopp, C. B. (1989). Regulation of distress and negative emotions: A developmental view. *Developmental Psychology, 25*, 343–354.

Kopp, C. B., & Kaler, S. R. (1989). Risk in infancy: Origins and implications. *American Psychologist, 44*, 224–230.

Kopta, S. M., Howard, K. I., Lowry, J. L., & Beutler, L. E. (1994). Patterns of symptomatic recovery in psychotherapy. *Journal of Consulting and Clinical Psychology, 62*, 1009–1016.

Kortenhaus, C. M., & Demarest, J. (1993). Gender role stereotyping in children's literature: An update. *Sex Roles, 28*, 219–232.

Koss, M. P. (1990). The women's mental health research agenda. *American Psychologist, 45*, 374–380.

Koss, M. P. (1993). Rape: Scope, impact, interventions, and public policy responses. *American Psychologist, 48*, 1062–1069.

Koss, M. P., Gidycz, C. A., & Wisniewski, N. (1987). The scope of rape: Incidence and prevalence of sexual aggression and victimization in a national sample of higher education students. *Journal of Consulting and Clinical Psychology, 55*, 162–170.

Kosslyn, S. M. (1975). Information representation in visual images. *Cognitive Psychology, 7*, 341–370.

Kosslyn, S. M. (1987). Seeing and imagining in the cerebral hemispheres: A computational approach. *Psychological Review, 94*, 148–175.

Koulack, D. (1991). *To catch a dream.* Albany: State University of New York Press.

Kozu, J. (1999). Domestic violence. *American Psychologist, 54*(1), 50–54.

Kozyk, J. C., Touyz, S. W., & Beumont, P. J. (1998). Is there a relationship between bulimia nervosa and hazardous alcohol use? *International Journal of Eating Disorders, 24*(1), 95–99.

Kramer, M. S., Cutler, N., Feighner, J., Shrivastava, R., Carman, J., Sramek, J. J., et al. (1998). Distinct mechanism for antidepressant activity by blockade of central substance P receptors. *Science, 281,* 1640–1644.

Krampe, R. T., & Ericsson, K. A. (1996). Maintaining excellence: Deliberate practice and elite performance in young and older pianists. *Journal of Experimental Psychology: General, 125*(4), 331–359.

Krantz, D. S., Contrada, R. J., Hill, D. R., & Friedler, E. (1988). Environmental stress and biobehavioral antecedents of coronary heart disease. *Journal of Consulting and Clinical Psychology, 56,* 333–341.

Krantz, D. S., Grunberg, N. E., & Baum, A. (1985). Health psychology. *Annual Review of Psychology, 36,* 349–383.

Kranzler, H. R., & Anton, R. F. (1994). Implications of recent neuropsychopharmacologic research for understanding the etiology and development of alcoholism. *Journal of Consulting and Clinical Psychology, 62,* 1116–1126.

Kranzler, J. H., & Jensen, A. R. (1991). The nature of psychometric g: Unitary process or a number of independent processes? *Intelligence, 15,* 397–422.

Kraut, R., Patterson, M., Lundmark, V., Kiesler, S., Mukopadhyay, T., & Scherlis, W. (1998). Internet paradox: A social technology that reduces social involvement and psychological well-being? *American Psychologist, 53*(9), 1017–1031.

Kreider, R. B., Fry, A. C., & O'Toole, M. L. (1998). Overtraining in sport. *International Journal of Sport Psychology, 27*(3), 269–285.

Krosnick, J. A. (1988). Attitude importance and attitude change. *Journal of Experimental Social Psychology, 24,* 240–255.

Krosnick, J. A., & Alwin, D. F. (1989). Aging and susceptibility to attitude change. *Journal of Personality and Social Psychology, 57,* 416–425.

Krosnick, J. A., Jussim, L. J., & Lynn, A. R. (1992). Subliminal conditioning of attitudes. *Personality and Social Psychology Bulletin, 18*(2), 152–162.

Kruley, P., Sciama, S. C., & Glenberg, A. M. (1994). On-line processing of textual illustrations in the visuospatial sketchpad: Evidence from dual-task studies. *Memory and Cogni tion, 22,* 261–272.

Kubey, R., & Csikszentmihalyi, M. (1990). *Television and the quality of life.* Hillsdale, NJ: Erlbaum.

Kübler-Ross, E. (1969). *On death and dying.* New York: Macmillan.

Kübler-Ross, E. (1975). *Death: The final stage of growth.* Englewood Cliffs, NJ: Prentice-Hall.

Kudoh, N., Tajima, H., Hatayama, T., Maruyama, K., Shoji, Y., Hayashi, T., & Nakanishi, M. (1991). Effects of room environment on human cognitive activities. *Tohoku Psychologica Folia, 50,* 45–54.

Kuhl, P. K., Andruski, J. E., Chistovich, I. A., Chistovich, L. A., Kozhevnikova, E. V., Ryskina, V. L., Stolyarova, E. I., Sundberg, U., & Lacerda, F. (1997). Cross-language analysis of phonetic units in language addressed to infants. *Science, 277,* 684–686.

Kuhl, P. K., Williams, K. A., Lacerda, F., Stevens, K. N., & Lindblom, B. (1992). Linguistic experience alters phonetic perception in infants by 6 months of age. *Science, 255,* 606–655.

Kuiper, N. A., & Martin, R. A. (1998). Laughter and stress in daily life: Relation to positive and negative affect. *Motivation and Emotion, 22*(2), 133–153.

Kutchins, H., & Kirk, S. A. (1997). *Making us crazy. DSM: The psychiatric bible and the creation of mental disorders.* New York: The Free Press.

Lachman, M. E., & James, J. B. (1997). *Multiple paths of midlife development. Studies on successful midlife development: The John D. and Catherine T. MacArthur Foundation series on mental health and development.* Chicago: The University of Chicago Press.

Lachman, M. E., & Weaver, S. L. (1998). Sociodemographic variations in the sense of control by domain: Findings from the MacArthur studies of midlife. *Psychology and Aging, 13*(4), 553–562.

Ladd, G. W. (1990). Having friends, keeping friends, making friends, and being liked by peers in the classroom: Predictors of children's early school adjustment? *Child Development, 61,* 1081–1100.

Laessle, R. G., Wurmser, H., & Pirke, K. M. (1997). A comparison of resting metabolic rate, self-rated food intake, growth hormone, and insulin levels in obese and nonobese preadolescents. *Physiology and Behavior, 61*(5), 725–729.

LaFerla, J. J., Anderson, D. L., & Schalch, D. S. (1978). Psychoendocrine response to sexual arousal in human males. *Psychosomatic Medicine, 40,* 166–172.

Lafferty, P., Beutler, L. E., & Crago, M. (1989). Differences between more and less effective psychotherapists: A study of select therapist variables. *Journal of Consulting and Clinical Psychology, 57,* 76–80.

Lahey, B. B., McNees, M. P., & McNees, M. C. (1973). Control of an obscene "verbal tic" through timeout in an elementary school classroom. *Journal of Applied Behavior Analysis, 6,* 101–104.

Lambert, A. J. (1995). Stereotypes and social judgment: The consequences of group variability. *Journal of Personality and Social Psychology, 68,* 388–403.

Landrine, H., Klonoff, E. A., & Brown-Collins, A. (1992). Cultural diversity and methodology in feminist psychology. *Psychology of Women Quarterly, 16,* 145–163.

Lang, P. J. (1994). The varieties of emotional experience: A meditation on James–Lange theory. *Psychological Review, 101,* 211–221.

Lange, C. G. (1922). *The emotions* (English translation). Baltimore: Williams & Wilkins. (Original work published 1885.)

Langer, E. J. (1989). *Mindfulness.* Reading, MA: Addison-Wesley.

Langer, E. J. (1992). Matters of mind: Mindfulness/mindlessness in perspective. *Consciousness and Cognition: An International Journal, 1*(4), 289–305.

Langer, E. J. (1993). A mindful education. *Educational Psychologist, 28*(1), 43–50.

Langer, E. J. (1997). *The power of mindful learning.* Reading, MA: Addison-Wesley.

Langlois, J. H., Ritter, J. M., Casey, R. J., & Sawin, D. B. (1995). Infant attractiveness predicts maternal behaviors and attitudes. *Developmental Psychology, 31,* 464–472.

Langlois, J. H., Ritter, J. M., Roggman, L. A., & Vaughn, L. S. (1991). Facial diversity and infant preferences for attractive faces. *Developmental Psychology, 27,* 79–84.

Langlois, J. H., Roggman, L. A., & Rieser-Danner, L. A. (1990). Infants' differential social responses to attractive and unattractive faces. *Developmental Psychology, 26,* 153–159.

Langman, B., & Cockburn, A. (1975). Sirhan's gun. *Harper's, 250,* 16–27.

Lapsley, D. K. (1993). Toward an integrated theory of adolescent ego development: The "new look" at adolescent egocentrism. *American Journal of Orthopsychiatry, 63*(4), 562–571.

Lapsley, D. K. (1996). *Moral psychology.* Boulder, CO: Westview.

Larrick, R. P., Morgan, J. N., & Nisbett, R. E. (1990). Teaching the use of cost–benefit reasoning in everyday life. *Psychological Science, 1,* 362–370.

Larson, R., & Ham, M. (1993). Stress and "storm and stress" in early adolescence: The relationship of negative events with dysphoric affect. *Developmental Psychology, 29,* 130–140.

Larson, R. W., Raffaelli, M., Richards, M. H., Ham, M., & Jewell, L. (1990). Ecology of depression in late childhood and early adolescence: A profile of daily states and activities. *Journal of Abnormal Psychology, 99,* 92–102.

Lassner, J. B., Matthews, K. A., & Stoney, C. M. (1994). Are cardiovascular reactors to asocial stress also reactors to social stress? *Journal of Personality and Social Psychology, 66,* 69–77.

Last, C. G., Hersen, M., Kazdin, A., Orvaschel, H., & Perrin, S. (1991). Anxiety disorders in children and their families. *Archives of General Psychiatry, 48,* 928–931.

Last, C. G., & Perrin, S. (1993). Anxiety disorders in African-American and white children. *Journal of Abnormal Child Psychology, 21,* 153–164.

Latané, B., & Darley, J. M. (1970). *The unresponsive bystander: Why doesn't he help?* New York: Meredith.

Latané, B., Williams, K., & Harkins, S. (1979). Many hands make light work: The causes and consequences of social loafing. *Journal of Personality and Social Psychology, 37,* 822–832.

Latham, G. P., Daghighi, S., & Locke, E. A. (1997). Implications of goal-setting theory for faculty motivation. In J. L. Bess et al. (Eds.), *Teaching well and liking it: Motivating faculty to teach effectively* (pp. 125–142). Baltimore, MD: Johns Hopkins University Press.

Laumann, E. O., Gagnon, J. H., Michael, R. T. & Michaels, S. (1994). *The social organization of sexuality: Sexual practices in the United States.* Chicago: The University of Chicago Press.

Laumann, E. O., Paik, A., & Rosen, R. C. (1999). Sexual dysfunction in the United States: Prevalence and predictors. *Journal of the American Medical Association, 281*(6), 537–544.

Laursen, B., Coy, K. C., & Collins, A. (1998). Reconsidering changes in parent–child conflict across adolescence: A meta-analysis. *Society for Research in Child Development, 69*(3), 817–832.

Lavie, P. (1996). *The enchanted world of sleep.* New Haven, CT and London: Yale University Press.

Lawler, E. E., & Porter, L. W. (1967). Antecedent attitudes of effective managerial performance. *Organizational Behavior and Human Performance, 2,* 122–142.

Lawler, J. J., & Elliot, R. (1996). Artificial intelligence in HRM: An experimental study of an expert system. *Journal of Management, 22*(1), 85–111.

Lazarus, A. A., & Fay, A. (1990). Brief psychotherapy: Tautology or oxymoron? In J. K. Zeig & S. G. Gilligan (Eds.), *Brief therapy myths, methods, and metaphors.* New York: Brunner/Mazel.

Lazarus, R. S. (1982). The psychology of stress and coping, with particular reference to Israel. In C. D. Spielberger, I. G. Sarason, & N. A. Milgram (Eds.), *Stress and anxiety* (Vol. 8). Washington, DC: Hemisphere.

Lazarus, R. S. (1984). The trivialization of distress. In B. L. Hammonds & C. J. Scheirer (Eds.), *Psychology and health: The master lecture series.* Washington, DC: American Psychological Association.

Lazarus, R. S. (1993). From psychological stress to the emotions: A history of changing outlooks. *Annual Review of Psychology, 44,* 1–21.

Lazarus, R. S., & Alfert, E. (1964). Short-circuiting of threat by experimentally altering cognitive appraisal. *Journal of Abnormal and Social Psychology, 69,* 195–205.

Lazarus, R. S., & DeLongis, A. (1983). Psychological stress and coping in aging. *American Psychologist, 38,* 245–254.

Leahey, T. H. (1992). The mythical revolutions of American psychology. *American Psychologist, 47,* 308–318.

Leaper, C. Anderson, K. J., & Sanders, P. (1998). Moderators of gender effects on parents' talk to their children: A meta-analysis. *Developmental Psychology, 34*(1), 3–27.

Lebow, J. L., & Gurman, A. S. (1995). Research assessing couple and family therapy. *Annual Review of Psychology, 46,* 27–57.

LeDoux, J. (1996). *The emotional brain: The mysterious underpinnings of emotional life.* New York: Simon and Schuster.

LeDoux, J. E. (1993). Emotional memory systems in the brain. *Behavioural Brain Research, 58,* 69–79.

LeDoux, J. E. (1995). Emotion: Clues from the brain. *Annual Review of Psychology, 46,* 209–235.

LeDoux, J. E., Romanski, L., & Xagoraris, A. (1989). Indelibility of subcortical emotional memories. *Journal of Cognitive Neuroscience, 1,* 238–243.

Lee, C., Ashford, S. J., & Bobko, P. (1990). Interactive effects of "Type A" behavior and perceived control on worker performance, job satisfaction, and somatic complaints. *Academy of Management Journal, 33,* 870–881.

Lefcourt, H. M. (1992). Durability and impact of the locus of control construct. *Psychological Bulletin, 112,* 411–414.

Lefcourt, H. M., & Davidson-Katz, K. (1991). Locus of control and health. In C. R. Snyder & D. R. Forsyth (Eds.),

Handbook of social and clinical psychology (pp. 246–266). New York: Pergamon.

Lefcourt, H. M., & Thomas, S. (1998). Humor and stress revisited. In W. Ruch et al. (Eds.), *The sense of humor: Explorations of a personality characteristic. Humor research: 3* (pp. 179–202). Berlin: Walter De Gruyter.

Leffler, C. T., & Dembert, M. L. (1998). Posttraumatic stress symptoms among U.S. Navy divers recovering TWA Flight 800. *Journal of Nervous and Mental Disease, 186*(9), 574–577.

Lefkowitz, M. M., Eron, L. D., Walder, L. O., & Huesmann, L. R. (1977). *Growing up to be violent.* New York: Pergamon.

Leibowitz, H. W. (1971). Sensory, learned, and cognitive mechanisms of size perception. *Annals of the New York Academy of Sciences, 1988,* 47–62.

Leikin, R., & Zaslavsky, O. (1997). Facilitating student interactions in mathematics in a cooperative learning setting. *Journal for Research in Mathematics Education, 28*(3), 331–354.

Leinbach, M. D., Hort, B. E., & Fagot, B. I. (1997). Bears are for boys: Metaphorical associations in young children's gender stereotypes. *Cognitive Development, 12,* 107–130.

Leiner, H. C., Leiner, A. L., & Dow, R. S. (1986). Does the cerebellum contribute to mental skills? *Behavioral Neuroscience, 100,* 443–454.

Lenneberg, E. H. (1967). *Biological foundations of language.* New York: Wiley.

Leon, M. (1992). The neurobiology of filial learning. *Annual Review of Psychology, 43,* 377–399.

Leonard, B. E. (1987). Stress, the immune system and mental illness. *Stress Medicine, 3*(4), 257–258.

Leonard, C. M., Lombardino, L. J., Mercado, L. R., Browd, S. R., Breier, J. I., & Agee, O. F. (1996). Cerebral asymmetry and cognitive development in children: A magnetic resonance imaging study. *American Psychological Society, 7*(2), 89–95.

Leonard-Barton, D. (1981). The diffusion of active residential solar energy equipment in California. In A. Shama (Ed.), *Marketing solar energy innovations* (pp. 243–257). New York: Praeger.

Lepine, J. P., & Bouchez, S. (1998). Epidemiology of depression in the elderly. *International Clinical Psychopharmacology, 13*(Suppl. 5), S7–S12.

Lepper, M. R., & Greene, D. (1978). Overjustification research and beyond: Toward a means–end analysis of intrinsic motivation. In M. R. Lepper & D. Greene (Eds.), *The hidden cost of reward.* Hillsdale, NJ: Erlbaum.

Lesch, K. P., Bengel, D., Heils, A., Sabol, S. Z., Greenberg, B. D., Petri, S., Benjamin, J., Müller, C. R., Hamer, D. H., & Murphy, D. L. (1996). Association of anxiety-related traits with a polymorphism in the serotonin transporter gene regulatory region. *Science, 274,* 1527–1531.

Leserman, J., Petitto, J. M., Perkins, D. O., Folds, J. D., Golden, R. N., et al. (1997). Severe stress, depressive symptoms, and changes in lymphocyte subsets in human immunodeficiency virus-infected men. A 2-year follow-up study. *Archives of General Psychiatry, 54*(3), 279–285.

Lessard, N., Paré, M., Lepore, F., & Lassonde, M. (1998). Early-blind human subjects localize sound sources better than sighted subjects. *Nature, 395,* 278–280.

Lester, B. M., & Dreher, M. (1989). Effects of marijuana use during pregnancy on newborn cry. *Child Development, 60,* 765–771.

LeVay, S. (1991). A difference in hypothalamic structure between heterosexual and homosexual men. *Science, 253,* 1034–1037.

LeVay, S., & Hamer, D. H. (1994, May). Evidence for a biological influence in male homosexuality. *Scientific American,* 44–49.

Levenson, R. W. (1992). Autonomic nervous system differences among emotions. *Psychological Science, 3,* 23–27.

Levenstein, S., Prantera, C., Varvo, V., & Arca, M. (1996). Long-term symptom patterns in duodenal ulcer: Psychosocial factors. *Journal of Psychosomatic Research, 41*(5), 465–472.

Levi, L. (1990). Occupational stress. *American Psychologist, 46,* 1142–1145.

Levin, D. J. (1990). *Alcoholism.* New York: Hemisphere.

Levin, J. S., & Taylor, R. J. (1997). Age differences in patterns and correlates of the frequency of prayer. *Gerontologist, 37*(1), 75–88.

Levine, E. L., Ash, R. A., Hall, H., & Sistrunk, F. (1983). Evaluation of job analysis methods by experienced job analysts. *Academy of Management Journal, 26,* 339–348.

Levine, J. A., Eberhardt, N. L., & Jensen, M. D. (1999). Role of nonexercise activity thermogenesis in resistance to fat gain in humans. *Science, 283,* 212–214.

Levine, M. (1998). Prevention and community. *American Journal of Community Psychology, 26*(2), 189–206.

LeVine, R. (1966). Sex roles and economic change in Africa. *Ethnology, 5,* 186–193.

Levine, R. L., & Stadtman, E. R. (1992). Oxidation of proteins during aging. *Generations, 16,* 39–42.

Levine, R. V., Martinez, T. S., Brase, G., & Sorenson, K. (1994). Helping in 36 U.S. cities. *Journal of Personality and Social Psychology, 67,* 69–82.

Levinson, D. J. (1978). *The seasons of a man's life.* New York: Knopf.

Levinson, D. J. (1980). Toward a conception of the adult life course. In N. J. Smelser & E. H. Erikson (Eds.), *Themes of work and love in adulthood.* Cambridge, MA: Harvard University Press.

Levinson, D. J. (1996). *The seasons of a woman's life.* New York: Alfred A. Knopf.

Levitt, M. J., Weber, R. A., Clark, M. C., & McDonnell, P. (1985). Reciprocity of exchange in toddler sharing behavior. *Developmental Psychology, 21,* 122–123.

Lewin, K. K. (1970). *Brief psychotherapy.* St. Louis, MO: Warren H. Green.

Lewinsohn, P. M. (1974). Classical and theoretical aspects of depression. In I. S. Calhoun, H. E. Adams, & K. M. Mitchell (Eds.), *Innovative treatment methods in psychopathology.* New York: Wiley Interscience.

Lewinsohn, P. M., Rohde, P., Klein, D. N., & Seeley, J. R. (1999). Natural course of adolescent major depressive disorder: I. Continuity into young adulthood. *Journal of the American Academy of Child and Adolescent Psychiatry, 38*(1), 56–63.

Lewinsohn, P. M., Rohde, P., Klein, D. N., Seeley, J. R., & Fischer, S. A. (1993). Age-cohort changes in the lifetime occurrence of depression and other mental disorders. *Journal of Abnormal Psychology, 102*(1), 110–120.

Lewinsohn, P. M., & Talkington, J. (1979). Studies on the measurement of unpleasant events and relations with depression. *Applied Psychological Measurement, 3,* 83–101.

Lewis, M. (1995). Self-conscious emotions. *American Scientist, 83,* 68–78.

Lewis, M. (1997). *Altering fate: Why the past does not predict the future.* New York: The Guilford Press.

Lewis, M. (1998). Altering fate: Why the past does not predict the future. *Psychological Inquiry, 9*(2), 105–108.

Lewis, M., & Feiring, C. (1989). Infant, mother, and mother–infant interaction behavior and subsequent attachment. *Child Development, 60,* 831–837.

Lidsky, T. I., Yablonski-Alter, E., Zuck, L. G., & Banerjee, S. P. (1997). Antipsychotic drug effects on glutamatergic activity. *Brain Research, 764*(1/2), 46–52.

Lidz, T. (1973). *The origin and treatment of schizophrenic disorders.* New York: Basic Books.

Liebrand, W. B. G., Messick, D. M., & Wolters, F. J. M. (1986). Why we are fairer than others: A cross-cultural replication and extension. *Journal of Experimental Social Psychology, 22,* 590–604.

Lilla, I., Szikriszt, E., Ortutay, J., Berecz, M., Gyoergy, F., & Attila, N. (1998). Psychological factors contributing to the development of coronary artery disease—a study of rigidity and the A-type behaviour pattern. *Psychiatria Hungarica, 13*(2), 169–180.

Lillo-Martin, D. (1997). The modular effects of sign language acquisition. In M. Marschark, P. Siple, et al. (Eds.), *Relations of language and thought* (pp. 62–109). New York: Oxford University Press.

Lilly, J. C. (1956). Mental effects of reduction of ordinary levels of physical stimuli in intact, healthy persons. *Psychiatric Research Reports, 5,* 1–28.

Linberg, M. A., Beggs, A. L., Chezik, D. D., & Ray, D. (1982). Flavor–toxicosis associations: Tests of three hypotheses of long delay learning. *Physiology and Behavior, 29,* 439–442.

Lindfors, O., Hannula, J., Aalber, V., Kaarento, K., Kaipainen, M., & Pylkkaenen, K. (1995). Assessment of the effectiveness of psychotherapy. *Psychiatria Fennica, 26,* 150–164.

Lindsay, D. S. (1993). Eyewitness suggestibility. *Current Directions in Psychological Science, 2,* 86–89.

Lindsey, K. P., & Paul, G. L. (1989). Involuntary commitments to public mental institutions: Issues involving the overrepresentation of blacks and assessment of relevant functioning. *Psychological Bulletin, 106,* 171–183.

Lindvall, O. (1991). Prospects of transplantation in human neurodegenerative diseases. *Trends in Neurosciences, 14,* 376–384.

Lindvall, O., Brundin, P., Widner, H., Rehncrona, S., Gustavi, B., Frackowiak, R., Leenders, K. L., Sawle, G., Rothwell, J. C., Marsden, C. D., & Bjorklund, A. (1990). Grafts of fetal dopamine neurons survive and improve motor function in Parkinson's disease. *Science, 247,* 374–577.

Linn, M. C., & Petersen, A. C. (1985). Emergence and characterization of sex differences in spatial ability: A meta-analysis. *Child Development, 56,* 1479–1498.

Lippincott, J. A., & Mierzwa, J. A. (1995). Propensity for seeking counseling services: A comparison of Asian and American undergraduates. *Journal of American College Health, 43*(5), 201–204.

Lips, H. (1994). Female powerlessness. In H. L. Radtke & H. J. Stam (Eds.), *Power/gender: Social relations in theory and practice.* London: Sage Publications.

Lipsey, M. W., & Wilson, D. B. (1993). The efficacy of psychological, educational, and behavioral treatment: Confirmation from meta-analysis. *American Psychologist, 48,* 1181–1209.

Livson, N., & Peskin, H. (1967). Prediction of adult psychological health in a longitudinal study. *Journal of Abnormal Psychology, 72*(6), 509–518.

Locher, P., Unger, R., Sociedade, P., & Wahl, J. (1993). At first glance: Accessibility of the physical attractiveness stereotype. *Sex Roles, 28,* 729–743.

Locke, E. A. (1996). Motivation through conscious goal setting. *Allied and Preventive Psychology, 5*(2), 117–124.

Locke, E. A., & Latham, G. P. (1990a). Work motivation: The high performance cycle. In U. Kleinbeck, H. Quast, H. Thierry, & H. Hacker (Eds.), *Work motivation.* Hillsdale, NJ: Erlbaum.

Locke, E. A., & Latham, G. P. (1990b). Work motivation and satisfaction: Light at the end of the tunnel. *Psychological Science, 1,* 240–246.

Loeber, R., & Stouthamer-Loeber, M. (1998). Development of juvenile aggression and violence: Some common misconceptions and controversies. *American Psychologist, 53*(2), 242–259.

Loehlin, J. C., McCrae, R. R., Costa, P. T., Jr., & John, O. P. Heritabilities of common and measure-specific components of the Big Five personality factors. *Journal of Research in Personality, 32*(4), 431–453.

Loewenstein, R. J. (1993). Dissociation, development, and the psychobiology of trauma. *Journal of the American Academy of Psychoanalysis, 21,* 581–603.

Loftus, E. F. (1979). The malleability of human memory. *American Scientist, 67,* 310–320.

Loftus, E. F. (1991). *Witness for the defense.* New York: St. Martin's.

Loftus, E. F. (1993). The reality of repressed memories. *American Psychologist, 48,* 518–537.

Loftus, E. F. (1997). Memory for a past that never was. *American Psychological Society, 6*(3), 60–65.

Lollis, S., Ross, H., & Leroux, L. (1996). An observational study of parents' socialization of moral orientation during sibling conflicts. *Merrill-Palmer Quarterly, 42,* 475–494.

Lombard, D. N., Lombard, T. N., & Winett, R. A. (1995). Walking to meet health guidelines: The effect of prompting frequency and prompt structure. *Health Psychology, 14,* 164–170.

Lore, R. K., & Schultz, L. A. (1993). Control of human aggression. *American Psychologist, 48,* 16–25.

Lorenz, F. O., Simons, R. L., & Conger, R. D. (1997). Married and recently divorced mothers' stressful events and distress: Tracing change across time. *Journal of Marriage and the Family, 59,* 219–232.

Lorenz, K. (1964). Ritualized fighting. In J. D. Carthy & F. J. Ebling (Eds.), *The natural history of aggression.* New York: Academic Press.

Lowe, M. R., Gleaves, D. H., & Murphy-Eberenz, K. P. (1998). The relation of dieting and bingeing in bulimia nervosa. *Journal of Abnormal Psychology, 107*(2), 263–271.

Lowell, E. L. (1952). The effect of need for achievement on learning and speed of performance. *Journal of Psychology, 33,* 31–40.

Lowenstein, R. J. (1993). Dissociation, development, and the psychobiology of trauma. *Journal of the American Academy of Psychoanalysis, 21*(4), 581–603.

Luborsky, L., Barber, J. P., & Crits-Christoph, P. (1990). Theory-based research for understanding the process of dynamic psychotherapy. *Journal of Consulting and Clinical Psychology, 58,* 281–287.

Lucidi, F., Devoto, A., Violani, C., Mastracci, P., & Bertini, M. (1997). Effects of different sleep duration on delta sleep in recovery nights. *Psychophysiology, 34,* 227–233.

Ludwick-Rosenthal, R., & Neufeld, W. J. (1988). Stress management during noxious medical procedures: An evaluative review of outcome studies. *Psychological Bulletin, 3,* 326–342.

Luecke-Aleksa, D., Anderson, D. R., Collins, P. A., & Schmitt, K. L. (1995). Gender constancy and television viewing. *Developmental Psychology, 31,* 773–780.

Luger, G. F., Bower, T. G. R., & Wishart, J. G. (1983). A model of the development of the early infant object concept. *Perception, 12,* 21–34.

Lundin, R. W. (1961). *Personality: An experimental approach.* New York: Macmillan.

Lundy, B., Field, T., McBride, C., Field, T., & Largie, S. (1998). Same-sex and opposite-sex best friend interactions among high school juniors and seniors. *Adolescence, 33*(130), 279–289.

Luttrell, W. (1989). Working-class women's ways of knowing: Effects of gender, race, and class. *Sociology of Education, 62*(1), 33–46.

Luus, C. A. E., & Wells, G. L. (1994). The malleability of eyewitness confidence: Co-witness and perseverance effects. *Journal of Applied Psychology, 79,* 714–723.

Lykken, D., & Tellegen, A. (1996). Happiness is a stochastic phenomenon. *American Psychological Association, 7*(3), 186–189.

Lykken, D. T. (1998) *A tremor in the blood: Uses and abuses of the lie detector.* New York: Plenum Press.

Lykken, D. T., McGue, M., Tellegen, A., & Bouchard, T. J., Jr. (1992). Emergenesis. *American Psychologist, 47,* 1565–1577.

Lynch, G., & Baudry, M. (1984). The biochemistry of memory: A new and specific hypothesis. *Science, 224,* 1057–1063.

Lynn, M., & Mynier, K. (1993). Effect of server posture on restaurant tipping. *Journal of Applied Social Psychology, 23,* 678–685.

Lynn, S. J. (1992). A non-state view of hypnotic involuntariness. *Contemporary Hypnosis, 9*(1), 21–27.

Lynn, S. J., Lock, T. G., Myers, B., & Payne, D. G. (1997). Recalling the unrecallable: Should hypnosis be used to recover memories in psychotherapy? *American Psychological Society, 6*(3), 79–83.

Lyons, M. J., Eisen, S. A., Goldberg, J., True, W., Lin, N., Meyer, J. M., Toomey, R., Faraone, S. V., Merla-Ramos, M., & Tsuang, M. T. (1998). A registry-based twin study of depression in men. *Archives of General Psychiatry, 55*(5), 468–472.

Lyons, M. J., True, W. R., Eisen, S. A., Goldberg, J., Meyer, J. M., Faraone, S. V., Eaves, L. J., & Tsuang, M. T. (1995). Differential heritability of adult and juvenile antisocial traits. *Archives of General Psychiatry, 52,* 906–915.

Lytton, H., & Romney, D. M. (1991). Parents' differential socialization of boys and girls: A meta-analysis. *Psychological Bulletin, 109,* 267–296.

Lyubomirsky, S., & Tucker, K. L. (1998). Implications of individual differences in subjective happiness for perceiving, interpreting, and thinking about life events. *Motivation and Emotion, 22*(2), 155–186.

Maas, J. B. (1998). *Power sleep.* New York: Villard.

Maccoby, E. E. (1988). Gender as a social category. *Developmental Psychology, 24,* 755–765.

Maccoby, E. E. (1998). *The two sexes: Growing up apart, coming together.* Cambridge, MA: Harvard University Press.

Mack, A., & Rock, I. (1998). *Inattentional blindness.* Cambridge, MA: MIT Press.

MacKay, N. J., & Covell, D. (1997). The impact of women in advertisements on attitudes toward women. *Sex Roles, 36*(9/10), 573–576.

MacLeod, C. M. (1991). Half a century of research on the Stroop effect: An integrative review. *Psychological Bulletin, 109,* 163–203.

MacWhinney, B. (1998). Models of the emergence of language. *Annual Review of Psychology, 49,* 199–227.

Maddux, J. E. (1995). Self-efficacy theory: An introduction. In J. E. Maddux (Ed.), *Self-efficacy, adaptation, and adjustment: Theory, research, and application* (pp. 3–33). New York: Plenum.

Maddux, J. E., & Meier, L. J. (1995). Self-efficacy and depression. In J. E. Maddux (Ed.), *Self-efficacy, adaptation, and adjustment: Theory, research, and application* (pp. 143–169). New York: Plenum.

Madigan, M. F., Jr., Dale, J. A., & Cross, J. D. (1997). No respite during sleep: Heart-rate hyperreactivity to rapid eye movement sleep in angry men classified as Type A. *Perceptual and Motor Skills, 85*(3, Pt. 2), 1451–1454.

Madrazo, I., Drucken-Colin, R., Diaz, V., Martinez-Mata, J., Toress, C., & Becerril, J. J. (1987). Open microsurgical autograft of adrenal medulla to the right caudate nucleus in two patients with intractable Parkinson's disease. *New England Journal of Medicine, 316,* 831–834.

Magdol, L., Moffitt, T. E., Caspi, A., & Silva, P. A. (1998). Developmental antecedents of partner abuse: A prospective-longitudinal study. *Journal of Abnormal Psychology, 107*(3), 375–389.

Magolda, M. B. (1990). Gender differences in epistemological development. *Journal of College Student Development, 31,* 555–561.

Maguire, E. A., Burgess, N., Donnett, J. G., Frackowiak, R. S. J., Frith, C. D., & O'Keefe, J. (1998). Knowing where and getting there: A human navigation network. *Science, 280,* 921–924.

Mahoney, M. J. (1977). Reflections on the cognitive–learning trend in psychotherapy. *American Psychologist, 32,* 5–13.

Mahoney, M. J. (1993). Introduction to special section: Theoretical developments in the cognitive psychotherapies. *Journal of Consulting and Clinical Psychology, 61,* 187–193.

Mahrer, A. R., & Nadler, W. P. (1986). Good moments in psychotherapy: A preliminary review, a list, and some promising research avenues. *Journal of Consulting and Clinical Psychology, 54,* 10–15.

Maier, N. R. F., & Klee, J. B. (1941). Studies of abnormal behavior in the rat: 17. Guidance versus trial and error and their relation to convulsive tendencies. *Journal of Experimental Psychology, 29,* 380–389.

Maier, S. F., & Watkins, L. R. (1998). Cytokines for psychologists: Implications of bidirectional immune-to-brain communication for understanding behavior, mood, and cognition. *Psychological Review, 105*(1), 83–107.

Maier, S. F., Watkins, L. R., & Fleshner, M. (1994). Psychoneuroimmunology: The interface between behavior, brain, and immunity. *American Psychologist, 49,* 1004–1017.

Malamuth, N. M., & Sockloskie, R. J. (1991). Characteristics of aggressors against women: Testing a model using a national sample of college students. *Journal of Consulting and Clinical Psychology, 59,* 670–681.

Malik, A., & Batra, P. (1998). Effect of crowding on a complex task. *Journal of Personality and Clinical Studies, 13*(1/2), 87–91.

Mamelak, M. (1991). A model for narcolepsy. *Canadian Journal of Psychology, 45,* 194–220.

Mangan, B. (1993). Dennett, consciousness, and the sorrows of functionalism. *Consciousness and Cognition, 2,* 1–17.

Manlove, J. (1998). The influence of high school dropout and school disengagement on the risk of school-age pregnancy. *Journal of Research on Adolescence, 8*(2), 187–220.

Mann, J. J., Malone, D. M., Diehl, D. J., Cooper, T. B., & Mintun, M. A. (1996). Demonstration in vivo of reduced serotonin reponsivity in the brain of untreated depressed patients. *American Journal of Psychiatry, 153*(2), 174–182.

Mann, J. J., Oquendo, M., Underwood, M. D., & Arango, V. (1999). The neurobiology of suicide risk: A review for the clinician. *Journal of Clinical Psychiatry, 60*(Suppl. 2), 7–11.

Mantzicopoulos, P. Y. (1997). The relationship of family variables to Head Start children's pre-academic competence. *Early Education & Development, 8*(4), 357–375.

Manuck, S. B., Cohen, S., Rabin, B. S., Muldoon, M. F., & Bachen, E. A. (1991). Individual differences in cellular immune response to stress. *Psychological Science, 2,* 111–115.

Manuck, S. B., Marsland, A. L., Kaplan, J. R., & Williams, J. K. (1995). The pathogenicity of behavior and its neuroendocrine mediation: An example from coronary artery disease. *Psychosomatic Medicine, 57,* 275–283.

March, J. S., Leonard, H. L., & Swedo, S. E. (1995). Obsessive–compulsive disorder. In J. S. March (Ed.), *Anxiety disorders in children and adolescents* (pp. 251–275). New York: Guilford.

Marcus, G. F., Vijayan, S., Bandi, R., & Vishton, P. M. (1999). Rule learning by seven-month-old infants. *Science, 283,* 77–79.

Maris, R., & Silverman, M. M. (1995). *Suicide prevention: Toward the year 2000.* New York: Guilford.

Markow, T. M. (1992). Genetics and developmental stability: An integrative conjecture on aetiology and neurobiology of schizophrenia. *Psychological Medicine, 22,* 295–305.

Markowitsch, H. J., & Tulving, E. (1994). Cognitive processes and cerebral cortical fundi: Findings from positron-emission tomography studies. *Proceedings of the National Academy of Sciences of the United States of America, 91,* 10507–10511.

Marks, I. M. (1977). Clinical phenomena in search of laboratory models. In J. D. Maser & M. E. P. Seligman (Eds.), *Psychopathology experimental models.* San Francisco: Freeman.

Marks, I. M. et al. (1986). *Behavioral psychotherapy: Pocketbook of clinical management.* Bristol, England: John Wright.

Marks, W. B., Dobell, W. H., & MacNichol, J. R. (1964). The visual pigments of single primate cones. *Science, 142,* 1181–1183.

Marlatt, G. A., Larimer, M. E., Baer, J. S., & Quigley, L. A. (1993). Harm reduction for alcohol problems: Moving beyond the controlled drinking. *Behavior Therapy, 24,* 461–504.

Marquis, D. P. (1931). Can conditioned responses be established in the newborn infant? *Journal of Genetic Psychology, 39,* 479–492.

Marschark, M., Yuille, J. C., Richman, C. L., & Hunt, R. R. (1987). The role of imagery in memory: On shared and distinctive information. *Psychological Bulletin, 102,* 28–41.

Marshall, G. N., Wortman, C. B., Vickers, R. R., Jr., Kusulas, J. W., & Hervig, L. K. (1994). The five-factor model of personality as a framework for personality–health research. *Journal of Personality and Social Psychology, 67,* 278–286.

Marshall, L. L., & Vitanza, S. A. (1994). Physical abuse in close relationships: Myths and realities. In A. L. Weber &

J. H. Harvey (Eds.), *Perspectives on close relationships* (pp. 263–284). Boston: Allyn & Bacon.

Marshall, W. A., & Tanner, J. M. (1969). Variations in the pattern of pubertal changes in girls. *Archives of Disease in Childhood, 44,* 291–303.

Martin, C., Hill, K. K., & Welsh, R. (1998). Adolescent pregnancy, a stressful life event: Cause and consequence. In T. W. Miller et al. (Eds.), *Children of trauma: Stressful life events and their effects on children and adolescents.* Madison, CT: International Universities Press.

Martin, R., & Haroldson, S. (1977). Effect of vicarious punishment on stuttering frequency. *Journal of Speech and Hearing Research, 20,* 21–26.

Martindale, C., Hines, D., Mitchell, L., & Covello, E. (1984). EEG alpha asymmetry and creativity. *Personality and Individual Differences, 5*(1), 77–86.

Masia, C. L., & Chase, P. N. (1997). Vicarious learning revisited: A contemporary behavior analytic interpretation. *Journal of Behavior Therapy and Experimental Psychiatry, 28*(1), 41–51.

Maslow, A. H. (1962). *Toward a psychology of being.* New York: Van Nostrand.

Maslow, A. H. (1969). Toward a humanistic biology. *American Psychologist, 24,* 734–735.

Masotto, C., & Racagni, G. (1995). Biological aspects of schizophrenia. *Rivista di Psichiatria, 30*(4), 34–46.

Masters, W. H., Johnson, V. E., & Kolodny, R. C. (1994). *Heterosexuality.* New York: HarperCollins.

Matarazzo, J. D. (1990). Psychological assessment versus psychological testing. *American Psychologist, 45,* 999–1017.

Matsui, T., & Onglatco, M. L. U. (1990). Relationships between employee quality circle involvement and need fulfillment in work as moderated by work type: A compensatory or a spillover model? In U. Kleinbeck, H. Quast, H. Thierry, & H. Hacker (Eds.), *Work motivation.* Hillsdale, NJ: Erlbaum.

Matsumoto, D. (1994). *People: Psychology from a cultural perspective.* Pacific Grove, CA: Brooks/Cole.

Matsumoto, D. (1996). *Culture and psychology,* Pacific Grove, CA: Brooks/Cole.

Matsumoto, D., & Kudoh, T. (1993). American–Japanese cultural differences in attributions of personality based on smiles. *Journal of Nonverbal Behavior, 17,* 231–243.

Matthews, K. A. (1988). Coronary heart disease and Type A behaviors: Update on and alternative to the Booth-Kewley and Friedman (1987) quantitative review. *Psychological Bulletin, 104,* 373–380.

Matthies, H. (1989). Neurobiological aspects of learning and memory. *Annual Review of Psychology, 40,* 381–404.

Maunsell, J. H. R. (1995). The brain's visual world: Representation of visual targets in the cerebral cortex. *Science, 270,* 764–769.

Mayer, J. D., & Salovey, P. (1997). What is emotional intelligence? In P. Salovey & D. J. Sluyter (Eds.), *Emotional development and emotional intelligence.* New York: Basic Books.

McAuley, E., Duncan, T. E., & McElroy, M. (1989). Self-efficacy cognitions and causal attributions for children's motor performance: An exploratory investigation. *Journal of Genetic Psychology, 150,* 65–73.

McBride, A. B. (1990). Mental health effects of women's multiple roles. *American Psychologist, 45,* 381–384.

McCandliss, B. D., Posner, M. I., & Given, T. (1997). Brain plasticity in learning visual words. *Cognitive Psychology, 33,* 88–110.

McCarty, D., Argeriou, M., Huebner, R. B., & Lubran, B. (1991). Alcoholism, drug abuse, and the homeless. *American Psychologist, 46,* 1139–1148.

McCaul, K. D., Jacobson, K., & Martinson, B. (1998). The effects of a state-wide media campaign on mammography screening. *Journal of Applied Social Psychology, 28*(6), 504–515.

McCauley, C. (1989). The nature of social influence in groupthink: Compliance and internalization. *Journal of Personality and Social Psychology, 57,* 250–260.

McClearn, G. E., Johansson, B., Berg, S., Pedersen, N. L., Ahern, F., Petrill, S. A., & Plomin, R. (1997). Substantial genetic influence on cognitive abilities in twins 80 or more years old. *Science, 276,* 1560–1563.

McClelland, D. C. (1958). Methods of measuring human motivation. In J. W. Atkinson (Ed.), *Motives in fantasy, action, and society.* Princeton, NJ: Van Nostrand.

McClelland, D. C. (1961). *The achieving society.* Princeton, NJ: Van Nostrand.

McClelland, D. C. (1986). Some reflections on the two psychologies of love. *Journal of Personality, 54,* 334–353.

McClelland, D. C. (1987). Characteristics of successful entrepreneurs. *Journal of Creative Behavior, 21,* 219–233.

McClelland, J. L. (1994). The organization of memory: A parallel distributed processing perspective. *Revue Neurologique, 150*(8/9), 570–579.

McClelland, J. L., McNaughton, B. L., & O'Reilly, R. C. (1995). Why there are complementary learning systems in the hippocampus and neocortex: Insights from the successes and failures of connectionist models of learning and memory. *Psychological Review, 102*(3), 419–437.

McClintock, M. K. (1971). Menstrual synchrony and suppression. *Nature, 229,* 244–245.

McCloskey, M., Wible, C. G., & Cohen, N. J. (1988). Is there a special flashbulb-memory mechanism? *Journal of Experimental Psychology: General, 117,* 171–181.

McConahay, J. B., & Hough, J. C. (1976). Symbolic racism. *Journal of Social Issues, 32*(2), 23–45.

McConkey, K. M., & Kinoshita, S. (1988). The influence of hypnosis on memory after one day and one week. *Journal of Abnormal Psychology, 97,* 48–53.

McCormick, E. J., Jeanneret, P. R., & Mecham, R. C. (1972). A study of job characteristics and job dimensions as based on the Position Analysis Questionnaire (PAQ) [Monograph]. *Journal of Applied Psychology, 56,* 347–368.

McCormick, L., Nielsen, T., Ptito, M., & Hassainia, F. (1997). REM sleep dream mentation in right hemispherectomized patients. *Neuropsychologia, 35*(5), 695–701.

McCrady, B. S. (1994). Alcoholics anonymous and behavior therapy: Can habits be treated as diseases? Can diseases be treated as habits? *Journal of Consulting and Clinical Psychology, 62,* 1159–1166.

McCrae, R. R., & Costa, P. T., Jr. (1987). Validation of the five-factor model of personality across instruments and observers. *Journal of Personality and Social Psychology, 52,* 81–90.

McCrae, R. R., & Costa, P. T., Jr. (1990). *Personality in adulthood.* New York: Guilford.

McCrae, R. R., & Costa, P. T., Jr. (1994). The stability of personality: Observations and evaluations. *Current Directions in Psychological Science, 3,* 173–175.

McCrae, R. R., Costa, P. T., Jr., Del Pilar, G. H., Rolland, J. P., & Parker, W. D. (1998). Cross-cultural assessment of the five-factor model: The revised NEO personality inventory. *Journal of Cross-Cultural Psychology, 29*(1), 171–188.

McDermott, K., & Roediger, H. L. (1996). Exact and conceptual repetition dissociate conceptual memory tests: Problems for transfer-appropriate processing theory. *Canadian Journal of Experimental Psychology, 50*(1), 57–71.

McDonaugh, G. R. (1992). *An examination of racial stereotypes: The differential effects of gender and social class on their content.* Dissertation research, Purdue University, West Lafayette, Indiana.

McFall, M. E., Mackay, P. W., & Donovan, D. M. (1991). Combat-related PTSD and psychosocial adjustment problems among substance abusing veterans. *Journal of Nervous and Mental Disease, 179,* 33–38.

McGaugh, J. L. (1990). Significance and remembrance: The role of neuromodulatory systems. *Psychological Science, 1,* 15–25.

McGill, M. E., & Slocum, J. W., Jr. (1998). A little leadership, please? *Organizational Dynamics, 26*(3), 39–49.

McGinty, D., & Szymusiak, R. (1988). Neuronal unit activity patterns in behaving animals: Brainstem and limbic system. *Annual Review of Psychology, 39,* 135–168.

McGlynn, S. M. (1990). Behavioral approaches to neuropsychological rehabilitation. *Psychological Bulletin, 108,* 420–441.

McKeachie, W. J. (1988). Teaching thinking. *Update: National Center for Research to Improve Postsecondary Teaching and Learning, 2,* 1.

McKeachie, W. J., Pintrich, P. R., & Lin, Y. (1985). Learning to learn. In G. d'Ydewalle (Ed.), *Cognition, information processing, and motivation.* New York: Elsevier–North Holland.

McKelvie, S. J. (1984). Relationship between set and functional fixedness: A replication. *Perceptual and Motor Skills, 58*(3), 996–998.

McKenzie, B. E., Tootell, H. E., & Day, R. H. (1980). Development of visual size constancy during the 1st year of human infancy. *Developmental Psychology, 16,* 163–174.

McLoyd, V. C. (1998). Socioeconomic disadvantage and child development. *American Psychologist, 53*(2), 185–204.

McLynn, F. (1997). *Carl Gustav Jung: A biography.* New York: St. Martin's Press.

McManus, I. C., & Bryden, M. P. (1991). Geschwind's theory of cerebral lateralization: Developing a formal, causal model. *Psychological Bulletin, 110,* 235–237.

McMinn, M. R., Lindsay, S. F., Hannum, L. E., & Troyer, P. K. (1990). Does sexist language reflect personal characteristics? *Sex Roles, 23,* 389–396.

McMinn, M. R., Troyer, P. K., Hannum, L. E., & Foster, J. D. (1991). Teaching nonsexist language to college students. *Journal of Experimental Education, 59,* 153–161.

McNally, R. J. (1994). Cognitive bias in panic disorder. *Current Directions in Psychological Science, 3,* 129–132.

McNally, R. J., Hornig, C. D., Otto, M. W., & Pollack, M. H. (1997). Selective encoding of threat in panic disorder: Application of a dual priming paradigm. *Behaviour Research and Therapy, 35*(6), 543–549.

McNeil, J. E., & Warrington, E. K. (1993). Prosopagnosia: A face-specific disorder. *The Quarterly Journal of Experimental Psychology, 46A*(1), 1–10.

McNeill, D. (1970). Explaining linguistic universals. In J. Morton (Ed.), *Biological and social factors in psycholinguistics.* London: Logos.

McReynolds, P. (1996). Lightner Witmer: A centennial tribute. *American Psychologist, 51,* 237–240.

McRoberts, C., Burlingame, G. M., & Hoag, M. J. (1998). Comparative efficacy of individual and group psychotherapy: A meta-analytic perspective. *Group Dynamics, 2*(2), 101–117.

Meadows, S. (1998). Children learning to think: Learning from others? Vygotskian theory and educational psychology. *Educational and Child Psychology, 15*(2), 6–13.

Mecklinger, A., & Muller, N. (1996). Dissociations in the processing of "what" and "where" information in working memory: An event-related potential analysis. *Journal of Cognitive Neuroscience, 8*(5), 453–473.

Medin, D. L. (1989). Concepts and conceptual structure. *American Psychologist, 44,* 1469–1481.

Mednick, S. A., Parnas, J., & Schulsinger, F. (1987). The Copenhagen high-risk project, 1962–1986. *Schizophrenia Bulletin, 13,* 485–495.

Meece, J. L., & Jones, G. (1996). Gender differences in motivation and strategy use in science: Are girls rote learners? *Journal of Research in Science Teaching, 33*(4), 393–406.

Meichenbaum, D. (1974). *Cognitive behavior modification.* Morristown, NJ: General Learning.

Meichenbaum, D. (1977). *Cognitive behavior modification.* New York: Plenum.

Meichenbaum, D., & Cameron, R. (1973). Training schizophrenics to talk to themselves: A means of developing attentional controls. *Behavior Therapy, 4,* 515–534.

Meinz, E. J., & Salthouse, T. A. (1997). The effects of age and experience on memory for visually presented music. *Journals of Gerontology Series B—Psychological Sciences and Social Sciences, 53B*(1), P60–P69.

Melton, G. B., Petrila, J., Poythress, N. G., & Slobogin, C. (1987). *Psychological evaluations for the courts.* New York: Guilford.

Melton, J. G. (1993). *Encyclopedia of American religions* (4th ed). Detroit, MI: Gale Research, Inc.

Meltzoff, A. N. (1988). Imitation of televised models by infants. *Child Development, 59,* 1221–1229.

Meltzoff, A. N. (1996). The human infant as imitative generalist: A 20-year progress report on infant imitation with implications for comparative psychology. In C. M. Heyes et al. (Eds.), *Social learning in animals: The roots of culture.* San Diego, CA: Academic Press.

Melville, J. (1977). *Phobias and compulsions.* New York: Penguin.

Melzack, R. (1990, February). The tragedy of needless pain. *Scientific American,* 27–33.

Melzack, R. (1993). Pain: Past, present and future. *Canadian Journal of Experimental Psychology, 47*(4), 615–629.

Melzack, R., & Wall, P. D. (1970). Psychophysiology of pain. *International Anesthesiology Clinics, 8,* 3–34.

Mercer, R. T., Nichols, E. G., & Doyle, G. C. (1989). *Transitions in a woman's life* (Vol. 12). New York: Springer.

Merton, R. K. (1949). Merton's typology of prejudice and discrimination. In R. M. MacIver (Ed.), *Discrimination and national welfare.* New York: Harper & Row.

Merzenich, M. M., Jenkins, W. M., Johnston, P., Schreiner, C., Miller, S. L., & Tallal, P. (1996). Temporal processing deficits of language-learning impaired children ameliorated by training. *Science, 271,* 77–81.

Messer, S. B., & Wachtel, P. L. (1997). The contemporary psychotherapeutic landscape: Issues and prospects. In P. L. Wachtel & S. B. Messer, (Eds.), *Theories of psychotherapy: Origins and evolution* (pp. 1–27). Washington, DC: American Psychological Association.

Metcalfe, J., Funnell, M., & Gazzaniga, M. S. (1995). Right-hemisphere memory superiority: Studies of a split-brain patient. *Psychological Science, 6,* 157–164.

Meyer, R. G., & Salmon, P. (1988). *Abnormal psychology* (2nd ed.). Boston: Allyn & Bacon.

Meyers-Levy, J., & Maheswaran, D. (1991). Exploring differences in males' and females' processing strategies. *Journal of Consumer Research, 18,* 63–70.

Michael, R. T., Wadsworth, J., Feinleib, H., Johnson, A. M., Laumann, E. O., & Wellings, K. (1998). Private sexual behavior, public opinion, and public health policy related to sexually transmitted diseases: A U.S.–British comparison. *American Journal of Public Health, 88*(5), 749–754.

Middaugh, S. J. (1990). On clinical efficacy: Why biofeedback does—and does not—work. *Biofeedback and Self-Regulation, 15,* 191–208.

Middleton, B., Arendt, J., & Stone, B. M. (1997). Complex effects of melatonin on human circadian rhythms in constant dim light. *Journal of Biological Rhythms, 12*(5), 467–477.

Mikhailova, N. G., Zukhar, A. V., Loseva, E. V., & Ermakova, I. V. (1991). Influence of transplantation of embryonal brain tissue (early periods) on reactions of avoidance of artificial and zoosocial stimuli in rats. *Neuroscience and Behavioral Physiology, 21,* 34–37.

Miklowitz, D. J. (1994). Family risk indicators in schizophrenia. *Schizophrenia Bulletin, 20,* 137–150.

Milgram, S. (1963). Behavioral study of obedience. *Journal of Abnormal and Social Psychology, 67,* 371–378.

Milgram, S. (1965). Liberating effects of group pressure. *Journal of Personality and Social Psychology, 1,* 127–134.

Millar, M. G., & Millar, K. (1990). Attitude change as a function of attitude type and argument type. *Journal of Personality and Social Psychology, 39,* 217–228.

Millar, M. G., & Millar, K. (1995). Negative affective consequences of thinking about disease detection behaviors. *Health Psychology, 14,* 141–146.

Miller, A. H. (1998). Neuroendocrine and immune system interactions in stress and depression. *Psychiatric Clinics of North America, 21*(2), 443–463.

Miller, B. C., McCoy, J. K., Olson, T. D., & Wallace, C. M. (1986). Parental discipline and control attempts in relation to adolescent sexual attitudes and behavior. *Journal of Marriage and the Family, 48*(3), 503–512.

Miller, C. T., & Myers, A. M. (1998). Conpensating for prejudice: How heavyweight people (and others) control outcomes despite prejudice. In J. K. Swim & C. Stangor (Eds.), *Prejudice: The target's perspective* (pp. 191–218). San Diego, CA: Academic Press.

Miller, E. K., Erickson, C. A., & Desimone, R. (1996). Neural mechanisms of visual working memory in prefrontal cortex of the macaque. *Journal of Neuroscience, 16*(16), 5154–5167.

Miller, G. A. (1956). The magical number seven plus or minus two: Some limits on our capacity for processing information. *Psychological Review, 63,* 81–97.

Miller, G. A. (1965). Some preliminaries to psycholinguistics. *American Psychologist, 20,* 15–20.

Miller, K. F., & Baillargeon, R. (1990). Length and distance: Do preschoolers think that occlusion brings things together? *Developmental Psychology, 26,* 103–114.

Miller, L. C. (1990). Intimacy and liking: Mutual influence and the role of unique relationships. *Journal of Personality and Social Psychology, 59,* 50–60.

Miller, M. E., & Bowers, K. S. (1993). Hypnotic analgesia: Dissociated experience or dissociated control? *Journal of Abnormal Psychology, 102,* 29–38.

Miller, N. E. (1944). Experimental studies of conflict. In J. M. Hunt (Ed.), *Personality and behavioral disorders* (Vol. 1). New York: Ronald Press.

Miller, N. E. (1959). Liberalization of basic S–R concepts: Extensions to conflict behavior, motivation, and social learning. In S. Koch (Ed.), *Psychology: A study of a science* (Vol. 2). New York: McGraw-Hill.

Miller, N. E. (1969). Learning of visceral and glandular responses. *Science, 163,* 434–445.

Miller, P. F., Light, K. C., Bragdon, E. E., Ballenger, M. N., Herbst, M. C., Maixner, W., Hinderliter, A. L., Atkinson, S. S., Koch, G. G., & Sheps, D. S. (1993). Beta-endorphin response to exercise and mental stress in patients with ischemic heart disease. *Journal of Psychosomatic Research, 37,* 455–465.

Miller, P. H., & Aloise, P. A. (1989). Young children's understanding of the psychological causes of behavior: A review. *Child Development, 60,* 257–285.

Miller, R. P., Cosgrove, J. M., & Doke, L. (1990). Motivating adolescents to reduce their fines in a token economy. *Adolescence, 25,* 97–104.

Miller, T. Q., Turner, C. W., Tindale, R. S., Posavac, E. J., & Dugoni, B. L. (1991). Reasons for the trend toward null findings in research on Type A behavior. *Psychological Bulletin, 110,* 469–485.

Milner, B. (1966). Amnesia following operation on the temporal lobes. In C. W. M. Whitty & O. L. Zangwill (Eds.), *Amnesia.* London: Butterworth.

Milner, B., Corkin, S., & Teuber, H. L. (1968). Further analysis of hippocampal amnesic syndrome: 14-year follow-up study of H. M. *Neuropsychologia, 6,* 215–234.

Milner, J. S., & Chilamkurti, C. (1991). Physical child abuse perpetrator characteristics: A review of the literature. *Journal of Interpersonal Violence, 6,* 345–366.

Milner, P. M. (1989). A cell assembly theory of hippocampal amnesia. *Neuropsychologia, 27,* 23–30.

Milner, P. M. (1991). Brain stimulation reward: A review. *Canadian Journal of Psychology, 45,* 1–36.

Miranda, S. M. (1994). Avoidance of groupthink meeting management using group support systems. *Small Group Research, 25,* 105–136.

Mischel, W. (1979). On the interface of cognition and personality: Beyond the person–situation debate. *American Psychologist, 34,* 740–754.

Mischel, W. (1983). Alternatives in the pursuit of the predictability and consistency of persons: Stable data that yield unstable interpretations. *Journal of Personality, 51,* 578–604.

Mischel, W., & Grusec, J. E. (1966). Determinants of the rehearsal and transmission of neutral and averse behaviors. *Journal of Personality and Social Psychology, 3,* 197–205.

Miserandino, M. (1998). Attributional retraining as a method of improving athletic performance. *Journal of Sport Behavior, 21*(3), 286–297.

Mishima, K., Okawa, M., Hishikawa, Y., Hozumi, S., Hori, H., & Takahashi, K. (1994). Morning bright light therapy for sleep and behavior disorders in elderly patients with dementia. *Acta Psychiatrica Scandinavica, 89,* 1–7.

Mishler, E. G., & Waxler, N. E. (1968). Family interaction processes and schizophrenia: A review of current theories. In E. G. Mishler & N. E. Waxler (Eds.), *Family processes and schizophrenia.* New York: Science House.

Mitler, M. M., Miller, J. C., Lipsitz, J. J., & Walsh, J. K. (1997). The sleep of long-haul truck drivers. *New England Journal of Medicine, 337*(11), 755–761.

Mittmann, N., Herrmann, N., Einarson, T. R., Busto, U. E., Lanctot, K. L., Liu, B. A., Shulman, K. I., Silver, I. L., Naranjo, C. A., & Shear, N. H. (1997). The efficacy, safety and tolerability of antidepressants in late life depression: A meta-analysis. *Journal of Affective Disorders, 46*(3), 191–217.

Moncrieff, J. (1997). Lithium: Evidence reconsidered. *British Journal of Psychiatry, 171,* 113–119.

Monroe, S. M., & Simons, A. D. (1991). Diathesis-stress theories in the context of life stress research: Implications for the depressive disorders. *Psychological Bulletin, 110,* 406–425.

Monroe, S. M., Simons, A. D., & Thase, M. E. (1991). Onset of depression and time to treatment entry: Roles of life stress. *Journal of Consulting and Clinical Psychology, 59,* 566–573.

Monteith, M. J., Zuwerink, J. R., & Devine, P. G. (1994). Prejudice and prejudice reduction: Classic challenges, contemporary approaches. In P. G. Devine (Ed.), *Social cognition: Impact on social psychology.* San Diego, CA: Academic Press, Inc.

Montepare, J. M., & Zebrowitz-McArthur, L. (1988). Impressions of people created by age-related qualities of their gaits. *Journal of Personality and Social Psychology, 55,* 547–556.

Montgomery, S. A., & Kasper, S. (1998). Depression: A long-term illness and its treatment. *International Clinical Psychopharmacology, 13*(6), S23–S26.

Montgomery-St. Laurent, T., Fullenkamp, A. M., & Fischer, R. B. (1988). A role for the hamster's flank gland in heterosexual communication. *Physiology and Behavior, 44,* 759–762.

Moore, T. E. (1995). Subliminal self-help auditory tapes: An empirical test of perceptual consequences. *Canadian Journal of Behavioural Science, 27*(1), 9–20.

Moorehouse, M. J. (1991). Linking maternal employment patterns to mother–child activities and children's school competence. *Developmental Psychology, 27,* 295–303.

Moorhead, G., Ference, R., & Neck, C. P. (1991). Group decision fiascoes continue: Space shuttle challenger and a revised groupthink framework. *Human Relations, 44*(6), 539–550.

Morgan, C. A., III, Kingham, P., Nicolaou, A., & Southwick, S. M. (1998). Anniversary reactions in Gulf War veterans: A naturalistic inquiry 2 years after the Gulf War. *Journal of Traumatic Stress, 11*(1), 165–171.

Morgan, D. G., & Stewart, N. J. (1998). High versus low density special care units: Impact on the behaviour of elderly residents with dementia. *Canadian Journal on Aging, 17*(2), 143–165.

Morgan, W. P. (1992). Hypnosis and sport psychology. In J. Rhue, S. J. Lynn, & I. Kirsch (Eds.), *Handbook of clinical hypnosis.* Washington, DC: American Psychological Association.

Morin, C. M., Stone, J., McDonald, K., & Jones, S. (1994). Psychological management of insomnia: A clinical replication series with 100 patients. *Behavior Therapy, 25,* 291–309.

Morren, M. (1998). Hostility as a risk factor for coronary heart disease. *Psycholoog, 33*(3), 101–108.

Morris, C. D., Bransford, J. D., & Franks, J. J. (1977). Levels of processing versus transfer appropriate processing. *Journal of Verbal Learning and Verbal Behavior, 16*(5), 519–533.

Morris, M. W., & Peng, K. (1994). Culture and cause: American and Chinese attributions for social and physical events. *Journal of Personality and Social Psychology, 67,* 949–971.

Morrison, J. W., Ispa, J. M., & Thornburg, K. R. (1994). African American college students' psychosocial development as related to care arrangements during infancy. *Journal of Black Psychology, 20,* 418–429.

Moser, E. I., Krobert, K. A., Moser, M. B., & Morris, R. G. (1998). Impaired spatial learning after saturation of long-term potentiation. *Science, 281,* 2038–2042.

Moskowitz, B. A. (1978, November). The acquisition of language. *Scientific American,* 92–108.

Mount, M. K., Barrick, M. R., & Stewart, G. L. (1998). Five-factor model of personality and performance in jobs involving interpersonal interactions. *Human Performance, 11*(2/3), 145–165.

Mroczek, D. K., & Kolarz, C. M. (1998). The effect of age on positive and negative affect: A developmental perspective on happiness. *Journal of Personality & Social Psychology, 75*(5), 1333–1349.

Mueser, K. T., Bellack, A. S., Morrison, R. L., & Wade, J. H. (1990). Gender, social competence, and symptomatology in schizophrenia: A longitudinal analysis. *Journal of Abnormal Psychology, 99,* 138–147.

Mukherjee, S., Sackeim, H. A., & Schnurr, D. B. (1994). Electroconvulsive therapy of acute manic episodes: A review. *American Journal of Psychiatry, 151,* 169–176.

Mullen, B., Anthony, T., Salas, E., & Driskell, J. E. (1994). Group cohesiveness and quality of decision making: An integration of tests of the groupthink hypothesis. *Small Group Research, 25,* 189–204.

Mullen, B. & Copper, C. (1994). The relation between group cohesiveness and performance: An integration. *Psychological Bulletin, 115,* 210–227.

Mulligan, N. W. (1996). The effects of perceptual interference at encoding on implicit memory, explicit memory, and memory for source. *Journal of Experimental Memory and Cognition, 22*(5), 1067–1087.

Muñoz, R. F., Hollon, S. D., McGrath, E., Rehm, L. P., & VandenBos, G. R. (1994). On the AHCPR *Depression in primary care* guidelines: Further considerations for practitioners. *American Psychologist, 49,* 42–61.

Murachver, T., Pipe, M. E., Gordon, R., & Owens, J. L. (1996). Do, show, and tell: Children's event memories acquired through direct experience, observation, and stories. *Child Development, 67*(6), 3029–3044.

Murphy, C. M., & O'Farrell, T. J. (1996). Marital violence among alcoholics. *American Psychological Society, 5*(6), 183–186.

Murphy, G. E., Wetzel, R. D., Robins, E., & McEvoy, L. (1992). Multiple risk factors predict suicide in alcoholism. *Archives of General Psychiatry, 49,* 459–463.

Murphy, S. M. (1990). Models of imagery in sport psychology: A review. *Journal of Mental Imagery, 14,* 153–172.

Murphy, S. M., & Jowdy, D. P. (1992). Imagery and mental practice. In Thelma S. Horn (Ed.), *Advances in sport psychology* (pp. 221–250). Champaign, IL: Human Kinetics.

Murray, H. A. (1938). *Explorations in personality.* New York: Oxford University Press.

Murray, J. B. (1995). Evidence for acupuncture's analgesic effectiveness and proposals for the physiological mechanisms involved. *Journal of Psychology, 129*(4), 443–461.

Myers, D. G., & Diener, E. (1995). Who is happy? *Psychological Science, 6,* 10–19.

Myerson, J., Rank, M. R., Raines, F. Q., & Schnitzler, M. A. (1998). Race and general cognitive ability: The myth of diminishing returns to education. *American Psychological Society, 9*(2), 139–142.

Naar, R. (1990). Psychodrama in short-term psychotherapy. In R. A. Wells & V. J. Giannetti (Eds.), *Handbook of the brief psychotherapies.* New York: Plenum.

Nace, E. P. (1987). *The treatment of alcoholism.* New York: Brunner/Mazel.

Nakkab, S. (1997). Adolescent sexual activity. *International Journal of Mental Health, 26*(1), 23–34.

Narrow, W. E., Regier, D. A., & Rae, D. S. (1993). Use of services by persons with mental and addictive disorders: Findings from the National Institute of Mental Health Epidemiologic Catchment Area Program. *Archives of General Psychiatry, 50,* 95–107.

Nash, M. (1987). What, if anything, is regressed about hypnotic age regression? A review of the empirical literature. *Psychological Bulletin, 102,* 42–52.

Nash, R. A. (1996). The serotonin connection. *Journal of Orthomolecular Medicine, 11*(1), 35–44.

Nass, C., Moon, Y., Fogg, B. J., & Reeves, B. (1995). Can computer personalities be human personalities? *International Journal of Human Computer Studies, 43*(2), 223–239.

Nathan, B. R., & Tippins, N. (1990). The consequences of halo "error" in performance ratings: A field study of the moderating effect of halo on test validation results. *Journal of Applied Psychology, 75,* 290–296.

Nathan, P. E. (1988). The addictive personality is the behavior of the addict. *Journal of Consulting and Clinical Psychology, 56,* 183–188.

Nathan, P. E., & Skinstad, A. H. (1987). Outcomes of treatment for alcohol problems: Current methods, problems, and results. *Journal of Consulting and Clinical Psychology, 55,* 332–340.

Nathans, J. (1989, February). The genes for color vision. *Scientific American,* 42–49.

National Council on Aging. (1998, September 28). Half of older Americans report they are sexually active; 4 in 10 want more sex, says new survey. Washington, DC: NCOA [On-line press release]. Available Internet: <http://www.ncoa.org/press/sexsurvey.htm>

National Research Council Panel on Research on Child Abuse and Neglect, Commission on Behavioral and Social Sciences and Education. (1993). *Understanding child abuse and neglect.* Washington, DC: National Academic Press.

Navon, D. (1990). How critical is the accuracy of an eyewitness's memory? Another look at the issue of lineup diagnosticity. *Journal of Applied Psychology, 75,* 506–510.

Neal, A. M., & Turner, S. M. (1991). Anxiety disorders research with African Americans: Current status. *Psychological Bulletin, 109,* 400–410.

Needham, A., Baillargeon, R., & Kaufman, L. (1997). Object segregation in infancy. *Advances in Infancy Research, 11*, 1–44.

Needleman, L. D., & Geller, E. S. (1992). Comparing interventions to motivate work-site collection of home-generated recyclables. *American Journal of Community Psychology, 20*, 775–785.

Neisser, U. (1967). *Cognitive psychology.* Englewood Cliffs, NJ: Prentice-Hall.

Neisser, U. (1992). Two themes in the study of cognition. In H. L Pick, Jr., P. van den Broek, & D. C. Knill (Eds.), *Cognition: Conceptual and methodological issues* (pp. 333–340). Washington, DC: American Psychological Association.

Neisser, U., Boodoo, G., Bouchard, T. J., Jr., Boykin, A. W., Brody, N., Ceci, S. J., Halpern, D. F., Loehlin, J. C., Perloff, R., Sternberg, R. J., & Urbina, S. (1996). Intelligence: Knowns and unknowns. *American Psychologist, 51*, 77–101.

Neitz, M. J. (1995). Feminist theory and religious experience. In R. W. Hood, Jr., et al. (Eds.), *Handbook of religious experience.* Birmingham, AL: Religious Education Press, Inc.

Nelson, B. A., & Stake, J. E. (1994). The Myers–Briggs type indicator personality dimensions and perceptions of quality of therapy relationships. *Psychotherapy, 31*, 449–455.

Nelson, D. L., McKinney, V. M., & Gee, N. R. (1998). Interpreting the influence of implicitly activated memories on recall and recognition. *Psychological Review, 105*(2), 299–324.

Nelson, K. (1993). The psychological and social origins of autobiographical memory. *Psychological Science, 4*, 7–14.

Nemeroff, C. B., Knight, D. L., Kirshnan, R. R., Slotkin, T. A., Bissette, G., Melville, M. L., & Blazer, D. G. (1988). Marked reduction in the number of platelet-tritiated imipramine binding sites in geriatric depression. *Archives of General Psychiatry, 45*, 919–923.

Nestler, E. J., & Aghajanian, G. K. (1997). Molecular and cellular basis of addiction. *Science, 278*, 58–63.

Neugarten, B. (1968). Adult personality: Toward a psychology of the life cycle. In B. Neugarten (Ed.), *Middle age and aging* (pp. 137–147). Chicago: University of Chicago Press.

Newcomb, A. F., & Bagwell, C. L. (1995). Children's friendship relations: A meta-analytic review. *Psychological Bulletin, 117*, 306–347.

Newcomb, M. D., & Bentler, P. M. (1989). Substance use and abuse among children and teenagers. *American Psychologist, 44*, 242–248.

Newcombe, N., & Huttenlocher, J. (1992). Children's early ability to solve perspective-taking problems. *Developmental Psychology, 28*, 635–643.

Newell, A., & Simon, H. A. (1972). *Human problem solving.* Englewood Cliffs, NJ: Prentice-Hall.

Newman, L. S., Duff, K. J., & Baumeister, R. F. (1997). A new look at defensive projection: Thought suppression, accessibility, and biased person perception. *Journal of Personality and Social Psychology, 72*(5), 980–1001.

NICHD Early Child Care Research Network. (1997). The effects of infant child care on infant–mother attachment security: Results of the NICHD study of early child care. *Child Development, 68*(5), 860–879.

Niehoff, D. (1999). *The biology of violence: How understanding the brain, behavior, and environment can break the vicious circle of aggression.* New York: The Free Press.

Nigg, J. T., & Goldsmith, H. H. (1994). Genetics of personality disorders: Perspectives from personality and psychopathology research. *Psychological Bulletin, 115*, 346–380.

Nilsson, K. M. (1990). The effect of subject expectations of "hypnosis" upon vividness of visual imagery. *The International Journal of Clinical and Experimental Hypnosis, 38*, 17–24.

Nisbett, R. E. (1972). Hunger, obesity, and the ventromedial hypothalamus. *Psychological Review, 79*, 433–453.

Nolen-Hoeksema, S. (1994). An interactive model for the emergence of gender differences in depression in adolescence. *Journal of Research on Adolescence, 4*(4), 519–534.

Nolen-Hoeksema, S., & Girgus, J. S. (1994). The emergence of gender differences in depression during adolescence. *Psychological Bulletin, 115*, 424–443.

Norman, D. A. (1990). *Design of everyday things.* New York: Doubleday.

Norman, R. A., Tataranni, P. A., Pratley, R., Thompson, D. B., Hanson, R. L., Prochazka, M., Baier, L., Ehm, M. G., Sakul, H., Foroud, T., Garvey, W. T., Burns D., Knowler, W. C., Bennett, P. H., Bogardus, C., & Ravussin, E. (1998). Autosomal genomic scan for loci linked to obesity and energy metabolism in Pima Indians. *American Journal of Human Genetics, 62*(3), 659–668.

Norris, J. (1989). Normative influence effects on sexual arousal to nonviolent sexually explicit material. *Journal of Applied Social Psychology, 19*, 341–352.

Noton, D., & Stark, L. (1971, June). Eye movements and visual perception, *Scientific American*, 35–44.

Notterman, J. M., & Drewry, H. N. (1993). *Psychology and education: Parallel and interactive approaches.* New York: Plenum.

Nyberg, L., Cabeza, R., & Tulving, E. (1996). PET studies of encoding and retrieval: The HERA model. *Psychonomic Bulletin and Review, 3*(2), 135–148.

O'Connor, F. L. (1998). The role of serotonin and dopamine in schizophrenia. *Journal of the American Psychiatric Nurses Association, 4*(4), S30–S34.

O'Donnell, C. R. (1995). Firearm deaths among children and youth. *American Psychologist, 50*, 771–776.

Ofshe, R. J., & Singer, M. T. (1994). Recovered-memory therapy and robust repression: Influence and pseudomemories. *The International Journal of Clinical and Experimental Hypnosis, 42*, 391–410.

Ogur, B. (1986). Long day's journey into night: Women and prescription drug abuse. *Women and Health, 11*, 99–115.

Okuda-Ashitaka, E., Minami, T., Tachibana, S., Yosihara, Y., Nishiuchi, Y., Kimura, T., & Ito, S. (1998). Nocistatin, a peptide that blocks nociceptin action in pain transmission. *Nature, 392*, 286–289.

Olds, J. (1955). Physiological mechanisms of reward. *Nebraska Symposium on Motivation, 3,* 73–139.

Olds, J. (1969). The central nervous system and the reinforcement of behavior. *American Psychologist, 24,* 114–132.

Olds, J., & Milner, P. (1954). Positive reinforcement produced by electrical stimulation of septal area and other regions of rat brain. *Journal of Comparative and Physiological Psychology, 47,* 419–427.

O'Leary, A. (1990). Stress, emotion, and human immune function. *Psychological Bulletin, 108,* 363–382.

O'Leary, K. D., Barling, J., Arias, I., Rosenbaum, A., Malone, J., & Tyree, A. (1989). Prevalence and stability of physical aggression between spouses: A longitudinal analysis. *Journal of Consulting and Clinical Psychology, 57,* 263–268.

Olio, K. A. (1994). Truth in memory. *American Psychologist, 49,* 442–443.

Olivardia, R., Pope, H. G., Jr., Mangweth, B., & Hudson, J. L. (1995). Eating disorders in college men. *American Journal of Psychiatry, 152,* 1279–1283.

Oliver, M. B., & Hyde, J. S. (1993). Gender differences in sexuality: A meta-analysis. *Psychological Bulletin, 114,* 29–51.

Olson, B., & Douglas, W. (1997). The family on television: Evaluation of gender roles in situation comedy. *Sex Roles, 36*(5/6), 409–427.

Olson, E. (1994). Female voices of aggression in Tonga. *Sex Roles, 30,* 237–248.

Ornstein, R. (1997). *The right mind: Making sense of the hemisphere.* New York: Harcourt Brace.

Ornstein, R. E. (1976). A science of consciousness. In P. R. Lee, R. E. Ornstein, D. Galin, A. Deikman, & C. T. Tart (Eds.), *Symposium on consciousness* (San Francisco, 1974). New York: Viking.

Ornstein, R. E. (1977). *The psychology of consciousness* (2nd ed.). New York: Harcourt Brace Jovanovich.

Ortega-Andeane, A. P. (1989). User participation in an environmental evaluation in the remodeling of hospital facilities. *Revista Mexicana de Psycologia, 6*(1), 45–54.

Osborne, J. W. (1997). Race and academic disidentification. *Journal of Educational Psychology, 89*(4), 728–735.

Osofsky, J. D. (1995). The effects of exposure to violence on young children. *American Psychologist, 50,* 782–788.

Ottati, V., Fishbein, M., & Middlestadt, S. E. (1988). Determinants of voters' beliefs about the candidates' stands on the issues: The role of evaluative bias heuristics and the candidates' expressed message. *Journal of Personality and Social Psychology, 55,* 517–529.

Overby, L. Y. (1990). A comparison of novice and experienced dancers' imagery ability. *Journal of Mental Imagery, 14,* 173–184.

Overmier, J. B. Learned helplessness: State of stasis of the art? In M. Sabourin, F. Craik, et al. (Eds.), *Advances in psychological science, Vol. 2: Biological and cognititve aspects* (pp. 301–315). Hove, England: Psychology Press/Erlbaum Taylor & Francis.

Overmier, J. B., & Gahtan, E. (1998). Psychoneuroimmunology: The final hurdle. *Integrative Physiological and Behavioral Science, 33*(2), 137–140.

Owen, A. M., Evans, A. C., & Petrides, M. (1996). Evidence for a two-stage model of spatial working memory processing within the lateral frontal cortex: A positron emission tomography study. *Cerebral Cortex, 6*(1) 31–38.

Pagano, R. W., Rose, R. M., Stivers, R. M., & Warrenburg, S. (1976). Sleep during transcendental meditation. *Science, 191,* 308–310.

Paikoff, R. L., & Brooks-Gunn, J. (1991). Do parent–child relationships change during puberty? *Psychological Bulletin, 110,* 47–66.

Paivio, A. (1971). *Imagery and verbal processes.* New York: Holt, Rinehart & Winston.

Palinkas, L. A., Russell, J., Downs, M. A., & Petterson, J. S. (1992). Ethnic differences in stress, coping, and depressive symptoms after the Exxon Valdez oil spill. *Journal of Nervous and Mental Disease, 180,* 287–295.

Paloutzian, R. F. (1996). *Invitation to the psychology of religion.* Boston: Allyn and Bacon.

Paloutzian, R. F., & Ellison, C. W. (1991). *Manual for the Spiritual Well-Being Scale.* Nyack, NY: Life Advance Inc.

Pantev, C., Oostenveld, R., Engelien, A., Ross, B., Roberts, L. E., & Hoke, M. (1998). Increased auditory critical representation in musicians. *Nature, 392,* 811–814.

Pantin, H. M., & Carver, C. S. (1982). Induced competence and the bystander effect. *Journal of Applied Social Psychology, 12,* 100–111.

Papini, M. R., & Bitterman, M. E. (1990). The role of contingency in classical conditioning. *Psychological Review, 97,* 396–403.

Paradis, C. M., Hatch, M., & Friedman, S. (1994). Anxiety disorders in African Americans: An update. *Journal of the National Medical Association, 86,* 609–612.

Park, H. S., Bauer, S. C., & Sullivan, L. M. (1998). Gender differences among top-performing elementary school students in mathematical ability. *Journal of Research and Development in Education, 31*(3), 133–141.

Parke, R. D. (1995). Fathers and families. In M. H. Bornstein (Ed.), *Handbook of parenting. Vol. III: Status and social conditions of parenting.* Mahwah, NJ: Lawrence Erlbaum Associates.

Parker, D. E. (1980, November). The vestibular apparatus. *Scientific American,* 118–135.

Parker, G., Roy, K., Hadzi-Pavlovic, D., & Pedic, F. (1992). Psychotic (delusional) depression: A meta-analysis of physical treatments. *Journal of Affective Disorders, 24,* 17–24.

Parker, L. E. (1993). When to fix it and when to leave: Relationships among perceived control, self-efficacy, dissent, and exit. *Journal of Applied Psychology, 78,* 949–959.

Parkin, A. J., Reid, T., & Russo, R. (1990). On the differential nature of implicit and explicit memory. *Memory and Cognition, 18,* 507–514.

Parrott, W. G., & Schulkin, J. (1993). Neuropsychology and the cognitive nature of the emotions. *Cognition and Emotion, 7,* 43–59.

Patrick, C. J. (1994). Emotion and psychopathy: Startling new insights. *Psychophysiology, 31,* 319–330.

Patrick, C. J., & Iacono, W. G. (1989). Psychopathy, threat, and polygraph test accuracy. *Journal of Applied Psychology, 74,* 347–355.

Pavlov, I. P. (1927). *Conditioned reflexes.* London: Oxford University Press.

Payne, D. G., Neuschatz, J. S., Lampinen, J. M., & Lynn, S. J. (1997). Compelling memory illusions: The characteristics of false memories. *American Psychological Society, 6*(3), 56–60.

Payne, J. W., Bettman, J. R., & Johnson, E. J. (1992). Behavioral decision research: A constructive processing perspective. *Annual Review of Psychology, 43,* 87–132.

Pearlmann, S. F. (1993). Late mid-life astonishment: Disruptions to identity and self-esteem. *Women and Therapy, 14,* 1–12.

Pedersen, D. M., & Wheeler, J. (1983). The Müller-Lyer illusion among Navajos. *Journal of Social Psychology, 121,* 3–6.

Pedersen, N. L., Plomin, R., & McClearn, G. E. (1994). Is there *g* beyond *g*? (Is there genetic influence on specific cognitive abilities independent of genetic influence on general cognitive ability?). *Intelligence, 18,* 133–143.

Pedersen, N. L., Plomin, R., Nesselroade, J. R., & McClearn, G. E. (1992). A quantitative genetic analysis of cognitive abilities during the second half of the life span. *Psychological Science, 3,* 346–353.

Pendergrast, M. (1997). Memo to Pope: Ask the real questions, please. *American Psychologist, 52,* 989–990.

Penfield, W. W. (1958). *The excitable cortex in conscious man.* Springfield, IL: Charles Thomas.

Penfield, W. W., & Jasper, H. (1954). *Epilepsy and the functional anatomy of the human brain.* Boston: Little, Brown.

Penfield, W. W., & Mathieson, G. (1974). Memory: Autopsy findings and comments on the role of hippocampus in experiential recall. *Archives of Neurology, 31,* 145–154.

Penfield, W. W., & Milner, B. (1958). Memory deficit produced by bilateral lesions in the hippocampal zone. *Archives of Neurological Psychiatry, 79,* 475–497.

Penfield, W. W., & Perot, P. (1963). The brain's record of auditory and visual experience. *Brain, 86,* 595–696.

Penn, D. L., Corrigan, P. W., Bentall, R. P., Racenstein, J. M., & Newman, L. (1997). Social cognition in schizophrenia. *Psychological Bulletin, 121*(1), 114–132.

Perkins, D. N., & Grotzer, T. A. (1997). Teaching intelligence. *American Psychologist, 52*(10), 1125–1133.

Perlin, M. L. (1996). The insanity defense: Deconstructing the myths and reconstructing the jurisprudence. In B. D. Sales & D. W. Shuman (Eds.), *Law, mental health, and mental disorder* (pp. 341–359). Pacific Grove, CA: Brooks/Cole Publishing Company.

Perner, J., & Ruffman, T. (1995). Episodic memory and autonoetic consciousness: Developmental evidence and a theory of childhood amnesia. *Journal of Experimental Child Psychology, 59*(3), 516–548.

Perrett, D. I., Lee, K. J., Penton-Voak, I., Rowland, D., Yoshikawa, S., Burt, D. M., Henzi, S. P., Castles, D. L., & Akamatsu, S. (1998). Effects of sexual dimorphism on facial attractiveness. *Nature, 394,* 884–887.

Persky, H. (1978). Plasma testosterone level and sexual behavior of couples. *Archives of Sexual Behavior, 7,* 157–173.

Persons, J. B., Thase, M. E., & Crits-Christoph, P. (1996). The role of psychotherapy in the treatment of depression. *Archives of General Psychiatry, 53,* 283–290.

Peselow, E. D., Sanfilipo, M. P., & Fieve, R. R. (1995). Relationship between hypomania and personality disorders before and after successful treatment. *American Journal of Psychiatry, 152,* 232–238.

Pesut, D. J. (1990). Creative thinking as a self-regulatory metacognitive process: A model for education, training and further research. *Journal of Creative Behavior, 24,* 105–110.

Peterson, C., & Seligman, M. E. P. (1984). Causal explanations as a risk factor for depression: Theory and evidence. *Psychological Review, 91,* 347–374.

Peterson, L. R., & Peterson, M. J. (1959). Short-term retention of individual verbal items. *Journal of Experimental Psychology, 58,* 193–198.

Petrill, S. A., Plomin, R., Berg, S., Johansoon, B., Pedersen, N. L., Ahern, F., & McClearn, G. E. (1998). The genetic and environmental relationship between general and specific cognitive abilities in twins age 80 and older. *Psychological Science, 9*(3), 183–189.

Pettigrew, T. F. (1997). The affective component of prejudice: Empirical support for the new view. In S. A. Tuch & J. K. Martin (Eds.), *Racial attitudes in the 1990s: Continuity and change* (pp. 76–90). New York: Praeger.

Pettigrew, T. F., Jackson, J. S., Brika, J. B., Lemaine, G., Meertens, R. W., Wagner, U., & Zick, A. (1998). Outgroup prejudice in Western Europe. In W. Stroebe, M. Hewstone, et al. (Eds.), *European Review of Social Psychology, Vol. 8.* (pp. 241–273). Chichester, England: John Wiley & Sons, Inc.

Petty, R. E., & Cacioppo, J. T. (1981). *Attitudes and persuasion: Classic and contemporary approaches.* Dubuque, IA: Wm. C. Brown.

Petty, R. E., & Cacioppo, J. T. (1985). The elaboration likelihood model of persuasion. In L. Berkowitz (Ed.), *Advances in experimental social psychology* (Vol. 19). New York: Academic.

Petty, R. E., Cacioppo, J. T., Strathman, A. J., & Priester, J. R. (1994). To think or not to think: Exploring two routes to persuasion. In S. Shavitt & T. C. Brock (Eds.), *Persuasion: Psychological insights and perspectives* (pp. 113–148). Boston: Allyn & Bacon.

Petty, R. E., Schumann, D. W., Richman, S. A., & Strathman, A. J. (1993). Positive mood and persuasion: Different roles for affect under high- and low-elaboration conditions. *Journal of Personality and Social Psychology, 64,* 5–20.

Pezdek, K., Finger, K., & Hodge, D. (1997). Planting false childhood memories: The role of event plausibility. *American Psychological Society, 8*(6), 437–441.

Pfister, H. P., & Muir, J. L. (1992). Prenatal exposure to predictable and unpredictable novelty stress and oxytocin treatment affects offspring development and behavior in rats. *International Journal of Neuroscience, 62,* 227–241.

Phares, V., & Compas, B. E. (1993). Fathers and developmental psychopathology. *Current Directions in Psychological Science, 2,* 162–165.

Phelps, J. A., Davis, J. O., & Schartz, K. M. (1997). Nature, nurture, and twin research strategies. *American Psychological Society, 6*(5), 117–120.

Phinney, J. S. (1996). When we talk about American ethnic groups, what do we mean? *American Psychologist, 51*(9), 918–927.

Piaget, J. (1932). *The moral judgment of the child.* London: Routledge & Kegan Paul.

Pinker, S. (1997). *How the mind works.* New York: W. W. Norton.

Pinker, S. (1999). *Words and rules.* New York: Basic Books.

Pinsof, W. M., Wynne, L. C., & Hambright, A. B. (1996). The outcomes of couple and family therapy: Findings, conclusions, and recommendations. *Psychotherapy, 33*(2), 321–331.

Pion, G. M., Mednick, M. T., Astin, H. S., Hall, C. C., Kenkel, M. B., Keita, G. P., et al. (1996). The shifting gender composition of psychology: Trends and implications for the discipline. *American Psychologist, 51*(5), 509–528.

Pittam, J., Gallois, C., Iwawaki, S., & Kroonenberg, P. (1995). Australian and Japanese concepts of expressive behavior. *Journal of Cross-Cultural Psychology, 26,* 451–473.

Pittenger, D. J. (1997). Reconsidering the overjustification effect: A guide to critical resources. *Teaching of Psychology, 23*(4), 234–236.

Plante, T. G., Boccaccini, M., & Andersen, E. (1998). Attitudes concerning professional issues impacting psychotherapy practice among members of the American Board of Professional Psychology. *Psychotherapy: Theory, Research and Practice, 35*(1), 34–42.

Plath, Sylvia. (1971). *The bell jar.* New York: HarperCollins.

Plihal, W., & Born, J. (1997). Effects of early and late nocturnal sleep on declarative and procedural memory. *Journal of Cognitive Neuroscience, 9*(4), 534–547.

Plomin, R. (1989). Environment and genes: Determinants of behavior. *American Psychologist, 44,* 105–111.

Plomin, R. (1994a). *Genetics and experience: The interplay between nature and nuture.* Thousand Oaks, CA: Sage.

Plomin, R. (1994b). Nature, nurture, and social development. *Social Development, 3,* 37–53.

Plomin, R., Fulker, D. W., Corley, R., & DeFries, J. C. (1997). Nature, nurture, and cognitive development from 1 to 16 years: A parent–offspring adoption study. *Psychological Science, 8*(6), 442–447.

Plomin, R., Petrill, S. A., & Cutting, A. L. (1996). What genetic research on intelligence tells us about the environment. *Journal of Biosocial Science, 28*(4), 587–606.

Plomin, R., Reiss, D., Hetherington, E. M., & Howe, G. W. (1994). Nature and nurture: Genetic contributions to measures of the family environment. *Developmental Psychology, 30,* 32–43.

Plotkin, W. B. (1980). The role of attributions of responsibility in the facilitation of unusual experiential states during alpha training: An analysis of the biofeedback placebo effect. *Journal of Abnormal Psychology, 89,* 67–78.

Plous, S. (1996). Attitudes toward the use of animals in psychological research and education. *American Psychologist, 51*(11), 1167–1180.

Plutchik, R. (1980). *Emotion: A psychoevolutionary synthesis.* New York: Harper & Row.

Pollack, W. (1998). *Real boys: Rescuing our sons from the myths of boyhood.* New York: Random House.

Pomerantz, E. M., Chaiken, S., & Tordesillas, R. S. (1995). Attitude strength and resistance processes. *Journal of Personality and Social Psychology, 69,* 408–419.

Pomerleau, A., Bolduc, D., Malcuit, G., & Cossette, L. (1990). Pink or blue: Environmental gender stereotypes in the first two years of life. *Sex Roles, 22,* 359–367.

Poole, D. A., Lindsay, D. S., Memon, A., & Bull, R. (1995). Psychotherapy and the recovery of memories of childhood sexual abuse: U.S. and British practitioners' opinions, practices, and experiences. *Journal of Clinical and Consulting Psychology, 63,* 426–437.

Pope, K. S. (1996). Memory, abuse, science. *American Psychologist, 51*(9), 957–974.

Porter, B. E., Leeming, F. C., & Dwyer, W. O. (1995). Solid waste recovery: A review of behavioral programs to increase recycling. *Environment and Behavior, 27,* 122–152.

Posner, M. I., DiGirolamo, G. J., & Fernandez-Duque, D. (1997). Brain mechanisms of cognitive skills. *Conscious Cognition, 6*(2/3), 267–290.

Posner, M. I., & Mitchell, R. F. (1967). Chronometric analysis of classification. *Psychological Review, 74,* 392–409.

Posner, M. I., & Pavese, A. (1998). Anatomy of word and sentence meaning. *Proceedings of the National Academy of Sciences, 95*(3), 899–905.

Post, R. M., Frye, M. A., Dnicoff, K. D., Leverich, G. S., Kimbrell, T. A., & Dunn, R. T. (1998). Beyond lithium in the treatment of bipolar illness. *Neuropsychopharmacology, 19*(3), 206–219.

Postmes, T. & Spears, R. (1998). Deindividuation and antinormative behavior: A meta-analysis. *Psychological Bulletin, 123*(3), 238–259.

Powell, B., & Steelman, L. C. (1996). Bewitched, bothered and bewildering: The use and misuse of state SAT and ACT scores. *Harvard Educational Review, 66*(1), 27–59.

Powers, P. C., & Geen, R. G. (1972). Effects of the behavior and the perceived arousal of a model on instrumental aggression. *Journal of Personality and Social Psychology, 23,* 175–184.

Powers, S. I., Hauser, S. T., & Kilner, L. A. (1989). Adolescent mental health. *American Psychologist, 44,* 200–208.

Powley, T. L. (1977). The ventromedial hypothalamic syndrome, satiety, and a cephalic phase hypothesis. *Psychological Review, 84,* 89–126.

Pratarelli, M. E., & McIntyre, J. A. (1994). Effects of social loafing on word recognition. *Perceptual and Motor Skills, 78,* 455–464.

Prather, J. E., & Minkow, N. V. (1991). Prescription for despair: Women and psychotropic drugs. In N. Van Den Bergh et al. (Eds.) *Feminist perspectives on addictions* (pp. 87–99). New York: Springer Publishing Co.

Pratkanis, A. R., Eskenazi, J., & Greenwald, A. G. (1994). What you expect is what you believe (but not necessarily what you get): A test of the effectiveness of subliminal self-help audiotapes. *Basic and Applied Social Psychology, 15,* 251–276.

Prelow, H. M., & Guarnaccia, C. A. (1997). Ethnic and racial differences in life stress among high school adolescents. *Journal of Counseling and Development, 75*(6), 442–450.

Premack, D. (1962). Reversibility of the reinforcement relation. *Science, 136,* 255–257.

Premack, D. (1965). Reinforcement theory. In D. Levine (Ed.), *Nebraska Symposium on Motivation* (Vol. 13, pp. 123–180). Lincoln: University of Nebraska Press.

Premack, D. (1971). Language in chimpanzees? *Science, 172,* 808–822.

Prentice-Dunn, S. (1991). Half-baked idea: Deindividuation and the nonreactive assessment of self-awareness. *Contemporary Social Psychology, 15,* 16–17.

Prinz, R. J., & Miller, G. E. (1994). Family-based treatment for childhood antisocial behavior: Experimental influences on dropout and engagement. *Journal of Consulting and Clinical Psychology, 62,* 654–660.

Prinz, R. N., Vitiello, M. V., Raskind, M. A., & Thorphy, M. J. (1990). Geriatrics: Sleep disorders and aging. *New England Journal of Medicine, 323,* 520–526.

Proshansky, H. M., & O'Hanlon, T. (1977). Environmental psychology: Origins and development. In D. Stokols (Ed.), *Perspectives on environment and behavior: Theory, research, and application.* New York: Plenum.

Prudic, J., Sackeim, H. A., & Devanand, D. P. (1990). Medication resistance and clinical response to electroconvulsive therapy. *Psychiatry Research, 31,* 287–296.

Puffer, S. M. (1987). Prosocial behavior, noncompliant behavior, and work performance among commission salespeople. *Journal of Applied Psychology, 72,* 615–621.

Pugh, K. R., Shaywitz, B. A., Shaywitz, S. E., et al. (1997). Predicting reading in performance from neuroimaging profiles: The cerebral basis of phonological effects in printed word identification. *Journal of Experimental Psychology: Human Perception and Performance, 23*(2), 299–318.

Puigserver, P., Wu, Z., Park, C. W., Graves, R., Wright, M., & Spiegelman, B. M. (1998). A cold-inducible co-activator of nuclear receptors linked to adaptive thermogenesis. *Cell, 92,* 829–839.

Punamäki, R. L., & Joustie, M. (1998). The role of culture, violence, and personal factors affecting dream content. *Journal of Cross-Cultural Psychology, 29*(2), 320–342.

Putnam, F. W., & Carlson, E. B. (1998). Trauma, memory, and dissociation. *Progress in Psychiatry, 54,* 27–55.

Putnam, F. W., Guroff, J. J., Silberman, E. K., Barban, L., & Post, R. M. (1986). The clinical phenomenology of multiple personality disorder: Review of 100 recent cases. *Journal of Clinical Psychiatry, 47,* 285–293.

Putnam, W. H. (1979). Hypnosis and distortions in eyewitness memory. *International Journal of Clinical and Experimental Hypnosis, 27,* 437–448.

Quigley, B., Gaes, G. G., & Tedeschi, J. T. (1989). Does asking make a difference? Effects of initiator, possible gain, and risk on attributed altruism. *Journal of Social Psychology, 129,* 259–267.

Quilitch, H. R., & Risley, T. R. (1973). The effects of play materials on social play. *Journal of Applied Behavior Analysis, 6,* 573–578.

Rabizadeh, S. et al. (1993). Induction of apoptosis by the low affinity NGF receptor. *Science, 261,* 345–348.

Rachlin, H. (1995). Things that are private and things that are mental. In J. T. Todd & E. K. Morris (Eds.), *Modern perspectives on B. F. Skinner and contemporary behaviorism* (pp. 179–183). Westport, CT: Greenwood.

Rafaeli, A. (1989). When clerks meet customers: A test of variables related to emotional expressions on the job. *Journal of Applied Psychology, 74,* 385–393.

Ragins, B. R., & Sundstrom, E. (1989). Gender and power in organizations: A longitudinal perspective. *Psychological Bulletin, 105,* 51–88.

Rahe, R. H. (1989). Recent life change stress and psychological depression. In T. W. Miller (Ed.), *Stressful life events.* Madison, WI: International Universities Press.

Raisman, G., Morris, R. J., & Zhou, C. F. (1987). Specificity in the reinnervation of adult hippocampus by embryonic hippocampal transplants. In F. J. Seil, E. Herbert, & B. M. Carlson (Eds.), *Progress in brain research* (Vol. 71, pp. 325–333). New York: Elsevier.

Ramey, C. T., & Ramey, S. L. (1998). Early intervention and early experience. *American Psychologist, 53*(2), 109–120.

Rao, S. C., Rainer, G., & Miller, E. K. (1997). Integration of what and where in the primate prefrontal cortex. *Science, 276,* 821–824.

Rapcsak, S. Z., Polster, M. R., Comer, J. F., & Rubens, A. B. (1994). False recognition and misidentification of faces following right hemisphere damage. *Cortex, 30*(4), 565–583.

Rapee, R. (1986). Differential response to hyperventilation in panic disorder and generalized anxiety disorder. *Journal of Abnormal Psychology, 95,* 24–28.

Rappaport, J., (1987). Terms of empowerment/exemplars of prevention: Toward a theory for community psychology. *American Journal of Community Psychology, 2,* 121–148.

Raskin, D. C. (1986). The polygraph in 1986: Scientific, professional and legal issues surrounding application and acceptance of polygraph evidence. *Utah Law Review, 29,* 29–75.

Raskin, D. C., Barland, G. H., & Podlesny, J. A. (1978). *Validity and reliability of detection of deception.* Washington, DC: National Institute of Law Enforcement and Criminal Justice.

Raskin, D. C., & Hare, R. D. (1978). Psychopathy and detection of deception in a prison population. *Psychophysiology, 15,* 126–136.

Ravussin, E., Lillioja, S., Knowler, W. C., Christin, L., Freymond, D., Abbott, W. G. H., Boyce, V., Howard, B. V., & Bogardus, C. (1988). Reduced rate of energy expenditure as a risk factor for body-weight gain. *New England Journal of Medicine, 318,* 467–472.

Rayner, K. (1998). Eye movements in reading and information processing: 20 years of research. *Psychological Bulletin, 124*(3), 372–422.

Rayner, K., & Pollatsek, A. (1992). Eye movements and scene perception. *Canadian Journal of Psychology, 46,* 342–376.

Raz, S., & Raz, N. (1990). Structural brain abnormalities in the major psychoses: A quantitative review of the evidence from computerized imaging. *Psychological Bulletin, 208,* 93–108.

Ree, M. J., & Earles, J. A. (1992). Intelligence is the best predictor of job performance. *Current Directions in Psychological Science, 1,* 86–89.

Ree, M. J., Earles, J. A., & Teachout, M. S. (1994). Predicting job performance: Not much more than g. *Journal of Applied Psychology, 79,* 518–524.

Reed, C. F. (1984). Terrestrial passage theory of the moon illusion. *Journal of Experimental Psychology: General, 113,* 489–516.

Reichle, E. D., Pollatsek, A., Fisher, D. L., & Rayner, K. (1998). Toward a model of eye movement control in reading. *Psychological Review, 105*(1), 125–157.

Reiger, D. A., Boyd, J. H., Burke, J. D., Rae, D. S., Myers, J. K., Kramer, M., Robins, L. N., George, L. K., Karno, M., & Locke, B. Z. (1988). One-month prevalence of mental disorders in the United States. *Archives of General Psychiatry, 45,* 977–986.

Reis, H. T., & Shaver, P. (1988). Intimacy as an interpersonal process. In S. Duck (Ed.), *Handbook of personal relationships: Theory, relationships and interventions.* Chichester, England: Wiley.

Reisenzein, R. (1983). The Schachter theory of emotion: Two decades later. *Psychological Bulletin, 94,* 239–264.

Reiss, D. (1995). Genetic influence on family systems: Implications for development. *Journal of Marriage and the Family, 57,* 543–560.

Reiss, D. (1997). Mechanisms linking genetic and social influences in adolescent development: Beginnning a collaborative search. *American Psychological Society,* 6(4), 100–105.

Reiss, D., & Price, R. H. (1996). National research agenda for prevention research: The National Institute of Mental Health Report. *American Psychologist, 51*(11), 1109–1115.

Renault, B., Signoret, J. L., Debruille, B., Breton, F., & Bolgert, F. (1989). Brain potentials reveal covert facial recognition in proposopagnosia. *Neuropsychologica, 27,* 905–912.

Repetti, R. L., Matthews, K. A., & Waldron, I. (1989). Employment and women's health. *American Psychologist, 44,* 1394–1401.

Reppucci, N. D., & Haugaard, J. J. (1989). Prevention of child sexual abuse. *American Psychologist, 44,* 1266–1275.

Rescorla, R. A. (1977). Pavlovian 2nd-order conditioning: Some implications for instrumental behavior. In H. Davis & H. Herwit (Eds.), *Pavlovian–operant interactions.* Hillsdale, NJ: Erlbaum.

Rescorla, R. A. (1978). Some implications of a cognitive perspective on Pavlovian conditioning. In S. H. Hulse, H. Fowler, & W. Honig (Eds.), *Cognitive process in animal behavior.* Hillsdale, NJ: Erlbaum.

Rescorla, R. A. (1988). Pavlovian conditioning: It's not what you think it is. *American Psychologist, 43,* 151–160.

Resnick, M. D., Bearman, P. S., Blum, R. W., Bauman, K. E., Harris, K. M., Jones, J., Tabor, J., Beuhring, T., Sieving, R. E., Shew, M., Ireland, M., Bearinger, L. H., & Udry, R. (1997). Protecting adolescents from harm: Findings from the National Longitudinal Study on Adolescent Health. *Journal of the American Medical Association, 278*(10), 823–831.

Resnick, R. J. (1997). A brief history of practice—expanded. *American Psychologist, 52*(4), 463–468.

Resnick, S. M. (1992). Positron emission tomography in psychiatric illness. *Psychological Science, 1,* 92–98.

Restak, R. M. (1994). *The modular brain: How new discoveries in neuroscience are answering age-old questions about memory, free will, consciousness, and personal identity.* New York: Macmillan.

Restle, F. (1970). Moon illusion explained on the basis of relative size. *Science, 167,* 1092–1096.

Reynolds, C. F., Frank, E., Perel, J. M., Imber, S. D., Cornes, C., et al. (1999). Nortryptyline and interpersonal psychotherapy as maintenance therapies for recurrent major depression: A randomized controlled trial in patients older than 59 years. *Journal of the American Medical Association, 281*(1), 39–45.

Rhode, D. L. (1997). *Speaking of sex: The denial of gender inequality.* Cambridge, MA: Harvard University Press.

Rhodes, N., & Wood, W. (1992). Self-esteem and intelligence affect influenceability: The mediating role of message reception. *Psychological Bulletin, 111,* 156–171.

Rice, G., Anderson, C., Risch, N., & Ebers, G. (1999). Male homosexuality: Absence of linkage to microsatellite markers at Xq28. *Science, 284,* 665–667.

Richardson, J. T. E., & Zucco, G. M. (1989). Cognition and olfaction: A review. *Psychological Bulletin, 105,* 352–360.

Richie, B. E. (1994). Gender entrapment: An exploratory study. In A. J. Dan et al. (Eds.), *Reframing women's health: Multidisciplinary research and practice* (pp. 219–232). Thousand Oaks, CA: Sage Publications.

Richman, A. L., Miller, P. M., & LeVine, R. A. (1992). Cultural and educational variations in maternal responsiveness. *Developmental Psychology, 28,* 614–621.

Riehle, A., Grun, S., Diesmann, M., & Aertsen, A. (1997). Spike synchronization and rate modulation differentially involved in motor cortical function. *Science, 278,* 1950–1953.

Rifai, A. H., George, C. J., Stack, J. A., Mann, J. J., & Reynolds, C. F. (1994). Hopelessness in suicide attempters after acute treatment of major depression in late life. *American Journal of Psychiatry, 151,* 1687–1690.

Rifai, A. H., Reynolds, C. F., & Mann, J. J. (1992). Biology of elderly suicide. *Suicide and Life Threatening Behavior, 22,* 48–61.

Ring, K., Wallston, K., & Corey, M. (1970). Mode of debriefing as a factor affecting subjective reaction to a Milgram-type obedience experiment: An ethical inquiry. *Representative Research in Social Psychology, 1,* 67–88.

Rips, L. J. (1990). Reasoning. *Annual Review of Psychology, 41,* 321–353.

Ritter, J. M., & Langlois, J. H. (1988). The role of physical attractiveness in the observation of adult–child interactions: Eye of the beholder or behavioral reality? *Developmental Psychology, 24,* 254–263.

Robberson, M. R., & Rogers, R. W. (1988). Beyond fear appeals: Negative and positive persuasive appeals to health and self-esteem. *Journal of Applied Social Psychology, 18,* 277–287.

Robbins, M., & Meyer, D. (1970). Motivational control of retrograde amnesia. *Journal of Experimental Psychology, 84,* 220–225.

Roberts, A. H., Kewman, D. G., Mercier, L., & Hovell, M. (1993). The power of nonspecific effects in healing: Implications for psychosocial and biological treatments. *Clinical Psychology Review, 13,* 375–391.

Roberts, B. W. (1997). Plaster or plasticity: Are adult work experiences associated with personality change in women? *Journal of Personality, 65*(2), 205–229.

Roberts, G. C. (1992). *Motivation in sport and exercise: Conceptual constraints and convergence.* (pp. 3–29). Champaign, IL: Human Kinetics.

Robinson, L. A., Berman, J. S., & Neimeyer, R. A. (1990). Psychotherapy for the treatment of depression: A comprehensive review of controlled outcome research. *Psychological Bulletin, 108,* 30–49.

Rock, I., & Palmer, S. (1990). The legacy of Gestalt psychology. *Scientific American, 263*(6), 84–90.

Rodin, J. (1981). Current status of the internal–external hypothesis for obesity: What went wrong? *American Psychologist, 36,* 361–372.

Rodin, J. (1986). Aging and health: Effects of the sense of control. *Science, 233,* 1271–1276.

Rodin, J., & Ickovics, J. R. (1990). Women's health. *American Psychologist, 45,* 1018–1034.

Rodin, J., & Salovey, P. (1989). Health psychology. *Annual Review of Psychology, 40,* 533–581.

Rodriguez, E., George, N., Lachaux, J. P., Martinerie, J., Renault, B., & Varela, F. J. (1999). Perception's shadow: Long-distance synchronization of human activity. *Nature, 397,* 430–433.

Roehrs, T., Timms, V., Zwyghuizen-Doorenbos, A., & Roth, T. (1989). Sleep extension in sleepy and alert normals. *Sleep, 12,* 449–457.

Rogers, C. R. (1951). *Client-centered therapy.* Boston: Houghton Mifflin.

Rogoff, B. & Morelli, G. (1989). Perspectives on children's development from cultural psychology. *American Psychologist, 44,* 343–348.

Romano, S. T., & Bordieri, J. E. (1989). Physical attractiveness stereotypes and students' perceptions of college professors. *Psychological Reports, 64,* 1099–1102.

Romans, S. E., Martin, J. L., Anderson, J. C., Herbison, G. P., & Mullen, P. E. (1995). Sexual abuse in childhood and deliberate self-harm. *American Journal of Psychiatry, 152,* 1336–1342.

Roose, S. P., Glassman, A. H., Attia, E., & Woodring, S. (1994). Comparative efficacy of selective serotonin reuptake inhibitors and tricyclics in the treatment of melancholia. *American Journal of Psychiatry, 151,* 1735–1739.

Roques, P., Lambin, M., Jeunier, B., & Strayer, F. F. (1997). Multivariate analysis of personal space in a primary school classroom. *Enfance, 4,* 451–468.

Rorty, M., Yager, J., & Rossotto, E. (1994). Childhood sexual, physical, and psychological abuse in bulimia nervosa. *American Journal of Psychiatry, 151,* 1122–1126.

Rosch, E. (1973). Natural categories. *Cognitive Psychology, 4,* 328–350.

Rosch, E. (1978). Principles of categorization. In E. Rosch & B. B. Lloyd (Eds.), *Cognition and categorization* (pp. 27–48). Hillsdale, NJ: Erlbaum.

Rose, S. A., & Feldman, J. F. (1995). Prediction of IQ and specific cognitive abilities at 11 years from infancy measures. *Developmental Psychology, 31,* 685–696.

Rose, S. D. (1991). The development and practice of group treatment. In M. Hersen, A. E. Kazdin, & A. S. Bellack (Eds.), *The clinical psychology handbook* (2nd ed.). New York: Pergamon.

Rosebush, P. A. (1998). Psychological intervention with military personnel in Rwanda. *Military Medicine, 163*(8), 559–563.

Rosenberg, H. (1993). Prediction of controlled drinking by alcoholics and problem drinkers. *Psychological Bulletin, 113,* 129–139.

Rosenberg, P. S. (1995). Scope of the AIDS epidemic in the United States. *Science, 270,* 1372–1375.

Rosenstock, I. M., & Kirscht, J. P. (1979). Why people seek health care. In G. C. Stone, F. Cohen, & N. E. Adler (Eds.), *Health psychology—a handbook.* San Francisco: Jossey-Bass.

Ross, H. S., & Lollis, S. P. (1987). Communication within infant social games. *Developmental Psychology, 2,* 241–248.

Ross, J. A., Haimes, D. H., & Hogaboam-Gray, A. (1998). Improving student helpfulness in cooperative learning groups. *Journal of Classroom Interaction, 31*(2), 13–22.

Ross, L., Bierbrauer, G., & Hoffman, S. (1976). The role of attribution processes in conformity and dissent. *American Psychologist, 31,* 148–157.

Ross, S. M., & Offermann, L. R. (1997). Transformational leaders: Measurement of personality attributes and work group performance. *Personality and Social Psychology Bulletin, 23*(10), 1078–1086.

Rothbart, M. K., Taylor, S. B., & Tucker, D. M. (1989). Right-sided facial asymmetry in infant emotional expression. *Neuropsychologia, 27,* 675–687.

Rothblum, E. D. (1990). Women and weight: Fad and fiction. *Journal of Psychology, 124*(1), 5–24.

Rothblum, E. D. (1992). Women and weight: An international perspective. In U. P. Gielen, L. L. Adler, et al. (Eds.), *Psychology in international perspective: 50 years of the International Council of Psychologists* (pp. 271–280). Amsterdam: Swets & Zeitlinger.

Rotter, J. B. (1990). Internal versus external control of reinforcement. *American Psychologist, 45,* 489–493.

Rowland, D. L., Greenleaf, W. J., Dorfman, L. J., & Davidson, J. M. (1993). Aging and sexual function in men. *Archives of Sexual Behavior, 22,* 545–558.

Rowland, N. E., Li, B. H., & Morien, A. (1996). Brain mechanisms and the physiology of feeding. In E. D. Capaldi et al. (Eds.), *Why we eat what we eat: The psychology of eating* (pp. 173–204). Washington, DC: American Psychological Association.

Roy, A., Neilsen, D., Rylander, G., Sarchiapone, M., & Segal, N. (1999). Genetics of suicide in depression. *Journal of Clinical Psychiatry, 60*(Suppl. 2), 12–17.

Roy, A., Segal, N. L., Ceterwall, B. S., & Robinette, C. D. (1991). Suicide in twins. *Archives of General Psychiatry, 48,* 29–32.

Ruback, R. B., Pandey, J., & Begum, H. A. (1997). Urban stressors in South Asia: Impact on male and female pedestrians in Delhi and Dhaka. *Journal of Cross-Cultural Psychology, 28*(1), 23–43.

Ruback, R. B., & Riad, J. K. (1994). The more (men), the less merry: Social density, social burden and social support. *Sex Roles, 30*(11/12), 743–763.

Ruchlin, H. S., & Morris, J. N. (1991). Impact of work on the quality of life in community-residing young elderly. *American Journal of Public Health, 81,* 498–500.

Rugg, M. D. (1996). Differential activation of the prefrontal cortex in successful and unsuccessful memory retrieval. *Brain, 119*(6), 2073–2083.

Ruggieri, V., Milizia, M., Sabatini, N., & Tosi, M. T. (1983). Body perception in relation to muscular tone at rest and tactile sensitivity. *Perceptual and Motor Skills, 56*(3), 799–806.

Rumbaugh, D. M., Gill, T. V., & Von Glaserfeld, E. D. (1973). Reading and sentence completion by a chimpanzee (Pan troglodytes). *Science, 182,* 731–733.

Rumbaugh, D. M., Savage-Rumbaugh, S., & Hegel, M. T. (1987). Summation in the chimpanzee (Pan troglodytes). *Journal of Experimental Psychology: Animal Behavior Processes, 13,* 107–115.

Rumiati, R. I., & Humphreys, G. W. (1997). Visual object agnosia without alexia or propagnosia: Arguments for separate knowledge stores. *Visual Cognition, 4*(2), 207–217.

Russell, J. A. (1994). Is there universal recognition of emotion from facial expression? A review of the cross-cultural studies. *Psychological Bulletin, 115,* 102–141.

Rustemli, A. (1991). Crowding effects of density and interpersonal distance. *The Journal of Social Psychology, 132,* 51–58.

Ryan, N. D., & Varma, D. (1998). Child and adolescent mood disorders: Experience with serotonin-based therapies. *Biological Psychiatry, 44*(5), 336–340.

Saffran, J., Aslin R., & Newport, E. (1996). Statistical learning by 8-month old infants. *Science, 274,* 1926–1928.

Sakata, S., Shinohara, J., Hori, T., & Sugimoto, S. (1995). Enhancement of randomness by flotation rest (restricted environmental stimulation technique). *Perceptual and Motor Skills, 80*(3, Pt. 1), 999–1010.

Sakitt, B., & Long, G. M. (1979). Cones determine subjective offset of a stimulus but rods determine total persistence. *Vision Research, 19,* 1439–1443.

Salminen, S., & Glad, T. (1992). The role of gender in helping behavior. *The Journal of Social Psychology, 132,* 131–133.

Salt, R. E. (1991). Affectionate touch between fathers and preadolescent sons. *Journal of Marriage and the Family, 53,* 545–554.

Salthouse, T. A. (1995). Selective influences of age and speed on associative memory. *American Journal of Psychology, 108,* 381–396.

Salthouse, T. A. (1999). Theories of cognition. In V. L. Bengtson, K. W. Schaie, et al. (Eds.), *Handbook of theories of aging* (pp. 196–208). New York: Springer Publishing Co.

Salzberg, H. C., & DePiano, F. A. (1980). Hypnotizability and task motivating suggestions: A further look at how they affect performance. *International Journal of Clinical and Experimental Hypnosis, 28,* 261–271.

Salzman, C. (1997). Update on the somatic treatment of depression in the older adult: Psychopharmacology and ECT. *Journal of Geriatric Psychiatry, 30*(2), 259–270.

Sanchez, J. I., & Fernandez, D. M. (1993). Acculturative stress among Hispanics: A bidimensional model of ethnic identification. *Journal of Applied Social Psychology, 23*(8), 654–668.

Sande, G. N., Goethals, G. R., & Radloff, C. E. (1988). Perceiving one's own traits and others: The multifaceted self. *Journal of Personality and Social Psychology, 54,* 13–20.

Sanders, G. S., & Simmons, W. L. (1983). Use of hypnosis to enhance eyewitness accuracy: Does it work? *Journal of Applied Psychology, 68,* 70–77.

Sanders, M. S., & McCormick, E. J. (1993). *Human factors in engineering and design* (7th ed.). New York: McGraw-Hill.

Sanders, R. J. (1985). Teaching apes to ape language: Explaining the imitative and nonimitative signing of a chimpanzee (Pan troglodytes). *Journal of Comparative Psychology, 99,* 197–210.

Santos, M. D., Leve, C., & Pratkanis, A. R. (1994). Hey buddy, can you spare seventeen cents? Mindful persuasion and the pique technique. *Journal of Applied Social Psychology, 224,* 755–764.

Sapp, M. (1996). Potential negative sequelae of hypnosis. *Australian Journal of Clinical Hypnotherapy and Hypnosis, 17*(2), 73–78.

Sarason, I. G., & Sarason, B. R. (1987). *Abnormal psychology: The problem of maladaptive behavior* (5th ed.). Englewood Cliffs, NJ: Prentice-Hall.

Sattler, J. M. (1992). *Assessment of children: Revised and updated* (3rd ed.). San Diego: Jerome M. Sattler.

Savage-Rumbaugh, S., Pate, J. L., Lawson, J., Smith, S. T., & Rosenbaum, S. (1983). Can a chimpanzee make a statement? *Journal of Experimental Psychology: General, 112,* 457–492.

Sawicki, S. (1988). Effective crisis intervention. *Adolescence, 23,* 83–88.

Saxe, L. (1994). Detection of deception: Polygraph and integrity tests. *Current Directions in Psychological Science, 3,* 69–73.

Scalaidhe, S. P., Wilson, F. A., & Goldman-Rakic, P. S. (1997). Areal segregation of face-processing neurons in prefrontal cortex. *Science, 278,* 1135–1138.

Scarr, S. (1998). American child care today. *American Psychologist, 53*(2), 95–108.

Scarr, S. & Eisenberg, M. (1993). Child care research: Issues, perspectives, and results. *Annual Review of Psychology, 44,* 613–644.

Scarr, S., Eisenberg, M., & Deater-Deckard, K. (1994). Measurement of quality in child care centers. *Early Childhood Research Quarterly, 9,* 131–151.

Scarr, S., Phillips, D., & McCartney, K. (1990). Facts, fantasies, and the future of child care in the United States. *Psychological Science, 1,* 26–35.

Scarr, S., & Weinberg, R. A. (1994). Educational and occupational achievements of brothers and sisters in adoptive and biologically related families. *Behavior-Genetics, 24*(4), 301–325.

Schachter, S., Goldman, R., & Gordon, A. (1968). Effects of fear, food deprivation, and obesity on eating. *Journal of Personality and Social Psychology, 10,* 91–97.

Schachter, S., & Singer, J. E. (1962). Cognitive, social, and physiological determinants of emotional state. *Psychological Review, 69,* 379–399.

Schacter, D. L. (1996). *Searching for memory: The brain, the mind, and the past.* New York: Basic Books.

Schacter, D. L. (1997). False recognition and the brain. *American Psychological Society, 6*(3), 65–70.

Schacter, D. L., Alpert, N. M., Savage, C. R., Rauch, S. L., & Albert, M. S. (1996). Conscious recollection and the human hippocampal formation: Evidence from positron emission tomography. *Proceedings of the National Academy of Sciences of the USA, 93,* 321–325.

Schacter, D. L., Kihlstrom, J. F., Kihlstrom, L. C., & Berren, M. B. (1989). Autobiographical memory in a case of multiple personality disorder. *Journal of Abnormal Psychology, 98,* 508–514.

Schafe, G. E., Sollars, S. I., & Bernstein, I. L. (1995). The CS-US interval and taste aversion learning: A brief look. *Behavioral Neuroscience, 109*(4), 799–802.

Schaie, K. W. (1993). The Seattle longitudinal studies of adult intelligence. *Current Directions in Psychological Science, 2,* 171–175.

Schaie, K. W. (1994). The course of adult intellectual development. *American Psychologist, 49,* 304–313.

Schaie, K. W., & Willis, S. L. (1986). *Adult development and aging* (2nd ed.). Boston: Little, Brown.

Schaller, M. (1991). Social categorization and the formation of group stereotypes: Further evidence for biased information processing in the perception of group-behavior correlations. *European Journal of Social Psychology, 21*(1), 25–35.

Schatzman, M. (1992). Freud: Who seduced whom? *New Scientist,* 34–37.

Schedlowski, M., Fluge, T., Richter, S., Tewes, U., Schmidt, R. W., et al. (1995). Beta-endorphin, but not substance P, is increased by acute stress in humans. *Psychoneuroendocrinology, 20*(1), 103–110.

Scheibel, A. B., Conrad, T., Perdue, S., Tomiyasu, U., & Wechsler, A. (1990). A quantitative study of dendrite complexity in selected areas of the human cerebral cortex. *Brain Cognition, 12,* 85–101.

Scheier, M. F., & Carver, C. S. (1993). On the power of positive thinking: The benefits of being optimistic. *Current Directions in Psychological Science, 2,* 26–30.

Schiff, M., Duyme, M., Dumaret, A., & Tomkiewicz, S. (1982). How much could we boost scholastic achievement and IQ scores? A direct answer from a French adoption study. *Cognition, 12,* 165–196.

Schiller, P. H. (1994). Area V4 of the primate visual cortex. *Current Directions in Psychological Science, 3,* 89–92.

Schinka, J. A., Dye, D. A., & Curtiss, G. (1997). Correspondence between five-factor and RIASEC models of personality. *Journal of Personality Assessment, 68*(2), 355–368.

Schlaug, G., Jäncke, L., Huang, Y., Staiger, J. F., & Steinmetz, H. (1995). Increased corpus callosum size in musicians. *Neuropsychologia, 33*(8), 1047–1055.

Schleifer, S. J., Keller, S. E., & Stein, M. (1987). Conjugal bereavement and immunity. *Israel Journal of Psychiatry and Related Sciences, 24*(1/2), 111–123.

Schmidt, D. F., & Boland, S. M. (1986). Structure of perceptions of older adults: Evidence for multiple stereotypes. *Psychology and Aging, 1,* 255–260.

Schmidt, F. L., & Hunter, J. E. (1998). The validity and utility of selection methods in personnel psychology: Practical and theoretical implications of 85 years of research findings. *Psychological Bulletin, 124*(2), 262–274.

Schmidt, F. L., Onex, D. S., & Hunter, J. E. (1992). Personnel selection. *Annual Review of Psychology, 43,* 627–670.

Schmidt, L. A., Fox, N. A., Rubin, K. H., & Sternberg, E. M. (1997). Behavioral and neuroendocrine responses in shy children. *Developmental Psychobiology, 30*(2), 127–140.

Schmidt, S. R. (1991). Can we have a distinctive theory of memory? *Memory and Cognition, 19,* 523–542.

Schmit, M. J., & Ryan, A. M. (1993). The big five in personnel selection: Factor structure in applicant and nonapplicant populations. *Journal of Applied Psychology, 78,* 966–974.

Schnur, E., Brooks-Gunn, J., & Shipman, V. C. (1992). Who attends programs serving poor children? The case of Head Start attendees and nonattendees. *Journal of Applied Developmental Psychology, 13,* 405–421.

Schoelmerich, A., Fracasso, M. P., Lamb, M. E., & Broberg, A. G. (1995). Interactional harmony at 7 and 10 months of age predicts security of attachment as measured by Q-sort ratings. *Social Development, 4*(1), 62–74.

Schooler, C., Neumann, E., Caplan, L. J., & Roberts, B. R. (1997). A time course analysis of Stroop interference and facilitation: Comparing normal individuals and individuals with schizophrenia. *Journal of Experimental Psychology: General, 126*(1), 19–36.

Schramke, C. J., & Bauer, R. M. (1997). State-dependent learning in older and younger adults. *Psychology and Aging, 12*(2), 255–262.

Schulberg, H. C., & Rush, A. J. (1994). Clinical practice guidelines for managing major depression in primary care practice: Implications for psychologists. *American Psychologist, 49,* 34–41.

Schusterman, R. J., & Gisiner, R. (1988). Artificial language comprehension in dolphins and sea lions: The essential cognitive skills. *Psychological Record, 38*(3), 311–348.

Schutte, N. S., Malouff, J. M., Post-Gorden, J. C., & Rodasta, A. L. (1988). Effects of playing video games on children's aggressive and other behaviors. *Journal of Applied Social Psychology, 18,* 454–460.

Schwartz, J. C., & Shaver, P. (1987). Emotions and emotion knowledge in interpersonal relations. *Advances in Personal Relationships, 1,* 197–241.

Schwartzman, A. E., Gold, D., Andres, D., Arbuckle, T. Y., & Chaikelson, J. (1987). Stability of intelligence: A 40-year follow-up. *Canadian Journal of Psychology, 41,* 244–256.

Schwarz-Stevens, K. S., & Cunningham, C. L. (1993). Pavlovian conditioning of heart rate and body temperature with morphine: Effects of CS duration. *Behavioral Neuroscience, 107,* 1039–1048.

Schweickert, R., & Boruff, B. (1986). Short-term memory capacity: Magic number or magic spell? *Journal of Experimental Psychology: Learning, Memory, and Cognition, 12,* 419–425.

Schweiger, U., Deuschle, M., Körner, A., Lammers, C. H., Schmider, J., Gotthardt, U., Holsboer, F., & Heuser, I. (1994). Low lumbar bone mineral density in patients with major depression. *American Journal of Psychiatry, 151,* 1691–1693.

Seamon, J. G., Luo, C. R., & Gallo, D. A. (1998). Creating false memories of words with or without recognition of list items. *American Psychological Society, 9*(1), 20–26.

Sears, D. O., & Kosterman, R. (1994). Mass media and political persuasion. In S. Shavitt & T. C. Brock (Eds.), *Persuasion: Psychological insights and perspectives* (pp. 251–278). Boston: Allyn & Bacon.

Segall, M. H., Lonner, W. J., & Berry, J. W. (1998). Cross-cultural psychology as a scholarly discipline: On the flowering of culture in behavioral research. *American Psychologist, 53*(10), 1101–1110.

Segerstrom, S. C., Taylor, S. D., Kemeny, M. E., & Fahey, J. L. (1998). Optimism is associated with mood, coping and immune change in response to stress. *Journal of Personality and Social Psychology, 74*(6), 1646–1655.

Seidenberg, M. S. (1997). Language acquisition and use: Learning and applying probabilistic constraints. *Science, 275,* 1599–1603.

Seif, M. N., & Atkins, A. L. (1979). Some defensive and cognitive aspects of phobias. *Journal of Abnormal Psychology, 88,* 42–51.

Sejnowski, T. J., Koch, C., & Churchland, P. S. (1988). Computational neuroscience. *Science, 24,* 1299–1306.

Seki, S. (1992). The visual image in mind and brain. *Scientific American, 267*(3), 68–76.

Selekman, M. D. (1993). Solution-oriented brief therapy with difficult adolescents. In S. Friedman (Ed.), *The new language of change: Constructive collaboration in psychotherapy* (pp. 138–157). New York: Guilford Press.

Seligman, M. E. P. (1975). *Helplessness.* San Francisco: Freeman.

Seligman, M. E. P. (1976). *Learned helplessness and depression in animals and humans.* Morristown, NJ: General Learning.

Seligman, M. E. P. (1988, August). *Learned helplessness.* G. Stanley Hall lecture at the American Psychological Association Convention, Atlanta.

Seligman, M. E. P. (1991). *Learned optimism.* New York: Knopf.

Seligman, M. E. P. (1995). The effectiveness of psychotherapy. *American Psychologist, 50,* 965–974.

Selkoe, D. J. (1992, September). Aging brain, aging mind. *Scientific American,* 135–142.

Sell, M. A., Ray, G. E., & Lovelace, L. N. (1995). Preschool children's comprehension of a Sesame Street video tape: The effects of repeated viewing and previewing instructions. *Educational Technology Research and Development, 43*(3), 49–60.

Sell, R. L., Wells, J. A., & Wypij, D. (1995). The prevalence of homosexual behavior and attraction in the United States, the United Kingdom and France: Results of national population-based samples. *Archives of Sexual Behavior, 24,* 235–248.

Selye, H. (1956). *The stress of life.* New York: McGraw-Hill.

Selye, H. (1976). *Stress in health and disease.* London: Butterworth.

Sengel, R. A., & Lovallo, W. R. (1983). Effects of cueing on immediate and recent memory in schizophrenics. *Journal of Nervous and Mental Disease, 171,* 426–430.

Sevcik, R. A., & Savage-Rumbaugh, E. S. (1994). Language comprehension and use by great apes. *Language and Communication, 14,* 37–58.

Severiens, S., & Ten-Dam, G. (1997). Gender and gender identity differences in learning styles. *Educational Psychology, 17*(1/2), 79–93.

Shadish, W. R., Montgomery, L. M., Wilson, P., Wilson, M. R., Bright, I., & Okwumabua, T. (1993). Effects of family and marital psychotherapies: A meta-analysis. *Journal of Consulting and Clinical Psychology, 61,* 992–1002.

Shallice, T., Fletcher, P., Frith, C. D., Grasby, P., Frackowiak, R. S. J., & Dolan, R. J. (1994). Brain regions associated with acquisition and retrieval of verbal episodic memory. *Nature, 368,* 633–635.

Shamir, B. (1992). Attribution of influence and charisma to the leader: The romance of leadership revisited. *Journal of Applied Social Psychology, 22,* 386–407.

Shanab, M. E., & Yahya, K. A. (1978). A cross-cultural study of obedience. *Bulletin of the Psychonomic Society, 11,* 267–269.

Shapiro, D. A., Barkham, M., Rees, A., Hardy, G. E., Reynolds, S., & Startup, M. (1994). Effects of treatment duration and severity of depression on the effectiveness of cognitive–behavioral and psychodynamic–interpersonal psychotherapy. *Journal of Consulting and Clinical Psychology, 62*, 522–534.

Sharabany, R., Gershoni, R., & Hofman, J. E. (1981). Girlfriend, boyfriend: Age and sex differences in intimate friendship. *Developmental Psychology, 17*, 800–808.

Sharit, J., & Czaja, S. J. (1999). Performance of a computer-based troubleshooting task in the banking industry: Examinating the effects of age, task experience, and cognitive abilities. *International Journal of Cognitive Ergonomics, 3*(1), 1–22.

Shatz, C. J. (1992, September). The developing brain. *Scientific American*, 61–67.

Shatz, M., & Gelman, R. (1973). The development of communication skills: Modifications in the speech of young children as a function of listener. *Monographs of the Society for Research in Child Development, 38*(2, Serial No. 152).

Shaw, G. M., Shapiro, R. Y., Lock, S., & Jacobs, L. R. (1998). Trends: Crime, the police, and civil liberties. *Public Opinion Quarterly*, 405–426.

Shaw, J. S., III, Bjork, R. A., & Handal, A. (1995). Retrieval-induced forgetting in an eyewitness-memory paradigm. *Psychonomic Bulletin and Review, 2*, 249–253.

Shaywitz, B. A., Shaywitz, S. E., Pugh, K. R., Constable, R. T., Skudlarski, P., Fulbright, R. K., Bronen, R. A., Fletcher, J. M., Shankweiler, D. P., Katz, L., & Gore, J. C. (1995). Sex differences in the functional organization of the brain for language. *Nature, 373*, 607–609.

Shaywitz, S. E. (1996). Dyslexia. *Scientific American, 275*(5), 98–104.

Shaywitz, S. E., Shaywitz, B. A., Pugh, K. R., Fullbright, R. K., & Constable, R. T. (1998). Functional disruption in the organization of the brain for reading in dyslexia. *Proceedings of the National Academy of Sciences, 95*(5), 2636–2641.

Shedler, J., & Block, J. (1990). Adolescent drug use and psychological health. *American Psychologist, 45*, 612–630.

Sheehan, P. W., & Tilden, J. (1983). Effects of suggestibility and hypnosis on accurate and distorted retrieval from memory. *Journal of Experimental Psychology: Learning, Memory and Cognition, 9*(2), 283–293.

Sheehy, G. (1995). *New passages: Mapping your life across time.* New York: Random House.

Sheehy, G. (1998). *Understanding men's passages: Discovering the new map of men's lives.* New York: Random House.

Sheeran, P., Abraham, C., & Orbell, S. (1999). Psychosocial correlates of heterosexual condom use: A meta-analysis. *Psychological Bulletin, 125*(1), 90–132.

Shefler, G., Dasberg, H., & Ben-Shakhar, G. (1995). A randomized controlled outcome and follow-up study of Mann's time-limited psychotherapy. *Journal of Consulting and Clinical Psychology, 63*, 585–593.

Shen, B., & McNaughton, B. L. (1996). Modeling the spontaneous reactivation of experience-specific hippocampal cell assemblies during sleep. *Hippocampus, 6*(6), 685–692.

Shepard, S., & Metzler, D. (1988). Mental rotation: Effects of dimensionality of objects and type of task. *Journal of Experimental Psychology: Human Perception and Performance, 14*, 3–11.

Shepperd, J. A. (1993). Productivity loss in performance groups: A motivation analysis. *Psychological Bulletin, 113*, 67–81.

Sher, L. (1998). The role of the immune system and infection in the effects of psychological factors on the cardiovascular system. *Canadian Journal of Psychiatry, 43*(9), 954–955.

Sheridan, M. S. (1985). Things that go beep in the night: Home monitoring for apnea. *Health and Social Work, 10*, 63–70.

Sherin, J. E., Shiromani, P. J., McCarley, R. W., & Saper, C. B. (1996). Activation of ventrolateral preoptic neurons during sleep. *Science, 271*, 216–219.

Sherman, M., & Key, C. B. (1932). The intelligence of isolated mountain children. *Child Development, 3*, 279–290.

Sherrington, R., Rogaev, E. I., Liang, Y., Rogaeva, E. A., Levesque, G., Ikeda, M., Chi, H., Lin, C., Li, G., Holman, K., Tsuda, T., Mar, L., Foncin, J. F., Bruni, A. C., Montesi, M. P., Sorbi, S., Rainero, I., Pinessi, L., Nee, L., Chumakov, I., Pollen, D., Brookes, A., Sanseau, P., Polinsky, R. J., Wasco, W., Da Silva, H. A. R., Haines, J. L., Pericak-Vance, M. A., Tanzi, R. E., Roses, A. D., Fraser, P. E., Rommens, J. M., & St. George-Hyslop, P. H. (1995). Cloning of a gene bearing missense mutations in early-onset familial Alzheimer's disease. *Nature, 375*, 754–760.

Shih, M., Pittinsky, T. L., & Ambady, N. (1999). Stereotype susceptibility: Identity salience and shifts in quantitative performance. *American Psychological Society, 10*(1), 80–81.

Shimamura, A. P., Berry, J. M., Mangels, J. A., Rusting, C. L., & Jurica, P. J. (1995). Memory and cognitive abilities in university professors: Evidence for successful aging. *Psychological Article, 6*, 271–277.

Shimamura, A. P., & Squire, L. R. (1986). Memory and metamemory: A study of the feeling-of-knowing phenomenon in amnesic patients. *Journal of Experimental Psychology: Learning, Memory, and Cognition, 12*, 452–460.

Shiner, R. L. (1998). How shall we speak of children's personalities in middle childhood? A preliminary taxonomy. *Psychological Bulletin, 124*(3), 308–332.

Shneidman, E. S. (1994). Clues to suicide, reconsidered. *Suicide and Life-Threatening Behavior, 24*, 395–397.

Shobe, K. K., & Kihlstrom, J. F. (1997). Is traumatic memory special? *Current Directions in Psychological Science, 6*(3), 70–74.

Shore, J. H., Vollmer, W. M., & Tatum, E. L. (1989). Community patterns of posttraumatic stress disorders. *Journal of Nervous and Mental Disease, 177*, 681–685.

Shum, M. S. (1998). The role of temporal landmarks in autobiographical memory processes. *Psychological Bulletin, 124*(3), 423–442.

Shute, V. J., Pellegrino, J. W., Hubert, L., & Reynolds. R. W. (1983). The relationship between androgen levels and human spatial abilities. *Bulletin of the Psychonomic Society, 21*, 465–468.

Si, G., Rethorst, S., & Willimczik, K. (1995). Causal attribution perception in sports achievement: A cross-cultural study on attributional concepts in Germany and China. *Journal of Cross-Cultural Psychology, 26,* 537–553.

Siegel, E. F. (1979). Control of phantom limb pain by hypnosis. *American Journal of Clinical Hypnosis, 21,* 285–286.

Siegel, J. M. (1990). Stressful life events and use of physician services among the elderly: The moderating role of pet ownership. *Journal of Personality and Social Psychology, 58,* 1081–1086.

Siegel, J. M., Aneshensel, C. S., Taub, B., Cantwell, D. P., & Driscoll, A. K. (1998). Adolescent depressed mood in a multiethnic sample. *Journal of Youth and Adolescence, 27*(4), 413–427.

Siegel, S. (1988). State dependent learning and morphine tolerance. *Behavioral Neuroscience, 102,* 228–232.

Siegel, S., & Allan, L. G. (1996). The widespread influence of the Rescorla-Wagner model. *Psychonomic Bulletin and Review, 3*(3), 314–321.

Sigelman, L. (1997). Blacks, whites, and the changing of the guard in black political leadership. In S. A. Tuch & J. K. Martin (Eds.), *Racial attitudes in the 1990s: Continuity and change.* Westport, CT: Praeger.

Sigman, M. (1995). Nutrition and child development: More food for thought. *Current Directions in Psychological Science, 4,* 52–55.

Silverman, B. G. (1992). Modeling and critiquing the confirmation bias in human reasoning. *IEEE Transactions on Systems, Man, and Cybernetics, 22*(5), 972–982.

Silverman, L. H. (1983). The subliminal psychodynamic activation method: Overview and comprehensive listing of studies. In J. Masling (Ed.), *Empirical studies of psychoanalytic theories* (Vol. 1, pp. 69–100). Hillsdale, NJ: Erlbaum.

Simonton, D. K. (1988). Age and outstanding achievement: What do we know after a century of research? *Psychological Bulletin, 104,* 251–267.

Simpson, J. A. (1990). Influence of attachment styles on romantic relationships. *Journal of Personality and Social Psychology, 59,* 971–980.

Singer, D. G., & Singer, J. L. (1990). *The house of make-believe.* Cambridge, MA: Harvard University Press.

Singer, L. M., Brodzinsky, D. M., Ramsay, D., Steir, M., & Waters, E. (1985). Mother–infant attachment in adoptive families. *Child Development, 56,* 1543–1551.

Singer, W. (1995). Development and plasticity of cortical processing architectures. *Science, 270,* 758–763.

Sinha, S. P., & Mukherjee, N. (1996). The effect of perceived cooperation on personal space requirements. *Journal of Social Psychology, 136*(5), 655–657.

Skaalvik, E. M., & Rankin, R. J. (1994). Gender differences in mathematics and verbal achievement, self-perception and motivation. *British Journal of Educational Psychology, 64,* 419–428.

Skinner, B. F. (1938). *The behavior of organisms.* New York: Appleton-Century-Crofts.

Skinner, B. F. (1948). Superstition in the pigeon. *Journal of Experimental Psychology, 38,* 168–172.

Skinner, B. F. (1988, June). Skinner joins aversives debate. *American Psychological Association APA Monitor,* 22.

Skinner, B. F. (1989). The origins of cognitive thought. *American Psychologist, 44,* 13–18.

Skoog, G., & Skoog, I. (1999). A 40-year follow-up of patients with obsessive-compulsive disorder. *Archives of General Psychiatry, 56,* 121–132.

Slaikeu, K. A. (1990). *Crisis intervention* (2nd ed.). Boston: Allyn & Bacon.

Smart, R., & Peterson, C. (1994). Stability versus transition in women's career development: A test of Levinson's theory. *Journal of Vocational Behavior, 45,* 241–260.

Smith, C. A. (1989). Dimensions of appraisal and physiological response in emotion. *Journal of Personality and Social Psychology, 56,* 339–353.

Smith, E. E. (1997). Working memory: A view from neuroimaging. *Cognitive Psychology, 33*(1), 5–42.

Smith, E. E., Jonides, J., Koeppe, R. A., & Awh, E. (1995). Spatial versus object working memory: PET investigations. *Journal of Cognitive Neuroscience, 7*(3), 337–356.

Smith, K. H., & Rogers, M. (1994). Effectiveness of subliminal messages in television commercials: Two experiments. *Journal of Applied Psychology, 79,* 866–874.

Smith, M. C. (1983). Hypnotic memory enhancement of witnesses: Does it work? *Psychological Bulletin, 94,* 387–407.

Smith, M. L., Glass, G. V., & Miller, T. I. (1980). *The benefits of psychotherapy.* Baltimore: Johns Hopkins University Press.

Smith, S. L., Wilson, B. J., Kunkel, D., Linz, D., Potter, J., Colvin, C. M., & Donnerstein, E. (1998). *National television violence study. Volume III.* London: Sage Publications.

Smyser, A. A. (1982). Hospices: Their humanistic and economic value. *American Psychologist, 37,* 1260–1262.

Sneed, C. D., McCrae, R. R., & Funder, D. C. (1998). Lay conceptions of the five-factor model and its indicators. *Personality & Social Psychology Bulletin, 24*(2), 115–126.

Snelders, H. J., & Lea, S. E. (1996). Different kinds of work, different kinds of pay: An examination of the overjustification effect. *Journal of Socio-Economics, 25*(4), 517–535.

Sniderman, P. M., & Tetlock, P. E. (1986). Symbolic racism: Problems of motive attribution in political analysis. *Journal of Social Issues, 42*(2), 129–150.

Snowden, L. R., & Cheung, F. K. (1990). Use of inpatient mental health services by members of ethnic minority groups. *American Psychologist, 45,* 347–355.

Snyder, C. R., & Higgins, R. L. (1988). Excuses: Their effective role in the negotiation of reality. *Psychological Bulletin, 104,* 23–35.

Snyder, D. K., Wills, R. M., & Grady-Fletcher, A. (1991). Long-term effectiveness of behavioral versus insight-oriented marital therapy: A 4-year follow-up study. *Journal of Consulting and Clinical Psychology, 59,* 138–141.

Snyder, S. H. (1980). Brain peptides as neurotransmitters. *Science, 209,* 976–983.

Soares, J. C., & Mann, J. (1997). The functional neuroanatomy of mood disorders. *Journal of Psychiatric Research, 31*(4), 393–432.

Sobell, M. B., & Sobell, L. C. (1982). Controlled drinking: A concept coming of age. In K. R. Blanstein & J. Polivy

(Eds.), *Self-control and self-modification of emotional behavior.* New York: Plenum.

Sogon, S., & Izard, C. (1987). Sex differences in emotion recognition by observing body movements: A case of American students. *Japanese Psychological Research, 29,* 89–93.

Solomon, G. F., Segerstrom, S. C., Grohr, P., Kemeny, M., & Fahey, J. (1997). Shaking up immunity: Psychological and immunologic changes after a natural disaster. *Psychosomatic Medicine, 59*(2), 114–127.

Solomon, P. R., Flynn, D., Mirak, J., Brett, M., Coslov, N., & Groccia, M. E. (1998). Five-year retention of the classically conditioned eyeblink response in young adult, middle-aged, and older humans. *Psychology and Aging, 13*(2), 186–192.

Solowij, N. (1998). *Cannabis and cognitive functioning.* Cambridge, England: Cambridge University Press.

Solso, R. L. (1979). *Cognitive psychology.* New York: Harcourt Brace Jovanovich.

Sommers-Flanagan, R., Sommers-Flanagan, J., & Davis, B. (1993). What's happening on music television? A gender role content analysis. *Sex Roles, 28,* 745–754.

Sonn, C. C., & Fisher, A. T. (1998). Sense of community: Community resilient responses to oppression and change. *Journal of Community Psychology, 26*(5), 457–472.

Sorce, J. F., & Emde, R. N. (1981). Mother's presence is not enough: Effect of emotional availability on infant exploration. *Developmental Psychology, 17,* 737–745.

Sosik, J. J., Kahai, S. S., & Avolio, B. J. (1998). Transformational leadership and dimensions of creativity: Motivating idea generation in computer-mediated groups. *Creativity Research Journal, 11*(2), 111–121.

Southwick, S. M., & Yehuda, R. (1993). The interaction between pharmacotherapy and psychotherapy in the treatment of posttraumatic stress disorder. *American Journal of Psychotherapy, 47,* 404–410.

Spangler, W. D. (1992). Validity of questionnaire and TAT measures of need for achievement: Two meta-analyses. *Psychological Bulletin, 112,* 140–154.

Spanos, N. P. (1983). The hidden observer as an experimental creation. *Journal of Personal and Social Psychology, 44*(1), 170–176.

Spanos, N. P. (1991). A sociocognitive approach to hypnosis. In S. J. Lynn & J. W. Rhue (Eds.), *Theories of hypnosis: Current models and perspectives* (pp. 324–361). New York: Guilford Press.

Spears, R., & Haslam, S. A. (1997). Stereotyping and the burden of cognitive load. In R. Spears (Ed.), *The social psychology of stereotyping and group life.* Oxford, England: Blackwell Publishers.

Specker, S., de Zwaan, M., Raymond, N., & Mitchell, J. (1994). Psychopathology in subgroups of obese women with and without binge eating disorder. *Comprehensive Psychiatry, 35,* 185–190.

Sperling, G. (1960). The information available in brief visual presentations. *Psychological Monographs, 15,* 201–293.

Sperry, R. W. (1985). Consciousness, personal identity, and the divided brain. In D. F. Benson & E. Zaidel (Eds.), *The dual brain: Hemispheric specialization in humans* (pp. 11–26). New York: Guilford.

Speth, C., & Brown, R. (1990). Effects of college students' learning styles and gender on their test preparation strategies. *Applied Cognitive Psychology, 4,* 189–202.

Sporer, S. L. (1993). Eyewitness identification accuracy, confidence, and decision times in simultaneous and sequential lineups. *Journal of Applied Psychology, 78,* 22–33.

Sporer, S. L., Penrod, S., Read, D., & Cutler, B. (1995). Choosing, confidence, and accuracy: A meta-analysis of the confidence-accuracy relation in eyewitness identification studies. *Psychological Bulletin, 118,* 315–327.

Sprecher, S. (1999). "I love you more today than yesterday": Romantic partners' perceptions of changes in love and related affect over time. *Journal of Personality and Social Psychology, 76*(1), 46–53.

Sprecher, S., Aron, A., Hatfield, E., Cortese, A., Potapova, E., & Levitskaya, A. (1992, July). *Love: American style, Russian style, and Japanese style.* Paper presented at the Sixth International Conference on Personal Relationships, Orono, Maine.

Sprecher, S., Sullivan, Q., & Hatfield, E. (1994). Mate selection preferences: Gender differences examined in a national sample. *Journal of Personality and Social Psychology, 66,* 1074–1080.

Sprock, J., & Yoder, C. Y. (1997). Women and depression: An update on the report of the APA Task Force. *Sex Roles, 36*(5/6), 269–303.

Squire, L. R. (1987). *Memory and brain.* New York: Oxford University Press.

Srinivas, K. (1996). Size and reflection effects in priming: A test of transfer-appropriate processing. *Memory and Cognition, 24*(4), 441–452.

Stagner, R. (1988). *A history of psychological theories.* New York: Macmillan.

Stajkovic, A. D., & Luthans, F. (1998). Self-efficacy and work-related performance: A meta-analysis. *Psychological Bulletin, 124*(2), 240–261.

Stake, J. E. (1997). Integrating expressiveness and instrumentality in real-life settings: A new perspective on the benefits of androgyny. *Sex Roles, 37*(7/8), 541–564.

Standing, L. (1973). Learning 10,000 pictures. *Quarterly Journal of Experimental Psychology, 25,* 207–222.

Standing, L., Conezio, J., & Haber, R. N. (1970). Perception and memory for pictures: Single-trial learning of 2500 visual stimuli. *Psychonomic Science, 19*(2), 73–74.

Stark, R. (1997). A taxonomy of religious experience. In B. Spilka, D. N. McIntosh, et al. (Eds.), *The psychology of religion: Theoretical approaches* (pp. 209–221). Boulder, CO: Westview Press.

Starkey, P. (1992). The early development of numerical reasoning. *Cognition, 43*(2), 93–126.

Stasson, M., & Fishbein, M. (1990). The relation between perceived risk and preventive action: A within-subject analysis of perceived driving risk and intentions to wear seatbelts. *Journal of Applied Social Psychology, 20,* 1541–1557.

Staszewski, J. J. (1987). The psychological reality of retrieval structures: An investigation of expert knowledge (doctoral dissertation, Cornell University, 1987). *Dissertation Abstracts International, 48,* 2168B.

Staszewski, J. J. (1988). Skilled memory and expert mental calculation. In M. T. H. Chi, R. Glaser, & M. J. Farr (Eds.), *The nature of expertise.* Hillsdale, NJ: Erlbaum.

Staub, E. (1996). Cultural-societal roots of violence. *American Psychologist, 51,* 117–132.

Steele, C. M. (1997). A threat in the air: How stereotypes shape intellectual identity and performance. *American Psychologist, 52*(6), 613–629.

Steele, C. M., & Aronson, J. (1995). Stereotype threat and the intellectual test performance of African Americans. *Journal of Personality and Social Psychology, 69,* 797–811.

Steele, C. M., & Josephs, R. A. (1990). Alcohol myopia. *American Psychologist, 45,* 921–933.

Stein, M. I. (1974). *Stimulating creativity.* New York: Academic.

Steinberg, L., Dornbusch, S. M., & Brown, B. B. (1992). Ethnic difference in adolescent achievement. *American Psychologist, 47,* 723–729.

Steinberg, L., Dornbusch, S. M., & Brown, B. B. (1993). Ethnic differences in adolescent achievement: An ecological perspective. *Annual Progress in Child Psychiatry and Child Development,* 528–543.

Steinberg, L., Lamborn, S. D., Darling, N., Mounts, N. S., & Dornbusch, S. M. (1994). Over-time changes in adjustment and competence among adolescents from authoritative, authoritarian, indulgent, and neglectful families. *Child Development, 65,* 754–770.

Steinberg, L., Lamborn, S. D., Dornbusch, S. M., & Darling, N. (1992). Impact of parenting practices on adolescent achievement: Authoritative parenting, school involvement, and encouragement to succeed. *Child Development, 63,* 1266–1281.

Steinberg, M. (1995). *Handbook for the assessment of dissociation: A clinical guide.* Washington, DC: American Psychiatric Press.

Steinberg, M., Cicchetti, D., Buchanan, J., Rakfeldt, J., & Rounsaville, B. (1994). Distinguishing between multiple personality disorder (dissociative identity disorder) and schizophrenia using the structured clinical interview for *DSM-IV* dissociative disorders. *Journal of Nervous and Mental Disease, 182,* 495–502.

Steiner, I. D. (1982). Heuristic models of groupthink. In M. Brandstatter, J. H. Davis, & G. Stocker-Kreichgauer (Eds.), *Group decision making.* New York: Academic.

Stephan, C. W., & Langlois, J. H. (1984). Baby beautiful: Adult attributions of infant competence as a function of infant attractiveness. *Child Development, 55,* 576–585.

Stephenson, J. S. (1985). *Death, grief, and mourning: Individual and social realities.* New York: Macmillan.

Steptoe, A., Kimball, J., & Basford, P. (1998). Exercise and the experience and appraisal of daily stressors: A naturalistic study. *Journal of Behavioral Medicine, 21*(4), 363–374.

Stern, K., & McClintock, M. K. (1998). Regulation of ovulation by human pheromones. *Nature, 392,* 126–127.

Sternberg, R. J. (1984). The Kaufman Assessment Battery for Children: An information-processing analysis and critique. *Journal of Special Education, 18,* 269–279.

Sternberg, R. J. (1985). *Beyond IQ.* Cambridge, England: Cambridge University Press.

Sternberg, R. J. (1986a). *Intelligence applied: Understanding and increasing your intellectual skills.* New York: Harcourt Brace Jovanovich.

Sternberg, R. J. (1986b). A triangular theory of love. *Psychological Review, 93,* 119–135.

Sternberg, R. J. (1995). For whom the bell curve tolls: A review of *The Bell Curve. Psychological Science, 6,* 257–261.

Sternberg, R. J. (1997a). The concept of intelligence and its role in lifelong learning and success. *American Psychologist, 52*(10), 1030–1037.

Sternberg, R. J. (1997b). *Thinking styles.* Cambridge, England: Cambridge University Press.

Sternberg, R. J. (1998). A balance theory of wisdom. *Review of General Psychology, 2*(4), 347–365.

Sternberg, R. J., & Lubart, T. I. (1993). Creative giftedness: A multivariate investment approach. *Gifted Child Quarterly, 37*(1), 7–15.

Sternberg, R. J., & Lubart, T. I. (1996). Investing in creativity. *American Psychologist, 51*(7), 677–688.

Sternberg, R. J., & Wagner, R. K. (1993). The g-ocentric view of intelligence and job performance is wrong. *Current Directions in Psychological Science, 2,* 1–4.

Sternberg, R. J., Wagner, R. K., Williams, W. M., & Horvath, J. A. (1995). Testing common sense. *American Psychologist, 50,* 912–927.

Sternberg, R. J., & Williams, W. M. (1997). Does the Graduate Record Examination predict meaningful success in the graduate training of psychologists? *American Psychologist, 52*(6), 630–641.

Sterrett, E. A. (1998). Use of a job club to increase self-efficacy: A case study of return to work. *Journal of Employment Counseling, 35*(2), 69–78.

Stewart, A. J., & Ostrove, J. M. (1998). Women's personality in middle age: Gender, history, and midcourse corrections. *American Psychologist, 53*(11), 1185–1194.

Stewart, A. J., & Vandewater, E. A. (1998). The course of generativity. In D. P. McAdams, E. de St. Aubin, et al. (Eds.), *Generativity and adult development: How and why we care for the next generation* (pp. 75–100). Washington, DC: American Psychological Association.

Stigler, J. W., & Baranes, R. (1988). Culture and mathematics learning. In E. Rothkopf (Ed.), *Review of Research in Education, 15* (pp. 253–306). Washington, DC: American Educational Research Association.

Stilwell, B. M., Galvin, M. R., Kopta, S. M., & Padgett, R. J. (1998). Moral volition: The fifth and final domain leading to an integrated theory of conscience understanding. *Journal of the American Academy of Child and Adolescent Psychiatry, 37*(2), 202–210.

Stimpson, D., Jensen, L., & Neff, W. (1992). Cross-cultural gender differences in preference for a caring morality. *Journal of Social Psychology, 132,* 317–322.

Stipek, D., Givvin, K. B., Aslmon, J. M., & MacGyvers, V. L. (1998). Can a teacher intervention improve classroom practices and student motivation in mathematics? *Journal of Experimental Education, 66*(4), 319–337.

Stitzer, M. L. (1988). Drug abuse in methadone patients reduced when rewards/punishments clear. *Alcohol, Drug Abuse, and Mental Health, 14,* 1.

Stoff, D. M., & Cairns, R. B. (1996). *Aggression and violence: Genetic, neurobiological, and biosocial perspectives.* Mahwah, NJ: Lawrence Erlbaum Associates, Inc.

Stokols, D. (1995). The paradox of environmental psychology. *American Psychologist, 50,* 821–837.

Stoléru, S., Grégoire, M. C., Gérard, D., Decety, J., Lafarge, E., Cinotti, L., Lavenne, F., LeBars, D., Vernet-Maury, E., Rada, H., Collet, C., Mazoyer, B., Forest, M. G., Magnin, F., Spira, A., & Comar, D. (1999). Neuroanatomical correlates of visually evoked sexual arousal in human males. *Archives of Sexual Behavior, 28*(1), 1–19.

Stone, J., Perry, Z. W., & Darley, J. M. (1997). "White men can't jump": Evidence for the perceptual confirmation of racial stereotypes following a basketball game. *Basic and Applied Social Psychology, 19*(3), 291–306.

Stone, J., Wiegand, A. W., Cooper, J., & Aronson, E. (1997). When exemplification fails: Hypocrisy and the motive for self-integrity. *Journal of Personality and Social Psychology, 72*(1), 54–65.

Stone, M. H. (1980). *The borderline syndromes.* New York: McGraw-Hill.

Stone, V. E., Nisenon, L., Eliassen, J. C., & Gazzaniga, M. S. (1996). Left hemisphere representations of emotional facial expressions. *Neuropsychologia, 34*(1), 23–29.

Strayer, D. L, & Kramer, A. R. (1990). Attentional requirements of automatic and controlled processing. *Journal of Experimental Psychology: Learning, Memory, and Cognition, 16,* 67–82.

Streissguth, A. P., Barr, H. M., & Martin, D. C. (1983). Maternal alcohol use and neonatal habituation assessed with the Brazelton Scale. *Child Development, 54,* 1109–1118.

Streissguth, A. P., Barr, H. M., Sampson, P. D., Darby, B. L., & Martin, D. C. (1989). IQ at age 4 in relation to maternal alcohol use and smoking during pregnancy. *Developmental Psychology, 25,* 3–11.

Strickland, B. R. (1992). Women and depression. *Psychological Science, 1,* 132–135.

Striegel-Moore, R. H., Silberstein, L. R., & Rodin, J. (1993). The social self in bulimia nervosa: Public self-consciousness, social anxiety, and perceived fraudulence. *Journal of Abnormal Psychology, 102*(2), 297–303.

Stringer, P. (1998). One night Vygotsky had a dream: "Children learning to think . . ." and implications for educational psychologists. *Educational and Child Psychology, 15*(2), 14–20.

Stritzke, W. G. K., Lang, A. R., & Patrick, C. J. (1996). Beyond stress and arousal: A reconceptualization of alcohol-emotion relations with reference to psychophysiological methods. *Psychological Bulletin, 120*(3), 376–395.

Stroop, J. R. (1935). Studies of interference in serial verbal reactions. *Journal of Experimental Psychology, 18,* 643–662.

Stuart, E. W., Shimp, T. A., & Engle, R. W. (1987). Classical conditioning of consumer attitudes: Four experiments in an advertising context. *Journal of Consumer Research, 14,* 334–349.

Sturges, J. S. (1994). Family dynamics. In J. L. Ronch, W. V. Ornum, & N. C. Stilwell (Eds.), *The counseling sourcebook: A practical reference on contemporary issues* (pp. 358–372). New York: Crossroad.

Styron, W. (1992). *Darkness visible: A memoir of madness.* New York: Vintage Books.

Suarez, E. C., & Williams, R. B. (1989). Situational determinants of cardiovascular and emotional reactivity in high and low hostile men. *Psychosomatic Medicine, 51,* 404–418.

Suddath, R. L, Christinson, G. W., Torrey, E. F., Casanova, M. F., & Weinberger, D. R. (1990). Anatomical abnormalities in the brains of monozygotic twins discordant for schizophrenia. *New England Journal of Medicine, 322,* 789–794.

Sue, S. (1988). Psychotherapeutic services for ethnic minorities. *American Psychologist, 43,* 301–308.

Suedfeld, P. (1990). Restricted environmental stimulation and smoking cessation: A 15-year progress report. *International Journal of the Addictions, 25,* 861–888.

Sullivan, P. F., Bulik, C. M., Fear, J. L., & Pickering, A. (1998). Outcome of anorexia nervosa: A case-control study. *American Journal of Psychiatry, 155*(7), 939–946.

Sulloway, F. J. (1996). *Born to rebel: Birth order, family dynamics, and creative lives.* New York: Pantheon Books.

Suls, J., & Wan, C. K. (1989a). Effects of sensory and procedural information on coping with stressful medical procedures and pain: A meta-analysis. *Journal of Consulting and Clinical Psychology, 57,* 372–379.

Suls, J., & Wan, C. K. (1989b). The relation between Type A behavior and chronic emotional distress: A meta-analysis. *Journal of Personality and Social Psychology, 57,* 503–512.

Suls, J., & Wan, C. K. (1993). The relationship between trait hostility and cardiovascular reactivity: A quantitative review and analysis. *Psychophysiology, 30,* 615–626.

Summers, T. P., & Hendrix, W. H. (1991). Modeling the role of pay equity perceptions: A field study. *Journal of Occupational Psychology, 64,* 145–157.

Sun, L.-C., & Roopnarine, J. L. (1996). Mother–infant, father–infant interaction and involvement in childcare and household labor among Taiwanese families. *Infant Behavior and Development, 19*(1), 121–129.

Sutker, P. B. & Allain, A. N. (1988). Issues in personality conceptualizations of addictive behaviors. *Journal of Consulting and Clinical Psychology, 56,* 172–182.

Sutker, P. B., Davis, J. M., Uddo, M., & Ditta, S. R. (1995). War zone stress, personal resources, and PTSD in Persian Gulf War returnees. *Journal of Abnormal Psychology, 104,* 444–452.

Suzuki, L. A., & Valencia, R. (1997). Race-ethnicity and measured intelligence: Educational implications. *American Psychologist, 52*(10), 1103–1114.

Swaab, D. F., & Hofman, M. A. (1995). Sexual differentiation of the human hypothalamus in relation to gender and sexual orientation. *Trends in Neuroscience, 18,* 264–270.

Swets, J. A. (1992). The science of choosing the right decision threshold in high-stakes diagnostics. *American Psychologist, 47,* 522–532.

Swim, J., Borgida, E., Maruyama, G., & Myers, D. G. (1989). Joan McKay versus John McKay: Do gender stereotypes bias evaluations? *Psychological Bulletin, 105,* 409–429.

Swim, J. K., Aikin, K. J., Hall, W. S., & Hunter, B. A. (1995). Sexism and racism: Old-fashioned and modern prejudices. *Journal of Personality and Social Psychology, 68,* 199–214.

Szasz, T. (1984). *The therapeutic state: Psychiatry in the mirror of current events* (p. 502). Buffalo, NY: Prometheus.

Szasz, T. (1987). *Insanity: The idea and its consequences.* New York: Wiley.

Szymanski, K., & Harkins, S. G. (1993). The effect of experimenter evaluation on self-evaluation within the social loafing paradigm. *Journal of Experimental Social Psychology, 29,* 268–286.

Tamminen, K. (1994). Religious experiences in childhood and adolescence: A view of religious development between the ages of 7 and 20. *International Journal for the Psychology of Religion, 4*(2), 61–85.

Tanda, G., Pontieri, F. E., & Di Chiara, G. (1997). Cannabinoid and heroin activation of mesolimbic dopamine transmission by a common μ_1 opioid receptor mechanism. *Science, 276,* 2048–2049.

Tarter, R. E., & Vanyukov, M. (1994). Alcoholism: A development disorder. *Journal of Consulting and Clinical Psychology, 62*(6), 1096–1107.

Tataranni, P. A., Young, J. B., Bogardus, C., & Ravussin, E. (1997). A low sympathoadrenal activity is associated with body weight gain and development of central adiposity in Pima Indian men. *Obesity Research, 5*(4), 341–347.

Taubes, G. (1998). As obesity rates rise, experts struggle to explain why. *Science, 280,* 1367–1368.

Taylor, S. E., Repetti, R. L., & Seeman, T. (1997). Health psychology: What is an unhealthy environment and how does it get under the skin? In J. T. Spence, J. M. Darley & D. J. Foss (Eds.), *Annual Review of Psychology, Vol. 48.* Palo Alto, CA: Annual Reviews, Inc.

Teevan, R. C., & McGhee, P. E. (1972). Childhood development of fear of failure motivation. *Journal of Personality and Social Psychology, 21,* 345–348.

Tempo, P. M., & Saito, A. (1996). Techniques of working with Japanese-American families. In G. Yeo, D. Gallagher-Thompson, et al. (Eds.), *Ethnicity and the dementias* (pp. 109–112). Washington, DC: Taylor & Francis.

Tennen, H., & Affleck, G. (1990). Blaming others for threatening events. *Psychological Bulletin, 108,* 209–232.

Tennov, D. (1981). *Love and limerance.* Briarcliffe Manor, NY: Stein & Day.

Terrace, H. S. (1979, November). How Nim Chimpski changed my mind. *Psychology Today,* 65–76.

Terrace, H. S. (1980). *Nim.* New York: Knopf.

Terrace, H. S. (1985). In the beginning was the "name." *American Psychologist, 40,* 1011–1028.

Teske, J. A. (1988). Seeing her looking at you: Acquaintance and variation in the judgment of gaze depth. *American Journal of Psychology, 101,* 239–257.

Tesser, A., & Beach, S. R. H. (1998). Life events, relationship quality, and depression: An investigation of judgment discontinuity in vivo. *Journal of Personality and Social Psychology, 74*(1), 36–52.

Thelen, E. (1994). Three-month-old infants can learn task-specific patterns of interlimb coordination. *Psychological Science, 5,* 280–285.

Theorell, T., Svensson, J., Knox, S., Waller, D., & Alvarez, M. (1986). Young men with high blood pressure report few recent life events. *Journal of Psychosomatic Research, 30,* 243–249.

Thomas, A., & Chess, S. (1977). *Temperament and development.* New York: Brunner/Mazel.

Thompson, R. F. (1991). Are memory traces localized or distributed? *Neuropsychologia, 29,* 571–582.

Thompson, R. F., & Krupa, D. J. (1994). Organization of memory traces in the mammalian brain. *Annual Review of Neuroscience, 17,* 519–549.

Thompson, S. C., Sobolew-Shubin, A., Galbraith, M. E., Schwankovsky, L., & Cruzen, D. (1993). Maintaining perceptions of control: Finding perceived control in low-control circumstances. *Journal of Personality and Social Psychology, 64,* 293–304.

Thompson, T. L., & Zerbinos, E. (1997). Television cartoons: Do children notice it's a boy's world? *Sex Roles, 37*(5/6), 415–432.

Tice, D. M., & Baumeister, R. F. (1985). Masculinity inhibits helping in emergencies: Personality does predict the bystander effect. *Journal of Personality and Social Psychology, 49,* 420–428.

Tice, D. M., & Baumeister, R. F. (1997). Longitudinal study of procrastination performance, stress, and health: The costs and benefits of dawdling. *American Psychological Society, 8*(6), 454–458.

Tilley, A., & Warren, P. (1983). Retrieval from semantic memory at different times of day. *Journal of Experimental Psychology: Learning, Memory, and Cognition, 9,* 718–724.

Timberlake, W., & Farmer-Dougan, V. A. (1991). Reinforcement in applied settings: Figuring out ahead of time what will work. *Psychological Bulletin, 110,* 379–391.

Tjosvold, D. (1987). Participation: A close look at its dynamics. *Journal of Management, 13,* 739–750.

Tomoyasu, N., Bovbjerg, D. H., & Jacobsen, P. B. (1996). Conditioned reactions to cancer chemotherapy: Percent reinforcement predicts anticipatory nausea. *Physiology & Behavior, 59*(2), 273–276.

Torrey, E. F., Bowler, A. E., Taylor, E. H., & Gottesman, I. I. (1994). *Schizophrenia and manic-depressive disorder: The biological roots of mental illness as revealed by the Landmark study of identical twins.* New York: Basic Books.

Tracy, J. A., Thompson, J. K., Krupa, D. J., & Thompson, R. F. (1998). Evidence of plasticity in the pontocerebellar conditioned stimulus pathway during classical conditioning of the eyeblink response in the rabbit. *Behavioral Neuroscience, 112*(2), 267–285.

Tracy, R. J., & Barker, C. H. (1994). A comparison of visual versus auditory imagery in predicting word recall. *Imagination, Cognition and Personality, 13,* 147–161.

Trappey, C. (1996). A meta-analysis of consumer choice and subliminal advertising. *Psychology and Marketing, 13*(5), 517–530.

Travis, C. B. (1988). *Women and health psychology: Biomedical issues.* Hillsdale, NJ: Erlbaum.

Trickett, P. K., & Putnam, F. W. (1993). Impact of child sexual abuse on females: Toward a developmental, psychobiological integration. *Psychological Science, 4,* 81–87.

Trickett, P. K., & Susman, E. J. (1988). Parental perceptions of child-rearing practices in physically abusive and nonabusive families. *Developmental Psychology, 24,* 270–276.

Trites, D., Galbraith, F. D., Sturdavent, M., & Leckwart, J. F. (1970). Influence of nursing-unit design on the activities and subjective feelings of nursing personnel. *Environment and Behavior, 2,* 203–234.

Tronick, E. Z. & Cohn, J. F. (1989). Infant–mother face-to-face interaction: Age and gender differences in coordination and the occurrence of miscoordination. *Child Development, 60,* 85–92.

Tronick, E. Z., Morelli, G. A., & Ivey, P. K. (1992). The Efe forager infant and toddler's pattern of social relationships: Multiple and simultaneous. *Developmental Psychology, 28,* 568–577.

True, W. R., Rice, J., Eisen, S. A., Heath, A. C., Goldberg, J., Lyons, M. J., & Nowak, J. (1993). A twin study of genetic and environmental contributions to liability for posttraumatic stress symptoms. *Archives of General Psychiatry, 50,* 257–264.

Trull, T. J., & Geary, D. C. (1997). Comparison of the Big-Five Factor structure across samples of Chinese and American adults. *Journal of Personality Assesssment, 69*(2), 324–341.

Tryon, W. W. (1998). A neural network explanation of posttraumatic stress disorder. *Journal of Anxiety Disorders, 12*(4), 373–385.

Tsai, M., & Uemura, A. (1988). Asian Americans: The struggles, the conflicts, and the successes. In P. Bronstein & K. Quina (Eds.), *Teaching a psychology of people.* Washington, DC: American Psychological Association.

Tuckman, A. (1996). Isn't it about time psychologists were granted prescription privileges? *Psychotherapy in Private Practice, 15*(2), 1–14.

Tukali-Williams, J., & Carrillo, J. (1995). The impact of psychosocial stressors on African-American and Latino preschoolers. *Journal of the National Medical Association, 87*(7), 473–478.

Tulving, E. (1993). What is episodic memory? *Current Directions in Psychological Science, 2,* 67–70.

Tulving, E., Kapur, S., Craik, F. I. M., Moscovitch, M., & Houle, S. (1994). Hemispheric encoding/retrieval asymmetry in episodic memory: Positron emission tomography findings. *Proceedings of the National Academy of Sciences USA, 91,* 2016–2020.

Tulving, E., Schacter, D. L., & Stark, H. A. (1982). Priming effects in word fragment completion are independent of recognition memory. *Journal of Experimental Psychology: Learning, Memory, and Cognition, 8,* 336–342.

Turk, D. C., Meichenbaum, D., & Genest, M. (1983). *Pain and behavioral medicine: A cognitive–behavioral perspective.* New York: Guilford Press.

Turkheimer, E. (1991). Individual and group differences in adoption studies of IQ. *Psychological Bulletin, 110,* 392–405.

Tversky, A., & Kahneman, D. (1973). Availability: A heuristic for judging frequency and probability. *Cognitive Psychology, 4,* 207–232.

Twenge, J. M. (1997). Changes in masculine and feminine traits over time: A meta-analysis. *Sex Roles, 36*(5/6), 305–309.

Tyler, T. R., & Schuller, R. A. (1991). Aging and attitude change. *Journal of Personality and Social Psychology, 61*(5), 689–697.

Tziner, A., & Murphy, K. R. (1999). Additional evidence of attitudinal influences in performance appraisal. *Journal of Business and Psychology, 13*(3), 407–419.

Uba, L. (1994). *Asian Americans: Personality patterns, identity, and mental health.* New York: Guilford.

Umberson, D., Wortman, C. B., & Kessler, R. C. (1992). Widowhood and depression: Explaining long-term gender differences in vulnerability. *Journal of Health and Social Behavior, 33,* 10–24.

Underwood, G. (1994). Subliminal perception on TV. *Nature, 370,* 103.

United States House of Representatives. (1997). Road Rage: Causes and dangers of aggressive driving. The Subcommittee on Surface Transportation Hearing. (Press Release).

Ursano, R. J., Fullerton, C. S., Kao, T., & Bhartiya, V. R. (1995). Longitudinal assessment of posttraumatic stress disorder and depression after exposure to traumatic death. *Journal of Nervous and Mental Disease, 183,* 36–42.

U.S. Department of Labor. (1998). *Equal pay: A thirty-five year perspective.* Available World Wide Web: <www.dol.gov/dol/wb/>

Vahava, O., Morell, R., Lynch, E. D., Weiss, S., Kagan, M. E., Ahituv, N., et al. (1998). Mutation in transcription factor POU4F3 associated with inherited progressive hearing loss in humans. *Science, 279,* 1950–1954.

Vaillant, G. E., & Milofsky, E. S. (1982). The etiology of alcoholism: A prospective view. *American Psychologist, 37,* 494–503.

Valenstein, E. S. (1998). *Blaming the brain: The truth about drugs and mental health.* New York: The Free Press.

Valins, S. (1966). Cognitive effects of false heart-rate feedback. *Journal of Personality and Social Psychology, 4,* 400–408.

Valins, S., & Baum, A. (1973). Residential group size, social interaction, and crowding. *Environment and Behavior, 5,* 421–435.

Valkenburg, P. M., & van der Voort, T. H. A. (1994). Influence of TV on daydreaming and creative imagination: A review of research. *Psychological Bulletin, 116,* 316–339.

Vandell, D. L., Henderson, V. K., & Wilson, K. S. (1988). A longitudinal study of children with day-care experiences of varying quality. *Child Development, 59,* 1286–1292.

Van Fleet, D. D., & Atwater, L. (1997). Gender-neutral names: Don't be so sure! *Sex Roles, 37*(1/2), 111–123.

Vargha-Khadem, F., Gadian, D. G., Watkins, K. E., Connelly, A., Van Paesschen, W., & Mishkin, M. (1997). Differential effects of early hippocampal pathology on episodic and semantic memory. *Science, 277,* 376–380.

Vartanian, L. R., & Powlishta, K. K. (1996). A longitudinal examination of the social-cognitive foundations of adolescent egocentrism. *Journal of Early Adolescence, 16*(2), 157–178.

Veenhoven, R. (1993). *Happiness in nations.* Rotterdam, Netherlands: Risbo.

Veniegas, R. C., & Peplau, L. A. (1997). Power and the quality of same-sex friendships. *Psychology of Women Quarterly, 21*(2), 279–297.

Verhaeghen, P., & Salthouse, T. A. (1997). Meta-analyses of age-cognition relations in adulthood: Estimates of linear and nonlinear age effects and structural models. *Psychological Bulletin, 122*(3), 231–249.

Vernon, P. (1979). *Intelligence: Heredity and environment.* San Francisco: W. H. Freeman.

Vinar, O. (1997). An attempt to prevent the sequelae of the posttraumatic stress disorder: Experience from the 1997 flood in Moravia. *Homeostasis in Health and Disease, 38*(4), 165–168.

Vitiello, M. V. (1989). *Unraveling sleep disorders of the aged.* Paper presented at the annual meeting of the Association of Professional Sleep Societies, Washington, DC.

Vogel, G. W. (1991). Sleep-onset mentation. In S. J. Ellman, J. S. Antrobus, et al. (Eds.), *The mind in sleep: Psychology and psychophysiology* (2nd ed.) (pp. 125–142). New York: John Wiley.

Von Senden, M. (1932). *Raum- und Gaestaltauffassung bei operierten: Blindgeborernin vor und nach der Operation.* Leipzig, Germany: Barth.

Vroom, V. H. (1964). *Work and motivation.* New York: Wiley.

Vroom, V. H. (1974). A new look at managerial decision making. *Organizational Dynamics, 5,* 66–80.

Vroom, V. H. (1997). Can leaders learn to lead? In R. P. Vecchio et al. (Eds.), *Leadership: Understanding the dynamics of power and influence in organizations* (pp. 278–291). Notre Dame, IN: University of Notre Dame Press.

Vroom, V. H., & Jago, A. G. (1995). Situation effects and levels of analysis in the study of leader participation. *Leadership Quarterly, 6*(2), 169–181.

Vroom, V. H., & Yetton, P. W. (1973). *Leadership and decision-making.* Pittsburgh: University of Pittsburgh Press.

Vroon, P. (1997). *Smell: The secret seducer.* New York: Farrar, Straus & Giroux.

Vygotsky, L. S. (1962). *Thought and language* (E. Hanfmann & G. Vakar, Eds. and Trans.). Cambridge, MA: MIT Press. (Original work published in 1934.)

Vygotsky, L. S. (1978). *Mind in society: The development of higher mental processes.* Cambridge, MA: Harvard University Press. (Original works published 1930, 1933, and 1935).

Wacholtz, E. (1996). Can we learn from the clinically significant face processing deficits prosopagnosia and Capgras delusion? *Neuropsychology Review, 6*(4), 203–257.

Waddington, J. L. (1993). Neurodynamics of abnormalities in cerebral metabolism and structure in schizophrenia. *Schizophrenia Bulletin, 19,* 55–69.

Wadsworth, J., McEwan, J., Johnson, A. M., Wellings, K., et al. (1995). Sexual health for women: Some findings of a large national survey discussed. *Sexual and Marital Therapy, 10*(2), 169–188.

Wagner, A. D., Schacter, D. L., Rotte, M., Koutstall, W., Maril, A., Dale, A. M., Rosen, B. R., & Buckner, R. L. (1998). Building memories: Remembering and forgetting of verbal experiences as predicted by brain activity. *Science, 281,* 1188–1192.

Wagner, R. K. (1997). Intelligence, training, and employment. *American Psychologist, 52*(10), 1059–1069.

Walker, E. A. (1989). Psychology and violence against women. *American Psychologist, 44,* 695–702.

Walker, E., Hoppes, E., Mednick, S., Emory, E., & Schulsinger, F. (1983). Environmental factors related to schizophrenia in psychophysiologically labile high-risk males. *Journal of Abnormal Psychology, 90,* 313–320.

Walker, L. E. (1999). Psychology and domestic violence around the world. *American Psychologist, 54*(1), 21–29.

Walker, L. J., & Pitts, R. C. (1998). Naturalistic conceptions of moral maturity. *Developmental Psychology, 34*(3), 403–419.

Walker-Andrews, A. S. (1986). Intermodal perception of expressive behaviors: Relation of eye and voice? *Developmental Psychology, 22,* 373 377.

Walker-Andrews, A. S. (1997). Infants' perception of expressive behavior: Differentiation of multimodal information. *Psychological Bulletin, 121*(3), 437–456.

Waller, N. G., & Shaver, P. R. (1994). The importance of nongenetic influences on romantic love styles: A twin-family study. *Psychological Science, 5,* 268–274.

Walsh, B. T., & Devlin, M. J. (1998). Eating disorders: Progress and problems. *Science, 280,* 1387–1390.

Walsh, V., & Cowey, A. (1998). Magnetic stimulation studies of visual cognition. *Trends in Cognitive Sciences, 2*(3), 103–110.

Walters, E. E., & Kendler, K. S. (1995). Anorexia nervosa and anorexic-like syndromes in a population-based female twin sample. *American Journal of Psychiatry, 152,* 64–67.

Walton, G. E., & Bower, T. G. R. (1993). Newborns form "prototypes" in less than 1 minute. *Psychological Science, 4,* 203–205.

Wampold, B. E., Monding, G. W., Moody, M., Stich, F., Benson, K., & Ahn, H. (1997). A meta-analysis of outcome studies comparing bona fide psychotherapies: Empirically, "all must have prizes." *Psychological Bulletin, 122*(3), 203–215.

Wandersman, A. H., & Hallman, W. K. (1993). Are people acting irrationally? *American Psychologist, 48,* 681–686.

Wandersman, A., & Nation, M. (1998). Urban neighborhoods and mental health: Psychological contributions to understanding toxicity, resilience, and interventions. *American Psychologist, 53*(6), 647–656.

Ware, R., Rytting, M., & Jenkins, D. (1994). The effect of stress on MBTI scores. *Journal of Psychological Type, 30,* 39–44.

Washton, A. M. (1989). *Cocaine addiction.* New York: Norton.

Watkins, M. J. (1990). Mediationism and the obfuscation of memory. *American Psychologist, 45,* 328–335.

Watson, J. B. (1924). *Behaviorism.* Chicago: University of Chicago Press.

Watson, J. B., & Rayner, R. (1920). Conditioned emotional reactions. *Journal of Experimental Psychology, 3,* 1–14.

Weaver, C. A., III (1993). Do you need a "flash" to form a flashbulb memory? *Journal of Experimental Psychology: General, 122,* 39–46.

Webb, W. B., & Agnew, H. W., Jr. (1975). The effects on subsequent sleep of an acute restriction of sleep length. *Psychophysiology, 12,* 367–370.

Webster, R. (1995). *Why Freud was wrong: Sin, science, and psychoanalysis.* New York: Basic Books.

Weidner, G., Friend, R., Ficarrotto, T. J., & Mendell, N. R. (1989). Hostility and cardiovascular reactivity to stress in women and men. *Psychosomatic Medicine, 51,* 36–45.

Weingartner, H. (1977). Human state-dependent learning. In B. T. Ho, D. Richards, & D. L. Chute (Eds.), *Drug discrimination and state-dependent learning.* New York: Academic.

Weingartner, H., Adefris, W., Eich, J. E., & Murphy, D. L. (1976). Encoding-imagery specificity in alcohol state-dependent learning. *Journal of Experimental Psychology, 2,* 83–87.

Weinstein, C. S., & Mignano, A. (1993). *Organizing the elementary school classroom: Lessons from research and practice.* New York: McGraw-Hill.

Weintraub, S. (1987). Risk factors in schizophrenia: The Stony Brook High-Risk Project. *Schizophrenia Bulletin, 13,* 439–443.

Weisfeld, G. E. (1993). The adaptive value of humor and laughter. *Ethology and Sociobiology, 14*(2), 141–169.

Weissman, M. M., Bland, R. C., Canino, G. J., Greewald, S., Hwu, H.-G., Joyce, P. R., Karam, E. G., Lee, C.-K., Lellouch, J., Lepine, J.-P., Newman, S. C., Rubio-Stipec, M., Wells, J. E., Wickramaratne, P. J., Wittchen, H.-U., & Yeh, E.-K. (1999). Prevalence of suicide ideation and suicide attempts in nine countries. *Psychological Medicine, 29*(1), 9–17.

Wells, G. L. (1993). What do we know about eyewitness identification? *American Psychologist, 48,* 553–571.

Wells, G. L., Luus, C. A. E., & Windschitl, P. D. (1994). Maximizing the utility of eyewitness identification evidence. *Current Directions in Psychological Science, 3,* 194–197.

Werler, M. M., Mitchell, A. A., & Shapiro, M. B. (1989). The relation of aspirin use during the first trimester of pregnancy to congenital cardiac defects. *New England Journal of Medicine, 321,* 1639–1642.

Wessels, H., Lamb, M. E., Hwang, C. P., & Broberg, A. G. (1997). Personality development between 1 and 8 years of age in Swedish children with varying child care experience. *International Journal of Behavioral Development, 21*(4), 771–794.

Wessinger, C. M., Fendrich, R., & Gazzaniga, M. S. (1997). Islands of residual vision in hemianopic patients. *Journal of Cognitive Neuroscience, 9*(2), 203–221.

West, M. A. (1980). Meditation and the EEG. *Psychological Medicine, 10,* 369–375.

West, M. A. (1982). Meditation and self-awareness: Physiological and phenomenological approaches. In G. Underwood (Ed.), *Aspects of consciousness: Vol. 3. Awareness and self-awareness.* London: Academic.

West, R. L. (1996). An application of prefrontal cortex function theory to cognitive aging. *Psychological Bulletin, 120*(2), 272–292.

Wetter, D. W., Fiore, M. C., Gritz, E. R., Lando, H. A., Stitzer, M. L., Hassleblad, V., & Baker, T. B. (1998). The Agency for Health Care Policy and Research smoking cessation clinical practice guideline: Findings and implications for psychologists. *American Psychologist, 53*(6), 657–669.

Wexler, B. E., & Cicchetti, D. V. (1992). The outpatient treatment of depression. *Journal of Nervous and Mental Disease, 180,* 277–286.

Wheeler, M. A., Stuss, D. T., & Tulving, E. (1997). Toward a theory of episodic memory: The frontal and autonoetic consciousness. *Psychological Bulletin, 121*(3), 331–354.

Whicker, K. M., Bol, L., & Nunnery, J. A. (1997). Cooperative learning in the secondary mathematics classroom. *Journal of Educational Research, 91*(1), 42–48.

Whisman, M. A. (1993). Mediators and moderators of change in cognitive therapy of depression. *Psychological Bulletin, 114,* 248–265.

Whisman, M. A., & Kwon, P. (1993). Life stress and dysphoria: The role of self-esteem and hopelessness. *Journal of Personality and Social Psychology, 65,* 1054–1060.

White, N. M., & Milner, P. M. (1992). The psychobiology of reinforcers. *Annual Review of Psychology, 43,* 443–471.

Whorf, B. L. (1956). *Language, thought, and reality: Selected writings of Benjamin Lee Whorf* (J. B. Carroll, Ed.). New York: Wiley.

Widiger, T. A., Frances, A. J., Pincus, H. A., Davis, W. W., & First, M. B. (1991). Toward an empirical classification for the *DSM-IV. Journal of Abnormal Psychology, 100,* 280–288.

Wiebe, D. J. (1991). Hardiness and stress moderation: A test of proposed mechanisms. *Journal of Personality and Social Psychology, 60,* 89–99.

Wiggins, J. S., & Trapnell, P. D. (1992). Personality structure: The return of the Big Five. In S. R. Briggs, R. Hogan, & W. H. Jones (Eds.), *Handbook of personality psychology.* Orlando, FL: Academic.

Williams, C. D. (1959). Case report: The elimination of tantrum behavior by extinction procedures. *Journal of Abnormal and Social Psychology, 59,* 269.

Williams, K., Harkins, S., & Latané, B. (1981). Identifiability as a deterrent to social loafing: Two cheering experiments. *Journal of Personality and Social Psychology, 40,* 303–311.

Williams, K. E., Chambless, D. L., & Steketee, G. (1998). Behavioral treatment of obsessive-compulsive disorder in African Americans: Clinical issues. *Journal of Behavior Therapy and Experimental Psychiatry, 29*(2), 163–170.

Williams, K. J., Suls, J., Alliger, G. M., Learner, S. M., & Wan, C. K. (1991). Multiple role juggling and daily mood states in working mothers: An experience sampling study. *Journal of Applied Psychology, 76,* 664–674.

Williams, L. M. (1994). Recall of childhood trauma: A prospective study of women's memories of child sexual abuse. *Journal of Consulting and Clinical Psychology, 62,* 1167–1176.

Williams, R. L. (1989). *The trusting heart: Great news about Type A behavior.* New York: Random House.

Williams, S. L., Kinney, P. J., & Falbo, J. (1989). Generalization of therapeutic changes in agoraphobia: The role of perceived self-efficacy. *Journal of Consulting and Clinical Psychology, 57,* 436–442.

Williams, W. M., & Ceci, S. J. (1997). Are Americans becoming more or less alike? Trends in race, class, and ability differences in intelligence. *American Psychologist, 52*(11), 1226–1235.

Williamson, R. C. (1991). *Minority languages and bilingualism: Case studies in maintenance and shift.* Norwood, NJ: Ablex.

Willoughby, J. C., & Glidden, L. M. (1995). Fathers helping out: Shared child care and marital satisfaction of parents of children with disabilities. *American Journal on Mental Retardation, 99,* 399–406.

Wilson, D. A., & Sullivan, R. M. (1994). Neurobiology of associative learning in the neonate: Early olfactory learning. *Behavioral and Neural Biology, 61,* 1–18.

Wilson, E. O. (1975). *Sociobiology: A new synthesis.* Cambridge, MA: Harvard University Press.

Wilson, E. O. (1998). *Consilience: The unity of knowledge.* New York: Alfred A. Knopf.

Wilson, F. A. W., & Goldman-Rakie, P. S. (1994). Viewing preferences of rhesus monkeys related to memory for complex pictures, colours and faces. *Behavioral Brain Research, 60,* 79–89.

Wilson, K. D. (1998). Issues surrounding the cognitive neuroscience of obsessive-compulsive disorder. *Psychonomic Bulletin and Review, 5*(2), 161–172.

Wilson, M. A., & McNaughton, B. L. (1994). Reactivation of hippocampal ensemble memories during sleep. *Science, 265,* 676–679.

Wing, R. R., Epstein, L. H., Nowalk, M. P., & Lamparski, D. M. (1986). Behavioral self-regulation in the treatment of patients with diabetes mellitus. *Psychological Bulletin, 99,* 78–89.

Wink, P., & Helson, R. (1993). Personality change in women and their partners. *Journal of Personality and Social Psychology, 65,* 597–605.

Winner, E. (1997). Exceptionally high intelligence and schooling. *American Psychologist, 52*(10), 1070–1081.

Witt, L. A., & Nye, L. G. (1992). Gender and the relationship between perceived fairness of pay or promotion and job satisfaction. *Journal of Applied Psychology, 77,* 910–917.

Wittrock, M. C. (1987, August 29). *The teaching of comprehension.* Thorndike Award Address, 1987 American Psychological Association annual meeting, New York.

Wodak, R., & Benke, G. (1997). Gender as a sociolinguistic variable: New perspectives on variation studies. In F. Coulmas (Ed.), *The handbook of sociolinguistics.* Oxford, England: Blackwell.

Wolpe, J. (1958). *Psychotherapy by reciprocal inhibition.* Stanford, CA: Stanford University Press.

Wong, R. O. L., Chernjavsky, A., Smith, S. J., & Shatz, C. J. (1995). Early functional neural networks in the developing retina. *Nature, 374,* 716–718.

Wood, J. M., Bootzin, R. R., Rosenhan, D., Nolen-Hoeksema, S., & Jourden, F. (1992). Effects of the 1989 San Francisco earthquake on frequency and content of nightmares. *Journal of Abnormal Psychology, 101,* 219–224.

Wood, J. M., Nezworski, M. T., & Stejskal, W. J. (1996). The comprehensive system for the Rorschach: A critical examination. *American Psychological Society, 7,* 3–10.

Wood, N. L., & Cowan, N. (1995). The cocktail party phenomenon revisited: Attention and memory in the classic selective listening procedure of Cherry (1953). *Journal of Experimental Psychology: General, 124,* 243–262.

Wood, W., Wong, F. Y., & Chachere, J. G. (1991). Effects of media violence on viewers' aggression in unconstrained social interaction. *Psychological Bulletin, 109,* 371–383.

Woods, C. J. P. (1996). Gender differences in moral development and acquisition: A review of Kohlberg's and Gilligan's models of justice and care. *Social Behavior and Personality, 24*(4), 375–384.

Woods, S. C., Seely, R. J., Porte D. P., Jr., & Schwartz, M. W. (1998). Signals that regulate food intake and energy homeostasis. *Science, 280,* 1378–1383.

Woodward, W. R. (1982). The "discovery" of social behaviorism and social learning theory, 1870–1980. *American Psychologist, 37,* 396–410.

Woody, E., & Sadler, P. (1998). On reintegrating dissociated theories: Comment on Kirsch and Lynn. *Psychological Bulletin, 123*(2), 192–197.

Worling, J. R. (1995). Sexual abuse histories of adolescent male sex offenders: Differences on the basis of the age and the gender of their victims. *Journal of Abnormal Psychology, 104,* 610–613.

Wright, L. (1997). *Twins and what they tell us about who we are.* New York: John Wiley and Sons.

Wright, W. (1999). *Born that way: Genes, behavior, personality.* New York: Alfred A. Knopf.

Wundt, W. (1896). *Lectures on human and animal psychology.* New York: Macmillian.

Wyatt, G. E. (1994). The sociocultural relevance of sex research: Challenges for the 1990s and beyond. *American Psychologist, 49,* 748–754.

Wynn, K. (1992). Addition and subtraction by human infants. *Letters to Nature, 358,* 749–750.

Wynn-Dancy, L. M., & Gillam, R. B. (1997). Accessing long-term memory: Metacognitive strategies and strategic action in adolescents. *Topics in Language Disorders, 18*(1), 32–44.

Wynne, L. C., Cole, R. E., & Perkins, P. (1987). University of Rochester child and family study: Risk research in progress. *Schizophrenia Bulletin, 13,* 463–467.

Wyszecki, G., & Stiles, W. S. (1967). *Color science: Concepts and methods, quantitative data, and formulas.* New York: Wiley.

Yamamoto, J., Rhee, S., & Chang, D. S. (1994). Psychiatric disorders among elderly Koreans in the United States. *Community Mental Health Journal, 30*(1), 17–27.

Yehuda, R., Schmeidler, J., Wainberg, M., Binder-Brynes, K., & Duvdevani, T. (1998). Vulnerability to posttraumatic stress disorder in adult offspring of Holocaust survivors. *American Journal of Psychiatry, 155*(9), 1163–1171.

Yoken, C., & Berman, J. S. (1984). Does paying a fee for psychotherapy alter the effectiveness of treatment? *Journal of Consulting and Clinical Psychology, 52,* 254–260.

York, J. L., & Welte, J. W. (1994). Gender comparisons of alcohol consumption in alcoholic and nonalcoholic populations. *Journal of Studies on Alcohol, 55,* 743–750.

Young, T. J., & French, L. A. (1993). Suicide and social status among Native Americans. *Psychological Reports, 73,* 461–462.

Youngstedt, S. D., O'Connor, P. J., & Dishman, R. K. (1997). The effects of acute exercise on sleep: A quantitative synthesis. *Sleep, 20*(3), 203–214.

Yousif, Y., & Korte, C. (1995). Urbanization, culture, and helpfulness: Cross-cultural studies in England and the Sudan. *Journal of Cross-Cultural Psychology, 26,* 474–489.

Zaidel, E., Aboitiz, F., Clarke, J., Kaiser, D., & Matteson, R. (1995). Sex differences in interhemispheric relations for language. In F. L. Kitterle (Ed.), *Hemispheric communication: Mechanisms and models* (pp. 85–175). Hillsdale, NJ: Erlbaum.

Zajonc, R. B. (1965). Social facilitation. *Science, 149,* 269–274.

Zajonc, R. B. (1984). On the primacy of affect. *American Psychologist, 39,* 117–123.

Zajonc, R. B., Murphy, S. T., & Inglehart, M. (1989). Feeling and facial efference: Implications of the vascular theory of emotion. *Psychological Review, 96,* 395–416.

Zakay, D., Hayduk, L. A., & Tsal, Y. (1992). Personal space and distance misperception: Implications of a novel observation. *Bulletin of the Psychonomic Society, 30,* 33–35.

Zangwill, O. L., & Blakemore, C. (1972). Dyslexia: Reversal of eye movements during reading. *Neuropsychologia, 10,* 371–373.

Zaragoza, M. S., & Mitchell, K. J. (1996). Repeated exposure to suggestion and the creation of false memories. *American Psychological Society, 7*(5), 294–300.

Zarcone, T. J., Branch, M. N., Hughes, C. E., & Pennypacker, H. S. (1997). Key pecking during extinction after intermittent or continuous reinforcement as a function of the number of reinforcers delivered during training. *Journal of the Experimental Analysis of Behavior, 67*(1), 91–108.

Zeki, S. (1992). The visual image in mind and brain. *Scientific American, 267*(3), 69–76.

Zhang, F., Shogo, E., Cleary, L. J., Eskin, A., & Byrne, J. H. (1997). Role of transforming growth factor-A in long-term synaptic facilitation in Aplysia. *Science, 275,* 1318–1320.

Zigler, E. F. (1987). Formal schooling for four-year-olds? No. *American Psychologist, 42,* 254–260.

Zigler, E. F. (1994). Reshaping early childhood intervention to be a more effective weapon against poverty. *American Journal of Community Psychology, 22,* 37–47.

Zigler, E. F. (1999). Head Start is not child care. *American Psychologist, 54*(2), 142.

Zigler, E. F., & Hodapp, R. M. (1991). Behavioral functioning in individuals with mental retardation. *Annual Review of Psychology, 42,* 29–50.

Zins, J. E., & Barnett, D. W. (1983). The Kaufman Assessment Battery for Children and school achievement: A validity study. *Journal of Psychoeducational Assessment, 1,* 235–241.

Zitrin, C. M. (1981). Combined pharmacological and psychological treatment of phobias. In M. Navissakalian & D. H. Barlow (Eds.), *Phobias: Psychological and pharmacological treatments.* New York: Guilford.

Zlotnick, C., Elkin, I., & Shea, M. T. (1998). Does the gender of a patient or the gender of a therapist affect the treatment of patients with major depression? *Journal of Consulting and Clinical Psychology, 66*(4), 655–659.

Zola-Morgan, S., Squire, L. R., & Mishkin, M. (1982). The neuroanatomy of amnesia: Amygdala–hippocampus versus temporal stem. *Science, 218,* 1337–1339.

Zuber, J. A., Crott, H. W., & Werner, J. (1992). Choice shift and group polarization: An analysis of the status of arguments and social decision schemes. *Journal of Personality and Social Psychology, 62,* 50–61.

Zuckerman, M. (1969). Variables affecting deprivation results and hallucinations, reported sensations, and images. In J. P. Zubek (Ed.), *Sensory deprivation.* New York: Appleton-Century-Crofts.

Zuckerman, M. (1990). Some dubious premises in research and theory on racial differences. *American Psychologist, 45,* 1297–1303.

Zuckerman, M. (1999). *Vulnerability to psychopathology: A biosocial model.* Washington, DC: American Psychological Association.

Zuckerman, M., Kuhlman, D. M., Joireman, J., Teta, P., & Kraft, M. (1993). A comparison of three structural models for personality: The big three, the big five, and the alternative five. *Journal of Personality and Social Psychology, 65,* 757–768.

Self-Test Answers

Chapter 1
1. D; 2. B; 3. C; 4. A; 5. D; 6. B; 7. C; 8. A; 9. C; 10. A

Chapter 2
1. D; 2. D; 3. C; 4. C; 5. A; 6. D; 7. C; 8. B; 9. D; 10. B

Chapter 3
1. D; 2. B; 3. A; 4. C; 5. B; 6. D; 7. B; 8. A; 9. B; 10. C

Chapter 4
1. C; 2. D; 3. A; 4. B; 5. A; 6. C; 7. C; 8. D; 9. B; 10. A

Chapter 5
1. A; 2. B; 3. A; 4. C; 5. A; 6. B; 7. B; 8. C; 9. C; 10. A; 11. D; 12. D; 13. D; 14. B; 15. B

Chapter 6
1. B, 2. A, 3. C, 4. A, 5. D, 6. B, 7. C, 8. D, 9. B, 10. C

Chapter 7
1. C; 2. B; 3. A; 4. B; 5. C; 6. D; 7. B; 8. D; 9. C; 10. B

Chapter 8
1. C; 2. A; 3. B; 4. B; 5. D; 6. A; 7. A; 8. D; 9. D; 10. B; 11. D; 12. B

Chapter 9
1. B; 2. A; 3. D; 4. C; 5. A; 6. C; 7. A; 8. B; 9. D; 10. C; 11. B; 12. B; 13. B; 14. A; 15. D

Chapter 10
1. C; 2. A; 3. B; 4. C; 5. D; 6. B; 7. A; 8. C; 9. A; 10. C

Chapter 11
1. B; 2. B; 3. C; 4. C; 5. D; 6. B; 7. D; 8. A; 9. D; 10. D; 11. C; 12. A; 13. C; 14. A; 15. C

Chapter 12
1. D; 2. C; 3. B; 4. D; 5. B; 6. D; 7. D; 8. B; 9. A; 10. D; 11. A; 12. D; 13. C; 14. A; 15. D

Chapter 13
1. C; 2. B; 3. A; 4. B; 5. D; 6. B; 7. D; 8. A; 9. C; 10. D; 11. C; 12. A

Chapter 14
1. A; 2. B; 3. D; 4. C; 5. D; 6. B; 7. D; 8. B; 9. B; 10. B; 11. D; 12. C

Credits

Figures and Tables

Chapter 3: FIGURE 3.1, p. 63: From Dowling, J. E., & Boycott, B. B. (1966). *Proceedings of the Royal Society* (London), B166, 80–111, Figure 7. Reprinted by permission. FIGURE 3.2, p. 64: From Pirenne, M. H. (1967). *Vision and the eye,* 32. London: Chapman and Hall, Ltd. Reprinted by permission. FIGURE 3.9, p. 75 (bottom right): From Beck, Jacob (1966). Effects of orientation and of shape similarity on perceptual grouping. *Perception and Psychophysics,* 1, 300–302. Reprinted by permission Psychonomic Society, Inc.

Chapter 7: TABLE 7.1, p. 189: Adapted from Gardner, H., & Hatch, T. (1989). Multiple intelligences go to school: Educational implications of the theory of multiple intelligences. *Educational Researcher, 18(8),* 6. Reprinted by permission of the authors with adaptation based on personal communication from H. Gardner (1996). TABLE 7.4, p. 195: Adapted from Sattler, Jerome M. (1992). *Assessment of children,* revised and updated, 3rd Edition, 79. San Diego: Sattler. Reprinted by permission.

Chapter 10: TABLE 10.4, p. 302: From the *Minnesota Multiphasic Personality Inventory.* Copyright © the University of Minnesota 1942, 1943 (renewed 1970). MMPI scale names reproduced by permission of the publisher.

Chapter 11: TABLE 11.3, p. 335: From Hendrick, C., & Hendrick, S. A theory and method of love. *Journal of Personality and Social Psychology, 50,* 392–402. Copyright © 1986 by the American Psychological Association. Reprinted with permission.

Chapter 12: TABLE 12.1, p. 343: From Kanner, A. D., Coyne, J. C., Schaefer, C., & Lazarus, R. S. (1981). Comparison of two modes of stress measurement: Daily hassles and uplifts versus major life events. *Journal of Behavioral Medicine, 4,* 1–39. Reprinted by permission of Kluwer Academic/Plenum Publishing Corp.

Chapter 13: TABLE 13.5, p. 383: From Meyer, Robert. G., & Salmon, Paul. *Abnormal psychology,* 2nd ed., p. 333 and the work of Edwin Shneidman and Norman Farberow. Copyright © 1988 by Allyn and Bacon. Reprinted by permission.

Chapter 14: TABLE 14.1, p. 396: From Mahrer, A. R., & Nadler, W. P. Good moments in psychotherapy: A preliminary review, a list, and some promising research avenues. *Journal of Consulting and Clinical Psychology, 54,* 10–15. Copyright © 1986 by the American Psychological Association. Adapted with permission. TABLE 14.4, p. 409: From Ellis, Albert, Ph.D., & Harper, Robert A., Ph.D. *A guide to rational living.* © 1989, 1961. Reprinted by permission.

Photos

Chapter 1: p. 1, Steve Winter/Black Star; p. 5, Courtesy of Neal E. Miller/Yale University; p. 12, AP/Wide World Photos; p. 17, Archives of the History of American Psychology/The University of Akron; p. 22 (top), National Library of Medicine; p. 22 (bottom), Ken Heyman/Woodfin Camp & Associates.

Chapter 2: p. 28, Charlyn Zlotnick/Woodfin Camp & Associates; p. 31, CNRI/SPI/Science Source/Photo Researchers; p. 37, Bob Daemmrich/The Image Works; p. 45, Robert Holmgren/Peter Arnold, Inc.; p. 52, Michael Gouverneur/Gamma Liaison.

Chapter 3: p. 57, Michael Justice/The Image Works; p. 59, PhotoDisc, Inc.; p. 61 (top left), David Harvey/Woodfin Camp & Associates; p. 61 (top right), PhotoDisc, Inc.; p. 61 (bottom), Benjamin Ailes; p. 71, Corbis/Digital Stock.

Chapter 4: p. 90, Ed Kashi; p. 95, Corbis/UPI; p. 96, Ted Spagna/Science Source/Photo Researchers; p. 102, David H. Wells/The Image Works; p. 105, Brian Phillips/The Image Works; p. 108, A. Lichtenstein/The Image Works.

Chapter 5: p. 117, Will Faller; p. 121, Archives of the History of American Psychology/The University of Akron; p. 127 (bottom left), AP/Wide World Photos; p. 127 (bottom right), Robert Brenner/PhotoEdit; p. 140, Will Faller; p. 143 (all), Photosynthesis Archives.

Chapter 6: p. 146, AP/Wide World Photos; p. 152, Brian Smith; p. 160, AP/Wide World Photos; p. 163, Harley Soltes/Seattle Times; p. 169, AP/Wide World Photos; p. 182, Susan Kuklin/Science Source/Photo Researchers.

Chapter 7: p. 186, Bob Daemmrich/The Image Works; p. 190, Steven Frisch/Stock, Boston; p. 196, Archives of the History of American Psychology/The University of Akron; p. 199, Brian Smith; p. 202, Alan Oddie/PhotoEdit; p. 204, Bob Daemmrich/The Image Works.

Chapter 8: p. 208, Kathy Ferguson/PhotoEdit; p. 212, Ed Lallo/Liaison International; p. 213, AP/Wide World Photos; p. 214, Richard Howard; p. 225, AP/Wide World Photos; p. 227, Michael Greenlar/The Image Works.

Chapter 9: p. 233, Will Hart; p. 237, Jean Shifrin/Associated Press/*The Atlanta Journal and Constitution;* p. 239, From Meltzoff, A. N., & Moore, M. K. "Imitation of facial and manual gestures by human neonates." *Science, 198, 75.* Copyright 1977 by American Association for the Advancement of Science; p. 249, Martin Rogers/Stock, Boston; p. 259, Will Hart; p. 273, Stephen Marks/Black Star; p. 275, Scott Thode/International Stock.

Chapter 10: p. 279, Brian Smith; p. 284, Prettyman/PhotoEdit; p. 287, Alon Reininger/Contact/Woodfin Camp & Associates; p. 292, Novastock/PhotoEdit; p. 293, Goldberg/Monkmeyer; p. 303, Lew Merrim/Monkmeyer.

Chapter 11: p. 307, Michael Newman/PhotoEdit; p. 310, Philip G. Zimbardo; p. 311, Bob Daemmrich/Stock, Boston; p. 319, Dorothy Littell Greco/The Image Works; p. 327, Drew Crawford/The Image Works; p. 330, PhotoDisc Inc.; p. 333, D. Perrett, I. Penton-Voak, M. Burk/University of St. Andrews/SPL/Science Source/Photo Researchers.

Chapter 12: p. 339, Rick Strange/Index Stock Imagery; p. 343 (top), Kaku Kurita/Gamma Liaison; p. 343 (bottom), Jonathan Nourok/PhotoEdit; p. 344, AP/Wide World Photos; p. 346, Courtesy of Hans Selye; p. 354, Bob Daemmrich/Stock, Boston.

Chapter 13: p. 362, Will Hart; p. 363, Seth Resnik/Stock, Boston; p. 364, Paul Carter/Register Guard/Sygma; p. 382, AP/Wide World Photos; p. 386, Gregory Rec/Gamma Liaison; p. 388, NIH/Science Source/Photo Researchers.

Chapter 14: p. 392, Will Hart; p. 395, Will Faller; p. 403, Copyright 1991 by The Estate of Frederick Perls/*The Gestalt Journal Press;* p. 407, Lori Adamski Peek/Tony Stone Images; p. 413, Will and Deni McIntyre/Science Source/Photo Researchers; p. 416, Louisa Preston.

Name Index

Subject Index